The history of Black Hawk County, Iowa, containing a history of the county, its cities, towns, &c., a biographical directory of citizens, war record of its volunteers in the late rebellion ... general and local statistics ... history of the Northwest,

publisher Western Historical Co.

THE

HISTORY

OF

BLACK HAWK COUNTY,

IOWA,

CONTAINING

A History of the County, its Cities, Towns, &c.,

A Biographical Directory of Citizens, War Record of its Volunteers in the late Rebellion, General and Local Statistics, Portraits of Early Settlers and Prominent Men, History of the Northwest, History of Iowa; Map of Black Hawk County, Constitution of the United States, Miscellaneous Matters, &c

ILLUSTRATED.

CHICAGO
WESTERN HISTORICAL COMPANY,

A699661

Culver Page Moyne & Co
PRINTERS
118 & 120 MONROE ST
CHICAGO

PREFACE.

LESS than half a century has rolled into eternity since the Indian title to any portion of the soil of Iowa was extinguished, and the Black Hawk Purchase permitted the resistless tide of emigration westward to flow across the Mississippi, and only thirty years ago the Winnebagoes reluctantly left their Iowa Reserve, the southern line of which was very near the northern part of Black Hawk County. Less than thirty-five years have elapsed since STURGIS and ADAMS built the first rude log cabins in the valley of the Cedar, and the first brave and hardy pioneers settled on the beautiful prairies of Black Hawk. But these fleeting years have been replete with eventful changes—of history that it has been the purpose of this work to gather, arrange and preserve for transmission to posterity as one of the almost countless chapters in the annals of this great country.

The task has been an arduous and responsible one. Some years had passed, after the first permanent settlements by STURGIS, ADAMS, HANNA, VIRDEN, MELROSE, MULLAN, NEWELL and others, before any written records were made; and of those who settled in the county in 1845, only one now remains to tell the story of their hardships and privations.

The compilers have been forced to depend upon the remembrances of the early settlers for many of the incidents recorded in the following pages. But memories fail with the accumulating burdens of years, and events that were vividly recalled ten or fifteen years ago, are now so nearly forgotten that they return with difficulty at the call of the historian. The reminiscences of JAMES NEWELL, one of the pioneers of Iowa as early as 1834–5, written by himself before his decease, kindly placed at the disposal of the historians by S. H. PACKARD, Esq., of Cedar Falls, have furnished some interesting and valuable matter for this work. Large numbers of circulars and letters addressed to Township Clerks and old settlers, asking for information for this work, have not been answered, with one or two honorable exceptions It has often occurred, also, that different individuals have given sincere and honest, but, nevertheless, conflicting, versions of the same events, and it has been a task of great delicacy to harmonize these conflicting statements This work has been done with much care and discrimination, with the sole purpose of arriving at the truth How well this task has been performed, the intelligent reader must judge It will be strange, indeed, if, in the multiplicity of names, dates and events no errors, no omissions be detected. The compilers do not dare hope that, in all its numerous and varied details, this work is absolutely correct, nor is it to be expected that it is beyond criticism; but it is hoped and believed that it will be found measurably correct and generally accurate and reliable. Great care has been constantly exercised in its preparation in the hope of making it a standard work of reference, as well as a volume of interest to the general reader.

Such as it shall be found, however, our work is done, our offering completed, and it remains for us to tender our acknowledgments to the people of Black Hawk County for the patronage that has enabled us to present them with this volume, and for the courtesy and kindness generally extended to our representatives, to whom has been intrusted the work of collecting and arranging the historical record herein presented to that posterity who, in the not far distant future, are to take the places of the fathers and mothers of to-day, so many of whose names are honorably recorded in the following pages.

Particularly do we desire to express our warmest thanks to those who have taken an interest in the work and who have so generously furnished valuable information, without whose aid this history of Black Hawk County could not have been so complete and accurate as it is hoped it will be found to be. To George W. Hanna, Esq , the oldest settler now living; to James Virden, Esq ; M. Parrott, Esq , of the *Iowa State Reporter,* W. H. Hartman, Esq, of the *Courier,* Snyder Bros., of the *Gazette;* S. Van Meter & Co., of the *Recorder,* S. H. Packard, Esq., Dr J. Wasson, of the *Progress,* to the county officers who have so courteously and kindly aided us and placed the official records of the county at our disposal, to the ministers and official representatives of the churches, lodges and societies, this paragraph of grateful appreciation and thanks is respectfully dedicated. We are also under obligations to Hon T. W Burdick, Member of Congress, for courtesies extended to our representatives.

In conclusion, we may be permitted to express the earnest hope that before twoscore more of years have passed, other and abler pens will have gathered and recorded the historic events that are to follow the close of this offering to the people of Black Hawk, that the history of the county may be preserved unbroken from generation to generation; and to this end public records, private journals and newspaper files should be carefully preserved.

PUBLISHERS.

September, 1878

CONTENTS.

HISTORICAL.

ILLUSTRATIONS.

LITHOGRAPHIC PORTRAITS.

BLACK HAWK COUNTY VOLUNTEERS.

CONTENTS

BIOGRAPHICAL TOWNSHIP DIRECTORY.

ABSTRACT OF IOWA STATE LAWS.

MISCELLANEOUS.

MAP OF
Black Hawk
COUNTY

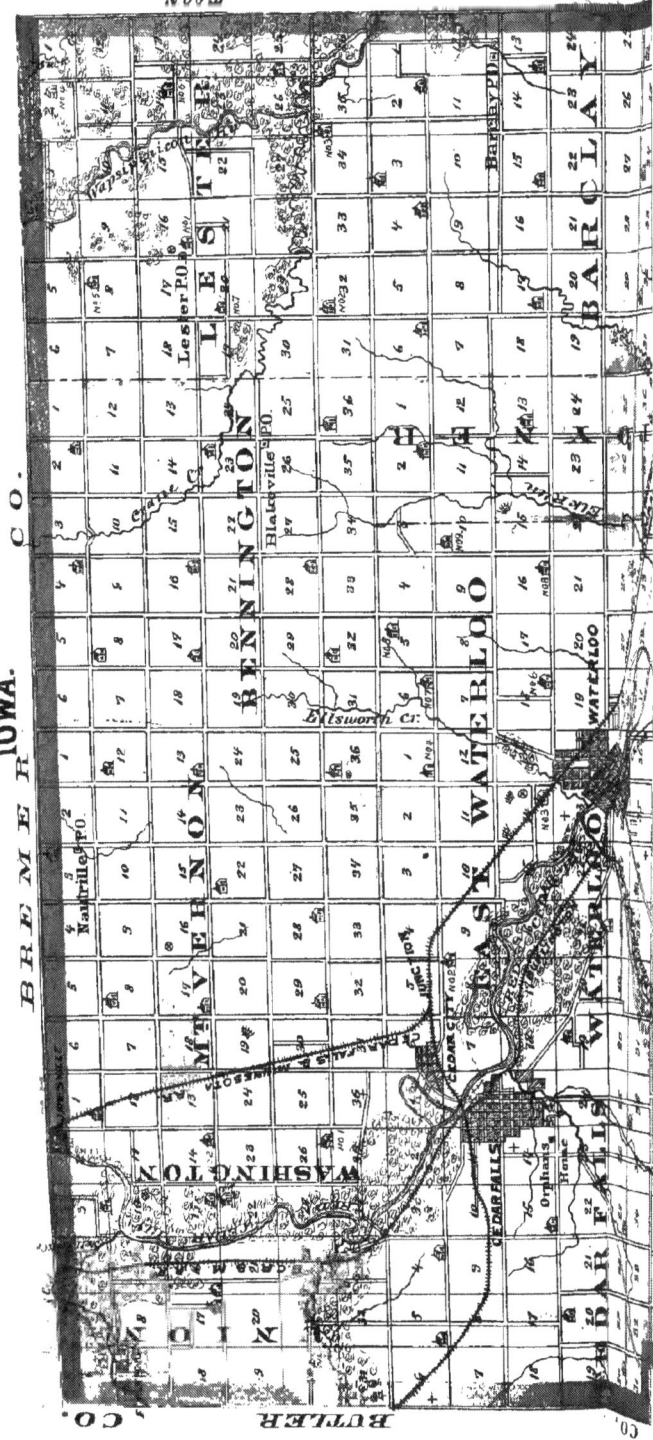

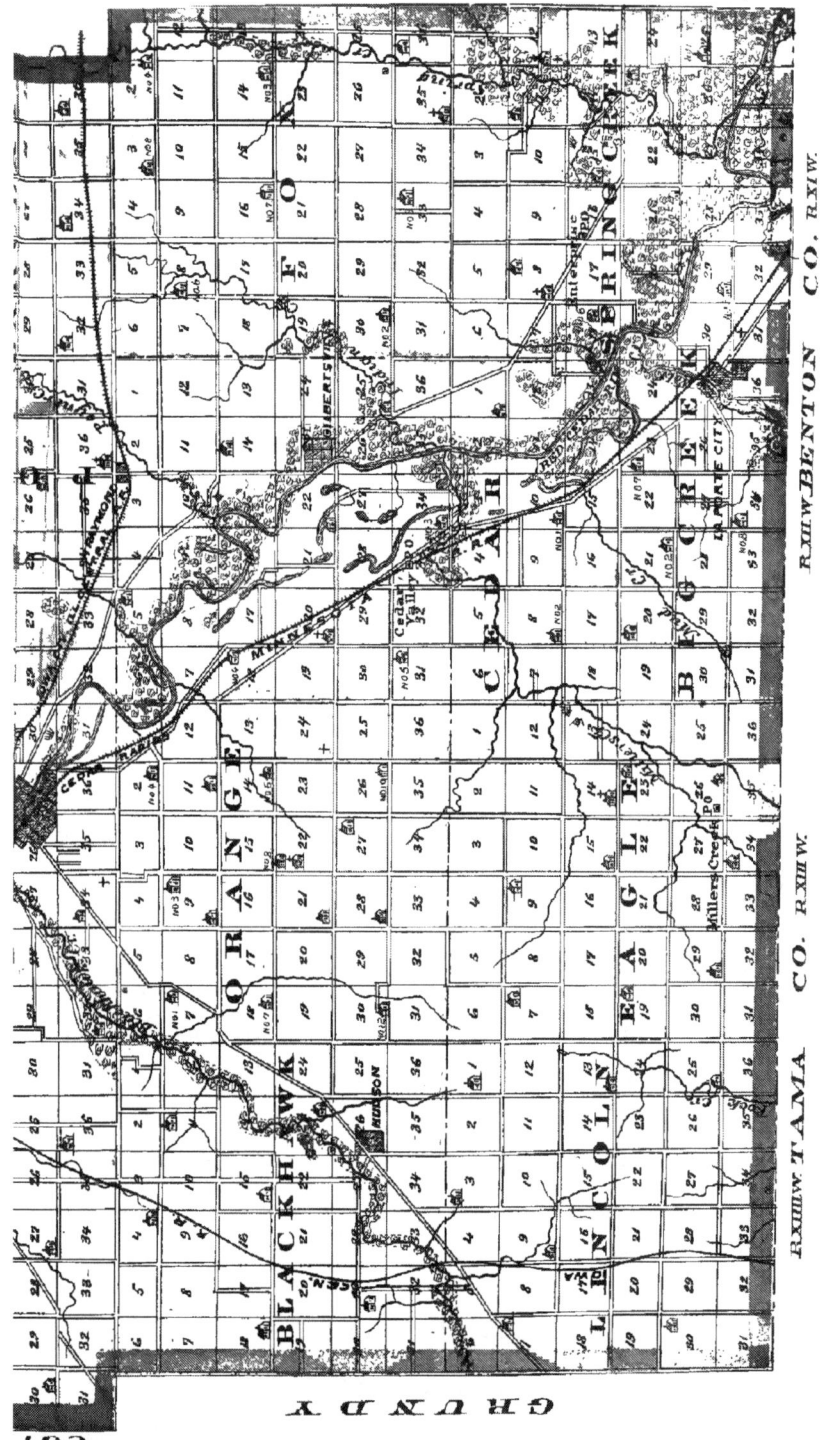

THE NORTHWEST TERRITORY.

GEOGRAPHICAL POSITION.

When the Northwestern Territory was ceded to the United States by Virginia in 1784, it embraced only the territory lying between the Ohio and the Mississippi Rivers, and north to the northern limits of the United States It coincided with the area now embraced in the States of Ohio, Indiana, Michigan, Illinois, Wisconsin, and that portion of Minnesota lying on the east side of the Mississippi River. The United States itself at that period extended no farther west than the Mississippi River; but by the purchase of Louisiana in 1803, the western boundary of the United States was extended to the Rocky Mountains and the Northern Pacific Ocean. The new territory thus added to the National domain, and subsequently opened to settlement, has been called the "New Northwest," in contradistinction from the old "Northwestern Territory."

In comparison with the old Northwest this is a territory of vast magnitude. It includes an area of 1,887,850 square miles; being greater in extent than the united areas of all the Middle and Southern States, including Texas. Out of this magnificent territory have been erected eleven sovereign States and eight Territories, with an aggregate population, at the present time, of 13,000,000 inhabitants, or nearly one third of the entire population of the United States.

Its lakes are fresh-water seas, and the larger rivers of the continent flow for a thousand miles through its rich alluvial valleys and far-stretching prairies, more acres of which are arable and productive of the highest percentage of the cereals than of any other area of like extent on the globe.

For the last twenty years the increase of population in the Northwest has been about as three to one in any other portion of the United States.

EARLY EXPLORATIONS.

In the year 1541, DeSoto first saw the Great West in the New World. He, however, penetrated no farther north than the 35th parallel of latitude. The expedition resulted in his death and that of more than half his army, the remainder of whom found their way to Cuba, thence to Spain, in a famished and demoralized condition. DeSoto founded no settlements, produced no results, and left no traces, unless it were that he awakened the hostility of the red man against the white man, and disheartened such as might desire to follow up the career of discovery for better purposes. The French nation were eager and ready to seize upon any news from this extensive domain, and were the first to profit by DeSoto's defeat. Yet it was more than a century before any adventurer took advantage of these discoveries.

In 1616, four years before the pilgrims "moored their bark on the wild New England shore," Le Caron, a French Franciscan, had penetrated through the Iroquois and Wyandots (Hurons) to the streams which run into Lake Huron, and in 1634, two Jesuit missionaries founded the first mission among the lake tribes. It was just one hundred years from the discovery of the Mississippi by DeSoto (1541) until the Canadian envoys met the savage nations of the Northwest at the Falls of St. Mary, below the outlet of Lake Superior. This visit led to no permanent result, yet it was not until 1659 that any of the adventurous fur traders attempted to spend a Winter in the frozen wilds about the great lakes, nor was it until 1660 that a station was established upon their borders by Mesnard, who perished in the woods a few months after. In 1665, Claude Allouez built the earliest lasting habitation of the white man among the Indians of the Northwest. In 1668, Claude Dablon and James Marquette founded the mission of Sault Ste. Marie at the Falls of St. Mary, and two years afterward, Nicholas Perrot, as agent for M. Talon, Governor General of Canada, explored Lake Illinois (Michigan) as far south as the present City of Chicago, and invited the Indian nations to meet him at a grand council at Sault Ste. Marie the following Spring, where they were taken under the protection of the king, and formal possession was taken of the Northwest. This same year Marquette established a mission at Point St. Ignatius, where was founded the old town of Michillimackinac.

During M. Talon's explorations and Marquette's residence at St. Ignatius, they learned of a great river away to the west, and fancied —as all others did then—that upon its fertile banks whole tribes of God's children resided, to whom the sound of the Gospel had never come. Filled with a wish to go and preach to them, and in compliance with a

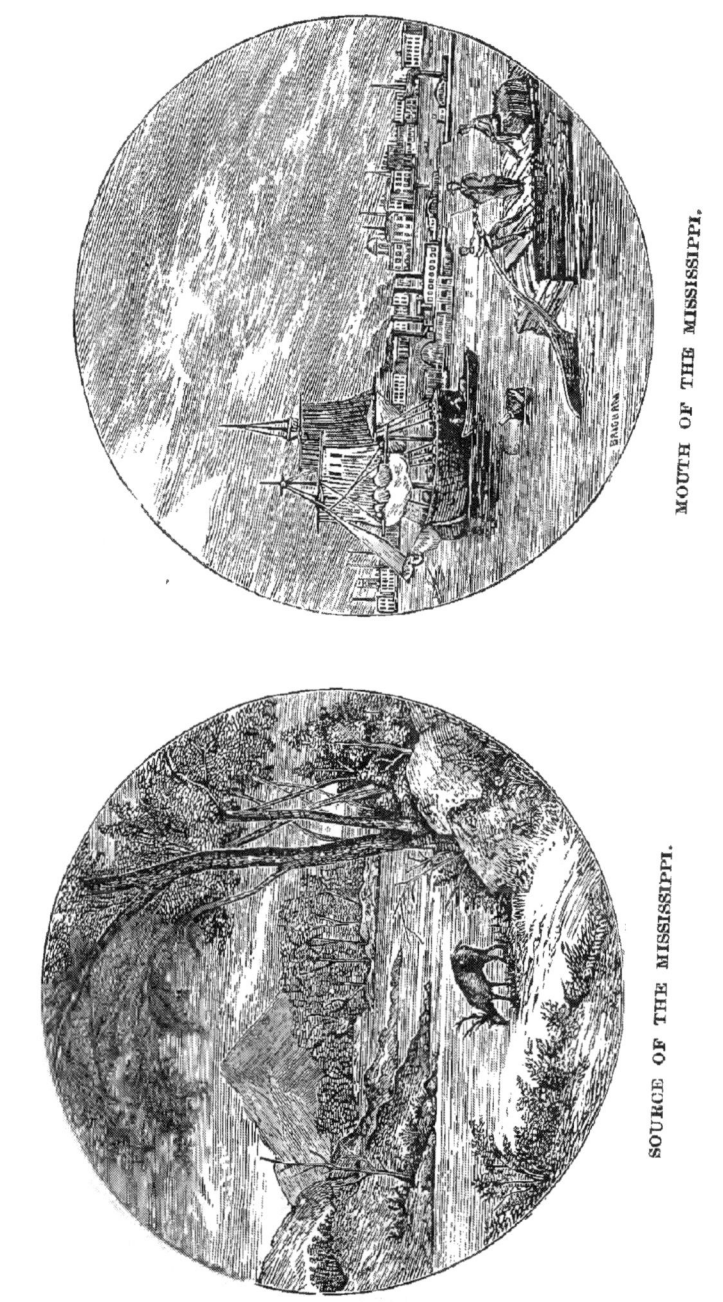

MOUTH OF THE MISSISSIPPI.

SOURCE OF THE MISSISSIPPI.

request of M. Talon, who earnestly desired to extend the domain of his king, and to ascertain whether the river flowed into the Gulf of Mexico or the Pacific Ocean, Marquette with Joliet, as commander of the expedition, prepared for the undertaking.

On the 13th of May, 1673, the explorers, accompanied by five assistant French Canadians, set out from Mackinaw on their daring voyage of discovery.' The Indians, who gathered to witness their departure, were astonished at the boldness of the undertaking, and endeavored to dissuade them from their purpose by representing the tribes on the Mississippi as exceedingly savage and cruel, and the river itself as full of all sorts of frightful monsters ready to swallow them and their canoes together. But, nothing daunted by these terrific descriptions, Marquette told them he was willing not only to encounter all the perils of the unknown region they were about to explore, but to lay down his life in a cause in which the salvation of souls was involved; and having prayed together they separated. Coasting along the northern shore of Lake Michigan, the adventurers entered Green Bay, and passed thence up the Fox River and Lake Winnebago to a village of the Miamis and Kickapoos. Here Marquette was delighted to find a beautiful cross planted in the middle of the town ornamented with white skins, red girdles and bows and arrows, which these good people had offered to the Great Manitou, or God, to thank him for the pity he had bestowed on them during the Winter in giving them an abundant " chase." This was the farthest outpost to which Dablon and Allouez had extended their missionary labors the year previous. Here Marquette drank mineral waters and was instructed in the secret of a root which cures the bite of the venomous rattlesnake. He assembled the chiefs and old men of the village, and, pointing to Joliet, said: " My friend is an envoy of France, to discover new countries, and I am an ambassador from God to enlighten them with the truths of the Gospel." Two Miami guides were here furnished to conduct them to the Wisconsin River, and they set out from the Indian village on the 10th of June, amidst a great crowd of natives who had assembled to witness their departure into a region where no white man had ever yet ventured. The guides, having conducted them across the portage, returned. The explorers launched their canoes upon the Wisconsin, which they descended to the Mississippi and proceeded down its unknown waters. What emotions must have swelled their breasts as they struck out into the broadening current and became conscious that they were now upon the bosom of the Father of Waters. The mystery was about to be lifted from the long-sought river. The scenery in that locality is beautiful, and on that delightful seventeenth of June must have been clad in all its primeval loveliness as it had been adorned by the hand of

Nature. Drifting rapidly, it is said that the bold bluffs on either hand "reminded them of the castled shores of their own beautiful rivers of France." By-and-by, as they drifted along, great herds of buffalo appeared on the banks. On going to the heads of the valley they could see a country of the greatest beauty and fertility, apparently destitute of inhabitants yet presenting the appearance of extensive manors, under the fastidious cultivation of lordly proprietors.

THE WILD PRAIRIE.

On June 25, they went ashore and found some fresh traces of men upon the sand, and a path which led to the prairie. The men remained in the boat, and Marquette and Joliet followed the path till they discovered a village on the banks of a river, and two other villages on a hill, within a half league of the first, inhabited by Indians. They were received most hospitably by these natives, who had never before seen a white person. After remaining a few days they re-embarked and descended the river to about latitude 33°, where they found a village of the Arkansas, and being satisfied that the river flowed into the Gulf of Mexico, turned their course up the river, and ascending the stream to the mouth of the Illinois, rowed up that stream to its source, and procured guides from that point to the lakes. "Nowhere on this journey," says Marquette, "did we see such grounds, meadows, woods, stags, buffaloes, deer, wildcats, bustards, swans, ducks, parroquets, and even beavers, as on the Illinois River." The party, without loss or injury, reached Green Bay in September, and reported their discovery—one of the most important of the age, but of which no record was preserved save Marquette's, Joliet losing his by the upsetting of his canoe on his way to Quebec. Afterward Marquette returned to the Illinois Indians by their request, and ministered to them until 1675. On the 18th of May, in that year, as he was passing the mouth of a stream—going with his boatmen up Lake Michigan—he asked to land at its mouth and celebrate Mass. Leaving his men with the canoe, he retired a short distance and began his devotions. As much time passed and he did not return, his men went in search of him, and found him upon his knees, dead. He had peacefully passed away while at prayer. He was buried at this spot Charlevoix, who visited the place fifty years after, found the waters had retreated from the grave, leaving the beloved missionary to repose in peace. The river has since been called Marquette

While Marquette and his companions were pursuing their labors in the West, two men, differing widely from him and each other, were preparing to follow in his footsteps and perfect the discoveries so well begun by him. These were Robert de La Salle and Louis Hennepin.

After La Salle's return from the discovery of the Ohio River (see the narrative elsewhere), he established himself again among the French trading posts in Canada. Here he mused long upon the pet project of those ages—a short way to China and the East, and was busily planning an expedition up the great lakes. and so across the continent to the Pacific, when Marquette returned from the Mississippi. At once the vigorous mind of LaSalle received from his and his companions' stories the idea that by following the Great River northward, or by turning up some of the numerous western tributaries, the object could easily be gained. He applied to Frontenac, Governor General of Canada, and laid before him the plan, dim but gigantic. Frontenac entered warmly into his plans. and saw that LaSalle's idea to connect the great lakes by a chain of forts with the Gulf of Mexico would bind the country so wonderfully together, give unmeasured power to France, and glory to himself, under whose administration he earnestly hoped all would be realized.

LaSalle now repaired to France, laid his plans before the King, who warmly approved of them, and made him a Chevalier. He also received from all the noblemen the warmest wishes for his success. The Chevalier returned to Canada, and busily entered upon his work. He at once rebuilt Fort Frontenac and constructed the first ship to sail on these fresh-water seas. On the 7th of August, 1679, having been joined by Hennepin, he began his voyage in the Griffin up Lake Erie. He passed over this lake, through the straits beyond, up Lake St. Clair and into Huron. In this lake they encountered heavy storms. They were some time at Michillimackinac, where LaSalle founded a fort, and passed on to Green Bay, the "Baie des Puans" of the French, where he found a large quantity of furs collected for him. He loaded the Griffin with these, and placing her under the care of a pilot and fourteen sailors,

LA SALLE LANDING ON THE SHORE OF GREEN BAY.

started her on her return voyage. The vessel was never afterward heard of. He remained about these parts until early in the Winter, when, hearing nothing from the Griffin, he collected all the men—thirty working men and three monks—and started again upon his great undertaking.

By a short portage they passed to the Illinois or Kankakee, called by the Indians, "Theakeke," *wolf*, because of the tribes of Indians called by that name, commonly known as the Mahingans, dwelling there. The French pronounced it *Kiakiki*, which became corrupted to Kankakee. "Falling down the said river by easy journeys, the better to observe the country," about the last of December they reached a village of the Illinois Indians, containing some five hundred cabins, but at that moment no inhabitants. The Seur de LaSalle being in want of some breadstuffs, took advantage of the absence of the Indians to help himself to a sufficiency of maize, large quantities of which he found concealed in holes under the wigwams. This village was situated near the present village of Utica in LaSalle County, Illinois. The corn being securely stored, the voyagers again betook themselves to the stream, and toward evening, on the 4th day of January, 1680, they came into a lake which must have been the lake of Peoria. This was called by the Indians *Pim-i-te-wi,* that is, *a place where there are many fat beasts.* Here the natives were met with in large numbers, but they were gentle and kind, and having spent some time with them, LaSalle determined to erect another fort in that place, for he had heard rumors that some of the adjoining tribes were trying to disturb the good feeling which existed, and some of his men were disposed to complain, owing to the hardships and perils of the travel. He called this fort " *Crevecœur* " (broken-heart), a name expressive of the very natural sorrow and anxiety which the pretty certain loss of his ship, Griffin, and his consequent impoverishment, the danger of hostility on the part of the Indians, and of mutiny among his own men, might well cause him. His fears were not entirely groundless. At one time poison was placed in his food, but fortunately was discovered.

While building this fort, the Winter wore away, the prairies began to look green, and LaSalle, despairing of any reinforcements, concluded to return to Canada, raise new means and new men, and embark anew in the enterprise. For this purpose he made Hennepin the leader of a party to explore the head waters of the Mississippi, and he set out on his journey. This journey was accomplished with the aid of a few persons, and was successfully made, though over an almost unknown route, and in a bad season of the year. He safely reached Canada, and set out again for the object of his search.

Hennepin and his party left Fort Crevecœur on the last of February, 1680. When LaSalle reached this place on his return expedition, he found the fort entirely deserted, and he was obliged to return again to Canada. He embarked the third time, and succeeded. Seven days after leaving the fort, Hennepin reached the Mississippi, and paddling up the icy stream as best he could, reached no higher than the Wisconsin River by the 11th of April. Here he and his followers were taken prisoners by a band of Northern Indians, who treated them with great kindness. Hennepin's comrades were Anthony Auguel and Michael Ako. On this voyage they found several beautiful lakes, and "saw some charming prairies." Their captors were the Isaute or Sauteurs, Chippewas, a tribe of the Sioux nation, who took them up the river until about the first of May, when they reached some falls, which Hennepin christened Falls of St. Anthony in honor of his patron saint. Here they took the land, and traveling nearly two hundred miles to the northwest, brought them to their villages. Here they were kept about three months, were treated kindly by their captors, and at the end of that time, were met by a band of Frenchmen,

BUFFALO HUNT.

headed by one Seur de Luth, who, in pursuit of trade and game, had penetrated thus far by the route of Lake Superior; and with these fellow-countrymen Hennepin and his companions were allowed to return to the borders of civilized life in November, 1680, just after LaSalle had returned to the wilderness on his second trip. Hennepin soon after went to France, where he published an account of his adventures.

The Mississippi was first discovered by De Soto in April, 1541, in his vain endeavor to find gold and precious gems. In the following Spring, De Soto, weary with hope long deferred, and worn out with his wanderings, he fell a victim to disease, and on the 21st of May died. His followers, reduced by fatigue and disease to less than three hundred men, wandered about the country nearly a year, in the vain endeavor to rescue themselves by land, and finally constructed seven small vessels, called brigantines, in which they embarked, and descending the river, supposing it would lead them to the sea, in July they came to the sea (Gulf of Mexico), and by September reached the Island of Cuba.

They were the first to see the great outlet of the Mississippi; but, being so weary and discouraged, made no attempt to claim the country, and hardly had an intelligent idea of what they had passed through.

To La Salle, the intrepid explorer, belongs the honor of giving the first account of the mouths of the river. His great desire was to possess this entire country for his king, and in January, 1682, he and his band of explorers left the shores of Lake Michigan on their third attempt, crossed the portage, passed down the Illinois River, and on the 6th of February, reached the banks of the Mississippi.

On the 13th they commenced their downward course, which they pursued with but one interruption, until upon the 6th of March they discovered the three great passages by which the river discharges its waters into the gulf. La Salle thus narrates the event:

" We landed on the bank of the most western channel, about three leagues (nine miles) from its mouth. On the seventh, M. de LaSalle went to reconnoiter the shores of the neighboring sea, and M. de Tonti meanwhile examined the great middle channel. They found the main outlets beautiful, large and deep On the 8th we reascended the river, a little above its confluence with the sea, to find a dry place beyond the reach of inundations. The elevation of the North Pole was here about twenty-seven degrees. Here we prepared a column and a cross, and to the column were affixed the arms of France with this inscription:

Louis Le Grand, Roi De France et de Navarre, regne , Le neuvieme Avril, 1682

The whole party, under arms, chanted the *Te Deum*, and then, after a salute and cries of *"Vive le Roi,"* the column was erected by M. de La Salle, who, standing near it, proclaimed in a loud voice the authority of the King of France. LaSalle returned and laid the foundations of the Mississippi settlements in Illinois, thence he proceeded to France, where another expedition was fitted out, of which he was commander, and in two succeeding voyages failed to find the outlet of the river by sailing along the shore of the gulf. On his third voyage he was killed, through the treachery of his followers, and the object of his expeditions was not accomplished until 1699, when D'Iberville, under the authority of the crown, discovered, on the second of March, by way of the sea, the mouth of the "Hidden River." This majestic stream was called by the natives "*Malbouchia*," and by the Spaniards, "*la Palissade*," from the great

TRAPPING.

number of trees about its mouth. After traversing the several outlets, and satisfying himself as to its certainty, he erected a fort near its western outlet, and returned to France.

An avenue of trade was now opened out which was fully improved. In 1718, New Orleans was laid out and settled by some European colonists. In 1762, the colony was made over to Spain, to be regained by France under the consulate of Napoleon. In 1803, it was purchased by the United States for the sum of fifteen million dollars, and the territory of Louisiana and commerce of the Mississippi River came under the charge of the United States. Although LaSalle's labors ended in defeat and death, he had not worked and suffered in vain. He had thrown open to France and the world an immense and most valuable country; had established several ports, and laid the foundations of more than one settlement there. " Peoria. Kaskaskia and Cahokia, are to this day monuments of LaSalle's labors; for, though he had founded neither of them (unless Peoria, which was built nearly upon the site of Fort Crevecœur,) it was by those whom he led into the West that these places were peopled and civilized. He was, if not the discoverer, the first settler of the Mississippi Valley, and as such deserves to be known and honored."

The French early improved the opening made for them. Before the year 1698, the Rev. Father Gravier began a mission among the Illinois, and founded Kaskaskia. For some time this was merely a missionary station, where none but natives resided, it being one of three such villages, the other two being Cahokia and Peoria. What is known of these missions is learned from a letter written by Father Gabriel Marest, dated "Aux Cascaskias, autrement dit de l Immaculate Conception de la Sainte Vierge, le 9 Novembre, 1712 " Soon after the founding of Kaskaskia, the missionary, Pinet, gathered a flock at Cahokia, while Peoria arose near the ruins of Fort Crevecœur. This must have been about the year 1700 The post at Vincennes on the Oubache river, (pronounced Wă-bă, meaning *summer cloud moving swiftly*) was established in 1702, according to the best authorities.* It is altogether probable that on LaSalle's last trip he established the stations at Kaskaskia and Cahokia. In July, 1701, the foundations of Fort Ponchartrain were laid by De la Motte Cadillac on the Detroit River. These stations, with those established further north, were the earliest attempts to occupy the Northwest Territory. At the same time efforts were being made to occupy the Southwest, which finally culminated in the settlement and founding of the City of New Orleans by a colony from England in 1718. This was mainly accomplished through the efforts of the famous Mississippi Company, established by the notorious John Law, who so quickly arose into prominence in France, and who with his scheme so quickly and so ignominiously passed away.

From the time of the founding of these stations for fifty years the French nation were engrossed with the settlement of the lower Mississippi, and the war with the Chicasaws, who had, in revenge for repeated

* There is considerable dispute about this date, some asserting it was founded as late as 1742 When the new court house at Vincennes was erected, all authorities on the subject were carefully examined, and , /02 fixed upon as the correct date. It was accordingly engraved on the corner-stone of the court house

injuries, cut off the entire colony at Natchez. Although the company did little for Louisiana, as the entire West was then called, yet it opened the trade through the Mississippi River, and started the raising of grains indigenous to that climate. Until the year 1750, but little is known of the settlements in the Northwest, as it was not until this time that the attention of the English was called to the occupation of this portion of the New World, which they then supposed they owned. Vivier, a missionary among the Illinois, writing from "Aux Illinois," six leagues from Fort Chartres, June 8, 1750, says: "We have here whites, negroes and Indians, to say nothing of cross-breeds. There are five French villages, and three villages of the natives, within a space of twenty-one leagues situated between the Mississippi and another river called the Kaskadaid (Kaskaskias). In the five French villages are, perhaps, eleven hundred whites, three hundred blacks and some sixty red slaves or savages. The three Illinois towns do not contain more than eight hundred souls all told. Most of the French till the soil; they raise wheat, cattle, pigs and horses, and live like princes. Three times as much is produced as can be consumed; and great quantities of grain and flour are sent to New Orleans." This city was now the seaport town of the Northwest, and save in the extreme northern part, where only furs and copper ore were found, almost all the products of the country found their way to France by the mouth of the Father of Waters. In another letter, dated November 7, 1750, this same priest says: "For fifteen leagues above the mouth of the Mississippi one sees no dwellings, the ground being too low to be habitable. Thence to New Orleans, the lands are only partially occupied. New Orleans contains black, white and red, not more, I think, than twelve hundred persons. To this point come all lumber, bricks, salt-beef, tallow, tar, skins and bear's grease; and above all, pork and flour from the Illinois. These things create some commerce, as forty vessels and more have come hither this year. Above New Orleans, plantations are again met with; the most considerable is a colony of Germans, some ten leagues up the river. At Point Coupee, thirty-five leagues above the German settlement, is a fort. Along here, within five or six leagues, are not less than sixty habitations. Fifty leagues farther up is the Natchez post, where we have a garrison, who are kept prisoners through fear of the Chickasaws. Here and at Point Coupee, they raise excellent tobacco. Another hundred leagues brings us to the Arkansas, where we have also a fort and a garrison for the benefit of the river traders. * * * From the Arkansas to the Illinois, nearly five hundred leagues, there is not a settlement. There should be, however, a fort at the Oubache (Ohio), the only path by which the English can reach the Mississippi. In the Illinois country are numberless mines, but no one to work them as they deserve." Father Marest, writing from the post at Vincennes in 1812, makes the same observation. Vivier also says: "Some individuals dig lead near the surface and supply the Indians and Canada. Two Spaniards now here, who claim to be adepts, say that our mines are like those of Mexico, and that if we would dig deeper, we should find silver under the lead; and at any rate the lead is excellent. There is also in this country, beyond doubt, copper ore, as from time to time large pieces are found in the streams."

HUNTING.

At the close of the year 1750, the French occupied, in addition to the lower Mississippi posts and those in Illinois, one at Du Quesne, one at the Maumee in the country of the Miamis, and one at Sandusky in what may be termed the Ohio Valley. In the northern part of the Northwest they had stations at St. Joseph's on the St. Joseph's of Lake Michigan, at Fort Ponchartrain (Detroit), at Michillimackanac or Massillimacanac, Fox River of Green Bay, and at Sault Ste. Marie. The fondest dreams of LaSalle were now fully realized. The French alone were possessors of this vast realm, basing their claim on discovery and settlement. Another nation, however, was now turning its attention to this extensive country, and hearing of its wealth, began to lay plans for occupying it and for securing the great profits arising therefrom.

The French, however, had another claim to this country, namely, the

DISCOVERY OF THE OHIO.

This "Beautiful" river was discovered by Robert Cavalier de La-Salle in 1669, four years before the discovery of the Mississippi by Joliet and Marquette.

While LaSalle was at his trading post on the St. Lawrence, he found leisure to study nine Indian dialects, the chief of which was the Iroquois. He not only desired to facilitate his intercourse in trade, but he longed to travel and explore the unknown regions of the West. An incident soon occurred which decided him to fit out an exploring expedition.

While conversing with some Senecas, he learned of a river called the Ohio, which rose in their country and flowed to the sea, but at such a distance that it required eight months to reach its mouth   In this statement the Mississippi and its tributaries were considered as one stream. LaSalle believing, as most of the French at that period did, that the great rivers flowing west emptied into the Sea of California, was anxious to embark in the enterprise of discovering a route across the continent to the commerce of China and Japan.

He repaired at once to Quebec to obtain the approval of the Governor. His eloquent appeal prevailed. The Governor and the Intendant, Talon, issued letters patent authorizing the enterprise, but made no provision to defray the expenses. At this juncture the seminary of St. Sulpice decided to send out missionaries in connection with the expedition, and LaSalle offering to sell his improvements at LaChine to raise money, the offer was accepted by the Superior, and two thousand eight hundred dollars were raised, with which LaSalle purchased four canoes and the necessary supplies for the outfit.

On the 6th of July, 1669, the party, numbering twenty-four persons, embarked in seven canoes on the St. Lawrence, two additional canoes carried the Indian guides. In three days they were gliding over the bosom of Lake Ontario. Their guides conducted them directly to the Seneca village on the bank of the Genesee, in the vicinity of the present City of Rochester, New York. Here they expected to procure guides to conduct them to the Ohio, but in this they were disappointed.

The Indians seemed unfriendly to the enterprise. LaSalle suspected that the Jesuits had prejudiced their minds against his plans. After waiting a month in the hope of gaining their object, they met an Indian

from the Iroquois colony at the head of Lake Ontario, who assured them
that they could there find guides, and offered to conduct them thence.

On their way they passed the mouth of the Niagara River, when they
heard for the first time the distant thunder of the cataract. Arriving

IROQUOIS CHIEF.

among the Iroquois, they met with a friendly reception, and learned
from a Shawanee prisoner that they could reach the Ohio in six weeks.
Delighted with the unexpected good fortune, they made ready to resume
their journey; but just as they were about to start they heard of the
arrival of two Frenchmen in a neighboring village. One of them proved
to be Louis Joliet, afterwards famous as an explorer in the West. He

had been sent by the Canadian Government to explore the copper mines on Lake Superior, but had failed, and was on his way back to Quebec. He gave the missionaries a map of the country he had explored in the lake region, together with an account of the condition of the Indians in that quarter. This induced the priests to determine on leaving the expedition and going to Lake Superior LaSalle warned them that the Jesuits were probably occupying that field, and that they would meet with a cold reception. Nevertheless they persisted in their purpose, and after worship on the lake shore, parted from LaSalle. On arriving at Lake Superior, they found, as LaSalle had predicted, the Jesuit Fathers, Marquette and Dablon, occupying the field.

These zealous disciples of Loyola informed them that they wanted no assistance from St Sulpice, nor from those who made him their patron saint; and thus repulsed, they returned to Montreal the following June without having made a single discovery or converted a single Indian.

After parting with the priests, LaSalle went to the chief Iroquois village at Onondaga, where he obtained guides, and passing thence to a tributary of the Ohio south of Lake Erie, he descended the latter as far as the falls at Louisville. Thus was the Ohio discovered by LaSalle, the persevering and successful French explorer of the West, in 1669.

The account of the latter part of his journey is found in an anonymous paper, which purports to have been taken from the lips of LaSalle himself during a subsequent visit to Paris. In a letter written to Count Frontenac in 1667, shortly after the discovery, he himself says that he discovered the Ohio and descended it to the falls. This was regarded as an indisputable fact by the French authorities, who claimed the Ohio Valley upon another ground. When Washington was sent by the colony of Virginia in 1753, to demand of Gordeur de St Pierre why the French had built a fort on the Monongahela, the haughty commandant at Quebec replied: " We claim the country on the Ohio by virtue of the discoveries of LaSalle, and will not give it up to the English. Our orders are to make prisoners of every Englishman found trading in the Ohio Valley."

ENGLISH EXPLORATIONS AND SETTLEMENTS.

When the new year of 1750 broke in upon the Father of Waters and the Great Northwest, all was still wild save at the French posts already described. In 1749, when the English first began to think seriously about sending men into the West, the greater portion of the States of Indiana, Ohio, Illinois, Michigan, Wisconsin, and Minnesota were yet under the dominion of the red men. The English knew, however, pretty conclusively of the nature of the wealth of these wilds. As early as 1710, Governor Spotswood, of Virginia, had commenced movements to secure the country west of the Alleghenies to the English crown. In Pennsylvania, Governor Keith and James Logan, secretary of the province, from 1719 to 1731, represented to the powers of England the necessity of securing the Western lands. Nothing was done, however, by that power save to take some diplomatic steps to secure the claims of Britain to this unexplored wilderness.

England had from the outset claimed from the Atlantic to the Pacific, on the ground that the discovery of the seacoast and its possession was a discovery and possession of the country, and, as is well known, her grants to the colonies extended "from sea to sea." This was not all her claim. She had purchased from the Indian tribes large tracts of land. This latter was also a strong argument. As early as 1684, Lord Howard, Governor of Virginia, held a treaty with the six nations. These were the great Northern Confederacy, and comprised at first the Mohawks, Oneidas, Onondagas, Cayugas, and Senecas. Afterward the Tuscaroras were taken into the confederacy, and it became known as the SIX NATIONS. They came under the protection of the mother country, and again in 1701, they repeated the agreement, and in September, 1726, a formal deed was drawn up and signed by the chiefs. The validity of this claim has often been disputed, but never successfully. In 1744, a purchase was made at Lancaster, Pennsylvania, of certain lands within the "Colony of Virginia," for which the Indians received £200 in gold and a like sum in goods, with a promise that, as settlements increased, more should be paid. The Commissioners from Virginia were Colonel Thomas Lee and Colonel William Beverly. As settlements extended, the promise of more pay was called to mind, and Mr. Conrad Weiser was sent across the mountains with presents to appease the savages. Col. Lee, and some Virginians accompanied him with the intention of sounding the Indians upon their feelings regarding the English. They were not satisfied with their treatment, and plainly told the Commissioners why. The English did not desire the cultivation of the country, but the monopoly of the Indian trade. In 1748, the Ohio Company was formed, and petitioned the king for a grant of land beyond the Alleghenies. This was granted, and the government of Virginia was ordered to grant to them a half million acres, two hundred thousand of which were to be located at once. Upon the 12th of June, 1749, 800,000 acres from the line of Canada north and west was made to the Loyal Company, and on the 29th of October, 1751, 100,000 acres were given to the Greenbriar Company. All this time the French were not idle. They saw that, should the British gain a foothold in the West, especially upon the Ohio, they might not only prevent the French settling upon it, but in time would come to the lower posts and so gain possession of the whole country. Upon the 10th of May, 1774, Vaudreuil, Governor of Canada and the French possessions, well knowing the consequences that must arise from allowing the English to build trading posts in the Northwest, seized some of their frontier posts, and to further secure the claim of the French to the West, he, in 1749, sent Louis Celeron with a party of soldiers to plant along the Ohio River, in the mounds and at the mouths of its principal tributaries, plates of lead, on which were inscribed the claims of France. These were heard of in 1752, and within the memory of residents now living along the "Oyo," as the beautiful river was called by the French. One of these plates was found with the inscription partly defaced. It bears date August 16, 1749, and a copy of the inscription with particular account of the discovery of the plate, was sent by DeWitt Clinton to the American Antiquarian Society, among whose journals it may now be found.* These measures did not, however, deter the English from going on with their explorations, and though neither party resorted to arms, yet the conflict was gathering, and it was only a question of time when the storm would burst upon the frontier settlements. In 1750, Christopher Gist was sent by the Ohio Company to examine its lands. He went to a village of the Twigtwees, on the Miami, about one hundred and fifty miles above its mouth He afterward spoke of it as very populous. From there he went down the Ohio River nearly to the falls at the present City of Louisville, and in November he commenced a survey of the Company's lands During the Winter, General Andrew Lewis performed a similar work for the Greenbriar Company. Meanwhile the French were busy in preparing their forts for defense, and in opening roads, and also sent a small party of soldiers to keep the Ohio clear. This party, having heard of the English post on the Miami River, early in 1652, assisted by the Ottawas and Chippewas, attacked it, and, after a severe battle, in which fourteen of the natives were killed and others wounded, captured the garrison. (They were probably garrisoned in a block house). The traders were carried away to Canada, and one account says several were burned. This fort or post was called by the English Pickawillany. A memorial of the king's ministers refers to it as " Pickawillanes, in the center of the territory between the Ohio and the Wabash. The name is probably some variation of Pickaway or Picqua in 1773, written by Rev. David Jones Pickaweke."

* The following is a translation of the inscription on the plate "In the year 1749, reign of Louis XV, King of France, we, Celeron, commandant of a detachment by Monsieur the Marquis of Gallisoniere, commander-in-chief of New France, to establish tranquility in certain Indian villages of these cantons, have buried this plate at the confluence of the Toradakoin, this twenty-ninth of July, near the river Ohio, otherwise Beautiful River, as a monument of renewal of possession which we have taken of the said river, and all its tributaries, inasmuch as the preceding Kings of France have enjoyed it, and maintained it by their arms and treaties, especially by those of Ryswick, Utrecht, and Aix La Chapelle."

This was the first blood shed between the French and English, and occurred near the present City of Piqua, Ohio, or at least at a point about forty-seven miles north of Dayton. Each nation became now more interested in the progress of events in the Northwest. The English determined to purchase from the Indians a title to the lands they wished to occupy, and Messrs. Fry (afterward Commander-in-chief over Washington at the commencement of the French War of 1775–1763), Lomax and Patton were sent in the Spring of 1752 to hold a conference with the natives at Logstown to learn what they objected to in the treaty of Lancaster already noticed, and to settle all difficulties. On the 9th of June, these Commissioners met the red men at Logstown, a little village on the north bank of the Ohio, about seventeen miles below the site of Pittsburgh. Here had been a trading point for many years, but it was abandoned by the Indians in 1750. At first the Indians declined to recognize the treaty of Lancaster, but, the Commissioners taking aside Montour, the interpreter, who was a son of the famous Catharine Montour, and a chief among the six nations, induced him to use his influence in their favor This he did, and upon the 13th of June they all united in signing a deed, confirming the Lancaster treaty in its full extent, consenting to a settlement of the southeast of the Ohio, and guaranteeing that it should not be disturbed by them. These were the means used to obtain the first treaty with the Indians in the Ohio Valley.

Meanwhile the powers beyond the sea were trying to out-manœuvre each other, and were professing to be at peace. The English generally outwitted the Indians, and failed in many instances to fulfill their contracts. They thereby gained the ill-will of the red men, and further increased the feeling by failing to provide them with arms and ammunition. Said an old chief, at Easton, in 1758: " The Indians on the Ohio left you because of your own fault. When we heard the French were coming, we asked you for help and arms, but we did not get them The French came, they treated us kindly, and gained our affections. The Governor of Virginia settled on our lands for his own benefit, and, when we wanted help, forsook us."

At the beginning of 1653, the English thought they had secured by title the lands in the West, but the French had quietly gathered cannon and military stores to be in readiness for the expected blow The English made other attempts to ratify these existing treaties, but not until the Summer could the Indians be gathered together to discuss the plans of the French. They had sent messages to the French, warning them away; but they replied that they intended to complete the chain of forts already begun, and would not abandon the field.

Soon after this, no satisfaction being obtained from the Ohio regarding the positions and purposes of the French, Governor Dinwiddie of Virginia determined to send to them another messenger and learn from them, if possible, their intentions. For this purpose he selected a young man, a surveyor, who, at the early age of nineteen, had received the rank of major, and who was thoroughly posted regarding frontier life. This personage was no other than the illustrious George Washington, who then held considerable interest in Western lands. He was at this time just twenty-two years of age. Taking Gist as his guide, the two, accompanied by four servitors, set out on their perilous march. They left Will's Creek on the 10th of November, 1753, and on the 22d reached the Monongahela, about ten miles above the fork. From there they went to Logstown, where Washington had a long conference with the chiefs of the Six Nations. From them he learned the condition of the French, and also heard of their determination not to come down the river till the following Spring. The Indians were non-committal, as they were afraid to turn either way, and, as far as they could, desired to remain neutral. Washington, finding nothing could be done with them, went on to Venango, an old Indian town at the mouth of French Creek. Here the French had a fort, called Fort Machault. Through the rum and flattery of the French, he nearly lost all his Indian followers. Finding nothing of importance here, he pursued his way amid great privations, and on the 11th of December reached the fort at the head of French Creek. Here he delivered Governor Dinwiddie's letter, received his answer, took his observations, and on the 16th set out upon his return journey with no one but Gist, his guide, and a few Indians who still remained true to him, notwithstanding the endeavors of the French to retain them. Their homeward journey was one of great peril and suffering from the cold, yet they reached home in safety on the 6th of January, 1754.

From the letter of St. Pierre, commander of the French fort, sent by Washington to Governor Dinwiddie, it was learned that the French would not give up without a struggle. Active preparations were at once made in all the English colonies for the coming conflict, while the French finished the fort at Venango and strengthened their lines of fortifications, and gathered their forces to be in readiness.

The Old Dominion was all alive. Virginia was the center of great activities, volunteers were called for, and from all the neighboring colonies men rallied to the conflict, and everywhere along the Potomac men were enlisting under the Governor's proclamation—which promised two hundred thousand acres on the Ohio. Along this river they were gathering as far as Will's Creek, and far beyond this point, whither Trent had come for assistance for his little band of forty-one men, who were working away in hunger and want, to fortify that point at the fork of the Ohio, to which both parties were looking with deep interest

"The first birds of Spring filled the air with their song; the swift river rolled by the Allegheny hillsides, swollen by the melting snows of Spring and the April showers. The leaves were appearing; a few Indian scouts were seen, but no enemy seemed near at hand; and all was so quiet, that Frazier, an old Indian scout and trader, who had been left by Trent in command, ventured to his home at the mouth of Turtle Creek, ten miles up the Monongahela But, though all was so quiet in that wilderness, keen eyes had seen the low intrenchment rising at the fork, and swift feet had borne the news of it up the river; and upon the morning of the 17th of April, Ensign Ward, who then had charge of it, saw upon the Allegheny a sight that made his heart sink—sixty batteaux and three hundred canoes filled with men, and laden deep with cannon and stores. * * * That evening he supped with his captor, Contrecœur, and the next day he was bowed off by the Frenchman, and with his men and tools, marched up the Monongahela."

The French and Indian war had begun. The treaty of Aix la Chapelle, in 1748, had left the boundaries between the French and English possessions unsettled, and the events already narrated show the French were determined to hold the country watered by the Mississippi and its tributaries; while the English laid claims to the country by virtue of the discoveries of the Cabots, and claimed all the country from Newfoundland to Florida, extending from the Atlantic to the Pacific. The first decisive blow had now been struck, and the first attempt of the English, through the Ohio Company, to occupy these lands, had resulted disastrously to them. The French and Indians immediately completed the fortifications begun at the Fork, which they had so easily captured, and when completed gave to the fort the name of DuQuesne. Washington was at Will's Creek when the news of the capture of the fort arrived. He at once departed to recapture it. On his way he entrenched himself at a place called the "Meadows," where he erected a fort called by him Fort Necessity. From there he surprised and captured a force of French and Indians marching against him, but was soon after attacked in his fort by a much superior force, and was obliged to yield on the morning of July 4th. He was allowed to return to Virginia.

The English Government immediately planned four campaigns; one against Fort DuQuesne; one against Nova Scotia; one against Fort Niagara, and one against Crown Point. These occurred during 1755-6, and were not successful in driving the French from their possessions. The expedition against Fort DuQuesne was led by the famous General Braddock, who, refusing to listen to the advice of Washington and those acquainted with Indian warfare, suffered such an inglorious defeat. This occurred on the morning of July 9th, and is generally known as the battle of Monongahela, or "Braddock's Defeat." The war continued with various vicissitudes through the years 1756-7; when, at the commencement of 1758, in accordance with the plans of William Pitt, then Secretary of State, afterwards Lord Chatham, active preparations were made to carry on the war. Three expeditions were planned for this year: one, under General Amherst, against Louisburg; another, under Abercrombie, against Fort Ticonderoga; and a third, under General Forbes, against Fort DuQuesne. On the 26th of July, Louisburg surrendered after a desperate resistance of more than forty days, and the eastern part of the Canadian possessions fell into the hands of the British. Abercrombie captured Fort Frontenac, and when the expedition against Fort DuQuesne, of which Washington had the active command, arrived there, it was found in flames and deserted. The English at once took possession, rebuilt the fort, and in honor of their illustrious statesman, changed the name to Fort Pitt.

The great object of the campaign of 1759, was the reduction of Canada. General Wolfe was to lay siege to Quebec, Amherst was to reduce Ticonderoga and Crown Point, and General Prideaux was to capture Niagara. This latter place was taken in July, but the gallant Prideaux lost his life in the attempt. Amherst captured Ticonderoga and Crown Point without a blow; and Wolfe, after making the memorable ascent to the Plains of Abraham, on September 13th, defeated Montcalm, and on the 18th, the city capitulated. In this engagement Montcalm and Wolfe both lost their lives. De Levi, Montcalm's successor, marched to Sillery, three miles above the city, with the purpose of defeating the English, and there, on the 28th of the following April, was fought one of the bloodiest battles of the French and Indian War. It resulted in the defeat of the French, and the fall of the City of Montreal. The Governor signed a capitulation by which the whole of Canada was surrendered to the English. This practically concluded the war, but it was not until 1763 that the treaties of peace between France and England were signed. This was done on the 10th of February of that year, and under its provisions all the country east of the Mississippi and north of the Iberville River, in Louisiana, were ceded to England. At the same time Spain ceded Florida to Great Britain.

On the 13th of September, 1760, Major Robert Rogers was sent from Montreal to take charge of Detroit, the only remaining French post in the territory. He arrived there on the 19th of November, and summoned the place to surrender. At first the commander of the post, Beletre, refused, but on the 29th, hearing of the continued defeat of the

French arms, surrendered. Rogers remained there until December 23d under the personal protection of the celebrated chief, Pontiac, to whom, no doubt, he owed his safety. Pontiac had come here to inquire the purposes of the English in taking possession of the country. He was assured that they came simply to trade with the natives, and did not desire their country. This answer conciliated the savages, and did much to insure the safety of Rogers and his party during their stay, and while on their journey home.

Rogers set out for Fort Pitt on December 23, and was just one month on the way. His route was from Detroit to Maumee, thence across the present State of Ohio directly to the fort. This was the common trail of the Indians in their journeys from Sandusky to the fork of the Ohio. It went from Fort Sandusky, where Sandusky City now is, crossed the Huron river, then called Bald Eagle Creek, to "Mohickon John's Town" on Mohickon Creek, the northern branch of White Woman's River, and thence crossed to Beaver's Town, a Delaware town on what is now Sandy Creek. At Beaver's Town were probably one hundred and fifty warriors, and not less than three thousand acres of cleared land. From there the track went up Sandy Creek to and across Big Beaver, and up the Ohio to Logstown, thence on to the fork.

The Northwest Territory was now entirely under the English rule. New settlements began to be rapidly made, and the promise of a large trade was speedily manifested. Had the British carried out their promises with the natives none of those savage butcheries would have been perpetrated, and the country would have been spared their recital.

The renowned chief, Pontiac, was one of the leading spirits in these atrocities. We will now pause in our narrative, and notice the leading events in his life. The earliest authentic information regarding this noted Indian chief is learned from an account of an Indian trader named Alexander Henry, who, in the Spring of 1761, penetrated his domains as far as Missillimacnac. Pontiac was then a great friend of the French, but a bitter foe of the English, whom he considered as encroaching on his hunting grounds. Henry was obliged to disguise himself as a Canadian to insure safety, but was discovered by Pontiac, who bitterly reproached him and the English for their attempted subjugation of the West. He declared that no treaty had been made with them; no presents sent them, and that he would resent any possession of the West by that nation. He was at the time about fifty years of age, tall and dignified, and was civil and military ruler of the Ottawas, Ojibwas and Pottawatamies.

The Indians, from Lake Michigan to the borders of North Carolina, were united in this feeling, and at the time of the treaty of Paris, ratified February 10, 1763, a general conspiracy was formed to fall suddenly

PONTIAC, THE OTTAWA CHIEFTAIN.

upon the frontier British posts, and with one blow strike every man dead. Pontiac was the marked leader in all this, and was the commander of the Chippewas, Ottawas, Wyandots, Miamis, Shawanese, Delawares and Mingoes, who had, for the time, laid aside their local quarrels to unite in this enterprise.

The blow came, as near as can now be ascertained, on May 7, 1763. Nine British posts fell, and the Indians drank, " scooped up in the hollow of joined hands," the blood of many a Briton.

Pontiac's immediate field of action was the garrison at Detroit. Here, however, the plans were frustrated by an Indian woman disclosing the plot the evening previous to his arrival. Everything was carried out, however, according to Pontiac's plans until the moment of action, when Major Gladwyn, the commander of the post, stepping to one of the Indian chiefs, suddenly drew aside his blanket and disclosed the concealed musket. Pontiac, though a brave man, turned pale and trembled. He saw his plan was known, and that the garrison were prepared. He endeavored to exculpate himself from any such intentions ; but the guilt was evident, and he and his followers were dismissed with a severe reprimand, and warned never to again enter the walls of the post.

Pontiac at once laid siege to the fort, and until the treaty of peace between the British and the Western Indians, concluded in August, 1764, continued to harass and besiege the fortress. He organized a regular commissariat department, issued bills of credit written out on bark, which, to his credit, it may be stated, were punctually redeemed. At the conclusion of the treaty, in which it seems he took 'no part, he went further south, living many years among the Illinois.

He had given up all hope of saving his country and race. After a time he endeavored to unite the Illinois tribe and those about St. Louis in a war with the whites. His efforts were fruitless, and only ended in a quarrel between himself and some Kaskaskia Indians, one of whom soon afterwards killed him. His death was, however, avenged by the northern Indians, who nearly exterminated the Illinois in the wars which followed.

Had it not been for the treachery of a few of his followers, his plan for the extermination of the whites, a masterly one, would undoubtedly have been carried out.

It was in the Spring of the year following Rogers' visit that Alexander Henry went to Missillimacnac, and everywhere found the strongest feelings against the English, who had not carried out their promises, and were doing nothing to conciliate the natives. Here he met the chief, Pontiac, who, after conveying to him in a speech the idea that their French father would awake soon and utterly destroy his enemies. said : " Englishman, although you have conquered the French, you have not yet conquered us! We are not your slaves! These lakes, these woods, these mountains, were left us by our ancestors. They are our inheritance, and we will part with them to none. Your nation supposes that we, like the white people, can not live without bread and pork and beef. But you ought to know that He, the Great Spirit and Master of Life, has provided food for us upon these broad lakes and in these mountains."

He then spoke of the fact that no treaty had been made with them, no presents sent them, and that he and his people were yet for war. Such were the feelings of the Northwestern Indians immediately after the English took possession of their country. These feelings were no doubt encouraged by the Canadians and French, who hoped that yet the French arms might prevail. The treaty of Paris, however, gave to the English the right to this vast domain, and active preparations were going on to occupy it and enjoy its trade and emoluments.

In 1762, France, by a secret treaty, ceded Louisiana to Spain, to prevent it falling into the hands of the English, who were becoming masters of the entire West. The next year the treaty of Paris, signed at Fontainbleau, gave to the English the domain of the country in question. Twenty years after, by the treaty of peace between the United States and England, that part of Canada lying south and west of the Great Lakes, comprehending a large territory which is the subject of these sketches, was acknowledged to be a portion of the United States; and twenty years still later, in 1803, Louisiana was ceded by Spain back to France, and by France sold to the United States.

In the half century, from the building of the Fort of Crevecœur by LaSalle, in 1680, up to the erection of Fort Chartres, many French settlements had been made in that quarter. These have already been noticed, being those at St. Vincent (Vincennes), Kohokia or Cahokia, Kaskaskia and Prairie du Rocher, on the American Bottom, a large tract of rich alluvial soil in Illinois, on the Mississippi, opposite the site of St. Louis.

By the treaty of Paris, the regions east of the Mississippi, including all these and other towns of the Northwest, were given over to England; but they do not appear to have been taken possession of until 1765, when Captain Stirling, in the name of the Majesty of England, established himself at Fort Chartres bearing with him the proclamation of General Gage, dated December 30, 1764, which promised religious freedom to all Catholics who worshiped here, and a right to leave the country with their effects if they wished, or to remain with the privileges of Englishmen. It was shortly after the occupancy of the West by the British that the war with Pontiac opened. It is already noticed in the sketch of that chieftain. By it many a Briton lost his life, and many a frontier settlement in its infancy ceased to exist. This was not ended until the year 1764, when, failing to capture Detroit, Niagara and Fort Pitt, his confederacy became disheartened, and, receiving no aid from the French, Pontiac abandoned the enterprise and departed to the Illinois, among whom he afterward lost his life.

As soon as these difficulties were definitely settled, settlers began rapidly to survey the country and prepare for occupation. During the year 1770, a number of persons from Virginia and other British provinces explored and marked out nearly all the valuable lands on the Monongahela and along the banks of the Ohio as far as the Little Kanawha. This was followed by another exploring expedition, in which George Washington was a party. The latter, accompanied by Dr. Craik, Capt. Crawford and others, on the 20th of October, 1770, descended the Ohio from Pittsburgh to the mouth of the Kanawha; ascended that stream about fourteen miles, marked out several large tracts of land, shot several buffalo, which were then abundant in the Ohio Valley, and returned to the fort.

Pittsburgh was at this time a trading post, about which was clustered a village of some twenty houses, inhabited by Indian traders. This same year, Capt. Pittman visited Kaskaskia and its neighboring villages. He found there about sixty-five resident families, and at Cahokia only forty-five dwellings. At Fort Chartres was another small settlement, and at Detroit the garrison were quite prosperous and strong. For a year or two settlers continued to locate near some of these posts, generally Fort Pitt or Detroit, owing to the fears of the Indians, who still maintained some feelings of hatred to the English. The trade from the posts was quite good, and from those in Illinois large quantities of pork and flour found their way to the New Orleans market. At this time the policy of the British Government was strongly opposed to the extension of the colonies west. In 1763, the King of England forbade, by royal proclamation, his colonial subjects from making a settlement beyond the sources of the rivers which fall into the Atlantic Ocean. At the instance of the Board of Trade, measures were taken to prevent the settlement without the limits prescribed, and to retain the commerce within easy reach of Great Britain.

The commander-in-chief of the king's forces wrote in 1769: " In the course of a few years necessity will compel the colonists, should they extend their settlements west, to provide manufactures of some kind for themselves, and when all connection upheld by commerce with the mother country ceases, an *independency* in their government will soon follow."

In accordance with this policy, Gov. Gage issued a proclamation in 1772, commanding the inhabitants of Vincennes to abandon their settlements and join some of the Eastern English colonies. To this they strenuously objected, giving good reasons therefor, and were allowed to remain. The strong opposition to this policy of Great Britain led to its change, and to such a course as to gain the attachment of the French population. In December, 1773, influential citizens of Quebec petitioned the king for an extension of the boundary lines of that province, which was granted, and Parliament passed an act on June 2, 1774, extending the boundary so as to include the territory lying within the present States of Ohio, Indiana, Illinois and Michigan.

In consequence of the liberal policy pursued by the British Government toward the French settlers in the West, they were disposed to favor that nation in the war which soon followed with the colonies; but the early alliance between France and America soon brought them to the side of the war for independence.

In 1774, Gov. Dunmore, of Virginia, began to encourage emigration to the Western lands. He appointed magistrates at Fort Pitt under the pretense that the fort was under the government of that commonwealth. One of these justices, John Connelly, who possessed a tract of land in the Ohio Valley, gathered a force of men and garrisoned the fort, calling it Fort Dunmore. This and other parties were formed to select sites for settlements, and often came in conflict with the Indians, who yet claimed portions of the valley, and several battles followed. These ended in the famous battle of Kanawha in July, where the Indians were defeated and driven across the Ohio

During the years 1775 and 1776, by the operations of land companies and the perseverance of individuals, several settlements were firmly established between the Alleghanies and the Ohio River, and western land speculators were busy in Illinois and on the Wabash. At a council held in Kaskaskia on July 5, 1773, an association of English traders, calling themselves the "Illinois Land Company," obtained from ten chiefs of the Kaskaskia, Cahokia and Peoria tribes two large tracts of land lying on the east side of the Mississippi River south of the Illinois. In 1775, a merchant from the Illinois Country, named Viviat, came to Post Vincennes as the agent of the association called the "Wabash Land Company." On the 8th of October he obtained from eleven Piankeshaw chiefs, a deed for 37,497,600 acres of land. This deed was signed by the grantors, attested by a number of the inhabitants of Vincennes, and afterward recorded in the office of a notary public at Kaskaskia. This and other land companies had extensive schemes for the colonization of the West; but all were frustrated by the breaking out of the Revolution. On the 20th of April, 1780, the two companies named consolidated under the name of the "United Illinois and Wabash Land Company." They afterward made strenuous efforts to have these grants sanctioned by Congress, but all signally failed.

When the War of the Revolution commenced, Kentucky was an unorganized country, though there were several settlements within her borders.

In Hutchins' Topography of Virginia, it is stated that at that time " Kaskaskia contained 80 houses, and nearly 1,000 white and black inhabitants — the whites being a little the more numerous. Cahokia contains 50 houses and 300 white inhabitants, and 80 negroes. There were east of the Mississippi River, about the year 1771 "—when these observations were made — " 300 white men capable of bearing arms, and 230 negroes."

From 1775 until the expedition of Clark, nothing is recorded and nothing known of these settlements, save what is contained in a report made by a committee to Congress in June, 1778. From it the following extract is made :

"Near the mouth of the River Kaskaskia, there is a village which appears to have contained nearly eighty families from the beginning of the late revolution. There are twelve families in a small village at la Prairie du Rochers, and near fifty families at the Kahokia Village. There are also four or five families at Fort Chartres and St. Philips, which is five miles further up the river."

St. Louis had been settled in February, 1764, and at this time contained, including its neighboring towns, over six hundred whites and one hundred and fifty negroes. It must be remembered that all the country west of the Mississippi was now under French rule, and remained so until ceded again to Spain, its original owner, who afterwards sold it and the country including New Orleans to the United States. At Detroit there were, according to Capt. Carver, who was in the Northwest from 1766 to 1768, more than one hundred houses, and the river was settled for more than twenty miles, although poorly cultivated—the people being engaged in the Indian trade. This old town has a history, which we will here relate.

It is the oldest town in the Northwest, having been founded by Antoine de Lamotte Cadillac, in 1701. It was laid out in the form of an oblong square, of two acres in length, and an acre and a half in width. As described by A. D. Frazer, who first visited it and became a permanent resident of the place, in 1778, it comprised within its limits that space between Mr. Palmer's store (Conant Block) and Capt. Perkins' house (near the Arsenal building), and extended back as far as the public barn, and was bordered in front by the Detroit River. It was surrounded by oak and cedar pickets, about fifteen feet long, set in the ground, and had four gates — east, west, north and south. Over the first three of these gates were block houses provided with four guns apiece, each a six-pounder. Two six-gun batteries were planted fronting the river and in a parallel direction with the block houses. There were four streets running east and west, the main street being twenty feet wide and the rest fifteen feet, while the four streets crossing these at right angles were from ten to fifteen feet in width.

At the date spoken of by Mr. Frazer, there was no fort within the enclosure, but a citadel on the ground corresponding to the present northwest corner of Jefferson Avenue and Wayne Street. The citadel was inclosed by pickets, and within it were erected barracks of wood, two stories high, sufficient to contain ten officers, and also barracks sufficient to contain four hundred men, and a provision store built of brick. The citadel also contained a hospital and guard-house. The old town of Detroit, in 1778, contained about sixty houses, most of them one story, with a few a story and a half in height. They were all of logs, some hewn and some round. There was one building of splendid appearance, called the "King's Palace," two stories high, which stood near the east gate. It was built for Governor Hamilton, the first governor commissioned by the British. There were two guard-houses, one near the west gate and the other near the Government House. Each of the guards consisted of twenty-four men and a subaltern, who mounted regularly every morning between nine and ten o'clock. Each furnished four sentinels, who were relieved every two hours. There was also an officer of the day, who performed strict duty. Each of the gates was shut regularly at sunset, even wicket gates were shut at nine o'clock, and all the keys were delivered into the hands of the commanding officer. They were opened in the morning at sunrise. No Indian or squaw was permitted to enter town with any weapon, such as a tomahawk or a knife. It was a standing order that the Indians should deliver their arms and instruments of every kind before they were permitted to pass the sentinel, and they were restored to them on their return. No more than twenty-five Indians were allowed to enter the town at any one time, and they were admitted only at the east and west gates. At sundown the drums beat, and all the Indians were required to leave town instantly. There was a council house near the water side for the purpose of holding council with the Indians. The population of the town was about sixty families, in all about two hundred males and one hundred females. This town was destroyed by fire, all except one dwelling, in 1805. After which the present "new" town was laid out.

On the breaking out of the Revolution, the British held every post of importance in the West. Kentucky was formed as a component part of Virginia, and the sturdy pioneers of the West, alive to their interests, and recognizing the great benefits of obtaining the control of the trade in this part of the New World, held steadily to their purposes, and those within the commonwealth of Kentucky proceeded to exercise their civil privileges, by electing John Todd and Richard Gallaway, burgesses to represent them in the Assembly of the parent state. Early in September of that year (1777) the first court was held in Harrodsburg, and Col. Bowman, afterwards major, who had arrived in August, was made the commander of a militia organization which had been commenced the March previous. Thus the tree of loyalty was growing. The chief spirit in this far-out colony, who had represented her the year previous east of the mountains, was now meditating a move unequaled in its boldness. He had been watching the movements of the British throughout the Northwest, and understood their whole plan. He saw it was through their possession of the posts at Detroit, Vincennes, Kaskaskia, and other places, which would give them constant and easy access to the various Indian tribes in the Northwest, that the British intended to penetrate the country from the north and south, and annihilate the frontier fortresses. This moving, energetic man was Colonel, afterwards General, George Rogers Clark. He knew the Indians were not unanimously in accord with the English, and he was convinced that, could the British be defeated and expelled from the Northwest, the natives might be easily awed into neutrality; and by spies sent for the purpose, he satisfied himself that the enterprise against the Illinois settlements might easily succeed. Having convinced himself of the certainty of the project, he repaired to the Capital of Virginia, which place he reached on November 5th. While he was on his way, fortunately, on October 17th, Burgoyne had been defeated, and the spirits of the colonists greatly encouraged thereby. Patrick Henry was Governor of Virginia, and at once entered heartily into Clark's plans. The same plan had before been agitated in the Colonial Assemblies, but there was no one until Clark came who was sufficiently acquainted with the condition of affairs at the scene of action to be able to guide them.

Clark, having satisfied the Virginia leaders of the feasibility of his plan, received, on the 2d of January, two sets of instructions—one secret, the other open—the latter authorized him to proceed to enlist seven companies to go to Kentucky, subject to his orders, and to serve three months from their arrival in the West. The secret order authorized him to arm these troops, to procure his powder and lead of General Hand at Pittsburgh, and to proceed at once to subjugate the country.

With these instructions Clark repaired to Pittsburgh, choosing rather to raise his men west of the mountains, as he well knew all were needed in the colonies in the conflict there. He sent Col. W. B. Smith to Holston for the same purpose, but neither succeeded in raising the required number of men! The settlers in these parts were afraid to leave their own firesides exposed to a vigilant foe, and but few could be induced to join the proposed expedition With three companies and several private volunteers, Clark at length commenced his descent of the Ohio, which he navigated as far as the Falls, where he took possession of and fortified Corn Island, a small island between the present Cities of Louisville, Kentucky, and New Albany, Indiana. Remains of this fortification may yet be found. At this place he appointed Col. Bowman to meet him with such recruits as had reached Kentucky by the southern route, and as many as could be spared from the station. Here he announced to the men their real destination. Having completed his arrangements, and chosen his party, he left a small garrison upon the island, and on the 24th of June, during a total eclipse of the sun, which to them augured no good, and which fixes beyond dispute the date of starting, he with his chosen band, fell down the river. His plan was to go by water as far as Fort Massac or Massacre, and thence march direct to Kaskaskia Here he intended to surprise the garrison, and after its capture go to Cahokia, then to Vincennes, and lastly to Detroit Should he fail, he intended to march directly to the Mississippi River and cross it into the Spanish country. Before his start he received two good items of information · one that the alliance had been formed between France and the United States; and the other that the Indians throughout the Illinois country and the inhabitants, at the various frontier posts, had been led to believe by the British that the " Long Knives " or Virginians, were the most fierce, bloodthirsty and cruel savages that ever scalped a foe. With this impression on their minds, Clark saw that proper management would cause them to submit at once from fear, if surprised, and then from gratitude would become friendly if treated with unexpected leniency.

The march to Kaskaskia was accomplished through a hot July sun, and the town reached on the evening of July 4. He captured the fort near the village, and soon after the village itself by surprise, and without the loss of a single man or by killing any of the enemy. After sufficiently working upon the fears of the natives, Clark told them they were at perfect liberty to worship as they pleased, and to take whichever side of the great conflict they would, also he would protect them from any barbarity from British or Indian foe. This had the desired effect, and the inhabitants, so unexpectedly and so gratefully surprised by the unlooked for turn of affairs, at once swore allegiance to the American arms, and when Clark desired to go to Cahokia on the 6th of July, they accompanied him, and through their influence the inhabitants of the place surrendered, and gladly placed themselves under his protection. Thus the two important posts in Illinois passed from the hands of the English into the possession of Virginia.

In the person of the priest at Kaskaskia, M. Gibault, Clark found a powerful ally and generous friend.   Clark saw that, to retain possession of the Northwest and treat successfully with the Indians within its boundaries, he must establish a government for the colonies he had taken. St. Vincent, the next important post to Detroit, remained yet to be taken before the Mississippi Valley was conquered.   M. Gibault told him that he would alone, by persuasion, lead Vincennes to throw off its connection with England.   Clark gladly accepted his offer, and on the 14th of July, in company with a fellow-townsman, M. Gibault started on his mission of peace, and on the 1st of August returned with the cheerful intelligence that the post on the "Oubache" had taken the oath of allegiance to the Old Dominion.   During this interval, Clark established his courts, placed garrisons at Kaskaskia and Cahokia, successfully re-enlisted his men, sent word to have a fort, which proved the germ of Louisville, erected at the Falls of the Ohio, and dispatched Mr. Rocheblave, who had been commander at Kaskaskia, as a prisoner of war to Richmond. In October the County of Illinois was established by the Legislature of Virginia, John Todd appointed Lieutenant Colonel and Civil Governor, and in November General Clark and his men received the thanks of the Old Dominion through their Legislature. ·

In a speech a few days afterward, Clark made known fully to the natives his plans, and at its close all came forward and swore allegiance to the Long Knives.   While he was doing this Governor Hamilton, having made his various arrangements, had left Detroit and moved down the Wabash to Vincennes intending to operate from that point in reducing the Illinois posts, and then proceed on down to Kentucky and drive the rebels from the West.   Gen. Clark had, on the return of M. Gibault, dispatched Captain Helm, of Fauquier County, Virginia, with an attendant named Henry, across the Illinois prairies to command the fort. Hamilton knew nothing of the capitulation of the post, and was greatly surprised on his arrival to be confronted by Capt. Helm, who, standing at the entrance of the fort by a loaded cannon ready to fire upon his assailants, demanded upon what terms Hamilton demanded possession of the fort.   Being granted the rights of a prisoner of war, he surrendered to the British General, who could scarcely believe his eyes when he saw the force in the garrison.

Hamilton, not realizing the character of the men with whom he was contending, gave up his intended campaign for the Winter, sent his four hundred Indian warriors to prevent troops from coming down the Ohio, and to annoy the Americans in all ways, and sat quietly down to pass the Winter. Information of all these proceedings having reached Clark, he saw that immediate and decisive action was necessary, and that unless he captured Hamilton, Hamilton would capture him. Clark received the news on the 29th of January, 1779, and on February 4th, having sufficiently garrisoned Kaskaskia and Cahokia, he sent down the Mississippi a "battoe," as Major Bowman writes it, in order to ascend the Ohio and Wabash, and operate with the land forces gathering for the fray.

On the next day, Clark, with his little force of one hundred and twenty men, set out for the post, and after incredible hard marching through much mud, the ground being thawed by the incessant spring rains, on the 22d reached the fort, and being joined by his "battoe,' at once commenced the attack on the post. The aim of the American backwoodsman was unerring, and on the 24th the garrison surrendered to the intrepid boldness of Clark. The French were treated with great kindness, and gladly renewed their allegiance to Virginia. Hamilton was sent as a prisoner to Virginia, where he was kept in close confinement. During his command of the British frontier posts, he had offered prizes to the Indians for all the scalps of Americans they would bring to him, and had earned in consequence thereof the title "Hair-buyer General," by which he was ever afterward known.

Detroit was now without doubt within easy reach of the enterprising Virginian, could he but raise the necessary force. Governor Henry being apprised of this, promised him the needed reinforcement, and Clark concluded to wait until he could capture and sufficiently garrison the posts. Had Clark failed in this bold undertaking, and Hamilton succeeded in uniting the western Indians for the next Spring's campaign, the West would indeed have been swept from the Mississippi to the Allegheny Mountains, and the great blow struck, which had been contemplated from the commencement, by the British.

"But for this small army of dripping, but fearless Virginians, the union of all the tribes from Georgia to Maine against the colonies might have been effected, and the whole current of our history changed."

At this time some fears were entertained by the Colonial Governments that the Indians in the North and Northwest were inclining to the British, and under the instructions of Washington, now Commander-in-Chief of the Colonial army, and so bravely fighting for American independence, armed forces were sent against the Six Nations, and upon the Ohio frontier, Col. Bowman, acting under the same general's orders, marched against Indians within the present limits of that State. These expeditions were in the main successful, and the Indians were compelled to sue for peace.

During this same year (1779) the famous "Land Laws" of Virginia were passed   The passage of these laws was of more consequence to the pioneers of Kentucky and the Northwest than the gaining of a few Indian conflicts. These laws confirmed in main all grants made, and guaranteed to all actual settlers their rights and privileges. After providing for the settlers, the laws provided for selling the balance of the public lands at forty cents per acre   To carry the Land Laws into effect, the Legislature sent four Virginians westward to attend to the various claims, over many of which great confusion prevailed concerning their validity. These gentlemen opened their court on October 13, 1779, at St. Asaphs, and continued until April 26, 1780, when they adjourned, having decided three thousand claims. They were succeeded by the surveyor, who came in the person of Mr. George May, and assumed his duties on the 10th day of the month whose name he bore. With the opening of the next year (1780) the troubles concerning the navigation of the Mississippi commenced. The Spanish Government exacted such measures in relation to its trade as to cause the overtures made to the United States to be rejected. The American Government considered they had a right to navigate its channel. To enforce their claims, a fort was erected below the mouth of the Ohio on the Kentucky side of the river. The settlements in Kentucky were being rapidly filled by emigrants. It was during this year that the first seminary of learning was established in the West in this young and enterprising Commonwealth.

The settlers here did not look upon the building of this fort in a friendly manner, as it aroused the hostility of the Indians. Spain had been friendly to the Colonies during their struggle for independence, and though for a while this friendship appeared in danger from the refusal of the free navigation of the river, yet it was finally settled to the satisfaction of both nations.

The Winter of 1779–80 was one of the most unusually severe ones ever experienced in the West. The Indians always referred to it as the "Great Cold"   Numbers of wild animals perished, and not a few pioneers lost their lives. The following Summer a party of Canadians and Indians attacked St. Louis, and attempted to take possession of it in consequence of the friendly disposition of Spain to the revolting colonies. They met with such a determined resistance on the part of the inhabitants, even the women taking part in the battle, that they were compelled to abandon the contest. They also made an attack on the settlements in Kentucky, but, becoming alarmed in some unaccountable manner, they fled the country in great haste.

About this time arose the question in the Colonial Congress concerning the western lands claimed by Virginia, New York, Massachusetts and Connecticut   The agitation concerning this subject finally led New York, on the 19th of February, 1780, to pass a law giving to the delegates of that State in Congress the power to cede her western lands for the benefit of the United States.   This law was laid before Congress during the next month, but no steps were taken concerning it until September 6th, when a resolution passed that body calling upon the States claiming western lands to release their claims in favor of the whole body. This basis formed the union, and was the first after all of those legislative measures which resulted in the creation of the States of Ohio, Indiana, Illinois, Michigan, Wisconsin and Minnesota   In December of the same year, the plan of conquering Detroit again arose.   The conquest might have easily been effected by Clark had the necessary aid been furnished him.   Nothing decisive was done, yet the heads of the Government knew that the safety of the Northwest from British invasion lay in the capture and retention of that important post, the only unconquered one in the territory.

Before the close of the year, Kentucky was divided into the Counties of Lincoln, Fayette and Jefferson, and the act establishing the Town of Louisville was passed.   This same year is also noted in the annals of American history as the year in which occurred Arnold's treason to the United States.

Virginia, in accordance with the resolution of Congress, on the 2d day of January, 1781, agreed to yield her western lands to the United States upon certain conditions, which Congress would not accede to, and the Act of Cession, on the part of the Old Dominion, failed, nor was anything farther done until 1783.   During all that time the Colonies were busily engaged in the struggle with the mother country, and in consequence thereof but little heed was given to the western settlements. Upon the 16th of April, 1781, the first birth north of the Ohio River of American parentage occurred, being that of Mary Heckewelder, daughter of the widely known Moravian missionary, whose band of Christian Indians suffered in after years a horrible massacre by the hands of the frontier settlers, who had been exasperated by the murder of several of their neighbors, and in their rage committed, without regard to humanity, a deed which forever afterwards cast a shade of shame upon their lives. For this and kindred outrages on the part of the whites, the Indians committed many deeds of cruelty which darken the years of 1771 and 1772 in the history of the Northwest.

During the year 1782 a number of battles among the Indians and frontiersmen occurred, and between the Moravian Indians and the Wyandots.   In these, horrible acts of cruelty were practised on the captives, many of such dark deeds transpiring under the leadership of the notorious frontier outlaw, Simon Girty, whose name, as well as those of his brothers, was a terror to women and children.   These occurred chiefly in the Ohio valleys.   Cotemporary with them were several engagements in Kentucky, in which the famous Daniel Boone engaged, and who, often by his skill and knowledge of Indian warfare, saved the outposts from cruel destruc-

INDIANS ATTACKING FRONTIERSMEN.

tion. By the close of the year victory had perched upon the American banner, and on the 30th of November, provisional articles of peace had been arranged between the Commissioners of England and her uncon-querable colonies. Cornwallis had been defeated on the 19th of October preceding, and the liberty of America was assured. On the 19th of April following, the anniversary of the battle of Lexington, peace was proclaimed to the army of the United States, and on the 3d of the next September, the definite treaty which ended our revolutionary struggle was concluded. By the terms of that treaty, the boundaries of the West were as follows: On the north the line was to extend along the center of the Great Lakes; from the western point of Lake Superior to Long Lake; thence to the Lake of the Woods; thence to the head of the Mississippi River; down its center to the 31st parallel of latitude, then on that line east to the head of the Appalachicola River; down its center to its junction with the Flint; thence straight to the head of St. Mary's River, and thence down along its center to the Atlantic Ocean.

Following the cessation of hostilities with England, several posts were still occupied by the British in the North and West. Among these was Detroit, still in the hands of the enemy. Numerous engagements with the Indians throughout Ohio and Indiana occurred, upon whose lands adventurous whites would settle ere the title had been acquired by the proper treaty.

To remedy this latter evil, Congress appointed commissioners to treat with the natives and purchase their lands, and prohibited the settlement of the territory until this could be done. Before the close of the year another attempt was made to capture Detroit, which was, however, not pushed, and Virginia, no longer feeling the interest in the Northwest she had formerly done, withdrew her troops, having on the 20th of December preceding authorized the whole of her possessions to be deeded to the United States. This was done on the 1st of March following, and the Northwest Territory passed from the control of the Old Dominion. To Gen. Clark and his soldiers, however, she gave a tract of one hundred and fifty thousand acres of land, to be situated any where north of the Ohio wherever they chose to locate them. They selected the region opposite the falls of the Ohio, where is now the dilapidated village of Clarksville, about midway between the Cities of New Albany and Jeffersonville, Indiana.

While the frontier remained thus, and Gen. Haldimand at Detroit refused to evacuate alleging that he had no orders from his King to do so, settlers were rapidly gathering about the inland forts. In the Spring of 1784, Pittsburgh was regularly laid out, and from the journal of Arthur Lee, who passed through the town soon after on his way to the Indian council at Fort McIntosh, we suppose it was not very prepossessing in appearance. He says:

"Pittsburgh is inhabited almost entirely by Scots and Irish, who live in paltry log houses, and are as dirty as if in the north of Ireland or even Scotland. There is a great deal of trade carried on, the goods being bought at the vast expense of forty-five shillings per pound from Philadelphia and Baltimore. They take in the shops flour, wheat, skins and money. There are in the town four attorneys, two doctors, and not a priest of any persuasion, nor church nor chapel."

Kentucky at this time contained thirty thousand inhabitants, and was beginning to discuss measures for a separation from Virginia. A land office was opened at Louisville, and measures were adopted to take defensive precaution against the Indians who were yet, in some instances, incited to deeds of violence by the British. Before the close of this year, 1784, the military claimants of land began to occupy them, although no entries were recorded until 1787.

The Indian title to the Northwest was not yet extinguished. They held large tracts of lands, and in order to prevent bloodshed Congress adopted means for treaties with the original owners and provided for the surveys of the lands gained thereby, as well as for those north of the Ohio, now in its possession. On January 31, 1786, a treaty was made with the Wabash Indians. The treaty of Fort Stanwix had been made in 1784. That at Fort McIntosh in 1785, and through these much land was gained. The Wabash Indians, however, afterward refused to comply with the provisions of the treaty made with them, and in order to compel their adherence to its provisions, force was used. During the year 1786, the free navigation of the Mississippi came up in Congress, and caused various discussions, which resulted in no definite action, only serving to excite speculation in regard to the western lands. Congress had promised bounties of land to the soldiers of the Revolution, but owing to the unsettled condition of affairs along the Mississippi respecting its navigation, and the trade of the Northwest, that body had, in 1783, declared its inability to fulfill these promises until a treaty could be concluded between the two Governments. Before the close of the year 1786, however, it was able, through the treaties with the Indians, to allow some grants and the settlement thereon, and on the 14th of September Connecticut ceded to the General Government the tract of land known as the "Connecticut Reserve," and before the close of the following year a large tract of land north of the Ohio was sold to a company, who at once took measures to settle it. By the provisions of this grant, the company were to pay the United States one dollar per acre, subject to a deduction of one-third for bad lands and other contingencies. They received 750,000 acres, bounded on the south by the Ohio, on the east by the seventh range of townships, on the west by the sixteenth range, and, on the north by a line so drawn as to make the grant complete without the reservations. In addition to this, Congress afterward granted 100,000 acres to actual settlers, and 214,285 acres as army bounties under the resolutions of 1789 and 1790.

While Dr. Cutler, one of the agents of the company, was pressing its claims before Congress, that body was bringing into form an ordinance for the political and social organization of this Territory. When the cession was made by Virginia, in 1784, a plan was offered, but rejected. A motion had been made to strike from the proposed plan the prohibition of slavery, which prevailed. The plan was then discussed and altered, and finally passed unanimously, with the exception of South Carolina. By this proposition, the Territory was to have been divided into states

A PRAIRIE STORM.

by parallels and meridian lines. This, it was thought, would make ten states, which were to have been named as follows — beginning at the northwest corner and going southwardly: Sylvania, Michigania, Chersonesus, Assenisipia, Metropotamia, Illenoia, Saratoga, Washington, Polypotamia and Pelisipia.

There was a more serious objection to this plan than its category of names,— the boundaries. The root of the difficulty was in the resolution of Congress passed in October, 1780, which fixed the boundaries of the ceded lands to be from one hundred to one hundred and fifty miles square These resolutions being presented to the Legislatures of Virginia and Massachusetts, they desired a change, and in July, 1786, the subject was taken up in Congress, and changed to favor a division into not more than five states, and not less than three. This was approved by the State Legislature of Virginia. The subject of the Government was again taken up by Congress in 1786, and discussed throughout that year and until July, 1787, when the famous "Compact of 1787" was passed, and the foundation of the government of the Northwest laid. This compact is fully discussed and explained in the history of Illinois in this book, and to it the reader is referred.

The passage of this act and the grant to the New England Company was soon followed by an application to the Government by John Cleves Symmes, of New Jersey, for a grant of the land between the Miamis. This gentleman had visited these lands soon after the treaty of 1786, and, being greatly pleased with them, offered similar terms to those given to the New England Company The petition was referred to the Treasury Board with power to act, and a contract was concluded the following year During the Autumn the directors of the New England Company were preparing to occupy their grant the following Spring, and upon the 23d of November made arrangements for a party of forty-seven men, under the superintendency of Gen Rufus Putnam, to set forward. Six boat-builders were to leave at once, and on the first of January the surveyors and their assistants, twenty-six in number, were to meet at Hartford and proceed on their journey westward ; the remainder to follow as soon as possible Congress, in the meantime, upon the 3d of October, had ordered seven hundred troops for defense of the western settlers, and to prevent unauthorized intrusions , and two days later appointed Arthur St Clair Governor of the Territory of the Northwest.

AMERICAN SETTLEMENTS

The civil organization of the Northwest Territory was now complete, and notwithstanding the uncertainty of Indian affairs, settlers from the East began to come into the country rapidly. The New England Company sent their men during the Winter of 1787–8 pressing on over the Alleghenies by the old Indian path which had been opened into Braddock's road, and which has since been made a national turnpike from Cumberland westward. Through the weary winter days they toiled on, and by April were all gathered on the Yohiogany, where boats had been built, and at once started for the Muskingum. Here they arrived on the 7th of that month, and unless the Moravian missionaries be regarded as the pioneers of Ohio, this little band can justly claim that honor.

Gen. St. Clair, the appointed Governor of the Northwest, not having yet arrived, a set of laws were passed, written out, and published by being nailed to a tree in the embryo town, and Jonathan Meigs appointed to administer them.

Washington in writing of this, the first American settlement in the Northwest, said: "No colony in America was ever settled under such favorable auspices as that which has just commenced at Muskingum. Information, property and strength will be its characteristics. I know many of its settlers personally, and there never were men better calculated to promote the welfare of such a community."

A PIONEER DWELLING.

On the 2d of July a meeting of the directors and agents was held on the banks of the Muskingum, "for the purpose of naming the new-born city and its squares." As yet the settlement was known as the "Muskingum," but that was now changed to the name Marietta, in honor of Marie Antoinette. The square upon which the block-houses stood was called "*Campus Martius;*" square number 19, "*Capitolium;*" square number 61, "*Cecilia;*" and the great road through the covert way, "*Sacra Via.*" Two days after, an oration was delivered by James M. Varnum, who with S. H. Parsons and John Armstrong had been appointed to the judicial bench of the territory on the 16th of October, 1787. On July 9, Gov. St. Clair arrived, and the colony began to assume form. The act of 1787 provided two district grades of government for the Northwest, under the first of which the whole power was invested in the hands of a governor and three district judges.   This was immediately formed upon the Governor's arrival, and the first laws of the colony passed on the 25th of July.   These provided for the organization of the militia, and on the next day appeared the Governor's proclamation, erecting all that country that had been ceded by the Indians east of the Scioto River into the County of Washington.   From that time forward, notwithstanding the doubts yet existing as to the Indians, all Marietta prospered, and on the 2d of September the first court of the territory was held with imposing ceremonies.

The emigration westward at this time was very great   The commander at Fort Harmer, at the mouth of the Muskingum, reported four thousand five hundred persons as having passed that post between February and June, 1788 — many of whom would have purchased of the "Associates," as the New England Company was called, had they been ready to receive them.

On the 26th of November, 1787, Symmes issued a pamphlet stating the terms of his contract and the plan of sale he intended to adopt.   In January, 1788, Matthias Denman, of New Jersey, took an active interest in Symmes' purchase, and located among other tracts the sections upon which Cincinnati has been built.   Retaining one-third of this locality, he sold the other two-thirds to Robert Patterson and John Filson, and the three, about August, commenced to lay out a town on the spot, which was designated as being opposite Licking River, to the mouth of which they proposed to have a road cut from Lexington.   The naming of the town is thus narrated in the "Western Annals":—" Mr. Filson, who had been a schoolmaster, was appointed to name the town, and, in respect to its situation, and as if with a prophetic perception of the mixed race that were to inhabit it in after days, he named it Losantiville, which, being interpreted, means : *ville*, the town ; *anti*, against or opposite to , *os*, the mouth ; *L.* of Licking."

Meanwhile, in July, Symmes got thirty persons and eight four-horse teams under way for the West.   These reached Limestone (now Maysville) in September, where were several persons from Redstone.   Here Mr. Symmes tried to found a settlement, but the great freshet of 1789 caused the "Point," as it was and is yet called, to be fifteen feet under water, and the settlement to be abandoned.   The little band of settlers removed to the mouth of the Miami.   Before Symmes and his colony left the "Point," two settlements had been made on his purchase.   The first was by Mr. Stiltes, the original projector of the whole plan, who, with a colony of Redstone people, had located at the mouth of the Miami, whither Symmes went with his Maysville colony.   Here a clearing had been made by the Indians owing to the great fertility of the soil. Mr. Stiltes with his colony came to this place on the 18th of November, 1788, with twenty-six persons, and, building a block-house, prepared to remain through the Winter. They named the settlement Columbia. Here they were kindly treated by the Indians, but suffered greatly from the flood of 1789.

On the 4th of March, 1789, the Constitution of the United States went into operation, and on April 30, George Washington was inaugurated President of the American people, and during the next Summer, an Indian war was commenced by the tribes north of the Ohio. The President at first used pacific means; but these failing, he sent General Harmer against the hostile tribes. He destroyed several villages, but

BREAKING PRAIRIE.

was defeated in two battles, near the present City of Fort Wayne, Indiana. From this time till the close of 1795, the principal events were the wars with the various Indian tribes. In 1796, General St. Clair was appointed in command, and marched against the Indians; but while he was encamped on a stream, the St. Mary, a branch of the Maumee, he was attacked and defeated with the loss of six hundred men.

General Wayne was now sent against the savages. In August, 1794, he met them near the rapids of the Maumee, and gained a complete victory. This success, followed by vigorous measures, compelled the Indians to sue for peace, and on the 30th of July, the following year, the treaty of Greenville was signed by the principal chiefs, by which a large tract of country was ceded to the United States.

Before proceeding in our narrative, we will pause to notice Fort Washington, erected in the early part of this war on the site of Cincinnati. Nearly all of the great cities of the Northwest, and indeed of the whole country, have had their *nuclei* in those rude pioneer structures, known as forts or stockades. Thus Forts Dearborn, Washington, Ponchartrain, mark the original sites of the now proud Cities of Chicago, Cincinnati and Detroit. So of most of the flourishing cities east and west of the Mississippi. Fort Washington, erected by Doughty in 1790, was a rude but highly interesting structure. It was composed of a number of strongly-built hewed log cabins. Those designed for soldiers' barracks were a story and a half high, while those composing the officers quarters were more imposing and more conveniently arranged and furnished. The whole were so placed as to form a hollow square, enclosing about an acre of ground, with a block house at each of the four angles.

The logs for the construction of this fort were cut from the ground upon which it was erected. It stood between Third and Fourth Streets of the present city (Cincinnati) extending east of Eastern Row, now Broadway, which was then a narrow alley, and the eastern boundary of of the town as it was originally laid out. On the bank of the river, immediately in front of the fort, was an appendage of the fort, called the Artificer's Yard. It contained about two acres of ground, enclosed by small contiguous buildings, occupied by workshops and quarters of laborers. Within this enclosure there was a large two-story frame house, familiarly called the "Yellow House," built for the accommodation of the Quartermaster General. For many years this was the best finished and most commodious edifice in the Queen City. Fort Washington was for some time the headquarters of both the civil and military governments of the Northwestern Territory.

Following the consummation of the treaty various gigantic land speculations were entered into by different persons, who hoped to obtain from the Indians in Michigan and northern Indiana, large tracts of lands. These were generally discovered in time to prevent the outrageous schemes from being carried out, and from involving the settlers in war. On October 27, 1795, the treaty between the United States and Spain was signed, whereby the free navigation of the Mississippi was secured.

No sooner had the treaty of 1795 been ratified than settlements began to pour rapidly into the West. The great event of the year 1796 was the occupation of that part of the Northwest including Michigan, which was this year, under the provisions of the treaty, evacuated by the British forces. The United States, owing to certain conditions, did not feel justified in addressing the authorities in Canada in relation to Detroit and other frontier posts. When at last the British authorities were called to give them up, they at once complied, and General Wayne, who had done so much to preserve the frontier settlements, and who, before the year's close, sickened and died near Erie, transferred his headquarters to the neighborhood of the lakes, where a county named after him was formed, which included the northwest of Ohio, all of Michigan, and the northeast of Indiana. During this same year settlements were formed at the present City of Chillicothe, along the Miami from Middletown to Piqua, while in the more distant West, settlers and speculators began to appear in great numbers. In September, the City of Cleveland was laid out, and during the Summer and Autumn, Samuel Jackson and Jonathan Sharpless erected the first manufactory of paper—the "Redstone Paper Mill"—in the West St. Louis contained some seventy houses, and Detroit over three hundred, and along the river, contiguous to it, were more than three thousand inhabitants, mostly French Canadians, Indians and half-breeds, scarcely any Americans venturing yet into that part of the Northwest.

The election of representatives for the territory had taken place, and on the 4th of February, 1799, they convened at Losantiville—now known as Cincinnati, having been named so by Gov. St. Clair, and considered the capital of the Territory—to nominate persons from whom the members of the Legislature were to be chosen in accordance with a previous ordinance This nomination being made, the Assembly adjourned until the 16th of the following September. From those named the President selected as members of the council, Henry Vandenburg, of Vincennes, Robert Oliver, of Marietta, James Findlay and Jacob Burnett, of Cincinnati, and David Vance, of Vanceville. On the 16th of September the Territorial Legislature met, and on the 24th the two houses were duly organized, Henry Vandenburg being elected President of the Council.

The message of Gov. St. Clair was addressed to the Legislature September 20th, and on October 13th that body elected as a delegate to Congress Gen. Wm. Henry Harrison, who received eleven of the votes cast, being a majority of one over his opponent, Arthur St Clair, son of Gen. St. Clair.

The whole number of acts passed at this session, and approved by the Governor, were thirty-seven—eleven others were passed, but received his veto. The most important of those passed related to the militia, to the administration, and to taxation. On the 19th of December this protracted session of the first Legislature in the West was closed, and on the 30th of December the President nominated Charles Willing Byrd to the office of Secretary of the Territory vice Wm Henry Harrison, elected to Congress The Senate confirmed his nomination the next day.

DIVISION OF THE NORTHWEST TERRITORY.

The increased emigration to the Northwest, the extent of the domain, and the inconvenient modes of travel, made it very difficult to conduct the ordinary operations of government, and rendered the efficient action of courts almost impossible. To remedy this, it was deemed advisable to divide the territory for civil purposes. Congress, in 1800, appointed a committee to examine the question and report some means for its solution. This committee, on the 3d of March, reported that:

"In the three western countries there has been but one court having cognizance of crimes, in five years, and the immunity which offenders experience attracts, as to an asylum, the most vile and abandoned criminals, and at the same time deters useful citizens from making settlements in such society. The extreme necessity of judiciary attention and assistance is experienced in civil as well as in criminal cases. * * * * To minister a remedy to these and other evils, it occurs to this committee that it is expedient that a division of said territory into two distinct and separate governments should be made; and that such division be made by a line beginning at the mouth of the Great Miami River, running directly north until it intersects the boundary between the United States and Canada"

The report was accepted by Congress, and, in accordance with its suggestions, that body passed an Act extinguishing the Northwest Territory, which Act was approved May 7 Among its provisions were these ·

"That from and after July 4 next, all that part of the Territory of the United States northwest of the Ohio River, which lies to the westward of a line beginning at a point on the Ohio, opposite to the mouth of the Kentucky River, and running thence to Fort Recovery, and thence north until it shall intersect the territorial line between the United States and Canada, shall, for the purpose of temporary government, constitute a separate territory, and be called the Indiana Territory."

After providing for the exercise of the civil and criminal powers of the territories, and other provisions, the Act further provides:

"That until it shall otherwise be ordered by the Legislatures of the said Territories, respectively, Chillicothe on the Scioto River shall be the seat of government of the Territory of the United States northwest of the Ohio River; and that St. Vincennes on the Wabash River shall be the seat of government for the Indiana Territory"

Gen. Wm. Henry Harrison was appointed Governor of the Indiana Territory, and entered upon his duties about a year later. Connecticut also about this time released her claims to the reserve, and in March a law was passed accepting this cession. Settlements had been made upon thirty-five of the townships in the reserve, mills had been built, and seven hundred miles of road cut in various directions. On the 3d of November the General Assembly met at Chillicothe Near the close of the year, the first missionary of the Connecticut Reserve came, who found no township containing more than eleven families. It was upon the first of October that the secret treaty had been made between Napoleon and the King of Spain, whereby the latter agreed to cede to France the province of Louisiana.

In January, 1802, the Assembly of the Northwestern Territory chartered the college at Athens. From the earliest dawn of the western colonies, education was promptly provided for, and as early as 1787, newspapers were issued from Pittsburgh and Kentucky, and largely read throughout the frontier settlements. Before the close of this year, the Congress of the United States granted to the citizens of the Northwestern territory the formation of a State government. One of the provisions of the "compact of 1787" provided that whenever the number of inhabitants within prescribed limits exceeded 45,000, they should be entitled to a separate government. The prescribed limits of Ohio contained, from a census taken to ascertain the legality of the act, more than that number, and on the 30th of April, 1802, Congress passed the act defining its limits, and on the 29th of November the Constitution of the new State of Ohio, so named from the beautiful river forming its southern boundary, came into existence. The exact limits of Lake Michigan were not then known, but the territory now included within the State of Michigan was wholly within the territory of Indiana.

Gen. Harrison, while residing at Vincennes, made several treaties with the Indians, thereby gaining large tracts of lands. The next year is memorable in the history of the West for the purchase of Louisiana from France by the United States for $15,000,000 Thus by a peaceful mode, the domain of the United States was extended over a large tract of country west of the Mississippi, and was for a time under the jurisdiction of the Northwest government, and, as has been mentioned in the early part of this narrative, was called the "New Northwest." The limits of this history will not allow a description of its territory. The same year large grants of land were obtained from the Indians, and the House of Representatives of the new State of Ohio signed a bill respecting the College Township in the district of Cincinnati.

Before the close of the year, Gen. Harrison obtained additional grants of lands from the various Indian nations in Indiana and the present limits of Illinois, and on the 18th of August, 1804, completed a treaty at St. Louis, whereby over 51,000,000 acres of lands were obtained from the aborigines. Measures were also taken to learn the condition of affairs in and about Detroit.

C. Jouett, the Indian agent in Michigan, still a part of Indiana Territory, reported as follows upon the condition of matters at that post:

"The Town of Detroit.—The charter, which is for fifteen miles square, was granted in the time of Louis XIV. of France, and is now, from the best information I have been able to get, at Quebec. Of those two hundred and twenty-five acres, only four are occupied by the town and Fort Lenault. The remainder is a common, except twenty-four acres, which were added twenty years ago to a farm belonging to Wm. Macomb. * * * A stockade incloses the town, fort and citadel. The pickets, as well as the public houses, are in a state of gradual decay. The streets are narrow, straight and regular, and intersect each other at right angles. The houses are, for the most part, low and inelegant."

During this year, Congress granted a township of land for the support of a college, and began to offer inducements for settlers in these wilds, and the country now comprising the State of Michigan began to fill rapidly with settlers along its southern borders. This same year, also, a law was passed organizing the Southwest Territory, dividing it into two portions, the Territory of New Orleans, which city was made the seat of government, and the District of Louisiana, which was annexed to the domain of Gen. Harrison.

On the 11th of January, 1805, the Territory of Michigan was formed, Wm. Hull was appointed governor, with headquarters at Detroit, the change to take effect on June 30. On the 11th of that month, a fire occurred at Detroit, which destroyed almost every building in the place. When the officers of the new territory reached the post, they found it in ruins, and the inhabitants scattered throughout the country. Rebuilding, however, soon commenced, and ere long the town contained more houses than before the fire, and many of them much better built.

While this was being done, Indiana had passed to the second grade of government, and through her General Assembly had obtained large tracts of land from the Indian tribes. To all this the celebrated Indian, Tecumthe or Tecumseh, vigorously protested, and it was the main cause of his attempts to unite the various Indian tribes in a conflict with the settlers. To obtain a full account of these attempts, the workings of the British, and the signal failure, culminating in the death of Tecumseh at the battle of the Thames, and the close of the war of 1812 in the Northwest, we will step aside in our story, and relate the principal events of his life, and his connection with this conflict.

TECUMSEH, THE SHAWANOE CHIEFTAIN.

TECUMSEH, AND THE WAR OF 1812.

This famous Indian chief was born about the year 1768, not far from the site of the present City of Piqua, Ohio. His father, Puckeshinwa, was a member of the Kisopok tribe of the Swanoese nation, and his mother, Methontaske, was a member of the Turtle tribe of the same people. They removed from Florida about the middle of the last century to the birthplace of Tecumseh. In 1774, his father, who had risen to be chief, was slain at the battle of Point Pleasant, and not long after Tecumseh, by his bravery, became the leader of his tribe. In 1795 he was declared chief, and then lived at Deer Creek, near the site of the present City of Urbana. He remained here about one year, when he returned to Piqua, and in 1798, he went to White River, Indiana. In 1805, he and his brother, Laulewasikan (Open Door), who had announced himself as a prophet, went to a tract of land on the Wabash River, given them by the Pottawatomies and Kickapoos. From this date the chief comes into prominence. He was now about thirty-seven years of age, was five feet and ten inches in height, was stoutly built, and possessed of enormous powers of endurance. His countenance was naturally pleasing, and he was, in general, devoid of those savage attributes possessed by most Indians. It is stated he could read and write, and had a confidential secretary and adviser, named Billy Caldwell, a half-breed, who afterward became chief of the Pottawatomies. He occupied the first house built on the site of Chicago. At this time, Tecumseh entered upon the great work of his life. He had long objected to the grants of land made by the Indians to the whites, and determined to unite all the Indian tribes into a league, in order that no treaties or grants of land could be made save by the consent of this confederation.

He traveled constantly, going from north to south, from the south to the north, everywhere urging the Indians to this step. He was a matchless orator, and his burning words had their effect.

Gen. Harrison, then Governor of Indiana, by watching the movements of the Indians, became convinced that a grand conspiracy was forming, and made preparations to defend the settlements. Tecumseh's plan was similar to Pontiac's, elsewhere described, and to the cunning artifice of that chieftain was added his own sagacity.

During the year 1809, Tecumseh and the prophet were actively preparing for the work. In that year, Gen. Harrison entered into a treaty with the Delawares, Kickapoos, Pottawatomies, Miamis, Eel River Indians and Weas, in which these tribes ceded to the whites certain lands upon the Wabash, to all of which Tecumseh entered a bitter protest, averring as one principal reason that he did not want the Indians to give up any lands north and west of the Ohio River

Tecumseh, in August, 1810, visited the General at Vincennes and held a council relating to the grievances of the Indians. Becoming unduly angry at this conference he was dismissed from the village and soon after departed to incite the southern Indian tribes to the conflict.

Gen Harrison determined to move upon the chief's headquarters at Tippecanoe, and for this purpose went about sixty-five miles up the Wabash, where he built Fort Harrison. From this place he went to the prophet's town, where he informed the Indians he had no hostile intentions, provided they were true to the existing treaties He encamped near the village early in October, and on the morning of November 7, he was attacked by a large force of the Indians, and the famous battle of Tippecanoe occurred. The Indians were routed and their town broken up. Tecumseh returning not long after, was greatly exasperated at his brother, the prophet, even threatening to kill him for rashly precipitating the war, and foiling his (Tecumseh's) plans

Tecumseh sent word to Gen Harrison that he was now returned from the South, and was ready to visit the President as had at one time previously been proposed Gen Harrison informed him he could not go as a chief, which method Tecumseh desired, and the visit was never made

In June of the following year, he visited the Indian agent at Fort Wayne. Here he disavowed any intention to make a war against the United States, and reproached Gen Harrison for marching against his people. The agent replied to this, Tecumseh listened with a cold indifference, and after making a few general remarks, with a haughty air drew his blanket about him, left the council house, and departed for Fort Malden, in Upper Canada, where he joined the British standard

He remained under this Government, doing effective work for the Crown while engaged in the war of 1812 which now opened He was, however, always humane in his treatment of the prisoners, never allowing his warriors to ruthlessly mutilate the bodies of those slain, or wantonly murder the captive

In the Summer of 1813, Perry's victory on Lake Erie occurred, and shortly after active preparations were made to capture Malden. On the 27th of September, the American army, under Gen. Harrison, set sail for the shores of Canada, and in a few hours stood around the ruins of Malden, from which the British army, under Proctor, had retreated to Sandwich, intending to make its way to the heart of Canada by the Valley of the Thames. On the 29th Gen. Harrison was at Sandwich, and Gen. McArthur took possession of Detroit and the territory of Michigan

On the 2d of October, the Americans began their pursuit of Proctor, whom they overtook on the 5th, and the battle of the Thames followed. Early in the engagement, Tecumseh who was at the head of the column of Indians was slain, and they, no longer hearing the voice of their chieftain, fled. The victory was decisive, and practically closed the war in the Northwest.

INDIANS ATTACKING A STOCKADE.

Just who killed the great chief has been a matter of much dispute; but the weight of opinion awards the act to Col. Richard M. Johnson, who fired at him with a pistol, the shot proving fatal.

In 1805 occurred Burr's Insurrection. He took possession of a beautiful island in the Ohio, after the killing of Hamilton, and is charged by many with attempting to set up an independent government. His plans were frustrated by the general government, his property confiscated and he was compelled to flee the country for safety.

In January, 1807, Governor Hull, of Michigan Territory, made a treaty with the Indians, whereby all that peninsula was ceded to the United States. Before the close of the year, a stockade was built about Detroit. It was also during this year that Indiana and Illinois endeavored to obtain the repeal of that section of the compact of 1787, whereby slavery was excluded from the Northwest Territory These attempts, however, all signally failed.

In 1809 it was deemed advisable to divide the Indiana Territory. This was done, and the Territory of Illinois was formed from the western part, the seat of government being fixed at Kaskaskia The next year, the intentions of Tecumseh manifested themselves in open hostilities, and then began the events already narrated

While this war was in progress, emigration to the West went on with surprising rapidity. In 1811, under Mr Roosevelt of New York, the first steamboat trip was made on the Ohio, much to the astonishment of the natives, many of whom fled in terror at the appearance of the " monster." It arrived at Louisville on the 10th day of October At the close of the first week of January, 1812, it arrived at Natchez, after being nearly overwhelmed in the great earthquake which occurred while on its downward trip.

The battle of the Thames was fought on October 6, 1813. It effectually closed hostilities in the Northwest, although peace was not fully restored until July 22, 1814, when a treaty was formed at Greenville, under the direction of General Harrison, between the United States and the Indian tribes, in which it was stipulated that the Indians should cease hostilities against the Americans if the war were continued. Such, happily, was not the case, and on the 24th of December the treaty of Ghent was signed by the representatives of England and the United States. This treaty was followed the next year by treaties with various Indian tribes throughout the West and Northwest, and quiet was again restored in this part of the new world.

On the 18th of March, 1816, Pittsburgh was incorporated as a city It then had a population of 8,000 people, and was already noted for its manufacturing interests. On April 19, Indiana Territory was allowed to form a state government At that time there were thirteen counties organized, containing about sixty-three thousand inhabitants. The first election of state officers was held in August, when Jonathan Jennings was chosen Governor The officers were sworn in on November 7, and on December 11, the State was formally admitted into the Union. For some time the seat of government was at Corydon, but a more central location being desirable, the present capital, Indianapolis (City of Indiana), was laid out January 1, 1825.

On the 28th of December the Bank of Illinois, at Shawneetown, was chartered, with a capital of $300,000. At this period all banks were under the control of the States, and were allowed to establish branches at different convenient points.

Until this time Chillicothe and Cincinnati had in turn enjoyed the privileges of being the capital of Ohio. But the rapid settlement of the northern and eastern portions of the State demanded, as in Indiana, a more central location, and before the close of the year, the site of Columbus was selected and surveyed as the future capital of the State Banking had begun in Ohio as early as 1808, when the first bank was chartered at Marietta, but here as elsewhere it did not bring to the state the hoped-for assistance. It and other banks were subsequently unable to redeem their currency, and were obliged to suspend.

In 1818, Illinois was made a state, and all the territory north of her northern limits was erected into a separate territory and joined to Michigan for judicial purposes. By the following year, navigation of the lakes was increasing with great rapidity and affording an immense source of revenue to the dwellers in the Northwest, but it was not until 1826 that the trade was extended to Lake Michigan, or that steamships began to navigate the bosom of that inland sea.

Until the year 1832, the commencement of the Black Hawk War, but few hostilities were experienced with the Indians. Roads were opened, canals were dug, cities were built, common schools were established, universities were founded, many of which, especially the Michigan University, have achieved a world wide-reputation. The people were becoming wealthy. The domains of the United States had been extended, and had the sons of the forest been treated with honesty and justice, the record of many years would have been that of peace and continuous prosperity.

BLACK HAWK AND THE BLACK HAWK WAR

This conflict, though confined to Illinois, is an important epoch in the Northwestern history, being the last war with the Indians in this part of the United States

Ma-ka-tai-me-she-kia-kiah, or Black Hawk, was born in the principal Sac village, about three miles from the junction of Rock River with the Mississippi, in the year 1767. His father's name was Py-e-sa or Pahaes, his grandfather's, Na-na-ma-kee, or the Thunderer. Black Hawk early distinguished himself as a warrior, and at the age of fifteen was permitted to paint and was ranked among the braves. About the year 1783, he went on an expedition against the enemies of his nation, the Osages, one

BLACK HAWK, THE SAC CHIEFTAIN.

of whom he killed and scalped, and for this deed of Indian bravery he was permitted to join in the scalp dance.   Three or four years after he, at the head of two hundred braves, went on another expedition against the Osages, to avenge the murder of some women and children belonging to his own tribe.   Meeting an equal number of Osage warriors, a fierce battle ensued, in which the latter tribe lost one-half their number.   The Sacs lost only about nineteen warriors   He next attacked the Cherokees for a similar cause   In a severe battle with them, near the present City of St' Louis, his father was slain, and Black Hawk, taking possession of the " Medicine Bag," at once announced himself chief of the Sac nation. He had now conquered the Cherokees, and about the year 1800, at the head of five hundred Sacs and Foxes, and a hundred Iowas, he waged war against the Osage nation and subdued it.   For two years he battled successfully with other Indian tribes, all of whom he conquered.

Black Hawk does not at any time seem to have been friendly to the Americans.   When on a visit to St Louis to see his " Spanish Father," he declined to see any of the Americans, alleging, as a reason, he did not want *two* fathers

The treaty at St Louis was consummated in 1804.   The next year the United States Government erected a fort near the head of the Des Moines Rapids, called Fort Edwards.   This seemed to enrage Black Hawk, who at once determined to capture Fort Madison, standing on the west side of the Mississippi above the mouth of the Des Moines River.   The fort was garrisoned by about fifty men   Here he was defeated.   The difficulties with the British Government arose about this time, and the War of 1812 followed   That government, extending aid to the Western Indians, by giving them arms and ammunition, induced them to remain hostile to the Americans.   In August, 1812, Black Hawk, at the head of about five hundred braves, started to join the British forces at Detroit, passing on his way the site of Chicago, where the famous Fort Dearborn Massacre had a few days before occurred.   Of his connection with the British Government but little is known.   In 1813 he with his little band descended the Mississippi, and attacking some United States troops at Fort Howard was defeated.

In the early part of 1815, the Indian tribes west of the Mississippi were notified that peace had been declared between the United States and England, and nearly all hostilities had ceased.   Black Hawk did not sign any treaty, however, until May of the following year.   He then recognized the validity of the treaty at St Louis in 1804.   From the time of signing this treaty in 1816, until the breaking out of the war in 1832, he and his band passed their time in the common pursuits of Indian life.

Ten years before the commencement of this war, the Sac and Fox

Indians were urged to join the Iowas on the west bank of the Father of Waters. All were agreed, save the band known as the British Band, of which Black Hawk was leader. He strenuously objected to the removal, and was induced to comply only after being threatened with the power of the Government This and various actions on the part of the white settlers provoked Black Hawk and his band to attempt the capture of his native village now occupied by the whites. The war followed. He and his actions were undoubtedly misunderstood, and had his wishes been acquiesced in at the beginning of the struggle, much bloodshed would have been prevented.

Black Hawk was chief now of the Sac and Fox nations, and a noted warrior. He and his tribe inhabited a village on Rock River, nearly three miles above its confluence with the Mississippi, where the tribe had lived many generations. When that portion of Illinois was reserved to them, they remained in peaceable possession of their reservation, spending their time in the enjoyment of Indian life. The fine situation of their village and the quality of their lands incited the more lawless white settlers, who from time to time began to encroach upon the red men's domain From one pretext to another, and from one step to another, the crafty white men gained a foothold, until through whisky and artifice they obtained deeds from many of the Indians for their possessions. The Indians were finally induced to cross over the Father of Waters and locate among the Iowas. Black Hawk was strenuously opposed to all this, but as the authorities of Illinois and the United States thought this the best move, he was forced to comply. Moreover other tribes joined the whites and urged the removal. Black Hawk would not agree to the terms of the treaty made with his nation for their lands, and as soon as the military, called to enforce his removal, had retired, he returned to the Illinois side of the river. A large force was at once raised and marched against him. On the evening of May 14, 1832, the first engagement occurred between a band from this army and Black Hawk's band, in which the former were defeated.

This attack and its result aroused the whites. A large force of men was raised, and Gen. Scott hastened from the seaboard, by way of the lakes, with United States troops and artillery to aid in the subjugation of the Indians On the 24th of June, Black Hawk, with 200 warriors, was repulsed by Major Demont between Rock River and Galena The American army continued to move up Rock River toward the main body of the Indians, and on the 21st of July came upon Black Hawk and his band, and defeated them near the Blue Mounds.

Before this action, Gen. Henry, in command, sent word to the main army by whom he was immediately rejoined, and the whole crossed the

Note —The above is the generally accepted version of the cause of the Black Hawk War, but in our History of Jo Daviess County Ill , we had occasion to go to the bottom of this matter, and have, we think, found the actual cause of the war, which will be found on page 157

Wisconsin in pursuit of Black Hawk and his band who were fleeing to the Mississippi. They were overtaken on the 2d of August, and in the battle which followed the power of the Indian chief was completely broken   He fled, but was seized by the Winnebagoes and delivered to the whites

On the 21st of September, 1832, Gen. Scott and Gov Reynolds concluded a treaty with the Winnebagoes, Sacs and Foxes by which they ceded to the United States a vast tract of country, and agreed to remain peaceable with the whites.   For the faithful performance of the provisions of this treaty on the part of the Indians, it was stipulated that Black Hawk, his two sons, the prophet Wabokieshiek, and six other chiefs of the hostile bands should be retained as hostages during the pleasure of the President.   They were confined at Fort Barracks and put in irons.

The next Spring, by order of the Secretary of War, they were taken to Washington   From there they were removed to Fortress Monroe, "there to remain until the conduct of their nation was such as to justify their being set at liberty "   They were retained here until the 4th of June, when the authorities directed them to be taken to the principal cities so that they might see the folly of contending against the white people   Everywhere they were observed by thousands, the name of the old chief being extensively known.   By the middle of August they reached Fort Armstrong on Rock Island, where Black Hawk was soon after released to go to his countrymen   As he passed the site of his birthplace, now the home of the white man, he was deeply moved.   His village where he was born, where he had so happily lived, and where he had hoped to die, was now another's dwelling place, and he was a wanderer.

On the next day after his release, he went at once to his tribe and his lodge.   His wife was yet living, and with her he passed the remainder of his days.   To his credit it may be said that Black Hawk always remained true to his wife, and served her with a devotion uncommon among the Indians, living with her upward of forty years

Black Hawk now passed his time hunting and fishing.   A deep melancholy had settled over him from which he could not be freed.   At all times when he visited the whites he was received with marked attention.   He was an honored guest at the old settlers' reunion in Lee County, Illinois, at some of their meetings, and received many tokens of esteem. In September, 1838, while on his way to Rock Island to receive his annuity from the Government, he contracted a severe cold which resulted in a fatal attack of bilious fever which terminated his life on October 3. His faithful wife, who was devotedly attached to him, mourned deeply during his sickness.   After his death he was dressed in the uniform presented to him by the President while in Washington.   He was buried in a grave six feet in depth, situated upon a beautiful eminence.   "The body was placed in the middle of the grave, in a sitting posture, upon a seat constructed for the purpose. On his left side, the cane, given him by Henry Clay, was placed upright, with his right hand resting upon it Many of the old warrior's trophies were placed in the grave, and some Indian garments, together with his favorite weapons.'

No sooner was the Black Hawk war concluded than settlers began rapidly to pour into the northern parts of Illinois, and into Wisconsin, now free from Indian depredations. Chicago, from a trading post, had grown to a commercial center, and was rapidly coming into prominence. In 1835, the formation of a State Government in Michigan was discussed, but did not take active form until two years later, when the State became a part of the Federal Union.

The main attraction to that portion of the Northwest lying west of Lake Michigan, now included in the State of Wisconsin, was its alluvial wealth. Copper ore was found about Lake Superior For some time this region was attached to Michigan for judiciary purposes, but in 1836 was made a territory, then including Minnesota and Iowa. The latter State was detached two years later. In 1848, Wisconsin was admitted as a State, Madison being made the capital. We have now traced the various divisions of the Northwest Territory (save a little in Minnesota) from the time it was a unit comprising this vast territory, until circumstances compelled its present division.

OTHER INDIAN TROUBLES.

Before leaving this part of the narrative, we will narrate briefly the Indian troubles in Minnesota and elsewhere by the Sioux Indians

In August, 1862, the Sioux Indians living on the western borders of Minnesota fell upon the unsuspecting settlers, and in a few hours massacred ten or twelve hundred persons. A distressful panic was the immediate result, fully thirty thousand persons fleeing from their homes to districts supposed to be better protected. The military authorities at once took active measures to punish the savages, and a large number were killed and captured. About a year after, Little Crow, the chief, was killed by a Mr Lampson near Scattered Lake. Of those captured, thirty were hung at Mankato, and the remainder, through fears of mob violence, were removed to Camp McClellan, on the outskirts of the City of Davenport. It was here that Big Eagle came into prominence and secured his release by the following order.

BIG EAGLE.

"Special Order, No 430.   "WAR DEPARTMENT,
      "ADJUTANT GENERAL'S OFFICE, WASHINGTON, Dec. 3, 1864.
      "Big Eagle, an Indian now in confinement at Davenport, Iowa,
will, upon the receipt of this order, be immediately released from confinement and set at liberty.
      "By order of the President of the United States.
"Official ·   "E. D TOWNSEND, *Ass't Adj't Gen*
      "CAPT JAMES VANDERVENTER, *Com'y Sub Vols.*
      "Through Com'g Gen'l, Washington, D. C "

Another Indian who figures more prominently than Big Eagle, and
who was more cowardly in his nature, with his band of Modoc Indians,
is noted in the annals of the New Northwest: we refer to Captain Jack.
This distinguished Indian, noted for his cowardly murder of Gen. Canby,
was a chief of a Modoc tribe of Indians inhabiting the border lands
between California and Oregon. This region of country comprises what
is known as the "Lava Beds." a tract of land described as utterly impenetrable, save by those savages who had made it their home.
      The Modocs are known as an exceedingly fierce and treacherous
race. They had, according to their own traditions, resided here for many
generations, and at one time were exceedingly numerous and powerful.
A famine carried off nearly half their numbers, and disease, indolence
and the vices of the white man have reduced them to a poor, weak and
insignificant tribe.
      Soon after the settlement of California and Oregon, complaints began
to be heard of massacres of emigrant trains passing through the Modoc
country. In 1847, an emigrant train, comprising eighteen souls, was entirely destroyed at a place since known as "Bloody Point." These occurrences caused the United States Government to appoint a peace commission,
who, after repeated attempts, in 1864. made a treaty with the Modocs,
Snakes and Klamaths, in which it was agreed on their part to remove to
a reservation set apart for them in the southern part of Oregon.
      With the exception of Captain Jack and a band of his followers, who
remained at Clear Lake, about six miles from Klamath, all the Indians
complied. The Modocs who went to the reservation were under chief
Schonchin. Captain Jack remained at the lake without disturbance
until 1869, when he was also induced to remove to the reservation. The
Modocs and the Klamaths soon became involved in a quarrel, and Captain
Jack and his band returned to the Lava Beds
      Several attempts were made by the Indian Commissioners to induce
them to return to the reservation, and finally becoming involved in a

difficulty with the commissioner and his military escort, a fight ensued, in which the chief and his l and were routed. They were greatly enraged, and on their retreat, before the day closed, killed eleven inoffensive whites.

The nation was aroused and immediate action demanded. A commission was at once appointed by the Government to see what could be done It comprised the following persons   Gen. E. R S. Canby, Rev. Dr. E. Thomas, a leading Methodist divine of California; Mr A. B. Meacham, Judge Rosborough, of California, and a Mr. Dyer, of Oregon After several interviews, in which the savages were always aggressive, often appearing with scalps in their belts, Bogus Charley came to the commission on the evening of April 10, 1873, and informed them that Capt Jack and his band would have a "talk" to-morrow at a place near Clear Lake, about three miles distant.   Here the Commissioners, accompanied by Charley, Riddle, the interpreter. and Boston Charley repaired. After the usual greeting the council proceedings commenced. On behalf of the Indians there were present: Capt Jack, Black Jim, Schnac Nasty Jim, Ellen's Man, and Hooker Jim.   They had no guns, but carried pistols.   After short speeches by Mr. Meacham, Gen. Canby and Dr. Thomas, Chief Schonchin arose to speak.   He had scarcely proceeded when, as if by a preconcerted arrangement, Capt. Jack drew his pistol and shot Gen. Canby dead.   In less than a minute a dozen shots were fired by the savages, and the massacre completed.   Mr. Meacham was shot by Schonchin, and Dr. Thomas by Boston Charley Mr Dyer barely escaped, being fired at twice.   Riddle, the interpreter, and his squaw escaped.   The troops rushed to the spot where they found Gen. Canby and Dr. Thomas dead, and Mr. Meacham badly wounded.   The savages had escaped to their impenetrable fastnesses and could not be pursued.

The whole country was aroused by this brutal massacre; but it was not until the following May that the murderers were brought to justice At that time Boston Charley gave himself up, and offered to guide the troops to Capt. Jack's stronghold.   This led to the capture of his entire gang, a number of whom were murdered by Oregon volunteers while on their way to trial.   The remaining Indians were held as prisoners until July when their trial occurred, which led to the conviction of Capt. Jack, Schonchin, Boston Charley, Hooker Jim, Broncho, *alias* One-Eyed Jim, and Slotuck, who were sentenced to be hanged.   These sentences were approved by the President, save in the case of Slotuck and Broncho whose sentences were commuted to imprisonment for life The others were executed at Fort Klamath, October 3, 1873.

These closed the Indian troubles for a time in the Northwest, and for several years the borders of civilization remained in peace.   They were again involved in a conflict with the savages about the country of the

CAPTAIN JACK, THE MODOC CHIEFTAIN.

Black Hills, in which war the gallant Gen Custer lost his life. Just now the borders of Oregon and California are again in fear of hostilities ; but as the Government has learned how to deal with the Indians, they will be of short duration. The red man is fast passing away before the march of the white man, and a few more generations will read of the Indians as one of the nations of the past.

The Northwest abounds in memorable places   We have generally noticed them in the narrative, but our space forbids their description in detail, save of the most important places. Detroit, Cincinnati, Vincennes, Kaskaskia and their kindred towns have all been described.   But ere we leave the narrative we will present our readers with an account of the Kinzie house, the old landmark of Chicago, and the discovery of the source of the Mississippi River, each of which may well find a place in the annals of the Northwest.

Mr John Kinzie, of the Kinzie house, represented in the illustration, established a trading house at Fort Dearborn in 1804.   The stockade had been erected the year previous, and named Fort Dearborn in honor of the Secretary of War.   It had a block house at each of the two angles, on the southern side a sallyport, a covered way on the north side, that led down to the river, for the double purpose of providing means of escape, and of procuring water in the event of a siege.

Fort Dearborn stood on the south bank of the Chicago River, about half a mile from its mouth.   When Major Whistler built it, his soldiers hauled all the timber, for he had no oxen, and so economically did he work that the fort cost the Government only fifty dollars   For a while the garrison could get no grain, and Whistler and his men subsisted on acorns.   Now Chicago is the greatest grain center in the world.

Mr Kinzie bought the hut of the first settler, Jean Baptiste Point au Sable, on the site of which he erected his mansion.   Within an inclosure in front he planted some Lombardy poplars, seen in the engraving, and in the rear he soon had a fine garden and growing orchard.

In 1812 the Kinzie house and its surroundings became the theater of stirring events.   The garrison of Fort Dearborn consisted of fifty-four men, under the charge of Capt. Nathan Heald, assisted by Lieutenant Lenai T. Helm (son-in-law to Mrs. Kinzie), and Ensign Ronan.   The surgeon was Dr Voorhees.   The only residents at the post at that time were the wives of Capt. Heald and Lieutenant Helm and a few of the soldiers, Mr. Kinzie and his family, and a few Canadian voyagers with their wives and children.   The soldiers and Mr. Kinzie were on the most friendly terms with the Pottawatomies and the Winnebagoes, the principal tribes around them, but they could not win them from their attachment to the British.

After the battle of Tippecanoe it was observed that some of the leading chiefs became sullen, for some of their people had perished in that conflict with American troops.

One evening in April, 1812, Mr. Kinzie sat playing his violin and his children were dancing to the music, when Mrs. Kinzie came rushing into the house pale with terror, and exclaiming, "The Indians! the Indians!" "What? Where?" eagerly inquired Mr. Kinzie. "Up at Lee's, killing and scalping," answered the frightened mother, who, when the alarm was given, was attending Mrs. Burns, a newly-made mother, living not far off.

KINZIE HOUSE.

Mr. Kinzie and his family crossed the river in boats, and took refuge in the fort, to which place Mrs. Burns and her infant, not a day old, were conveyed in safety to the shelter of the guns of Fort Dearborn, and the rest of the white inhabitants fled. The Indians were a scalping party of Winnebagoes, who hovered around the fort some days, when they disappeared, and for several weeks the inhabitants were not disturbed by alarms.

Chicago was then so deep in the wilderness, that the news of the declaration of war against Great Britain, made on the 19th of June, 1812, did not reach the commander of the garrison at Fort Dearborn till the 7th of August. Now the fast mail train will carry a man from New York to Chicago in twenty-seven hours, and such a declaration might be sent, every word, by the telegraph in less than the same number of minutes.

PRESENT CONDITION OF THE NORTHWEST.

Preceding chapters have brought us to the close of the Black Hawk war, and we now turn to the contemplation of the growth and prosperity of the Northwest under the smile of peace and the blessings of our civilization.   The pioneers of this region date events back to the deep snow

A REPRESENTATIVE PIONEER.

of 1831, no one arriving here since that date taking first honors.   The inciting cause of the immigration which overflowed the prairies early in the '30s was the reports of the marvelous beauty and fertility of the region distributed through the East by those who had participated in the Black Hawk campaign with Gen. Scott.   Chicago and Milwaukee then had a few hundred inhabitants, and Gurdon S. Hubbard's trail from the former city to Kaskaskia led almost through a wilderness.   Vegetables and clothing were largely distributed through the regions adjoining the lakes by steamers from the Ohio towns. There are men now living in Illinois who came to the state when barely an acre was in cultivation, and a man now prominent in the business circles of Chicago looked over the swampy, cheerless site of that metropolis in 1818 and went south ward into civilization. Emigrants from Pennsylvania in 1830 left behind

LINCOLN MONUMENT, SPRINGFIELD, ILLINOIS.

them but one small railway in the coal regions, thirty miles in length, and made their way to the Northwest mostly with ox teams, finding in Northern Illinois petty settlements scores of miles apart, although the southern portion of the state was fairly dotted with farms. The water courses of the lakes and rivers furnished transportation to the second great army of immigrants, and about 1850 railroads were pushed to that extent that the crisis of 1837 was precipitated upon us, from the effects of which the Western country had not fully recovered at the outbreak of the war. Hostilities found the colonists of the prairies fully alive to the demands of the occasion, and the honor of recruiting

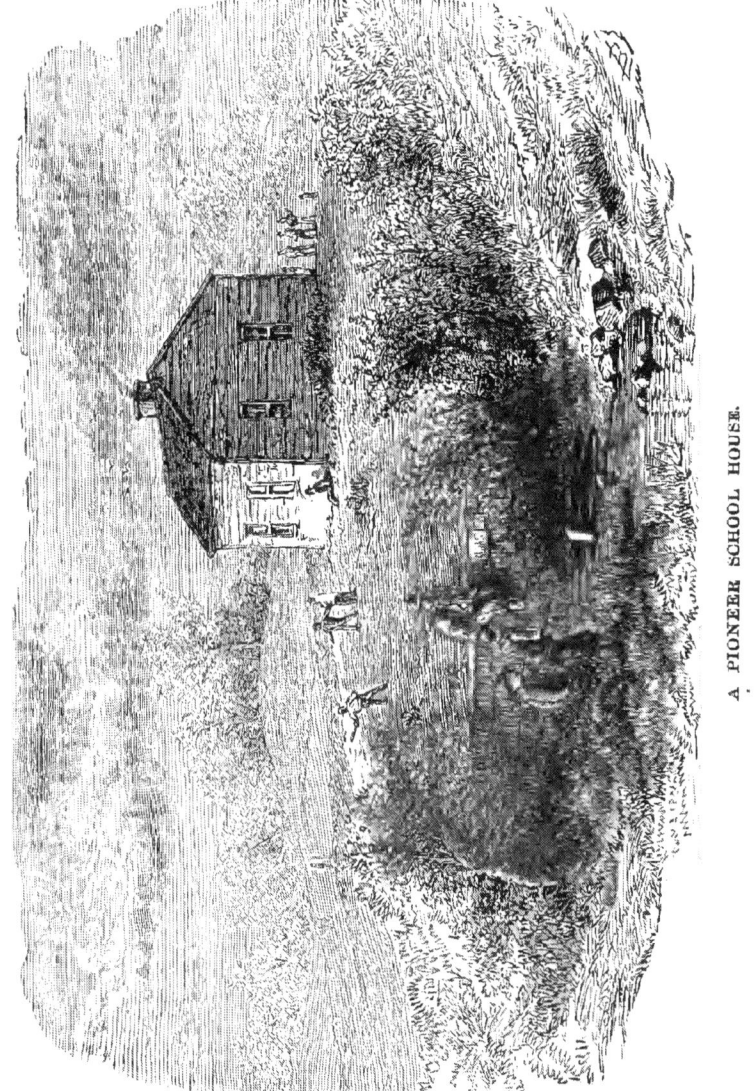

A PIONEER SCHOOL HOUSE.

the vast armies of the Union fell largely to the Governors of the Western States. The struggle, on the whole, had a marked effect for the better on the new Northwest, giving it an impetus which twenty years of peace would not have produced. In a large degree, this prosperity was an inflated one; and, with the rest of the Union, we have since been compelled to atone therefor by four years of depression of values, of scarcity of employment, and loss of fortune   To a less degree, however, than the manufacturing or mining regions has the West suffered during the prolonged panic now so near its end.   Agriculture, still the leading feature in our industries, has been quite prosperous through all these dark years, and the farmers have cleared away many incumbrances resting over them from the period of fictitious values.   The population has steadily increased, the arts and sciences are gaining a stronger foothold, the trade area of the region is becoming daily more extended, and we have been largely exempt from the financial calamities which have nearly wrecked communities on the seaboard dependent wholly on foreign commerce or domestic manufacture.

At the present period there are no great schemes broached for the Northwest, no propositions for government subsidies or national works of improvement, but the capital of the world is attracted hither for the purchase of our products or the expansion of our capacity for serving the nation at large.   A new era is dawning as to transportation, and we bid fair to deal almost exclusively with the increasing and expanding lines of steel rail running through every few miles of territory on the prairies. The lake marine will no doubt continue to be useful in the warmer season, and to serve as a regulator of freight rates; but experienced navigators forecast the decay of the system in moving to the seaboard the enormous crops of the West.   Within the past five years it has become quite common to see direct shipments to Europe and the West Indies going through from the second-class towns along the Mississippi and Missouri

As to popular education, the standard has of late risen very greatly, and our schools would be creditable to any section of the Union.

More and more as the events of the war pass into obscurity will the fate of the Northwest be linked with that of the Southwest, and the next Congressional apportionment will give the valley of the Mississippi absolute control of the legislation of the nation, and do much toward securing the removal of the Federal capitol to some more central location.

Our public men continue to wield the full share of influence pertaining to their rank in the national autonomy, and seem not to forget that for the past sixteen years they and their constituents have dictated the principles which should govern the country.

In a work like this, destined to lie on the shelves of the library for generations, and not doomed to daily destruction like a newspaper, one can not indulge in the same glowing predictions, the sanguine statements of actualities that fill the columns of ephemeral publications.   Time may bring grief to the pet projects of a writer, and explode castles erected on a pedestal of facts.   Yet there are unmistakable indications before us of the same radical change in our great Northwest which characterizes its history for the past thirty years. Our domain has a sort of natural geographical border, save where it melts away to the southward in the cattle raising districts of the southwest.

Our prime interest will for some years doubtless be the growth of the food of the world, in which branch it has already outstripped all competitors, and our great rival in this duty will naturally be the fertile plains of Kansas, Nebraska and Colorado, to say nothing of the new empire so rapidly growing up in Texas. Over these regions there is a continued progress in agriculture and in railway building, and we must look to our laurels. Intelligent observers of events are fully aware of the strides made in the way of shipments of fresh meats to Europe, many of these ocean cargoes being actually slaughtered in the West and transported on ice to the wharves of the seaboard cities. That this new enterprise will continue there is no reason to doubt. There are in Chicago several factories for the canning of prepared meats for European consumption, and the orders for this class of goods are already immense. English capital is becoming daily more and more dissatisfied with railway loans and investments, and is gradually seeking mammoth outlays in lands and live stock. The stock yards in Chicago, Indianapolis and East St. Louis are yearly increasing their facilities, and their plant steadily grows more valuable. Importations of blooded animals from the progressive countries of Europe are destined to greatly improve the quality of our beef and mutton Nowhere is there to be seen a more enticing display in this line than at our state and county fairs, and the interest in the matter is on the increase.

To attempt to give statistics of our grain production for 1877 would be useless, so far have we surpassed ourselves in the quantity and quality of our product. We are too liable to forget that we are giving the world its first article of necessity — its food supply. An opportunity to learn this fact so it never can be forgotten was afforded at Chicago at the outbreak of the great panic of 1873, when Canadian purchasers, fearing the prostration of business might bring about an anarchical condition of affairs, went to that city with coin in bulk and foreign drafts to secure their supplies in their own currency at first hands. It may be justly claimed by the agricultural community that their combined efforts gave the nation its first impetus toward a restoration of its crippled industries, and their labor brought the gold premium to a lower depth than the government was able to reach by its most intense efforts of legislation and compulsion. The hundreds of millions about to be disbursed for farm products have already, by the anticipation common to all commercial nations, set the wheels in motion, and will relieve us from the perils so long shadowing our efforts to return to a healthy tone.

Manufacturing has attained in the chief cities a foothold which bids fair to render the Northwest independent of the outside world. Nearly

GREAT IRON BRIDGE OF C. R. I. & P. R.R., CROSSING MISSISSIPPI RIVER AT DAVENPORT.

our whole region has a distribution of coal measures which will in time support the manufactures necessary to our comfort and prosperity. As to transportation, the chief factor in the production of all articles except food, no section is so magnificently endowed, and our facilities are yearly increasing beyond those of any other region.

The period from a central point of the war to the outbreak of the panic was marked by a tremendous growth in our railway lines, but the depression of the times caused almost a total suspension of operations. Now that prosperity is returning to our stricken country we witness its anticipation by the railroad interest in a series of projects, extensions, and leases which bid fair to largely increase our transportation facilities. The process of foreclosure and sale of incumbered lines is another matter to be considered   In the case of the Illinois Central road, which formerly transferred to other lines at Cairo the vast burden of freight destined for the Gulf region, we now see the incorporation of the tracks connecting through to New Orleans, every mile co-operating in turning toward the northwestern metropolis the weight of the inter-state commerce of a thousand miles or more of fertile plantations.   Three competing routes to Texas have established in Chicago their general freight and passenger agencies.   Four or five lines compete for all Pacific freights to a point as as far as the interior of Nebraska.   Half a dozen or more splendid bridge structures have been thrown across the Missouri and Mississippi Rivers by the railways.   The Chicago and Northwestern line has become an aggregation of over two thousand miles of rail, and the Chicago, Milwaukee and St. Paul is its close rival in extent and importance   The three lines running to Cairo *via* Vincennes form a through route for all traffic with the states to the southward.   The chief projects now under discussion are the Chicago and Atlantic, which is to unite with lines now built to Charleston, and the Chicago and Canada Southern, which line will connect with all the various branches of that Canadian enterprise.   Our latest new road is the Chicago and Lake Huron, formed of three lines, and entering the city from Valparaiso on the Pittsburgh, Fort Wayne and Chicago track   The trunk lines being mainly in operation, the progress made in the way of shortening tracks, making air-line branches, and running extensions does not show to the advantage it deserves, as this process is constantly adding new facilities to the established order of things.   The panic reduced the price of steel to a point where the railways could hardly afford to use iron rails, and all our northwestern lines report large relays of Bessemer track.   The immense crops now being moved have given a great rise to the value of railway stocks, and their transportation must result in heavy pecuniary advantages.

Few are aware of the importance of the wholesale and jobbing trade of Chicago.   One leading firm has since the panic sold $24,000,000 of dry goods in one year, and they now expect most confidently to add seventy per cent. to the figures of their last year's business   In boots and shoes and in clothing, twenty or more great firms from the east have placed here their distributing agents or their factories; and in groceries

Chicago supplies the entire Northwest at rates presenting advantages over New York.

Chicago has stepped in between New York and the rural banks as a financial center, and scarcely a banking institution in the grain or cattle regions but keeps its reserve funds in the vaults of our commercial institutions. Accumulating here throughout the spring and summer months, they are summoned home at pleasure to move the products of the prairies. This process greatly strengthens the northwest in its financial operations, leaving home capital to supplement local operations on behalf of home interests.

It is impossible to forecast the destiny of this grand and growing section of the Union. Figures and predictions made at this date might seem ten years hence so ludicrously small as to excite only derision.

PIONEERS' FIRST WINTER.

CHICAGO.

It is impossible in our brief space to give more than a meager sketch of such a city as Chicago, which is in itself the greatest marvel of the Prairie State.   This mysterious, majestic, mighty city, born first of water, and next of fire; sown in weakness, and raised in power; planted among the willows of the marsh, and crowned with the glory of the mountains; sleeping on the bosom of the prairie, and rocked on the bosom of the sea,

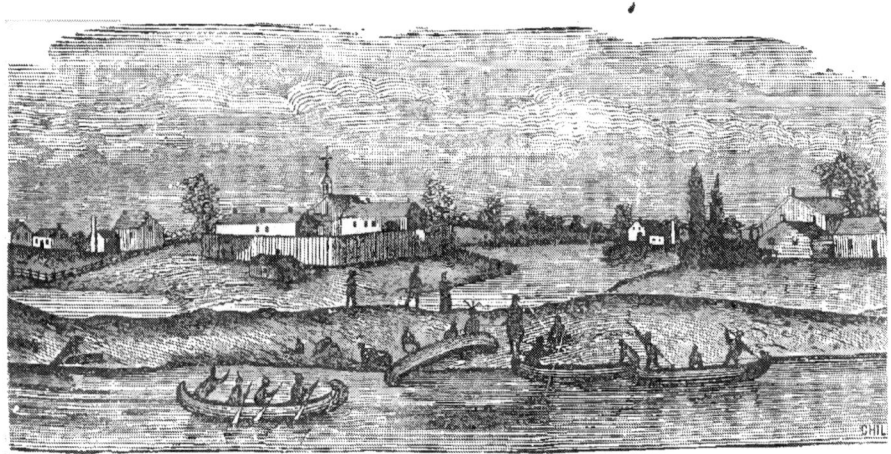

CHICAGO IN 1833.

the youngest city of the world, and still the eye of the prairie, as Damascus, the oldest city of the world, is the eye of the desert.   With a commerce far exceeding that of Corinth on her isthmus, in the highway to the East; with the defenses of a continent piled around her by the thousand miles, making her far safer than Rome on the banks of the Tiber;

with schools eclipsing Alexandria and Athens: with liberties more conspicuous than those of the old republics; with a heroism equal to the first Carthage, and with a sanctity scarcely second to that of Jerusalem—set your thoughts on all this, lifted into the eyes of all men by the miracle of its growth, illuminated by the flame of its fall, and transfigured by the divinity of its resurrection, and you will feel, as I do, the utter impossibility of compassing this subject as it deserves. Some impression of her importance is received from the shock her burning gave to the civilized world

When the doubt of her calamity was removed, and the horrid fact was accepted, there went a shudder over all cities, and a quiver over all lands. There was scarcely a town in the civilized world that did not shake on the brink of this opening chasm. The flames of our homes reddened all skies. The city was set upon a hill, and could not be hid All eyes were turned upon it. To have struggled and suffered amid the scenes of its fall is as distinguishing as to have fought at Thermopylæ, or Salamis, or Hastings, or Waterloo, or Bunker Hill.

Its calamity amazed the world, because it was felt to be the common property of mankind.

The early history of the city is full of interest, just as the early history of such a man as Washington or Lincoln becomes public property, and is cherished by every patriot.

Starting with 560 acres in 1833, it embraced and occupied 23,000 acres in 1869, and, having now a population of more than 500,000, it commands general attention.

The first settler—Jean Baptiste Pointe au Sable, a mulatto from the West Indies—came and began trade with the Indians in 1796. John Kinzie became his successor in 1804, in which year Fort Dearborn was erected.

A mere trading-post was kept here from that time till about the time of the Blackhawk war, in 1832. It was not the city. It was merely a cock crowing at midnight. The morning was not yet. In 1833 the settlement about the fort was incorporated as a town. The voters were divided on the propriety of such corporation, twelve voting for it and one against it. Four years later it was incorporated as a city, and embraced 560 acres.

The produce handled in this city is an indication of its power. Grain and flour were imported from the East till as late as 1837. The first exportation by way of experiment was in 1839. Exports exceeded imports first in 1842. The Board of Trade was organized in 1848, but it was so weak that it needed nursing till 1855. Grain was purchased by the wagon-load in the street.

I remember sitting with my father on a load of wheat, in the long line of wagons along Lake street, while the buyers came and untied the bags, and examined the grain, and made their bids. That manner of business had to cease with the day of small things. Now our elevators will hold 15,000,000 bushels of grain. The cash value of the produce handled in a year is $215,000,000, and the produce weighs 7,000,000 tons or 700,000 car loads. This handles thirteen and a half ton each minute, all the year round. One tenth of all the wheat in the United States is handled in Chicago. Even as long ago as 1853 the receipts of grain in Chicago exceeded those of the goodly city of St Louis, and in 1854 the exports of grain from Chicago exceeded those of New York and doubled those of St. Petersburg, Archangel, or Odessa, the largest grain markets in Europe.

The manufacturing interests of the city are not contemptible. In 1873 manufactories employed 45,000 operatives; in 1876, 60,000. The manufactured product in 1875 was worth $177,000,000.

No estimate of the size and power of Chicago would be adequate that did not put large emphasis on the railroads. Before they came thundering along our streets canals were the hope of our country. But who ever thinks now of traveling by canal packets? In June, 1852, there were only forty miles of railroad connected with the city. The old Galena division of the Northwestern ran out to Elgin. But now, who can count the trains and measure the roads that seek a terminus or connection in this city? The lake stretches away to the north, gathering in to this center all the harvests that might otherwise pass to the north of us If you will take a map and look at the adjustment of railroads, you will see, first, that Chicago is the great railroad center of the world, as New York is the commercial city of this continent; and, second, that the railroad lines form the iron spokes of a great wheel whose hub is this city. The lake furnishes the only break in the spokes, and this seems simply to have pushed a few spokes together on each shore. See the eighteen trunk lines, exclusive of eastern connections.

Pass round the circle, and view their numbers and extent. There is the great Northwestern, with all its branches, one branch creeping along the lake shore, and so reaching to the north, into the Lake Superior regions, away to the right, and on to the Northern Pacific on the left, swinging around Green Bay for iron and copper and silver, twelve months in the year, and reaching out for the wealth of the great agricultural belt and isothermal line traversed by the Northern Pacific. Another branch, not so far north, feeling for the heart of the Badger State. Another pushing lower down the Mississippi—all these make many connections, and tapping all the vast wheat regions of Minnesota, Wisconsin, Iowa, and all the regions this side of sunset. There is that elegant road, the Chicago, Burlington & Quincy, running out a goodly number of

OLD FORT DEARBORN, 1830.

PRESENT SITE OF LAKE STREET BRIDGE, CHICAGO, IN 1833.

branches, and reaping the great fields this side of the Missouri River. I can only mention the Chicago, Alton & St. Louis, *our* Illinois Central, described elsewhere, and the Chicago & Rock Island. Further around we come to the lines connecting us with all the eastern cities The Chicago, Indianapolis & St. Louis, the Pittsburgh, Fort Wayne & Chicago, the Lake Shore & Michigan Southern, and the Michigan Central and Great Western, give us many highways to the seaboard. Thus we reach the Mississippi at five points, from St. Paul to Cairo and the Gulf itself by two routes. We also reach Cincinnati and Baltimore, and Pittsburgh and Philadelphia, and New York. North and south run the water courses of the lakes and the rivers, broken just enough at this point to make a pass. Through this, from east to west, run the long lines that stretch from ocean to ocean.

This is the neck of the glass, and the golden sands of commerce must pass into our hands Altogether we have more than 10,000 miles of railroad, directly tributary to this city, seeking to unload their wealth in our coffers. All these roads have come themselves by the infallible instinct of capital. Not a dollar was ever given by the city to secure one of them, and only a small per cent. of stock taken originally by her citizens, and that taken simply as an investment Coming in the natural order of events, they will not be easily diverted,

There is still another showing to all this. The connection between New York and San Francisco is by the middle route. This passes inevitably through Chicago. St. Louis wants the Southern Pacific or Kansas Pacific, and pushes it out through Denver, and so on up to Cheyenne But before the road is fairly under way, the Chicago roads shove out to Kansas City, making even the Kansas Pacific a feeder, and actually leaving St. Louis out in the cold. It is not too much to expect that Dakota, Montana, and Washington Territory will find their great market in Chicago.

But these are not all. Perhaps I had better notice here the ten or fifteen new roads that have just entered, or are just entering, our city. Their names are all that is necessary to give. Chicago & St. Paul, looking up the Red River country to the British possessions, the Chicago, Atlantic & Pacific; the Chicago, Decatur & State Line; the Baltimore & Ohio; the Chicago, Danville & Vincennes; the Chicago & LaSalle Railroad, the Chicago, Pittsburgh & Cincinnati; the Chicago and Canada Southern; the Chicago and Illinois River Railroad. These, with their connections, and with the new connections of the old roads, already in process of erection, give to Chicago not less than 10,000 miles of new tributaries from the richest land on the continent. Thus there will be added to the reserve power, to the capital within reach of this city, not less than $1,000,000,000.

Add to all this transporting power the ships that sail one every nine minutes of the business hours of the season of navigation ; add, also, the canal boats that leave one every five minutes during the same time—and you will see something of the business of the city.

THE COMMERCE OF THIS CITY

has been leaping along to keep pace with the growth of the country around us. In 1852, our commerce reached the hopeful sum of $20,000,000. In 1870 it reached $400,000,000. In 1871 it was pushed up above $450,000,000. And in 1875 it touched nearly double that.

One-half of our imported goods come directly to Chicago Grain enough is exported directly from our docks to the old world to employ a semi-weekly line of steamers of 3,000 tons capacity This branch is not likely to be greatly developed Even after the great Welland Canal is completed we shall have only fourteen feet of water. The great ocean vessels will continue to control the trade.

The banking capital of Chicago is $24,431,000. Total exchange in 1875, $659,000,000. Her wholesale business in 1875 was $294,000,000. The rate of taxes is less than in any other great city.

The schools of Chicago are unsurpassed in America. Out of a population of 300,000 there were only 186 persons between the ages of six and twenty-one unable to read. This is the best known record.

In 1831 the mail system was condensed into a half-breed, who went on foot to Niles, Mich., once in two weeks, and brought back what papers and news he could find. As late as 1846 there was often only one mail a week. A post-office was established in Chicago in 1833, and the postmaster nailed up old boot-legs on one side of his shop to serve as boxes for the nabobs and literary men.

It is an interesting fact in the growth of the young city that in the active life of the business men of that day the mail matter has grown to a daily average of over 6,500 pounds It speaks equally well for the intelligence of the people and the commercial importance of the place. that the mail matter distributed to the territory immediately tributary to Chicago is seven times greater than that distributed to the territory immediately tributary to St. Louis.

The improvements that have characterized the city are as startling as the city itself. In 1831, Mark Beaubien established a ferry over the river, and put himself under bonds to carry all the citizens free for the privilege of charging strangers. Now there are twenty-four large bridges and two tunnels.

In 1833 the government expended $30,000 on the harbor. Then commenced that series of manœuvers with the river that has made it one of the world's curiosities. It used to wind around in the lower end of the town, and make its way rippling over the sand into the lake at the foot of Madison street They took it up and put it down where it now is. It was a narrow stream, so narrow that even moderately small crafts had to go up through the willows and cat's tails to the point near Lake street bridge, and back up one of the branches to get room enough in which to turn around

In 1844 the quagmires in the streets were first pontooned by plank roads, which acted in wet weather as public squirt-guns Keeping you out of the mud, they compromised by squirting the mud over you. The wooden-block pavements came to Chicago in 1857. In 1840 water was delivered by peddlers in carts or by hand. Then a twenty-five horse-power engine pushed it through hollow or bored logs along the streets till 1854, when it was introduced into the houses by new works. The first fire-engine was used in 1835, and the first steam fire-engine in 1859. Gas was utilized for lighting the city in 1850. The Young Men's Christian Association was organized in 1858, and horse railroads carried them to their work in 1859. The museum was opened in 1863 The alarm telegraph adopted in 1864. The opera-house built in 1865. The city grew from 560 acres in 1833 to 23,000 in 1869. In 1834, the taxes amounted to $48.90, and the trustees of the town borrowed $60 more for opening and improving streets. In 1835, the legislature authorized a loan of $2,000, and the treasurer and street commissioners resigned rather than plunge the town into such a gulf

Now the city embraces 36 square miles of territory, and has 30 miles of water front, besides the outside harbor of refuge, of 400 acres, inclosed by a crib sea-wall. One-third of the city has been raised up an average of eight feet, giving good pitch to the 263 miles of sewerage. The water of the city is above all competition. It is received through two tunnels extending to a crib in the lake two miles from shore. The closest analysis fails to detect any impurities, and, received 35 feet below the surface, it is always clear and cold. The first tunnel is five feet two inches in diameter and two miles long, and can deliver 50,000,000 of gallons per day. The second tunnel is seven feet in diameter and six miles long, running four miles under the city, and can deliver 100,000,000 of gallons per day. This water is distributed through 410 miles of water-mains.

The three grand engineering exploits of the city are: First, lifting the city up on jack-screws, whole squares at a time, without interrupting the business, thus giving us good drainage; second, running the tunnels under the lake, giving us the best water in the world; and third, the turning the current of the river in its own channel, delivering us from the old abominations, and making decency possible. They redound about equally to the credit of the engineering, to the energy of the people, and to the health of the city.

That which really constitutes the city, its indescribable spirit, its soul, the way it lights up in every feature in the hour of action, has not been touched. In meeting strangers, one is often surprised how some homely women marry so well. Their forms are bad, their gait uneven and awkward, their complexion is dull, their features are misshapen and mismatched, and when we see them there is no beauty that we should desire them. But when once they are aroused on some subject, they put on new proportions. They light up into great power. The real person comes out from its unseemly ambush, and captures us at will. They have power. They have ability to cause things to come to pass. We no longer wonder why they are in such high demand. So it is with our city. ,

There is no grand scenery except the two seas, one of water, the other of prairie. Nevertheless, there is a spirit about it, a push, a breadth, a power, that soon makes it a place never to be forsaken. One soon ceases to believe in impossibilities. Balaams are the only prophets that are disappointed. The bottom that has been on the point of falling out has been there so long that it has grown fast. It can not fall out. It has all the capital of the world itching to get inside the corporation.

The two great laws that govern the growth and size of cities are, first, the amount of territory for which they are the distributing and receiving points; second, the number of medium or moderate dealers that do this distributing. Monopolists build up themselves, not the cities. They neither eat, wear, nor live in proportion to their business. Both these laws help Chicago.

The tide of trade is eastward—not up or down the map, but across the map. The lake runs up a wingdam for 500 miles to gather in the business. Commerce can not ferry up there for seven months in the year, and the facilities for seven months can do the work for twelve. Then the great region west of us is nearly all good, productive land. Dropping south into the trail of St. Louis, you fall into vast deserts and rocky districts, useful in holding the world together. St. Louis and Cincinnati, instead of rivaling and hurting Chicago, are her greatest sureties of dominion. They are far enough away to give sea-room,—farther off than Paris is from London,—and yet they are near enough to prevent the springing up of any other great city between them.

St. Louis will be helped by the opening of the Mississippi, but also hurt. That will put New Orleans on her feet, and with a railroad running over into Texas and so West, she will tap the streams that now crawl up the Texas and Missouri road. The current is East, not North, and a seaport at New Orleans can not permanently help St. Louis.

Chicago is in the field almost alone, to handle the wealth of one-fourth of the territory of this great republic. This strip of seacoast divides its margins between Portland, Boston, New York, Philadelphia, Baltimore and Savannah, or some other great port to be created for the South in the next decade. But Chicago has a dozen empires casting their treasures into her lap. On a bed of coal that can run all the machinery of the world for 500 centuries; in a garden that can feed the race by the thousand years; at the head of the lakes that give her a temperature as a summer resort equaled by no great city in the land, with a climate that insures the health of her citizens; surrounded by all the great deposits of natural wealth in mines and forests and herds, Chicago is the wonder of to-day, and will be *the city of the future.*

MASSACRE AT FORT DEARBORN.

During the war of 1812, Fort Dearborn became the theater of stirring events. The garrison consisted of fifty-four men under command of Captain Nathan Heald, assisted by Lieutenant Helm (son-in-law of Mrs. Kinzie) and Ensign Ronan. Dr. Voorhees was surgeon. The only residents at the post at that time were the wives of Captain Heald and Lieutenant Helm, and a few of the soldiers, Mr. Kinzie and his family, and a few Canadian *voyageurs,* with their wives and children. The soldiers and Mr. Kinzie were on most friendly terms with the Pottawattamies and Winnebagos, the principal tribes around them, but they could not win them from their attachment to the British.

One evening in April, 1812, Mr. Kinzie sat playing on his violin and his children were dancing to the music, when Mrs. Kinzie came rushing into the house, pale with terror, and exclaiming: "The Indians! the Indians!" "What? Where?" eagerly inquired Mr. Kinzie. "Up at Lee's, killing and scalping," answered the frightened mother, who, when the alarm was given, was attending Mrs. Barnes (just confined) living not far off. Mr. Kinzie and his family crossed the river and took refuge in the fort, to which place Mrs. Barnes and her infant not a day old were safely conveyed. The rest of the inhabitants took shelter in the fort. This alarm was caused by a scalping party of Winnebagos, who hovered about the fort several days, when they disappeared, and for several weeks the inhabitants were undisturbed.

On the 7th of August, 1812, General Hull, at Detroit, sent orders to Captain Heald to evacuate Fort Dearborn, and to distribute all the United States property to the Indians in the neighborhood—a most insane order. The Pottawattamie chief, who brought the dispatch, had more wisdom than the commanding general. He advised Captain Heald not to make the distribution. Said he: "Leave the fort and stores as they are, and let the Indians make distribution for themselves, and while they are engaged in the business, the white people may escape to Fort Wayne."

RUINS OF CHICAGO.

Captain Heald held a council with the Indians on the afternoon of the 12th, in which his officers refused to join, for they had been informed that treachery was designed—that the Indians intended to murder the white people in the council, and then destroy those in the fort. Captain Heald, however, took the precaution to open a port-hole displaying a cannon pointing directly upon the council, and by that means saved his life

Mr. Kinzie, who knew the Indians well, begged Captain Heald not to confide in their promises, nor distribute the arms and munitions among them, for it would only put power into their hands to destroy the whites. Acting upon this advice, Heald resolved to withhold the munitions of war; and on the night of the 13th, after the distribution of the other property had been made, the powder, ball and liquors were thrown into the river, the muskets broken up and destroyed.

Black Partridge, a friendly chief, came to Captain Heald, and said: "Linden birds have been singing in my ears to-day: be careful on the march you are going to take." On that dark night vigilant Indians had crept near the fort and discovered the destruction of their promised booty going on within. The next morning the powder was seen floating on the surface of the river. The savages were exasperated and made loud complaints and threats.

On the following day when preparations were making to leave the fort, and all the inmates were deeply impressed with a sense of impending danger, Capt. Wells, an uncle of Mrs. Heald, was discovered upon the Indian trail among the sand-hills on the borders of the lake, not far distant, with a band of mounted Miamis, of whose tribe he was chief, having been adopted by the famous Miami warrior, Little Turtle. When news of Hull's surrender reached Fort Wayne, he had started with this force to assist Heald in defending Fort Dearborn. He was too late Every means for its defense had been destroyed the night before, and arrangements were made for leaving the fort on the morning of the 15th.

It was a warm bright morning in the middle of August. Indications were positive that the savages intended to murder the white people; and when they moved out of the southern gate of the fort, the march was like a funeral procession. The band, feeling the solemnity of the occasion, struck up the Dead March in Saul.

Capt. Wells, who had blackened his face with gun-powder in token of his fate, took the lead with his band of Miamis, followed by Capt. Heald, with his wife by his side on horseback. Mr. Kinzie hoped by his personal influence to avert the impending blow, and therefore accompanied them, leaving his family in a boat in charge of a friendly Indian, to be taken to his trading station at the site of Niles, Michigan, in the event of his death.

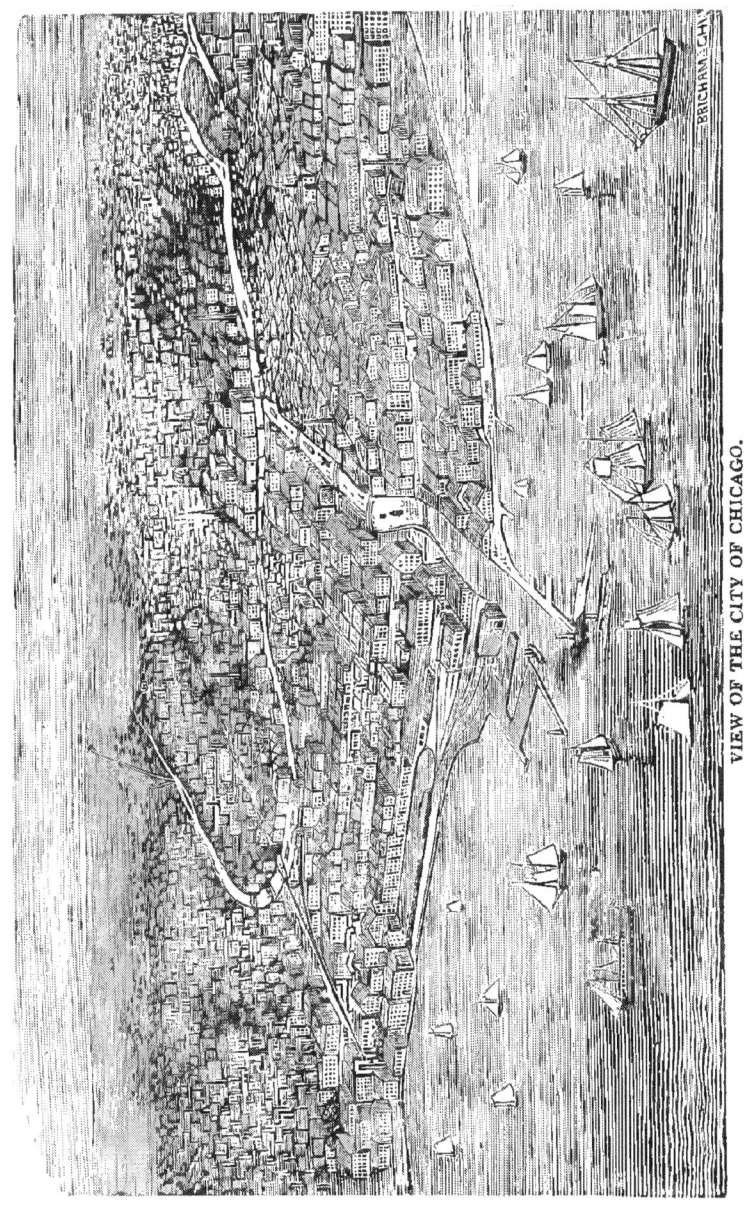

VIEW OF THE CITY OF CHICAGO.

The procession moved slowly along the lake shore till they reached the sand-hills between the prairie and the beach, when the Pottawattamie escort, under the leadership of Blackbird, filed to the right, placing those hills between them and the white people. Wells, with his Miamis, had kept in the advance. They suddenly came rushing back, Wells exclaiming, "They are about to attack us; form instantly." These words were quickly followed by a storm of bullets, which came whistling over the little hills which the treacherous savages had made the covert for their murderous attack. The white troops charged upon the Indians, drove them back to the prairie, and then the battle was waged between fifty-four soldiers, twelve civilians and three or four women (the cowardly Miamis having fled at the outset) against five hundred Indian warriors. The white people, hopeless, resolved to sell their lives as dearly as possible. Ensign Ronan wielded his weapon vigorously, even after falling upon his knees weak from the loss of blood. Capt. Wells, who was by the side of his niece, Mrs. Heald, when the conflict began, behaved with the greatest coolness and courage. He said to her, "We have not the slightest chance for life. We must part to meet no more in this world. God bless you." And then he dashed forward. Seeing a young warrior, painted like a demon, climb into a wagon in which were twelve children, and tomahawk them all, he cried out, unmindful of his personal danger, "If that is your game, butchering women and children, I will kill too." He spurred his horse towards the Indian camp, where they had left their squaws and papooses, hotly pursued by swift-footed young warriors, who sent bullets whistling after him. One of these killed his horse and wounded him severely in the leg. With a yell the young braves rushed to make him their prisoner and reserve him for torture. He resolved not to be made a captive, and by the use of the most provoking epithets tried to induce them to kill him instantly. He called a fiery young chief a *squaw*, when the enraged warrior killed Wells instantly with his tomahawk, jumped upon his body, cut out his heart, and ate a portion of the warm morsel with savage delight!

In this fearful combat women bore a conspicuous part. Mrs. Heald was an excellent equestrian and an expert in the use of the rifle. She fought the savages bravely, receiving several severe wounds. Though faint from the loss of blood, she managed to keep her saddle. A savage raised his tomahawk to kill her, when she looked him full in the face, and with a sweet smile and in a gentle voice said, in his own language, "Surely you will not kill a squaw!" The arm of the savage fell, and the life of the heroic woman was saved.

Mrs. Helm, the step-daughter of Mr. Kinzie, had an encounter with a stout Indian, who attempted to tomahawk her. Springing to one side, she received the glancing blow on her shoulder, and at the same instant seized the savage round the neck with her arms and endeavored to get hold of his scalping knife, which hung in a sheath at his breast. While she was thus struggling she was dragged from her antagonist by another powerful Indian, who bore her, in spite of her struggles, to the margin of the lake and plunged her in To her astonishment she was held by him so that she would not drown, and she soon perceived that she was in the hands of the friendly Black Partridge, who had saved her life.

The wife of Sergeant Holt, a large and powerful woman, behaved as bravely as an Amazon. She rode a fine, high-spirited horse, which the Indians coveted, and several of them attacked her with the butts of their guns, for the purpose of dismounting her ; but she used the sword which she had snatched from her disabled husband so skillfully that she foiled them ; and, suddenly wheeling her horse, she dashed over the prairie, followed by the savages shouting, " The brave woman ! the brave woman ! Don't hurt her ! ' They finally overtook her, and while she was fighting them in front, a powerful savage came up behind her, seized her by the neck and dragged her to the ground. Horse and woman were made captives. Mrs. Holt was a long time a captive among the Indians, but was afterwards ransomed.

In this sharp conflict two-thirds of the white people were slain and wounded, and all their horses, baggage and provision were lost. Only twenty-eight straggling men now remained to fight five hundred Indians rendered furious by the sight of blood. They succeeded in breaking through the ranks of the murderers and gaining a slight eminence on the prairie near the Oak Woods. The Indians did not pursue, but gathered on their flanks, while the chiefs held a consultation on the sand-hills, and showed signs of willingness to parley. It would have been madness on the part of the whites to renew the fight; and so Capt. Heald went forward and met Blackbird on the open prairie, where terms of surrender were soon agreed upon. It was arranged that the white people should give up their arms to Blackbird, and that the survivors should become prisoners of war, to be exchanged for ransoms as soon as practicable. With this understanding captives and captors started for the Indian camp near the fort, to which Mrs. Helm had been taken bleeding and suffering by Black Partridge, and had met her step-father and learned that her husband was safe

A new scene of horror was now opened at the Indian camp. The wounded, not being included in the terms of surrender, as it was interpreted by the Indians, and the British general, Proctor, having offered a liberal bounty for American scalps, delivered at Malden, nearly all the wounded men were killed and scalped, and the price of the trophies was afterwards paid by the British government.

THE STATE OF IOWA.

GEOGRAPHICAL SITUATION.

The State of Iowa has an outline figure nearly approaching that of a rectangular parallelogram, the northern and southern boundaries being nearly due east and west lines, and its eastern and western boundaries determined by southerly flowing rivers—the Mississippi on the east, and the Missouri, together with its tributary, the Big Sioux, on the west. The northern boundary is upon the parallel of forty-three degrees thirty minutes, and the southern is approximately upon that of forty degrees and thirty-six minutes. The distance from the northern to the southern boundary, excluding the small prominent angle at the southeast corner, is a little more than two hundred miles. Owing to the irregularity of the river boundaries, however, the number of square miles does not reach that of the multiple of these numbers; but according to a report of the Secretary of the Treasury to the United States Senate, March 12, 1863, the State of Iowa contains 35,228,200 acres, or 55,044 square miles. When it is understood that all this vast extent of surface, except that which is occupied by our rivers, lakes and peat beds of the northern counties, is susceptible of the highest cultivation, some idea may be formed of the immense agricultural resources of the State. Iowa is nearly as large as England, and twice as large as Scotland: but when we consider the relative area of surface which may be made to yield to the wants of man, those countries of the Old World will bear no comparison with Iowa.

TOPOGRAPHY.

No complete topographical survey of the State of Iowa has yet been made. Therefore all the knowledge we have yet upon the subject has been obtained from incidental observations of geological corps, from barometrical observations by authority of the General Government, and levelings done by railroad engineer corps within the State.

Taking into view the facts that the highest point in the State is but a little more than twelve hundred feet above the lowest point, that these two points are nearly three hundred miles apart, and that the whole State is traversed by gently flowing rivers, it will be seen that in reality the State of Iowa rests wholly within, and comprises a part of, a vast plain, with no mountain or hill ranges within its borders.

A clearer idea of the great uniformity of the surface of the State may be obtained from a statement of the general slopes in feet per mile, from point to point, in straight lines across it:

From the N E corner to the S E corner of the State .. ....1 foot 1 inch per mile
From the N E corner to Spirit Lake   ....   . . .5 feet 5 inches per mile
From the N W corner to Spirit Lake ....   5 feet 0 inches per mile.
From the N. W corner to the S W. corner of the State .. ..2 feet 0 inches per mile.
From the S W corner to the highest ridge between the two
     great rivers (in Ringgold County)...   .   4 feet 1 inch per mile
From the dividing ridge in the S E corner of the State .....5 feet 7 inches per mile
From the highest point in the State (near Spirit Lake) to the
     lowest point in the State (at the mouth of Des Moines   •
     River)   . ..   .4 feet 0 inches per mile

It will be seen, therefore, that there is a good degree of propriety in regarding the whole State as a part of a great plain, the lowest point of which within its borders, the southeast corner of the State, is only 444 feet above the level of the sea. The average height of the whole State above the level of the sea is not far from eight hundred feet, although it is more than a thousand miles inland from the nearest sea coast. These remarks are, of course, to be understood as applying to the surface of the State as a whole. When we come to consider its surface feature in detail, we find a great diversity of surface by the formation of valleys out of the general level, which have been evolved by the action of streams during the unnumbered years of the terrace epoch.

It is in the northeastern part of the State that the river valleys are deepest; consequently the country there has the greatest diversity of surface, and its physical features are most strongly marked.

DRAINAGE SYSTEM

The Mississippi and Missouri Rivers form the eastern and western boundaries of the State, and receive the eastern and western drainage of it.

The eastern drainage system comprises not far from two-thirds of the entire surface of the State. The great watershed which divides these two systems is formed by the highest land between those rivers along the whole length of a line running southward from a point on the northern boundary line of the State near Spirit Lake, in Dickinson County, to a nearly central point in the northern part of Adair County.

From the last named point, this highest ridge of land, between the two great rivers, continues southward, without change of character, through Ringgold County into the State of Missouri; but southward from that point, in Adair County, it is no longer the great watershed From that point, another and lower ridge bears off more nearly southeastward, through the counties of Madison, Clarke, Lucas and Appanoose, and becomes itself the great watershed.

RIVERS.

All streams that rise in Iowa rise upon the incoherent surface deposits, occupying at first only slight depressions in the surface, and scarcely perceptible. These successively coalesce to form the streams.

The drift and bluff deposits are both so thick in Iowa that its streams not only rise upon their surface, but they also reach considerable depth into these deposits alone, in some cases to' a depth of nearly two hundred feet from the general prairie level.

The majority of streams that constitute the western system of Iowa drainage run, either along the whole or a part of their course, upon that peculir deposit known as bluff deposit. Their banks are often, even of the small streams, from five to ten feet in height, quite perpendicular, so that they make the streams almost everywhere unfordable, and a great impediment to travel across the open country where there are no bridges.

The material of this deposit is of a slightly yellowish ash color, except where darkened by decaying vegetation, very fine and silicious, but not sandy, not very cohesive, and not at all plastic. It forms excellent soil, and does not bake or crack in drying, except limy concretions, which are generally distributed throughout the mass, in shape and size resembling pebbles; not a stone or pebble can be found in the whole deposit. It was called "silicious marl" by Dr. Owen, in his geological report to the General Government, and its origin referred to an accumulation of sediment in an ancient lake, which was afterward drained, when its sediment became dry land. Prof Swallaw gives it the name of "bluff," which is here adopted; the term Lacustral would have been better. The peculiar properties of this deposit are that it will stand securely with a precipitous front two hundred feet high, and yet is easily excavated with a spade. Wells dug in it require only to be walled to a point just above the water line. Yet, compact as it is, it is very porous, so that water which falls on its surface does not remain, but percolates through it; neither does it accumulate within its mass, as it does upon the surface of and within the drift and the stratified formations.

The bluff deposit is known to occupy a region through which the Missouri runs almost centrally, and measures, as far as is known, more than two hundred miles in length and nearly one hundred miles in width The thickest part yet known in Iowa is in Fremont County, where it reaches two hundred feet. The boundaries of this deposit in Iowa are nearly as follows. Commencing at the southeast corner of Fremont County, follow up the watershed between the East Nishnabotany and the West Tarkio Rivers to the southern boundary of Cass County; thence to the center of Audubon County; thence to Tip Top Station, on the Chicago & Northwestern Railway; thence by a broad curve westward to the northwest corner of Plymouth County.

This deposit is composed of fine sedimentary particles, similar to that which the Missouri River now deposits from its waters, and is the same which that river did deposit in a broad depression in the surface of the drift that formed a lake-like expansion of that river in the earliest period of the history of its valley.   That lake, as shown by its deposit, which now remains, was about one hundred miles wide and more than twice as long.   The water of the river was muddy then, as now, and the broad lake became filled with the sediment which the river brought down, before its valley had enough in the lower portion of its course to drain it.   After the lake became filled with the sediment, the valley below became deepened by the constant erosive action of the waters, to a depth of more than sufficient to have drained the lake of its first waters ; but the only effect then was to cause it to cut its valley out of the deposits its own muddy waters had formed   Thus along the valley of that river, so far as it forms the western boundary of Iowa, the bluffs which border it are composed of that sediment known as bluff deposit, forming a distinct border along the broad, level flood plain, the width of which varies from five to fifteen miles, while the original sedimentary deposit stretches far inland.

All the rivers of the western system of drainage, except the Missouri itself, are quite incomplete as rivers, in consequence of their being really only branches of other larger tributaries of that great river , or, if they empty into the Missouri direct, they have yet all the usual characteristics of Iowa rivers, from their sources to their mouths.

Chariton and Grand Rivers both rise and run for the first twenty-five miles of their courses upon the drift deposit alone.   The first strata that are exposed by the deepening valleys of both these streams belong to the upper coal measures, and they both continue upon the same formation until they make their exit from the State (the former in Appanoose County, the latter in Ringgold County), near the boundary of which they have passed nearly or quite through the whole of that formation to the middle coal measures   Their valleys gradually deepen from their upper portions downward, so that within fifteen or twenty miles they have reached a depth of near a hundred and fifty feet below the general level of the adjacent high land.   When the rivers have cut their valleys down through the series of limestone strata, they reach those of a clayey composition   Upon these they widen their valleys and make broad flood plains (commonly termed " bottoms "), the soil of which is stiff and clayey, except where modified by sandy washings.

A considerable breadth of woodland occupies the bottoms and valley sides along a great part of their length ; but their upper branches and tributaries are mostly prairie streams.

Platte River —This river belongs mainly to Missouri   Its upper branches pass through Ringgold County, and, with the west fork of the Grand River, drain a large region of country.

Here the drift deposit reaches its maximum thickness on an east and west line across the State, and the valleys are eroded in some instances to a depth of two hundred feet, apparently, through this deposit alone.

The term " drift deposit" applies to the soil and sub-soil of the greater part of the State, and in it alone many of our wells are dug and our forests take root.   It rests upon the stratified rocks.   It is composed of clay, sand, gravel and boulders, promiscuously intermixed, without stratification, varying in character in different parts of the State

The proportion of lime in the drift of Iowa is so great that the water of all our wells and springs is too "hard" for washing purposes; and the same substance is so prevalent in the drift clays that they are always found to have sufficient flux when used for the manufacture of brick

One Hundred and Two River is represented in Taylor County, the valleys of which have the same general character of those just described.   The country around and between the east and west forks of this stream is almost entirely prairie

Nodaway River —This stream is represented by east, middle and west branches.   The two former rise in Adair County, the latter in Cass County These rivers and valleys are fine examples of the small rivers and valleys of Southern Iowa.   They have the general character of drift valleys, and with beautiful undulating and sloping sides   The Nodaways drain one of the finest agricultural regions in the State, the soil of which is tillable almost to their very banks.   The banks and the adjacent narrow flood plains are almost everywhere composed of a rich, deep, dark loam

Nishnabotany River —This river is represented by east and west branches, the former having its source in Anderson County, the latter in Shelby County Both these branches, from their source to their confluence—and also the main stream, from thence to the point where it enters the great flood plain of the Missouri—run through a region the surface of which is occupied by the bluff deposit.   The West Nishnabotany is probably without any valuable mill sites. In the western part of Cass County, the East Nishnabotany loses its identity by becoming abruptly divided up into five or six different creeks.   A few good mill sites occur here on this stream.   None, however, that are thought reliable exist on either of these rivers, or on the main stream below the confluence, except, perhaps, one or two in Montgomery County.   The valleys of the two branches, and the intervening upland, possess remarkable fertility.

Boyer River.—Until it enters the flood plain of the Missouri, the Boyer runs almost, if not quite, its entire course through the region occupied by the bluff deposit, and has cut its valley entirely through it along most of its passage   The only rocks exposed are the upper coal measures, near Reed's mill, in Harrison County   The exposures are slight, and are the most northerly now known in Iowa.   The valley of this river has usually gently sloping sides, and an indistinctly defined flood plain.   Along the lower half of its course the adjacent upland presents a surface of the billowy character, peculiar to the bluff deposit. The source of this river is in Sac County.

Soldier River.—The east and middle branches of this stream have their source in Crawford County, and the west branch in Ida County. The whole course of this river is through the bluff deposit. It has no exposure of strata along its course.

Little Sioux River.—Under this head are included both the main and west branches of that stream, together with the Maple, which is one of its branches. The west branch and the Maple are so similar to the Soldier River that they need no separate description. The main stream has its boundary near the northern boundary of the State, and runs most of its course upon drift deposit alone, entering the region of the bluff deposit in the southern part of Cherokee County. The two principal upper branches, near their source in Dickinson and Osceola Counties, are small prairie creeks, with indistinct valleys. On entering Clay County, the valley deepens, and at their confluence has a depth of one hundred feet, which still further increases until along the boundary line between Clay and Buena Vista Counties, it reaches a depth of two hundred feet. Just as the valley enters Cherokee County, it turns to the southward and becomes much widened, with its sides gently sloping to the uplands. When the valley enters the region of the bluff deposit, it assumes the billowy appearance. No exposures of strata of any kind have been found in the valley of the Little Sioux or any of its branches.

Floyd River.—This river rises upon the drift in O'Brien County, and flowing southward enters the region of the bluff deposit a little north of the center of Plymouth County. Almost from its source to its mouth it is a prairie stream, with slightly sloping valley sides, which blend gradually with the uplands. A single slight exposure of sandstone of cretaceous age occurs in the valley near Sioux City, and which is the only known exposure of rock of any kind along its whole length. Near this exposure is a mill site, but farther up the stream it is not valuable for such purposes.

Rock River.—This stream passes through Lyon and Sioux Counties. It was evidently so named from the fact that considerable exposures of the red Sioux quartzite occur along the main branches of the stream in Minnesota, a few miles north of our State boundary. Within this State the main stream and its branches are drift streams, and strata are exposed. The beds and banks of the streams are usually sandy and gravelly, with occasional boulders intermixed.

Big Sioux River.—The valley of this river, from the northwest corner of the State to its mouth, possesses much the same character as all the streams of the surface deposits. At Sioux Falls, a few miles above the northwest corner of the State, the stream meets with remarkable obstructions from the presence of Sioux quartzite, which outcrops directly across the stream, and causes a fall of about sixty feet within a distance of half a mile, producing a series of cascades. For the first twenty-five miles above its mouth, the valley is very broad, with a broad, flat flood plain, with gentle slopes occasionally showing indistinctly defined terraces. These terraces and valley bottoms constitute some of the finest agricultural land of the region. On the Iowa side of the valley the upland presents abrupt bluffs, steep as the materials of which they are composed will stand, and from one hundred to nearly two hundred feet high above the stream At rare intervals, about fifteen miles from its mouth, the cretaceous strata are found exposed in the face of the bluffs of the Iowa side. No other strata are exposed along that part of the valley which borders our State, with the single exception of Sioux quartzite at its extreme northwestern corner. Some good mill sites may be secured along that portion of this river which borders Lyon County, but below this the fall will probably be found insufficient and the location for dams insecure

Missouri River.—This is one of the muddiest streams on the globe, and its waters are known to be very turbid far toward its source. The chief peculiarity of this river is its broad flood plains, and its adjacent bluff deposits. Much the greater part of the flood plain of this river is upon the Iowa side, and continuous from the south boundary line of the State to Sioux City, a distance of more than one hundred miles in length, varying from three to five miles in width This alluvial plain is estimated to contain more than half a million acres of land within the State, upward of four hundred thousand of which are now tillable.

The rivers of the eastern system of drainage have quite a different character from those of the western system. They are larger, longer and have their valleys modified to a much greater extent by the underlying strata For the latter reason, water-power is much more abundant upon them than upon the streams of the western system.

Des Moines River.—This river has its source in Minnesota, but it enters Iowa before it has attained any size, and flows almost centrally through it from northwest to southeast, emptying into the Mississippi at the extreme southeastern corner of the State It drains a greater area than any river within the State. The upper portion of it is divided into two branches known as the east and west forks These unite in Humboldt County. The valleys of these branches above their confluence are drift-valleys, except a few small exposures of subcarboniferous limestone about five miles above their confluence. These exposures produce several small mill-sites The valleys vary from a few hundred yards to half a mile in width, and are the finest agricultural lands In the northern part of Webster County, the character of the main valley is modified by the presence of ledges and low cliffs of the subcarboniferous limestone and gypsum. From a point a little below Fort Dodge to near Amsterdam, in Marion County, the river runs all the way through and upon the lower coal-measure strata. Along this part of its course the flood-plain varies from an eighth to half a mile or more in width. From Amsterdam to Ottumwa the subcarboniferous limestone appears at intervals in the valley sides Near Ottumwa, the subcarboniferous rocks pass beneath the river again, bringing down the coal-measure strata into its bed; but they rise again from it in the extreme northwestern part of Van Buren County, and subcarboniferous strata resume and keep their place along the valley to the north of the river. From Fort Dodge to the northern part of Lee County, the strata of the lower coal measures are present in the valley. Its flood plain is frequently sandy, from the debris of the sandstone and sandy shales of the coal measures produced by their removal in the process of the formation of the valley

The principal tributaries of the Des Moines are upon the western side. These are the Raccoon and the three rivers, viz.. South, Middle and North Rivers The three latter have their source in the region occupied by the upper coal-measure limestone formation, flow eastward over the middle coal measures, and enter the valley of the Des Moines upon the lower coal measures These streams, especially South and Middle Rivers, are frequently bordered by high, rocky cliffs. Raccoon River has its source upon the heavy surface deposits of the middle region of Western Iowa, and along the greater part of its course it has excavated its valley out those deposits and the middle coal measures alone. The valley of the Des Moines and its branches are destined to become the seat of extensive manufactures in consequence of the numerous mill sites of immense power, and the fact that the main valley traverses the entire length of the Iowa coal fields.

Skunk River.—This river has its source in Hamilton County, and runs almost its entire course upon the border of the outcrop of the lower coal measures, or, more properly speaking, upon the subcarboniferous limestone, just where it begins to pass beneath the coal measures by its southerly and westerly dip. Its general course is southeast. From the western part of Henry County, up as far as Story County, the broad, flat flood plain is covered with a rich deep clay soil, which, in time of long-continued rains and overflows of the river, has made the valley of Skunk River a terror to travelers from the earliest settlement of the country There are some excellent mill sites on the lower half of this river, but they are not so numerous or valuable as on other rivers of the eastern system.

Iowa River.—This river rises in Hancock County, in the midst of a broad, slightly undulating drift region. The first rock exposure is that of subcarboniferous limestone, in the southwestern corner of Franklin County. It enters the region of the Devonian strata near the southwestern corner of Benton County, and in this it continues to its confluence with the Cedar in Louisa County. Below the junction with the Cedar, and for some miles above that point, its valley is broad, and especially on the northern side, with a well marked flood plain. Its borders gradually blend with the uplands as they slope away in the distance from the river The Iowa furnishes numerous and valuable mill sites.

Cedar River.—This stream is usually understood to be a branch of the Iowa, but it ought, really, to be regarded as the main stream. It rises by numerous branches in the northern part of the State, and flows the entire length of the State, through the region occupied by the Devonian strata and along the trend occupied by that formation.

The valley of this river, in the upper part of its course, is narrow, and the sides slope so gently as to scarcely show where the lowlands end and the uplands begin. Below the confluence with the Shell Rock, the flood plain is more distinctly marked and the valley broad and shallow. The valley of the Cedar is one of the finest regions in the State, and both the main stream and its branches afford abundant and reliable mill sites.

Wapsipinnicon River.—This river has its source near the source of the Cedar, and runs parallel and near it almost its entire course, the upper half upon the same formation—the Devonian. In the northeastern part of Linn County, it enters the region of the Niagara limestone, upon which it continues to the Mississippi. It is one hundred miles long, and yet the area of its drainage is only from twelve to twenty miles in width. Hence, its numerous mill sites are unusually secure.

Turkey River.—This river and the Upper Iowa are, in many respects, unlike other Iowa rivers. The difference is due to the great depth they have eroded their valleys and the different character of the material through which they have eroded. Turkey River rises in Howard County, and in Winneshiek County, a few miles from its source, its valley has attained a depth of more than two hundred feet, and in Fayette and Clayton Counties its depth is increased to three and four hundred feet. The summit of the uplands, bordering nearly the whole length of the valley, is capped by the Maquoketa shales. These shales are underlaid by the Galena limestone, between two and three hundred feet thick. The valley has been eroded through these, and runs upon the Trenton limestone. Thus, all the formations along and within this valley are Lower Silurian. The valley is usually narrow, and without a well-marked flood plain. Water power is abundant, but in most places inaccessible.

Upper Iowa River.—This river rises in Minnesota, just beyond the northern boundary line, and enters our State in Howard County before it has attained any considerable size. Its course is nearly eastward until it reaches the Mississippi. It rises in the region of the Devonian rocks, and flows across the outcrops, respectively, of the Niagara, Galena and Trenton limestone, the lower magnesian limestone and Potsdam sandstone, into and through all of which, except the last, it has cut its valley, which is the deepest of any in Iowa. The valley sides are, almost everywhere, high and steep, and cliffs of lower magnesian and Trenton limestone give them a wild and rugged aspect. In the lower part of the valley, the flood plain reaches a width sufficient for the location of small farms, but usually it is too narrow for such purposes. On the higher surface, however, as soon as you leave the valley you come immediately upon a cultivated country. This stream has the greatest slope per mile of any in Iowa, consequently it furnishes immense water power. In some places, where creeks come into it, the valley widens and affords good locations for farms. The town of Decorah, in Winneshiek County, is located in one of these spots, which makes it a lovely location; and the power of the river and the small spring streams around it offer fine facilities for manufacturing. This river and its tributaries are the only trout streams in Iowa.

Mississippi River.—This river may be described, in general terms, as a broad canal cut out of the general level of the country through which the river flows It is bordered by abrupt hills or bluffs. The bottom of the valley ranges from one to eight miles in width. The whole space between the bluffs is occupied by the river and its bottom, or flood plain only, if we except the occasional terraces or remains of ancient flood plains, which are not now reached by the highest floods of the river. The river itself is from half a mile to nearly a mile in width There are but four points along the whole length of the State where the bluffs approach the stream on both sides. The Lower Silurian formations compose the bluffs in the northern part of the State, but they gradually disappear by a southerly dip, and the bluffs are continued successively by the Upper Silurian, Devonian, and subcarboniferous rocks, which are reached near the southeastern corner of the State.

Considered in their relation to the present general surface of the state, the relative ages of the river valley of Iowa date back only to the close of the glacial epoch, but that the Mississippi, and all the rivers of Northeastern Iowa, if no others, had at least a large part of the rocky portions of their valleys eroded by pre-glacial, or perhaps even by palæozoic rivers, can scarcely be doubted.

LAKES

The lakes of Iowa may be properly divided into two distinct classes. The first may be called *drift lakes*, having had their origin in the depressions left in the surface of the drift at the close of the glacial epoch, and have rested upon the undisturbed surface of the drift deposit ever since the glaciers disappeared. The others may be properly termed *fluvatile* or *alluvial lakes*, because they have had their origin by the action of rivers while cutting their own valleys out from the surface of the drift as it existed at the close of the glacial epoch, and are now found resting upon the alluvium, as the others rest upon the drift By the term alluvium is meant the deposit which has accumulated in the valleys of rivers by the action of their own currents. It is largely composed of sand and other coarse material, and upon that deposit are some of the best and most productive soils in the State. It is this deposit which form the flood plains and deltas of our rivers, as well as the terraces of their valleys

The regions to which the drift lakes are principally confined are near the head waters of the principal streams of the State. We consequently find them in those regions which lie between the Cedar and Des Moines Rivers, and the Des Moines and Little Sioux. No drift lakes are found in Southern Iowa. The largest of the lakes to be found in the State are Spirit and Okoboji, in

Dickinson County; Clear Lake, in Cerro Gordo County; and Storm Lake, in Bunea Vista County.

Spirit Lake.—The width and length of this lake are about equal, and it contains about twelve square miles of surface, its northern border resting directly on the boundary of the State. It lies almost directly upon the great watershed Its shores are mostly gravelly, and the country about it fertile

Okoboji Lake.—This body of water lies directly south of Spirit Lake, and has somewhat the shape of a horse-shoe, with its eastern projection within a few rods of Spirit Lake, where it receives the outlet of the latter. Okoboji Lake extends about five miles southward from Spirit Lake, thence about the same distance westward, and then bends northward about as far as the eastern projection. The eastern portion is narrow, but the western is larger, and in some places a hundred feet deep. The surroundings of this and Spirit Lake are very pleasant. Fish are abundant in them, and they are the resort of myriads of water fowl.

Clear Lake.—This lake is situated in Cerro Gordo County, upon the watershed between the Iowa and Cedar Rivers. It is about five miles long, and two or three miles wide, and has a maximum depth of only fifteen feet. Its shores and the country around it are like that of Spirit Lake.

Storm Lake.—This body of water rests upon the great water shed in Buena Vista County. It is a clear, beautiful sheet of water, containing a surface area of between four and five square miles.

The outlets of all these drift-lakes are dry during a portion of the year, except Okoboji.

Walled Lakes—Along the water sheds of Northern Iowa great numbers of small lakes exist, varying from half a mile to a mile in diameter. One of the lakes in Wright County, and another in Sac, have each received the name of "Walled Lake," on account of the existence of embankments on their borders, which are supposed to be the work of ancient inhabitants. These embankments are from two to ten feet in height, and from five to thirty feet across. They are the result of natural causes alone, being referable to the periodic action of ice, aided, to some extent, by the force of the waves. These lakes are very shallow, and in winter freeze to the bottom, so that but little unfrozen water remains in the middle. The ice freezes fast to everything upon the bottom, and the expansive power of the water in freezing acts in all directions from the center to the circumference, and whatever was on the bottom of the lake has been thus carried to the shore, and this has been going on from year to year, from century to century, forming the embankments which have caused so much wonder.

SPRINGS.

Springs issue from all formations, and from the sides of almost every valley, but they are more numerous, and assume proportions which give rise to the name of sink-holes, along the upland borders of the Upper Iowa River, owing to the peculiar fissured and laminated character and great thickness of the strata of the age of the Trenton limestone which underlies the whole region of the valley of that stream.

No mineral springs, properly so called, have yet been discovered in Iowa, though the water of several artesian wells is frequently found charged with soluble mineral substances.

ORIGIN OF THE PRAIRIES.

It is estimated that seven-eighths of the surface of the State was prairie when first settled. They are not confined to level surfaces, nor to any particular variety of soil, for within the State they rest upon all formations, from those of the Azoic to those of the Cretaceous age, inclusive. Whatever may have been their *origin*, their present existence in Iowa is not due to the influence of climate, nor the soil, nor any of the underlying formations. The real cause is the prevalence of the annual fires. If these had been prevented fifty years ago, Iowa would now be a timbered country. The encroachment of forest trees upon prairie farms as soon as the bordering woodland is protected from the annual prairie fires, is well known to farmers throughout the State.

The soil of Iowa is justly famous for its fertility, and there is probably no equal area of the earth's surface that contains so little untillable land, or whose soil has so high an average of fertility. Ninety-five per cent of its surface is tillable land.

GEOLOGY.

The soil of Iowa may be separated into three general divisions, which not only possess different physical characters, but also differ in the mode of their origin These are drift, bluff and alluvial, and belong respectively to the deposits bearing the same names. The drift occupies a much larger part of the surface of the State than both the others. The bluff has the next greatest area of surface, and the alluvial least.

All soil is disintegrated rock. The drift deposit of Iowa was derived, to a considerable extent, from the rocks of Minnesota; but the greater part of Iowa drift was derived from its own rocks, much of which has been transported but a short distance In general terms the *constant* component element of the drift soil is that portion which was transported from the north, while the *inconstant* elements are those portions which were derived from the adjacent or underlying strata. For example, in Western Iowa, wherever that cretaceous formation known as the Nishnabotany sandstone exists, the soil contains more sand than elsewhere. The same may be said of the soil of some parts of the State occupied by the lower coal measures, the sandstones and sandy shales of that formation furnishing the sand

In Northern and Northwestern Iowa, the drift contains more sand and gravel than elsewhere. This sand and gravel was, doubtless, derived from the cretaceous rocks that now do, or formerly did, exist there, and also in part from the conglomerate and pudding-stone beds of the Sioux quartzite.

In Southern Iowa, the soil is frequently stiff and clayey. This preponderating clay is doubtless derived from the clayey and shaly beds which alternate with the limestones of that region.

The bluff soil is that which rests upon, and constitutes a part of, the bluff deposit. It is found only in the western part of the State, and adjacent to the Missouri River Although it contains less than one per cent of clay in its composition, it is in no respect inferior to the best drift soil

The alluvial soil is that of the flood plains of the river valleys, or bottom lands. That which is periodically flooded by the rivers is of little value for agricultural purposes; but a large part of it is entirely above the reach of the highest floods, and is very productive

The stratified rocks of Iowa range from the Azoic to the Mesozoic, inclusive; but the greater portion of the surface of the State is occupied by those of the Palæozoic age. The table below will show each of these formations in their order:

SYSTEMS AGES	GROUPS PERIODS	FORMATIONS EPOCHS	THICKNESS IN FEET
Cretaceous..	Post Tertiary ..	*Drift*	10 to 200
	Lower Cretaceous	*Inoceramous bed..*	50
		Woodbury Sandstone and Shales	130
		Nishnabotany Sandstone...... . . .	100
	Coal Measures.	Upper Coal Measures	200
		Middle Coal Measures	200
Carboniferous.. ...		Lower Coal Measures .	200
	Subcarboniferous	St Louis Limestone . .	75
		Keokuk Limestone.....	90
		Burlington Limestone . . .	196
		Kinderhook beds.........	175
Devonian	Hamilton.	Hamilton Limestone and Shales	200
Upper Silurian	Niagara	Niagara Limestone	350
	Cincinnati	Maquoketa Shales	80
	Trenton	Galena Limestone	250
		Trenton Limestone.	200
Lower Silurian.. .		St Peter's Sandstone	80
	Primordial.	Lower Magnesian Limestone	250
		Potsdam Sandstone.	300
Azoic	Huronian	Sioux Quartzite . ...|	50

THE AZOIC SYSTEM.

The Sioux quartzite is found exposed in natural ledges only upon a few acres in the extreme northwest corner of the State, upon the banks of the Big Sioux River, for·which reason the specific name of Sioux Quartzite has been given them It is an intensely hard rock, breaks in splintery fracture, and a color varying, in different localities, from a light to deep red. The process of metamorphism has been so complete throughout the whole formation that the rock is almost everywhere of uniform texture. The dip is four or five degrees to the northward, and the trend of the outcrop is eastward and westward. This rock may be quarried in a few rare cases, but usually it cannot be secured in dry forms except that into which it naturally cracks, and the tendency is to angular pieces.   It is absolutely indestructible.

LOWER SILURIAN SYSTEM
PRIMORDIAL GROUP

Potsdam Sandstone.—This formation is exposed only in a small portion of the northeastern portion of the State.   It is only to be seen in the bases of the bluffs and steep valley sides which border the river there.   It may be seen underlying the lower magnesian limestone, St. Peter s sandstone and Trenton limestone, in their regular order, along the bluffs of the Mississippi from the northern boundary of the State as far south as Guttenburg, along the Upper Iowa for a distance of about twenty miles from its mouth, and along a few of the streams which empty into the Mississippi in Allamakee County.

It is nearly valueless for economic purposes.

No fossils have been discovered in this formation in Iowa.

Lower Magnesium Limestone —This formation has but little greater geographical extent in Iowa than the Potsdam sandstone.   It lacks a uniformity of texture and stratification, owing to which it is not generally valuable for building purposes

The only fossils found in this formation in Iowa are a few traces of crinoids, near McGregor.

St. Peter's Sandstone —This formation is remarkably uniform in thickness throughout its known geographical extent; and it is evident it occupies a large portion of the northern half of Allamakee County, immediately beneath the drift

TRENTON GROUP

Trenton Limestone.—With the exception of this, all the limestones of both Upper and Lower Silurian age in Iowa are magnesian limestones—nearly pure dolomites   This formation occupies large portions of Winnesheik and Allamakee Counties and a portion of Clayton.   The greater part of it is useless for economic purposes, yet there are in some places compact and evenly bedded layers, which afford fine material for window caps and sills

In this formation, fossils are abundant, so much so that, in some places, the rock is made up of a mass of shells, corals and fragments of tribolites, cemented by calcareous material into a solid rock.   Some of these fossils are new to science and peculiar to Iowa.

The Galena Limestone.—This is the upper formation of the Trenton group. It seldom exceeds twelve miles in width, although it is fully one hundred and fifty miles long.   The outcrop traverses portions of the counties of Howard, Winnesheik, Allamakee, Fayette, Clayton, Dubuque and Jackson.   It exhibits its greatest development in Dubuque County.   It is nearly a pure dolomite, with a slight admixture of silicious matter.   It is usually unfit for dressing, though sometimes near the top of the bed good blocks for dressing are found. This formation is the source of the lead ore of the Dubuque lead mines. The lead region proper is confined to an area of about fifteen miles square in the vicinity of Dubuque. The ore occurs in vertical fissures, which traverse the rock at regular intervals from east to west; some is found in those which have a north and south direction. The ore is mostly that known as Galena, or sulphuret of lead, very small quantities only of the carbonate being found with it.

CINCINNATI GROUP

Maquoketa Shales.—The surface occupied by this formation is singularly long and narrow, seldom reaching more than a mile or two in width, but more than a hundred miles in length. Its most southerly exposure is in the bluffs of the Mississippi near Bellevue, in Jackson County, and the most northerly yet recognized is in the western part of Winnesheik County. The whole formation is largely composed of bluish and brownish shales, sometimes slightly arenaceous, sometimes calcareous, which weather into a tenacious clay upon the surface, and the soil derived from it is usually stiff and clayey. Its economic value is very slight.

Several species of fossils which characterize the Cincinnati group are found in the Maquoketa shales, but they contain a larger number that have been found anywhere else than in these shales in Iowa, and their distinct faunal characteristics seem to warrant the separation of the Maquoketa shales as a distinct formation from any others of the group.

UPPER SILURIAN SYSTEM.
NIAGARA GROUP

Niagara Limestone.—The area occupied by the Niagara limestone is nearly one hundred and sixty miles long from north to south, and forty and fifty miles wide.

This formation is entirely a magnesian limestone, with in some places a considerable proportion of silicious matter in the form of chert or coarse flint. A large part of it is evenly bedded, and probably affords the best and greatest amount of quarry rock in the State. The quarries at Anamosa, LeClaire and Farley are all opened in this formation.

DEVONIAN SYSTEM.
HAMILTON GROUP

Hamilton Limestone.—The area of surface occupied by the Hamilton limestone and shales is fully as great as those by all the formations of both Upper and Lower Silurian age in the State. It is nearly two hundred miles long and from forty to fifty miles broad. The general trend is northwestward and southeastward.

Although a large part of the material of this formation is practically quite worthless, yet other portions are valuable for economic purposes; and having a large geographical extent in the State, is one of the most important formations, in a practical point of view. At Waverly, Bremer County, its value for the production of hydraulic lime has been practically demonstrated. The heavier and more uniform magnesian beds furnish material for bridge piers and other material requiring strength and durability.

All the Devonian strata of Iowa evidently belong to a single epoch, and referable to the Hamilton, as recognized by New York geologists.

The most conspicuous and characteristic fossils of this formation are brachiopod, mollusks and corals. The coral Acervularia Davidsoni occurs near Iowa City, and is known as "Iowa City Marble," and "bird's-eye marble."

CARBONIFEROUS SYSTEM.

Of the three groups of formations that constitute the carboniferous system, viz., the subcarboniferous, coal measures and permian, only the first two are found in Iowa.

SUBCARBONIFEROUS GROUP.

The area of the surface occupied by this group is very large. Its eastern border passes from the northeastern part of Winnebago County, with considerable directness in a southeasterly direction to the northern part of Washington County. Here it makes a broad and direct bend nearly eastward, striking the Mississippi River at Muscatine. The southern and western boundary is to a considerable extent the same as that which separates it from the coal field. From the southern part of Pocahontas County it passes southeast to Fort Dodge, thence to Webster City, thence to a point three or four miles northeast of Eldora, in Hardin County, thence southward to the middle of the north line of Jasper County, thence southeastward to Sigourney, in Keokuk County, thence to the northeastern corner of Jefferson County, thence sweeping a few miles eastward to the southeast corner of Van Buren County. Its area is nearly two hundred and fifty miles long, and from twenty to fifty miles wide.

The Kinderhook Beds.—The most southerly exposure of these beds is near the mouth of Skunk River, in Des Moines County. The most northerly now known is in the eastern part of Pocahontas County, more than two hundred miles distant. The principal exposures of this formation are along the bluffs which border the Mississippi and Skunk Rivers, where they form the eastern and northern boundary of Des Moines County, along English River, in Washington County; along the Iowa River, in Tama, Marshall, Hamlin and Franklin Counties; and along the Des Moines River, in Humboldt County.

The economic value of this formation is very considerable, particularly in the northern portion of the region it occupies. In Pocahontas and Humboldt Counties it is almost invaluable, as no other stone except a few boulders are found here. At Iowa Falls the lower division is very good for building purposes. In Marshall County all the limestone to be obtained comes from this formation, and the quarries near LeGrand are very valuable. At this point some of the layers are finely veined with peroxide of iron, and are wrought into ornamental and useful objects.

In Tama County, the oolitic member is well exposed, where it is manufactured into lime.   It is not valuable for building, as upon exposure to atmosphere and frost, it crumbles to pieces.

The remains of fishes are the only fossils yet discovered in this formation that can be referred to the sub-kingdom VERTEBRATA; and so far as yet recognized, they all belong to the order selachians.

Of ARTICULATES, only two species have been recognized, both of which belong to the genus *phillipsia.*

The sub-kingdom MOLLUSCA is largely represented.

The RADIATA are represented by a few crinoids, usually found in a very imperfect condition.   The sub-kingdom is also represented by corals.

The prominent feature in the life of this epoch was molluscan; so much so in fact as to overshadow all other branches of the animal kingdom.   The prevailing classes are: *lamellibranchiates,* in the more arenaceous portions; and brachiopods, in the more calcareous portions.

No remains of vegetation have been detected in any of the strata of this formation.

The Burlington Limestone.—This formation consists of two distinct calcareous divisions, which are separated by a series of silicious beds.   Both divisions are eminently crinoidal.

The southerly dip of the Iowa rocks carries the Burlington limestone down, so that it is seen for the last time in this State in the valley of Skunk River, near the southern boundary of Des Moines County.   The most northerly point at which it has been recognized is in the northern part of Washington County. It probably exists as far north as Marshall County.

This formation affords much valuable material for economic purposes.   The upper division furnishes excellent common quarry rock.

The great abundance and variety of its fossils—*crinoids*—now known to be more than three hundred, have justly attracted the attention of geologists in all parts of the world.

The only remains of vertebrates discovered in this formation are those of fishes, and consist of teeth and spines; bone of bony fishes, like those most common at the present day, are found in these rocks.   On Buffington Creek, in Louisa County, is a stratum in an exposure so fully charged with these remains that it might with propriety be called bone breccia.

Remains of articulates are rare in this formation.   So far as yet discovered, they are confined to two species of tribolites of the genus *phillipsia*

Fossil shells are very common.

The two lowest classes of the sub-kingdom radiata are represented in the genera *zaphrentis,* amplexus and syringapora, while the highest class—echinoderms—are found in most extraordinary profusion.

The Keokuk Limestone —It is only in the four counties of Lee, Van Buren, Henry and Des Moines that this formation is to be seen

In some localities the upper silicious portion of this formation is known as the Geode bed. It is not recognizable in the northern portion of the formation, nor in connection with it where it is exposed, about eighty miles below Keokuk.

The geodes of the Geode bed are more or less spherical masses of silex, usually hollow and lined with crystals of quartz   The outer crust is rough and unsightly, but the crystals which stud the interior are often very beautiful. They vary in size from the size of a walnut to a foot in diameter

The economic value of this formation is very great.   Large quantities of its stone have been used in the finest structures in the State, among which are the post offices at Dubuque and Des Moines.   The principal quarries are along the banks of the Mississippi, from Keokuk to Nauvoo

The only vertebrate fossils found in the formation are fishes, all belonging to the order selachians, some of which indicate that their owners reached a length of twenty-five or thirty feet.

Of the articulates, only two species of the genus *phillipsia* have been found in this formation.

Of the mollusks, no cephalopods have yet been recognized in this formation in this State ; gasteropods are rare ; brachiopods and polyzoans are quite abundant.

Of radiates, corals of genera zaphrentes, amplexus and aulopera are found, but crinoids are most abundant.

Of the low forms of animal life, the protozoans, a small fossil related to the sponges, is found in this formation in small numbers.

The St Louis Limestone —This is the uppermost of the subcarboniferous group in Iowa.   The superficial area it occupies is comparatively small, because it consists of long, narrow strips, yet its extent is very great.   It is first seen resting on the geode division of the Keokuk limestone, near Keokuk.   Proceeding northward, it forms a narrow border along the edge of the coal fields in Lee, Des Moines, Henry, Jefferson, Washington, Keokuk and Mahaska Counties.   It is then lost sight of until it appears again in the banks of Boone River, where it again passes out of view under the coal measures until it is next seen in the banks of the Des Moines, near Fort Dodge.   As it exists in Iowa, it consists of three tolerably distinct subdivisions—the magnesian, arenaceous and calcareous.

The upper division furnishes excellent material for quicklime, and when quarries are well opened, as in the northwestern part of Van Buren County, large blocks are obtained.   The sandstone, or middle division, is of little economic value   The lower or magnesian division furnishes a valuable and durable stone, exposures of which are found on Lick Creek, in Van Buren County, and on Long Creek, seven miles west of Burlington

Of the fossils of this formation, the vertebrates are represented only by the remains of fish, belonging to the two orders, selachians and ganoids   The articulates are represented by one species of the trilobite, genus *phillipsia*, and two ostracoid, genera, *cythre* and *beyricia* The mollusks distinguish this formation more than any other branch of the animal kingdom Radiates are exceedingly rare, showing a marked contrast between this formation and the two preceding it

The rocks of the subcarboniferous period have in other countries, and in other parts of our own country, furnished valuable minerals, and even coal, but in Iowa the economic value is confined to its stone alone

The Lower Silurian, Upper Silurian and Devonian rocks of Iowa are largely composed of limestone. Magnesia also enters largely into the subcarboniferous group. With the completion of the St Louis limestone, the production of the magnesian limestone seems to have ceased among the rocks of Iowa.

Although the Devonian age has been called the age of fishes, yet so far as Iowa is concerned, the rocks of no period can compare with the subcarboniferous in the abundance and variety of the fish remains, and, for this reason, the Burlington and Keokuk limestones will in the future become more famous among geologists, perhaps, than any other formations in North America.

It will be seen that the Chester limestone is omitted from the subcarboniferous group, and which completes the full geological series. It is probable the whole surface of Iowa was above the sea during the time of the formation of the Chester limestone to the southward about one hundred miles.

At the close of the epoch of the Chester limestone, the shallow seas in which the lower coal measures were formed again occupied the land, extending almost as far north as that sea had done in which the Kinderhook beds were formed, and to the northeastward its deposits extended beyond the subcarboniferous groups, outlines of which are found upon the next, or Devonian rock

THE COAL-MEASURE GROUP

The coal-measure group of Iowa is properly divided into three formations, viz , the lower, middle and upper coal measures, each having a vertical thickness of about two hundred feet.

A line drawn upon the map of Iowa as follows, will represent the eastern and northern boundaries of the coal fields of the State : Commencing at the southeast corner of Van Buren County, carry the line to the northeast corner of Jefferson County by a slight easterly curve through the western portions of Lee and Henry Counties. Produce this line until it reaches a point six or eight miles northward from the one last named, and then carry it northwestward, keeping it at about the same distance to the northward of Skunk River and its north branch that it had at first, until it reaches the southern boundary of Marshall County, a little west of its center. Then carry it to a point three or four miles northeast from Eldora, in Hardin County, thence west-ward to a point a little north of Webster City, in Hamilton County; and thence further westward to a point a little north of Fort Dodge, in Webster County.

Lower Coal Measures.—In consequence of the recedence to the southward of the borders of the middle and upper coal measures, the lower coal measures alone exist to the eastward and northward of Des Moines River. They also occupy a large area westward and southward of that river, but their southerly dip passes them below the middle coal measures at no great distance from the river

No other formation in the whole State possesses the economic value of the lower coal measures   The clay that underlies almost every bed of coal furnishes a large amount of material for potters' use.   The sandstone of these measures is usually soft and unfit, but in some places, as near Red Rock, in Marion County, blocks of large dimensions are obtained which make good building material, samples of which can be seen in the State Arsenal, at Des Moines. On the whole, that portion of the State occupied by the lower coal measures, is not well supplied with stone.

But few fossils have been found in any of the strata of the lower coal meas-ures, but such animal remains as have been found are without exception of marine origin.

Of fossil plants found in these measures, all probably belong to the class *acrogens.*   Specimens of *calamites,* and several species of ferns, are found in all of the coal measures, but the genus *lepidodendron* seems not to have existed later than the epoch of the middle coal measures.

Middle Coal Measures.—This formation within the State of Iowa occupies a narrow belt of territory in the southern central portion of the State, embrac-ing a superficial area of about fourteen hundred square miles.   The counties more or less underlaid by this formation are Guthrie, Dallas, Polk, Madison, Warren, Clarke, Lucas, Monroe, Wayne and Appanoose.

This formation is composed of alternating beds of clay, sandstone and lime-stone, the clays or shales constituting the bulk of the formation, the limestone occurring in their bands, the lithological peculiarities of which offer many con-trasts to the limestones of the upper and lower coal measures.   The formation is also characterized by regular wave-like undulations, with a parallelism which indicates a widespread disturbance, though no dislocation of the strata have been discovered

Generally speaking, few species of fossils occur in these beds.   Some of the shales and sandstone have afforded a few imperfectly preserved land plants—three or four species of ferns, belonging to the genera.   Some of the carbonif-erous shales afford beautiful specimens of what appear to have been sea-weeds Radiates are represented by corals   The mollusks are most numerously repre-sented.   *Trilobites* and *ostracoids* are the only remains known of articulates.

Vertebrates are only known by the remains of *salachians*, or sharks, and ganoids

Upper Coal Measures —The area occupied by this formation in Iowa is very great, comprising thirteen whole counties, in the southwestern part of the State. It adjoins by its northern and eastern boundaries the area occupied by the middle coal measures.

The prominent lithological features of this formation are its limestones, yet it contains a considerable proportion of shales and sandstones. Although it is known by the name of upper coal measures, it contains but a single bed of coal, and that only about twenty inches in maximum thickness.

The limestone exposed in this formation furnishes good material for building as in Madison and Fremont Counties. The sandstones are quite worthless No beds of clay for potter's use are found in the whole formation.

The fossils in this formation are much more numerous than in either the middle or lower coal measures. The vertebrates are represented by the fishes of the orders selachians and ganoids. The articulates are represented by the trilobites and ostracoids. Mollusks are represented by the classes *cephalapoda, gasteropoda, lamelli, branchiata, brachiapoda* and *polyzoa*. Radiates are more numerous than in the lower and middle coal measures. Protogoans are represented in the greatest abundance, some layers of limestone being almost entirely composed of their small fusiform shells.

CRETACEOUS SYSTEM

There being no rocks, in Iowa, of permian, triassic or jurassic age, the next strata in the geological series are of the cretaceous age. They are found in the western half of the State, and do not dip, as do all the other formations upon which they rest, to the southward and westward, but have a general dip of their own to the north of westward, which, however, is very slight. Although the actual exposures of cretaceous rocks are few in Iowa, there is reason to believe that nearly all the western half of the State was originally occupied by them; but being very friable, they have been removed by denudation, which has taken place at two separate periods. The first period was during its elevation from the cretaceous sea, and during the long tertiary age that passed between the time of that elevation and the commencement of the glacial epoch The second period was during the glacial epoch, when the ice produced their entire removal over considerable areas

It is difficult to indicate the exact boundaries of these rocks; the following will approximate the outlines of the area

From the northeast corner to the southwest corner of Kossuth County; thence to the southeast corner of Guthrie County; thence to the southeast corner of Cass County; thence to the middle of the south boundary of Montgomery County; thence to the middle of the north boundary of Pottawattamie County; thence to the middle of the south boundary of Woodbury County;

thence to Sergeant's bluffs, up the Missouri and Big Sioux Rivers to the northwest corner of the State, eastward along the State line to the place of beginning

All the cretaceous rocks in Iowa are a part of the same deposits farther up the Missouri River, and in reality form their eastern boundary.

Nishnabotany Sandstone —This rock has the most easterly and southerly extent of the cretaceous deposits of Iowa, reaching the southeastern part of Guthrie County and the southern part of Montgomery County. To the northward, it passes beneath the Woodbury sandstones and shales, the latter passing beneath the inoceramus, or chalky, beds   This sandstone is, with few exceptions, almost valueless for economic purposes

The only fossils found in this formation are a few fragments of angiospermous leaves.

Woodbury Sandstones and Shales.—These strata rest upon the Nishnabotany sandstone, and have not been observed outside of Woodbury County, hence their name. Their principal exposure is at Sergeant's Bluffs, seven miles below Sioux City.

This rock has no value except for purposes of common masonry.

Fossil remains are rare. Detached scales of a lepidoginoid species have been detected, but no other vertebrate remains. Of remains of vegetation, leaves of *salix* meekii and sassafras cretaceum have been occasionally found.

Inoceramus Beds.—These beds rest upon the Woodbury sandstones and shales. They have not been observed in Iowa, except in the bluffs which border the Big Sioux River in Woodbury and Plymouth Counties. They are composed almost entirely of calcareous material, the upper portion of which is extensively used for lime. No building material is to be obtained from these beds; and the only value they possess, except lime, are the marls, which at some time may be useful on the soil of the adjacent region.

The only vertebrate remains found in the cretaceous rocks are the fishes Those in the inoceramus beds of Iowa are two species of squoloid selachians, or cestratront, and three genera of teliosts.   Molluscan remains are rare.

PEAT.

Extensive beds of peat exist in Northern Middle Iowa, which, it is estimated, contain the following areas:

Counties	Acres
Cerro Gordo	1,500
Worth	2,000
Winnebago	2,000
Hancock	1,500
Wright	500
Kossuth	700
Dickinson	80

Several other counties contain peat beds, but the character of the peat is inferior to that in the northern part of the State   The character of the peat

named is equal to that of Ireland. The beds are of an average depth of four
feet. It is estimated that each acre of these beds will furnish two hundred and
fifty tons of dry fuel for each foot in depth. At present, owing to the sparse-
ness of the population, this peat is not utilized; but, owing to its great distance
from the coal fields and the absence of timber, the time is coming when their
value will be realized, and the fact demonstrated that Nature has abundantly
compensated the deficiency of other fuel.

GYPSUM

The only deposits of the sulphates of the alkaline earths of any economic
value in Iowa are those of gypsum at and in the vicinity of Fort Dodge, in
Webster County. All others are small and unimportant. The deposit occupies
a nearly central position in Webster County, the Des Moines River running
nearly centrally through it, along the valley sides of which the gypsum is seen
in the form of ordinary rock cliff and ledges, and also occurring abundantly in
similar positions along both sides of the valleys of the smaller streams and of
the numerous ravines coming into the river valley.

The most northerly known limit of the deposit is at a point near the mouth
of Lizard Creek, a tributary of the Des Moines River, and almost adjoining
the town of Fort Dodge. The most southerly point at which it has been
found exposed is about six miles, by way of the river, from this northerly point
before mentioned. Our knowledge of the width of the area occupied by it is
limited by the exposures seen in the valleys of the small streams and in the
ravines which come into the valley within the distance mentioned. As one goes
up these ravines and minor valleys, the gypsum becomes lost beneath the overlying drift. There can be no doubt that the different parts of this deposit, now
disconnected by the valleys and ravines having been cut through it, were originally connected as a continuous deposit, and there seems to be as little reason
to doubt that the gypsum still extends to considerable distance on each side of
the valley of the river beneath the drift which covers the region to a depth of
from twenty to sixty feet.

The country round about this region has the prairie surface approximating
a general level which is so characteristic of the greater part of the State, and
which exists irrespective of the character or geological age of the strata beneath,
mainly because the drift is so deep and uniformly distributed that it frequently
almost alone gives character to the surface. The valley sides of the Des Moines
River, in the vicinity of Fort Dodge, are somewhat abrupt, having a depth there
from the general level of the upland of about one hundred and seventy feet,
and consequently presents somewhat bold and interesting features in the landscape.

As one walks up and down the creeks and ravines which come into the
valley of the Des Moines River there, he sees the gypsum exposed on
either side of them, jutting out from beneath the drift in the form of

ledges and bold quarry fronts, having almost the exact appearance of ordinary limestone exposures, so horizontal and regular are its lines of stratification, and so similar in color is it to some varieties of that rock. The principal quarries now opened are on Two Mile Creek, a couple of miles below Fort Dodge.

The reader will please bear in mind that the gypsum of this remarkable deposit does not occur in "heaps" or "nests," as it does in most deposits of gypsum in the States farther eastward, but that it exists here in the form of a regularly stratified, continuous formation, as uniform in texture, color and quality throughout the whole region, and from top to bottom of the deposit as the granite of the Quincy quarries is. Its color is a uniform gray, resulting from alternating fine horizontal lines of nearly white, with similar lines of darker shade. The gypsum of the white lines is almost entirely pure, the darker lines containing the impurity. This is at intervals barely sufficient in amount to cause the separation of the mass upon those lines into beds or layers, thus facilitating the quarrying of it into desired shapes. These bedding surfaces have occasionally a clayey feeling to the touch, but there is nowhere any intercalation of clay or other foreign substance in a separate form. The deposit is known to reach a thickness of thirty feet at the quarries referred to, but although it will probably be found to exceed this thickness at some other points, at the natural exposures, it is seldom seen to be more than from ten to twenty feet thick.

Since the drift is usually seen to rest directly upon the gypsum, with nothing intervening, except at a few points where traces appear of an overlying bed of clayey material without doubt of the same age as the gypsum, the latter probably lost something of its thickness by mechanical erosion during the glacial epoch, and it has, doubtless, also suffered some diminution of thickness since then by solution in the waters which constantly percolate through the drift from the surface. The drift of this region being somewhat clayey, particularly in its lower part, it has doubtless served in some degree as a protection against the diminution of the gypsum by solution in consequence of its partial imperviousness to water. If the gypsum had been covered by a deposit of sand instead of the drift clays, it would have no doubt long since disappeared by being dissolved in the water that would have constantly reached it from the surface. Water merely resting upon it would not dissolve it away to any extent, but it rapidly disappears under the action of running water. Where little rills of water at the time of every rain run over the face of an unused quarry, from the surface above it, deep grooves are thereby cut into it, giving it somewhat the appearance of melting ice around a waterfall. The fact that gypsum is now suffering a constant, but, of course, very slight, diminution, is apparent in the fact the springs of the region contain more or less of it in solution in their waters. An analysis of water from one of these springs will be found in Prof Emery's report

Besides the clayey beds that are sometimes seen to rest upon the gypsum, there are occasionally others seen beneath them that are also of the same age, and not of the age of the coal-measure strata upon which they rest.

Age of the Gypsum Deposit.—In neither the gypsum nor the associated clays has any trace of any fossil remains been found, nor has any other indication of its geological age been observed, except that which is afforded by its stratigraphical relations; and the most that can be said with certainty is that it is newer than the coal measures, and older than the drift   The indications afforded by the stratigraphical relations of the gypsum deposit of Fort Dodge are, however, of considerable value

As already shown, it rests in that region directly and unconformably upon the lower coal measures; but going southward from there, the whole series of coal-measure strata from the top of the subcarboniferous group to the upper coal measures, inclusive, can be traced without break or unconformability. The strata of the latter also may be traced in the same manner up into the Permian rocks of Kansas; and through this long series, there is no place or horizon which suggests that the gypsum deposit might belong there

Again, no Tertiary deposits are known to exist within or near the borders of Iowa to suggest that the gypsum might be of that age, nor are any of the palæozoic strata newer than the subcarboniferous unconformable upon each other as the other gypsum is unconformable upon the strata beneath it.   It therefore seems, in a measure, conclusive, that the gypsum is of Mesozoic age, perhaps older than the Cretaceous

Lithological Origin.—As little can be said with certainty concerning the lithological origin of this deposit as can be said concerning its geological age, for it seems to present itself in this relation, as in the former one, as an isolated fact.   None of the associated strata show any traces of a double decomposition of pre-existing materials, such as some have supposed all deposits of gypsum to have resulted from.   No considerable quantities of oxide of iron nor any trace of native sulphur have been found in connection with it, nor has any salt been found in the waters of the region   These substances are common in association with other gypsum deposits, and are regarded by some persons as indicative of the method of or resulting from their origin as such.   Throughout the whole region, the Fort Dodge gypsum has the exact appearance of a sedimentary deposit.   It is arranged in layers like the regular layers of limestone, and the whole mass, from top to bottom, is traced with fine horizontal laminæ of alternating white and gray gypsum, parallel with the bedding surfaces of the layers, but the whole so intimately blended as to form a solid mass   The darker lines contain almost all the impurity there is in the gypsum, and that impurity is evidently sedimentary in its character.   From these facts, and also from the further one that no trace of fossil remains has been detected in the gypsum, it seems not unreasonable to entertain the opinion that the gypsum of Fort Dodge originated as a chemical precipitation in comparatively still waters which were saturated with sulphate of lime and destitute of life, its stratification and impurities being deposited at the same time as clayey impurities which had been held suspended in the same waters

Physical Properties —Much has already been said of the physical properties or character of this gypsum, but as it is so different in some respects from that of other deposits, there are yet other matters worthy of mention in connection with those. According to the results of a complete and exhaustive analysis by Prof. Emery, the ordinary gray gypsum contains only about eight per cent of impurity; and it is possible that the average impurity for the whole deposit will not exceed that proportion, so uniform in quality is it from to top to bottom and from one end of the region to the other

When it is remembered that plaster for agricultural purposes is sometimes prepared from gypsum that contains as much as thirty per cent. of impurity, it will be seen that ours is a very superior article for such purposes   The impurities are also of such a character that they do not in any way interfere with its value for use in the arts   Although the gypsum rock has a gray color, it becomes quite white by grinding, and still whiter by the calcining process necessary in the preparation of plaster of Paris.   These tests have all been practically made in the rooms of the Geological Survey, and the quality of the plaster of Paris still further tested by actual use and experiment.   No hesitation, therefore, is felt in stating that the Fort Dodge gypsum is of as good a quality as any in the country, even for the finest uses.

In view of the bounteousness of the primitive fertility of our Iowa soils, many persons forget that a time may come when Nature will refuse to respond so generously to our demand as she does now, without an adequate return. Such are apt to say that this vast deposit of gypsum is valueless to our commonwealth, except to the small extent that it may be used in the arts.   This is undoubtedly a short-sighted view of the subject, for the time is even now rapidly passing away when a man may purchase a new farm for less money than he can re-fertilize and restore the partially wasted primitive fertility of the one he now occupies.   There are farms even now in a large part of the older settled portions of the State that would be greatly benefited by the proper application of plaster, and such areas will continue to increase until it will be difficult to estimate the value of the deposit of gypsum at Fort Dodge.   It should be remembered, also, that the inhabitants of an extent of country adjoining our State more than three times as great as its own area will find it more convenient to obtain their supplies from Fort Dodge than from any other source.

For want of direct railroad communication between this region and other parts of the State, the only use yet made of the gypsum by the inhabitants is for the purposes of ordinary building stone.   It is so compact that it is found to be comparatively unaffected by the frost, and its ordinary situation in walls of houses is such that it is protected from the dissolving action of water, which can at most reach it only from occasional rains, and the effect of these is too slight to be perceived after the lapse of several years.

One of the citizens of Fort Dodge, Hon. John F Duncombe, built a large, fine residence of it in 1861, the walls of which appear as unaffected by exposure and as beautiful as they were when first erected. It has been so long and successfully used for building stone by the inhabitants that they now prefer it to the limestone of good quality, which also exists in the immediate vicinity. This preference is due to the cheapness of the gypsum, as compared with the stone.   The cheapness of the former is largely due to the facility with which it is quarried and wrought   Several other houses have been constructed of it in Fort Dodge, including the depot building of the Dubuque & Sioux City Railroad.   The company have also constructed a large culvert of the same material to span a creek near the town, limestone only being used for the lower courses, which come in contact with the water.   It is a fine arch, each stone of gypsum being nicely hewn, and it will doubtless prove a very durable one   Many of the sidewalks in the town are made of the slabs or flags of gypsum which occur in some of the quarries in the form of thin layers.   They are more durable than their softness would lead one to suppose   They also possess an advantage over stone in not becoming slippery when worn.

The method adopted in quarrying and dressing the blocks of gypsum is peculiar, and quite unlike that adopted in similar treatment of ordinary stone Taking a stout auger-bit of an ordinary brace, such as is used by carpenters, and filing the cutting parts of it into a peculiar form, the quarryman bores his holes into the gypsum quarry for blasting, in the same manner and with as great facility as a carpenter would bore hard wood.   The pieces being loosened by blasting, they are broken up with sledges into convenient sizes, or hewn into the desired shapes by means of hatchets or ordinary chopping axes, or cut by means of ordinary wood-saws.   So little grit does the gypsum contain that these tools, made for working wood, are found to be better adapted for working the former substance than those tools are which are universally used for working stone.

MINOR DEPOSITS OF SULPHATE OF LIME.

Besides the great gypsum deposit of Fort Dodge, sulphate of lime in the various forms of fibrous gypsum, selenite, and small, amorphous masses, has also been discovered in various formations in different parts of the State, including the coal measure shales near Fort Dodge, where it exists in small quantities, quite independently of the great gypsum deposit there   The quantity of gypsum in these minor deposits is always too small to be of any practical value, and frequently minute.   They usually occur in shales and shaly clays, associated with strata that contain more or less sulphuret of iron (iron pyrites). Gypsum has thus been detected in the coal measures, the St Louis limestone, the cretaceous strata, and also in the lead caves of Dubuque.   In most of these cases it is evidently the result of double decomposition of iron pyrites and carbonate of lime, previously existing there ; in which cases the gypsum is of course not an original deposit as the great one at Fort Dodge is supposed to be.

The existence of these comparatively minute quantities of gypsum in the shales of the coal measures and the subcarboniferous limestone which are exposed within the region of and occupy a stratigraphical position beneath the great gypsum deposits, suggests the possibility that the former may have originated as a precipitate from percolating waters, holding gypsum in solution which they had derived from that deposit in passing over or through it. Since, however, the same substance is found in similar small quantities and under similar conditions in regions where they could have had no possible connection with that deposit, it is believed that none of those mentioned have necessarily originated from it, not even those that are found in close proximity to it.

The gypsum found in the lead caves is usually in the form of efflorescent fibers, and is always in small quantity. In the lower coal-measure shale near Fort Dodge, a small mass was found in the form of an intercalated layer, which had a distinct fibrous structure, the fibers being perpendicular to the plane of the layer. The same mass had also distinct, horizontal planes of cleavage at right angles with the perpendicular fibers. Thus, being more or less transparent, the mass combined the characters of both fibrous gypsum and selenite. No anhydrous sulphate of lime (*anhydrite*) has been found in connection with the great gypsum deposit, nor elsewhere in Iowa, so far as yet known.

SULPHATE OF STRONTIA.
(*Celestine*)

The only locality at which this interesting mineral has yet been found in Iowa, or, so far as is known, in the great valley of the Mississippi, is at Fort Dodge   It occurs there in very small quantity in both the shales of the lower coal measures and in the clays that overlie the gypsum deposit, and which are regarded as of the same age with it. The first is just below the city, near Rees' coal bank, and occurs as a layer intercalated among the coal measure shales, amounting in quantity to only a few hundred pounds' weight. The mineral is fibrous and crystalline, the fibers being perpendicular to the plane of the layer. Breaking also with more or less distinct horizontal planes of cleavage, it resembles, in physical character, the layer of fibro-crystalline gypsum before mentioned. Its color is light blue, is transparent and shows crystaline facets upon both the upper and under surfaces of the layer; those of the upper surface being smallest and most numerous   It breaks up readily into small masses along the lines of the perpendicular fibers or columns. The layer is probably not more than a rod in extent in any direction and about three inches in maximum thickness. Apparent lines of stratification occur in it, corresponding with those of the shales which imbed it.

The other deposit was still smaller in amount, and occurred as a mass of crystals imbedded in the clays that overlie the gypsum at Cummins' quarry in the valley of Soldier Creek, upon the north side of the town. The mineral is in this case nearly colorless, and but for the form of the separate crystals would closely resemble masses of impure salt. The crystals are so closely aggregated that they enclose but little impurity in the mass, but in almost all cases their fundamental forms are obscured. This mineral has almost no real practical value, and its occurrence, as described, is interesting only as a mineralogical fact.

SULPHATE OF BARYTA.
(Barytis, Heavy Spar)

This mineral has been found only in minute quantities in Iowa. It has been detected in the coal-measure shales of Decatur, Madison and Marion Counties, the Devonian limestone of Johnson and Bremer Counties and in the lead caves of Dubuque. In all these cases, it is in the form of crystals or small crystalline masses.

SULPHATE OF MAGNESIA.
(Epsomite)

Epsomite, or native epsom salts, having been discovered near Burlington, we have thus recognized in Iowa all the sulphates of the alkaline earths of natural origin; all of them, except the sulphate of lime, being in very small quantity. Even if the sulphate of magnesia were produced in nature, in large quantities, it is so very soluble that it can accumulate only in such positions as afford it complete shelter from the rains or running water The epsomite mentioned was found beneath the overhanging cliff of Burlington limestone, near Starr's mill, which are represented in the sketch upon another page, illustrating the subcarboniferous rocks. It occurs in the form of efflorescent encrustations upon the surface of stones and in similar small fragile masses among the fine debris that has fallen down beneath the overhanging cliff. The projection of the cliff over the perpendicular face of the strata beneath amounts to near twenty feet at the point where epsomite was found. Consequently the rains never reach far beneath it from any quarter The rock upon which the epsomite accumulates is an impure limestone, containing also some carbonate of magnesia, together with a small proportion of iron pyrites in a finely divided condition. It is doubtless by double decomposition of these that the epsomite results. By experiments with this native salt in the office of the Survey, a fine article of epsom salts was produced, but the quantity that might be annually obtained there would amount to only a few pounds, and of course is of no practical value whatever, on account of its cheapness in the market.

CLIMATOLOGY.

No extended record of the climatology of Iowa has been made, yet much of great value may be learned from observations made at a single point. Prof T. S. Parvin, of the State University, has recorded observations made from 1889 to the present time. Previous to 1860, these observations were made at Muscatine.   Since that date, they were made in Iowa City.   The result is that the atmospheric conditions of the climate of Iowa are in the highest degree favorable to health.

The highest temperature here occurs in August, while July is the hottest month in the year by two degrees, and January the coldest by three degrees

The mean temperature of April and October most nearly corresponds to the mean temperature of the year, as well as their seasons of Spring and Fall, while that of Summer and Winter is best represented in that of August and December

The period of greatest heat ranges from June 22d to August 31st, the next mean time being July 27th.   The lowest temperature extends from December 16th to February 15th, the average being January 20th—the range in each case being two full months.

The climate of Iowa embraces the range of that of New York, Pennsylvania, Ohio, Indiana and Illinois.   The seasons are not characterized by the frequent and sudden changes so common in the latitudes further south.   The temperature of the Winters is somewhat lower than States eastward, but of other seasons it is higher.   The atmosphere is dry and invigorating.   The surface of the State being free at all seasons of the year from stagnant water, with good breezes at nearly all seasons, the miasmatic and pulmonary diseases are unknown.   Mortuary statistics show this to be one of the most healthful States in the Union, being one death to every ninety-four persons.   The Spring, Summer and Fall months are delightful; indeed, the glory of Iowa is her Autumn, and nothing can transcend the splendor of her Indian Summer, which lasts for weeks, and finally blends, almost imperceptibly, into Winter.

HISTORY OF THE STATE OF IOWA.

DISCOVERY AND OCCUPATION

Iowa, in the symbolical and expressive language of the aboriginal inhabitants, is said to signify "The Beautiful Land," and was applied to this magnificent and fruitful region by its ancient owners, to express their appreciation of its superiority of climate, soil and location. Prior to 1803, the Mississippi River was the extreme western boundary of the United States. All the great empire lying west of the "Father of Waters," from the Gulf of Mexico on the south to British America on the north, and westward to the Pacific Ocean was a Spanish province. A brief historical sketch of the discovery and occupation of this grand empire by the Spanish and French governments will be a fitting introduction to the history of the young and thriving State of Iowa, which, until the commencement of the present century, was a part of the Spanish possessions in America.

Early in the Spring of 1542, fifty years after Columbus discovered the New World, and one hundred and thirty years before the French missionaries discovered its upper waters, Ferdinand De Soto discovered the mouth of the Mississippi River at the mouth of the Washita After the sudden death of De Soto, in May of the same year, his followers built a small vessel, and in July, 1543, descended the great river to the Gulf of Mexico

In accordance with the usage of nations, under which title to the soil was claimed by right of discovery, Spain, having conquered Florida and discovered the Mississippi, claimed all the territory bordering on that river and the Gulf of Mexico. But it was also held by the European nations that, while discovery gave title, that title must be perfected by actual possession and occupation. Although Spain claimed the territory by right of first discovery, she made no effort to occupy it, by no permanent settlement had she perfected and held her title, and therefore had forfeited it when, at a later period, the Lower Mississippi Valley was re-discovered and occupied by France

The unparalleled labors of the zealous French Jesuits of Canada in penetrating the unknown region of the West, commencing in 1611, form a history of no ordinary interest, but have no particular connection with the scope of the present work, until in the Fall of 1665. Pierre Claude Allouez, who had entered Lake Superior in September, and sailed along the southern coast in search of copper, had arrived at the great village of the Chippewas at Chegoincegon. Here a grand council of some ten or twelve of the principal Indian nations was held The Pottawatomies of Lake Michigan, the Sacs and Foxes of the West, the Hurons from the North, the Illinois from the South, and the Sioux from the land of the prairie and wild rice, were all assembled there. The Illinois told the story of their ancient glory and about the noble river on the banks of which they dwelt.   The Sioux also told their white brother of the same great river, and Allouez promised to the assembled tribes the protection of the French nation against all their enemies. native or foreign

The purpose of discovering the great river about which the Indian nations had given such glowing accounts appears to have originated with Marquette, in 1669   In the year previous, he and Claude Dablon had established the Mission of St Mary's, the oldest white settlement within the present limits of the State of Michigan.   Marquette was delayed in the execution of his great undertaking, and spent the interval in studying the language and habits of the Illinois Indians, among whom he expected to travel.

About this time, the French Government had determined to extend the dominion of France to the extreme western borders of Canada.   Nicholas Perrot was sent as the agent of the government, to propose a grand council of the Indian nations, at St. Mary's.

When Perrot reached Green Bay, he extended the invitation far and near; and, escorted by Pottawatomies, repaired on a mission of peace and friendship to the Miamis, who occupied the region about the present location of Chicago

In May, 1671, a great council of Indians gathered at the Falls of St. Mary, from all parts of the Northwest, from the head waters of the St. Lawrence, from the valley of the Mississippi and from the Red River of the North. Perrot met with them, and after grave consultation, formally announced to the assembled nations that their good French Father felt an abiding interest in their welfare, and had placed them all under the powerful protection of the French Government.

Marquette, during that same year, had gathered at Point St Ignace the remnants of one branch of the Hurons.   This station, for a long series of years, was considered the key to the unknown West.

The time was now auspicious for the consummation of Marquette's grand project.   The successful termination of Perrot's mission, and the general friendliness of the native tribes, rendered the contemplated expedition much less perilous   But it was not until 1673 that the intrepid and enthusiastic priest was finally ready to depart on his daring and perilous journey to lands never trod by white men.

The Indians, who had gathered in large numbers to witness his departure, were astounded at the boldness of the proposed undertaking, and tried to discourage him, representing that the Indians of the Mississippi Valley were cruel and bloodthirsty, and would resent the intrusion of strangers upon their domain. The great river itself, they said, was the abode of terrible monsters, who could swallow both canoes and men

But Marquette was not to be diverted from his purpose by these fearful reports.   He assured his dusky friends that he was ready to make any sacrifice, even to lay down his life for the sacred cause in which he was engaged. 'He prayed with them; and having implored the blessing of God upon his undertaking, on the 13th day of May, 1673, with Joliet and five Canadian-French voyageurs, or boatmen, he left the mission on his daring journey.   Ascending Green Bay and Fox River, these bold and enthusiastic pioneers of religion and discovery proceeded until they reached a Miami and Kickapoo village, where Marquette was delighted to find "a beautiful cross planted in the middle of the town, ornamented with white skins, red girdles and bows and arrows, which these good people had offered to the Great Manitou, or God, to thank Him for the pity He had bestowed on them during the Winter, in having given them abundant chase."

This was the extreme point beyond which the explorations of the French missionaries had not then extended. Here Marquette was instructed by his Indian hosts in the secret of a root that cures the bite of the venomous rattlesnake, drank mineral water with them and was entertained with generous hospitality. He called together the principal men of the village, and informed them that his companion, Joliet, had been sent by the French Governor of Canada to discover new countries, to be added to the dominion of France; but that he, himself, had been sent by the Most High God, to carry the glorious religion of the Cross; and assured his wondering hearers that on this mission he had no fear of death, to which he knew he would be exposed on his perilous journeys

Obtaining the services of two Miami guides, to conduct his little band to the Wisconsin River, he left the hospitable Indians on the 10th of June. Conducting them across the portage, their Indian guides returned to their village, and the little party descended the Wisconsin, to the great river which had so long been so anxiously looked for, and boldly floated down its unknown waters

On the 25th of June, the explorers discovered indications of Indians on the west bank of the river and landed a little above the mouth of the river now known as Des Moines, and for the first time Europeans trod the soil of Iowa. Leaving the Canadians to guard the canoes, Marquette and Joliet boldly followed the trail into the interior for fourteen miles (some authorities say six), to an Indian village situate on the banks of a river, and discovered two other villages, on the rising ground about half a league distant. Their visit, while it created much astonishment, did not seem to be entirely unexpected, for there was a tradition or prophecy among the Indians that white visitors were to come to them. They were, therefore, received with great respect and hospitality, and were cordially tendered the calumet or pipe of peace They were informed that this band was a part of the Illini nation and that their village was called Mon-in-gou-ma or Moingona, which was the name of the river on which it stood This, from its similarity of sound, Marquette corrupted into Des Moines (Monk's River), its present name.

Here the voyagers remained six days, learning much of the manners and customs of their new friends. The new religion they boldly preached and the authority of the King of France they proclaimed were received without hostility or remonstrance by their savage entertainers. On their departure, they were accompanied to their canoes by the chiefs and hundreds of warriors. Marquette received from them the sacred calumet, the emblem of peace and safeguard among the nations, and re-embarked for the rest of his journey.

It is needless to follow him further, as his explorations beyond his discovery of Iowa more properly belong to the history of another State

In 1682, La Salle descended the Mississippi to the Gulf of Mexico, and in the name of the King of France, took formal possession of all the immense region watered by the great river and its tributaries from its source to its mouth, and named it Louisiana, in honor of his master, Louis XIV. The river he called "Colbert," after the French Minister, and at its mouth erected a column and a cross bearing the inscription, in the French language,

"LOUIS THE GREAT, KING OF FRANCE AND NAVARRE, REIGNING APRIL 9TH, 1682."

At the close of the seventeenth century, France claimed, by right of discovery and occupancy, the whole valley of the Mississippi and its tributaries, including Texas, as far as the Rio del Norte.

The province of Louisiana stretched from the Gulf of Mexico to the sources of the Tennessee, the Kanawha, the Allegheny and the Monongahela on the east, and the Missouri and the other great tributaries of the Father of Waters on the west   Says Bancroft, "France had obtained, under Providence, the guardianship of this immense district of country, not, as it proved, for her own benefit, but rather as a trustee for the infant nation by which it was one day to be inherited "

By the treaty of Utrecht, France ceded to England her possessions in Hudson's Bay, Newfoundland and Nova Scotia.   France still retained Louisiana, but the province had so far failed to meet the expectations of the crown and the people that a change in the government and policy of the country was deemed indispensable.   Accordingly, in 1711, the province was placed in the hands of a Governor General, with headquarters at Mobile.   This government was of brief duration, and in 1712 a charter was granted to Anthony Crozat, a wealthy merchant of Paris, giving him the entire control and monopoly of all the trade and resources of Louisiana.   But this scheme also failed. Crozat met with no success in his commercial operations; every Spanish harbor on the Gulf was closed against his vessels; the occupation of Louisiana was deemed an encroachment on Spanish territory, Spain was jealous of the ambition of France.

Failing in his efforts to open the ports of the district, Crozat "sought to develop the internal resources of Louisiana, by causing trading posts to be opened, and explorations to be made to its remotest borders   But he actually accomplished nothing for the advancement of the colony.   The only prosperity which it ever possessed grew out of the enterprise of humble individuals, who had succeeded in instituting a little barter between themselves and the natives, and a petty trade with neighboring European settlements After a persevering effort of nearly five years, he surrendered his charter in August, 1717."

Immediately following the surrender of his charter by Crozat, another and more magnificent scheme was inaugurated · The national government of France was deeply involved in debt, the colonies were nearly bankrupt, and John Law appeared on the scene with his famous Mississippi Company, as the Louisiana branch of the Bank of France.   The charter granted to this company gave it a legal existence of twenty-five years, and conferred upon it more extensive powers and privileges than had been granted to Crozat.   It invested the new company with the exclusive privilege of the entire commerce of Louisiana, and of New France, and with authority to enforce their rights.   The Company was authorized to monopolize all the trade in the country; to make treaties with the Indians, to declare and prosecute war; to grant lands, erect forts, open mines of precious metals, levy taxes, nominate civil officers, commission those of the army, and to appoint and remove judges, to cast cannon, and build and equip ships of war   All this was to be done with the paper currency of John Law's Bank of France.   He had succeeded in getting His Majesty the French King to adopt and sanction his scheme of financial operations both in France and in the colonies, and probably there never was such a huge financial bubble ever blown by a visionary theorist   Still, such was the condition of France that it was accepted as a national deliverance, and Law became the most powerful man in France.   He became a Catholic, and was appointed Comptroller General of Finance.

Among the first operations of the Company was to send eight hundred emigrants to Louisiana, who arrived at Dauphine Island in 1718.

In 1719, Philipe Francis Renault arrived in Illinois with two hundred miners and artisans. The war between France and Spain at this time rendered it extremely probable that the Mississippi Valley might become the theater of Spanish hostilities against the French settlements; to prevent this, as well as to extend French claims, a chain of forts was begun, to keep open the connection between the mouth and the sources of the Mississippi. Fort Orleans, high up the Mississippi River, was erected as an outpost in 1720.

The Mississippi scheme was at the zenith of its power and glory in January, 1720, but the gigantic bubble collapsed more suddenly than it had been inflated, and the Company was declared hopelessly bankrupt in May following France was impoverished by it, both private and public credit were overthrown, capitalists suddenly found themselves paupers, and labor was left without employment. The effect on the colony of Louisiana was disastrous

While this was going on in Lower Louisiana, the region about the lakes was the theater of Indian hostilities, rendering the passage from Canada to Louisiana extremely dangerous for many years. The English had not only extended their Indian trade into the vicinity of the French settlements, but through their friends, the Iroquois, had gained a marked ascendancy over the Foxes, a fierce and powerful tribe, of Iroquois descent, whom they incited to hostilities against the French. The Foxes began their hostilities with the siege of Detroit in 1712, a siege which they continued for nineteen consecutive days, and although the expedition resulted in diminishing their numbers and humbling their pride, yet it was not until after several successive campaigns, embodying the best military resources of New France, had been directed against them, that were finally defeated at the great battles of Butte des Morts, and on the Wisconsin River, and driven west in 1746

The Company, having found that the cost of defending Louisiana exceeded the returns from its commerce, solicited leave to surrender the Mississippi wilderness to the home government Accordingly, on the 10th of April, 1732, the jurisdiction and control over the commerce reverted to the crown of France. The Company had held possession of Louisiana fourteen years. In 1735, Bienville returned to assume command for the King

A glance at a few of the old French settlements will show the progress made in portions of Louisiana during the early part of the eighteenth century As early as 1705, traders and hunters had penetrated the fertile regions of the Wabash, and from this region, at that early date, fifteen thousand hides and skins had been collected and sent to Mobile for the European market.

In the year 1716, the French population on the Wabash kept up a lucrative commerce with Mobile by means of traders and voyageurs. The Ohio River was comparatively unknown.

In 1746, agriculture on the Wabash had attained to greater prosperity than in any of the French settlements besides, and in that year six hundred barrels of flour were manufactured and shipped to New Orleans, together with considerable quantities of hides, peltry, tallow and beeswax.

In the Illinois country, also, considerable settlements had been made, so that, in 1730, they embraced one hundred and forty French families, about six hundred "converted Indians," and many traders and voyageurs.

In 1753, the first actual conflict arose between Louisiana and the Atlantic colonies. From the earliest advent of the Jesuit fathers, up to the period of which we speak, the great ambition of the French had been, not alone to preserve their possessions in the West, but by every possible means to prevent the slightest attempt of the English, east of the mountains, to extend their settlements toward the Mississippi   France was resolved on retaining possession of the great territory which her missionaries had discovered and revealed to the world   French commandants had avowed their purpose of seizing every Englishman within the Ohio Valley

The colonies of Pennsylvania, New York and Virginia were most affected by the encroachments of France in the extension of her dominion, and particularly in the great scheme of uniting Canada with Louisiana. To carry out this purpose, the French had taken possession of a tract of country claimed by Virginia, and had commenced a line of forts extending from the lakes to the Ohio River. Virginia was not only alive to her own interests, but attentive to the vast importance of an immediate and effectual resistance on the part of all the English colonies to the actual and contemplated encroachments of the French.

In 1753, Governor Dinwiddie, of Virginia, sent George Washington, then a young man just twenty-one, to demand of the French commandant "a reason for invading British dominions while a solid peace subsisted." Washington met the French commandant, Gardeur de St Pierre, on the head waters of the Alleghany, and having communicated to him the object of his journey, received the insolent answer that the French would not discuss the matter of right, but would make prisoners of every Englishman found trading on the Ohio and its waters   The country, he said, belonged to the French, by virtue of the discoveries of La Salle, and they would not withdraw from it.

In January, 1754, Washington returned to Virginia, and made his report to the Governor and Council   Forces were at once raised, and Washington, as Lieutenant Colonel, was dispatched at the head of a hundred and fifty men, to the forks of the Ohio, with orders to "finish the fort already begun there by the Ohio Company, and to make prisoners, kill or destroy all who interrupted the English settlements."

On his march through the forests of Western Pennsylvania, Washington, through the aid of friendly Indians, discovered the French concealed among the rocks, and as they ran to seize their arms, ordered his men to fire upon them, at the same time, with his own musket, setting the example. An action lasting about a quarter of an hour ensued; ten of the Frenchmen were killed, among them Jumonville, the commander of the party, and twenty-one were made prisoners   The dead were scalped by the Indians, and the chief, bearing a tomahawk and a scalp, visited all the tribes of the Miamis, urging them to join the Six Nations and the English against the French. The French, however, were soon re-enforced, and Col. Washington was compelled to return to Fort Necessity. Here, on the 3d day of July, De Villiers invested the fort with 600 French troops and 100 Indians. On the 4th, Washington accepted terms of capitulation, and the English garrison withdrew from the valley of the Ohio

This attack of Washington upon Jumonville aroused the indignation of France, and war was formally declared in May, 1756, and the "French and Indian War" devastated the colonies for several years   Montreal, Detroit and all Canada were surrendered to the English, and on the 10th of February, 1763, by the treaty of Paris—which had been signed, though not formally ratified by the respective governments, on the 3d of November, 1762—France relinquished to Great Britain all that portion of the province of Louisiana lying on the east side of the Mississippi, except the island and town of New Orleans   On the same day that the treaty of Paris was signed, France, by a secret treaty, ceded to Spain all her possessions on the west side of the Mississippi, including the whole country to the head waters of the Great River, and west to the Rocky Mountains, and the jurisdiction of France in America, which had lasted nearly a century, was ended.

At the close of the Revolutionary war, by the treaty of peace between Great Britain and the United States, the English Government ceded to the latter all the territory on the east side of the Mississippi River and north of the thirty-first parallel of north latitude. At the same time, Great Britain ceded to Spain all the Floridas, comprising all the territory east of the Mississippi and south of the southern limits of the United States

At this time, therefore, the present State of Iowa was a part of the Spanish possessions in North America, as all the territory west of the Mississippi River was under the dominion of Spain That government also possessed all the territory of the Floridas east of the great river and south of the thirty-first parallel of north latitude The Mississippi, therefore, so essential to the prosperity of the western portion of the United States, for the last three hundred miles of its course flowed wholly within the Spanish dominions, and that government claimed the exclusive right to use and control it below the southern boundary of the United States

The free navigation of the Mississippi was a very important question during all the time that Louisiana remained a dependency of the Spanish Crown, and as the final settlement intimately affected the status of the then future State of Iowa, it will be interesting to trace its progress

The people of the United States occupied and exercised jurisdiction over the entire eastern valley of the Mississippi, embracing all the country drained by its eastern tributaries, they had a natural right, according to the accepted international law, to follow these rivers to the sea, and to the use of the Mississippi River accordingly, as the great natural channel of commerce. The river was not only necessary but absolutely indispensable to the prosperity and growth of the western settlements then rapidly rising into commercial and political importance. They were situated in the heart of the great valley, and with wonderfully expansive energies and accumulating resources, it was very evident that no power on earth could deprive them of the free use of the river below them, only while their numbers were insufficient to enable them to maintain their right by force Inevitably, therefore, immediately after the ratification of the treaty of 1783, the Western people began to demand the free navigation of the Mississippi—not as a favor, but as a right In 1786, both banks of the river, below the mouth of the Ohio, were occupied by Spain, and military posts on the east bank enforced her power to exact heavy duties on all imports by way of the river for the Ohio region. Every boat descending the river was forced to land and submit to the arbitrary revenue exactions of the Spanish authorities Under the administration of Governor Miro, these rigorous exactions were somewhat relaxed from 1787 to 1790; but Spain held it as her right to make them Taking advantage of the claim of the American people. that the Mississippi should be opened to them, in 1791, the Spanish Government concocted a scheme for the dismemberment of the Union. The plan was to induce the Western people to separate from the Eastern States by liberal land grants and extraordinary commercial privileges

Spanish emissaries, among the people of Ohio and Kentucky, informed them that the Spanish Government would grant them favorable commercial privileges, provided they would secede from the Federal Government east of the mountains. The Spanish Minister to the United States plainly declared to his confidential correspondent that, unless the Western people would declare their independence and refuse to remain in the Union, Spain was determined never to grant the free navigation of the Mississippi.

By the treaty of Madrid, October 20, 1795, however, Spain formally stipulated that the Mississippi River, from its source to the Gulf, for its entire width, should be free to American trade and commerce, and that the people of the United States should be permitted, for three years, to use the port of New Orleans as a port of deposit for their merchandise and produce, duty free.

In November, 1801, the United States Government received, through Rufus King, its Minister at the Court of St. James, a copy of the treaty between Spain and France, signed at Madrid March 21, 1801, by which the cession of Louisiana to France, made the previous Autumn, was confirmed.

The change offered a favorable opportunity to secure the just rights of the United States, in relation to the free navigation of the Mississippi, and ended the attempt to dismember the Union by an effort to secure an independent government west of the Alleghany Mountains. On the 7th of January, 1803, the American House of Representatives adopted a resolution declaring their " unalterable determination to maintain the boundaries and the rights of navigation and commerce through the River Mississippi, as established by existing treaties."

In the same month, President Jefferson nominated and the Senate confirmed Robert R. Livingston and James Monroe as Envoys Plenipotentiary to the Court of France, and Charles Pinckney and James Monroe to the Court of Spain, with plenary powers to negotiate treaties to effect the object enunciated by the popular branch of the National Legislature. These envoys were instructed to secure, if possible, the cession of Florida and New Orleans, but it does not appear that Mr. Jefferson and his Cabinet had any idea of purchasing that part of Louisiana lying on the *west* side of the Mississippi In fact, on the 2d of March following, the instructions were sent to our Ministers, containing a plan which expressly left to France " all her territory on the west side of the Mississippi" Had these instructions been followed, it might have been that there would not have been any State of Iowa or any other member of the glorious Union of States west of the " Father of Waters"

In obedience to his instructions, however, Mr. Livingston broached this plan to M. Talleyrand, Napoleon's Prime Minister, when that courtly diplomatist quietly suggested to the American Minister that France *might* be willing to cede the *whole French domain* in North America to the United States, and asked how much the Federal Government would be willing to give for it. Livingston intimated that twenty millions of francs might be a fair price. Talleyrand thought that not enough, but asked the Americans to "think of it " A few days later, Napoleon, in an interview with Mr. Livingston, in effect informed the American Envoy that he had secured Louisiana in a contract with Spain for the purpose of turning it over to the United States for a mere nominal sum He had been compelled to provide for the safety of that province by the treaty, and he was "anxious to give the United States a magnificent bargain for a mere trifle." The price proposed was one hundred and twenty-five million francs. This was subsequently modified to fifteen million dollars, and on this basis a treaty was negotiated, and was signed on the 30th day of April, 1803.

This treaty was ratified by the Federal Government, and by act of Congress, approved October 31, 1803, the President of the United States was authorized to take possession of the territory and provide for it a temporary government. Accordingly, on the 20th day of December following on behalf of the President, Gov. Claiborne and Gen. Wilkinson took possession of the Louisiana purchase, and raised the American flag over the newly acquired domain, at New Orleans. Spain, although it had by treaty ceded the province to France in 1801, still held *quasi* possession, and at first objected to the transfer, but withdrew her opposition early in 1804

By this treaty, thus successfully consummated, and the peaceable withdrawal of Spain, the then infant nation of the New World extended its dominion west of the Mississippi to the Pacific Ocean, and north from the Gulf of Mexico to British America.

If the original design of Jefferson's administration had been accomplished, the United States would have acquired only that portion of the French territory lying east of the Mississippi River, and while the American people would thus have acquired the free navigation of that great river, all of the vast and fertile empire on the west, so rich in its agricultural and inexhaustible mineral resources, would have remained under the dominion of a foreign power. To Napoleon's desire to sell the whole of his North American possessions, and Livingston's act transcending his instructions, which was acquiesced in after it was done, does Iowa owe her position as a part of the United States by the Louisiana purchase.

By authority of an act of Congress, approved March 26, 1804, the newly acquired territory was, on the 1st day of October following, divided · that part lying south of the 33d parallel of north latitude was called the Territory of Orleans, and all north of that parallel the District of Louisiana, which was placed under the authority of the officers of Indiana Territory, until July 4, 1805, when it was organized, with territorial government of its own, and so remained until 1812, when the Territory of Orleans became the State of Louisiana, and the name of the Territory of Louisiana was changed to Missouri. On the 4th of July, 1814, that part of Missouri Territory comprising the present State of Arkansas, and the country to the westward, was organized into the Arkansas Territory.

On the 2d of March, 1821, the State of Missouri, being a part of the Territory of that name, was admitted to the Union. June 28, 1834, the territory west of the Mississippi River and north of Missouri was made a part of the Territory of Michigan; but two years later, on the 4th of July, 1836, Wisconsin Territory was erected, embracing within its limits the present States of Iowa, Wisconsin and Minnesota.

By act of Congress, approved June 12, 1838, the

TERRITORY OF IOWA

was erected, comprising, in addition to the present State, much the larger part of Minnesota, and extending north to the boundary of the British Possessions.

THE ORIGINAL OWNERS.

Having traced the early history of the great empire lying west of the Mississippi, of which the State of Iowa constitutes a part, from the earliest discovery to the organization of the Territory of Iowa, it becomes necessary to give some history of

THE INDIANS OF IOWA

According to the policy of the European nations, possession perfected title to any territory. We have seen that the country west of the Mississippi was first discovered by the Spaniards, but afterward, was visited and occupied by the French It was ceded by France to Spain, and by Spain back to France again, and then was purchased and occupied by the United States.   During all that time, it does not appear to have entered into the heads or hearts of the high contracting parties that the country they bought, sold and gave away was in the possession of a race of men who, although savage, owned the vast domain before Columbus first crossed the Atlantic.   Having purchased the territory, the United States found it still in the possession of its original owners, who had never been dispossessed; and it became necessary to purchase again what had already been bought before, or forcibly eject the occupants; therefore, the history of the Indian nations who occupied Iowa prior to and during its early settlement by the whites, becomes an important chapter in the history of the State, that cannot be omitted

For more than one hundred years after Marquette and Joliet trod the virgin soil of Iowa, not a single settlement had been made or attempted; not even a trading post had been established   The whole country remained in the undisputed possession of the native tribes, who roamed at will over her beautiful and fertile prairies, hunted in her woods, fished in her streams, and often poured out their life-blood in obstinately contested contests for supremacy   That this State so aptly styled "The Beautiful Land," had been the theater of numerous, fierce and bloody struggles between rival nations, for possession of the favored region, long before its settlement by civilized man, there is no room for doubt. In these savage wars, the weaker party, whether aggressive or defensive, was either exterminated or driven from their ancient hunting grounds.

In 1673, when Marquette discovered Iowa, the Illini were a very powerful people, occupying a large portion of the State; but when the country was again visited by the whites, not a remnant of that once powerful tribe remained on the west side of the Mississippi, and Iowa was principally in the possession of the Sacs and Foxes, a warlike tribe which, originally two distinct nations, residing in New York and on the waters of the St. Lawrence, had gradually fought their way westward, and united, probably, after the Foxes had been driven out of the Fox River country, in 1846, and crossed the Mississippi.   The death of Pontiac, a famous Sac chieftain, was made the pretext for war against the Illini, and a fierce and bloody struggle ensued, which continued until the Illinois were nearly destroyed and their hunting grounds possessed by their victorious foes.   The Iowas also occupied a portion of the State for a time, in common with the Sacs, but they, too, were nearly destroyed by the Sacs and Foxes, and, in "The Beautiful Land," these natives met their equally warlike foes, the Northern Sioux, with whom they maintained a constant warfare for the possession of the country for many years

When the United States came in possession of the great valley of the Mississippi, by the Louisiana purchase, the Sacs and Foxes and Iowas possessed the entire territory now comprising the State of Iowa.   The Sacs and Foxes, also, occupied the most of the State of Illinois.

The Sacs had four principal villages, where most of them resided, viz. · Their largest and most important town—if an Indian village may be called such—and from which emanated most of the obstacles and difficulties encountered by the Government in the extinguishment of Indian titles to land in this region, was on Rock River, near Rock Island; another was on the east bank of the Mississippi, near the mouth of Henderson River; the third was at the head of the Des Moines Rapids, near the present site of Montrose, and the fourth was near the mouth of the Upper Iowa.

The Foxes had three principal villages, viz ·   One on the west side of the Mississippi, six miles above the rapids of Rock River, another about twelve miles from the river, in the rear of the Dubuque lead mines, and the third on Turkey River.

The Iowas, at one time identified with the Sacs, of Rock River, had withdrawn from them and become a separate tribe. Their principal village was on the Des Moines River, in Van Buren County, on the site where Iowaville now stands. Here the last great battle between the Sacs and Foxes and the Iowas was fought, in which Black Hawk, then a young man, commanded one division of the attacking forces. The following account of the battle has been given

' Contrary to long established custom of Indian attack, this battle was commenced in the day time, the attending circumstances justifying this departure from the well settled usages of Indian warfare. The battle field was a level river bottom, about four miles in length, and two miles wide near the middle, narrowing to a point at either end. The main area of this bottom rises perhaps twenty feet above the river, leaving a narrow strip of low bottom along the shore, covered with trees that belted the prairie on the river side with a thick forest, and the immediate bank of the river was fringed with a dense growth of willows. Near the lower end of this prairie, near the river bank, was situated the Iowa village. About two miles above it and near the middle of the prairie is a mound, covered at the time with a tuft of small trees and underbrush growing on its summit. In the rear of this little elevation or mound lay a belt of wet prairie, covered, at that time with a dense growth of rank, coarse grass. Bordering this wet prairie on the north, the country rises abruptly into elevated broken river bluffs, covered with a heavy forest for many miles in extent, and in places thickly clustered with undergrowth, affording a convenient shelter for the stealthy approach of the foe.

" Through this forest the Sac and Fox war party made their way in the night and secreted themselves in the tall grass spoken of above, intending to remain in ambush during the day and make such observations as this near proximity to their intended victim might afford, to aid them in their contemplated attack on the town during the following night. From this situation their spies could take a full survey of the village, and watch every movement of the inhabitants, by which means they were soon convinced that the Iowas had no suspicion of their presence.

" At the foot of the mound above mentioned, the Iowas had their race course, where they diverted themselves with the excitement of horse racing, and schooled their young warriors in cavalry evolutions. In these exercises mock battles were fought, and the Indian tactics of attack and defense carefully inculcated, by which means a skill in horsemanship was acquired rarely excelled. Unfortunately for them this day was selected for their equestrian sports, and wholly unconscious of the proximity of their foes, the warriors repaired to the race ground, leaving most of their arms in the village and their old men and women and children unprotected.

" Pash-a-po-po, who was chief in command of the Sacs and Foxes, perceived at once the advantage this state of things afforded for a complete surprise of his now doomed victims, and ordered Black Hawk to file off with his young warriors through the tall grass and gain the cover of the timber along the river bank, and with the utmost speed reach the village and commence the battle, while he remained with his division in the ambush to make a simultaneous assault on the unarmed men whose attention was engrossed with the excitement of the races. The plan was skillfully laid and most dexterously executed. Black Hawk with his forces reached the village undiscovered, and made a furious onslaught upon the defenseless inhabitants, by firing one general volley into their midst, and completing the slaughter with the tomahawk and scalping knife, aided by the devouring flames with which they enveloped the village as soon as the fire brand could be spread from lodge to lodge.

" On the instant of the report of fire arms at the village the forces under Pash-x-po-po leaped from their couchant position in the grass and sprang tiger-like upon the astonished and unarmed Iowas in the midst of their racing sports. The first impulse of the latter naturally led them to make the utmost speed toward their arms in the village, and protect if possible their wives and children from the attack of their merciless assailants. The distance from the place of attack on the prairie was two miles, and a great number fell in their flight by the bullets and tomahawks of their enemies, who pressed them closely with a running fire the whole way, and the survivors only reached their town in time to witness the horrors of its destruction. Their whole village was in flames, and the dearest objects of their lives lay in slaughtered heaps amidst the devouring element, and the agonizing groans of the dying, mingled with the exulting shouts of the victorious foe, filled their hearts with maddening despair. Their wives and children who had been spared the general massacre were prisoners, and together with their arms were in the hands of the victors, and all that could now be done was to draw off their shattered and defenseless forces, and save as many lives as possible by a retreat across the Des Moines River, which they effected in the best possible manner, and took a position among the Soap Creek Hills "

The Sacs and Foxes, prior to the settlement of their village on Rock River, had a fierce conflict with the Winnebagoes, subdued them and took possession of their lands. Their village on Rock River, at one time, contained upward of sixty lodges, and was among the largest Indian villages on the continent. In 1825, the Secretary of War estimated the entire number of the Sacs and Foxes at 4,600 souls. Their village was situated in the immediate vicinity of the upper rapids of the Mississippi, where the beautiful and flourishing towns of Rock Island and Davenport are now situated. The beautiful scenery of the island, the extensive prairies, dotted over with groves; the picturesque bluffs along the river banks, the rich and fertile soil, producing large crops of corn, squash and other vegetables, with little labor; the abundance of wild fruit, game, fish, and almost everything calculated to make it a delightful spot for an Indian village, which was found there, had made this place a favorite home of the Sacs, and secured for it the strong attachment and veneration of the whole nation

North of the hunting grounds of the Sacs and Foxes, were those of the Sioux, a fierce and warlike nation, who often disputed possession with their rivals in savage and bloody warfare. The possessions of these tribes were mostly located in Minnesota, but extended over a portion of Northern and Western Iowa to the Missouri River Their descent from the north upon the hunting grounds of Iowa frequently brought them into collision with the Sacs and Foxes; and after many a conflict and bloody struggle, a boundary line was established between them by the Government of the United States, in a treaty held at Prairie du Chien, in 1825. But this, instead of settling the difficulties, caused them to quarrel all the more, in consequence of alleged trespasses upon each other's side of the line. These contests were kept up and became so unrelenting that, in 1830, Government bought of the respective tribes of the Sacs and Foxes, and the Sioux, a strip of land twenty miles in width, on both sides of the line, and thus throwing them forty miles apart by creating between them a "neutral ground," commanded them to cease their hostilities Both the Sacs and Foxes and the Sioux, however, were allowed to fish and hunt on this ground unmolested, provided they did not interfere with each other on United States territory. The Sacs and Foxes and the Sioux were deadly enemies, and neither let an opportunity to punish the other pass unimproved

In April, 1852, a fight occurred between the Musquaka band of Sacs and Foxes and a band of Sioux, about six miles above Algona, in Kossuth County, on the west side of the Des Moines River. The Sacs and Foxes were under the leadership of Ko-ko-wah, a subordinate chief, and had gone up from their home in Tama County, by way of Clear Lake, to what was then the "neutral ground" At Clear Lake, Ko-ko-wah was informed that a party of Sioux were encamped on the west side of the East Fork of the Des Moines, and he determined to attack them With sixty of his warriors, he started and arrived at a point on the east side of the river, about a mile above the Sioux encampment, in the night, and concealed themselves in a grove, where they were able to discover the position and strength of their hereditary foes. The next morning, after many of the Sioux braves had left their camp on hunting tours, the vindictive Sacs and Foxes crossed the river and suddenly attacked the camp. The conflict was desperate for a short time, but the advantage was with the assailants, and the Sioux were routed Sixteen of them, including some of their women and children, were killed, and a boy 14 years old was captured. One of the Musquakas was shot in the breast by a squaw as they were rushing into the Sioux's camp. He started to run away, when the same brave squaw shot him through the body, at a distance of twenty rods, and he fell dead. Three other Sac braves were killed. But few of the Sioux escaped The victorious party hurriedly buried their own dead, leaving the dead Sioux above ground, and made their way home, with their captive, with all possible expedition

PIKE'S EXPEDITION

Very soon after the acquisition of Louisiana, the United States Government adopted measures for the exploration of the new territory, having in view the conciliation of the numerous tribes of Indians by whom it was possessed, and, also, the selection of proper sites for the establishment of military posts and trading stations. The Army of the West, Gen James Wilkinson commanding, had its headquarters at St Louis From this post, Captains Lewis and Clark, with a sufficient force, were detailed to explore the unknown sources of the Missouri, and Lieut Zebulon M Pike to ascend to the head waters of the Mississippi. Lieut. Pike, with one Sergeant, two Corporals and seventeen privates, left the military camp, near St Louis, in a keel-boat, with four months' rations. on the 9th day of August, 1805 On the 20th of the same month, the expedition arrived within the present limits of Iowa, at the foot of the Des Moines Rapids, where Pike met William Ewing, who had just been appointed Indian Agent at this point, a French interpreter and four chiefs and fifteen Sac and Fox warriors.

At the head of the Rapids, where Montrose is now situated, Pike held a council with the Indians, in which he addressed them substantially as follows: "Your great Father, the President of the United States, wished to be more intimately acquainted with the situation and wants of the different nations of red people in our newly acquired territory of Louisiana, and has ordered the General to send a number of his warriors in different directions to take them by the hand and make such inquiries as might afford the satisfaction required." At the close of the council he presented the red men with some knives, whisky and tobacco

Pursuing his way up the river, he arrived, on the 23d of August, at what is supposed, from his description, to be the site of the present city of Burlington, which he selected as the location of a military post He describes the place as being " on a hill, about forty miles above the River de Moyne Rapids, on the west side of the river, in latitude about 41° 21' north The channel of the river runs on that shore, the hill in front is about sixty feet perpendicular; nearly level on top, four hundred yards in the rear is a small prairie fit for gardening, and immediately under the hill is a limestone spring, sufficient for the consumption of a whole regiment." In addition to this description, which corresponds to Burlington, the spot is laid down on his map at a bend in the river, a short distance below the mouth of the Henderson which pours its waters into the Mississippi from Illinois The fort was built at Fort Madison, but from the distance, latitude, description and map furnished by Pike, it could not have been the place selected by him, while all the circumstances corroborate the opinion that the place he selected was the spot where Burlington is now located, called by the early voyagers on the Mississippi, "Flint Hills."

On the 24th, with one of his men, he went on shore on a hunting expedition, and following a stream which they supposed to be a part of the Mississippi, they were led away from their course. Owing to the intense heat and tall grass, his two favorite dogs, which he had taken with him, became exhausted and he left them on the prairie, supposing that they would follow him as soon as they should get rested, and went on to overtake his boat Reaching the river, he waited some time for his canine friends, but they did not come, and as he deemed it inexpedient to detain the boat longer, two of his men volunteered to go in pursuit of them, and he continued on his way up the river, expecting that the two men would soon overtake him   They lost their way, however, and for six days were without food, except a few morsels gathered from the stream, and might have perished, had they not accidentally met a trader from St. Louis, who induced two Indians to take them up the river, and they overtook the boat at Dubuque.

At Dubuque, Pike was cordially received by Julien Dubuque, a Frenchman. who held a mining claim under a grant from Spain   Dubuque had an old field piece and fired a salute in honor of the advent of the first Americans who had visited that part of the Territory. Dubuque, however, was not disposed to publish the wealth of his mines, and the young and evidently inquisitive officer obtained but little information from him.

After leaving this place, Pike pursued his way up the river, but as he passed beyond the limits of the present State of Iowa, a detailed history of his explorations on the upper waters of the Mississippi more properly belongs to the history of another State.

It is sufficient to say that on the site of Fort Snelling, Minnesota, at the mouth of the Minnesota River, Pike held a council with the Sioux, September 23, and obtained from them a grant of one hundred thousand acres of land On the 8th of January, 1806, Pike arrived at a trading post belonging to the Northwest Company, on Lake De Sable, in latitude 47°. At this time the then powerful Northwest Company carried on their immense operations from Hudson's Bay to the St Lawrence; up that river on both sides, along the great lakes to the head of Lake Superior, thence to the sources of the Red River of the north and west, to the Rocky Mountains, embracing within the scope of their operations the entire Territory of Iowa. After successfully accomplishing his mission, and performing a valuable service to Iowa and the whole Northwest, Pike returned to St. Louis, arriving there on the 30th of April, 1806

INDIAN WARS.

The Territory of Iowa, although it had been purchased by the United States, and was ostensibly in the possession of the Government, was still occupied by the Indians, who claimed title to the soil by right of ownership and possession Before it could be open to settlement by the whites, it was indispensable that the Indian title should be extinguished and the original owners removed.   The accomplishment of this purpose required the expenditure of large sums of money and blood, and for a long series of years the frontier was disturbed by Indian wars, terminated repeatedly by treaty, only to be renewed by some act of oppression on the part of the whites or some violation of treaty stipulation.

As previously shown, at the time when the United States assumed the control of the country by virtue of the Louisiana purchase, nearly the whole State was in possession of the Sacs and Foxes, a powerful and warlike nation, who were not disposed to submit without a struggle to what they considered the encroachments of the pale faces.

Among the most noted chiefs, and one whose restlessness and hatred of the Americans occasioned more trouble to the Government than any other of his tribe, was Black Hawk, who was born at the Sac village, on Rock River, in 1767   He was simply the chief of his own band of Sac warriors, but by his energy and ambition he became the leading spirit of the united nation of Sacs and Foxes, and one of the prominent figures in the history of the country from 1804 until his death.   In early manhood he attained some distinction as a fighting chief, having led campaigns against the Osages, and other neighboring tribes   About the beginning of the present century he began to appear prominent in affairs on the Mississippi. Some historians have added to the statement that "it does not appear that he was ever a great general, or possessed any of the qualifications of a successful leader"   If this was so, his life was a marvel. How any man who had none of the qualifications of a leader became so prominent as such, as he did, indicates either that he had some ability, or that his cotemporaries, both Indian and Anglo-Saxon, had less than he   He is said to have been the "victim of a narrow prejudice and bitter ill-will against the Americans," but the impartial historian must admit that if he was the enemy of the Americans, it was certainly not without some reason.

It will be remembered that Spain did not give up possession of the country to France on its cession to the latter power, in 1801, but retained possession of it, and, by the authority of France, transferred it to the United States, in 1804. Black Hawk and his band were in St. Louis at the time, and were invited to be present and witness the ceremonies of the transfer, but he refused the invitation, and it is but just to say that this refusal was caused probably more from regret that the Indians were to be transferred from the jurisdiction of the Spanish authorities than from any special hatred toward the Americans.   In his life he says : "I found many sad and gloomy faces because the United States were about to take possession of the town and country.   Soon after the Americans came, I took my band and went to take leave of our Spanish father The Americans came to see him also.   Seeing them approach, we passed out of one door as they entered another, and immediately started in our canoes for our village, on Rock River, not liking the change any more than our friends appeared to at St Louis.   On arriving at our village, we gave the news that strange people had arrived at St. Louis, and that we should never see our Spanish father again.   The information made all our people sorry."

On the 3d day of November, 1804, a treaty was concluded between William Henry Harrison, then Governor of Indiana Territory, on behalf of the United States, and five chiefs of the Sac and Fox nation, by which the latter, in consideration of two thousand two hundred and thirty-four dollars' worth of goods then delivered, and a yearly annuity of one thousand dollars to be paid in goods at just cost, ceded to the United States all that land on the east side of the Mississippi, extending from a point opposite the Jefferson, in Missouri, to the Wisconsin River, embracing an area of over fifty-one millions of acres.

To this treaty Black Hawk always objected and always refused to consider it binding upon his people   He asserted that the chiefs or braves who made it had no authority to relinquish the title of the nation to any of the lands they held or occupied ; and, moreover, that they had been sent to St Louis on quite a different errand, namely, to get one of their people released, who had been imprisoned at St. Louis for killing a white man

The year following this treaty (1805), Lieutenant Zebulon M Pike came up the river for the purpose of holding friendly councils with the Indians and selecting sites for forts within the territory recently acquired from France by the United States   Lieutenant Pike seems to have been the first American whom Black Hawk ever met or had a personal interview with, and he was very much prepossessed in Pike's favor.   He gives the following account of his visit to Rock Island.

"A boat came up the river with a young American chief and a small party of soldiers.   We heard of them soon after they passed Salt River   Some of our young braves watched them every day, to see what sort of people he had on board.   The boat at length arrived at Rock River, and the young chief came on shore with his interpreter, and made a speech and gave us some presents   We in turn presented them with meat and such other provisions as we had to spare. We were well pleased with the young chief.   He gave us good advice, and said our American father would treat us well.''

The events which soon followed Pike's expedition were the erection of Fort Edwards, at what is now Warsaw, Illinois, and Fort Madison, on the site of the present town of that name, the latter being the first fort erected in Iowa   These movements occasioned great uneasiness among the Indians.   When work was commenced on Fort Edwards, a delegation from their nation, headed by some of their chiefs, went down to see what the Americans were doing, and had an interview with the commander; after which they returned home apparently satisfied.   In like manner, when Fort Madison was being erected, they sent down another delegation from a council of the nation held at Rock River.   According to Black Hawk's account, the American chief told them that he was building a house for a trader who was coming to sell them goods cheap, and that the soldiers were coming to keep him company—a statement which Black Hawk says they distrusted at the time, believing that the fort was an encroachment upon their rights, and designed to aid in getting their lands away from them.

It has been held by good American authorities, that the erection of Fort Madison at the point where it was located *was* a violation of the treaty of 1804 By the eleventh article of that treaty, the United States had a right to build a fort near the mouth of the Wisconsin River; by article six they had bound themselves '' that if any citizen of the United States or any other white persons should form a settlement upon their lands, such intruders should forthwith be removed.''   Probably the authorities of the United States did not regard the establishment of military posts as coming properly within the meaning of the term ''settlement,'' as used in the treaty   At all events, they erected Fort Madison within the territory reserved to the Indians, who became very indignant.   Not long after the fort was built, a party led by Black Hawk attempted its destruction.   They sent spies to watch the movements of the garrison, who ascertained that the soldiers were in the habit of marching out of the fort every morning and evening for parade, and the plan of the party was to conceal themselves near the fort, and attack and surprise them when they were outside.   On the morning of the proposed day of attack, five soldiers came out and were fired upon by the Indians, two of them being killed.   The Indians were too hasty in their movement, for the regular drill had not yet commenced.   However, they kept up the attack for several days, attempting the old Fox strategy of setting fire to the fort with blazing arrows; but finding their efforts unavailing, they soon gave up and returned to Rock River.

When war was declared between the United States and Great Britain, in 1812, Black Hawk and his band allied themselves with the British, partly because he was dazzled by their specious promises, and more probably because they had been deceived by the Americans.   Black Hawk himself declared that they were ''forced into the war by being deceived.''   He narrates the circumstances as follows: '' Several of the chiefs and head men of the Sacs and Foxes were called upon to go to Washington to see their Great Father.   On their return, they related what had been said and done   They said the Great Father wished them, in the event of a war taking place with England, not to interfere on either side, but to remain neutral.   He did not want our help, but wished us to hunt and support our families, and live in peace.   He said that British traders would not be permitted to come on the Mississippi to furnish us with goods, but that we should be supplied with an American trader.   Our chiefs then told him that the British traders always gave them credit in the Fall for guns, powder and goods, to enable us to hunt and clothe our families He repeated that the traders at Fort Madison would have plenty of goods; that we should go there in the Fall and he would supply us on credit, as the British traders had done "

Black Hawk seems to have accepted of this proposition, and he and his people were very much pleased. Acting in good faith, they fitted out for their Winter's hunt, and went to Fort Madison in high spirits to receive from the trader their outfit of supplies. But, after waiting some time, they were told by the trader that he would not trust them. It was in vain that they pleaded the promise of their great father at Washington. The trader was inexorable; and, disappointed and crestfallen, they turned sadly toward their own village. "Few of us," says Black Hawk, "slept that night; all was gloom and discontent. In the morning, a canoe was seen ascending the river; it soon arrived bearing an express, who brought intelligence that a British trader had landed at Rock Island with two boats loaded with goods, and requested us to come up immediately, because he had good news for us, and a variety of presents. The express presented us with tobacco, pipes and wampum. The news ran through our camp like fire on a prairie. Our lodges were soon taken down, and all started for Rock Island. Here ended all hopes of our remaining at peace, having been forced into the war by being deceived."

He joined the British, who flattered him, styled him "Gen. Black Hawk," decked him with medals, excited his jealousies against the Americans, and armed his band; but he met with defeat and disappointment, and soon abandoned the service and came home.

With all his skill and courage, Black Hawk was unable to lead all the Sacs and Foxes into hostilities to the United States. A portion of them, at the head of whom was Keokuk ("the Watchful Fox"), were disposed to abide by the treaty of 1804, and to cultivate friendly relations with the American people. Therefore, when Black Hawk and his band joined the fortunes of Great Britain, the rest of the nation remained neutral, and, for protection, organized, with Keokuk for their chief. This divided the nation into the "War and the Peace party."

Black Hawk says he was informed, after he had gone to the war, that the nation, which had been reduced to so small a body of fighting men, were unable to defend themselves in case the Americans should attack them, and having all the old men and women and children belonging to the warriors who had joined the British on their hands to provide for, a council was held, and it was agreed that Quash-qua-me (the Lance) and other chiefs, together with the old men, women and children, and such others as chose to accompany them, should go to St Louis and place themselves under the American chief stationed there. They accordingly went down, and were received as the "friendly band" of the Sacs and Foxes, and were provided for and sent up the Missouri River. On Black Hawk's return from the British army, he says Keokuk was introduced to him as the war chief of the braves then in the village. He inquired how he had become chief, and was informed that their spies had seen a large armed force going toward Peoria, and fears were entertained of an attack upon the village; whereupon a council was held, which concluded to leave the village and cross over to the west side of the Mississippi. Keokuk had been standing at the door of the lodge where the council was held, not being allowed to enter on account of never having killed an enemy, where he remained until Wa-co-me came out. Keokuk asked permission to speak in the council, which Wa-co-me obtained for him   Keokuk then addressed the chiefs , he remonstrated against the desertion of their village, their own homes and the graves of their fathers, and offered to defend the village   The council consented that he should be their war chief.   He marshaled his braves, sent out spies, and advanced on the trail leading to Peoria, but returned without seeing the enemy   The Americans did not disturb the village, and all were satisfied with the appointment of Keokuk

Keokuk, like Black Hawk, was a descendant of the Sac branch of the nation, and was born on Rock River, in 1780.   He was of a pacific disposition, but possessed the elements of true courage, and could fight, when occasion required, with a cool judgment and heroic energy.   In his first battle, he encountered and killed a Sioux, which placed him in the rank of warriors, and he was honored with a public feast by his tribe in commemoration of the event.

Keokuk has been described as an orator, entitled to rank with the most gifted of his race   In person, he was tall and of portly bearing ; in his public speeches, he displayed a commanding attitude and graceful gestures, he spoke rapidly, but his enunciation was clear, distinct and forcible ; he culled his figures from the stores of nature and based his arguments on skillful logic   Unfortunately for the reputation of Keokuk, as an orator among white people, he was never able to obtain an interpreter who could claim even a slight acquaintance with philosophy   With one exception only, his interpreters were unacquainted with the elements of their mother-tongue   Of this serious hindrance to his fame, Keokuk was well aware, and retained Frank Labershure, who had received a rudimental education in the French and English languages, until the latter broke down by dissipation and died   But during the meridian of his career among the white people, he was compelled to submit his speeches for translation to uneducated men, whose range of thought fell below the flights of a gifted mind, and the fine imagery drawn from nature was beyond their power of reproduction.   He had sufficient knowledge of the English language to make him sensible of this bad rendering of his thoughts, and often a feeling of mortification at the bungling efforts was depicted on his countenance while speaking   The proper place to form a correct estimate of his ability as an orator was in the Indian council, where he addressed himself exclusively to those who understood his language, and witness the electrical effect of his eloquence upon his audience

Keokuk seems to have possessed a more sober judgment, and to have had a more intelligent view of the great strength and resources of the United States, than his noted and restless cotemporary, Black Hawk.   He knew from the first that the reckless war which Black Hawk and his band had determined to carry on could result in nothing but defeat and disaster, and used every argument against it.   The large number of warriors whom he had dissuaded from following Black Hawk became, however, greatly excited with the war spirit after Stillman's defeat, and but for the signal tact displayed by Keokuk on that occasion, would have forced him to submit to their wishes in joining the rest of the warriors in the field   A war-dance was held, and Keokuk took part in it, seeming to be moved with the current of the rising storm.   When the dance was over, he called the council to prepare for war.   He made a speech, in which he admitted the justice of their complaints against the Americans.   To seek redress was a noble aspiration of their nature   The blood of their brethren had been shed by the white man, and the spirits of their braves, slain in battle, called loudly for vengeance.   "I am your chief," he said, "and it is my duty to lead you to battle, if, after fully considering the matter, you are determined to go.   But before you decide on taking this important step, it is wise to inquire into the chances of success." He then portrayed to them the great power of the United States, against whom they would have to contend, that their chance of success was utterly hopeless. "But," said he, "if you do determine to go upon the war-path, I will agree to lead you, on one condition, viz.· that before we go, we will kill all our old men and our wives and children, to save them from a lingering death of starvation, and that every one of us determine to leave our homes on the other side of the Mississippi."

This was a strong but truthful picture of the prospect before them, and was presented in such a forcible light as to cool their ardor, and cause them to abandon the rash undertaking.

But during the war of 1832, it is now considered certain that small bands of Indians, from the west side of the Mississippi, made incursions into the white settlements, in the lead mining region, and committed some murders and depredations.

When peace was declared between the United States and England, Black Hawk was required to make peace with the former, and entered into a treaty at Portage des Sioux, September 14, 1815, but did not "touch the goose-quill to it until May 13, 1816, when he smoked the pipe of peace with the great white chief," at St. Louis This treaty was a renewal of the treaty of 1804, but Black Hawk declared he had been deceived, that he did not know that by signing the treaty he was giving away his village. This weighed upon his mind, already soured by previous disappointment and the irresistible encroachments of the whites, and when, a few years later, he and his people were driven from their possessions by the military, he determined to return to the home of his fathers

It is also to be remarked that, in 1816, by treaty with various tribes, the United States relinquished to the Indians all the lands lying north of a line drawn from the southernmost point of Lake Michigan west to the Mississippi, except a reservation five leagues square, on the Mississippi River, supposed then to be sufficient to include all the mineral lands on and adjacent to Fever River, and one league square at the mouth of the Wisconsin River

THE BLACK HAWK WAR

The immediate cause of the Indian outbreak in 1830 was the occupation of Black Hawk's village, on the Rock River, by the whites, during the absence of the chief and his braves on a hunting expedition, on the west side of the Mississippi. When they returned, they found their wigwams occupied by white families, and their own women and children were shelterless on the banks of the river. The Indians were indignant, and determined to repossess their village at all hazards, and early in the Spring of 1831 recrossed the Mississippi and menacingly took possession of their own cornfields and cabins. It may be well to remark here that it was expressly stipulated in the treaty of 1804, to which they attributed all their troubles, that the Indians should not be obliged to leave their lands until they were sold by the United States, and it does not appear that they occupied any lands other than those owned by the Government. If this was true, the Indians had good cause for indignation and complaint But the whites, driven out in turn by the returning Indians, became so clamorous against what they termed the encroachments of the natives, that Gov. Reynolds, of Illinois, ordered Gen Gaines to Rock Island with a military force to drive the Indians again from their homes to the west side of the Mississippi. Black Hawk says he did not intend to be provoked into war by anything less than the blood of

some of his own people : in other words, that there would be no war unless it should
be commenced by the pale faces. But it was said and probably thought by the military commanders along the frontier that the Indians intended to unite in a general
war against the whites, from Rock River to the Mexican borders   But it does not
appear that the hardy frontiersmen themselves had any fears, for their experience had been that, when well treated, their Indian neighbors were not dangerous Black Hawk and his band had done no more than to attempt to repossess the
the old homes of which they had been deprived in their absence. No blood
had been shed. Black Hawk and his chiefs sent a flag of truce, and a new
treaty was made, by which Black Hawk and his band agreed to remain forever
on the Iowa side and never recross the river without the permission of the
President or the Governor of Illinois. Whether the Indians clearly understood
the terms of this treaty is uncertain   As was usual, the Indian traders had
dictated terms on their behalf, and they had received a large amount of provisions, etc., from the Government, but it may well be doubted whether the
Indians comprehended that they could never revisit the graves of their fathers
without violating their treaty   They undoubtedly thought that they had agreed
never to recross the Mississippi with hostile intent. However this may be, on
the 6th day of April, 1832, Black Hawk and his entire band, with their women
and children, again recrossed the Mississippi in plain view of the garrison of
Fort Armstrong, and went up Rock River. Although this act was construed
into an act of hostility by the military authorities, who declared that Black
Hawk intended to recover his village, or the site where it stood, by force ; but
it does not appear that he made any such attempt, nor did his apearance
create any special alarm among the settlers. They knew that the Indians never
went on the war path encumbered with the old men, their women and their
children.

The *Galenian*, printed in Galena, of May 2, 1832, says that Black Hawk
was invited by the Prophet and had taken possession of a tract about forty
miles up Rock River ; but that he did not remain there long, but commenced
his march up Rock River   Capt. W. B. Green, who served in Capt. Stephenson's company of mounted rangers, says that "Black Hawk and his band
crossed the river with no hostile intent, but that his band had had bad luck in
hunting during the previous Winter, were actually in a starving condition, and
had come over to spend the Summer with a friendly tribe on the head waters of
the Rock and Illinois Rivers, by invitation from their chief   Other old settlers, who all agree that Black Hawk had no idea of fighting, say that he came
back to the west side expecting to negotiate another treaty, and get a new
supply of provisions   The most reasonable explanation of this movement, which
resulted so disastrously to Black Hawk and his starving people, is that, during
the Fall and Winter of 1831–2, his people became deeply indebted to their
favorite trader at Fort Armstrong (Rock Island). They had not been fortunate
in hunting, and he was likely to lose heavily, as an Indian debt was outlawed
in one year   If, therefore, the Indians could be induced to come over, and the
fears of the military could be sufficiently aroused to pursue them, another treaty
could be negotiated, and from the payments from the Government the shrewd
trader could get his pay.   Just a week after Black Hawk crossed the river, on
the 13th of April, 1832, George Davenport wrote to Gen Atkinson. "I am
informed that the British band of Sac Indians are determined to make war on
the frontier settlements.   *   *   *   From every information that I have
received, I am of the opinion that the intention of the British band of Sac
Indians is to commit depredations on the inhabitants of the frontier."   And

yet, from the 6th day of April until after Stillman's men commenced war by firing on a flag of truce from Black Hawk, no murders nor depredations were committed by the British band of Sac Indians

It is not the purpose of this sketch to detail the incidents of the Black Hawk war of 1832, as it pertains rather to the history of the State of Illinois. It is sufficient to say that, after the disgraceful affair at Stillman's Run, Black Hawk, concluding that the whites, refusing to treat with him, were determined to exterminate his people, determined to return to the Iowa side of the Mississippi. He could not return by the way he came, for the army was behind him, an army, too, that would sternly refuse to recognize the white flag of peace. His only course was to make his way northward and reach the Mississippi, if possible, before the troops could overtake him, and this he did, but, before he could get his women and children across the Wisconsin, he was overtaken, and a battle ensued   Here, again, he sued for peace, and, through his trusty Lieutenant, "the Prophet," the whites were plainly informed that the starving Indians did not wish to fight, but would return to the west side of the Mississippi, peaceably, if they could be permitted to do so   No attention was paid to this second effort to negotiate peace, and, as soon as supplies could be obtained, the pursuit was resumed, the flying Indians were overtaken again eight miles before they reached the mouth of the Bad Axe, and the slaughter (it should not be dignified by the name of battle) commenced   Here, overcome by starvation and the victorious whites, his band was scattered, on the 2d day of August, 1832   Black Hawk escaped, but was brought into camp at Prairie du Chien by three Winnebagoes. He was confined in Jefferson Barracks until the Spring of 1833, when he was sent to Washington, arriving there April 22. On the 26th of April, they were taken to Fortress Monroe, where they remained till the 4th of June, 1833, when orders were given for them to be liberated and returned to their own country. By order of the President, he was brought back to Iowa through the principal Eastern cities. Crowds flocked to see him all along his route, and he was very much flattered by the attentions he received. He lived among his people on the Iowa River till that reservation was sold, in 1836, when, with the rest of the Sacs and Foxes, he removed to the Des Moines Reservation, where he remained till his death, which occurred on the 3d of October, 1838.

INDIAN PURCHASES, RESERVES AND TREATIES.

At the close of the Black Hawk War, in 1832, a treaty was made at a council held on the west bank of the Mississippi, where now stands the thriving city of Davenport, on grounds now occupied by the Chicago, Rock Island & Pacific Railroad Company, on the 21st day of September, 1832   At this council, the United States were represented by Gen. Winfield Scott and Gov. Reynolds, of Illinois   Keokuk, Pash-a-pa-ho and some thirty other chiefs and warriors of the Sac and Fox nation were present. By this treaty, the Sacs and Foxes ceded to the United States a strip of land on the eastern border of Iowa fifty miles wide, from the northern boundary of Missouri to the mouth of the Upper Iowa River, containing about six million acres. The western line of the purchase was parallel with the Mississippi. In consideration of this cession, the United States Government stipulated to pay annually to the confederated tribes, for thirty consecutive years, twenty thousand dollars in specie, and to pay the debts of the Indians at Rock Island, which had been accumulating for seventeen years and amounted to fifty thousand dollars, due to Davenport & Farnham, Indian traders   The Government also generously donated to the Sac and Fox women and children whose husbands and fathers had fallen in the Black Hawk war, thirty-five beef cattle, twelve bushels of salt, thirty barrels of pork, fifty barrels of flour and six thousand bushels of corn.

This territory is known as the "Black Hawk Purchase."   Although it was not the first portion of Iowa ceded to the United States by the Sacs and Foxes, it was the first opened to actual settlement by the tide of emigration that flowed across the Mississippi as soon as the Indian title was extinguished.   The treaty was ratified February 13, 1833, and took effect on the 1st of June following, when the Indians quietly removed from the ceded territory, and this fertile and beautiful region was opened to white settlers.

By the terms of the treaty, out of the Black Hawk Purchase was reserved for the Sacs and Foxes 400 square miles of land situated on the Iowa River, and in-lcuding within its limits Keokuk's village, on the right bank of that river.   This tract was known as "Keokuk's Reserve," and was occupied by the Indians until 1836, when, by a treaty made in September between them and Gov. Dodge, of Wisconsin Territory, it was ceded to the United States   The council was held on the banks of the Mississippi, above Davenport, and was the largest assemblage of the kind ever held by the Sacs and Foxes to treat for the sale of lands   About one thousand of their chiefs and braves were present, and Keokuk was their leading spirit and principal speaker on the occasion.   By the terms of the treaty, the Sacs and Foxes were removed to another reservation on the Des Moines River, where an agency was established for them at what is now the town of Agency City

Besides the Keokuk Reserve, the Government gave out of the Black Hawk Purchase to Antoine Le Claire, interpreter, in fee simple, one section of land opposite Rock Island, and another at the head of the first rapids above the island, on the Iowa side   This was the first land title granted by the United States to an individual in Iowa

Soon after the removal of the Sacs and Foxes to their new reservation on the Des Moines River, Gen. Joseph M Street was transferred from the agency of the Winnebagoes, at Prairie du Chien, to establish an agency among them   A farm was selected, on which the necessary buildings were erected, including a comfortable farm house for the agent and his family, at the expense of the Indian Fund   A salaried agent was employed to superintend the farm and dispose of the crops   Two mills were erected, one on Soap Creek and the other on Sugar Creek.   The latter was soon swept away by a flood, but the former remained and did good service for many years.   Connected with the agency were Joseph Smart and John Goodell, interpreters   The latter was interpreter for Hard Fish's band   Three of the Indian chiefs, Keokuk, Wapello and Appanoose, had each a large field improved, the two former on the right bank of the Des Moines, back from the river, in what is now "Keokuk's Prairie," and the latter on the present site of the city of Ottumwa. Among the traders connected with the agency were the Messrs Ewing, from Ohio, and Phelps & Co., from Illinois, and also Mr. J. P. Eddy, who established his post at what is now the site of Eddyville

The Indians at this agency became idle and listless in the absence of their natural and wonted excitements, and many of them plunged into dissipation. Keokuk himself became dissipated in the latter years of his life, and it has been reported that he died of *delirium tremens* after his removal with his tribe to Kansas

In May, 1843, most of the Indians were removed up the Des Moines River, above the temporary line of Red Rock, having ceded the remnant of their lands in Iowa to the United States on the 21st of September, 1837, and on the 11th of October, 1842. By the terms of the latter treaty, they held possession of the "New Purchase" till the Autumn of 1845, when the most of them were removed to their reservation in Kansas, the balance being removed in the Spring of 1846.

1 *Treaty with the Sioux*—Made July 19, 1815, ratified December 16, 1815' This treaty was made at Portage des Sioux, between the Sioux of Minnesota and Upper Iowa and the United States, by William Clark and Ninian Edwards, Commissioners, and was merely a treaty of peace and friendship on the part of those Indians toward the United States at the close of the war of 1812

2 *Treaty with the Sacs* — A similar treaty of peace was made at Portage des Sioux, between the United States and the Sacs, by William Clark, Ninian Edwards and Auguste Choteau, on the 13th of September, 1815, and ratified at the same date as the above In this, the treaty of 1804 was re-affirmed, and the Sacs here represented promised for themselves and their bands to keep entirely separate from the Sacs of Rock River, who, under Black Hawk, had joined the British in the war just then closed

3 *Treaty with the Foxes* —A separate treaty of peace was made with the Foxes at Portage des Sioux, by the same Commissioners, on the 14th of September, 1815, and ratified the same as the above, wherein the Foxes re-affirmed the treaty of St Louis, of November 3, 1804, and agreed to deliver up all their prisoners to the officer in command at Fort Clark, now Peoria, Illinois

4 *Treaty with the Iowas* —A treaty of peace and mutual good will was made between the United States and the Iowa tribe of Indians, at Portage des Sioux, by the same Commissioners as above, on the 16th of September, 1815, at the close of the war with Great Britain, and ratified at the same date as the others

5 *Treaty with the Sacs of Rock River*—Made at St Louis on the 13th of May, 1816, between the United States and the Sacs of Rock River, by the Commissioners, William Clark, Ninian Edwards and Auguste Choteau, and ratified December 30, 1816 In this treaty, that of 1804 was re established and confirmed by twenty-two chiefs and head men of the Sacs of Rock River, and Black Hawk himself attached to it his signature, or, as he said, "touched the goose quill"

6 *Treaty of 1824* —On the 4th of August, 1824, a treaty was made between the United States and the Sacs and Foxes, in the city of Washington, by William Clark, Commissioner, wherein the Sac and Fox nation relinquished their title to all lands in Missouri and that portion of the southeast corner of Iowa known as the "Half-Breed Tract" was set off and reserved for the use of the half-breeds of the Sacs and Foxes, they holding title in the same manner as Indians Ratified January 18, 1825

7 *Treaty of August 19, 1825* —At this date a treaty was made by William Clark and Lewis Cass, at Prairie du Chien, between the United States and the Chippewas, Sacs and Foxes, Menomonees, Winnebagoes and a portion of the Ottawas and Pottawatomies In this treaty, in order to make peace between the contending tribes as to the limits of their respective hunting grounds in Iowa, it was agreed that the United States Government should run a boundary line between the Sioux, on the north, and the Sacs and Foxes, on the south, as follows

Commencing at the mouth of the Upper Iowa River, on the west bank of the Mississippi, and ascending said Iowa River to its west fork ; thence up the fork to its source , thence crossing the fork of Red Cedar River in a direct line to the second or upper fork of the Des Moines River , thence in a direct line to the lower fork of the Calumet River, and down that river to its junction with the Missouri River

8. *Treaty of 1830* — On the 15th of July, 1830, the confederate tribes of the Sacs and Foxes ceded to the United States a strip of country lying south of the above line, twenty miles in width; and extending along the line aforesaid from the Mississippi to the Des Moines River The Sioux also, whose possessions were north of the line, ceded to the Government, in the same treaty, a like strip on the north side of the boundary Thus the United States, at the ratification of this treaty, February 24, 1831, came into possession of a portion of Iowa forty miles wide, extending along the Clark and Cass line of 1825, from the Mississippi to the Des Moines River This territory was known as the "Neutral Ground," and the tribes on either side of the line were allowed to fish and hunt on it unmolested till it was made a Winnebago reservation, and the Winnebagoes were removed to it in 1841.

9 *Treaty with the Sacs and Foxes and other Tribes* —At the same time of the above treaty respecting the "Neutral Ground" (July 15, 1830), the Sacs and Foxes, Western Sioux, Omahas, Iowas and Missouris ceded to the United States a portion of the western slope of Iowa, the boundaries of which were defined as follows: Beginning at the upper fork of the Des Moines River, and passing the sources of the Little Sioux and Floyd Rivers, to the fork of the first creek that falls into the Big Sioux, or Calumet, on the east side , thence down said creek and the Calumet

River to the Missouri River; thence down said Missouri River to the Missouri State line above the Kansas, thence along said line to the northwest corner of said State, thence to the high lands between the waters falling into the Missouri and Des Moines, passing to said high lands along the dividing ridge between the forks of the Grand River, thence along said high lands or ridge separating the waters of the Missouri from those of the Des Moines, to a point opposite the source of the Boyer River, and thence in a direct line to the upper fork of the Des Moines, the place of beginning

It was understood that the lands ceded and relinquished by this treaty were to be assigned and allotted, under the direction of the President of the United States, to the tribes then living thereon, or to such other tribes as the President might locate thereon for hunting and other purposes In consideration of three tracts of land ceded in this treaty, the United States agreed to pay to the Sacs three thousand dollars, to the Foxes, three thousand dollars, to the Sioux, two thousand dollars, to the Yankton and Santie bands of Sioux, three thousand dollars; to the Omahas, two thousand five hundred dollars; and to the Ottoes and Missouris, two thousand five hundred dollars—to be paid annually for ten successive years In addition to these annuities, the Government agreed to furnish some of the tribes with blacksmiths and agricultural implements to the amount of two hundred dollars, at the expense of the United States, and to set apart three thousand dollars annually for the education of the children of these tribes It does not appear that any fort was erected in this territory prior to the erection of Fort Atkinson on the Neutral Ground, in 1840–41

This treaty was made by William Clark, Superintendent of Indian affairs, and Col Willoughby Morgan, of the United States First Infantry, and came into effect by proclamation, February 24, 1831

10 *Treaty with the Winnebagoes* —Made at Fort Armstrong, Rock Island, September 15, 1832, by Gen Winfield Scott and Hon John Reynolds, Governor of Illinois In this treaty the Winnebagoes ceded to the United States all their land lying on the east side of the Mississippi, and in part consideration therefor the United States granted to the Winnebagoes, to be held as other Indian lands are held, that portion of Iowa known as the Neutral Ground The exchange of the two tracts of country was to take place on or before the 1st day of June, 1833 In addition to the Neutral Ground, it was stipulated that the United States should give the Winnebagoes, beginning in September, 1833, and continuing for twenty-seven successive years, ten thousand dollars in specie, and establish a school among them, with a farm and garden, and provide other facilities for the education of their children, not to exceed in cost three thousand dollars a year, and to continue the same for twenty-seven successive years Six agriculturists, twelve yoke of oxen and plows and other farming tools were to be supplied by the Government

11 *Treaty of 1832 with the Sacs and Foxes* —Already mentioned as the Black Hawk purchase

12 *Treaty of 1836*, with the Sacs and Foxes, ceding Keokuk's Reserve to the United States, for which the Government stipulated to pay thirty thousand dollars, and an annuity of ten thousand dollars for ten successive years, together with other sums and debts of the Indians to various parties

13 *Treaty of 1837* — On the 21st of October, 1837, a treaty was made at the city of Washington, between Carey A Harris, Commissioner of Indian Affairs, and the confederate tribes of Sacs and Foxes, ratified February 21, 1838, wherein another slice of the soil of Iowa was obtained, described in the treaty as follows: "A tract of country containing 1,250,000 acres, lying west and adjoining the tract conveyed by them to the United States in the treaty of September 21, 1832 It is understood that the points of termination for the present cession shall be the northern and southern points of said tract as fixed by the survey made under the authority of the United States, and that a line shall be drawn between them so as to intersect a line extended westwardly from the angle of said tract nearly opposite to Rock Island, as laid down in the above survey, so far as may be necessary to include the number of acres hereby ceded, which last mentioned line, it is estimated, will be about twenty-five miles "

This piece of land was twenty-five miles wide in the middle, and ran off to a point at both ends, lying directly back of the Black Hawk Purchase, and of the same length

14 *Treaty of Relinquishment* —At the same date as the above treaty, in the city of Washington, Carey A Harris, Commissioner, the Sacs and Foxes ceded to the United States all their right and interest in the country lying south of the boundary line between the Sacs and Foxes and Sioux, as described in the treaty of August 19, 1825, and between the Mississippi and Missouri Rivers, the United States paying for the same one hundred and sixty thousand dollars The Indians also gave up all claims and interests under the treaties previously made with them, for the satisfaction of which no appropriations had been made

15 *Treaty of 1842* —The last treaty was made with the Sacs and Foxes October 11, 1842, ratified March 23, 1843 It was made at the Sac and Fox agency (Agency City), by John Chambers, Commissioner on behalf of the United States In this treaty the Sac and Fox Indians "ceded to the United States all their lands west of the Mississippi to which they had any claim or title." By the terms of this treaty they were to be removed from the country at the expiration of three years, and all who remained after that were to move at their own expense. Part of them were removed to Kansas in the Fall of 1845, and the rest the Spring following.

SPANISH GRANTS

While the territory now embraced in the State of Iowa was under Spanish rule as a part of its province of Louisiana, certain claims to and grants of land were made by the Spanish authorities, with which, in addition to the extinguishment of Indian titles, the United States had to deal. It is proper that these should be briefly reviewed

Dubuque.—On the 22d day of September, 1788, Julien Dubuque, a Frenchman, from Prairie du Chien, obtained from the Foxes a cession or lease of lands on the Mississippi River for mining purposes, on the site of the present city of Dubuque. Lead had been discovered here eight years before, in 1780, by the wife of Peosta Fox, a warrior, and Dubuque's claim embraced nearly all the lead bearing lands in that vicinity. He immediately took possession of his claim and commenced mining, at the same time making a settlement. The place became known as the "Spanish Miners," or, more commonly, "Dubuque's Lead Mines."

In 1796, Dubuque filed a petition with Baron de Carondelet, the Spanish Governor of Louisiana, asking that the tract ceded to him by the Indians might be granted to him by patent from the Spanish Government. In this petition, Dubuque rather indefinitely set forth the boundaries of this claim as "about seven leagues along the Mississippi River, and three leagues in width from the river," intending to include, as is supposed, the river front between the Little Maquoketa and the Tete des Mertz Rivers, embracing more than twenty thousand acres. Carondelet granted the prayer of the petition, and the grant was subsequently confirmed by the Board of Land Commissioners of Louisiana.

In October, 1804, Dubuque transferred the larger part of his claim to Auguste Choteau, of St. Louis, and on the 17th of May, 1805, he and Choteau jointly filed their claims with the Board of Commissioners. On the 20th of September, 1806, the Board decided in their favor, pronouncing the claim to be a regular Spanish grant, made and completed prior to the 1st day of October, 1800, only one member, J. B. C. Lucas, dissenting.

Dubuque died March 24, 1810. The Indians, understanding that the claim of Dubuque under their former act of cession was only a permit to occupy the tract and work the mines during his life, and that at his death they reverted to them, took possession and continued mining operations, and were sustained by the military authority of the United States, notwithstanding the decision of the Commissioners. When the Black Hawk purchase was consummated, the Dubuque claim thus held by the Indians was absorbed by the United States, as the Sacs and Foxes made no reservation of it in the treaty of 1832.

The heirs of Choteau, however, were not disposed to relinquish their claim without a struggle. Late in 1832, they employed an agent to look after their interests, and authorized him to lease the right to dig lead on the lands. The miners who commenced work under this agent were compelled by the military to abandon their operations, and one of the claimants went to Galena to institute legal proceedings, but found no court of competent jurisdiction, although he did bring an action for the recovery of a quantity of lead dug at Dubuque, for the purpose of testing the title. Being unable to identify the lead, however, he was non-suited

By act of Congress, approved July 2, 1836, the town of Dubuque was surveyed and platted. After lots had been sold and occupied by the purchasers, Henry Choteau brought an action of ejectment against Patrick Malony, who held land in Dubuque under a patent from the United States, for the recovery of seven undivided eighth parts of the Dubuque claim, as purchased by Auguste Choteau in 1804. The case was tried in the District Court of the United States for the District of Iowa, and was decided adversely to the plaintiff. The case was carried to the Supreme Court of the United States on a writ of error, when it was heard at the December term, 1853, and the decision of the lower court was affirmed, the court holding that the permit from Carondolet was merely a lease or permit to work the mines, that Dubuque asked, and the Governor of Louisiana granted, nothing more than the "peaceable possession" of certain lands obtained from the Indians; that Carondelet had no legal authority to make such a grant as claimed, and that, even if he had, this was but an "inchoate and imperfect title."

Giard —In 1795, the Lieutenant Governor of Upper Louisiana granted to Basil Giard five thousand eight hundred and sixty acres of land, in what is now Clayton County, known as the "Giard Tract." He occupied the land during the time that Iowa passed from Spain to France, and from France to the United States, in consideration of which the Federal Government granted a patent of the same to Giard in his own right His heirs sold the whole tract to James H. Lockwood and Thomas P. Burnett, of Prairie du Chien, for three hundred dollars.

Honori —March 30, 1799, Zenon Trudeau, Acting Lieutenant Governor of Upper Louisiana, granted to Louis Honori a tract of land on the site of the present town of Montrose, as follows: "It is permitted to Mr. Louis (Fresson) Henori, or Louis Honore Fesson, to establish himself at the head of the rapids of the River Des Moines, and his establishment once formed, notice of it shall be given to the Governor General, in order to obtain for him a commission of a space sufficient to give value to such establishment, and at the same time to render it useful to the commerce of the peltries of this country, to watch the Indians and keep them in the fidelity which they owe to His Majesty."

Honori took immediate possession of his claim, which he retained until 1805. While trading with the natives, he became indebted to Joseph Robedoux, who obtained an execution on which the property was sold May 13, 1803, and was purchased by the creditor. In these proceedings the property was described as being "about six leagues above the River Des Moines." Robedoux died soon after he purchased the proprerty. Auguste Choteau, his executor, disposed of the Honori tract to Thomas F. Reddeck, in April, 1805, up to which time Honori continued to occupy it. The grant, as made by the Spanish government, was a league square, but only one mile square was confirmed by the United States. After the half-breeds sold their lands, in which the Honori grant was included, various claimants resorted to litigation in attempts to invalidate the title of the Reddeck heirs, but it was finally confirmed by a decision of the Supreme Court of the United States in 1839, and is the oldest legal title to any land in the State of Iowa.

THE HALF-BREED TRACT

Before any permanent settlement had been made in the Territory of Iowa, white adventurers, trappers and traders, many of whom were scattered along the Mississippi and its tributaries, as agents and employes of the American Fur Company, intermarried with the females of the Sac and Fox Indians, producing a race of half-breeds, whose number was never definitely ascertained. There were some respectable and excellent people among them, children of men of some refinement and education. For instance: Dr. Muir, a gentleman educated at Edinburgh, Scotland, a surgeon in the United States Army, stationed at a military post located on the present site of Warsaw, married an Indian woman, and reared his family of three daughters in the city of Keokuk Other examples might be cited, but they are probably exceptions to the general rule, and the race is now nearly or quite extinct in Iowa

A treaty was made at Washington, August 4, 1824, between the Sacs and Foxes and the United States, by which that portion of Lee County was reserved to the half-breeds of those tribes, and which was afterward known as "The Half-Breed Tract." This reservation is the triangular piece of land, containing about 119,000 acres, lying between the Mississippi and Des Moines Rivers. It is bounded on the north by the prolongation of the northern line of Missouri This line was intended to be a straight one, running due east, which would have caused it to strike the Mississippi River at or below Montrose; but the surveyor who run it took no notice of the change in the variation of the needle as he proceeded eastward, and, in consequence, the line he run was bent, deviating more and more to the northward of a direct line as he approached the Mississippi, so that it struck that river at the lower edge of the town of Fort Madison. "This erroneous line," says Judge Mason, "has been acquiesced in as well in fixing the northern limit of the Half-Breed Tract as in determining the northern boundary line of the State of Missouri" The line thus run included in the reservation a portion of the lower part of the city of Fort Madison, and all of the present townships of Van Buren, Charleston, Jefferson, Des Moines, Montrose and Jackson

Under the treaty of 1824, the half-breeds had the right to occupy the soil, but could not convey it, the reversion being reserved to the United States. But on the 30th day of January, 1834, by act of Congress, this reversionary right was relinquished, and the half-breeds acquired the lands in fee simple This was no sooner done, than a horde of speculators rushed in to buy land of the half-breed owners, and, in many instances, a gun, a blanket, a pony or a few quarts of whisky was sufficient for the purchase of large estates. There was a deal of sharp practice on both sides; Indians would often claim ownership of land by virtue of being half-breeds, and had no difficulty in proving their mixed blood by the Indians, and they would then cheat the speculators by selling land to which they had no rightful title On the other hand, speculators often claimed land in which they had no ownership. It was diamond cut diamond, until at last things became badly mixed. There were no authorized surveys, and no boundary lines to claims, and, as a natural result, numerous conflicts and quarrels ensued.

To settle these difficulties, to decide the validity of claims or sell them for the benefit of the real owners, by act of the Legislature of Wisconsin Territory, approved January 16, 1838, Edward Johnstone, Thomas S. Wilson and David Brigham were appointed Commissioners, and clothed with power to effect these objects The act provided that these Commissioners should be paid six dollars a day each The commission entered upon its duties and continued until the next session of the Legislature, when the act creating it was repealed, invalidating all that had been done and depriving the Commissioners of their pay. The repealing act, however, authorized the Commissioners to commence action against the owners of the Half-Breed Tract, to receive pay for their services, in the District Court of Lee County. Two judgments were obtained, and on execution the whole of the tract was sold to Hugh T. Reid, the Sheriff executing the deed. Mr Reid sold portions of it to various parties, but his own title was questioned and he became involved in litigation. Decisions in favor of Reid and those holding under him were made by both District and Supreme Courts, but in December, 1850, these decisions were finally reversed by the Supreme Court of the United States in the case of Joseph Webster, plaintiff in error, vs. Hugh T. Reid, and the judgment titles failed. About nine years before the "judgment titles" were finally abrogated as above, another class of titles were brought into competition with them, and in the conflict between the two, the final decision was obtained These were the titles based on the "decree of partition" issued by the United States District Court for the Territory of Iowa, on the 8th of May, 1841, and certified to by the Clerk on the 2d day of June of that year. Edward Johnstone and Hugh T Reid, then law partners at Fort Madison, filed the petition for the decree in behalf of the St Louis claimants of half-breed lands Francis S Key, author of the Star Spangled Banner, who was then attorney for the New York Land Company, which held heavy interests in these lands, took a leading part in the measure, and drew up the document in which it was presented to the court. Judge Charles Mason, of Burlington, presided The plan of partition divided the tract into one hundred and one shares and arranged that each claimant should draw his proportion by lot, and should abide the result, whatever it might be The arrangement was entered into, the lots drawn, and the plat of the same filed in the Recorder's office, October 6, 1841. Upon this basis the titles to land in the Half-Breed Tract are now held.

EARLY SETTLEMENTS

The first permanent settlement by the whites within the limits of Iowa was made by Julien Dubuque, in 1788, when, with a small party of miners, he settled on the site of the city that now bears his name, where he lived until his death. in 1810 Louis Honori settled on the site of the present town of Montrose, probably in 1799. and resided there until 1805, when his property passed into other hands. Of the Giard settlement, opposite Prairie du Chien, little is known, except that it was occupied by some parties prior to the commencement of the present century, and contained three cabins in 1805. Indian traders, although not strictly to be considered settlers, had established themselves at various points at an early date A Mr. Johnson, agent of the American Fur Company, had a trading post below Burlington, where he carried on traffic with the Indians some time before the United States possessed the country. In 1820, Le Moliese, a French trader, had a station at what is now Sandusky, six miles above Keokuk, in Lee County. In 1829, Dr. Isaac Gallaud made a settlement on the Lower Rapids, at what is now Nashville.

The first settlement in Lee County was made in 1820, by Dr. Samuel C Muir, a surgeon in the United States army, who had been stationed at Fort Edwards, now Warsaw, Ill, and who built a cabin where the city of Keokuk now stands. Dr. Muir was a man of strict integrity and irreproachable character. While stationed at a military post on the Upper Mississippi, he had married an Indian woman of the Fox nation. Of his marriage, the following romantic account is given

The post at which he was stationed was visited by a beautiful Indian maiden—whose native name, unfortunately, has not been preserved—who, in her dreams, had seen a white brave unmoor his canoe, paddle it across the river and come directly to her lodge. She felt assured, according to the superstitious belief of her race, that, in her dreams, she had seen her future husband, and had come to the fort to find him Meeting Dr Muir, she instantly recognized him as the hero of her dream, which, with childlike innocence and simplicity, she related to him Her dream was, indeed, prophetic Charmed with Sophia's beauty, innocence and devotion, the doctor honorably married her, but after a while, the sneers and gibes of his brother officers—less honorable than he, perhaps—made him feel ashamed of his dark-skinned wife, and when his regiment was ordered down the river, to Bellefontaine, it is said he embraced the opportunity to rid himself of her, and left her, never expecting to see her again, and little dreaming that she would have the courage to follow him   But, with her infant child, this intrepid wife and mother started alone in her canoe, and, after many days of weary labor and a lonely journey of nine hundred miles, she, at last, reached him   She afterward remarked, when speaking of this toilsome journey down the river in search of her husband, "When I got there I was all perished away—so thin'"   The doctor, touched by such unexampled devotion, took her to his heart, and ever after, until his death, treated her with marked respect   She always presided at his table with grace and dignity, but never abandoned her native style of dress   In 1819-20, he was stationed at Fort Edward, but the senseless ridicule of some of his brother officers on account of his Indian wife induced him to resign his commission

After building his cabin, as above stated, he leased his claim for a term of years to Otis Reynolds and John Culver, of St Louis, and went to La Pointe, afterward Galena, where he practiced his profession for ten years, when he returned to Keokuk   His Indian wife bore to him four children—Louise (married at Keokuk, since dead), James, (drowned at Keokuk), Mary and Sophia   Dr Muir died suddenly of cholera, in 1832, but left his property in such condition that it was soon wasted in vexatious litigation, and his brave and faithful wife, left friendless and penniless, became discouraged, and, with her children, disappeared, and, it is said, returned to her people on the Upper Missouri

Messrs. Reynolds & Culver, who had leased Dr. Muir's claim at Keokuk, subsequently employed as their agent Mr. Moses Stillwell, who arrived with his family in 1828, and took possession of Muir's cabin   His brothers-in-law, Amos and Valencourt Van Ansdal, came with him and settled near.

His daughter, Margaret Stillwell (afterward Mrs Ford) was born in 1831, at the foot of the rapids, called by the Indians Puch-a-she-tuck, where Keokuk now stands   She was probably the first white American child born in Iowa.

In 1831, Mr. Johnson, Agent of the American Fur Company, who had a station at the foot of the rapids, removed to another location, and, Dr. Muir having returned from Galena, he and Isaac R. Campbell took the place and buildings vacated by the Company and carried on trade with the Indians and half-breeds   Campbell, who had first visited and traveled through the southern part of Iowa, in 1821, was an enterprising settler, and besides trading with the natives carried on a farm and kept a tavern

Dr. Muir died of cholera in 1832

In 1830, James L and Lucius H Langworthy, brothers and natives of Vermont, visited the Territory for the purpose of working the lead mines at Dubuque   They had been engaged in lead mining at Galena, Illinois, the former from as early as 1824.   The lead mines in the Dubuque region were an object of great interest to the miners about Galena, for they were known to be rich in lead ore   To explore these mines and to obtain permission to work them was therefore eminently desirable

In 1829, James L Langworthy resolved to visit the Dubuque mines   Crossing the Mississippi at a point now known as Dunleith, in a canoe, and swimming his horse by his side, he landed on the spot now known as Jones Street Levee   Before him spread out a beautiful prairie, on which the city of Dubuque now stands.   Two miles south, at the mouth of Catfish Creek, was a village of Sacs and Foxes.   Thither Mr Langworthy proceeded, and was well received by the natives   He endeavored to obtain permission from them to mine in their hills, but this they refused.   He, however, succeeded in gaining the confidence of the chief to such an extent as to be allowed to travel in the interior for three weeks and explore the country.   He employed two young Indians as guides, and traversed in different directions the whole region lying between the Maquoketa and Turkey Rivers   He returned to the village, secured the good will of the Indians, and, returning to Galena, formed plans for future operations, to be executed as soon as circumstances would permit

In 1830, with his brother, Lucius H., and others, having obtained the consent of the Indians, Mr Langworthy crossed the Mississippi and commenced mining in the vicinity around Dubuque.

At this time, the lands were not in the actual possession of the United States. Although they had been purchased from France, the Indian title had not been extinguished, and these adventurous persons were beyond the limits of any State or Territorial government. The first settlers were therefore obliged to be their own law-makers, and to agree to such regulations as the exigencies of the case demanded. The first act resembling civil legislation within the limits of the present State of Iowa was done by the miners at this point, in June, 1830. They met on the bank of the river, by the side of an old cottonwood drift log, at what is now the Jones Street Levee, Dubuque, and elected a Committee, consisting of J. L. Langworthy, H. F. Lander, James McPhetres, Samuel Scales, and E M. Wren. This may be called the first Legislature in Iowa, the members of which gathered around that old cottonwood log, and agreed to and reported the following, written by Mr. Langworthy, on a half sheet of coarse, unruled paper, the old log being the writing desk :

We, a Committee having been chosen to draft certain rules and regulations (laws) by which we as miners will be governed, and having duly considered the subject, do unanimously agree that we will be governed by the regulations on the east side of the Mississippi River,* with the following exceptions, to wit

ARTICLE I   That each and every man shall hold 200 yards square of ground by working said ground one day in six

ARTICLE II   We further agree that there shall be chosen, by the majority of the miners present, a person who shall hold this article, and who shall grant letters of arbitration on application having been made, and that said letters of arbitration shall be obligatory on the parties so applying.

The report was accepted by the miners present, who elected Dr. Jarote, in accordance with Article 2   Here, then, we have, in 1830, a primitive Legislature elected by the people, the law drafted by it being submitted to the people for approval, and under it Dr. Jarote was elected first Governor within the limits of the present State of Iowa   And it is to be said that the laws thus enacted were as promptly obeyed, and the acts of the executive officer thus elected as duly respected, as any have been since

The miners who had thus erected an independent government of their own on the west side of the Mississippi River continued to work successfully for a long time, and the new settlement attracted considerable attention.   But the west side of the Mississippi belonged to the Sac and Fox Indians, and the Government, in order to preserve peace on the frontier, as well as to protect the Indians in their rights under the treaty, ordered the settlers not only to stop mining, but to remove from the Indian territory.   They were simply intruders. The execution of this order was entrusted to Col Zachary Taylor, then in command of the military post at Prairie du Chien, who, early in July, sent an officer to the miners with orders to forbid settlement, and to command the miners to remove within ten days to the east side of the Mississippi, or they would be driven off by armed force   The miners, however, were reluctant about leaving the rich "leads" they had already discovered and opened, and were not disposed to obey the order to remove with any considerable degree of alacrity.   In due time, Col Taylor dispatched a detachment of troops to enforce his order.   The miners, anticipating their arrival, had, excepting three, recrossed the river, and from the east bank saw the troops land on the western shore   The three who had lingered a little too long were, however, permitted to make their escape

---

* Established by the Superintendent of U S Lead Mines at Fever River

unmolested. From this time, a military force was stationed at Dubuque to prevent the settlers from returning, until June, 1832. The Indians returned, and were encouaged to operate the rich mines opened by the late white occupants.

In June, 1832, the troops were ordered to the east side to assist in the annihilation of the very Indians whose rights they had been protecting on the west side. Immediately after the close of the Black Hawk war, and the negotiations of the treaty in September, 1832, by which the Sacs and Foxes ceded to the United States the tract known as the "Black Hawk Purchase," the settlers, supposing that now they had a right to re-enter the territory, returned and took possession of their claims, built cabins, erected furnaces and prepared large quantities of lead for market. Dubuque was becoming a noted place on the river, but the prospects of the hardy and enterprising settlers and miners were again ruthlessly interfered with by the Government, on the ground that the treaty with the Indians would not go into force until June 1, 1833, although they had withdrawn from the vicinity of the settlement. Col. Taylor was again ordered by the War Department to remove the miners, and in January, 1833, troops were again sent from Prairie du Chien to Dubuque for that purpose This was a serious and perhaps unnecessary hardship imposed upon the settlers. They were compelled to abandon their cabins and homes in mid-winter. It must now be said, simply, that "red tape" should be respected. The purchase had been made, the treaty ratified, or was sure to be; the Indians had retired, and, after the lapse of nearly fifty years, no very satisfactory reason for this rigorous action of the Government can be given.

But the orders had been given, and there was no alternative but to obey. Many of the settlers recrossed the river, and did not return; a few, however, removed to an island near the east bank of the river, built rude cabins of poles, in which to store their lead until Spring, when they could float the fruits of their labor to St. Louis for sale, and where they could remain until the treaty went into force, when they could return Among these were James L Langworthy, and his brother Lucius, who had on hand about three hundred thousand pounds of lead.

Lieut Covington, who had been placed in command at Dubuque by Col Taylor, ordered some of the cabins of the settlers to be torn down, and wagons and other property to be destroyed. This wanton and inexcusable action on the part of a subordinate clothed with a little brief authority was sternly rebuked by Col. Taylor, and Covington was superseded by Lieut George Wilson, who pursued a just and friendly course with the pioneers, who were only waiting for the time when they could repossess their claims

June 1, 1833, the treaty formally went into effect, the troops were withdrawn, and the Langworthy brothers and a few others at once returned and resumed possession of their home claims and mineral prospects, and from this time the first permanent settlement of this portion of Iowa must date. Mr. John P. Sheldon was appointed Superintendent of the mines by the Government, and a system of permits to miners and licenses to smelters was adopted, similar to that which had been in operation at Galena, since 1825, under Lieut. Martin Thomas and Capt. Thomas C. Legate. Substantially the primitive law enacted by the miners assembled around that old cottonwood drift log in 1830 was adopted and enforced by the United States Government, except that miners were required to sell their mineral to licensed smelters and the smelter was required to give bonds for the payment of six per cent. of all lead manufactured to the Government. This was the same rule adopted in the United States mines on Fever River in

Illinois, except that, until 1830, the Illinois miners were compelled to pay 10 per cent tax   This tax upon the miners created much dissatisfaction among the miners on the west side as it had on the east side of the Mississippi.   They thought they had suffered hardships and privations enough in opening the way for civilization, without being subjected to the imposition of an odious Government tax upon their means of subsistence, when the Federal Government could better afford to aid than to extort from them.   The measure soon became unpopular   It was difficult to collect the taxes, and the whole system was abolished in about ten years.

During 1833, after the Indian title was fully extinguished, about five hundred people arrived at the mining district, about one hundred and fifty of them from Galena.

In the same year, Mr. Langworthy assisted in building the first school house in Iowa, and thus was formed the nucleus of the now populous and thriving City of Dubuque   Mr. Langworthy lived to see the naked prairie on which he first landed become the site of a city of fifteen thousand inhabitants, the small school house which he aided in constructing replaced by three substantial edifices, wherein two thousand children were being trained, churches erected in every part of the city, and railroads connecting the wilderness which he first explored with all the eastern world   He died suddenly on the 13th of March, 1865, while on a trip over the Dubuque & Southwestern Railroad, at Monticello, and the evening train brought the news of his death and his remains

Lucius H. Langworthy, his brother, was one of the most worthy, gifted and influential of the old settlers of this section of Iowa.   He died, greatly lamented by many friends, in June, 1865.

The name Dubuque was given to the settlement by the miners at a meeting held in 1834

In 1832, Captain James White made a claim on the present site of Montrose. In 1834, a military post was established at this point, and a garrison of cavalry was stationed here, under the command of Col Stephen W Kearney.   The soldiers were removed from this post to Fort Leavenworth, Kansas, in 1837

During the same year, 1832, soon after the close of the Black Hawk War, Zachariah Hawkins, Benjamin Jennings, Aaron White, Augustine Horton, Samuel Gooch, Daniel Thompson and Peter Williams made claims at Fort Madison.   In 1833, these claims were purchased by John and Nathaniel Knapp, upon which, in 1835, they laid out the town.   The next Summer, lots were sold   The town was subsequently re-surveyed and platted by the United States Government

At the close of the Black Hawk War, parties who had been impatiently looking across upon "Flint Hills," now Burlington, came over from Illinois and made claims   The first was Samuel S White, in the Fall of 1832, who erected a cabin on the site of the city of Burlington   About the same time, David Tothero made a claim on the prairie about three miles back from the river, at a place since known as the farm of Judge Morgan   In the Winter of that year, they were driven off by the military from Rock Island, as intruders upon the rights of the Indians, and White's cabin was burnt by the soldiers. He retired to Illinois, where he spent the Winter, and in the Summer, as soon as the Indian title was extinguished, returned and rebuilt his cabin.   White was joined by his brother-in-law, Doolittle, and they laid out the original town of Burlington in 1834.

All along the river borders of the Black Hawk Purchase settlers were flocking into Iowa   Immediately after the treaty with the Sacs and Foxes, in September, 1832, Col. George Davenport made the first claim on the spot where the thriving city of Davenport now stands. As early as 1827, Col. Davenport had established a flatboat ferry, which ran between the island and the main shore of Iowa, by which he carried on a trade with the Indians west of the Mississippi In 1833, Capt. Benjamin W. Clark moved across from Illinois, and laid the foundation of the town of Buffalo, in Scott County, which was the first actual settlement within the limits of that county. Among other early settlers in this part of the Territory were Adrian H. Davenport, Col. John Sullivan, Mulligan and Franklin Easly, Capt. John Coleman, J M. Camp, William White, H. W. Higgins, Cornelius Harrold, Richard Harrison, E H. Shepherd and Dr. E S. Barrows

The first settlers of Davenport were Antoine LeClaire, Col George Davenport, Major Thomas Smith, Major William Gordon, Philip Hambough, Alexander W McGregor, Levi S. Colton, Capt James May and others Of Antoine LeClaire, as the representative of the two races of men who at this time occupied Iowa, Hon. C. C. Nourse, in his admirable Centennial Address, says: "Antoine LeClaire was born at St Joseph, Michigan, in 1797. His father was French, his mother a granddaughter of a Pottowatomie chief In 1818, he acted as official interpreter to Col Davenport, at Fort Armstrong (now Rock Island). He was well acquainted with a dozen Indian dialects, and was a man of strict integrity and great energy. In 1820, he married the granddaughter of a Sac chief. The Sac and Fox Indians reserved for him and his wife two sections of land in the treaty of 1833, one at the town of LeClaire and one at Davenport. The Pottawatomies, in the treaty at Prairie du Chien, also reserved for him two sections of land, at the present site of Moline, Ill. He received the appointment of Postmaster and Justice of the Peace in the Black Hawk Purchase, at an early day. In 1833, he bought for $100 a claim on the land upon which the original town of Davenport was surveyed and platted in 1836. In 1836, LeClaire built the hotel, known since, with its valuable addition, as the LeClaire House. He died September 25, 1861."

In Clayton County, the first settlement was made in the Spring of 1832, on Turkey River, by Robert Hatfield and William W Wayman. No further settlement was made in this part of the State till the beginning of 1836.

In that portion now known as Muscatine County, settlements were made in 1834, by Benjamin Nye, John Vanater and G. W Kasey, who were the first settlers E E. Fay, William St. John, N. Fullington, H Reece, Jona Pettibone, R P. Lowe, Stephen Whicher, Abijah Whiting, J. E Fletcher, W. D. Abernethy and Alexis Smith were early settlers of Muscatine.

During the Summer of 1835, William Bennett and his family, from Galena, built the first cabin within the present limits of Delaware County, in some timber since known as Eads' Grove

The first post office in Iowa was established at Dubuque in 1833. Milo H Prentice was appointed Postmaster.

The first Justice of the Peace was Antoine Le Claire, appointed in 1833, as "a very suitable person to adjust the difficulties between the white settlers and the Indians still remaining there."

The first Methodist Society in the Territory was formed at Dubuque on the 18th of May, 1834, and the first class meeting was held June 1st of that year.

The first church bell brought into Iowa was in March, 1834.

The first mass of the Roman Catholic Church in the Territory was celebrated at Dubuque, in the house of Patrick Quigley, in the Fall of 1833.

The first school house in the Territory was erected by the Dubuque miners in 1833

The first Sabbath school was organized at Dubuque early in the Summer of 1834

The first woman who came to this part of the Territory with a view to permanent residence was Mrs. Noble F Dean, in the Fall of 1832

The first family that lived in this part of Iowa was that of Hosea T. Camp, in 1832.

The first meeting house was built by the Methodist Episcopal Church, at Dubuque, in 1834.

The first newspaper in Iowa was the Dubuque *Visitor*, issued May 11th, 1836. John King, afterward Judge King, was editor, and William C. Jones, printer.

The pioneers of Iowa, as a class, were brave, hardy, intelligent and enterprising people.

As early as 1824, a French trader named Hart had established a trading post, and built a cabin on the bluffs above the large spring now known as "Mynster Spring," within the limits of the present city of Council Bluffs, and had probably been there some time, as the post was known to the employes of the American Fur Company as *Lacote de Hart*, or "Hart's Bluff." In 1827, an agent of the American Fur Company, Francis Guittar, with others, encamped in the timber at the foot of the bluffs, about on the present location of Broadway, and afterward settled there. In 1839, a block house was built on the bluff in the east part of the city. The Pottawatomie Indians occupied this part of the State until 1846-7. when they relinquished the territory and removed to Kansas. Billy Caldwell was then principal chief. There were no white settlers in that part of the State except Indian traders, until the arrival of the Mormons under the lead of Brigham Young. These people on their way westward halted for the Winter of 1846-7 on the west bank of the Missouri River, about five miles above Omaha, at a place now called Florence. Some of them had reached the eastern bank of the river the Spring before, in season to plant a crop In the Spring of 1847, Young and a portion of the colony pursued their journey to Salt Lake, but a large portion of them returned to the Iowa side and settled mainly within the limits of Pottawattamie County. The principal settlement of this strange community was at a place first called "Miller's Hollow," on Indian Creek, and afterward named Kanesville, in honor of Col Kane, of Pennsylvania, who visited them soon afterward The Mormon settlement extended over the county and into neighboring counties, wherever timber and water furnished desirable locations. Orson Hyde, priest, lawyer and editor, was installed as President of the Quorum of Twelve, and all that part of the State remained under Mormon control for several years. In 1846, they raised a battalion, numbering some five hundred men, for the Mexican war. In 1848, Hyde started a paper called the *Frontier Guardian*, at Kanesville. In 1849, after many of the faithful had left to join Brigham Young at Salt Lake, the Mormons in this section of Iowa numbered 6,552, and in 1850, 7,828, but they were not all within the limits of Pottawattamie County. This county was organized in 1848, all the first officials being Mormons. In 1852, the order was promulgated that all the true believers should gather together at Salt Lake. Gentiles flocked in, and in a few years nearly all the first settlers were gone

May 9, 1843, Captain James Allen, with a small detachment of troops on board the steamer Ione, arrived at the present site of the capital of the State, Des Moines. The Ione was the first steamer to ascend the Des Moines River to this point The troops and stores were landed at what is now the foot of

Court avenue, Des Moines, and Capt Allen returned in the steamer to Fort Sanford to arrange for bringing up more soldiers and supplies. In due time they, too, arrived, and a fort was built near the mouth of Raccoon Fork, at its confluence with the Des Moines, and named Fort Des Moines. Soon after the arrival of the troops, a trading post was established on the east side of the river, by two noted Indian traders named Ewing, from Ohio

Among the first settlers in this part of Iowa were Benjamin Bryant, J B. Scott, James Drake (gunsmith), John Sturtevant, Robert Kinzie, Alexander Turner, Peter Newcomer, and others.

The Western States have been settled by many of the best and most enterprising men of the older States, and a large immigration of the best blood of the Old World, who, removing to an arena of larger opportunities, in a more fertile soil and congenial climate, have developed a spirit and an energy peculiarly Western. In no country on the globe have enterprises of all kinds been pushed forward with such rapidity, or has there been such independence and freedom of competition. Among those who have pioneered the civilization of the West, and been the founders of great States, none have ranked higher in the scale of intelligence and moral worth than the pioneers of Iowa, who came to the territory when it was an Indian country, and through hardship, privation and suffering, laid the foundations of the populous and prosperous commonwealth which to-day dispenses its blessings to a million and a quarter of people From her first settlement and from her first organization as a territory to the present day, Iowa has had able men to manage her affairs, wise statesmen to shape her destiny and frame her laws, and intelligent and impartial jurists to administer justice to her citizens ; her bar, pulpit and press have been able and widely influential ; and in all the professions, arts, enterprises and industries which go to make up a great and prosperous commonwealth, she has taken and holds a front rank among her sister States of the West.

TERRITORIAL HISTORY.

By act of Congress, approved October 31, 1803, the President of the United States was authorized to take possession of the territory included in the Louisiana purchase, and provide for a temporary government. By another act of the same session, approved March 26, 1804, the newly acquired country was divided, October 1, 1804 into the Territory of Orleans, south of the thirty-third parallel of north latitude, and the district of Louisiana, which latter was placed under the authority of the officers of Indiana Territory.

In 1805, the District of Louisiana was organized as a Territory with a government of its own. In 1807, Iowa was included in the Territory of Illinois, and in 1812 in the Territory of Missouri When Missouri was admitted as a State, March 2, 1821, " Iowa," says Hon. C. C. Nourse, " was left a political orphan," until by act of Congress, approved June 28, 1834, the Black Hawk purchase having been made, all the territory west of the Mississippi and north of the northern boundary of Missouri, was made a part of Michigan Territory. Up to this time there had been no county or other organization in what is now the State of Iowa, although one or two Justices of the Peace had been appointed and a post office was established at Dubuque in 1833. In September, 1834, however, the Territorial Legislature of Michigan created two counties on the west side of the Mississippi River, viz.: Dubuque and Des Moines, separated by a line drawn westward from the foot of Rock Island. These counties were partially organized. John King was appointed Chief Justice of Dubuque County, and Isaac Leffler, of Burlington, of Des Moines County. Two Associate Justices, in each county, were appointed by the Governor

On the first Monday in October, 1835, Gen George W Jones, now a citizen of Dubuque, was elected a Delegate to Congress from this part of Michigan Territory. On the 20th of April, 1836, through the efforts of Gen. Jones, Congress passed a bill creating the Territory of Wisconsin, which went into operation, July 4, 1836, and Iowa was then included in

THE TERRITORY OF WISCONSIN,

of which Gen. Henry Dodge was appointed Governor; John S. Horner, Secretary of the Territory; Charles Dunn, Chief Justice; David Irwin and William C. Frazer, Associate Justices

September 9, 1836, Governor Dodge ordered the census of the new Territory to be taken. This census resulted in showing a population of 10,531 in the counties of Dubuque and Des Moines. Under the apportionment, these two counties were entitled to six members of the Council and thirteen of the House of Representatives. The Governor issued his proclamation for an election to be held on the first Monday of October, 1836, on which day the following members of the First Territorial Legislature of Wisconsin were elected from the two counties in the Black Hawk purchase

Dubuque County.—Council: John Fally, Thomas McKnight, Thomas Mc-Crancy. *House ·* Loring Wheeler, Hardin Nowlan, Peter Hill Engle, Patrick Quigley, Hosea T. Camp.

Des Moines County.—Council: Jeremiah Smith, Jr., Joseph B. Teas, Arthur B Ingram *House:* Isaac Leffler, Thomas Blair, Warren L. Jenkins, John Box, George W. Teas, Eli Reynolds David R Chance.

The first Legislature assembled at Belmont, in the present State of Wisconsin, on the 25th day of October, 1836, and was organized by electing Henry T. Baird President of the Council. and Peter Hill Engle, of Dubuque, Speaker of the House. It adjourned December 9, 1836.

The second Legislature assembled at Burlington, November 10, 1837. Adjourned January 20, 1838   The third session was at Burlington, commenced June 1st, and adjourned June 12, 1838.

During the first session of the Wisconsin Territorial Legislature, in 1836, the county of Des Moines was divided into Des Moines, Lee, Van Buren, Henry, Muscatine and Cook (the latter being subsequently changed to Scott) and defined their boundaries   During the second session, out of the territory embraced in Dubuque County, were created the counties of Dubuque, Clayton, Fayette, Delaware, Buchanan, Jackson, Jones, Linn, Clinton and Cedar, and their boundaries defined, but the most of them were not organized until several years afterward, under the authority of the Territorial Legislature of Iowa.

The question of a separate territorial organization for Iowa, which was then a part of Wisconsin Territory, began to be agitated early in the Autumn of 1837   The wishes of the people found expression in a convention held at Burlington on the 1st of November, which memorialized Congress to organize a Territory west of the Mississippi, and to settle the boundary line between Wisconsin Territory and Missouri   The Territorial Legislature of Wisconsin, then in session at Burlington, joined in the petition.   Gen George W Jones, of Dubuque, then residing at Sinsinawa Mound, in what is now Wisconsin, was Delegate to Congress from Wisconsin Territory, and labored so earnestly and successfully, that " An act to divide the Territory of Wisconsin, and to establish the Territorial Government of Iowa," was approved June 12, 1838, to take effect and be in force on and after July 3, 1838   The new Territory embraced "all that part of the present Territory of Wisconsin which lies west of the Mississippi River, and west of a line drawn due north from the head water or sources of the Mississippi to the territorial line "   The organic act provided for a Governor, whose term of office should be three years, and for a Secretary, Chief Justice, two Associate Justices, and Attorney and Marshal, who should serve four years, to be appointed by the President, by and with the advice and consent of the Senate.   The act also provided for the election, by the white male inhabitants, citizens of the United States, over twenty-one years of age, of a House of Representatives, consisting of twenty-six members, and a Council, to consist of thirteen members.   It also appropriated $5,000 for a public library, and $20,000 for the erection of public buildings.

President Van Buren appointed Ex-Governor Robert Lucas, of Ohio, to be the first Governor of the new Territory.   William B. Conway, of Pittsburgh, was appointed Secretary of the Territory; Charles Mason, of Burlington, Chief Justice, and Thomas S. Wilson, of Dubuque, and Joseph Williams, of Pennsylvania, Associate Judges of the Supreme and District Courts; Mr. Van Allen, of New York, Attorney; Francis Gehon, of Dubuque, Marshal; Augustus C Dodge, Register of the Land Office at Burlington, and Thomas Mc Knight, Receiver of the Land Office at Dubuque   Mr. Van Allen, the District Attorney, died at Rockingham, soon after his appointment, and Col Charles Weston was appointed to fill his vacancy   Mr. Conway, the Secretary, also died at Burlington, during the second session of the Legislature, and James Clarke, editor of the *Gazette*, was appointed to succeed him.

Immediately after his arrival, Governor Lucas issued a proclamation for the election of members of the first Territorial Legislature, to be held on the 10th of September, dividing the Territory into election districts for that purpose, and appointing the 12th day of November for meeting of the Legislature to be elected, at Burlington

The first Territorial Legislature was elected in September and assembled at Burlington on the 12th of November, and consisted of the following members:

Council.—Jesse B Brown, J. Keith, E. A. M Swazey, Arthur Ingram, Robert Ralston, George Hepner, Jesse J. Payne, D. B. Hughes, James M Clark, Charles Whittlesey, Jonathan W. Parker, Warner Lewis, Stephen Hempstead.

House—William Patterson, Hawkins Taylor, Calvin J. Price, James Brierly, James Hall, Gideon S. Bailey, Samuel Parker, James W. Grimes, George Temple, Van B Delashmutt, Thomas Blair, George H Beeler,* William G Coop, William H. Wallace, Asbury B. Porter, John Frierson, William L. Toole, Levi Thornton, S. C. Hastings, Robert G. Roberts, Laurel Summers,† Jabez A Burchard, Jr., Chauncey Swan, Andrew Bankson, Thomas Cox and Hardin Nowlin

Notwithstanding a large majority of the members of both branches of the Legislature were Democrats, yet Gen. Jesse B. Browne (Whig), of Lee County, was elected President of the Council, and Hon. William H Wallace (Whig), of Henry County, Speaker of the House of Representatives—the former unanimously and the latter with but little opposition.   At that time, national politics

---

* Cyrus S Jacobs, who was elected for Des Moines County, was killed in an unfortunate encounter at Burlington before the meeting of the Legislature, and Mr Beeler was elected to fill the vacancy

† Samuel R, Murray was returned as elected from Clinton County, but his seat was successfully contested by Burchard

were little heeded by the people of the new Territory, but in 1840, during the Presidential campaign, party lines were strongly drawn

At the election in September, 1838, for members of the Legislature, a Congressional Delegate was also elected. There were four candidates, viz : William W. Chapman and David Rohrer, of Des Moines County ; B. F Wallace, of Henry County, and P. H. Engle, of Dubuque County. Chapman was elected, receiving a majority of thirty-six over Engle

The first session of the Iowa Territorial Legislature was a stormy and exciting one. By the organic law, the Governor was clothed with almost unlimited veto power. Governor Lucas seemed disposed to make free use of it, and the independent Hawkeyes could not quietly submit to arbitrary and absolute rule, and the result was an unpleasant controversy between the Executive and Legislative departments. Congress, however, by act approved March 3, 1839, amended the organic law by restricting the veto power of the Governor to the two-thirds rule, and took from him the power to appoint Sheriffs and Magistrates.

Among the first important matters demanding attention was the location of the seat of government and provision for the erection of public buildings, for which Congress had appropriated $20,000. Governor Lucas, in his message, had recommended the appointment of Commissioners, with a view to making a central location. The extent of the future State of Iowa was not known or thought of   Only on a strip of land fifty miles wide, bordering on the Mississippi River, was the Indian title extinguished, and a central location meant some central point in the Black Hawk Purchase   The friends of a central location supported the Governor's suggestion. The southern members were divided between Burlington and Mount Pleasant, but finally united on the latter as the proper location for the seat of government. The central and southern parties were very nearly equal, and, in consequence, much excitement prevailed. The central party at last triumphed, and on the 21st day of January, 1839, an act was passed, appointing Chauncey Swan, of Dubuque County ; John Ronalds, of Louisa County, and Robert Ralston, of Des Moines County, Commissioners, to select a site for a permanent seat of Government within the limits of Johnson County.

Johnson County had been created by act of the Territorial Legislature of Wisconsin, approved December 21, 1837, and organized by act passed at the special session at Burlington in June, 1838, the organization to date from July 4th, following. Napoleon, on the Iowa River, a few miles below the future Iowa City, was designated as the county seat, temporarily.

Then there existed good reason for locating the capital in the county. The Territory of Iowa was bounded on the north by the British Possessions ; east, by the Mississippi River to its source ; thence by a line drawn due north to the northern boundary of the United States ; south, by the State of Missouri, and west, by the Missouri and White Earth Rivers   But this immense territory was in undisputed possession of the Indians, except a strip on the Mississippi, known as the Black Hawk Purchase   Johnson County was, from north to south, in the geographical center of this purchase, and as near the east and west geographical center of the future State of Iowa as could then be made, as the boundary line between the lands of the United States and the Indians, established by the treaty of October 21, 1837, was immediately west of the county limits.

The Commissioners, after selecting the site, were directed to lay out 640 acres into a town, to be called Iowa City, and to proceed to sell lots and erect public buildings thereon, Congress having granted a section of land to be selected by the Territory for this purpose. The Commissioners met at Napoleon, Johnson County, May 1, 1839, selected for a site Section 10, in Township 79 North of Range 6 West of the Fifth Principal Meridian, and immediately surveyed it and laid off the town. The first sale of lots took place August 16, 1839. The site selected for the public buildings was a little west of the geographical center of the section, where a square of ten acres on the elevated grounds overlooking the river was reserved for the purpose. The capitol is located in the center of this square. The second Territorial Legislature, which assembled in November, 1839, passed an act requiring the Commissioners to adopt such plan for the building that the aggregate cost when complete should not exceed $51,000, and if they had already adopted a plan involving a greater expenditure they were directed to abandon it Plans for the building were designed and drawn by Mr. John F Rague, of Springfield, Ill., and on the 4th day of July, 1840, the corner stone of the edifice was laid with appropriate ceremonies Samuel C Trowbridge was Marshal of the day, and Gov. Lucas delivered the address on that occasion.

When the Legislature assembled at Burlington in special session, July 13. 1840, Gov. Lucas announced that on the 4th of that month he had visited Iowa City, and found the basement of the capitol nearly completed A bill authorizing a loan of $20,000 for the building was passed, January 15, 1841, the unsold lots of Iowa City being the security offered, but only $5,500 was obtained under the act.

THE BOUNDARY QUESTION.

The boundary line between the Territory of Iowa and the State of Missouri was a difficult question to settle in 1838, in consequence of claims arising from taxes and titles, and at one time civil war was imminent. In defining the boundaries of the counties bordering on Missouri, the Iowa authorities had fixed a line that has since been established as the boundary between Iowa and Missouri The Constitution of Missouri defined her northern boundary to be the parallel of latitude which passes through the rapids of the Des Moines River. The lower rapids of the Mississippi immediately above the mouth of the Des Moines River had always been known as the Des Moines Rapids, or "the rapids of the Des Moines River." The Missourians (evidently not well versed in history or geography) insisted on running the northern boundary line from the rapids in the Des Moines River, just below Keosauqua, thus taking from Iowa a strip of territory eight or ten miles wide Assuming this as her northern boundary line, Missouri attempted to exercise jurisdiction over the disputed territory by assessing taxes, and sending her Sheriffs to collect them by distraining the personal property of the settlers. The Iowans, however, were not disposed to submit, and the Missouri officials were arrested by the Sheriffs of Davis and Van Buren Counties and confined in jail. Gov. Boggs, of Missouri, called out his militia to enforce the claim and sustain the officers of Missouri. Gov. Lucas called out the militia of Iowa, and both parties made active preparations for war. In Iowa, about 1,200 men were enlisted, and 500 were actually armed and encamped in Van Buren County, ready to defend the integrity of the Territory. Subsequently, Gen. A. C Dodge, of Burlington, Gen. Churchman, of Dubuque, and Dr. Clark, of Fort Madison, were sent to Missouri as envoys plenipotentiary, to effect, if possible, a peaceable adjustment of the difficulty. Upon their arrival, they found that the County Commissioners of Clarke County, Missouri, had rescinded their order for the collection of the taxes, and that Gov. Boggs had despatched messengers to the Governor of Iowa proposing to submit an agreed case to the Supreme Court of the United States for the final settlement of the boundary question. This proposition was declined, but afterward Congress authorized a suit to settle the controversy, which was instituted, and which resulted in a judgment for Iowa. Under this decision, William G Miner, of Missouri, and Henry B. Hendershott were appointed Commissioners to survey and establish the boundary. Mr. Nourse remarks that "the expenses of the war on the part of Iowa were never paid, either by the United States or the Territorial Government The patriots who furnished supplies to the troops had to bear the cost and charges of the struggle."

The first legislative assembly laid the broad foundation of civil equality, on which has been constructed one of the most liberal governments in the Union Its first act was to recognize the equality of woman with man before the law by providing that "no action commenced by a single woman, who intermarries during the pendency thereof, shall abate on account of such marriage." This principle has been adopted by all subsequent legislation in Iowa, and to-day woman has full and equal civil rights with man, except only the right of the ballot.

Religious toleration was also secured to all, personal liberty strictly guarded, the rights and privileges of citizenship extended to all white persons, and the purity of elections secured by heavy penalties against bribery and corruption. The judiciary power was vested in a Supreme Court, District Court, Probate Court, and Justices of the Peace. Real estate was made divisible by will, and intestate property divided equitably among heirs. Murder was made punishable by death, and proportionate penalties fixed for lesser crimes. A system of free schools, open for every class of white citizens, was established. Provision was made for a system of roads and highways. Thus under the territorial organization, the country began to emerge from a savage wilderness, and take on the forms of civil government

By act of Congress of June 12, 1838, the lands which had been purchased of the Indians were brought into market, and land offices opened in Dubuque and Burlington. Congress provided for military roads and bridges, which greatly aided the settlers, who were now coming in by thousands, to make their homes on the fertile prairies of Iowa—"the Beautiful Land." The fame of the country had spread far and wide; even before the Indian title was extinguished, many were crowding the borders, impatient to cross over and stake out their claims on the choicest spots they could find in the new Territory. As soon as the country was open for settlement, the borders, the Black Hawk Purchase, all along the Mississipi, and up the principal rivers and streams, and out over the broad and rolling prairies, began to be thronged with eager land hunters and immigrants, seeking homes in Iowa. It was a sight to delight the eyes of all comers from every land—its noble streams, beautiful and picturesque hills and valleys, broad and fertile prairies extending as far as the eye could reach, with a soil surpassing in richness anything which they had ever seen. It is not to be wondered at that immigration into Iowa was rapid, and that within less than a decade from the organization of the Territory, it contained a hundred and fifty thousand people.

As rapidly as the Indian titles were extinguished and the original owners removed, the resistless tide of emigration flowed westward. The following extract from Judge Nourse's Centennial Address shows how the immigrants gathered on the Indian boundary, ready for the removal of the barrier:

In obedience to our progressive and aggressive spirit, the Government of the United States made another treaty with the Sac and Fox Indians, on the 11th day of August, 1842, for the remaining portion of their land in Iowa The treaty provided that the Indians should retain possession of all the lands thus ceded until May 1, 1843, and should occupy that portion of the ceded territory west of a line running north and south through Redrock, until October 11, 1845 These tribes, at this time, had their principal village at Ot-tum-wa-no, now called Ottumwa. As soon as it became known that the treaty had been concluded, there was a rush of immigration to Iowa, and a great number of temporary settlements were made near the Indian boundary, waiting for the 1st day of May As the day approached, hundreds of families encamped along the line, and their tents and wagons gave the scene the appearance of a military expedition. The country beyond had been thoroughly explored, but the United States military authorities had prevented any settlement or even the making out of claims by any monuments whatever

To aid them in making out their claims when the hour should arrive, the settlers had placed piles of dry wood on the rising ground, at convenient distances, and a short time before twelve o'clock of the night of the 30th of April, these were lighted, and when the midnight hour arrived, it was announced by the discharge of firearms The night was dark, but this army of occupation pressed forward, torch in hand, with axe and hatchet, blazing lines with all manner of curves and angles When daylight came and revealed the confusion of these wonderful surveys, numerous disputes arose, settled generally by compromise, but sometimes by violence Between midnight of the 30th of April and sundown of the 1st of May, over one thousand families had settled on their new purchase

While this scene was transpiring, the retreating Indians were enacting one more impressive and melancholy The Winter of 1842–43 was one of unusual severity, and the Indian prophet, who had disapproved of the treaty, attributed the severity of the Winter to the anger of the Great Spirit, because they had sold their country Many religious rites were performed to atone for the crime When the time for leaving Ot-tum-wa-no arrived, a solemn silence pervaded the Indian camp, and the faces of their stoutest men were bathed in tears; and when their cavalcade was put in motion, toward the setting sun, there was a spontaneous outburst of frantic grief from the entire procession

The Indians remained the appointed time beyond the line running north and south through Redrock The government established a trading post and military encampment at the Raccoon Fork of the Des Moines River, then and for many years known as Fort Des Moines Here the red man lingered until the 11th of October, 1845, when the same scene that we have before described was re-enacted, and the wave of immigration swept over the remainder of the " New Purchase " The lands thus occupied and claimed by the settlers still belonged in fee to the General Government The surveys were not completed until some time after the Indian title was extinguished After their survey, the lands were publicly proclaimed or advertised for sale at public auction Under the laws of the United States, a pre-emption or exclusive right to purchase public lands could not be acquired until after the lands had thus been publicly offered and not sold for want of bidders Then, and not until then, an occupant making improvements in good faith might acquire a right over others to enter the land at the minimum price of $1 25 per acre The " claim laws " were unknown to the United States statutes They originated in the " eternal fitness of things," and were enforced, probably, as belonging to that class of natural rights not enumerated in the constitution, and not impaired or disparaged by its enumeration

The settlers organized in every settlement prior to the public land sales, appointed officers, and adopted their own rules and regulations Each man's claim was duly ascertained and recorded by the Secretary It was the duty of *all* to attend the sales The Secretary bid off the lands of each settler at $1 25 per acre The others were there, to see, first, that he did his duty and bid in the land, and, secondly, to see that *no one else bid* This, of course, sometimes led to trouble, but it saved the excitement of competition, and gave a formality and degree of order and regularity to the proceedings they would not otherwise have attained As far as practicable, the Territorial Legislature recognized the validity of these " claims " upon the public lands, and in 1839 passed an act legalizing their sale and making their transfer a valid consideration to support a promise to pay for the same (Acts of 1843, p 456) The Supreme Territorial Court held this law to be valid (See Hill v Smith, 1st Morris Rep 70) The opinion not only contains a decision of the question involved, but also contains much valuable erudition upon that " spirit of Anglo-Saxon liberty ' which the Iowa settlers unquestionably inherited in a direct line of descent from the said " Anglo-Saxons " But the early settler was not always able to pay even this dollar and twenty-five cents per acre for his land

Many of the settlers had nothing to begin with, save their hands, health and courage and their family jewels, " the pledges of love," and the " consumers of bread." It was not so easy to accumulate money in the early days of the State, and the " beautiful prairies," the " noble streams," and all that sort of poetic imagery, did not prevent the early settlers from becoming discouraged.

An old settler, in speaking of the privations and trials of those early days, says :

Well do the " old settlers ' of Iowa remember the days from the first settlement to 1840 Those were days of sadness and distress The endearments of home in another land had been broken up, and all that was hallowed on earth, the home of childhood and the scenes of youth, we severed, and we sat down by the gentle waters of our noble river, and often "hung our harps on the willows"

Another, from another part of the State, testifies.

There was no such thing as getting money for any kind of labor. I laid brick at $3 00 per thousand, and took my pay in anything I could eat or wear   I built the first Methodist Church at Keokuk, 42x60 feet, of brick, for $600, and took my pay in a subscription paper, part of which I never collected, and upon which I only received $50 00 in money   Wheat was hauled 100 miles from the interior, and sold for 37½ cents per bushel

Another old settler, speaking of a later period, 1843, says:

Land and everything had gone down in value to almost nominal prices   Corn and oats could be bought for six or ten cents a bushel, pork, $1 00 per hundred, and the best horse a man could raise sold for $50 00   Nearly all were in debt, and the Sheriff and Constable, with legal processes, were common visitors at almost every man's door   These were indeed "the times that tried men's souls"

"A few," says Mr. Nourse, "who were not equal to the trial, returned to their old homes, but such as had the courage and faith to be the worthy founders of a great State remained, to more than realize the fruition of their hopes, and the reward of their self-denial."

On Monday, December 6, 1841, the fourth Legislative Assembly met, at the new capital, Iowa City, but the capitol building could not be used, and the Legislature occupied a temporary frame house, that had been erected for that purpose, during the session of 1841-2   At this session, the Superintendent of Public Buildings (who, with the Territorial Agent, had superseded the Commissioners first appointed), estimated the expense of completing the building at $33,330, and that rooms for the use of the Legislature could be completed for $15,600.

During 1842, the Superintendent commenced obtaining stone from a new quarry, about ten miles northeast of the city.   This is now known as the "Old Capitol Quarry," and contains, it is thought, an immense quantity of excellent building stone.   Here all the stone for completing the building was obtained, and it was so far completed, that on the 5th day of December, 1842, the Legislature assembled in the new capitol   At this session, the Superintendent estimated that it would cost $39,143 to finish the building.   This was nearly $6,000 higher than the estimate of the previous year, notwithstanding a large sum had been expended in the meantime.   This rather discouraging discrepancy was accounted for by the fact that the officers in charge of the work were constantly short of funds.   Except the congressional appropriation of $20,000 and the loan of $5,500, obtained from the Miners' Bank, of Dubuque, all the funds for the prosecution of the work were derived from the sale of the city lots (which did not sell very rapidly), from certificates of indebtedness, and from scrip, based upon unsold lots, which was to be received in payment for such lots when they were sold.   At one time, the Superintendent made a requisition for bills of iron and glass, which could not be obtained nearer than St Louis   To meet this, the Agent sold some lots for a draft, payable at Pittsburgh, Pa, for which he was compelled to pay twenty-five per cent exchange.   This draft, amounting to $507, that officer reported to be more than one-half the cash actually handled by him during the entire season, when the disbursements amounted to very nearly $24,000.

With such uncertainty, it could not be expected that estimates could be very accurate.   With all these disadvantages, however, the work appears to have been prudently prosecuted, and as rapidly as circumstances would permit.

Iowa remained a Territory from 1838 to 1846, during which the office of Governor was held by Robert Lucas, John Chambers and James Clarke.

STATE ORGANIZATION.

By an act of the Territorial Legislature of Iowa, approved February 12, 1844, the question of the formation of a State Constitution and providing for the election of Delegates to a convention to be convened for that purpose was submitted to the people, to be voted upon at their township elections in April following. The vote was largely in favor of the measure, and the Delegates elected assembled in convention at Iowa City, on the 7th of October, 1844 On the first day of November following, the convention completed its work and adopted the first State Constitution

The President of the convention, Hon. Shepherd Leffler, was instructed to transmit a certified copy of this Constitution to the Delegate in Congress, to be by him submitted to that body at the earliest practicable day It was also provided that it should be submitted, together with any conditions or changes that might be made by Congress, to the people of the Territory, for their approval or rejection, at the township election in April, 1845

The boundaries of the State, as defined by this Constitution, were as follows :

Beginning in the middle of the channel of the Mississippi River, opposite mouth of the Des Moines River, thence up the said river Des Moines, in the middle of the main channel thereof, to a point where it is intersected by the Old Indian Boundary line, or line run by John C Sullivan, in the year 1816 ; thence westwardly along said line to the " old " northwest corner of Missouri, thence due west to the middle of the main channel of the Missouri River ; thence up in the middle of the main channel of the river last mentioned to the mouth of the Sioux or Calumet River, thence in a direct line to the middle of the main channel of the St Peters River, where the Watonwan River—according to Nicollet's map—enters the same, thence down the middle of the main channel of said river to the middle of the main channel of the Mississippi River ; thence down the middle of the main channel of said river to the place of beginning

These boundaries were rejected by Congress, but by act approved March 3, 1845, a State called Iowa was admitted into the Union, provided the people accepted the act, bounded as follows :

Beginning at the mouth of the Des Moines River, at the middle of the Mississippi, thence by the middle of the channel of that river to a parallel of latitude passing through the mouth of the Mankato or Blue Earth River, thence west, along said parallel of latitude, to a point where it is intersected by a meridian line seventeen degrees and thirty minutes west of the meridian of Washington City ; thence due south, to the northern boundary line of the State of Missouri, thence eastwardly, following that boundary to the point at which the same intersects the Des Moines River, thence by the middle of the channel of that river to the place of beginning.

These boundaries, had they been accepted, would have placed the northern boundary of the State about thirty miles north of its present location, and would have deprived it of the Missouri slope and the boundary of that river. The western boundary would have been near the west line of what is now Kossuth County. But it was not so to be. In consequence of this radical and unwelcome change in the boundaries, the people refused to accept the act of Congress and rejected the Constitution at the election, held August 4, 1845, by a vote of 7,656 to 7,235.

A second Constitutional Convention assembled at Iowa City on the 4th day of May, 1846, and on the 18th of the same month another Constitution for the new State with the present boundaries, was adopted and submitted to the people for ratification on the 3d day of August following, when it was accepted , 9,492 votes were cast " for the Constitution," and 9,036 " against the Constitution "

The Constitution was approved by Congress, and by act of Congress approved December 28, 1846, Iowa was admitted as a sovereign State in the American Union.

Prior to this action of Congress, however, the people of the new State held an election under the new Constitution on the 26th day of October, and elected Oresel Briggs, Governor; Elisha Cutler, Jr, Secretary of State; Joseph T. Fales, Auditor, Morgan Reno, Treasurer; and members of the Senate and House of Representatives.

At this time there were twenty-seven organized counties in the State, with a population of nearly 100,000, and the frontier settlements were rapidly pushing toward the Missouri River The Mormons had already reached there

The first General Assembly of the State of Iowa was composed of nineteen Senators and forty Representatives. It assembled at Iowa City, November 30, 1846, about a month *before* the State was admitted into the Union.

At the first session of the State Legislature, the Treasurer of State reported that the capitol building was in a very exposed condition, liable to injury from storms, and expressed the hope that some provision would be made to complete it, at least sufficiently to protect it from the weather The General Assembly responded by appropriating $2,500 for the completion of the public buildings At the first session also arose the question of the re-location of the capital The western boundary of the State, as now determined, left Iowa City too far toward the eastern and southern boundary of the State; this was conceded Congress had appropriated five sections of land for the erection of public buildings, and toward the close of the session a bill was introduced providing for the re-location of the seat of government, involving to some extent the location of the State University, which had already been discussed. This bill gave rise to a deal of discussion and parliamentary maneuvering, almost purely sectional in its character. It provided for the appointment of three Commissioners, who were authorized to make a location as near the geographical center of the State as a healthy and eligible site could be obtained; to select the five sections of land donated by Congress, to survey and plat into town lots not exceeding one section of the land so selected; to sell lots at public sale, not to exceed two in each block Having done this, they were then required to suspend further operations, and make a report of their proceedings to the Governor The bill passed both Houses by decisive votes, received the signature of the Governor, and became a law. Soon after, by "An act to locate and establish a State University," approved February 25, 1847, the unfinished public buildings at Iowa City, together with the ten acres of land on which they were situated, were granted for the use of the University, reserving their use, however, by the General Assembly and the State officers, until other provisions were made by law.

The Commissioners forthwith entered upon their duties, and selected four sections and two half sections in Jasper County Two of these sections are in what is now Des Moines Township, and the others in Fairview Township, in the southern part of that county. These lands are situated between Prairie City and Monroe, on the Keokuk & Des Moines Railroad, which runs diagonally through them. Here a town was platted, called Monroe City, and a sale of lots took place Four hundred and fifteen lots were sold, at prices that were not considered remarkably remunerative. The cash payments (one-fourth) amounted to $1,797 43, while the expenses of the sale and the claims of the Commissioners for services amounted to $2,206.57. The Commissioners made a report of their proceedings to the Governor, as required by law, but the location was generally condemned.

When the report of the Commissioners, showing this brilliant financial operation, had been read in the House of Representatives, at the next session, and while it was under consideration, an indignant member, afterward known as the eccentric Judge McFarland, moved to refer the report to a select Committee of Five, with instructions to report " how much of said city of Monroe was under water and how much was burned " The report was referred, without the instructions, however, but Monroe City never became the seat of government. By an act approved January 15, 1849, the law by which the location had been made was repealed and the new town was vacated, the money paid by purchasers of lots being refunded to them. This, of course, retained the seat of government at Iowa City, and precluded, for the time, the occupation of the building and grounds by the University.

At the same session, $3,000 more were appropriated for completing the State building at Iowa City   In 1852, the further sum of $5,000 and in 1854 $4,000 more were apppropriated for the same purpose, making the whole cost $123,000, paid partly by the General Government and partly by the State, but principally from the proceeds of the sale of lots in Iowa City.

But the question of the permanent location of the seat of government was not settled, and in 1851 bills were introduced for the removal of the capital to Pella and to Fort Des Moines. The latter appeared to have the support of the majority, but was finally lost in the House on the question of ordering it to its third reading.

At the next session, in 1853, a bill was introduced in the Senate for the removal of the seat of government to Fort Des Moines, and, on final vote, was just barely defeated. At the next session, however, the effort was more successful, and on the 15th day of January, 1855, a bill re-locating the capital within two miles of the Raccoon Fork of the Des Moines, and for the appointment of Commissioners, was approved by Gov. Grimes. The site was selected in 1856, in accordance with the provisions of this act, the land being donated to the State by citizens and property-holders of Des Moines. An association of citizens erected a building for a temporary capitol, and leased it to the State at a nominal rent

The third Constitutional Convention to revise the Constitution of the State assembled at Iowa City, January 19, 1857. The new Constitution framed by this convention was submitted to the people at an election held August 3, 1857, when it was approved and adopted by a vote of 40,311 " for " to 38,681 " against," and on the 3d day of September following was declared by a proclamation of the Governor to be the supreme law of the State of Iowa

Advised of the completion of the temporary State House at Des Moines, on the 19th of October following, Governor Grimes issued another proclamation, declaring the City of Des Moines to be the capital of the State of Iowa

The removal of the archives and offices was commenced at once and continued through the Fall.   It was an undertaking of no small magnitude , there was not a mile of railroad to facilitate the work, and the season was unusually disagreeable. Rain, snow and other accompaniments increased the difficulties; and it was not until December, that the last of the effects—the safe of the State Treasurer, loaded on two large " bob-sleds "—drawn by ten yoke of oxen was deposited in the new capital It is not imprudent now to remark that, during this passage over hills and prairies, across rivers, through bottom lands and timber, the safes belonging to the several departments contained large sums of money, mostly individual funds, however. Thus, Iowa City ceased to be the capital of the State, after four Territorial Legislatures, six State Legislatures and three

Constitutional Conventions had held their sessions there   By the exchange, the old capitol at Iowa City became the seat of the University, and, except the rooms occupied by the United States District Court, passed under the immediate and direct control of the Trustees of that institution

Des Moines was now the permanent seat of government, made so by the fundamental law of the State, and on the 11th day of January, 1858, the seventh General Assembly convened at the new capital.   The building used for governmental purposes was purchased in 1864   It soon became inadequate for the purposes for which it was designed, and it became apparent that a new, large and permanent State House must be erected.   In 1870, the General Assembly made an appropriation and provided for the appointment of a Board of Commissioners to commence the work.   The board consisted of Gov. Samuel Merrill, ex officio, President ; Grenville M. Dodge, Council Bluffs ; James F. Wilson, Fairfield ; James Dawson, Washington ; Simon G. Stein, Muscatine ; James O. Crosby, Gainsville, Charles Dudley, Agency City ; John N. Dewey, Des Moines ; William L. Joy, Sioux City ; Alexander R. Fulton, Des Moines, Secretary.

The act of 1870 provided that the building should be constructed of the best material and should be fire proof ; to be heated and ventilated in the most approved manner ; should contain suitable legislative halls, rooms for State officers, the judiciary, library, committees, archives and the collections of the State Agricultural Society, and for all purpoees of State Government, and should be erected on grounds held by the State for that purpose   The sum first appropriated was $150,000 ; and the law provided that no contract should be made, either for constructing or furnishing the building, which should bind the State for larger sums than those at the time appropriated.   A design was drawn and plans and specifications furnished by Cochrane & Piquenard, architects, which were accepted by the board, and on the 23d of November, 1871, the corner stone was laid with appropriate ceremonies   The estimated cost and present value of the capitol is fixed at $2,000,000

From 1858 to 1860, the Sioux became troublesome in the northwestern part of the State.   These warlike Indians made frequent plundering raids upon the settlers, and murdered several families.   In 1861, several companies of militia were ordered to that portion of the State to hunt down and punish the murderous thieves   No battles were fought, however, for the Indians fled when they ascertained that systematic and adequate measures had been adopted to protect the settlers

"The year 1856 marked a new era in the history of Iowa   In 1854, the Chicago & Rock Island Railroad had been completed to the east bank of the Mississippi River, opposite Davenport   In 1854, the corner stone of a railroad bridge, that was to be the first to span the "Father of Waters," was laid with appropriate ceremonies at this point   St Louis had resolved that the enterprise was unconstitutional, and by writs of injunction made an unsuccessful effort to prevent its completion.   Twenty years later in her history, St. Louis repented her folly, and made atonement for her sin by imitating our example. On the 1st day of January, 1856, this railroad was completed to Iowa City. In the meantime, two other railroads had reached the east bank of the Mississippi—one opposite Burlington, and one opposite Dubuque—and these were being extended into the interior of the State   Indeed, four lines of railroad had been projected across the State from the Mississippi to the Missouri, having eastern connections   On the 15th of May, 1856, the Congress of the United States passed an act granting to the State, to aid in the construction of railroads, the public lands in alternate sections, six miles on either side of the proposed lines An extra session of the General Assembly was called in July of this year, that disposed of the grant to the several companies that proposed to complete these enterprises. The population of our State at this time had increased to 500,000. Public attention had been called to the necessity of a railroad across the continent The position of Iowa, in the very heart and center of the Republic, on the route of this great highway across the continent, began to attract attention Cities and towns sprang up through the State as if by magic. Capital began to pour into the State, and had it been employed in developing our vast coal measures and establishing manufactories among us, or if it had been expended in improving our lands, and building houses and barns, it would have been well. But all were in haste to get rich, and the spirit of speculation ruled the hour.

"In the meantime, every effort was made to help the speedy completion of the railroads Nearly every county and city on the Mississippi, and many in the interior, voted large corporate subscriptions to the stock of the railroad companies, and issued their negotiable bonds for the amount." Thus enormous county and city debts were incurred, the payment of which these municipalities tried to avoid upon the plea that they had exceeded the constitutional limitation of their powers. The Supreme Court of the United States held these bonds to be valid; and the courts by mandamus compelled the city and county authorities to levy taxes to pay the judgments These debts are not all paid even yet, but the worst is over and ultimately the burden will be entirely removed

The first railroad across the State was completed to Council Bluffs in January, 1871. The others were completed soon after. In 1854, there was not a mile of railroad in the State. In 1874, twenty years after, there were 3,765 miles in successful operation.

GROWTH AND PROGRESS.

When Wisconsin Territory was organized, in 1836, the entire population of that portion of the Territory now embraced in the State of Iowa was 10,531 The Territory then embraced two counties, Dubuque and Des Moines, erected by the Territory of Michigan, in 1834 From 1836 to 1838, the Territorial Legislature of Wisconsin increased the number of counties to sixteen, and the population had increased to 22,859. Since then, the counties have increased to ninety-nine, and the population, in 1875, was 1,366,000. The following table will show the population at different periods since the erection of Iowa Territory:

Year.	Population	Year	Population	Year	Population
1838	22,589	1852	230,713	1869	1,040,819
1840	43,115	1854	326,013	1870	1,191,727
1844	75,152	1856	519,055	1873	1,251,333
1846	97,588	1859	638,775	1875	1,366,000
1847	116,651	1860	674,913	1876	..
1849	152,988	1863	701,732	1877	...
1850	191,982	1865	754,699		
1851	204,774	1867	902,040		

The most populous county in the State is Dubuque Not only in population, but in everything contributing to the growth and greatness of a State has Iowa made rapid progress. In a little more than thirty years, its wild but beautiful prairies have advanced from the home of the savage to a highly civilized commonwealth, embracing all the elements of progress which characterize the older States.

Thriving cities and towns dot its fair surface; an iron net-work of thousands of miles of railroads is woven over its broad acres; ten thousand school houses, in which more than five hundred thousand children are being taught the rudiments of education, testify to the culture and liberality of the people; high schools, colleges and universities are generously endowed by the State; manufactories spring up on all her water courses, and in most of her cities and towns

Whether measured from the date of her first settlement, her organization as a Territory or admission as a State, Iowa has thus far shown a growth unsurpassed, in a similar period, by any commonwealth on the face of the earth; and, with her vast extent of fertile soil, with her inexhaustible treasures of mineral wealth, with a healthful, invigorating climate; an intelligent, liberty-loving people, with equal, just and liberal laws, and her free schools. the future of Iowa may be expected to surpass the most hopeful anticipations of her present citizens.

Looking upon Iowa as she is to-day—populous, prosperous and happy—it is hard to realize the wonderful changes that have occurred since the first white settlements were made within her borders. When the number of States was only twenty-six, and their total population about twenty millions, our republican form of government was hardly more than an experiment, just fairly put upon trial. The development of our agricultural resources and inexhaustible mineral wealth had hardly commenced Westward the "Star of Empire" had scarcely started on its way. West of the great Mississippi was a mighty empire, but almost unknown, and marked on the maps of the period as "The Great American Desert."

Now, thirty-eight stars glitter on our national escutcheon, and forty-five millions of people, who know their rights and dare maintain them, tread American soil, and the grand sisterhood of States extends from the Gulf of Mexico to the Canadian border, and from the rocky coast of the Atlantic to the golden shores of the Pacific.

THE AGRICULTURAL COLLEGE AND FARM.

Ames, Story County.

The Iowa State Agricultural College and Farm were established by an act of the General Assembly, approved March 22, 1858. A Board of Trustees was appointed, consisting of Governor R P Lowe, John D Wright, William Duane Wilson, M. W. Robinson, Timothy Day, Richard Gaines, John Pattee, G. W. F Sherwin, Suel Foster, S. W Henderson, Clement Coffin and E G. Day; the Governors of the State and President of the College being ex officio members. Subsequently the number of Trustees was reduced to five. The Board met in June, 1859, and received propositions for the location of the College and Farm from Hardin, Polk, Story and Boone, Marshall, Jefferson and Tama Counties. In July, the proposition of Story County and some of its citizens and by the citizens of Boone County was accepted, and the farm and the site for the buildings were located In 1860–61, the farm-house and barn were erected. In 1862, Congress granted to the State 240,000 acres of land for the endowment of schools of agriculture and the mechanical arts, and 195,000 acres were located by Peter Melendy, Commissioner, in 1862–3 George W. Bassett was appointed Land Agent for the institution. In 1864, the General Assembly appropriated $20,000 for the erection of the college building.

In June of that year, the Building Committee, consisting of Suel Foster, Peter Melendy and A. J. Bronson, proceeded to let the contract   John Browne, of Des Moines, was employed as architect, and furnished the plans of the building, but was superseded in its construction by C. A. Dunham.   The $20,000 appropriated by the General Assembly were expended in putting in the foundations and making the brick for the structure.   An additional appropriation of $91,000 was made in 1866, and the building was completed in 1868.

Tuition in this college is made by law forever free to pupils from the State over sixteen years of age, who have been resident of the State six months previous to their admission.   Each county in the State has a prior right of tuition for three scholars from each county; the remainder, equal to the capacity of the college, are by the Trustees distributed among the counties in proportion to the population, and subject to the above rule.   All sale of ardent spirits, wine or beer are prohibited by law within a distance of three miles from the college, except for sacramental, mechanical or medical purposes.

The course of instruction in the Agricultural College embraces the following branches: Natural Philosophy Chemistry, Botany, Horticulture, Fruit Growing, Forestry, Animal and Vegetable Anatomy, Geology, Mineralogy, Meteorology, Entomology, Zoology, the Veterinary Art, Plane Mensuration, Leveling, Surveying, Bookkeeping, and such Mechanical Arts as are directly connected with agriculture; also such other studies as the Trustees may from time to time prescribe, not inconsistent with the purposes of the institution

The funds arising from the lease and sale of lands and interest on investments are sufficient for the support of the institution.   Several College Societies are maintained among the students, who publish a monthly paper.   There is also an " out-law " called the " *ATA*, Chapter Omega."

The Board of Trustees in 1877 was composed of C. W Warden, Ottumwa, Chairman; Hon Samuel J. Kirkwood, Iowa City; William B Treadway, Sioux City; Buel Sherman, Fredericksburg, and Laurel Summers, Le Claire. E. W. Starten, Secretary; William D. Lucas, Treasurer.

Board of Instruction.—A. S. Welch, LL. D , President and Professor of Psychology and Philosophy of Science , Gen. J. L. Geddes, Professor of Military Tactics and Engineering; W. H Wynn, A M , Ph D., Professor of English Literature; C. E Bessey, M. S., Professor of Botany, Zoology, Entomology; A. Thompson, C E , Mechanical Engineering and Superintendent of Workshops; F. E. L Beal, B. S., Civil Engineering, T E. Pope, A. M , Chemistry; M Stalker, Agricultural and Veterinary Science; J L Budd, Horticulture; J. K. Macomber, Physics , E W. Stanton, Mathematics and Political Economy; Mrs. Margaret P. Stanton, Preceptress, Instructor in French and Mathematics.

THE STATE UNIVERSITY.

Iowa City, Johnson County.

In the famous Ordinance of 1787, enacted by Congress before the Territory of the United States extended beyond the Mississippi River, it was declared that in all the territory northwest of the Ohio River, " Schools and the means of education shall forever be encouraged " By act of Congress, approved July 20, 1840, the Secretary of the Treasury was authorized " to set apart and reserve from sale, out of any of the public lands within the Territory of Iowa, to which the Indian title has been or may be extinguished, and not otherwise appropriated, a quantity of land, not exceeding the entire townships, for the use and support of a university within said Territorry when it becomes a State, and for no other use or purpose whatever , to be located in tracts of not less than an entire section, corresponding with any of the large divisions into which the public land are authorized to be surveyed "

William W. Dodge, of Scott County, was appointed by the Secretary of the Treasury to make the selections. He selected Section 5 in Township 78, north of Range 3, east of the Fifth Principal Meridian, and then removed from the Territory. No more lands were selected until 1846, when, at the request of the Assembly, John M. Whitaker of Van Buren County, was appointed, who selected the remainder of the grant except about 122 acres

In the first Constitution, under which Iowa was admitted to the Union, the people directed the disposition of the proceeds of this munificent grant in accordance with its terms, and instructed the General Assembly to provide, as soon as may be, effectual means for the improvement and permanent security of the funds of the university derived from the lands

The first General Assembly, by act approved February 25, 1847, established the "State University of Iowa " at Iowa City, then the capital of the State, "with such other branches as public convenience may hereafter require " The "public buildings at Iowa City, together with the ten acres of land in which they are situated," were granted for the use of said university, *provided*, however, that the sessions of the Legislature and State offices should be held in the capitol until otherwise provided by law   The control and management of the University were committed to a board of fifteen Trustees, to be appointed by the Legislature, five of whom were to be chosen biennially.   The Superintendent of Public Instruction was made President of this Board.   Provisions were made for the disposal of the two townships of land, and for the investment of the funds arising therefrom.   The act further provides that the University shall never be under the exclusive control of any religious denomination whatever," and as soon as the revenue for the grant and donations amounts to $2,000 a year, the University should commence and continue the instruction, free of charge, of fifty students annually.   The General Assembly retained full supervision over the University, its officers and the grants and donations made and to be made to it by the State

Section 5 of the act appointed James P. Carleton, H. D. Downey, Thomas Snyder, Samuel McCrory, Curtis Bates, Silas Foster, E. C Lyon, James H. Gower, George G Vincent, Wm G Woodward, Theodore S. Parvin, George Atchinson, S. G. Matson, H W. Starr and Ansel Briggs, the first Board of Trustees.

The organization of the University at Iowa City was impracticable, however, so long as the seat of government was retained there

In January, 1849, two branches of the University and three Normal Schools were established.   The branches were located—one at Fairfield, and the other at Dubuque, and were placed upon an equal footing, in respect to funds and all other matters, with the University established at Iowa City "This act," says Col Benton, "created *three* State Universities, with equal rights and powers, instead of a 'University with such branches as public convenience *may hereafter demand*,' as provided by the Constitution."

The Board of Directors of the Fairfield Branch consisted of. Barnet Ristine, Christian W. Slagle, Daniel Rider, Horace Gaylord, Bernhart Henn and Samuel S. Bayard.   At the first meeting of the Board, Mr. Henn was elected President, Mr Slagle Secretary, and Mr. Gaylord Treasurer.   Twenty acres of land were purchased, and a building erected thereon, costing $2,500

This building was nearly destroyed by a hurricane, in 1850, but was rebuilt more substantially, all by contributions of the citizens of Fairfield. This branch never received any aid from the State or from the University Fund, and by act approved January 24, 1853, at the request of the Board, the General Assembly terminated its relation to the State.

The branch at Dubuque was placed under the control of the Superintendent of Public Instruction, and John King, Caleb H. Booth, James M. Emerson, Michael J. Sullivan, Richard Benson and the Governor of the State as Trustees. The Trustees never organized, and its existence was only nominal.

The Normal Schools were located at Andrew, Oskaloosa and Mount Pleasant, respectively. Each was to be governed by a board of seven Trustees, to be appointed by the Trustees of the University. Each was to receive $500 annually from the income of the University Fund, upon condition that they should educate eight common school teachers, free of charge for tuition, and that the citizens should contribute an equal sum for the erection of the requisite buildings. The several Boards of Trustees were appointed At Andrew, the school was organized Nov. 21, 1849; Samuel Ray, Principal; Miss J. S. Dori, Assistant. A building was commenced and over $1,000 expended on it, but it was never completed. At Oskaloosa, the Trustees organized in April, 1852 This school was opened in the Court House, September 13, 1852, under the charge of Prof. G. M. Drake and wife. A two story brick building was completed in 1853, costing $2,473. The school at Mount Pleasant was never organized. Neither of these schools received any aid from the University Fund, but in 1857 the Legislature appropriated $1,000 each for those at Oskaloosa and Andrew, and repealed the law authorizing the payment of money to them from the University Fund. From that time they made no further effort to continue in operation.

At a special meeting of the Board of Trustees, held February 21, 1850, the "College of Physicians and Surgeons of the Upper Mississippi," established at Davenport, was recognized as the "College of Physicians and Surgeons of the State University of Iowa," expressly stipulating, however, that such recognition should not render the University liable for any pecuniary aid, nor was the Board to have any control over the property or management of the Medical Association. Soon after, this College was removed to Keokuk, its second session being opened there in November, 1850. In 1851, the General Assembly confirmed the action of the Board, and by act approved January 22, 1855, placed the Medical College under the supervision of the Board of Trustees of the University, and it continued in operation until this arrangement was terminated by the new Constitution, September 3, 1857

From 1847 to 1855, the Board of Trustees was kept full by regular elections by the Legislature, and the Trustees held frequent meetings, but there was no effectual organization of the University. In March, 1855, it was partially opened for a term of sixteen weeks. July 16, 1855, Amos Dean, of Albany, N. Y, was elected President, but he never entered fully upon its duties The University was again opened in September, 1855, and continued in operation until June, 1856, under Professors Johnson, Welton, Van Valkenburg and Guffin

In the Spring of 1856, the capital of the State was located at Des Moines; but there were no buildings there, and the capitol at Iowa City was not vacated by the State until December, 1857.

In June, 1856, the faculty was re-organized, with some changes, and the University was again opened on the third Wednesday of September, 1856.

There were one hundred and twenty-four students—eighty-three males and forty-one females—in attendance during the year 1856–7, and the first regular catalogue was published

At a special meeting of the Board, September 22, 1857, the honorary degree of Bachelor of Arts was conferred on D. Franklin Wells. This was the first degree conferred by the Board.

Article IX, Section 11, of the new State Constitution, which went into force September 3, 1857, provided as follows .

The State University shall be established at one place, without branches at any other place; and the University fund shall be applied to that institution, and no other

Article XI, Section 8, provided that

The seat of Government is hereby permanently established, as now fixed by law, at the city of Des Moines, in the county of Polk, and the State University at Iowa City, in the county of Johnson

The new Constitution created the Board of Education, consisting of the Lieutenant Governor, who was ex officio President, and one member to be elected from each judicial district in the State. This Board was endowed with "full power and authority to legislate and make all needful rules and regulations in relation to common schools and other educational institutions," subject to alteration, amendment or repeal by the General Assembly, which was vested with authority to abolish or re-organize the Board at any time after 1863

In December, 1857, the old capitol building, now known as Central Hall of the University, except the rooms occupied by the United States District Court, and the property, with that exception, passed under the control of the Trustees, and became the seat of the University. The old building had had hard usage, and its arrangement was illy adapted for University purposes. Extensive repairs and changes were necessary, but the Board was without funds for these purposes

The last meeting of the Board, under the old law, was held in January, 1858 At this meeting, a resolution was introduced, and seriously considered, to exclude females from the University; but it finally failed.

March 12, 1858, the first Legislature under the new Constitution enacted a new law in relation to the University, but it was not materially different from the former. March 11, 1858, the Legislature appropriated $3,000 for the repair and modification of the old capitol building, and $10,000 for the erection of a boarding house, now known as South Hall.

The Board of Trustees created by the new law met and duly organized April 27, 1858, and determined to close the University until the income from its fund should be adequate to meet the current expenses, and the buildings should be ready for occupation. Until this term, the building known as the "Mechanics' Academy" had been used for the school The Faculty, except the Chancellor (Dean), was dismissed, and all further instruction suspended, from the close of the term then in progress until September, 1859. At this meeting, a resolution was adopted excluding females from the University after the close of the existing term; but this was afterward, in August, modified, so as to admit them to the Normal Department

At the meeting of the Board, August 4, 1858, the degree of Bachelor of Science was conferred upon Dexter Edson Smith, being the first degree conferred upon a student of the University. Diplomas were awarded to the members of the first graduating class of the Normal Department as follows: Levi P. Aylworth, Cellina H Aylworth, Elizabeth L. Humphrey, Annie A Pinney and Sylvia M. Thompson

An "Act for the Government and Regulation of the State University of Iowa," approved December 25, 1858, was mainly a re-enactment of the law of March 12, 1858, except that changes were made in the Board of Trustees, and manner of their appointment This law provided that both sexes were to be admitted on equal terms to all departments of the institution, leaving the Board no discretion in the matter.

The new Board met and organized, February 2, 1859, and decided to continue the Normal Department only to the end of the current term, and that it was unwise to re-open the University at that time; but at the annual meeting of the Board, in June of the same year, it was resolved to continue the Normal Department in operation; and at a special meeting, October 25, 1859, it was decided to re-open the University in September, 1860 Mr Dean had resigned as Chancellor prior to this meeting, and Silas Totten, D. D , LL D., was elected President, at a salary of $2,000, and his term commenced June, 1860

At the annual meeting, June 28, 1860, a full Faculty was appointed, and the University re-opened, under this new organization, September 19, 1860 (third Wednesday), and at this date the actual existence of the University may be said to commence

August 19, 1862. Dr. Totten having resigned, Prof Oliver M Spencer was elected President and the honorary degree of Doctor of Laws was conferred upon Judge Samuel F Miller, of Keokuk.

At the commencement, in June, 1863, was the first class of graduates in the Collegiate Department

The Board of Education was abolished March 19, 1864, and the office of Superintendent of Public Instruction was restored; the General Assembly resumed control of the subject of education, and on March 21, an act was approved for the government of the University. It was substantially the same as the former law, but provided that the Governor should be ex officio President of the Board of Trustees   Until 1858, the Superintendent of Public Instruction had been ex officio President. During the period of the Board of Education, the University Trustees were elected by it, and elected their own President.

President Spencer was granted leave of absence from April 10, 1866, for fifteen months, to visit Europe; and Prof. Nathan R. Leonard was elected President *pro tem.*

The North Hall was completed late in 1866.

At the annual meeting in June, 1867, the resignation of President Spencer (absent in Europe) was accepted, and Prof. Leonard continued as President *pro tem.*, until March 4, 1868, when James Black, D. D., Vice President of Washington and Jefferson College, Penn , was elected President. Dr Black entered upon his duties in September, 1868.

The Law Department was established in June, 1868, and, in September following, an arrangement was perfected with the Iowa Law School, at Des Moines, which had been in successful operation for three years, under the management of Messrs George G. Wright, Chester C Cole and William G Hammond, by which that institution was transferred to Iowa City and merged in the Law Department of the University. The Faculty of this department consisted of the President of the University, Hon Wm. G. Hammond, Resident Professor and Principal of the Department, and Professors G. G. Wright and C. C. Cole.

Nine students entered at the commencement of the first term, and during the year ending June, 1877, there were 103 students in this department

At a special meeting of the Board, on the 17th of September, 1868, a Committee was appointed to consider the expediency of establishing a Medical Department. This Committee reported at once in favor of the proposition, the Faculty to consist of the President of the University and seven Professors, and recommended that, if practicable, the new department should be opened at the commencement of the University year, in 1869–70. At this meeting, Hon Ezekiel Clark was elected Treasurer of the University

By an act of the General Assembly, approved April 11, 1870, the "Board of Regents" was instituted as the governing power of the University, and since that time it has been the fundamental law of the institution. The Board of Regents held its first meeting June 28, 1870. Wm. J. Haddock was elected Secretary, and Mr. Clark, Treasurer

Dr. Black tendered his resignation as President, at a special meeting of the Board, held August 18, 1870, to take effect on the 1st of December following. His resignation was accepted

The South Hall having been fitted up for the purpose, the first term of the Medical Department was opened October 24, 1870, and continued until March, 1871, at which time there were three graduates and thirty-nine students

March 1, 1871, Rev. George Thacher was elected President of the University. Mr. Thacher accepted, entered upon his duties April 1st, and was formally inaugurated at the annual meeting in June, 1861.

In June, 1874, the "Chair of Military Instruction" was established, and the President of the United States was requested to detail an officer to perform its duties. In compliance with this request, Lieut. A. D. Schenck, Second Artillery, U S A, was detailed as "Professor of Military Science and Tactics," at Iowa State University, by order of the War Department, August 26, 1874, who reported for duty on the 10th of September following. Lieut. Schenck was relieved by Lieut James Chester, Third Artillery, January 1, 1877

Treasurer Clark resigned November 3, 1875, and John N. Coldren elected in his stead.

At the annual meeting, in 1876, a Department of Homœopathy was established.

In March, 1877, a resolution was adopted affiliating the High Schools of the State with the University

In June, 1877, Dr. Thacher's connection with the University was terminated, and C. W. Slagle, a member of the Board of Regents, was elected President.

In 1872, the ex officio membership of the Superintendent of Public Instruction was abolished; but it was restored in 1876. Following is a catalogue of the officers of this important institution, from 1847 to 1878:

TRUSTEES OR REGENTS.

PRESIDENTS.

	FROM	TO
James Harlan, Superintendent Public Instruction, ex officio..	1847	1848
Thomas H Benton, Jr,, Superintendent Public Instruction, ex officio	1848	1854
James D Eads, Superintendent Public Instruction, ex officio . . .	1854	1857
Maturin L Fisher, Superintendent Public Instruction, ex officio	1857	1858
Amos Dean, Chancellor, ex officio	1858	1859
Thomas H Benton, Jr	1859	1863
Francis Springer	1863	1864
William M Stone, Governor, ex officio	1864	1868
Samuel Merrill, Governor ex officio	1868	1872
Cyrus C Carpenter, Governor, ex officio	1872	1876
Samuel J Kirkwood, Governor, ex officio.	1876	1877
Joshua G Newbold, Governor, ex officio	1877	1878
John H Gear	1878	. ...

VICE PRESIDENTS.

	FROM	TO
Silas Foster	1847	1851
Robert Lucas	1851	1853
Edward Connelly	1854	1855
Moses J Morsman	1855	1858

SECRETARIES

Hugh D Downey	1847	1851
Anson Hart	1851	1857
Elijah Sells	1857	1858
Anson Hart	1858	1864
William J. Haddock	1864	

TREASURERS

Morgan Reno, State Treasurer, ex officio	1847	1850
Israel Kister, State Treasurer ex officio.	1850	1852
Martin L Morris, State Treasurer, ex officio	1852	1855
Henry W Lathrop	1855	1862
William Crum	1862	1868
Ezekiel Clark	1868	1876
John N. Coldren	1876	...

PRESIDENTS OF THE UNIVERSITY

Amos Dean, LL D.	1855	1858
Silas Totten, D D , LL. D	1860	1862
Oliver M Spencer, D D.*	1862	1867
James Black, D D	1868	1870
George Thacher, D D.	1871	1877
C W. Slagle	1877	

The present educational corps of the University consists of the President, nine Professors in the Collegiate Department, one Professor and six Instructors in Military Science ; Chancellor, three Professors and four Lecturers in the Law Department; eight Professor Demonstrators of Anatomy; Prosector of Surgery and two Lecturers in the Medical Department, and two Professors in the Homœopathic Medical Department

STATE HISTORICAL SOCIETY.

By act of the General Assembly, approved January 28, 1857, a State Historical Society was provided for in connection with the University. At the commencement, an appropriation of $250 was made, to be expended in collecting, embodying, and preserving in an authentic form a library of books, pamphlets, charts, maps, manuscripts, papers, paintings, statuary, and other materials illustrative of the history of Iowa ; and with the further object to rescue from oblivion the memory of the early pioneers ; to obtain and preserve various accounts of their exploits, perils and hardy adventures ; to secure facts and statements relative to the history and genius, and progress and decay of the Indian tribes of Iowa ; to exhibit faithfully the antiquities and past and present resources of the State, to aid in the publication of such collections of the Society as shall from time to time be deemed of value and interest ; to aid in binding its books, pamphlets, manuscripts and papers, and in defraying other necessary incidental expenses of the Society.

There was appropriated by law to this institution, till the General Assembly shall otherwise direct, the sum of $500 per annum. The Society is under the management of a Board of Curators, consisting of eighteen persons, nine of whom are appointed by the Governor, and nine elected by the members of the Society. The Curators receive no compensation for their services. The annual meeting is provided for by law, to be held at Iowa City on Monday preceding the last Wednesday in June of each year.

The State Historical Society has published a series of very valuable collections, including history, biography, sketches, reminiscences, etc., with quite a large number of finely engraved portraits of prominent and early settlers, under the title of " Annals of Iowa."

THE PENITENTIARY.

Located at Fort Madison, Lee County

The first act of the Territorial Legislature, relating to a Penitentiary in Iowa, was approved January 25, 1839, the fifth section of which authorized the Governor to draw the sum of $20,000 appropriated by an act of Congress approved July 7, 1838, for public buildings in the Territory of Iowa It provided for a Board of Directors of three persons elected by the Legislature, who should direct the building of the Penitentiary, which should be located within one mile of the public square, in the town of Fort Madison, Lee County, provided Fort Madison should deed to the directors a tract of land suitable for a site, and assign them, by contract, a spring or stream of water for the use of the Penitentiary. To the Directors was also given the power of appointing the Warden, the latter to appoint his own assistants

The first Directors appointed were John S. David and John Claypole They made their first report to the Legislative Council November 9, 1839. The citizens of the town of Fort Madison had executed a deed conveying ten acres of land for the building site. Amos Ladd was appointed Superintendent of the building June 5, 1839. The building was designed of sufficient capacity to contain one hundred and thirty eight convicts, and estimated to cost $55,933 90. It was begun on the 9th of July, 1839; the main building and Warden's house were completed in the Fall of 1841. Other additions were made from time to time till the building and arrangements were all complete according to the plan of the Directors.   It has answered the purpose of the State as a Penitentiary for more than thirty years, and during that period many items of practical experience in prison management have been gained.

It has long been a problem how to conduct prisons, and deal with what are called the criminal classes generally, so as to secure their best good and best subserve the interests of the State   Both objects must be taken into consideration in any humanitarian view of the subject.   This problem is not yet solved, but Iowa has adopted the progressive and enlightened policy of humane treatment of prisoners and the utilization of their labor for their own support.   The labor of the convicts in the Iowa Penitentiary, as in most others in the United States, is let out to contractors, who pay the State a certain stipulated amount therefor, the State furnishing the shops, tools and machinery, as well as the supervision necessary to preserve order and discipline in the prison.

While this is an improvement upon the old solitary confinement system, it still falls short of an enlightened reformatory system that in the future will treat the criminal for mental disease and endeavor to restore him to usefulness in the community. ' The objections urged against the contract system of disposing of the labor of prisoners, that it brings the labor of honest citizens into competition with convict labor at reduced prices, and is disadvantageous to the State, are not without force, and the system will have no place in the prisons of the future.

It is right that the convict should labor.   He should not be allowed to live in idleness at public expense   Honest men labor , why should not they? Honest men are entitled to the fruits of their toil; why should not the convict as well?   The convict is sent to the Penitentiary to secure public safety   The State deprives him of his liberty to accomplish this purpose and to punish him for violations of law, but, having done this, the State wrongs both itself and the criminal by confiscating his earnings , because it deprives his family of what justly belongs to them, and an enlightened civilization will ere long demand that the prisoner in the penitentiary, after paying a fair price for his board, is as justly entitled to his net earnings as the good citizen outside its walls, and his family, if he has one, should be entitled to draw his earnings or stated portion of them at stated periods   If he has no family, then if his net earnings should be set aside to his credit and paid over to him at the expiration of his term of imprisonment, he would not be turned out upon the cold charities of a somewhat pharisaical world, penniless, with the brand of the convict upon his brow, with no resource save to sink still deeper in crime. Let Iowa, " The Beautiful Land," be first to recognize the rights of its convicts to the fruits of their labor ; keep their children from the alms-house, and place a powerful incentive before them to become good citizens when they return to the busy world again.

ADDITIONAL PENITENTIARY.

Located at Anamosa, Jones County.

By an act of the Fourteenth General Assembly, approved April 23, 1872, William Ure, Foster L. Downing and Martin Heisey were constituted Commissioners to locate and provide for the erection and control of an additional Penitentiary for the State of Iowa.   These Commissioners met on the 4th of the following June, at Anamosa, Jones County, and selected a site donated by the citizens, within the limits of the city.   L. W. Foster & Co , architects, of Des Moines, furnished the plan, drawings and specifications, and work was commenced on the building on the 28th day of September, 1872.   May 13, 1873, twenty convicts were transferred to Anamosa from the Fort Madison Penitentiary.   The entire enclosure includes fifteen acres, with a frontage of 663 feet.

IOWA HOSPITAL FOR THE INSANE.

Mount Pleasant, Henry County.

By an act of the General Assembly of Iowa, approved January 24, 1855, $4,425 were appropriated for the purchase of a site, and $50,000 for building an Insane Hospital, and the Governor (Grimes), Edward Johnston, of Lee County, and Charles S. Blake, of Henry County, were appointed to locate the institution and superintend the erection of the building.   These Commissioners located the institution at Mt. Pleasant, Henry County. A plan for a building designed to accommodate 300 patients, drawn by Dr Bell, of Massachusetts, was accepted, and in October work was commenced under the superintendence of Mr. Henry Winslow.   Up to February 25, 1858, and including an appropriation made on that date, the Legislature had appropriated $258,555.67 to this institution, but the building was not finished ready for occupancy by patients until March 1, 1861.   The Trustees were Maturin L. Fisher, President, Farmersburg ; Samuel McFarland, Secretary, Mt. Pleasant ; D. L.

McGugin, Keokuk; G. W. Kincaid, Muscatine; J. D. Elbert, Keosauqua; John B. Lash and Harpin Riggs, Mt. Pleasant   Richard J. Patterson, M. D., of Ohio, was elected Superintendent; Dwight C. Dewey, M. D, Assistant Physician; Henry Winslow, Steward; Mrs Catharine Winslow, Matron. The Hospital was formally opened March 6, 1861, and one hundred patients were admitted within three months.   About 1865, Dr. Mark Ranney became Superintendent   April 18, 1876, a portion of the hospital building was destroyed by fire.   From the opening of the Hospital to the close of October, 1877, 3,584 patients had been admitted. Of these, 1,141 were discharged recovered, 505 discharged improved, 589 discharged unimproved, and 1 died; total discharged, 2,976, leaving 608 inmates   During this period, there were 1,384 females admitted, whose occupation was registered "domestic duties;" 122, no occupation; 25, female teachers, 11, seamstresses; and 25, servants. Among the males were 916 farmers, 394 laborers, 205 without occupation, 39 cabinet makers, 23 brewers, 31 clerks, 26 merchants, 12 preachers, 18 shoemakers, 13 students, 14 tailors, 13 teachers, 14 agents, 17 masons, 7 lawyers, 7 physicians, 4 saloon keepers, 3 salesmen, 2 artists, and 1 editor.   The products of the farm and garden, in 1876, amounted to $13,721.26.

   Trustees, 1877 —T. Whiting, President, Mt Pleasant; Mrs. E M Elliott, Secretary, Mt Pleasant; William C. Evans, West Liberty; L E Fellows, Lansing; and Samuel Klein, Keokuk; Treasurer, M. Edwards, Mt Pleasant.

   Resident Officers.—Mark Ranney, M. D., Medical Superintendent; H. M. Bassett, M D. First Assistant Physician; M Riordan, M. D., Second Assistant Physician; Jennie McCowen, M. D, Third Assistant Physician; J W Henderson, Steward. Mrs. Martha W. Ranney, Matron; Rev. Milton Sutton, Chaplain.

HOSPITAL FOR THE INSANE.

Independence, Buchanan County.

   In the Winter of 1867–8, a bill providing for an additional Hospital for the Insane was passed by the Legislature, and an appropriation of $125,000 was made for that purpose   Maturin L. Fisher, of Clayton County; E G. Morgan, of Webster County, and Albert Clark, of Buchanan County, were appointed Commissioners to locate and supervise the erection of the Building   Mr Clark died about a year after his appointment, and Hon. G. W. Bemis, of Independence, was appointed to fill the vacancy.

   The Commissioners met and commenced their labors on the 8th day of June, 1868, at Independence.   The act under which they were appointed required them to select the most eligible and desirable location, of not less than 320 acres, within two miles of the city of Independence, that might be offered by the citizens free of charge to the State.   Several such tracts were offered, but the Commissioners finally selected the south half of southwest quarter of Section 5; the north half of northeast quarter of Section 7; the north half of northwest quarter of Section 8, and the north half of northeast quarter of Section 8, all in Township 88 north, Range 9 west of the Fifth Principal Meridian. This location is on the west side of the Wapsipinicon River, and about a mile from its banks, and about the same distance from Independence

   Col. S. V. Shipman, of Madison, Wis, was employed to prepare plans, specifications and drawings of the building, which, when completed, were submitted to Dr. M. Ranney, Superintendent of the Hospital at Mount Pleasant, who suggested several improvements.   The contract for erecting the building was awarded to Mr. David Armstrong, of Dubuque, for $88,114 The contract was signed November 7, 1868, and Mr Armstrong at once commenced work. Mr George Josselyn was appointed to superintend the work. The main buildings were constructed of dressed limestone, from the quarries at Anamosa and Farley. The basements are of the local granite worked from the immense boulders found in large quantities in this portion of the State

In 1872, the building was so far completed that the Commissioners called the first meeting of the Trustees, on the 10th day of July of that year. These Trustees were Maturin L. Fisher, Mrs P. A. Appleman, T. W. Fawcett, C. C Parker, E. G. Morgan, George W. Bemis and John M Boggs. This board was organized, on the day above mentioned, by the election of Hon. M. L Fisher, President, Rev J G. Boggs, Secretary, and George W Bemis, Treasurer, and, after adopting preliminary measures for organizing the local government of the hospital, adjourned to the first Wednesday of the following September. A few days before this meeting, Mr. Boggs died of malignant fever, and Dr. John G. House was appointed to fill the vacancy. Dr. House was elected Secretary. At this meeting, Albert Reynolds, M D , was elected Superintendent; George Josselyn, Steward, and Mrs. Anna B. Josselyn, Matron. September 4, 1873, Dr. Willis Butterfield was elected Assistant Physician The building was ready for occupancy April 21, 1873.

In the Spring of 1876, a contract was made with Messrs. Mackay & Lundy, of Independence, for furnishing materials for building the outside walls of the two first sections of the south wing, next to the center building, for $6,250. The carpenter work on the fourth and fifth stories of the center building was completed during the same year, and the wards were furnished and occupied by patients in the Fall.

In 1877, the south wing was built, but it will not be completed ready for occupancy until next Spring or Summer (1878).

October 1, 1877, the Superintendent reported 322 patients in this hospital, and it is now overcrowded

The Board of Trustees at present (1878) are as follows: Maturin L. Fisher, President, Farmersburg; John G. House, M. D , Secretary, Independence; Wm G. Donnan, Treasurer, Independence , Erastus G Morgan, Fort Dodge; Mrs Prudence A. Appleman, Clermont; and Stephen E. Robinson, M. D , West Union.

RESIDENT OFFICERS.

Albert Reynolds, M D , Superintendent; G. H. Hill, M. D., Assistant Physician, Noyes Appleman, Steward, Mrs. Lucy M. Gray, Matron

IOWA COLLEGE FOR THE BLIND.
Vinton, Benton County.

In August, 1852, Prof. Samuel Bacon, himself blind, established an Institution for the Instruction of the Blind of Iowa, at Keokuk.

By act of the General Assembly, entitled " An act to establish an Asylum for the Blind," approved January 18, 1853, the institution was adopted by the State, removed to Iowa City, February 3d, and opened for the reception of pupils April 4, 1853, free to all the blind in the State.

The first Board of Trustees were James D Eads, President; George W McClary, Secretary; James H. Gower, Treasurer; Martin L. Morris, Stephen Hempstead, Morgan Reno and John McCaddon. The Board appointed Prof.

Samuel Bacon, Principal; T. J. McGittigen, Teacher of Music, and Mrs Sarah K. Bacon, Matron. Twenty-three pupils were admitted during the first term

In his first report, made in 1854, Prof Bacon suggested that the name should be changed from "Asylum for the Blind," to that of "Institution for the Instruction of the Blind " This was done in 1855, when the General Assembly made an annual appropriation for the College of $55 per quarter for each pupil. This was subsequently changed to $3,000 per annum, and a charge of $25 as an admission fee for each pupil, which sum, with the amounts realized from the sale of articles manufactured by the blind pupils, proved sufficient for the expenses of the institution during Mr. Bacon's administration Although Mr Bacon was blind, he was a fine scholar and an economical manager, and had founded the Blind Asylum at Jacksonville, Illinois. As a mathematician he had few superiors.

On the 8th of May, 1858, the Trustees met at Vinton, and made arrangements for securing the donation of $5,000 made by the citizens of that town.

In June of that year, a quarter section of land was donated for the College, by John W O. Webb and others, and the Trustees adopted a plan for the erection of a suitable building In 1860, the plan was modified, and the contract for enclosing let to Messrs. Finkbine & Lovelace, for $10,420.

In August, 1862, the building was so far completed that the goods and furniture of the institution were removed from Iowa City to Vinton, and early in October, the school was opened there with twenty-four pupils. At this time, Rev. Orlando Clark was Principal

In August, 1864, a new Board of Trustees were appointed by the Legislature, consisting of James McQuin, President; Reed Wilkinson, Secretary; Jas Chapin, Treasurer; Robert Gilchrist, Elijah Sells and Joseph Dysart, organized and made important changes. Rev. Reed Wilkinson succeeded Mr. Clark as Principal Mrs. L. S. B. Wilkinson and Miss Amelia Butler were appointed Assistant Teachers; Mrs. N. A. Morton, Matron.

Mr. Wilkinson resigned in June, 1867, and Gen James L Geddes was appointed in his place. In September, 1869, Mr Geddes retired, and was succeeded by Prof S A Knapp. Mrs S C Lawton was appointed Matron, and was succeeded by Mrs M. A. Knapp Prof. Knapp resigned July 1, 1875, and Prof. Orlando Clark was elected Principal, who died April 2, 1876, and was succeeded by John B. Parmalee, who retired in July, 1877, when the present incumbent, Rev. Robert Carothers, was elected.

Trustees, 1877–8.—Jeremiah L Gay, President, S. H. Watson, Treasurer; H C Piatt, Jacob Springer, C L. Flint and P F Sturgis.

Faculty—Principal, Rev. Robert Carothers, A. M ; Matron, Mrs. Emeline E. Carothers, Teachers, Thomas F McCune, A. B., Miss Grace A. Hill, Mrs. C A Spencer, Miss Mary Baker, Miss C. R Miller, Miss Lorana Mattice, Miss A. M McCutcheon; Musical Director, S O Spencer

The Legislative Committee who visited this institution in 1878 expressed their astonishment at the vast expenditure of money in proportion to the needs of the State. The structure is well built, and the money properly expended; yet it was enormously beyond the necessities of the State, and shows an utter disregard of the fitness of things. The Committee could not understand why $282,000 should have been expended for a massive building covering about two and a half acres for the accommodation of 130 people, costing over eight thousand dollars a year to heat it, and costing the State about five hundred dollars a year for each pupil.

INSTITUTION FOR THE DEAF AND DUMB.

Council Bluffs, Pottawattomie County

The Iowa Institution for the Deaf and Dumb was established at Iowa City by an act of the General Assembly, approved January 24, 1855.   The number of deaf mutes then in the State was 301; the number attending the Institution, 50.   The first Board of Trustees were: Hon. Samuel J Kirkwood, Hon. E. Sells, W. Penn Clarke, J. P. Wood, H. D. Downey, William Crum, W E. Ijams, Principal.   On the resignation of Mr. Ijams, in 1862, the Board appointed in his stead Mr Benjamin Talbot, for nine years a teacher in the Ohio Institution for the Deaf and Dumb.   Mr. Talbot was ardently devoted to the interests of the institution and a faithful worker for the unfortunate class under his charge.

A strong effort was made, in 1866, to remove this important institution to Des Moines, but it was located permanently at Council Bluffs, and a building rented for its use   In 1868, Commissioners were appointed to locate a site for, and to superintend the erection of, a new building, for which the Legislature appropriated $125,000 to commence the work of construction   The Commissioners selected ninety acres of land about two miles south of the city of Council Bluffs.   The main building and one wing were completed October 1, 1870, and immediately occupied by the Institution.   February 25, 1877, the main building and east wing were destroyed by fire; and August 6 following, the roof of the new west wing was blown off and the walls partially demolished by a tornado.   At the time of the fire, about one hundred and fifty pupils were in attendance   After the fire, half the classes were dismissed and the number of scholars reduced to about seventy, and in a week or two the school was in running order.

The Legislative Committee which visited this Institution in the Winter of 1857–8 was not well pleased with the condition of affairs, and reported that the building (west wing) was a disgrace to the State and a monument of unskillful workmanship, and intimated rather strongly that some reforms in management were very essential

Trustees, 1877–8.—Thomas Officer, President; N. P. Dodge, Treasurer, Paul Lange, William Orr, J. W. Cattell

Superintendent, Benjamin Talbot, M. A.   Teachers, Edwin Southwick, Conrad S. Zorbaugh, John A Gillespie, John A. Kennedy, Ellen J. Israel, Ella J Brown, Mrs H. R. Gillespie; Physician, H W Hart, M. D ; Steward, N. A. Taylor, Matron, Mary B Swan.

SOLDIERS' ORPHANS' HOMES

Davenport, Cedar Falls, Glenwood.

The movement which culminated in the establishment of this beneficent institution was originated by Mrs. Annie Wittenmeyer, during the civil war of 1861–65.   This noble and patriotic lady called a convention at Muscatine, on the 7th of October 1863, for the purpose of devising measures for the support and education of the orphan children of the brave sons of Iowa, who had fallen in defense of national honor and integrity.   So great was the public interest in the movement that there was a large representation from all parts of the State on the day named, and an association was organized called the Iowa State Orphan Asylum.

The first officers were · President, William M Stone ; Vice Presidents, Mrs G. G. Wright, Mrs. R L Cadle, Mrs. J. T. Hancock, John R. Needham, J W. Cattell, Mrs. Mary M. Bagg ; Recording Secretary, Miss Mary Kibben, Corresponding Secretary, Miss M. E. Shelton ; Treasurer, N. H. Brainerd; Board of Trustees, Mrs. Annie Wittenmeyer, Mrs C B Darwin, Mrs. D. T. Newcomb, Mrs. L. B Stephens, O. Fayville, E. H. Williams, T. S. Parvin, Mrs. Shields, Caleb Baldwin, C. C. Cole, Isaac Pendleton, H. C. Henderson.

The first meeting of the Trustees was held February 14, 1864, in the Representative Hall, at Des Moines.   Committees from both branches of the General Assembly were present and were invited to participate in their deliberations Gov Kirkwood suggested that a home for disabled soldiers should be connected with the Asylum.   Arrangements were made for raising funds.

At the next meeting, in Davenport, in March, 1864, the Trustees decided to commence operations at once, and a committee, of which Mr. Howell, of Keokuk, was Chairman, was appointed to lease a suitable building, solicit donations, and procure suitable furniture.   This committee secured a large brick building in Lawrence, Van Buren County, and engaged Mr. Fuller, of Mt. Pleasant, as Steward.

At the annual meeting, in Des Moines, in June, 1864, Mrs. C. B. Baldwin, Mrs. G G. Wright, Mrs. Dr. Horton, Miss Mary E Shelton and Mr. George Sherman were appointed a committee to furnish the building and take all necessary steps for opening the "Home," and notice was given that at the next meeting of the Association, a motion would be made to change the name of the Institution to Iowa Orphans' Home.

The work of preparation was conducted so vigorously that on the 13th day of July following, the Executive Committee announced that they were ready to receive the children   In three weeks twenty-one were admitted, and the number constantly increased, so that, in a little more than six months from the time of opening, there were seventy children admitted, and twenty more applications, which the Committee had not acted upon—all orphans of soldiers

Miss M. Elliott, of Washington, was appointed Matron. She resigned, in February, 1865, and was succeeded by Mrs. E. G. Platt, of Fremont County.

The "Home" was sustained by the voluntary contributions of the people, until 1866, when it was assumed by the State   In that year, the General Assembly provided for the location of several such "Homes" in the different counties, and which were established at Davenport, Scott County; Cedar Falls, Black Hawk County, and at Glenwood, Mills County

The Board of Trustees elected by the General Assembly had the oversight and management of the Soldiers' Orphans' Homes of the State, and consisted of one person from each county in which such Home was located, and one for the State at large, who held their office two years, or until their successors were elected and qualified.   An appropriation of $10 per month for each orphan actually supported was made by the General Assembly.

The Home in Cedar Falls was organized in 1865, and an old hotel building was fitted up for it   Rufus C., Mary L. and Emma L. Bauer were the first children received, in October, and by January, 1866, there were ninety-six inmates.

October 12, 1869, the Home was removed to a large brick building, about two miles west of Cedar Falls, and was very prosperous for several years, but in 1876, the General Assembly established a State Normal School at Cedar Falls and appropriated the buildings and grounds for that purpose.

By "An act to provide for the organization and support of an asylum at Glenwood, in Mills County, for feeble minded children," approved March 17, 1876, the buildings and grounds used by the Soldiers' Orphans' Home at that place were appropriated for this purpose. By another act, approved March 15, 1876, the soldiers' orphans, then at the Homes at Glenwood and Cedar Falls, were to be removed to the Home at Davenport within ninety days thereafter, and the Board of Trustees of the Home were authorized to receive other indigent children into that institution, and provide for their education in industrial pursuits.

STATE NORMAL SCHOOL.

Cedar Falls, Black Hawk County.

Chapter 129 of the laws of the Sixteenth General Assembly, in 1876, established a State Normal School at Cedar Falls, Black Hawk County, and required the Trustees of the Soldiers' Orphans' Home to turn over the property in their charge to the Directors of the new institution

The Board of Directors met at Cedar Falls June 7, 1876, and duly organized by the election of H. C. Hemenway, President; J. J. Toleston, Secretary, and E. Townsend, Treasurer. The Board of Trustees of the Soldiers' Orphans' Home met at the same time for the purpose of turning over to the Directors the property of that institution, which was satisfactorily done and properly receipted for as required by law. At this meeting, Prof. J. C. Gilchrist was elected Principal of the School.

On the 12th of July, 1876, the Board again met, when executive and teachers' committees were appointed and their duties assigned. A Steward and a Matron were elected, and their respective duties defined.

The buildings and grounds were repaired and fitted up as well as the appropriation would admit, and the first term of the school opened September 6, 1876, commencing with twenty-seven and closing with eighty-seven students. The second term closed with eighty-six, and one hundred and six attended during the third term.

The following are the Board of Directors, Board of Officers and Faculty:

Board of Directors —H C. Hemenway, Cedar Falls, President, term expires 1882; L D. Lewelling, Salem, Henry County, 1878, W. A. Stow, Hamburg, Fremont County, 1878; S G. Smith, Newton, Jasper County, 1880; E H Thayer, Clinton, Clinton County, 1880; G S. Robinson, Storm Lake, Buena Vista County, 1882

Board of Officers.—J. J Toleston, Secretary; E. Townsend, Treasurer; William Pattes, Steward; Mrs. P. A. Schermerhorn, Matron—all of Cedar Falls

Faculty.—J. C. Gilchrist, A. M., Principal, Professer of Mental and Moral Philosophy and Didactics; M W. Bartlett, A. M., Professor of Languages and Natural Science; D. S. Wright, A. M., Professor of Mathematics; Miss Frances L. Webster, Teacher of Geography and History; E. W. Burnham, Professor of Music

ASYLUM FOR FEEBLE MINDED CHILDREN.

Glenwood, Mills County.

Chapter 152 of the laws of the Sixteenth General Assembly, approved March 17, 1876, provided for the establishment of an asylum for feeble minded children at Glenwood, Mills County, and the buildings and grounds of the

Soldiers' Orphans' Home at that place were to be used for that purpose. The asylum was placed under the management of three Trustees, one at least of whom should be a resident of Mills County   Children between the ages of 7 and 18 years are admitted   Ten dollars per month for each child actually supported by the State was appropriated by the act, and $2,000 for salaries of officers and teachers for two years.

Hon J W. Cattell, of Polk County ; A J Russell, of Mills County, and W. S Robertson, were appointed Trustees, who held their first meeting at Glenwood, April 26, 1876   Mr Robertson was elected President, Mr Russell, Treasurer, and Mr. Cattell, Secretary.   The Trustees found the house and farm which had been turned over to them in a shamefully dilapidated condition   The fences were broken down and the lumber destroyed or carried away, the windows broken, doors off their hinges, floors broken and filthy in the extreme, cellars reeking with offensive odors from decayed vegetables, and every conceivable variety of filth and garbage ; drains obstructed, cisterns broken, pump demoralized, wind-mill broken, roof leaky, and the whole property in the worst possible condition   It was the first work of the Trustees to make the house tenable.   This was done under the direction of Mr Russell   At the request of the Trustees, Dr. Charles T. Wilbur, Superintendent of the Illinois Asylum, visited Glenwood, and made many valuable suggestions, and gave them much assistance

O W Archibald, M. D., of Glenwood, was appointed Superintendent, and soon after was appointed Secretary of the Board, vice Cattell, resigned. Mrs S. A. Archibald was appointed Matron, and Miss Maud M. Archibald, Teacher.

The Institution was opened September 1, 1876 , the first pupil admitted September 4, and the school was organized September 10, with only five pupils, which number had, in November, 1877, increased to eighty-seven   December 1, 1876, Miss Jennie Van Dorin, of Fairfield, was employed as a teacher and in the Spring of 1877, Miss Sabina J. Archibald was also employed

THE REFORM SCHOOL.
Eldora, Hardin County.

By "An act to establish and organize a State Reform School for Juvenile Offenders," approved March 31, 1868, the General Assembly established a State Reform School at Salem, Lee (Henry) County , provided for a Board of Trustees, to consist of one person from each Congressional District. For the purpose of immediately opening the school, the Trustees were directed to accept the proposition of the Trustees of White's Iowa Manual Labor Institute, at Salem, and lease, for not more than ten years, the lands, buildings, etc., of the Institute, and at once proceed to prepare for and open a reform school as a temporary establishment.

The contract for fitting up the buildings was let to Clark & Haddock, September 21, 1868, and on the 7th of October following, the first inmate was received from Jasper County   The law provided for the admission of children of both sexes under 18 years of age   In 1876, this was amended, so that they are now received at ages over 7 and under 16 years.

April 19, 1872, the Trustees were directed to make a permanent location for the school, and $45,000 was appropriated for the erection of the necessary buildings.   The Trustees were further directed, as soon as practicable, to organize a school for girls in the buildings where the boys were then kept.

The Trustees located the school at Eldora, Hardin County. and in the Code of 1873, it is permanently located there by law.

The institution is managed by five Trustees, who are paid mileage, but no compensation for their services.

The object is the reformation of the children of both sexes, under the age of 16 years and over 7 years of age, and the law requires that the Trustees shall require the boys and girls under their charge to be instructed in piety and morality, and in such branches of useful knowledge as are adapted to their age and capacity, and in some regular course of labor, either mechanical, manufacturing or agricultural, as is best suited to their age, strength, disposition and capacity, and as may seem best adapted to secure the reformation and future benefit of the boys and girls

A boy or girl committed to the State Reform School is there kept, disciplined, instructed, employed and governed, under the direction of the Trustees, until he or she arrives at the age of majority, or is bound out, reformed or legally discharged. The binding out or discharge of a boy or girl as reformed, or having arrived at the age of majority, *is a complete release* from all penalties incurred by conviction of the offense for which he or she was committed.

This is one step in the right direction In the future, however, still further advances will be made, and the right of every individual to the fruits of their labor, even while restrained for the public good, will be recognized

FISH HATCHING ESTABLISHMENT.

Near Anamosa, Jones County

The Fifteenth General Assembly, in 1874, passed " An act to provide for the appointment of a Board of Fish Commissioners for the construction of Fishways for the protection and propagation of Fish," also ' An act to provide for furnishing the rivers and lakes with fish and fish spawn " This act appropriated $3,000 for the purpose. In accordance with the provisions of the first act above mentioned, on the 9th of April, 1874, S B Evans of Ottumwa, Wapello County , B. F. Shaw of Jones County, and Charles A Haines, of Black Hawk County, were appointed to be Fish Commissioners by the Governor · These Commissioners met at Des Moines, May 10, 1874, and organized by the election of Mr. Evans, President; Mr. Shaw, Secretary and Superintendent, and Mr. Haines, Treasurer.

The State was partitioned into three districts or divisions to enable the Commissioners to better superintend the construction of fishways as required by law That part of the State lying south of the Chicago, Rock Island & Pacific Railroad was placed under the especial supervision of Mr. Evans , that part between that railroad and the Iowa Division of the Illinois Central Railroad, Mr Shaw, and all north of the Illinois Central Railroad, Mr Haines At this meeting, the Superintendent was authorized to build a State Hatching House , to procure the spawn of valuable fish adapted to the waters of Iowa , hatch and prepare the young fish for distribution, and assist in putting them into the waters of the State.

In compliance with these instructions, Mr. Shaw at once commenced work, and in the Summer of 1874, erected a " State Hatching House" near Anamosa, 20x40 feet, two stories , the second story being designed for a tenement , the first story being the "hatching room." The hatching troughs are supplied with water from a magnificent spring four feet deep and about ten feet in diameter, affording an abundant and unfailing supply of pure running water During the first year, from May 10, 1874, to May 10, 1875, the Commissioners distributed within the State 100,000 Shad, 300,000 California Salmon, 10,000 Bass, 80,000 Penobscot (Maine) Salmon, 5,000 land-locked Salmon, 20,000 of other species.

By act approved March 10, 1876, the law was amended so that there should be but one instead of three Fish Commissioners, and B. F Shaw was appointed, and the Commissioner was authorized to purchase twenty acres of land, on which the State Hatching House was located near Anamosa

In the Fall of 1876, Commissioner Shaw gathered from the sloughs of the Mississippi, where they would have been destroyed, over a million and a half of small fish, which were distributed in the various rivers of the State and turned into the Mississippi.

In 1875–6, 533,000 California Salmon, and in 1877, 303,500 Lake Trout were distributed in various rivers and lakes in the State. The experiment of stocking the small streams with brook trout is being tried, and 81,000 of the speckled beauties were distributed in 1877. In 1876, 100,000 young eels were distributed. These came from New York and they are increasing rapidly.

At the close of 1877, there were at least a dozen private fish farms in successful operation in various parts of the State. Commissioner Shaw is enthusiastically devoted to the duties of his office and has performed an important service for the people of the State by his intelligent and successful operations

The Sixteenth General Assembly passed an act in 1878, prohibiting the catching of any kind of fish except Brook Trout from March until June of each year. Some varieties are fit for food only during this period.

THE PUBLIC LANDS.

The grants of public lands made in the State of Iowa, for various purposes, are as follows :

        1   The 500,000 Acre Grant
        2   The 16th Section Grant
        3   The Mortgage School Lands
        4   The University Grant
        5   The Saline Grant
        6.   The Des Moines River Grant
        7   The Des Moines River School Lands
        8   The Swamp Land Grant
        9   The Railroad Grant
       10   The Agricultural College Grant

I.   THE FIVE HUNDRED THOUSAND ACRE GRANT.

When the State was admitted into the Union, she became entitled to 500,000 acres of land by virtue of an act of Congress, approved September 4, 1841, which granted to each State therein specified 500,000 acres of public land for internal improvements ; to each State admitted subsequently to the passage of the act, an amount of land which, with the amount that might have been granted to her as a Territory, would amount to 500,000 acres. All these lands were required to be selected within the limits of the State to which they were granted.

The Constitution of Iowa declares that the proceeds of this grant, together with all lands then granted or to be granted by Congress for the benefit of schools, shall constitute a perpetual fund for the support of schools throughout the State. By an act approved January 15, 1849, the Legislature established a board of School Fund Commissioners, and to that board was confided the selection, care and sale of these lands for the benefit of the School Fund. Until 1855, these Commissioners were subordinate to the Superintendent of Public Instruction, but on the 15th of January of that year, they were clothed with exclusive authority in the management and sale of school lands. The office of School Fund Commissioner was abolished March 23, 1858, and that officer in each county was required to transfer all papers to and make full settlement with the County Judge. By this act, County Judges and Township Trustees were made the agents of the State to control and sell the sixteenth sections; but no further provision was made for the sale of the 500,000 acre grant until April 3d, 1860, when the entire management of the school lands was committed to the Boards of Supervisors of the several counties

II.   THE SIXTEENTH SECTIONS.

By the provisions of the act of Congress admitting Iowa to the Union, there was granted to the new State the sixteenth section in every township, or where that section had been sold, other lands of like amount for the use of schools. The Constitution of the State provides that the proceeds arising from the sale of these sections shall constitute a part of the permanent School Fund   The control and sale of these lands were vested in the School Fund Commissioners of the several counties until March 23, 1858, when they were transferred to the County Judges and Township Trustees, and were finally placed under the supervision of the County Boards of Supervisors in January, 1861.

III.   THE MORTGAGE SCHOOL LANDS.

These do not belong to any of the grants of land proper. They are lands that have been mortgaged to the school fund, and became school lands when bid off by the State by virtue of a law passed in 1862. Under the provisions of the law regulating the management and investment of the permanent school fund, persons desiring loans from that fund are required to secure the payment thereof with interest at ten per cent. per annum, by promissory notes endorsed by two good sureties and by mortgage on unincumbered real estate, which must be situated in the county where the loan is made, and which must be valued by three appraisers   Making these loans and taking the required securities was made the duty of the County Auditor, who was required to report to the Board of Supervisors at each meeting thereof, all notes, mortgages and abstracts of title connected with the school fund, for examination.

When default was made of payment of money so secured by mortgage, and no arrangement made for extension of time as the law provides, the Board of Supervisors were authorized to bring suit and prosecute it with diligence to secure said fund; and in action in favor of the county for the use of the school fund, an injunction may issue without bonds, and in any such action, when service is made by publication, default and judgment may be entered and enforced without bonds. In case of sale of land on execution founded on any such mortgage, the attorney of the board, or other person duly authorized, shall, on behalf of the State or county for the use of said fund, bid such sum as the interests of said fund may require, and if struck off to the State the land shall be held and disposed of as the other lands belonging to the fund   These lands are known as the Mortgage School Lands, and reports of them, including description and amount, are required to be made to the State Land Office.

IV   UNIVERSITY LANDS.

By act of Congress, July 20, 1840, a quantity of land not exceeding two entire townships was reserved in the Territory of Iowa for the use and support of a university within said Territory when it should become a State.   This land was to be located in tracts of not less than an entire section, and could be used for no other purpose than that designated in the grant   In an act supplemental to that for the admission of Iowa, March 3, 1845, the grant was renewed, and it was provided that the lands should be used "solely for the purpose of such university, in such manner as the Legislature may prescribe."

Under this grant there were set apart and approved by the Secretary of the Treasury, for the use of the State, the following lands ·

		ACRES
In the Iowa City Land District, Feb 26, 1849		20,150 49
In the Fairfield Land District, Oct 17, 1849		9,685 20
In the Iowa City Land District, Jan 28, 1850		2,571 81
In the Fairfield Land District, Sept 10, 1850 . .		3,198 20
In the Dubuque Land District, May 19, 1852		10,552 24
Total		45,957 94

These lands were certified to the State November 19, 1859.   The University lands are placed by law under the control and management of the Board of Trustees of the Iowa State University.   Prior to 1865, there had been selected and located under 282 patents, 22 892 acres in sixteen counties, and 23,036 acres unpatented, making a total of 45,928 acres

V.—SALINE LANDS.

By act of Congress, approved March 3, 1845, the State of Iowa was granted the use of the salt springs within her limits not exceeding twelve By a subsequent act, approved May 27, 1852, Congress granted the springs to the State in fee simple, together with six sections of land contiguous to each, to be disposed of as the Legislature might direct.   In 1861, the proceeds of these lands then to be sold were constituted a fund for founding and supporting a lunatic asylum, but no sales were made   In 1856, the proceeds of the saline lands were appropriated to the Insane Asylum, repealed in 1858.   In 1860, the saline lands and funds were made a part of the permanent fund of the State University   These lands were located in Appanoose, Davis, Decatur, Lucas, Monroe, Van Buren and Wayne Counties

VI.—THE DES MOINES RIVER GRANT.

By act of Congress, approved August 8, 1846, a grant of land was made for the improvement of the navigation of Des Moines River, as follows:

Be it enacted by the Senate and House of Representatives of the United States of America in Congress assembled, That there be, and hereby is, granted to said Territory of Iowa, for the purpose of aiding said Territory to improve the navigation of the Des Moines River from its mouth to the Raccoon Fork (so called) in said Territory, one equal moiety, in alternate sections, of the public lands (remaining unsold and not otherwise disposed of, incumbered or appropriated), in a strip five miles in width on each side of said river, to be selected within said Territory by an agent or agents to be appointed by the Governor thereof, subject to the approval of the Secretary of the Treasury of the United States

Sec 2 *And be it further enacted,* That the lands hereby granted shall not be conveyed or disposed of by said Territory, nor by any State to be formed out of the same, except as said improvement shall progress; that is, the said Territory or State may sell so much of said lands as shall produce the sum of thirty thousand dollars, and then the sales shall cease until the Governor of said Territory or State shall certify the fact to the President of the United States that one-half of said sum has been expended upon said improvements, when the said Territory or

State may sell and convey a quantity of the residue of said lands sufficient to replace the amount expended, and thus the sales shall progress as the proceeds thereof shall be expended, and the fact of such expenditure shall be certified as aforesaid

Sec 8 *And be it further enacted*, That the said River Des Moines shall be and forever remain a public highway for the use of the Government of the United States, free from any toll or other charge whatever, for any property of the United States or persons in their service passing through or along the same *Provided always*, That it shall not be competent for the said Territory or future State of Iowa to dispose of said lands, or any of them, at a price lower than, for the time being, shall be the minimum price of other public lands.

Sec 4 *And be it further enacted*, That whenever the Territory of Iowa shall be admitted into the Union as a State, the lands hereby granted for the above purpose shall be and become the property of said State for the purpose contemplated in this act, and for no other *Provided* the Legislature of the State of Iowa shall accept the said grant for the said purpose " Approved Aug 8, 1846

By joint resolution of the General Assembly of Iowa, approved January 9, 1847, the grant was accepted for the purpose specified. By another act, approved February 24, 1847, entitled "An act creating the Board of Public Works, and providing for the improvement of the Des Moines River," the Legislature provided for a Board consisting of a President, Secretary and Treasurer, to be elected by the people This Board was elected August 2, 1847, and was organized on the 22d of September following. The same act defined the nature of the improvement to be made, and provided that the work should be paid for from the funds to be derived from the sale of lands to be sold by the Board.

Agents appointed by the Governor selected the sections designated by "odd numbers" throughout the whole extent of the grant, and this selection was approved by the Secretary of the Treasury. But there was a conflict of opinion as to the extent of the grant. It was held by some that it extended from the mouth of the Des Moines only to the Raccoon Forks; others held, as the agents to make selection evidently did, that it extended from the mouth to the head waters of the river. Richard M. Young, Commissioner of the General Land Office, on the 23d of February, 1848, construed the grant to mean that "the State is entitled to the alternate sections within five miles of the Des Moines River, throughout the whole extent of that river within the limits of Iowa " Under this construction, the alternate sections above the Raccoon Forks would, of course, belong to the State; but on the 19th of June, 1848, some of these lands were, by proclamation, thrown into market On the 18th of September, the Board of Public Works filed a remonstrance with the Commissioner of the General Land Office. The Board also sent in a protest to the State Land Office, at which the sale was ordered to take place. On the 8th of January, 1849, the Senators and Representatives in Congress from Iowa also protested against the sale, in a communication to Hon. Robert J. Walker, Secretary of the Treasury, to which the Secretary replied, concurring in the opinion that the grant extended the whole length of the Des Moines River in Iowa.

On the 1st of June, 1849, the Commissioner of the General Land Office directed the Register and Receiver of the Land Office at Iowa City " to withhold from sale all lands situated in the odd numbered sections within five miles on each side of the Des Moines River above the Raccoon Forks " March 13, 1850, the Commissioner of the General Land Office submitted to the Secretary of the Interior a list "showing the tracts falling within the limits of the Des Moines River grant, above the Raccoon Forks, etc., under the decision of the Secretary of the Treasury, of March 2, 1849," and on the 6th of April following, Mr. Ewing, then Secretary of the Interior, reversed the decision of Secretary Walker, but ordered the lands to be withheld from sale until Con-

gress could have an opportunity to pass an explanatory act.   The Iowa authorities appealed from this decision to the President (Taylor), who referred the
matter to the Attorney General (Mr. Johnson).   On the 19th of July, Mr.
Johnson submitted as his opinion, that by the terms of the grant itself, it extended to the very source of the Des Moines, but before his opinion was published President Taylor died.   When Mr. Tyler's cabinet was formed, the
question was submitted to the new Attorney General (Mr Crittenden), who, on
the 30th of June, 1851, reported that in his opinion the grant did not extend
above the Raccoon Forks.   Mr. Stewart, Secretary of the Interior, concurred
with Mr. Crittenden at first, but subsequently consented to lay the whole subject before the President and Cabinet, who decided in favor of the State

October 29, 1851, Mr. Stewart directed the Commissioner of the General
Land Office to "submit for his approval such lists as had been prepared, and to
proceed to report for like approval lists of the alternate sections claimed by the
State of Iowa above the Raccoon Forks, as far as the surveys have progressed,
or may hereafter be completed and returned."   And on the following day, three
lists of these lands were prepared in the General Land Office.

The lands approved and certified to the State of Iowa under this grant, and
all lying above the Raccoon Forks, are as follows:

By Secretary Stewart, Oct 30, 1851 .... , ... 81,707 93 acres
                        March 10, 1852 ....143,908 37   "
By Secretary McLellan, Dec. 17, 1853..... ..   . . 33,142 43   "
                        Dec 30, 1853 . ... 12,818 51   "

      Total .... 271,572 24 acres

The Commissioners and Register of the Des Moines River Improvement, in
their report to the Governor, November 30, 1852, estimates the total amount of
lands then available for the work, including those in possession of the State and
those to be surveyed and approved, at nearly a million acres.   The indebtedness
then standing against the fund was about $108,000, and the Commissioners
estimated the work to be done would cost about $1,200,000.

January 19, 1853, the Legislature authorized the Commissioners to sell
"any or all the lands which have or may hereafter be granted, for not less than
$1,300,000."

On the 24th of January, 1853, the General Assembly provided for the election of a Commissioner by the people, and appointed two Assistant Commissioners, with authority to make a contract, selling the lands of the Improvement
for $1,300,000.   This new Board made a contract, June 9, 1855, with the Des
Moines Navigation & Railroad Company, agreeing to sell *all* the lands donated
to the State by Act of Congress of August 8, 1846, which the State had not
sold prior to December 23, 1853, for $1,300,000, to be expended on the im-
provement of the river, and in paying the indebtedness then due   This contract was duly reported to the Governor and General Assembly

By an act approved January 25, 1855, the Commissioner and Register of
the Des Moines River Improvement were authorized to negotiate with the Des
Moines Navigation & Railroad Company for the purchase of lands in Webster
County which had been sold by the School Fund Commissioner as school lands,
but which had been certified to the State as Des Moines River lands, and had,
therefore, become the property of the Company, under the provisions of its
contract with the State.

March 21, 1856, the old question of the extent of the grant was again raised
and the Commissioner of the General Land Office decided th. it was limited to

the Raccoon Fork. Appeal was made to the Secretary of the Interior, and by him the matter was referred to the Attorney General, who decided that the grant extended to the northern boundary of the State; the State relinquished its claim to lands lying along the river in Minnesota, and the vexed question was supposed to be finally settled.

The land which had been certified, as well as those extending to the northern boundary within the limits of the grant, were reserved from pre-emption and sale by the General Land Commissioner, to satisfy the grant of August 8, 1846, and they were treated as having passed to the State, which from time to time sold portions of them prior to their final transfer to the Des Moines Navigation & Railroad Company, applying the proceeds thereof to the improvement of the river in compliance with the terms of the grant. Prior to the final sale to the Company, June 9, 1854, the State had sold about 327,000 acres, of which amount 58,830 acres were located above the Raccoon Fork. The last certificate of the General Land Office bears date December 30, 1853

After June 9th, 1854, the Des Moines Navigation & Railroad Company carried on the work under its contract with the State. As the improvement progressed, the State, from time to time, by its authorized officers, issued to the Company, in payment for said work, certificates for lands. But the General Land Office ceased to certify lands under the grant of 1846. The State had made no other provision for paying for the improvements, and disagreements and misunderstanding arose between the State authorities and the Company.

March 22, 1858, a joint resolution was passed by the Legislature submitting a proposition for final settlement to the Company, which was accepted. The Company paid to the State $20,000 in cash, and released and conveyed the dredge boat and materials named in the resolution; and the State, on the 3d of May, 1858, executed to the Des Moines Navigation & Railroad Company fourteen deeds or patents to the lands, amounting to 256,703 64 acres. These deeds were intended to convey all the lands of this grant certified to the State by the General Government not previously sold, but, as if for the purpose of covering any tract or parcel that might have been omitted, the State made another deed of conveyance on the 18th day of May, 1858 These fifteen deeds, it is claimed, by the Company, convey 266,108 acres, of which about 53,367 are below the Raccoon Fork, and the balance, 212,741 acres, are above that point.

Besides the lands deeded to the Company, the State had deeded to individual purchasers 58,830 acres above the Raccoon Fork, making an aggregate of 271,- 571 acres, deeded above the Fork, all of which had been certified to the State by the Federal Government.

By act approved March 28, 1858, the Legislature donated the remainder of the grant to the Keokuk, Fort Des Moines & Minnesota Railroad Company, upon condition that said Company assumed all liabilities resulting from the Des Moines River improvement operations, reserving 50,000 acres of the land in security for the payment thereof, and for the completion of the locks and dams at Bentonsport, Croton, Keosauqua and Plymouth. For every three thousand dollars' worth of work done on the locks and dams, and for every three thousand dollars paid by the Company of the liabilities above mentioned, the Register of the State Land Office was instructed to certify to the Company 1,000 acres of the 50,000 acres reserved for these purposes. Up to 1865, there had been presented by the Company, under the provisions of the act of 1858, and allowed, claims amounting to $109,579.37, about seventy-five per cent. of which had been settled

After the passage of the Act above noticed, the question of the extent of the original grant was again mooted, and at the December Term of the Supreme Court of the United States, in 1859–60, a decision was rendered declaring that the grant did *not* extend above Raccoon Fork, and that all certificates of land *above* the Fork had been issued without authority of law and were, therefore, void (see 23 How., 66).

The State of Iowa had disposed of a large amount of land without authority, according to this decision, and appeal was made to Congress for relief, which was granted on the 3d day of March, 1861, in a joint resolution relinquishing to the State all the title which the United States then still retained in the tracts of land along the Des Moines River above Raccoon Fork, that had been improperly certified to the State by the Department of the Interior, and which is now held by *bona fide* purchasers under the State of Iowa

In confirmation of this relinquishment, by act approved July 12, 1862, Congress enacted :

That the grant of lands to the then Territory of Iowa for the improvement of the Des Moines River, made by the act of August 8, 1846, is hereby extended so as to include the alternate sections (designated by odd numbers) lying within five miles of said river, between the Raccoon Fork and the northern boundary of said State, such lands are to be held and applied in accordance with the provisions of the original grant, except that the consent of Congress is hereby given to the application of a portion thereof to aid in the construction of the Keokuk, Fort Des Moines & Minnesota Railroad, in accordance with the provisions of the act of the General Assembly of the State of Iowa, approved March 22, 1858 And if any of the said lands shall have been sold or otherwise disposed of by the United States before the passage of this act, except those released by the United States to the grantees of the State of Iowa, under joint resolution of March 3, 1861, the Secretary of the Interior is hereby directed to set apart an equal amount of lands within said State to be certified in lieu thereof, *Provided*, that if the State shall have sold and conveyed any portion of the lands lying within the limits of the grant the title of which has proved invalid, any lands which shall be certified to said State in lieu thereof by virtue of the provisions of this act, shall inure to and be held as a trust fund for the benefit of the person or persons, respectively, whose titles shall have failed as aforesaid

The grant of lands by the above act of Congress was accepted by a joint resolution of the General Assembly, September 11, 1862, in extra session. On the same day, the Governor was authorized to appoint one or more Commissioners to select the lands in accordance with the grant. These Commissioners were instructed to report their selections to the Registrar of the State Land Office The lands so selected were to be held for the purposes of the grant, and were not to be disposed of until further legislation should be had D W Kilburne, of Lee County, was appointed Commissioner, and, on the 25th day of April, 1864, the General Land Officer authorized the selection of 300,000 acres from the vacant public lands as a part of the grant of July 12, 1862, and the selections were made in the Fort Dodge and Sioux City Land Districts.

Many difficulties, controversies and conflicts, in relation to claims and titles, grew out of this grant, and these difficulties were enhanced by the uncertainty of its limits until the act of Congress of July, 1862. But the General Assembly sought, by wise and appropriate legislation, to protect the integrity of titles derived from the State.   Especially was the determination to protect the actual settlers, who had paid their money and made improvements prior to the final settlement of the limits of the grant by Congress.

VII.—THE DES MOINES RIVER SCHOOL LANDS.

These lands constituted a part of the 500,000 acre grant made by Congress in 1841; including 28,378 46 acres in Webster County, selected by the Agent of the State under that grant, and approved by the Commissioner of the General Land Office February 20, 1851.   They were ordered into the market June 6,

1853, by the Superintendent of Public Instruction, who authorized John Tol-man, School Fund Commissioner for Webster County, to sell them as school lands. Subsequently, when the act of 1846 was construed to extend the Des Moines River grant above Raccoon Fork, it was held that the odd numbered sections of these lands within five miles of the river were appropriated by that act, and on the 30th day of December, 1853, 12,813 51 acres were set apart and approved to the State by the Secretary of the Interior, as a part of the Des Moines River grant January 6, 1854, the Commissioner of the General Land Office transmitted to the Superintendent of Public Instruction a certified copy of the lists of these lands, indorsed by the Secretary of the Interior. Prior to this action of the Department, however, Mr. Tolman had sold to indi-vidual purchasers 3,194 28 acres as school lands, and their titles were, of course, killed. For their relief, an act, approved April 2, 1860, provided that, upon application and proper showing, these purchasers should be entitled to draw from the State Treasury the amount they had paid, with 10 per cent interest, on the contract to purchase made with Mr. Tolman. Under this act, five appli-cations were made prior to 1864, and the applicants received, in the aggregate, $949.53.

By an act approved April 7, 1862, the Governor was forbidden to issue to the Dubuque & Sioux City Railroad Company any certificate of the completion of any part of said road, or any conveyance of lands, until the company should execute and file, in the State Land Office, a release of its claim—first, to cer-tain swamp lands; second, to the Des Moines River Lands sold by Tolman; third, to certain other river lands. That act provided that "the said company shall transfer their interest in those tracts of land in Webster and Hamilton Counties heretofore sold by John Tolman, School Fund Commissioner, to the Register of the State Land Office in trust, to enable said Register to carry out and perform said contracts in all cases when he is called upon by the parties interested to do so, before the 1st day of January, A. D. 1864.

The company filed its release to the Tolman lands, in the Land Office, Feb-ruary 27, 1864, at the same time entered its protest that it had no claim upon them, never had pretended to have, and had never sought to claim them. The Register of the State Land Office, under the advice of the Attorney General, decided that patents would be issued to the Tolman purchasers in all cases where contracts had been made prior to December 23, 1853, and remaining uncanceled under the act of 1860 But before any were issued, on the 27th of August, 1864, the Des Moines Navigation & Railroad Company commenced a suit in chancery, in the District Court of Polk County, to enjoin the issue of such patents. On the 30th of August, an *ex parte* injunction was issued. In January, 1868, Mr. J. A. Harvey, Register of the Land Office, filed in the court an elaborate answer to plaintiffs' petition, denying that the company had any right to or title in the lands. Mr. Harvey's successor, Mr. C. C. Carpen-ter, filed a still more exhaustive answer February 10, 1868. August 3, 1868, the District Court dissolved the injunction. The company appealed to the Supreme Court, where the decision of the lower court was affirmed in December, 1869.

VIII.—SWAMP LAND GRANT.

By an act of Congress, approved March 28, 1850, to enable Arkansas and other States to reclaim swampy lands within their limits, granted all the swamp and overflowed lands remaining unsold within their respective limits to the several States. Although the total amount claimed by Iowa under this act does not exceed 4,000,000 acres, it has, like the Des Moines River and some of the land grants, cost the State considerable trouble and expense, and required a deal of legislation   The State expended large sums of money in making the selections, securing proofs, etc., but the General Government appeared to be laboring under the impression that Iowa was not acting in good faith ; that she had selected a large amount of lands under the swamp land grant, transferred her interest to counties, and counties to private speculators, and the General Land Office permitted contests as to the character of the lands already selected by the Agents of the State as "swamp lands"   Congress, by joint resolution Dec 18, 1856, and by act March 3, 1857, saved the State from the fatal result of this ruinous policy.   Many of these lands were selected in 1854 and 1855, immediately after several remarkably wet seasons, and it was but natural that some portions of the selections would not appear swampy after a few dry seasons. Some time after these first selections were made, persons desired to enter parcels of the so-called swamp lands and offering to prove them to be dry   In such cases the General Land Office ordered hearing before the local land officers, and if they decided the land to be dry, it was permitted to be entered and the claim of the State rejected.   Speculators took advantage of this.   Affidavits were bought of irresponsible and reckless men, who, for a few dollars, would confidently testify to the character of lands they never saw   These applications multiplied until they covered 3,000,000 acres.   It was necessary that Congress should confirm all these selections to the State, that this gigantic scheme of fraud and plunder might be stopped.   The act of Congress of March 3, 1857, was designed to accomplish this purpose.   But the Commissioner of the General Land Office held that it was only a qualified confirmation, and under this construction sought to sustain the action of the Department in rejecting the claim of the State, and certifying them under act of May 15, 1856, under which the railroad companies claimed all swamp land in odd numbered sections within the limits of their respective roads.   This action led to serious complications.   When the railroad grant was made, it was not intended nor was it understood that it included any of the swamp lands.   These were already disposed of by previous grant.   Nor did the companies expect to receive any of them, but under the decisions of the Department adverse to the State the way was opened, and they were not slow to enter their claims.   March 4, 1862, the Attorney General of the State submitted to the General Assembly an opinion that the railroad companies were not entitled even to contest the right of the State to these lands, under the swamp land grant   A letter from the Acting Commissioner of the General Land Office expressed the same opinion, and the General Assembly by joint resolution, approved April 7, 1862, expressly repudiated the acts of the railroad companies, and disclaimed any intention to claim these lands under any other than the act of Congress of Sept. 28, 1850.   A great deal of legislation has been found necessary in relation to these swamp lands.

IX.—THE RAILROAD GRANT.

One of the most important grants of public lands to Iowa for purposes of internal improvement was that known as the "Railroad Grant," by act of Congress approved May 15, 1856.   This act granted to the State of Iowa, for the purpose of aiding in the construction of railroads from Burlington, on the Mississippi River, to a point on the Missouri River, near the mouth of Platte River; from the city of Davenport, via Iowa City and Fort Des Moines to

Council Bluffs; from Lyons City northwesterly to a point of intersection with the main line of the Iowa Central Air Line Railroad, near Maquoketa; thence on said main line, running as near as practicable to the Forty-second Parallel; across the said State of Iowa to the Missouri River; from the city of Dubuque to a point on the Missouri River, near Sioux City, with a branch from the mouth of the Tete des Morts, to the nearest point on said road, to be completed as soon as the main road is completed to that point, every alternate section of land, designated by odd numbers, for six sections in width on each side of said roads. It was also provided that if it should appear, when the lines of those roads were definitely fixed, that the United States had sold, or right of preemption had attached to any portion of said land, the State was authorized to select a quantity equal thereto, in alternate sections, or parts of sections, within fifteen miles of the lines so located. The lands remaining to the United States within six miles on each side of said roads were not to be sold for less than the double minimum price of the public lands when sold, nor were any of said lands to become subject to private entry until they had been first offered at public sale at the increased price.

Section 4 of the act provided that the lands granted to said State shall be disposed of by said State only in the manner following, that is to say: that a quantity of land not exceeding one hundred and twenty sections for each of said roads, and included within a continuous length of twenty miles of each of said roads, may be sold; and when the Governor of said State shall certify to the Secretary of the Interior that any twenty continuous miles of any of said roads is completed, then another quantity of land hereby granted, not to exceed one hundred and twenty sections for each of said roads having twenty continuous miles completed as aforesaid, and included within a continuous length of twenty miles of each of such roads, may be sold; and so from time to time until said roads are completed, and if any of said roads are not completed within ten years, no further sale shall be made, and the lands unsold shall revert to the United States "

At a special session of the General Assembly of Iowa, by act approved July 14, 1856, the grant was accepted and the lands were granted by the State to the several railroad companies named, provided that the lines of their respective roads should be definitely fixed and located before April 1, 1857; and provided further, that if either of said companies should fail to have seventy-five miles of road completed and equipped by the 1st day of December, 1859, and its entire road completed by December 1, 1865, it should be competent for the State of Iowa to resume all rights to lands remaining undisposed of by the company so failing.

The railroad companies, with the single exception of the Iowa Central Air Line, accepted the several grants in accordance with the provisions of the above act, located their respective roads and selected their lands. The grant to the Iowa Central was again granted to the Cedar Rapids & Missouri River Railroad Company, which accepted them.

By act, approved April 7, 1862, the Dubuque & Sioux City Railroad Company was required to execute a release to the State of certain swamp and school lands, included within the limits of its grant, in compensation for an extension of the time fixed for the completion of its road.

A careful examination of the act of Congress does not reveal any special reference to railroad *companies*. The lands were granted to the *State*, and the act evidently contemplate the sale of them *by the* State, and the appropriation of the proceeds to aid in the construction of certain lines of railroad within its limits.   Section 4 of the act clearly defines the authority of the State in disposing of the lands.

Lists of all the lands embraced by the grant were made, and certified to the State by the proper authorities   Under an act of Congress approved August 3, 1854, entitled *"An act to vest in the several States and Territories the title in fee of the lands which have been or may be certified to them,"* these certified lists, the originals of which are filed in the General Land Office, conveyed to the State "the fee simple title to all the lands embraced in such lists that are of the character contemplated" by the terms of the act making the grant, and "intended to be granted thereby; but where lands embraced in such lists are not of the character embraced by such act of Congress, and were not intended to be granted thereby, said lists, so far as these lands are concerned, shall be perfectly null and void; and no right, title, claim or interest shall be conveyed thereby." Those certified lists made under the act of May 15, 1856, were forty-three in number, viz · For the Burlington & Missouri River Railroad, nine; for the Mississippi & Missouri Railroad, 11; for the Iowa Central Air Line, thirteen; and for the Dubuque & Sioux City Railroad, ten.   The lands thus approved to the State were as follows:

Burlington & Missouri River R R	. 287,095 84 acres
Mississippi & Missouri River R R	. 774,674 36 "
Cedar Rapids & Missouri River R R . .	775,454 19 "
Dubuque & Sioux City R. R...	. 1,226,558.32 "

A portion of these had been selected as swamp lands by the State, under the act of September 28, 1850, and these, by the terms of the act of August 3, 1854, could not be turned over to the railroads unless the claim of the State to them as swamp was first rejected   It was not possible to determine from the records of the State Land Office the extent of the conflicting claims arising under the two grants, as copies of the swamp land selections in some of the counties were not filed of record.   The Commissioner of the General Land Office, however, prepared lists of the lands claimed by the State as swamp under act of September 28, 1850, and also claimed by the railroad companies under act of May 15, 1856, amounting to 553,293 33 acres, the claim to which as swamp had been rejected by the Department   These were consequently certified to the State as railroad lands.   There was no mode other than the act of July, 1856, prescribed for transferring the title to these lands from the State to the companies   The courts had decided that, for the purposes of the grant, the lands belonged to the State, and to her the companies should look for their titles   It was generally accepted that the act of the Legislature of July, 1856, was all that was necessary to complete the transfer of title.   It was assumed that all the rights and powers conferred upon the State by the act of Congress of May 14, 1856, were by the act of the General Assembly transferred to the companies; in other words, that it was designed to put the companies in the place of the State as the grantees from Congress—and, therefore, that which perfected the title thereto to the State perfected the title to the companies by virtue of the act of July, 1856.   One of the companies, however, the Burlington & Missouri River Railroad Company, was not entirely satisfied with this construction.   Its managers thought that some further and specific action of the State authorities in addition to the act of the Legislature was necessary to complete their title.   This induced Gov. Lowe to attach to the certified lists his official certificate, under the broad seal of the State.   On the 9th of November, 1859, the Governor thus certified to them (commencing at the Missouri River) 187,207.44 acres, and December 27th, 48,775.70 acres, an aggregate of 231,073.14 acres.   These were the only lands under the grant that were certified by the State authorities with any design of perfecting the title already vested in the company by the act of July, 1856 The lists which were afterward furnished to the company were simply certified by the Governor as being correct copies of the lists received by the State from the United States General Land Office. These subsequent lists embraced lands that had been claimed by the State under the Swamp Land Grant.

It was urged against the claim of the Companies that the effect of the act of the Legislature was simply to substitute them for the State as parties to the grant. 1st. That the lands were granted to the State to be held in trust for the accomplishment of a specific purpose, and therefore the State could not part with the title until that purpose should have been accomplished. 2d. That it was not the intention of the act of July 14, 1856, to deprive the State of the control of the lands, but on the contrary that she should retain supervision of them and the right to withdraw all rights and powers and resume the title conditionally conferred by that act upon the companies in the event of their failure to complete their part of the contract. 3d. That the certified lists from the General Land Office vested the title in the State only by virtue of the act of Congress approved August 3, 1854. The State Land Office held that the proper construction of the act of July 14, 1856, when accepted by the companies, was that it became a *conditional contract* that might ripen into a positive sale of the lands as from time to time the work should progress, and as the State thereby became authorized by the express terms of the grant to sell them

This appears to have been the correct construction of the act, but by a subsequent act of Congress, approved June 2, 1864, amending the act of 1856, the terms of the grant were changed, and numerous controversies arose between the companies and the State.

The ostensible purpose of this additional act was to allow the Davenport & Council Bluffs Railroad "to modify or change the location of the uncompleted portion of its line," to run through the town of Newton, Jasper County, or as nearly as practicable to that point The original grant had been made to the State to aid in the construction of railroads within its limits and not to the companies, but Congress, in 1864, appears to have been utterly ignorant of what had been done under the act of 1856, or, if not, to have utterly disregarded it. The State had accepted the original grant. The Secretary of the Interior had already certified to the State all the lands intended to be included in the grant within fifteen miles of the lines of the several railroads. It will be remembered that Section 4, of the act of May 15, 1856, specifies the manner of sale of these lands from time to time as work on the railroads should progress, and also provided that "if any of said roads are not completed within ten years, no *further* sale shall be made, and the lands *unsold shall revert to the United States*" Having vested the title to these lands in trust, in the State of Iowa, it is plain that until the expiration of the ten years there could be no reversion, and the State, not the United States, must control them until the grant should expire by limitation. The United States authorities could not rightfully require the Secretary of the Interior to certify directly to the companies any portion of the lands already certified to the State. And yet Congress, by its act of June 2, 1864, provided that whenever the Davenport & Council Bluffs Railroad Company should file in the General Land Office at Washington a map definitely showing such new location, the Secretary of the Interior should cause to be certified and conveyed to said Company, from time to time, as the road progressed, out of any of the lands belonging to the United States, not sold, reserved, or otherwise disposed of, or to which a pre-emption claim or right of homestead had not attached, and on which a *bona fide* settlement and improvement had not been made under color of title derived from the United States or from the State of Iowa, within six miles of such newly located line, an amount of land per mile equal to that originally authorized to be granted to aid in the construction of said road by the act to which this was an amendment.

The term "out of any lands *belonging to the United States,* not sold, reserved or otherwise disposed of, etc ," would seem to indicate that Congress did intend to grant lands already granted, but when it declared that the Company should have an amount per mile *equal* to that originally *authorized to be granted,* it is plain that the framers of the bill were ignorant of the real terms of the original grant, or that they designed that the United States should *resume* the title it had already parted with two years before the lands could revert to the United States under the original act, which was not repealed.

A similar change was made in relation to the Cedar Rapids & Missouri Railroad, and dictated the conveyance of lands in a similar manner.

Like provision was made for the Dubuque & Sioux City Railroad, and the Company was permitted to change the location of its line between Fort Dodge and Sioux City, so as to secure the best route between those points; but this change of location was not to impair the right to the land granted in the original act, nor did it change the location of those lands.

By the same act, the Mississippi & Missouri Railroad Company was authorized to transfer and assign all or any part of the grant to any other company or person, "if, in the opinion of said Company, the construction of said railroad across the State of Iowa would be thereby sooner and more satisfactorily completed; but such assignee should not in any case be released from the liabilities and conditions accompanying this grant, nor acquire perfect title in any other manner than the same would have been acquired by the original grantee."

Still further, the Burlington & Missouri River Railroad was not forgotten, and was, by the same act, empowered to receive an amount of land per mile equal to that mentioned in the original act, and if that could not be found within the limits of six miles from the line of said road, then such selection might be made along such line within twenty miles thereof out of any public lands belonging to the United States, not sold, reserved or otherwise disposed of, or to which a pre-emption claim or right of homestead had not attached.

Those acts of Congress, which evidently originated in the "lobby," occasioned much controversy and trouble. The Department of the Interior, however, recognizing the fact that when the Secretary had certified the lands to the State, under the act of 1856, that act divested the United States of title, under the vesting act of August, 1854, refused to review its action, and also refused to order any and all investigations for establishing adverse claims (except in pre-emption cases), on the ground that the United States had parted with the title, and, therefore, could exercise no control over the land

May 12, 1864, before the passage of the amendatory act above described, Congress granted to the State of Iowa, to aid in the construction of a railroad from McGregor to Sioux City, and for the benefit of the McGregor Western Railroad Company, every alternate section of land, designated by odd numbers, for ten sections in width on each side of the proposed road, reserving the right to substitute other lands whenever it was found that the grant infringed upon pre-empted lands, or on lands that had been reserved or disposed of for any other purpose. In such cases, the Secretary of the Interior was instructed to select, in lieu, lands belonging to the United States lying nearest to the limits specified

X —AGRICULTURAL COLLEGE AND FARM LANDS.

An Agricultural College and Model Farm was established by act of the General Assembly, approved March 22, 1858. By the eleventh section of the act, the proceeds of the five-section grant made for the purpose of aiding in the erection of public buildings was appropriated, subject to the approval of Congress, together with all lands that Congress might thereafter grant to the State for the purpose, for the benefit of the institution. On the 23d of March, by joint resolution, the Legislature asked the consent of Congress to the proposed transfer. By act approved July 11, 1862, Congress removed the restrictions imposed in the "five-section grant," and authorized the General Assembly to make such disposition of the lands as should be deemed best for the interests of the State. By these several acts, the five sections of land in Jasper County certified to the State to aid in the erection of public buildings under the act of March 3, 1845, entitled "An act supplemental to the act for the admission of the States of Iowa and Florida into the Union," were fully appropriated for the benefit of the Iowa Agricultural College and Farm. The institution is located in Story County. Seven hundred and twenty-one acres in that and two hundred in Boone County were donated to it by individuals interested in the success of the enterprise

By act of Congress approved July 2, 1862, an appropriation was made to each State and Territory of 30,000 acres for each Senator and Representative in Congress, to which, by the apportionment under the census of 1860, they were respectively entitled. This grant was made for the purpose of endowing colleges of agriculture and mechanic arts.

Iowa accepted this grant by an act passed at an extra session of its Legislature, approved September 11, 1862, entitled "An act to accept of the grant, and carry into execution the trust conferred upon the State of Iowa by an act of Congress entitled 'An act granting public lands to the several States and Territories which may provide colleges for the benefit of agriculture and the mechanic arts,' approved July 2, 1862." This act made it the duty of the Governor to appoint an agent to select and locate the lands, and provided that none should be selected that were claimed by any county as swamp lands. The agent was required to make report of his doings to the Governor, who was instructed to submit the list of selections to the Board of Trustees of the Agricultural College for their approval One thousand dollars were appropriated to carry the law into effect. The State, having two Senators and six Representatives in Congress, was entitled to 240,000 acres of land under this grant, for the purpose of establishing and maintaining an Agricultural College Peter Melendy, Esq., of Black Hawk County, was appointed to make the selections, and during August, September and December, 1863, located them in the Fort Dodge, Des Moines and Sioux City Land Districts December 8, 1864, these selections were certified by the Commissioner of the General Land Office, and were approved to the State by the Secretary of the Interior December 13, 1864. The title to these lands was vested in the State in fee simple, and conflicted with no other claims under other grants

The agricultural lands were approved to the State as 240,000.96 acres; but as 35,691.66 acres were located within railroad limits, which were computed at the rate of two acres for one, the actual amount of land approved to the State under this grant was only 204,309.30 acres, located as follows·

In Des Moines Land District	6,804 96 acres.
In Sioux City Land District	59,025.37 "
In Fort Dodge Land District..	138,478 97 "

By act of the General Assembly, approved March 29, 1864, entitled, " An act authorizing the Trustees of the Iowa State Agricultural College and Farm to sell all lands acquired, granted, donated or appropriated for the benefit of said college, and to make an investment of the proceeds thereof," all these lands were granted to the Agricultural College and Farm, and the Trustees were authorized to take possession, and sell or lease them.   They were then, under the control of the Trustees, lands as follows ·

Under the act of July 2, 1852.	204,309.80 acres
Of the five-section grant.	3,200 00 "
Lands donated in Story County	721 00 "
Lands donated in Boone County	200 00 "
Total.	208,430 30 acres

The Trustees opened an office at Fort Dodge, and appointed Hon. G. W. Bassett their agent for the sale of these lands.

THE PUBLIC SCHOOLS.

The germ of the free public school system of Iowa, which now ranks second to none in the United States, was planted by the first settlers   They had migrated to the " The Beautiful Land " from other and older States, where the common school system had been tested by many years' experience, bringing with them some knowledge of its advantages, which they determined should be enjoyed by the children of the land of their adoption. The system thus planted was expanded and improved in the broad fields of the West, until now it is justly considered one of the most complete, comprehensive and liberal in the country

Nor is this to be wondered at when it is remembered humble log school houses were built almost as soon as the log cabin of the earliest settlers were occupied by their brave builders.   In the lead mining regions of the State, the first to be occupied by the white race, the hardy pioneers provided the means for the education of their children even before they had comfortable dwellings for their families.   School teachers were among the first immigrants to Iowa Wherever a little settlement was made, the school house was the first united public act of the settlers; and the rude, primitive structures of the early time only disappeared when the communities had increased in population and wealth, and were able to replace them with more commodious and comfortable buildings. Perhaps in no single instance has the magnificent progress of the State of Iowa been more marked and rapid than in her common school system and in her school houses, which, long since, superseded the log cabins of the first settlers   To-day, the school houses which everywhere dot the broad and fertile prairies of Iowa are unsurpassed by those of any other State in the great Union.   More especially is this true in all her cities and villages, where liberal and lavish appropriations have been voted, by a generous people, for the erection of large, commodious and elegant buildings, furnished with all the modern improvements, and costing from $10,000 to $60,000 each   The people of the State have expended more than $10,000,000 for the erection of public school buildings.

The first house erected in Iowa was a log cabin at Dubuque, built by James L Langworthy and a few other miners, in the Autumn of 1833   When it was completed, George Cabbage was employed as teacher during the Winter of 1833–4, and thirty-five pupils attended his school.   Barrett Whittemore taught the second term with twenty-five pupils in attendance.   Mrs. Caroline Dexter commenced teaching in Dubuque in March, 1836. She was the first female teacher there, and probably the first in Iowa. In 1839, Thomas H. Benton, Jr., afterward for ten years Superintendent of Public Instruction, opened an English and classical school in Dubuque. The first tax for the support of schools at Dubuque was levied in 1840

Among the first buildings erected at Burlington was a commodious log school house in 1834, in which Mr. Johnson Pierson taught the first school in the Winter of 1834–5.

The first school in Muscatine County was taught by George Bumgardner, in the Spring of 1837, and in 1839, a log school house was erected in Muscatine, which served for a long time for school house, church and public hall The first school in Davenport was taught in 1838. In Fairfield, Miss Clarissa Sawyer, James F. Chambers and Mrs. Reed taught school in 1839.

When the site of Iowa City was selected as the capital of the Territory of Iowa, in May, 1839, it was a perfect wilderness The first sale of lots took place August 18, 1839, and before January 1, 1840, about twenty families had settled within the limits of the town; and during the same year, Mr Jesse Berry opened a school in a small frame building he had erected, on what is now College street

The first settlement in Monroe County was made in 1843, by Mr. John R Gray, about two miles from the present site of Eddyville; and in the Summer of 1844, a log school house was built by Gray, William V. Beedle, C. Renfro, Joseph McMullen and Willoughby Randolph, and the first school was opened by Miss Urania Adams. The building was occupied for school purposes for nearly ten years. About a year after the first cabin was built at Oskaloosa, a log school house was built, in which school was opened by Samuel W. Caldwell in 1844.

At Fort Des Moines, now the capital of the State, the first school was taught by Lewis Whitten, Clerk of the District Court in the Winter of 1846–7, in one of the rooms on " Coon Row," built for barracks

The first school in Pottawattomie County was opened by George Green, a Mormon, at Council Point, prior to 1849; and until about 1854, nearly, if not quite, all the teachers in that vicinity were Mormons.

The first school in Decorah was taught in 1853, by T. W Burdick, then a young man of seventeen. In Osceola, the first school was opened by Mr. D. W. Scoville The first school at Fort Dodge was taught in 1855, by Cyrus C. Carpenter, since Governor of the State. In Crawford County, the first school house was built in Mason's Grove, in 1856, and Morris McHenry first occupied it as teacher.

During the first twenty years of the history of Iowa, the log school house prevailed, and in 1861, there were 893 of these primitive structures in use for school purposes in the State Since that time they have been gradually disappearing In 1865, there were 796; in 1870, 336, and in 1875, 121

Iowa Territory was created July 3, 1838. January 1, 1839, the Territorial Legislature passed an act providing that " there shall be established a common school, or schools in each of the counties in this Territory, which shall be open and free for every class of white citizens between the ages of five and twenty-one years." The second section of the act provided that " the County Board shall, from time to time, form such districts in their respective counties whenever a petition may be presented for the purpose by a majority of the voters resident within such contemplated district " These districts were governed by boards of trustees, usually of three persons; each district was required to maintain school at least three months in every year, and later, laws were enacted providing for county school taxes for the payment of teachers, and that whatever additional sum might be required should be assessed upon the parents sending, in proportion to the length of time sent.

When Iowa Territory became a State, in 1846, with a population of 100,-000, and with 20,000 scholars within its limits, about four hundred school districts had been organized. In 1850, there were 1,200, and in 1857, the number had increased to 3,265.

In March, 1858, upon the recommendation of Hon. M. L. Fisher, then Superintendent of Public Instruction, the Seventh General Assembly enacted that "each civil township is declared a school district," and provided that these should be divided into sub-districts This law went into force March 20, 1858, and reduced the number of school districts from about 3,500 to less than 900.

This change of school organization resulted in a very material reduction of the expenditures for the compensation of District Secretaries and Treasurers An effort was made for several years, from 1867 to 1872, to abolish the sub-district system. Mr Kissell, Superintendent, recommended, in his report of January 1, 1872, and Governor Merrill forcibly endorsed his views in his annual message.   But the Legislature of that year provided for the formation of independent districts from the sub-districts of district townships.

The system of graded schools was inaugurated in 1849; and new schools, in which more than one teacher is employed, are universally graded.

The first official mention of Teachers' Institutes in the educational records of Iowa occurs in the annual report of Hon. Thomas H. Benton, Jr , made December 2, 1850, who said, "An institution of this character was organized a few years ago, composed of the teachers of the mineral regions of Illinois, Wisconsin and Iowa.   An association of teachers has, also, been formed in the county of Henry, and an effort was made in October last to organize a regular institute in the county of Jones ' At that time—although the beneficial influence of these institutes was admitted, it was urged that the expenses of attending them was greater than teachers with limited compensation were able to bear   To obviate this objection, Mr. Benton recommended that "the sum of $150 should be appropriated annually for three years, to be drawn in installments of $50 each by the Superintendent of Public Instruction, and expended for these institutions " He proposed that three institutes should be held annually at points to be designated by the Superintendent

No legislation in this direction, however, was had until March, 1858, when an act was passed authorizing the holding of teachers' institutes for periods not less than six working days, whenever not less than thirty teachers should desire. The Superintendent was authorized to expend not exceeding $100 for any one institute, to be paid out by the County Superintendent as the institute might direct for teachers and lecturers, and one thousand dollars was appropriated to defray the expenses of these institutes

December 6, 1858, Mr Fisher reported to the Board of Education that institutes had been appointed in twenty counties within the preceding six months, and more would have been, but the appropriation had been exhausted.

The Board of Education at its first session, commencing December 6, 1858, enacted a code of school laws which retained the existing provisions for teachers' institutes.

In March, 1860, the General Assembly amended the act of the Board by appropriating " a sum not exceeding fifty dollars annually for one such institute, held as provided by law in each county.'

In 1865, Mr Faville reported that "the provision made by the State for the benefit of teachers' institutes has never been so fully appreciated, both by the people and the teachers, as during the last two years"

By act approved March 19, 1874, Normal Institutes were established in each county, to be held annually by the County Superintendent   This was regarded as a very decided step in advance by Mr. Abernethy, and in 1876 the Sixteenth General Assembly established the first permanent State Normal School at Cedar Falls, Black Hawk County, appropriating the building and property of the Soldiers' Orphans' Home at that place for that purpose.   This school is now "in the full tide of successful experiment."

The public school system of Iowa is admirably organized, and if the various officers who are entrusted with the educational interests of the commonwealth are faithful and competent, should and will constantly improve.

" The public schools are supported by funds arising from several sources. The sixteenth section of every Congressional Township was set apart by the General Government for school purposes, being one-thirty-sixth part of all the lands of the State.   The minimum price of these lands was fixed at one dollar and twenty-five cents per acre.   Congress also made an additional donation to the State of five hundred thousand acres, and an appropriation of five per cent. on all the sales of public lands to the school fund   The State gives to this fund the proceeds of the sales of all lands which escheat to it; the proceeds of all fines for the violation of the liquor and criminal laws.   The money derived from these sources constitutes the permanent school fund of the State, which cannot be diverted to any other purpose   The penalties collected by the courts for fines and forfeitures go to the school fund in the counties where collected The proceeds of the sale of lands and the five per cent. fund go into the State Treasury, and the State distributes these proceeds to the several counties according to their request, and the counties loan the money to individuals for long terms at eight per cent. interest, on security of land valued at three times the amount of the loan, exclusive of all buildings and improvements thereon.   The interest on these loans is paid into the State Treasury, and becomes the available school fund of the State   The counties are responsible to the State for all money so loaned, and the State is likewise responsible to the school fund for all moneys transferred to the counties   The interest on these loans is apportioned by the State Auditor semi-annually to the several counties of the State, in proportion to the number of persons between the ages of five and twenty-one years. The counties also levy an annual tax for school purposes, which is apportioned to the several district townships in the same way.   A district tax is also levied for the same purpose.   The money arising from these several sources constitutes the support of the public schools, and is sufficient to enable every sub-district in the State to afford from six to nine months' school each year."

The taxes levied for the support of schools are self-imposed   Under the admirable school laws of the State, no taxes can be legally assessed or collected for the erection of school houses until they have been ordered by the election of the district at a school meeting legally called   The school houses of Iowa are, the pride of the State and an honor to the people   If they have been sometimes built at a prodigal expense, the tax payers have no one to blame but themselves   The teachers' and contingent funds are determined by the Board of Directors under certain legal restrictions.   These boards are elected annually, except in the independent districts, in which the board may be entirely changed every three years   The only exception to this mode of levying taxes for support of schools is the county school tax, which is determined by the County Board of Supervisors. The tax is from one to three mills on the dollar; usually, however, but one   Mr. Abernethy, who was Superintendent of Public Instruction from 1872 to 1877, said in one of his reports.

There is but little opposition to the levy of taxes for the support of schools, and there would be still less if the funds were always properly guarded and judiciously expended However much our people disagree upon other subjects, they are practically united upon this The opposition of wealth has long since ceased to exist, and our wealthy men are usually the most liberal in their views and the most active friends of popular education They are often found upon our school boards, and usually make the best of school officers. It is not uncommon for Boards of Directors, especially in the larger towns and cities, to be composed wholly of men who represent the enterprise, wealth and business of their cities

At the close of 1877, there were 1,086 township districts, 3,138 independent districts and 7,015 sub-districts   There were 9,948 ungraded and 476 graded schools, with an average annual session of seven months and five days. There were 7,348 male teachers employed, whose average compensation was $34 88 per month, and 12,518 female teachers, with an average compensation of $28 69 per month

The number of persons between the ages 5 and 21 years, in 1877, was 567.859; number enrolled in public schools, 421,163; total average attendance, 251,372, average cost of tuition per month, $1.62.   There are 9,279 frame, 671 brick, 257 stone and 89 log school houses, making a grand total of 10,296, valued at $9,044,973.   The public school libraries number 17,329 volumes. Ninety-nine teachers' institutes were held during 1877   Teachers' salaries amounted to $2,953,645   There was expended for school houses, grounds, libraries and apparatus, $1,106,788, and for fuel and other contingencies, $1,136,995, making the grand total of $5,197,428 expended by the generous people of Iowa for the support of their magnificent public schools in a single year.   The amount of the permanent school fund, at the close of 1877, was $3,462,000.   Annual interest, $276,960

In 1857, there were 3,265 independent districts, 2,708 ungraded schools, and 1,572 male and 1,424 female teachers.   Teachers' salaries amounted to $198,142, and the total expenditures for schools was only $364,515   Six hundred and twenty-three volumes were the extent of the public school libraries twenty years ago, and there were only 1,686 school houses, valued at $571,064.

In twenty years, teachers' salaries have increased from $198,142, in 1857, to $2,953,645 in 1877.   Total school expenditures, from $364,515 to $5,197,428

The significance of such facts as these is unmistakable.   Such lavish expenditures can only be accounted for by the liberality and public spirit of the people, all of whom manifest their love of popular education and their faith in the public schools by the annual dedication to their support of more than one per cent. of their entire taxable property; this, too, uninterruptedly through a series of years, commencing in the midst of a war which taxed their energies and resources to the extreme, and continuing through years of general depression in business—years of moderate yield of produce, of discouragingly low prices, and even amid the scanty surroundings and privations of pioneer life   Few human enterprises have a grander significance or give evidence of a more noble purpose than the generous contributions from the scanty resources of the pioneer for the purposes of public education.

POLITICAL RECORD.

TERRITORIAL OFFICERS.

Governors—Robert Lucas, 1838–41; John Chambers, 1841–45; James Clarke, 1845

Secretaries—William B Conway, 1838, died 1839; James Clarke, 1839; O H. W. Stull, 1841; Samuel J Burr, 1843, Jesse Williams, 1845

Auditors—Jesse Williams, 1840; Wm. L. Gilbert, 1843 · Robert M. Secrest, 1845

Treasurers—Thornton Bayliss, 1839, Morgan Reno, 1840

Judges—Charles Mason, Chief Justice, 1838; Joseph Williams, 1838; Thomas S. Wilson, 1838.

Presidents of Council—Jesse B. Browne, 1838–9, Stephen Hempstead, 1839–40, M Bainridge, 1840–1; Jonathan W. Parker, 1841–2; John D. Elbert, 1842–3; Thomas Cox, 1843–4, S. Clinton Hastings, 1845, Stephen Hempstead, 1845–6.

Speakers of the House—William H Wallace, 1838–9, Edward Johnston, 1839–40; Thomas Cox, 1840–1, Warner Lewis, 1841–2, James M. Morgan, 1842–3; James P Carleton, 1843–4, James M. Morgan, 1845; George W. McCleary, 1845–6.

First Constitutional Convention, 1844—Shepherd Leffler, President, Geo. S. Hampton, Secretary

Second Constitutional Convention, 1846—Enos Lowe, President, William Thompson, Secretary

OFFICERS OF THE STATE GOVERNMENT

Governors—Ansel Briggs, 1846 to 1850; Stephen Hempstead, 1850 to 1854, James W. Grimes, 1854 to 1858, Ralph P Lowe, 1858 to 1860; Samuel J. Kirkwood, 1860 to 1864; William M. Stone, 1864 to 1868; Samuel Morrill, 1868 to 1872; Cyrus C. Carpenter, 1872 to 1876; Samuel J. Kirkwood, 1876 to 1877; Joshua G. Newbold, Acting, 1877 to 1878, John H. Gear, 1878 to ——.

Lieutenant Governor—Office created by the new Constitution September 3, 1857—Oran Faville, 1858–9; Nicholas J Rusch, 1860–1; John R. Needham, 1862–3; Enoch W. Eastman, 1864–5; Benjamin F. Gue, 1866–7, John Scott, 1868–9; M. M. Walden, 1870–1, H. C. Bulis, 1872–3; Joseph Dysart, 1874–5; Joshua G Newbold, 1876–7; Frank T. Campbell, 1878–9

Secretaries of State—Elisha Cutler, Jr., Dec. 5, 1846, to Dec 4, 1848; Josiah H. Bonney, Dec. 4, 1848, to Dec. 2, 1850; George W. McCleary, Dec 2, 1850, to Dec. 1, 1856; Elijah Sells, Dec. 1, 1856, to Jan. 5, 1863, James Wright, Jan. 5, 1863, to Jan. 7, 1867; Ed. Wright, Jan. 7, 1867, to Jan 6, 1873; Josiah T. Young, Jan. 6, 1873, to ——.

Auditors of State—Joseph T. Fales, Dec. 5, 1846, to Dec 2, 1850; William Pattee, Dec. 2, 1850, to Dec 4, 1854; Andrew J. Stevens, Dec. 4, 1854, resigned in 1855; John Pattee, Sept. 22, 1855, to Jan. 3, 1859; Jonathan W. Cattell, 1859 to 1865; John A. Elliot, 1865 to 1871; John Russell, 1871 to 1875; Buren R. Sherman, 1875 to ——.

Treasurers of State—Morgan Reno, Dec 18, 1846, to Dec. 2, 1850, Israel Kister, Dec. 2, 1850, to Dec 4, 1852, Martin L. Morris, Dec. 4, 1852, to Jan. 2, 1859; John W. Jones, 1859 to 1863; William H. Holmes, 1863 to

1867 ; Samuel E Rankin, 1867 to 1873 ; William Christy, 1873 to 1877 ; George W Bemis, 1877 to ——

Superintendents of Public Instruction—Office created in 1847—James Harlan, June 5, 1845 (Supreme Court decided election void), Thomas H Benton, Jr., May 23, 1844, to June 7, 1854 ; James D Eads, 1854–7 ; Joseph C. Stone, March to June, 1857 , Maturin L. Fisher, 1857 to Dec , 1858, when the office was abolished and the duties of the office devolved upon the Secretary of the Board of Education.

Secretaries of Board of Education—Thomas H Benton, Jr., 1859–1863 ; Oran Faville, Jan 1, 1864. Board abolished March 23, 1864.

Superintendents of Public Instruction—Office re-created March 23, 1864— Oran Faville, March 28, 1864, resigned March 1, 1867 , D. Franklin Wells, March 4, 1867, to Jan , 1870 ; A S. Kissell, 1870 to 1872 ; Alonzo Abernethy, 1872 to 1877 , Carl W Von Coelln, 1877 to ——.

State Binders—Office created February 21, 1855—William M Coles, May 1, 1855, to May 1, 1859, Frank M. Mills, 1859 to 1867 ; James S. Carter, 1867 to 1870, J. J. Smart, 1870 to 1874 ; H A Perkins, 1874 to 1875 , James J Smart, 1875 to 1876 ; H. A. Perkins, 1876 to ——

Registers of the State Land Office—Anson Hart, May 5, 1855, to May 13, 1857 ; Theodore S. Parvin, May 13, 1857, to Jan. 3, 1859 ; Amos B. Miller, Jan. 3, 1859, to October, 1862 ; Edwin Mitchell, Oct 31, 1862, to Jan 5, 1863 ; Josiah A Harvey, Jan. 5, 1863, to Jan. 7, 1867 ; Cyrus C. Carpenter, Jan. 7, 1867, to January, 1871 , Aaron Brown, January, 1871, to to January, 1875 , David Secor, January, 1875, to ——.

State Printers— Office created Jan 3, 1840—Garrett D. Palmer and George Paul, 1849, William H. Merritt, 1851 to 1853 ; William A. Hornish, 1853 (resigned May 16, 1853); Mahoney & Dorr, 1853 to 1855 ; Peter Moriarty, 1855 to 1857 ; John Teesdale, 1857 to 1861 ; Francis W Palmer, 1861 to 1869 ; Frank M. Mills, 1869 to 1870 ; G. W. Edwards, 1870 to 1872 ; R. P. Clarkson, 1872 to ——.

Adjutants General—Daniel S. Lee, 1851–5 ; Geo. W. McCleary, 1855–7 , Elljah Sells, 1857 , Jesse Bowen, 1857–61 , Nathaniel Baker, 1861 to 1877 ; John H. Looby, 1877 to ——

Attorneys General—David C. Cloud, 1853–56 ; Samuel A. Rice, 1856–60 , Charles C. Nourse, 1861–4 ; Isaac L. Allen, 1865 (resigned January, 1866); Frederick E. Bissell, 1866 (died June 12, 1867), Henry O'Connor, 1867–72 ; Marsena E Cutts, 1872–6 , John F. McJunkin, 1877

Presidents of the Senate—Thomas Baker, 1846–7 ; Thomas Hughes, 1848 ; John J Selman, 1848–9 ; Enos Lowe, 1850–1 ; William E. Leffing-well, 1852–3 , Maturin L Fisher, 1854–5 ; William W. Hamilton, 1856–7. Under the new Constitution, the Lieutenant Governor is President of the Senate.

Speakers of the House—Jesse B. Brown, 1847–8 ; Smiley H Bonhan, 1849–50 , George Temple, 1851–2 ; James Grant, 1853–4 ; Reuben Noble, 1855–6 ; Samuel McFarland, 1856–7 ; Stephen B. Sheledy, 1858–9 , John Edwards, 1860–1 , Rush Clark, 1862–3 ; Jacob Butler, 1864–5 ; Ed. Wright, 1866–7 , John Russell, 1868–9 , Aylett R Cotton, 1870–1 ; James Wilson, 1872–3, John H. Gear, 1874–7 ; John Y. Stone, 1878.

New Constitutional Convention, 1859—Francis Springer, President ; Thos. J Saunders, Secretary.

STATE OFFICERS, 1878.

John H. Gear, Governor; Frank T Campbell, Lieutenant Governor; Josiah T. Young, Secretary of State; Buren R. Sherman, Auditor of State, George W Bemis, Treasurer of State; David Secor, Register of State Land Office; John H. Looby, Adjutant General; John F. McJunken, Attorney General; Mrs. Ada North, State Librarian; Edward J Holmes, Clerk Supreme Court; John S. Runnells, Reporter Supreme Court; Carl W. Von Coelln, Superintendent Public Instruction, Richard P. Clarkson, State Printer, Henry A. Perkins, State Binder: Prof. Nathan R Leonard, Superintendent of Weights and Measures, William H. Fleming, Governor's Private Secretary, Fletcher W Young, Deputy Secretary of State; John C. Parish, Deputy Auditor of State; Erastus G Morgan, Deputy Treasurer of State; John M. Davis, Deputy Register Land Office; Ira C. Kling, Deputy Superintendent Public Instruction.

THE JUDICIARY.
SUPREME COURT OF IOWA.

Chief Justices.—Charles Mason, resigned in June, 1847; Joseph Williams, Jan , 1847, to Jan., 1848, S. Clinton Hastings, Jan ,1848, to Jan., 1849; Joseph Williams, Jan , 1849, to Jan. 11, 1855; Geo. G Wright, Jan. 11, 1855, to Jan., 1860 , Ralph P. Lowe, Jan., 1860, to Jan 1, 1862; Caleb Baldwin, Jan , 1862, to Jan., 1864; Geo. G. Wright, Jan , 1864, to Jan., 1866 , Ralph P. Lowe, Jan ,1866, to Jan , 1868; John F. Dillon, Jan., 1868, to Jan , 1870; Chester C. Cole, Jan. 1, 1870, to Jan 1, 1871; James G. Day, Jan. 1, 1871, to Jan. 1, 1872; Joseph M. Beck, Jan. 1, 1872, to Jan. 1, 1874; W E. Miller, Jan. 1, 1874, to Jan. 1, 1876, Chester C Cole, Jan. 1, 1876, to Jan 1, 1877, James G. Day, Jan. 1, 1877, to Jan. 1, 1878; James H. Rothrock, Jan. 1, 1878

Associate Judges.—Joseph Williams; Thomas S Wilson, resigned Oct., 1847; John F. Kinney, June 12, 1847, resigned Feb. 15, 1854; George Greene, Nov. 1, 1847, to Jan 9, 1855; Jonathan C. Hall, Feb. 15, 1854, to succeed Kinney, resigned, to Jan., 1855; William G. Woodward, Jan. 9, 1855; Norman W. Isbell, Jan. 16, 1855, resigned 1856; Lacen D. Stockton, June 3, 1856, to succeed Isbell, resigned, died June 9, 1860; Caleb Baldwin, Jan. 11, 1860, to 1864; Ralph P Lowe, Jan. 12, 1860; George G. Wright, June 26, 1860, to succeed Stockton, deceased, elected U S Senator, 1870; John F. Dillon, Jan. 1, 1864, to succeed Baldwin, resigned, 1870, Chester C. Cole, March 1, 1864, to 1877; Joseph M. Beck, Jan. 1, 1868, W. E. Miller, October 11, 1864, to succeed Dillon, resigned; James G. Day, Jan. 1, 1871, to succeed Wright.

SUPREME COURT, 1878.

James H. Rothrock, Cedar County, Chief Justice; Joseph M Beck, Lee County, Associate Justice; Austin Adams, Dubuque County, Associate Justice, William H. Seevers, Oskaloosa County, Associate Justice; James G. Day, Fremont County, Associate Justice

CONGRESSIONAL REPRESENTATION.
UNITED STATES SENATORS.

(The first General Assembly failed to elect Senators.)
George W. Jones, Dubuque, Dec 7, 1848–1858; Augustus C. Dodge, Burlington, Dec. 7, 1848–1855; James Harlan, Mt. Pleasant, Jan 6, 1855–1865; James W. Grimes, Burlington, Jan. 26, 1858–died 1870; Samuel J. Kirkwood, Iowa City, elected Jan 13, 1866, to fill vacancy caused by resignation of James

Harlan ; James Harlan, Mt. Pleasant, March 4, 1866–1872 ; James B Howell, Keokuk, elected Jan 20, 1870, to fill vacancy caused by the death of J. W. Grimes—term expired March 3d; George G. Wright, Des Moines, March 4, 1871–1877 , William B Allison, Dubuque, March 4, 1872 , Samuel J. Kirkwood, March 4, 1877.

MEMBERS OF HOUSE OF REPRESENTATIVES

Twenty-ninth Congress—1846 to 1847.—S. Clinton Hastings; Shepherd Leffler.

Thirtieth Congress—1847 to 1849.—First District, William Thompson , Second District, Shepherd Leffler.

Thirty-first Congress—1849 to 1851.—First District, First Session, Wm. Thompson, unseated by the House of Representatives on a contest, and election remanded to the people First District, Second Session, Daniel F Miller. Second District, Shepherd Leffler.

Thirty-second Congress—1851 to 1853.—First District, Bernhart Henn Second District, Lincoln Clark.

Thirty-third Congress—1853 to 1855.—First District, Bernhart Henn. Second District, John P. Cook.

Thirty-fourth Congress—1855 to 1857 —First District, Augustus Hall. Second District, James Thorington.

Thirty-fifth Congress—1857 to 1859 —First District, Samuel R. Curtis. Second District, Timothy Davis.

Thirty-sixth Congress—1859 to 1861.—First District, Samuel R. Curtis. Second District, William Vandever

Thirty-seventh Congress—1861 to 1863.—First District, First Session, Samuel R. Curtis.* First District, Second and Third Sessions, James F Wilson. Second District, William Vandever

Thirty-eighth Congress—1863 to 1865.—First District, James F. Wilson. Second District, Hiram Price Third District, William B. Allison Fourth District, Josiah B Grinnell. Fifth District, John A. Kasson. Sixth District, Asahel W Hubbard.

Thirty-ninth Congress—1865 to 1867.—First District, James F. Wilson ; Second District, Hiram Price; Third District, William B Allison ; Fourth District, Josiah B. Grinnell ; Fifth District, John A Kasson ; Sixth District, Asahel W Hubbard

Fortieth Congress—1867 to 1869.—First District, James F. Wilson ; Second District, Hiram Price ; Third District, William B. Allison, Fourth District, William Loughridge; Fifth District, Grenville M. Dodge , Sixth District, Asahel W. Hubbard

Forty-first Congress—1869 to 1871.—First District, George W. McCrary ; Second District, William Smyth ; Third District, William B. Allison ; Fourth District, William Loughridge , Fifth District, Frank W. Palmer ; Sixth District, Charles Pomeroy

Forty-second Congress—1871 to 1873 —First District, George W. McCrary ; Second District, Aylett R. Cotton ; Third District, W. G Donnan , Fourth District, Madison M Waldon ; Fifth District, Frank W Palmer ; Sixth District, Jackson Orr

Forty-third Congress—1873 to 1875.—First District, George W. McCrary ; Second District, Aylett R. Cotton ; Third District, William Y. Donnan , Fourth District, Henry O. Pratt ; Fifth District, James Wilson ; Sixth District,

---

* Vacated seat by acceptance of commission as Brigadier General, and J F Wilson chosen his successor

William Loughridge; Seventh District, John A. Kasson; Eighth District, James W McDill; Ninth District, Jackson Orr

Forty-fourth Congress—1875 to 1877.—First District, George W. McCrary; Second District, John Q. Tufts; Third District, L L. Ainsworth; Fourth District, Henry O Pratt; Fifth District, James Wilson; Sixth District, Ezekiel S. Sampson; Seventh District, John A. Kasson; Eighth District; James W. McDill; Fifth District, Addison Oliver

*Forty-fifth Congress—1877 to 1879 —*First District, J. C Stone; Second District, Hiram Price; Third District, T. W. Burdick, Fourth District, H. C. Deering; Fifth District, Rush Clark; Sixth District, E S. Sampson, Seventh District, H. J B. Cummings; Eighth District, W F. Sapp; Ninth District, Addison Oliver.

WAR RECORD.

The State of Iowa may well be proud of her record during the War of the Rebellion, from 1861 to 1865. The following brief but comprehensive sketch of the history she made during that trying period is largely from the pen of Col. A. P. Wood, of Dubuque, the author of "The History of Iowa and the War," one of the best works of the kind yet written

"Whether in the promptitude of her responses to the calls made on her by the General Government, in the courage and constancy of her soldiery in the field, or in the wisdom and efficiency with which her civil administration was conducted during the trying period covered by the War of the Rebellion, Iowa proved herself the peer of any loyal State The proclamation of her Governor, responsive to that of the President, calling for volunteers to compose her First Regiment, was issued on the fourth day after the fall of Sumter At the end of only a single week, men enough were reported to be in quarters (mostly in the vicinity of their own homes) to fill the regiment. These, however, were hardly more than a tithe of the number who had been offered by company commanders for acceptance under the President's call So urgent were these offers that the Governor requested (on the 24th of April) permission to organize an additional regiment. While awaiting an answer to this request, he conditionally accepted a sufficient number of companies to compose two additional regiments. In a short time, he was notified that both of these would be accepted Soon after the completion of the Second and Third Regiments (which was near the close of May), the Adjutant General of the State reported that upward of one hundred and seventy companies had been tendered to the Governor to serve against the enemies of the Union.

"Much difficulty and considerable delay occured in fitting these regiments for the field. For the First Infantry a complete outfit (not uniform) of clothing was extemporized—principally by the volunteered labor of loyal women in the different towns—from material of various colors and qualities, obtained within the limits of the State. The same was done in part for the Second Infantry. Meantime, an extra session of the General Assembly had been called by the Governor, to convene on the 15th of May. With but little delay, that body authorized a loan of $800,000, to meet the extraordinary expenses incurred, and to be incurred, by the Executive Department, in consequence of the new emergency. A wealthy merchant of the State (Ex-Governor Merrill, then a resident of McGregor) immediately took from the Governor a contract to supply a complete outfit of clothing for the three regiments organized, agreeing to receive, should the Governor so elect, his pay therefor in State bonds at par. This contract he executed to the letter, and a portion of the clothing (which was manufactured in Boston, to his order) was delivered at Keokuk, the place at which the troops had rendezvoused, in exactly one month from the day on which the contract had been entered into.   The remainder arrived only a few days later. This clothing was delivered to the regiment, but was subsequently condemned by the Government, for the reason that its color was gray, and blue had been adopted as the color to be worn by the national troops.

Other States also clothed their troops, sent forward under the first call of President Lincoln, with gray uniforms, but it was soon found that the confederate forces were also clothed in gray, and that color was at once abandoned by the Union troops.   If both armies were clothed alike, annoying if not fatal mistakes were liable to be made.

But while engaged in these efforts to discharge her whole duty in common with all the other Union-loving States in the great emergency, Iowa was compelled to make immediate and ample provision for the protection of her own borders, from threatened invasion on the south by the Secessionists of Missouri, and from danger of incursions from the west and northwest by bands of hostile Indians, who were freed from the usual restraint imposed upon them by the presence of regular troops stationed at the frontier posts.   These troops were withdrawn to meet the greater and more pressing danger threatening the life of the nation at its very heart.

To provide for the adequate defense of her borders from the ravages of both rebels in arms against the Government and of the more irresistible foes from the Western plains, the Governor of the State was authorized to raise and equip two regiments of infantry, a squadron of cavalry (not less than five companies) and a battalion of artillery (not less than three companies)   Only cavalry were enlisted for home defense, however, "but," says Col. Wood, "in times of special danger, or when calls were made by the Unionists of Northern Missouri for assistance against their disloyal enemies, large numbers of militia on foot often turned out, and remained in the field until the necessity for their services had passed.

" The first order for the Iowa volunteers to move to the field was received on the 13th of June.   It was issued by Gen Lyon, then commanding the United States forces in Missouri.   The First and Second Infantry immediately embarked in steamboats, and moved to Hannibal.   Some two weeks later, the Third Infantry was ordered to the same point.   These three, together with many other of the earlier organized Iowa regiments, rendered their first field service in Missouri   The First Infantry formed a part of the little army with which Gen. Lyon moved on Springfield, and fought the bloody battle of Wilson's Creek.   It received unqualified praise for its gallant bearing on the field.   In the following month (September), the Third Iowa, with but very slight support, fought with honor the sanguinary engagement of Blue Mills Landing; and in November, the Seventh Iowa, as a part of a force commanded by Gen. Grant, greatly distinguished itself in the battle of Belmont, where it poured out its blood like water—losing more than half of the men it took into action.

" The initial operations in which the battles referred to took place were followed by the more important movements led by Gen Grant, Gen. Curtis, of this State, and other commanders, which resulted in defeating the armies defending the chief strategic lines held by the Confederates in Kentucky, Tennessee, Missouri and Arkansas, and compelling their withdrawal from much of the territory previously controlled by them in those States.   In these and other movements, down to the grand culminating campaign by which Vicksburg was captured and the Confederacy permanently severed on the line of the Mississippi River, Iowa troops took part in steadily increasing numbers. In the investment and siege of Vicksburg, the State was represented by thirty regiments and two batteries, in addition to which, eight regiments and one battery were employed on the outposts of the besieging army. The brilliancy of their exploits on the many fields where they served won for them the highest meed of praise, both in military and civil circles Multiplied were the terms in which expression was given to this sentiment, but these words of one of the journals of a neighboring State, 'The Iowa troops have been heroes among heroes,' embody the spirit of all.

" In the veteran re-enlistments that distinguished the closing months of 1863 above all other periods in the history of re-enlistments for the national armies, the Iowa three years' men (who were relatively more numerous than those of any other State) were prompt to set the example of volunteering for another term of equal length, thereby adding many thousands to the great army of those who gave this renewed and practical assurance that the cause of the Union should not be left without defenders

"In all the important movements of 1864–65, by which the Confederacy was penetrated in every quarter, and its military power finally overthrown, the Iowa troops took part. Their drum-beat was heard on the banks of every great river of the South, from the Potomac to the Rio Grande, and everywhere they rendered the same faithful and devoted service, maintaining on all occasions their wonted reputation for valor in the field and endurance on the march.

" Two Iowa three-year cavalry regiments were employed during their whole term of service in the operations that were in progress from 1863 to 1866 against the hostile Indians of the western plains. A portion of these men were among the last of the volunteer troops to be mustered out of service The State also supplied a considerable number of men to the navy, who took part in most of the naval operations prosecuted against the Confederate power on the Atlantic and Gulf coasts, and the rivers of the West.

" The people of Iowa were early and constant workers in the sanitary field, and by their liberal gifts and personal efforts for the benefit of the soldiery, placed their State in the front rank of those who became distinguished for their exhibitions of patriotic benevolence during the period covered by the war Agents appointed by the Governor were stationed at points convenient for rendering assistance to the sick and needy soldiers of the State, while others were employed in visiting, from time to time, hospitals, camps and armies in the field, and doing whatever the circumstances rendered possible for the health and comfort of such of the Iowa soldiery as might be found there.

" Some of the benevolent people of the State early conceived the idea of establishing a Home for such of the children of deceased soldiers as might be left in destitute circumstances. This idea first took form in 1863, and in the following year a Home was opened at Farmington, Van Buren County, in a building leased for that purpose, and which soon became filled to its utmost capacity. The institution received liberal donations from the general public, and also from the soldiers in the field. In 1865, it became necessary to provide increased accommodations for the large number of children who were seeking the benefits of its care. This was done by establishing a branch at Cedar Falls, in Black Hawk County, and by securing, during the same year, for the use of the parent Home, Camp Kinsman near the City of Davenport. This property was soon afterward donated to the institution, by act of Congress.

" In 1866, in pursuance of a law enacted for that purpose, the Soldiers' Orphans' Home (which then contained about four hundred and fifty inmates) became a State institution, and thereafter the sums necessary for its support were appropriated from the State treasury A second branch was established at Glenwood, Mills County. Convenient tracts were secured, and valuable improvements made at all the different points. Schools were also established, and employments provided for such of the children as were of suitable age. In all ways the provision made for these wards of the State has been such as to challenge the approval of every benevolent mind. The number of children who have been inmates of the Home from its foundation to the present time is considerably more than two thousand

" At the beginning of the war, the population of Iowa included about one hundred and fifty thousand men presumably liable to render military service The State raised, for general service, thirty-nine regiments of infantry, nine regiments of cavalry, and four companies of artillery, composed of three years' men ; one regiment of infantry, composed of three months' men ; and four regiments and one battalion of infantry, composed of one hundred days' men. The original enlistments in these various organizations, including seventeen hundred and twenty-seven men raised by draft, numbered a little more than sixty-nine thousand The re-enlistments, including upward of seven thousand veterans, numbered very nearly eight thousand. The enlistments in the regular army and navy, and organizations of other States, will, if added, raise the total to upward of eighty thousand The number of men who, under special enlistments, and as militia, took part at different times in the operations on the exposed borders of the State, was probably as many as five thousand.

" Iowa paid no bounty on account of the men she placed in the field. In some instances, toward the close of the war, bounty to a comparatively small amount was paid by cities and towns. On only one occasion—that of the call of July 18, 1864—was a draft made in Iowa This did not occur on account of her proper liability, as established by previous rulings of the War Department, to supply men under that call, but grew out of the great necessity that there existed for raising men The Government insisted on temporarily setting aside, in part, the former rule of settlements, and enforcing a draft in all cases where subdistricts in any of the States should be found deficient in their supply of men. In no instance was Iowa, as a whole, found to be indebted to the General Government for men, on a settlement of her quota accounts."

It is to be said to the honor and credit of Iowa that while many of the loyal States, older and larger in population and wealth, incurred heavy State debts for the purpose of fulfilling their obligations to the General Government, Iowa, while she was foremost in duty, while she promptly discharged all her obligations to her sister States and the Union, found herself at the close of the war without any material addition to her pecuniary liabilities incurred before the war commenced Upon final settlement after the restoration of peace, her claims upon the Federal Government were found to be fully equal to the amount of her bonds issued and sold during the war to provide the means for raising and equipping her troops sent into the field, and to meet the inevitable demands upon her treasury in consequence of the war.

NUMBER OF TROOPS FURNISHED BY THE STATE OF IOWA DURING THE WAR OF THE REBELLION, TO JANUARY 1, 1865.

No Regiment	No of men	No Regiment	No of men.
1st Iowa Infantry	959	39th Iowa Infantry..	933
2d " "	1,247	40th " "	900
3d " "	1,074	41st Battalion Iowa Infantry	294
4th " "	1,184	44th Infantry (100-days men)	867
5th " "	1,037	45th " " "	912
6th " "	1,013	46th " " "	892
7th " "	1,138	47th " " "	884
8th " "	1,027	48th Battalion "	346
9th " "	1,090	1st Iowa Cavalry	1,478
10th " "	1,027	2d " "	1,394
11th " "	1,022	3d " "	1,360
12th " "	981	4th " "	1,227
13th " "	989	5th " "	1,245
14th " "	840	6th " "	1,125
15th " "	1,196	7th " "	562
16th " "	919	8th " "	1,234
17th " "	956	9th " "	1,178
18th " "	875	Sioux City Cavalry*	93
19th " "	985	Co A, 11th Penn Cavalry	87
20th " "	925	1st Battery Artillery.	149
21st " "	980	2d " "	123
22d " "	1,008	3d " "	142
23d " "	961	4th " "	152
24th " "	979	1st Iowa African Infantry, 60th U S†	903
25th " "	995	Dodge's Brigade Band	14
26th " "	919	Band of 2d Iowa Infantry	10
27th " "	940	Enlistments as far as reported to Jan 1, 1864, for the older Iowa regiments	2,765
28th " "	956		
29th " "	1,005	Enlistments of Iowa men in regiments of other States, over	2,500
30th " "	978		
31st " "	977		
32d " "	925	Total.	61,653
33d " "	985	Re-enlisted Veterans for different Regiments	7,202
34th " "	953		
35th " "	984	Additional enlistments	6,664
36th " "	986		
37th " "	914	Grand total as far as reported up to Jan 1, 1865	75,519
38th " "	910		

This does not include those Iowa men who veteranized in the regiments of other States, nor the names of men who enlisted during 1864, in regiments of other States

* Afterward consolidated with Seventh Cavalry

† Only a portion of this regiment was credited to the State

NUMBER OF CASUALTIES AMONG OFFICERS OF IOWA REGIMENTS DURING THE WAR.

REGIMENT OR BATTERY	Killed In action	Killed Accidentally	Killed Total	Died Of wounds	Died Of disease	Died By drowning	Died Total	Discharged For disability	Discharged Cause unknown	Discharged Total	Wounded In action	Wounded Accidentally	Wounded Total	Resigned	Dismissed	Total casualties	Captured	Transferred To Vel. Res. Corps	Transferred By appointment	Transferred Total
First Cavalry	1		1	1	2		3	1		1	4		4	34	3	46	1		3	3
Second Cavalry	1		1		2		2		2	2	12		12	25	3	45	5		5	5
Third Cavalry	3		3	2	4		6		5	5	9		9	39	1	63	4		3	3
Fourth Cavalry	3		3		6		6		6	6	8		7	31	2	55	8		2	2
Fifth Cavalry	5		5		2		2		1	1	6		6	35	2	51	8			
Sixth Cavalry					2		2		1	1	1		1	15	2	21				
Seventh Cavalry					3		3		2	2	2		2	15	1	23			1	1
Eighth Cavalry	1		1		3		3		2	2	10		10	23	2	41	22		1	1
Ninth Cavalry	3		3		1		1		1	1				25		30		1	1	2
Artillery, First Battery					2		2		2	2				6		10				
Artillery, Second Battery																	No casualt's rep			
Artillery, Third Battery	1		1		2		2				1		1	4		8	1		1	1
Artillery, Fourth Battery														1						
First Infantry	1		1		2		2	1		1	1		1			5				
Second Infantry	6		6	3	2		5		2	2	23		23	25		61	1	1	8	9
Second Veteran Infantry	2		2		1		1				3		3	3		9	1		1	1
Second and Third Infantry (consolidated)	1		1		1		1				1		1	3		6			1	1
Third Infantry	2		2	3			3		1	1	35		35	40		81	8		2	2
Third Veteran Infantry	2		2													2				
Fourth Infantry	3		3		5		5				16		16	34	1	59	7		5	5
Fifth Infantry	4		4	3	3		6	2	4	6	17		17	28	1	63	6		5	5
Sixth Infantry	7		7	1	3		4	1	2	3	18		18	32	2	67	12		3	3
Seventh Infantry	4		4	3	2		5		3	3	22		22	37	3	73	9	1	1	1
Eighth Infantry	8		8	1	2		3		2	2	14		14	30	2	57	6		7	7
Ninth Infantry	6		6		4		6		4	4	24	2	26	26		72	12	1	3	4
Tenth Infantry	6		6		2		2	2		2	16		16	32		58	9		6	6
Eleventh Infantry	6		6	2	1		3	2		2	11		11	25		47	1		1	1
Twelfth Infantry	3		3	1	8		8		3	3	13	2	13	19	3	45	22		5	5
Thirteenth Infantry	2		2	4	3	1	7	1		1	19		19	36	1	65	4		4	4

Fourteenth Infantry
Fourteenth Residuary Battalion
Fifteenth Infantry
Sixteenth Infantry
Seventeenth Infantry
Eighteenth Infantry
Nineteenth Infantry
Twentieth Infantry
Twenty-first Infantry
Twenty-second Infantry
Twenty-third Infantry
Twenty-fourth Infantry
Twenty-fifth Infantry
Twenty-sixth Infantry
Twenty-seventh Infantry
Twenty-eighth Infantry
Twenty-ninth Infantry
Thirtieth Infantry
Thirty-first Infantry
Thirty-second Infantry
Thirty-third Infantry
Thirty-fourth Infantry
Thirty-fourth [34th and 38th] consolidated
Thirty-fifth Infantry
Thirty-sixth Infantry
Thirty-seventh Infantry
Thirty-eighth Infantry
Thirty-ninth Infantry
Fortieth Infantry
Forty-fourth Infantry
Forty-fifth Infantry
Forty-sixth Infantry
Forty-seventh Infantry
Forty-eighth Infantry (battalion)
First Colored Regiment of Iowa (60th U. S.)

Total.........

NUMBER OF CASUALTIES AMONG ENLISTED MEN OF IOWA REGIMENTS DURING THE WAR.

REGIMENT OR BATTERY	KILLED			DIED					DISCHARGED			WOUNDED			Missing	Total Casualties	Captured	TRANSFERRED		
	In Action	Accidentally	Total	Of Wounds	Of Disease	By Suicide	By Drowning	Total	For Disability	Cause Unknown	Total	In Action	Accidentally	Total				To V.R. Corps	By Appointment	Total
First Cavalry	34	8	42	20	187	1	4	212	187	16	203	81	3	84	2	543	21	14	22	36
Second Cavalry	37	3	40	28	191		3	222	140	29	169	158	3	161	10	602	73	26	11	37
Third Cavalry	58	4	62	19	224		2	245	220	85	305	155	2	157	1	770	141	24	7	31
Fourth Cavalry	37	4	41	11	186		4	201	151	82	233	108	4	112	3	590	90	25	8	33
Fifth Cavalry	36	6	42	7	127	1	2	137	172	51	223	47	3	50		452	209	14	3	17
Sixth Cavalry	16	3	19	5	59		4	70	70	16	86	15	3	18		198		3	5	6
Seventh Cavalry	37	8	45	2	92	2	7	101	228	18	246	4	1	8		402			5	8
Eighth Cavalry	24	3	27	10	91		4	104	49	15	64	75	2	77	2	274	237	20		20
Ninth Cavalry	5	1	6	3	162	1	3	175	54	8	62	13	2	15		258	1	3	1	11
Artillery, 1st Battery	7		7		51			54	25	9	84	28	1	29		124		3	1	3
Artillery, 2d Battery	1		1		29			80	16		16	14	1	15		62		3	1	6
Artillery, 3d Battery	2	1	3	1	33			34	23	3	26	15	1	16		79	1	3		
Artillery, 4th Battery					5			6	11		11					17				
*Independent Company Sioux City Cavalry											7					7				
†Company A, 11th Pennsylvania Cavalry	1		4		4		1	4	3							5				
Dodge's Brigade Band																				
First Infantry	12		12	5	7		4	13	187	191	203	137		137	3	165	18		6	15
Second Infantry	55	3	58	17	107		4	128	187	2	328	244	1	245		758	18	9	1	1
Second Veteran Infantry	11		11	3	11		2	14	14	14	3	41		41	10	69	18	5	3	8
Second and Third Consolidated Infantry	4		4		27			27	163	67	28	8		8		67	85	13	4	17
Third Infantry	52	3	55	28	99		2	129	163	146	230	333	2	335		749	23		2	2
Third Veteran Infantry	17		17	1	9			10		15	1				5	28	44	30	2	32
Fourth Infantry	57	1	58	51	237		2	290	152	146	298	319	3	322		973	96	45	2	47
Fifth Infantry	59	1	60	29	90			120	222	15	237	278	4	282	5	699	54	15		7
Sixth Infantry	102		102	30	124		2	154	211	47	258	328	3	331	3	855	73	21	7	22
Seventh Infantry	94		94	35	135		1	172	180	108	288	210	4	214	8	885	882	24	18	84
Eighth Infantry	49	1	50	44	137		1	182	245	63	308	354	5	331	1	761	23	23		24
Ninth Infantry	76	2	78	57	208		1	266	243	26	269	354	4	359		973				
Tenth Infantry	56	1	57	35	134		1	170	137	115	252	257	4	261		739	16	41	5	48

Regiment	1	2	3	4	5	6	7	8	9	10	11	12	13	14	15	16	17	18	19	20
Eleventh Infantry	54	1	55	25	148		1	174	121	30	151	220	6	226	7	610	59	26	11	87
Twelfth Infantry	80	1	30	32	243		1	276	124	133	257	208		209		768	382	19	3	22
Thirteenth Infantry	65	1	66	34	182		1	217	192	77	269	290	4	294	6	852	84	15	15	30
Fourteenth Infantry	27	1	28	23	122			145	137	53	190	162		162	1	526	249	13	10	23
Fourteenth Residuary Battalion					3					4	11					11		1	1	2
Fifteenth Infantry	52		52	78	194		2	274	270	32	302	392	2	394		1029	78	18	6	27
Sixteenth Infantry	57		57	82	217			249	160	49	289	289	1	290	14	819	242	21	6	27
Seventeenth Infantry	43		43	18	97		1	116	129	93	222	225		225	8	614	264	28	3	26
Eighteenth Infantry	26	2	28	7	109		3	119	222	6	228	73	1	74		449	68	5	5	10
Nineteenth Infantry	58		53	33	91		6	130	183	5	188	190	5	191		562	204	27	13	40
Twentieth Infantry	8		8	5	130		7	142	157	14	163	43	3	46		339	10	36	5	38
Twenty-first Infantry	37	1	38	29	157		2	188	189	8	158	147	3	150	2	581	20	49	5	54
Twenty-second Infantry	53	1	54	52	126		2	180	150	8	177	245	3	245		634	79	40	2	42
Twenty-third Infantry	39		39	30	196		2	228	171	6	123	122	2	126		570	8	41	1	42
Twenty-fourth Infantry	58	1	69	53	197		3	253	200	4	204	240	3	248	2	761	72	48	6	54
Twenty-fifth Infantry	39		39	22	199			219	120	18	198	162	3	164	4	564	17	16	8	69
Twenty-sixth Infantry	40	2	42	29	204		8	236	140	68	141	140	4	143		562	24	69		69
Twenty-seventh Infantry	7			14	162		4	180	184	16	202	132	2	185	6	530	82	40	5	45
Twenty-eighth Infantry	52		52	24	180		1	206	166	7	182	242	2	246	10	696	89	33	10	43
Twenty-ninth Infantry	19	2	21	17	248			266	117	13	124	97	8	99		511	53	31	6	87
Thirtieth Infantry	39		40	24	233			257	129	38	142	202		205	2	646	19	46	1	47
Thirty-first Infantry	11		11	16	261			277	137	10	175	77	1	77		540	13	72		72
Thirty-second Infantry	56	1	56	33	203		1	287	156	34	166	182	2	133		589	93	27	6	88
Thirty-third Infantry	25	1	26	37	166		3	236	109	27	143	166		168	7	580	78	18	10	28
Thirty-fourth Infantry	4		4	2	228		1	231	286		313	13	2	13		561	3	22		22
Thirty-fourth consolidated Battalion Infantry [34th and 38th] Infantry consolidated		2		2	10				3	7	3				3	6				
Thirty-fifth Infantry	23	2	25	19	182		1	12	29	17	86	12		14		66	15	51	14	65
Thirty-sixth Infantry	35		35	24	226		1	208	172	30	189	93	2	93		510	437	17	6	23
Thirty-seventh Infantry	3		3		141		1	251	187	9	191	142		142	2	619		2		2
Thirty-eighth Infantry	1		1		310		1	142	326	34	356		3			503		8	4	12
Thirty-ninth Infantry	33		34	21	119		1	311	108	4	117	2		2		431	203	12	3	15
Fortieth Infantry	5		5	10	179		5	141	89		123	105		108		406	2	20	6	26
*Forty-first Infantry (battalion)					2			194	117		121	41	1	41		361				
Forty-fourth Infantry		1	1	1	14			2	15		15					17				
Forty-fifth Infantry		2	2		17			14								15				
Forty-sixth Infantry		2	2	2	23			19				1		1		22	3	1		1
Forty-seventh Infantry		1	1	1	45			24								28				
Forty-eighth Infantry					4			46								47				
First African Infantry [60th U S]	4	1	5	1	831		5	337	40	40	40	1		1		383		1		1
	1940	78	2017	1199	8695	8	109	10011	8005	1982	9987	8180	112	8282	1115	30394	4489	1264	281	1545

* Before transferred to 7th Iowa Cavalry † Partial returns

POPULATION OF IOWA,

By Counties

COUNTIES	AGGREGATE					
	1875.	1870.	1860.	1850.	1840.	Voters.
Adair	7045	3982	984	.. ..	.... ..	1616
Adams . . .	7832	4614	1533	.. .. .	.. .. .	1727
Allamakee . .	19158	17868	12237	777	.	3653
Appanoose	2370	16456	11931	3181	... .	527
Audubon	17405	1212	454	....	.. .. ..	3679
Benton ... . .,.	28807	22454	8496	672	......	4778
Black Hawk .. .	22918	21706	8244	135	. .	4877
Boone	17251	14584	4232	735	. .	3515
Bremer..	13220	12528	4915	....	....	2656
Buchanan	17315	17034	7906	517	....	3890
Buena Vista	3561	1585	57	....	. .	817
Buncombe*	....	....	....	... . .	....	....
Butler	11734	9951	3724	.. ..	....	2598
Calhoun	3185	1602	147	.. . .. .	. .	681
Carroll..	5760	2451	281	....	. .	1197
Cass	10552	5464	1612	....	....	2422
Cedar	17879	19731	12949	3941	1253	3934
Cerro Gordo	6685	4722	940	. . . .	... . .	1526
Cherokee....	4249	1967	58	. . ..	....	1001
Chickasaw.	11400	10180	4336	. . . .	....	2392
Clarke	10118	8735	5427	79	... .	2213
Clay	3559	1523	52	. . . .	... . .	868
Clayton	27184	27771	20728	3873	1101	5272
Clinton	34295	35357	18938	2822	821	5569
Crawford....	6039	2530	383	....	.. . .	1244
Dallas............... .	14386	12019	5244	854	... . .	3170
Davis	15757	15565	13764	7264	....	3448
Decatur	13249	12018	8677	965	....	2882
Delaware	16893	17432	11024	1759	168	3662
Des Moines	35415	27256	19611	12988	5577	6654
Dickinson	1748	1389	180	... .	.	894
Dubuque......	43845	38969	31164	10841	3059	8759
Emmett	1436	1392	105	... .	. ...	299
Fayette....	20515	16973	12073	825	. .	4637
Floyd	13100	10768	3744	....	....	2884
Franklin	6558	4738	1309	.. .	.. .. .	1374
Fremont	13719	11173	5074	1244	.. .	2998
Greene	7028	4627	1374	. . . .	....	1622
Grundy	8134	6399	793	....	.	1525
Guthrie	9638	7061	3058	.. . . .	.. ..	2339
Hamilton . . .	7701	6055	1699	. ...	.	1455
Hancock	1482	999	179	. .	. .	303
Hardin	15029	13684	5440	......	....	3215
Harrison	11818	8931	3621	. .	... .	2658
Henry	21594	21468	18701	8707	3772	4641
Howard	7875	6282	3168	....	. .	1712
Humboldt	3455	2596	332	......	. .	695
Ida	794	226	43	. ..	... .	172
Iowa.	17456	16644	8029	822	... . .	3576
Jackson	23061	22619	18493	7210	1411	4901
Jasper	24128	22116	9883	1280	....	5289
Jefferson	17127	17839	15038	9904	2773	3721
Johnson	24654	24898	17573	4472	1491	5225
Jones	19168	19731	13306	3007	471	4180

* In 1862, name changed to Lyon

POPULATION OF IOWA—Concluded.

COUNTIES	AGGREGATE					
	1875.	1870.	1860.	1850.	1840.	Voters.
Keokok	20488	19484	13271	4822	...	4202
Kossuth	3765	3351	416	....	....	773
Lee	33913	38210	29232	18861	6093	6709
Linn	31815	28852	18947	5444	1373	7274
Louisa	12499	12877	10370	4939	1927	2899
Lucas	11725	10388	5766	471	....	2464
Lyon*.	1139	221	....	....	......	287
Madison	16030	13884	7339	1179	.....	2632
Mahaska	23718	22508	14816	5989	....	5287
Marion	24094	24436	16813	5482	.. ..	4988
Marshall	19629	17576	6015	338	....	4445
Mills	10555	8718	4481	....		2365
Mitchell	11523	9582	3409	.. . ..	. .	2838
Monona	2267	3654	832	....	. ...	1292
Monroe	12811	12724	8612	2884	....	2743
Montgomery	10889	5934	1256	..	.....	2485
Muscatine	21623	21688	16444	5731	1942	6588
O'Brien	2349	715	8	.. .	.. ..	595
Osceola	1778	.. . ..	. ...	.... .		498
Page	14274	9975	4419	551	.....	3222
Palo Alto	2728	1336	132	..	....	556
Plymouth	5282	2199	148	.	....	1136
Pocahontas	2249	1446	103	... .. .	.. .	464
Polk	31558	27857	11625	4513	.... .	6842
Pottawattomie	21665	16893	4968	7828	....	4392
Poweshiek	16482	15581	5668	615	.....	3634
Ringgold..	7546	5691	2923	....	. .	1496
Sac	2873	1411	246	....		657
Scott	39768	38599	25959	5986	2140	7109
Shelby.	5664	2540	818	.... .	...	1084
Sioux	3720	576	10	. . .	..	637
Story	13111	11651	4051	. ...	..	2574
Tama	18771	16131	5285	8	.	3911
Taylor	10418	6989	3590	204	....	2282
Union	8827	6986	2012	.. . .	.	1924
Van Buren	17980	17672	17081	12270	6146	3893
Wapello	18541	22346	14618	8471	....	3923
Warren	19269	17980	10281	961	.. ..	4168
Washington	23865	18952	14285	4957	1594	5346
Wayne	13978	11287	6409	340	....	2947
Webster	13114	10484	2504			8747
Winnebago	24233	1562	168	... . .	... .	4117
Winneshiek	2986	23570	13942	546	.... .	406
Woodbury..	8568	6172	1119	.....	....	1776
Worth	4908	2892	756	....	....	763
Wright	3244	2392	653	. . .	....	694
Total.	1353118	1191792	674913	192214	48112	284557

* Formerly Buncombe

ILLINOIS.

Length, 380 miles, mean width about 156 miles. Area, 55,410 square miles, or 35,462,400 acres. Illinois, as regards its surface, constitutes a table-land at a varying elevation ranging between 350 and 800 feet above the sea level; composed of extensive and highly fertile prairies and plains. Much of the south division of the State, especially the river-bottoms, are thickly wooded. The prairies, too, have oasis-like clumps of trees scattered here and there at intervals. The chief rivers irrigating the State are the Mississippi—dividing it from Iowa and Missouri—the Ohio (forming its south barrier), the Illinois, Wabash, Kaskaskia, and Sangamon, with their numerous affluents. The total extent of navigable streams is calculated at 4,000 miles. Small lakes are scattered over various parts of the State. Illinois is extremely prolific in minerals, chiefly coal, iron, copper, and zinc ores, sulphur and limestone. The coal-field alone is estimated to absorb a full third of the entire coal-deposit of North America. Climate tolerably equable and healthy; the mean temperature standing at about 51° Fahrenheit As an agricultural region, Illinois takes a competitive rank with neighboring States, the cereals, fruits, and root-crops yielding plentiful returns; in fact, as a grain-growing State, Illinois may be deemed, in proportion to her size, to possess a greater area of lands suitable for its production than any other State in the Union. Stock-raising is also largely carried on, while her manufacturing interests in regard of woolen fabrics, etc., are on a very extensive and yearly expanding scale. The lines of railroad in the State are among the most extensive of the Union. Inland water-carriage is facilitated by a canal connecting the Illinois River with Lake Michigan, and thence with the St. Lawrence and Atlantic. Illinois is divided into 102 counties; the chief towns being Chicago, Springfield (capital), Alton, Quincy, Peoria, Galena, Bloomington, Rock Island, Vandalia, etc. By the new Constitution, established in 1870, the State Legislature consists of 51 Senators, elected for four years, and 153 Representatives, for two years; which numbers were to be decennially increased thereafter to the number of six per every additional half-million of inhabitants. Religious and educational institutions are largely diffused throughout, and are in a very flourishing condition. Illinois has a State Lunatic and a Deaf and Dumb Asylum at Jacksonville; a State Penitentiary at Joliet; and a Home for

Soldiers' Orphans at Normal. On November 30, 1870, the public debt of the State was returned at $4,870,937, with a balance of $1,808,833 unprovided for. At the same period the value of assessed and equalized property presented the following totals: assessed, $840,031,703; equalized $480,664,058. The name of Illinois, through nearly the whole of the eighteenth century, embraced most of the known regions north and west of Ohio. French colonists established themselves in 1673, at Cahokia and Kaskaskia, and the territory of which these settlements formed the nucleus was, in 1763, ceded to Great Britain in conjunction with Canada, and ultimately resigned to the United States in 1787. Illinois entered the Union as a State, December 3, 1818; and now sends 19 Representatives to Congress. Population, 2,539,891, in 1870.

INDIANA.

The profile of Indiana forms a nearly exact parallelogram, occupying one of the most fertile portions of the great Mississippi Valley. The greater extent of the surface embraced within its limits consists of gentle undulations rising into hilly tracts toward the Ohio bottom. The chief rivers of the State are the Ohio and Wabash, with their numerous affluents. The soil is highly productive of the cereals and grasses—most particularly so in the valleys of the Ohio, Wabash, Whitewater, and White Rivers. The northeast and central portions are well timbered with virgin forests, and the west section is notably rich in coal, constituting an offshoot of the great Illinois carboniferous field. Iron, copper, marble, slate, gypsum, and various clays are also abundant. From an agricultural point of view, the staple products are maize and wheat, with the other cereals in lesser yields ; and besides these, flax, hemp, sorghum, hops, etc., are extensively raised. Indiana is divided into 92 counties, and counts among her principal cities and towns, those of Indianapolis (the capital), Fort Wayne, Evansville, Terre Haute, Madison, Jeffersonville, Columbus, Vincennes, South Bend, etc. The public institutions of the State are many and various, and on a scale of magnitude and efficiency commensurate with her important political and industrial status. Upward of two thousand miles of railroads permeate the State in all directions, and greatly conduce to the development of her expanding manufacturing interests. Statistics for the fiscal year terminating October 31, 1870, exhibited a total of receipts, $3,896,541 as against disbursements, $3,532,406, leaving a balance, $364,135 in favor of the State Treasury. The entire public debt, January 5, 1871, $3,971,000. This State was first settled by Canadian voyageurs in 1702, who erected a fort at Vincennes; in 1763 it passed into the hands of the English, and was by the latter ceded to the United States in 1783. From 1788 till 1791, an Indian warefare prevailed. In 1800, all the region west and north of Ohio (then formed into a distinct territory) became merged in Indiana. In 1809, the present limits of the State were defined, Michigan and Illinois having previously been withdrawn. In 1811, Indiana was the theater of the Indian War of Tecumseh, ending with the decisive battle of Tippecanoe. In 1816 (December 11), Indiana became enrolled among the States of the American Union. In 1834, the State passed through a monetary crisis owing to its having become mixed up with railroad, canal, and other speculations on a gigantic scale, which ended, for the time being, in a general collapse of public credit, and consequent bankruptcy. Since that time, however, the greater number of the public works which had brought about that imbroglio — especially the great Wabash and Erie Canal — have been completed, to the great benefit of the State, whose subsequent progress has year by year been marked by rapid strides in the paths of wealth, commerce, and general social and political prosperity. The constitution now in force was adopted in 1851. Population, 1,680,637.

IOWA.

In shape, Iowa presents an almost perfect parallelogram; has a length, north to south. of about 300 miles, by a pretty even width of 208 miles, and embraces an area of 55,045 square miles, or 35,228,800 acres. The surface of the State is generally undulating, rising toward the middle into an elevated plateau which forms the "divide" of the Missouri and Mississippi basins. Rolling prairies, especially in the south section, constitute a regnant feature, and the river bottoms, belted with woodlands, present a soil of the richest alluvion. Iowa is well watered, the principal rivers being the Mississippi and Missouri, which form respectively its east and west limits, and the Cedar, Iowa, and Des Moines, affluents of the first named. Mineralogically, Iowa is important as occupying a section of the great Northwest coal field, to the extent of an area estimated at 25,000 square miles. Lead, copper, zinc, and iron, are also mined in considerable quantities. The soil is well adapted to the production of wheat, maize, and the other cereals; fruits, vegetables, and esculent roots; maize, wheat, and oats forming the chief staples. Wine, tobacco, hops, and wax, are other noticeable items of the agricultural yield. Cattle-raising, too, is a branch of rural industry largely engaged in. The climate is healthy, although liable to extremes of heat and cold. The annual gross product of the various manufactures carried on in this State approximate, in round numbers, a sum of $20,000,000. Iowa has an immense railroad system, besides over 500 miles of water-communication by means of its navigable rivers. The State is politically divided into 99 counties, with the following centers of population: Des Moines (capital), Iowa City (former capital), Dubuque, Davenport, Burlington, Council Bluffs, Keokuk, Muscatine, and Cedar Rapids. The State institutions of Iowa—religious, scholastic, and philanthropic — are on a par, as regards number and perfection of organization and operation, with those of her Northwest sister States, and education is especially well cared for, and largely diffused. Iowa formed a portion of the American territorial acquisitions from France, by the so-called Louisiana purchase in 1803, and was politically identified with Louisiana till 1812, when it merged into the Missouri Territory; in 1834 it came under the Michigan organization, and, in 1836, under that of Wisconsin. Finally, after being constituted an independent Territory, it became a State of the Union, December 28, 1846. Population in 1860, 674,913; in 1870, 1,191,792, and in 1875, 1,353,118.

MICHIGAN.

United area, 56,243 square miles, or 35,995,520 acres. Extent of the Upper and smaller Peninsula — length, 316 miles; breadth, fluctuating between 36 and 120 miles The south division is 416 miles long, by from 50 to 300 miles wide. Aggregate lake-shore line, 1,400 miles. The Upper, or North, Peninsula consists chiefly of an elevated plateau, expanding into the Porcupine mountain-system, attaining a maximum height of some 2,000 feet Its shores along Lake Superior are eminently bold and picturesque, and its area is rich in minerals, its product of copper constituting an important source of industry. Both divisions are heavily wooded, and the South one, in addition, boasts of a deep, rich, loamy soil, throwing up excellent crops of cereals and other agricultural produce. The climate is generally mild and humid, though the Winter colds are severe. The chief staples of farm husbandry include the cereals, grasses, maple sugar, sorghum, tobacco, fruits, and dairy-stuffs. In 1870, the acres of land in farms were: improved, 5,096,939; unimproved woodland, 4,080,146; other unimproved land, 842,057. The cash value of land was $398,240,578; of farming implements and machinery, $13,711,979. In 1869, there were shipped from the Lake Superior ports, 874,582 tons of iron ore, and 45,762 of smelted pig, along with 14,188 tons of copper (ore and ingot). Coal is another article largely mined. Inland communication is provided for by an admirably organized railroad system, and by the St Mary's Ship Canal, connecting Lakes Huron and Superior. Michigan is politically divided into 78 counties; its chief urban centers are Detroit, Lansing (capital), Ann Arbor, Marquette, Bay City, Niles, Ypsilanti, Grand Haven, etc. The Governor of the State is elected biennially. On November 30, 1870, the aggregate bonded debt of Michigan amounted to $2,385,028, and the assessed valuation of land to $266,929,278, representing an estimated cash value of $800,000,000. Education is largely diffused and most excellently conducted and provided for. The State University at Ann Arbor, the colleges of Detroit and Kalamazoo, the Albion Female College, the State Normal School at Ypsilanti, and the State Agricultural College at Lansing, are chief among the academic institutions. Michigan (a term of Chippeway origin, and signifying "Great Lake), was discovered and first settled by French Canadians, who, in 1670, founded Detroit, the pioneer of a series of trading-posts on the Indian frontier. During the " Conspiracy of Pontiac," following the French loss of Canada, Michigan became the scene of a sanguinary struggle between the whites and aborigines. In 1796, it became annexed to the United States, which incorporated this region with the Northwest Territory, and then with Indiana Territory, till 1803, when it became territorially independent. Michigan was the theater of warlike operations during the war of 1812 with Great Britain, and in 1819 was authorized to be represented by one delegate in Congress; in 1837 she was admitted into the Union as a State, and in 1869 ratified the 15th Amendment to the Federal Constitution. Population, 1,184,059.

WISCONSIN.

It has a mean length of 260 miles, and a maximum breadth of 215. Land area, 53,924 square miles, or 34,511,360 acres Wisconsin lies at a considerable altitude above sea-level, and consists for the most part of an upland plateau, the surface of which is undulating and very generally diversified. Numerous local eminences called mounds are interspersed over the State, and the Lake Michigan coast-line is in many parts characterized by lofty escarped cliffs, even as on the west side the banks of the Mississippi form a series of high and picturesque bluffs. A group of islands known as The Apostles lie off the extreme north point of the State in Lake Superior, and the great estuary of Green Bay, running far inland, gives formation to a long, narrow peninsula between its waters and those of Lake Michigan. The river-system of Wisconsin has three outlets — those of Lake Superior, Green Bay, and the Mississippi, which latter stream forms the entire southwest frontier, widening at one point into the large watery expanse called Lake Pepin Lake Superior receives the St. Louis, Burnt Wood, and Montreal Rivers; Green Bay, the Menomonee, Peshtigo, Oconto, and Fox; while into the Mississippi empty the St. Croix, Chippewa, Black, Wisconsin, and Rock Rivers. The chief interior lakes are those of Winnebago, Horicon, and Court Oreilles, and smaller sheets of water stud a great part of the surface The climate is healthful, with cold Winters and brief but very warm Summers. Mean annual rainfall 31 inches The geological system represented by the State, embraces those rocks included between the primary and the Devonian series, the former containing extensive deposits of copper and iron ore. Besides these minerals, lead and zinc are found in great quantities, together with kaolin, plumbago, gypsum, and various clays. Mining, consequently, forms a prominent industry, and one of yearly increasing dimensions. The soil of Wisconsin is of varying quality, but fertile on the whole, and in the north parts of the State heavily timbered. The agricultural yield comprises the cereals, together with flax, hemp, tobacco, pulse, sorgum, and all kinds of vegetables, and of the hardier fruits. In 1870, the State had a total number of 102,904 farms, occupying 11,715,321 acres, of which 5,899,343 consisted of improved land, and 3,437,442 were timbered. Cash value of farms, $300,414,064; of farm implements and machinery, $14,239,364. Total estimated value of all farm products, including betterments and additions to stock, $78,027,032; of orchard and dairy stuffs, $1,045,933; of lumber, $1,327,618; of home manufactures, $338,423; of all live-stock, $45,310,882. Number of manufacturing establishments, 7,136, employing 39,055 hands, and turning out productions valued at $85,624,966. The political divisions of the State form 61 counties, and the chief places of wealth, trade, and population, are Madison (the capital), Milwaukee, Fond du Lac, Oshkosh, Prairie du Chien, Janesville, Portage City, Racine, Kenosha, and La Crosse. In 1870, the total assessed valuation reached $333,209,838, as against a true valuation of both real and personal estate aggregating $602,207,329. Treasury receipts during 1870, $886,-696, disbursements, $906,329. Value of church property, $4,749,983. Education is amply provided for. Independently of the State University at Madison, and those of Galesville and of Lawrence at Appleton, and the colleges of Beloit, Racine, and Milton, there are Normal Schools at Platteville and Whitewater. The State is divided into 4,802 common school districts, maintained at a cost, in 1870, of $2,094,160. The charitable institutions of Wisconsin include a Deaf and Dumb Asylum, an Institute for the Education of the Blind, and a Soldiers' Orphans' School. In January, 1870, the railroad system ramified throughout the State totalized 2,779 miles of track, including several lines far advanced toward completion. Immigration is successfully encouraged by the State authorities, the larger number of yearly new-comers being of Scandinavian and German origin. The territory now occupied within the limits of the State of Wisconsin was explored by French missionaries and traders in 1639, and it remained under French jurisdiction until 1703, when it became annexed to the British North American possessions. In 1796, it reverted to the United States, the government of which latter admitted it within the limits of the Northwest Territory, and in 1809, attached it to that of Illinois, and to Michigan in 1818. Wisconsin became independently territorially organized in 1836, and became a State of the Union, March 3, 1847. Population in 1870, 1,064,985, of which 2,113 were of the colored race, and 11,521 Indians, 1,206 of the latter being out of tribal relations.

MINNESOTA.

Its length, north to south, embraces an extent of 380 miles; its oreadth one of 250 miles at a maximum. Area, 84,000 square miles, or 54,760,000 acres. The surface of Minnesota, generally speaking, consists of a succession of gently undulating plains and prairies, drained by an admirable water-system, and with here and there heavily-timbered bottoms and belts of virgin forest The soil, corresponding with such a superfices, is exceptionally rich, consisting for the most part of a dark, calcareous sandy drift intermixed with loam. A distinguishing physical feature of this State is its riverine ramifications, expanding in nearly every part of it into almost innumerable lakes—the whole presenting an aggregate of water-power having hardly a rival in the Union. Besides the Mississippi — which here has its rise, and drains a basin of 800 miles of country — the principal streams are the Minnesota (334 miles long), the Red River of the North, the St. Croix, St. Louis, and many others of lesser importance; the chief lakes are those called Red, Cass, Leech, Mille Lacs, Vermillion, and Winibigosh. Quite a concatenation of sheets of water fringe the frontier line where Minnesota joins British America, culminating in the Lake of the Woods. It has been estimated, that of an area of 1,200,000 acres of surface between the St. Croix and Mississippi Rivers, not less than 73,000 acres are of lacustrine formation. In point of minerals, the resources of Minnesota have as yet been very imperfectly developed; iron, copper, coal, lead — all these are known to exist in considerable deposits; together with salt, limestone, and potter's clay. The agricultural outlook of the State is in a high degree satisfactory; wheat constitutes the leading cereal in cultivation, with Indian corn and oats in next order. Fruits and vegetables are grown in great plenty and of excellent quality. The lumber resources of Minnesota are important; the pine forests in the north region alone occupying an area of some 21,000 square miles, which in 1870 produced a return of scaled logs amounting to 313,116,416 feet. The natural industrial advantages possessed by Minnesota are largely improved upon by a railroad system. The political divisions of this State number 78 counties; of which the chief cities and towns are: St. Paul (the capital), Stillwater, Red Wing, St. Anthony, Fort Snelling, Minneapolis, and Mankato. Minnesota has already assumed an attitude of high importance as a manufacturing State; this is mainly due to the wonderful command of water-power she possesses, as before spoken of. Besides her timber-trade, the milling of flour, the distillation of whisky, and the tanning of leather, are prominent interests, which in 1869, gave returns to the amount of $14,831,043.

Education is notably provided for on a broad and catholic scale, the entire amount expended scholastically during the year 1870 being $857,- 816; while on November 30 of the preceding year the permanent school fund stood at $2,476,222 Besides a University and Agricultural College, Normal and Reform Schools flourish, and with these may be mentioned such various philanthropic and religious institutions as befit the needs of an intelligent and prosperous community. The finances of the State for the fiscal year terminating December 1, 1870, exhibited a balance on the right side to the amount of $136,164, being a gain of $44,000 over the previous year's figures. The earliest exploration of Minnesota by the whites was made in 1680 by a French Franciscan, Father Hennepin, who gave the name of St. Antony to the Great Falls on the Upper Mississippi In 1763, the Treaty of Versailles ceded this region to England. Twenty years later, Minnesota formed part of the Northwest Territory transferred to the United States, and became herself territorialized independently in 1849. Indian cessions in 1851 enlarged her boundaries, and, May 11, 1857, Minnesota became a unit of the great American federation of States. Population, 439,706.

NEBRASKA

Maximum length, 412 miles; extreme breadth, 208 miles. Area, 75,905 square miles, or 48,636,800 acres. The surface of this State is almost entirely undulating prairie, and forms part of the west slope of the great central basin of the North American Continent. In its west division, near the base of the Rocky Mountains, is a sandy belt of country, irregularly defined. In this part, too, are the "dunes," resembling a wavy sea of sandy billows. as well as the Mauvaises Terres, a tract of singular formation, produced by eccentric disintegrations and denudations of the land. The chief rivers are the Missouri, constituting its entire east line of demarcation; the Nebraska or Platte, the Niobrara, the Republican Fork of the Kansas, the Elkhorn, and the Loup Fork of the Platte. The soil is very various, but consisting chiefly of rich, bottomy loam, admirably adapted to the raising of heavy crops of cereals. All the vegetables and fruits of the temperate zone are produced in great size and plenty. For grazing purposes Nebraska is a State exceptionally well fitted, a region of not less than 23,000,000 acres being adaptable to this branch of husbandry. It is believed that the, as yet, comparatively infertile tracts of land found in various parts of the State are susceptible of productivity by means of a properly conducted system of irrigation. Few minerals of moment have so far been found within the limits of

Nebraska, if we may except important saline deposits at the head of Salt Creek in its southeast section. The State is divided into 57 counties, independent of the Pawnee and Winnebago Indians, and of unorganized territory in the northwest part. The principal towns are Omaha, Lincoln (State capital), Nebraska City, Columbus, Grand Island, etc. In 1870, the total assessed value of property amounted to $53,000,000, being an increase of $11,000,000 over the previous year's returns. The total amount received from the school-fund during the year 1869–70 was $77,999. Education is making great onward strides, the State University and an Agricultural College being far advanced toward completion. In the matter of railroad communication, Nebraska bids fair to soon place herself on a par with her neighbors to the east. Besides being intersected by the Union Pacific line, with its off-shoot, the Fremont and Blair, other tracks are in course of rapid construction. Organized by Congressional Act into a Territory, May 30, 1854, Nebraska entered the Union as a full State, March 1, 1867. Population, 122,993.

HUNTING PRAIRIE WOLVES IN AN EARLY DAY.

CONSTITUTION OF THE UNITED STATES OF AMERICA AND ITS AMENDMENTS.

We, the people of the United States, in order to form a more perfect union, establish justice, insure domestic tranquillity, provide for the common defense, promote the general welfare, and secure the blessings of liberty to ourselves and our posterity, do ordain and establish this Constitution for the United States of America.

ARTICLE I.

SECTION 1. All legislative powers herein granted shall be vested in a Congress of the United States, which shall consist of a Senate and House of Representatives.

SEC. 2. The House of Representatives shall be composed of members chosen every second year by the people of the several states, and the electors in each state shall have the qualifications requisite for electors of the most numerous branch of the State Legislature.

No person shall be a representative who shall not have attained to the age of twenty-five years, and been seven years a citizen of the United States, and who shall not, when elected, be an inhabitant of that state in which he shall be chosen.

Representatives and direct taxes shall be apportioned among the several states which may be included within this Union, according to their respective numbers, which shall be determined by adding to the whole number of free persons, including those bound to service for a term of years, and excluding Indians not taxed, three-fifths of all other persons. The actual enumeration shall be made within three years after the first meeting of the Congress of the United States, and within every subsequent term of ten years, in such manner as they shall by law direct. The number of Representatives shall not exceed one for every thirty thousand, but each state shall have at least one Representative; and until such enumeration shall be made the State of New Hampshire shall be entitled to choose three, Massachusetts eight, Rhode Island and Providence Plantations one, Connecticut five, New York six, New Jersey four, Pennsylvania eight, Delaware one, Maryland six, Virginia ten, North Carolina five, and Georgia three.

When vacancies happen in the representation from any state, the Executive authority thereof shall issue writs of election to fill such vacancies

The House of Representatives shall choose their Speaker and other officers, and shall have the sole power of impeachment.

SEC. 3 The Senate of the United States shall be composed of two Senators from each state, chosen by the Legislature thereof for six years; and each Senator shall have one vote.

Immediately after they shall be assembled in consequence of the first election, they shall be divided as equally as may be into three classes. The seats of the Senators of the first class shall be vacated at the expiration of the second year, of the second class at the expiration of the fourth year, and of the third class at the expiration of the sixth year, so that one-third may be chosen every second year; and if vacancies happen by resignation or otherwise, during the recess of the Legislature of any state, the Executive thereof may make temporary appointments until the next meeting of the Legislature, which shall then fill such vacancies.

No person shall be a Senator who shall not have attained to the age of thirty years and been nine years a citizen of the United States, and who shall not, when elected, be an inhabitant of that state for which he shall be chosen.

The Vice-President of the United States shall be President of th Senate, but shall have no vote unless they be equally divided.

The Senate shall choose their other officers, and also a President *pro tempore*, in the absence of the Vice-President, or when he shall exercise the office of President of the United States

The Senate shall have the sole power to try all impeachments. When sitting for that purpose they shall be on oath or affirmation. When the President of the United States is tried the Chief Justice shall preside. And no person shall be convicted without the concurrence of two-thirds of the members present.

Judgment, in cases of impeachment, shall not extend further than to removal from office, and disqualification to hold and enjoy any office of honor, trust, or profit under the United States; but the party convicted shall nevertheless be liable and subject to indictment, trial, judgment, and punishment according to law.

SEC 4. The times, places and manner of holding elections for Senators and Representatives shall be prescribed in each state by the Legislature thereof; but the Congress may at any time by law make or alter such regulations, except as to the places of choosing Senators.

The Congress shall assemble at least once in every year, and such meeting shall be on the first Monday in December, unless they shall by law appoint a different day.

SEC. 5. Each house shall be the judge of the election, returns, and qualifications of its own members, and a majority of each shall constitute a quorum to do business; but a smaller number may adjourn from day to day, and may be authorized to compel the attendance of absent members in such manner and under such penalties as each house may provide.

Each house may determine the rules of its proceedings, punish its members for disorderly behavior, and, with the concurrence of two-thirds, expel a member.

Each house shall keep a journal of its proceedings, and from time to time publish the same, excepting such parts as may, in their judgment, require secrecy; and the yeas and nays of the members of either house on any question shall, at the desire of one-fifth of those present, be entered on the journal.

Neither house, during the session of Congress, shall, without the consent of the other, adjourn for more than three days, nor to any other place than that in which the two houses shall be sitting.

SEC. 6. The Senators and Representatives shall receive a compensation for their services, to be ascertained by law, and paid out of the treasury of the United States. They shall in all cases, except treason, felony, and breach of the peace, be privileged from arrest during their attendance at the session of their respective houses, and in going to and returning from the same; and for any speech or debate in either house they shall not be questioned in any other place.

No Senator or Representative shall, during the time for which he was elected, be appointed to any civil office under the authority of the United States, which shall have been created, or the emoluments whereof shall have been increased during such time; and no person holding any office under the United States, shall be a member of either house during his continuance in office

SEC. 7. All bills for raising revenue shall originate in the House of Representatives; but the Senate may propose or concur with amendments as on other bills.

Every bill which shall have passed the House of Representatives and the Senate, shall, before it becomes a law, be presented to the President the United States; if he approve he shall sign it, but if not he shall return it, with his objections, to that house in which it shall have originated, who shall enter the objections at large on their journal, and proceed to reconsider it. If, after such reconsideration two-thirds of that house shall agree to pass the bill, it shall be sent, together with the objections, to the other house, by which it shall likewise be reconsidered, and if approved by two-thirds of that house, it shall become a law. But in all such cases the votes of both houses shall be determined by yeas and nays, and the names of the persons voting for and against the bill shall be entered on the journal of each house respectively. If any bill shall not be returned by the President within ten days (Sundays excepted), after it shall have been presented to him, the same shall be a law, in like manner as if he had signed it, unless the Congress, by their adjournment, prevent its return, in which case it shall not be a law.

Every order, resolution, or vote to which the concurrence of the Senate and House of Representatives may be necessary (except on a question of adjournment), shall be presented to the President of the United States, and before the same shall take effect shall be approved by him, or, being disapproved by him, shall be re-passed by two-thirds of the Senate and House of Representatives, according to the rules and limitations prescribed in the case of a bill.

SEC. 8. The Congress shall have power—

To lay and collect taxes, duties, imposts and excises, to pay the debts, and provide for the common defense and general welfare of the United States; but all duties, imposts, and excises shall be uniform throughout the United States;

To borrow money on the credit of the United States;

To regulate commerce with foreign nations, and among the several States, and with the Indian tribes;

To establish a uniform rule of naturalization, and uniform laws on the subject of bankruptcies throughout the United States;

To coin money, regulate the value thereof, and of foreign coin, and fix the standard of weights and measures;

To provide for the punishment of counterfeiting the securities and current coin of the United States,

To establish post offices and post roads;

To promote the progress of sciences and useful arts, by securing, for limited times, to authors and inventors, the exclusive right to their respective writings and discoveries;

To constitute tribunals inferior to the Supreme Court;

To define and punish piracies and felonies committed on the high seas, and offenses against the law of nations;

To declare war, grant letters of marque and reprisal, and make rules concerning captures on land and water,

To raise and support armies, but no appropriation of money to that use shall be for a longer term than two years;

To provide and maintain a navy;

To make rules for the government and regulation of the land and naval forces;

To provide for calling forth the militia to execute the laws of the Union, suppress insurrections, and repel invasions;

To provide for organizing, arming and disciplining the militia, and for governing such part of them as may be employed in the service of the United States, reserving to the states respectively the appointment of the officers, and the authority of training the militia according to the discipline prescribed by Congress;

To exercise legislation in all cases whatsoever over such district (not exceeding ten miles square) as may, by cession of particular states, and the acceptance of Congress, become the seat of the government of the United States, and to exercise like authority over all places purchased by the consent of the Legislature of the state in which the same shall be, for the erection of forts, magazines, arsenals, dock yards, and other needful buildings; and

To make all laws which shall be necessary and proper for carrying into execution the foregoing powers, and all other powers vested by this Constitution in the government of the United States, or in any department or officer thereof,

Sec 9. The migration or importation of such persons as any of the states now existing shall think proper to admit, shall not be prohibited by the Congress prior to the year one thousand eight hundred and eight, but a tax or duty may be imposed on such importation, not exceeding ten dollars for each person.

The privilege of the writ of habeas corpus shall not be suspended, unless when in cases of rebellion or invasion the public safety may require it.

No bill of attainder or *ex post facto* law shall be passed.

No capitation or other direct tax shall be laid, unless in proportion to the census or enumeration hereinbefore directed to be taken.

No tax or duty shall be laid on articles exported from any state

No preference shall be given by any regulation of commerce or revenue to the ports of one state over those of another; nor shall vessels bound to or from one state be obliged to enter, clear, or pay duties in another.

No money shall be drawn from the Treasury, but in consequence of appropriations made by law; and a regular statement and account of the receipts and expeditures of all public money shall be published from time to time.

No title of nobility shall be granted by the United States: and no person holding any office of profit or trust under them, shall, without the consent of the Congress, accept of any present, emolument, office, or title of any kind whatever, from any king, prince, or foreign state.

SEC. 10. No state shall enter into any treaty, alliance, or confederation, grant letters of marque and reprisal; coin money; emit bills of credit; make anything but gold and silver coin a tender in payment of debts; pass any bill of attainder, *ex post facto* law, or law impairing the obligation of contracts, or grant any title of nobility.

No state shall, without the consent of the Congress, lay any imposts or duties on imports or exports, except what may be absolutely necessary for executing its inspection laws, and the net produce of all duties and imposts laid by any state on imports or exports, shall be for the use of the Treasury of the United States; and all such laws shall be subject to the revision and control of the Congress.

No state shall, without the consent of Congress, lay any duty on tonnage, keep troops or ships of war in time of peace, enter into any agreement or compact with another state, or with a foreign power, or engage in war, unless actually invaded, or in such imminent danger as will not admit of delay.

ARTICLE II.

SECTION 1. The Executive power shall be vested in a President of the United States of America. He shall hold his office during the term of four years, and, together with the Vice-President chosen for the same term, be elected as follows:

Each state shall appoint, in such manner as the Legislature thereof may direct, a number of Electors, equal to the whole number of Senators and Representatives to which the state may be entitled in the Congress; but no Senator or Representative, or person holding an office of trust or profit under the United States, shall be appointed an Elector.

[* The Electors shall meet in their respective states, and vote by ballot for two persons, of whom one at least shall not be an inhabitant of the same state with themselves. And they shall make a list of all the persons voted for, and of the number of votes for each; which list they shall sign and certify, and transmit, sealed, to the seat of the government of the United States, directed to the President of the Senate. The President of the Senate shall, in the presence of the Senate and House of Representatives, open all the certificates, and the votes shall then be counted. The person having the greatest number of votes shall be the President, if such number be a majority of the whole number of Electors appointed; and if there be more than one who have such majority, and have an equal number of votes, then the House of Representatives shall immediately choose by ballot one of them for President; and if no person have a majority, then from the five highest on the list the said House shall in like manner choose the President. But in choosing the President, the vote shall be taken by states, the representation from each state having one vote; a quorum for this purpose shall consist of a member or members from two-thirds of the states, and a majority of all the states shall be necessary to a choice. In every case, after the choice of the President,

---

* This clause between brackets has been superseded and annulled by the Twelfth amendment

the person having the greatest number of votes of the Electors shall be the Vice-President. But if there should remain two or more who have equal votes, the Senate shall choose from them by ballot the Vice-President.]

The Congress may determine the time of choosing the Electors, and the day on which they shall give their votes; which day shall be the same throughout the United States.

No person except a natural born citizen, or a citizen of the United States at the time of the adoption of this Constitution, shall be eligible to the office of President; neither shall any person be eligible to that office who shall not have attained the age of thirty-five years, and been fourteen years a resident within the United States.

In case of the removal of the President from office, or of his death, resignation, or inability to discharge the powers and duties of the said office, the same shall devolve on the Vice-President, and the Congress may by law provide for the case of removal, death, resignation, or inability, both of the President and Vice-President, declaring what officer shall then act as President, and such officer shall act accordingly, until the disability be removed, or a President shall be elected.

The President shall, at stated times, receive for his services a compensation which shall neither be increased nor diminished during the period for which he shall have been elected, and he shall not receive within that period any other emolument from the United States or any of them.

Before he enters on the execution of his office, he shall take the following oath or affirmation:

"I do solemnly swear (or affirm) that I will faithfully execute the office of President of the United States, and will, to the best of my ability, preserve, protect, and defend the Constitution of the United States."

SEC. 2. The President shall be commander in chief of the army and navy of the United States, and of the militia of the several states, when called into the actual service of the United States; he may require the opinion, in writing, of the principal officer in each of the executive departments, upon any subject relating to the duties of their respective offices, and he shall have power to grant reprieves and pardon for offenses against the United States, except in cases of impeachment.

He shall have power, by and with the advice and consent of the Senate, to make treaties, provided two-thirds of the Senators present concur; and he shall nominate, and by and with the advice of the Senate, shall appoint ambassadors, other public ministers and consuls, judges of the Supreme Court, and all other officers of the United States whose appointments are not herein otherwise provided for, and which shall be established by law; but the Congress may by law vest the appointment of such inferior officers as they think proper in the President alone, in the courts of law, or in the heads of departments.

The President shall have power to fill up all vacancies that may happen during the recess of the Senate, by granting commissions which shall expire at the end of their next session.

SEC. 3. He shall from time to time give to the Congress information of the state of the Union, and recommend to their consideration such measures as he shall judge necessary and expedient; he may on extraordinary occasions convene both houses, or either of them. and in case of disagreement between them, with respect to the time of adjournment, he may adjourn them to such time as he shall think proper; he shall receive ambassadors and other public ministers, he shall take care that the laws be faithfully executed, and shall commission all the officers of the United States.

SEC. 4. The President, Vice-President, and all civil officers of the United States, shall be removed from office on impeachment for, and conviction of, treason, bribery, or other high crimes and misdemeanors.

ARTICLE III.

SECTION I. The judicial power of the United States shall be vested in one Supreme Court, and such inferior courts as the Congress may from time to time ordain and establish. The Judges, both of the Supreme and inferior courts, shall hold their offices during good behavior, and shall, at stated times, receive for their services a compensation, which shall not be diminished during their continuance in office.

SEC. 2. The judicial power shall extend to all cases, in law and equity, arising under this Constitution, the laws of the United States, and treaties made, or which shall be made, under their authority; to all cases affecting ambassadors, other public ministers, and consuls, to all cases of admiralty and maritime jurisdiction; to controversies to which the United States shall be a party, to controversies between two or more states; between a state and citizens of another state; between citizens of different states, between citizens of the same state claiming lands under grants of different states, and between a state or the citizens thereof, and foreign states, citizens, or subjects.

In all cases affecting ambassadors, other public ministers, and consuls, and those in which a state shall be a party, the Supreme Court shall have original jurisdiction.

In all the other cases before mentioned, the Supreme Court shall have appellate jurisdiction, both as to law and fact, with such exceptions and under such regulations as the Congress shall make.

The trial of all crimes, except in cases of impeachment, shall be by jury, and such trial shall be held in the state where the said crimes shall have been committed; but when not committed within any state, the trial shall be at such place or places as the Congress may by law have directed.

SEC. 3. Treason against the United States shall consist only in levying war against them, or in adhering to their enemies, giving them aid and comfort. No person shall be convicted of treason unless on the testimony of two witnesses to the same overt act, or on confession in open court.

The Congress shall have power to declare the punishment of treason but no attainder of treason shall work corruption of blood, or forfeiture except during the life of the person attainted.

ARTICLE IV.

SECTION 1. Full faith and credit shall be given in each state to the public acts, records, and judicial proceedings of every other state. And the Congress may, by general laws, prescribe the manner in which such acts, records, and proceedings shall be proved, and the effect thereof.

Sec. 2. The citizens of each state shall be entitled to all privileges and immunities of citizens in the several states.

A person charged in any state with treason, felony, or other crime, who shall flee from justice and be found in another state, shall, on demand of the executive authority of the state from which he fled, be delivered up, to be removed to the state having jurisdiction of the crime.

No person held to service or labor in one state, under the laws thereof escaping into another, shall, in consequence of any law or regulation therein, be discharged from such service or labor, but shall be delivered up on the claim of the party to whom such service or labor may be due.

Sec. 3. New states may be admitted by the Congress into this Union; but no new state shall be formed or erected within the jurisdiction of any other state; nor any state be formed by the junction of two or more states, or parts of states, without the consent of the Legislatures of the states concerned, as well as of the Congress.

The Congress shall have power to dispose of and make all needful rules and regulations respecting the territory or other property belonging to the United States; and nothing in this Constitution shall be so construed as to prejudice any claims of the United States or of any particular state.

Sec. 4. The United States shall guarantee to every state in this Union a republican form of government, and shall protect each of them against invasion, and on application of the Legislature, or of the Executive (when the Legislature can not be convened), against domestic violence.

ARTICLE V.

The Congress, whenever two-thirds of both houses shall deem it necessary, shall propose amendments to this Constitution, or, on the application of the Legislatures of two-thirds of the several states, shall call a convention for proposing amendments, which, in either case, shall be valid to all intents and purposes as part of this Constitution, when ratified by the Legislatures of three fourths of the several states, or by conventions in three-fourths thereof, as the one or the other mode of ratification may be proposed by the Congress. Provided that no amendment which may be made prior to the year one thousand eight hundred and eight shall in any manner affect the first and fourth clauses in the ninth section of the first article; and that no state, without its consent, shall be deprived of its equal suffrage in the Senate.

ARTICLE VI.

All debts contracted and engagements entered into before the adoption of this Constitution shall be as valid against the United States under this Constitution as under the Confederation.

This Constitution, and the laws of the United States which shall be made in pursuance thereof, and all treaties made, or which shall be made, under the authority of the United States, shall be the supreme law of the land; and the Judges in every state shall be bound thereby, anything in the Constitution or laws of any state to the contrary notwithstanding.

The Senators and Representatives before mentioned, and the members of the several state Legislatures, and all executive and judicial officers, both of the United States and of the several states, shall be bound by oath or affirmation to support this Constitution, but no religious test shall ever be required as a qualification to any office or public trust under the United States.

ARTICLE VII.

The ratification of the Conventions of nine states shall be sufficient for the establishment of this Constitution between the states so ratifying the same.

Done in convention by the unanimous consent of the states present, the seventeenth day of September, in the year of our Lord one thousand seven hundred and eighty-seven, and of the independence of the United States of America the twelfth. In witness whereof we have hereunto subscribed our names

GEO. WASHINGTON,
President and Deputy from Virginia.

New Hampshire.
JOHN LANGDON,
NICHOLAS GILMAN.

Massachusetts.
NATHANIEL GORHAM,
RUFUS KING.

Connecticut.
WM. SAM'L JOHNSON,
ROGER SHERMAN.

New York.
ALEXANDER HAMILTON.

New Jersey.
WIL. LIVINGSTON,
WM. PATERSON,
DAVID BREARLEY,
JONA. DAYTON.

Pennsylvania.
B. FRANKLIN,
ROBT. MORRIS,
THOS. FITZSIMONS,
JAMES WILSON,
THOS. MIFFLIN,
GEO. CLYMER,
JARED INGERSOLL,
GOUV. MORRIS.

Delaware.
GEO. READ,
JOHN DICKINSON,
JACO BROOM,
GUNNING BEDFORD, JR.,
RICHARD BASSETT.

Maryland.
JAMES M'HENRY,
DANL. CARROLL,
DAN. OF ST. THOS. JENIFER.

Virginia.
JOHN BLAIR,
JAMES MADISON, JR.

North Carolina.
WM. BLOUNT,
HU. WILLIAMSON,
RICH'D DOBBS SPAIGHT.

South Carolina.
J. RUTLEDGE,
CHARLES PINCKNEY,
CHAS. COTESWORTH PINCKNEY,
PIERCE BUTLER.

Georgia.
WILLIAM FEW,
ABR BALDWIN.

WILLIAM JACKSON, *Secretary.*

ARTICLES IN ADDITION TO AND AMENDATORY OF THE CONSTITUTION OF THE UNITED STATES OF AMERICA.

Proposed by Congress and ratified by the Legislatures of the several states, pursuant to the fifth article of the original Constitution.

ARTICLE I.

Congress shall make no law respecting an establishment of religion, or prohibiting the free exercise thereof; or abridging the freedom of speech, or of the press; or the right of the people peaceably to assemble, and to petition the Government for a redress of grievances.

ARTICLE II.

A well regulated militia being necessary to the security of a free state, the right of the people to keep and bear arms shall not be infringed.

ARTICLE III.

No soldier shall, in time of peace, be quartered in any house without the consent of the owner, nor in time of war but in a manner to be prescribed by law.

ARTICLE IV.

The right of the people to be secure in their persons, houses, papers, and effects against unreasonable searches and seizures, shall not be violated; and no warrants shall issue but upon probable cause, supported by oath or affirmation, and particularly describing the place to be searched and the persons or things to be seized.

ARTICLE V.

No person shall be held to answer for a capital or otherwise infamous crime, unless on a presentment or indictment of a Grand Jury, except in cases arising in the land or naval forces, or in the militia when in actual service in time of war or public danger; nor shall any person be subject for the same offense to be twice put in jeopardy of life or limb; nor shall be compelled in any criminal case to be a witness against himself, nor be deprived of life, liberty, or property, without due process of law; nor shall private property be taken for public use, without just compensation.

ARTICLE VI.

In all criminal prosecutions, the accused shall enjoy the right to a speedy and public trial, by an impartial jury of the state and district wherein the crime shall have been committed, which district shall have been previously ascertained by law, and to be informed of the nature and cause of the accusation; to be confronted with the witnesses against him; to have compulsory process for obtaining witnesses in his favor; and to have the assistance of counsel for his defense.

ARTICLE VII.

In suits at common law, where the value in controversy shall exceed twenty dollars, the right of trial by jury shall be preserved, and no fact tried by a jury shall be otherwise re-examined in any court of the United States than according to the rules of the common law.

ARTICLE VIII.

Excessive bail shall not be required, nor excessive fines imposed, nor cruel and unusual punishments inflicted.

ARTICLE IX.

The enumeration, in the Constitution, of certain rights, shall not be construed to deny or disparage others retained by the people.

ARTICLE X.

The powers not delegated to the United States by the Constitution, nor prohibited by it to the states, are reserved to the states respectively, or to the people.

ARTICLE XI.

The judicial power of the United States shall not be construed to extend to any suit in law or equity commenced or prosecuted against one of the United States by citizens of another state, or by citizens or subjects of any foreign state.

ARTICLE XII.

The Electors shall meet in their respective states and vote by ballot for President and Vice-President, one of whom, at least, shall not be an inhabitant of the same state with themselves; they shall name in their ballots the person to be voted for as president, and in distinct ballots the person voted for as Vice-President, and they shall make distinct lists of all persons voted for as President, and of all persons voted for as Vice-President, and of the number of votes for each, which list they shall sign and certify, and transmit sealed to the seat of the government of the United States, directed to the President of the Senate. The President of the Senate shall, in presence of the Senate and House of Representatives, open all the certificates, and the votes shall then be counted. The person having the greatest number of votes for President shall be the President, if such number be a majority of the whole number of Electors appointed; and if no person have such majority, then from the persons having the highest number not exceeding three on the list of those voted for as President, the House of Representatives shall choose immediately, by ballot, the President. But in choosing the President, the votes shall be taken by States, the representation from each state having one vote; a quorum for this purpose shall consist of a member or members from two-thirds of the states, and a majority of all the states shall be necessary to a choice. And if the House of Representatives shall not choose a President whenever the right of choice shall devolve upon them, before the fourth day of March next following, then the Vice-President shall act as President, as in the case of the death or other constitutional disability of the President. The person having the greatest number of votes as Vice-President, shall be the Vice-President, if such number be the majority of the whole number of electors appointed, and if no person have a major-

ity, then from the two highest numbers on the list, the Senate shall choose the Vice-President; a quorum for the purpose shall consist of two-thirds of the whole number of Senators, and a majority of the whole number shall be necessary to a choice. But no person constitutionally ineligible to the office of President shall be eligible to that of Vice-President of the United States.

ARTICLE XIII.

SECTION 1. Neither slavery nor involuntary servitude, except as a punishment for crime, whereof the party shall have been duly convicted, shall exist within the United States, or any place subject to their jurisdiction.

SEC. 2. Congress shall have power to enforce this article by appropriate legislation.

ARTICLE XIV.

SECTION 1. All persons born or naturalized in the United States and subject to the jurisdiction thereof, are citizens of the United States, and of the state wherein they reside. No state shall make or enforce any law which shall abridge the privileges or immunities of citizens of the United States; nor shall any state deprive any person of life, liberty, or property, without due process of law, nor deny to any person within its jurisdiction the equal protection of the laws.

SEC. 2. Representatives shall be appointed among the several states according to their respective numbers, counting the whole number of persons in each state, excluding Indians not taxed; but when the right to vote at any election for the choice of Electors for President and Vice-President of the United States, Representatives in Congress, the executive and judicial officers of a state, or the members of the Legislature thereof, is denied to any of the male inhabitants of such state, being twenty-one years of age and citizens of the United States, or in any way abridged except for participation in rebellion or other crimes, the basis of representation therein shall be reduced in the proportion which the number of such male citizens shall bear to the whole number of male citizens twenty-one years of age in such state.

SEC. 3. No person shall be a Senator or Representative in Congress, or Elector of President and Vice-President, or hold any office, civil or military, under the United States, or under any state, who, having previously taken an oath as a Member of Congress, or as an officer of the United States, or as a member of any state Legislature, or as an executive or judicial officer of any state to support the Constitution of the United States, shall have engaged in insurrection or rebellion against the same, or given aid or comfort to the enemies thereof. But Congress may by a vote of two-thirds of each house, remove such disability.

SEC. 4. The validity of the public debt of the United States authorized by law, including debts incurred for payment of pensions and bounties for services in suppressing insurrection or rebellion, shall not be questioned. But neither the United States nor any state shall pay any debt or obligation incurred in the aid of insurrection or rebellion against the United States, or any loss or emancipation of any slave, but such debts, obligations, and claims shall be held illegal and void.

ARTICLE XV.

SECTION 1. The right of citizens of the United States to vote shall not be denied or abridged by the United States, or by any State, on account of race, color, or previous condition of servitude.

VOTE FOR GOVERNOR, 1877, AND PRESIDENT, 1876.

COUNTIES.	1877. Governor.				1876. President.		COUNTIES.	1877. Governor.				1876. President.	
	Rep.	Dem.	Gr.	Pro.	Rep.	Dem.		Rep.	Dem.	Gr.	Pro.	Rep.	Dem.
Adair	982	151	581	15	1334	693	Johnson	1884	2345	18	273	2345	3563
Adams	876	397	485	38	1376	626	Jones	1868	1218	14	68	2591	1763
Allamakee	1547	1540	69	36	1709	1646	Keokuk	1772	1526	322	105	2364	1862
Appanoose	1105	1049	729	82	1711	1419	Kossuth	463	236	13	89	638	227
Audubon	410	352	26	......	427	352	Lee	2157	2863	350	299	3160	3682
Benton	1432	712	567	449	2901	1356	Linn	2524	2316	75	685	4331	2917
Black Hawk	1780	1111	95	244	2979	1592	Louisa	1328	817	89	108	1920	1008
Boone	1612	981	466	10	2918	1305	Lucas	1263	804	103	12	1478	1644
Bremer	1180	682	196	1	1737	757	Lyon	261	17	9	14	262	46
Buchanan	1290	769	725	223	2227	1416	Madison	1792	1077	616	56	2248	1538
Buena Vista	747	192	161	20	770	200	Mahaska	1823	1046	1011	696	3221	1701
Butler	1453	758	19	95	1828	780	Marion	1976	1866	760	95	2736	2804
Calhoun	418	75	171	74	622	196	Marshall	1448	837	389	504	3056	1189
Carroll	633	744	141	11	799	771	Mills	1435	1102	98	28	1452	1165
Cass	1692	839	116	30	1876	979	Mitchell	1396	459	35	36	1663	671
Cedar	1315	1093	206	446	2328	1445	Monona	580	110	432	9	713	304
Cerro Gordo	903	348	72	40	1274	448	Monroe	1034	928	247	26	1418	1246
Cherokee	662	74	383	86	864	176	Montgomery	1122	441	532	47	1740	759
Chickasaw	1279	1107	37	94	1574	1090	Muscatine	1753	1775	171	387	2523	2075
Clark	1054	267	813	19	1405	816	O'Brien	306	21	201	14	463	118
Clay	617	16	20	67	567	94	Osceola	295	40	13	33	329	59
Clayton	1873	1779	66	167	2692	2621	Page	1166	508	348	293	2248	861
Clinton	2444	2327	286	66	3654	3308	Palo Alto	311	357	......	3	343	333
Crawford	808	651	19	111	1043	638	Plymouth	779	487	77	39	835	502
Dallas	1541	215	1241	80	2136	752	Pocahontas	370	93	44	36	374	141
Davis	893	1231	803	12	1586	1631	Polk	3171	1885	1353	94	4321	2382
Decatur	1269	961	810	19	1647	1282	Pottawattamie	2223	2059	218	121	2565	2414
Delaware	1226	1143	32	525	2233	1466	Poweshiek	1496	882	429	346	2509	1083
Des Moines	2315	1384	767	6	3325	2917	Ringgold	964	71	671	47	1246	422
Dickinson	197	8	......	12	259	48	Sac	656	128	177	13	661	168
Dubuque	1687	3415	406	53	2798	4977	Scott	3031	1963	309	37	3816	2859
Emmett	213	28	......	......	246	36	Shelby	888	689	3	16	807	631
Fayette	1933	1067	889	27	3029	1709	Sioux	436	132	49	......	439	220
Floyd	1233	208	162	30	2032	751	Story	1260	344	644	187	1843	579
Franklin	1311	336	16	10	1178	379	Tama	1426	833	196	133	2337	1317
Fremont	1250	1331	334	......	1658	1682	Taylor	1326	293	868	......	1727	678
Greene	1031	215	551	27	1310	510	Union	899	516	830	63	1238	795
Grundy	909	504	......	8	1099	417	Van Buren	1499	1305	301	130	2113	1661
Guthrie	1160	496	864	21	1434	629	Wapello	1710	1929	1265	290	2582	2412
Hamilton	842	265	422	57	1187	425	Warren	1726	944	742	101	2439	1315
Hancock	340	95	29	2	281	99	Washington	1687	1221	303	112	2467	1508
Hardin	1492	661	238	154	2152	980	Wayne	1316	832	404	3	1692	1341
Harrison	1348	86?	523	19	1557	1386	Webster	860	127	1421	47	1299	987
Henry	1770	424	1041	140	2309	1485	Winnebago	544	40	......	......	498	89
Howard	551	647	201	519	1194	600	Winneshiek	2074	1009	279	238	2759	1617
Humboldt	382	149	115	64	523	188	Woodbury	1109	867	226	9	1034	997
Ida	321	84	104	......	212	57	Worth	628	132	8	14	703	149
Iowa	1132	1120	642	228	1870	1348	Wright	391	166	117	98	574	184
Jackson	1619	1966	224	15	2126	2486							
Jasper	1977	1154	1015	268	3375	1804	Totals	121546	79853	34228	10639	1713??	112127
Jefferson	1396	753	576	169	2166	1449	Majorities	42198	......	......	......	59211	......

Total vote, 1877, 245,766, 1876 (including 940 Greenback), 292,943.

VOTE FOR CONGRESSMEN, 1876.

District.	Rep.	Dem.	R. Maj.	Total.	Maj. '74.	District.	Rep.	Dem.	R. Maj.	Total.	Maj. '74.
I	17188	14814	2374	32002	D. 1863	VII	19496	11688	7808	31184	R. 2300
II	16430	14683	1766	31122	R. 657	VIII	19358	15236	4122	34594	R. 2127
III	17423	16100	1323	33623	D. 63	IX	19563	10583	8980	30146	R. 5849
IV	20770	9379	11391	30149	R. 3824						
V	19274	11154	8120	30428	R. 6245						
VI	18778	14719	4059	33497	R. 2724		168289	118356	49933	*292111	......

Total vote, 1874, 184,640; aggregate Republican majority, 24,524. *Including 6,466 Greenback votes.

Practical Rules for Every Day Use.

How to find the gain or loss per cent. when the cost and selling price are given.

RULE.—Find the difference between the cost and selling price, which will be the gain or loss.

Annex two ciphers to the gain or loss, and divide it by the cost price ; the result will be the gain or loss per cent.

How to change gold into currency.

RULE.—Multiply the given sum of gold by the price of gold.

How to change currency into gold.

Divide the amount in currency by the price of gold.

How to find each partner's share of the gain or loss in a copartnership business.

RULE.—Divide the whole gain or loss by the entire stock, the quotient will be the gain or loss per cent

Multiply each partner's stock by this per cent , the result will be each one's share of the gain or loss.

How to find gross and net weight and price of hogs.

A short and simple method for finding the net weight, or price of hogs, when the gross weight or price is given, and vice versa.

NOTE—It is generally assumed that the gross weight of Hogs diminished by 1-5 or 20 per cent. of itself gives the net weight and the net weight increased by ¼ or 25 per cent. of itself equals the gross weight.

To find the net weight or gross price.

Multiply the given number by .8 (tenths.)

To find the gross weight or net price.

Divide the given number by 8 (tenths.)

How to find the capacity of a granary, bin, or wagon-bed.

RULE.—Multiply (by short method) the number of cubic feet by 6308, and point off ONE decimal place—the result will be the correct nswer in bushels and tenths of a bushel.

For only an approximate answer, multiply the cubic feet by 8, and point off one decimal place.

How to find the contents of a corn-crib.

RULE.—Multiply the number of cubic feet by 54, short method, or by 4½ ordinary method, and point off ONE decimal place—the result will be the answer in bushels

How to find the contents of a cistern or tank.

RULE.—Multiply the square of the mean diameter by the depth (all in feet) and this product by 5681 (short method), and point off ONE decimal place—the result will be the contents in barrels of 31½ gallons.

How to find the contents of a barrel or cask.

RULE.—Under the square of the mean diameter, write the length (all in inches) in REVERSED order, so that its UNITS will fall under the TENS; multiply by short method, and this product again by 430; point off one decimal place, and the result will be the answer in wine gallons.

How to measure boards.

RULE.—Multiply the length (in feet) by the width (in inches) and divide the product by 12—the result will be the contents in square feet.

How to measure scantlings, joists, planks, sills, etc.

RULE.—Multiply the width, the thickness, and the length together (the width and thickness in inches, and the length in feet), and divide the product by 12—the result will be square feet.

How to find the number of acres in a body of land.

RULE.—Multiply the length by the width (in rods), and divide the product by 160 (carrying the division to 2 decimal places if there is a remainder), the result will be the answer in acres and hundredths.

When the opposite sides of a piece of land are of unequal length, add them together and take one-half for the mean length or width.

How to find the number of square yards in a floor or wall.

RULE.—Multiply the length by the width or height (in feet), and divide the product by 9, the result will be square yards.

How to find the number of bricks required in a building.

RULE.—Multiply the number of cubic feet by 22½.

The number of cubic feet is found by multiplying the length, height nd thickness (in feet) together.

Bricks are usually made 8 inches long, 4 inches wide, and two inches thick, hence, it requires 27 bricks to make a cubic foot without mortar, but it is generally assumed that the mortar fills 1-6 of the space.

How to find the number of shingles required in a roof.

RULE.—Multiply the number of square feet in the roof by 8, if the shingles are exposed 4½ inches, or by 7 1-5 if exposed 5 inches

To find the number of square feet, multiply the length of the roof by twice the length of the rafters.

To find the length of the rafters, at ONE–FOURTH pitch, multiply the width of the building by .56 (hundredths), at ONE–THIRD pitch, by .6 (tenths); at TWO–FIFTHS pitch, by .64 (hundredths), at ONE–HALF pitch, by 71 (hundredths). This gives the length of the rafters from the apex to the end of the wall, and whatever they are to project must be taken into consideration.

NOTE—By ¼ or ½ pitch is meant that the apex or comb of the roof is to be ¼ or ½ the width of the building higher than the walls or base of the rafters

How to reckon the cost of hay.

RULE.—Multiply the number of pounds by half the price per ton, and remove the decimal point three places to the left.

How to measure grain.

RULE.—Level the grain; ascertain the space it occupies in cubic feet; multiply the number of cubic feet by 8, and point off one place to the left.

NOTE—Exactness requires the addition to every three hundred bushels of one extra bushel

The foregoing rule may be used for finding the number of gallons, by multiplying the number of bushels by 8.

If the corn in the box is in the ear, divide the answer by 2, to find the number of bushels of shelled corn, because it requires 2 bushels of ear corn to make 1 of shelled corn.

Rapid rules for measuring land without instruments.

In measuring land, the first thing to ascertain is the contents of any given plot in square yards; then, given the number of yards, find out the number of rods and acres.

The most ancient and simplest measure of distance is a step. Now, an ordinary-sized man can train himself to cover one yard at a stride, on the average, with sufficient accuracy for ordinary purposes.

To make use of this means of measuring distances, it is essential to walk in a straight line; to do this, fix the eye on two objects in a line straight ahead, one comparatively near, the other remote, and, in walking, keep these objects constantly in line.

Farmers and others by adopting the following simple and ingenious contrivance, may always carry with them the scale to construct a correct yard measure

Take a foot rule, and commencing at the base of the little finger of the left hand, mark the quarters of the foot on the outer borders of the left arm, pricking in the marks with indelible ink.

To find how many rods in length will make an acre, the width being given.

RULE.—Divide 160 by the width, and the quotient will be the answer

How to find the number of acres in any plot of land, the number of rods being given.

RULE.—Divide the number of rods by 8, multiply the quotient by 5, and remove the decimal point two places to the left.

The diameter being given, to find the circumference.

RULE —Multiply the diameter by 3 1-7.

How to find the diameter, when the circumference is given.

RULE —Divide the circumference by 3 1-7.

To find how many solid feet a round stick of timber of the same thickness throughout will contain when squared.

RULE.—Square half the diameter in inches, multiply by 2, multiply by the length in feet, and divide the product by 144.

General rule for measuring timber, to find the solid contents in feet.

RULE.—Multiply the depth in inches by the breadth in inches, and then multiply by the length in feet, and divide by 144.

To find the number of feet of timber in trees with the bark on.

RULE.—Multiply the square of one-fifth of the circumference in inches, by twice the length, in feet, and divide by 144. Deduct 1-10 to 1-15 according to the thickness of the bark.

Howard s new rule for computing interest.

RULE.—The reciprocal of the rate is the time for which the interest on any sum of money will be shown by simply removing the decimal point two places to the left; for ten times that time, remove the point one place to the left; for 1-10 of the same time, remove the point three places to the left.

Increase or diminish the results to suit the time given.

NOTE —The reciprocal of the rate is found by **inverting** the rate , thus 3 per cent. per month, inverted, becomes ⅓ of a month, or 10 days

When the rate is expressed by one figure, always write it thus: 3-1, three ones.

Rule for converting English into American currency.

Multiply the pounds, with the shillings and pence stated in decimals, by 400 plus the premium in fourths, and divide the product by 90.

U. S. GOVERNMENT LAND MEASURE.

A township—36 sections each a mile square.

A section—640 acres.

A quarter section, half a mile square—160 acres.

An eighth section, half a mile long, north and south, and a quarter of a mile wide—80 acres.

A sixteenth section, a quarter of a mile square—40 acres.

The sections are all numbered 1 to 36, commencing at the north-east corner.

The sections are divided into quarters, which are named by the cardinal points. The quarters are divided in the same way. The description of a forty acre lot would read: The south half of the west half of the south-west quarter of section 1 in township 24, north of range 7 west, or as the case might be; and sometimes will fall short and sometimes overrun the number of acres it is supposed to contain.

The nautical mile is 795 4-5 feet longer than the common mile.

SURVEYORS' MEASURE.

7 92-100 inches		make 1 link.
25 links		" 1 rod.
4 rods		" 1 chain.
80 chains		" 1 mile.

NOTE —A chain is 100 links, equal to 4 rods or 66 feet.

Shoemakers formerly used a subdivision of the inch called a barleycorn; three of which made an inch.

Horses are measured directly over the fore feet, and the standard of measure is four inches—called a hand

In Biblical and other old measurements, the term span is sometimes used, which is a length of nine inches.

The sacred cubit of the Jews was 24.024 inches in length.

The common cubit of the Jews was 21.704 inches in length.

A pace is equal to a yard or 36 inches.

A fathom is equal to 6 feet.

A league is three miles, but its length is variable, for it is strictly speaking a nautical term, and should be three geographical miles, equal to 3.45 statute miles, but when used on land, three statute miles are said to be a league.

In cloth measure an aune is equal to 1¼ yards, or 45 inches.

An Amsterdam ell is equal to 26.796 inches.

A Trieste ell is equal to 25.284 inches.

A Brabant ell is equal to 27.116 inches.

HOW TO KEEP ACCOUNTS.

Every farmer and mechanic, whether he does much or little business, should keep a record of his transactions in a clear and systematic manner. For the benefit of those who have not had the opportunity of acquiring a primary knowledge of the principles of book-keeping, we here present a simple form of keeping accounts which is easily comprehended, and well adapted to record the business transactions of farmers, mechanics and laborers.

1875.	A. H. JACKSON.	Dr.	Cr.
Jan 10	To 7 bushels Wheat _____ at $1.25	$8 75	
" 17	By shoeing span of Horses _____		$2 50
Feb. 4	To 14 bushels Oats _____ at $ 45	6 30	
" 4	To 5 lbs. Butter _____ at .25	1 25	
March 8	By new Harrow _____		18 00
" 8	By sharpening 2 Plows _____		40
" 13	By new Double-Tree _____		2 25
" 27	To Cow and Calf _____	48 00	
April 9	To half ton of Hay _____	6 25	
" 9	By Cash _____		25 00
May 6	By repairing Corn-Planter _____		4 75
" 24	To one Sow with Pigs _____	17 50	
July 4	By Cash, to balance account _____		35 15
		$88 05	$88 05

1875.	CASSA MASON.	Dr.	Cr.
March 21	By 3 days' labor _____ at $1 25		$3 75
" 21	To 2 Shoats _____ at 3 00	$6 00	
" 23	To 18 bushels Corn _____ at .45	8 10	
May 1	By 1 month's Labor _____		25 00
" 1	To Cash _____	10 00	
June 19	By 8 days' Mowing _____ at $1.50		12 00
" 26	To 50 lbs. Flour _____	2 75	
July 10	To 27 lbs. Meat _____ at $ .10	2 70	
" 29	By 9 days' Harvesting _____ at 2 00		18 00
Aug 12	By 6 days' Labor _____ at 1.50		9 00
" 12	To Cash _____	20 00	
Sept. 1	To Cash -to balance account _____	18 20	
		$67 75	$67 75

INTEREST TABLE

A Simple Rule for Accurately Computing Interest at Any Given Per Cent for Any Length of Time

Multiply the *principal* (amount of money at interest) by the *time reduced to days*, then divide this *product* by the *quotient* obtained by dividing 360 (the number of days in the interest year) by the *per cent* of interest, and *the quotient thus obtained* will be the required interest

ILLUSTRATION

Require the interest of $462 50 for one month and eighteen days at 6 per cent   An interest month is 30 days, one month and eighteen days equal 48 days $462 50 multiplied by 48 gives $222 0000, 360 divided by 6 (the per cent of interest) gives 60, and $222 0000 divided by 60 will give you the exact interest, which is $3 70   If the rate of interest in the above example were 12 per cent, we would divide the $222 0000 by 30 (because 360 divided by 12 gives 30), if 4 per cent, we would divide by 90, if 8 per cent., by 45   and in like manner for any other per cent.

Solution

$$
\begin{array}{r}
\$462\ 50 \\
48 \\
\hline
370000 \\
185000 \\
\hline
\end{array}
$$

b)360

60)$222 0000($3 70
180

420
420
00

MISCELLANEOUS TABLE.

12 units, or things, 1 Dozen..	196 pounds, 1 Barrel of Flour	24 sheets of paper, 1 Quire
12 dozen, 1 Gross	200 pounds, 1 Barrel of Pork	20 quires paper 1 Ream
20 things, 1 Score	56 pounds, 1 Firkin of Butter	4 ft wide, 4 ft high, and 8 ft long, 1 Cord Wood.

NAMES OF THE STATES OF THE UNION, AND THEIR SIGNIFICATIONS.

Virginia.—The oldest of the States, was so called in honor of Queen Elizabeth, the "Virgin Queen," in whose reign Sir Walter Raleigh made his first attempt to colonize that region.

Florida.—Ponce de Leon landed on the coast of Florida on Easter Sunday, and called the country in commemoration of the day, which was the Pasqua Florida of the Spaniards, or "Feast of Flowers."

Louisiana was called after Louis the Fourteenth, who at one time owned that section of the country.

Alabama was so named by the Indians, and signifies "Here we Rest."

Mississippi is likewise an Indian name, meaning "Long River."

Arkansas, from Kansas, the Indian word for "smoky water." Its prefix was really *arc*, the French word for "bow."

The *Carolinas* were originally one tract, and were called "Carolana," after Charles the Ninth of France.

Georgia owes its name to George the Second of England, who first established a colony there in 1732.

Tennessee is the Indian name for the "River of the Bend," *i. e.*, the Mississippi which forms its western boundary .

Kentucky is the Indian name for "at the head of the river"

Ohio means "beautiful;" *Iowa*, "drowsy ones;" *Minnesota*, "cloudy water," and *Wisconsin*, "wild-rushing channel."

Illinois is derived from the Indian word *illini*, men, and the French suffix *ois*, together signifying "tribe of men."

Michigan was called by the name given the lake, *fish-weir*, which was so styled from its fancied resemblance to a fish trap.

Missouri is from the Indian word "muddy," which more properly applies to the river that flows through it.

Oregon owes its Indian name also to its principal river.

Cortes named *California.*

Massachusetts is the Indian for "The country around the great hills."

Connecticut, from the Indian Quon-ch-ta-Cut, signifying "Long River."

Maryland, after Henrietta Maria, Queen of Charles the First, of England.

New York was named by the Duke of York.

Pennsylvania means "Penn's woods," and was so called after William Penn, its orignal owner.

Delaware after Lord De La Ware.

New Jersey, so called in honor of Sir George Carteret, who was Governor of the Island of Jersey, in the British Channel.

Maine was called after the province of Maine in France, in compliment of Queen Henrietta of England, who owned that province.

Vermont, from the French word *Vert Mont*, signifying Green Mountain

New Hampshire, from Hampshire county in England. It was formerly called Laconia.

The little State of *Rhode Island* owes its name to the Island of Rhodes in the Mediterranean, which domain it is said to greatly resemble.

Texas is the American word for the Mexican name by which all that section of the country was called before it was ceded to the United States.

POPULATION OF THE UNITED STATES.

STATES AND TERRITORIES	Total Population
Alabama	996,992
Arkansas	484,471
California	560,247
Connecticut	537,454
Delaware	125,015
Florida	187,748
Georgia	1,184,109
Illinois	2,539,891
Indiana	1,680,637
Iowa	1,191,792
Kansas	364,399
Kentucky	1,321,011
Louisiana	726,915
Maine	626,915
Maryland	780,894
Massachusetts	1,457,351
Michigan	1,184,059
Minnesota	439,706
Mississippi	827,922
Missouri	1,721,295
Nebraska	122,993
Nevada	42,491
New Hampshire	318,300
New Jersey	906,096
New York	4,382,759
North Carolina	1,071,361
Ohio	2,665,260
Oregon	90,923
Pennsylvania	3,521,791
Rhode Island	217,353
South Carolina	705,606
Tennessee	1,258,520
Texas	818,579
Vermont	330,551
Virginia	1,225,163
West Virginia	442,014
Wisconsin	1,054,670
Total States	**38,113,253**
Arizona	9,658
Colorado	39,864
Dakota	14,181
District of Columbia	131,700
Idaho	14,999
Montana	20,595
New Mexico	91,874
Utah	86,786
Washington	23,955
Wyoming	9,118
Total Territories	**442,730**
Total United States	**38,555,983**

POPULATION OF FIFTY PRINCIPAL CITIES.

CITIES	Aggregate Population
New York, N Y	942,292
Philadelphia, Pa	674,022
Brooklyn, N Y	396,009
St. Louis, Mo	310,864
Chicago, Ill	298,977
Baltimore, Md	267,354
Boston, Mass	250,526
Cincinnati, Ohio	216,239
New Orleans, La	191,418
San Francisco, Cal	149,473
Buffalo, N Y	117,714
Washington, D C	109,199
Newark, N J	105,059
Louisville, Ky	100,753
Cleveland, Ohio	92,829
Pittsburg, Pa	86,076
Jersey City, N J	82,546
Detroit, Mich	79,577
Milwaukee, Wis	71,440
Albany, N Y	69,422
Providence, R I	68,904
Rochester, N. Y	62,386
Allegheny, Pa.	53,180
Richmond, Va	51,038
New Haven, Conn	50,840
Charleston, S C	48,956
Indianapolis, Ind	48,244
Troy, N Y	46,465
Syracuse, N Y	43,051
Worcester, Mass	41,105
Lowell, Mass	40,928
Memphis, Tenn	40,226
Cambridge, Mass	39,634
Hartford, Conn	37,180
Scranton, Pa	35,092
Reading, Pa	33,930
Paterson, N J	33,579
Kansas City, Mo	32,260
Mobile, Ala	32,034
Toledo, Ohio	31,584
Portland, Me	31,413
Columbus, Ohio	31,274
Wilmington, Del	30,841
Dayton, Ohio	30,473
Lawrence, Mass	28,921
Utica, N Y	28,804
Charlestown, Mass	28,828
Savannah, Ga	28,235
Lynn, Mass	28,283
Fall River, Mass	26,766

POPULATION OF THE UNITED STATES.

STATES AND TERRITORIES	Area in square Miles	POPULATION 1870	POPULATION 1875.	Miles R R 1872	STATES AND TERRITORIES	Area in square Miles.	POPULATION 1870.	POPULATION 1875	Miles R R 1872
States					*States*				
Alabama	50,722	996,992		1,671	Pennsylvania	46,000	3,521,791		5,113
Arkansas	52,198	484 471		25	Rhode Island	1,306	217,353	258,239	136
California	188 981	560,247		1,012	South Carolina	29,385	705,606	925,145	1,201
Connecticut	4 674	537,454		820	Tennessee	45,600	1,258,520		1,520
Delaware	2,120	125,015		227	Texas	237,504	818,579		865
Florida	59,268	187,748		466	Vermont	10 212	330,551		675
Georgia	58,000	1,184,109		2,108	Virginia	40,904	1,225,163		1,490
Illinois	55,410	2,539,591		5,904	West Virginia	23,000	442,014		485
Indiana	33,809	1,680 637		3 529	Wisconsin	53,924	1,054,670	1,236,729	1,725
Iowa	55,045	1,191 792	1,350,544	3 150					
Kansas	81,318	364,399	528,349	1,760	*Total States*	1,950,171	38 113,253		59,587
Kentucky	37,600	1,321,011		1,123					
Louisiana	41,346	726,915	857,039	539	*Territories*				
Maine	31,776	626,915		871	Arizona	113,916	9,658		
Maryland	11,184	780,894		820	Colorado	104,500	39,864		392
Massachusetts	7,800	1,457,351	1,651,912	1,606	Dakota	147,490	14,181		
Michigan*	56,451	1,184,059	1,334,031	3,295	Dist of Columbia	60	131,700		*
Minnesota	83,531	439 706	598,429	1,512	Idaho	90,932	14,999		
Mississippi	47,156	827,922		990	Montana	143,776	20,595		
Missouri	65,350	1,721,295		2,580	New Mexico	121 201	91,874		
Nebraska	75,995	123,993	246,280	828	Utah	80,056	86,786		375
Nevada	112,090	42,491	52,540	593	Washington	69,944	23,955		
New Hampshire	9,280	318 300		790	Wyoming	93,107	9,118		498
New Jersey	8 320	906,096	1,026,502	1 265					
New York	47,000	4,382,759	4,705,208	4,470	*Total Territories*	965,032	442,730		1,265
North Carolina	50,704	1,071 361		1,190					
Ohio	39,964	2,665,260		3,740	Aggregate of U S	2,915,203	38,555,983		60,852
Oregon	95,244	90,923		159					

* Last Census of Michigan taken in 1874   * Included in the Railroad Mileage of Maryland

PRINCIPAL COUNTRIES OF THE WORLD;

POPULATION AND AREA.

COUNTRIES	Population	Date of Census	Area in Square Miles	Inhabitants to Square Mile	CAPITALS	Population.
China	446,500 000	1871	3,741,846	119 3	Pekin	1,648,800
British Empire	226,817,108	1871	4,677,432	48 6	London	3,251,800
Russia	81,925,440	1871	8,003,778	10 2	St. Petersburg	667,000
United States with Alaska	38,925,600	1870	2,603,884	7 78	Washington	109,199
France	36,469,800	1866	204 091	178 7	Paris	1,825,300
Austria and Hungary	35,904,400	1869	240 348	149 4	Vienna	833,900
Japan	34,785,300	1871	149,399	232 8	Yeddo	1,554,900
Great Britain and Ireland	31,817,100	1871	121 315	262 3	London	3,251,800
German Empire	29,906,092	1871	160,207	187	Berlin	825,400
Italy	27,482,921	1871	118 847	230 9	Rome	244,484
Spain	16 642,000	1867	195,775	85	Madrid	332,050
Brazil	10,000,000		3,253,029	3 07	Rio Janeiro	420,000
Turkey	16,463,000		672,621	24 4	Constantinople	1,075,000
Mexico	9,173,000	1869	761,526		Mexico	210,300
Sweden and Norway	5,921,500	1870	292,871	20	Stockholm	136,900
Persia	5,000,000	1870	635,964	7 8	Teheran	120,000
Belgium	5,021,300	1866	11,373	441 5	Brussels	314,100
Bavaria	4,861,400	1871	29,292	165 9	Munich	169,500
Portugal	3,995,200	1868	34,494	115 8	Lisbon	224,063
Holland	3,688,300	1870	12,680	290 9	Hague	90,100
New Grenada	3,000,000	1870	357,157	8 4	Bogota.	45,000
Chili	2,000,000	1869	132,616	15 1	Santiago	115,405
Switzerland	2,669,100	1870	15,992	166 9	Berne	36,000
Peru	2,500,000	1871	471,838	5 3	Lima	100,100
Bolivia	2,000,000		497,321	4	Chuquisaca	25,000
Argentine Republic	1,812,000	1869	871,848	2 1	Buenos Ayres	177,800
Wurtemburg	1,818,500	1871	7,533	241 4	Stuttgart	91,600
Denmark	1,784 700	1870	14,753	120 9	Copenhagen	162,042
Venezuela	1,500,000		368,238	4 2	Caraccas	47,000
Baden	1,461,400	1871	5,912	247	Carlsruhe	36,600
Greece	1,457 900	1870	19,353	75 3	Athens	43,400
Guatemala	1,180,000	1871	40,870	28 9	Guatemala	40,000
Ecuador	1,300,000		218,928	5 9	Quito	70,000
Paraguay	1,000,000	1871	63,787	15 6	Asuncion	48,000
Hesse	823,138		2,969	277	Darmstadt	30,000
Liberia	718,000	1871	9,576	74 9	Monrovia	3,000
San Salvador	600,000	1871	7,335	81 8	Sal Salvador	15,000
Haytl	572,000		10,205	56	Port au Prince	20,000
Nicaragua	350,000	1871	58,171	6	Managua	10,000
Uruguay	300,000	1871	66,723	6 5	Monte Video	44,500
Honduras	350,000	1871	47,092	7 4	Comayagua	12,000
San Domingo	136,000		17,827	7 6	San Domingo	20,000
Costa Rica	165 000	1870	21,505	7 7	San Jose	2,000
Hawaii	62 950		7 633	80	Honolulu	7,633

STATISTICS OF AGRICULTURE OF IOWA (CENSUS OF 1875.)

COUNTIES.	No of Acres of Improved Land	No of Acres Unimproved Land	No of Acres under Cultivation in 1874	Spring Wheat		Winter Wheat		Indian Corn		Oats		Value of Products of Farm in Dollars
				No of Acres	No of Bushels Harv't'd	No of Acres	No of Bushels Harv't'd	No of Acres	No of Bushels Harv't'd	No of Acres	No of Bushels Harv't'd	
Appanoose	161053	161069	125188	9606	77789	1049	10688	64871	2335243	13758	387346	$1611987
Alamakee	134787	156821	109388	61880	987639	181	1964	24925	905920	12776	442829	1415769
Audubon	21146	23819	15986	6878	89235	10	97	9225	391855	788	33253	184158
Adams	65159	43735	54352	17947	281376	7	174	25474	959777	3951	141293	695318
Adair	83182	55680	66265	27550	485014	70	3500	30860	1402428	4455	159789	828171
Buena Vista	33118	37034	27010	15514	162737			7888	232281	2791	67089	207828
Benton	297518	58911	239408	99406	1848666	7	280	83244	3328921	15490	445070	2664995
Boone	158987	71810	108642	32505	429257	11	84	46151	1596752	10401	404620	1018458
Butler	149498	58908	124877	57907	779167	20	700	39685	1270878	13827	421719	1209785
Bremer	145967	47001	104910	48878	644796			28754	1026641	14259	518571	1144620
Black Hawk	213025	150881	181256	89981	1108024			55592	1989590	16804	536196	1898424
Buchanan	19056	71418	157210	64291	812342			48831	1511250	17481	556209	2615949
Clay	37059	39919	93875	17481	153159			8797	180120	4496	98796	123848
Cherokee	54638	28974	45412	81698	401507			9459	315215	3545	115595	95019
Cass	110864	45304	92785	40123	676209			40583	1901062	9079	176251	1284899
Crawford	58058	283414	15262	24000	324894			17957	646653	2902	99156	433357
Cedar	248860	41417	166485	40467	640544	28	295	28224	2845923	20243	675887	2806149
Cerro Gordo	52980	309695	46648	28199	415463			9512	283449	7199	225097	501617
Clayton	212291	151908	179622	86883	1305125	1347	21080	37918	1471268	20024	669895	2061793
Clinton	299655	57887		65683	1010345	12	428	89297	3061388	28704	702059	3049049
Chickasaw	96504	94772	74104	40162	643519	8	63	16821	514279	11744	446300	894656
Carroll	58065	309744	39159	26756	340161	8	20	16014	550041	8288	107577	451366
Clarke	99694	50487	78503	17968	217090	7	55	39066	1580260	12337	867648	7054987
Calhoun	26996		26618	11040	109881	10	150	10856	351120	2998	72182	221613
Davis	150998	116008	131597	5378	80993	5379	56405	62127	2115569	13643	345707	1606000
Decatur	115751	87172	93275	8211	77169	817	12239	50484	1763140	10555	844551	1024541
Dubuque	187831	98561	146244	49240	634185	84	1720	67118	1702391	25115	648322	1636132
Des Moines	143685	58165	97818	10615	113396	8688	117810	103924	2307988	9242	287592	1772992
Delaware	472029	62305	181887	80401	71728	5	50	56150	1690895	20577	632113	1693814
Dickinson	15770	29850	11961	5701	25822			8188	44455	2408	37292	150318
Dallas	132485	57765	114625	29256	446848	7	188	57682	2484598	9987	585124	1503047
Emmet	9989	25588	8387	3911	1510			2197	14278	1549	8241	15244
Floyd	147098	82190	110708	62067	941489			25462	642448	15481	487729	1367977
Fayette	179301	98156	133758	60779	886670	48	968	37091	1296880	20770	704407	1508127
Franklin	59859	43046	65590	81096	455909			24068	758985	9532	328679	777106
Fremont	115907	198882	108059	15229	208901	841	16625	73845	1703985	5419	179645	1046066
Grundy	146099	47926	135108	67384	978807			40175	1482562	11786	401948	1593977
Green	59940	49688	52328	19291	257760	2	44	769087	789027	4227	120948	620905
Guthrie	87259	47820	76392	27489	393574	22	360	83902	1669184	4145	153505	792461
Hardin	128831	39990	97765	38464	497251			41304	1879961	10982	358945	1069627
Humboldt	29114	36808	27015	13046	20902			9998	297381	8974	90944	200001
Howard	115823	171048	61871	36115	582303			9916	807912	10310	340266	784409
Harrison	94848	387451	72287	25948	143701	84	1200	44720	1620192	8440	69149	786677
Hancock	10452	841615	9005	4899	70008			8067	57899	1853	48316	89405
Hamilton	68966	39935	52050	20676	294680			20941	670781	6108	188262	32782
Henry	182080	50249	110831	15026	180220	9041	113203	62672	2415670	13399	358221	1765670
Ida	7292	9494	6514	3108	48815			2801	108485	455	14060	748221
Iowa	291041	89857	158488	48410	670247	36	1080	92518	2713880	11758	319071	2003049
Jackson	199290	142401	142401	43515	550000	491	7942	58962	1665518	28652	621156	1750091
Johnson	241021	71257	193019	45306	666779	100	1274	77142	3158178	17760	532197	2447875
Jasper	278881	179752	216940	79926	1107150			100217	4325889	15267	532239	2916898
Jones	206907	63298	140484	36090	462479	81	409	65429	1909534	13260	464824	1856416
Jefferson	167389	66979	125590	16237	164904	6192	66739	55061	1695510	14005	446128	1590040
Keokuk	208125	98999	149672	32278	868528	148	1363	75697	3327282	15382	447658	1919728
Kossuth	31550	48793	25895	10798	13189	140		9781	119771	6148	27897	105306
Lee	183832	78692	138580	10851	72624	15400	200407	59963	2190806	11817	279089	1681518
Lucas	108952	59757	88857	18954	153587	81	929	47022	1902530	12565	342164	1080654
Lyon	15872	818811	12766	8182	76742		64	2645	10396	3477	18789	82651
Linn	281118	82649	175655	52178	656597	12	160	91778	3499928	22670	585648	2590052
Louisa	161007	52922	100066	19784	199939	1388	16267	49842	2184658	6792	175765	1665799
Mitchell	126884	70176	94193	65584	1063811			11274	411961	14078	542662	1591878
Mahaska	282398	122190	150366	34862	995582	205	2697	88775	3768209	16846	498248	2195785
Marion	199669	82779	158214	45136	549668	189	2212	84680	8835068	10987	335746	2181946
Mills	141512	53604	99897	24985	342961	82	843	59543	1538976	6528	232689	1003509
Madison	161998	158709	137879	37559	538914	25	484	69494	2953880	8743	285109	1709030
Monroe	102215	78206	91730	11638	101418	268	5584	45575	1789916	11512	241081	938962
Marshall	223786	47552	117803	69696	1125389	21	200	87899	2808256	18611	465245	2868278
Monona	52242	56278	39641	15534	189811			21577	818888	2304	66475	447565
Muscatine	178945	48882	129599	82875	416471	63	629	54760	1715973	13821	405852	1747906
Montgomery	104639	50807	86028	1581	551559	8	188	99251	1441457	5322	201685	1072127
O'Brien	33626	32070	28434	14904	157526			6579	106052	8107	56921	191542
Osceola	18490	21406	14651	8769	74757			5510	17279	1390	26829	69581
Polk	207689	55841	140450	87686	563389	21	394	71497	3272040	12188	317641	2140028
Pochahontas	21928	55572	19219	7494	30174			8961	229262	2541	40494	112366
Pottawattomie	124680	419489	90679	33369	688971	63	475	47258	1750038	6278	168081	1252829
Poweshiek	209889	48697	171589	57812	762826			86748	8571105	11418	833565	2393022
Page	156782	175471	115484	22589	955792	1220	20235	71886	2290048	9758	346507	1293469
Plymouth	58288	51912	44379	33028	442786	10	16D	10097	175778	4811	120487	484123
Palo Alto	18517	82225	16679	8606	23209	925		6641	142957	2979	46859	96618
Ringgold	18400	58329	50878	10926	78951	125	1762	35618	1145987	4118	253007	1115782
Scott	285515	19123	185742	47898	762315	40	618	59071	2226846	15915	525868	3041873
Story	149649	43874	99837	26658	830897	8	20	51279	1788477	11273	348265	1083748
Shelby	53180	69826	47290	22029	517944			17674	689556	2254	71676	573026
Sioux	80624	367894	83615	22998	251288			6780	82088	4591	45096	166980
Sac	81838	47201	24179	11056	110094		10	8662	279716	8085	6599	288880
Taylor	102561	285515	79142	15446	208818	244	9068	48260	1419680	8718	269657	908478
Tama	255182	90222	214941	97013	1437807			78251	2842855	18574	984469	2816405
Union	57005	83216	45836	10586	141188	53	960	24068	1180980	6127	187748	624260
Van Buren	153674	89526	113269	7455	58808	10928	121854	60211	1528622	12596	955698	1499586
Wayne	147768	86795	117685	10975	76346	143	1286	85625	2405187	13242	967396	1861878
Warren	194255	167178	158737	42177	654679	61	910	80280	3561385	8391	281510	2208592
Winneshiek	246140	181670	259469	112175	1819485			27185	977814	24307	8218508	2265252
Woodbury	44179	57097	39097	16248	2.8875			11647	490871	8072	91647	298209
Worth	48927	45957	82157	23092	410487			8530	122291	4445	161557	896506
Washington	225176	55552	157384	41646	469679	1439	14198	78265	2832241	15701	458820	2095264
Webster	97238	61744	70910	30554	991051	5		28713	917911	7491	202498	788342
Winnebago	17589	80625	12421	8039	162281	11	270	1374	52425	1827	45109	140219
Wright	95518	82387	28957	13829	196166			10089	281821	4184	135176	288685
Wapello	150209	63491	135178	17368	157585	1617	16159	57085	2148781	11570	298590	1453319

ABSTRACT OF IOWA STATE LAWS.

BILLS OF EXCHANGE AND PROMISSORY NOTES.

Upon negotiable bills, and notes payable in this State, grace shall be allowed according to the law merchant. All the above mentioned paper falling due on Sunday, New Year's Day, the Fourth of July, Christmas, or any day appointed or recommended by the President of the United States or the Governor of the State, as a day of fast or thanksgiving, shall be deemed as due on the day previous. No defense can be made against a negotiable instrument (assigned before due) in the hands of the assignee without notice, except fraud was used in obtaining the same. To hold an indorser, due diligence must be used by suit against the maker or his representative. Notes payable to person named or to order, in order to absolutely transfer title, must be indorsed by the payee Notes payable to bearer may be transferred by delivery, and when so payable, every indorser thereon is held as a guarantor of payment, unless otherwise expressed.

In computing interest or discount on negotiable instruments, a month shall be considered a calendar month or twelfth of a year, and for less than a month, a day shall be figured a thirtieth part of a month. Notes only bear interest when so expressed; but after due, they draw the legal interest, even if not stated.

INTEREST.

The legal rate of interest is six per cent. Parties may agree, in writing, on a rate not exceeding ten per cent If a rate of interest greater than ten per cent. is contracted for, it works a forfeiture of ten per cent to the school fund, and only the principal sum can be recovered.

DESCENT.

The personal property of the deceased (except (1) that necessary for payment of debts and expenses of administration; (2) property set apart to widow, as exempt from execution; (3) allowance by court, if necessary, of twelve months' support to widow, and to children under fifteen years of age), including life insurance, descends as does real estate.

One-third in value (absolutely) of all estates in real property, possessed by husband at any time during marriage, which have not been sold on execution or other judicial sale, and to which the wife has made no relinquishment of her right, shall be set apart as her property, in fee simple, if she survive him.

The same share shall be set apart to the surviving husband of a deceased wife.

The widow's share cannot be affected by any will of her husband's, unless she consents, in writing thereto, within six months after notice to her of provisions of the will.

The provisions of the statutes of descent apply alike to surviving husband or surviving wife

Subject to the above, the remaining estate of which the decedent died siezed, shall in absence of other arrangements by will, descend

First. To his or her children and their descendants in equal parts; the descendants of the deceased child or grandchild taking the share of their deceased parents in equal shares among them.

Second. Where there is no child, nor descendant of such child, and no widow or surviving husband, then to the parents of the deceased in equal parts; the surviving parent, if either be dead, taking the whole, and if there is no parent living, then to the brothers and sisters of the intestate and their descendants

Third When there is a widow or surviving husband, and no child or children, or descendants of the same, then one-half of the estate shall descend to such widow or surviving husband, absolutely; and the other half of the estate shall descend as in other cases where there is no widow or surviving husband, or child or children, or descendants of the same.

Fourth If there is no child, parent, brother or sister, or descendants of either of them, then to wife of intestate, or to her heirs, if dead, according to like rules.

Fifth If any intestate leaves no child, parent, brother or sister, or descendants of either of them, and no widow or surviving husband, and no child, parent, brother or sister (or descendant of either of them) of such widow or surviving husband, it shall escheat to the State.

WILLS AND ESTATES OF DECEASED PERSONS.

No exact form of words are necessary in order to make a will good at law Every male person of the age of twenty-one years, and every female of the age of eighteen years, of sound mind and memory, can make a valid will; it must be in writing, signed by the testator, or by some one in his or her presence, and by his or her express direction, and attested by two or more competent witnesses Care should be taken that the witnesses are not interested in the will. Inventory to be made by executor or administrator within fifteen days from date of letters testamentary or of administration. Executors' and administrators' compensation on amount of personal estate distributed, and for proceeds of sale of real estate, five per cent for first one thousand dollars, two and one-half per cent on overplus up to five thousand dollars, and one per cent on overplus above five thousand dollars, with such additional allowance as shall be reasonable for extra services

Within *ten days* after the receipt of letters of administration, the executor or administrator shall give such *notice of appointment* as the court or clerk shall direct

Claims (other than preferred) must be filed *within one year* thereafter, are forever barred, *unless the claim is pending* in the District or Supreme Court, or *unless peculiar circumstances* entitle the claimant to equitable relief.

Claims are *classed* and *payable* in the following order:

1. Expenses of administration.
2. Expenses of last sickness and funeral.
3. Allowance to widow and children, if made by the court.
4. Debts preferred under laws of the United States
5. Public rates and taxes.
6. Claims filed within six months after the *first publication* of the notice given by the executors of their appointment.
7. All other debts.
8. Legacies

The *award*, or property which must be *set apart to the widow, in her own right,* by the executor, includes all personal property which, in the hands of the deceased, as head of a family, would have been *exempt from execution.*

TAXES

The owners of personal property, on the first day of January of each year, and the owners of real property on the first day of November of each year, *are liable* for the taxes thereon.

The following property is exempt from taxation, viz.:

1. The property of the United States and of this State, including university, agricultural, college and school lands and all property leased to the State; property of a county, township, city, incorporated town or school district when devoted entirely to the public use and not held for pecuniary profit; public grounds, including all places for the burial of the dead, fire engines and all implements for extinguishing fires, with the grounds used exclusively for their buildings and for the meetings of the fire companies; all public libraries, grounds and buildings of literary, scientific, benevolent, agricultural and religious institutions, and societies devoted solely to the appropriate objects of these institutions, not exceeding 640 acres in extent, and not leased or otherwise used with a view of pecuniary profit; and all property leased to agricultural, charitable institutions and benevolent societies, and so devoted during the term of such lease, *provided,* that all deeds, by which such property is held, shall be duly filed for record before the property therein described shall be omitted from the assessment

2. The books, papers and apparatus belonging to the above institutions; used solely for the purposes above contemplated, and the like property of students in any such institution, used for their education

3. Money and credits belonging exclusively to such institutions and devoted solely to sustaining them, but not exceeding in amount or income the sum prescribed by their charter.

4. Animals not hereafter specified, the wool shorn from sheep, belonging to the person giving the list, his farm produce harvested within one year previous to the listing, private libraries not exceeding three hundred dollars in value; family pictures, kitchen furniture, beds and bedding requisite for each family, all wearing apparel in actual use, and all food provided for the family, but no person from whom a compensation for board or lodging is received or expected, is to be considered a member of the family within the intent of this clause

5. The polls or estates or both of persons who, by reason of age or infirmity, may, in the opinion of the Assessor, be unable to contribute to the public

revenue; such opinion and the fact upon which it is based being in all cases reported to the Board of Equalization by the Assessor or any other person, and subject to reversal by them

6. The farming utensils of any person who makes his livelihood by farming, and the tools of any mechanic, not in either case to exceed three hundred dollars in value.

7. Government lands entered or located or lands purchased from this State, should not be taxed for the year in which the entry, location or purchase is made.

There is also a suitable exemption, in amount, for planting fruit trees or forest trees or hedges.

Where buildings are destroyed by fire, tornado or other unavoidable casualty, after being assessed for the year, the Board of Supervisors may rebate taxes for that year on the property destroyed, *if same has not been sold for taxes, and if said taxes have not been delinquent for thirty days* at the time of destruction of the property, and the rebate shall be allowed for such loss only as is not covered by insurance.

All other property is subject to taxation Every inhabitant of full age and sound mind shall assist the Assessor in listing all taxable property of which he is the owner, or which he controls or manages, either as agent, guardian, father, husband, trustee, executor, accounting officer, partner, mortgagor or lessor, mortgagee or lessee

Road beds of railway corporations shall not be assessed to owners of adjacent property, but shall be considered the property of the companies for purposes of taxation, nor shall real estate used as a public highway be assessed and taxed as part of adjacent lands whence the same was taken for such public purpose.

The property of railway, telegraph and express companies shall be listed and assessed for taxation as the property of an individual would be listed and assessed for taxation. Collection of taxes made as in the case of an individual.

The Township Board of Equalization shall meet first Monday in April of each year. Appeal lies to the Circuit Court.

The County Board of Eqalization (the Board of Supervisors) meet at their regular session in June of each year. Appeal lies to the Circuit Court

. Taxes become delinquent February 1st of each year, payable, without interest or penalty, at any time before March 1st of each year

Tax sale is held on first Monday in October of each year.

Redemption may be made at any time within three years after date of sale, by paying to the County Auditor the *amount* of sale, and *twenty per centum* of such amount immediately added as *penalty, with ten per cent. interest per annum* on the whole amount thus made from the day of sale, and also all subsequent taxes, interest and costs paid by purchaser after March 1st of each year, and a similar *penalty* of twenty per centum added as before, with ten per cent. *interest* as before.

If *notice* has been given, by purchaser, of the date at which the redemption is limited, the cost of same is added to the redemption money. Ninety days' notice is required, by the statute, to be published by the purchaser or holder of certificate, to terminate the right of redemption.

●

JURISDICTION OF COURTS
DISTRICT COURTS

have jurisdiction, general and original, both civil and criminal, except in such cases where Circuit Courts have exclusive jurisdiction. District Courts have *exclusive supervision* over courts of Justices of the Peace and Magistrates, in criminal matters, on appeal and writs of error

CIRCUIT COURTS

have jurisdiction, general and original, with the District Courts, in all civil actions and special proceedings, and *exclusive jurisdiction* in all appeals and writs of error from inferior courts, in civil matters And *exclusive jurisdiction* in matters of estates and general probate business.

JUSTICES OF THE PEACE

have jurisdiction in civil matters where $100 or less is involved. By consent of parties, the jurisdiction may be extended to an amount not exceeding $300. They have jurisdiction to try and determine all public offense less than felony, committed within their respective counties, in which *the fine*, by law, does not exceed *$100* or *the imprisonment thirty days.*

LIMITATION OF ACTIONS.

Action for injuries to the person or reputation; for a stutute penalty; and to enforce a mechanics' lien, must be brought in two (2) years.

Those against a public officer within three (3) years.

Those founded on unwritten contracts; for injuries to property; for relief on the ground of fraud; and all other actions not otherwise provided for, within five (5) years.

Those founded on written contracts, on judgments of any court (except those provided for in next section), and for the recovery of real property, within ten (10) years

Those founded on judgment of any court of record in the United States, within twenty (20) years.

All above limits, except those for penalties and forfeitures, are extended in favor of minors and insane persons, until one year after the disability is removed —time during which defendant is a non-resident of the State shall not be included in computing any of the above periods.

Actions for the recovery of real property, sold for non-payment of taxes, must be brought within five years after the Treasurer's Deed is executed ◢ and recorded, except where a minor or convict or insane person is the owner, and they shall be allowed five years after disability is removed, in which to bring action.

JURORS.

All qualified electors of the State, of good moral character, sound judgment, and in full possession of the senses of hearing and seeing, are competent jurors in their respective counties.

United States officers, practicing attorneys, physicians and clergymen, acting professors or teachers in institutions of learning, and persons disabled by bodily infirmity or over sixty-five years of age, are exempt from liability to act as jurors.

Any person may be excused from serving on a jury when his own interests or the public's will be materially injured by his attendance, or when the state of his health or the death, or sickness of his family requires his absence.

CAPITAL PUNISHMENT

was restored by the Seventeenth General Assembly, making it optional with the jury to inflict it or not.

A MARRIED WOMAN

may convey or incumber real estate, or interest therein, belonging to her; may control the same or contract with reference thereto, as other persons may convey, encumber, control or contract.

She may own, acquire, hold, convey and devise property, as her husband may

Her husband is not liable for civil injuries committed by her.

She may convey property to her husband, and he may convey to her.

She may constitute her husband her attorney in fact.

. EXEMPTIONS FROM EXECUTION.

A resident of the State and head of a family may hold the following property exempt from execution: All wearing apparel of himself and family kept for actual use and suitable to the condition, and the trunks or other receptacles necessary to contain the same; one musket or rifle and shot-gun, all private libraries, family Bibles, portraits, pictures, musical instruments, and paintings not kept for the purpose of sale, a seat or pew occupied by the debtor or his family in any house of public worship; an interest in a public or private burying ground not exceeding one acre, two cows and a calf, one horse, unless a horse is exempt as hereinafter provided; fifty sheep and the wool therefrom, and the materials manufactured from said wool, six stands of bees; five hogs and all pigs under six months, the necessary food for exempted animals for six months; all flax raised from one acre of ground, and manufactures therefrom, one bedstead and necessary bedding for every two in the family; all cloth manufactured by the defendant not exceeding one hundred yards, household and kitchen furniture not exceeding two hundred dollars in value; all spinning wheels and looms · one sewing machine and other instruments of domestic labor kept for actual use, the necessary provisions and fuel for the use of the family for six months; the proper tools, instruments, or books of the debtor, if a farmer, mechanic, surveyor, clergyman, lawyer, physician, teacher or professor; the horse or the team, consisting of not more than two horses or mules, or two yokes of cattle, and the wagon or other vehicle, with the proper harness or tackle, by the use of which the debtor, if a physician, public officer, farmer, teamster or other laborer. habitually earns his living, and to the debtor. if a printer, there shall also be exempt a printing press and the types, furniture and material necessary for the use of such printing press, and a newspaper office to the value of twelve hundred dollars; the earnings of such debtor, or those of his family, at any time within ninety days next preceding the levy

Persons unmarried and not the head of a family, and non-residents, have

There is also exempt, to a head of a family, a homestead, not exceeding forty acres; or, if inside city limits, one-half acre with improvements, value not limited. The homestead is liable for all debts contracted prior to its acquisition as such, and is subject to mechanics' liens for work or material furnished for the same

An article, otherwise exempt, is liable, on execution, for the purchase money thereof

Where a debtor, if a head of a family, has started to leave the State, he shall have exempt only the ordinary wearing apparel of himself and family, and other property in addition, as he may select, in all not exceeding seventy-five dollars in value.

A policy of life insurance shall inure to the separate use of the husband or wife and children, entirely independent of his or her creditors

ESTRAYS.

An unbroken animal shall not be taken up as an estray between May 1st and November 1st, of each year, unless the same be found within the lawful enclosure of a householder, who alone can take up such animal, unless some other person gives him notice of the fact of such animal coming on his place; and if he fails, within five days thereafter, to take up such estray, any other householder of the township may take up such estray and proceed with it as if taken on his own premises, provided he shall prove to the Justice of the Peace such notice, and shall make affidavit where such estray was taken up.

Any swine, sheep, goat, horse, neat cattle or other animal distrained (for damage done to one's enclosure), when the owner is not known, shall be treated as an estray

Within five days after taking up an estray, notice, containing a full description thereof, shall be posted up in three of the most public places in the township; and in ten days, the person taking up such estray shall go before a Justice of the Peace in the township and make oath as to where such estray was taken up, and that the marks or brands have not been altered, to his knowledge. The estray shall then be appraised, by order of the Justice, and the appraisement, description of the size, age, color, sex, marks and brands of the estray shall be entered by the Justice in a book kept for that purpose, and he shall, within ten days thereafter, send a certified copy thereof to the County Auditor.

When the appraised value of an estray does not exceed five dollars, the Justice need not proceed further than to enter the description of the estray on his book, and if no owner appears within six months, the property shall vest in the finder, if he has complied with the law and paid all costs.

Where appraised value of estray exceeds five and is less than ten dollars, if no owner appears in nine months, the finder has the property, if he has complied with the law and paid costs.

An estray, legally taken up, may be used or worked with care and moderation.

If any person unlawfully take up an estray, or take up an estray and fail to comply with the law regarding estrays, or use or work it contrary to above, or work it before having it appraised, or keep such estray out of the county more than five days at one time, before acquiring ownership, such offender shall forfeit to the county twenty dollars, and the owner may recover double damages with costs

If the owner of any estray fail to claim and prove his title for one year after the taking up, and the finder shall have complied with the law, a complete title vests in the finder.

But if the owner appear within eighteen months from the taking up, prove his ownership and pay all costs and expenses, the finder shall pay him the appraised value of such estray, or may, at his option, deliver up the estray

WOLF SCALPS

A bounty of one dollar is paid for wolf scalps.

MARKS AND BRANDS.

Any person may adopt his own mark or brand for his domestic animals, and have a description thereof recorded by the Township Clerk

No person shall adopt the recorded mark or brand of any other person residing in his township

DAMAGES FROM TRESPASS.

When any person's lands are enclosed by a *lawful* fence, the owner of any domestic animal injuring said lands is liable for the damages, and the damages may be recovered by suit against the owner, or may be made by distraining the animals doing the damage; and if the party injured elects to recover by action against the owner, no appraisement need be made by the Trustees, as in case of distraint.

When trespassing animals are distrained within twenty-four hours, Sunday not included, the party injured shall notify the owner of said animals, if known; and if the owner fails to satisfy the party within twenty-four hours thereafter, the party shall have the township Trustees assess the damage, and notice shall be posted up in three conspicuous places in the township, that the stock, or part thereof, shall, on *the tenth day after posting the notice*, between the hours of 1 and 3 P. M., be sold to the highest bidder, to satisfy said damages, with costs

Appeal lies, within twenty days, from the action of the Trustees to the Circuit Court.

Where stock is restrained, by police regulation or by law, from running at large, any person injured in his improved or cultivated lands by any domestic animal, may, by action against the owner of such animal, or by distraining such animal, recover his damages, whether the lands whereon the injury was done were inclosed by a lawful fence or not.

FENCES.

A lawful fence is fifty-four inches high, made of rails, wire or boards, with posts not more than ten feet apart where rails are used, and eight feet where boards are used, substantially built and kept in good repair, or any other fence which, in the opinion of the Fence Viewers, shall be declared a lawful fence—provided the lower rail, wire or board be not more that twenty nor less than sixteen inches from the ground.

The respective owners of lands enclosed with fences shall maintain partition fences between their own and next adjoining enclosure so long as they improve them in equal shares, unless otherwise agreed between them.

If any party neglect to maintain such partition fence as he should maintain, the Fence Viewers (the township Trustees), upon complaint of aggrieved party, may, upon due notice to both parties, examine the fence, and, if found insufficient, notify the delinquent party, *in writing*, to repair or re-build the same within such time as they judge reasonable.

If the fence be not repaired or rebuilt accordingly. the complainant may do so, and the same being adjudged sufficient by the Fence Viewers, and the value thereof, with their fees, being ascertained and certified under their hands, the complainant may demand of the delinquent the sum so ascertained, and if the same be not paid in one month after demand, may recover it with one per cent a month interest, by action.

In case of disputes, the Fence Viewers may decide as to who shall erect or maintain partition fences, and in what time the same shall be done; and in case any party neglect to maintain or erect such part as may be assigned to him, the aggrieved party may erect and maintain the same, and recover double damages.

No person, not wishing his land inclosed, and not using it otherwise than in common, shall be compelled to maintain any partition fence, but when he uses or incloses his land otherwise than in common, he shall contribute to the partition fences.

Where parties have had their lands inclosed in common, and one of the owners desires to occupy his separate and apart from the other, and the other refuses to divide the line or build a sufficient fence on the line when divided, the Fence Viewers may divide and assign, and upon neglect of the other to build as ordered by the Viewers, the one may build the other's part and recover as above

And when one incloses land which has lain uninclosed, he must pay for one-half of each partition fence between himself and his neighbors.

Where one desires to lay not less than twenty feet of his lands, adjoining his neighbor, out to the public to be used in common, he must give his neighbor six months' notice thereof.

Where a fence has been built on the land of another through mistake, the owner may enter upon such premises and remove his fence and material within six months after the division line has been ascertained. Where the material to build such a fence has been taken from the land on which it was built, then, before it can be removed, the person claiming must first pay for such material to the owner of the land from which it was taken, nor shall such a fence be removed at a time when the removal will throw open or expose the crops of the other party; a reasonable time must be given beyond the six months to remove crops.

MECHANICS' LIENS.

Every mechanic, or other person who shall do any labor upon, or furnish any materials, machinery or fixtures for any building, erection or other improvement upon land, including those engaged in the construction or repair of any work of internal improvement, by virtue of any contract with the owner, his agent, trustee, contractor, or sub-contractor, shall have a lien, on complying with the forms of law, upon the building or other improvement for his labor done or materials furnished

It would take too large a space to detail the manner in which a sub-contractor secures his lien. He should file, within thirty days after the last of the labor was performed, or the last of the material shall have been furnished, with the Clerk of the District Court a true account of the amount due him, after allowing all credits, setting forth the time when such material was furnished or labor performed, and when completed, and containing a correct description of the property sought to be charged with the lien, and the whole verified by affidavit.

A principal contractor must file such an affidavit within ninety days, as above

Ordinarily, there are so many points to be examined in order to secure a mechanics' lien, that it is much better, unless one is accustomed to managing such liens, to consult at once with an attorney.

Remember that the proper time to file the claim is ninety days for a principal contractor, thirty days for a sub-contractor, as above; and that actions to enforce these liens must be commenced within two years, and the rest can much better be done with an attorney

ROADS AND BRIDGES.

Persons meeting each other on the public highways, shall give one half of the same by turning to the right.   All persons failing to observe this rule shall be liable to pay all damages resulting therefrom, together with a fine, not exceeding five dollars

The prosecution must be instituted on the complaint of the person wronged.

Any person guilty of racing horses, or driving upon the public highway, in a manner likely to endanger the persons or the lives of others, shall, on conviction, be fined not exceeding one hundred dollars or imprisoned not exceeding thirty days.

It is a misdemeanor, without authority from the proper Road Supervisor, to break upon, plow or dig within the boundary lines of any public highway.

The money tax levied upon the property in each road district in each township (except the general Township Fund, set apart for purchasing tools, machinery and guide boards), whether collected by the Road Supervisor or County Treasurer, shall be expended for highway purposes in that district, and no part thereof shall be paid out or expended for the benefit of another district.

The Road Supervisor of each district, is bound to keep the roads and bridges therein, in as good condition as the funds at his disposal will permit; to put guide boards at cross roads and forks of highways in his district; and when notified in writing that any portion of the public highway, or any bridge is unsafe, must in a reasonable time repair the same, and for this purpose may call out any or all the able bodied men in the district, but not more than two days at one time, without their consent

Also, when notified in writing, of the growth of any Canada thistles upon vacant or non-resident lands or lots, within his district, the owner, lessee or agent thereof being unknown, shall cause the same to be destroyed

Bridges when erected or maintained by the public, are parts of the highway, and must not be less than sixteen feet wide.

A penalty is imposed upon any one who rides or drives faster than a walk across any such bridge

The manner of establishing, vacating or altering roads, etc., is so well known to all township officers, that it is sufficient here to say that the first step is by petition, filed in the Auditor's office, addressed in substance as follows :

The Board of Supervisors of ——— County · The undersigned asks that a highway, commencing at ——— and running thence ——— and terminating at ———, be established, vacated or altered (as the case may be)

When the petition is filed, all necessary and succeeding steps will be shown and explained to the petitioners by the Auditor.

ADOPTION OF CHILDREN.

Any person competent to make a will can adopt as his own the minor child of another   The consent of both parents, if living and not divorced or separated, and if divorced or separated, or if unmarried, the consent of the parent lawfully having the custody of the child; or if either parent is dead, then the consent of the survivor, or if both parents be dead, or the child have been and remain abandoned by them, then the consent of the Mayor of the city where the child is living, or if not in the city, then of the Clerk of the Circuit Court of the county shall be given to such adoption by an instrument in writing, signed by party or parties consenting, and stating the names of the parties, if known, the name of the child, if known, the name of the person adopting such child, and the residence of all, if known, and declaring the name by which the child is thereafter to be called and known, and stating, also, that such child is given to the person adopting, for the purpose of adoption as his own child.

The person adopting shall also sign said instrument, and all the parties shall acknowledge the same in the manner that deeds conveying lands shall be acknowledged.

The instrument shall be recorded in the office of the County Recorder.

SURVEYORS AND SURVEYS

There is in every county elected a Surveyor known as County Surveyor, who has power to appoint deputies, for whose official acts he is responsible.   It is the duty of the County Surveyor, either by himself or his Duputy, to make all surveys that he may be called upon to make within his county as soon as may be after application is made.   The necessary chainmen and other assistance must be employed by the person requiring the same to be done, and to be by him paid, unless otherwise agreed; but the chainmen must be disinterested persons and approved by the Surveyor and sworn by him to measure justly and impartially   Previous to any survey, he shall furnish himself with a copy of the field notes of the original survey of the same land, if there be any in the office of the County Auditor, and his survey shall be made in accordance therewith

Their fees are three dollars per day.   For certified copies of field notes, twenty-five cents.

SUPPORT OF POOR.

The father, mother and children of any poor person who has applied for aid, and who is unable to maintain himself by work, shall, jointly or severally, maintain such poor person in such manner as may be approved by the Township Trustees

In the absence or inability of nearer relatives, the same liability shall extend to the grandparents, if of ability without personal labor, and to the male grandchildren who are of ability, by personal labor or otherwise.

The Township Trustees may, upon the failure of such relatives to maintain a poor person, who has made application for relief, apply to the Circuit Court for an order to compel the same

Upon ten days' notice, in writing, to the parties sought to be charged, a hearing may be had, and an order made for entire or partial support of the poor person.

Appeal may be taken from such judgment as from other judgments of the Circuit Court.

When any person, having any estate, abandons either children, wife or husband, leaving them chargeable, or likely to become chargeable, upon the public for support, upon proof of above fact, an order may be had from the Clerk of the Circuit Court, or Judge, authorizing the Trustees or the Sheriff to take into possession such estate.

The Court may direct such personal estate to be sold, to be applied, as well as the rents and profits of the real estate, if any, to the support of children, wife or husband.

If the party against whom the order is issued return and support the person abandoned, or give security for the same, the order shall be discharged, and the property taken returned

The mode of relief for the poor, through the action of the Township Trustees, or the action of the Board of Supervisors, is so well known to every township officer, and the circumstances attending applications for relief are so varied, that it need now only be said that it is the duty of each county to provide for its poor, no matter at what place they may be

LANDLORD AND TENANT.

A tenant giving notice to quit demised premises at a time named, and afterward holding over, and a tenant or his assignee willfully holding over the premises after the term, and after notice to quit, shall pay double rent.

Any person in possession of real property, with the assent of the owner, is presumed to be a tenant at will until the contrary is shown.

Thirty days' notice, in writing, is necessary to be given by either party before he can terminate a tenancy at will; but when, in any case, a rent is reserved payable at intervals of less than thirty days, the length of notice need not be greater than such interval between the days of payment. In case of tenants occupying and cultivating farms, the notice must fix the termination of the tenancy to take place on the 1st day of March, except in cases of field tenants or croppers, whose leases shall be held to expire when the crop is harvested, provided, that in case of a crop of corn, it shall not be later than the 1st day of December, unless otherwise agreed upon But when an express agreement is made, whether the same has been reduced to writing or not, the tenancy shall cease at the time agreed upon, without notice.

But where an express agreement is made, whether reduced to writing or not, the tenancy shall cease at the time agreed upon, without notice.

If such tenant cannot be found in the county, the notices above required may be given to any sub-tenant or other person in possession of the premises; or, if the premises be vacant, by affixing the notice to the principal door of the building or in some conspicuous position on the land, if there be no building.

The landlord shall have a lien for his rent upon all the crops grown on the premises, and upon any other personal property of the tenant used on the premises during the term, and not exempt from execution, for the period of one year after a year's rent or the rent of a shorter period claimed falls due; but such lien shall not continue more than six months after the expiration of the term

The lien may be effected by the commencement of an action, within the period above prescribed, for the rent alone; and the landlord is entitled to a writ of attachment, upon filing an affidavit that the action is commenced to recover rent accrued within one year previous thereto upon the premises described in the affidavit.

WEIGHTS AND MEASURES.

Whenever any of the following articles shall be contracted for, or sold or delivered, and no special contract or agreement shall be made to the contrary, the weight per bushel shall be as follows, to-wit:

Apples, Peaches or Quinces,	48	Sand	130
Cherries, Grapes, Currants or Gooseberries,	40	Sorghum Seed	30
Strawberries, Raspberries or Blackberries,	32	Broom Corn Seed	30
Osage Orange Seed	32	Buckwheat	52
Millet Seed	45	Salt	50
Stone Coal	80	Barley	48
Lime	80	Corn Meal	48
Corn in the ear	70	Castor Beans	46
Wheat	60	Timothy Seed	45
Potatoes	60	Hemp Seed	44
Beans	60	Dried Peaches	33
Clover Seed	60	Oats	33
Onions	57	Dried Apples	24
Shelled Corn	56	Bran	20
Rye	56	Blue Grass Seed	14
Flax Seed	56	Hungarian Grass Seed	45
Sweet Potatoes	46		

Penalty for giving less than the above standard is treble damages and costs and five dollars addition thereto as a fine.

DEFINITION OF COMMERCIAL TERMS.

$—— means dollars, being a contraction of U. S., which was formerly placed before any denomination of money, and meant, as it means now, United States Currency.

£—— means *pounds*, English money.

@ stands for *at* or *to*; ℔ for *pounds*, and bbl. for *barrels*; ℔ for *per* or *by the*. Thus, Butter sells at 20@30c ℔ ℔, and Flour at $8@$12 ℔ bbl.

% for *per cent*, and # for *number*.

May 1. Wheat sells at $1.20@$1.25, "seller June" *Seller June* means that the person who sells the wheat has the privilege of delivering it at any time during the month of June.

Selling *short*, is contracting to deliver a certain amount of grain or stock, at a fixed price, within a certain length of time, when the seller has not the stock on hand. It is for the interest of the person selling "short" to depress the market as much as possible, in order that he may buy and fill his contract at a profit. Hence the "shorts" are termed "bears."

Buying *long*, is to contract to purchase a certain amount of grain or shares of stock at a fixed price, deliverable within a stipulated time, expecting to make a profit by the rise in prices. The "longs" are termed "bulls," as it is for their interest to "operate" so as to "toss" the prices upward as much as possible

NOTES

Form of note is legal, worded in the simplest way, so that the amount and time of payment are mentioned.

$100.   CHICAGO, Ill., Sept. 15, 1876.

Sixty days from date I promise to pay to E. F. Brown or order, one hundred dollars, for value received.   L D. LOWRY

A note to be payable in anything else than money needs only the facts substituted for money in the above form.

ORDERS

Orders should be worded simply, thus:

Mr. F H COATS·   CHICAGO, Sept. 15, 1876.

Please pay to H. Birdsall twenty-five dollars, and charge to
                                        F. D. SILVA.

RECEIPTS.

Receipts should always state when received and what for, thus:

$100   CHICAGO, Sept 15, 1876

Received of J W Davis, one hundred dollars, for services rendered in grading his lot in Fort Madison, on account.

                                        THOMAS BRADY

If receipt is in full, it should be so stated.

BILLS OF PURCHASE.

W. N. MASON,   SALEM, Illinois, Sept. 18, 1876.
                    Bought of A. A. GRAHAM
4 Bushels of Seed Wheat, at $1 50   ....$6 00
2 Seamless Sacks   "   30...   60
                                        _____
                    Received payment, $6 60
                                        A. A. GRAHAM.

CONFESSION OF JUDGMENT.

$——.   ——, Iowa, ——, 18—.

—— after date — promises to pay to the order of ——, —— dollars, at ——, for value received, with interest at ten per cent. per annum after —— until paid. Interest payable ——, and on interest not paid when due, interest at same rate and conditions

A failure to pay said interest, or any part thereof, within 20 days after due, shall cause the whole note to become due and collectable at once

If this note is sued, or judgment is confessed hereon, $——shall be allowed as attorney fees

No. —.   P. O ——,   ——.

                    CONFESSION OF JUDGMENT

— vs. —. In —— Court of —— County, Iowa, ——, of —— County, Iowa, do hereby confess that —— justly indebted to ——, in the sum of —— dollars, and the further sum of $—— as attorney fees, with interest thereon at ten per cent from ——, and — hereby confess judgment against —— as defendant in favor of said ——, for said sum of $——, and $—— as attorney fees, hereby authorizing the Clerk of the —— Court of said county to enter up judgment for said sum against —— with costs, and interest at 10 per cent. from ——, the interest to be paid ——.

Said debt and judgment being for ——.

It is especially agreed, however, That if this judgment is paid within twenty days after due, no attorney fees need be paid. And —— hereby sell, convey and release all right of homestead we now occupy in favor of said —— so far as this judgment is concerned, and agree that it shall be liable on execution for this judgment.

Dated ——, 18—.

—— ——.

—— ——.

THE STATE OF IOWA, }
—— County. }

—— being duly sworn according to law, depose and say that the foregoing statement and Confession of Judgment was read over to ——, and that — understood the contents thereof, and that the statements contained therein are true, and that the sums therein mentioned are justly to become due said —— as aforesaid.

—— ——.

Sworn to and subscribed before me and in my presence by the said —— this —— day of ——, 18—. —— ——, Notary Public

ARTICLES OF AGREEMENT.

An agreement is where one party promises to another to do a certain thing in a certain time for a stipulated sum. Good business men always reduce an agreement to writing, which nearly always saves misunderstandings and trouble. No particular form is necessary, but the facts must be clearly and explicitly stated, and there must, to make it valid, be a reasonable consideration.

GENERAL FORM OF AGREEMENT

THIS AGREEMENT, made the Second day of June, 1878, between John Jones, of Keokuk, County of Lee, State of Iowa, of the first part, and Thomas Whiteside, of the same place, of the second part—

WITNESSETH, that the said John Jones, in consideration of the agreement of the party of the second part, hereinafter contained, contracts and agrees to and with the said Thomas Whiteside, that he will deliver in good and marketable condition, at the Village of Melrose, Iowa, during the month of November, of this year, One Hundred Tons of Prairie Hay, in the following lots, and at the following specified times, namely, twenty-five tons by the seventh of November, twenty-five tons additional by the fourteenth of the month, twenty-five tons more by the twenty-first, and the entire one hundred tons to be all delivered by the thirtieth of November.

And the said Thomas Whiteside, in consideration of the prompt fulfillment· of this contract, on the part of the party of the first part, contracts to and agrees with the said John Jones, to pay for said hay five dollars per ton, for each ton as soon as delivered.

In case of failure of agreement by either of the parties hereto, it is hereby stipulated and agreed that the party so failing shall pay to the other, One Hundred dollars, as fixed and settled damages.

In witness whereof, we have hereunto set our hands the day and year first above written.   JOHN JONES,
THOMAS WHITESIDE.

AGREEMENT WITH CLERK FOR SERVICES

THIS AGREEMENT, made the first day of May, one thousand eight hundred and seventy-eight, between Reuben Stone, of Dubuque, County of Dubuque, State of Iowa, party of the first part, and George Barclay, of McGregor, County of Clayton, State of Iowa, party of the second part—

WITNESSETH, that said George Barclay agrees faithfully and diligently to work as clerk and salesman for the said Reuben Stone, for and during the space of one year from the date hereof, should both live such length of time, without absenting himself from his occupation, during which time he, the said Barclay, in the store of said Stone, of Dubuque, will carefully and honestly attend, doing and performing all duties as clerk and salesman aforesaid, in accordance and in all respects as directed and desired by the said Stone.

In consideration of which services, so to be rendered by the said Barclay, the said Stone agrees to pay to said Barclay the annual sum of one thousand dollars, payable in twelve equal monthly payments, each upon the last day of each month; provided that all dues for days of absence from business by said Barclay, shall be deducted from the sum otherwise by the agreement due and payable by the said Stone to the said Barclay.

Witness our hands.   REUBEN STONE.
GEORGE BARCLAY.

BILLS OF SALE.

A bill of sale is a written agreement to another party, for a consideration to convey his right and interest in the personal property. *The purchaser must take actual possession of the property, or* the bill of sale *must be acknowledged and recorded.*

COMMON FORM OF BILL OF SALE.

KNOW ALL MEN by this instrument, that I, Louis Clay, of Burlington, Iowa, of the first part, for and in consideration of Five Hundred and Ten Dollars, to me paid by John Floyd, of the same place, of the second part, the receipt whereof is hereby acknowledged, have sold, and by this instrument do convey unto the said Floyd, party of the second part, his executors, administrators and assigns, my undivided half of ten acres of corn, now growing on the arm of Thomas Tyrell, in the town above mentioned; one pair of horses, sixteen sheep, and five cows, belonging to me and in my possession at the farm aforesaid; to have and to hold the same unto the party of the second part, his executors and assigns forever. And I do, for myself and legal representatives, agree with the said party of the second part, and his legal representatives, to warrant and defend the sale of the afore-mentioned property and chattels unto the said party of the second part, and his legal representatives, against all and every person whatsoever.

In witness whereof, I have hereunto affixed my hand, this tenth day of October, one thousand eight hundred and seventy-six.

LOUIS CLAY.

NOTICE TO QUIT.

To John Wontpay·

You are hereby notified to quit the possession of the premises you now occupy to wit:

[*Insert Description.*]

on or before thirty days from the date of this notice.

Dated January 1, 1878.   Landlord

[*Reverse for Notice to Landlord*]

GENERAL FORM OF WILL FOR REAL AND PERSONAL PROPERTY.

I, Charles Mansfield, of the Town of Bellevue, County of Jackson, State of Iowa, being aware of the uncertainty of life, and in failing health, but of sound mind and memory, do make and declare this to be my last will and testament, in manner following, to-wit:

First. I give, devise and bequeath unto my eldest son, Sidney H Mansfield, the sum of Two Thousand Dollars, of bank stock, now in the Third National Bank, of Cincinnati, Ohio, and the farm owned by myself, in the Township of Iowa, consisting of one hundred and sixty acres, with all the houses, tenements and improvements thereunto belonging; to have and to hold unto my said son, his heirs and assigns, forever.

Second. I give, devise and bequeath to each of my two daughters, Anna Louise Mansfield and Ida Clara Mansfield, each Two Thousand Dollars in bank stock in the Third National Bank of Cincinnati, Ohio; and also, each one quarter section of land, owned by myself, situated in theTownship of Fairfield, and recorded in my name in the Recorder's office, in the county where such land is located   The north one hundred and sixty acres of said half section is devised to my eldest daughter, Anna Louise.

Third I give, devise and bequeath to my son, Frank Alfred Mansfield, five shares of railroad stock in the Baltimore & Ohio Railroad, and my one hundred and sixty acres of land, and saw-mill thereon, situated in Manistee, Michigan, with all the improvements and appurtenances thereunto belonging, which said real estate is recorded in my name, in the county where situated.

Fourth. I give to my wife, Victoria Elizabeth Mansfield, all my household furniture, goods, chattels and personal property, about my home, not hitherto disposed of, including Eight Thousand Dollars of bank stock in the Third National Bank of Cincinnati, Ohio, fifteen shares in the Baltimore & Ohio Railroad, and the free and unrestricted use, possession and benefit of the home farm so long as she may live, in lieu of dower, to which she is entitled by law —said farm being my present place of residence.

Fifth. I bequeath to my invalid father, Elijah H Mansfield, the income from rents of my store building at 145 Jackson street, Chicago, Illinois, during the term of his natural life.   Said building and land therewith to revert to my said sons and daughters in equal proportion, upon the demise of my said father.

Sixth. It is also my will and desire that, at the death of my wife, Victoria Elizabeth Mansfield, or at any time when she may arrange to relinquish her life interest in the above mentioned homestead, the same may revert to my above named children, or to the lawful heirs of each.

And lastly   I nominate and appoint as the executors of this, my last will and testament, my wife, Victoria Elizabeth Mansfield, and my eldest son, Sidney H. Mansfield

I further direct that my debts and necessary funeral expenses shall be paid from moneys now on deposit in the Savings Bank of Bellevue, the residue of such moneys to revert to my wife, Victoria Elizabeth Mansfield, for her use forever.

In witness whereof, I, Charles Mansfield, to this my last will and testament, have hereunto set my hand and seal, this fourth day of April, eighteen hundred and seventy-two.

CHARLES MANSFIELD

Signed, and declared by Charles Mansfield, as and for his last will and testment, in the presence of us, who, at his request, and in his presence, and in the presence of each other, have subscribed our names hereunto as witnesses thereof.

PETER A. SCHENCK, Dubuque, Iowa,
FRANK E. DENT, Bellevue, Iowa.

CODICIL.

Whereas I, Charles Mansfield, did, on the fourth day of April, one thousand eight hundred and seventy-two, make my last will and testament, I do now, by this writing, add this codicil to my said will, to be taken as a part thereof

Whereas, by the dispensation of Providence, my daughter, Anna Louise, has deceased, November fifth, eighteen hundred and seventy-three ; and whereas, a son has been born to me, which son is now christened Richard Albert Mansfield, I give and bequeath unto him my gold watch, and all right, interest and title in lands and bank stock and chattels bequeathed to my deceased daughter, Anna Louise, in the body of this will.

In witness whereof, I hereunto place my hand and seal, this tenth day of March, eighteen hundred and seventy-five   CHARLES MANSFIELD.

Signed, sealed, published and declared to us by the testator, Charles Mansfield, as and for a codicil to be annexed to his last will and testament.   And we, at his request, and in his presence, and in the presence of each other, have subscribed our names as witnesses thereto, at the date hereof.

FRANK E. DENT, Bellevue, Iowa,
JOHN C. SHAY, Bellevue, Iowa.

(Form No. 1.)

SATISFACTION OF MORTGAGE.

STATE OF IOWA, } ss
—— County, }

I, ——, of the County of ——, State of Iowa, do hereby acknowledge that a certain Indenture of ——, bearing date the —— day of ——, A D. 18—, made and executed by —— and ——, his wife, to said —— on the following described Real Estate, in the County of ——, and State of Iowa, to-wit · (here insert description) and filed for record in the office of the Recorder of the County of ——, and State of Iowa, on the —— day of ——

A. D. 18——, at —— o'clock M.; and recorded in Book —— of Mortgage Records, on page ——, is redeemed, paid off, satisfied and discharged in full.

————— [SEAL.]

STATE OF IOWA, ⎫
—— County,   ⎬ ss.
           ⎭

Be it Remembered, That on this —— day of ——, A. D. 18——, before me the undersigned, a —————— in and for said county, personally appeared ——, to me personally known to be the identical person who executed the above (satisfaction of mortgage) as grantor, and acknowledged —— signature thereto to be —— voluntary act and deed.

Witness my hand and ———————— seal, the day and year last above written.   —————.

ONE FORM OF REAL ESTATE MORTGAGE.

KNOW ALL MEN BY THESE PRESENTS: That ——, of —— County, and State of ——, in consideration of —————— dollars, in hand paid by ——————— of —————— County, and State of ——, do hereby sell and convey unto the said —— the following described premises, situated in the County ————, and State of ——, to wit: (here insert description,) and —— do hereby covenant with the said ———————— that —— lawfully seized of said premises, that they are free from incumbrance, that —— have good right and lawful authority to sell and convey the same; and —— do hereby covenant to warrant and defend the same against the lawful claims of all persons whomsoever To be void upon condition that the said ———————— shall pay the full amount of principal and interest at the time therein specified, of —— certain promissory note for the sum of —— dollars.

One note for $————, due ————, 18——, with interest annually at —— per cent.
One note for $————, due ————, 18——, with interest annually at —— per cent.
One note for $————, due ————, 18——, with interest annually at —— per cent.
One note for $————, due ————, 18——, with interest annually at —— per cent.

And the said Mortgagor agrees to pay all taxes that may be levied upon the above described premises. It is also agreed by the Mortgagor that if it becomes necessary to foreclose this mortgage, a reasonable amount shall be allowed as an attorney's fee for foreclosing. And the said ———————— hereby relinquishes all her right of dower and homestead in and to the above described premises.

Signed to —— day of ——, A. D. 18——.

——— ———.
——— ———.

[Acknowledge as in Form No. 1.]

SECOND FORM OF REAL ESTATE MORTGAGE.

THIS INDENTURE, made and executed —— by and between ———— of the county of —— and State of ——, part of the first part, and ———— of the county of —— and State of —— party of the second part, *Witnesseth*, that the said part of the first part, for and in consideration of the sum of —— dollars, paid by the said party of the second part, the receipt of which is hereby acknowledged, have granted and sold, and do by these presents, grant, bargain, sell, convey and confirm, unto the said party of the second part, —— heirs and assigns forever, the certain tract or parcel of real estate situated in the county of —— and State of ——, described as follows, to-wit:

(Here insert description)

The said part of the first part represent to and covenant with the part of the second part, that he have good right to sell and convey said premises, that they are free from encumbrance and that he will warrant and defend them against the lawful claims of all persons whomsoever, and do expressly hereby release all rights of dower in and to said premises, and relinquish and convey all rights of homestead therein.

This Instrument is made, executed and delivered upon the following conditions, to-wit :

First. Said first part agree to pay said —— or order ——————————

Second. Said first part further agree as is stipulated in said note, that if he shall fail to pay any of said interest when due, it shall bear interest at the rate of ten per cent. per annum, from the time the same becomes due, and this mortgage shall stand as security for the same.

Third Said first part further agree that he will pay all taxes and assessments levied upon said real estate before the same become delinquent, and if not paid the holder of this mortgage may declaie the whole sum of money herein secured due and collectable at once, or he may elect to pay such taxes or assessments, and be entitled to interest on the same at the rate of ten per cent. per annum, and this mortgage shall stand as security for the amount so paid.

Fourth. Said first part further agree that if he fail to pay any of said money, either principal or interest, within —— days after the same becomes due , or fail to conform or comply with any of the foregoing conditions or agreements, the whole sum herein secured shall become due and payable at once, and this mortgage may thereupon be foreclosed immediately for the whole of said money, interest and costs

Fifth. Said part further agree that in the event of the non-payment of either principal, interest or taxes when due, and upon the filing of a bill of foreclosure of this mortgage, an attorney's fee of —— dollars shall become due and payable, and shall be by the court taxed, and this mortgage shall stand as security therefor, and the same shall be included in the decree of foreclosure and shall be made by the Sheriff on general or special execution with the other money, interest and costs, and the contract embodied in this mortgage and the note described herein, shall in all respects be governed, constructed and adjudged by the laws of ————, where the same is made. The foregoing conditions being performed, this conveyance to be void, otherwise of full force and virtue

—— ——,
—— ——

[Acknowledge as in form No. 1.]

FORM OF LEASE

THIS ARTICLE OF AGREEMENT, Made and entered into on this —— day of ——, A. D. 187–, by and between ————————, of the county of ——————, and State of Iowa, of the first part, and ————————, of the county of ——————, and State of Iowa. of the second part. witnesseth that the said party of the first part has this day leased unto the party of the second part the following described premises, to wit :

[Here insert description]

for the term of ———— from and after the — day of ——, A. D. 187–, at the ———— rent of ———— dollars, to be paid as follows, to wit:

[Here insert Terms]

And it is further agreed that if any rent shall be due and unpaid, or if default be made in any of the covenants herein contained, it shall then be lawful for the said party of the first part to re-enter the said premises, or to destrain for such rent; or he may recover possession thereof, by action of forcible entry and detainer, notwithstanding the provision of Section 3,612 of the Code of 1873; or he may use any or all of said remedies.

And the said party of the second part agrees to pay to the party of the first part the rent as above stated, except when said premises are untenantable by reason of fire, or from any other cause than the carelessness of the party of the second part, or persons —— family, or in —— employ, or by superior force and inevitable necessity. And the said party of the second part covenants that —— will use the said premises as a ————, and for no other purposes whatever, and that —— especially will not use said premises, or permit the same to be used, for any unlawful business or purpose whatever; that —— will not sell, assign, underlet or relinquish said premises without the written consent of the lessor, under penalty of a forfeiture of all —— rights under this lease, at the election of the party of the first part; and that ———— will use all due care and diligence in guarding said property, with the buildings, gates, fences, trees, vines, shrubbery, etc., from damage by fire, and the depredations of animals; that —— will keep buildings, gates, fences, etc , in as good repair as they now are, or may at any time be placed by the lessor, damages by superior force, inevitable necessity, or fire from any other cause than from the carelessness of the lessee, or persons of —— family, or in —— employ, excepted ; and that at the expiration of this lease, or upon a breach by said lessee of any of the said covenants herein contained, —— will, without further notice of any kind, quit and surrender the possession and occupancy of said premises in as good condition as reasonable use, natural wear and decay thereof will permit, damages by fire as aforesaid, superior force, or inevitable necessity, only excepted.

In witness whereof, the said parties have subscribed their names on the date first above written.

In presence of

———— ————   ———— ————

FORM OF NOTE.

$————   ———— —, 18—.

On or before the — day of ——, 18—, for value received, I promise to pay ———— ———— or order, ———— dollars, with interest from date until paid, at ten per cent. per annum, payable annually, at ————. Unpaid interest shall bear interest at ten per cent per annum On failure to pay interest within —— days after due, the whole sum, principal and interest, shall become due at once.

———— ————

CHATTEL MORTGAGE.

KNOW ALL MEN BY THESE PRESENTS: That —— of —— County, and State of—— in consideration of —— dollars, in hand paid by ——, of —— County and State of —— do hereby sell and convey unto the said —— the following described personal property, now in the possession of ——in the county —— and State of ——, to wit:

[Here insert Description]

And —— do hereby warrant the title of said property, and that it is free from any incumbrance or lien. The only right or interest retained by grantor in and to said property being the right of redemption as herein provided. This conveyance to be void upon condition that the said grantor shall pay to said grantee, or his assigns, the full amount of principal and interest at the time therein specified, of —— certain promissory notes of even date herewith, for the sum of —— dollars,

One note for $——, due——, 18—, with interest annually at —— per cent.
One note for $——, due——, 18—, with interest annually at —— per cent.
One note for $——, due——, 18—, with interest annually at —— per cent.
One note for $——, due——, 18—, with interest annually at —— per cent.

The grantor to pay all taxes on said property, and if at any time any part or portion of said notes should be due and unpaid, said grantee may proceed by sale or foreclosure to collect and pay himself the unpaid balance of said notes, whether due or not, the grantor to pay all necessary expense of such foreclosure, including $—— Attorney's fees, and whatever remains after paying off said notes and expenses, to be paid over to said grantor.

Signed the —— day of ——, 18—.   ——— ———.

[Acknowledged as in form No. 1.]   ——— ———.

WARRANTY DEED.

KNOW ALL MEN BY THESE PRESENTS: That —— of —— County and State of ——, in consideration of the sum of —— Dollars, in hand paid by —— of ——, County and State of ——, do hereby sell and convey unto the said —— and to —— heirs and assigns, the following described premises, situated in the County of ——, State of Iowa, to-wit:

[Here insert description]

And I do hereby covenant with the said —— that — lawfully seized in fee simple, of said premises, that they are free from incumbrance; that — ha good right and lawful authority to sell the same, and — do hereby covenant to warrant and defend the said premises and appurtenances thereto belonging, against the lawful claims of all persons whomsoever; and the said —— hereby relinquishes all her right of dower and of homestead in and to the above described premises.

Signed the —— day of ——, A. D. 18—.

IN PRESENCE OF

—— ——   —— ——
—— ——
—— ——   —— ——
—

QUIT-CLAIM DEED.

KNOW ALL MEN BY THESE PRESENTS: That ——, of —— County, State of ——, in consideration of the sum of —— dollars, to — in hand paid by ——, of —— County, State of ——, the receipt whereof — do hereby acknowledge, have bargained, sold and quit-claimed, and by these presents do bargain, sell and quit-claim unto the said —— and to — heirs and assigns forever, all — right, title, interest, estate, claim and demand, both at law and in equity, and as well in possession as in expectancy, of, in and to the following described premises, to wit · [here insert description] with all and singular the hereditaments and appurtenances thereto belonging.

Signed this —— day of ——, A D. 18—.

SIGNED IN PRESENCE OF

—— ——   —— ——

—— ——   —— ——

—— ——   [Acknowledged as in form No. 1.]

BOND FOR DEED.

KNOW ALL MEN BY THESE PRESENTS: That —— of —— County, and State of —— am held and firmly bound unto —— of —— County, and State of ——, in the sum of —— Dollars, to be paid to the said ——, his executors or assigns, for which payment well and truly to be made, I bind myself firmly by these presents. Signed the —— day of —— A D. 18 —

The condition of this obligation is such, that if the said obligee shall pay to said obligor, or his assigns, the full amount of principal and interest at the time therein specified, of — certain promissory note of even date herewith, for the sum of —— Dollars,

One note for $——, due ——, 18 —, with interest annually at — per cent.
One note for $——, due ——, 18 —, with interest annually at — per cent.
One note for $——, due ——, 18 —, with interest annually at — per cent.

and pay all taxes accruing upon the lands herein described, then said obligor shall convey to the said obligee, or his assigns, that certain tract or parcel of real estate, situated in the County of —— and State of Iowa, described as follows, to wit: [here insert description,] by a Warranty Deed, with the usual covenants, duly executed and acknowledged

If said obligee should fail to make the payments as above stipulated, or any part thereof, as the same becomes due, said obligor may at his option, by notice to the obligee terminate his liability under the bond and resume the possession and absolute control of said premises, time being the essence of this agreement.

On the fulfillment of the above conditions this obligation to become void, otherwise to remain in full force and virtue; unless terminated by the obligor as above stipulated.

—— ——

[Acknowledge as in form No. 1.]

CHARITABLE, SCIENTIFIC AND RELIGIOUS ASSOCIATIONS.

Any three or more persons of full age, citizens of the United States, a majority of whom shall be citizens of this State, who desire to associate themselves for benevolent, charitable, scientific, religious or missionary purposes, may make, sign and acknowledge, before any officer authorized to take the acknowledgments of deeds in this State, and have recorded in the office of the Recorder of the county in which the business of such society is to be conducted, a certificate in writing, in which shall be stated the name or title by which such society shall be known, the particular business and objects of such society, the number of Trustees, Directors or Managers to conduct the same, and the names of the Trustees, Directors or Managers of such society for the first year of its existence.

Upon filing for record the certificate, as aforesaid, the persons who shall have signed and acknowledged such certificate, and their associates and successors, shall, by virtue hereof, be a body politic and corporate by the name stated in such certificate, and by that they and their successors shall and may have succession, and shall be persons capable of suing and being sued, and may have and use a common seal, which they may alter or change at pleasure; and they and their successors, by their corporate name, shall be capable of taking, receiving, purchasing and holding real and personal estate, and of making by-laws for the management of its affairs, not inconsistent with law.

The society so incorporated may, annually or oftener, elect from its members its Trustees, Directors or Managers at such time and place, and in such manner as may be specified in its by-laws, who shall have the control and management of the affairs and funds of the society, a majority of whom shall be a quorum for the transaction of business, and whenever any vacancy shall happen among such Trustees, Directors or Managers, by death, resignation or neglect to serve, such vacancy shall be filled in such manner as shall be provided by the by-laws of such society. When the body corporate consists of the Trustees, Directors or Managers of any benevolent, charitable, literary, scientific, religious or missionary institution, which is or may be established in the State, and which is or may be under the patronage, control, direction or supervision of any synod, conference, association or other ecclesiastical body in such State, established agreeably to the laws thereof, such ecclesiastical body may nominate and appoint such Trustees, Directors or Managers, according to usages of the appointing body, and may fill any vacancy which may occur among such Trustees, Directors or Managers; and when any such institution may be under the patronage, control, direction or supervision of two or more of such synods, conferences, associations or other ecclesiastical bodies, such bodies may severally nominate and appoint such proportion of such Trustees, Directors or Managers as shall be agreed upon by those bodies immediately concerned. And any vacancy occurring among such appointees last named, shall be filled by the synod, conference, association or body having appointed the last incumbent

In case any election of Trustees, Directors or Managers shall not be made on the day designated by the by-laws, said society for that cause shall not be dissolved, but such election may take place on any other day directed by such by-laws.

Any corporation formed under this chapter shall be capable of taking, holding or receiving property by virtue of any devise or bequest contained in any last will or testament of any person whatsoever; but no person leaving a wife, child or parent, shall devise or bequeath to such institution or corporation more than one-fourth of his estate after the payment of his debts, and such device or bequest shall be valid only to the extent of such one-fourth.

Any corporation in this State of an academical character, the memberships of which shall consist of lay members and pastors of churches, delegates to any synod, conference or council holding its annual meetings alternately in this and one or more adjoining States, may hold its annual meetings for the election of officers and the transaction of business in any adjoining State to this, at such place therein as the said synod, conference or council shall hold its annual meetings; and the elections so held and business so transacted shall be as legal and binding as if held and transacted at the place of business of the corporation in this State.

The provisions of this chapter shall not extend or apply to any association or individual who shall, in the certificate filed with the Recorder, use or specify a name or style the same as that of any previously existing incorporated society in the county.

The Trustees, Directors or stockholders of any existing benevolent, charitable, scientific, missionary or religious corporation, may, by conforming to the requirements of Section 1095 of this chapter, re-incorporate themselves or continue their existing corporate powers, and all the property and effects of such existing corporation shall vest in and belong to the corporation so re-incorporated or continued.

INTOXICATING LIQUORS.

No intoxicating liquors (alcohol, spirituous and vinous liquors), except wine manufactured from grapes, currants or other fruit grown in the State, shall be manufactured or sold, except for mechanical, medicinal, culinary or sacramental purposes; and even such sale is limited as follows:

Any citizen of the State, except hotel keepers, keepers of saloons, eating houses, grocery keepers and confectioners, is permitted to buy and sell, within the county of his residence, such liquors for such mechanical, etc, purposes only, provided he shall obtain the consent of the Board of Supervisors. In order to get that consent, he must get a certificate from a majority of the electors of the town or township or ward in which he desires to sell, that he is of good moral character, and a proper person to sell such liquors.

If the Board of Supervisors grant him permission to sell such liquors, he must give bonds, and shall not sell such liquors at a greater profit than thirty-three per cent on the cost of the same. Any person having a permit to sell, shall make, on the last Saturday of every month, a return in writing to the Auditor of the county, showing the kind and quantity of the liquors purchased by him since the date of his last report, the price paid, and the amount of freights paid on the same; also the kind and quantity of liquors sold by him since the date of his last report; to whom sold; for what purpose and at what price; also the kind and quantity of liquors on hand; which report shall be sworn to by the person having the permit, and shall be kept by the Auditor, subject at all times to the inspection of the public

No person shall sell or give away any intoxicating liquors, including wine or beer, to any minor, for any purpose whatever, except upon written order of parent, guardian or family physician; or sell the same to an intoxicated person or a person in the habit of becoming intoxicated.

Any person who shall mix any intoxicating liquor with any beer, wine or cider, by him sold, and shall sell or keep for sale, as a beverage, such mixture, shall be punished as for sale of intoxicating liquor.

But nothing in the chapter containing the laws governing the sale or prohibiting the sale of intoxicating liquors, shall be construed to forbid the sale by the importer thereof of foreign intoxicating liquor, imported under the authority of the laws of the United States, regarding the importation of such liquors, and in accordance with such laws; provided that such liquor, at the time of the sale by the importer, remains in the original casks or packages in which it was by him imported, and in quantities not less than the quantities in which the laws of the United States require such liquors to be imported, and is sold by him in such original casks or packages, and in said quantities only

All payment or compensation for intoxicating liquor sold in violation of the laws of this State, whether such payments or compensation be in money, goods, lands, labor, or anything else whatsoever, shall be held to have been received in violation of law and equity and good conscience, and to have been received upon a valid promise and agreement of the receiver, in consideration of the receipt thereof, to pay on demand, to the person furnishing such consideration, the amount of the money on the just value of the goods or other things.

All sales, transfers, conveyances, mortgages, liens, attachments, pledges and securities of every kind, which, either in whole or in part, shall have been made on account of intoxicating liquors sold contrary to law, shall be utterly null and void.

Negotiable paper in the hands of holders thereof, in good faith, for valuable consideration, without notice of any illegality in its inception or transfer, however, shall not be affected by the above provisions. Neither shall the holder of land or other property who may have taken the same in good faith, without notice of any defect in the title of the person from whom the same was taken, growing out of a violation of the liquor law, be affected by the above provision.

Every wife, child, parent, guardian, employer, or other person, who shall be injured in person or property or means of support, by an intoxicated person, or in consequence of the intoxication, has a right of action against any person who shall, by selling intoxicating liquors, cause the intoxication of such person, for all damages actually sustained as well as exemplary damages.

For any damages recovered, the personal and real property (except homestead, as now provided) of the person against whom the damages are recovered, as well as the premises or property, personal or real, occupied and used by him, with consent and knowledge of owner, either for manufacturing or selling intoxicating liquors contrary to law, shall be liable.

The only other exemption, besides the homestead, from this sweeping liability, is that the defendant may have enough for the support of his family for six months, to be determined by the Township Trustee.

No ale, wine, beer or other malt or vinous liquors shall be sold within two miles of the corporate limits of any municipal corporation, except at wholesale, for the purpose of shipment to places outside of such corporation and such two-mile limits. The power of the corporation to prohibit or license sale of liquors not prohibited by law is extended over the two miles.

No ale, wine, beer or other malt or vinous liquors shall be sold on the day on which any election is held under the laws of this State, within two miles of the place where said election is held; except only that any person holding a permit may sell upon the prescription of a practicing physician

SUGGESTIONS TO THOSE PURCHASING BOOKS BY SUBSCRIPTION.

The business of *publishing books by subscription*, having so often been brought into disrepute by agents making representations and declarations *not authorized by the publisher*, in order to prevent that as much as possible, and that there may be more general knowledge of the relation such agents bear to their principal, and the law governing such cases, the following statement is made:

A subscription is in the *nature of a contract* of mutual promises, by which the subscriber agrees to *pay a certain sum* for the work described, the *consideration is concurrent* that the publisher shall *publish the book named,* and deliver the same, for which the subscriber is to pay the price named. *The nature and character of the work is described by the prospectus and sample shown.* These should be *carefully examined before subscribing*, as they are the basis and consideration of the promise to pay, and not the too *often exaggerated statements of the agent*, who is *merely employed* to *solicit subscriptions*, for which he is usually *paid a commission* for each subscriber, and has *no authority to change or alter* the conditions upon which the subscriptions are authorized to be made by the publisher. Should the *agent assume* to agree to make the subscription conditional or *modify or change the agreement of the publisher*, as set out by the prospectus and sample, in order to *bind the principal*, the *subscriber* should see that such condition or changes are stated *over or in connection with his signature*, so that the publisher may have notice of the same.

All persons making contracts in reference to matters of this kind, or any other business, should remember *that the law as written is,* that they can *not be altered, varied or rescinded verbally, but if done at all, must be done in writing.* It is therefore *important* that all *persons contemplating subscribing should distinctly understand that all talk before or after the subscription is made, is not admissible as evidence, and is no part of the contract.*

Persons employed to solicit subscriptions are known to the trade as canvassers. They are agents *appointed to do a particular business in a prescribed mode,* and *have no authority* to do it any other way to the prejudice of their principal, nor can they bind their principal in any other matter. They *can not collect money*, or agree that payment may be made in *anything else but money.* They *can not extend* the time of payment *beyond the time of delivery,* nor *bind their principal* for the *payment of expenses* incurred in their business.

It would save a great deal of trouble, and often serious loss, if persons, *before signing* their names to any subscription book, or any written instrument, would *examine carefully what it is;* if they can not read themselves call on some one disinterested who can.

TABULAR STATEMENT,

Showing the Valuation and Tax Levied in Black Hawk County, Iowa, from the Year 1877.

Names of Townships or Cities	Total Assessed Valuation	Total Equalized Value by County Board	Total Equalized Value by State Board	Poll Tax	State Tax	County Tax	School Tax	Poor Tax	Bridge Tax	Bond Tax	Insane Tax	Teachers' Tax	Contingent Tax	School House Tax	Corporation Tax	Total
Fox	$1706 25	$1564 67	$1857 08	$83 50	$371 46	$742 96	$185 74	$185 74	$557 82	$232 18	$92 87	$1508 68	$404 01	$445 74		$2461 69
Cedar	1702 57	1681 76	2320 76	53 00	464 29	928 68	232 16	232 16	696 44	290 18	116 08		511 89			6431 30
Orange	1871 63	2028 68	2556 89	96 00	611 39	1022 78	255 69	255 69	707 08	919 62	127 85		108 47			3867 49
Black Hawk	1898 78	1896 68	2997 96	84 00	459 66	919 12	229 78	229 78	689 34	287 21	114 89	530 88	213 97	213 97		3653 03
Spring Creek	1708 22	1708 22	2139 37	70 50	427 34	855 89	213 97	213 19	641 91	267 47	106 99	427 94	374 12	457 21		3654 62
Big Creek	1464 75	1614 89	2120 72	55 50	424 24	848 47	212 12	212 12	636 35	265 14	106 06	1593 89	220 80	1104 01		5185 22
La Porte	881 58	881 68	1108 98	83 50	220 80	441 60	110 40	110 40	381 20	138 00	55 20	1046 81	268 01		662 41	4527 18
Eagle	1609 91	1690 91	1946 24	59 50	389 33	788 66	194 67	194 67	584 00	243 33	97 33	866 18	86 16			3763 79
Lincoln	1611 43	1863 64	1853 64	64 00	370 76	741 50	185 37	185 37	556 13	231 72	92 68	1297 63	648 82	92 69		4467 17
East Waterloo	2132 48	2188 40	3131 06	105 00	626 30	1252 60	313 16	313 15	939 45	391 43	156 68	1947 38	1237 00	444 36		7727 29
East Waterloo City	2739 99	3059 30	3909 71	264 00	782 03	1604 06	391 02	391 02	1173 05	488 77	195 51	5278 70	3323 63	3910 16	3910 16	21672 11
West Waterloo City	3317 26	3761 46	4696 88	243 50	939 41	1878 82	409 71	469 71	1409 11	687 13	234 85	2348 53	460 71	3622 79	4607 06	17269 33
Cedar Falls City	3276 31	3695 52	4569 20	237 00	913 85	1827 71	456 92	456 92	1370 78	571 17	228 46	7996 21	3885 88	1142 32	5016 19	24211 41
Lester	1429 52	1429 52	1767 73	94 00	353 64	707 29	176 82	176 82	530 46	221 03	88 41	1691 39	707 29	405 64		6052 79
Bennington	1665 87	1727 51	2086 57	62 00	417 37	884 74	208 69	208 69	626 06	260 86	104 34	1252 13	208 69			4392 26
Mt Vernon	1779 86	1795 13	2270 22	81 00	464 16	908 83	227 08	227 08	681 25	283 85	113 53	1330 17	664 18			4870 63
Washington	811 23	811 23	1136 11	52 50	227 21	454 44	113 61	113 61	340 83	142 00	66 81	560 28	284 81			2346 10
Union	710 57	710 57	1103 87	44 50	220 83	441 67	110 42	110 42	331 95	137 98	56 21	386 46	165 63	110 42		2114 79
Barclay	1965 92	1880 84	2559 99	108 00	612 03	1024 07	256 01	256 01	768 05	320 00	128 08	1151 99	768 05			6287 22
cyber	1916 14	1831 33	2314 97	104 00	464 13	926 26	231 56	231 56	694 71	289 49	116 78	1177 06	477 08			4711 13
cedar Falls	2165 59	2263 14	2323 83	108 50	646 87	1293 73	223 44	223 44	970 30	404 29	161 72	1285 53	626 38	151 52		6290 72
Waterloo	1170 89	1203 07	1695 27	35 00	339 17	678 34	169 48	169 48	508 75	211 99	84 79	525 30	373 64	397 75		3433 79
Total	$38514 91	$40386 71	$52621 65	$2278 50	$10686 78	$21071 62	$5267 90	$5267 90	$15803 72	$6584 84	$2683 96	$34107 09	$15900 80	$12484 73	$13271 15	$146440 91

PUBLISHER & PROPRIETOR OF THE WATERLOO COURIER

HISTORY OF BLACK HAWK COUNTY.

THE Indian title to the territory in Iowa west of the Black Hawk Purchase and south of the neutral ground at Winnebago Reserve was not extinguished until 1837, and the beautiful valley of the Red Cedar, a portion of which is now embraced in the limits of Black Hawk County, was the favorite hunting ground of the Sacs and Foxes. Nor did they relinquish it entirely when they ceded "the Beautiful Land" to the United States. For years, wandering bands roved through this region, and were occasionally very troublesome to the few white settlers who ventured to establish homes in the smiling wilderness.

BOUNDARIES AND CIVIL DIVISIONS.

Black Hawk County was created and its boundaries defined by act of the Territorial Legislature of Iowa, approved February 17, 1843, and attached to Delaware County for judicial and revenue purposes.

Black Hawk County contains sixteen Congressional townships, viz.: Townships Nos. 87, 88, 89 and 90 north of Ranges 11, 12, 13 and 14 west. These are divided into eighteen civil townships, as follows· Spring Creek, all of Township 87, Range 11, lying north of the Cedar River; Fox, Township 88, Range 11, Barclay, Township 89, Range 11; Lester, Township 90, Range 11; Bennington, Township 90, Range 12; Poyner, a strip two and one-half sections wide on east of Township 89, Range 12, all of Township 88, Range 12, on east side of Cedar River, except west half of Section 4, and Sections 5 and 6, and that part of Township 87, Range 12, lying east of the river (a township about fifteen miles long and two and a half miles wide), Cedar, that part of Township 88, Range 12, west of Cedar River and that part of the north half of Township 87, Range 12, that lies west of the river; Big Creek, south half of Township 87, Range 12, and that part of Township 87, Range 11, which lies south of the Red Cedar River; Eagle, Township 87, Range 13, Orange, Township 88, Range 13; Waterloo, that part of Township 89, Range 13, and Township 89, Range 12, south of the Red Cedar, East Waterloo, that part of Township 89, Range 13, north and east of the Red Cedar, except Sections 6 and 7, that part of Township 89, Range 12, not included in Poyner east of the river, and Sections 6, 5 and west half of Section 4, Township 88, Range 12; Mount Vernon, Township 90, Range 13, Washington, east half of Township 90, Range 14; Union, west half of Township 90, Range 14, Cedar Falls, Township 89, Range 14, and Sections 6 and 7, Township 89, Range 13; Black Hawk, Township 88, Range 14; Lincoln, Township 87, Range 14.

LOCATION.

Black Hawk County lies chiefly in the lovely and fertile valley of the Red Cedar River—the garden and granary of the State—unsurpassed on the Amer-

ican continent for beauty of scenery and fertility of soil.   The general surface
presents an undulating prairie, with an elevation slightly less than surrounding
counties.   The soil is a deep black, vegetable, sandy mold or loam, well adapted to withstand both droughts and floods.   Wheat and corn are the chief products, but all grasses, grain and vegetables grown in the latitude can be raised
to perfection here.   Recently, however, the people of the county are devoting
more attention to the dairy.

STREAMS.

The Red Cedar runs diagonally through the center of the county from northwest to southeast, a beautiful river about two hundred yards wide and an average depth of two feet   Its waters are clear, and, in this county, flow mostly
over a rocky, gravelly bed, having an average fall of two feet six inches.

The Wapsipinicon flows through the township of Lester.

Crane Creek flows through Bennington and Lester, and loses itself in the
Wapsipinicon.

Black Hawk Creek drains the southwest, pouring its waters into the Cedar
just above Waterloo

Miller's Creek, Beaver Creek, Mud Creek, Prairie Creek and other small
streams empty into the Cedar from the west, and Ellsworth, Elk Run, Poyner,
Indian and Spring Creeks from the east.

TIMBER.

Originally, the proportion of timber was about one acre to fourteen acres of
prairie.   Nearly all of that standing when the county was first settled has been cut
off, but much of the land it covered has come up with second growth and many
groves have been planted by the settlers, so that the supply has increased rather
than diminished.

It is said that the banks of the river were formerly covered in many places with
groves of red cedar trees, from which fact the river took its name.   A large
portion of this valuable timber, however, was cut and rafted to St. Louis, before
the advance guard of civilization began to settle in this beautiful valley, by
bands of adventurers, some of whom continued their depredations after the
removal of the Indians and after the white settlers began to occupy their hunting grounds.   One of these was Charles Dyer, who had a peculiarly formed
hump-back, looking, as some of the early settlers described him, "as if he had
shouldered himself."   Dyer continued his work of plunder to such an extent that
the white settlers determined to drive him from the county   They assembled,
and visited his shanty in a body to deal with him in accordance with pioneer
custom; but the gentleman whom they desired to see was not at home.   After
due deliberation—as they knew that Dyer could not read a note of warning if
they left one for him—they stripped the bark from a large tree in front of his
rude cabin, and, with a bit of charcoal, one of their number sketched upon the
naked trunk a picture of the hump-back, which they riddled with bullets.   The
likeness was unmistakable, and it is said Dyer understood it, as he quietly disappeared.   It is not known when the event occurred or where Dyer's cabin was
located

THE GEOLOGICAL FORMATION

of the Red Cedar Valley is full of interest to the careful student of natural history   Most of the county is underlaid with Devonian rock, generally of the
Hamilton group, although the Chemung appears in the western part.   Much of
the rock is magnésian limestone, suitable for building purposes, while in other

localities it is entirely unfit for use. Fossils are numerous, and everywhere the limestone rock abounds with corals, sea-weeds, shells, spines, teeth, etc., of ganoid fishes, as well as teeth of those reptiles and fishes that abounded during the old red sandstone era

There are also evidences of vegetable life prior to the deposits constituting the present prairie. Ancient soil and timber are found in digging wells, generally twenty-five to thirty feet below the present surface.

Beautiful specimens of spar are frequently found, and agates and cornelians are occasionally picked up along the river banks.

Boulders of granite, schist, quartz and greenstone scattered over the prairie are evidences that this was a part of the great drift region. Much of the limestone, when burned, makes excellent lime, while good brick-clay and sand are abundant and well distributed throughout the county.

The climate is remarkably salubrious. Malarious diseases are rare. Winters are cold and long, but the cold is steady and the air pure and invigorating.

The county is peculiarly adapted to grazing—the long Winter being the only drawback.

EARLY SETTLEMENT.

The first "pale-face" to enter the domain of the Sacs and Foxes, in that portion of the valley of the Cedar now embraced within the limits of Black Hawk County, was, so far as is now known, G. Paul Somaneux, a Frenchman, who located at the Falls of the Cedar in the Spring or early Summer of 1837, and commenced trafficking with the natives. For some reason, probably not caring to spend the Winter alone, surrounded by "no gentler" neighbors than Indians, he left his encampment in the Fall of that same year. Although his first stay was so brief, Somaneux must probably be considered the pioneer settler of Black Hawk County, for he returned ten years after his first visit or stay, and in the Winter of 1847–48, in company with A. J. Taylor, trapped above Sturgis' Falls. During the following Summer of 1848, Somaneux worked for Overman & Co. In the Fall of that year, he trapped along the Shell Rock, and early in the Winter of 1848–49, made a claim and built a cabin where the village of Cedar City now stands. He is said to have been a very devout Catholic, having been reared by a Catholic priest at Detroit, Mich., and very rarely uttered a profane word. He died at his cabin in the Fall of 1850, and was buried on the bank of the slough, near by. Leaving no known heirs, his estate was administered by John T. Barrick.

ROBERT STUART.

Somaneux was not the only white man who came to the Cedar Valley in 1837. Robert Stuart, an elderly man, said to have been a surveyor, spent the Summer of 1837 in the vicinity of the Falls, engaged in trading with the Indians. Stuart's testimony remains, that the Summer of 1837 was extremely wet. The river, according to his statement, having risen to higher water than it has ever reached since that time.

In 1855, Stuart was at Cedar Falls; while there an evangelist visited the place and held meetings in the school house every evening during the week, and announced three discourses on the Sabbath. He drew large audiences, and it was understood that a collection was to be taken up in his behalf, on Sunday afternoon. The house was crowded as usual, Bob Stuart, the pioneer of 1837, was among the audience, the sermon was long and Stuart got tired. He was near the door and determined to leave; he rose to his feet and deliberately marched up the aisle toward the preacher   Every eye was upon him, for he was over six feet high, gaunt, stoop-shouldered, grizzly, and dressed as a frontiersman, he halted at the desk, thrust his bony hand deep into his trousers, fished up a ten-cent piece, which he turned over on the open Bible with a muscular slap, and exclaimed, "Here's my sheer!" turned on his heel and passed out of the door, leaving both preacher and congregation paralyzed with astonishment

A man named Osborn, who afterward settled in the southern part of Cedar County, hunted at the forks of the Cedar prior to 1845, but in what year is not now known.

From 1837 to 1844, a period of seven years, there are no traces of white occupation of any portion of the territory of this county. It does not seem probable, however, that this beautiful valley could have been so long overlooked by the roving frontier traders and trappers known to have had their tramping grounds in this region.   Although the Sacs and Foxes had ceded this region to the United States in 1837, so that south of the neutral line it was open to white occupation, they had not left their old hunting grounds.   The south line of the neutral ground, starting from a point on the left bank of the Des Moines River, 37 miles 70.50 chains below the second or upper fork of the same, and running a course north 70 deg. 15 min. east, passed very near the forks of the Cedar, and very near the northwest corner of the county of Black Hawk, as subsequently laid out.

This line was surveyed by James Craig, under instructions from the Superintendent of Indian Affairs, April 9, 1833.   North of this line, from 1833 to 1848, the Winnebago Indians had their Reserve, a strip forty miles wide, from the Des Moines River to the Mississippi.   Along this line Indian traders and an occasional settler located.   In 1840, Franklin Wilcox, with his family and his brother Nathaniel, settled just south of the line surveyed by Craig, in Fayette County; and a few miles east on the Volga, in 1841, George Culver built a log trading-post that is still standing.

With these facts in view, and with the knowledge that white men lived on the bank of the Cedar in 1837, it is difficult to believe that from that date to 1844, this lovely valley was untrodden by any save Indian feet.   It seems almost certain that other traders lived in succeeding Summers where Somaneux and Stuart tarried in 1837, but there are no evidences remaining to verify this belief.

In the Spring of 1844, however, William Chambers, a genuine specimen of the Western frontiersman, from Louisa County, established himself at the Falls of the Cedar, built a cabin, and engaged in trading with the Indians   The cabin which he occupied (whether he or some previous trader built it, is not so clear), stood on the south bank of the Cedar at the head of the Falls.   The south end of the Dubuque & Pacific Railroad bridge at Cedar Falls is very near the spot where Chambers lived, "monarch of all he surveyed," in the Summer of 1844.   It is not known whether Chambers made any "claim," as understood by Western pioneers.   If he did, he abandoned it in the Fall, when he is said to have returned to his home in Louisa County, and never returned to make any permanent settlement.

FIRST PERMANENT SETTLEMENT

The next visitors at this point were destined to make a more permanent location.   In March, 1845, William Sturgis, a farmer from Michigan, and his wife, and Erasmus D Adams, a cabinet maker from Ohio then living in Johnson

County, made a trip up the valley of the Red Cedar, in search of homes and a desirable water-power   Arrived at the point where Chambers had lived the previous year, they were charmed by the romantic beauty of the spot, and, with an eye to business, appreciating its adaptability for a town site in the future, they determined to remain and make claims.   Mr. Sturgis claimed the north part of the present town of Cedar Falls, including the mill site, and Adams selected his claim farther south, near what is now called Dry Run

Sturgis built a double log cabin on the bank of the river, and broke five acres of prairie   Adams built a cabin on his claim, about two miles from Mr Hanna's, and also broke about five acres.   This breaking by Sturgis and Adams was the first breaking done in Black Hawk County.   "Adams soon returned to Iowa City," says George W. Hanna, the only settler of 1845 now living in the county.   "Sturgis had some hands, and commenced getting out timber for a mill, but his family got sick, and he and his family went back to Iowa City again, leaving a Dutchman to work his claim, and not intending to return until other settlers came in.   The man he left had a claim where Hon. Jeremiah Gay now lives (on Miller's Creek), and the creek took its name from him "   To Mrs. Sturgis must be accorded the credit of being the pioneer white woman of Black Hawk County   "In the Fall," says Mr. Hanna, "Sturgis and his wife, and Adams, and his wife and his little boy John, came back and occupied the cabins they had built in the Spring previous "

The Chambers' cabin was yet standing as he had left it, but soon after Sturgis and Adams moved to their claims in the Fall, it singularly enough tumbled into the river   By what mysterious agency this result was produced is not known, but it is said that Sturgis had a theory upon which the phenomenon was to be explained; but he never, so far as is known, made the explanation.

When the mill was built and the town of Cedar Falls was laid out, Sturgis' cabin proved to be near the upper end of the race, at the foot of Washington street, where it remained until, a few years ago, it was removed to give place to a more permanent and graceful building.

In May or June, 1845, John Hamilton and his sons, also from Johnson County, arrived and made claims near Sturgis and Adams · They brought a team and breaking-plow with them, and broke some prairie.   The Hamiltons did not remain long.   Becoming dissatisfied, they abandoned their claims, returned to Johnson County, and left Sturgis and Adams the only white men in the county, whose nearest white neighbors were at Quasqueton, Buchanan County, and Fremont (Vinton), Benton County.

They, too, had gone when, on the 18th day of July, 1845, George W. Hanna, with his wife and two children and his wife's brother, John Melrose, arrived and located on Section 20, Town 89, Range 13, about half-way between Sturgis' Falls and Prairie Rapids.   If Mrs. Sturgis is fairly entitled to the honor of being the first white woman in the county, Mrs. Hanna has the honor of being the first to permanently settle here

In the Fall, about the time Sturgis and Adams moved in, William Virden and his family, consisting of his wife and little daughter, settled about half a mile southeast of Hanna's cabin, on what in 1878 is known as the "Glover Farm."   The four families of Hanna, Sturgis, Adams and Virden, numbering thirteen souls, comprised the entire permanent population of Black Hawk County in the Winter of 1845–6.   Mr. Sturgis made some progress with his dam across the Cedar at the head of the Falls during the Fall, but owing to the difficulty in obtaining "hands," the work progressed very slowly.

Capt. Boone, of Missouri, visited Iowa in the Summer of 1836, and in the Fall of that year gave James Newell, then living in the vicinity of Muscatine, a glowing description of the region about the three forks of the Cedar, through which he had passed some years before in command of a squad of eleven soldiers, marching from Council Bluffs to Prairie du Chien. So much pleased had Boone been with the beauty of the surroundings that he halted his party there for four days, and spent the time in hunting and fishing

In the Spring of 1845, James Newell and Harris Wilson started out from the vicinity of Muscatine to visit the country along the upper part of Cedar River. At Marion, they were informed that the last settler northward lived seventeen miles out, and that after they passed that lonely cabin they must keep a sharp look-out, for the Fall before the Indians had robbed two brothers named Ward who had been trapping along the Cedar. The two explorers met James Chambers as they proceeded northwestward, who told them it was a fine country along the Cedar, but that no white man could live there in safety because it was neutral ground for the Sacs, Foxes, Winnebagoes and Sioux, The first night in Black Hawk County, the two men camped near where Gilbertsville was afterward laid out. Near where Waterloo now stands, they crossed an Indian trail leading from Fort Atkinson to Indiantown, on the Iowa River, which crossed the Cedar at the rapids above. The men left the ford to the left, and came to the Cedar again near where Janesville now stands, where they crossed and explored the country between the Cedar and the Shellrock. While camping in the vicinity, a heavy rain occurred They forded the Shellrock with great difficulty, and in crossing the Cedar the water filled their wagon-box. Wilson was hardly satisfied with the forks of the Cedar, but Newell had made up his mind to settle there. Returning, Wilson was better pleased with the land north of the Rapids, where Sturgis had just made his claim, but objected to the whole country as being too far from Muscatine.

The two travelers decided they must visit Sturgis, and on the way Newell picked up a piece of coal, which Wilson suggested had been carried thither by ice.

Arriving opposite Sturgis Rapids, they found a small canoe at the eddy below, into which they got, Newell rowing When they reached the main current, Wilson became frightened and stretched himself in the bottom of the boat, whimpering, praying and begging Newell to set him on shore. When they reached the south bank, Wilson sprang out and remarked that he'd "be d—d if Newell would get him in that boat again." They did not find Sturgis, and had nothing to do but to return to camp That evening, Wilson visited the bank of the second bottom, and found flood-wood about seven feet higher than their camping ground, which convinced him he did not want to settle there

The following Fall, 1845, Newell returned to the forks of the Cedar, called "Turkey Foot Forks" by the Indians, accompanied by his brother Robert, Walter Fillman and Joseph Brown, but was much incommoded on the way by an attack of ague. His companions built him a cabin, and, not fancying the region, they soon returned down the river, Newell going back with them, fully determined to return to his claim as soon as possible

TRESPASSING ON THE PUBLIC LANDS.

In January, 1846, James Newell and Hugh Rawdon started up the Cedar, with the intention of cutting cedar logs and rafting them down They engaged Charles Hinkley, of Benton County, to go with them as guide. They found the Dickersons cutting logs near the mouth of Big Creek The Dickersons informed them that " Cedar " Johnson had begun cutting eight miles above Big Creek in 1844.

They found Johnson's cabin and moved in without ceremony, sending Rawdon back for grain for the teams

Johnson heard that his cabin was occupied, and sent word up the river for the party to vacate, or to " prepare their wooden jackets," for he intended to shoot them at sight   But the little party kept at work till they had cut and hauled logs enough for a raft eighty-four yards long   About this time they were visited by John Sturgis, who stayed one night with them   When Newell was about ready to start, Johnson came up in a wagon, with two hands.   His desire for human blood was not so great as when he was at Cedar Rapids   Johnson went into the grove, saw that it was badly slashed, and returned to the cabin, where, after being invited in by Newell, he expostulated mildly about Newell's occupying his cabin, and gave Newell to understand that he intended to sue him for the value of the logs   Newell remarks concerning this, " that it would be a d—d pretty case—two thieves going to law about property they were stealing from the Government "

The latter part of March came, and the water being too low for rafting, Newell started for home in a canoe down the Cedar, sold his place and made his preparations to move to Black Hawk County   He reached his cabin May 19, 1846.   He mentions that his wagon broke down at Poyner Creek, and that Clark and Giles, of Quasqueton, passed by without offering to help him   He had sold his share of the raft, and was enabled to go to farming in earnest as soon as he reached his claim   In spite of the crows, he raised 500 bushels of corn, one hundred of which he sold to the Indians at a dollar a bushel.

Wolves were very numerous around Newell's cabin in the Fall of 1846, killing off all his chickens but one rooster, whose gills turned white with fear To save his life, they had to take him in the cabin of nights.

In January or February, 1847, James Chambers made Newell a visit   He was going northward with a load of pork, driving up the river on the ice.

June 1, 1846, James Virden came to visit his brother William and see the country, and was so well pleased that he made a claim and broke some prairie on the east side of the Cedar, at Prairie Rapids, on Section 23, Township 89, Range 13, just above the original town plat of Waterloo, but he did not build a cabin until the Fall of the next year.   June 24, Charles Mullan and family, wife and two children (Mrs. Mullan was a sister of James and William Virden), located on the west side of the river, opposite Prairie Rapids, and built a log cabin on the northwest quarter of Section 26, Township 89, Range 13   The first actual settler near the future city, Andrew Jackson Taylor, and his family, settled at Sturgis Falls about the same time.   E. G   Young settled at Turkey Foot Forks, near Newell's, in the Fall of 1846, and two Williams families settled in the vicinity   Mr Sturgis continued work on his dam during this year, but did not succeed in completing it

THE FIRST SCHOOL

on the territory of the future county of Black Hawk was " kept " at Sturgis Falls, during the Summer of 1846, by Mrs. A. J. Taylor, with six scholars, who doubtless acquired the rudiments of knowledge under Mrs. Taylor's tuition just as readily and thoroughly as the pupils of a generation later with infinitely better advantages have done.

The first election occurred in August, 1846 (see " First Election " on succeeding pages).

It is said that when the Winter of 1846–7 set in, there were ten white families in the entire area of Black Hawk County, now so densely populated.

Berry Way and another young man, well-known thieves from the Lower Cedar, made a trip through Black Hawk County in March, 1846, stopping at Newell's logging camp over night. The next morning, they proceeded up the Cedar, spent the night with "Big Wave," a Winnebago Chief, and to requite that chief's hospitality, stole two valuable horses from him before daylight next morning About twenty of Big Wave's band pursued them, and found them at a singing school near Center Point They threatened to shoot the trio, but the settlers interfered and persuaded the Indians it would be best to place the thieves under arrest and let the law take its course The scoundrels were accordingly confined in jail at Marion, but soon after escaped

In December, 1846, Winnesheik, the head chief of the Winnebagoes, paid Newell a visit, accompanied by Big Wave and 250 men and women. The Indians camped for the Winter in the grove near Newell's. In February, 1847, a band of Pottawatomies, 250 in number, came and camped on the Cedar also, soon after which, both bands celebrated their meeting with a feast and dance In the Spring, the Indians broke camp to make sugar, the Winnebagoes going up the Shell Rock, and the Pottawatomies coming down the Cedar toward Sturgis Rapids.

INDIAN RAID.

It is said that during the first year of the settlement, probably in 1846, the Sioux made a raid down the Cedar, and surprised and killed nine Winnebagoes near Newell's Ford, on Turkey Foot Forks The next year, the Winnebagoes surprised a camp of Sioux about twenty-five miles above, while the braves were absent hunting, and killed twenty-seven squaws and papooses. Mr. James Virden, however, thinks that originally the twenty-seven squaws and papooses were a Sioux brave and a boy, only two, increased to twenty-seven by the lapse of years

In Febuary, 1847, the Overmans and John T Barrich came to Sturgis Falls. Sturgis was trying to build a dam and mill, but his resources were very limited, and he finally concluded to sell, and during the next Fall did sell, to John W. Overman, D. C. Overman and Barrick, his claim of 280 acres of land, including the mill site and improvements, for $2,200, Barrick borrowing $500 of James Newell to make part payment for his share of the purchase. The new firm pushed the work with such energy that early in 1848 they had the saw-mill—the first in the county—in operation, and in 1850, in a shed addition to the saw-mill, the company put in one run of stones cut from a granite bowlder in the vicinity. This was the first grist-mill in the county, and was of great service to the settlers who patronized it for a hundred miles north and west.

COULDN'T SCARE HIM

About 1847, Moses Bates, from Western Indiana, located on Section 14, Township 87, Range 11 (Spring Creek Township), on the bank of Spring Creek. Bates appears to have been connected with the gang of prairie bandits, and was a "hard case" On one occasion he went to the cabin of Henry Gray, who had settled near him. Abruptly entering his neighbor's house, he roughly inquired of Gray if he knew who his visitor was. Gray said he had that honor, whereupon Bates, who was armed with a rifle, tomahawk, three revolvers and a bowie-knife, informed his quiet neighbor that he might have just three days to pack up his "traps" and leave the county. Gray, however, did not belong to a timid family; he didn't "scare" worth a cent. His trusty rifle was hanging just over his head. He coolly took it down, "drew a bead" on his surly neighbor and exclaimed, "D——n you, Bates, I'll give *you* just three *minutes* to get out from here. Git!" It is needless to add that before the three minutes had expired, Bates had placed himself at a safe distance from Gray's rifle.

On another occasion a German from Allamakee County, in search of some horses that had been stolen, found them in Bates' possession There were other evidences of Bates' propensity to appropriate to his own use the property of others, without rendering compensation, and about a dozen stalwart settlers gathered, took the offender into the woods, stripped him and tied him securely to a tree. The men then prudently formed a ring with their *backs* to the center while the irate owner of the stolen horses applied a liberal dose of hickory to his bare back. Bates afterward had his castigator arrested, but as there were no witnesses who had *seen* him chastised, he was unable to maintain his accusation. Bates sold out to John Clark in 1852, and removed to Boone County, where he died

Soon after Bates, Peyton Culver and John Robinson settled near him on the southwest quarter of Section 14, and commenced building a saw-mill on Spring Creek, but abandoned the project, and after remaining a year or two removed to Marysville.

The years 1848 and 1849 were uneventful, and the population of the county did not increase very rapidly. Among those who sought homes in Black Hawk during these two years were William Pennell, H. H Meredith, J. L. Kirkpatrick, Geo. Philpot, Jonathan R Pratt, Edwin Brown and Samuel Newell

A VENGEFUL SAVAGE.

In the Spring of 1848, after the Indians had been collected at Fort Atkinson prior to their removal to Minnesota, one of them, "Very Good" Johnson, returned to Turkey Foot Forks, and falling in with Paul Somaneux, got drunk and quareled with him. Somaneux gave him more whisky and paddled up the river to his camp Johnson went to Newell's house, breathing vengeance toward Somaneux. He then started off, and meeting George Newell in the river bottom, after threatening Somaneux, fired at George, one of the buck-shot grazing his skull. George ran to the house, and had just got a satisfactory bead on Mr Johnson, when Mrs Newell caught hold of the gun and drew him in the house. His brother Thomas coming along just then, saw Johnson in the act of leveling his gun on George again. Thomas snatched the piece from the Indian, and took it into the house, Johnson following There Thomas took the drunken vagabond in hand and inflicted a punishment that left him with a couple of fractured ribs, which made him roar for mercy. The impudence of Johnson was sublime On his way to his camping place up the river he met James Newell, who, being struck with the scamp's woe-begone appearance, asked him what was the matter Johnson's only answer was a grunt. Noticing that the scamp had his blanket wrapped around his noble form although the weather was hot, Newell snatched it off, when it was very evident what ailed the vagabond The Indian, in reply to Newell's questioning look, merely said, "Two ribs—Thomas no good," and made off. Had Newell known of the affray it is probable the Indian would have had more bones broken

"BLACK HAWK STORE."

During the Summer of 1850, Andrew Mullarky removed from Independence to Sturgis' Falls, brought a small stock of goods and opened a store He occupied a small building on the north side of First street, which served for both store and residence   This was soon named the "Black Hawk Store," the first in the county, and, like the mill, drew custom for a hundred miles north and west

POPULATION IN 1850.

In 1850, according to the United States census of that year, there were 26 families in the county, with a total population of 135 persons , 75 males and 60 females.   The whole number of children attending school was four, and there were two births and two deaths during that year.   There were 389 acres of improved land , farming implements valued at $655 , 15 horses, 39 cows, 28 oxen, 41 head of other cattle, 40 sheep and 183 hogs.   The entire productions of the county in that year were 160 bushels of wheat, 2,150 bushels of corn, 100 bushels of oats, 75 bushels buckwheat, 120 pounds of wool, 3,364 pounds of maple sugar, and 615 pounds of honey.   In 1852 the population had increased to 315

FIRST BIRTHS, WEDDINGS AND DEATHS.

The first white child born in the county was Jennette, daughter of William Sturgis, born Oct 1, 1846   The first white male child was Henry F. Adams son of E. D. Adams, who was born three days after Jennette Sturgis.   The third birth was Emily Hanna, March 7, 1847

The first wedding, so far as can now be ascertained, was that of James Virden and Charlotte Pratt, at the house of Jonathan R. Pratt at Cedar City.   The license was obtained from the County Judge of Buchanan County, Feb. 25, 1851, and the wedding took place on the 27th, George W. Hanna, Justice of the Peace, officiating.   The records of Buchanan County show the following marriages under that jurisdiction, viz :   David S. Pratt and Miss Jane Sturgis, license issued Sept. 16, married by Edwin Brown, Justice of the Peace, September 21, 1851 ; James S Hampton and Mary Ann Payne, license dated June 22, married June 27, 1852, by George W Hanna, Justice of the Peace; Marquis L Knapp and Mary Streeter, licensed Sept. 3, married Sept. 5, 1852, by G. W. Hanna, Justice of the Peace, James Keeler, Jr. and Cornelia Streeter, married Sept 21, 1852, by James Keeler, Justice of the Peace; Adam Shigley and Aurelia S Harwood, license issued June 13, 1853, married June 14, by Benoni Harris, local preacher.

The first marriage of any resident of Black Hawk, however, was that of James Newell   His wife died June 2, 1847, and his family, one an infant born May 21, 1847, needed the care of a mother ; accordingly he found Mrs. Howard in Cedar County, and married her there, Nov. 7, 1847.

The first death was James Monroe Hanna, infant son of George W and Mary Hanna, who died Oct. 18, 1845   The second was Mrs. James Newell, June 2, 1847.   The third death, so far as is known, was that of Mary Virden, 2 years old, daughter of William Virden, whose clothes took fire accidentally, and she was so badly burned that she died soon after, in 1848.

In 1847, Rev. Mr. Collins, a missionary of the Methodist Episcopal Church, visited the region and held religious services in Mr. Mullan's cabin at " Prairie Rapids" and at other places in the county where there were any settlers to listen to him.   Rev. Mr. Johnson, also a Methodist, preached to the pioneers of Black Hawk a little later in the same year

It is perhaps a little singular that no post office was established in Black Hawk County until Jan. 3, 1850, when Dempsey C. Overman was appointed Postmaster at Cedar Falls.   The arrival of the first mail was quite an event, but for some time the mails were so small that the Postmaster used to carry the letters in his hat, delivering them as he happened to meet the persons addressed It is not known that there were any other carrier deliveries in the State at that time, and Mr. Overman may be called the Pioneer Letter Carrier of Iowa. The mails were carried on horseback by Thomas W. Case, and the receipts of the first quarter were $2 50 It was nearly two years after the establishment of the first post office at Cedar Rapids before the second one was established at Waterloo In the Summer or Fall of 1851, Charles Mullan circulated a petition for a post office at Prairie Rapids, or "Prairie Rapids Crossing," as the little hamlet was then called, and asking for the appointment of Charles Mullan as Postmaster The petition had seven signatures The petitioners had not agreed upon a name for the post office, but left the selection to Mr. Mullan, who, when he took the petition to Cedar Falls to be indorsed by the postmaster there, looked through the list of post offices in the United States to find a name. He found Waterloo, was pleased with it, selected it, and in due time the necessary papers were received, dated December 29, 1851. The post office being named Waterloo, the town and township were designated by the same name

In 1851, Mr. John T. Barrick had disposed of his interest in the mill property to the Overmans, Edwin Brown and Dr H H Meredith. This change brought into the combination considerable capital, which was at once applied to developing the water-power. The race was increased in width and depth, and the brush dam was replaced with one of logs and plank, and soon after a three-story flouring mill was erected. But this was not all.

A town plat was surveyed, and the little settlement for the first time received the name of Cedar Falls. The plat was not recorded, however, and two years later the town was again surveyed and recorded as Independence. John R Cameron purchased the first lot, on the southeast corner of Main and Second streets, on which he erected a frame building for a store, which is still standing. The first frame dwelling was that of Samuel Wick, on First street, near Main At the time the plat was made, there were nine log cabins and forty inhabitants in the new town of Cedar Falls

The first lawyer to settle in the county was Samuel Wick. He settled at Cedar Falls, and was there in 1850. The first lawyer at Waterloo was John Randall.

When Black Hawk County was created, in 1843, it was attached to Delaware County; but in 1845 it was attached to Benton County, and in 1846. states Geo W. Hanna, Esq, under Benton jurisdiction, an election was held at the house of E D. Adams, near the Falls At this election, Geo W Hanna, E D. Adams and John Melrose were the judges, and William Sturgis and a man from Benton County, whose name is forgotten, were the clerks George W. Hanna, E. D. Adams and John Melrose were elected Justices of the Peace at this election, who held their offices for five years, as Mr Hanna states that after that first election, in 1846, there was none held until 1851.

The first action of the County Commissioners of Buchanan County, relating to Black Hawk, was recorded April 14, 1851, when the following entry was made:

Application of Black Hawk County and Bremer County to be set off into separate election precincts allowed Black Hawk to be one, and Bremer to be one, and election ordered on the 28th day of April inst , at ———— in Black Hawk County, and at J H Messinger's in Bremer

Under this order, the second election in Black Hawk County was held at the house of John T Barrick. There are no records of the meeting, but it is remembered that 'Squire Hanna was re-elected Justice of the Peace, and Edwin

Brown was elected Justice of the Peace, and John Melrose and Norman Williams, Constables

The first assessment rolls of Buchanan County on which the names of Black Hawk settlers appear, were made in 1851, when the following citizens of Black Hawk were assessed, viz.. E D Adams, F. Davenport, D S. Pratt, D. S. Pratt & Co., William Virden, Overman & Co ,—— Brown, D. C. Overman, E Brown, J. Morgan, Mahlon Lupton, F. Hohmer, A. Mullarky, George Philpot, David Davis, G. W Hanna, J. Melrose, John Virden, R. Jones, L Downing, William Sturgis, Henry S. Crumrine, James Wadell, C. Mullan, Geo. Ellis, Hiram Hampton, James Virden, G B. White, John Crumrine, J. L. Kirkpatrick, J. H. Pennell, Chas. McCaffree, Thomas Pinner, A. Nims, Moses Bates, O H Hadon (Hayden), — Layseur, J H. McRoberts, John Clark, Isaac Virden, O H. Wilson, S. Wick, Perrin Lathrop, J. R. Pratt, Thomas Newell, S S. Knapp, M. L. Knapp, C F Jaquith, Benj. Knapp, Elbridge (G.) Young, A C Finney, John Fairbrother, W. W. Payne, J. T. Barrick, S. T Vail.

In 1850, a man named Brown settled on Section 22, Township 87, Range 11 (Spring Creek), and Henry Gray located in the northeast part of the township in 1851; and in 1852, Charles Sturtevant, Edmund Sawyer, Henry Gipe, William Gipe, Jesse Shimer and D B. Seeter settled in the same township

About 1850, a supply of flour and meal became a matter of no small importance to the little settlement at Sturgis' Rapids (Cedar Falls) There was no grist-mill in the county, and very little grain raised. The Mississippi River was the nearest point at which supplies of that essential commodity could be obtained. John T Barrick was chosen to go for such supplies, the country affording plenty of meat in the wild game that was here in abundance. He accordingly made the journey to Muscatine, but was much delayed by high water, there having been a great deal of rain. He was able in about five weeks to return as far as Big Creek, where the city of La Porte now stands He found the creek impassable, on account of its height, with a large camp of Indians waiting on its banks for the return of their hunters, who had gone out on a buffalo chase He tried in vain to procure the assistance of the Indians in crossing the swollen stream They would assist with their canoes if he would give them half of his flour, which he refused to do, though offering to pay them liberally for their assistance In the mean time the hunters returned, after a successful chase, and learning the situation of our hero, they also attempted to enforce the tribute which their comrades had demanded , but failing in negotiations, they took him prisoner and took his team from the vicinity, but did not attempt to pilfer his flour. The second day they became tired of holding him, and set him across the creek with orders to leave Returning to Sturgis' Rapids, he procured the assistance of some mutual friends and returned for his team and wagon. After some parleying and considerable pay, the team was brought back, his load ferried across, his wagon floated over, and they successfully started on the road to their settlement, where they arrived in due time, and thus another Indian massacre was happily avoided.

About this time, some men, supposed to be horse-thieves, having built a small cabin near the bank of the river, spent the Winter in cutting cedar timber for fence posts and piling it on the river bank preparatory to rafting it to St. Louis. The settlement at Sturgis' Rapids being aware of the fact, and not fancying such near neighbors, made a raid upon the timber thieves, burned their cabin and timber, stampeded their teams, and drove them from the country.

In 1851, O. M Hayden opened a farm on Miller's Creek, near Cedar Valley, where he remained some twenty years   Soon after, George Cook settled where La Porte now stands, followed soon after by John G. Forbes, two miles above, James Blanzy, John Walker, Robert Harris, Lewis Smith Eldridge, Joseph and William Boun, in that immediate vicinity and near La Porte, John Dees, James Hamer, Byron Stewart and Jesse Wasson, who laid out the town of La Porte.

Amasa Nims located on Section 26, Township 89, Range 12, in 1850, but sold his claim to Benjamin Winsett in 1852, and removed from the township

BRADFORD LAYS IN ITS PORK.

In the Spring of 1851, James Newell, at Turkey Foot Forks, had twenty-five head of swine stray away.   He searched for them far and wide, but could not find them.   In the Fall, he heard that they were in the vicinity of where Waverly now stands; but when he went up, they were half way to Bradford   A settler named Forest proposed that if Newell would bring him some corn, he would feed them to keep them tame.   Newell went home, and, as soon as he could, took a large load of new corn to Forest's cabin, but he had just sold out and had made a new claim about a mile off   Newell drove to Forest's new cabin, but he was not at home   Newell carried the corn into the cabin, and went home.   When the first snow fell, late in November, Newell started with some men to gather and kill his swine.   On the way he met an acquaintance who told him that Forest had sold the hogs to the people of Bradford, that two loads had been killed, and the remainder would be slaughtered that day.   Newell, in his narrative, says, "Well, I knew the jig was up; for there was not a man in the place you could collect a dollar of, if there was either law or gospel there, and there was neither."

The Third General Assembly, by a joint resolution approved Feb 5, 1851, instructed the Iowa Senators and requested her Representatives in Congress to use their influence to secure to the people of the State forty-six additional mail routes, among them were, (19) from Cedar Falls in Black Hawk County, to Fort Clark on the Des Moines River; (29) from Centerville in Fayette County, by way of Cedar Falls in Black Hawk County, to the county seat of Marshall County

By act of the Third General Assembly, approved Feb. 5, 1851, State roads were provided for in Black Hawk County as follows:

James Allensworth, of Linn County, John Alexander, of Benton County, and David S. Pratt, of Black Hawk, were appointed to locate and establish a State road from Center Point in Linn County, on the most practicable route to Marysville in Benton County, thence in a northwesterly direction *via* the residence of James Virden to the Big Woods near the residence of John H. Messenger, to Rice's old trading house.

Thomas W. Close and Isaac L. Hathaway, of Buchanan County, and Andrew Mullarky, of Black Hawk County, were appointed to lay out and establish a State road from Independence to Cedar Falls.

John Barrick, Edwin Brown and David S. Pratt were appointed to locate a State road from Cedar Falls in Black Hawk County, to the county seat of Marshall County.

Samuel Davis, Benjamin Knapp and Daniel Parker, to locate a State road from Cedar Falls to Fort Clark.

Charles Mullen, James Virden and William Pennell to locate a State road from Independence to intersect the road from Cedar Rapids to Cedar Falls, at or near the residence of Charles Mullen.

By an act approved Feb 5, 1851, Black Hawk, Bremer, Butler and Grundy were attached to Buchanan for judicial, election and revenue purposes.

The first entries of land in each township in the county, made at the United States Land Office, are as follows·

Township 90, Range 11 (Lester)—Joseph Potterf entered a part of Section 36, July 21, 1851; Caspar Rowse entered a part of Sec. 14, July 23, 1851; David S Wilson, H. W. Sanford, Frederick E. Bissell, George Counts, John Somers, Alvin S McDowell and John Stobie entered land in this township in 1852.

Township 90, Range 12 (Bennington)—Allen C. Fuller entered a part of Sec 36, July 20, 1854. Nearly all the land in this township was entered in 1855.

Township 90, Range 13 (Mt. Vernon)—William Bergin entered a part of Sec 3, July 21, 1852; Thomas Gordon entered a part of Sec. 3; William Joshua, Barney and William Kern entered in 1852.

Township 90, Range 14 (Washington and Union) — James W. True entered July 18, 1850, Benjamin Knapp entered a part of Sec. 27, Nov. 1, 1850; James Newell entered Jan. 18, 1851; John Fairbrother, C. H Wilson, Valorious Thomas, E. G. Young, C. F. Jaquith, Wm. Kern, John C. Higginson, James L. Cumons, Margaret Roberts, Simon Wyatt, Jr, James Sween, Alfred Goss, Solomon S. Knapp, James Carlisle, S. M Knapp, Jesse Morgan and others, entered in 1851.

Township 89, Range 11 (Barclay)—Joseph Potterf entered a part of Sec. 13, and Edward Momey entered a part of Sec. 12, June 16, 1851.

Township 89, Range 12 (partly in Poyner and partly in East Waterloo)— John Crumrine entered a part of Secs. 31 and 32, Dec. 5, 1850, Caleb H. Booth, John L. Kirkpatrick and Joseph M. Pennell entered in 1852.

Township 89, Range 13 (Waterloo and East Waterloo)—Alvin R. Dunton entered parts of Secs 22 and 23, July 24, 1847; George W. Hanna entered a part of Sec. 17 and the northeast fractional half of Sec. 26, July 26, 1847; John Hersley entered a part of Sec 21, Sept. 13, 1849; James Waddell entered a part of Sec. 6; Wm. M. Dean, John M. McDonald, H. S. Crumrine, Lyman Downing entered in 1850, and Andrew Mullarky, John Adams, Norman W Tottingham, Richard Goodwin, Oscar Virden, S. B. Philpot, James Wilson, America Mullan, William Virden, Cephas Clearwater, Peter Powers and Jacob Witten entered in 1852.

Township 89, Range 14 (Cedar Falls)—William Sturgis entered a part of Sec. 12, Oct. 9, 1847; Jackson Taylor entered in 1849; George Philpot entered in 1850

Township 88, Range 11 (Fox)—Frederick E. Bissell entered Sept. 29, 1852, John A Dunham entered a part of Sec 19, Nov. 10, 1852.

Township 88, Range 12 (Poyner and Cedar)—H. W. Sanford entered Feb. 1, 1850; Samuel Owens entered a part of Sec. 6, June 6, 1850.

Township 88, Range 13 (Orange)—Samuel Owens entered Jan. 6, 1850.

Township 88, Range 14 (Black Hawk)—Robert A. Jones entered Dec. 17, 1851.

Township 87, Range 11 (Spring Creek)—Moses Bates entered parts of Secs 11, 12 and 14, Sept. 11, 1849.

Township 87, Range 12 (Cedar and Big Creek)—David Baker entered a part of Sec. 3, and Samuel D. Warner entered a part of Sec. 15, Jan. 2, 1852; Otto F. Hayden entered a part of Sec. 2, July 10, 1852.

Township 87, Range 13 (Eagle)—Joseph H. Mead and Cicero Close entered Sec. 13, Jan. 3, 1854

Township 87, Range 14 (Lincoln)—Madison E Hollister and Watson V Coe entered July 5, 1854.

In April, 1851, the County Commissioners of Buchanan County erected Black Hawk County into a voting precinct, and ordered an election. In August of that year, the County Commissioners were superseded by a County Judge. March 1, 1852, the County Court of Buchanan divided Black Hawk County into two voting precincts, as follows:

Ordered, By the Court, that that portion of Black Hawk County lying west of Cedar River and north of Black Hawk Creek compose one precinct, to be called Cedar Falls Precinct, that an election be held in said precinct on the first Monday in April next, at the house of A Mullarky, and the Court appoints D C Overman, E D Adams and Edwin Brown Judges of said Election And it is

Further Ordered, By the Court that all that portion of Black Hawk County lying east of the Cedar River, together with that portion lying west of Cedar River and south of Black Hawk Creek, shall compose one precinct to be called Black Hawk Precinct, that an election shall be held in said precinct on the first Monday in April next, at the house of Jeremiah Pratt and the Court appoints Jeremiah Pratt, Charles Mullan and Samuel Wick Judges of said Election

O H P ROSZELL, County Judge

Evidently some error occurred in the above order, or the people were not satisfied with the action of the Court, for on the 8th of March, one week later, the orders of the 1st were revoked, and Judge Roszell

Ordered, That all that portion of Black Hawk County lying north of the correction line* and west of the Cedar River compose one precinct to be called Black Hawk Precinct, and that an election be held in said precinct on the first Monday in April next, at the house of Andrew Mullarky, and Edwin Brown, E D Adams and Samuel Wick are hereby appointed Judges of Election

It is further ordered, That all that part of Black Hawk County south of Black Hawk Creek and west of Cedar River, together with all that portion south of the correction line and east of Cedar River, shall compose one precinct to be called Cedar Precinct, and that an election shall be held in said precinct on the first Monday in April next, at the house J A Durham, and Charles Mullan, J. A. Durham and Moses Bates are hereby appointed Judges of Election

There are no records to show that elections were held at the places and times designated, except that on the 3d day of May, 1852, Judge Roszell ordered the payment of the Judges of Election aforesaid, from which it is to be inferred that the elections took place.

Cedar Precinct was divided Oct. 2, 1852, by order of the County Court of Buchanan Co., as follows:

Ordered, By the Court, that the precinct called Cedar Precinct, in Black Hawk County, be divided, and that part lying west of Cedar River shall form one precinct to be called Cedar Precinct, and that portion lying east of Cedar River shall form a new precinct to be called Prairie Precinct, and the Court orders an election to be held in said precinct on the 2d day of November next, at the house of John A Durham, for the purpose of voting for Presidential Electors

It is further ordered, By the Court, that Prairie Precinct extend one mile north of the correction line, and be bounded on the north by the Section line running parallel with the correction line, at a distance of one mile north of said correction line

There are no records of this election, no poll books are to be found either in Buchanan or Black Hawk County archives, but it is said that the first election was held at the house of Benjamin Winset, and that James H. Hampton was elected Clerk; Nathan Poyner, Justice of the Peace, and T Van Eaton, Constable.

Among the ancient papers preserved in the office of the County Auditor, are lists of real and personal property in Prairie Precinct, Black Hawk Co, made in the Spring of 1853, from which the following names of residents are

---

* The correction line falls at the south line of the tier of townships numbered 89

compiled : Benjamin Winset, John Clark, Felix G. Walker, T. B. Van Eaton, Wilson Sawyer, Edmund Sawyer, Thomas Poyner & Co., John Perry, Joseph Perry, William Pennell, Mispah S. Oxley, George McConnell, Charles McCaffrey, Michael Lanning, Stephen Howell, John Helton, Steven Helton, J. H. Hampton, Daniel Walker, Henry Gray, D. G. Ellis, Jacob Bunting, Barney Bouck, George Arthur, Elizabeth Crumrine, George Clark, Henry Clark.

June 26, 1852, the County Court of Buchanan Co. levied a tax on the taxable property of the county of Buchanan, and counties attached, viz.: Black Hawk, Bremer, Butler and Grundy. The tax was one and one-half mills on the dollar for State purposes, four mills for county, one-half mill for schools and one mill for roads.

March 16, 1853, Charles Mullan was appointed Justice of the Peace to fill a vacancy till the April election   June 30, a vacancy having occurred in the office of Justice of the Peace in and for the county of Black Hawk, by the removal from said county, of George W Hanna, the Court appointed George W. Christy to serve till August, 1853

By act approved Jan. 22, 1853, the counties of Dubuque, Delaware, Clayton, Allamakee, Winnesheik, Fayette, Buchanan, Black Hawk, Bremer, Chickasaw and Howard were constituted the Second Judicial Circuit.

By act approved January 22, 1853, E. L Adams, of Black Hawk, Daniel Preeley, of Buchanan, and H D. Wood, of Delaware, were appointed to locate a State road from Cedar Falls, *via* Greeley settlement, and Richardson's Grove, in Buchanan, Turner's Mill, Eads' Grove and Dickson settlement to Buena Vista, in Clayton County.

E. A Bunn, of Black Hawk, John Blunt, of Chickasaw, and W. C Stanberry, of Benton, were appointed to locate a State road from Fremont (Vinton), Benton County, to Waterloo; thence to John H. Messenger's, in Bremer County ; thence to Bradford, in Chickasaw County.

James Newell, Jesse Morgan and William Payne were appointed to locate a State road from Cedar Falls through Beaver and Gohen Groves, in Butler County, through Babas Grove, in Floyd County, thence to Clear Lake.

By joint resolution, January 22, 1853, the Legislature asked for a mail route from the county seat of Black Hawk County to Fort Dodge , for extra line from Dubuque to Cedar Falls, in Black Hawk County, by a four horse coach three times a week

The first store in Waterloo was opened by Nelson Fancher in 1853, in a log cabin near the present residence of G. R Crittenden.

By the appointment of 1853, the counties of Fayette, Chickasaw, Butler, Bremer, Black Hawk, Grundy, Franklin, Cerro Gordo, Floyd, Howard, Mitchell and Worth were constituted the third district, entitled to one representative.

LOCATION OF THE COUNTY SEAT

Section 1 of " An Act to locate the seat of justice of Black Hawk County," approved January 22, 1853, provided, " That A J Lowe, of Delaware County, S. S McClure and Edward Brewer, of the County of Buchanan, be and they are hereby appointed Commissioners to locate and establish the seat of justice of Black Hawk County. Said Commissioners, or any two of them, shall meet at the house of E. D. Adams, in Black Hawk County, on the first Monday of May next, or within two months thereafter, as a majority of them may agree, in pursuance of their duties," etc.   By the same act, the counties of Bremer,

Grundy and Butler were attached to Black Hawk for judicial, election and revenue purposes.

On the 9th day of June, A D 1853, the Commissioners met at the house of E. D. Adams, in the village of Cedar Falls, and performed their duties under the law The following report appears of record on the minute book of the County Judge of Buchanan County ·

A Record of Commissioners' proceedings, locating the county seat of Black Hawk

A J Lowe, S S McClure, Edward Brewer, Commissioners, sworn on the 6th day of June, 1853, before O H P Roszell, County Judge of Buchanan We, the undersigned Commissioners, appointed by an act of the Legislature of the State of Iowa, approved Jan 22, 1853, to locate and establish the county seat of Black Hawk County, would respectfully report that, after complying with the requisitions of the law in relation thereto, we met at the place specified, and within the time required by said act, and proceeded to examine said county, and on mature deliberation, after said examination, have selected certain lots, hereinafter designated, in the village of Cedar Falls, in said county of Black Hawk, which said lots are now deeded by the proprietors of said village to the county, and are described as follows Lots 2 and 3, in Block 4 , Lots 1, 2 3 and 4, in Block 15 , Lots 6 and 7, in Block 11 , Lots 6 and 7, in Block 12 , Lots 6 and 7, in Block 13 , Lots 6 and 7, in block 23 , Lots 6 and 7, in Block 24 , Lots 2 and 7, in Block 33 , Lots 3, 6 and 7, in Block 34 , Lots 3 and 6, in Block 35 , Lots 3 and 7, in Block 32 , Lots 2 and 3, in Block 25 , Lots 2 and 3, in Block 22 , Lots 2 and 3, in Block 36 , Lots 6 and 7, in Block 37 Lots 6 and 7, in Block 38 , Lots 3 and 6, in Block 30 , Lots 3 and 6, in Block 29 , Lots 3 and 6, in Block 28 , Lots 3 and 6, in Block 27 , Lots 3 and 6, in Block 31 , Lots 2 and 7, in Block 26 , Lots 2 and 7, in Block 19 , Lot 2, in Block 14 in the village of Cedar Falls, in Black Hawk County, Iowa , also Lots 1, 2 and 10, in Block 4 , and Lots 3, 4 and 5, in Block 3, in Dean and Garrison's addition to the said village of Cedar Falls, in Black Hawk County, Iowa, and designate the said lots collectively by the name of Cedar Falls, county seat of Black Hawk County Signed, A J LOWE, ⎫
S S McCLURE, ⎬ *Commissioners*
EDWARD BREWER, ⎭

ORGANIZATION OF THE COUNTY.

The county seat having been authoritatively located, the people of the county began to think about organization, and justly considered themselves capable of running county machinery of their own. The following entry on the records of Buchanan County, made Jan. 30, 1853, indicates that a petition was circulated for an organizing election very soon after the location of the county seat

A majority of the legal voters of Black Hawk County having petitioned for the calling of an election in said county for the election of county officers, it is thereupon ordered that an election be held in said county on the first Monday in August next, for the election of county officers in and for said county, to wit A County Judge, Sheriff, Clerk of District Court, Recorder and County Surveyor, for the term of two years from that date, as the law provides, also a Prosecuting Attorney, for the term of one year , and a School Fund Commissioner, and a Drainage Commissioner, to hold their respective offices until the first Monday in April, 1853 [4?]

The first election was unquestionably held as ordered above, but the poll books and tally lists are not to be found They were returned to the County Judge of Buchanan County, and by him turned over, with other documents, to the county authorities of Black Hawk after the election, as appears of record, but they are not accessible. It would be interesting to know the names of the persons who organized this county a quarter of a century ago.

At that first election, however, held on the first Monday in August, 1853, the following officers were elected, viz : County Judge, Jonathan R. Pratt ; Treasurer and Recorder, Aaron Dow : Clerk of the District Court, John H. Brooks ; Prosecuting Attorney, William L. Christie : Sheriff, John Virden : School Fund Commissioner, H H. Fowler ; Drainage Commissioner, Norman Jackson ; Coroner, Edmund Butterfield ; County Surveyor, Charles Mullan.

It is said that there was no person in the county at that time authorized to administer the oath of office to the new county officers ; consequently, on the

c

9th day of August, Mr Pratt, County Judge elect, went to Independence, where the oath of office was duly administered to him by the County Judge of Buchanan County, O. H. P. Roszell.

The first recorded act of the first County Court of Black Hawk County was the administering of the oath of office to the other county officers elect, on the 17th day of August, on which day all their official bonds were filed and approved, and they entered upon the discharge of their official duties   Black Hawk County was now completely organized, with a government of its own.

July 4, 1853, was celebrated by the people of the county at Waterloo   A brush tent or arbor was erected on the bank of the river, above Mill Square. The Declaration of Independence was read ; speeches made by John Virden, John H Brooks and others ; a picnic dinner by the assembled multitude ; after which, the usual patriotic toasts were read and appropriate responses made.

The first tax levy was made by Judge Pratt, August 28, 1853, when the Court

Ordered, That a tax of six mills on the dollar be levied, for county purposes, including the support of the poor, and with a poll tax of fifty cents on all able-bodied men not over fifty years of age , and for the support of schools, one and one-half mills on the dollar , one mill on a dollar for road purposes , one and a quarter mills on the dollar for State purposes—making a total of eight and three-fourths mills on the dollar

The total amount of taxable property at that time, including the " unseated " land, and also including the other counties attached to Black Hawk for revenue purposes, was $91,608.58.

Amount of county tax	$642 92
Whole amount of State tax.	110 27
Whole amount of road tax .	80 11
Whole amount of school tax	39 78
Total....	$873 08

The first marriage after the organization of the county was that of Henry Clark and Sarah Winset.   Mr. Clark had considerable difficulty in obtaining the requisite license   He came up to Waterloo, forded the river, found the Clerk of the Court, John H. Brooks, who informed the anxious young man that the County Judge was the proper authority to issue marriage licenses.   Judge Pratt lived at Cedar City, but he, said the sympathizing Brooks, was absent from home, and it was very doubtful whether the necessary papers were accessible   At the earnest solicitation of Mr. Clark, Mr. Brooks accompanied him to Cedar City, when they found that Judge Pratt was not only away from home, but that his trunk was locked.   Inside that trunk was the paper Clark wanted. The Clerk was equal to the emergency, however, with a knife for a screwdriver he soon removed the lock, found the necessary paper, which he made out and delivered to Clark on the 27th day of September, 1853.   On the 29th, the couple were joined in matrimony, at Spring Creek, Rev. C. N Moberly officiating on the happy occasion.

CITIES AND TOWNS

Cedar Falls, located on Sections 8 and 9, Town 89, Range 14, John M. Overman, Phebe J. Overman, William P Overman, Harriet C. Overman, Demcy C Overman and Edwin Brown, proprietors.   Acknowledged April 12, 1853, and ordered to be recorded, by O H. P. Roszell, County Judge of Buchanan County, April 26, 1853.   Twenty-five additions have been made to the original plat.

Waterloo, located on Sections 23, 24, 25 and 26, Town 89, Range 13   Plat filed for record June 24, 1854.   Surveyed and platted by Charles Mullan.

County Surveyor George W. Hanna, Mary Hanna, Lewis Hallock, Lady A. Hallock, Charles Mullan and America Mullen, John H. Brooks, Lucinda Brooks, proprietors on west side, and Jonathan R Piatt, James Virden, Charlotte Virden, B M. Cooley on both sides Their several acknowledgments were made, the first in December, 1853. Twenty-six additions have been made to the original plat.

Gilbertsville, located on Sections 23, 22 and west half, northeast quarter Section 27, Town 88, Range 12 Surveyed and platted by John W. Holmes, July 2, 1856 John Chambaud and John Felton, proprietors.

Ottawa, located on north half of southwest quarter of Section 25, Town 87, Range 12 John Dees and Nancy Dees, proprietors. Surveyed by Joseph Owen. Acknowledged November 6, 1854. Filed for record November 6, 1854.

Barclay, located on northwest quarter Section 13, Town 89, Range 11. Surveyed by D A Sovereign, August 8, 1854. James Barclay, Lucinda Barclay, proprietors. Filed for record April 7, 1855.

Janesville, located on the northwest of northeast of Section 2, Town 90, Range 14. Surveyed July 24, 1855, by George W Miller. Mary Ann Fairbrother and Hiram Fairbrother, proprietors. Filed for record January 12, 1856.

Brooklin, located in Black Hawk and Benton Counties. Surveyed April 3, 1856, by Newell Colby, County Surveyor of Benton County. H. N. Brooks, proprietor. Filed for record June 22, 1860

Cedar City, located on south half of Section 6, Town 89, Range 13. Surveyed by George W. Miller, County Surveyor. William M. Dean and Sarah Dean, proprietors. Filed for record May 16, 1856.

Hudson, located on west half of Section 26, Town 88, Range 14 Surveyed June 15, 1857, by William L Miller, Deputy County Surveyor. John L. Alline, Mary Alline and Asaph Sergeant, proprietors. Filed for record June 24, 1857.

La Porte City, on south half of Section 25, Town 87, Range 12. Surveyed by Wesley Whipple, Surveyor, January 5, 1855. Jesse Wasson, Junia Wasson, W. Catlin and Rozella Catlin, proprietors. Filed for record July 16, 1855. At least twelve additions have been made to the original plat.

Warren, located on southeast quarter Section 16, Town 87, Range 11 (Spring Creek). Surveyed October 11, 1855, by George W. Miller, County Surveyor. Warren Rankins, Eliza J. Rankins, proprietors. Filed October 15, 1855. Fees not paid and never recorded Good crops are raised on the site of this town

Raymond, located on Sections 2 and 3, Town 88, Range 12, was surveyed by John Ball, County Surveyor, April 11, 1866 Edward E. McStay, proprietor. Filed for record June 14, 1867.

Finchford, located on Section 7, Town 90, Range 14 Surveyed, June, 1869, by Edwin Rodenberger, County Surveyor Lewis Goings, Elizabeth Goings, proprietors. Filed for record June 11, 1872.

Florence City, was the high-sounding name of a town laid out on Section 35, Town 87, Range 11, on Cedar River, March 5, 1855 The plat of the town was presented to the County Court for approval, with a petition asking that it might be recorded, but the Judge refused to order it recorded on account of alleged informalities.

October 3, 1853. Ordered by Judge Pratt, that the County Court sessions be held at the office of L D. C Maggart, in the village of Cedar Falls.

FERRIES.

The Red Cedar is a shallow stream, easily and safely forded in many places in ordinary stages of water; but something more was necessary, bridges were out of the question at that time, and a ferry appeared to be one of the essential wants of the little community, and an enterprising settler was ready to supply it, as appears from the following entry in the County Court records of October 12, 1853.

Now, to wit, this day, Samuel L May makes application for a license to erect and keep a ferry at Waterloo across Cedar River at said place, and on proof that the legal notice has been given, by posting up as the law directs, and, also, the said applicant having filed the bonds required by law in a penalty of $200 and bonds being approved by the court, whereupon the court grant to said Samuel L May the exclusive right to keep and run a ferry boat or boats on the Cedar River, at Waterloo, and this privilege to extend one mile each way, up and down the river from Waterloo, for ten years from this date, if so long the applicant shall attend and cause to be kept in good order, and in all respects comply with the requirements of the law in regard to ferries, and the court prescribe the following rates of toll to be charged, and no greater, to wit. For each footman, 5 cents, man and horse, 15 cents, one horse and buggy, 20 cents, two horses and wagon, 25 cents; two horses and carriage, 25 cents, four horses and wagon, 50 cents, two yokes of oxen and wagon, 50 cents, neat cattle, per head, 10 cents, horses, per head, 10 cents; sheep, per head, 3 cents, hogs, per head. 3 cents   The said May is to ferry free of charge all persons going to or returning from meetings on the Sabbath, and all voters going to or returning from elections held at Waterloo   J R PRATT, *County Judge*

Mr May established his ferry at a point a little above the present dam.

April 3, 1855, the County Court granted a license to Benoni H Butterfield to run a ferry across Cedar River from Tenth street, Waterloo (just below the Court House)   This franchise extended a mile down the river.   On the 23d day of August, of the same year, Mr Butterfield sold his license to Lewis Hallock for $700

June 5, 1855, a license was granted to Benjamin Barnes to run a ferry across the Cedar River, at or near Section 29, Town 87, Range 11.

In 1857, Messrs. Lake & Bullock established a steam ferry above the dam at Waterloo, and operated it for a short time; but the boat was unwieldy, ran over the dam two or three times, and finally laid itself upside down near the livery stable, on the bank of the river, which terminated the experiment.

August 8, 1854, the County Court granted a license to J. R. Cameron to run a ferry across Cedar River opposite the village of Cedar Falls.

SALE OF COUNTY LOTS IN CEDAR FALLS.

November 22, 1853, Judge Pratt ordered that the fifty-six lots in the village of Cedar Falls, donated to the county by the people of that town, "be offered for sale at public vendue on the 24th day of December next, for the purpose of raising a fund to erect a building for county offices; thirty days' notice to be given of the sale, by posting up notices."

On the day appointed, December 24, 1853, eleven lots were sold as follows.

To John Melrose, Lot No 2, Block 4, for..   ....$17 00 paid
To John Hartman, Lot No 3, Block 4, for ... . 19 00 paid
To Lewis Hallick, Lot No. I, Block 15, for ....   38 00 paid $24 60
To W Claton, Lot No 2, Block 15, for... ... ...   21 00 paid.
To J A Dunham, Lot No 3 Block 15, for... .... 14 00 paid
To John R Cameron, Lot No 4, Block 15, for... .. ..   . . 10 50 paid
To John T Barrick, Lot No 6, Block 11, for.... . ....   .   9 00 paid
To John R Cameron, Lot No 7, Block 11, for . .   . .   9 75 paid
To L Barrick, Lot No 2, Block 19, for... .... 20 00 paid
To L. D C Maggart, Lot No. 7, Block 19, for .....   .   16 00 paid.
To Henry Melin, Lot No 3, Block 28, for   .... .   .   9 00 paid.
                                                       ———— $188 25
March 4, 1854, sold to E D Adams six lots for 60 00

January 2, 1854, the Court appointed William L Christy "Agent, for the purpose of examining and selecting the overflowed and swamp lands in the county of Black Hawk, and State of Iowa, and report to this office by the first day of March next."

January 1, 1854, by order of the County Court, C F Jaquith was paid $15 33 for rent of a room for use of the county.

WASHINGTON TOWNSHIP.

Among the earlier and more important duties devolving upon the County Judge was that of carving the county into civil townships; and this has been done in some cases without regard to Congressional township lines   The creation of these townships constitutes one of the more interesting portions of the history of the county, and the transcript from the records will be new to many of the residents of the county who settled here after the civil divisions were made.

First among these was the following: On petition of Benjamin Knapp and others, the County Court made the following:

It is Ordered, That the inhabitants of Congressional Township 90 north of Range 14 west, be organized as a township of Black Hawk County, under the name of Washington   *   *

And it is further Ordered, That the first township election in the town of Washington be held on the first Monday of April next, at the house of Delos Jordan in said township, and that the following town officers be then and there elected, to wit   Three Trustees, one Town Clerk, two Constables, two Justices of the Peace, one Assessor and one Supervisor of Roads, and that an order be issued to Benjamin Knapp, of said town, for such election, and that Benjamin Knapp, Christopher Wilson and John Knapp are appointed Judges of Election

It is also Ordered, That the Congressional Township 90 north, Range 13 west, be attached to and be a part of the township of Washington for revenue, election and judicial purposes, with all privileges of the citizens of Washington Township   J R PRATT, *County Judge*
Feb 6, 1854

At the first election in the township, on the first Monday in April, 1856, John Wallin Hitchcock, James Newell and Valorus Thomas were elected Trustees, E. G. Young, Clerk; John Knapp and J. Ackerson, Justices of the Peace; W. J Sherman and Elijah Eggers, Constables.

The first settlers in this township were James Newell and Elbridge G. Young

A school was taught by William Dean in James Newell's house, in the Winter of 1850–51.

CEDAR FALLS TOWNSHIP.

On petition of John R Cameron and others, it was

Ordered, That the inhabitants of said township (89—14) be organized as a township of the county of Black Hawk, by the name of CEDAR FALLS, and

It is further Ordered, That the first election thereof be held on the first Monday of April next, at the house of Andrew Mullarky, and that John R Cameron, Henry Mellin and Luther L Pease be Judges of said election

Feb 6, 1854   J. R PRATT, *County Judge.*

At the election on the first Monday in April following, Henry Mellin and George Philpot were elected Justices of the Peace; Elias Overman, Andrew Mullarky and C. F Jaquith, Trustees; E. D. Adams, Clerk; J. R. Cameron, Assessor; J. W. Maggart and T. M Taylor, Constables.

WATERLOO TOWNSHIP.

February 7, 1864, the petition of Edward Butterfield and other citizens in Congressional Township No 89 north, Range 13 west, praying for it to be made into a civil township, was presented and the following order passed:

It is Ordered, That the inhabitants of said Congressional Township be organized as a township of the county of Black Hawk, under the name of Waterloo, and

It is further Ordered, That the first town election in the township of Waterloo be held on the first Monday of April next after the date hereof, at the school house in the village of Waterloo, in said township, and that the following township officers be then and there elected, to wit: Three Trustees, one Clerk, two Constables, two Justices of the Peace, one Assessor, one Supervisor of Roads, and such other County and State officers as are to be elected at the next April election, and that a warrant be issued to James Virden, for such election of said Township, and that James Virden, H N Ayers and Samuel L May be Judges of said election

Order dated Feb 7, 1854   JOHN H BROOKS, *Clerk*

And it is further Ordered, That two tiers of sections on the north side of Township 88, Range 12, be attached to the township of Waterloo, for election, judicial and revenue purposes

                                                          J R PRATT, *County Judge*

At the election ordered above, Morrison Bailey and Charles Mullan were elected Justices of the Peace, John L. Kirkpatrick, Martin Bailey and H. N. Ayers, Trustees ; C W. Buffum, Clerk ; John Melrose, Assessor

The first settler was George W. Hanna, in 1845, followed by James Virden and Charles Mullan, in 1846

HELENA TOWNSHIP.

February 7, 1854, Helena was organized by the following order

It is Ordered, That the inhabitants of Congressional Township 89 north, Range 12 west, be organized as a township of said county by the name of Helena, under the laws of this State , and that said town be attached to the town of Waterloo for all election, judicial and revenue purposes ; *Provided,* That the inhabitants thereof shall be allowed to vote for the town officers of said town of Waterloo

It is also Ordered, That the Congressional Towns 89 north, Range 11 west ; 88 north, Ranges 13 and 14 west, and two miles off the north side of Town 88 in Range 12 west, be attached to Waterloo

February 7, on petition of N S. Jackson and others, Township 88 north, Ranges 13 and 14 west, was attached to Waterloo for election and judicial purposes.

This township was never organized

LESTER TOWNSHIP

On petition of A. S. McDowell and others, the following order was passed .

It is Ordered, That the inhabitants of Congressional Towns 89 and 90 north in Range 11 west, and Town 90 north in Range 12 west, be organized into a township by the name of Lester, and that the first election for said township be held at the house of A S McDowell, * * * * and that A S McDowell, E S Wheeler and J R Owens be Judges of said election

                                                          J R PRATT, *County Judge*

At the election so ordered, Alonzo W. Barber, Thomas Wilson and E. S Wheeler were elected Trustees ; E S. Wheeler, Clerk ; Jonathan R. Owens and James Barkley, Justices of the Peace.

PRECINCT NO. 1—(MILLER'S CREEK TOWNSHIP.)

Beside creating townships, the County Court exercised its authority and ingenuity in the creation of election precincts, composed of several Congressional townships and parts of townships.   February 7, 1854, the Court

Ordered, That the inhabitants of the following Congressional towns, viz 87 north of Range 14, 87 north of Range 13 , and all that part of Congressional townships, viz 87 north of Range 12 and 87 north of Range 11 lying west of the Cedar River , and all that part of Congressional Town 88 north of Range 12 lying west of the Cedar River and south of a line running through said town from the Cedar River to the west boundary thereof, and on the south line of Section 7, be organized as an election precinct of the county of Black Hawk under the name of Precinct No 1, and that the first election thereof be held on the first Monday of April next after the date hereof, at the house of John G Forbes, in said precinct   *   *   *   *   And that John G. Forbes, O H Hayden and J R Points be the Judges of said Election

Although no order of court appears changing the name, the above territory appears to be recognized in subsequent records as "Miller's Creek Township," to which an election was held on the first Monday in April following, when Thomas R. Points, John C. Walker and Michael Bunting were elected Trustees; John G. Forbes, Clerk; Joseph Bown, Assessor; John C. Reeves, Justice of the Peace, and R. C Harris and John King, Constables.

PRECINCT NO. 2—(SPRING CREEK TOWNSHIP.)

It is hereby ordered, That the inhabitants of that part of Congressional Township 88 north of Range 12 lying east of the Cedar River, and south of a line running east from said river to the east line of said township, and south of Section 12, and those parts of Congressional Towns 87 north of Range 11 and 87 north of Range 12 lying east of the Cedar River, and of Congressional Town 88 north of Range 11, in said county, be organized as an election precinct of said county, under the name of Precinct No 2, and that the first election thereof be held on the first Monday of April next after the date hereof, at the house of E Sawyer　*　*　*　*　* And that B Winsett, John Clark and Stephen Evans be the Judges of said Election
February 7, 1854

Like Precinct No 1, or "Miller's Creek," Precinct No. 2 appears in other and subsequent records as Spring Creek Township; and an election was reported in such a township on the first Monday in April, 1854, when there were about thirty votes polled, and Stephen Evans and Isaac Skinner were elected Justices; Edward Wood, Charles N Moberly and John Clark, Township Trustees; Henry Gipe, Clerk, James H. Hampton, Assessor, Henry Clark and John Blackford, Constables.

The first sermon in this township was preached by Rev. C. N Moberly, a Methodist minister, in 1853.

Peyton Culver taught the first school, in 1854. He had eight or nine pupils.

BUTLER PRECINCT.

There is no preceding order creating Butler County into a precinct or township, but it is evident that there was such, as appears from the following order:

STATE OF IOWA, BLACK HAWK COUNTY, ss, *To M B Wamsley* You are hereby requested to give due notice of the election which is to be held in Butler Precinct on the first Monday of April next, for the purpose of electing the following officers Three Trustees, one Clerk, two Constables, two Justices of the Peace, one Assessor, and to vote for such other State officers as are to be elected on said day　　　　　　　J R PRATT, *County Judge*
March 8, 1854.

JURORS CALLED.

Under date of March 11, 1854, the following entry appears of record·

Warrant has this day been issued to the Sheriff of said county to notify the Judges of the several election districts of said county to return to this office the following number of names as Jurors from the several election districts, viz　　From Washington, 21, Waterloo, 57, Cedar Falls, 22, Spring Creek, 24, Miller's Creek, 19; Lester, 7

In the above order, it is evident that Precinct No. 1 is called "Miller's Creek," and No. 2 "Spring Creek."

April 4, 1854, John H. Brooks, Clerk of the District Court, resigned, and on the 20th of the same month the following order appears of record:

Be it known, That on the 20th day of April, 1854, Luther L Peas was, by the County Court, appointed Clerk of the District Court of Black Hawk County, Iowa Luther L Peas having given bonds according to law, and on the above date appointed and was sworn and duly qualified according to law, and entered upon the duties of said office
　　　　　　　J R PRATT, *County Judge*

In the matter of the petition of Robert Stuart and others asking that the County Court of Black Hawk County attach so much of Congressional Township 90, Range 14, as lies west of Cedar River and south of Beaver Creek to Township 89, Range 14, for election purposes, it is thereupon *Ordered*, That the prayer of said petition be granted and the same be made a part of the record of said Township 89, Range 14, as relates thereto
June 17, 1854　　　　　　　L L PEAS, *Clerk*

The first dam across Cedar River was built at Cedar Falls in 1847–8, the second at Waterloo, by James Eggers. June 20, 1854, Mr. Eggers received permission from the County Court to construct a dam across the Cedar at the village of Waterloo, in accordance with an act of the Territorial Legislature of Iowa, approved February 15, 1843, Mr. Eggers having filed a bond in the sum of $2,000, according to law. He located his dam a short distance above the one that in 1878 dams the waters of the river, built it of logs and brush, and in three weeks after he received his permit he had a dam that raised the water two feet.

POYNER'S CREEK TOWNSHIP.

On petition of Nathan Fancher and others, it was

Ordered, That all that part of Township 87, Range 12, laying east of Cedar River, and all that part of Township 88, Range 12, lying south of Elk River and east of Cedar River, and one mile of the west side of Township 88, Range 11, and the whole of Township 89, R. 11, and all that part of Township 89, Range 12, east of Elk Run, shall constitute the township of Poyner's Creek, and that the election will be held at the house of Nathan Poyner

June 20, 1854   J. R. PRATT, *County Judge*

The Township 89, Range 11, was afterward ceded to Barclay.

Previous to this time, a portion of the above territory was a part of Precinct No. 2, or Spring Creek Township

At the first election of record, in April, 1855, M. S Oxley, Benjamin Brown and Job Engle were Judges, and J. H. Hampton and J. C. Engle, Clerks. Nathan Poyner and I. T. Corwin were elected Justices of the Peace, W W Engle and T. B. Vaneaton, Constables.

The township was named in honor of Rev. Nathan Poyner, a Baptist clergyman, who settled here in 1853. It is said that he used to hold religious services under a large oak tree near his cabin.

The first settlement was made by Amasa Nims, in 1850, on Section 26, Township 88, Range 12; but he sold to Benjamin Winsett in 1852; and during that year, John Perry, Joseph Perry and George Arthur settled in the township Rev Nathan Poyner, Thomas Poyner, Edmund Sawyer and John Van Etton came in 1853. John Morgan, a soldier in the Black Hawk war in 1832, settled near the mouth of Poyner's Creek in 1854. John Chamband and John Felton came the same year and founded the town of Gilbertsville

The first marriage was that of Henry Clark and Sarah J. Winsett, in 1853. The first death, that of Mrs. Nathan Poyner, in the Spring of 1853.

The first school house was built on Section 25, Township 88, Range 12, in District No. —, and the first school taught during the same year.

There are ten school houses in the township, and two churches—one Catholic Church, at Gilbertville, Rev. John Nemmert, Pastor; and one Methodist Church, at Raymond, Rev. Mr. Alden, Pastor.

Township officers, 1878: J. P. Kieffer, Clerk ; W. Waterfield, E. Marble and J. Dobson, Trustees ; J. P. Kieffer and E. Marble, Justices of the Peace.

PIONEER JURISPRUDENCE.

The dockets of the earlier Justices of the Peace, of Cedar Falls Township, in which were most of the cases tried in the county prior to 1855, were lost by fire some years ago, and the dates and many details of the primitive administration of justice cannot now be obtained.

Among the cases remembered, was one trial at Cedar Falls, wherein A. F. Brown, counsel for the defense, made application for a change of venue and moved that the cause be tried before a Justice in Hardin County, which application was duly granted.

Another Justice, it is said, assumed jurisdiction of an application for a divorce, and even went so far as to order the amount of alimony and make provision for the custody of the children.

One of the early marriages was solemnized by R. P. Speer, Justice of the Peace. During the progress of the ceremony, the blushing lady discovered, to her dismay, that she was standing on the unlucky side, and requested the Justice to wait till the mistake could be rectified. "Keep right hold, just as you are, ma'am," commanded the custodian of the peace and dignity of Iowa; "for, by G—d, we'll soon be through with this job." The Justice was not going to allow trifles to hamper him in the discharge of his pleasing duty

A citizen had committed an assault upon a gentleman from Vaterland, for which he was arrested and taken before the nearest Justice, without a warrant. The hour was late and the weather was hot when they appeared before the magistrate. He was roused from his sleep and appeared in his office without dressing. He called for a statement of the case, which was given. Without making out either complaint or warrant, the Justice announced judgment upon the prisoner as follows: "I fine you one dollar, and, by ——, if you ever hit a Dutchman again without drawing blood, I'll fine you ten dollars!" The fine was paid and His Honor adjourned court

A lot of whisky was seized at Cedar Falls in the early years of the town. The owner of the contraband goods, through his attorney, obtained a change of venue to Justice Knapp, of Washington Township. Whisky, witnesses, owners, and attorneys all appeared on the day fixed. The defense demanded a jury, which was impaneled; the case was tried and submitted. After being out a reasonable time, the jurors sent word to Justice Knapp that they could not agree, for some of them were not sufficiently convinced as to the identity of the fluid with the article mentioned in the information, and that it would be necessary to inspect the casks more thoroughly than had been done. Accordingly, a twelve-quart tin pail was filled with the liquor, a dipper placed therein, and the sample conveyed to the thirsty jury by the Constable. The Justice, not knowing but the jury might have an arduous task before them, allowed the attorneys, witnesses and spectators to partake of what was left, which was as refreshing to their throats as "a great rock in a desert land" to a sun-burnt traveler The result was that the spirit of the law in that case made and provided, was fully carried out. To the lasting credit of the legal profession, which is always regarded as able to take care of itself, it is said that all the attorneys engaged in the case got back to Cedar Falls before any of the witnesses.

Mr. Francis Cox relates the particulars of his own arrest while removing to Cedar Falls, in October, 1854 For a day before reaching the eastern limit of Black Hawk County, a party with ox teams had been close to him on the journey. He was gradually drawing ahead of them, on the second day, when Mr. Cox, in looking back, saw that the prairie was on fire, set, no doubt, by the men with the ox teams Toward night, Mr Cox was confronted by the Sheriff, who politely informed him he was under arrest for setting the grass on fire Some settler had gone to Waterloo and had made the complaint The Sheriff and his prisoners, the ox-drivers having been also arrested, proceeded to a Justice of the Peace not far off, who heard the case and promptly discharged Mr. Cox He not being able to give evidence as to the fact of the others having set the fire, although fully convinced in his own mind, they were also discharged. Although the effort of the complaining witness was a failure, there is no doubt that it was of advantage in that vicinity, as it would have the effect of deterring others from needlessly exposing houses and grain stacks to the dangers of prairie fires.

A pertinacious liquor dealer of Cedar Falls was frequently arrested for selling liquor contrary to statute Some of the people of Cedar Falls, believing that a saloon was a necessary factor in the growth of the community, and being generous with their money, would usually assess themselves and pay his fines. On one occasion he was fined five dollars and costs for a new offense. One of his friends, who was attending the trial, inquired the total cost Having been informed by the Justice, he counted up the number of friends present, figured up the pro rata to each, and paid his share, promptly followed by the rest. To make it as easy as possible, the Justice and the witnesses contributed their own fees.

The Judge of the Second Judicial District appointed a term of court in Black Hawk County on the 27th day of June, A. D. 1854, and on that day court was duly opened at Cedar Falls in the school house then standing on the block now occupied by the Baptist Church Present, Hon Thomas S. Wilson, Judge, Luther L Peas,, Clerk, John Virden, Sheriff.

On the same day, a petit jury was impaneled as follows · Jesse Shimer, James Hampton, Thomas R. Points, Joseph Brown, Zimri Streeter, J. D. Dewey, William H Virden, J C Hubbard and Myron Smith No grand jury was summoned.

The first case entered was that of Mathew Bevard vs John A. Dunham, attachment In this case, D. L. Deyo appeared as attorney for plaintiff, but it appears to have been settled and plaintiff's demand paid previous to the term of court, and was ordered to be stricken from the docket.

The second entry was the petition of Emeline Peterson vs. William Peterson for divorce; but the petitioner failed to appear, and the suit was discontinued at her costs.

The other cases entered at this term were G. W. Burton vs L. D. C. Maggart, D. C Overman vs. John H Brooks, J R. Pratt vs. William True, Henry Mellin vs Covil & Butterfield.

On motion of D S Wilson, William H. McClure, a practicing attorney of the State of New York, was admitted to practice in the courts of Iowa.

The jury was discharged and the court adjourned, having been in session one day

There appear to have been present at the first term of court in Black Hawk County, D. S. Wilson, Esq., of Dubuque, D. L. Deyo, of Independence and William H McClure, the latter being admitted to practice in the morning.

The census of Black Hawk County for 1854 shows a total population of 2,488, of which 1,385 were males and 1,103 females. There were 603 voters, 523 militia men, and 14 aliens.

MT. VERNON TOWNSHIP.

Sept 19, 1854 —It is ordered by the County Court that Township 90, Range 13, be organized a civil township by the name of Mt Vernon, for all the purposes of a township of Black Hawk County (Attest) MARTIN BAILEY, Clerk

The county record does not show that any township officers or Judges of Election were appointed, but from other sources it is understood that the first Trustees were · Frederick Pattee, Henry Cole and S. S. Knapp, appointed by the County Court. These Trustees appointed Abraham Eyestone, Township Clerk, and Wallace Pattee, Road Supervisor.

The first township election appears to have been held at the house of Wallace Pattee, April 2, 1855, when Joel Hiser and Randolph Leland were elected Justices; Thomas Gordon and Frederick Pattee, Trustees, Wallace Pattee, Assessor; A. Eyestone, Clerk. Mr. Leland refused to qualify, and in August following, Alpheus Lawrence was elected to fill the vacancy, and Moses W St. John was elected Constable

The first settlement in this township, it is said, was made by a Mr. Allen, on the northeast quarter of Section 4, in the Summer of 1852, although the record of original entries shows that William Bergin entered a part of Section 3, July 21, 1852 Allen sold to Isaac McCaffrey in 1854 William Hogan settled in northeast quarter of Section 3 in 1853, and his daughter Rebecca and Elihu Thorpe were married the following Autumn by Rev. Jonathan Goforth, being the first marriage in the township. George Housch settled on Section 4, and Thomas Gordon on Section 3, in 1853. Joel Hiser built a cabin and broke some prairie on the southwest quarter of Section 4, in 1854, and returned to Western Virginia and married in the following Winter. The following settlers located in 1854. Abraham Eyestone on Section 30; Moses W. St. John, Section 27, Alpheus Lawrence, southeast quarter of Section 27; Joseph Thomas, northeast quarter of Section 1, S. S. Knapp, Section 29, Wallace Pattee, Section 5. The township was named Mt. Vernon by S S. Knapp.

The first child born was a son to Mr. and Mrs. R. L. Leland in the Spring of 1855, and Clement Leeper, son of Jacob Leeper, was born in the following August

In 1855, Milton Smith built a tavern on the Independence, Janesville and Waverly road, on the southwest corner of Section 1. This was well known to the early settlers as the "Seven-Mile House." Smith sold it to Charles Gibbs the same Fall. One warm summer's night the next year, it is said that while Mr Gibbs was asleep a wild cat bit his big toe. Two large cottonwoods mark the spot where the old house stood.

The first independent school district was formed in 1856. A Presbyterian society was organized in 1856 by Rev. Mr. Colwell, services being held in Mrs. Cleaver's house on the southwest quarter of Section 1. A Methodist Church was organized in November of the same year by Rev A. N. Odell

The first grove meeting in the township, and probably in the county, was held in the only natural grove in the township, on the northwest corner of Section 3, in 1857. A Grange of Patrons of Husbandry was organized at the King school house in 1870.

May 29, 1871, at a special election, the proposition for a tax to aid in building the Grinnell, Cedar Falls & Winona Railroad was defeated by twelve majority. At another trial on the 24th of June, however, the proposition was carried by a majority of eighteen; but the road was not built, and the people saved their money. Mt. Vernon Township is considered one of the best in the county for farming

On the 30th of September, 1854, twenty-six of the Cedar Falls town lots belonging to the county were sold. from which about $400 was realized.

October 30, A. F Brown was appointed Prosecuting Attorney to fill a vacancy

November 13, the question of incorporation was submitted to the voters of the town of Waterloo. The election resulted in its favor, and another election was appointed by the County Court to accept Articles of Incorporation, but for some informality in the proceedings the project was abandoned.

INDIAN PANICS.

The hardy pioneers of Black Hawk County, like most others who endured the toils, privations and hardships of frontier life when they were brought into frequent and disagreeable contact with the Indians, who were being slowly but surely crowded toward the setting sun by the active encroachments of the Anglo-Saxon race, have many thrilling stories to tell of their experiences.

During the years 1853-4, the settlers in this and neighboring counties were frequently alarmed by reports of Indian depredations and massacres north and west of here Every few weeks settlers would come in from a distance and tell the most wonderful stories of hair-breadth escapes from cruel deaths by blood-thirsty savages, of houses burned and stock driven off. But investigation invariably demonstrated that all these alleged frightful occurrences were utterly without foundation

For some time the relations existing between the Sioux and Winnebagoes, living in the neighborhood had not been friendly, which finally culminated in an outbreak in which a Winnebago boy was killed. The news of this affair rapidly spread, gaining strength as it was told by one excited and thoroughly scared settler to another, until by the time it had reached Black Hawk County it was reported that hundreds of painted warriors were marching down the valley murdering and burning everything before them The people became fearfully excited, and many fled with their families and what little household stuff they could carry, finding safety in the more thickly settled counties or in the adjoining States. A company was raised in Cedar Falls, and under command of Capt. E. Brown and Lieuts. A F Brown and W H. McClure, went out to reconnoiter the enemy, going as far as Floyd County, where they learned, to their great joy and greater chagrin, that it was all a hoax and no hostile Indians were within hundreds of miles. Others went from Waterloo and Independence ; while at Janesville and some other places they hastily constructed rude forts or stockades, and put themselves in the best possible shape to make a strong defense against the blood-thirsty savages

Mr James Virden, who lived in the grove at the upper end of Waterloo, was awakened one night by a man from near Waverly, who informed him that the Indians were coming, killing and burning everything in their path, and warning him to pack up and flee to a place of safety. Mr. Virden had passed through two or three "scares," and took but little stock in the story. He asked the man in, and finally prevailed upon him to go to bed. It the morning settlers began arriving on foot, horseback and in wagons, and the yard and surrounding grove were soon filled with the fleeing settlers. Mr Virden, Charles Mullan and one or two others mounted their horses and started up the river on a reconnoissance After a day's ride, failing to discover any signs of Indians, they returned, and their reports reassured the runaways, who started at once for their homes

These sensational reports had a bad effect upon the timid, and several families left here and went to Linn County, then supposed to be thickly settled and safe

At the supreme agony of the scare, says Mr Streeter, who had just got the main part of his house up and inclosed, fifty persons stayed all night with him , and he says his house was so full he could not step between the sleeping fugitives that night. Many of them had buried their valuables before starting, and some of them, when they got over their fright and returned, could not remember where they had dug and hid their property. The danger became more imminent as the news was carried eastward, and by the time it had got to Dubuque, 6,000 Sioux warriors were rampaging down the Cedar with the besom of death and desolation.

Some very ludicrous incidents are told in connection with this bloodless war On the return of the company to Cedar Falls, one of their number, to signalize the victory, rode his horse into the office of the Carter House, around the stove and out again, whereupon his comrades fired a salute in honor of his bravery, rousing the whole town A settler of the name of Rucker and his wife were so badly frightened by the firing of this salute, supposing it to be the realization of what they had so long intensely feared, that they left everything and rushing out ran sixteen miles that night At Waterloo, several of the timid left, and after spending a few weeks in Illinois, or some other supposed safe locality, returned.

Among others thus leaving was Greenleaf Glidden and family, living on the west side. After spending a short time in Linn County, Mr. Glidden returned and resumed his home here. The night of his return there was a wedding in town (Isaac Virden and Eliza May being the parties interested), and the boys had made arrangements to give the newly-married couple a *charivari*. Soon after Glidden went to bed the clan assembled with cow-bells, pans and various instruments more noted for noise than melody, and the first general break-out of the din aroused Mr. Glidden, who was probably dreaming of Indians, and when he sprang from his bed the general hub-bub and clatter only confirmed him in the belief that the Indians had surely come, and were killing all the inhabitants. Hastily *burying his grindstone*, which was evidently a highly cherished possession, and throwing his feather bed and household traps into his wagon, he hitched up his horses and started at full speed for the land of safety, alarming the settlers as he went He made a halt at Abraham Turner's, below town, told his blood-curdling tale, and warned them to flee. While he was talking he glanced backward toward town, expecting probably to see the flames of the burning houses, but instead saw several dark objects approaching at a rapid gait, and with a cry, almost of despair, he shouted, "They are coming! Here they are!" and putting the whip to his team he once more started on his journey at a break-neck speed A lady at Turner's was so alarmed at Glidden's story that she started at once for some place where she would be safe, and wandered around all night in the sloughs and wet grass in her night clothes. The dark objects that had so suddenly and terribly frightened Mr. Glidden, turned out to be a number of colts that had followed the flying team Glidden continued his journey until he reached the river, and finding he could not ford it in safety in the dark, was compelled to remain there until morning, when the nature of the "scare" was ascertained, and afterward afforded many a hearty laugh.

RELOCATION OF THE COUNTY SEAT

Like most other counties in this part of Iowa, Black Hawk has had its "county seat fight," but it came early, and was finally settled

As previously stated, the seat of justice was located at Cedar Falls by Commissioners appointed by the Legislature in 1853; but this action was not entirely satisfactory, partly, perhaps because it was too far removed from the geographical center, and partly because Waterloo, which was near the center, was ambitious to bear the honor of being the shire town

It is in tradition that an attempt of some kind to change the location of the county seat was made in 1854, but the exact nature cannot be ascertained. It is said that certain citizens of Waterloo went up to Cedar Falls for that purpose, and that a general melee was the result. In an account of the affair published in the *Iowa State Reporter*, May 26, 1875, the local historian remarks : "Something stronger than Cedar River water was used. and after steam was up, the citizens of thatt own procured some eggs and opened fire on the invaders. O. E. Hardy sported a plug hat that afforded a prominent mark for the egg men, and the hat was badly damaged, and the Waterloo force was driven from the field " the result was This was a "Waterloo defeat ;" but the Waterloo force did not propose to give it up, and when the General Assembly convened the following Winter the matter was presented with so much success, that they secured the passage of "An act to authorize the qualified electors of the County of Black Hawk to vote on the removal of the county seat of said county," approved . January 19, 1855. Section 1 of this act provided ·

That there shall be a poll opened at the usual place of voting in the several organized townships in Black Hawk County, on the first Monday in April next, for the purpose of allowing the qualified electors of said county to vote for or against the removal of the county seat of said county

Section 2 provided that the ballots of the electors should have written or printed thereon the word " Cedar Falls " or " Waterloo," and that place having the greater number of votes should be the county seat

Provided, that if Waterloo should receive the greater number, the county seat should remain at Cedar Falls until July 4, 1855 and thereafter at Waterloo In the event of removal, the County Judge was instructed to refund the purchase money to such persons as had purchased lots in Cedar Falls, with interest thereon from date of purchase

On the 5th of March, 1855, Moses W. Chapman presented a petition to the County Court, asking that a town plat called " Florence City," located in the southeast part of the county, be approved and recorded ; but owing to a deficiency in the proof the petition was denied

On the same day, H. H. Meredith and others presented a petition to the County Court, asking that the question of the removal of the county seat to Florence City, might be submitted to the people at the ensuing April election Mr Meredith and others of the petitioners were residents of Cedar Falls, and this petition was designed to create a division, through which it was hoped that the county seat might be retained at that place. The consideration of this petition was postponed by the Court to the 19th of March, when the Judge denied the prayer of the petitioners for reasons, 1st, that it was in conflict with the act of January 19, and 2d, that Florence City was a place unknown to the Court.

Ordered to show cause At the second term of the District Court, held at Cedar Falls March 26, T S Wilson, J presiding, on petition of H H Meredith and others, it was ordered that " the County Judge of Black Hawk County show cause before me at chambers, ten days after the date hereof, why the prayer of said petitioners should not be granted, and such other order made and entered as may seem fit and proper in the premises "

Before the day appointed, however, the people of the county had made answer at the polls, and nothing further of this matter appears of record

At the election held April 2, 1855, the question of removal was submitted as provided by the act of January 19, and resulted as follows: Whole number of ballots cast, 648 ; "Waterloo," received 388 ; "Cedar Falls," 260.

April 11, the County Court entered of record the following :

WHEREAS, The election on the removal of the county seat of Black Hawk County, held April 2, 1855, resulted in a majority of 128 for Waterloo over Cedar Falls,

Ordered, By the Court that proclamation be this day made, that on the 4th day of July, A D 1855, the county seat of Black Hawk County shall cease at Cedar Falls, and that the several county offices required to be kept at the county seat shall thereafter be held at Waterloo

There are those who aver to this day that the vote as cast was not free from the taint of fraud. It was asserted after election, that the advocates and managers for Waterloo imported votes from Benton County, who made the counter-assertion that Cedar Falls generously accorded the numerous strangers then stopping at that place with the intention of buying lands further west, the freedom of the town as citizens of Black Hawk County.

In May following this action, County Judge Pratt was taken sick and only a few days before he died he issued an order locating the county seat on the Public Square on the east side; and it is said that when he came to affix the seal of his office to the order he was so weak that he was at first unable to make the impression   He refused assistance, however, being fearful that some question might be raised as to the legality of the proceeding, and finally, by putting almost his whole strength on the seal, succeeded in affixing it to the order.   On the 1st of June following he died, and John Randall, then Prosecuting Attorney, having been appointed to fill a vacancy March 20, became *ex officio* County Judge

But the opponents of removal were determined to fight it to the bitter end. On the 21st day of June, 1855, they applied to Hon. William G. Woodward, one of the Judges of the Supreme Court, and obtained a writ of injunction restraining the removal, which was served very early on the 4th of July   On the 16th of July an appropriation of $50 was made by the County Court to aid in defraying the expenses attending the efforts to have the injunction dissolved, the order giving as a reason for the appropriation "that the injunction was obtained in violation of law, and injurious to the interests of the county."

The injunction was soon afterward dissolved by Judge Woodward, and an order issued for the removal of all the books, papers and documents to Waterloo, which was done on the 27th day of July.   The county officers established themselves in the second story of Hubbard's brick store, on Commercial street, between Fifth and Sixth.

The general election of August, 1855, was now close at hand, Mr. Randall, Acting Judge, was a candidate for the office of County Judge   There was a strong feeling in Waterloo between the people on the east and west sides of the river in relation to the location of the Court House   The citizens of the west side were active in their efforts to secure the county building on their side of the river.   Acting Judge Randall in order to advance his interests in the pending canvass, rescinded the order of his predecessor locating the county seat on the east side, and agreed that if he should be elected he would submit the question of location to a vote of the people of the whole county   This was evidently satisfactory for Randall was elected, and afterward issued a proclamation for a special election to be held on the 10th day of December, 1855, to decide upon which side of the river in Waterloo the prospective Court House should be erected   At this election, 731 ballots were cast, of which 467 were for the east side and 264 for the side that would pay the most money for the location and erection of the county buildings, the proposition being submitted in that form.   This decided the matter in favor of the east side of the town, but the definite location was a matter that was yet within the sole control of the County Judge

Cedar Falls, though defeated the year before, could yet annoy Waterloo. Her citizens were not disposed to forgive their upstart neighbors for removing the county seat and if they could not prevent Waterloo from keeping it they were going to have it just as far to one side as possible   So the vote of Cedar Falls was cast with substantial unanimity for East Waterloo

By act approved January 9, 1855, Palmer F. Newton, of Fayette County, and T. E. Turner, of Buchanan, were appointed to locate a State road from

Cedar Falls to Janesville and Waverly, in Bremer County, thence to St. Charles, Floyd County, thence to Osage, Mitchell County.

January 24, Wm H McClure, of Black Hawk County, Henry H Griffith, of Polk, and Thomas S Griffin, of Woodbury, were appointed to locate a State road from Cedar Falls, by Fort Dodge, in Webster County, to near the mouth of the Big Sioux River, in Woodbury County.

By act approved January 25, 1855, the counties of Dubuque, Delaware, Buchanan, Black Hawk and Bremer were constituted the Second Judicial District, and terms of court established in Black Hawk on the first Monday after the third Monday in March and September of each year.

By act of January 25, 1855, the Counties of Linn, Benton, Black Hawk and Buchanan were constituted the Twenty-fifth Senatorial District, entitled to one Senator. Black Hawk and Buchanan were constituted the Forty-first Representative District, entitled to one Representative.

The Omnibus Road Bill, approved January 24, 1855, provided for the appointment of Commissioners to locate State roads, as follows:

James B Kelsey and Thomas B. Stone, of Linn County, and Harrison Bristol, of Benton, to locate a road from Cedar Rapids, via Bear Creek Mill and Vinton, to Cedar Falls.

William P. Hammon, of Bremer, Samuel Sufficool, of Buchanan, and O P Harwood, of Floyd, to locate a road from Independence, via Barclay, Waverly, St. Charles and Floyd Center, to the State line, in Mitchell County

John T. Barroch, ——— Boone and Cornelius Beal, to locate a road from Cedar Falls, via Hardin City and New Castle, to Fort Dodge.

By joint resolution approved January 18, 1855, the Legislature of Iowa asked for additional mail facilities in Black Hawk County, as follows:

From Des Moines, via Nevada, Minerva Grove Henry Grove and Eldora, to Cedar Falls, in Black Hawk County, in two-horse coaches, once a week.

From Cedar Falls, via Hardin City and New Castle, to Fort Dodge, in two-horse coaches, once a week.

BLACK HAWK TOWNSHIP.

March 2, 1855, upon petition of John Virden and others, it was

Ordered by the Court, That Townships 87 and 88 north of Range 14 west be organized a civil township of Black Hawk County, by the name of Black Hawk Township, and that the first election therein be held at the house of ——— * * * (record sayeth not).
                                   (Attest)   MARTIN BAILEY, *Clerk*

The first election in Black Hawk Township was held at the house of Byron Sergeant, April 2, 1855, and the poll book contained the names of eleven voters A. J. Tapp, Oliver Hughes and John D. Ferris were elected Trustees, Byron Sergeant, Township Clerk. B. Sergeant and N. L. Pratt, Justices of the Peace; D M Ward, Assessor, J D. Ferris and H. H. DeWitt, Constables.

Hiram Luddington has the credit of building the first house in this township, in the Fall of 1852, on the southeast side of Black Hawk Creek, where the town of Hudson was afterward located.

John D Ferris built the second house, during the same Fall, about two miles below Luddington

The first cabin on the other side of the creek was built of home-made shingles, crotches, slabs and sod, by G. Osman.

The first school house was built in the Spring of 1855, located about seven miles southwest of Waterloo, in which Miss Asenath Worthington taught the first school, during the following Summer, at $10 a month, with fifteen scholars enrolled.

Matt. Parrott.

WATERLOO

Rev. Mr Gilmore preached the first sermon, in 1855

Warren Baldwin was the first blacksmith.

Algernon Ferris was the first child born in the township.

In 1858, a bridge was built across Black Hawk Creek, by D W. Young and others. It was a rude structure, about sixty feet long, built of poles, rails and slough grass, with crotches for piles and piers ; but it served a good purpose for a time

The town of Hudson is in this township.

In 1861, Township 87, Range 14, was set off as a new township, and called Lincoln.

BARCLAY TOWNSHIP

March 2, 1855, Barclay Township was created by the following order :

On application of James Barclay and others, it is ordered by the Court that Township 89 north of Range 11 west be organized a civil township, for all the purposes of a civil township of Black Hawk County, in this State

At the election, William C. Morton, C A. Foye and Charles L. Coon were Judges, and James Barclay and Ira Beckford, Clerks, of the election   James Barclay was elected Clerk ; William C Morton and James Barclay, Justices of the Peace.

DISTRICT COURT.

The second term of the District Court was held at Cedar Falls March 26, 1855. Present, Hon. T S Wilson, Judge of Second Judicial District, Martin Bailey, Clerk ; John Virden, Sheriff, and John Randall, Prosecuting Attorney

At this term, the first grand jury was impaneled, as follows : Henry Sherman, Foreman ; Benjamin Knapp, Pleasant Morris, E. G Young, John Wilson, Stephen Evans. Henry Gipe, M S. Oxley, Jesse Shimer, Michael Bunting, William Fisher, C. H. Wilson, R. P. Speer, L L. Pease and B F. White.

S. H Packard, Jr, and Safford W. Rawson, practicing attorneys, of the State of New York, were admitted to practice law in the courts of Iowa.

The grand jury reported that no bill was found in the case of State vs John M. Cowen for larceny, and State vs. Charles Brooks, Jr., William Campbell, Joseph Kinsell and Preston Herrington, and defendants were discharged in both cases. It is said that Cowen came here with horses for sale, and while here indulged in a little private speculation by breaking into the store of B J. Capwell & Co, and stealing a shot bag partially filled with silver, and a bead purse with a number of bills of various denominations. He was held to bail for the crime. deposited the amount himself, and left for parts unknown.

Martin Bailey, Clerk of the Court, was appointed a General Commissioner to take depositions in all cases pertaining to the business of this Court, to report at next term

The first record of declaration of intention to become a citizen of the United States was made by Grounder Osman, a native of Norway, May 31, 1855. Walter McNally entered his intentions about the same time   The first naturalization papers were issued to Andrew H. Kennedy, a native of Scotland .

The September (1858) term of court was held at Waterloo, the new county seat, September 25, in Capwell's Hall, which was then unfinished, and the seats for spectators consisted of boards placed on nail kegs and other temporary contrivances   William M Newton, J O Williams and W. L Christy were admitted on certificates to practice, and B E. Baker was admitted to the bar after examination by I S. Woodward and F. H. Webster.

D

The first bill of indictment reported by the grand jury of the county was against Hamilton Acres, for seduction. The defendant was held to bail in $300. At the next term, *nolle pros.* entered on the ground that there was no ground for prosecution.

March 2, 1855, all that part of Grundy County north of the correction line was established an election precinct of Black Hawk County, and the first election ordered to be held at the house of Silas Peck

March 6, 1856, it was ordered that all that part of Grundy County lying south of the correction line be organized into an election precinct, and that the first election be held at the house of Thomas G Copp. A. W. Lawrence, T. G. Hoxie and T. G Copp were appointed Judges of Election, and the precinct named Palermo Township.

June 30, 1855, John M. Harper was appointed an agent to sell liquors at Waterloo, under an act of the General Assembly, approved Jan. 22, 1855

July 17, 1855, the Court ordered a warrant for $75 to be drawn in favor of John M Harper, County Liquor Agent, to pay for a bill of liquors purchased by him

July 19th, George N. Minor was appointed as such agent for Cedar Falls, and a warrant for $115 ordered to be drawn in his favor by Martin Bailey, Acting County Judge

Martin Bailey, Clerk of the Court, resigned August 24, 1855, and Morrison Bailey was appointed to fill the vacancy.

January 17, 1856, the office of Treasurer and Recorder was declared vacant, and Francis B. Davison was appointed to fill the vacancy.

ADALINE TOWNSHIP.

March 3, 1856, the County Court ordered the organization of Adaline Township, with the following boundaries: Commencing at the northeast corner of Congressional Township 88 north of Range 14, running thence east on the line of said Township 88, Range 13, to the bank of Cedar River, until it intersects the west line of Township 88, Range 12, thence south along section line to the southwest corner of said last mentioned township, thence west on the north line of Township 87, Range 13, to the southeast corner of Township 88, Range 14; thence north to place of beginning. An election was ordered for April 7, but no place of holding it appears in the order

The Judges of the election held April 7, 1856, were Loring B Shepard, James Munger and John Parker; Clerks, William L. Manning and John F. Darling. At this election Obadiah Sineaweaver was elected Clerk, William L Manning and John Parker, Justices of the Peace

While there is no order of the County Court changing the name of the Township of Adaline, yet in the records of the general election in August following its organization, Orange is substituted, and James Munger, W H. Wiswell and L. B. Shepard were Judges, and O. P. Sineaweaver and Dyer Reed, Clerks

CEDAR TOWNSHIP.

March 12, 1856:

It is hereby Ordered, that all of that part of Congressional Township 88 north of Range 12 west, in Black Hawk County, Iowa which lies west of the Cedar River, and all of that part of Township 87 north of Range 12 west, in the said county, which lies west of the said river and north of a line running east and west through the center of said township, be and the same are hereby organized into a township for election and other purposes, to be known and designated as Cedar Township, and that the first election in the said Cedar Township be held at the store of Jesse Wasson, on the first Monday in April next

At the first election, April 7, 1856, Bradford W Clark, N P. Clark and John P. Romack were Judges; and L. H. Mead and T. R Points, Clerks B. S. Doxey was elected Township Clerk; Joseph H Mead, Justice of the Peace, and Clarke K. White and Norman P. Clark, Constables

BIG CREEK TOWNSHIP.

On the same day in which Cedar Township was created, viz., March 12, 1856, the following appears of record:

And it is further Ordered, That all of that part of Township 87 north of Range 12 west, in said county, which lies south of a line running east and west through the center of the same, and all of that part of Township 87 north of Range 11 west, which lies south and west of the Cedar River, be and the same is hereby organized into a township for election and other purposes, to be known and designated as Big Creek Township, and that the first election in the said Big Creek Township be held on the first Monday in April, at the house of Thomas R Points

The two townships of Cedar and Big Creek appear to have been slightly mixed in the contest. The election in Cedar was ordered at the house of J Wasson, and J. Wasson was elected Justice of the Peace in Big Creek. The election in Big Creek was ordered at the house of Thomas R. Points, and T R. Points was Clerk of the election in Cedar

At the first election in Big Creek Township, James Hammer, Christian Good and S P. Cooper were Judges, and S. N. Knowles and J. Wasson, Clerks. John Shawner was elected Clerk, and C Good and Jesse Wasson, Justices of the Peace

THE COURT HOUSE

On the 10th day of December, 1855, the Court House was ordered to be built, when erected, on the east side of the river; but no further steps were taken and the first recorded action of the County Court after that time was on the 3d day of March, 1856, as follows·

WHEREAS, The said county of Black Hawk has no Court House or other building or room in which to transact the general business of the county, consequently having to rent all rooms now used for such purposes, and there being a surplus of funds on hand now in the treasury of said county not appropriated, and the county being in need of a Court House;

It is hereby Ordered, That the surplus money now in the treasury of said county, or which may hereafter be collected into said treasury for the year 1855, be appropriated for the erection of a Court House in the village of Waterloo, in said county And that said county further incur the responsibility of an additional expense, which, in connection with the surplus money in the treasury, or which may be as aforesaid, will amount to $13,000 And, in case such surplus, as above, does not amount to the said $13,000, the balance above what said surplus may be, shall be paid from the first surplus money in the treasury of the said county not otherwise required or appropriated And until there be such a surplus in said county treasury, the bonds or warrants of said county be given to the amount of said deficiency

And it is further Ordered, That a contract or provision be made by said county of Black Hawk, for the erection of such Court House in the said village of Waterloo, during the present year of 1856

J RANDALL, *County Judge*

March 7, 1856, a contract was made with Giles M. Tinker, for the erection of a Court House. The contract price was $12,747 61; but as to the nature of the building to be erected the records of the County Court are silent.

Having entered into a contract for building a Court House, it became necessary for Judge Randall to determine where, on the east side, it should be located. This was under his control, although under the pledges made prior to his election, the people thought they might have some voice in the matter. But the event proved that the County Judge was abundantly able to locate the building without advice or assistance from anybody, however public confidence might be betrayed and abused.   He took the responsibility, it appears, for the following entry of record, May 24, 1856 ·

WHEREAS, It being necessary to make a location of the county building or Court House, the erection of which has been provided by contract with Giles M Tinker, in the village of Waterloo,
It is hereby Ordered, That the location of a Court House for Black Hawk County, in the State of Iowa, be this day made, and that it be upon Block 20, in the village of Waterloo, county of Black Hawk, State of Iowa, and that the Court House be erected thereon, now contracted for with Giles M Tinker, and the said location was this day made as above
J RANDALL, *County Judge*

The official record, however, does not show the general indignation of the people over this one-sided location ; but there was no remedy.   The County Judge was an autocrat, when he elected to exercise to its full extent the power vested in him   It is now generally understood that certain town lots in which Mr. Randall had an interest, influenced Judge Randall in making this selection ; dim visions perhaps of a bridge across the Red Cedar at that point, and consequently an entire change of location of the business of the town.   Speculation was rampant, and it is said that river lots on the west side, opposite Randall's location of the Court House, sold for $500 in gold.   But the location of the bridge on Fourth street punctured the glittering bauble, and permanently fixed the business part of the city a number of blocks up the river.

Many changes and alterations were made in the original plans, before the building was completed, and, by the time the expensive job was completed, the contractor had received more than double the contract price, or about $27,000, for his work.   It is a problem to the uninitiated how so much money could have been put into that building.   It is said that the fence around the lot on which the building stands, although looking so modest and unpretentious, cost nearly $2,200.   Lumber, of course, had to be hauled from Dubuque; but even that does not account for the excessive cost.   The inference is rather strong that there was some "jobbery" in connection with it   The Court House was completed and occupied by the county officials May 4, 1857.

September 9, 1856, the County Court ordered an election to be held on the 10th day of September, to decide whether the county should take $200,000 stock in the Dubuque & Pacific Railroad, at that time being agitated   The election was held and resulted in the affirmative, whereupon the company agreed to pass through the county via Waterloo and Cedar Falls, making their stations within one mile of the center of said towns, and to cross the Cedar River at or near the village of Waterloo.   The agreement was signed by J. P. Farley, President   For some reason, this contract was not consummated , the bonds were printed, but the County Judge refused to sign and issue them, and the line of the road was afterward changed to its present location.

January 19, 1856, George Bishop, S. P Brainard and George H. Bemis, practicing attorneys of Illinois and New York, were admitted to practice in the courts of Iowa.

September 22, 1856, Nathaniel Huntington, from Indiana, and James S George, from Illinois, were admitted to practice in Iowa Courts.

March 23, 1857, William J. Ackley, from New York, was admitted to practice , also Mr Lannbard, D J. Coleman, and Sylvester Bagg.

By the apportionment of 1857, Black Hawk County was made the Sixth Representative District, entitled to one Representative.

January 28, 1857, James M. Noble, of Delaware; H. B Martin and John F. Duncan, of Webster, were appointed to locate a State road from Cedar Falls, via Webster City and Fort Dodge, to Sioux City.

On the 6th day of July, A. D. 1857, Andrew J. Yancey was shot and killed by Jacob Harmon, while holding his plow, in Spring Creek Township. On the 20th of October, the grand jury, George Ordway, foreman, presented a true bill of indictment against Harmon. October 22d, the accused was arraigned and pleaded not guilty The prosecution was conducted by Sylvester Bagg, J. M. Preston and S. W Rawson, and Newton & Brainard, George Bishop and Pierce appeared for the defense. The jury was composed of John Hackett, J M. Benjamin, O. O. St. John, J. L Alline, S. R Crittenden, James Merwin, Charles E Balkeour, William W Wiswall, Randall Churchill, Augustin Beaucham, George P. Pratt and Charles Singleterry. After a patient hearing, on the morning of October 24, the jury returned a verdict of "guilty of murder in the second degree." A motion for a new trial was overruled, and Harmon was sentenced to be confined in the Penitentiary at hard labor for a period of eleven years.

The first divorce decreed was in the case of Eliza Barber vs. Orson Barber, October 21, 1857.

July 21, 1857, Francis B. Davison, Assignee of G M Tinker, filed his account of extra work done on the Court House, to the amount of $2,745.98.

UNION TOWNSHIP.

February 1, 1858, on petition of Randall Churchill and others, it was

Ordered, That that part of Township No 90 north of Range 14 west, in said county, which lies west of the center of the main channel of the Cedar River, be set off and become a separate township for all the purposes for which civil townships are organized in the different counties of this State, to be known and designated by the name of Union Township, and bounded as follows Commencing at the northwest corner of Township 89 north of Range 14 west, thence running east on the township line to the center of the main channel of the Cedar River, thence up the said river on the line of the center of the channel thereof to the forks of the same, thence up the center of the main channel of the east branch to the north line of said Township 90, Range 14, thence west on the said township line to the northwest corner of Black Hawk County, thence south on the west line of said county the place of beginning, and that the first election in said Union Township be held at the school house in District No. 3, at the usual time of holding the April election, 1858, and that a warrant be issued to John Hackett for the notice of said election

At the election under the above order J A Webster, D G. Jones and James Bennett were Judges, and Albert E B. Lamb, Clerk of the election. J. D Gilkey and Randall Churchill were elected Justices of the Peace; N. S. Bails, Township Clerk; Harrison Newell, Constable.

August 9, 1858, on petition of Benj Knapp and others, the County Judge ordered the records in relation to the division of Washington and Union Townships corrected so as to stand dividing said townships by the center section-line running north and south.

BENNINGTON TOWNSHIP.

February 1, 1858, on petition of Nathan Harwood and others, of Lester Township, praying for the setting-off and organizing of Township 90, Range 12, which was then a part of Lester, it was

Ordered, That the prayer of said petitioners be granted, and that said Township No 90, Range 12, be organized into a separate and distinct township of the said Black Hawk County, for all the purposes for which townships are organized in the several counties of the State of Iowa; that the same be known and designated by the name of "Bennington Township," and that the first election therein be held at the house of B G Updike, at the usual time of holding the April elections, A. D 1858, and that a warrant be issued to B G Updike for the notice of said election.

At this first election, the Judges were Samuel Buck, Charles M. Bower and Thomas S Thamer; the Clerks were Isaac K. Vanderberg and Harlan P.

Homer   Thomas S Homer and John E. Burlaw were elected Justices of the
Peace; Isaac K Vanderberg, Clerk; Hiram E. Bundy and Daniel Faulkner,
Constables

EAGLE TOWNSHIP.

March 1, 1858, on petition of Owen McMannus and others, Eagle Township was organized, with boundaries as follows : Commencing at the northwest
corner of Township No 87, north of Range 12 west, thence running west
along the township line, between Townships 87 and 88, to the northeast corner
of Township 87 north, Range 14 west; thence south along the township line
between Townships 88 and 87, to the southwest corner of Township 88 north,
Range 14 west; thence east along the county line between the counties of Black
Hawk and Bremer to the southwest corner of Township No. 87 north, Range
12 west, thence north to the place of beginning

The first election was ordered at the house of Calvin Eighmey. At the
usual April election, 1858, the warrant was issued to Owen McMannus   At
this election, N. P. Camp, C. W. Eighmey and Michael Mitchell were Judges,
and Owen McMannus, Clerk   N. P. Camp and M Mitchell were elected Justices
of the Peace, O. McMannus, Township Clerk; and James Sheon and Joseph
Millage, Constables

The burial ground on Section 7, containing one acre, was donated for this
purpose in 1874 by Wm. H. Thompson and wife   The neighbors generally
contributed for fencing, etc , which was done November 18, 1874.   William P
Thompson, P. B. Ross and Peter McNally are the Trustees.   Up to August,
1878, only three graves have been filled, which indicates a very healthy
neighborhood.

At the term of the District Court, March 12, 1858, William Pattee was
admitted to the bar.

March 13, Sylvester Bagg, Esq , introduced a series of ninety-five Rules of
Practice in the District Court, which were adopted by the Court   On the same
day, the Court appointed William H. McClure Prosecuting Attorney in place
of William Haddock, absent from duty.   The grand jury returned a true bill
of indictment against Haddock for willfully neglecting his duty as prosecuting
officer.   The defendant was arrested and brought into court, asked for a continuance and resigned his office; whereupon the Acting Prosecuting Attorney,
McClure, entered a *nolle pros.*

September 13, 1858, Samuel Owens was admitted to practice

April 25, 1859, Joseph Taylor was indicted for passing counterfeit money,
tried and found guilty.

FOX TOWNSHIP.

May 3, 1858, Fox Township was set off from Spring Creek Township by
the County Court, in answer to the petition of A B. Mather and others, being
Congressional Township 88 north, Range 11 west, and the place of holding the
first election, the house of Theodore L Williams; the time, at the usual April
election, 1859—afterward changed to October, 1858

At the first township election, in October, Andrew Murphy, Aaron L,
Burgess and C. W Corwin were Judges, and A. B. Mather and Silas I. Pettit,
Clerks.   A B. Mather and M S Oxley were elected Justices of the Peace;
Lewis Shroyer and C W Corwin, Constables; C. W. Corwin, Township Clerk;
S. I Pettit, Assessor.   It is supposed that Stephen Howell, from Indiana,
was the first to settle in this township, locating in the southeastern part   His
son, James Howell, was the first child born in the township.

The first breaking was done on the southeast quarter of the southeast quarter of Section 36, in the Fall of 1852. It was done with three yokes of oxen, by Henry Gray, Stephen Howell and Peter Cox

The first school house was built on the northwest corner of Section 36, about 1856. The building was of logs, contract price, $110.

The first sermon was preached by Rev. Stephen Howell in the log school house in the Spring of 1857. A Methodist Class was organized in 1869 by Rev. W H. Holland, with a membership of twenty-six.

EAST WATERLOO TOWNSHIP.

May 5, 1858, S P. Brainard presented a petition to the court, praying for a division of Waterloo Township by a line running along the channel of the Cedar River, and that the eastern part thereof be organized a new township by the name of Wellington The matter was laid over, however, until the July term, when the Judge ordered the question to be submitted to the people, to be voted on at the Court House the first Monday in August, 1858. When the people of the eastern part of the township petitioned, they doubted their ability to carry it; but when the day came for the election a rain had swollen the Cedar to the highest point, and not a man from the west side appeared to disturb or make afraid Sixty votes were cast, all of them in favor of the division The election was held on the first Monday of August, 1858. It was accordingly divided, and that portion lying east of the river was newly organized and named East Waterloo, and the first election thereof ordered to take place at the Court House on the second Tuesday of October, and a warrant was issued to A. G Hastings, a Constable, to post notices therefor.

The election was held. O E Shipman, Myron Smith and Isaac Young were the Judges, and Charles D. Young and Morrison Bailey were the Clerks of the election William Armstrong and William P. Bunn were elected Justices of the Peace; La Fayette Norris and A G. Hastings, Constables, Chas. D. Gray, Town Clerk; Isaac Young, Assessor.

An now, to wit, on this 8th day of October, A D 1860, is produced from the files of this court the petition of John G Park and others, asking for a division of Big Creek Township, in Black Hawk County and the court being fully advised, ordered that the prayer of the petition be granted, and that all that part of Township 87 north, Range 11 west, in said county lying west and south of the Cedar River, and now forming a part of Big Creek Township, be detached from said Big Creek Township, and that it be and the same is attached to and made a part of Spring Creek Township for all the purposes for which civil townships are organized in the several counties of the State of Iowa, so that Spring Creek Township shall be composed of the entire territory of Township 87 north, Range 11 west, in Black Hawk County, State of Iowa

THE CEDAR RIVER RAMPANT.

The season of 1858 is remarkable for the high water which prevailed in the Cedar The *Iowa State Register* of July 24, 1858, said · "During the last few days, one of the most deluging rain-storms that have ever occurred West took place in the valley of the Cedar, which has had the effect of raising the river to a prodigious height. We learn from the Black Hawk County *Democrat*, printed at Cedar Falls, that the rain fell during one night in sheets, and at daylight the sluiceway across Main street was found to be unable to carry off the water which fell in the upper part of the town It burst over the street and finally found its way by Fourth and Fifth streets to the river The amount of damage is estimated as high as $1,500. The cellars in that neighborhood were all filled, and the fences and out-houses along the path of the torrent were all swept away The foundation wall of Mr. Bishop's store caved in, and the wall of Messrs. Fox & Henry's new building lost its perpendicularity.   The bridge over Dry Run went off, and that portion of the village known as Germantown was entirely submerged.

At Cedar City the water overflowed the town and swept away a two-story building, which was seen sailing down the river at Waterloo

At Waterloo about 200 feet of the embankment of the Dubuque & Pacific Railroad was swept away, and the water poured in torrents through two of the ravines on the west side, making havoc with wood and lumber piles, and inundating the lower portion of the town   Below Waterloo, the river overflowed its banks for a wide extent

Two weeks after the first freshet, another heavy storm occurred, which created a higher freshet than before, and two weeks later, still another flood occurred.

July 19, 1858, two young ladies—Miss Case and Miss Cusen—were drowned in the river at Waterloo.   On the 20th, James Dyer was drowned in the bayou near Cedar City, and a man was drowned while attempting to cross the river at Gilbertville, about the same time.

RAILROAD CONVENTION.

In 1858, the people of the Cedar Valley were much agitated by the various railroad projects presented to them, and nearly every scheme met with favor. Among others was the building of a road from Cedar Rapids up the valley of the Cedar to Minnesota, and on the 15th of July, 1858, a Cedar River Valley Railroad convention was held at Waverly, Bremer County, which continued in session two days   A large number of delegates from Black Hawk, Linn, Benton, Floyd, Chickasaw and Mitchell Counties were in attendance, and L. B. Crocker, President of the Chicago, Iowa & Nebraska Railroad Company, was present to give proper direction to the deliberations of the convention.

Judge Maxwell, of Bremer County, was President of the convention Among the Vice Presidents were Morris Case and William H McClure, of Black Hawk, and Robert Gilchrist, of Benton   Among the editors selected for Secretaries were W. W. Harford, of the Vinton *Eagle*, and W. W. Haddock, of the Waterloo *Register*.

A Committee on Resolutions reported in favor of the organization of an independent company, composed of stockholders and Directors along the line of the road; also for the commencement and completion of the road as soon as possible.   During the discussion of this report, the delegates from Cedar Falls presented a proposition for the junction of the Cedar Falls and Minnesota with the Cedar Valley project, and labored hard to effect their purpose; but the convention flatly refused to enter into any such arrangement, and determined to make the Cedar Valley Company entirely independent, and to run their line upon the straightest and most economical line from Cedar Rapids to the State line, crossing the Cedar River at Waterloo, thence to Janesville, leaving Cedar Falls to the left, on the west side of the river.

Articles of incorporation were drafted and adopted, and a Board of Directors elected, among whom were Sheldon Fox and George W Couch, of Black Hawk; J. C. Traer and Alex. Runyen, of Benton; L. B. Crocker, of New York; Charles Walker, William J. McAlpine, of Chicago, and Franklin Steele, of Minnesota.   The Board of Directors elected L. B. Crocker, President; W. P. Harmon, of Bremer, Vice President; S. C. Bever, of Linn, Treasurer; W. W. Walker, Secretary, and Milo Smith, Chief Engineer.

The editor of the Waterloo *Register*, in the report of this convention, said: "By this it will be seen that the railroad policy of Cedar Valley is definitely settled, although we have no doubt it will be some time * * * before we shall have the pleasure of riding over the road But * * it is to be built sometime, and upon the air-line principle as nearly as may be. Much will depend upon the people along the Valley, as they are to grade and tie the road themselves, without any assistance from abroad."

STEAMBOAT NAVIGATION

In 1858, a steamboat of about one hundred tons capacity was built by citizens of Cedar Rapids for the Upper Cedar traffic, and named the "Black Hawk" That year is noted for the extreme high water, and almost all the season the Cedar was high enough for steamboat purposes. A boat was already running down the river from Cedar Rapids, and the intention was to connect with it there, although the freight had to be transferred on account of the dam.

On the 8th of October, the "Black Hawk" made its appearance at Waterloo amid the wildest excitement of its citizens, who fired salutes, ran up flags, and made other demonstrations of joy. The first landing was effected below the island, and subsequently the boat was moved up to the bank near the livery stables. The boat was a stern-wheeler, with J. J. Snouffer, of Cedar Rapids, as Captain, and the first trip up was of several days' duration, as obstructions had to be removed from the channel, and frequent stoppages were made to procure wood, etc.

On the day following his arrival, Capt. Snouffer gave a free excursion to the citizens for a trip down the river. In the evening the citizens returned the compliment by giving the Captain and the officers of the boat a grand banquet at Capwell's Hall, at which were speeches, toasts, responses and congratulations, and, presumably, the good cheer induced dreams of a custom house here, with direct trade established with all European ports.

The news of the arrival of the steamboat excited the citizens of Cedar Falls almost as much as those of Waterloo. The dam across the river at the latter place, however, was an effectual bar to any advance up the river, and the people of the former town did not relish the idea of having Waterloo stand at the head of navigation. Delegations were sent to interview the Captain, and strong threats were made of tearing out the dam and raising Cain generally. But the Captain made a trial trip, with Andrew Mullarky, of Cedar Falls, at the bow to point out the way, and after spending several hours, it was demonstrated that the boat could not even reach the dam, and the citizens up above had to relinquish the idea of being a port of entry.

Two or three trips were made before the close of navigation, and the boat was a great help to the town. Salt, which had formerly been sold at $8.00 per barrel, with only fifty cents profit, dropped down to $4.00, and other bulky articles in the same proportion Freights from Chicago were reduced to seventy cents per hundred, which was very low for that time Waterloo became the headquarters for the salt trade for all the points north and west.

In 1859, trips were resumed and continued until the water got so low that it was impossible to make the ascent The last trip the boat had to be unloaded at Gilbertville and her cargo then hauled by wagon to Waterloo. The boat was afterward taken back to Cedar Rapids, and what became of it is not known in this locality.

THE LAST INDIAN COUNCIL.

The last meeting of the Indian tribes in this vicinity was on the 5th of August, 1858   Little Priest, a Winnebago Chief, with his band, had arrived at the forks of the Cedar late in July, and sent a messenger requesting the Pottawatomies to meet him.   The Pottawatomies arrived opposite Janesville, and were ferried over, the river being very high   The Pottawatomie braves formed in battle array less than a mile north of James Newell's house, and marched toward the Winnebago tents in a column twelve deep, breaking into a circle every hundred yards, and firing their guns and beating drums.   When they reached the Winnebago camp, they fired a salute and dismounted, the squaws taking care of the horses.   A great feast was then served in a bower erected for the purpose   That night the Indians had a dance, witnessed by many of the white settlers.   The next morning a council was held in the bower, which lasted about an hour, followed by a speech from Little Priest, about twenty minutes long, followed by the pipe being lighted by the Pottawatomie Chief, who passed it to Little Priest, and it went from mouth to mouth all round the tent.   A lot of goods were then distributed   By this time numerous visitors had arrived from Waverly, Janesville, Cedar Falls and Waterloo, who asked to see a war dance, which the Indians refused, saying that they were to leave in half an hour   They packed up at once, and were all gone in the time announced.

LETTER FROM A WINNEBAGO.

While speaking of the Indians and their final disappearance from Black Hawk County, it may be well to remark that if the Indians never forgave an enemy, they seldom forgot a friend.

The friendship between James Newell and the Winnebagoes was never disturbed, except in 1847, when one of the Indians stole a horse from Newell and sold the animal to a man named Way, a noted character of Benton County. Newell allowed himself to be fooled by another Indian, who offered, if Newell would give him a horse pistol, a blanket and one or two other articles, to go down to Way's, steal the horse and bring him back   Newell let him have the articles, and the Indian came back, in about a week, minus horse, pistol, blanket, and his own property as well.   He did not get the horse as he had promised, but had enjoyed a huge drunk in Benton County.

The following letter from Bradford L. Porter, one of the Winnebago Chiefs, to Newell is well worth reading, as it shows better than anything the historian can say the high regard the Indians had for this hardy, energetic pioneer:

MAY 25TH, 1864, WINNEBAGO AGENCY

My Dear Friend—To James Newell   I received your letter the 24th of this month   I was very glad to hear from you   My family, they like to go back to your place now very much   I have been tell them I will try go back soon ever I get money enough to start with   You stated to me you wanted to know if we are going to remove again or not   I think we shall remove to Big Sioux River some time next Fall   We don't know yet what time it may be—may be not until quite late, and may be some time this Summer, soon we get our payments—money and goods   Soon we get our money and goods, we shall start all down the river   Let the Agent stay here alone if he can do better may be without us this Summer   Our Agent he is down below yet, waiting for the steamboat come up the river so to he put all his goods on, provisions and all, fetch all right up with him at once   The boats they can't do much now   Since last week river beginning to rise about two feet now   They say going to be fifteen steamboats come up on this river very soon now for the Government   I have nothing of importance to write to you this time   My family they all well now, we are doing very good now, so far, my family and my brothers   I got my brother's wife in the school with me, I allow her forty dollars a month, she can get plenty to eat now   The next time you write to me be sure find out about how all the people feel toward the Winnebagoes tribes about coming to Big Sioux River, toward in your State of Iowa   If you think there is any danger for me coming back toward your place again, you just let me know how it go be   We can't live in this place, so we can't raise anything to eat   The Indians (the Sioux) they won't let our tribes hunt for one mile from agency, so all we got eat we get from Government   The chiefs they don't like it soon   The Winnebagoes got to no money and no goods, and can't live in to such country where can't raise no corn   I want you to see to the people how they feel toward how our father at Washington has to use us   I can't use to the whites people to any such way Now I am going close   Give my respects to all your family, hoping see each other some of these days   You please send me some postage stamps if you got any, we can't get any very easy , since we got up the river too far one postage stamp cost to us twenty-five cents apiece

My dear, good friend, I will bid to you good-by to you   I hope God will bless you   Your good friend,
                                                                          BRADFORD L PORTER

To James Newell,

By act of the General Assembly, approved March 26, 1860, the petty dukedoms created by the County Judge system that had been on trial for ten years, were abolished.   The powers of the County Judge were restricted to the exercise of probate powers, and the government of the county was vested in a Board of Supervisors, consisting of one from each civil township, to be elected in October, and to assume the duties of their office in January following   The act went into effect July 4, 1860   The Supervisors were elected in the several townships at the October election, and the first Board of Supervisors of Black Hawk met at the office of the Clerk of the District Court, January 7, 1861, and was composed of the following members, viz.: M H. Moore, Waterloo Township; C. F. Jaquith, Cedar Falls , M Bailey, East Waterloo; Jesse Wasson, Big Creek , J B Orr, Spring Creek ; Levi Washburn, Poyner; S. P Babcock, Orange, F S Tewksbury, Black Hawk ; D. W Jordan, Washington ; H. P. Homer, Bennington ; Oscar Dunton, Barclay, D. E Chapin, Fox, James Hempseed, Lester ; John Hackett, Union , Gillson Gardner, Eagle ; J H Mead, Cedar; Jefferson Jaquith, Mount Vernon   M. Bailey was elected Chairman.

THE JAIL.

Among the first matters presented to the Board of Supervisors was a petition asking that an appropriation be made for the erection of a County Jail, which was presented January 9, and referred to the Committee on County Buildings and Property.   The petitioners probably considered a jail a necessary adjunct of civilization, and that every well-ordered county should have one   For eight years they had been deprived of the safety supposed to be guaranteed to a community by suitable provisions for restraining its lawless members, and the time had come when the want must be supplied.

After due deliberation, and with an eye to economy, on the 10th of January, 1861, the committee reported as follows:

To the Board of Supervisors of Black Hawk County

Your committee to whom was referred the petition of C D Gray and others, asking this Board to take immediate steps to procure some suitable place for the confinement of criminals, beg leave to report as follows   We find that the county is entirely without any sufficient place for the safe-keeping of public offenders, and that the county is continuously subject to very heavy bills of expense in procuring temporary places for the safe-keeping of such persons, demanding, as your committee believe, immediate action on the part of this Board to make some suitable arrangements therefor   We would therefore recommend that the room in the basement of the north corner of the Court House originally contemplated for that purpose, be put in such condition as will meet the demands in the case

Your committee have not yet determined what, in their opinion, would be the best mode of doing the same, but would recommend that in case the report of this committee be adopted, a special committee be appointed, whose duty it shall be to superintend the work, and that they be instructed to limit their expenditures to four hundred dollars   All of which is respectfully submitted
                                                    J WASSON,
                                                    D E CHAMPLIN, } Committee
                                                    M H MOORE

If there had been extravagant expenditures in the construction of the Court House, the committee were determined that there should be none in providing a jail   The Board, however, evidently thinking that a four hundred dollar jail would be rather too cheap an affair, amended the report by substituting " six hundred " for " four hundred" dollars as the maximum cost of the county jail As thus amended the report was accepted and the recommendations of the committee were adopted.   The next day, however, this action was reconsidered and the report was further amended by substituting "east " in place of "north," so that it should read " the room in the basement of the east corner," etc., and as thus amended was again adopted.   The Chairman of the Board appointed Messrs. Wasson, Champlin and Moore as the Special Committee to supervise the work.

June 7, 1861, Mr Moore reported to the Board that work was to be commenced forthwith, and on the 2d day of September of the same year the committee reported that they had caused to be built in the basement, as designated, two cells and one outer room, at a total cost of $391 48.

This was providing the county with a jail at a trifling expense , but it is questionable whether it is sound policy or true economy to have jails connected with Court Houses   Fayette County built a lock-up in one corner of her Court House, and the result was that a prisoner in escaping set fire to the building, and the county had to build a new Court House, besides losing many valuable records and papers that cannot be replaced   A fire is liable to originate in the Black Hawk County Jail, and the county be subjected to irreparable loss in consequence.   Basements of Court Houses are not the best possible locations for jails.

In April, 1861, commenced the war of the rebellion, and Black Hawk County was one of the foremost in the State to respond to the call of the President, a more extended account of which will be found under the head of " War Record."

LINCOLN TOWNSHIP.

June 6, 1861, by resolution, the Board of Supervisors set off Congressional Township 87 north of Range 14 west, from Black Hawk Township, as a new civil division of the county, called Lincoln Township, in which an election for township officers was ordered to be held on the second Tuesday in October following.   At this election Samuel B. Roberts, Samuel Gibson and H Beckwith were Judges, and Samuel Marston and William Wrought, Clerks, of the election William Wrought, Samuel Gibson and J. Huckel were elected Trustees.

It is said that the township received its name from the fact that at the Presidential election in 1860, there were fifteen voters in the township, every one of whom voted for Abraham Lincoln.

The first settler in this township was Samuel Gibson.

The Zion Baptist Church of Lincoln was organized in Eagle Township, on January 3, 1869, by Rev J W. Thompson, with ten members.   William P Thompson was its first and only Clerk.   In the Winter of 1869–70, a protracted meeting was held, during which twenty-one were added, and L. H. Thompson licensed to preach.   June 15, 1870, a council met with the church and recognized it.   Rev. D S. Starr, of Cedar Falls, preached on the occasion   March 10, 1872, the place of meeting was changed to the school house, in sub-district No 4, Lincoln Township   Present membership, forty.

January 8, 1862, by order of the Board, all that portion of East Waterloo Township lying in Township 88, Range 13, was attached to Orange Township.

January 9, 1862, all that portion of Congressional Township 87, Range 11, lying south of Cedar River—then a portion of Spring Creek—was attached to Big Creek Township; and all that portion of Township 87, Range 12, lying on the east side of Cedar River—then a portion of Poyner Township—was attached to Spring Creek. But in June, the latter action was revoked, and the land re-annexed to Poyner Township

The Board met in special session February 27, 1863, to pass resolutions of respect to the memory of John Hackett, a member of the Board, who had died a short time previous.

The Board of Supervisors early began to devise measures for providing for the support of those who were so unfortunate as to become objects of public charity The purchase of a County Poor Farm, for the purpose of furnishing a comfortable home for this class, and also to furnish them with employment whereby they might earn at least a portion of the cost of their support, was considered advisable; but the Board did not wish to take the responsibility of appropriating public moneys for the purpose, without first submitting the question to the people. Accordingly, on the 8th day of June, 1865, a resolution was adopted, as follows:

Resolved, That the Clerk of this Board be instructed to give legal notice to the voters of Black Hawk County, Iowa, that, at the next general election, in October next, a proposition will be submitted to said voters, authorizing the Board of Supervisors of said Black Hawk County to appropriate from the funds of said county a sum not to exceed $10,000 (ten thousand dollars), for the purpose of purchasing real estate in the name of the county of Black Hawk, Iowa, and improving the same, to be used for the benefit and purpose of supporting the paupers of the said county of Black Hawk.

The election was held, as ordered, and resulted in favor of the proposed appropriation, by a vote of 1,125 to 273.

January 4, 1866, the Board of Supervisors adopted the following resolution:

Resolved, That a committee of three be appointed by the Board to select lands within the county of Black Hawk, State of Iowa, not to exceed 200 acres, and improve the same, in the name of said county of Black Hawk, for the purpose and to be used for the support of the paupers of said county of Black Hawk, said purchase to be made with moneys to be appropriated by said county, as voted at the general election of said county, not to exceed $10,000 And the Clerk of this Board be authorized to issue county warrants, bearing 10 per cent interest, for the same, to said Committee of Three, not to exceed $10,000

The committee was to be paid $2 50 per day.

Messrs C. May, A. A. Alline and H W. Abbey were appointed as the committee provided in the above resolution , but for some reason they resigned on the same day on which they were appointed, and a new committee, consisting of William Gilchrist, N Hitchcock and A Vittam, was elected This committee was further authorized to employ a suitable person for Superintendent of the Poor Farm, when it should be ready for occupancy.

June 5, 1866, the committee reported that it had examined a number of farms, but had selected and purchased the farm owned by Mr Russell, on the west side of the Cedar River, containing 120 acres, at $30 per acre ; and that Mr. Russell had executed a warranty deed of the premises , that the committee had requested the Clerk to issue bonds therefor, but it was discovered that the Board had no legal authority to issue bonds, and Mr. Russell refused to accept the warrants provided for by the resolution of January 4 This was the official record.

The report was accepted and the committee discharged It is said that this bargain was not consummated because Mr Russell refused to take county warrants *at their face;* he would take them at a discount, but the committee were not authorized to comply with this demand.

The purchase of a farm appears to have been abandoned with this failure to consummate the trade with Mr Russell   But on the 5th day of September, another committee was appointed, consisting of Messrs. William Gilchrist, D. E. Champlin and C May, "to purchase a lot, not exceeding twenty acres, for poor purposes.

September 5, 1866, a committee was appointed to purchase a lot not exceeding twenty acres for poor purposes ; Wm. Gilchrist, D. E. Champlin and C. May, Committee.

Tuesday, January 8, 1867, this Committee reported that they had purchased the private residence of Mr Gilchrist (Block 21, Lots 1, 2, 3 and 4), for $3,500. Mr Gilchrist was a member of the Purchasing Committee and it is said succeeded in making a bargain advantageous to himself, with himself.

January 8, 1868, the Directors of the Poor House (Samuel D Shaw and W. F Bunn) reported that an addition to the house had been built at a cost of $1,320.68.

A portion of the county poor are provided for at this house, but many are relieved by Township Trustees and by the county in addition to those then furnished with a home at the County Poor House   The first Superintendent was H. A Henderson, who served until 1877, when he was succeeded by George K. Beal.

January 9, 1867, on petition of citizens, the Board ordered that that portion of East Waterloo Township known as Cedar City be annexed to Cedar Falls Township

On Saturday, July 21, 1866, the people of Black Hawk County were excited by the startling intelligence that a little girl 3½ years old, daughter of Mr Barney E Wheeler, of Lester Township, had unaccountably disappeared. About 9 o'clock A. M. of that day, she and her brother, several years older, went to carry some water to their father who was at work in the field about sixty rods from the house.   Their errand performed, the children started to return to the house   The little girl was a little slow in her movements, and her brother became impatient and went home, leaving her to take her time.   Mrs. Wheeler asked him where he left his sister, and he told her, "at the edge of the cornfield."   As the little one did not come in, her mother went out to the spot where the little boy said he left her, but she was not there.   Mr. Wheeler was called from his work, and both commenced search, having become thoroughly alarmed ; but no trace of the lost one could be found.   The neighborhood was alarmed, and by 3 o'clock P M. all the neighbors in the vicinity were engaged in the search.   During that night men were stationed all around the houses for several miles who were listening eagerly to hear the cries of the child.   The next morning two men said they thought they heard cries near a slough in the vicinity, but a thorough search in that locality revealed nothing.   On Sunday, the whole county was aroused and at least 200 people, mostly on horseback, were engaged in the search, but not a trace of the missing child could be found.   It was as if the little one had been removed from the face of the earth. On Monday the excitement and sympathy for the mysteriously bereaved family became intense   All work was thrown aside, for everybody felt that to aid in the search for the lost one was a sacred duty   From all parts of the county, and from Bremer, the people gathered.   From twenty-five to one hundred men went every day from Waterloo alone, and for ten days the most vigorous search was maintained.   The county was swept for miles by mounted men and men on foot, and every foot of ground supposed to be carefully examined.   Several large fields of grain were trampled down, and the prairie grass and hazel brush flattened to the ground for miles, but yet no trace of the lost one. The most exaggerated reports were in circulation. Now, a lightning rod man had seen a child crying at the road side, and now, somebody had seen her with two men in a wagon traveling northward; now, she had been seen and described by a lady in Fayette County; anon, was heard from in Minnesota. " One thing is evident," said the Waterloo *Courier* of the 2d of August, " the child must be some distance from home, for everything has been searched within four or five miles around the house." Mr. Wheeler, although a poor man, offered $300 reward for information that would lead to the discovery of his daughter. As the people became satisfied that the child had been spirited away and would not be found in the vicinity of home, the search was abandoned; but Mr. Wheeler continued to follow the rumors as long as his money held out. George Barker, of Lester, followed the trail of the team driven by a man who had been seen with the child, to the Mississippi River at Dubuque, and visited every ferry and crossing from that point to the mouth of Yellow River, but was compelled to return home without discovering any trace of the object of his search.

On Saturday morning, November 3d, Mr. Siple, a neighbor of the Wheelers, was engaged in trapping near his house, when his attention was attracted to a little clump of hazel bushes surrounded by some tall grass, by the singular conduct of his dog. Here, upon examination, he found the bones of a child, the clothing, however, was in a good state of preservation and enabled him to identify the remains as those of the little child who had so mysteriously disappeared more than three months before The spot was about one-fourth of a mile from Mr Siple's house, and only about a mile and a quarter from Mr. Wheeler's; and it is among the mysteries that are difficult to solve to understand how the spot could have escaped discovery during the minute and extended search made in July and August.

January 11, 1867, the county authorities authorized the County Treasurer to pay a bounty of 10 cents for each pocket-gopher scalp presented These little pests had become so numerous and so injurious to the agricultural interests of the county, that for several years about $1,000 annually was paid out for bounties on these little animals

June 10, 1875, the Board of Supervisors authorized the payment of a bounty of 10 cents for each gray and 5 cents for each striped gopher presented during a term of sixty days.

The first bridge across the Cedar in this county was built by subscription by G. W Couch, contractor. It was constructed on wooden piers, and was opened to the public in September, 1859. In 1864 or '65, two spans of this bridge fell and were replaced; but in the freshet soon afterward, the entire structure was swept away June 6, 1866, the County Board appropriated $5,000 to build a new bridge across the river at this point, which was completed in 1867 at a cost of $9,269.75 Four years afterward, in 1871, it was found necessary to provide for a better and more permanent structure, and August 16, 1871, the County Supervisors

Ordered, That the sum of $8,000, or so much thereof as may be necessary, be appropriated out of the bridge fund to build necessary abutments, and not more than four piers, for a new bridge on the site of the present bridge across the Cedar River, in the city of Waterloo, and that the Board of Supervisors act in Committee of the Whole to receive proposals, and let the contract in whole or in part for furnishing material and for building said abutments and piers

September 6, 1871, in the matter of the Waterloo bridge, the Board not having authority to appropriate more than $12,000 for any one bridge, and having already appropriated $8,000 for building the abutments and piers, submitted the question of appropriating $18,000 for the superstructure to a vote of the people, at the general election on the second Tuesday in October, 1871.

September 9, 1871, on petition of the citizens of Waterloo, it was ordered that the east end of the new bridge be at the center of the county road, and that the west end be at the center of Bridge street, as near as practicable

December 4, 1871, a canvass of the election showed that there were 892 votes for the appropriation for Waterloo bridge, and 912 against said appropriation Appropriation lost

January 3, 1872, the Board appropriated $4,700 (the limit allowed by law) for Waterloo bridge

Feb. 17, 1872, an appropriation of $14,000 was made for the construction of the Waterloo bridge, and A. T. Weatherwax, H. B. Allen, and L. A. Cobb, were authorized to receive proposals for the building of the same. This Committee was instructed to report the proposals to the County Bridge Commission, who were authorized to award the same.

The contract was awarded to the Ohio Bridge Company, and April 11, 1872, a further appropriation of $1,900 was made.   Work was commenced on the bridge and completed in the Summer and Fall of 1872, probably in September, as on the 4th of that month the Board ordered warrants to be drawn in favor of the Ohio Bridge Company in payment for building the Waterloo bridge.

IRON BRIDGE AT CEDAR FALLS.

December 17, 1872, $11,000 was appropriated for an iron bridge at Cedar Falls, the County Bridge Commissioners to award the contract, and G. B. Van Saun, A. S. Smith and E. Townsend appointed to superintend the building of the same.

June 12, 1868, the Committee on County Buildings and Property reported as follows:

*   *   *   We would further recommend to this Board the building of a house or the procuring of one suitable for the Sheriff to live in, near the jail, that he may be better prepared to take charge of the jail and prevent the escape of prisoners—said house to cost not more than $1,000   *   *

A T Webster,
S A Cobb,
D E Champlin,
Committee

This report was laid on the table until next session, but on the 10th of September was taken up and adopted.   The site for the proposed house was designated as the northeast corner of the Court House lot, by the Board, and Messrs. D. E. Champlin and W. F. Brown were appointed to superintend its erection. Work was commenced at once, and pushed so energetically that the Sheriff's domicile was completed in December, 1868.

Three children, sons of Israel Scroggy, of Cedar Township, were drowned Feb 16, 1869, in a small pond about eighty rods north of the Doxie School House   It was at noon, and the boys of the school were engaged in throwing a ball across the pond, the teacher, George S. Bishop, participating.   The teacher threw the ball, which William and Wesley Scroggy ran out upon the pond to catch, when the ice broke, letting them into the water, which was six or eight feet deep   Abram ran out to try and save them, but was pulled in by William. An effort was made by another boy, named Johnson, to get them out, but it was a failure   After being in the water three-quarters of an hour, the boys were taken out by Thomas Doxie and Abraham Turner.

S. A. Bishop

NURSERYMAN
CEDAR FALLS.

The following unique document is found in the early probate records of Benton County, and is given *verbatim et literatim.*

STATE OF IOWA, BENTON COUNTY, ss   This is to certify that I hereby commit the guardianship of Lidia Ann Willard to Jackson Taylor, until she attains the age of eighteen years of age if he should so long live, if not otherwise ordered by the Judge of Probate of said County and the Jackson Tailor to have full power and authority to sue for demand of and have all powers granted to guardians by law.   Given under my hand and seal this the 7th day of May, A D 1847, James Mitchel Judge of Probate of Benton Co, State of Iowa

JAMES MITCHEL, *Judge of Probate*

Know all men by these presents that I, Jackson Tailor and Erasmus D Adams are helde and stands firmly bound to the people of the State of Iowa for the use of Lidia Ann Willard in the sum of fifty dollars   The condition of the above obligation is such that if the above bound Jackson Tailor, who has been appointed guardian for Lidiann Willard shal fithfully discharge the office and trust of such guardian according to law and shall render a fair and just acc of his said guardianship to the Court of Probate for the County of Benton from time to time as he shal thereto be required by said Courte and comply with all orders of said Courte lawfully made relative to the goods chattels and moneys of such minor and render and pay to such all moneys goods and chattels title, papers and effects which may come to the hands or possession of such guardian belonging to such minor when such minor shall thereto be entitled or to any subsequent guardian should such Courte so direct this obligation shall be void or otherwise to remain in full force and virtue this the ——— day of May 1847

JACKSON TAILOR,   [Seal]
ERASMUS D ADAMS,   [Seal]

Approved by the Judge of Probate James Michel this the 28th day of May, 1847

JAMES MITCHEL, *Judge of Probate*

Filde this the 28th day of May, 1847

I do hereby certify that the foregoing is a true coppy of the papers that came to my possession in the office of Probate Court in the Guardianship of Lydia Ann Willard, ward of Jackson Tailor

Given under my hand this 20th day of Jan A D 1852

JOHN S FORSYTH, *County Judge*

POST OFFICES AND POSTMASTERS

Cedar Falls.—Demsey C. Overman, Jan. 3, 1850; Edwin Brown, Nov. 11, 1851; Andrew Mullarky, April 14, 1853; Sylvester H. Packard, Sept. 16, 1856; Robt. P Speer, March 2, 1858; Andrew Mullarky, March 29, 1858; Geo M Harris, March 20, 1861; Henry A. Perkins, March 14, 1865; Wm. H. McClure, Aug 20, 1866; Fred. Boehmler, March 20, 1867; Wm. M. Morrison, May 13, 1869; Chas W. Snyder, Jan. 13, 1876.'

Waterloo.—Chas. Mullan, Dec. 29, 1851; Levi Aldrich, Aug 12, 1854; Julius C. Hubbard, March 23, 1855, Seneca Cleveland, July 1, 1861; Jeremiah P. Evans, Nov. 2, 1866; Horace Barron, March 20, 1867; Miss Marion Champlin, March 26, 1869; Wm H. Hartman, March 10, 1873; Wm. H. Hartman (re-appointed), March 16, 1877.

Eliza.—D. G Ellis, May 20, 1852; John G. Forbes, Jan. 12, 1853; Nathan S. Merrill, Dec. 24, 1855; discontinued Nov. 18, 1856.

Enterprise.—Daniel B. Feeter, Sept 27, 1853; Hutchinson M Smith, July 23, 1862; Wm. Fike, Nov. 16, 1870; Harriet Smith, Nov. 19, 1872.

Elk Run.—Daniel G. Ellis, Oct. 1, 1853; discontinued July 18, 1856.

Knox.—Manuel E Mallo, June 15, 1855.   Changed to *Gilbertville.*—Augustus Kammann, June 3, 1858; Benj. Winsett, Aug. 10, 1859; Peter Felton, Sept. 13, 1861; Benj. Winsett, Dec. 13, 1865, Matthew Miller, Oct 6, 1873.

La Porte City —Jesse Wasson, July 18, 1855; Lewis Turner, December 28, 1857, Wm L. Fox, February 10, 1858; Cyrus C. Charles, May 2, 1861, Geo. W Hayzlett, April 13, 1863, Thomas Bunton, October 16. 1863; Geo. W Hayzlett, March 12, 1868; John R. Stebbins, January 9, 1874

E

Barclay —Israel B. Cowan, September 5, 1855 , Jacob Wolf, November 27, 1855; James Muncey, October 12, 1858 , Adam Giget, July 1, 1863; James Muncey, August 25, 1864 , Edward Basse, March 26, 1867.

Cedar Valley —Thomas R. Points, March 28, 1856; Philander T Mead, July 17, 1856; Cicero Close, July 9, 1857; Jeremiah Gay, December 22, 1867 ; Cicero C. Close, March 1, 1870

Blakeville.—Barzilar G. Updike, June 18, 1856 : James Rodgers, May 11, 1865

Lester.—John Cook, July 24, 1856; Jonathan R Owen, October 21, 1859; Levi J Schrack, January 28, 1862 . Shirburn D. Presba, October 17, 1867 ; Chas. A Harrington, January 21, 1868 , Samuel H Kayler, June 2, 1873.

Hudson.—Lyman Pierce, July 30, 1857; Rufus W. Wass, January 28, 1864 , Philander B. Curtiss, July 13, 1874.

Miller's Creek.—Elizabeth Roberts, March 3, 1870 , Hannah Bateman, March 21, 1871.

Mullarky's Grove —Joshua A Hooker, March 15, 1858; George L. Zabriskie, May 14, 1849; Levi Washburn, September 9, 1861   Changed to *Raymond*, February 27, 1862

Raymond —Harvey T. Hume, December 10, 1863; Geo. Edginton, June 2, 1865; Henry D. Gould, September 27, 1865; Levi B Cook, October 12, 1869 , Elva C Walsh, November 30, 1875.

Filkin's Grove.—John T Mills, June 17, 1858. Discontinued September 20, 1858.

Perry Valley.—T. W. Boardman, November 13, 1858   Changed to Buchanan County.

East Waterloo —Roswell Baker, November 13, 1858; Samuel P. Brainard, February 4, 1860 ; James A Fry, July 6, 1861; discontinued March 27, 1862.

Energy —Aaron L Burgess, December 30, 1861; discontinued November 13, 1863.

Finchford —George W Collins, November 16, 1870 ; John Ferguson, July 19, 1872; Milton G Finch, April 21, 1873

Sunny Side.—John B Masters, November 11, 1873 , Mrs Ellen Walker, December 17, 1873 , Geo. Frink, November 16, 1874. Now in Buchanan County.

Nantville.—Thomas H. Fitch, September 16, 1861. Late in Bremer County.

ECLIPSE OF THE SUN.

Cedar Falls being within the line of totality of the great eclipse of August 7, 1869, observers for the Smithsonian Institution were sent hither from Dubuque. From their report the following extract is made:

At the store of Wise & Bryant, the average temperature, in the shade, before the eclipse was 74°, which, at the period of totality, fell to 67°

At the Orphans' Home, the first contact was at 8 o'clock 53 minutes and 9½ seconds , last contact, 5 o'clock 53 minutes and 42 seconds; duration, 2 hours 32½ seconds. Total phase lasted 68¾ seconds, with a variation from 71 seconds, at one and a half miles southeast of the Orphans' Home, to 51 seconds in the city

The corona was well defined   The moments of immersion and emersion of the sun were startlingly instantaneous, and were of such thrilling interest to behold as to require no ordinary power of attention to secure accuracy in recording the period of duration. During the time, dew deposited plentifully on the grass

At the southwest, the darkness was of the blackest character, while at the northeast, through a lurid haze, trees could be seen basking in the dim sunlight in the vicinity of Janesville, ten or twelve miles distant.

The best description was furnished by an amateur observer, Hon. Peter Melendy, who says:

We had chosen for our point of observation one of the highest in Black Hawk County, where we could get a full view of Cedar Falls and the surrounding country   From the elevated position selected, we could count four hundred distinct farm houses, and could discover objects in five counties, viz , Black Hawk, Grundy Butler, Bremer and Buchanan   It is claimed, also, that, in favorable and clear weather, the woods near Independence, thirty miles off, can be seen with the naked eye   *   *   *   *   *   *

When the sun was about half hidden by the dark disk of the moon, our attention was called to the appearance of the sky in the north. A gloom was thrown over all the landscape, and the sky was of a deep, dense, black blue—particularly the horizon—as if a terrible storm was approaching   The trees in the distance had lost their lively verdure, the golden wheat fields had a dull, sickly color, and the gradual approach of darkness became impressive   The sunlight in the south and southeast had become much weakened , it had that unearthly greenish and reddish, gloomy, sickly, faint aspect, making the contrast between the sky in the north and in the south very great   It appeared as if the sky was descending to the ground and the horizon contracting   As we could see for miles to the north and east, the sight was grand, beautiful, inspiring awe and wonder

As the eclipse advanced to within a few seconds of the total observation, the scene became intensely interesting, particularly at the north.   The big woods and the timber in the valley of the Cedar had lost their beautiful verdure, and looked like outlines of dark pictures in an unfamiliar country   It was a magnificent sight , not quite as dark as night, but it appeared as if the sky at the north was putting on a deep blue black , the sky to the south, near the horizon, was a brownish yellow.   *   *   *   *   *   *

We look around us now on the countenances of those of our party   All wear a look of wonder and anxiety, watching for the approach of the moon's shadow   Suddenly, one of the party shouted "There it is ' the shadow !'"   The awful shadow of the moon was approaching us at a velocity of a mile a second from the west, as a dark, vast mass or column, or cloud, as the description had been given us.   How grand this sight was, as the mighty shadow swept onward to the east'

The approach and recession of the shadow was not uniform, but dark stripes appeared fluttering across the landscape and the edges appeared tremulous , and one of our party, who was looking at the eclipse just as the last visible ray disappeared says it is like a flicker of a candle going out   It seemed but a second before we were immersed in the shadow, and as near as we could calculate, the shadow was thirty to forty seconds passing over, from the time when first seen until it had passed away

Now comes the grand sight ! In an instant the panorama is changed   The dark clouds that were at the north changed positions to the south, which was as black as the darkness of night   To the north and northeast, covering one-third of the visible horizon, we could see objects plainly beyond the disk on the distant landscape   All above is of a deep blue, or black , to the south and southwest, a deep jet black, while at the north, a mellow, faint yellowish or brimstone color, and beautiful, the wheat fields waving with the golden grain, the varied hues of green, with the white farm houses dotted here and there, appeared   Above us, now, were the twinkling stars, glittering in all their glory, in the broad, dark zone—night—with the stars above us to south and west of us , and to the north and east of us, ten or twelve miles, old Sol shining on the landscape, and the dark, deep shadow sleeping on the southwest in all its blackness   What a variety of views we can take in with one scanning of the eye !   Around and over us, we cannot describe it   At this moment we have to the southeast, south and west, the blackness of a terrible storm , to the north, the distant objects have a fine yellow hue, and to the east, a fine purple color, and the deep blue overhead, with stars peeping out, with the sun entirely hid, with the beautiful faint crown of light apparently surrounding the moon, with the faint streaks, like jets of flame, are seen protruding from the edge.   The coolness was great, as the temperature had fallen some twenty degrees

The sight was certainly much finer from our point of observation than farther to the center , for we had the effect of the totality a sufficient length of time to get the full benefit of it, with the addition of seeing the sunlight on the distant parts of the landscape beyond the northern boundary ; and as the restoration began, the landscape became more beautiful, the striking contrast of the glorious and sublime spectacle of the light on the distant landscape as it began to play among the golden fields and the distant hills and forests, it were as if a flood of grateful and cheering brightness had fallen into the Cedar Valley with a sweet, mellow tinge and power beyond description   It was a sudden and amazing change from the dark and gloomy appearance of a few moments before

THE CIRCUIT COURT.

By an act of the General Assembly of Iowa, entitled " An act to establish Circuit and General Term Courts, and to define the powers and duties thereof," approved April 3, 1868, each Judicial District in the State was divided into two circuits, and the office of Circuit Judge was created to be elected at the general election in November, 1868, for a term of four years   Circuit Courts were endowed with exclusive jurisdiction of all probate matter, and of all actions and proceedings in which County Judges have previously had jurisdiction, and also in all appeals and writs of error from Justices' Courts, Mayors' Courts, and all other inferior tribunals, either in civil or criminal cases, and concurrent jurisdiction with the District Court in foreclosures, etc   The counties of Buchanan, Black Hawk and Grundy were constituted the second circuit of the Ninth Judicial District; and terms were established in Black Hawk on the first Monday in February, fourth Monday in June, first Monday in October and fifth Monday in November for the year 1869

The first term of the Circuit Court in Black Hawk County was held at the Court House, February 1, 1869, present, Sylvester Bagg, Judge presiding; W. F Brown, Sheriff, and G A. Eberhart, Clerk.

The office of County Judge was abolished; but that officer became *ex officio* County Auditor

COUNTY AUDITOR

By an act entitled " An act to provide for the election of County Auditors, and define their powers and duties, and making County Judges *ex officio* County Auditors," approved April 7, 1868, it was provided that at the general election preceding the expiration of the term of office of County Judges then in office, a County Auditor should be elected, whose term of office should commence on the 1st of January thereafter and continue two years.   After January 1, 1869, the County Judge was made *ex officio* County Auditor until the election and qualification of such office   The County Auditor was made Clerk of the Board of Supervisors, etc   Under this act, Daniel W Foote, County Judge, became *ex officio* County Auditor of Black Hawk January 1, 1869, and was elected his own successor

COUNTY SUPERVISOR.

By " An act to amend Article 2 of Chapter 22 of the revision of 1860," etc., approved April 14, 1870, the cumbrous Board of Township Supervisors was abolished and a Board of three County Supervisors established instead, to be elected at the general election in 1870, and assumed the control of county affairs on the first Monday in January, 1871.   Under the act in October, 1870, Cicero Close, George B Van Saun and A. T. Weatherwax were elected, who assembled in January, 1871, and organized by the election of Cicero Close, Chairman   At the November election, 1872, the people voted that the number of Supervisors of Black Hawk County should be increased to seven.   The additional members thus added were elected in October, 1873, and took their seats in January, 1874.

CRIMINAL CASES.

One of the most noted criminal cases in the annals of Black Hawk County was the attempted murder of 'Byron Wright at Cedar City, by Almira Stickley, January 6, 1873   Mr. Wright was teaching the public school at that village, and was, up to that date, boarding with Mrs Stickley, at the solicitation of her daughter   Finding the place unpleasant, he had decided to remove to Mr. Kingsley's, and had notified the Stickleys of the proposed change on the morning noted above, just before starting to his school   He had slept late that morning and did not wait for breakfast.   At recess, he returned to Mrs. Stickley's for something to eat, and while eating his lunch, Almira Stickley approached from behind and fired a revolver at his head, the bullet penetrating his brain. Wright rose from the table, fell to the floor, regained his feet and attempted to leave the room, but was prevented by Richard George, a lover of Almira's. He then went to the window for air, and while standing there, was shot in the left side of the head by George. Almira and George then drove hurriedly to Cedar Falls, and the girl excitedly related to James Taggart what they had done. The pair were arrested a few minutes afterward.

Wright was able to stagger to the school house and tell what had befallen him. He was taken to Mr Davidson's house, and the next day was removed to Waterloo.

The subsequent statement of the Stickleys was that Almira was in love with Wright, and was determined to marry or kill him, in which she was abetted by the mother. George had been anxious to secure the girl for some time, and his motive for becoming an accomplice in the attempted murder is apparent. The bullet in Wright's head was not extracted till the following August.

Mrs. Stickley was convicted at Vinton in March, 1873, for complicity in the attempt to murder Wright, and sentenced to the penitentiary for nine years. Almira was sentenced to the Reform School for one year.

Wright afterward removed to Johnson County and married. He obtained a situation in the Iowa City public school, but soon after became insane. He was harmless in his insanity, and was allowed to remain at Waterloo, whither his friends took him. As predicted at the time he was shot, he died from the effects of the wound July 26, 1875.

The Stickleys appealed from the judgment of Judge Shane, and were for some time at large on bail, pending the decision of the appeal, which was adverse to them. Their bail then surrendered them to undergo the sentence pronounced.

George had previously forfeited his bail and had fled the State.

On the morning of April 5, 1873, the body of an infant was found in Cedar River, below Cedar Falls. April 29th, William Riley and Ursula Spangler were indicted for the murder of the child. Miss Spangler took change of venue to Bremer County. Riley was tried in Black Hawk, and on the 3d day of October, 1873, Judge D. S. Wilson rendered judgment that the said William Riley be imprisoned at hard labor in the penitentiary of the State of Iowa, at Fort Madison, for the term of his lifetime, or life, and that he pay the costs of the prosecution, taxed at $227.

INCIDENTS AND CASUALTIES.

The farmers of Washington Township in the Spring of 1860 manufactured about $1,500 worth of maple sugar and syrup. The same community sowed over a thousand acres of wheat the same season.

Christopher Close, of Cedar Township, lost a new house, almost completed, by fire August 15, 1860, caused by the tinners who were putting on the eaves-troughs, allowing a soldering iron to ignite some shavings. The building had cost about $1,500.

The residence of George Tuttle, of Mount Vernon, was destroyed by fire Jan. 13, 1865, the loss being about $500.

Sept 19, 1869, John Geyer, of Mount Vernon Township, was killed by a blow from a stick of wood in the hands of Henry Burke, at the house of Conrad Paul, where a party had assembled. Both had been drinking.

April 21, 1872, Michael Ulrich, of Washington Township, committed suicide by shooting himself in the breast with a gun. He was 25 years old, and left a wife and one child.

William Graves, who lived with his mother about four miles north of Cedar Falls, while out hunting on Sunday, Aug 11, 1872, was accidentally killed by his own gun. He had been lying down, and on arising the contents of the gun were lodged in his breast.

Jan. 31, 1873, the dwelling of L. B. Corwin, seven miles northwest of Cedar Falls, was destroyed by fire, the loss being $600, partially covered by insurance

James Anderson, of Washington Township, Oct 6, 1875, lost his dwelling, worth about $4,000, by fire

Jan. 28, 1876, John Carroll, of Washington Township, was thrown from a loaded wagon and killed by one of the forward wheels crushing his skull before he could extricate himself

George Emmert, a young man living near La Porte, was fatally stabbed by Samuel Pray Feb. 7, 1876. All were attending church. Pray and his companions had been pulling Emmert's hair, and on his objecting they dared him out to fight. In the scuffle which followed, Emmert was stabbed in the lungs, dying in eight minutes

Otto Kutter, of German, committed suicide in the cemetery at Waterloo by shooting himself in the breast with a pistol, Oct 1, 1876

In May, 1868, Mr. Jacob Hoffman discovered a deposit of peat six miles northwest of Waterloo

COUNTY OFFICERS.

County Judges —Jonathan R. Pratt, 1853, died June 1855, John Randall, 1855–7; Julius C. Hubbard, 1857–9; George W Couch, 1860–61 (confined to Probate duties after 1861); S. D Shaw, 1862–7, Daniel W. Foote, 1868–9 (office abolished January 1, 1870).

Treasurers and Recorders.—Aaron Dow, 1853–5; O. E. Hardy, 1855, January, 1856, Francis B Davidson, 1856–7; A. C. Bunnell, 1857–65.

Treasurers.—John Elwell, 1866–7; R. A. Whitaker, 1868–75; David B. Washburn, 1876.

Recorders.—James W McClure, 1865–72, C. B. Stillson, 1873

Clerks of District Courts.—John H. Brooks, 1853, resigned April 4, 1854; Luther L Peas, 1854; Martin Bailey, 1854–5; Morrison Bailey, 1855–6; J B Severance, 1856–60; Dempster J. Coleman, 1861–6; A G Eberhart, 1867–72; J. C. Gates, 1873.

Sheriffs —John Virden, 1853–5; Benjamin F. Thomas, 1855–7; John Elwell, 1857–9–60 and '61; W. F. Brown, 1862–73; George W Hayzlett, 1874.

Prosecuting Attorneys —William L. Christie, 1853, R. P Spear, 1854, A. F. Brown, 1854, John Randall, 1854–5; William Haddock, 1855–6; Wm. H McClure, 1856; S. W. Rawson, 1857 (superseded by District Attorney).

School Fund Commissioners.—H. H. Fowler, 1853–4; Stephen A. Bishop, 1854 (office abolished in 1855).

County Surveyors.—Charles Mullan, 1853–5, George W. Miller, 1855–9; M L. Tracey, 1860–62; Geo. W. Miller, 1863–5, J Ball, 1866–7; E. A Snyder, 1868–73; E Rodenberger, 1874.

Drainage Commissioners.—Norman L. Jackson, 1853–5; Thomas R Points, 1855–7; J. W Holmes, 1857–9; Jacob Wolf, 1860; A. G. Bannister, 1861–2; S. R. Crittenden, 1863–5, J. A Loatwell, 1866. (Office abolished

Superintendents of Schools.—Truman Steed, 1859–61; M H. Moore, 1862–3; George Ordway, 1864–5; J. C. Gates, 1866–7, Seymour Gookins, 1868–9; E. G Miller, 1870, A. H Nye, 1870–71; W. H. Brinkerhoff, 1872–3; A. F. Townsend, 1874–5; James S George, 1876.

County Auditor.—Daniel W Foote, 1870.

Deputies.—J C. Gates, 1870–72: W. A. Cottrell, 1873

SUPERVISORS—(TOWNSHIP SYSTEM).

For 1861.—M. Bailey, Chairman; C F. Jaquith, M H Moore, Jesse Wassen, J. B Orr, Levi Washburn, S. P. Babcock, F S. Tewksbury, D. W Jordan, H. P. Homer, Oscar Dunton, D E. Champlin, James Hempseed, John Hackett, Gardiner, J. H Mead, J Jaquith.

1862.—M. H Moore, Chairman, F B. Carpenter, O O St.' John, J. Wasson, J. B. Orr, L. Washburn, L. B. Sheppard, F. S Tewksbury, D. W. Jordan, W. W. Hutton, Oscar Dunton, D. E. Champlin, James Hempseed, John Hackett, Gardiner, J. H Mead, Charles Pierce, Horace Beckwith.

1863.—M. H. Moore, Chairman; L. B. Sheppard, W. W. Hutton, D. E. Champlin, G. Gardner, H Beckwith, J Hackett, D. W. Jordan, O. O. St. John, Jacob Wolf, I. T Corwin, Byron Sargent, Simeon Clark, J. H. Potts, O. M. Hayden, Geo. Bishop, D. W. Jordan. John Hachett died in February, and I. D Gilkey was appointed.

1864.—M H. Moore, Chairman; C. May, G. Bishop, I. T Corwin, D. W. Jordan, B. Sargent, B. G. Updike, J. Wolf, D E Champlin, J. H. Potts, I. D. Gilkey, O. M. Hayden, H M. Bailey, A. Vittam, L. B. Sheppard, John McManus, William Rolph, S. Clark

1865.—M. H. Moore, Chairman; C. May, William Gilchrist, Wm. Rolph, Josiah Jackson, I T Corwin. L B Sheppard, O. Hughes, H W. Abbey, B. G. Updike, James Sandiland, D E. Champlin, P. S Canfield, I. D. Gilkey, John Bird, Nelson Hitchcock, H. M. Bailey, Albert Vittam.

1866.—D. E. Champlin, Chairman, James S George, C May, Wm. Gilchrist, Wm. Rolph, Josiah Jackson, I. T. Corwin, C. P. Nichols, A. A Alline, H. W. Abbey, W. H Hutton, James Sandiland, P. S Canfield, L. Goings, Damon Mott, N Hitchcock, H. M Bailey, A Vittam

1867.—A. A. Alline, Chairman; J. S. George, C. May, Wm Gilchrist, T. H. Elwell, Josiah Jackson, I. T. Corwin, C P. Nichols, L. P. Holt, W. W. Hutton, James Sandiland, R. S. Wooster, J. M. Northrup, I. D. Gilkey, D Mott, N Hitchcock, A T Webster, A. Vittam.

1868.—Byron Culver, Chairman; N S. Boyles, D. E. Champlin, L. A. Cobb, N Hitchcock, L P. Holt, J Jackson, S. H Rownd, J Sandiland, G. F. Ward, I. T. Corwin, James Hempseed, H. P. Homer, G W. Humphrey, H J. McCord, D. Mott, C. P. Nichols, A. T. Webster, H. J. McCord.

1869.—Cicero Close, Chairman; J. D Abbott, N. S. Boyles, D. E Champlin, L A Cobb, I. T. Corwin, G. W Humphrey, H. P Homer, I. D. Gilkey, Josiah Jackson, H J McCord, Damon Mott, Alonzo Norris, Charles Robinson, Samuel H. Rownd, Byron Sargent, L. B. Sheppard, Jesse Wasson, A. T. Webster.

1870 —C. Close, Chairman, J. D. Abbott, Urias Caskel, D. E. Champlin, L A. Cobb, I. T Corwin, J. L. Finch, Daniel Fish, G. W. Hayzlett, E. C. Humphrey, Josiah Jackson, Jefferson Jaquith, Caleb May, H. J. McCord. C. B. Miller, Alonzo Norris, Charles Robinson, S. H. Rownd, Byron Sargent.

COUNTY SYSTEM.

1871 —Cicero Close, Chairman, George B. Van Saun, A. T Weatherwax.

1872.—A. T Weatherwax, Chairman; C Close and G. B. Van Saun.

1873 —Cicero Close, Chairman; A. T. Weatherwax, A. T. Webster. (Increased to seven by vote of the people October, 1872)

1874 —A. T. Weatherwax, Chairman; A. T. Webster, N. Hitchcock, D. B. Washburn, H. J. McCord, H W Jenney, Caleb May.

1875,—Caleb May, Chairman, J. C. Burnham, H W Jenney, H. J. McCord, D. B. Washburn, A. T. Weatherwax, A. T. Webster.

1876 —H J. McCord, Chairman; H. W Jenney, Jefferson Jaquith, J. C. Burnham, H. B. Eighmey, A. T. Weatherwax, C. May.

1877.—H. J. McCord, Chairman; C. May, John McQuilken, H. W. Jenney, A T Weatherwax, B. J. Rodemer, Jefferson Jaquith

1878 —H W Jenney, Chairman, I. T Corwin, J. Jaquith, C. May, John McQuilken, Samuel Owens, B. J. Rodemer

MEMBERS OF THE LEGISLATURE

Senate —A. F. Brown, 1860-1-2-3, Coker F. Clarkson, 1864-5; James B. Powers, 1866-7-8-9; George W Couch, 1870-71; John H Leavitt, 1872-3; Edward G. Miller, 1876-7; H. C. Hemenway, 1878-9

House of Assembly —Morrison Bailey, 1856-7, Zimri Streeter, 1858-9-'60-61, Warner H. Curtis, 1862-3; Cicero Close, 1864-5-6-7; George Ordway, 1868-9, T. B. Carpenter, 1870-71; Cicero Close, 1872-3; Charles B Campbell, 1874-5; Harlan P. Homer, 1876-7; H. C Hemenway, 1876-7; Lore Alford, 1878; Jeremiah L. Gay, 1878.

EDUCATIONAL.

The first schools taught in Black Hawk County were private or subscription schools. Their accommodations, as may be readily supposed, were not good Sometimes they were taught in small log houses erected for the purpose. Stoves and such heating apparatus as are in use now were unknown A mud and stick chimney in one end of the building, with earthen hearth, with a fire-place wide enough and deep enough to take in a four-foot back log, and smaller wood to match, served for warming purposes in Winter and a kind of conservatory in Summer. For windows, part of a log was cut out in either side, and maybe a few panes of eight by ten glass set in, or, just as likely as not, the aperture would be covered over with greased paper. Writing benches were made of wide planks, or, maybe, puncheons resting on pins or arms driven into two-inch auger holes bored into the logs beneath the windows. Seats were made out of thick planks or puncheons, flooring was made of the same kind of stuff. Everything was rude and plain, but many of America's greatest men have gone out from just such school houses to grapple with the world and make a name for themselves, and names that come to be an honor to their country. In other cases, private rooms and parts of private houses were utilized as school houses, but the furniture was just as plain.

But all these things are changed now. A log school house in Iowa is a rarity. Their places are filled with handsome frame or brick structures The rude furniture has also given way, and the old school books, the "Popular Reader," the "English Reader" (the finest literary compilation ever known in American schools), and "Webster's Elementary Spelling Book," are superseded by others of greater pretensions. The old spelling classes and spelling matches have followed the old school houses, until they are remembered only in name Of her school system, Iowa can justly boast. It has sent out a large number of representative men whose names are as familiar to the nation as they are in the histories of the counties and neighborhoods in which they once lived. While the State has extended such fostering care to the interests of education, the several counties have been no less zealous and watchful in the management of this vital interest. And Black Hawk County forms no exception to the rule. The school houses and their furnishings are in full keeping with the spirit of the law that provides for their maintenance and support. The teachers rank high among the other thousands of teachers in the State; and the several County Superintendents, since the office of Superintendent was made a part of the school system, have been chosen with especial reference to their fitness for the position

It is impossible to find any reports of educational matters in this county prior to 1858, when the Seventh General Assembly passed "An act for the Public Instruction of the State of Iowa," and organized the present school system By this act, which went into force March 20, 1858, each civil township was made a school district, and the number of districts and district officers was thus greatly reduce t By the same act, the office of County Superintendent of Schools was created, and appropriations made in aid of Teachers' Institutes

The first Teachers' Institute held in the county, of which any recollection remains, was at Cedar Falls, October 8-13, 1860, conducted by J L Enos, of Cedar Rapids Those in attendance were. T. Steed, L J Hammond, W. C. Porter, R. C. Hall, J. S Livingston, E. B Lamb, W H. Merwin, Peter Livingston, T. H Leshe, Dr. John Kerr, E H. Wilcox, Wilbur F. Poor, Jennie Gardner, Anna Gardner, E. A Leshe, Alice Doolittle, Sarah A Dougherty, Lois A Dunham, Anna E Jaynes, N. Collins, E. A. McStay, Anna Bullock, Mary E. Pratt, Mary A Barnard, M J. Collier, Mrs D. C. Overman, Mrs. Joseph Chase, Phebe Tondro, Susan McNalley, Emma Hall, W. Garrison, L. F. Barnard, W. W Engle, M. J. Engle, M W Collins, Eliza Dixon, M J. McStay. The officers chosen for the ensuing year were: J. M White, President, E. B. Lamb, Vice President, L. F Barnard, Secretary ; T. Steed, Treasurer ; Mrs. D. C. Overman, L. J. Hammond, E H Wilcox Executive Committee.

Between October 5, 1860, and October 4. 1861, there were 70 public schools in Black Hawk County ; number of pupils attending school, 2,347 , number of teachers—males, 44 , females, 64 ; average weekly compensation to males, $5.21 ; to females, $3.16 ; amount paid teachers during year, $6,353.60 The total population of the county in 1860 was 8,244

The following abstracts from the Superintendent's reports for 1860, 1867 and 1877 will show the progress of the educational interests of the county, since the period when records are accessible:

	1860	1867	1877
Township Districts...	17	22	11
Independent Districts			56
Sub-Districts	71	114	81
Ungraded schools			136
Graded schools			5
Number of schools	78	108	141
Average duration—months			7 58
Number of male teachers	6	54	84
Number of female teachers	12	139	197
Average compensation—males, per week	$6 46	$7 50	month $35 34
Average compensation—females, per week	8 08	6 25	" 29 88
Number of persons between ages of 5 and 21 years—males	1,461	3,307	4,380
Number of persons between ages of 5 and 21 years—females	1,371	3,225	4,188

Pupils enrolled	2,108	6,080	6,172
Average attendance	1,275	3,403	4,281
Cost of tuition per pupil—Summer, per week	22	21 } month, $1 32	
Winter, "	38	27 }	
School houses—frame	25	72	127
brick		4	10
stone	3	5	10
logs	7	9	
Value of school houses	$8,695 25	$84,088	$170,150
Value of apparatus	49 50	2,139 20	3,249
Number of volumes in libraries	32	32	61
Total expense for paid teachers	4,132 74	18,978 78	47,030 86

Following is the Financial Statement for 1877.

SCHOOL HOUSE FUND

Total receipts during the year	$47,511 23
Paid for school houses and sites	5,425 42
Paid on bonds and interest	35,134 31
On hand	6,951 50

CONTINGENT FUND

Total receipts	$25,696 67
Paid rent for school houses	1 60
Paid repairs for school houses	3,197 90
Paid for fuel	4,887 87
Paid Secretaries	642 66
Paid Treasurers	527 15
Paid records and apparatus	913 56
Paid various purposes	6,932 44
On hand	8,743 49

TEACHERS' FUND

Total receipts	$79,655 94
Paid teachers	47,030 86
On hand	32,625 08
Number of teachers receiving certificates of first grade	54
Number of teachers receiving certificates of second grade	129
Number of teachers receiving certificates of third grade	98
Total number of certificates granted	281
Number of applicants rejected	118
Number of applicants examined	899
Average of applicants, male	.25
Average of applicants, female	23
No experience in teaching, males	7
No experience in teaching, females	35
Taught less than one year, males	39
Taught less than one year, females	49
Number of schools visited by County Superintendent	142
Number of visits	187
Educational meetings held	3
Appeals decided	1
Compensation of Supt from October 1, 1876 to Oct 1, 1877	$1,232
Number of private schools	4
Number of private school teachers	19
Number of pupils in private schools	370

A Teachers' Normal Institute was held at Waterloo, commencing March 26, 1877, continuing two weeks. E. Baker, Conductor; J. K Sweeney, M. F. Avery, T R. Hamlin and Miss M McCowen, Assistant Instructors; C. W. Van Coelln and J. C. Gilchrist, Lecturers. Total number of teachers in attendance, 205—41 gentlemen and 164 ladies.

Graded Schools of 1877.—Cedar Falls. Male teachers, 3; female teachers, 12; J McNaughton, Principal, salary $1,200. East Waterloo: Female teachers, 10; J. K. Sweeney, Principal, salary $1,200. La Porte City: Female teachers, 4 ; E M. Sharon, Principal, salary $680. Waterloo: Female teachers, 9 ; Prof. W. H. Robertson, Principal, salary $1,390

The private schools are: Prairie Home Female Seminary—Miss A. Fields, Principal; 4 teachers employed; 65 pupils. Conservatory of Music—E. W. Burnham, Principal, teachers, 3. Our Lady of Victory (Catholic)—Lady Crescentia, Principal; teachers, 5 ; pupils, 145

The present efficient Superintendent of Schools is James S George, Esq., and the present condition of the schools in the county is thus summarized in his last annual report :

> The raising of the grades of certificates has produced a very beneficial effect upon teachers and schools
>
> It has incited our teachers to more application and study, and I can plainly see that they are giving much closer attention to their school work   I find the people generally in favor of elevating the standard of their teachers and schools , and I also meet, in my efforts to accomplish this much-to-be desired end, not a little opposition from teachers   I have been sorely tried in a few instances by teachers and their relatives asking, and even demanding, particular favors   I have been forced to the conclusion that nepotism is, perhaps, as common here as in many other parts of the State , but by the strict observance of law and official instructions, I have it in a great measure under subjection
>
> We held our Normal Institute this year last Spring, having an attendance of 205 members, and it proved in all respects a success   The attendance would have been much greater had it not been for prevailing sickness at the time, and that a number of schools were in session.   The State Normal School is in a very prosperous condition, but is much in need of more room   An appropriation should be made by the State this Winter for its enlargement
>
> The State can well feel proud of this institution, and should give liberally toward its encouragement and support
>
> In the compiling of my report, I have labored, as usual, under great embarrassments in procuring prompt and correct reports from school Secretaries and Treasurers
>
> The difficulty will continue to occur until the Legislature afford to the Superintendent some relief   The law as it now is, renders him completely powerless , and if he is refused reports by these officers, he has no efficient way provided to enforce compliance with the law   I often wonder why our law makers are so dilatory and lax concerning these important r gulations   It is to be hoped that our Legislature will act wisely and promptly in this matter

STATE NORMAL SCHOOL

On page 201 of this work will be found a brief account of the inception of this institution, which promises to be such an important adjunct to the common school system of Iowa.

It is needless to say that the people of Black Hawk County fully appreciate the establishment of the Normal School in their midst.

The first Commencement Exercises were held on Wednesday, June 27, 1877. There were six applicants for graduation, but two of the number were denied diplomas on account of their youth, though they were allowed to participate in the exercises   The subjects discussed by the class were as follows ·

Maude Gilchrist, Cedar Falls, '' Progression the Law of the Human Race ;'' R O. Benton, Mason City, "Superstitions ;'' Mary Flagler, Cedar Falls, " Public Sentiment;'' Ada Coates, Green Mountain, ''The Triumph of Peace;'' Eva M. Donohue, Mason City, "The Value of Character ;'' David K. Bond, Hopkinton, " Penn and Lycurgus.''

The average attendance by terms during the Normal year was ninety.

At the Commencement of 1878 (July 11), the orations were: "Civilization," Loren E Churchill, Finchford; " Vicissitudes of a Poet's Life," Maude Gilchrist , "Safety Lies in a Medium," David K. Bond, Hopkinton ; " Misanthropy," Rome O. Benton, Mason City.

The number of students in attendance during the past year was 237, of whom 153 were ladies.   There are two literary societies—the Philomathean and the Alpha—both of which are heartily sustained by the students.

The officers chosen by the Trustees for the coming two years are: S. G Smith, President, J. J. Tolerton, Vice President; E Townsend, Treasurer; W. C Bryant, Secretary.

The faculty for 1878–9 is as follows · J. C. Gilchrist, A M, Principal, and Professor of Mental Philosophy, Moral Philosophy and Didactics, M W. Bartlett, A. M., Professor of Ancient Languages and Natural Science, D. S. Wright, A. M, Professor of Mathematics and Ancient Literature; Miss S. Laura Ensign, Teacher of Geography, History, Botany, et al.; Miss Mary E. Bradley, Teacher of Drawing, Penmanship and Bookkeeping; William Pattee, Steward, and Mrs. Parsons, Matron.

Students seeking admission to this school are required to be, if males, at least 17, and, if females, at least 16 years of age; to produce a certificate of good moral character, signed by some responsible person; to sign a statement of their intention in good faith to follow the business of teaching in the public schools of the State; to produce a certificate showing that the applicant has passed the examination required to obtain a teacher's certificate of the lowest grade, and that he has been appointed to the school   Such examination and appointment must be made, and such certificate is signed by the Superintendent of Schools for the county in which the applicant resides   Students need not hesitate to correspond with the institution before this appointment, or even if failing to get it.

Each county is entitled to one student for every four thousand inhabitants, or part thereof; but admission will not be refused to any applicant who can be admitted without prejudice to the rights of others under the apportionment. Practically, the school is open to all.

Students not intending to become teachers can enter the school, provided there are accommodations untaken by student teachers; but such students must pay tuition at the rate of two dollars ($2.00) per month.

THE PRESS.

Cedar Falls Banner —In 1854, it became necessary that Cedar Falls and Black Hawk County should have a newspaper.   Accordingly, Wm H McClure and Dr. Meredith purchased at Tipton a six-column hand press and the necessary outfit of material, both having seen hard service, but capable of more, and on the 11th of July, the first number of the Cedar Falls *Banner* was issued. A. F. Brown was the editor; Samuel C. Dunn and Joseph Farley, printers The sheet was a six-column folio, "independent in all things" In October following, Dr. Meredith sold his share to S. H Packard, Esq., who assumed the editorial duties.   McClure & Packard afterward sold the concern to Hill & Ball, who were succeeded by Wm. H Hartman, in 1857 or 1858, who soon after removed the concern to Waterloo and began the publication of the Waterloo *Courier*.

The *Banner* had a circulation of about six hundred, copies being sent to every State in the Union, and one or two to China.   It was a most useful little paper, and was of material help in calling attention to the natural advantages of Iowa as a home for immigrants and attracting settlers hither.

A file of the *Banner* was kept, and was introduced in evidence in a case being tried at Waterloo some years ago.   Its owner, who prized it highly, not finding it convenient to take the bulky package home with him, left it in the Clerk's office for a more convenient occasion.   The Clerk conscientiously used up the entire file for kindling fires, very much to the regret of all the early settlers.

The *Cedar Falls Gazette* was given to the expectant citizens of that town for the first time on Friday, March 16, 1860, by H. A. and G. D. Perkins, publishers and editors. In the "Salutatory" the editors say, "We come with a strong determination to work with a will for your interests, to leave no honorable means untried to enhance your prosperity, promote your interests, and give publicity to the many natural and artificial advantages with which this point is favored." The politics of the new paper was defined to be in accord with the Republican platform of 1856. The paper was a folio sheet, seven columns to the page. Four years afterward, it was enlarged one column to the page. During the war, George D., the younger brother, enlisted in the volunteer service, but was discharged for disability, after a year's service. In 1865, Henry A. Perkins was appointed Postmaster of Cedar Falls. July 13, 1866, the brothers sold the paper and material to Rev. S. B. Goodenow, who had just withdrawn from the Independence *Guardian*. This gentleman retained control till March 22, 1867, when he disposed of the property to Mr. C. W. Snyder, of Clinton, and A. C. Holt, of Cedar Falls. Mr. Holt remained in the paper till the Summer of 1868, when he disposed of his interest to E. A. Snyder. Early in 1869, the Snyder Brothers sold to George K. Shaw and L. D. Tracy. In two short weeks the partners quarreled, and the firm was dissolved, C. W. Snyder buying out Shaw, who took possession of the *Grundy County Atlas*. For two or three weeks the *Atlas* and the *Gazette* were fairly sulphureous with epithets, the doughty Shaw, among other things, challenging Rev. Mr. Tracy to fight a duel with him. The latter gentleman retired April 15, 1869, when E. A. Snyder again stepped into his old place. The Snyder Brothers continued its ownership till 1877, when Mr. Merchant purchased of them a one-third interest, and the firm still remains the same. The *Gazette* has always been regarded as one of the very best newspapers in Iowa, being always courteous and fair in political matters, and most painstaking and industrious in its local department.

The *Northwest Democrat* was established by a stock company at Cedar Falls, and the first number issued in June, 1862. Its first editor was a decided partisan, and his management drew down on the sheet the ire of the Republican portion of the community to the extent of threatening to suppress the paper. Early in 1863, the owners of the paper decided to conclude its brief life till the kindly touches of time should allay the bitter feeling then existing.

The Cedar Falls *Recorder* was begun in October, 1872, by S. G. Sherburne. It was a good sized quarto sheet, Democratic in politics. Mr. Sherburne remained as proprietor till February, 1874, when he sold out to H. C. Shaver, who had been foreman of the office. In November, 1875, Mr. Shaver sold to L. Hawkins, who converted it into a semi-religious paper; but finding the experiment a hazardous one, he disposed of the property, six weeks afterward, to J. B. Abbott & Co., who made it a Republican paper. It soon passed back to H. C. Shaver, who changed its politics to its original position. In May, 1877, I. Van Metre purchased a half interest, and assumed editorial control. The *Recorder* is now an eight-column folio sheet, all printed at home, and has a large circulation among the Democracy of Black Hawk County. The office is on the first floor of No. 1 Main street. The proprietors are now arranging to have the presses run by water power from the mill race, which can be supplied very cheaply.

Two other journals have been published at Cedar Falls—the *Record*, by A. C. Holt, in 1866, and the *Real Estate Journal*, by T. L. French & Co., two or three years after. Both were advertising papers.

The *Iowa State Register and Waterloo Herald* made its appearance on Saturday, December 15, 1855, Wm Haddock, editor and proprietor. It was an eight-column folio, and, for the time, a very handsome and creditable sheet. In his salutation to his readers, the editor says: "In politics, our paper will be independent, and not merely neutral;" and further on, that he is a firm believer in "the doctrine of State rights, and that the South ought to be permitted to hold slaves unmolested so long as there is no help for it under the Constitution" But he was opposed to extending slavery into the territories, and in the struggle growing out of the Kansas-Nebraska bill, the paper took Republican grounds, and then, like most independent journals, was everything by turns and nothing long

In the latter part of its life, the paper missed frequent issues, the business of the office was neglected, and dissatisfaction was manifested by the patrons in various ways, in hopes of spurring up the publisher to better things; but all without avail. After repeated threats of encouraging the starting of another paper, the citizens did finally extend material aid to Hartman & Ingersoll, which resulted in establishing the *Courier*, which soon proved a formidable competitor. In October, 1859, the *Register* was discontinued, and the material was sold to parties in Waverly, who were about to start a Democratic paper there

The *Waterloo Courier* —In August, 1858, W. H. Hartman, then a young man "chock-full of days' works," and ambitious of winning fame and wealth as a newspaper publisher, resurrected the defunct *Banner*, at Cedar Falls, and in November following, Geo. D Ingersoll became associated with him. They made a desperate struggle to keep it waving; but times were tight, money scarce, and the publishers, finding it hard to live on faith and corn meal alone, suspended the paper again, and on Christmas Day, 1858, moved the material to Waterloo, where, on January 18, 1859, the *Courier* was born. It was first issued as a seven-column folio Patronage was light, and it was only by the most rigid economy that both ends were made to meet. On the 1st of January, 1860, the paper was enlarged to an eight-column sheet, the death of the *Register* making such enlargement possible and necessary. In September of the same year, Hartman bought out Ingersoll, and the *Courier* continued with him as sole proprietor until November 14, 1864, when J W. Logan became half owner. In 1865, the paper was again enlarged by adding an extra column to the page, and other improvements were made In April, 1871, Hartman & Logan sold out the entire establishment to Aldrich & Woodruff, but in October of the same year, Mr. Hartman again became part owner by purchasing Mr. Aldrich's interest On February 5, 1874, Mr. Woodruff sold out to A J Felt, and the firm name was changed to Felt & Hartman. On the 16th of April following, the paper was again enlarged and changed to a seven-column quarto. August 16, 1875, Mr. Hartman purchased Mr. Felt's interest, and since that date, has been sole editor and proprietor.

The early years of the *Courier* were full of troubles and struggles for existence; but now it is considered one of the best newspaper properties in the interior of the State, and it is blessed with a patronage which insures its publisher a good, liberal income.

The Iowa State Reporter, next in order, was started May 13, 1868, by H. Q. Nicholson, and was then almost the only paper in the State issued in quarto form It was started as a Democratic paper, although Black Hawk was one of the strong Republican counties of the State, giving only 841 Democratic votes out of 3,421 cast at the election of that year But the paper was neatly printed, ably edited, and its publisher soon worked up a list of about 1,000 subscribers, and a handsome advertising patronage. In November, 1868, Mr Nicholson was called East by the serious illness of his father, and during his absence the paper was continued by the boys in the office so long as there were any coal piles in the neighborhood and the paper dealers had faith enough to send on white paper. When these two supplies were cut off, the paper had to stop, but the boys were full of grit to the end, and in their last number let themselves down with the following explanation:

" Owing to the rapidly increasing business which an appreciating community is bestowing upon us, we find it necessary to remove our material and machinery to more capacious quarters. Therefore, we shall be compelled, however reluctantly, to suspend the publication of the *Reporter* for a few weeks, as our machinery is so heavy and extensive that the change cannot be effected without incurring the above suspension "

But the suspension was a permanent one, so far as Mr Nicholson was concerned. His father died December 20, 1868, which made it impossible for him to return and resume its publication On February 11, 1869, the material and subscription list were purchased by Smart & Parrott At that time the office was in the building on Fourth street, now occupied by Seaman & Son, and was too small and inconvenient for printing office purposes The new proprietors secured a lease of the rear rooms in the second story of Union Hall Block, but did not commence the publication of the *Reporter* again until the office was moved to the new location, which was in April, and on the 14th of that month the *Reporter* again appeared, but as a Republican paper.

On the 31st of May, 1871, the paper was enlarged to a six-column quarto, and other improvements made, and at that time it was the largest newspaper in the county.

The next era in the life of the *Reporter* was October 16, 1872, when the establishment was moved from Union Block into the building specially erected for its occupancy, on Sycamore street.

On June 18, 1873, a change was made in the firm, James L. Girton becoming a partner, and the firm name was changed to Smart, Parrott & Co. On March 17, 1875, J. J. Smart sold out his interest to J P. Sherman, and the firm name was changed to Parrott, Girton & Sherman, who are the present publishers.

Der Deutsch Amerikaner.—The first number of this paper was issued August 29, 1872, one side English and the other German. It was published by a company and edited by A. Schill. On the 1st of January, 1873, Mr. Martin Blim became proprietor and editor, and on the 21st of February following, discontinued the English part of his paper, making it exclusively German. It is enjoying a fair degree of prosperity, and its subscription list is constantly increasing.

The La Porte *Progress* was established November 30, 1870, by Dr Jesse Wasson It was a seven-column folio, Independent in politics, and edited with ability In February, 1872, the *Progress* was enlarged to eight columns It is now edited by its original editor, Dr. Wasson, and in politics is Democratic

The La Porte City *Republican* first appeared in July, 1852, W H. Brinkerhoff, editor and publisher. After struggling against fate for eleven long, weary months, the *Republican* succumbed to the inevitable, and suspended for want of adequate support.

Burroughs' Journal was first started in Streator, Ill., by Rev. J. W. Burroughs, but was removed to Raymond, Black Hawk County, Iowa, in July, 1874 It is a six-column quarto paper, devoted to the discussion of religious topics, mainly. It is published weekly, and is printed at Raymond.

RAILROADS.

Dubuque & Pacific Railroad —The necessity for railroads was felt by the early settlers of Iowa to be a vital one, and whenever a project was presented to any settlement, it was sure to meet hearty welcome. In 1854, a preliminary survey was made for a line westward, by the Dubuque & Pacific Company, then just organized, and the people of Black Hawk County felt that the hour of their prosperity was near at hand; while the residents of Waterloo and Cedar Falls saw in the future the thriving cities that have sprung up. But the company, having limited capital, and the people east of Black Hawk being able to do but little, the road progressed very slowly.

To insure the building of the Dubuque & Pacific Road to Cedar Falls, the inhabitants contributed freely by donations of cash and lands, and also by taking stock; the principal contributors being the Overmans, Brown, Dr Meredith, Mullarky and others : the amount in all being about $100,000.

The county of Black Hawk was asked to aid the enterprise by subscribing to the capital stock of the company to the amount of $200,000, and the people voted to do so. The bonds were prepared and are still preserved in the county archives as a memento of railroad excitement and the sanguine hopes of the people It is said that the County Judge at that time (1856) refused to sign these bonds, and consequently they were never issued. The reasons for this refusal are not clearly apparent; but it is said that the city of Waterloo became largely identified with the Burlington, Cedar Rapids & Minnesota Railroad, which was probably thought to be of more importance to that city than the Dubuque & Pacific. In consequence of their refusal to comply with the terms of the agreement, it is alleged that the line of the road, after being partially graded and designed to cross the Cedar in the city of Waterloo, was changed to its present route, and the depots established north of the city

The track of the Dubuque & Pacific, or Sioux City, Railroad reached the water-tank, within eighty rods of the depot, at Cedar Falls, March 29, 1861, and the first regular train arrived on the following Monday. To celebrate the auspicious event that enabled Cedar Falls to shake hands with the outside world, the people of the town made extensive preparations. The Committee of Reception contained 128 citizens The celebration was had on Thursday, April 11th, the guests from Dubuque and other towns being met at the depot by a long procession of citizens, who, giving three hearty cheers, bound a chaplet of evergreens filled with mottoes over the locomotive, and assembled with the guests in the depot building, where an address of welcome was made by Hon A. F Brown, in behalf of the city, and felicitously responded to by Herman Gelpke, President of the road.   Other speeches followed from Col. Sessions, of Cedar Falls, Platt Smith, of Dubuque, and Hon J. B Grinnell, of Poweshiek County.

The invited guests, sixty-three in number, were then conducted to the American House, then presided over by J. L. Wilcox, where a bountiful supper was provided.   This disposed of, the following toasts were responded to as indicated:

The President and Directors of the Dubuque & Sioux City Railroad—Herman Gelpke.

The Four Great Cities of the Northern Confederacy—Cedar Falls, Dubuque, Chicago and New York—Platt Smith

Our Guests—For the first time we greet you, welcome collectively to our festive board, may it not be the last—Hon A. F Brown.

The Flag of Our Union—C T Smeed, of Waverly

The Press, the Intellectual Elevator of the World—D A Mahoney.

Iowa, Her Past and Her Future—Hon J B. Grinnell.

The Cedar Falls & Minnesota Railroad—Edwin Brown

The Communication between Dubuque and Cedar Falls—Its Change from the Coach to the Locomotive—Hon Zimri Streeter

The Pioneers of Iowa—Hon Wm P Harmon, of Waverly.

A grand ball followed the banquet, the Germania Band, of Dubuque, furnishing the music

The extension of the Dubuque & Sioux City Road from Cedar Falls westward, began late in the season of 1864

Cedar Falls & Minnesota Railroad—May 7, 1860, the stockholders of the Cedar Falls & Minnesota Railway Company chose the following as Directors for the ensuing year: R. B. Mason, J F. English, E Brown, E. Edgerton, J M Overman, S A Bishop, A. S Smith, William Ward, Chester Butterfield, J Barrick, D. Wiltse, J. D Jenkins, A. Mullarky. R B. Mason was made President the same day.

The work of grading began in the Fall of 1860, and about forty miles were made ready for the ties the following year.

The following were the Directors of the company, as elected in May, 1861. R B Mason, Chicago; E. Brown, J. M. Overman, S. A. Bishop, A S. Smith, E Edgerton, Cedar Falls, W P. Harmon, Bremer County, S Harwood, R. M. Matthews, M. G Cook, Floyd County; J. F English, A Hitchcock, S. Clawson, Mitchell County

The Articles of Incorporation were amended early in 1864, and by the change the company was enabled to remove its place of business to Dubuque

Track-laying was begun on this line in 1864, the road reaching Waverly the same season; but so insufficient was the grade and so hastily was the work done, that the running of trains was abandoned for a time the following Spring

The people of Cedar Falls were much disappointed in losing this road, which they had counted on so much The company had been formed originally as an appendage of the Dubuque & Pacific Company, and to buy its iron it had to lease the line to the Dubuque Company. Hence, when the Dubuque Company decreed that the Cedar Falls road should begin nearly two miles east of that town, there was nothing to do but to submit

Iowa Central Railroad.—Many miles of grading were done on the "Iowa Central Railroad" during the Autumn of 1865, beginning at Cedar Falls and working southward. The company was organized on the 5th of January previous Ground was broken September 19th, with elaborate ceremonies, and speeches by Hon. David Morgan, who threw the first shovelful, Hon. B. F. Gue, of Fort Dodge; Wm. E. McMaster, of New York; C. C. Carpenter, of Fort Dodge; Alfred Phillips, of Tama County; Capt Babcock, of Chickasaw County; Judge Palmer, of Butler County; Mr. Chase, of Mitchell County. Letters were also read from W R. Marshall, of St. Paul, and Hon. J. B. Grinnell, of Poweshiek County. But the discovery of coal and fire clay in Hardin County induced capitalists to foster the "plug" started from Ackley about the same time, which was also called then the "Iowa Central," and the people of Cedar Falls were unable to obtain funds for completing their line, which still remains unfinished.

Burlington, Cedar Rapids & Minnesota Railroad.—In August, 1870, the people of Cedar Falls voted a tax of five per cent. to aid in the construction of the Burlington, Cedar Rapids & Minnesota Railroad, conditional on the track being laid to the city by January 1, 1871. Other towns along the line voted similar aid, and Waterloo gave material assistance in subscriptions, etc.

The construction train of the Burlington, Cedar Rapids & Minnesota road reached Cedar Falls on Wednesday, November 30, 1870, and the first passenger train next day, just a month in advance of the time agreed upon by the officers of that company

F

THE BLACK HAWK COUNTY AGRICULTURAL SOCIETY

The first meeting for the organization of an agricultural society in this county was held at the Clerk's office in Waterloo August 30, 1856 G A. Knowles was Chairman of the meeting, and S. W Rawson, Secretary. At this meeting, a Constitution was adopted and the following officers elected ·

President, George Ordway, Vice Presidents, G A Knowles, Z Streeter, B Winset; Corresponding Secretary, S W. Rawson; Recording Secretary, J. O Williams; Treasurer, O E Hardy Executive Committee—L. Kennicutt, S. R Crittenden, James Barclay, C K White, James Dunkerton, S Webster, Benjamin Knapp, M. S. Oxley, M. W. Chapman, William Kent and Byron Sargent.

The Executive Committee was authorized to make arrangements for a fair, but the first exhibition was not held until October 1, 1857, when it took place at the Court House. The records do not show the premiums awarded, but the Treasurer's first annual report gives the receipts from all sources as amounting to $100. The attendance was quite large for the time, and the exhibition a meritorious one One of the principal attractions was an immense squash vine, bearing 1,100 pounds of "fruit," exhibited by T. B and B. S. Doxey.

During the fair, the organization was perfected, and the officers same as above continued for another year, except that James Evans was elected Treasurer, and J. H Sherrill, L C Sanborn and J. H. Mead were added to the Executive Committee

The second fair was on the West Side, the following year The vegetables, fine arts, pickles, needle work, preserves, etc., were in the basement of the Congregational church, and the stock and cumbersome articles were on the bluff, somewhere near Fowler's greenhouse

The grounds of the Society were purchased in 1865, but had been occupied for several years before the purchase for the exhibition of stock, etc., and the Court House was used for an exhibition hall The grounds cost $2,175. Cost of fitting up, fences and improvements, about $1,600. Fairs have been held every year and have generally been successful.

The following are the Presidents of the Society from its organization to 1878, viz.· George Ordway, 1856–8; J H Sherrill, 1859, ——— ———, 1860; O. O. St. John, 1861–4; Cicero Close, 1865, John Elwell, 1866; C. A. Farwell, 1867, P McIsaac, 1868–70, A Cottrell, 1871, Byron Sargent, 1872; A. Cottrell, 1873–4; Albert Whitney, 1875; H B. Allen, 1876–8.

Officers, 1878—H. B. Allen, President; W. H. Palmer, J Gay, Vice Presidents; R A. Whitaker, Secretary; C C. Close, Treasurer Directors—W. A Wilson, Bennington; A C Bratnober, Barclay, Philip Bonesteel, Lester; John Struble, Black Hawk, Samuel Gilson, Lincoln; John Osborn, Big Creek; William Winters, Mt. Vernon; William M. Fields, Cedar Falls; Ethan Allen, Orange, W H. Leavitt, Cedar, John Engle, Poyner; N. B. Choate, East Waterloo; George Clark, Spring Creek; J C. Gunn, Eagle; George Newell, Union; W H. Young, Fox, John Tennyson, Washington, and J. A. Fowler, Waterloo.

THE CEDAR VALLEY DISTRICT JOINT STOCK AGRICULTURAL ASSOCIATION

was organized in 1856, through the influence and labors of Hon. Peter Melendy, who was chosen the first President, which office he filled for more than ten years. This society held annual exhibitions on their grounds at Cedar Falls and accomplished much to advance the agricultural interests of the county.

The records of the Association were burned several years since, but a few items respecting it are gleaned from various sources.

When the first number of the Cedar Falls *Gazette* was issued, March 16, 1860, this Association had subscribed $1,300 for the purpose of purchasing and fitting up grounds.

Something over 200 premiums were awarded at the fourth annual fair at Cedar Falls, which was held September 18-20, 1860.

The officers of the Cedar Valley Association for 1861 were · Peter Melendy, President; A S Smith, Vice President, J. B. Powers, Secretary, S A. Bishop, Treasurer; H C Overman, Benj. Knapp, A Mullarky, Directors.

In May, 1872, a basis of agreement was reached between the officers of the Black Hawk County Agricultural Society on one hand and the Cedar Valley District Association on the other. for a practical union of the two societies The agreement was that a horse fair should be held in each alternate year at Waterloo and Cedar Falls, and an agricultural fair in the city not having the horse fair.

PATRONS OF HUSBANDRY.

In 1872-3, when the organization known as the Patrons of Husbandry swept like a tidal wave over the entire West, Black Hawk County did not escape. Granges were organized in every township, and many honest farmers indulged in the most sanguine dreams of the benefit to accrue from the institution. "The original and leading idea of the Grange," says Mr. Stevens, of Delaware County, himself a prominent and influential member of the Order, "was to secure social advantages; but in 1873, the leading idea among our farmers was business, or pecuniary benefit. Hence, Granges were crowded with anxious farmers, cherishing the illusory ideas of immediately bettering their circumstances, of the sooner clearing their farms from mortgages or securing a competency for the accomplishment of other cherished purposes through some mysterious influence of the organization. They did not realize that all changes or reforms proceed slowly. '

Under this delusive faith that the organization was destined to work an immediate and wonderful revolution in their financial condition, the husbandmen of Black Hawk, in common with those of the whole State, rushed into the Granges until the institution became a power which, had it been wisely and judiciously directed, might have accomplished something in the desired direction.

In this county, not only were subordinate Granges established in every township, but a county council was organized to centralize and utilize the power evoked. A Grange store was established at Waterloo and a Grange elevator was started on the east side of the river.

But the new broom, although it swept clean at first, did not bring about the miraculous reforms anticipated. Its managers did not realize the tremendous power they had invoked, and it controlled them, and crumbled because it was not controlled and directed Those who had anticipated such immediate and tremendous results, soon became disgusted; were not satisfied with the slow reforms the organization might legitimately be expected to produce, and abandoned the institution nearly as rapidly as they had entered it, forgetting the lesson they every day receive—that plants of the most rapid growth are generally the first to decay

In 1878, only a few Granges maintain a feeble existence in the county The county council, it is said, maintains its organization, but is dormant. The Grange store at Waterloo is being closed up, and the Grangers no longer have an elevator.

BLACK HAWK COUNTY MEDICAL ASSOCIATION

This is, comparatively, a young society, having been organized but two years—August 4, 1876. The charter members are as follows. J. M Ball, graduate W. R. College, Cleveland, Ohio, 1846; S W Pierce, graduate Vermont Medical College, 1856; D W Crouse, graduate Chicago Medical College, 1864; S. Vandervaart, graduate Holland College, Netherlands, 1842; D. B. Colcord, graduate Bellevue Hospital Medical College, 1875, William Robinson, graduate Berkshire Medical College, 1844; O S Knox, graduate Albany Medical College, 18—, J. M. Lanning, graduate Rush Medical College, 1862; J J. Wasson, graduate La Porte City Medical College, 1847; H. W. Brown, graduate Geneva Medical College, 1866; D W. Crouse, graduate Long Island Medical College, 1869; W. Eddy, graduate Michigan University Medical College, 1863, G J Mack, graduate Bellevue Medical College, 1872.

The first officers were: J M. Ball, President, S N Pierce, Vice President, J. M Lanning, Secretary and Treasurer; Drs. Ball, Pierce and Crouse, Board of Censors.

Their present officers· S. N. Pierce, President; J. M. Lanning, Vice President; A. D. Bedford, Secretary and Treasurer; Drs Crouse, Eddy and Bedford, Board of Censors.

The association meets on the first Friday in each alternate month.

THE FARMERS' MUTUAL FIRE INSURANCE COMPANY

was organized in 1873, by Wm Strayer, S. H Miller, Jos. S. Strickler, J. W Leeper, J. M. Bandfield, J. H. Jeffers, S B Vinton, J. W. Miller, Thos. Heitter, Cornelius Miller, J. H Mead, Matthew Simons, Chas. Lichty, J. M. Saylor, A L. Eyestone, D. A. Miller, Sam'l J. Metz, H. C Glasgow, S B. Beekly, L B Berkley, A A. Miller, M V B. Turner, Chas. Heller, C. M Mishler, Chas A. Hesse, O Virden, John Palmer, L R Peifer, Samuel Cain, S. G Leversee, Michael Beachley, John M Lichty, Chas. Asquith, Jonas Flickinger, Wesley S Stokes, Levi Strayer, August Boldt, John Asquith, James Holmes, G. W. Strayer and Gilson Gardner.

The method of doing business is very simple and practical. When any member of the association shall sustain a loss or damage by fire, he shall, within ten days after such loss, deliver to the Secretary a particular statement in writing of such loss or damage, signed by him, and verified by his oath or affirmation, and also, if required, by proper vouchers, and stating also the whole cash value of the property lost or damaged, how the building was occupied, and by whom, at the time of the loss, how the fire originated, as far as he knows or believes, and that the fire occurred by misfortune, and without fraud or evil practice; also, declare whether any insurance existed thereon in any other company, and if so, what amount; and if required, submit to a full examination

The Secretary shall, within ten days after receiving a statement of a loss by fire or lightning, call a meeting of the Board of Directors, giving notice to persons interested, of the time and place of meeting. The Board, after examining into the cause and amount of said loss, and being satisfied that the claim is just, shall levy a *pro rata* tax on the amount of protection afforded each member of this Company, and no assessment shall be made unless a loss occurred

WATERLOO

This city, the largest in the State west of Dubuque and north of the line of the Chicago & North-Western Railway, is located on the east side of Township 89, Range 13, nearly in the geographical center of Black Hawk County, of which it is the county seat, is beautifully situated on both banks of the Cedar River, at a point where the timber handsomely opens out into a fine rolling prairie, forming a site as perfectly adapted for the location of a large and healthful city as if it had been specially planned by the Creator for that purpose. The business and residence portion of the town are about equally divided by the river, and are situated on ground which, in the lowest portion, is just above the ordinary high water, and, gradually rising as it recedes, affords some quite elevated and commanding building sites a few blocks back from the business streets, which run parallel with the river on the west side, and at right angles with it on the east, which have only a sufficient grade to afford good drainage. The town is regularly laid out, with most of the streets running parallel and at right angles with the river, which here runs in nearly a southeast direction, although some portion of the east side is laid out north and south. The general appearance and character of the improvements are good, fully equal with those of Eastern towns that possess no larger population. Some really handsome business blocks adorn the principal streets on either side, while the generality of the residences are neat and tasty in their appearance, with a few that are truly palatial in design, external finish and arrangements, surrounded by grounds that cannot fail to attract the attention and secure the approval of the most unobserving. The river, which is here some nine hundred feet in width, has good banks and a solid lime rock bottom, over which the water, clear as crystal, flows in sufficient quantities to afford motive power sufficient to drive almost any amount of machinery. This power, which is among the best, has, though but partially improved, already done much to advance the business prosperity of the town, and is destined at no very distant day to be of still greater value in encouraging manufactures and other material interests, without which no Western town can secure or hold a large business.

FIRST SETTLERS.

In June, 1846, James Virden, then a young man, a Kentuckian by birth, selected a claim on the east side of the river at Prairie Rapids, on Section 23, Township 89, Range 13, just above the original plat of the town of Waterloo. He did some breaking in that season, but did not build a cabin until the next year. About a month later, Charles Mullan and family arrived, and located on the west side of the northwest quarter of Section 26, northwest of the original town plat. Mr. Mullan was from Illinois, and became the first Postmaster at Waterloo, and the first County Surveyor of Black Hawk. He died in August, 1874, at the age of 63 years.

July 26, 1847, George W. Hanna entered Lots Nos. 1, 2 and 3, of Section 26, being that part of the east half of the northeast quarter of Section 26 not covered by the river, and was the first entry of lands on which Waterloo was afterward laid out. In the Spring of 1852, Mr. Hanna built a cabin on the west bank of the river, which was the first house built on the original town plat. It stood about one hundred and fifty feet west of the race bridge on Bridge street, on the site of a building that, in 1878, is called "Nauman's Office," and was occupied in the following Winter by Adam Shipley. The second building on the first town plat was a rude shanty built by Samuel Aldrich, on the east bank of the river, at the corner of Third and Water streets, in the Fall of 1852; and the third by Adam Shipley.

Prior to December, 1851, the place was called Prairie Rapids, or Prairie Rapids Crossing; but at that time the post office was established, and the name selected for it, by Mr. Mullan, was Waterloo   The first platting of the present town site was done in the Fall of 1853, by Charles Mullan, G. W. Hanna and John H. Brooks, and was the westerly portion of the original plat on the West Side.   As originally surveyed in 1853, the town was laid out with due regard to the Government survey, and the streets were laid parallel with the Section lines.   In the Spring of 1854, Lewis Hallock, who owned the balance of the land now in the original plat on that side, joined with Mullan & Hanna, and J. R. Pratt, B. M. Cooley and James Virden, who were the owners of the land on the East Side, had a plat made early in 1854, and then all the parties joined, and the united plat was recorded June 24, 1854.

The Mullan part of the plat of Lots 1, 2 and 3 of Section 26, 89, 13. being the fractional east half of the northeast quarter of Section 26, was pre-empted in 1846, but was not entered until the 3d of May, 1852   Hallock's part of the original plat, on the West Side, was entered by himself February 25, 1853, Lots 5 and 6, Section 25, being on southwest of northwest quarter of that section.   Brooks' part was entered by W J. Barney June 24, 1853, and conveyed to Brooks August 11th, of the same year.

J. R. Pratt's part of the original plat, on the East Side, was entered by Isaac Carr on the 3d of May, 1852, and conveyed to Pratt June 4, 1853.   Cooley's part was entered by George Plaisted June 25, 1852, and purchased by Cooley June 7, 1854 Part of Virden's property was entered by himself January 10, 1853, and the remainder, by W. J Barney May 18, 1853, and conveyed to Virden April 7, 1854.

Since the original plat was made in 1854, a large number of additions have been made, and the primitive town comprises but a small portion of the present thriving city of Waterloo.

THE FIRST HOTEL

In 1853, Adam Shigley had built a story and a half log cabin, about 16x24 feet, on the west bank of the river, near the ferry landing, near the corner of Second street and Cedar avenue.   This was opened as a boarding house and sort of a tavern by Seth Lake, in the Fall of 1853; but it was a primitive affair, and the accommodations exceedingly meager

Very soon after the first survey of the town plat was made, in the Fall of 1853, Jared and —— Emerson, brothers, lumbermen, from Wisconsin, pur-chased Lot 3, Block 8, on the west side of Commercial street, and commenced laying up the walls of a log cabin   But before it was completed they sold out to Solomon Ayers, who completed the building and lived in it during the Win-ter of 1853–4, keeping some boarders, as boarders were plenty and boarding houses few and far between at that time   The next Spring, in April, 1854, Ayers sold to Henry Sherman, who opened the cabin as a tavern, and called it the "Sherman House," which was practically the first hotel in Water-loo.

In the Fall of 1854, he built an imposing two-story frame addition, on the southeast of the original structure   In this building was "the School Section," which those who stopped at the Sherman House in those days may perhaps remember.   The "School Section" was one large room in the loft, in which a dozen or fifteen beds were placed. These beds were numbered from one to fifteen, under Groat's management. It is said that when strangers came, the landlord would very consequentially direct the boy to show the gentleman up to No 10, for instance "Is that a single room?" the guest would query "Certainly, sir! certainly sir!" The guest would vanish under the guidance of the factotum, with a tallow candle, but dismayed at finding fifteen beds in "his single room," each one, perhaps, except the one assigned to him, with two occupants, he would rush down stairs and salute the landlord with, "I thought you said sir, that my room was a single one," only to return with a crest-fallen air to his dormitory when the landlord blandly returned for answer, "Well, is there more than one room up there?"

Besides "the School Section," there was another dormitory with five or six beds in it that was called "the Prairie," the entrance to which was only about three feet high, and which guests entered on their hands and knees.

Sherman was genial, and kept a very fair house for those pioneer times. The old settlers tell numerous humorous stories, however, about the Sherman House and its jolly landlord. Perhaps some of the old settlers may remember Charley McCloud, the tailor, who used to wait on the table for his board. The markets in 1854-5 were not very liberally supplied, but when there were strangers at the table, Charley would politely accost them with "Beef steak, mutton chop, or salt pork, sir?" "I'll take a bit of steak, well done, sir" "All right, sir, in one minute." And away the enterprising waiter would hurry for a plate of fried pork, for he knew that was all the larder afforded; and it was amusing to witness his gravity when he returned with a plate of greasy pork, and handed it to the disappointed guest with "I'm very sorry, sir, but the steak's all out"

In 1856, the house was leased by M. T Williams, familiarly known in this region as "Dad" Williams, and a partner named Eichelberger, who changed its name to Tremont House Mr. Williams' brother, Henry D., came soon after, and became the popular Clerk of the Tremont Eichelberger sold his interest to —— Day, and Day to Fuller, and at the expiration of their lease Sherman again became landlord, and the house was again known as the "Sherman" Soon afterward, he leased to B. F Thomas, under whose administration it was the "Franklin House" Thomas was followed successively by —— Groat, Joseph Henry and —— Cormick, when Sherman resumed possession and again changed the name to the Sherman House. Sherman was followed by C. Brubacker. In April, 1864, Robert W. Chapman and Henry D. Williams purchased the premises and changed the name to the "Central House" In May, 1865, Chapman & Williams removed the "School Section" to the rear, converted it into a kitchen, and erected a three story addition in its former place. In the Spring of 1869, Williams purchased his partner's interest and became sole proprietor, but in 1872, leased to J. J Sanford, and in 1873, sold to his brother, John H. Williams. Should any patron of the old "Sherman," "Tremont" or "Franklin" desire to revive old memories by a glimpse of the "School Section" or the "Prairie," Mr. Williams, of the "Central" will take pleasure in gratifying their wish.

The first tavern on the east side was of logs, built by Samuel L May, on the corner of Fourth and Sycamore street, on which, in 1878, stands Burnham's Block, and was kept by that gentleman until his death in the Winter 1855-6, when it was closed for a short time. It was afterward reopened by Job Engle, succeeded in a short time by his son, John C. Engle, and still later by Asa Shinn

The second hotel was built by Myron Smith, in 1855–6. It was a small frame structure, on Water street, corner of Fifth, where the Key City House now stands.

STORES.

The first store in Waterloo was opened by Nelson Fancher, in 1853, in a log cabin on Third street, Lot 10, Block 2. He afterward sold out to Geo. W. Hanna, who removed to a log building, near where the square brick house is, on Lot 1, Block 1. Henry Kent had a store, in 1854, near the present residence of John Elwell. The ferry landing was in the vicinity of these first stores. In May, 1854, B J Capwell & Co. opened a store in a log building fourteen feet square, on the corner of Block 8, below the Sherman House. Mr. Capwell states that he paid $250 for his corner, which probably included Lots 1 and 2. He found seventeen buildings on the site of Waterloo when he arrived in 1854.

Geo B Pratt and James Virden built and opened the first store on the East Side in 1853, at the corner of Fourth and Water streets. In 1854, Samuel Aldrich opened a grocery on Sycamore street, which was known as "Uncle Sam's Grocery." The public was attracted by a sign, which, although not very artistic, was certainly novel, and read as follows. " Uncle Sam's Grocery; Rough and Reddy. Walk In. Don't be Alarmed ! "

Whitney & Martin opened a store in the same year, and in 1855, S P. Brainard opened a general stock.

MILLS

The first mill was a saw-mill, run by horse power, which was located near where the City Mill now stands, on the West Side, and was put in operation in 1854.

The first movement made toward improving the water-power was made by James Eggers, who, having received permission from the County Court June 20, 1854, immediately commenced constructing a log and brush dam, a little above the present one, and in three weeks after obtaining the permit he had a dam sufficiently high to raise the water two feet.

In 1855, Eggers built and operated a saw-mill. The building is still standing, and is occupied as a furniture factory.

The first flouring-mill was erected in 1856 by G. W. Couch & Co, who commenced grinding early the following Spring. C A. Farwell hauled the water-wheel for this mill from Rock Island, Ill, and the buhrs from Iowa City.

The mill was started with only one run of stones, but another was put in shortly afterward for grinding corn and feed. Previous to the erection of this mill, the settlers were obliged to go to Cedar Falls to mill; and before the mill there was built, Cedar Rapids was the nearest point. This first mill is still standing on the West Side, and is known as the "Waterloo Mill"

The first mill on the East Side was a one-story building, erected by W & E Mears in 1855–6. In 1857, a second story was added, and the machinery for a grist-mill was put in. This mill is still standing, above the "Cedar Mill."

A ferry was established by Samuel L Way in the Fall of 1853. (See "Ferries" in County History, page 326)

PROFESSIONAL, ETC.

The first lawyer to locate in Waterloo was John Randall, who afterward, when County Judge, located the Court House; for which act he has been and will continue to be held in remembrance by the people of the town and county.

The first physician in Waterloo was Dr. —— McKinley, who located here in 1853. He was considered skillful in his profession, and is remembered as an excellent violin player. He did not remain here permanently, removing to Texas in 1854 or '55

The first celebration of the nation's birthday was in 1853 About 200 people gathered on that occasion An arbor was built of brush on the river bank, just above Mill Square, under which tables were spread and a picnic dinner provided Among the speakers were John Virden and John H. Brooks

The next year, 1854, preparations were made for a big time. Various committees were appointed, and a free dinner promised: but before the time appointed there was a "split," and the result was two celebrations—one at the Sherman House, where Edmund Miller read the Declaration of Independence and George Ordway stirred up the American eagle; and the other at or near the Public Square, where G W. Miller and Rev. S W. Ingham performed like services for their country. It is said that Mr Sherman had a flag, the only one in town; but the others, not to be outdone, manufactured one out of unbleached sheeting and red cambric, forty feet long, which floated triumphantly on the appointed day.

In 1855, another grand celebration was held in Virden's Grove, a barbecue in the form of an ox roasted whole being the principal attraction There was also a "horse company," which went through with all sorts of tactics and performed many maneuvers not recognized in military works, to the great edification of the assembled multitude. The barbecue was not a success, the ox being burnt on the outside and much too "rare done" on the inside—an illustration of the old adage that "too many cooks spoil the broth." S W Rawson, Esq , delivered the oration on this occasion, and the instrumental music was furnished by Mason Hale and Elijah Balcom.

The first dance in the town was in Dr. McKinley's log house, 12x14 feet, on the evening of July 4, 1854. It is said that the beauty and fashion of the city were out in full force on that occasion The ball-room stood opposite the present residence of Judge Bagg.

The first bank was opened by A P. Hosford and Edmund Miller, in 1854. Their banking house was a one-story frame building, about 16x24 feet, on the southwest side of Commercial street, above the Sherman House, about where Forry's drug store stands in 1878. April 9, 1855, there was a surplus of $1,200 in the county treasury, which, by order of the County Court the Treasurer was authorized to deposit with Hosford & Miller "on their giving ample security by notes and bonds." J. H. Leavitt, who came to Waterloo in 1854, opened his bank on the opposite side of the street in 1856 William Hammond and R Russell were also engaged in banking in Waterloo at an early day

On the East Side, the first bank was opened in 1867, by C. A. Farwell on the corner of Sycamore and Bridge streets, on the ground now occupied by the First National Bank. This bank was established in February, 1865, on the West Side, with M. H. Moore, President, and G W. Couch, Cashier. It was removed to its present location in February, 1874.

The *Iowa State Register and Waterloo Herald*, was the first paper published in Waterloo The first number bears date of December 8, 1845. A copy, the first sheet printed, was secured by F. S. Washburn, and is preserved by his widow Some extracts from this first paper are entitled to a place in the history of Waterloo. Following the salutatory, in which the editor returns thanks for favors received, is an article headed "Bridge at Waterloo," which he says "is one of the greatest wants of the present time," and concerning which there was considerable discussion, it being a question whether it should be built by subscription or by the county. The subscription plan was evidently the most feasible, as the paper announced that "some $4,000 had already been subscribed," and argued in favor of the construction of a "durable and capacious bridge, with side walks on each side, and room enough between for two teams to pass with ease." Following this is a description of a steam saw-mill then being built F S Washburn. The editor, having attended the raising, pronounced it a jolly affair. The building was fifty feet long by thirty-six feet wide, two stories high, and was to contain a muley, rotary and lath saw and shingle machine, the whole to be operated by a thirty-horse-power engine. The building was about thirty rods above the old railroad crossing, and in 1863 was taken down and the material used in the construction of elevator "B," at the Central Depot. The machinery was used in a mill at Elk Run, and afterward taken to Minnesota

Then comes an article on the "Stage Facilities of Waterloo," starting out with the assertion that "perhaps no place in the West is better favored with conveniences of going everywhere, than Waterloo." The stages left the Sherman House at 6 o'clock every morning for the south; 9 o'clock for the east; and at 2 o'clock in the afternoon for the north and west; and the editor congratulates "our citizens" in having such superior traveling accommodations. The heading of the next article is quite metropolitan; it reads: "Waterloo—Its Population, Business Position and Prospects." It states that the population, taken the week previous, was 903 souls; of which number, 657 were on the West Side, and 246 on the East Side. The article goes on to illustrate the growth of the town, by saying that the year before the population was but 300, and that in the last of June in that year, the census showed 714 inhabitants, and saying that in one year Waterloo had trebled its population It then proceeded to state, "one year ago there were but three stores here; now there are seventeen, among which are dry goods, hardware, stove and tinware, groceries, clothing, bakery, druggists, cabinet, etc., etc. There are 20 carpenter, 3 blacksmith shops, 1 harness shop, 2 shoemaker shops, 1 wagon shop, 2 livery stables and 1 millinery shop, there are also 6 brick makers, 6 attorneys and 4 ministers We have three school houses, two of which are District schools, and one, a Seminary;" and, after discussing various other topics, the article concludes: "Nature has done everything for Waterloo, and her future residents will doubtless do the rest. We now want industry, shrewd management and capital, which will make it one of the largest cities in the interior of the State. As to the two first requisites, we have a large share of those, and we have some of the latter but there is a chance for the investment of any amount of capital to good advantage."

A sale of East Waterloo lots, belonging to the estate of the late Judge Pratt, took place on the 3d, 4th and 5th of December, which was largely attended Bidders were present from New Hampshire, Massachusetts, New York, Wisconsin and other States One hundred and nineteen lots were sold amounting to $15,527. The largest price for a single lot was $200, and one-third of the mill property was sold for $4,067.

A literary society was in existence at that early day, a meeting of which was announced for Friday evening, at which the question for discussion was to be "Do the signs of the times indicate the speedy dissolution of the Union?"

A notice of the "first ball of the season" also appears. This ball was at Capwell's new brick hall, then just completed, below the Sherman House, on the corner of Commercial and Fifth streets. The paper remarks that "all the dancers appeared to be in fine spirits, and no doubt felt highly delighted to feel that the enterprise of Capwell & Co. had supplied a suitable place for their amusement For balls and concerts the hall is well adapted, and we have no doubt it will be well patronized."

November 29, 1855, a Democratic County Convention was held, the proceedings of which were reported in the *Register*. George Ordway was President; S. P. Brainard, Vice President; W H. McClure, Benjamin Winset and S. D. McDowell participated in the proceedings. The resolutions were short and explicit, but read queerly. Among them were the following:

Resolved, That in the main we approve of the administration of Franklin Pierce
Resolved, That the repeal of the Missouri Compromise is just and democratic in its spirit
Resolved, That we adhere firmly to the principles of Jefferson and his illustrious compatriots
Resolved, That we maintain the doctrines of Free Trade and State Rights
Resolved, That we ignore the organization of secret societies in party politics in general, and the party called Know-Nothings in particular

The third term of the Waterloo Seminary was announced to commence in January, 1856 The building was located on the corner of Ninth and Bluff streets, J B. Hewett was proprietor; Otis Daggett, Principal; and Chloe Severance (since Mrs W. Miller), Assistant.

George Ordway started a nursery, a mile or two west of the town, in 1855, and his advertisement appeared in the first paper. Hosford & Miller (A. P. Hosford and Edmund Miller) advertised lands for sale, insurance business, etc, Randall & Miller (J. Randall and G. W Miller), land surveyors and agents Samuel Dearer was stone and brick mason; Williams & Worcester, house, sign and carriage painters; T. H. & J. Elwell, hardware and groceries; B J Capwell & Co., general merchandise; S. P. Brainard advertised his store on the East Side.

The highest water ever known in the Cedar River, at Waterloo, was on the 1st of August, 1858. During the whole season the river was very high, overflowing its banks and stopping the mills. The town was simply a group of islands, and boats sailed about in the streets. The supply of flour in town became exhausted, and for several days the people dieted on hulled corn. George Ordway went to La Porte City after something to eat, and after two days' hard work, by boat and wagon, he succeeded in reaching the submerged city of his home with eight hundred pounds of flour

During that wet season, twenty years ago, most of the business men of Waterloo went bare-footed, and generally with their trousers legs rolled up above their knees In this way they went to church on Sunday, pushing the skiffs, in which the women were, before them through the sloughs Boots and shoes and stockings were at a discount in 1858.

During the season of high water, the current in the river was very rapid, but near the west shore was a large eddy extending for some distance down stream up to the mill In this eddy, or circular current, the townspeople amused themselves in boating. Paddling into the stream at the mill, boats were swept swiftly down the turbulent stream, when, drifting into the eddy, they were carried back again to the point of starting

On Monday, July 19, 1858, William Fiske, Melissa L. Corson, 16 years old, daughter of Charles Corson, and Ellen Case, about the same age, daughter of W Case, crossed the river in a skiff, from the east to the west side, to enjoy the pleasing circular boat-riding with others. After a time they started to return, were drifting down stream, when Fiske's brother, who was standing on shore, shouted to him to use his oars or the boat would be swept on to the island —"Lover's Retreat"—over which the water was about four feet deep. Fiske heeded the caution and commenced rowing, but the boat struck an unseen snag just above the head of the island, instantly capsized, precipitating the occupants into the water. The young ladies were swept under and were drowned Fiske managed to reach a tree on the island, to which he clung until he was rescued in an insensible condition by Dr. McFatrich As soon as he recovered suffi ciently to speak, he asked if the girls were saved, and when told that they were drowned, his intellect gave way and he became insane.

Several weeks afterward, funeral services were held at the Court House by Rev. A. G Eberhart, and a few days afterward the decomposed remains of the un fortunate girls were found in the timber skirting the river about three miles be low the accident Their bodies had become entangled in the thick brush into which they had been swept by the flood, and when the water subsided they rested there, the bones dropping to the ground as the bodies decomposed. They were discovered by a party of men who were traveling through the timber in that vicinity, whose dog brought to them a woman's shoe in which were the remains of a human foot. The shoe was identified as belonging to Miss Case, and after a brief search her remains were found as above described The remains of Miss Corson were found soon afterward, and were identified by a gold chain she wore when she was drowned

The first railroad train on the Dubuque & Sioux City Railroad arrived at Waterloo March 11, 1861 On the Burlington road, trains began to run in Oc tober, 1870

A meeting was held at "Cap's" Hall, Waterloo, August 15, 1861, to con sider the Swamp Land Contract entered into by the County Judge, and a com mittee, composed of C. Mullan, S. D. McDowell and Mr Shaw, was appointed to investigate the transaction.

A "New York Festival" was held at Waterloo, January 22, 1862, with a supper at the Cedar Valley House. The toasts were responded to by Rev. J. Bidlington, Seth Newman, H. C. Raymond, T L. Bowman, S. C. Barber, Rev. O. W Merrill, H. F Peebles, George D Perkins and J. B. Powers

On Saturday, September 22, 1866, the first span on the west end of the bridge across Cedar River at Waterloo, fell into the river, carrying with it three two-horse teams and a single team Mr. Hutton, Supervisor from Bennington, was standing directly over the first pier when the bridge parted, and he was pre cipitated into the pier and was injured severely Several horses were killed. Workmen were engaged in repairing the bridge, which had become unsafe, and they had stretched a rope across to prevent passing, but this was removed by one of the teamsters, who thought he knew better than they whether the bridge was safe. He lost one of his horses and his load of wheat

The Waterloo Woolen Mill was built in 1866, by Messrs. Beck & Nauman, at a cost of $49,000, with Charles Blossburg as Superintendent. The mill com menced running in the Spring of 1867, and was kept in operation, at a sacrifice, until 1875, when it was sold to the Union Mill Company for $11,000. By this company it was rented to Holmes, Emerson & Frances, by whom it was operated until March, 1878. Since that date, it has not been in operation, and can be rented for $800 per annum.

The Waterloo Mill Company was organized in the Fall of 1867. Among the principal stockholders were Hon. S. Bagg, John Elwell, A Hungerford, R. Marson and G W. Couch, the last-named being President. Their mill on the

West Side was built in 1868–9. Seneca Cleaveland was the architect, and William Butterfield, millwright.

The Cedar Mill Company was organized about the same time, perhaps a little before the Waterloo Company, and its mill was built on the East Side in 1867–8. The principal stockholders were W. O. Richards, A Spencer, Nelson Fancher, J Engle and E J. Messinger. Mr. Spencer was President.

In 1873, the Waterloo Mill Company and Cedar Mill Company were consolidated under the name of the Union Mills Company, with T. H Elwell, President, and W. L. Illingworth, Secretary. President in 1878, A. T. Lane, Mr Illingworth still remains Secretary. This company owns twenty-three-twenty-fourths of the Mill Square and splendid water power, the other twenty-fourth being owned by Daniel & Slade, manufacturers of furniture. The Union Mills have 12 run of flouring stones, and manufacture daily 250 barrels of flour, 200 of which are shipped. Three runs of stones for grinding feed turn out 600 car loads of feed annually.

Gem Lodge, I. O of G T., was organized May 1, 1868, with W. W Engle, W. C T.

POLITICAL RECORD

In the Spring of 1854, the town of Waterloo was surveyed and platted, and appears of record. At the November term of the County Court that year, a petition was presented asking the court to order an election, to vote upon the question of incorporation The election was ordered for Monday, the 13th day of November. At the December Term the same year, it is certified that a majority of the votes cast were for incorporation; and another election was ordered on the 13th of January, 1855, for the purpose of choosing three persons to draft Articles of Incorporation, and that is the last entry It is understood, however, that subsequently it was found there had been irregularities in the proceedings, and the matter was dropped in consequence.

After this ineffectual attempt to attain to city honors, the matter was frequently agitated and one or two petitions circulated and presented to the County Court; but none blossomed into another vote until 1868, when, on the 26th day of May, a petition signed by R A Whitaker, H. J. Jenny and thirty-eight others was presented to the County Court, asking for the incorporation of Waterloo as a city of the second class, describing the territory designed to be included within the limits of the corporation, and requesting the court to take requisite steps to order a vote. Whereupon, Judge Daniel W. Foote appointed Samuel D. Shaw, P. J. Siberling, W G. Burbee, Andrew Thompson and Robert Robinson Commissioners to call an election 'of the qualified voters to decide upon the question.

On the 29th of May, the Commissioners issued the notice for an election at Central House, on Monday, the 22d day of June, at which election 679 votes were cast, 372 being in favor of incorporation and 305 against

On the 23d day of June, after certifying the returns, it was ordered and decreed by the court that as a majority of the votes had been cast in favor of incorporation, and the provisions of the law had been complied with, the city of Waterloo was incorporated as a city of the second class.

On the 29th day of June, the Commissioners issued a notice for an election of officers, to be held at the Commercial Hotel (on the East Side), on Monday, the 20th day of July, at which time the following officers were elected: Mayor, R A. Whitaker; Marshal, S M. Hoff; Treasurer, C. A. Farwell, Solicitor, Lewis Lichty, Clerk, J. S. George. Trustees—First Ward, H B. Allen, G.

Conger; Second Ward, W. A. Crowther, John Hilferty; Third Ward, Sullivan Day, F. E Cutler; Fourth Ward, R. D. Titcomb, Allen Spencer.

The first ordinance passed by the new City Council was one fixing the rates for licenses for circuses and menageries.

On the 1st day of March. 1869, the first regular election for city officers was held, R. A. Whitaker being elected Mayor, Marshal, J P. Evans, Treasurer, C. A. Farwell; Solicitor, Lewis Lichty, Clerk, Lewis Lichty; Assessor, A. C. Bunnell   Trustees—First Ward, H W Jenney, Henry Nauman; Second Ward, L. C. Barber, C. W. Champlin, Third Ward, F. E. Cutler, Sullivan Day; Fourth Ward, D. E Champlin, R. D. Titcomb.

OFFICERS OF THE CITY OF WATERLOO FROM 1870 TO 1878.

Mayors—R. A. Whitaker, 1868–72; Lewis Lichty, 1873–6; Matt Parrott, 1876–

Clerks—Lewis Lichty, 1869–72, William Galloway, 1873, J. H. Kuhns, 1874.

Treasurers—J H Leavitt, 1870–71, H Nauman, 1872–3; C. A. Farwell, 1876; John W Krupfle, 1877; A. C. Bunnell, 1878.

Marshals—J. P. Evans, 1870–72; James Ellis, 1873; J P Evans, 1874–5; H H Saunders, 1876–7, H. W. Jenney, 1878.

Trustees for 1870—First Ward, H W. Jenney, A T Lusch; Second Ward, J H Preston, C. W. Champlin; Third Ward, H. E. Cutler, H. M. Crittenden; Fourth Ward, R. D Titcomb, W Russell

For 1871—First Ward, A T Lusch, G. W. Barnes; Second Ward, J. H. Preston, J. S George; Third Ward, H. M Crittenden, H. B. Gifford, Fourth Ward, W W. Russell. O. E. Hardy.

For 1872—First Ward, G. W Barnes, L. A Cobb; Second Ward; J S. George, William Hammond; Third Ward, H. M Crittenden, C. G Ankeny; Fourth Ward, W W Russell, T. W. Place (elected to fill vacancy of O E. Hardy, who resigned March 1, 1872).

For 1873—First Ward, G. W Barnes, L. A. Cobb, Second Ward, Wm. Hammond, J. A. Fowler; Third Ward, H. M. Crittenden, Matt Parrott; Fourth Ward, T W Place, A C. Bratnober, resigned May 7th, and W. Russell elected to fill vacancy.

For 1874—First Ward, G. W Barnes, R. Russell; Second Ward, J. A. Fowler, J Taylor: Third Ward, Matt Parrott, John McCabe, Fourth Ward, T W. Place, W. Russell.

For 1875—First Ward, R. Russell, G W. Barnes; Second Ward, J. Taylor, Frank Neely (resigned November 3d, and W. A. Crouther, elected to fill vacancy); Third Ward, John McCabe, M Ricker; Fourth Ward, Adam Rosgen, Andrew Thompson (to fill vacancy), W. Russell (resigned end of first year), D. B. Stanton (resigned April 5th).

For 1876—First Ward, G W. Barnes, Frank Neely, Second Ward, W A. Crowther, James Ellis; Third Ward, M. Ricker, John Palfreyman; Fourth Ward, Adam Rosgen, D. R Weaver

For 1877—First Ward, Frank Neely, H Nauman; Second Ward, James Ellis, G. J. Mack; Third Ward, John Palfreyman, F. S. Morrill; Fourth Ward, D. R. Weaver (resigned November 7th), Louis Lichty (elected to fill vacancy), T W. Place.

For 1878—First Ward, H. Nauman, Frank Neely; Second Ward, G. J. Mack, C. J. Maynard; Third Ward, F. S. Morrill (resigned May 8), John T. Moran, W. W Miller; Fourth Ward, T. W. Place, Lewis Lichty.

EDUCATIONAL.

The first school house in Waterloo was about 16x22 feet, built of logs, on Lot 8, Block 7, on Jefferson street, between Fourth and Main. It was standing until 1877, when it was removed to give place to a brick stable It was erected in the Spring of 1853, and the first school in it was kept by Miss Eliza May, afterward Mrs. Isaac Virden This log school house was used on the Sabbath for church, the Baptists, Presbyterians and Methodists occupying it alternately.

In 1860, a school house was built on the site the present one now occupies.

March 19, 1866, in accordance with an order of the Township Trustees, an election was held making West Waterloo an independent school district, and electing the following Board · S. D. Shaw, President; I S Shaw, Vice President, E R Ware, Secretary, D. W. Foote, Treasurer, P. J. Barber, P Smith, D. B. Stanton, Directors

In 1871, the present school house was built by Jacob Reichards; cost nearly $20,000, and was first under the care of Mr. Hood, Principal The present Principal is W. H Robertson.

The first school on the East Side was taught by O. E Hardy, in the Winter of 1854–5, in a house then occupied by Myron Smith, but which was afterward a part of the Key City House Afterward, Hardy transferred the school to a small building in the rear of Colburn & Geddes' marble shops

The Know-Nothings of that day used to assemble in the same building, which was subsequently used for a store by James Evans.

The first school house on this side was a grout building, erected in 1855, on what is called Church Donation Block It was used as a school house until 1862. Schools were thereafter taught in private buildings until 1864, when a brick school house of four rooms was erected on Block 40, in which C. O. Knepper taught the first school

The Independent School District of East Waterloo, was organized in April, 1866, with the following first Board O E Hardy, President, Lewis Lichty, Vice President R. A. Whitaker, Secretary; M H. Voorhees, Treasurer.

The primary school house in the Third Ward was built in the Fall of 1869, and Miss Hattie Wainwright employed as one of the first teachers

The present school building on Block 76, Fourth Ward, was built in 18—, and its first Principal was Prof. J K. Sweeney, who still occupies the position

Prairie Home Seminary —In 1862, Miss Anna Field, a graduate of Mt. Holyoke Seminary, erected a large and handsome brick building at the head of Main street, designed both for school and dwelling purposes, and in the same year opened the " Prairie Home Female Seminary," which became widely and popularly known as an excellent and well-managed institution It continued as a female seminary until 1874, when young men were admitted and " Female" was dropped from the name The average attendance for the past year was about forty-five. Common school branches are principally taught. Miss Field is still the Principal of the seminary

Iowa State Conservatory of Music —Established in 1877, by E. W Burnham. It is conducted in the second and third stories of Burnham's Opera House, where everything is admirably adapted for the purpose. The Conservatory employs two learned musicians as teachers, and has an average of about one hundred students

Burnham's Opera House.—Erected in Fall of 1877, and, although not possessing the external grace and beauty of some similar edifices, its interior is singularly adapted to the purposes for which it was built. Its stage is one of the largest in the State, and the main hall has a seating capacity of 1,000 people. The scenery was painted by F. L. Lowell & Co, of Chicago The Opera House was opened by the Emma Abbott Concert Troupe, in November, 1877

The Cedar River Institute.—Established in Waterloo about 1875, by Mrs. C. L Billings, who was an excellent teacher, but was compelled to suspend on account of ill health, at the close of 1877.

Our Lady of Victory —The school of the above name is located at Waterloo, and is conducted by the Sisters of Charity, B. V. M It was first opened in August, 1872, and has proved quite a prosperous venture. As is the rule in Catholic schools, special attention is given here to music, languages and deportment (See Catholic Church.)

RELIGIOUS

First Baptist Church.—A Baptist Church was organized in 1853, without any regular Pastor The first service was held in a log school house near the residence of George R. Crittenden. Rev Mr. Bicknell, a local minister, and Elder Knapp, of Cedar Falls, held services occasionally.

The first Pastor was Rev J C. Miller. Under his pastorate, services were held in what is now known as Capwell's Hall

In September, 1857, Rev A. G Eberhart commenced his labors with the Church, and on the 12th day of April following, the society was incorporated under the laws of Iowa. The original incorporators were Nelson Ayers, T I Messick, Henry Sherman, Nehemiah J. Randolph, William C. Clough, Rufus Ordway and Reuben Rush.

During the first few months of Mr. Eberhart's ministry, services were held in what was then known as Benight's Hall. Soon after the society was incorporated, they purchased their present house of worship of the Presbyterian society. Mr. Eberhart remained with the Church some four years, and left it in a very prosperous condition.

Rev. Frank Miller succeeded Mr. Eberhart as Pastor, remaining only a short time, and was followed by Rev C. Billings Smith, who continued with the Church some two years. After Mr. Smith's resignation, Rev. William L. Hunter supplied the pulpit some time before his ordination, and after it, remained with the Church nearly four years as its Pastor. He had the pleasure of seeing the Church increase largely in numbers and influence. He was followed by Rev. William Tilley, who remained one year, and was succeeded by Rev. E. K. Cressey, who resigned after terminating his first year. Rev. A. G Eberhart was again called, but was obliged to resign in a short time on account of ill health. Rev. A. A. Russell followed Mr. Eberhart, but his labors were soon brought to a close on account of failing health He was succeeded by the present Pastor, Rev Richard Garton

The Church records were burned with the house of Dr A. B. Mason, therefore we cannot give the number received into the church by baptism and otherwise during the twenty-two years of its existence.

The present membership is about two hundred and fifty. The church and society are in a very prosperous condition, sustaining one of the largest Sabbath schools in the place, with a large library. The Church now numbers about three hundred and fifty

The present officers are as follows : Pastor, Rev. Robert Garton ; Deacons, E G Baker, H. M Van Buren, H. N. Ayers, Samuel Hall, C. P. Jones, A.

CEDAR FALLS

J. Edwards; Clerk, E. V. Hayden, Treasurer. J Taylor; Collector, C F Morrill; Trustees, D. F Crouse, Robert Williams, John Sine, J. E Chapman, A. J. Edwards, S. Bagg, I. Taylor, Sabbath School Superintendent, H. T Roberts; Assistant Superintendent, G D. Frink Connected with the church is a Woman's Foreign Missionary Society, officered as follows: Mrs. D. F. Crouse, President; Mrs C K. Howe, Vice President, Mrs. D. B. Ames, Secretary; Mrs W. H H. Becker, Treasurer. The Ladies' Benevolent Society: Mrs. D. Z Hartman, President; Mrs. Kate Frink, Vice President; Mrs W H. H. Becker, Secretary; Mrs. Frank Ricker, Treasurer; and also the Young Ladies' Home Mission Society: President, Miss Sadie Waychoff, Vice President, Miss O. Right; Secretary, Miss T. Magnis The Church is in a prosperous condition

The Congregational Church.—At a meeting convened at the school house in Waterloo on Saturday evening, August 23, 1856, by those interested in the principles of Congregationalism, Rev. Oliver Emerson, agent of the American Missionary Association, was called to the chair, and John H. Leavitt was chosen Clerk.

As a result of this meeting, a council was called for the purpose of organizing a church, September 24th, of same year, Rev. G H. Woodward, of Toledo, Moderator, and Rev. A Graves, of York, Scribe. The meeting was held in the log school house.

The council were unwilling to advise an increase in the number of churches in town without prayerful consideration of the subject. But this was before the slavery question had been settled by the war, and when some branches of the Presbyterian system were maintaining a complicity with "the slave power," and also at a period of the adoption of the "Church Extension Scheme," which finally resulted in breaking up the old union principles between Congregationalists and Presbyterians.

Had the present comity and good feeling between the two denominations existed twenty years ago, it is very doubtful if the Congregational Church of Waterloo had been organized Among reasons given for the formation of the new society (many of which are now dead issues and not wisely revived), the originators say, "We wish to adhere to the faith of our fathers, because a departure from it by so many of our brethren has injured the cause of truth, by giving occasion to the representation that this course is a confession on their part that their principles are not worth maintaining."

In an account of the organization, a writer in the Congregational *Herald* says: "The village of Waterloo is beautifully located on the Cedar River, about ninety miles from the Mississippi, on the line of the Dubuque & Pacific Railroad. Two and a half years since, it consisted of a dozen log cabins. It now embraces more than twelve hundred souls, and is rapidly increasing in population and wealth. In illustration of the rapidity with which the village and vicinity are advancing, it may be stated that five saw-mills are constantly in motion to supply building material, besides a large quantity of fine lumber brought from the Mississippi. The little Church now organized are in pressing need of a faithful minister, they think themselves able to pay one-half his salary, and, with assistance for a short time, will be able to assume his entire support."

The original members were: Abram P. Hosford, J. P White, Cynthia White, L. B Worcester and wife, and John H Leavitt. The Deacons first chosen were J P. White and L. C. Sanborn. The first Clerk was John H Leavitt, and first Pastor, Rev T S La Due The society first held its meetings in the old log school house on Jefferson street, afterward, in Benight's Hall, corner Fourth and Commercial streets, and in Capwell's Hall, corner Fifth and Commercial

In December, 1856, the Church was duly and wisely incorporated, "for the purpose of taking charge of the financial interests of the Church," "the incorporation to commence January 1, 1857, and continue twenty years, with the right of renewal." The incorporators were. A. P. Hosford, L. B. Worcester, L. C Sanborn, J P. White and J. H. Leavitt. There is no record of any infirmity or inadequacy of this body politic to provide for its own wants and interests.

The present site of the church was occupied in 1857, the lower part of the edifice being used till 1862, when the upper part was finished and occupied without essential change till 1872, when both stories were thrown into one, and an extension of twenty feet added. The first pipe organ was brought to Waterloo by E. W Burnham, Esq., in 1864, and placed in this church. It is a small but sweet-toned instrument, and now adorns the Congregational Church at Independence. Mr. Burnham purchased the great organ in 1872, which is rented by the society In 1869, the society built a commodious parsonage on the corner of Washington and Fourth streets, this was first occupied by Dr Geo. Thacher, Pastor, subsequently President of Iowa State University. According to the records, the first member admitted to the Church upon profession of faith, was Mrs. Wheeler, now Mrs. Wm. Robinson. The first baptism of adults was Mary Manwell, and of infants, Roger Leavitt

The ministers who have supplied the Church, are as follows· Revs Thomas S La Due, John S Whittlesey, Orville W. Merrill, Smith B. Goodenow, Edward S Palmer, W H Marble, George Thacher, D. D , late President of the State University, Alfred A. Ellsworth and Henry S DeForest The pastorate of the latter terminated in April, 1878, since which time the Church has been destitute of a Pastor.

The Deacons have been : A. P. Hosford, L. C Sanborn, L. B. Worcester, J. P White, H A. Lane, M L. Burnham and J. H. Goodrich.

Clerks—John H Leavitt, O W Merrill, H. A. Lane, C. T. Ingersoll, H. Belden, J. H. Goodrich and M. K Cross

The Sunday school was not organized till the second or third year after the Church, and has been superintended, for one year or more, by H A. Lane, A. P Hosford, Geo Ordway, J. H. Leavitt, H. W. Knapp, F. E. Churchill, C. W Von Coelln, Dr G J. Mack, and others for a shorter term

The Church now numbers about 230, the Sabbath school, 150. The officers of the Church and society are· Pastor. ——. —— ——; Deacons, Dr M. L Burnham, J. H. Goodrich, Esq., Mr Henry A. Lane ; Clerk of the Church, Rev. M. K. Cross, Superintendent of Sunday school, Dr G G. Mack ; Secretary, Schuyler Mitchell ; Librarian, E. S. Cobb

The first Trustees of the society. incorporated April 16, 1874, were: J. H. Leavitt, G W. Gilbert, N S Hungerford ; Clerk of the society, J H. Preston. Present Trustees· W. W. Forry, Dr. G J Mack and C. P. Hunt, Clerk, J. H Preston

St Mark's Episcopal Church —The first Episcopal service ever held in Waterloo was on Sunday, Aug 3, 1856, at which time Rt. Rev H. W. Lee, then Bishop of the Diocese of Iowa, made his first visit to this place Services were held in the morning at Capwell's Hall, on the West Side. and in the Grout school house, on the East Side, in the afternoon. In the evening, a meeting was held at Capwell's Hall, and an organization of a parish effected under the name of St Thomas'.

The names of the persons subscribing to the Articles of Association were Charles Fiske, James S. George, J. C. Hubbard, J. H. Wilkins, William Haddock and Edmund Miller, and the first vestry elected consisted of the above gentlemen, with the exception of Mr. Haddock. Mr George is the only one of the above now a resident of Waterloo.

The first officiating minister was Benjamin R Gifford, who commenced his labors the following year, the society holding its services in Day's Hall, on the East Side. Mr. Gifford remained with the society until some time in 1859. Services were also held at Capwell's Hall, on the West Side, and at the Court House occasionally, until the completion of Russell's Hall, when that was secured by lease

Rev. W. F. Lloyd succeeded to the rectorship in 1860, and held regular services in Russell's Hall, and continued as Rector until 1864. At a meeting held April 6, 1863, the name of the parish was changed from St. Thomas' to St. Mark's, for irregularities in the organization under the former name At the termination of Mr. Lloyd's term the society was without a Rector for some time, occasional services being held by Rev Henry C. Kinney, who also officiated at Cedar Falls.

Rev. W. T. Campbell was called in October, 1866, and remained with the parish for about one year, services still being held in Russell's Hall. In June, 1867. Rev. S. D. Day was called to minister to the parish, and in the year following, the present church edifice was commenced. The Building Committee consisted of the Rector, R. Russell and A. T. Lusch. The foundation was not finished until late, and the frame was raised Sept. 21, 1868. The work was prosecuted as fast as possible, much of the plastering and inside work being completed during the Winter.

The ladies belonging to the society rendered valuable and efficient services in raising funds, and through their exertions most of the adornments were procured

The first service held in the church was held in the latter part of February, 1869, Mr. Day preaching the first sermon to a very large congregation. He retained his connection with the parish until 1871.

For several months after Mr. Day's removal, the parish was without a Rector Rev. J. E Ryan was called late in 1871, but did not commence his labors until January, 1872, and is still the Rector.

R Russell was elected a member of the vestry in May, 1858, and has been continued in that office ever since—over seventeen years. Jas S. George was a member from the organization until 1865, and for a number of years was Clerk J. P. Evans also had a long service as Vestryman C. A Farwell was first elected in 1861, and continued a member of the vestry until 1868. Messrs. William Snowden, H. B. Allen, R A. Whitaker, J. L Cooley, H. W. Sill and Morris Case were among the earlier members of the vestry. Rev. Mr. Ryan is still presiding.

First Methodist Episcopal Church.—Among the first Methodists of this city were Mr. James Virden, George W. Hanna and Mrs Mullan In 1852, there was a regular appointment for "circuit" preaching at James Virden's house on the East Side. Waterloo was made a station in 1855. Rev. A Coleman was Presiding Elder, and Rev S. W. Ingham, Pastor Mr Ingham was a local minister, much beloved, and an earnest preacher. When the first school house was built, the preaching service was held there.

During the year, an extensive revival occurred, and over one hundred were added to the society A Mr. Daggett, who taught the school, and who was a local preacher in the church, rendered the Pastor efficient and in the work. The meetings during the revival were held in the old brick seminary, corner of Bluff and Ninth streets, West Side. Among others who joined the Church, as the fruit of the revival, were Mr Benjamin Stewart and wife, and Mrs. G. W Miller, who still remain in the society.

Rev J. G. Witted was appointed to the station in 1856, and occupied as the place of worship the stone hall then owned by John McD. Benight, now occupied as an office by Dr. Mack. The salary of the Pastor at that time was $760, and all paid. This certainly was much to the credit of the society.

The following persons composed the Board of Stewards for that year: John McD. Benight, Guy R. Benight, G. W Hanna, Stephen Bush, Benj. Stewart and Mr. Hewett E. V Cooley and John C. McIlmoil were Class Leaders.

In 1857, Rev. Mr Sessions was Pastor, with the services held in Capwell's brick hall. A good revival was enjoyed this year. He was followed by Rev. H. Hood, for the year 1858, and Rev E A. Hill, in 1859, succeeded Mr. Hood. In 1860-61 Rev. R Ridlington was Pastor. During his pastorate, the society prepared to build a house of worship, and before his removal the lot was purchased and the foundation laid. The Trustees of the society at this time were: Stephen Bush, Edmund Miller, G. W. Hanna, H. C. Drew, Benj, Stewart and Isaac Parmenter.

Rev Mr. Holmes followed Mr. Ridlington, in 1862, and this year the church was inclosed In 1863, Rev Wm M. Sampson was appointed Pastor, but remained only a part of the year, the Rev. Dr. Thomas filling out the time.

The basement of the church was occupied during the Winter of 1863-4, and in the Autumn of 1864, Rev. Bishop Scott presided over the deliberations of the Upper Iowa Conference, which met in this city, and held its sessions in the basement. At the close of the Conference, Rev. Dr. John Bowman became Pastor During his year of service the society was divided and the Church on the East Side was formed and their house of worship erected.

Rev. S A. Lee was the minister for 1865-6, and during his pastorate the church building was finished and dedicated, and the society was blessed with a gracious revival.

Dr. Fairall followed Mr. Lee for the year 1867. Rev. U. Eberhart served as Pastor during 1868-9. In 1870-71, Rev. D Sheffer was the minister, and the society was favored with a good revival. In 1872, Rev W. Frank Paxton was appointed Presiding Elder, and Rev. S. A. Lee returned as the Pastor. Rev W P. Watkins was appointed Pastor for 1873.

In October, 1874, Rev J. T. Crippen was transferred from the Central New York Conference and stationed over this Church, which then had a membership of about one hundred and eighty. The society owns a comfortable church and parsonage, upon which there is no indebtedness. The Sunday school is in a prosperous condition, with a library, to which has been recently added one hundred dollars worth of books G. W. Miller is Superintendent, and I. M Hay, Assistant

The following compose the present Board of Church officials ·

Trustees—C. Brubacher J. S Glover, D. W. Foote, J. P. Hummill, W P. Strayer, G W. Miller and Samuel Deaner

Stewards—J. S. Glover, C. Brubacher, H. S. Van Buren, B. McCormick, A. Anderson, 1. Hossman, W T. Spencer, Benj. Stewart and I. M. Hay.

Class Leaders—W. P. Carpenter and W. W. Evans.

Following Mr. Crippen came Rev. Mr Allen, who came in 1876 and stayed until 1877, when the present Pastor, Rev. H O. Pratt, took charge

East Side Methodist Church.—At an early day, it became apparent that the division of the city by the river would necessitate the organization of a second M E. Church, one on the east side, in addition to the one already in operation on the west side of the Cedar river.   Accordingly, the records show that a Board of Trustees was organized and Articles of Incorporation adopted as early as March 22, 1861, by the following citizens : J.'W. Hankinson, G. R Benight, D. B. Gilbert, Joseph Gorrell, J. W. Ayres, Albert R. Hale and David Edwards.   Also that at their first meeting a church was proposed and discussed.

At their second meeting, June 16, 1862, J S Barbee, A. C. Bunnell and Thomas Brooks were elected instead of Messrs. Benight, Gilbert and Edwards, and a committee was appointed to inquire into the feasibility of securing church room in connection with the school building then about to be erected in East Waterloo   That being impracticable, at their next meeting, February 21, 1865, it was resolved to proceed immediately to take necessary steps to build a church The new members of the Board were E. P. Albee, Wm Gilchrist, R A Whitaker and George W Hawver.   Messrs. Barbee, Hankinson and Hawver, were the Committee to estimate the cost, and Messrs. Hankinson, Gilchrist and Albee were to supervise the erection of said building   The size resolved upon was 36x58.   Proposals were received, and J. S. Barbee was assigned the contract.   The church was finished and dedicated by Rev Dr. Kynett, in September, 1865, and Mr. Barbee settled with in October, 1865, paying him in full $4,600.   Some of the subscriptions were not paid and had to be advanced, for which a mortgage was given, which mortgage and interest, amounting to some $1,300, was finally raised and paid in September, 1873, freeing the property from all incumbrance

The parsonage, which, with the furniture, is valued at $2,500, was built in 1869, under the ministry of Rev. E. L Miller, the Building Committee consisting of Edmund Miller, A. C. Bunnell and William Gilchrist.

The first Sunday school met in a frame building on the bank of the river, known as Evans' Building, officered by John W. Ayers and J. W. Hankinson, at which time J. G. Witted, the sailor-preacher, was Pastor of the M. E. Church in Waterloo; thence to the Court House, with A. C. Bunnell, Superintendent. Afterward, Day's Hall was the Sunday school room, said hall being a brick building on the site where the *Reporter* Block now stands.   The Sunday school remained in Day's Hall until removed to the new church, in September, 1865.

Johnson B Hewitt was the first Class Leader, a devout and useful man, whose life was finally sacrificed on the altar of his country   Following him in that sub-pastorate were E. P. Albee and A C. Bunnell, successively.

Among the early members, besides the first mentioned Trustees and their families, were Mrs Polly May, Mrs E. Virden, Mrs. E. Doxey, and Mrs J. Higgins and daughter.

The Upper Iowa Conference held its sessions in Waterloo, in 1864.   The venerable Bishop Scott presided, and was the guest of Edmund Miller.

At that session, Rev. John Bowman was appointed Pastor, under whose ministry the first church was erected.   Since then, the following ministers have served as Pastors : Revs R. N. Earhart, J B. Casebeer, E L. Miller, H. S. Church, G. W. Brindell, and Rev. J. R. Berry, now closing with his third and final year in this city.   Under his pastorate the Church has had great prosperity ; over 130 members have been added to the Church, and a new and beautiful church erected at a cost of $18,000   The corner stone was laid July 4, 1877, by Rev W. H. Perrine, D. D., of Albion, Mich.   The building was finished and dedicated Dec. 30, 1877, by Rev. Bishop E G. Andrews, D. D

DESCRIPTION OF THE CHURCH.

The building is in Gothic style The foundations are of stone, rustic ashlar, superstructure of brick, tastefully trimmed with terra cotta and white brick The form of the building is nearly that of a Greek cross; the main axis, the entire length of the foundation, being 104 feet, the transverse axis 67 feet There are 3 gables, each 50 feet from the base, with rear gable of 30 feet elevation The tower, with double front, is 14 feet square, 53 feet above water table, surmounted by a mansard roof, 18 feet, making the total height of tower, from level of street, 76 feet. The apex of the entire roof is finished in iron cresting, with finials at corners In each gable there is a large triple-sashed window 9x20 feet, in Gothic form, supported by side windows of similar style, 2x8 feet. There are three double and two single entrances, all surmounted by Gothic arches

The interior wood-work is finished in white and black walnut The entire building is wainscoted in white, with base and rail in black. The ceiling is panel-work of white, with rails in black and sham trusses in white walnut, likewise pews, chancel and choir, all finished in Gothic style. The front projection contains the lecture or Sabbath school room, and is 27x45 feet, with class-room adjoining, 15x15 feet, and separated by folding doors. The transepts contain the main auditorium, 45x62 feet, with front vestibule, 11x11 feet, and north vestibule, 6x15 feet The chancel is a semi-circle, 9x18 feet, at the rear of which is the orchestra, 6x18 feet, and back of this the organ loft, 8x18 feet. At the rear of the building, on each side, is a vestibule, 5x9 feet, leading from the auditorium to the parlors, and also connecting with outside entrances The parlors are 14 feet square, connected by folding doors.

The pews are arranged in a semi-circle, the aisles radiating from a center just back of the pulpit. By this excellent plan every auditor in every pew in the house directly faces the speaker There are 105 pews, with seating accommodations for 450 persons. By a simple and ingenious arrangement, the baseboard around the whole auditorium is hinged so that it can be easily raised and form a seat, thus adding about 150 more to the seating capacity. The lecture-room, while it is directly in front of the pulpit, is separated from the main room by sliding doors of ground glass. These are hung on weights and can be dropped easily into the basement, thereby throwing the two rooms together and making an auditorium in extreme length 62x87 feet, and capable of seating 900 persons.

The principal windows are in memory of Mr. Edmund Miller, a former member and Trustee of the church, and were presented by his widow and sisters.

First Presbyterian Church.—The First Presbyterian Church of Waterloo was organized by Rev N. C. Robinson, on the 17th day of September, 1854, with a membership of six, viz : George Ordway, Mrs George Ordway, Mrs. Marilla Beauchine, Mrs. Alvira Barrett, Zimri Streeter and Mrs. Charlotte Lake Mr. Robinson continued to preach to the Church once in two or three weeks until late in the Fall of 1854, when he accepted a call to the church in Vinton.

In the Fall of 1854, Rev James M. Phillips commenced his labors at Waterloo, Cedar Falls and Janesville; residing at Cedar Falls, and continued to preach at Waterloo once in two weeks for about one year

Mr Phillips was succeeded in the Fall of 1856 by Rev Moses Robinson, who devoted his whole time to this society, and during his ministry of about one year, the erection of a church was commenced.

Rev. James Harrison, still a much esteemed and honored resident of Waterloo, was the next Pastor of the church, commencing his labors in the Summer of 1856 and continuing until the Spring of 1868. At that time, Rev. William Fithian assumed the pastorate, and continued for several months in charge.

The first church building, now occupied by the Baptist society, was commenced in 1856, but was not finished until the following year, and was dedicated in the Fall. When the society began planning for the edifice the country was in a flourishing condition, settlers were coming in rapidly, money was comparatively plenty, and no one expected a sudden change, such as followed. The society planned for the future, and built accordingly; but when the financial crash of 1857 came, could not fulfill their engagements. Aid that had been promised in the East failed to come, owing to a bank failure, property began to depreciate and members to scatter. With all these discouraging surroundings, it was thought best to sell the property, which was accordingly done. After the sale of the church, the society was for a long time without a Pastor, and its usual services were suspended.

During the years 1860 and 1861, occasional services were held, and a small part of the time regularly once in two weeks, conducted by Rev. James M. Phillips, of Cedar Falls, and Rev. David Blakely, who then resided near Waterloo, on a farm, and by occasional supplies.

Late in the year 1864, Rev. Stephen Phelps, now a resident of Vinton, commenced his labors with this Church in Russell Hall, and continued to labor with great acceptability till his health failed, in the Spring of 1869, when he resigned his pastorate. The present pleasant and commodious brick church on the corner of Fourth and Jefferson streets, was erected during the Summer of 1867, and dedicated free of debt in November of that year. The building was not completed without a struggle, and only with the assistance of contributions from abroad, and a donation from the Church Erection Committee of the Presbyterian Church. Prominent among the contributors was Myron Phelps, Esq., of Lewistown, Ill., father of Pastor Phelps, a most exemplary and Christian man, who gave over $1,000.

In the Summer of 1869, Rev. A. R. Olney, just graduated at Union Theological Seminary, New York, commenced his labors as Pastor of this church, and continued with them one year. He was succeeded by Rev W. W. Thorp in the Fall of 1870. During the year 1871, funds were raised for the purchase of a pipe organ, and an addition was built in the rear for an " organ loft " and Pastor's study, with session room, etc. The advent of the organ was celebrated with a concert at the church on the evening of November 22, 1871, at which the superior merits of the instrument were fully demonstrated.

Early in 1873, Mr. Thorp tendered his resignation, to take effect the first Sunday in March. After his departure, there were only occasional services until in August, 1873, when Rev. I. E. Carey commenced his labors. Since that time the pulpit of the Church has been filled by Rev. Mr. Carey, Rev. A. K. Baird, Rev. Geo R. Carroll and Rev. Rockwood McQuesten, the present Pastor. The present Elders are · W. C. Morris, A. W. Morrill, E. A. Raymond, W. H Curtis, R. F Sulzer and George Ordway ; W. C. Morris, Clerk.

The members on the church record now numbers about 107. The Sunday school, Prof. W. H. Robertson, Superintendent, averages about 100 pupils, and the library contains about 300 volumes ; E. A. Raymond, Librarian.

The Catholic Church —The first Catholics are believed to have located in Waterloo in the year 1852 or 1853. For a year or two, they were visited occasionally by Rev. Fathers Slattery and Baumgartner, the latter of whom then resided at Gilbertville. About this time, Waterloo and the surrounding missions were given in charge of Rev John Sheil, who fixed his residence in Waverly, Bremer County, and for some years attended to the spiritual wants of the few Catholics scattered through the surrounding counties.

In 1856, through the exertions of Mr. B Kelly, two lots were purchased, and the first church edifice erected on the corner of Mulberry and Third streets, East Side.

In the Spring of 1867, Rev. Mr. Shiel was succeeded in the mission by Rev. M. Flavin, who remained only one year, and in the Spring of 1868, was succeeded in turn by Rev. P. J. R Murphy, who, like his predecessors, resided in Waverly He continued in charge of the missions until the time of his death, which occurred in August, 1869. During the Summer of 1868, Father Murphy caused the church to be enlarged to its present size On the 23d of October, 1869, Rev N F Scallan, the present Pastor, arrived in the city, and became the first resident Pastor of the chuich. In the Spring of 1870, the pastoral residence, a neat frame structure, was erected near the church

In September, 1871, one-fourth of a block was purchased on the corner of Mulberry and Second streets, and the foundations laid for a Catholic school building, which was completed in August of the following year. This building, known as the School of Our Lady of Victory, is 50x50 feet, two stories high. It affords a residence to the Sisters of Charity, B V M , who have charge of the school, and ample accommodations for 250 pupils. The Sisters opened school August 26, 1872, and the attendance has generally averaged 200 pupils The number of teachers constantly employed is five, which may be increased at any time the number of pupils may demand it. The branches taught include all those usually comprised in an academic course. Pupils of any denomination may be admitted, but are always required to conform to the external usages of the institution.

The congregation of St. Joseph's Church numbers, at present, somewhat over one hundred families, who are already taking steps toward the erection of a new and more commodious church

Evangelical Association—In the year 1857, the Cedar Valley country was taken up as a mission field by the Illinois Conference of the Evangelical Association, and that year Jacob Schœffle and J Mohr were sent by said Conference to seek the German settlers in these regions, and preach the Gospel of Christ among them ; and as far as we can learn, Schœffle was the first German missionary who passed through Waterloo. Finding no opening in this place, he passed on to Cedar Falls, where he found an open door.

In the following year, H. Kleinsorge, as successor to Schœffle, took up Waterloo as an appointment ; but his mission field being too large, extending from La Porte City north into Bremer County, west into Hardin County, and to Fort Dodge, and the Germans then but few in Waterloo, he did not preach here very often.

In 1861, H Hinze was sent to this mission, but he only preached occasionally in Waterloo. C. Pfile, also from the same Conference, visited Waterloo at intervals Then followed Jacob Kieper, from the same Conference, who preached several times in Waterloo, during the year 1863.

In 1864, C. Berner was sent to this field of labor. A Conference had been organized in Iowa, and, as the mission territory was more divided, he could pay more attention to Waterloo, and preached more regularly. The services were held in a hall owned by J. D. Weaver, formerly Day's Hall ; but up to this time no church had been organized.

In the month of May, 1865, Joseph Harlacher emigrated from Wisconsin and joined the Iowa Conference, and was by the same appointed to Cedar Falls and adjoining appointments. He commenced to preach regularly in Waterloo in that year, in the above mentioned hall. About this time, several families, members of the Evangelical Association, had moved to Waterloo from Illinois, and the same Fall the first Church of this order in Waterloo, consisting of about ten members, was organized by Mr. Harlacher. Preaching was continued in Weaver's Hall for some time, but later in the same year it was changed to Champlin's Hall. In this location, the religious meetings were held for several years, during which period the church was strengthened by several revivals, a goodly number being converted and added to the Church.

In the year 1870, while C. H. Egge had charge of the society, a house of worship was erected, in which the society still worship, with a membership of about fifty. For the present, the society conduct their worship altogether in the German language. A Sabbath school is also held every Sabbath morning, at $9\frac{1}{2}$ o'clock, in the German language. The Superintendent at present is Peter Jacobe. The present Pastor of the Church is Rev. N. Shook.

German Lutheran Church.—The first services of this society were held in the basement of the Congregational Church, commencing in 1866. Rev. Mr. Durchner was the minister, and divided his time between Cedar Falls and Waterloo, preaching alternate Sundays at each place. Some time in 1877, Beck & Nauman's Hall was leased as a place of worship, Rev. Mr. Foelch succeeding Durchner, and preaching on alternate Sundays for several years.

Articles of Incorporation were adopted July 1, 1869, under the name of "The Lutheran Church of Waterloo," the object being, as stated therein, "To secure the worship of God, and promote religion and morality among the German population in the vicinity of Waterloo." The incorporators named were John Nauman, D. Kruse, Henry Vogel, Charles F. Sury, Godfried Hartman and Conrad Bochringer. The first Trustees were Charles F Sury, Godfried and Conrad Bochringer.

Rev. Joseph Westenberger was the first regular Pastor of the society, commencing his labors in 1872. Under his administration, the present church edifice was commenced and finished It is a brick structure, 30x56 feet on the ground, and is located on Jefferson street, between Third and Main. Work was commenced in July, 1872, and the building was occupied in October following. It has a seating capacity of about two hundred, and cost $2,500. To the credit of the society, which is one of the smallest in the city, is to be mentioned the fact that all the building expenses have been paid and the property is free from debt.

Rev. William Burhreng was called in January, 1874, and left in July of the same year. Rev. Mr. Foelch, from Cedar Falls, filled the office until November, 1875, when Rev. Chris Mordorf, the present Pastor, came. He is assisted by Henry Schurz.

May 26, 1878, these gentlemen established a school at the parsonage, teaching both American and German languages. They have fifty-two scholars

A Sunday school was organized about the time services commenced, the Pastor acting as Superintendent.

Free-Will Baptist Church.—On the 22d day of January, 1867, the following-named persons were organized into a Free-Will Baptist Church in this city: Rev. D. E. Champlin, Mrs L. Champlin, Mr. and Mrs. S. V. R. Slade, Mr. L Ellis, Mr and Mrs. J. H. Bowers, Mr. and Mrs. P. McStay, Mrs A. Heisrodt, Miss J Hubbard and Miss M. J. Heisrodt.

The first meetings of the above organization were held in Champlin Hall; but in the following year, the present church edifice was erected, situated on the corner of La Fayette and Main streets, and dedicated on the 29th day of November, 1868, Rev. O. E. Baker, of Wilton College, preaching the dedicatory sermon The Church has not enjoyed the privilege of constant pastoral care, although able and earnest men, including the Revs. D. E. Champlin, C B Messer and O E Baker have rendered it efficient service.

In January, 1874, a call was extended to its present Pastor, the Rev J. J Hall, late of C. H. Spurgeon's College, London, England, who, having accepted the invitation, commenced his labors with the Church the following March. Under his labors the Church enjoyed considerable progress, the membership having increased from thirty-five to seventy persons.

Rev. O. E Baker, who had previously preached for the Church as a temporary supply, became Pastor August 1, 1876

Considerable additions have been made to the Church membership of late The Church maintains a flourishing Sabbath school, conducted for several years by S. V. R. Slade, and for the past year by E. Cleveland A valuable library and other Sabbath school helps are liberally furnished the school

The Free Baptist Church announce as their distinguishing principles—one Lord, one faith, one baptism, free will, free salvation, free communion, free church government, free pews, free speech, free men.   Pastor, Rev O. E Baker.

Universalist Society —Universalist services were first held in 1868, at which time Rev. R G Hamilton preached regularly in Lincoln Hall   He removed to Clinton the following year, and then for several years there were no regular services

In 1873, Rev J. J. Austin, who formerly had charge of a large church in Indiana ; but his health failing him, he came to Waterloo, partly to regain his lost health and partly on business for himself and others. Shortly after his arrival here, he commenced preaching occasionally in Union Hall. About this time, the society re-organized and held regular services and a Sunday school, and in the Spring of 1875, it was incorporated and purchased a fine lot on the East Side.

Not long after this, the Society ceased to hold regular services, and have not, as yet, commenced active work.   They are, however, looking hopefully to the future

Free Methodist Church —This Church was organized in 1874, with a membership of thirty-two, and first held services in a building on the bank of the river, on the East Side. Rev. J. W Dake was the Pastor in charge.

In 1875, the society built a church edifice on the East Side. The Church has been presided over by the following Pastors, in the order named, succeeding Mr Dake: Revs. Crawford, Buss, Scott and Rev. C. E Herroun, the present minister.   The membership is now about fifteen.

The Church of the Brethren.—The Church of the Brethren was organized in 1855, by John Speicher, Elder.   The first meetings were in private houses The points of belief are faith, repentance, conversion, holy communion, washing of feet, kiss of charity, anointing the sick with oil in the name of the Lord, etc   The original members were from Germany, and the first church in this country was established in Germantown, Penn., about one hundred years ago.

The society at Waterloo was first supplied by Elders E. K and Benjamin Beuchlay, who continued until early in 1878, when Rev. John Wise came, who is still presiding   The society now meets in a hall formerly known as Capwell's Hall, which is nicely furnished for church purposes

The Church of Christ was first organized in this city, with a small membership, in the year 1855. It was re-organized in 1872, and met regularly in the Free Baptist Church every Sunday afternoon, for a short time. There has never been any settled Pastor, and the society is not meeting at all at present.

MASONIC.

Waterloo Lodge, No. 105.—This Lodge was organized under a dispensation issued by Grand Master Sanford to Timothy Rowell, Ephraim Mears, S P Brainard, Wm McCall, P W. Ingham, V. V Locey, John McIlmoil and H E Hurlburt, authorizing them to open a Lodge of Masons in this city. The charter was granted in June, 1857

The first officers elected were: Timothy Rowell, W. M., Ephraim Mears, S W , S P. Brainard, J. W.; V V. Locey, Secretary; H. E Hurlburt, Treasurer; John McIlmoil. S. D ; Wm NcCall, J. D.; S. W. Ingham, Tiler.

The first hall occupied by the Lodge was the upper story of J C. Hubbard's store, just below Wood's Block In 1862, the Lodge was removed to the Althouse Building on Bridge street, and in November, 1868, another move was made to the third story of Pardee's Building, which is still occupied

The first "jewels" were made of tin. The first candidate initiated was J C. Hubbard, and the second, J. W. Hankinson. The Masters of the Lodge, after Rowell, were· S P. Brainard, who served five years in that capacity , G W. Couch, R A Whitaker, T A. Covert, A. D Griffin and Frank Neely

The present officers are as follows· H H. Saunders, W M., H. L Shutts, S W.; H C Roberts, J. W., Henry Nauman, Treasurer, G A. Eberhart, Secretary; Charles Shirland, S. D.; Jos Bennett, Jr., J D.; G R. Crittenden, S S.· John V. Smith, J S., John Jackson, Tiler.

Victory Lodge, No. 296.—On the 3d of October, 1870, Grand Master Scott issued a dispensation to about thirty members demitting from Waterloo Lodge to organize a new Lodge, which was accordingly organized and named as above. The charter was issued in June, 1871.

The officers named in the dispensation, and who were continued through the first year, were R. A. Whitaker, W M , and who has occupied the position till 1878, J W McClure, S. W., Matt Parrott, J. W.; Lewis Lichty, Secretary; D. B Stanton, Treasurer, which position he still holds; E Ellis, S. D , D. M. Crouse, J D , H J. Main, Tiler.

The first room occupied by Victory Lodge was the second story of the building now occupied by Rider & Bailey, and in 1873, arrangements were made with M. L. Burnham for the third story of his block, which he added that year. The new room was furnished throughout in the most elegant manner The first meeting in the new room was held January 2, 1874.

The present (1878) officers are as follows: Matt Parrott, W. M , J. Mosher, S W.; C Ragan, J. W: A. W. Morrill, Treasurer, A. I Breckinridge, Secretary; D Robey, S D , F. S. Morrill, J. D , J C. Elwell, S. S; I E. Chapman. J S ; H. Lampe, Tiler.

Tabernacle Chapter, No. 52, R. A. M.—Chartered October 17, 1870, with Frank Neely as High Priest. The Chapter holds its meetings in the hall of Waterloo Lodge The present officers are: R A. Whitaker, H P , Chancy Maynard, K.; H L Shutts, Scribe, James Ellis, Treasurer, D. R. Weaver, Secretary.

Ascalon Commandery, No. 25, K T.—Instituted December 5, 1875, by O. P Waters. from Burlington. And the following first officers were elected: Frank Neely, E. C.; D B. Stanton, G ; J P. Sherman, C. G.; Matt Parrott, P., L

H. Cobb, Treasurer; H. W. Jenny, Recorder. Its present officers are · Frank Neely, E. C.; L Sharpless, G., I. A. Shipman, C. G; Matt Parrott, P.; H. L. Shutts, Treasurer; R. A. Whitaker, Recorder The Commandery numbers, at this date, thirty-one members. It meets the first Thursday in each month

An Eastern Star Lodge was instituted in 1873, but survived only a few years.

ODD FELLOWS.

Black Hawk Lodge, No. 72.—This Lodge was instituted at Waterloo, Iowa, in the second story of J. C. Hubbard's store, since known as the American House, on the 5th day of June, 1855. The ceremonies of institution were performed by Special D. D G. M Benjamin Rupert, of Dubuque. The charter members were J. C Hubbard, Oren E. Hardy, W. K Worcester, John McD. Benight and Henry Sherman. The Lodge started with a fair membership, having received several additions on the night of institution, and continued to flourish until the memorable hard times of 1857–8, when, it being impossible for most of the members to spare money to pay their dues, it was determined, though very reluctantly, to surrender their charter until better times, which was accordingly done. They, however, paid their G L dues, and paid their rent with their carpet, stove, chairs, etc., so that they went down honorably. It was no doubt a source of much sorrow to the small band of brothers to be thus compelled, by circumstances beyond their control, to give up the ship of F., L and T; but it was the best they could do

This first attempt, however, though rather short lived, was not to be the end of Odd Fellowship in Waterloo; for in a few years we find a *change* had come over the finances of the country, indicative of better times. Other men who were members of the triple-linked fraternity began to appear upon the scene, and they, after some consultation with others who had taken part in the first attempt, determined to begin again and to make it successful. Accordingly, in the year 1867, the Lodge was re-instituted in the upper story of the building then used as a saloon by G Althouse, with A. C Bunnell, O E Hardy, J C. Hubbard, T Wiley and B J. Capwell as petitioners. They received their same old seal and the same charter, which, we omitted to state, was granted October 11, 1855, by Martin Heisey, Grand Master; William Garrett, of Burlington, Grand Secretary.

W Russell was the originator of the revival, and to him is the Lodge largely indebted for its present prosperity. The re-organization occurred June 2, 1867. The ceremonies were again conducted by Benjamin Rupert, who was at that time Grand Master of the State.

In the Fall of that same year the Lodge was moved from Althouse's building to the hall formerly occupied, over J. C. Hubbard's store. When the building of Pardee & Bro. was finished they removed into the third story; from there to the second story of M. H. Barker's building, East Side; from there to the third story on the opposite corner, owned by M. L. Burnham. They now occupy a hall over Shutt & Barber's drug store, which is elegantly and tastefully fitted up. Their present officers are · S F. Walker, N. G., George Purdie, V G.; R. Lester, Secretary; Harvey, P. S.; J. D. Weaver, Treasurer. The Lodge meets every Wednesday evening.

Waterloo Encampment, No. 51, was instituted at Waterloo on the 8th day of February, 1871, with W. Russell, L. F. Walker, A. Ohler, D. M. Crouse, S Wells, R. Robinson and R. McDonald as charter members. The charter was granted the 10th day of January, 1871, by E. W. Hartman. Grand Patriarch, and William Garrett. Grand Scribe. The ceremonies of institution were conducted by Benjamin Rupert, of Dubuque, Special Grand Patriarch. The Camp started favorably, and has flourished and prospered in the practice of Faith, Hope and Charity. It has had one off-shoot, to wit: Parkersburg Camp, No. 62, the charter members of which were members of Waterloo, No. 51. This is the most beautiful branch of the Order, and, like the subordinate Lodge, always keeps its "latch-string" hanging outside to visiting brothers, and hospitality is never refused to those who adhere to the Golden Rule.

The present officers are: J. D Weaver, Chief; R. Lester, H. P., J. Davis, S. W.; D. B. Smith, J. W.; Harvey Smith, Scribe, L. F Walker, F. S; G. Hartman, Treasurer The Lodge meets the first and third Tuesday of each month

A O. OF U. W.

Waterloo Lodge, No 26, was organized by D. D. G. M. W. H. W. Holman, from Dubuque, May 11, 1875, with the following charter members: R A Whitaker, A. J. Edwards, I. W Ghrist, Lewis Lichty, J. H. Kuhns, E. Swank, D. R Weaver, A. B. Vanbolkenburg, M. Partridge, D. B Stanton, G W. Hazlitt, H. W Brown, C B. Stilson, H Lampe, H. Lindley, H Hirst. The Lodge was first officered as follows L. Lichty, P. M. W.; R. A. Whitaker, M. W.; A. J. Edwards, F.; J. H. Kuhns, O; D. R. Weaver, G; C. B. Stilson, Rec., E Swank, Financier, M. Partridge, Receiver; H. Lampe, O W; A J. Edwards, Lewis Lichty and C. B. Stilson, Trustees. The present (1878) officers are: S. J. Hoot, P. M. W., H. T. Roberts, M W.; J. T. Burkett, F; H. Lampe, O; C. C. Bigsbey, G.; C. B. Stilson, Rec; R. A. Whitaker, Financier; H. Hirst, Receiver; J. A. Smith, I. W.; H. H. Lewelyn, O W.; G H Robinson, G. F Roberts and A. J. Edwards, Trustees; G. H. Roberts and B. Banton, Medical Examiners. The present membership all told is 75. The Lodge meets every Tuesday evening, in Victory Hall.

Goethe Lodge, No. 95, was the next Lodge of this order organized in Waterloo It was instituted Jan. 26, 1877, by D. D. G. M. W. H. W. Holman, now of Independence; is made up principally of German citizens, of whom the following were charter members: Prof Frederick Barth, Godfred Hartman, H. H. Bezold, Henry Eifert, Tobias Wiley, Kasper Weis, Antony Dusman, John Christian, Martin Grady, Matthias Tittman, Constantine Stein, Charles Adler, Benhart Kinstler, Marcus Kahler, Frank Beck, Edward Fisher The following were its first officers Henry H. Bezold, P. M. W; Frederick Barth, M. W.; Tobias Wiley, F.; Godfred Hartman, O.; Henry Eifert, G.; Charles Adler, Rec.; Marcus Kahler, Financier; Kasper Weis, Receiver, Edward Fisher, I. W., Frank Beck, O. W., Martin Grady, Antony Dusmann, M. Tittman, Trustees. At present it is under the management of the following corps of officers: H. H. Bezold, P. M W.; G. Hartman, M W; G. A. Hermann, F; Mathias Tittman, O; H. Eifert, Rec.; Frank Beck, G.; F Kramer, Financier; Kasper Weis, Receiver; M. Grady, I. W., Fred. Ischer, Jr., O. W.; R. Lester, H. H. Bezold and E. Fisher, Trustees. The Lodge meets every Thursday evening in Odd Fellows' Hall, numbers 36 members and is prosperous.

Courier Lodge, No 145.—This Lodge was organized Jan. 16, 1868, by H. H Bezold, D. D. G. M W., of Waterloo, with the following charter members M. V. Adams, W H. H Becker, M. C. Brown, S. Coburn, J H. Crippen, G. R Crittenden, P S. Dorlan, G. A Eberhart, J A. Fowler, C. P

Hunt, W. H Hartman, S. B. Hitt, S M Hoff, C P Jones, Lewis Libby, W. C Munger, H L. Shutts, S. E. Rider, J. Q A. Rider, H D. Smith, A. B Thomas

First officers—P. M W., A. B. Thomas; M W, H L. Shutts; F, S E. Rider; O., S P. Hitt; Recorder, G A Eberhart; Receiver, J Q. A. Rider; Financier, J A. Fowler; Guide, M V. Adams; I. W, P. S. Dorland; O W., W. C. Munger; Trustees, W H. Hartman, C P Jones, H. D Smith. Present officers are—P. M W., H. L. Shutts; M. W., J. W. Richards, F., S. E Rider; O., S M Huff; Guide, M V Adams, Recorder, G A. Eberhart; Financier, M. C. Brown; Receiver, J. Q. A. Rider; I.W., J. C. Munson; O, W P. Dorlan, Trustees—same as last term. Lodge meets every Wednesday evening in Masonic Hall Lodge now numbers 57 members, and is in good condition

I O OF G T.

Waterloo Lodge, No 39.—This Lodge was organized August 25, 1875, with the following charter members. William Galloway, Lee Peppers, Mrs R Lester, J. B. Emerson, Frank Steinor, George Lichty, Mrs. J. C Powell, W G. McLaughlin, Charles Fancher, Mrs Peppers, J C Gates, Charles Brindell, Mary Averill, Thomas Gwynne, Henry Griffin, Mrs. F. Kinney, J J. Hall, Lillie Garbrandt, Albert Lane, J P. Reed, W Thrower. Mrs McGlaughlin, W O Richards, Jenny Colby, Mary Balke, J. Moshier, Fred. Pendleton, Frank Crippen, David Geddes, Mrs. J. R Hammond, Wm. Kinney, O. P Carrott, Cora Spencer, A. J. Breckenridge, Emma McKroy, E R Travis, R Lester. Julia Lacy, T A. Rose, Mrs. J. Richards, Elizabeth McClure, E. F Merwin, Mrs. E F. Merwin. Its first officers were as follows: W. O. Richards, W C T ; Mrs. Mary Peppers, W V. T.; J. J. Hall, W. O ; J V. Reed, W. S.: Ralph Hurd, W A. S., Wm. Galloway, W. F S.; Mrs. Mary Averall, W.T ; A I. Breckenridge, W. M, Lillian Garbrant, W. D. M ; Jennie Colby, W. I. G.; J B Emerson, W. O. G., David Geddes, W R H. S, Julia Richards, W. L. H S.; Thomas Gwynne, P W. C. T. The officers at this writing are· A. D. Bedford, W. C. T.; Jennie Moyer, W L H S.; Hattie Hankinson, W. R. H. S ; Wm. Johnson, W. S., Emma McCormack, W. A. S., W. A. Van Ordan, W. F. S., Carrie Thomas, W. T., Ruth Hurd, W C ; T. Gwynne, P W C.T, O. P. Carroll, W. M.; Emma Wright, W. D M., Emma Dull, W. V T ; Alice Demick, W.I. G ; J. L. Newhard, W. O G.; Linda Ragan, Organist. The Lodge meets every Friday evening.

FIRE DEPARTMENT.

The first fire company in Waterloo was the Waterloo Hook and Ladder Company, No 1, organized April 2, 1861 Its first officers were as follows: R. W. Chapman, Foreman ; M Maverick, First Assistant; H. D. Williams, Second Assistant; Horace Barron, Secretary. It numbered about forty active members, among whom were· R. W. Chapman, T. Wiley, George R. Crittenden, C. K. White, James Gifford, George P Peck, W. Russell, T. A Covert, John Elwell, H. Hallock, Fred. Chapman, M. H. Barker, O. Alexander, B H. Hoover, L. F. Walker, J Garbrant, John Hilferty, S M. Hoff, D. C. Cook, H. M. Goodhue, R H. Morrow, John Hubbard, Ed Webster and J. H Leavitt This company used a hook and ladder truck made under the direction of their Foreman, R W. Chapman, at a cost of $60.

In 1867, they turned their apparatus over to the German Hook and Ladder Company, which was organized in August of that year, with officers as follows:

T. Wiley, Foreman; D. Kruse, First Assistant; John Nauman, Second Assistant; John Bressler, Secretary; John Redenbach, Treasurer.   The first fire was in the old warehouse on Mill Square, in 1869, where they held the fire in check until the arrival of the engine.   Mr Wiley says, at this fire he acted as Foreman, Assistant and company, himself and Mr. Fuller doing most of the work.

In 1873, they sold their old cart to the city of Iowa Falls for $100, and had a new one built by Hitt & Chapman at a cost of $250, which they run at the present time   They have a full set of extension ladders made at the same time In times of fire theirs is the post of danger and of honor.   They must climb to the roof, enter the burning building and clear away the wreck so that the engines can do efficient service; and they have always shown themselves equal to the task.   Their present officers are T. Wiley, Foreman; Lewis Miller, First Assistant; E. Miller, Second Assistant; Kasper Weis, Secretary; John Nauman, Treasurer; G. Vulger, Steward.

Red Jacket Engine and Hose Company, No. 1, was the first engine company organized in this city   In 1868, money was raised by private subscription, and R. W. Chapman was appointed by the citizens to purchase a fire engine   Mr. Chapman went to Chicago, and for $1,000 purchased the Red Jacket.   This engine had a peculiar interest for Mr. Chapman   It was built in 1849 by L. Button, of Waterford, N. Y., for Fulton, No. 3, of Utica, of which company Mr Chapman, was the first Foreman.   It was sold to the Chicago Fire Department in 1853, and used by No 4, of that city, for a number of years   When the city began using steamers it was abandoned, and Mr. Chapman found it covered with dust and rubbish, stowed away in an old lumber room in the engine house   He at once bought it and brought it to Waterloo.

A company was formed in January, 1869, of which R. W. Chapman was Foreman; G. R. Crittenden, First Assistant; D. C Cook, Second Assistant; John Hilferty, Secretary, G P. Beck, Treasurer.   Charles Berg, Steward, H. W. Jenney, Foreman of Hose, Fred. Chapman, Assistant.   Their Constitution was adopted January 1, 1869, and approved by the City Council February 10, of the same year.   Their first place of meeting was in Wood's Block. On the completion of Capwell's Building they moved into that, which they occupied until the city built their present engine house, in September, 1872.   Here they have a fine hall, neatly decorated with appropriate pictures, mostly the gift of that firm friend of the firemen, Charles S. Champlin, of Hudson, N. Y, who has done much for the Waterloo boys.   He has presented them at different times, with a number of drawings of his own which show great skill; also with a company register, officers' belts, trumpets, etc.   He will always be held in grateful remembrance by our firemen, and is an honorary member of both engine companies.

The first fire of any consequence that the Red Jacket played on, was at the warehouse on Mill Square, where they did excellent service in saving surrounding property

In 1870, the Red Jacket Cornet Band was formed, H. W. Jenney, H. Hallock and R. W. Chapman signing a note for $200 on behalf of the company to purchase the instruments.

In 1874, the company, considering their hose cart too small, sent Messrs. Chapman, Beck and Crittenden to Dubuque to purchase a larger one.   They purchased a Silsby four-wheeled cart, made to carry 800 feet of hose, for $150. It was brought home, painted and varnished by Hitt & Chapman and delivered to the hose company.

The Red Jacket Company has an engine, two hose carts and 1,050 feet of hose. The present officers are as follows. G W. Barnes, Foreman ; R. Lester, First Assistant, Silas Lichty, Second Assistant: F. W. Beck, Secretary ; G. P Beck, Treasurer, John Smith, Foreman of the Hose, G. Hollister, First Assistant, Mart. Adams, Steward.

Early in 1871, it became evident that another engine was necessary for the East Side, and R. W. Chapman, then Chief Engineer, was appointed with W. Russell to purchase one. They purchased from the city of Janesville, Wis., an engine built by L Button, in 1855. The price paid was $600, and $150 for 500 feet of hose. This was brought home, and L F. Walker, M. H. Barker, J, Garbrant, John Hubbard, W Russell, J. Fressle, B S Doxey, Thomas Watts. J. P. Weeks, M Hannon and Wm. Barker withdrew from the Red Jacket, and A Rosgen from the Hook and Ladder Company, and, on February 3, 1871, formed the Water Witch Engine and Hose Co., No. 2.

Its first officers were · L. F Walker, Foreman ; J. Garbrant, First Assistant; John Hubbard, Second Assistant ; W Russell, Secretary ; A. Rosgen, Treasurer ; J. Fressle, Steward ; M. H. Barker, Foreman of Hose ; Wm. Barker, Assistant.

The first time they were called out was early in the Spring of the same year, when the Mayor of Cedar Falls telegraphed for help, saying their city was on fire. The engine was at once loaded, and the run from here to Cedar Falls was made in seven minutes, and in thirty-eight from the time of the first alarm, the Water Witch had a stream on the fire and did good service in checking the flames.

Their first place of meeting was in A. Rosgen's harness shop, but in September, 1871, their present engine house was built In 1874, the building was raised and a capacious hall built over the engine room, the city furnishing the material and the boys doing the work. They have a fine hall, the walls of which are adorned with pictures presented by Chas S Champlin.

They have an engine second to none, a hose cart and 800 feet of hose, and as fine a company as ever manned a brake. They have now on their rolls about fifty men, with officers as follows : A. G. Dunham, Foreman ; E. J. Light, First Assistant, C I Daly, Second Assistant ; John Holden, Secretary ; Ponsford, Treasurer G F Dunham, Foreman of Hose ; Warren Brown, First Assistant ; Michael Fouch, Steward

Red Jacket Co, No. 1, 60 men, Water Witch Co., No. 2, 50 men, Hook and Ladder Co., 25 men ; total 135 men.

The city has two fire engines, three hose carts and 1,850 feet of hose ; is well supplied with public cisterns in all parts of the city, with the Cedar River running through the center, and is as well prepared to fight fire as any city in the State Waterloo has been very fortunate in the past, and has never had a sweeping fire

R. W. Chapman was the first Chief Engineer, but held the position but one year, elected in 1869.

The Department is now under the charge of George P. Beck, Chief Engineer (since 1870); L. F Walker, First Assistant; John Nauman, Second Assistant.

Hope Engine Company.—About three years ago, Clarence Hollister, an ingenious lad of 18, thought he could make a hand fire engine, tried it and succeeded The box containing the apparatus is between three and four feet long, and of proportionate width and depth. The hose nozzle is three-eighths of an inch in diameter. It was kept as a curiosity till June 1st, when a company of boys, averaging 12 years old, was organized to man it. Herbert George is

Foreman, Edwin Miller is Assistant, and the other members are Henry Williams, Fayette Place, Allen Newton, Charles Newton, W Covert, George Beck, B Hitt, D. Hay and E Shaffer. The boys are handsomely uniformed and meet twice a week for drill. The little engine, as manned by the boys, throws a stream horizontally over 100 feet

The moral might be deduced that the boys are safer on the street with the "Hope" than without any central point of discipline. The corollary is plain that these handsome youths will grow up to be the officers of the other companies, with a training as reliable as instinct for their duties

WATERLOO LIBRARY ASSOCIATION.

November 18, 1865, the citizens of Waterloo held a meeting for the purpose of establishing a library George Ordway was Chairman, and James W Logan, Secretary of the meeting. A constitution was adopted and subscriptions made At an adjourned meeting December 4, 1865, the subscribers met at Dr Mason's office and elected permanent officers, as follows. President, George W. Couch; Vice President, R A. Whitaker; Secretary, James W. Logan; Treasurer, A. T Lusch; Librarian, Dr A B Mason; Investing Committee, P. McIsaacs, Dr. C T Ingersoll, J W Logan, to which were afterward added George Ordway and Dr Mason. The library was first opened in Dr Mason's office, December 2, 1867. Capt (now Judge) S Bagg was elected President of the Association, and the records do not indicate any election since

For several years the library was kept in active operation, and had on its shelves over a thousand volumes.

Dr. Mason was succeeded by Judge D. W. Foote, as Librarian, afterward, Henry Harrison and Dr Williams acted, for short terms, in that capacity; and then came a time when the library took care of itself, the books became scattered and many of them lost. In 1877, President Bagg and Secretary Logan appointed William G. Burbee Librarian, with instructions to collect the scattered volumes July, 1878, Mr. Burbee had succeeded in collecting between 400 and 500 volumes, which are stored in his carpenter shop, on Fifth street, of no use to anybody. There should be interest enough taken in this Association in this active town to revive the organization and make the Library a permanently useful institution.

FLORAL HILL GREEN HOUSE.

One of the institutions of Waterloo, is the "Floral Hill Green House," established, or rather commenced, in 1872, by J. A. Fowler, for many years well known as a prominent railroad man Mr. Fowler has a magnificent collection of house and garden plants, and his green house is one of the most extensive in the West Mr. Fowler, however, has devoted especial attention to the cultivation of the strawberry, and is hybridizing and originating new varieties, in which he has been very successful He procures the best varieties, and in the flowering season conveys the pollen from one plant to another by means of a feather, and does not depend upon the uncertain action of insects to accomplish this purpose. He has succeeded in producing a strawberry $8\frac{1}{2}$ inches in circumference, as large as a respectable-sized tomato. Another variety he has produced, called the "Iowa Prolific," is a marvel as an illustration of the power of intelligence to improve on nature One of these plants produced 236 berries, and 70 quarts were produced on a little plat of ground 4x8 feet Mr. Fowler is not satisfied yet, is continuing his experiments, and expects to produce strawberries as large as the largest tomatoes if his life is spared. So mote it be. He is unquestionably one of the most intelligent and successful strawberry culturists in the United States.

CEDAR FALLS

The first settlement of Black Hawk County having been made at Cedar Falls, its history up to the time of organizing the county includes almost the whole of the county's early history. For this reason, no mention is made here of the first eight years of Cedar Falls, fuller particulars being given elsewhere

A small town site was laid out at the mills in 1851, for the convenience of those employed about the mills, and for such others as chose to settle; but no effort was made to build up a town until 1853, when a new plat was made and recorded in Buchanan County.

In 1853, a school district was organized at Cedar Falls, the Board being: S. A. Bishop, President; E. D. Adams, Secretary; J. M. Overman, Treasurer. A house was built, by subscription, the same year During 1853, John R. Cameron built a store

When it became a settled fact that Black Hawk County was to be organized, the people at Cedar Falls and vicinity differed from those in the southern and eastern parts of the county. The people at Cedar Falls petitioned the Legislature for an act submitting the question of locating the county seat to a vote of the people; while Waterloo, on the other hand, petitioned for the appointment of Commissioners to locate the site. The petition of Waterloo was granted

But when the Commissioners chosen by the Legislature met to discharge their duty, they decided to make the location at Cedar Falls; and the red cedar stake that marked the spot for the future buildings was driven, amid great rejoicing, by the people of Cedar Falls. The Overmans had contributed fifty building lots, the avails of which were to be applied toward erecting buildings.

The election for officers took place, and Black Hawk County set up keeping house at Cedar Falls, in August, 1853 The officers took the second story of Andrew Mullarky's store, now occupied by Pickton & Landgraf

In the Fall of this year, Cedar Falls boasted a population of of 300, but it is believed this was too large an estimate.

February 22, 1854, the ladies gave a festival dinner at the school house, the proceeds of which were applied to purchasing a bell, which was immediately sent for, secured and swung It is now in the belfry of one of the new school houses. It is probable that this was the first bell ever brought west of Dubuque

In 1854, the town claimed 450 inhabitants. Many new houses were built, a hotel was erected, and, July 11th, the first number of the Cedar Falls *Banner*, the only paper, save one, between Cedar Falls and Dubuque, was issued by Meredith & McClure.

During this year, John R. Cameron established a ferry, a much needed convenience to the town.

The reader is referred to the general history for particulars concerning the stampede that took place in September of this year, caused by a report that the Sioux were coming down the valley, scalping all the whites they could find. It is sufficient to say here that the men of Cedar Falls showed themselves to be brave men; and had there proven to have been real cause for the alarm, they would no doubt have acquitted themselves with credit.

Aside from the struggle which resulted in the loss of the county seat, in 1855, the history of Cedar Falls until 1859 was comparatively uneventful. Like all new Western towns, it experienced a severe blow in the hard times of 1857; but such were the real attractions of the place, the town overcame the stringency of the panic sooner and easier than most other places. It was a period of growth throughout.

A STEAMBOAT FOR CEDAR FALLS.

In 1858, the people of Cedar Falls were much exercised over the fact that Waterloo was in steamboat communication with Cedar Rapids; but what was still more galling to them, Waterloo business men could get freight from Chicago for 70 cents a hundred, which was drawing trade to their bustling, ambitious town, right past Cedar Falls, which had hitherto held the supremacy over all other towns on the Upper Cedar. Something must be done, or Cedar Falls would be undone.

The first move was in this wise: Andrew Mullarky went down to Waterloo, went on board the little steamer Black Hawk, and offered Captain Snouffer a handsome sum to run his boat against the Waterloo dam. The Cedar had been declared by Congress to be a navigable stream, and the head of navigation had been established about 40 rods below the dam at Cedar Falls. Consequently, the dam at Waterloo was there in violation of law and the riparian rights of Cedar Falls. To bunt the boat against the Waterloo dam, even if it did no injury to the dam, would be conclusive evidence against its owners in the United States Courts, and they would either be compelled to remove it or construct a navigable canal around it. The Captain ordered his engineer to put on all steam and started the boat in the direction of the dam, but when he reached the "ripple" he could not "make it," either on account of its swiftness or the deep draught of the boat. This was discouraging to Mullarky, who returned home and reported his want of success. A public meeting was held to deliberate upon the unhappy situation of Cedar Falls, sitting forlorn at the head of navigation, six miles from a steamboat, and a mill-dam between

This meeting was well attended. It was resolved to buy a steamboat of light draught to ply between Cedar Rapids and Cedar Falls, and W. P. Overman and Sheldon Fox were deputed to visit the Mississippi River and negotiate for a craft.

A subscription paper in the nature of a contract was drawn up, empowering Sheldon Fox and W. P. Overman to purchase a suitable boat. In case they were not permitted to pass the dam at Cedar Rapids, they were to be paid all reasonable expenses during the delay at that place after the first week, not exceeding $10 a day. As soon as passage could be effected at Cedar Rapids, the boat was to proceed to Waterloo, where the expenses of delay were to be paid as at Cedar Rapids. In case the subscription was absorbed, the subscribers held themselves further liable for any excess.

The document is dated July 10, 1859, and the contributors were Sheldon Fox, W. P. Overman, Peter Melendy, Van Saun & Hunt, A. Mullarky, M. Rosenbaum & Co, J. M. Overman & Co., A. F. Brown, J. M. Benjamin, Timothy Mullarky, E. B. Hatch, W. P. Taubman, John W. Inman, J. H. Wilson, G. M. Harris, M. H. Creague, John R. Cameron, John G. Arbuckle, Francis Cox, L. D. Lampman, A. S. Smith, E. Brown, G. W. Smith, E. D. Adams, Samuel Berry, J. H. Boehmler, A. Henderson, C. H. Mullarky, L. P. Hammond, Cyrus Ashley, Graves & Bagley, E. Hodgin, W. H. Phelps, Giles Mabee, J.

M. Maggart, Caleb May, Henry Millen, G. W. Henry, Charles G. Miller, John M Harland, Mahlon Freeman, Luke Shimers, Peter Geyen, S. Wilson, W. H. Sessions, John Hartman, Joseph Sartori, J W Bonnell, F A. Bryant, Benj Graham, Chester Sawyer.   The subscription amounted to $1,530.

The Committee visited Dubuque, Davenport and Muscatine—found plenty of boats for sale, but could not agree on the price for such as were suitable to their wants   They accordingly returned home for instructions, by which time the water was falling in the Cedar, and Captain Snouffer was beginning to find it troublesome to reach Waterloo, even

The prospects for the railroad from Dubuque were also brightening, for work had been resumed and the western terminus was only fifty miles away   So the project was abandoned, and is now almost forgotten by those who were most actively engaged in it.

Cedar Falls, as described in the first issue of the *Gazette*, March 16, 1860, before the completion of the Dubuque & Pacific Railway to the town, claimed 1,600 inhabitants, probably an excessive estimate   The flouring-mill of J M. Overman & Co was in operation, drawing custom from Bremer, Butler, Webster, Hardin, Floyd, Chickasaw and Franklin Counties, and even from Blue Earth County, Minn.   The same firm owned a saw-mill.

Edwin Brown had just erected another flouring-mill of about the same size as the older one, both of which were built of stone, five stories high.   The other manufactories on the bank of the Cedar were D C. Porter & Co.'s chair and bedstead factory, a planing-mill owned by the same firm, and a saw-mill owned by Edwin Brown   There were beside, two steam saw-mills, one owned by A. S. Smith, and the other by Rounds, Wilson & Morrison.   Of those engaged in merchandising, T. B. & H. H. Carpenter owned a brick store   Andrew Mullarky's brick store was 22x70, three stories high, and W. A. Winslow's building was about the same size and height.   Overman & Brown had shortly before completed a three-story building, 44x80 feet, three stories high, the upper story fitted up as a public hall.

The second issue of the *Gazette* mentioned the school exhibition, under the management of Mr. L. J. Hammond, Principal of the Public School.   This occasion was enlivened by music from the Cedar Falls Brass Band, Henry Overman, leader, and songs from the Glee Club, composed of Mrs. Pierce, Mrs Clark, Miss Abbott, Miss Crosby, Mr. Van Saun and Mr H. Cooper.   Hammond, in 1876, had degenerated into a produce buyer at Joliet, Illinois, where he had become a heavy shipper of dressed hogs and poultry.

May 7th, the people of Cedar Falls, for the first time, received mail matter mailed at Dubuque the same morning, the railroad having been completed to Jessup, twenty miles east.

The 4th of July, 1860, was celebrated in the evening by an exhibition of flowers and vegetables at Horticultural Hall.   D. J Coleman read the Declaration of Independence, followed by J. B Powers, Esq., with an essay on " Human Life "

September 6th, a great Republican mass meeting was held at Cedar Falls. The local chronicler estimated the crowd at 5,000 persons.   Delegations came from Floyd, Bremer and Butler Counties   Speeches were made by Hon. T. Drummond, of Vinton ; Judge C. A. Newcomb, of West Union ; Hon. S. P. Adams, of Dubuque ; Hon John A Kasson, of Des Moines ; Hon W. B. Fairfield, of Charles City ; and F W Palmer, Esq , of Dubuque.   The music was furnished by three bands.   The time not consumed by speeches was occupied by a grand procession, made splendid with mottoes and banners

A "New England Association" was formed at Cedar Falls in February, 1861, with W. H Sessions as President Erastus Edgerton, Vice President; A. S. Smith, Treasurer; W. H Nichols, Secretary.

The members of Black Hawk Lodge, No 65, A., F. & A M., celebrated Washington's birthday in 1861 by a supper at the Western Hotel J. B. Powers made the address A Bible was presented to theLodge by the ladies attending, their spokeswoman being Mrs John M. Cameron.

Early in March, the "Ranch,' as it was called by the old settlers, was torn down. This building, erected by Mr. Taubman, in 1853, had been used for a boarding house. tailor shop, law office, saloon, Justice's office, and surveyor's office, all at the same time

Miss Mary Holmes, who had resided in Iowa since 1855, died at Cedar Falls on Sunday, April 7th, of apoplexy. at the age of 67 over years

Sixty-six buildings were erected in Cedar Falls in 1861, prior to August 2d.

The Ladies' Aid Society was formed December 16th—Mrs. Di Bryant, President; Mrs Doolittle, Vice President; Mrs J. B Powers, Secretary, Mrs. A. S Mitts. Corresponding Secretary; Mrs H C Wright, Treasurer

The California Association was organized December 21st—L. L. Cook, President; H. H Meredith, Vice President, O Bradley, Secretary; D. D. Devine, Corresponding Secretary, J. M Overman, Treasurer A festival was held on the 23d of January following

About the same time, a notice appeared on the streets, of which this is said to be a literal copy ·

POSEY COUNTIANS The natives of Posey County, Ind , will meet at the Lime-Kiln on Christmas, for the purpose of having a Tare Pukes, Hoosiers, Suckers, Badgers, Buckeyes and Hawkeyes are invited to participate All natives of Posey County that have fathers will act as Committee of Arrangements MANY NATIVES

The following week (December 28th), the Empire State Club was organized —Hon. Zimri Streeter, President; Albert Allen, Vice President; Jas. Miller, Secretary, A. Henderson, Treasurer

During February and March, 1862, the people of Cedar Falls received their mails with great irregularity, owing to severe storms March 19th, the train was "snowed in" two miles this side of Independence. The agent employed a gentleman, who was visiting Iowa, to carry the mail through. He got a team and drove to Waterloo, but the horses were exhausted and could go no further Nobody at Waterloo cared to send his horses even as far as Cedar Falls, and the contract was completed with a yoke of oxen.

Clement Vogt, a comparative stranger in Cedar Falls, was found dead in the river, on the East Side, June 18, 1862. The verdict of the jury was that he came to his death by accident; but many believed he had committed suicide. He had disappeared from the Inman House three months before

The peace of the State of Iowa was broken on Sunday, March 8, 1863, at the Carter House, by Lieut Fitzroy Sessions assaulting Stilson Hutchins, now Editor of the Washington (D C) *Post*, but then one of the editors of the Des Moines *Journal*. During the war, Hutchins had published a misstatement in regard to Lieut Sessions, charging him with having instigated an attempt to mob the Dubuque *Herald* office. Hutchins was staying at the Carter House, at the date given above, and was followed into the hall by Sessions, who, after ascertaining that he was the author of the libel, called for a retraction. This Hutchins refused to make. Fitz then passed his hand across Hutchins' face, which brought on a battle with fists, in which the latter was considerably worsted; though his punishment had no effect in modifying his perverse politics or restraining his violent expressions, either on the stump or at the editor's desk.

The first step taken to build a school house of sufficient dimensions for the district of Cedar Falls was at a public meeting held July 6, 1863, at which time it was voted to apply the Teachers' Fund then on hand toward the building

The first occasion on which Black Hawk Lodge, A , F & A. M., was called upon to perform the burial rite was on Thursday, August 22, 1863, the deceased being William Cox, a young man of excellent character, who had been married only two months before

The telegraph line from Dubuque to Cedar Falls was completed December 9, 1863.

Andrew Mullarky, the pioneer merchant of Cedar Falls, was drowned in the mill-race, near the saw-mill, December 12, 1863. His body was recovered within ten minutes after his first call for help, but too late to restore life. He was about 47 years old, and had resided in Black Hawk County since 1850

The walls of the school house were laid and the roof put on during 1864, under the supervision of J. Q. A. Crosby, who had contracted to do the work The brick work was relet to Joseph Johnson, and the carpenter work to William Ray and Joseph Godfrey

On the reception of the news of McClellan's nomination for the Presidency, in 1864, the Democracy of Cedar Falls felt it incumbent upon them to burn a little powder. Two anvils were procured, and after about the third round, which was terrifically loud, the artillerists looked around for the top anvil, which they could not find. Being of cast iron, it had burst into a hundred fragments; but, with almost miraculous good fortune, not a man had been hurt by the flying pieces

Sept 14, 1864, the frame of the Baptist Church fell to the ground with a great ci ash, owing to its being insufficiently stayed H Wallace, of Independence, the contractor, and Henry Bogart, of Cedar Falls, were at work on the cupola, sixty feet above the ground. Wallace spoke to his companion, but himself clung to the frame, until it fell to within ten or fifteen feet of the ground, when he jumped down without injury. Mr Bogart jumped inside of the cupola, probably intending to clamber down before it fell, but missed his grasp, and fell on the sidewalk head first, breaking his neck in the fall. He was picked up insensible and lived only a few minutes The coroner's jury censured Wallace for gross negligence. Mr. Bogart was buried next day with Masonic honors. Wallace claimed, a few days afterward, in a published statement, that the building was ordinarily secure, and that the accident was due to a high wind prevailing at the time.

Within a few weeks after this tragic event, a stranger victimized Townsend & Knapp out of some $1,600 in cash by means of a forged draft, and N. McClellan, a grain buyer at Cedar Falls, disappeared, having obtained of Mr Case, of Cedar Falls, about $1,400 on a railroad receipt. He also obtained $1,000 from Richmond & Jackson, of Dubuque

John Garrison, who settled at Cedar Falls in 1852, died Jan 18, 1865, at the advanced age of nearly 93 years. Mr. Garrison was a native of New Jersey. Mr. Garrison's life was an adventurous and busy one, and most of it was spent in the ever-shifting Western frontiers. Mr G became a Free Mason in Ohio in 1812, and while living in Detroit was one of the petitioners for the Grand Lodge of Michigan, of which Lewis Cass was first Grand Master He was a charter member, and the first W. M. of Black Hawk Lodge, which body followed his remains to their last resting-place, the funeral sermon being preached by Rev John Bowman

Miss McGarvey was drowned in Dry Run, near Cedar Falls, March 19, 1865, by being precipitated from a falling bridge

W. W Stanton, of Cedar Falls, employed as a fireman on the Dubuque & Sioux City Road, was injured by the locomotive being thrown from the track near Farley, April 30, 1865, from the effects of which he died next day

June 27, 1865, is remembered for the heavy rain that fell during the night, by which great damage was done to crops, fences, etc   The track of the Dubuque & Sioux City Road was washed out in many places between Dyersville and New Hartford, and the telegraph line broken badly.   No mail was received at Cedar Falls from the East till the following Wednesday, which was carried through on wagons under charge of N. C. Deering, then Special Agent of the Post Office Department.   It was over three weeks before the damage done to the railway track was repaired and trains began running

ORPHANS' HOME AT CEDAR FALLS

On pages 199–200, will be found a brief account of the origin of the Orphans' Home Association.   The following paragraph will show that the people of Cedar Falls, very early in the existence of the Association, had earned for themselves a very high place in the regard of the officers of the Association

Nov. 7, 1864, at a meeting of the people of Cedar Falls, addressed by Rev. P P. Ingalls, agent for the "Iowa State Orphan Asylum," about twenty soldiers' orphans were called out one by one, and some one in the audience requested to pay for a life membership in the child's behalf.   Five hundred and twenty dollars was pledged on the spot.   Before adjourning, an auxiliary society was formed, with Rev C. Waterbury, President; Revs. A. G. Eberhart, L. B Fifield, R. Norton, —— Bernner, Vice Presidents; G. M Harris, Treasurer, H A Perkins, Secretary.

At a meeting at the Orphan's Home Association, held at Des Moines, June 7, 1865, the committee to whom had been referred the question of establishing another temporary Home, expressed the opinion that it should te located in the northern, or at least the central, part of the State.   They further said.

We recommend that the selection of such Home shall be referred to a committee of five, whose duty it shall be to visit in person the several locations asking the establishment, or where, in their opinion, a suitable building can be obtained, and make a careful examination thereof, that they have power to take, receive and conclude contracts or bargains with individuals or associations representing the several localities, with the view of receiving and realizing for the benefit of the Association, as large an amount in donations or subscriptions as possible, and that after making such examinations, receiving such propositions and making such contracts, they be authorized and empowered to make the location, with full power to conclude all contracts and agreements, subject, however, to the approval and satisfaction of the Board of Trustees, or a majority of those present at any meeting called for that purpose   We recommend that this committee shall proceed to act as promptly and as speedily as possible, so as to secure at an early day the advantages of another Home

The recommendation was adopted, and Hon. Ralph P Lowe, Hon. John A. Parvin, Hon John A. Elliott, Mrs. M W. Porter and Mrs. H E J. Boardman were appointed a committee to carry out the resolution.

Meantime, the people of Cedar Falls were actively laboring to secure its location here; and, shortly after being advised of the above action by the Association, a committee was appointed, consisting of Dr S. N. Pierce, A Morrison and S. A. Bishop, to solicit funds for the purpose of erecting a suitable building for the new Home.   The committee visited Cedar Falls late in July, and, finding the community all alive for the project, resolved to recommend that the new Orphans' Home be located here   In their report, the committee say, among other things .

We found here a building that had been used for a hotel, situated in the outer lines of the town, sufficiently capacious to accommodate the officers of the Home and some eighty-five orphans, beside the kitchen and dining room and one other room sufficiently large, perhaps, to afford instruction to fifty pupils   In addition to this, there are, on an adjoining lot, a frame building which would answer for a wash house, and a brick tenement of twelve rooms, which would accommodate, comfortably, forty orphans, both of which, it is understood, could be made available for the use of the Home   To obtain immediate possession and use of the hotel building specified, some four or five hundred dollars would have to be advanced to a party or parties in possession claiming some interest in the same   The amount the citizens of the town propose to pay   Before it could be occupied as a Home, considerable repair would have to be made and some changes in the removal and enlargement of the stable, and some other improvements, amounting to, say, $500, more or less   This amount the lessor, who is a non-resident, would allow to be deducted from the first rents, which would be $300 the first year and $450 per annum thereafter   This expenditure for repairs the citizens of the place will advance in the first instance, until they can be reimbursed out of the rents paid

In connection with this Home, forty or eighty acres of cultivated land may be had, from half to one mile distant, at the customary rent, for the use thereof   Should more school room be required than can be furnished by the building in question, it is understood that the basement of the Presbyterian Church, which is close by, can be had for that purpose. Commissary supplies and provender for stock may be had in abundance, and as cheaply, perhaps, as in any other portion of the State

In other respects, the location is an eligible one, accessible, perhaps, as any other one point can be for the orphans in the northern portion of the State, situated in the midst of a kind people and surrounded by good moral and religious opportunities and advantages   It is proper to state that the rent of the brick and frame buildings spoken of on the adjoining lot will be from $225 to $250, and that it was supposed that the rent of the land would be about $2 per acre, making the rent of forty acres and all the buildings spoken of about $675 to $700 per annum

The Association accepted the proffer of the people of Cedar Falls, and, by resolution, proceeded to fit up the building for use early in September, which was duly accomplished.

The first officers and employes of the Orphans' Home were: Arthur Morrison, Superintendent ; Mrs. E. G. Platt, Matron ; Dr. S. N. Pierce, Surgeon ; Mrs E L. Yokoner, Nurse ; John H Rownd, Steward , Mrs Sarah H Wells, Miss H. J. Blodgett, Teachers , Miss M. Cates, Miss Nellie Mead, Mrs. Rachel Jairdine, Seamstress ; Mrs John H Rownd, Chief Cook

Lizzie Ward, aged 6 years, was the first inmate to die at the Home, May 23, 1866

Frank Case, an insurance agent, settled in Cedar Falls in 1864, and during the following Summer married an estimable young lady of the place   In July, 1865, it was ascertained that Case was an unprincipled scoundrel, the young lady he had just married being his tenth wife.   Case was accordingly arrested on the complaint of the young woman's father, and was committed for the crime of bigamy on the 10th of August   The same night he put an end to his worse than worthless life by hanging himself

In November, 1865, work was resumed on the unfinished school building. The Board had been fearful that if they voted the tax necessary to complete it in proper shape, they would thereby become personally liable in case any taxpayer saw fit to contest the matter.   To obviate this contingency an indemnifying bond was signed by fifty citizens in the sum of $3,000

Nov. 30, 1865, a package of $1,250 was stolen from the office of the Dubuque & Sioux City Railroad at Cedar Falls, which had been got ready to send on the train going east.

Dr. H. H. Meredith, who settled at Cedar Falls in 1853, died of cancer Dec 28, 1865, at the age of 48 years   He was buried with Masonic honors the following day.

The school house was dedicated to the work of education Jan 5, 1866, with addresses by Prof. A. S Kissell, of Chicago, Revs. L B Fifield, Eberhart, True and Kinney. The building, completed and furnished, cost not far from $23,000. The corps of instructors installed in the building were: G. A Graves, Principal; Miss J. H Harris, Assistant, Miss S V Harlacher, First Primary; Miss E. A Moulton, Second Primary, Miss K. C Goodenow, First Intermediate; Miss S E Miller, Second Intermediate

The Cedar Falls Starch Manufactory was incorporated about April 1, 1866, with Jacob Cole as President, J M Overman, Vice President; J. M. Benjamin, Treasurer, H. C Hunt, Secretary, A G Thompson, E. Townsend, Geo A. Baker, W. S. Garrison, Jesse Cooper, Directors.

A determined effort was made by the people of Cedar Falls to suppress the traffic in intoxicating liquors in March, 1866. Soon afterward, three barns, belonging to Messrs Barnum, May and Wilson respectively, were set on fire and destroyed, and the prevalent opinion was that they had been fired by some one among the prosecuted saloon keepers

The building of a woolen factory at Cedar Falls was first projected in 1863. A Mr. Blasburg visited the town and made arrangements with J. M Overman & Co to erect the building and he would put in the machinery and lease the building. The scheme fell through at that time; but in 1865, M. Collins & Co. began the erection of the Cedar Falls Woolen Mill, and had it completed in June, 1866.

The high water in August, 1866, washed out the supports of the old bridge and one of the spans fell with its own weight into the water below.

A re-union of the veteran soldiers of Cedar Falls and vicinity was held Dec. 21, 1866, under the auspices of Post No 38, Grand Army of the Republic The address was given by Gen M. M. Trumbull, of Waterloo.

A little boy, son of Dr. S N. Pierce, of Cedar Falls, was drowned in the Cedar Feb 5, 1867, by falling through a hole in the ice His body was found near the woolen mill next day

John Callen, who resided six miles south of Cedar Falls, started for home in the storm of March 12, 1867, leaving Cedar Falls in the evening. He was found three days afterward about half a mile from home, having perished with the cold. He had fastened the driving lines so tightly to the sled stakes that the horses were unable to move, one of them having its feet badly frozen.

July 16, 1867, a destructive fire occurred at Cedar Falls, caused, it was believed, by the explosion of a lamp in T. Hazlett's store. Several buildings were destroyed. Immediately after the fire, a call was made for a public meeting for the purpose of organizing a fire company.

The meeting was held on the 23d, at which time eighty-five citizens enrolled themselves into a company, and the meeting by resolution requested the City Council to pass an ordinance governing the newly created organization.

The death of Mrs Peter Melendy occurred Aug 6, 1867. This lady was a most excellent wife and mother, beloved by a large circle of friends, among whom she had lived so many years.

Asa Southwell, who had resided in Cedar Falls about four months, was arrested by officers from Detroit, Mich., February 27, 1868, for complicity in manufacturing counterfeit money. A considerable sum in two and ten dollar bills, all counterfeit, was found with his wife.

Another fire occurred March 19, 1868, the total loss being $3,500. The organization of the fire company, several months before, had proved abortive.

A Normal Musical Institute was held at Cedar Falls, beginning on Monday, October 19, 1868, and continuing three weeks. The Instructors were. J. W. Suffern, of Chicago, I. H Bunn, of Cedar Falls, and Miss Pitkin, of Cleveland, Ohio. The exercises closed with a concert, at the M. E. Church, on the evening of November 6th.

The organization of the Musical Association of Cedar Falls was effected during the Institute, with S C. Cotton as President; A. L Nichols, Vice President; H. C Hunt, Treasurer; H F. Adams, Secretary; I. H. Bunn, Conductor; A. G. Chapin, Assistant Conductor. About fifty persons enrolled themselves as members.

The Musical Convention in November, 1869, was attended by over two hundred and fifty persons, guests being present from several neighboring counties. Prof George F. Root, of Chicago, officiated as Conductor, assisted by Prof. Matthews. The receipts, after paying expenses, were over $300.

A son of Mrs. Stephen Kellogg, living at Cedar Falls Junction, was killed at Janesville, November 1, 1870. In company with two other boys, he had left home, and was riding north on the train. At Janesville, the boys had got off, and when the train started, young Kellogg attempted to jump upon the tender, but fell, and one arm and leg were severed by the wheels.

Cedar Falls Grange, Patrons of Husbandry, was formed in November, 1870. The first officers were · Peter Melendy, Master, R. P. Spear, Lecturer; E. Murdock, Overseer; Josiah Thompson, Steward; J Bradley, Assistant Steward, C W Snyder, Secretary; L O Howland, Treasurer; F N Chase, Gate Keeper.

After several futile movements in the direction of fire protection, a chemical steam fire engine was tested in Cedar Falls, February 15, 1870, and was soon after, by the Council, ordered to be shipped to the factory as not having sufficient capacity.

A Farmers' Institute was held at Cedar Falls, December 19th to the 25th, 1870, with President Welch, Prof Geo. W Jones, Prof. James Matthews, of the Iowa Agricultural College, in attendance as Instructors. Others from abroad were · Dr. Sprague, Des Moines; R A Richardson, Fayette; J H. Bacon, Washington; E R. Shankland, Jacob Rich, Dubuque, Rev. Z. Cook, Minnesota; J. C. Abbott, Clarksville; M Bryant, Bremer County, G. E. Fitch, New Hartford; Mr Collar, Butler County. The Institute was well attended by the farmers of Black Hawk County, and adjournment was made to meet in January, 1871

At the adjourned meeting. John Grinnell, of Clayton County, discussed fruit growing; essays were read by R. P. Spear and William Winters.

March 9, 1871, Cedar Falls, still without organized means of fire protection, was again visited by the fiend of conflagration The loss consisted of the Overman Block and two adjoining buildings. The loss was estimated to be about $75,000, distributed among Wilson Brothers, Miller, Wilson & Co, G. L Mills, Thompson & Co, J. H. Stanley, Warren Pierce, Cabinet Makers' Union, Hunt & Howland, George Sampter, Wise & Bryant, Charles Loose and L. B Crosby. The Public Library was destroyed, and the Odd Fellows lost their newly purchased furniture, etc

A dispatch was sent to Waterloo for help, which was responded to by the arrival of the fire engine "Water Witch, No. 2," on a special train, within three-qarters of an hour after the beginning of the fire By the exertions of the men accompanying the Water Witch the fire was prevented from doing more destruction.

Considerable damage was done by a violent gale of wind April 8, 1871, which fanned sparks into flame, whereby John Egmire, six miles south of Cedar Falls, lost $1,500 worth of barn and shed buildings Frederick Numan, of Mount Vernon Township, lost his stables, fences and hay. A farmer near Blakeville, in Bennington, George Boulton, near Willoughby, and Henry Bluhn, five miles south of Cedar Falls, all experienced similar losses. S. S Knapp had a lot of wood burned north of Cedar Falls.

The City Council, at its meeting May 3, 1871, contracted with Mr. King, agent of the Silsby Company, to purchase an engine of their manufacture, at a cost of $6,000 The engine was received May 25th, but, after a thorough trial on the two following days, it was decided by the Council to purchase a larger sized machine from the same company, at an added cost of $1,000.

The school fund of Black Hawk County was increased $315.69 June 17, 1871, by the finding of the body of a Norwegian, lying dead under a shed in Lamb, Byng & Co.'s lumber yard at Cedar Falls. No clue to his name or abiding place was found upon his body.

Another considerable fire broke out in Cedar Falls on Sunday, October 8, 1871, causing a loss of about $40,000, distributed among S Wilson, G. B. Van Saun, Woolen Mills Company and Cabinet Makers' Union Wilson & Van Saun's flouring-mill and the woolen-mill were burned to the foundations, as well as several other buildings, the latter of small value

Phœnix Hall was completed in the Fall of 1871. This room is 44x80 feet in size, 20 feet high The stage is 16x44, and has a drop curtain 26x17 feet. There are two side entrances.

John O'Brien was killed February 23, 1872, by a moving train, near Cedar Falls According to the verdict of the Coroner's jury, he was intoxicated and had lain down on the track.

A fire was discovered, in the evening of March 16, 1872, in Mrs. Mullarky's building, which was, with great difficulty, suppressed The loss to the owner of the building and to T. Hazlett, who occupied it for a dry goods store, was several thousand dollars. In the same fire, S. H. Packard lost his law library and the Cornet Band lost their instruments. The next night, another fire started in the Severin Block, under the store of Pilcher & Pennock, in which L. H. Severin, Pilcher & Pennock, B. Thorpe, Jr., Stearns & Odell, Joseph Sartori, Thompson & Co and Price Brothers lost about $20,000, largely insured.

The residence of T L. French was destroyed by fire July 14, 1872. It had cost about $24,000, and was insured for only $4,000.

Mrs. D. H. Kingsley, of Cedar Falls, was drowned July 24, 1872. She was with a picnic party, near the Cedar, and, after dinner, with other ladies, went into the river for a bath, and lost her life in trying to rescue her sister, who had got into deep water

A notice having appeared in the *Gazette* that there would be services in the Episcopal Church on Sunday, October 20, 1872, a congregation respectable in numbers were in attendance at the usual hour. A youthful face appeared in the pulpit, and the boyish frame was draped in the canonical vestments Part of the congregation, recognizing the features of young Burlingame, indignantly left the church; but others, supposing him to be a young divinity student, remained A choir of young misses rendered the music The prayer was decorously said, and the text announced, "Let your light so shine," etc. The pseudo-divine then exhorted the congregation on the necessity of employing a Pastor, and on the shame of allowing the church to remain unoccupied The next morning, the companions of the 17-year-old lad asked him for a reason for his prank, and were told by him that "it was too d—n bad that such a nice little church should be without a Pastor"

The iron bridge now spanning the river at Cedar Falls was put in place in the Winter of 1872–3, and cost, besides the piers, $13,075, of which amount Cedar Falls contributed $2,500 Its length is 347 feet The builders were the Wrought Iron Bridge Co , Canton, Ohio

John E. Stearns departed from life February 2, 1873. at the age of 63 years He settled in Cedar Falls in 1856, where he resided continuously till his death

Hans Christenson and Christen Olsen, both Danes, were drowned in the Cedar, at the dam, May 24, 1873.   They had got into a boat, which was just launched   It floated into the current, and, reaching the dam, the men jumped out and were swept into the boiling eddy below, beyond the reach of helping hands.

Emma Case, a young lady of Cedar Falls, died June 9, 1874, from the effects of a dose of corrosive sublimate, taken in a state of derangement caused by typhoid fever

The First National Bank of Cedar Falls was established in the Summer of 1874, with a capital of $100,000

Conductor A W. Putnam, of the Burlington Road, was run over by the tender of his own train, October 20, 1874, at the Cedar Falls depot.   His foot caught in the frog of the track as he was getting off the tender, which backed over him before he could extricate himself.

James Newell, a resident of Black Hawk County since 1846, died at Cedar Falls, at the age of 66, about June 1, 1875.   He was born and reared in Belmont County, Ohio. but had resided in Iowa for about forty years.   He was a giant in size, having weighed 350 pounds , but for several years prior to his death had weighed a hundred pounds less.

MUNICIPAL GOVERNMENT

February 19, 1857, on petition of E A Arnold and seventy-six others, the County Court ordered an election to be held at Cedar Falls, to decide whether said town should or should not be incorporated   The election was held, according to order, on Wednesday, February 25, 1857, at the office of D. J. Coleman, and resulted affirmatively. A second election was then ordered to be held at the same place, on March 17th, to choose three persons to draft a charter or Articles of Incorporation. At this election, R P Speer, Wm H McClure and D J Coleman were chosen as such committee, and their labors were indorsed by a unanimous vote of the election of the village, June 18, 1857.

The officers chosen under the charter were . J. M. Overman, Mayor , Geo. C. Dean, Recorder , J M Benjamin, Treasurer , J M S Hodgsdon, Marshal

The prime object of the organization was not so much for police control as to provide ways and means for building a bridge across the Cedar   The great tidal wave of immigration was bearing an immense number of settlers to Black Hawk County, and to Cedar Falls as well   The ferry-boat started by John R Cameron was too slow for Cedar Falls, was a disadvantage to its business, and a bridge must take its place.   Accordingly, the town officers contracted for the erection of a bridge, and issued bonds for payment.

The bridge, as originally erected, was 340 feet in length, with a transverse width of 16 feet.   A toll-keeper was appointed, and an office erected for him. The citizens soon afterward became dissatisfied with paying tolls, and one night a crowd collected, tore down the office and threw it into the river.   When hard times began to press, the scrip commenced depreciating, and some eight or ten thousand dollars of the notes passed into the hands of Andrew Mullarky, who traded goods for them at fifty cents on the dollar. Other scrip depreciated still more To avoid settlement and to postpone payment of the debt became the settled policy of the town For several years, the town officers were elected with this object in view, and a masterly inactivity was preserved regarding the bridge debt. Mullarky at last sought relief in the courts and obtained judgment, after which bonds were issued in lieu of the former due bills

The Mayors succeeding J. M Overman, under the village organization, were Edwin Brown, William H. Philpot, C. F Jaquith and M W. Chapman

In March, 1865, Cedar Falls having under the State law become a city of the second class, officers were elected as follows: T B Carpenter, Mayor; J. T. Knapp, Treasurer, J B. Powers, Solicitor; F. Sessions, Marshal. The Trustees were: First Ward—John H Brown, S A. Bishop, Second Ward— James V Bird, James Williams; Third Ward—Caleb May, M. W Chapman, Fourth Ward—Byron Culver, Josiah Thompson

The Mayors since that time have been: Albert Allen, 1866; F. A. Bryant, 1867-8-9; E Townsend, 1870-71; A. S. Smith, 1872-3; F. F. Butler, 1874-5; B Culver, 1876-7.

The city officers for 1878 are: A. S. Smith, Mayor; C. C. Knapp, Treasurer; S. H Packard, Clerk; A. D. Polk, Solicitor; Lanfear Knapp, Assessor, H. M. Adams, J. F. Zeising, S Hubbard, P. D. Mornin, W. H. Stickney, L. H. Barnes, W. T. Williams, G. H. Boemhler, Aldermen; Jefferson Sager, Marshal.

EDUCATIONAL.

Reference has been made in the preceding pages to the first matters pertaining to the schools of Cedar Falls. There are now two large and commodious buildings owned by the district and occupied for school purposes, besides two smaller structures—one on the North Side—the cost of all being between $40,000 and $50,000

For the school year ending in June last, the schools have been supervised by Prof. J. McNaughton, a well-known and able teacher. The teachers, with the positions occupied, are given herewith: High School, S. Laura Ensign, Principal; Rev F. Humphreys, Assistant; B. F. Landis, First Grammar; Dora Tucker, Second Grammar; Emma Smith, Third Grammar, Jennie Read, Fourth Grammar; Alice Carpenter, Mary Reihl, First Primary, Eva Barber, Josie Lawrence, Second Primary; Lucinda Hall, Ella Fox, Third Primary; Mary Flagler, Alice Miller, Fourth Primary. C. W. Rownd had charge of the Mixed school on the North Side.

The School Board for 1878 is as follows: F. F. Butler, President; S Wilson, E Townsend, I. D. Gilkey, P. J. Kaynor, D. T. Choat, Directors, A D Polk, Secretary; R. A Davison, Treasurer.

The district is now free from debt

RELIGIOUS.

Methodist.—The evangelists of this belief are pretty sure to be a little in advance of the ministers of other denominations in carrying the Word into the wilderness; and it is a tradition that Rev. Mr. Reed organized a class on the Upper Cedar soon after its settlement; nor would it be strange if Rev. Simeon Clark, a well-known character in the eastern counties, had preached along the Cedar while hunting bee trees.

The origin of the churches at Cedar Falls and Waterloo was the organization of a society east of the former place in 1851, by Rev Asbury Collins Cedar Falls Circuit was established by Conference in the Fall of 1853, and Rev. Messrs. Ingham and Smith were appointed to the charge About the same time a class was organized at Cedar Falls Revs Burley and Kendall rode the circuit in 1854–5, and were succeeded by Rev. P E Brown Rev. S Alger was appointed in 1856, but resigned. Rev Edwin Lamb succeeded him, but died soon after, and the year was filled out by Rev Hiram Hood.

Cedar Falls was made a station in 1857, Rev. Rufus Ricker taking charge. Rev. W. F Paxton came in 1859 Although he was a fine preacher and an energetic preacher, he is best remembered for the dashing style in which he got his wife. Miss Dimheart was teaching in the public school, and Rev. Mr Paxton had become decidedly smitten. A gentleman arrived from Wisconsin, expecting to marry her Rev. Frank heard that he had come, and on what errand. He drove over to the school house, got her into his buggy. proceeded to Waterloo, and married her off-hand

Rev David Poor followed in 1861, during whose stay a church was built, succeeded by Rev Landon Taylor and Rev L. D. Tracy Rev John Bowman came in the Fall of 1862, and remained two years. During his pastorate, the society having outgrown the old church, another was built of brick The new building was dedicated Sunday. Dec 4, 1864, the sermon being preached by Rev A. J Kynett to a large audience. The notables present were Rev Messis. Wm Brush, Wm Fawcett, John Van Anda and the Presiding Elder, R Norton The remaining indebtedness on the church, about $2,800, was provided for during the day.

Rev R. Norton filled the station from 1864 to 1866, succeeded by Rev. J. G. Dimmett, Rev. R. W. Keeler, Rev. D. Sheffer, Rev. A. B. Kendig, Rev. R. D. Parsons and Rev J. H Rhea, who is now in charge

The Church has a membership of about 350

The Sabbath school was organized in 1857, by withdrawal from the Union Sabbath school, managed under the joint care of the Presbyterian, Baptist and Methodist Churches. The Sabbath school is managed by five officers and twenty-five teachers, and has an average attendance of over two hundred pupils.

Baptist —This Church was organized in the Fall of 1854, by Rev. L. Knapp, who held regular services for about two years, when he removed to Joliet, Ill July 31, the society had a meeting at the school house, at which time the members resolved to place the Church on a sound footing, and to seek recognition from the other Churches, which was accomplished August 28. Rev. Mr Dean, of New Hartford, preached to the little band till November 21, when Rev W. K. Walton was invited to become the Pastor, who was ordained Dec. 23, and remained in charge till Nov. 21, 1860. He was succeeded by Rev. H. E Bailey Rev. A. G. Eberhart became Pastor Sept. 1, 1862, and remained till Nov. 27, 1867. His was a prosperous ministry, for the Church was largely increased, twenty-six being received into fellowship at one meeting

The society had bought the old school house and converted it into a parsonage in 1854. During Mr Eberhart's stay the church was built It was dedicated in 1863

Following Elder Eberhart, came Elders D. N. Mason, Star and W. H. Stifler, covering a period of about eight years.

Rev. G. W. Wisselius became Pastor June 23, 1876, but resigned December 10. A difficulty had arisen between him and the Church, which was the cause of much local and newspaper comment. He was succeeded by Rev. L.

T. Bush, who is still in charge   He was formally installed March 4, 1877, having been called from a position in the Cedar Valley Seminary.

The Sabbath school was organized in 1859 (May 8)

Presbyterian.—The beginning of this Church dates from March 18, 1855, when the society was organized under the ministration of Rev J. M. Phillips, with seven members, all of them now dead.   Rev Mr Phillips remained till Oct 17, 1858, services being held usually in Mullarky's Hall during his stay.   Rev. William Porterfield was installed Pastor Dec. 31, 1858, and withdrew Oct. 14, 1861, leaving an unpleasant impression behind him   The church was built during his stay, which was dedicated in October of that year, the Synod being in session at Cedar Falls during the time

Rev. Stephen Waterbury became Pastor Dec. 9, 1861, and remained just three years   Rev. Albert True presided from May 21, 1865, to Jan 6, 1867, followed by Rev D. Russell from April 7, 1867, to March 28, 1869, during whose stay a considerable revival was experienced.

Rev. S M. Griffith was called to the pulpit July 16, 1869, and ministered till August 31, 1872, leaving a good reputation behind him. .

Rev. A. J Compton remained only a short time—from Oct. 11, 1872, to May 11, 1873.   On the latter date, Rev A B Goodale assumed charge of the Church, and remained a little over four years.   Mr Goodale, who had been a missionary in the East Indies, proved a valuable Pastor, for the membership of the Church was considerably increased during his stay.

Rev. John Wood, the present Pastor, took charge Sept 3, 1877

The present membership is about one hundred and sixty.   The Synod has held two sessions here, and the Presbytery three.

The Sabbath school is very large, there being about two hundred and fifty pupils, taught by nineteen teachers.

St. Patrick's. Catholic.—This is one of the oldest societies in Cedar Falls. The first mass was celebrated by Rev. Father McGinnis, at the house of Andrew Mullarky, in January, 1855, and in the evening of that day he lectured at the school house   The main occasion for this visit was the recent birth of Elizabeth E. Mullarky (Mrs A H. Morrill), Father McGinnis having been summoned to administer the rite of confirmation.

In May of that year, Bishop Loras, accompanied by another clergyman, visited Cedar Falls and provided for regular services, which were conducted for several months, by Rev. Mr Brady, succeeded by Rev. Mr Slattery.   In 1856, Father Shields assumed charge, and in 1857, during his pastorate, a church was built on Washington street, just above Seventh.   Father Shields died at Waverly, in 1870, and was succeeded by Father McLaughlin, followed by Father Gunn, who remained three years, and added a residence to the church property.   His successors were Rev. Messrs. O'Dowd, Flavin and Ryan.   Next came Father Smith, under whose energetic management a splendid church was built.

The corner stone was laid Aug 11, 1876.   Mass was celebrated by Rev. Mr. Smith, assisted by Rev. Messrs. Scallon, of Waterloo, and Niemers, of Gilbertville.   This was followed by a procession to the location of the new church, succeeded by a sermon preached by Rev. Mr Smith, and the placing of the stone.

The edifice, which was erected near the former one, was dedicated Nov. 4, by Rt. Rev. John Hennessy.   Mass was said in the forenoon by Rev. Mr. Smith, assisted by several pastors of neighboring churches.   The services lasted far into the afternoon, the sermon being preached by Bishop Hennessy, with his accustomed eloquence and power   The music was supplied by the choir from the church at Waterloo.

Notwithstanding that a severe snow storm was prevailing, the spacious church was densely crowded, visitors being in attendance from the churches in the vicinity of Cedar Falls

Next morning a large number were confirmed at the church by the Bishop in person.

There are about eighty families connected with St. Patrick's

There is a small Sabbath school, under the direction of Father Smith

St. Luke's Episcopal —This society was organized in the Spring of 1855, by Rev James Keeler, at the school house.   Rev James Gifford succeeded Mr Keeler the following year, preaching alternately at Cedar Falls and Waterloo.   Rev Walter Loyd followed in 1861.

Rev. H. C. Kinney assumed charge in 1864.   He soon returned to New York, married, and brought his bride to Cedar Falls   By the free use of Mrs Kinney's money and his own hard work the church was built   Mr and Mrs. Kinney remained till 1869, leaving poorer in purse than when they came, but with a tender remembrance of them by all his parishioners.   Rev Ezra Isaacs occupied the pulpit for a short time in 1873

Rev. F. Humphreys took pastoral charge in 1873, and remained until the Winter of 1877–78, when he was succeeded by Rev. Dr. Estabrook, of Independence

A Sabbath school has been maintained since the organization of the Church

German Lutheran —A society of this Church was organized in the Summer of 1865, by Rev. B. Durschner.   Services were held in the Presbyterian Church for a year; but by the exertions of Mr. Durschner and the substantial help of Mr Bœhrler (deceased), the society had a church of its own in the Fall of 1866.

Rev L Lish accepted a call to the Church in the Spring of 1867, and remained till July, 1868, followed by the present Pastor, Rev. B. Fœlsch, who came directly hither from Germany   Mr Fœlsch began by holding morning and evening services every Sabbath, and heard a Bible class every Wednesday evening, besides preaching, for a time, on alternate Sabbath afternoons at Waterloo.

In the Spring of 1871, the Woman's Missionary Society was organized.

The congregation numbers about sixty families   Two hundred children have been baptized, and about sixty confirmed, since the organization of the Church.

German Evangelical.—The first services of this faith were held at the old school house in 1857, by Rev. Messrs. Shafely and More, who preached three or four times   Rev Mr. Phile visited Cedar Falls every three or four weeks, during 1859, usually preaching in dwelling-houses.   Rev Henry Klinsorge came in 1860 and remained one year   Rev. Henry Hinser came in 1861, remaining two years, under whose pastorate a revival was held, resulting in fifty additions to the society.   A church was also built during his pastorate.   His successors were Rev Jacob Keiber, two years; Rev. Mr Bernner, one year; Rev. Mr. Harlacher, two years; Rev. Mr. Schultz, two years; Rev. Jacob Nuhn, one year, Rev. Mr. Harlacher, three years; Rev Mr. Klinsorge, two years; Rev Mr. Bernner, in 1875, who still remains.   During this time the Church grew from a mission to a circuit, and from that to a station.

Another church was built in 1876, and the old church was converted into a day school room   The new building is 36x64 feet, with spire 114 feet high,

WATERLOO

and cost $6,500. The dedication ceremonies were held on Sunday, December 24th, the sermon being preached by Bishop Esher, of Chicago.

The membership of the society is quite large

A Sabbath school was organized about the year 1869

Danish Lutheran.—This society was organized in 1871, by Rev. A. S. Neilson, who settled in Cedar Falls the same year. The project for a building was entered on in the following year. The edifice was dedicated September 7, 1873, the sermon being preached by the Pastor. The building is 40x60 feet in size, with vestibule and spire, and cost about $4,000. It is located toward the southwestern portion of the city. The membership is about seventy.

Miss Neilson, daughter of the Pastor, teaches school which is held in connection with the Church, and is under the supervision of the Pastor

Another church of the same faith is situated about eight miles southwest of the city, over which Rev. Mr Neilson has pastoral charge, also.

Congregational Church.—In accordance with letters missive, a Council met at the Congregational Hall in Cedar Falls, July 7, 1860, to consider the question of organizing a Congregational Church. The ministers attending were: J R. Nutting, Bradford; J. C. Holbrook, Dubuque; H. N Gates, Earlville; I Russell, Buffalo Grove; O Emerson, Twelve Mile-Creek; O. W Merrill, Waterloo. Revs J R. Upton and L. B Fifield attended, though not as members.

The following day—Sunday—the Church at Cedar Falls was organized, with seventeen members—six males and eleven females. The sermon was preached by Rev Mr. Holbrook, and the fellowship of the churches extended by Rev. H. N Gates.

Rev. L. B. Fifield, of Manchester, was invited to become Pastor, which he did at that time, and remained until June 10, 1870. Mr. Fifield was an excellent preacher, his matter being better than his manner. He was a studious, bookish man, reserved in manner, and made acquaintances slowly. One peculiarity was his inattention, on the street, to his acquaintances, frequently passing without seeming to see them

The society, in 1862, purchased the building which had been erected by the Methodists

The Church received help, until 1872, from the Home Missionary Society, when, through the exertions of the present Pastor, Rev. C Gibbs, who assumed charge shortly after Mr Fifield's withdrawal, the society became self-supporting.

The present membership is about ninety; there having been, in all, about two hundred names borne on the Church book

The Sabbath school was organized in 1860. Its Superintendents have been G. N. Miner, James Miller and W. C Bryant. About one hundred and thirty pupils attend.

Universalist.—A society of this faith was organized several years ago, but soon afterward became inactive. Rev. Mr. Hines now holds regular services, and the prospect is excellent for a stable organization. Services are held at Phœnix Hall.

A Sabbath school has recently been organized, with Mrs. Charles Overman as Superintendent. Six or seven teachers instruct the pupils, who are about fifty in number.

The Cemetery Association of Cedar Falls was organized in February, 1865, with G B Van Saun for President; J B Powers, Secretary; Albert Allen, Treasurer; S A. Bishop, T. B. Carpenter, A. S Smith, Byron Culver, Directors

I

FIRE DEPARTMENT.

Cedar Falls Engine Company, No. 1, held its first meeting early in May, 1871. At the meeting held May 19th, 1871, officers were elected, as follows: G. B. Van Saun, Foreman; F A. Hotchkiss, Assistant Foreman; N Rodenbach, Hose Captain, P. Boehmler, Assistant, C C Knapp, Secretary; L. N Fabrick, Treasurer. May 25th, after consultation with the City Council, J. A Fosdick was elected Engineer.

June 8th, a committee was chosen to ascertain the cost of suitable uniform, and report thereon

A public parade was made on the afternoon of February 22, 1872, followed by a festival, at Mullarky's Hall, in the evening.

June 7, 1877, the company met, to make arrangements for attending the funeral of F. Anschutz, which took place the following day, at which time thirty-two members took place in the procession.

The present officers are as follows: M. Hammond, Foreman, E. M. Stead, Assistant, Jacob Boehmler, Hose Captain; Robert Strachan, Assistant; C. H Rodenbach, Secretary; C W Odell, Treasurer, J A. Fosdick, Engineer, John Costelo, Assistant, S. M Lamb, Stoker, Daniel Corrigan, Assistant

The company holds frequent meetings for business and drill; and, the members being young men of high character, the *morale* is excellent. The membership is about fifty.

The engine is a Silsby, and has always been reliable in time of need Its capacity is very great.

This is the only company for fire duty in Cedar Falls

PUBLIC LIBRARY.

The Cedar Valley Horticultural and Literary Association was organized February 18, 1859, with P Melendy as President, D C. Overman, Vice President; J H Brown, Treasurer, G. M. Harris, Secretary. February 24th, W W. Beebe, of Dubuque, gave an address before the society on " The Best Method of Growing Fruit Trees in Northern Iowa." In the following Autumn, the society had accumulated a library of about five hundred volumes, and had made arrangements to provide a cabinet of fossils, minerals, insects, curiosities and relics. Weekly discussions were had on horticultural topics; the reading room was opened on Monday afternoon, and books could be borrowed on Saturday. Three floral exhibitions were given during 1860. The society, which had had a very healthy existence, in spite of the war feeling and the constant efforts put forth by the citizens of Cedar Falls, terminated its existence Jan 6, 1865, by giving way to the " Library Association of Cedar Falls," which was organized at the same meeting, with Peter Melendy as President, G. B. Van Saun, Vice President, S. N. Pierce, Secretary and Librarian; George D. Perkins, Financial Secretary; John H Brown, Treasurer. The old society turned over to the new its library, numbering about five hundred volumes A few weeks after, $100 worth of new books were ordered by the society.

The books were destroyed in the fire of March 9, 1871, but the society proceeded to secure another supply. The library has been generally well patronized.

MASONIC.

Black Hawk Lodge, No 65, A., F. and A M.—Organized in 1853. In 1862, S A Bishop, one of the charter members, served as Grand Treasurer; Geo.

B. Van Saun served as Junior Grand Master in 1872, and is now Representative near the Grand Lodge for the Grand Lodge of Michigan

During the Masonic year ending May 1, 1878, one candidate was initiated, two were passed and three were raised. Two were admitted to membership and two demitted. The present membership is seventy-two S. Vandervaart is W. M; R. O. Beeson, Secretary.

Meets Monday evening on or before full moon.

Valley Chapter, No. 20, R. A. M, was organized under dispensation November 3, 1857, with James Keeler as M. E. H. P., John Garrison, E. K.; S. H. Packard, E. S.; M. Simons, Treasurer; John H. Brown, Secretary, Charles R. Arnold, C. H.; Robert Lapsley, P. S., S. P. Brainard, R. A. C., S. A. Bishop, G. M., 3d V.; John Hartman, G. M., 2d V.

The charter was issued in October, 1858.

S. H. Packard has served one year as Treasurer of the Grand Chapter.

Baldwin Commandery, No. 10, K. T.—The dispensation for this body was issued by W. E. Leffingwell, Grand Commander, December 15, 1866, and the Commandery was organized and instituted by E. A. Guilbert, D. G. Commander, April 3, 1867. The charter was issued November 13, 1867. and the officers chosen were: G. B. Van Saun, E. C., S. A. Bishop, Gen.; E. Townsend, C. G.; A. G. Thompson, Prel., J. M. Benjamin, Treasurer, S. H. Packard, Recorder; Frank Neely, S. W.; A. B. Sessions, J. W.; L. N. Fabrick, Std. Br., E. A. Haskill, Swd. Br.; P. Pickton, W.; J. G. Dimmitt, S. P. Pickton was Grand Warden in 1873, and G. B. Van Saun is now R. E. Grand Commander of Iowa.

ODD FELLOWSHIP

Cedar Falls Lodge, No. 71, I. O. O. F. was established Oct. 10, 1855 Among its charter members were Dr. H. H. Meredith, B. B. Smith, Andrew Kennedy and J. M. Benjamin.

The Lodge has maintained a healthy though not rapid growth A few years ago, the furniture and other property of the Lodge were destroyed by fire This loss has been replaced and the Lodge is now comfortably placed in the third story of the building one door south of Phœnix Block

There have been two deaths from the membership—that of Christian Sherer in 1876, and that of J. W. Galloway in October, 1877.

The principal officers for the last half of 1878 are: James Hatfield, N. G.; O. B. Wood, V. G.; Z. T. Phillips, Perm. Sec.; A. J. Norris, Rec. Sec.; Z. McNally, Treas.

The Lodge meets every Thursday evening There are sixty-four members.

Cedar Valley Lodge, No. 223, I. O. O. F. was instituted by dispensation Feb. 1, 1872. The members named in the warrant are Henry Pheiffer, Jacob Pheiffer, Sebastian Klaus, Jacob Geier, F. Bepler, Adam Close, Philip Hopp, Morris Lippold, Charles Hesse and John Collman. The charter was granted Oct. 17, 1872.

The present officers are: Adam Close, N. G.; Henry Pheiffer, V. G.; George Flockdicker, Per. Sec.; Jacob Pheiffer, Treas.; Abram White, R. S. to N. G., Loyal Ravel, L. S. to N. G.; Paul Gehring, Cond.; John Case, Warden; Jacob Geiler, I. G.

The Lodge meets on Wednesday evenings, and has about thirty-five members. The society has $800 invested in addition to its joint ownership in hall fixtures.

UNITED WORKMEN.

Cedar Falls Lodge, No. ——, *A O. U. W* was organized Oct. 23, 1875, with the following as officers · S H. Packard, P M. W , R. O. Beeson, M W ; Phil. Boehmler, Foreman ; Francis Cox, Overseer ; T. F. Beswick, Guide; L. O Howland, Recorder, S. N. Pierce, Financier ; W P Overman, Receiver; H. C. Shaver, I. W., F. H. Hurd, O W.; T. F. Beswick, Francis Cox, F. A. Hotchkiss, Trustees

One death has occurred in the history of the Lodge—that of Christian Sherer, Aug. 17, 1876. The insurance policy of $2,000 was paid Sept 20th.

The present officers are. J. W. Sturtevant, P M. W., Francis Cox, M. W , M Davis, Foreman; T J. Tiller, Overseer, M C Stitler, Guide, F A. Hotchkiss, Recorder ; C. C Shockey, Financier ; C. C. Knapp, Receiver, J E Bates, I W , G. H Thorpe, O. W , E. Townsend, R. O. Beeson, G Leland, Trustees.

The Lodge has about seventy members, and has a considerable accumulation of funds

Meet in Odd Fellows' Hall on Tuesday evening of each week.

LA PORTE CITY.

This pleasant town was located on the south half of Section 25, Township 87, Range 12 (Big Creek), was surveyed by Wesley Whipple, June 5, 1855, plat filed for record July 16, 1855, by the proprietors, Jesse Wasson, Junia Wasson, W Catlin and Rosella Catlin At least. a dozen additions have been made to the original plat. The town was named by Dr. Wasson in honor of La Porte, Ind., where he had previously lived.

The first settler in town was Dr. J. Wasson, who built the first building on the town plat, on the corner of Main and Locust streets. in April, 1855. It was designed as a storehouse and was opened as such, with a stock of goods, in May following ; but he occupied a portion of it for a dwelling until he completed his house, which he built during the ensuing Summer.

Among the early settlers were G. Bishop, the first attorney in the new town , W. L. Fox, R. Montray, W C Kennedy, R. A. Brooks and George Cook.

The first saw-mill was erected by Dr. Wasson in 1856, on Big Creek, near the present railroad bridge.

The first grist-mill was built by Lewis Turner in 1855–6, about 200 feet above the present mill. This mill was burned about 1860, and was not restored until 1864–5, when T. H Elwell built another about 200 feet below the site of the old one. Elwell's mill was and is one of the best flouring-mills in Iowa, has four runs of stone, is supplied with all the most approved machinery and modern improvements, and manufactures the highest grades of flour, and supplies the bakers of Vinton, Waterloo and Cedar Falls Mr. Elwell sold an interest in the mill property to his son-in-law, Babcock, and the mill was run by Elwell & Babcock Since Mr. Babcock's decease, there has been no change in the firm name, Mrs Babcock retaining her interest.

In 1856, John Rolph and W. L. Fox built a story-and-a-half building, 12x 12 feet, in the brush, on the east side of Main street, near Commercial, every stick of timber in which, says Mr Fox, was taken from public lands The upper floor of this building was designed as a paint shop by Mr. Rolph , the lower floor was supplied with a few rude benches, and in that same Summer the first school in town was opened in it by Miss Hattie Fleming (now Mrs. James Fosdick)

The first school house was built of logs on School House Square   The second was a frame building, built in 1863–4, on the same site.   Near this, a brick school house was erected in 1871–2, and both are now occupied for school purposes. The Principal is W. H Butler, with an Assistant Principal and four teachers

John Thompson was the first blacksmith who struck the first ringing blows on the anvil in La Porte, in a log shop, near the corner of Commercial and Main streets

MUNICIPAL RECORD.

October 7, 1870, G. W Hayzlett, Jasper Parks and thirty-nine others presented a petition to the Circuit Court, praying for the incorporation of La Porte City An election was ordered, and held at the "Kennebec House" (now the National), January 31, 1871, which resulted—110 votes "for incorporation" and 75 votes "against incorporation," and on the 11th day of February, 1871, the Court declared the town of La Porte City duly incorporated.

B. S. Stanton, George Waltz, Hiram Goodwin, C. T. Ingersoll, William Chapple, Commissioners appointed by the Court, called an election on the 6th day of March, 1871, for the election of officers.   The election resulted as follows.   Mayor, R J. McQuilken, Recorder, W. H. Brinkerhoff; Trustees, G. W. Hayzlett, W A. Walker, William Chapple, John Hilferty and W L. Fox   The municipal government was duly organized March 11, and its first act was the adoption of rules of order.   April 1, T. H. Cole was elected Marshal and Henry Chapple Treasurer, and April 15, O. G. Young was elected Street Commissioner

1872.—R J McQuilken, Mayor : W H. Brinkerhoff, Recorder ; G. W. Hayzlett, W. A. Walker, J. R Stebbins, B S. Stanton and William Chapple, Trustees.

1873.—R. J. McQuilken, Mayor ; J R Stebbins, Recorder, W H Brinkerhoff, W A. Walker, B S. Stanton, George Banger and R. M. Lane, Trustees.

1874.—R. J McQuilken, Mayor , Henry Chapple, Recorder , R. M Lane, George Waltz, George Banger, W. H. McKee and John M Wright, Trustees.

1875.—Jesse Wasson, Mayor ; E. K. McGogy, Recorder, Jacob Wagner, Robert M Lane, G. A. Watson, John M. Wright and W. H. McKee, Trustees.

1876.—J. Wasson, Mayor : E. K McGogy, Recorder ; R J McQuilken, W. A. Walker, John H Fisher, William Rolph and George Banger, Trustees.

1877.—J. Wasson, Mayor ; B A. Chapin, Recorder ; R. J. McQuilken, John H. Fisher, Henry Sharon, W. A. Walker and George Banger, Trustees.

1878.—William A. Walker, Mayor ; B. A Chapin, Recorder ; John H. Fisher, John E. Eberhart, Nelson Taylor, Adam Keller and William Hamilton, Trustees; T. L. Reed, Marshal ; George Cramer, Street Commissioner , C. T. Ingersoll, Treasurer ; John McQuilken, Assessor.

Dr. Jesse Wasson was not only the first settler, but was first Justice of the Peace. and first Postmaster.   He individually paid for the delivery of the mail the first year, as it was not on a regular mail route.

The first established road through the town was the State road, from Vinton to Cedar Falls, in May, 1855.

The first iron bridge built in the county was one thrown across Big Creek, in this town, in 1867, at a cost of $4,500, and in 1874 a substantial "Howe Truss" bridge was built across the Cedar River, nearly opposite the town, which cost over $7,000.

In May, 1865, the town contained 600 inhabitants, 2 churches, 1 school house, 3 groceries, 4 dry goods stores, 1 boot and shoe shop, 3 hotels, 2 drug stores, 1 furniture store, 1 hardware store, 1 news depot, 3 millinery stores, 1 confectionery shop, 2 blacksmiths, 1 carriage shop, 1 photograph gallery, 1 grist-mill

In 1875, its business interests were represented by 5 dry goods stores, 4 groceries, two drug and book stores, 1 hardware store, 3 agricultural implement stores, 5 elevators, 1 large flouring-mill with 3 run of stones, 2 livery stables, 5 millinery stores, 4 restaurants and bakeries, two meat markets, 2 wagon makers, 4 blacksmiths, 2 lumber yards, 5 doctors, 3 lawyers, 1 newspaper and printing office, and 1,200 inhabitants.

The first newspaper was the *Progress,* established by Dr J Wasson, in November, 1870. The office was in a building on the corner of Main and Locust streets, which occupied the site of the pioneer building erected in the Spring of 1855. Jan 12, 1872, the office was burned and the material destroyed, but with characteristic energy Dr Wasson very soon obtained a new outfit, which he put in the basement of the building now occupied by the *Progress,* a short distance northwest of the old office The paper has prospered under Dr. Wasson's management, and he is now erecting a large stone building on the site of the office that was burned, in which the *Progress* will find business quarters

July 17, 1878, Company E of the First Regiment of Iowa National Guards was organized at La Porte. The officer sare · Captain, Chas. A. Bishop; First Lieutenant, John Connor; Second Lieutenant, B. A. Chapin The company has its full quota of men, and will soon receive a supply of breech loading rifles.

The population of La Porte, in 1878, is about fifteen hundred. It has 4 churches, 2 school houses, 5 dry goods stores, 3 groceries, 3 boot and shoe stores, 4 hotels, 2 hardware stores, 3 drug stores, 2 lumber yards, 1 bank, 5 elevators, 1 newspaper and printing office, etc., etc.

RELIGIOUS.

Methodist Episcopal Church——This Church was organized in 1856 or 1857, and was first supplied by Rev Mr. Hollinsworth, then of Vinton. Their meetings were first held in a private building on the west side of Big Creek, and afterward in dwellings and school house, until 1872, when a church edifice was erected on Block 10, in Wasson's Addition, which was dedicated by Rev. John Clinton, from Mount Vernon A Sabbath school was instituted at the time of the organization of the Church, and A N Day was its first Superintendent. A Ladies' Aid Society and the Young People's Mite Society were organized some time after the organization of the Church. Rev. J. H. Gilrouth is the present Pastor in charge, who, assisted by Mr. John Fisher, also has charge of the Sabbath school.

The Seventh-Day Adventists, La Porte City —This Church was organized and built its church (28x74) in 1861, with Amos Amburn as Elder, and Benjamin Leach, Deacon (who were not regularly ordained, however, until 1866) The society held meeting three times a week In 1868, they sold their church to the Presbyterians. since which time services have been held in private houses The Sabbath school was organized in 1861, and Amos Amburn appointed as first Superintendent. A Vigilance Missionary Society was organized November 21, 1877, with the object to further the interests of the Church. Its officers elected and still serving are as follows: President, John King; Vice President, Otis Mitchell; Secretary and Treasurer, Amos Amburn The association meets once a week

Evangelical Association—The early history of this Church at La Porte is identified with that of the Waterloo Church, it being a part of the same until 1873, when the work was divided and the La Porte Church became independent. A church was built in 1868, and dedicated by Bishop Long, from Illinois (now occupied by the American Evangelical Association) Until 1874, the American and German societies were united, but in that year they were divided, the German division having purchased the Presbyterian Church in 1873 The first German Pastor after the separation was Rev. Mr Egge, who was followed successively by Revs Eckhart, Echer, Shook, and the present Pastor, N. Knoll. The Sunday school was started in 1870, with T. Lunerman as Superintendent. The present Superintendent is Mr. C Trepp. A nice parsonage is now nearly finished, near the church. The American society still occupies the church purchased in 1868. Their first Pastor was Rev A. Wagner. The present Pastor is Rev. Wm J Hahn, who occupies the parsonage built near the church in 1872 The Sunday school is under the supervision of Mr. Joseph Susong.

Presbyterian Church —The first public services by this denomination were held by Rev. N. C Robinson, in November, 1857, in a log cabin which stood on Commercial stceet, near Mr. Walker's present residence The Church was organized November 4, 1867, by a council consisting of Rev. Luther Dodd and R Wylie, Ruling Elder. The first members were James McQuilken, T. L Mayes, R. J. McQuilken, Jennie H. McQuilken, John McQuilken, William P. Mayes and Annie Mayes. Rev. J A Hoyt was first Pastor, and James McQuilken and T. L. Mayes Ruling Elders. In 1868, the society purchased the church built by the Adventists, about 1861, and occupied it until 1873, when they sold it to the German Evangelical society, reserving the privilege of occupying it for morning services until the 1st of November.

In June, 1873, Dr C T Ingersoll, R J. McQuilken and B. S. Stanton were appointed a committee to select and purchase a site for a new church edifice, who soon afterward reported that they had selected lots on the corner of First and Sycamore streets, which were purchased for $400. J T. Wagner, an architect, drafted a plan for the building. which was accepted, and a Building Committee appointed, consisting of C. T Ingersoll, B. S Stanton, R J. McQuilken, F S. Boynton and F. M Thompson. Work was commenced in July, 1873, and the vestry was completed ready for occupation in the last part of November, 1873 The church proper was completed and dedicated on the last Sabbath in November, 1874, the dedicatory sermon being preached by Rev. Stephen Phelps, of Vinton. The building is 60x36 feet, and cost, including the site, $8,372.74.

After Mr. Hoyt's pastorate, Rev N. C. Robinson occupied the pulpit about six months, when Rev. D S Morgan became Pastor, who was succeeded by Rev. J. A. Donahey, who retired April 1, 1878. Since that time, the Church has been destitute of a settled Pastor, but the pulpit is regularly supplied by Rev W R. Stewart The present officers of the Church are. Ruling Elders, S. White, T L. Mayes, R R McQuilken, Samuel McQuilken, P E. Triem and R J. McQuilken; Trustees, B S Stanton, J R. Stebbins and John McQuilken.

MASONIC.

Trowel Lodge, No. 216, A , F & A M—Organized U D. dated March 26, 1867. The organization was effected very soon afterward. The petitioners for dispensation were George W Dickinson, G. W Hayzlett, George Raines,

O. A. Phillips, F S. Boynton, R. C. Heath and Hubbard Moore.   George W. Dickinson was first W M , and George W Hayzlett, S. W.

About a year afterward, the Lodge was regularly instituted under charter dated June 3, 1868.   The first officers under charter were George W. Dickinson, W. M ; G. W Hayzlett, S W.; William Chapple, J W.; B. S. Stanton, Treasurer, Jesse Wasson, Secretary; William Cooper. S. D.; R. C. Heath, J. D., Miller Edsil, Tiler. Bro. Dickinson served as W M until May, 1870, when G W. Hayzlett succeeded him, and the succession has been John S Eberhart, Nelson Taylor and J C. Bauman.   The Secretaries of the Lodge since its institution under charter, have been J. Wasson, W. H. Brinkerhoff, C F Swallow, J. Wasson, J. E. Babcock and J. Wasson.

The officers elected in 1878 are J. C. Bauman, W M.; James Norton, S. W., James Van Dyne, J W ; J. Wasson, Secretary; B. S. Stanton, Treasurer

I. O. O F.

La Porte Lodge, No 229, was organized in Masonic Hall, La Porte City, December 1, 1871, by W. P. Overman, D D. G. M , assisted by a large delegation from Cedar Falls, with five charter members, as follows . Charles Waite, William G. Goodwin, D. W. Dalton, Henry Chapple and W. H McKee The first officers were C Waite, N G., Henry Chapple, V. G., William G. Goodwin, Secretary, and D. W. Dalton, Treasurer. The present officers are William C. Fritz, N. G ; John McQuilken, V G ; Henry Chapple, Secretary; and John Waite, Treasurer.

The Lodge meets every Friday evening in Masonic Hall, corner Main and Commercial streets.   Present membership, twenty-one.

A. O. U. W.

Shield Lodge, No 127, organized August, 1877, with the following charter members, viz.; B. A. Chapin, E. M Sharon, Nelson Taylor, B. S. Stanton, George Husted, Dr. J. B. Darling, John S. Eberhart, Henry Sharon, Henry Chapple, William B. Clark, William Rolph, J D. Hudson, Charles Berry, C. A. Bishop, G. S. Bishop, John McQuilken, James McPhail, H. J Preble and Adam Keller.

First officers · B A Chapin, P M. W.; E. M. Sharon, M. W.; Nelson Taylor, General Foreman; John McQuilken, Overseer; G. S. Bishop, Recorder; John S Eberhart, F ; B. S. Stanton, Receiver.

Officers, July, 1878 · Nelson Taylor, P M. W., John S. Eberhart, M. W.; William Rolph, G. F., B. A. Chapin, Recorder, H J. Preble, O ; H. Chapple, F.; B. S. Stanton, Receiver.

Present membership, seventeen.

CEDAR CITY.

The first settler on the site of Cedar City was Paul Somaneux, who built a cabin there in 1847–48.   The town is located near the east bank of the Cedar River, on south half of Section 6, 89, 13, and was laid out in 1856 by William M. Dean.   Prior to the advent of railroads, it was a town of some importance. In 1865, it had a population of about 200, and had a hotel, a school house, two breweries, two stores, etc.   When the railroad was built, however, its business was drawn to the neighboring town of Cedar Falls, and now there are but few evidences remaining of its former prosperity.

Just west of Cedar City, on the flat, is where Newell and his companion camped when returning from the Upper Cedar in the Spring of 1845; and when Somaneux decided to make a claim, he could find no more suitable spot than where Cedar City now stands.   He lived here, accordingly, when not engaged in trapping, till 1851, when he died   Mr Newell has recorded that the honest Frenchman sent for him when he felt death approaching. and, with Newell, went carefully over his little accounts with the few neighbors at Cedar Falls.

Cedar City has been prominent only since the advent of the railway, from the notoriety derived from the attempted murder of Byron Wright by Almira Stickles, an account of which is given elsewhere.

It is hardly likely that the town can regain its former thrift, owing to the fact that Cedar Falls has ample room to spread out on the south side of the river, and it will remain only as another little landmark of the restless energy of 1856, that marked out town plats all over the West, where town lots would not sell to amplify their projectors' bank accounts

GILBERTVILLE.

This town was located on Sections 22, 23 and 27, Township 88, Range 12, in Poyner Township, John Chamboud and John Felton, proprietors.   The county records show that it was platted in 1856, but it seems probable that it was laid out at least a year or two prior to that date.   In a sketch of this town, published in the *Iowa State Reporter* in 1875, it is stated that in 1854 John Chamboud and John Felton came into the township and founded the city of Gilbertville.   As Rome was called the "seven-hilled city," Gilbertville might be called the "sand-hill city," provided it ever assumed such proportions.   The question has often been asked, why a town was laid out on such a barren place. The only reason to be given is that the good land had been entered before this, and the rock bottom and fall in the river made it a suitable place for a mill, which was much needed.   A mill was built on the west bank and run by steam for two or three years.   Arrangements were also in progress for the building of a dam and ferry, when the accidental death of John Felton, by drowning, put a stop to the work   Felton and two other men were out in a boat stretching a cable across the river for the ferry, when in some manner the boat was caught by the rope, upset and all thrown into the water.   Two of the men were rescued, but Felton was unable to swim and was drowned before assistance could be given him.

Messrs. Chamboud and Felton were well calculated to carry out the plans which they had made together, the former possessing good planning talent, and the latter great executive ability   One was theoretical and the other practical, and working well together, but neither calculated to do much alone.

The city was a magnificent one—on paper.   It was extensively laid out in blocks, lots, streets and avenues on both sides of the Cedar River.   There were seventy-eight blocks subdivided into 714 lots on the east side, and 120 blocks on the west side.   The plat represented a beautiful city possessing unequaled natural advantages.   It showed a large public square in the center, a beautiful lake in the center of the square, a nice pleasure boat in the center of the lake, with a party of pleasure seekers on board the boat enjoying a sail.   Such a magnificent plat was well calculated to give one an exalted opinion of the place; but, says the writer of the sketch above alluded to, "I must confess I was *somewhat* disappointed when I came to visit it for the first time. June 10, 1856 I drove into town with three yoke of heavy cattle to a light loaded wagon. I had crossed many sloughs without getting sloughed, but in Gilbertville I got sanded—stuck in the deep sand. I had to put my shoulder to the wheel and call on Hercules to help and whip the cattle

Mr. Chamboud, the projector of this magnificent enterprise, took his plat and went to Dubuque to sell lots and to induce emigration to his new city. Christopher Kelley was pleased with the glittering prospect He sold his possessions in Dubuque and invested the proceeds in seven lots in the "sand-hill city" of the Cedar. On his arrival, however, Kelley's wrath was righteously kindled, and there was some pretty loud and pretty hard talk; but he was in for it, he had invested his all in lots in a paper city; his hopes and his money were all sunk together, and he was obliged to remain to watch the spot where they had disappeared. Nicholas Bowden also invested in town lots after a careful examination of the plat; but when he came to examine his Gilbertville property it is said that he gave free vent to his rage without being very fastidious in his language. John Fagan was very cautious; he didn't want to invest until he had seen the spot He did not place implicit reliance in Chamboud's plat, and with Joseph Mathews he came out to see. They were in a hurry (perhaps being fearful that the lots would be all sold before they could get back) and made the journey from Dubuque to Gilbertville in a day and a half, Mr. Fagan coming on foot and Mathews on horseback. They came, saw and returned to Dubuque, but concluded not to invest

For a few years, the city grew rapidly. Chamboud, Kammon & Felton opened a store with a general assortment, well adapted to the wants of the country. Nicholas Bowden also opened a small store, but did not continue long. John Snyder had the first blacksmith shop, in 1855, and the first in the township. John Eickelberg, now a resident of Waterloo, started a wagon shop soon after.

In 1857, Peter Felton started a steam saw-mill on the Cedar bottom, under the bluff, on some vacant lots. In the Summer of 1858, the top of the smokestack was visible above the water of the Cedar. The next season he moved it out of the bottom and set it in the center of the public square, and where the lake was represented to be on the plat, and then had to dig a well twelve feet deep right in the middle of the lake to get water to supply the engine.

Many people who owned land in the vicinity built in town, but finding it inconvenient they removed the buildings to their farms.

In the early settlement of the place, it supported a small brewery and tannery, but they soon ceased operations. A few years after, two small distilleries existed for a short time. In 1856, a small Catholic Church was erected and used until 1868, when a larger one was built, which was destroyed by wind in 1874. Another church was built and dedicated early in 1875.

In 1875, Gilbertville had two stores, three saloons, a post office, one blacksmith shop, and the main street was solid, containing nineteen families and ninety-eight inhabitants. In 1878, there is a blacksmith shop, a saloon or two and a store

RAYMOND.

This is a small village and station on the Illinois Central Railroad (originally Dubuque & Pacific). It is situated on the northwest quarter of the northwest quarter of Section 2, and the northeast quarter of the northeast quarter of Section 3, Township 88, Range 12, and is about in the center of Poyner Township. It was surveyed by John Ball, County Surveyor, for Edward E McStay, proprietor, April 11, 1866, plat filed for record Jan 14, 1867, at 10 o'clock A. M. Edmund Miller built a house and an elevator in 1860, the first building in the place. Porter M. Chaffee built and opened the first store in 1865. In 1875, it had one elevator, one dry goods and grocery, and one drug store, depot, telegraph and post office, and one blacksmith shop and one hotel

In 1878, there are one store, one blacksmith shop, one hotel, depot and post office, elevator, two churches, one school house.

The school house was built in the Fall of 1866 It is a small frame school house, and it is not remembered who taught the first school in it.

The Church of Christ (Advent) was organized December, 1873, by Rev J W Burroughs, editor of *Burroughs' Journal*, with forty-one members Incorporated in 1874, and bought one-half of the Wesleyan Methodist Church Dr. B. Banton, C. L Shaw and William Wheeler are the Trustees. Rev. Mr Burroughs is Pastor.

Raymond Circuit M. E. Church —The region occupied by the Raymond Circuit of the M E Church has long enjoyed the preaching of the Methodist itinerant; but in the year 1869 it was formed into a charge by itself, under the labors of Rev. W. O. Glassner, then a supernumerary member of Upper Iowa Conference

It was formed from parts of Jessup and Brandon Circuits, taking Raymond and Pleasant Valley appointments from the former, and Mount Pleasant Church and society in Spring Creek Township from the latter Indian Creek appointment was afterward added. The whole had a membership of about one hundred

Its name first appears in the minutes of the Upper Iowa Annual Conference for the year 1870

The following have been appointed its Pastors: 1870–71. W. S. R. Burnett; 1872, S N Howard; 1873, A. Critchfield; 1874, Joseph Cook; 1875, Geo. W Rogers; 1876–77, B. D. Alden; 1878, —.

Under the energetic labors of Rev W S. R. Burnett, a convenient parsonage was built in Raymond in 1871.

Under the administration of Rev. S. N. Howard, the neat church edifice occupied by the society in Raymond was erected and dedicated Aug. 10, 1873

The present membership of the charge is 133.

HUDSON.

This little rural hamlet was surveyed and platted by George W. Miller, June 15, 1857, John L. Alline and Asaph Sergeant, proprietors. It was located on the west half of Section 26, Township 88, Range 14 (Black Hawk), on the southeast side of Black Hawk Creek, eight miles southwest of Waterloo

Through it passed the Waterloo and Eldora road, a great wagon thoroughfare, over which mail stages made semi-weekly trips

About the time this line was projected, which was probably before the plat was made or recorded, speculation was rife and everybody wanted all the land they could see.

For two years, the little village of Hudson had flattering prospects. During that time, there were erected seven dwellings—one brick, one log and five frame; two hotels, one brick and one frame, one frame store, on the corner of Fifth and Washington streets, Asaph Sergeant, proprietor, and one blacksmith shop

The town has had within its limits two hotels, two shoe shops, general assortment store, post office, blacksmith shop, cabinet maker's shop, Methodist parsonage, a shingle machine, and a milliner's shop in every house.   There is a sawmill one-quarter of a mile distant, built by Tewksbury Bros., in 1857-8.   The mill-dam was made of logs and brush   This was afterward converted into a flouring-mill, which was run successfully

Extra brick were made on the Worthington farm, two miles north   The brick used in the erection of the two building in Hudson, were made on this farm   Some of Black Hawk Township brick are in Waterloo edifices.

On the 4th of July, 1857, the first celebration was held in the village of Hudson, "not on Bunker Hill," but on the Public Square, where the good flag of our Union boldly wafted in the gentle breeze and bid defiance to the red men.

The city fathers were extremely wise, were never humbugged by a lightning rod company, street railway company, nor even by a gas company   There never were any bank suspensions in the town.

The town has now nearly as many buildings as it had in its palmier days. There are two blacksmith shops and a machine for making barbed wire fencing, which is run by horse power.   A store is now being built in town by Deacon H. A. Lane, of Waterloo, who expects to open it with a stock of goods required by farmers, in August, 1878.   There are seven families living in the town.   About half a mile away is a tavern.

"Jockey Town," is the name given, by Mr. Bonesteel, to a little cluster of houses about a mile northeast of Hudson, while he was trading horses with the residents.

BARCLAY.

A small village located on Camp Creek, about twelve miles northeast of Waterloo   It was laid out on the northwest quarter of Section 13, Township 89, Range 11, Barclay Township, August 8, 1854, by James Barclay.   In 1865, it contained two stores, a saw-mill, a large tavern and about 100 inhabitants; but with the advent of railroads, which attracted business to other points, this little village, like many another in the West, dwindled away, until now there are only a blacksmith shop and a post office there.   The ruins of the old steam saw-mill are yet to be seen.

JANESVILLE.

This town is mainly in Bremer County, but a town plat was made on the northwest quarter of the northeast quarter of Section 2, Township 90, Range 14, in 1855, by Mary Ann and Hiram Fairbrother

FINCHFORD.

In Union Township, a small hamlet containing a good flouring-mill, two or three stores, a hotel, blacksmith shop and school house.   It is a mile and a half from Finchford Station, on the Burlington, Cedar Rapids & Northern Railroad, where there is another school house.

The town was laid out on Section 7, Township 90, Range 14, by Lewis Goings, in 1872.

WAR HISTORY.

The people of the Northern States have just reason to be proud of the glorious record they made during the dark and bloody days when crimson-handed rebellion threatened the life of the nation. When war was forced upon the country by rebels in arms against the Government, the people were quietly pursuing the even tenor of their way, doing whatever their hands found to do—working the mines, making farms or cultivating those already made, erecting homes, building shops, founding cities and towns, building mills and factories—in short, the country was alive with industry and hopes for the future. The people were just recovering from the depression and losses incident to the financial panic of 1857. The future looked bright and promising, and the industrious and patriotic sons and daughters of the Free States were buoyant with hope, looking forward to the perfecting of new plans for the ensurement of comfort and competence in their declining years; they little heeded the mutterings and threatenings of treason's children, in the Slave States of the South True sons and descendants of the heroes of the "times that tried men's souls" —the struggle for American independence—they never dreamed that there was even one so base as to dare attempt the destruction of the Union of their fathers —a government baptized with the best blood the world ever knew While immediately surrounded with peace and tranquillity, they paid but little attention to the rumored plots and plans of those who lived and grew rich from the sweat and toil, blood and flesh of others—aye, even trafficked in the offspring of their own loins. Nevertheless, the war came, with all its attendant horrors.

April 12, 1861, Fort Sumter, at Charleston, South Carolina, Maj. Anderson, U. S. A., Commandant, was fired upon by rebels in arms. Although basest treason, this first act in the bloody reality that followed was looked upon as the mere bravado of a few hot-heads—the act of a few fire-eaters whose sectional bias and freedom and hatred was crazed by the excessive indulgence in intoxicating potations. When, a day later, the news was borne along the telegraph wires that Maj Anderson had been forced to surrender to what had first been regarded as a drunken mob, the patriotic people of the North were startled from their dreams of the future, from undertakings half completed, and made to realize that behind that mob there was a dark, deep and well-organized purpose to destroy the Government, rend the Union in twain, and out of its ruins erect a slave oligarchy, wherein no one would dare question their right to hold in bondage the sons and daughters of men whose skins were black, or who, perchance, through practices of lustful natures, were half or quarter removed from the color that God, for His own purposes, had given them. But they "reckoned without their host." Their dreams of the future, their plans for the establishment of an independent confederacy, were doomed from their inception to sad and bitter disappointment

Immediately upon the surrender of Fort Sumter, Abraham Lincoln—America's martyr President, who, but a few short weeks before, had taken the oath of office as the nation's Chief Executive, issued a proclamation calling for 75,000 volunteers for three months.   The last word had scarcely been taken from the electric wires before the call was filled.   Men and money were counted out by hundreds and thousands   The people who loved their whole Government could not give enough   Patriotism thrilled and vibrated and pulsated through every heart.   The farm, the workshop, the office, the pulpit, the bar, the bench, the college, the school house, every calling offered its best men, their lives and fortunes in defense of the Government's honor and unity.   Party lines were for the time ignored   Bitter words, spoken in moments of political heat, were forgotten and forgiven, and, joining hands in a common cause, they repeated the oath of America's soldier-statesman: "*By the great Eternal, the Union must and shall be preserved'*"

Seventy-five thousand men were not enough to subdue the rebellion.   Nor were ten times that number   The war went on, and call followed call, until it began to look as if there would not be men enough in all the Free States to crush out and subdue the monstrous war traitors had inaugurated.   But to every call for either men or money, there was a willing and ready response. And it is a boast of the people that, had the supply of men fallen short, there were women brave enough, daring enough, patriotic enough, to have offered themselves as sacrifices on their country's altar.   Such were the impulses, motives and actions of the patriotic men of the North, among whom the sons of Black Hawk County made a conspicuous and praiseworthy record.   Of the offerings made by these people during the great and final struggle between freedom and slavery it is the purpose now to write.

April 14, A D 1861, Abraham Lincoln, President of the United States, issued the following .

PROCLAMATION

WHEREAS, The laws of the United States have been and now are violently opposed in several States, by combinations too powerful to be suppressed in the ordinary way , I therefore call for the militia of the several States of the Union, to the aggregate number of 75,000, to suppress said combinations and execute the laws   I appeal to all loyal citizens to facilitate and aid in this effort to maintain the laws and the integrity of the perpetuity of the popular government, and redress wrongs long enough endured   The first service assigned to the forces, probably, will be to repossess the forts, places and property which have been seized from the Union   Let the utmost care be taken, consistent with the object, to avoid devastation, destruction, interference with the property of peaceful citizens in any part of the country , and I hereby command persons composing the aforesaid combination to disperse within twenty days from date

I hereby convene both Houses of Congress for the 4th day of July next, to determine upon measures for public safety which the interest of the subject demansd

ABRAHAM LINCOLN,
President of the United States

WM H SEWARD, *Secretary of State*

The gauntlet thrown down by the traitors of the South was accepted—not, however, in the spirit with which insolence meets insolence—but with a firm, determined spirit of patriotism and love of country.   The duty of the President was plain, under the Constitution and the laws, and above and beyond all, the people, from whom political power is derived, demanded the suppression of the rebellion, and stood ready to sustain the authority of their representatives and executive officers

The absence of the files of newspapers in Waterloo, from 1861 to 1864, renders it impossible for the historian to do full justice to the spirit and patriotism of this people in the early days of America's gigantic and bloody struggle against rebellion, and their liberal contributions to maintain the integrity of this

glorious Union.   It is a proud record, for from their midst went out brave sol
diers, to aid in the grand struggle for the maintenance and perpetuity of
Republican institutions.

A union of lakes, a union of lands,
A union that none can sever,
A union of hearts, a union of hands—
The American Union forever

Never before in the world's history was witnessed such an uprising of the masses,
such unanimity of sentiment, such willingness to sacrifice life and money on the
altar of patriotism

When the first companies were being raised, measures were inaugurated and
carried out to raise money by subscription for the support of the families of the
volunteers.   But there were so many calls for men, and the number and needs
of these families whose providers had gone to defend the life of the nation, that
it became an impossibility for private purses, however willing their holders, to
supply all the demand, and the county authorities made frequent and liberal
appropriations from the public treasury for that purpose   Private liberality
still continued.   This money was raised in the midst of the excitement of war,
when the exigencies of the times demanded it, and the generous people never
thought to inquire how much was given.   Aside from the sums appropriated by
county authority, no account was ever kept   Had there been, the sum would
now seem almost fabulous.

A volunteer military company was organized at Cedar Falls in February,
1861, with J. B. Smith as Captain; C. D Billings, First Lieutenant, W
Francis, Second Lieutenant, F Sessions, C H. Mullarky, W Hamel, F. H
Cooper, Sergeants; William McCoy, John Brown, George Leland, J. Rosenbaum, Corporals.   The company bore on its roster sixty names   The name
adopted was "Pioneer Grays."

Late in April, 1861, the Pioneer Grays began to prepare for marching to
the front, under the following order :

ADJUTANT GENERAL'S OFFICE, IOWA CITY, April 18, 1861
J B Smith, Captain of the Pioneer Grays

SIR—The President of the United States has made a requisition upon Iowa for a regiment
of volunteers, to defend the Government against traitors and rebels in arms

The Governor has directed me to call on you, and to request you to fill up your ranks to the
number of not less than seventy-eight men, including officers; and if that number should be
exceeded, there will be no objection to it   ,When your number is completed, your company will
proceed to elect a Captain and two Lieutenants, and transmit the result to this office, when the
officers will be immediately commissioned

As soon as your company is organized and officers are elected, unless you get other orders
from the Governor, let the men go home, holding themselves in readiness to march at a moment's
warning   They must be at the rendezvous by the 20th of May, at the farthest, and may be
called sooner at the proper time   You will be notified when and where to meet to be mustered
into the service, and will be furnished with funds for all expenses from that time until received
by the United States officers

The United States will furnish arms and accouterments for the use of the regiment

I am very respectfully your obedient servant,

J BOWEN
Adjutant General of the Militia of Iowa

The company met at their armory on the evening of the 20th, and adopted
the following resolutions by a vote of fifty to three .

WHEREAS, The Government of the United States, in the peaceful exercise of its rights, has
been threatened by rebellion and insurrection in some of the States, by armed mobs seizing the
Government property and holding it in defiance of law, in refusing in those States to execute
the laws of Congress, made under and by virtue of the Constitution of the United States ,
attacking their army when peacefully occupying their forts and other property, and destroying
the same , therefore,

Resolved, 1st, That we condemn in the severest terms the actions of those engaged in the insurrection, and all who sympathize with them, as unpatriotic, disloyal and traitorous to the country

Resolved, 2d. That the General Government ought to be sustained by every true and loyal citizen, and that we hereby pledge ourselves as a company to rally to the support of the Star Spangled Banner at any and all times when the country shall need our services

Resolved, 3d, That we cheerfully tender to the Governor of Iowa the services of the Pioneer Grays, at such times as he shall deem it expedient to demand our aid, and earnestly entreat him to accept the same

Resolved, 4th, That the Secretary be requested to forward a certified copy of these resolutions to the Hon Samuel J Kirkwood, Governor of the State, and that they be published in the Cedar Falls *Gazette*

A large national flag, bearing the motto, "Our Flag, We will Defend It," was then hanging across the street by a cord passing from the Carter House to the Overman Block When the resolutions had been adopted, the boys marched out, formed a square under the flag and gave three cheers for the banner, followed by three more for their country. A piece of music was played by the Cornet Band, after which the crowd gave three cheers for the Grays— the offering of Cedar Falls on their country's altar.

The resolutions given above were transmitted to the Governor, and in response the following was received ·

DAVENPORT, April 24, 1861

J Jay Layman, Esq , Cedar Falls

DEAR SIR—The Governor has received a copy of the proceedings of your Company, the sentiments of which, he instructs me to say, he highly approves The regiment called for by the Government has already been filled up and accepted. He requests me to say that you should report to the Adjutant General's office a roll of your Company and to hold your Company in readiness for a future call   I am truly yours,

J BOWEN, *Adjutant General*

W. J. Steel was the first man to leave Cedar Falls for the war He was a member of a Chicago cavalry company which had been accepted and ordered into camp Mentioning the fact that he was ordered to rejoin his company, and that he was going on the next train, the Grays turned out and escorted him to the depot, where the patriotic good-by was said between him and each member of the Grays as the train came in that was to carry him from his new-found home

Late in May came the order to march, from the Adjutant General, to which the following was supplementary :

ATTENTION, GRAYS '—All those who have enrolled themselves with the Pioneer Grays, of Cedar Falls, are hereby notified that they must report themselves to the Commanding Officer at once, as the Company should drill daily until the time of departure The citizens of the town are furnishing a fatigue uniform for each member The Company will *positively leave* on the cars *Tuesday morning* [June 4th]   J B SMITH, *Captain*

FITZROY SESSIONS, *Orderly.*

During the same week a contribution was raised among the citizens of the town to assist in the maintenance of the families of those who were so soon to go This fund amounted to over $800, and was separate from the uniform fund, which was $300 more

But little else was now thought of by the community till the close of the day that marked their departure. Sunday afternoon, Rev L B. Fifield addressed the Grays at Overman's Hall. At noon on Monday, the recruits from Waverly and vicinity arrived, accompanied by 350 citizens from that town, and were received in front of the Overman Block At 3 o'clock, Capt. M. M. Trumbull, of Butler County, reached town with his company, the Union Guards, and for a time each command seemed to be trying to outcheer the other After remaining half an hour, the Butler boys resumed their march toward Waterloo, where they were to be joined by some twenty-five or more recruits.   The Grays then chose their permanent officers

Monday night another meeting was held at Overman's Hall, and the crowded audience was addressed by J. B Powers, Esq , Hon Z. Streeter, D Allen, Esq., A. J. Felt, of Bradford, Rev Mr. Porterfield and Mr. Jackson, the latter one of the Floyd County volunteers.   The parting address was made by W H. Nichols, Esq.

Tuesday morning, five thousand people assembled for the final farewell One touching incident at the depot will suffice for this   A wife, whose sobbing children were clinging to her skirts, entreated her husband not to go   Three men standing by, each begged the brave fellow to let them take his place, but with patriotic fortitude he gently released his almost fainting wife, and boarded the train.   The train moved out amid shouts and sobs, the excitement had culminated, and by noon the town had such repose as follows a burial service on a Sabbath afternoon

If the members of Company K were sent away with sadness of heart, caused by the reflection that they had left hosts of true friends behind them, they were fully recompensed by their reception on their arrival at home on Saturday, April 2, 1864, nearly three years after their departure.   A brief address was made at the depot by Rev J. S Eberhart, after which the veterans marched to Overman's Hall, where they were formally welcomed by Rev. L. B. Fifield, who, for the town, had dedicated them to their country's service.   A bountiful supper was then served by the patriotic women at Cedar Falls, at Horticultural Hall, and at its close the boys felt that for them the "days of danger, nights of waking," were over and done

At the June session of the Board of Supervisors, on the 8th day of June, 1861, Jesse Wasson introduced the following ·

WHEREAS, Certain States of this Union are in rebellion against the laws and government of the United States, and with force of arms are attempting to subvert our beloved institutions, and, whereas, this rebellion has become so extensive and formidable as to seriously threaten the very existence of our national institutions , and, whereas, the President of the United States, in view of the imminent perils which now hang over the nation, has called upon all good, loyal citizens to defend the Union, assist in executing the laws and protect the nation's property, therefore,

Resolved, That the strong arm of national power should crush all such attempts at treason, even at the cannon's mouth, and that the time has now come to solve the problem whether we have a Government capable of sustaining itself against its foes , that all good and loyal citizens should heartily unite to defend the Union against the attacks of its enemies, whether foreign or domestic , that every order-loving and law-abiding citizen should regard as enemies the citizens of all the seceded States while in arms against the Government , and not until they have returned to their former allegiance and made restitution for these aggressions will we hail them as we have heretofore done , that we look at the unanimity that now prevails throughout all the loyal States of this Union in the present crisis, with joy, and that in the suppression of this rebellion we will not act as partisans but as *patriots,* as good loyal citizens , forgetting all proclivities, we will stand by the *Ship of State,* the Constitution and the maintenance of the *laws,* and by no act of ours will we show sympathy with *treason,* nor will we allow it to go unpunished, but will do our utmost to transmit the fair fabric of our beloved institutions to the remotest posterity , that we believe the best and only sure remedy for *treason* and *rebellion,* now so prevalent in some States in this Union, is powder and lead for the ranks and *hemp* for the leaders

That we will sustain the President of the United States in his efforts to maintain the supremacy of the laws and our national existence, that we will sustain the Governor of this State in the prompt and efficient manner in which he has responded to the call of the National Government , that we will march under no other banner but the Stars and Stripes , that we will know no other country but the Union , that we will carry the Star Spangled Banner throughout the length and breadth of this Union until it spreads its fluttering folds over the battlements of Fort Sumter, retrieved in honor and its glory untarnished

The resolution was unanimously adopted.   On the same day the Board passed a resolution appropriating $500 for the relief of the families of volunteers who had enlisted or should enlist during the progress of the strife.   The Clerk reported Oct. 15, 1861, that $110 had been drawn for said purposes, whereupon Mr. Wasson moved the further appropriation of $110 to be added to the original appropriation, which was carried

A special session of the Board was held August 22, 1861, at which resolutions expressing the most patriotic sentiments were passed by the Board of Supervisors, and by them it was made the duty of each Supervisor to ascertain the wants and necessities of the wives and families of volunteers in their respective townships, and upon his report relief was to be furnished such families by the county, the maximum amount not to exceed $5 per month for the wife and $1.50 for each child.

[The Board drew pay and mileage for their extra labors in this patriotic cause]

The following resolution was read by the Clerk at the September meeting, 1862, having been passed at a mass meeting held in Waterloo :

Resolved, That it is the sentiment of this meeting that the Board of Supervisors of Black Hawk County should make an appropriation of $5 per month to the family of each volunteer in the county, and that the Clerk be requested to lay this resolution before the Board at their next session

It was referred to a special committee, who reported favorably, but was not adopted by the Board.

Sept. 5th, the Board passed a resolution which, after its various amendments, provided for the payment of "four & $16\frac{2}{3}$-100 dollars " to the families of " soldiers," excluding commissioned officers '

At the October session, 1862, the Clerk reported a total of $899.56 expended for the relief of soldiers' families, drawn by townships as follows   Waterloo, $212.16 ; East Waterloo, $145 60 ; Lester, $30.12 ; Mount Vernon, $12 48 , Washington, $12.48 ; Union, $8.32 ; Barclay, $12.48 ; Poyner, $37.44 ; Fox, $4 16 ; Cedar, $8.32 ; Orange, $24.96 ; Black Hawk, $16.64 ; Spring Creek, $112.32 , Big Creek, $45 76 ; Cedar Falls, $216.32.

At an adjourned meeting, held December 7, 1863, the Board ordered a bounty of $200 to be paid to each volunteer who had or should enlist under the then last call for men.

January 6, 1864, the Board ordered that families receiving the $200 should be excluded from receiving aid from the Volunteer Fund

September 6, 1864, on motion of B. Sergeant, the Clerk was authorized to issue county warrants to veteran volunteers, for bounty of $200 each, upon the certificate of the Captain or any officer of higher grade than Captain, that they had enlisted as veteran volunteers and been credited to Black Hawk, previous to January 7, A. D. 1864.

January 4, 1865, a committee was appointed to draft resolutions in the matter of raising a bounty for volunteers to fill the call for soldiers, consisting of Messrs. Corwin, Abbey and Gilkey, who presented the following :

Resolved, That the Clerk of this Board be authorized and he is hereby directed to issue a county warrant for $400 to each volunteer recruit or drafted man who shall enlist or be drafted under the present call of the President of the United States for 300,000 men, on the said volunteer or drafted man filing with said Clerk a certificate from the Provost Marshal that the said volunteer or drafted man has been accepted and mustered into the service of the United States and credited to the county of Black Hawk

Resolved, That the Clerk of this Board shall not issue warrants (for the said purpose of paying enlisted volunteers or drafted men) to any one township of said county of Black Hawk, to exceed $400 for each man of the number that may be assigned to each of the several townships, but issue warrants of $400 to each man of the number that may be assigned to each of the several townships and raised by volunteers or draft and complying with the foregoing resolution by presenting a certificate as aforesaid

Carried.

As long as the war continued, money was ready—men were ready. Men of wealth furnished the former, and the less affluent filled the ranks—furnished the brawn, the muscle, the bravery, the sinews of war Oftentimes, the former furnished not only their share of money, but shouldered their muskets and followed the starry flag, as well.

Having noticed the financial sacrifices and the readiness of the wealthier part of the people to contribute liberally and continuously of their means, we come now to the volunteer soldiery And of these, what can we say? What vivid words can the pen employ that will do justice to their heroic valor, to their unequaled and unparalleled bravery and endurance? Home and home comforts, wives and little ones, fathers, mothers, sisters, brothers, were all given up for life and danger on the fields of battle—for exposure, fatigue, disease and death, at the point of the bayonet or at the cannon's mouth But little they recked for all these, but boldly and bravely went out with their lives in their hands, to meet and to conquer the foes of the Union, maintain its supremacy and vindicate its honor and its integrity. No more fitting tribute to their patriotic valor can be offered than a full and complete record. so far as it is possible to make it, embracing the names, the terms of enlistment, the battles in which they were engaged, and all the minutiæ of their military lives. It will be a wreath of glory encircling every brow—a precious memento which each and every one of them earned, gloriously earned, in defense of their and our common country.

WAR RECORD OF BLACK HAWK COUNTY.

TAKEN PRINCIPALLY FROM ADJUTANT GENERAL'S REPORTS

ABBREVIATIONS.

Adjt.	Adjutant	I V I	Iowa Volunteer Infantry
Art.	Artillery	kld	killed
Bat	Battle or Battalion	Lieut.	Lieutenant
Col	Colonel	Maj	Major
Capt	Captain	m o	mustered out
Corp	Corporal	prmtd	promoted
Comsy	Commissary	prisr	prisoner
com	commissioned	Regt	Regiment
cav	cavalry	re-e	re-enlisted
captd	captured	res	resigned
desrtd	deserted	Sergt	Sergeant
disab	disabled	trans	transferred
died	discharged	vet	veteran
e	enlisted	V R C	Veteran Reserve Corps
excd	exchanged	wd	wounded
Inf	infantry	hon died	honorably discharged
inv	invalid		

THIRD INFANTRY

The Third Regiment was raised, drilled and sent to the front about August 1, 1861 Its first engagement was at Blue Mills, Mo., September 18, 1861 Fought gallantly at Shiloh two days, the second day under command of Lieut Crosley, the regimental officers being off duty or wounded At Metamora, October 5, 1862, the regiment suffered heavily On its way to join Gen Grant, before Vicksburg, the Third was attacked by guerrillas, and had fourteen men wounded Participated in the operations at Vicksburg July 12, 1863, it went into battle at Johnson, Miss., with 241 men, and lost 114 killed, wounded and missing Participated in the Meridian expedition, arriving there February 3, 1864, and next day tore up fifteen miles of railroad Near Atlanta, did good service, July 28th Greatly reduced in numbers, the survivors re enlisted, forming three companies, and consolidated with the Second Infantry

Surg Daniel M Cool, com asst. surg June 21, 1861, prmtd surg April 8, 1862, resd Sept 4, 1862
Adjt Fitzroy Seamons, com 1st lieut Co K June 3, 1861, prmtd adjt. June 26, 1861, resd October 16, 1862
Sergt Maj R W Montague, e May 20, 1861, died Nov 15, 1862
Hosp Steward John J Fry, e. May 21 1861

Company A.

Blasberry, Chas , e April 4, 1864
Smith, John T , e April 4, 1864, kld July 21, 1864

Company B.

Tusing, Noah , e Dec 10, 1863, died May 29, 1864.

Company I.

Second Lieut G A Eberhart, com June 5, 1861, resd May 1, 1862
Second Lieut Daniel W Foote, com Aug 10, 1862, wd at Blue Mills and Metamora, resd Aug 21, 1863
Sergt R Miller, e May 20, 1861, kld at Jackson, Miss
Sergt Henry Crittenden, e May 20, 1861
Corp Matthew Toule, e May 20, 1861, wd at Jackson, Miss., and died at Jefferson Barracks Aug 12, 1863
Musician Chas E Balcomb, e May 20, 1861, wd at Blue Mills
Bullock, Howard, e May 20, 1861, wd at Shiloh
Brott, A E , e May 20, 1861
Collins, Geo W , e Nov 10, 1861
Collins, C C., e May 20, 1861, died at St Louis May 3, 1863
Dorland, Peter S , e May 20, 1861, wd at Blue Mills, died Sept. 5, 1862
Dutcher, Wheaton, e May 20, 1861, kld July 12, 1863, in battle at Jackson, Miss
DeWolf, George W , e May 20, 1861, died Dec 20, 1861, disab
Dodd, J B P , e May 20, 1861, wd at Blue Mills
Eberhart. Geo E , e May 20, 1861
Frost, James M , e Jan 4, 1864
Garrett, George F , e May 20, 1861
Gates, S B , e May 20, 1861
Livingston, Peter, e May 20, 1861
Peppers, William L , e May 20, 1861, wd twice at Blue Mills
Stocken, John C., e May 20, 1861, wd at Shiloh
Shaw, H B , e, May 20, 1861, wd at Metamora
Starr, Hiram, e Nov 10, 1861
Short, S L , e May 20, 1861, wd at Shiloh, died April 7, 1862
Shipman, William W , e Dec 6, 1861, died at St. Louis Jan 3, 1862
Thorn, S B , e May 20, 1861
Washburn, L T , e May 20, 1861, wd at Blue Mills, died Sept 18, 1861
White, Joseph B , e May 20, 1861, died Feb 9, 1862
White, Nelson, e May 20, 1861

Company K.

Capt. John B Smith, com June 8, 1861, resd June 14, 1864
First Lieut William B Hamill, e as sergt May 21, 1861, prmtd 1st lieut Nov 15, 1861, wd at Shiloh, resd April 20, 1864
Second Lieut Charles H Mullarky, com June 3, 1861, resd Nov 30, 1861
Second Lieut. John Wayne, e as sergt May 21, 1861, prmtd 2d lieut Dec 1, 1861, wd and captd at bat Shiloh Feb 1, 1863
Second Lieut John T Boggs, e as private May 21, 1861, sergt , then 2d lieut April 3, 1863
Sergt Gilbert H Pulver, e May 21, 1861, wd at Shiloh, trans to Inv Corps
Sergt George H Merrill, e. May 21, 1861, wd at Shiloh, died Oct. 25, 1862
Sergt Samuel L Taggart, e May 21, 1861, wd at Shiloh, prmtd to capt and A A G, U S Vols
Sergt George W Briggs, e May 21, 1861, died Feb 9, 1862
Sergt. H J. Denton, e May 21, 1861
Corp Jesse Cooper, e May 21, 1861
Corp W F Schenck, e May 21, 1861, died at Jackson Dec 23, 1862
Corp Edward Reniger, e May 21, 1861, trans to Co B, 7th inf
Corp R. Van Ransselaer, e May 21, 1861, wd at Shiloh
Corp G E Ellsworth, e May 21, 1861, wd at Jackson
Corp Levi M Langstaff, e May 21, 1861
Corp Walter W Wood, e May 21, 1861
Corp Wm H Nickolls, e May 21, 1861
Corp Chas H Boehmler, e May 21, 1861
Musician G B Thayer, e May 21, 1861, wd at Jackson, died Sept 12, 1863
Musician F A Thyne, e May 21, 1861, wd at Jackson, died June 11, 1864, wds
Wagoner L Young, e May 21, 1861
Wagoner S O Hammond, e May 21, 1861

Allen, Moses, e May 21, 1861, vet. Jan 4, 1864, captd at Canton, died at Andersonville
Allen, Hiram, e Jan 4, 1864
Brown, A E , e May 21, 1861, wd at Shiloh, died April 10, 1862
Ball, R J , e May 21, 1861, died April 2, 1862
Bullis, C H , e May 21, 1861, died June 16, 1862, at St Louis
Brownell, J H , e May 21, 1861, kld at battle of Blue Mills
Bennett, A J , e May 21, 1861, died for disability Feb 28, 1862
Burke, Patrick, e May 21, 1861
Baker, James H , e May 21, 1861
Briggs, Wallace, e May 21, 1861, wd at Shiloh, died Sept 19, 1862
Cutler, D B , e May 21, 1861
Cain, Martin A , e May 21, 1861
Davenport, R W , e May 21, 1861, died Dec. 6, 1861
Dickey, A N , e May 21, 1861
Daniels, James M , e May 21, 1861
Dignan, John, e May 21, 1861, died March 31, 1862, disab
Dawson P B , e May 21, 1861
Fisk, William H , e May 21, 1861, died Dec. 6, 1861.
Griggs, Freeman, e May 21, 1861, died Dec 29, 1862
Griggs, Luther, e May 21, 1861, kld accidentally Dec 2, 1861
Groom, E., e May 21, 1861
Grove, Samuel, e May 21, 1861, wd at Jackson, died Oct. 9, 1863
Gillett, M F , e May 21, 1861 died April 24, 1862
Gosting, William E , e May 21, 1861
Hubbard, A O , e. May 21, 1861
Hasselton, R C, e May 21, 1861, died Jan 12, 1862, at Quincy
Jackson, Z E , e May 21, 1861
Jones, C , e May 21, 1861, wd at Shiloh, died Oct 19, '62
Johnston, J B , e May 21, 1861
Jefferson, E H , e May 21, 1861, wd at Shiloh, trans to Invalid Corps
King, H H , e May 21, 1861
Leveraee, Austin, e May 21, 1861, wd at Jackson
Lawrence, A G , e May 21, 1861, died Sept 18, 1862.
Laird, John Q , e May 21, 1861, died May 5, 1862, at Pittsburg Landing
Merrill, John T , e May 21, 1861
Morris, George W , e May 21, 1861
Mabie, D M , e May 21, 1861
Matlack, E , e May 21, 1861, deserted Nov 8, 1861
McElroy, William, e May 21, 1861, deserted Sept 14, '61
McRoberts, John, e May 21, 1861, died April 29, 1862
Mook, Joseph
Moury, George W , e May 21, 1861, kld at Shiloh
Moulton, C C , e May 21, 1861, wd at Shiloh, died. Sept 24, 1862
Orchard, George, e May 21, 1861
Parmalee, Junius, e May 21, 1861
Philpot, John, e May 21, 1861
Philpot. George J , e May 21, 1861
Peyton, William, e May 21, 1861
Potts, John, e May 21, 1861, died April 12, 1862
Pattee, John W , e May 21, 1861
Rambeck, M , e May 21, 1861
Rider, W S , e May 21, 1861
Ross, Joseph A , e May 21, 1861, wd at Shiloh, died April 10, 1862
Snyder, P W , e May 21, 1861
Skillen, B F , e May 21, 1861
Shields, Edward, e May 21, 1861, captd at Canton, Miss
Sabin, George H , e May 21, 1861, deserted Nov 9, 1861
Tyrell, F M , e May 21, 1861, missing at Shiloh
Taylor, B E , e May 21, 1861
Troutner, John F , e May 21, 1861
Tracy, Samuel J , e May 21, 1861
Tuthill, George, e May 21, 1861
West, Darius B , e. May 21, 1861
West, Thomas P , e May 21, 1861
Wolcott, Norman M , e May 21, 1861, wd at Shiloh, died Sept 26, 1862
Watson, George H , e May 21, 1861, wd at Shiloh, died Sept 19, 1862
Wemple, Charles E , e May 21, 1861, died Feb. 28, 1862
Wemple, Albert H., e May 21, 1861

UNKNOWN

Ayres, J D , e Dec 10, 1863
Brubacher, D , e Dec 14, 1863
Filkins, William, e, Dec 10, 1863
Nash, C P , e Dec 11, 1863
Wilder, William, e Dec 10, 1863.

SECOND CONSOLIDATED INFANTRY

(Second and Third)

Company A.

First Lieut Jesse Cooper, com July 8, 1864, from 3d vet inf, died March 23, 1865
Second Lieut Chas Boehmler, e June 8, 1861, prmt 2d lieut. March 24, 1865
Corp Danl M Mabie, e June 8, 1861, vet Jan 4, 1864
Boehmler, Jacob, e April 4, 1864
Boehmler, Edw, e April 4, 1864
Daniel, Jas M, e June 8, 1861, vet Jan 18, 1864
Hoyt, E F, e April 4, 1864
Maggart, Jas M, e April 4, 1864
Nichols, Wm H, e Jan 8, 1861, vet. Jan 4, 1864
Rambach, M, e Jan 8, 1861, vet Jan 4, 1864
Rhorssen, Henry, e April 4, 1864
Rothermal, Geo, e April 4, 1864

Company F.

Corp Geo W Collins, e Jan 8, 1861, vet Dec 27, 1863.
Musician C E Balcom, e Jan 8, 1861, vet. Jan 4, 1864
Brott A E, e Jan 8, 1864, vet. Dec 17, 1863
Brewbecker, D, e Dec. 14, 1863
Eberhart, Geo E., e Jan 8, 1861, vet Jan 4, 1864
Loatwell, Jas., e Jan 8, 1861, vet. Dec 27, 1863, died May 26, 1865
White, Nelson, e Jan 8, 1861, vet Jan 4, 1864, kld at Atlanta

NINTH INFANTRY

In July, 1861, the day after the battle of Bull Run, Hon William Vandever tendered to the Secretary of War a regiment of volunteers, to be recruited in his district His offer was accepted, and he at once resigned, returned to Iowa and went energetically to work The first company went into rendezvous at Dubuque, early in August, and the regiment was raised and mustered into service September 24, 1861 Immediately after being mustered in, the regiment was ordered to St Louis, where it went into camp of instruction at Benton Barracks In October it was assigned to railroad guard duty January 22, 1862, the Ninth joined the Army of the Southwest at Rolla, under Brig Gen Samuel R Curtis, and was made a portion of the Second Brigade, which was placed under the command of Col Vandever The army marched in pursuit of the rebel Gen Price, and February 15, entered Springfield, but Price was gone, and Curtis pursued At a skirmish at Sugar Creek, near the line between Missouri and Arkansas, the Ninth was first under fire and behaved like veterans, charging and driving a force three times their number March 4th, Col Vandever, with a portion of his brigade, went to Huntsville, fifteen miles, and while here received dispatches from Gen Curtis that Price had been heavily reinforced, that forty thousand rebels, under Van Dorn, were advancing northward, and ordering him to rejoin the army at Pea Ridge, at once To avoid the rebel army, Col Vandever marched forty-one miles on the 6th, fording White River and several other streams on the way, arriving at headquarters at 6 P M, and participated in the two days' battle of Pea Ridge The brigades commanded by Col Vandever and Col Dodge stood the brunt of the battle They were handled with remarkable skill and coolness, and fought with a valor never surpassed in the war history of the world "The Fourth and Ninth Iowa," says Gen Curtis, "won imperishable honors" In his report of the battle, Col Vandever makes especial mention of Lieut Col Herron, Maj Coyle, Adj William Scott, Capts Dripe (who was killed), Turner, Bull, Carpenter, Bevins (killed), Washburn, Moore and Cankadden, and Lieuts Kelsey, Riley, Jones, Neff, Tindale, Rice (killed), Baker, Beebe, Leverich, Crane, McGee, McKenzie, Fellows, Claflin and Inman, and Sergt Maj Foster, of the Ninth The regiment went into camp at Helena, Ark, about the middle of July, and remained five months December 28th and 29th, the regiment was under fire in the battle of Chickasaw Bayou The year 1864 was brilliantly commenced by the Ninth by the campaign of Arkansas Post After destroying the works there, the regiment encamped near Young's Point, La, for many weary weeks The regiment participated in the siege of Vicksburg, was a part of Sherman's army in pursuit of Joe Johnston, was in the battle above the clouds at Lookout Mountain On the 1st of May, 1885, the regiment entered upon the Atlanta campaign, and for four months participated in all the labors, battles and skirmishes of the famous march through the Carolinas, and was a portion of the Iowa Brigade which captured Columbia. The gallant Ninth always fought with bravery when there was any fighting to do

Company B.

Long, Daniel R., e Aug 30, 1861, vet Jan 1, 1864, captd at Dallas, Ga
Long, Geo W, e Dec 12, 1863, kld at Dallas, Ga

Company C.

Van Wie, John, e Dec 14, 1863

Company C.

Capt Fred S Washburn, com Sept 16, 1861, wd three times at Vicksburg, May 22, 1863, and died at home of wds June 16, 1863
Capt Jno P Bowman, e as sergt Aug 11, 1861, prmtd 1st lieut May 29, 1863, prmtd capt Sept 17, 1863, m o Oct 26, 1864, term expired
Second Lieut. Henry L Peacock, e as sergt Aug 20, 1861, prmtd 2d lieut May 12, 1862, res Aug 3, 1863
Corp Otis G Day, e Aug 3, 1861, prmtd sergt of Hay den's Bat Oct 7 1861
Corp H Kilbourn, e July 28, 1861, wd at Ringgold, Ga
Allman, Jas B, e July 28, 1861, wd at Pea Ridge, died at Waterloo
Branniger, H S, e Aug 26, 1861, vet Jan 1, 1864, prmtd corp
Balkcom D E, e Aug 20, 1861, died Dec 20, 1861
Brewater, Jas P, vet Jan 1, 1864
Branniger, Jas M, e Sept 16, 1861, died at Waterloo March 13, 1864
Clark, F J, e Aug 20, 1861, wd at Pea Ridge, killed at Kenesaw Mt
Dunaboo, A, e Aug 20, 1861, vet Jan 1, 1864, wd at Vicksburg and Kingston, Ga
Estell, Hiram, e Aug 16, 1861, wd at Pea Ridge, died at Springfield, Mo
Hill, Jas D, e Aug 20, 1861, died Sept 30, 1862, disab
Heath, F H, e Aug 20, 1861, died March 28, 1862, of wds received at Pea Ridge
Hurlbut, S B, vet Jan 1, '64, captd at Lynch Creek, Ga
Klock, Geo, e Aug 30, 1861, vet Jan 1, 1864
Little, Sardie, e Sept 6, 1861, died
Lockerby, Nelson, Aug 15, 1861, died June 23, '62, disab
Mitchell, C H, e Aug 12, 1861
Parker, Jos, e Aug 10, 1861, kld at Pea Ridge
Price, Anthony, e Aug 24, 1861, died ae Vicksburg
Parker, Wm H, e Aug 20, 1861, died Nov 12, 1861 in Pacific, Mo
Jordan, M L, e Aug 19, 1861, vet Jan 1, 1864
St John, Jas N, e Aug 24, 1861, vet Jan 1, 1864
Symons, O E, vet Jan 1, 1864

Company I.

First Lieut. Jos G Inman, com 2d lieut Sept 18, 1861, prmtd 1st lieut June 14, 1862, resd Feb 15, 1863

TWELFTH INFANTRY

The Twelfth Regiment was recruited late in the Summer of 1861, and organized at Camp Union, Dubuque, Iowa, and mustered into the service of the United States November 25, 1861, by Capt Washington, Thirteenth United States Infantry

The first active service was at Fort Donelson, where it was assigned to Cook's Brigade of Smith's Division, and was engaged in the battles of the 13th, 14th and 15th of February, which resulted in the capture of the Fort and its garrison on the 16th

At Shiloh, the Twelfth was brigaded with the Second, Seventh and Fourteenth Iowa regiments, called the Iowa Brigade, commanded by Gen Tuttle, Second Iowa Infantry, Gen W H Wallace commanding the Division, and were in position near a field beyond Gen Hurlbut's headquarters Here it remained in line of battle from 6 o'clock A M until about 4 P M, during which time the enemy made several bold charges, and was repulsed with great loss in killed and wounded

The Twelfth and Fourteenth being in support of a battery, and having no orders to fall back, and not having notice that the left had given way, were allowed to be surrounded, and, after several hours' desperate fighting, in which three or four regiments contended against the whole rebel force, the Twelfth having its commanding officer, Col Woods, severely wounded, with sixteen men killed and ninety seven wounded, with all hopes of retreat or succor cut off, was obliged to surrender at 6 o'clock P M Number of men captured from the regiment, about 400

The men of the Eighth, Twelfth and Fourteenth Iowa Regiments who were not captured, were organized into a regiment called the "Union Brigade," of which regiment the Twelfth formed Companies E and K

The Union Brigade was engaged and took a very prominent part in the battle of Corinth, October 3d and 4th, 1862, the Twelfth Iowa losing three killed and twenty-five wounded out of eighty men engaged After pursuing the enemy as far as Ripley, Miss, the regiment returned to Corinth, where it was engaged in building fortifications, until December 18, 1862, when orders were received from the War Department discontinuing the organization known as the Union Brigade, and ordering the men of the Eighth, Twelfth and Fourteenth Iowa to proceed to Davenport, Iowa, to re-organize their regiments, prisoners having been paroled October 18, 1862, and exchanged November 10, 1862

The detachment of the Twelfth Iowa arrived at Jackson, Tenn, where it was found that Forrest had destroyed the railroad from Uniontown and was threatening Jackson The detachment was at once ordered to the defense of the place, and remained four days, when it was ordered to open the railroad to Columbus, Ky, which delayed the detachment until the 4th of January It arrived at Columbus on that day and was ordered once more to Davenport, where it arrived on the 7th of January, 1863, and from there it was ordered, on the 27th of March, to proceed to St Louis, Mo, there to rejoin the regiment, and as soon as organized, was ordered to report to Gen Grant in the field, near Vicksburg, Miss, and served during the entire siege, participating in all the principal engagements until the 22d of June, when it was sent to Black River, to guard the rear from an attack by Johnston Vicksburg surrendered July 4th

The Twelfth was engaged in the battle near Tupelo, Miss, on 13th, 14th and 15th of July, '64, losing nine men killed, fifty-four wounded and one missing out of 200 engaged

In June, 1864, Companies A and F, numbering fifty-five men, under command of Capt J R C Hunter, and Company A, while stationed at the mouth of White River, Ark, were attacked by 800 rebels of Marmaduke's command, about daylight on the 22d of June, but taking refuge behind a slight stockade, they repulsed the enemy, he leaving twenty killed and mortally wounded on the field The loss of Companies A and F was one killed and four wounded

The regiment fought bravely in the battle of Nashville, and received special mention by brigade and division commanders for good service

The regiment marched in pursuit of Hood, with the army, to Clinton, on the Tennessee River, thence by steamer to Eastport, Miss, arriving there on the 7th of January, 1865

From Eastport, the regiment was ordered to New Orleans, then embarked with the forces under Gen Canby, on the expedition against Mobile, was in the front line during the siege of Spanish Fort, which was the last service rendered by the regiment

During its service, the gallant Twelfth was in twenty three battles, was under fire 112 days, and had ninety-five men killed in battle

Company B.

First Lieut. John H Borger, com 2d lieut Oct 17, 1861, prmtd to 1st lieut Oct 3, 1862, m o Nov 23, 1864
Andrews, H R, e Oct 12, 1861, captd at Shiloh
Griffin, Lawrence, e Oct 12, 1861, deserted at Camp Union Oct. 23, 1861
Monk, Frederick, e Oct 7, 1861, captd at Shiloh

Company E.

Capt William Haddock, com Oct. 29, 1861, missing a[t] battle of Shiloh, com maj 9th cav May 28, 1863
First Lieut John Elwell, com Oct 29, 1861, captd at Shiloh and escaped, resd July 12, 1862
First Lieut James Stewart, e as sergt Sept 25, 1861, captd at Shiloh, prmtd to 2d lieut March 6, 1863, prmtd to 1st lieut May 28, 1863, died at Memphis July 4, 1864, of wds received from citizen of Memphis
First Lieut Charles R Switzer, e Oct 3, 1861, prmtd to 1st lieut April 20, 1866

Second Lieut John W Shumaker, e as corp Oct 12, '61, wd at Fort Donelson, vet Dec. 25, 1863, prmtd to 2d lieut. May 28, 1863, m o Dec 1, 1864
Sergt Patrick Duke, e Sept 25, 1861, died Aug 5, 1862
Sergt Charles Cook, e Oct 11, 1861, captd at Jackson
Corp John T Smith, e Oct 11, 1861, died at Baltimore, Md., Nov 10, 1862
Corp P P Carpenter, e Sept 25, 1861, died Jan. 31, 1862, at St Louis
Corp James Andrews, e Oct 19, 1861, died May 22, 1862, disab
Corp William Hamilton, e Oct 6 1861, died Jan 24, '62
Musician Oliver Lichty, e Oct 20, 1861, vet Dec 25, 1863
Biller, Anthony, e Oct 13, 1861, wd at Shiloh, vet. Dec 25, 1863, prmtd to corp.
Bird, Joshua, e Oct 15, 1861, captd at Shiloh, vet Dec 25, 1863
Bailey, Geo, e Oct 6, 1861, died May 3, 1862, at Keokuk
Bradfield, John, e Oct 4, 1861, died April 26, 1862, at Pittsburg
Church, Nathan, e Oct 14, 1861, died May 14, 1862
Cooley, Franklin, e Oct 28, 1861, died Jan 2, 1862, at St. Louis
Fuller, I W, e Oct 29, 1861, kld at Shiloh
Gorral, John W, e May 5, 1864, died Oct 13, 1864, at Memphis
Grady, Joseph, e Oct 17, 1861, vet. Dec 25, 1863
Holden, George R, e Oct 4, 1861, captd at Shiloh, vet Dec 25, 1863, kld, at Tupelo, Miss, July 12, 1864.
Howrey, Jacob, e Oct. 13, 1861, wd at Shiloh, died April 19, 1862
Hart, P N, e Oct. 13, 1861
Harrison, H J, e Oct 28, 1861, died April 1, 1862
King, E A, e Oct 8, 1861, wd at Fort Donelson, died July, 1862, disab
Koch, J F, e Oct 3, 1861, captd at Shiloh, died May 8, 1862, at Montgomery, Ala.
Lichey, Samuel J, e Oct 10, 1861, wd and captd at Shiloh, died at Macon, Ga, Oct 10, 1862
Leech, W P, e Oct 4, 1861, died at St Louis May, 1862
Moore, W S, e Nov 14, 1861, died July 12, 1862
Morris, C D, e Oct 6, 1861, captd at Shiloh, vet Dec 25, 1863
Minium, D., e Oct. 9, 1861
Manson, James, e Nov 18, 1861, died Jan 19, 1862
Meers, George W, e Nov 14, 1861, died March, 1862, at Dubuque
Ochs, Charles, e Oct 10, 1861, died April 4, 1862, disab
Porter, Thomas, e Oct 4, 1861, wd and captd at Shiloh, died
Pauley, William L, e Oct. 4, 1861, kld at Shiloh
Perry, A B, e. Oct 12, 1861, captd at Shiloh
Reed, Z, e Sept 23, 1861, died June 9, 1862, disab
Sherman, William H, e Oct 28, 1861 captd at Shiloh, died at Camp Woods Sept 12, 1863
Schrack David, e. Oct 6, 1861, wd at Corinth, died Feb 17, 1863
Strong, B, e Jan 4, 1864
Sawyer, Edmund, e Oct 6, 1861 died May 1862.
Shroger, Nathaniel, e Dec 28, 1861, died July 16, 1862, disab
Thompson, John P, e Oct. 22, 1861, wd. at Shiloh, died April 20, 1862
Talbot, Allen E, e Oct 11, 1861, captd at Shiloh, vet Dec 25, 1863
Watkins, Isaac, e Sept 25, 1861, vet. Dec 25, 1863

Company F.

Kironner, Michael, e Oct. 31, 1861, captd at Shiloh
Wigton, Thomas J, e Oct 1 1861, died April 4, 1862, at Savannah, Tenn

UNKNOWN

Griffin, Daniel, e Dec 31, 1864.
Lawrence, William, e Dec 7, 1864
Miller, John, e Dec 10, 1864
Rockwell, William, e Oct 15, 1864

SIXTEENTH INFANTRY.

The Sixteenth Regiment Iowa Volunteers left Davenport March 20, 1862, and was at the battles of Shiloh April 6th and 7th, when it met with heavy loss, took part in the siege of Corinth, also was in the battle of Iuka, September 19, 1862

After this, the regiment was engaged in the two-days fight at Corinth, October 3d and 4th, and was variously employed in marching from point to point, as their services were required in their department, and at all times were found ready to do their duty

They were engaged in many sharp conflicts, until March 17, 1864, when they started for Davenport, Iowa, on veteran furlough

On May 3d, the boys again resumed their knapsacke and arrived at Clifton, Tenn , about the middle of the month, and on the 27th of June, a part of the regiment were engaged in the attack on Kenesaw Mountain, meeting with heavy loss. The regiment was under fire from June 14th to July 2d, was in the battles at Atlanta, July 20th, 21st and 22d, meeting with heavy losses, which reduced the regiment to less than 100 men present for duty

Afterward, the regiment being increased to 450 men by an exchange of prisoners and drafted men, they started from Atlanta, November 15th, for Savannah, where they arrived December 10th, where they were engaged in the siege of the city until its evacuation

On January 6, 1865, they started for Beaufort, S C., and were actively engaged in the campaign in the Carolinas, and finally camped at Raleigh on the 6th of April, where they remained till May 2d The war being closed, they marched for Washington, where they took part in the grand review May 24, 1865

Company B

John Claussen, e as sergt. Sept. 20, 1861, wd at Shiloh and Corinth, vet. Feb 23, 1864, prmtd 2d lieut Nov 16, 1864,

Company G.

Atthue, Henry, e Dec 10, 1863
Bowers, H J C, e Dec 20, 1863, capt at Atlanta
Krommelbein, John e Dec 22, 1863, wd Nickajack Creek, died at Marietta, Ga
Lichtenheim, J J, e Dec 12, 1863
Miller, Lewis, e Dec 10, 1863
Mueller, Lewis, e Dec 10, 1863, capt at Atlanta
Schlicht, E A G, e Dec 7, 1863, capt. at Atlanta

Company H.

Baker, Reuben, e Feb 27, 1862, died July 14, 1862, disab.

Company I.

Capt. Henry D Wilhams, comd 1st lieut Feb 7, 1862, wd at Iuka, prmtd capt Nov 14, 1862
Capt Hugh Skelling, e, as Sergt Nov 30, 1861, capt at Iuka, prmtd 1st lieut Feb 13, 1863, prmtd capt April 9, 1863, wd at Nickajack Creek, m o Jan 19, 1865, term ex
Capt Martin Lott, e as sergt. Dec 2, 1861, prmtd 2d lieut April 19, 1863, captd in Atlanta, prmtd capt. Dec. 8, 1864
First Lieut. Isaac C Munger, e sergt Dec 16, 1861, capt. at Atlanta, prmtd 1st lieut, May 25, 1865
Sergt Geo N Hall, e Dec 14, 1861, vet Jan 5, 1864, trans to V R C
Corp. W P Hubbard, e Jan 29, 1862, vet Jan. 29, 1864, captd at Atlanta
Corp Wm Spencer, e Nov 28, 1862, died June 28, 1862, of wds received at Shiloh
Corp Geo Crumrine, e Dec 9, 1861 vet Jan 5, 1864, captd at Atlanta
Brown, J W, e Dec 18, 1863
Bowers, Chas H, e Dec. 2, 1862, vet. Dec 22, 1863, wd at Kenesaw Mt
Brubaker, Jno., e Feb 29, 1864
Bannister, Wm, e Dec 9, 1862, died Dec. 10, 1862, disab
Blake E., e Feb 23, 1864, wd at Nickajack Creek
Bowers, F E, e Jan 13, 1862, wd at Shiloh, died at Savannah, Tenn
Brooks Wm E, e Dec 9, 1861, captd at Atlanta
Brott, Wm H, e Jan 14, 1862 died Nov 28, 1863
Dengis, J A, e Dec 29, 1862
Griffith, W, e Jan 9, 1862, died at Keokuk, Nov 14, 1862
Higgins, Freeman, e Dec 9, 1861
Johnson, Jas W, e Dec 4, 1861
Keith, B K., e Nov 30, 1861
Lowell, A J, e Feb 29, 1864
Lake, C D, e Feb 19, 1862, died Nov 12, 1862
Lichly, Charles, e Dec 4, 1861, died Oct 4, 1862
McDowell, Martin, e Jan 8, 1862, died Jan 28, 1863, disab
Motts, G, e Dec 29, 1863, captd at Atlanta
Morgan, Thomas, e Dec 13, 1861, died July 26, 1862
McCumber, D, e Jan 30, 1862, died at Corinth
Odell, Jas E, e Feb 24, 1862, died Dec 22, 1862

Wellover, John H, e Dec 16, 1861, vet Jan 5, 1864
Evans, Ira, Dec 14, 1863
Kennedy, B, e Dec 25, 1863, captd. at Atlanta, died at Andersonville
Walther, Jacob, e Dec 19, 1863
Whitbeck, Robt., e Feb 3, 1863

TWENTY-FIRST INFANTRY

Went into service under Col Samuel Merrill, since Governor of Iowa Was engaged at Hartsville, Mo, January 11, 1863 Was at Port Gibeon, losing sixteen men Was again engaged at Black River Bridge, losing eighty-three. Was in charge on Fort Beauregard Was at capture of Vicksburg after which was ordered to New Orleans and thence to Texas March 5, 1865, was transferred to Mobile and served in engagement in that vicinity Was at Fort Blakely Was sent up Red River and thence to Baton Rouge, La., where it was mustered out July 15, 1865

Quartermaster Sergt J P Hamilton, e March 12, 1862

Company A.

Second Lieut Jeremiah W Brown, e as sergt March 15, 1862, prmtd 2d lieut Aug 2, 1862, resd. Feb 2, 1863
Sergt. Hiram Buel, e March 15, 1862, wd at Vicksburg, died Sept 18, 1863
Sergt Eli Wood, e March 19, 1862, died at Memphis
Sergt, J L Wheeler, e March 20, 1862, wd at Vicksburg
Corp Robt Moore, e March 20, 1862, kld at Jackson Miss
McCloud, John, e March 19, 1862, died June 27, 1864
Adams, John Q., e June 4, 1862, died Aug 6, 1862
Beecher, Ira, e June 4, 1862
Kinney, James, e June 4, 1862, died Sept., 1864
Lichly, M O, e June 4, 1862
Lawless, Peter, e Aug 21, 1862
McCrary, Lewis, e June 4, 1862, captd at Beaver Creek, Mo
McDonough, Patrick, e June 4, 1862, wd at Jackson, Miss
Moore, Robt, e June 4, 1862
Nearey, Edward, e June 4, 1862
Purkins, L., e June 4, 1862, died Aug 25, 1862
Stearns, Geo, e June 29, 1862, wd at Black River Bridge, Miss
Wood, Eli, e March 19, 1862

Company C.

First Lieut Frank Dale, com Aug 20, 1862, resd Feb 17, 1864
Corp John E Watson, e Aug 14, 1862, captd at Vicksburg
Mathews, John W, e Aug 14, 1862
Miner, H M, e Aug 14, 1862

Company E.

Blanchard, 1 D, e Dec 29, 1863

Company F.

McNally, Wm J, Aug 22, 1862

THIRTY-FIRST INFANTRY.

[NOTE —This regiment was mustered out at Louisville, Ky , June 27, 1865]

Was mustered into service at Davenport, by Capt Hendershott, on the 13th of October, 1862, and under command of Col William Smyth took transport and moved down the river November 1st, arriving at Helena, Ark., the 20th inst On the 27th of the same month, they started on an expedition to the Cold Water River, in Mississippi, returning to Helena December 7th Two weeks later, they started on the Yazoo River expedition, and the regiment was partially engaged in the battle at Chickasaw Bayou, on the 27th, 28th and 29th of December

On the 2d of January, 1863, they started for a point near Arkansas Post, where they arrived on the 9th inst, and on the night of the 10th marched through swamps and mire to the rear of the enemy's works, where, on the 11th, they hotly engaged in the capture of the place

From this point, the regiment was ordered to Young's Point, La., where they remained in camp until April 2d, when they moved again up the river to Greenville, Miss , and, after some skirmishing and considerable foreging for mules, cattle, horses, hogs, and even negroes, returned to Young's Point on the 26th of the same month From here they moved with Grant's whole army toward Grand Gulf, arriving May 7th, when they again moved toward Jackson, Miss The regiment was under fire at Raymond, on the 12th, was at the taking of Jackson, on the 14th , and again under fire at Black River, on the 16th, reaching the rear of Vicksburg on the 18th, where it was engaged on the 22d in a terrible but successful charge on the enemy's works, and was from this time steadily under fire till the fall of Vicksburg, on the 4th day of July

The regiment, under Gen Sherman, started for Jackson, Miss , on the 6th of July, being under fire until the second evacuation of that place, when it was moved to Canton, Miss., when it was again engaged, when it went into camp at Black River until the 22d of September From here it moved to Vicksburg, thence to Memphis, thence to Corinth, Miss., where it remained till October 11, thence marched to Iuka, and to Cherokee on the 20th, and on the morning of the 21st had a severe engagement with rebel cavalry On the 26th and 27th, had a running fight with the enemy, again returning to Cherokee Station On the 24th of November, was in the battle of Lookout Mountain, and on the following day, had equally hard fighting at Mission Ridge, and on the 27th, was again engaged at Ringgold and Taylor's Hills, where the regiment suffered severely Here they remained until December 1, when, moving by way of Chattanooga, and Bridgeport, they reached Woodville, Ala , on the 27th inst., and went into Winter quarters, where they remained until the 1st day of May, 1864

On the morning of May 1, moved east, reaching Snake Gap, Ga , on the 9th inst , where they encountered the enemy in force On the 13th, had a severe fight at Resaca, in which Lieut Col Jenkins was severely wounded The regiment laid in camp at Kingston, Ga., from the night of the 19th, until the morning of the 23d, awaiting supplies, then moved on, encountering the enemy at Dallas, on the night of the 26th, and the following morning, after a short but sharp conflict, the enemy was driven back , and again, on the 28th, the enemy charging on their works, were driven back The fighting lasted during the 29th, 30th and 31st On the 1st of June, the regiment moved to New Hope Church and occupied rifle pits, under fire of the enemy, until the 6th, when the regiment moved to Ackworth, remaining there until the 10th, when they marched to Big Shanty, ten miles distant, again engaging the enemy in force Guarded wagon train until the 16th, when they moved into rifle pits near Kenesaw Mountain, and were constantly under fire until the evening of July 3d, when the enemy evacuated Kenesaw Mountain

July 4th, they again encountered the enemy at Chattahoochie River, and, building works, remained under fire until the 11th, when they moved to Roswell, Ga From here they went to Vining Station, thence to a point near Atlanta. August 26th, they moved toward Jonesboro, on the Macon Railroad On the 31st, the enemy made a desperate fight, and the regiment was again under fire until the 2d of September, when Jonesboro was evacuated On October 1, the regiment, with a large portion of Sherman's army, moved north in pursuit of Hood, skirmishing with him at Resaca, Snake Gap, Little River, etc , after this, went to Atlanta, November 15th, thence into the heart of Georgia Marching about fifteen miles per day, they reached the rear of Savannah, on the 10th of December, 1864, and ten days later the whole army entered that city By this victory the army was severed into three parts, and the enemy compelled to loosen its grasp over a vast territory The Thirty-first was actively engaged in the North Carolina campaigns from this time till March 8th, when Gen Grant's famous dispatch, " Let us finish the job now," was announced, when the final blow was soon struck, and the year which promised to be so full of bloody strife was the end of the war of the rebellion

The Thirty-first was mustered out of service at Louisville June 27, 1865, and came to Davenport, where they were paid off and disbanded

Lieut. Col Theodore Stimming, com 1st lieut Co B Oct 13, 1862, prmtd maj March 31, 1863, prmtd lieut col May 27, 1865, m o as maj
Adjt. Jos Rosenbaum, e as sergt Co B August 6, 1862, prmtd adjt. June 17, 1865, m o as q m sergt
Q M John W Gilman, e as private Aug 6, 1862, prmtd 2d lieut Co B March 31, 1863, prmtd 1st lieut June 9, 1863, prmtd q m July 11, 1863

Company B.

Capt Robert B P Speer, com Oct 13, 1862, resd. Sept 17, 1864
Capt Henry E Williams, e as private Aug 6, 1862, prmtd, 2d lieut prmtd 1st lieut. July 11, 1863, prmtd capt. Sept 18, 1864
First Lieut Edward Townsend, com 2d lieut. Oct 13, 1862, prmtd 1st sergt March 31, 1863, resd June 8, 1863
First Lieut Thomas G Salisbury, e as 1st sergt Aug 6, 1862, wd at Missionary Ridge, prmtd 2d lieut March 26, 1864, prmt 1st lieut Sept 18, 1864.
Second Lieut Corydon Smith, e as private Aug 6, 1862, com 2d lieut Aug 24, 1863, com canceled
Sergt. Orlando Bradley, e Aug 6, 1862, died at Memphis
Sergt G D Streeter, e Aug 8, 1862, died Nov 14, 1865
Sergt N N Blakeslee, e Aug 1, 1862, wd at Resaca, died May 31, 1864
Corp Geo L Stearns, e Aug 7, 1862
Corp Wm W Carpenter, e Aug 1, 1862
Corp John F Manser, e Aug 6, 1862
Corp Spence Fellows, e Aug 12, 1862, wd at Missionary Ridge
Corp S E Pratt, e Aug 3, 1862, died at St Louis
Corp John W Ray, e Aug 10, 1862
Corp F Davenport, e Aug 13, 1862, died Sept 9, 1863, disab
Corp D H Sessions, e July 29, 1862
Corp Geo Bawn, e Aug 15, 1862, died at Dallas, Ga
Corp Erasmus Wilson, e Aug 10, 1862
Corp Chas Seavey, e Aug 15, 1862, died at Vicksburg
Musician Noel P Orcutt, e Aug 15, 1862
Musician Wm Harter, e July 29, 1862, died Sept. 9, '63, disab
Wagoner F D Streeter, e Aug 7, '62, capt Aug 28, '63
Anderson, Geo W , e Feb 18, 1864
Brown, Edwin, e Aug 7, 1862, died Feb 23, 1863, disab
Berry, Samuel, e Aug 6, 1862
Burke, James W , e Aug 12, 1862, died at Chattanooga
Barry, Wm , e Aug 14, 1862, died at Black River, Miss
Brandon, Buel, e Aug 13, 1862
Caldwell, Henry, e Aug. 14, 1862, trans to V R C
Cooper, H T , e Aug 12, 1862
Clayton, W D , e Dec 30, 1864
Cowing, J , e Aug. 13, 1862, died Dec 23, 1863
Clough, John H , e Dec 18, 1862, wd , died at Dallas, Ga
Crosby, E P , e Aug 8, 1862, died July 15, 1863, disab
Crandall, W A , e Aug 8, 1862, died Jan 11, 1863, disab.
Culver, E B , e Aug 12, 1862, died at Young's Point, La
Cowles, G O , e. Aug 15, 1862
Cummings, C E , e Aug 11, 1862
Clay, C H., e Aug 14, 1862.
Davenport, R W , e Aug 14, 1862, trans to V R C Feb 16, 1864
Dawding, John T , e Dec 22, 1864
Eyestone, A D , e Aug 14, 1862
Ford, Ward, e Aug 14, 1862, died April 23, 1863, disab
Fitkin, F F , e Aug 8, 1862
Fox, O C., e Jan 2, 1864
Gilman, John W , e Aug 6, 1862, prmtd, com sergt
Griggs, L , e Jan 3, 1864
Galleon, E , e Aug 12, 1862
Gries, J A , e Dec 24, 1864
Graham, E , e Aug 14, 1862, trans to V R C
Graham, T B., e Aug 12, 1862, trans to Inv Corps Sept 1, 1863
Hotckiss, S T , e Aug 6, 1862
Hildt, A , e Jan 3, 1864, kld at Big Shanty, Ga
Hoagland, Wm V , e Aug 8, 1862
Height, H , e Jan 4, 1864
Hayward, L D , e Aug 2, 1862, died Feb 26, 1863, disab.
Hotchkin, James K , e Jan 2, 1864
Hartsough, D , e Aug 13, 1862, died on hospital boat June 27, 1863
Humbert, S B , e Aug 12, 1862
Harrington, G , e Aug 13, 1862
Jacob, Frederick, e Aug 14, 1862, died Jan. 1, '66, disab
Knowles, Leonard, e Aug 8, 1862, wd at Vicksburg
Kinsey, David, e Aug 2, 1862
Ladd, L W , e Aug 14, 1862, died at Memphis
Lusch, Charles, e Aug 12, 1862, died at Vicksburg
McCartney, M , e Jan 3, 1863.
Mills, Jos , e Aug 12, 1862
Montgomery, D C , e Jan 4, 1864
Moore, A , e Aug 13, 1862, died Feb 15, 1864, disab
Morrison, J A , e Aug 9, 1862
Moulton, Wm , e Aug 12, 1862, died Sept 17, 1863, disab
Mensch, H S., e Aug 14, 1862, died June 20, '64, disab
Martin, E , e Feb 5, 1864

Overman, Elias, e Aug 6, 1862
Orcutt, D M , e Aug 7, 1862, wd at Missionary Ridge
Peterson, F L , e Jan 3, 1864
Perry, H C , e Aug 9, 1862, kld at Dallas, Ga
Parmenter, John, e Dec. 23, 1863
Perkins, G D , e Aug 12, 1862, died Jan 12, 1863
Phinney, E A , e Dec 21, 1863
Prouty, W M , e Aug 2, 1862
Porquett, H , e Jan 4, 1864
Porter, Elias D , e Dec 31, 1863, died at Savannah, Ga
Philpot, Chas P , e. Aug 2, 1862, captd , died at Andersonville.
Pattee, M A , e Aug 6 1862, died Jan 12, 1863
Palmer, Wm H , e Aug 13, 1862, wd at Kenesaw Mt
Quimby, M , e Aug 6, 1862, died at Memphis
Rarrick, John, e Feb 10, 1864, captd
Rattray, C , e Aug 6, 1862
Rockwood, A , e Jan 2, 1864
Round, Samuel, e Aug 12, 1862, died Sept 17, '63, disab
Reed, L T , e Aug 12, 1862
Rath, John, e Aug 7, 1862
Rholeder, H C , e Aug 7, 1861
Rucker, Levi, e Aug 10, 1862, died at Nashville
Rath, Geo J , e Aug 10, 1862, kld in battle of Missionary Ridge
Rownd, John H , e Aug 12 1862, wd
Richardson, James R , e Aug 14, 1862, wd at Arkansas Post, trans to Inv Corps
Smith, Corydon, e Aug 6, 1862
Stitoeler, David, e Aug 10, 1862
Steinbach, Lewis, e Aug 12, 1862, died at Black River Bridge, Miss.
Schermerhorn, W S , e Jan 1, 1864
Sellon, Jerome, e Aug 12, 1862, died March 17, 1863, disab
Smelser, Ephraim, e Aug 12, 1862, kld on a plantation in South Carolina while foraging
Shucker, A K , e Aug 14, 1862
Smith, E , e Aug 12, 1862
Tabor, H H , e. Dec 7, 1863, trans to V R C May 10, 1865
Tracy, M. L., e Aug 6, 1862, captd in South Carolina
Tyrells, John, e Dec 12, 1863, died at Snake Gap, Ga
Tondro, L W , e Aug 12, 1862, wd at Vicksburg, died Oct 2, 1863, disab
Vandemark, P C , e Aug 12, 1862
Van Norden, John J , e Aug 15, 1862
Watson, Jas , e Feb 12, 1864, kld at Dallas, Ga
Worcester, A , e Aug 8, 1862
Williams, W T , e Dec 24, 1864
Williams, H E , e Aug 6, 1862
Webster, Wm W , e Feb 6, 1864
Welle, Erastus, e Aug, 7, 1862, died Jan 21, 1863, at St Louis
Webster, C I , e Feb 6, 1864
Yocom, Martin L., e Aug 12, 1862, died March 12, 1863, disab
Young, Alfred, e Aug 14, 1862

Company C.

Capt John Cook, com Oct. 13, 1862, died at Helena, Ark , Nov 22, 1862
Capt Chauncey J Maynard, com 1st lieut Oct 13, 1862, prmtd. capt Nov 23, 1862, resd Jan 30, 1863
Capt Levi W Herring, e as corp Aug 9, 1862, prmtd capt. Dec 30, 1864
First Lieut Joseph T Hedinger, com 2d lieut Oct 13, 1862, prmtd 1st lieut Nov 23, 1862, resd July 15, 1863
First Lieut Thos C Bird, e as 1st sergt Aug 2, 1862, prmtd. 2d lieut March 31, 1863, prmtd 1st lieut July 16, 1863, wd twice at Missionary Ridge Aug 14, 1864
Second Lieut Jonas P Ward, e as private Aug 20, 1862, wd at Kenesaw Mt , prmtd. 2d lieut July 16, 1863, kld in action at Atlanta Aug 7, 1864
Sergt Royal A Brooks, e Aug 5, 1862, died at St Louis May 24, 1863
Sergt Jesse Munson, e Aug 4, 1862, died Aug 7, 1863, disab
Sergt William McCrory, e Aug 15, 1862, wd at Lookout Mt
Sergt Samuel M Howrey, e Aug 12, 1862, wd and died at Milliken's Bend
Sergt Purdy I Wood, e July 14, 1862, died at Milliken's Bend, La
Corp F M Geren, e Aug 7, 1862, died , disab
Corp Joseph B White, e Aug 22, 1862, trans to Inv Corps Sept 3, 1863

Corp Joseph L Weaver, e. Aug 15, 1862, wd
Corp John N Hale, e Aug 8, 1862, wd. at Lookout Mt., died at Chattanooga
Corp James Burns, Jr , e Aug 7, 1862, died at Young's Point, La
Corp R C Tunison, e Aug 11, 1862
Corp H J Plantz, e Aug 7, 1862
Corp Wm , A Whitaker, e Aug. 2, 1862, died on steamer City of Memphis
Corp. W J Brunson, e July 8, 1862, died at Vicksburg
Wagoner C K Hale, e. Aug 20, 1862, died April 28, 1863, disab
Ackerman, James H , e Aug 11, 1862, wd at Arkansas Post, died April 13, 1863, disab
Brown, I K , e Aug 7, 1862, died April 15, 1863, disab
Bressler, John, e Aug 4, 1862, wd Jan 26, 1863
Brown, Joseph, e Aug 9, 1862, died Dec 16, 1862, at St Louis
Brechner, John, e Aug 13, 1862
Brunn Charles, e Aug 29, 1862
Brechner, Aaron, e Aug 15, 1862
Baker, George, e Aug 18, 1862
Carnes, J C , e Aug 5, 1862, wd at Kenesaw Mt , died at Chattanooga
Coger, Samuel E , e Aug 7, 1862
Cram, Brainard, e Aug 14, 1862, died at St Louis
Cumrine, John H , e Aug 6, 1862
Carney, S E , e Aug 23, 1862
Dees, John A , e Aug. 11, 1862, trans to Inv Corps
Debare, Joseph, e Aug 11, 1862, died at Milliken's Bend.
Debare, Geo W , e Aug 8, 1862
Edwards, Jas B , e Aug 8, 1862
Frundt, John H , e Aug 13, 1862
Foye, Chas A., e Aug 11, 1862
Gardner, Joel, e Aug 22, 1862, died Aug 17, 1863, disab
Hastings, A G , e July 14, 1862, trans to regular army Sept 3, 1863
Hall, R S , e. July 26, 1862
Hollenbeck, J F , e Aug 14, 1862, captd , died at Richmond, Va, while prisr
Hale, S W , e Aug 7, 1862, died at Young's Point, La.
Hayes, Henry, e Aug 8, 1862, died Oct 24, 1863, disab
Hollenshead, Levi, e Aug 20, 1862, died at Jefferson Barracks, Mo
Job, Robt G , e Aug 12, 1862, died at Woodville, Ala
Jackson, Joseph, e Aug 14, 1862, died Jan 14, 1863, at Arkansas Post
Knapp, Geo R , e Aug 20, 1862
Linderman, C., e Aug 13, 1862, died at Vicksburg
Lockerby, Jason, e Aug 18, 1862, trans to 33d Co , 1st Bat Inv Corps, Aug 1, 1863
Jackerby, Geo W , e Aug 18, 1862, trans to 33d Co , 1st Bat Inv Corps, Aug 1, 1863
Letter, Wm , e Aug 18, 1862
Lantz, Jacob, e Aug 5, 1862, wd at Vicksburg and Lookout Mt
McColl, Alexander, e Aug 15, 1862 died March 20, 1863, disab
Millard, L B , e July 18, 1862
Mears, Wm , Aug 2, 1862
Mitchell, Joseph, e Aug 4, 1862
Munger, E S , e Aug 20, 1862, trans to Inv Corps April 30, 1864
Muchmore, S., e Aug 11, 1862, trans to Inv Corps Sept 1, 1863
Madden, Thomas, e Aug 20, 1862
Munger, Jas H , e Aug 22, 1862, trans to Inv Corps Sept 1, 1863
Nocton, D W , e July 14, 1862
Owens, E M , e. July 9, 1862
Pearsant, H , e Aug 15, 1862, wd at Arkansas Post, died at Nashville
Porter, Henry, e Aug 11, 1862
Pierce, H F , e Aug 20, 1862
Ritzman, Chas , e July 16, 1862, trans to Inv Corps Sept. 1, 1863
Rice, Horace, e Aug 7, 1862, died at Young's Point, La
Rice, S , e Aug 7, 1862, died in Black Hawk Co July 18, 1863
Shuler, Geo , e July 10, 1862
Smith, S R., e Aug 11, 1862, wd at Kenesaw Mountain, died. June 13, 1865, disab
Scott, G S , e Aug 11, 1862, wd at Dallas, Ga,, trans. to V R C Dec 21, 1864
Stickley, Robert, e Aug 22, 1862
Thomas, B A , e Aug 5, 1862, died at Young's Point, La
Tunison, R C , e Aug 7, 1862, trans to Inv Corps Sept. 1, 1863
Turner, G H., e Aug 6, 1862

Vaughn, John, e July 11, 1862, died at Nashville, on hospital boat
Wright, Thomas, e July 14, 1862
White, M E, e Aug 14, 1862, died
Walls, Simon, e Aug 12, 1862
Warner, J A, e Aug 20, 1862, died Aug 17, 1863, disab
Ward, J P, e Aug 20, 1862
Ward, Erick, e Aug 20, 1862, wd at Vicksburg, died May 10, 1864

Company D.

Capt. Geo W Dearth, com Oct 13, 1862, from private 3d battery, res Sept 10, 1864
Capt Robert J McQuilkin, e as corp. Aug 15, 1862, prmtd 2d lieut Feb 14, 1863, prmtd 1st lieut Feb 19, 1863, prmtd capt. Sept 21, 1864
First Lieut Francis M Thompson, com Oct 13, 1862, from private 3d battery, resd Feb. 18, 1863
First Lieut. Francis H Lacey, e as corp Aug 15, 1862, prmtd 2d lieut. Feb 19, 1863, prmtd 1st lieut Sept 21, 1864
Second Lieut Henry B Webster, com Oct 13, 1862, resd Dec 29, 1862
Sergt T J Rogers, e Aug 14, 1862, died Jan 28, 1863, at Young's Point, La
Sergt. E F Smith, e Aug 7, 1862
Sergt E M Ashley, e Aug 7, 1862
Sergt Michael Lanning, e. July 25, 1862
Sergt William Duncan, e Aug 4, 1862
Corp R J McQuilkin, e Aug 15, 1862
Corp V Edal, e July 23, 1862
Corp Jos E Moore, e Aug 9, 1862, trans to 123d Co, 1st battery Inv Corps
Corp Wm H H Hill, e Aug 7, 1862, died March 30, '63
Corp Martin S Hill, e Aug 7, 1862.
Corp H L Smelser, e Aug 15, 1862, died at St. Louis
Corp C M Turner, e Aug 15, 1862, died May 7, 1863, disab
Corp. A M Talcoa, e Aug 15, 1862, trans to 123d Co, 1st Bat Inv Corps
Corp. A Amborn, e Aug 9, 1862, wd at Ringgold, Ga, died June 16, 1864, wds
Corp M E Torner, e Aug 15, 1862
Corp Wm H Barnea, e Aug 9, 1862, died at Vicksburg
Corp George Grattenberger, e Aug 14, 1862, died May 20, 1863, disab
Musician John W Sherman, e Aug. 15, 1862, trans to Inv Corps Sept 1, 1863
Musician John L Cotton, e Oct. 20, 1862, died June 22, 1863, disab
Wagoner S Harvey, e Aug 16, 1862, died Aug 24, 1863
Wagoner H P Searl, e Aug 9, 1862, died Jan 25, 1863, at Young's Point, La
Bence, Michael, e July 24, 1862, died Sept 7, 1863, disab
Chase, James, e Aug 15, 1862, died May 23, 1862, disab
Cotten, Allen, e July 23, 1862, died Nov 25, 1862, disab,
Cotten, F M, e Oct. 20, 1862, died Feb 24, 1863, Young's Point, La

Company D.

Cotten, Noah, e Aug 8, 1862, trans to Invalid Corps Nov 20, 1863
Crowell, Thao Aug 2, 1862, died at Memphis
Cooper, C E, e July 25. 1862, died at Memphis
Current, A W, e Aug 8, 1862, died at Memphis
Duncan, C a Aug 4, 1862, died at Young's Point, La
Dingman, Wm L, e July 24, 1862, captd at Claysville, Ala., died at Andersonville while prisr
Dingman, A J, e Aug 15, 1862, died at Memphis
Dodson, B R, e Aug 14, 1862
Engledow J M., e July 23, 1862, reptd died at St. Louis, Mo, Feb, 1863
Engledow, Wm, e July 23, 1862
Engledow, Samuel, e Aug 16, 1862, died at St Louis
Estal, James, e Aug 5, 1862, died on hospital boat
Frisbey, P W, e Aug 12, 1862, wd at Arkansas Post, died March 11, 1863
Forbes, Jos A, e Aug 12, 1862
George, John S, e July 30, 1862
Griffin, S F, e Aug 2, 1862, died Feb 23, 1863, disab
Husman, Joseph, e July 23, 1862
Hayes, Geo S., e July 29, '62, died at Young's Point, La
Hill, Geo B, e Aug 2, 1862
Hutsman, Harm, e Aug 9, '62, died at Young's Point, La
Hayes, Thos R, e Aug 15, 1862
Hackett, Geo L, e Aug 15, 1862
Howitt, F, e Aug 15, 1862
Harmon, R E, e Aug 4, '62, died at Young's Point, La
Harmon, Wm N, e Aug 15, 1862
Hasket, Wm T, e Aug 15, 1862

Isenhower, N H., e July 23, 1862
Isenhower, D L., e July 30, 1862.
Isenhower, Nelson, e Aug 15, 1862, died at Memphis
Jones, David A, e Aug 8, 1862
Kennicott, G F W, e July 24, 1862, died. Aug 5, 1863, disab
Kennicott, E S, e July 24, 1862
King, Isaac C., e Aug. 31, 1862, died Oct, 14, 1863, at Raymond
Ketring, Wm D, e Aug 8, 1862, died at Keokuk
Kingsberry, John, e Aug 9, 1862
King, James, e Aug 9, 1862, died Sept 7, 1863, disab
Knowles, W, a. July 25, 1862
Ludlow, S V K, e July 23, 1862
Lane, Isaac, e July 23, 1862, wd. at Arkansas Post
Lane, Samuel, e July 23, 1862
Lamb, Wm, e July 31, 1862, died at St Louis
Long, S R, e Aug 9, 1862
Lamb, E V, e Aug 4, 1862, died at Memphis
McKee, Christopher, e July 25, '62, died at Nashville
Mitchell, D M, e Aug 7, 1862
Minard, Jas, e Aug 14, 1862
McNamara, Jno e Aug 12, 1862, wd
Orr, G, e Aug 15, 1862, died at Keokuk
O'Reardon, M, e Aug 4, 1862.
Peterson, Richard, e Dec. 2, 1864
Perry, Jas., e Aug 9, 1862
Perry, Jno W, e Aug 8, 1862, died Jan. 28, 1863, at Young's Point, La
Rundall, I D, e July 24, 1862, trans to Inv Corps
Ritchey, M, e Dec 2, 1864
Shroyer, John W, e Aug 8, 1862, trans to Inv Corps Sept 1, 1863
Somers, A C, e July 24, 1862, trans to Inv Corps Sept. 1, 1863
Searl, Quimby, e July 26, 1862, trans to Inv Corps Sept. 3, 1863
Smelser, Wm, e Aug 15, 1862
Smith, W W, e Aug 2, 1862, trans to Inv Corps, April 30, 1864
Southerland A., e Aug 4, 1862, trans to Inv Corps, Dec 1, 1863
Smelser, John, e Aug 15, 1862
Stevens, Henry, e Aug 8, 1862
Taylor, C B., e Aug 4, 1862, died Nov 8, 1862, at Davenport
Urmy, E W, e Aug 9, 1862
Vanschoick, Edward, e Aug 15, 1862, died April 14, '65
Wright, Joseph C, e July 24, 1862, trans to Inv Corps, Aug 1, 1863
Williams, James, e Aug 5, '62, died at Young's Point, La
Williams, A, e July 25, 1862, died Feb 27, 1863
Wolf, W, e Aug 8, 1862
Wheeler, C W H, e. Aug 15, 1862

UNKNOWN

Ranson, T D, e Aug 20, 1862

THIRTY-SECOND INFANTRY.

The Thirty-second Infantry was organized at Dubuque October 6, 1862, and on 15th and 17th was moved to Davenport Left Davenport November 21st, for St. Louis, Mo November 25th, Companies B, C, E, H, I and K, with Regimental Headquarters, went to New Madrid, Mo, and Companies A, D, F and G, for Cape Girardeau, Mo, and were so separated until March 4, 1864 The New Madrid portion left December 29th, for Fort Pillow, Tenn, April 1, 1863, Company B was ordered to Fulton, Tenn, and on June 20th, the detachment was ordered to Columbus, Ky July 1st, Company C was mounted and attached to the Forth Missouri Cavalry September 1st, Companies H and K were ordered to Island No 10, January 15, 1864, Company C was dismounted; January 20th, the detachment left Columbus for Vicksburg, Miss, and assigned to Second Brigade, Third Division, 16th A C, February 3d, marched with Gen Sherman's forces, to Meridian, Miss, and returned March 4th The detachment under Col Eberhart, garrisoned at Cape Girardeau until March 14, 1863, when it took a scout to Bloomington, Mo, and returned on the 24th, on 28th, joined in pursuit of Marmaduke's forces, returning May 5th, July 10, 1863, moved to Bloomington, Mo, and was assigned to Reserve Brigade, First Cavalry Division, on 19th, moved southward, arriving at Clarendon, Ark, August 8th, leaving on 13th, on gunboats, going to mouth of Red River Companies A and K captured two confederate transports In destroying pontoon bridges, lost several men in an engagement On 16th, drove enemy's pickets to Harrison's Landing, joined division on 18th August 27th, had 160 men which were put in wagons, found enemy and repulsed them, and reached Little Rock September 11th with hardly a man fit for duty, on account of two months of such fearful exposure and hardships, arrived at Memphis February 6th, and at Vicksburg the 9th, and there joined the balance of regiment On 10th, started for Red River, and disembarked at Limeport, La Assisted in the capture of Fort De Russey On 16th, camped at Alexandria, La., and marched to Grand Ecore April 3d On 7th, marched for Shreveport, and was attacked at Pleasant Hill, loss, thirty-eight killed, 116 wounded, fifty six missing After several tedious marches, went in camp at Memphis June 16th June 24th, went to Moscow, Tenn , and on the 27th to La Grange July 14th, was attacked by enemy at Tupelo, and on the 15th, at Old Town Creek Arrived in Holly Springs August 4th, and Memphis, 30th From September 6th to October 18th, was on the move, and landed at St Louis On the 25th, moved by transports to Nashville, Tenn In battle of Nashville, the Thirty-second did nobly, capturing Burguchoud's battery of five guns and fifty prisoners December 31, 1864, embarked for Eastport, Miss

The regiment traveled 5,594 miles, 2,332 on foot Aggregate mustered into service, 911 Has received, since muster in, 277 recruits Lost 93 men in battle, 177 by disease, 122 discharged, 29 transferred and 1 missing

Col Gustavus A Eberhart, com maj Sept 19, 1862, prmtd. lieut. col April 10, 1864, com col May 28, 1864, m o as lieut col
Asst. Surg Jesse Wasson, com Sept 18, 1862, resd March 7, 1863
Q. M Morrison Bailey, e as sergt Aug 12, 1862, prmtd q m Aug 2, 1864
Com Sergt J R Millard, Aug 11, 1862

Company B.

Palmer, S W , e. Dec 30, 1863
Sussong, Henry, e Dec 22, 1863

Company C.

Capt Hubert F Peables, cnm Oct 8, 1862, wd and captd in battle Pleasant Hill, La , April 9, and died of wds April 25, 1864
Capt Henry C Raymond, com 1st lieut Oct 8, 1862, prmtd capt April 26, 1864
First Lieut. Benj F Thomas, com 2d lieut Oct 8, 1862, prmtd 1st lieut April 26, 1864
Second Lieut Patrick Molsaacs, e as sergt Aug 14, 1862, prmtd 2d lieut April 26, 1864, res Jan 19, 1865
Second Lieut Wellington Russell, e as corp Aug 14, 1862, prmtd 2d lieut Aug 1, 1865, m o as sergt
Sergt C K White, e Aug 9, 1862, died April 20, 1865
Sergt J H Cutter, e Aug 14, 1862, died Dec 18, 1863
Sergt D W. Albaugh, e Aug 13, 1862, kld at Nashville
Sergt N R. Ordway, e Aug 8, 1862
Sergt Jno M Wood, e Aug 5, 1862, diw July 6, 1865
Sergt C Bennett, e Aug 9, 1862, wd and captd at Pleasant Hill, died April 10, 1864
Corp H T Roberts, e Aug 9, 1862
Corp C P Hunt, e Aug 11, 1862, wd at Pleasant Hill, died Jan 25, 1865
Corp John LaBarre, e Aug 13, 1862, died May 19, 1866
Corp Ora Alexander, e. Aug 12, 1862
Corp Wm Prouty, e Aug. 14, 1862, kld at Lake Chicot, Ark , June 6, 1864
Corp Wm Nichols, e Aug 22, 1862, died at Waterloo April 9, 1864
Corp F Williams, e Aug 6, 1862, wd at Nashville, died July 26, 1865
Corp E. B Williams, e Aug 14, 1862
Musician E S Lechty, e Aug 14, 1862, died at Waterloo Oct 18, 1863
Musician E M Balcom, e Aug 22, 1862, trans to 24th Mo. Aug 12, 1863
Wagoner Jas F McFarland, e Aug 14, 1862, wd at Pleasant Hill, died April 18, 1864
Atkinson, Thomas, e Aug 9, 1862, trans to Inv Corps Nov 20, 1863
Brown, 1 V G W , e Aug 8, 1862, died at Fort Pillow, Tenn
Brooks, Jno H , e March 24, 1864
Brooke, E., e Aug 11, 1862
Becker, I H , e Dec 22, 1863
Backus, Jno W , e Aug 15, 1862, died May 29, '63, disab.

Boyd, A , e Dec 31, 1863
Bowers, E S , e Aug 14, 1862
Baldwin, Jas , e Dec 30, 1863, died at Vicksburg
Baldwin, A T , e Aug 14, 1862, wd at Pleasant Hill, La
Benight, C W , e Dec 23, 1863
Bowen, Wm H , e Aug 22, 1862, die May 26, 1865, disab
Crapo, Jos , e March 31, 1864, died in Memphis
Corson, N M , e Aug 7, 1862
Campbell, Wm W , e Dec 14, 1863
Couch, H , Jr , e Aug 8, 1862, died at Columbus, Ky
Clark, C A , e Aug 9, 1862
Conley, Jas L., e Aug 12, 1862, trans to V B C Jan 11, 1865
Clark, Geo D., e Aug 13, 1862
Colvin, Wm , e Aug 14, 1862
Clark, Robt , e Aug 14, 1862, died May 29, 1863
Cleveland, Chas., e Aug 14, '82, wd at Pleasant Hill, La
Chapman, Henry, e Aug 21, 1862, died in Memphis
Duke, Z J , e Aug 11, 1862, wd at Pleasant Hill
Donley, Levi, e Aug 14, 1862.
Doxey, T B , e Aug 14, 1862, wd at Pleasant Hill
Emmitt, Jno., e Aug 9 1862
Ellis, Luther e Aug 13, 1862
Fiske, Augustus, e Aug 12, 1862, died. Oct. 3, 1863
Fulkins, C B , e Aug 14, 1862, died at Pleasant Hill
Felton, J W , e Dec 31, 1863, died in Mound City, Ill
Flood, Edwd , e Aug 22, 1862, kld in Canton, Miss
Goodwin, H J , e, Oct 24 1864, died in Memphis
Harvey, S , e Aug 8, 1862
Highsmith, A B , e Jan 4, 1864.
Heffer, Jesse, e Aug 20, 1862, captd in Pleasant Hill
Hewett, B , e Aug 22, 1862, wd and captd at Pleasant Hill, died there April 10, 1864.
Jackson, Jno, L., e Aug 14, 1862
Jolls, Levi, e Aug 14, 1862
Kellogg, Jacob B , e Aug 9, 1862
Lemon, A , e Dec 18, 1863
Lichey, J M , e Aug 14, 1862, wd at Nashville and died Dec 21, 1864.
Mills, W H , e June 13, 1864, died at Cairo, Ill
Meyer, August, e Aug 9, 1862
Miller, A W , e Feb 9, 1864
Martindale, L , e Aug 9, 1862, died at Memphis
Marquand, T F , e Feb 9, 1864
McCormick, B , e Aug 13, 1862, wd at Pleasant Hill, La
McCall, Alex , e Feb. 20, 1864
Meyers, J L., e Aug 14, 1862, died at Jefferson Barracks, Mo
Moore, E A , e Aug 22, 1862, died March 5, 1864.
Miller, Levi, e Aug 14, 1862
Matthews, G F , e Aug 14, 1862
Ohler, Adam, e Aug 14, 1862
Palmer, S W , e Jan 4, 1864, wd and captd. at Pleasant Hill, La , died May 13, 1864
Page Alva, e Aug 5, 1862
Phillis, John S , e Aug 7, 1862
Palmer, George N , e Aug 11, 1862
Parmenter, A W , e Aug 12, 1862
Philipps, D F , e. Aug 14, 1862, died at Fort Pillow, Tenn
Rich, H , e Feb 10, 1864
Rice, Z , e Aug 5, 1862, died March 20, 1863
Rathbun, Warren, e Aug 11, 1862
Redfield, L L , e Aug 14, 1862
Redfield, James A , e Dec. 14, 1863, died at New Orleans
Richardson, John N , e Aug 22, 1862, died May 30, 1863
Risden, Charles, e. Aug 22, 1862
Shaffer, Frederick, e Aug 9, 1862
Switzer, William D , e Aug 11, 1862, died Jan 24, 1865
Switzer, F , e Aug 22, 1862
Scott, Uriah, e Aug 12, 1862
Shaw, Charles, e Aug 14, 1862, wd and captd at Pleasant Hill, La.
Shaffer, C , e Aug 14 1862, died at Nashville
Shaffer, F , e Aug 14, 1862
Thompson, A J W , e Aug 14, 1862
Trowbridge, ———, e Feb 24, 1864
Trask, A , e Aug 22, 1862
Voorhees Eugene, e Dec 21, 1863
Vogle, Henry, e Aug 11, 1862
Virden, Isaac, e Jan 4, 1864
White, Charles, e Aug 7, 1862
Worthington, A , e Aug 11, 1862
Whipple, F T , e Aug 12, 1862, died at Memphis
Ward, John N , e Aug 12, 1862
Webster E W , e Aug 13, 1862, wd at Pleasant Hill
Wiltse, Charles, e Aug 22, 1862
Young, John H , e Aug 11, 1862
Brainard, E C , Aug 27, 1862

Company D.

Sussong, Henry, e Dec 10, 1863
Blackman, E L , e Jan 4, 1864
Carter, F J , e Jan 4, 1864
Chaffin, G H., e Feb 11, 1864
Fugue, William E , e Jan 4, 1864
Homback, J D., Jan 11, 1864

Company E.

Churchill, Jas N , e Aug 13, 1862
Clayton, Dow, e Aug 12, 1862 wd and captd at Pleasant Hill
James, L D , e Dec 23, 1863, kld at Pleasant Hill, La
Kitterman, I N , e. Dec 23, 1863, captd at Pleasant Hill
Lewis, Chas. , e Aug 12, 1862, captd at Pleasant Hill, La., died at Tyler, Texas
Morse, E A , e Dec. 23, 1863, died at Memphis
Patten, Delos, e Dec. 14, 1863, kld at Pleasant Hill
Rosebrough, J M , e Dec 23, 1863, died at Vicksburg
Sperry, John, e Aug 20, 1862

Company G.

Belcher, Jas L , e Dec 24, 1863, died Aug 3, 1864

UNKNOWN

Buker, I A , e Dec 22, 1863
Longaker, D M , e Oct 19, 1864
Smith, Robt , e Oct 17, 1864

THIRTY-SEVENTH INFANTRY.

This regiment was known as the "Gray Beard Regiment," from the fact that nearly or quite every member was over forty-five years of age The regiment was formed during the Summer of 1862

The Thirty-seventh was assigned to guard duty at St Louis, afterward at Alton, then at Rock Island From there it went to Memphis, Tenn , and Holly Spring, Ark , where regular duty was performed It was in numerous skirmishes, but no battles No man from Linn County was killed in an engagement By doing duty as guards of rebel prisoners, the Thirty-seventh relieved another regiment of younger men It was in the service about three years, but our informant, Mr Hergeshamer, private in Company A, is unable to give exact dates

Company A.

First Lieut Jno McCall, e as sergt Sept 21, 1862, prmtd 1st lieut June 27, 1863, resd Nov 6, 1863
Second Lieut Julius C Hubbard, com Dec 15, 1862, resd May 3, 1863
Corp Jos Weaver, e Sept 8, 1862
Corp Sardies Little, e Oct 1, 1862, died May 21, 1863
Corp Lyman Pierce, e Oct 8, 1862 died Oct 12, 1864
Wagoner Jno Hays, e Sept 7, 1862
Boston, Wm H , e Oct 22, 1862, died Nov 30, 1864
Baker, Anthony, e Oct 5, 1862
Bullis, Gideon, e Sept. 22, 1862, died March 13, 1864, at Rock Island, Ill
Byford, Jno R , e Nov 15, 1862
Carey, A , e Sept 20, 1862, died Nov 2, 1863
Caignay, M , e Sept 18, 1862
Haswell, N , e Oct 8, 1862, died , May 8, 1863
Harris, Joe J , e Sept 19, 1862
Harris, Benj , e Sept 5, 1862, died May 21, 1863
Moore, Samuel , e Oct 4, 1862, died May 24, 1865
McCrackan, H , e Sept. 22, 1862
Markell, Eli , e Sept 8, 1862, died May 8, 1863
McCord, T , e Sept 3, 1862
Miller, Wm H , e Sept 20, 1862, died Jan 2, 1865
Nash, Joseph, e Sept 6, 1862
Norton, Lyman, e Sept 5, 1862, died July 31, 1863
Outcanit, F , e Sept. 8, 1862, died April 4, 1863
Reed, Warren, e Nov 1862, died May 30, 1863
Sergeant, A , e Oct 2, 1862, died Nov 9, 1864
Sperry, Lewis, e Sept 8, 1862, died May 14, 1865
Whitbeck, Andrew, e Sept 26, 1863, died April 2, 1865
Wood, Chauncey, e Sept 2, 1862, died May 8, 1865
Washburn, H , e Oct 1, 1862, died Nov 19, 1863

Company H.

Cole, H A., e Oct 1, 1863, died Jan 12, 1862, at Muscatine

Company K.

Wood, Chauncey, e Sept 2, 1863, died May 8, 1865

UNKNOWN

Cagnay, M , e Sept 16, 1862

FORTY-FIRST INFANTRY

Q. M S Chester B Stilson, e. Sept 23, 1862

Company A.

Capt Francis H Cooper, com 1st lieut Oct 23, 1861, prmtd capt Sept 1, 1862
Sergt. Jno M S Hodgdon, e Sept 25, 1861
Sergt Robert Wright, e Sept. 24, 1861
Corp E F Sawyer, e Sept 24, 1861
Corp Jacob F Kylar, e Oct 1, 1861
Corp D A Babcock, e Oct 1, 1861
Corp Jas R Michael, e Sept 28, 1861
Alvord, Chas , e Sept 26, 1861
Clark Wm M , e Sept 26, 1861
Coburn, Wm , e Sept 26, 1861
Dexter, R , e Nov 5, 1861
Dawson, F , e Sept, 26, 1861
Grow, Wm , e Nov 5, 1861
Henry, A , e Sept 30, 1861
Harris, L M , e Nov 12, 1861
Johnson, Theo , e Sept 28, 1861
Ryan, D , e Sept 28, 1861
Sawyer, E F , e Sept 24, 1861
Trumbo, Geo , e Oct 7, 1862
Woodward, Henry, e Sept 28, 1861

FORTY-SEVENTH INFANTRY.

Company D.

First Lieut Arthur E McHugh, comd 2d lieut, June 4, 1864, prmtd 1st lieut Aug 17, 1864
Sergt. John F Clarke, e Sept. 6, 1861
Corp James D Hill, e Sept 7, 1861
Corp O. D Boyles, e Sept 11, 1861 died at Helena, Ark , Aug 12 1864
Corp Geo S Jackson, e Sept 9, 1861
Boyle, L W , e Sept 17, 1861
Baldwin, John H , e Sept 4, 1861
Cox, Acton , e Sept. 9, 1861
Cotton, John L , e Sept 5, 1861
Cooley, Lewis F , e Sept 5, 1861
Dorlau, Frank, e Sept. 14, 1861
Finley, David, e Sept 7, 1861
Good, John C , e Sept 5, 1861
Helferty, Daniel, e Sept 5, 1861
Hallen, David, e Sept 16, 1861
Hesse, Frank, e Sept 10, 1861
McCullough, H , e Sept 3, 1861
Mullen, C W , e Sept 21, 1861
Morgan, Thos e Sept 4, 1861
Morgan, Jacob B , e Sept. 4, 1861
McWilhams, R , e Sept 17, 1861
Payn, E S., e Sept 9, 1861
Trant, Cyrus, e Sept 9, 1861
White, F W , e Sept 5, 1861
Dick, Jas C , e Sept 24, 1861

FIRST CAVALRY

The First Cavalry was recruited during the Summer of 1861 Its services began during the following Winter Its first action was at Silver Creek, Mo , where the rebel camp was attacked and routed In February, 1862, a detachment from the First helped surprise and capture Gen Price at Warsaw. Another detachment had a brush with guerrillas near Montevallo in the following April. During the next few months, the regiment had skirmishes with rebels near Clinton, Big Creek, Clear Creek and Newtonia December 7th, the first and third battalions participated in the battle at Prairie Grove That month the command assisted at the capture of Van Buren, where a number of steamboats, several hundred prisoners and a large amount of stores fall into the hands of our forces April 28, 1863, the most of the regiment was concerned in a night attack upon a portion of Marmaduke's forces, breaking up the camp and inflicting heavy loss

August 26th and 27th, the regiment did gallant service at White River From September 10th until the following January, the First was stationed at Little Rock April 24, 1864 the command repulsed a charge of the enemy at Mono River, and had a share in the battle at Jenkins' Ferry on the 30th The regiment continued doing scout service until January, 1865, when they were sent to Dardanelle, and had a brush with Col Cooper, driving him off the field They went thence to Pine Bluff, and to Memphis From this place they made two incursions into Mississippi After the war closed, much to the disappointment of the men, the regiment was ordered to Texas under Custer On the route, two or three of the regiment committed some depredations on the inhabitants, contrary to specific orders from Gen Custer, who was in command A few of the men were detected and ordered to be flogged This order created much bitterness of feeling toward Custer, which had hardly disappeared when he met tragic death on the plains

Company B.

Carney, Geo R, e July 18, 1861
Chase, John M, e Aug 16, 1862

Company C.

Sergt. Horace Barron, June 13, 1861, died June, 1862, disab
Sergt A A Allne, e June 13, 1861
Sergt Saml M Hoff, e July 13, 1861
Corp J Q. Hanna, e June 13, 1861
Corp S M Hoff, e July 13, 1861
Corp V Gilbert, e June 13, 1861, died at Little Rock, Ark
Ayres, James, c Dec 14, 1863
Boston, James C, e June 13, 1861, died Feb 14, 1863, disab
Labarre, Theo, e June 13, 1861, died Jan 26, 1863, Forsyth, Mo
Simmons, C M, died Sept 21, 1861, vet Jan 5, 1864
Cobb, D K, e Aug 10, 1861, vet Jan 5, 1864, died at St Joseph, Mo
Clark, Wm, e Aug 10, 1861, died July, 15, 1862
Clark, John F, e Aug 10, 1861, died June 15, 1861
Leilcer, Coe, e Aug 10, 1861, vet Jan 5, 1864
Simmons, L N, e Aug 10, 1861, deserted June 21, 1863
Pocock, C, e Aug 11, 1861, vet Jan 5, 1864
Terwilliger, David, e Aug 15, 1861

Company L.

Kayes, S, vat Jan 5, 1864
Dodd, J B, P, e May 20, 1861, vet Jan 5, 1864
Davis, Geo H, vet Jan 5, 1864, died July 5, 1864

UNKNOWN

Brownson, L H, e Feb 16, 1864
Babcock, C J, e Jan 4, 1864
Blood, A C, e Jan 2, 1864
Forts, John B., e Jan 2, 1864
Holding, Nelson, e Jan 2, 1864
Kingsbury, Geo H e Dec 30, 1864
Pennock, M J, e Jan 2, 1864
Rhoades, L W, e Dec 31, 1863
Watson, Geo A, e Dec 24, 1863
Wilkins, Owen, a Dec 31, 1863

FOURTH CAVALRY

Company B.

Barnes, Geo S., a Dec 4, 1863
Cutshell, S L., e Oct 1, 1863.
Cimbine, L, e Dec. 16, 1863, drowned or Napoleon, Ark
Conklin, A G, e Dec 21, 1863, died at St Louis
Dunton, Wm A, Sept 3, 1864, died at Atlanta.
Guger, John, e Dec 21, 1863
Gates, W H, e Oct. 1, 1863
Hemer, L., a. Dec 17, 1863
Luddic, Jacob, e Dec 19, 1863, wd near Memphis
Rust, F, Jr, e Dec 21, 1863
Shaffer, E, e Nov 26, 1863, died at Atlanta
Shuler, Jos., e Dec 20, 1863
Schaffer, C, e Sept. 3, 1864, wd near Memphis, died June 13, 1865, disab
Schaffer, A, e Dec 10, 1863, wd and died at Memphis
Schrack, L J, e Dec 19, 1863
Schrack, Theo, e Dec 21, 1863, captd near Memphis Dec 14, 1864

Schrack, S J, e Dec 21, 1863, wd near Memphis
Tracy, A A, e Oct 1, 1863, captd at Ripley, Miss., died at Annapolis, Md
Tuffs, Chas W, e Nov 2, 1861
Warner, Jno A, e Dec 26, 1863
Young, J C., e Dec. 26, 1863
Young, Jacob C., e Sept 25, 1861

Company E.

Barnes, Geo S, e Dec 4, 1863
Shroyer, Lewis, e Dec 16, 1863
Shimer, A M, e Dec 21, 1863

Company H.

Rowley, L C, e Dec 22, 1863
Thoroman, N B, e Dec 22, 1863

SEVENTH CAVALRY

Company A.

Groom, Wm H, e April 16, 1864

Company B.

Alder, Philip, e March 17, 1863
Alder, Wm., e March 17, 1863
Dodd, Wm, e March 17, 1863
Eaton, Samuel, e March 16, 1863
Marsh, Wm H e Feb. 8, 1864
Perkins, L T, e March 17, 1863
Sileby, Edward, e March 12, 1863

Company C.

Gallup, Wm M., e Dec 19, 1863

Company E.

Com Sergt Chas Oche, e March 14, 1863
Corp Wm Hamilton, e March 7, 1863
Farrier P Duke, e March 14, 1863, died, disab
Cronright, Thomas, e May 11, 1863
Maddock, Jos R., e April 1, 1863
Rice, Wm, e May 9, 1863

Company F.

Sergt F W Fenstermaker, e March 19, 1863
Corp Levi Donley, e March 4, 1863, died at Fort Kearney, C T
Corp H W Brundage, e May 7, 1863, kld at Julesburg, C T
Wagoner A Donley, e Feb 1, 1863
Burk, Thomas, e March 18, 1863, died Aug 31, '63, disab.
Hardesty, Jos, e March 17, 1863, died at Davenport, Iowa, Aug 21, 1863
Shanewise, F, e March 14, 1863
Starr, Wm, e March 18, 1863
Starr, Hiram, e May 8, 1863
Tucker, Wm, e April 20, 1863
Younett, A, e March 18, 1863

Company H.

Corp Thos Turner, e June 8, 1863
Boyd, Henry, e June 6, 1863
Glidden, John, e Oct 18, 1864.
Hughs, Lee M, e June 25, 1863
Hall, H H G, e Oct 22, 1864.
Johnston, A, e June 7, 1863
Rice, H P, e Sept. 29, 1864
Turner, M V B, e June 29, '63, wd at Crow Creek, Ark

Company K.

Capt. Francis H Cooper, com Sept. 1, 1862
First Lieut. Wallace Pattee, com 2d lieut Sept 1, 1862, prmtd 1st lieut June 1, 1865
Second Lieut Robert Wright, e as sergt, com 2d lieut June 1, 1865, resd Jan 5, 1865
Q. M S James R Michael, e Sept. 28, 1861
Sergt John M E Hodgdon, e Sept. 28, 1861, vet Feb 28, 1864
Sergt H P Leland, e Sept 24, 1861, vet Feb 28, 1864
Sergt J F Kyler, Oct 1, 1861, vet Feb 28, 1864
Corp E F Sawyer, e Sept 24, 1861, vet Feb 28, 1864
Corp Geo Trumbo, e. Oct 7, 1861
Farrier Wilson M Clark, e Sept 28, '61, vet Feb 28, '64.

Adams, Wm , e Jan 4, 1864
Alvord, Chas , e Sept. 26, 1861, vet. Feb 28, 1864
Babcock, D A , e Oct 1, 1861
Coburn, Wm , e Sept 26, 1861
Dawson, F A , e Sept 26, 1861, vet Feb 28, 1864
Dexter, R. S., e Nov 5, 1861, vet. Feb 28, 1864
Gross, W H , e Sept. 27, 1861
Harris, L M , e Nov 12, 1861
Pattee, A C., vet Feb 29, 1864
Henry, A , e Sept 30, 1861
Johnson, Thao , Sept 28, 1861, vet. Feb 28, 1864
Moody, C D , Dec 22, 1863
Ryan, Daniel, e Sept 26, 1861, vet. Feb 28, 1864
Stilson, C B , e Sept 24, 1861
Wiltse, N P , e Jan 4, 1864
Woodward, H D , e Sept 28, 1861, vet. Feb 28, 1864

NINTH CAVALRY.

[NOTE — *This Regiment was mustered out at Little Rock, Ark , Feb 28, 1866*]

This regiment, Col Matthew M Trumbull, was the last of the three-year regiments recruited in Iowa It was organized at Davenport, November 30, 1863, and ordered to Arkansas, where it remained performing heavy scouting, guard and garrison duty until the close of the war

Col Matthew M Trumbull, com Sept 24, 1863, brev brig gen U S V March 13, 1865
Maj Wm Haddock, com Nov 3, 1863, prmtd capt Co E, 12th Inf, resd Sept 13, 1864
Maj John Wayne, com Oct. 17, 1863, prmtd maj Sept 14, 1864
Surg Jesse Wasson, com Oct. 19, 1863, resd Jan 27, 1865
Adjt. Ward B Sherman, com commy Nov 5, 1863, from private Co G, 13th Inf, prmtd adjt Sept 4, 1864, resd April 1, 1865

Company C.

Sergt Daniel G Ellis, e Aug 11, 1863
Corp Jas M Morgan, e Sept 29, 1863
Adams, H N., e March 9, 1864
Gaston, John, e July 4, 1863
Geiste, Chas H , Sept. 24, 1863, died at St Louis, Mo
Harding, Hiram, e Oct 24, 1863
Johnson, Richard, e June 29, 1863.
Kock, Wm , e Sept 24, 1863

Company G.

Trump, W Champlin, e Sept. 2, 1863
Bennett, Windsor, e Aug 28, 1863
Franklin, Wm , e Aug 21, 1863
Hurlbut, S B
Hayward, George, e July 4, 1863
Wilson, James H , e Aug 15, 1863

UNASSIGNED

McCardle, James, e Oct 25, 1864.
Raymond, Albert, e Feb 29, 1864
Smith, John, e Feb 22, 1864.

FIRST BATTERY LIGHT ARTILLERY

Corp Thos Filkin
Baker, David, e Oct 24, 1864
Barnascone, David, e as vet Jan 2, 1864
Johnson, H B , Dec 26, 1863
Lockerby, Geo W , died June 3, 1862
Martin, Peter, died at Davenport July 2, 1864
Morrison, Samuel, died at Corinth, Miss
Rice, Wm A , e Dec 14, 1863
Round, Geo W , died Nov 28, 1862, disab
Smith, J , e Dec. 14, 1863
Williams, Richard, died Jan 19, 1862 at St Louis
Spencer, F , e as vet Jan 2, 1864.

SECOND BATTERY LIGHT ARTILLERY

Buffington, C , e as vet March 23, 1864

THIRD BATTERY LIGHT ARTILLERY

[NOTE — *This battery was mustered out at Davenport Oct 3, 1865*]

This battery was organized by Capt M M Hayden under special authority from the Secretary of War, during the months of August and September, 1861, at Dubuque, under the name of the Dubuque Battery, and was attached to the Ninth Regiment Iowa Voluntary Infantry, Col William Vandever commanding On the 3d of September, 1861, the first detachment of the battery was mustered in by Capt Washington, William H McClure, of Cedar Falls, Iowa, being mustered as First Lieutenant, under whose charge the detachment was placed in Camp Union, near Dubuque

The battery was speedily filled up by recruits, and on the 24th of the same month the final muster-in as a battery took place, the following officers having been chosen Captain, M M Hayden , Senior First Lieutenant, W H McClure, Junior First Lieutenant, M C Wright, Senior Second Lieutenant, W H Cromer, Junior Second Lieutenant, Jerome Bailey The battery, with the Ninth Iowa Infantry, left Camp Union, on the steamer Canada, September 26th, for St Louis Were immediately marched to Benton Barracks (than in process of completion) Requisitions for guns, horses and harness were made

On the 13th of November, they were ordered to Pacific City, Mo , where they remained during the greater part of the Winter Guns and equipments were received about the 1st of December

The battery consisted of four six-pounder bronze guns and two twelve-pounder howitzers On the 25th of January, they moved by rail to Rolla, where they were assigned under Gen Curtis On the 28th of the same month, they marched from Rolla in the direction of Lebanon

February 9th, marched to Springfield, Mo Participated in the famous race after Price's fleeing army, making some almost unprecedented marches, and ending in the battle of Pea Ridge

The suddenness of their final attack, with the meagerness of our support, compelled us to leave two of our guns upon the field These guns however, were not abandoned until they were spiked, and every horse had been killed and every man serving with them either killed or wounded We fell back some 400 yards, where, support coming to our aid, we kept up fire with the remaining guns until darkness put an end to the engagement

Our entire loss in the two days' engagement was two men killed, two officers and fifteen men wounded, twenty-three horses killed and three guns captured, and fired, during the engagement, over 1,200 rounds of ammunition.

Marched to Batesville, Ark Arrived at Helena July 12th, and made several reconnaissances from that point. Was in the Little Rock expedition

In January, 1864, the battery re-enlisted and went home Returned in May and received new guns and outfit and did efficient service during the rest of the war

Sr First Lieut. Wm. H McClure, com Sept 16, 1861, wd at Pea Ridge March 7, 1862, resd Sept 3, 1862
Jr First Lieut Otis G Day, e as sergt, Aug 3, 1861, prmtd ar 2d lieut May 1, 1862, prmtd, jr 1st lieut Sept 4, 1862, m o April 30, 1863
Corp David C Baker, died at Helena, Ark
Adams, John Q., e Feb 23, 1864
Adams, Wm , e Jan 4, 1864
Benton, Thos., wd at Pea Ridge, died Aug 27, 1862
Curtis, W T , e Dec 19, 1863
Chase, Wm J , e as vet. Feb 1, 1864
Deeming, Geo , e as vet Dec 22, 1863
Dorlan, T J
Dolph, Edward M
Eidson, Barney, e as vet Dec 22, 1863
Eaton, Julius M
Ferguson, Jos J , died Oct 12, 1863, disab
Gallarno, Geo , e Jan 13, 1864, died Sept. 23, 1864, at Little Rock, Ark
Gilley, S , e Oct 14, 1864.
Headley, A B , died on steamer D A January
Herring, F C , e Feb 26, 1864
Hurlburt, Samuel B
Harkness, David
Headley, Wm E., e as corp. Dec 22, 1863
Kelley, M B , e Feb 2, 1864, died at Little Rock, Ark
Knapp, Samuel M , died at Cassville, Mo
Lindsay, J W , e as vet Dec 22, 1863

Leversee, Charles
Mitchell, O A , e as vet Dec. 22, 1863
Munger, A , e as vet. Dec 22, 1863
Moody, O D , e Dec 22, 1863, died March 28, 1865, disab
Maddock, Jos R , wd at Pea Ridge, died Dec 17, 1862, disab
McCardle, Patrick , e as vet Dec 22, 1863
Overman, C M , e April 20, 1864
Preble, H J , prmtd Q. M S., vet. Dec 22, 1863
Patrick, Chas , e Oct 14, 1864
Parker, C J , died July 17, 1862, on str D A January
Riddle, J M , e Oct 17, 1864
Reynolds, E B , wd at Pea Ridge, died May 8, 1864
Steele, Robert J , e as vet Dec 22, 1863
Scott, H E., e Jan 2, 1864
Shreves, J C
Shroyer, Jas M , e Oct 14, 1864
Sisson, George W
Turner, J A , e Feb 3, 1864
Thompson, F M., wd at Pea Ridge, Ark
Tronin, L , e Oct 14, 1864
Waters, Geo T
Wiltse, N T , e. Jan 4, 1864
Wynn, A , e Jan 4, 1864
Warren, A , e Jan 4, 1864
Walters, Geo I , e as vet Dec 22, 1863

MISCELLANEOUS.

First Iowa Infantry.

Butler, G W , e Jan 4, 1864, m o Aug 25, 1861
McManis, H J , e April 24, 1861, m o Aug 25, 1861

Fifth Infantry.

Rice, W A , e June 24, 1861, wd at Iuka, m o Aug 18, 1864
Sergt. Keisy S Marlin, e July 1, 1861, prmtd surgeon 20th inf, m o Aug 18, 1864.
Musician D Sawyer, e July 1, 1861, m o Aug 18, 1864.
Crawford, Wm , e July 1, 1861, m o Aug 18, 1864
Marlin, J W., e July 1, 1861, m o Aug 18, 1864
Puckett, T C., e. July 1, 1861, m o Aug 18, 1864
Snider, H W , e July 1, 1861, m o Aug 18, 1864
Snider, John , e July 1, 1861, m o Aug 18, 1864
Williams, W , e. July 1, 1861, m o Aug 18, 1864
Williams, M , e July 1, 1861, m o Aug 18, 1864
Knowles, B A , e. July 15, 1861, wd at Iuka, m o Aug 18, 1864.
Martin, B H , e July 15, 1861, m o Aug 18, 1864
Purington, Curtis , e July 24, 1861, m o Aug 18, 1864
Wilson, P D , e July 24, 1861, prmtd to corp, m o Aug 18, 1864

Sixth Infantry.

Bullock, Gilbert, e June 24, 1861, m o July 21, 1865
Eaton, Samuel, e. June 24, 1861, m o. July 21, 1865.

Seventh Infantry.

Albertson, F D , e July 8, 1861, vet Dec. 24, 1863, m o July 12, 1865
Thomas, J S , e July 8, 1861, vet. Dec 24, 1863, m o. July 12, 1865

Eighth Infantry.

Loyd, Jos S., e Oct. 19, 1864, m o April 20, 1868
Lamb, Daniel, e Nov 18, 1864, m o April 20, 1866

Thirteenth Infantry.

Brown, A S , e Sept 27, 1861, m o July 21, 1865
Gipe, John H , e Sept 27, 1861, m o July 21, 1865
Pray, Robt J , e. Sept 27, 1861, m o July 21, 1865

Fourteenth Infantry.

First Lieut Francis H Cooper, com. Oct 23, 1861, trans to 7th cav Sept 4, 1862, m o June 22, 1866
Davidson, C F , e Nov 6, 1862, died Sept 6, 1863
Ontoult, Fred , e May 7, 1863, m o June 22, 1866.

Seventeenth Infantry.

Second Lieut David C Montgomerie, prmtd 2d lieut , m o July 25, 1865

Eighteenth Infantry.

Barker Geo W , e July 2, 1862, m o July 20, 1865

Nineteenth Infantry.

Asst Surg M C Lathrop, com July 11, 1863, resd Oct 26, 1863, to accept promotion in 4th Eng O D A

Twentieth Infantry.

Asst. Surg Keisey S Martin, com Oct 1, 1862, m o July 8, 1866
Schemerhorn, Wm S , e Jan 4, 1864

Thirty-eighth Infantry.

Chesley, Jno H , e Aug 22, 1862, m o Aug 15, 1865
Reynolds, D D , e Jan 9, 1863, m o Aug 15, 1865

Thirty-fourth and Thirty-eighth Infantry Consolidated.

Chesley, Jno H , e. Aug 22, 1862, m o. Aug 15, 1865

Thirty-ninth Infantry.

Null, Jas , e Feb 24, 1864, m o June 5, 1865
Wood, F M , e Feb 27, 1864, m o. June 5, 1865
Welle, Isaac S , e Feb 24, 1864, m o June 5, 1865

Forty-second Infantry.

Heath, Chas K , e Aug 4, 1861
Lockeby, Jason, e Aug 4, 1861
Starr, Benj , e. Aug 4, 1861

Forty-fourth Infantry.

Corp Perry Newell, e May 11, 1864.

Second Cavalry

Savage, Chas , e Dec 22, 1863, m o Sept. 19, 1865
Thayer, E S , e Sept 3, 1864, m o Sept. 19, 1865
Brown, Geo W , e Jan 5, 1864, died Aug , 1864
Burroughs, S , e Aug 4, 1861, deserted July 8, 1862

Fifth Cavalry.

Beeson, R O , m o Aug 11, 1865
McCalmut, Peter, deserted Nov 16, 1862
Corp Jas B. Wolf, e July 1, 1861, from Co. E, 5th inf, m o. Aug 11, 1865
Williams Mahlon, e July 1, 1861, from Co E 5th inf, vet. Jan 5, 1864, m o. Aug 11, 1865
Corp Nicholas Eisenhauer, e June 24, 1861, vet., April 11, 1864, m o Aug. 11, 1865
Martin, B H., e June 24, 1861, vet , Feb. 6, 1864, m o Aug 11, 1865
Martin, J G , e June 24, 1861, vet , Jan 5, 1864, m o. Aug 11, 1865
Purington, C B., e June 24, 1861, vet., Feb 7, 1864, m o Aug 11, 1865

Sixth Cavalry.

Craven, Gersham, e. Dec 15, 1862, m o Oct 17, 1865
Nocton, Wm J e Nov 11, 1862, m o Oct. 17, 1865
Stickley, Jesse, e Nov 19, 1862, m o Oct 17, 1865
Teamster Jno R Maulson, e Sept. 16, 1862, m o Oct 17, 1865
Creighton, M , e Oct 15, 1862, m o Oct. 17, 1865
Eberhart, B E., e Oct 16, 1862, m o Oct. 17, 1865
Hoague, O B., e Dec 15, 1862, m o Oct 17, 1865
Miller, J L "G," e Oct 15, 1864, m o Oct 17, 1865
Meyers, H B , e Oct. 19, 1864, m o Oct. 17, 1865

Eighth Cavalry.

Farrier Robt Bellingham, e Oct 10, 1864, m o Aug 13, 1865
Farrier U Betterly, e Dec. 5, 1864, m o Aug 13, 1865
Farrier Chester Mehan, e Aug 5, 1863, m o Aug 13, '65
Shirl, Jerry, e July 1, 1863, m o Oct. 13, 1865
Corp S Rathbone, e July 6, 1863, m o Aug 13, 1865
Knowlton, C. F, e July 25, 1863, m o. Aug 13, 1865
Peeters, Isaac M , e Aug 11, 1863, m o Aug 13, 1865
Rowley, Eli M., e Aug. 11, 1863, m o Aug 13, 1865
Rahe, Wm , e July 20, 1863, m o. Aug. 13, 1865

First Iowa Infantry (African Descent).

Corp Wm H. Webster, e Sept 8, 1863

Engineer Regiment of the West.

Musician Eugene Mengoz, Aug 28, 1861, died Oct 24, '62
Artificer Jne Brietoph, e Aug 28 1861
Artificer Clement Catoie, e Sept 20, 1861
Artificer Michael Gilly, e Sept 28, 1861
Golegly, Patrick e Sept. 14, 1861
Mengoz, Francois, e Sept 30, 1861
Blanchard, John e Sept 14, 1861
Harrington, Jas., e Sept 14, 1864

Seventh Illinois Cavalry.

Scott, H K , e Jan 2, 1864
Scott, John H , e Jan 2, 1864

Ninth Illinois Cavalry.

Brown, E , e Nov 12, 1861

Second Missouri Cavalry (Merrill Horse).

Dow, Simen , e Aug 18, 1862

Eleventh Pennsylvania Cavalry.

First Bugler C D Mach , e Sept 16, 1862
Farrier Jas Hunter, e Oct 11, 1862
Brown, Jno F , e Sept 28, 1861
Chandler, Starling, e Sept 28, 1861
Forbes, Jae W , e Sept 16, 1861
Frost, Wm , e Sept. 28, 1861
Kimble, Jacob, e Sept 16, 1861, died May, 1862
Brown, Jno F , e Nov 14, 1863 ,

Eighteenth Michigan Infantry.

Shcermerhorn, Wm , e Jan 4, 1864

For four years and more, the notes of the fife and drum and bugle and the tramp of armed hosts were continually heard, from the Atlantic to the Pacific, from the Gulf of Mexico to British North America, and the clash of arms was borne northward on every breeze from the sunny but blood-drenched plains of the South For four years and more, "grim-visaged war" had waved its crimsoned banners over the fair fabric the Fathers had erected, in a vain endeavor to hurl it from its foundations In this terrible and gigantic struggle, Black Hawk had borne its full part, and many a brave volunteer from its beautiful prairies had laid down his life on the battle field or starved to death in the rebel slaughter pens at Andersonville and Macon

But now Sherman and his "brave boys in blue" had made their memorable and historic march to the sea, Lee had surrendered to the victorious army of the Union under Grant, the war was ended, peace restored, the Union preserved in its integrity, and the patriotic sons of Black Hawk who were spared to witness the final victory of the armies of the Union returned to their homes to receive grand ovations and tributes of honor from friends and neighbors who had eagerly and jealously and anxiously watched and followed them wherever the varying fortunes of war had called them.

Exchanging their soldiers' uniforms for citizens' dress, most of them fell back to their old avocations—on the farm, in the mines, at the forge, the bench, in the shop, in the office, or at whatever else their hands found to do. Their noble deeds, in the hour of their country's peril, are now and always will be dear to the hearts of the people whom they so faithfully served. Brave men are always honored, and no class of citizens are entitled to greater respect than the brave volunteers of Black Hawk County, not simply because they were soldiers, but because, in their association with their fellow men, their walk is upright, and their character and honesty without reproach.

> Their country first, their glory and their pride,
> Land of their hopes—land where their fathers died,
> When in the right, they'll keep their honor bright,
> When in the wrong, they'll die to set it right

The wondrous deeds of daring and glorious achievements of the Army of the Union, during the great war of the rebellion, will always be dearly cherished by all patriotic hearts But there are scenes, incidents and accidents, the memory of which will shade with sadness the bright reflections engendered by the contemplation of a heroism, devotion and sacrifice the like of which the world never saw before But the memory of those who fell in the stupendous struggle is still familiar to the present people of Black Hawk County , and fifty years hence, when the fathers and mothers of to-day shall have passed on to their eternal home, they will be remembered by posterity more as matters of tradition than of absolute written history.

BIOGRAPHICAL DIRECTORY.

agt	agent
carp	carpenter
clk	clerk
Co	company or county
dlr	dealer
far	farmer
gro	grocer
I V A	Iowa Volunteer Artillery
I V C	Iowa Volunteer Cavalry
I V I	Iowa Volunteer Infantry
lab	laborer
mach	machinist
mech	mechanic
mer	merchant
mfr	manufacturer
mkr	maker
P O	Post Office
prop	proprietor
S or Sec	Section
st	street
supt	superintendent
Treas	Treasurer

WATERLOO CITY.

(P O WATERLOO)

ABLE, MADISON, laborer

Ackler, W J., retired

Adrian, Philip, gardener

Adrian, William, laborer

Alexander, O, carpenter

Alford, L, attorney.

ALLEN, HENRY B., President First National Bank in Waterloo, was born in Lewis Co, N Y, May 8, 1833, moved to Watertown, N Y, with parents, where he was educated, and then went to Lowville, Lewis Co, N Y., and studied law with Judge Brown, came to Dubuque in the Fall of 1855, and on March 1, 1857, came to this city, where he married Mary C Nowlin on August 11, 1857; she was born in Dubuque, Iowa, in 1836, Hattie M, born Nov 17, 1858, and Mary D, May 8, 1863, are their children.

Althouse, John, wagon maker.

Ames, D B, laborer

Ampfard, P, farmer, Sec 8

Anderson, E., hog merchant

Andrews, V S, hides

Annibal, W W, wagon maker

Austin, J. G, minister

Aplin, Robert C, shoemaker

Arthur, Alex., merchant

Austin, J J, minister

Averill, John, miller

Ayers, Homer, teamster

Ayers, H N, minister.

Ayers, Nelson, deacon

BAGG, S, Hon, Judge of Circuit Court

Bailey, H. A, merchant.

Baldwin, C W, engineer I C R R.

BALL, JAMES M., physician and surgeon; born in Steubenville, Jefferson Co, Ohio, in 1812 Married Katurah Ford in 1831, she was born in Jefferson Co, Ohio, in 1813 The subject of this sketch received his primary education in his native county, and commenced the study of medicine with William Farmer, M. D., and graduated in Cleveland, Ohio. Emigrated in 1849, to Monroe, Greene Co., Wis., where he was commissioned Assistant Surgeon of the 31st Wis. V I; was detached from his regiment by order of Gen Van Cleve, to take charge of a hospital and fit others for refugees, in Murfreesboro, ordered to report to his regiment, and in July, 1864, obtained leave of absence of Gen Sherman, soon after his return home he was commissioned Surgeon of the 44th Wis. V I, but being unfit for field duty, was ordered to Camp Randall, Madison, Wis., making primary examinations,

I

was ordered to report to Gen Thomas, at Nashville, Tenn., ordered to report to Gen Palmer, and he to Gen. Meredith, at Paducah, Tenn, where he was appointed Surgeon in charge of that post, and soon after of the district of Paducah, in September, 1865, was mustered out of service, and came to Waverly, Iowa, in 1866, and to this city in 1872

Ballow, A E, harness maker.

Ballow, Fred B, harness maker.

BALLIETT & WELD, dealers in jewelry, Logan House Block, Fourth st., East Side. C O Balliett was born in Northumberland Co, Penn, and came to this county in 1867, moved to Niagara Co, N Y, and returned here in 1872 W R Weld was born in St Joseph Co, Mich, in 1844, and married Minnie E. Trobridge in 1870, she was born in Monroe Co, N Y, in 1847, they came to this county in April, 1872, settling in this city May 1, 1872, commenced their present business

Barnburger, D, druggist

Banning, John

BENSON, BANTON, physician and surgeon, born in Baltimore Co, Md, Jan 20, 1828, went with parents to Monroe Co., N Y, in 1845, where he was educated Married Mary Doggett in 1854, she was born in Monroe Co, N Y, in 1827, and died May 26, 1861 Came to Dubuque Co, Iowa, in 1866, where he studied medicine in the office of Dr Clark, went to Raymond, this county, in 1868. where he practiced his profession Married Mary Smith in August. 1869, she was born in Saratoga Co, N Y, Herman and Willie are their children

Barber, P. J, physician

Barber, Earl, druggist

Barden, L, money loaner

Barker, M H, carpenter.

Barker, W. J. machinist.

BARNES, GEORGE W., dealer in farming implements, garden, field and flower seeds, corner of Fourth and Jefferson streets, was born in Chemung Co, N Y, in 1840 Emigrated to Sycamore, De Kalb Co, Ill, in 1858, came to this county, settling in Cedar Falls, in 1868, where he married Alfer-

etta Ray April 5, 1868, she was born in Ashtabula Co., Ohio Mr Barnes commenced business in this city in 1869

Barrent, John. carpenter

BARRETT, WILLIAM, proprietor of the Logan House, was born in Orange Co, Vt, Jan 7, 1827, when quite young he, with his parents, moved to Genesee Co, N. Y., and to Baldwinstown, Wis., in 1844, moved to Anamosa, Iowa, in 1852, and the year following to New York City, and from the latter place to California, where he resided until Feb, 1868, when he went to Geneva, Wis, taking charge of the Lake House After going to Chicago and residing seven months, he moved to Charles City, Iowa, as proprietor of the Union House, after residing in Decorah, Iowa, ten months, he came to this county May 20, 1875 Married Nellie Martin in Nov, 1865, she was born on Long Island Feb 1, 1846; Lulu, 3 years old, is their adopted daughter

Barro, Caspar, saloon

Barro, George, laborer.

Barrows, D A, saloon

Bates. A M, sewing machine agent

BATES, WILLIAM, dealer in butter and eggs, East Side, was born in Joe Daviess Co, Ill, Aug 5, 1847. Married Salona J Harper March 4, 1868, she was born in Grant Co, Wis, in Dec, 1848 After residing in Hazel Green, Wis, for many years, they came to this county, settling in this city in 1867, and commenced his business the year following He enlisted in the 16th Wis V I in 1864, and was honorably discharged in 1865 Eddie A, Florence V, and Kittie are the children

Beal, Albert, patent rights

BECK, FRANK, dealer in boots and shoes, Fourth street, was born in Baltimore, Md, in 1835, and married Margaret Lewis in 1858, she was born in Germany Emigrated to Ohio in 1836, with his parents. and, after going to Dayton, Ohio, emigrated to Dubuque, Iowa, and came to this county in 1864, settling in this city; commenced his present business in June of that year

BECK, G. P., of the firm of Beck & Nauman, dealers in all kinds of pine lumber, lath and shingles, sash, doors, moldings and all sizes of fanning mills, was born in Bavaria July 20, 1832, emigrated to this country with parents in 1832, first settling in Virginia, moved to Dayton, Ohio in 1844, where he married Albertina Shulan Sept 20, 1853, she was born in Stuttgart Feb. 20, 1832, they emigrated to this county in 1856, first settling in this city. Anna W, F W, Malinda, Emma, George, Rosetta, John and Philip are their children

Becker, Charles, laborer
Becker, N E, shoemaker
Becker, W H H, painter
Beefle, N A, retired
Bell, Daniel, carpenter
Bender, Andrew, laborer
Benedict, D. A, music dealer.
Bennett, Joseph, merchant.
Bentz, John, butcher.
Berkley, L B., laborer
Berry, J. R, minister.
Bezold, H H, attorney
Bickley, G G, physician
Bigsby, Charles C, street sprinkler.
Bixby, L L, laborer
Black, William G, mason
Blenis, S, I C R R
Blim, Adam, brewer.
BLIM, MARTIN, editor of *Der Deutsch Amerikaner*, and insurance agent and notary public, was born in Germany Jan 8, 1841 Married Theresa Ordner Jan 27, 1864, she was born in Austria. Mr. Blim emigrated to this country in 1860, settling in Stephenson Co, Ill., and came to this county in March, 1861, commenced the editorship of above paper in 1873
Blim, Peter, furniture.
Blitch, Jacob, laborer
Bloeser, George, saloon
Blowers, William, barber.
Blum, Joseph, shoemaker.
Bogardus, J. A., laborer
Boice, Horace, attorney
Bouck, G. B, butcher
Brainard P. E, livery
Breckinridge, A J, insurance agent
Brodereck, Thomas, laborer.
Brooks, L. L, dry goods
Brott, W B, carpenter.
Brott, W H, auctioneer
Brown, H. S
Brown, H W, physician.

Brown, Willis, saloon.
BROWN, W. F., grain and coal dealer at Raymond, P O Waterloo, born in Kennebec Co, Me in 1823; he moved to Philadelphia, Penn in 1848, to Iowa and Dubuque in 1855, to Waterloo in 1857 He was married in 1850 to Miss Cyntha Rich, from Maine, they have had eight children, five living—Ella R, Elnor E, Tinnie, Walter E and Iola Mr B owns 160 acres of land, valued at $4,500, also three village properties in Waterloo, and two in Dysart, Tama, Co. He has held the office of County Sheriff for twelve years, School Director five years, Township Assessor two years His family reside in Waterloo, he rents the elevator at Raymond and carries on the grain and coal trade, he lost his right arm, in the Fall of 1856, in Dubuque, while engaged with machinery
Brubacher, C, clerk
Brubacher, Elias, restaurant
Brunn, D H, laborer
Buck, Luther, gardener
Bucknell, Elias, baker
Bundy, P S, gardener
BUNNELL, A. C., City Treasurer; was born in Cayuga Co, N Y, Dec. 18, 1818 Married Jane Inman, who was born in Wilkinsburg, Penn, they moved to Racine, Wis, in 1837, in 1854, came to Cedar Falls, this county, and to this city in 1857, when he was elected to his present office, which he held for eight years, and re-elected at the last election
Bunnell, Joseph, agricultural
Bumgardner, W, labor
BURBEE, WILLIAM G., carpenter, joiner and builder, was born in Oswego Co, N. Y, on Sept 16, 1823, and moved to Walworth Co in 1848, and in 1849, emigrated to Janesville, Rock Co, Wis, and married Eliza Fitch May 17, 1853, she was born in Trumbull Co, Wis, Nov 24, 1838, they came to this county in 1855, settling in this city Charles W and Frank H are their children Has been Treasurer of this city for fourteen years
Burger, Martin, laborer
Burkett, John, miller
Burkett, J T., millwright
Burnell, A L., laborer

Burnham, E W , music teacher.

Burnham, M L , druggist

Burroughs, D W , retired bailiff

Burroughs, Stephen, printer

BUSER, J. S., photographer, West Side, born in Lycoming Co , Penn , in 1845, and emigrated to Grant Co , Wis , in 1858, where he resided until going to Warren, Ill , engaging in business with his brother , after one year, he went to Fulton, Ill , and to Cedar Rapids, Iowa, Monroe, Wis , where he bought a gallery, and from which place he came to this county in 1873, where he has been engaged in business

Button, Benj , express agent

Butterfield, N , teamster.

Buttrick, Willard, shoemaker

CAFFALL, O G , grain dealer
Calkins, Porter, painter.

Camp, Edward, clerk

Campwell, B J , coal merchant

Cardey, Robert, machinist

Carey, W W , blacksmith

CASCADEN, THOMAS, dealer in agricultural implements, West Side , born in Ireland June 23, 1835 , moved to Canada and to this county in August, 1868, and married Amanda L Smith in May, 1868, and again married Annie L. Mayes in April, 1874, she was born in Ohio. Mr C moved to Cedar Falls, and then to this city , has been engaged in foundry and agricultural implements trade since his arrival here

Chadwick, T , stone quarry and farmer

Chaffee, P M , grocer

Chapman, I. E , foreman machine shop.

Chapin, W A , merchant

Chase, Chas , foreman, I C. R. R

Chevalier, Alfred, painter

Chevalier, Charles, machinist.

Chevalier, D. T , engineer I. C R R

CHRISTIE, T., grain dealer at Illinois Central Depot, born in Scotland in 1839 , came to Canada in 1853, and Traer, in Tama Co , in 1863, and to this county in 1864 Married Mary Collins in 1876, who was born in Salem, Mass Mr Christie commenced his present business in 1866, and bought his present elevator in 1874.

Christopher, Robert, laborer

Cleveland, E. W , cracker factory

CLINGER, JAMES, dealer in coal and wood , office cor of Fourth and Bluff

sts , was born in Mifflin Co , Penn., in 1814 Married Hannah Condo in 1840, she was born in Centre Co , Penn , in 1819 , they moved to Greene Co , Wis., in 1855, and came to this county in 1865, settling in this city

COBB, DANIEL, livery stable, Fifth and Commercial sts. , was born in Windham Co , Vt , April 14 1805 Married Julia A. Rathbone Oct 17, 1827 , she was born in Milo, Saratoga Co , N. Y , Nov 8, 1808 , when quite young, Mr Cobb moved with his parents to Worcester Co , Mass , and after two years moved to Westmoreland, Cheshire Co , N H , and after seven years went to Saratoga Springs, N Y , and then to Cattaraugus Co , and Erie Co , and Yorkshire, N Y , after residing in Macomb Co , Mich , and Genesee Co , N Y , Allegany , N Y., and Ohio, he came to this county from Allegany Co , N Y , arriving May 5, 1859

COBB, LUCIUS A., retired lumber merchant, was born in Windham Co , N H , Aug 30, 1821 Married H A Ellsworth Nov 3, 1860 , she was born in Hardwick, Vt , moved to Saratoga Springs, N Y and to Cattaraugus Co , N Y , emigrating to Jackson Co., Iowa in 1853, and on Nov 5, 1855, came to this county, settling in this city

COBB, W. S., retired farmer, was born in Westmoreland Co , N. H., on June 9, 1824. Married A E Lingenfelter March 5, 1847; she was born in Victory, N Y , moved to Saratoga Springs, and to Cattaraugus Co , N Y, where he was married, and then came to this county in October, 1856, settling in Cedar Township on Sec. 6 , came to this city in 1866 Ravilla and Edgar S. are their children

Coburn, S , boots and shoes

Colby, L W , restaurant.

Colladay, F , hardware

Collier, C. F., conductor, I. C R R

Conger, G , stock dealer

Conger, Hiram, Street Commissioner

Conger, P H , retired

Connelly, John, machinist.

Connelly, Lawrence, laborer.

Conway, James, laborer

COOLEY, JAMES L., real estate agent in Waterloo, was born in Hart ford, Conn , Aug 1, 1826 , emigrated to Kane Co , Ill., in 1846, and in 1858, came to this county, settling in this city, where he has been engaged in the grain trade Enlisted in the 32d I. V I in 1862, serving in the army of the Cumberland until discharged in 1865 , in 1878, was elected Overseer of the Poor and Township Trustee Married Sarah Lichty, who was born in Kane Co , Ill., in 1846

Coons, Jacob, Justice of the Peace.

Cordell, Alfred, miller

CORWIN, C. W., Assistant Marshal and Notary Public , was born in Tompkins Co , N Y , in 1834 , emigrated to Lake Co., Ill., in 1847, and to this county in 1857, settling in Fox Township Married Alice McStay in 1860, who was born in Dundee , they came to this city in 1864. Willard H is their only child.

Cornell, Wm , minister

Cottrell, W. A , Deputy Auditor

Couch, Carl F , attorney

COWIN, E. F., attorney at law , was born in Cleveland, Ohio, Sept. 28, 1847 , received his education in his native city, and, after attending the Law School at Ann Arbor, Mich , he was admitted to the bar in Ohio Sept 6, 1869 Came to this county June 28, 1870

Cox, G W., painter

Craig, Wm , plaster and stone mason

CRIPPEN, J. H., physician and surgeon , was born in Decatur, Otsego Co , N Y , April 9, 1850 Moved to Ithaca, Tompkins Co , N Y ; commenced the study of medicine with E B. Nash, M. D , of Courtland, N Y.. and graduated at the Hahnemann Medical College in Philadelphia in 1872 , commenced the practice of medicine in Ithaca, N Y , came to this county in Jan , 1874 Married Minnie M Clingman April 10, 1877 , she was born in Greene Co., Wis , Jan 5,1857

Crooker, Charles E , drayman.

Crotty, L R , livery

Crouse. D F , physician

Crouse, D W , physician

Crouse, Henry, physician

Crowley, I R , prop. Key City Hotel

Crowther, W A , Justice of the Peace.

Cutler, D A , short-hand reporter.

CUTLER, F. E., hardware , born in Canada August 1, 1843. Married Hattie A Lautenslager May 22, 1877 , she was born in Niagara Co , N Y , May 8, 1843 Emigrated to this country in 1850 , settled in Niagara Co , N Y., and, in 1866, came to this city , commenced his business in 1872.

Cutler, W H , retired.

Curry, W H , laborer

Curtis, W H , attorney

DAHL, FRED , machinist

Daugherty, P F , conductor, I. C. R R

Davis, Joshua, blacksmith

Davis, Wm H , blacksmith.

Day, Sullivan, speculator

Deener, Samuel, mason

DEMMEL BROS., meat market on Commercial st , were born in Germany ; came to this country in 1866, settling in Pittsburgh, Penn , and then moved to Freeport, Ill , came to this city in 1873 , they built, in 1876, a building 23x70, two stories high, fitting it up for their market ; it is regarded as the finest meat market west of Chicago

Deuel, Judson, I C R R

Depew, Levi, painter

Dunsmonde, John F , I C R R

Dobson, William, railroad yard master.

Donavan, Daniel, I C R R

Dorlan, Peter, mason

Doxey, B S , railroad man

Dubois, Uriah, cabinet maker

Duke, John C , miller

Dull, Josiah, carpenter.

Dunham, A G., carpenter.

Dunham, M L , carpenter

Dunwald, H J , grocer

Durland, J. C , lime kiln

ECK, LEONARD, grocer

Eddy, E. M.

Eddy, Wm , physician

Edman, Thomas C , teamster.

Edwards, A J , clerk in Recorder's office.

Edgington, W. W , Deputy Sheriff

Eggleston, A M , merchant

Eggleston, Harry, machinist.

Eickelberg, John, wagon maker.

Ellis, Ebenezer, carpenter

Ellis, James, retired merchant

Elwell, Joseph C., attorney

Ercanbrack, S., tailor

EVANS, J. P., dealer in staple and fancy groceries, tobacco and cigars, Fourth street, West Side, was born in Hillsboro Co, N. H, May 25, 1812, moved with his parents to Abbottsford, Lower Canada, in 1822, at the age of 21, emigrated to Berrien Co Mich, and after two years' residence there, and in Edwardsburg, Cass Co, he married Eliza A Booth in 1838, she was born in Utica, N Y., they came to Dubuque, Iowa, on Nov 2, 1839, and to this city in 1861, served as Marshal of this city six years, commenced his present business in May, 1877 Mrs Adeline M, Mrs Josephine Fuller, Mrs Emma Lush and Frank H are their children

Ewald, Wm, manufacturer of pop.

FARNSWORTH, E W, laborer.

FANCHER, NELSON, grain dealer, warehouse at Burlington Depot, was born in Delaware Co, Ohio, June 28, 1826, in the Fall of 1841, he came to Dubuque, and went to California in 1850, but returned to this State, and settled in this city in 1853, and in the same year commenced keeping a general store in this city, afterward, he was engaged in farming in Poyner Township, but in 1868 returned to this city and commenced his present business Married Elizabeth Virden May 25, 1854, she was born in Edwards Co., Ill, June, 1834

FARWELL, C. A., insurance and real estate agent, born in Bennington Co, Vt, Sept. 7, 1832, moved to Genesee Co, N Y., with his parents in 1837. and to Chautauqua Co, N. Y., in 1850, after going to California, he came to this city in March, 1856, where he married Mary P Evans Oct. 20, 1860, she was born in New Orleans May 22, 1841

Faulkner, Wm, carpenter.

Fay, Thomas, laborer

Fernbach, A., hotel proprietor

Fenstermaker, James, harness maker.

Fenstermaker, S. W, machinist,

Finnerty, Joseph, nurseryman

Flanagan, D A, lime burner

Foote, D W, County Auditor

Fountain, J P, laborer

Fowler, C F, nurseryman

Fowler, G V, nursery

FOWLER, J. A., fruit dealer

Fowler, Ralph P, butter dealer

FOWLER BROS. & PLACE, manufacturers of cheese, factory on West Side Richard Place, born in Herkimer Co, N Y., in 1822 Married Sarah Talbot, who was born in Onondaga Co, N Y Mr Place moved to Onondaga Co, where he resided until after marriage, when he went to Herkimer Co, N Y, came to this county in the Spring of 1873, and took charge of the factory, they made about 40,000 pounds the first year, and have increased to 175,000 pounds George A, Dora A., Harris, Talbert and Fayette are their children

Frank, A H, grain merchant

FRANK, M., proprietor of the old reliable clothing house of Waterloo, Iowa, he is the fashionable merchant tailor and clothier, and dealer in furnishing goods, hats and caps, trunks and valises, Commercial st, born in Cincinnati, Ohio, in 1848, and came to this county in 1865 Married Anna Beck in December, 1876, she was born in Dayton, Ohio, in 1855, they have one child—Jessie. Mr Frank has gained an enviable reputation on account of having good goods for *"one price."* This was the first clothing house in this city for some years after their opening in 1865.

Freet, W. S, shoemaker

Frink, George D., conductor

Fuller, H. A., agricultural implements

Fuoss, Jacob, plasterer

GABLE, O, ticket agent, I. C. R R

Galloway, Jos C, attorney

Garbrant, Jacob, blacksmith

Garton, Richard, minister

Gates, J C, Clerk District Court

Geddes, D H, marble factory

GEORGE, JAMES S., County Superintendent of Schools, was born in Yorkshire, England, April 27, 1833, Mr George, with his father, left England in June, 1836, arriving in Rockford, Ill, the following September; he was educated at Jubilee College, Peoria, Ill., after which he went to Ottawa, Ill, in the Fall of 1851, teaching school, and where he married Mary J Quirk May 8, 1861, she was born in Belvidere, N J, Feb 24, 1839, came to this county in 1856 Elected on the Republican ticket for County Superintendent

GILBERT, G. W., dealer in dry goods, born in Tioga Co, N Y., July 10, 1833 Married Sarah M. Jenks, April 12, 1858, who was born in Worcester, Mass Emigrated to Fort Dodge in the Fall of 1855, the following year, he went to Algona, Iowa, and in the Fall of 1857, went to Waverly, N Y, where he married, came to this city in in Aug, 1858

Godard, H , engineer, I C R R
Glover, John S , merchant.
Goodman, A , machinist
Goodman, S , butcher
Goodrich, James H , insurance agent
Gould, D R , engineer, I C R R
Gregg, J W , mason.
Groves, William, livery
Gwynne, John A , merchant.
Gwynne, J B , furniture
Gwynne, Thomas, furniture.

HACKER, FRED, machines.

Hacker, James, hardware
Hacker, Joe, machines.
Haffa, Daniel, carpenter
Haffa, J W , carpenter.
Hale, Enoch, carriage maker
Hall, F F
Halstead, E E.
Hamilton, Wm , jeweler
Hammond, Wm , retired merchant

HANKINSON, J. W., representing the Northwestern Life Insurance Co , of Milwaukee, Wis , office corner Sycamore and Fourth sts , was born in Montgomery Co , N. Y., May 17, 1820 Married Mary J. Mason, who was born in Dutchess Co , N Y., April 1, 1828 , moved to Canada West in 1836, and in the Fall of the same year, went to Detroit, Mich., coming to Rockford, Ill , in 1843 , emigrated to this county in 1856, settling in this city, was engaged here in the mercantile trade, but abandoned it in a few years for his present business, which he has followed sixteen years. Hattie J , born Dec 27, 1854, is their only child

Haner, S , cabinet maker
Hannon, Morris, smith.

HARBIN, GEO. W. & CO., wholesale dealers in drugs, medicines, and retail books and stationery, Logan House Block East Side. The senior partner was born in Ripley Co , Ind , in 1842, emigrated to Washington Co , Iowa, in 1858, where he enlisted in the 24th Iowa V I., in Aug , 1862, and honorably discharged in Aug , 1865, came to this city in 1869 , commenced his present business in this city in July, 1869, and has been a practical druggist since 1857, learning the business in Indiana Married A J Snyder in 1867 , she was born in Cincinnati, Ohio, in 1841 , their children are Charles, Willie, Jessie L and Ella M F. M Robinson, the junior partner of the firm, was born in Wood Co , Ohio, March 15, 1852, came to this county in 1868, with his mother, and went into partnership with Mr Harbin, about three months since.

Harmon, A. W., railroad
Harper, M C , engineer
Hartman, G , saloon

HARTMAN, WILLIAM H. There are but few newspaper men in the State, who have so long and faithfully occupied an editorial chair as has William H Hartman, the founder and one of the present editors and proprietors of the *Waterloo Courier.* He was born in Allentown, Penn , Aug. 27, 1838 When he was 2 years of age, his parents removed to Tiffin, Ohio, where he lived until he was 14 years old Received what educational advantages the common schools of Ohio offered at that time In 1850, he came to Iowa with his parents, who located at Anamosa Soon after they arrived in Iowa, *The Anamosa News,* the first paper ever published in Jones County, was established, and young William was employed as junior devil, rolling the first edition ever published in that county He remained in that office several years, and then, starting on a tramp He worked in Delhi, Dubuque, Tiffin (Ohio) and other places, arriving at Waterloo in March, 1858, finding employment for the first four or five months in the offices of the *Iowa State Register* and *Waterloo Herald* He then went to Cedar Falls and attempted to instill new life into the *Banner,* which had previously suspended. After working hard for several months he became convinced that it was not a paying institution, and, in company with George D Ingersoll, purchased the office, removed it to Waterloo, and Jan 18, 1859, issued the first number of the *Waterloo Courier*, which after passing through many struggles in its early existence, has now become one of the best paying newspaper offices in the interior of the State, and is blessed with a liberal and constantly increasing patronage. Politically, Mr Hartman has always been an earnest and able defender of the Republican party and its principles, personally and through the columns of the *Courier*, lending material aid to the party in the county. In March, 1873, he was appointed and commissioned Postmaster at Waterloo, and has since performed the duties of that responsible office to the general satisfaction of the public, not excepting those on the East Side, who were bitterly opposed to his appointment

Hartnett, J , conductor, I C R R.

Harkong, N., policeman

Harvey, C W , patent right dealer.

Hay, D G , grocery

Hay, I M , clothing

Hatch, E. E , machinist

Hatch, H D , bookkeeper.

Hawkins, G., clerk hotel

Hawkins, G H , clerk

Hayden, E V , railroad

Hayes, B D , carriage trimmer

Hayes, F S , blacksmith.

Hazleton, F , machinist

Hazlett, G W , Sheriff

Heiserodt, A M , Constable

Higgins, Freeman, carpenter

Hirsh, Henry, clerk

Hitchcock, Nelson, miller

HITT, E. R., manufacturer of buggies, on Commercial st. , was born in Delaware Co , N Y., in August, 1836 ; he went to Ashtabula Co , Ohio, where he learned his trade—that of blacksmith —and returned to Broome Co., N. Y , where he married Elizabeth Smith in September, 1855 , she was born in Worcester, Otsego Co., N Y , in 1836 , they went to Lake Co , Ohio, where Mr Hitt was foreman of C G Whitman's manufactory for three years , and then Hamden, Geauga Co , Ohio, in 1861, where he was commissioned First Lieu-

tenant of Co B, 42d Ohio V I. After his discharge from the service, he went to Hillsdale Co , Mich, and to this city in 1870, commencing his business two years last Fall

Hoff, George A., merchant.

Hoff, J E , merchant

Hoff, J G , merchant

Hoff, Samuel, policeman

Holdiman, D , carpenter.

Holderman, Wm , machinist.

Holden, C B , R R

Holden, John O , clerk I C. R. R

Hollister, C C , teamster

Hollister, J. J , street sprinkler

Holmes, Frank, laborer

Holzer, Albert, groceryman.

Hooper, Joseph, machinist

Hoot, S G., shoemaker

Hoover, B H , laundryman

Hough, Daniel, merchant.

HOWARD, GEORGE W., attorney at law and capitalist, was born in Maine, and after residing there about twenty-eight years, he emigrated to Chickasaw Co , Iowa, where he resided until the late war, when he was commissioned as Major of the 27th I V I in 1862, and during the war was Acting Lieut Colonel, and during the last year took command of his regiment. After returning from the war, he came to this county, arriving in the Summer of 1866. He was admitted to the Bar in 1854 His office is at the corner of Bridge and Commercial streets.

Howe, C. K , traveling agent

HUME, DANIEL E., dealer in horses, was born in Monroe Co , N Y , Jan 24, 1830 , moved with parents to Orleans Co , N. Y , when 6 years old, and where he married Susan Smith on April 5, 1858 , April 16, 1859, they came to this county, settling in Poyner Township , they moved to this city in 1873.

Hummel, J P , blacksmith.

Hummel, R , blacksmith

Hungerford, N S , clerk

Hunt, L S , machinist.

Hurd, James, wheat buyer.

Husted, James L., attorney.

ILLINGWORTH, W. L., miller.

Ischei, Fred , Jr., machinist

Israel, E E , merchant
Israel, E H , merchant.
JACKSON, ALVIN, lumber merchant.

Jackson, John, carpenter
Jackson, Wm , Sr., wagon maker
Jacoby, Peter, agricultural implements
Jenkins, Enoch, retired preacher
Jenney, H W., Marshal.
Johnson Emmons, banker
JOHNSTON, J. S. & CO., manufacturers of plows, cultivators, harrows, and farming implements in general The senior partner of the firm was born in England in 1832, and came to this country, settling in New York, moved to this county from Rockford, Ill., in Feb. 1878, commencing their business at that time They have a small but well-regulated factory near the Illinois Central Railroad Depot C A Johnson is the junior partner.
Johnston, W S , butcher
Jones, C P , bridge builder.
Judd W B , physician
KEENAN, PATRICK

Kur, S A , machinist
Kellogg, D C, proprietor bus line
KELLOGG, T. N., proprietor of bus line ; was born in Vernon, Oneida Co , N Y., in 1826, when very young, his parents moved to Rome, N Y , where he resided for many years, and where he married the daughter of Jeptha Madison, of that place ; they came to Dubuque in 1856, and to Cedar Falls, this county, where he was engaged in dry goods trade, and after selling this business, came to this city
Kelly, B , grocery.
Kelsey, J H , speculator
Kennedy, W. C , grain buyer
Ketchum, F. E., conductor, I C R R
Kimble, Henry, teamster
Kimble, Jeremiah, teamster
Kinstler B , merchant.
Kistner, Frank, shoemaker
Kistner, Fred, shoemaker
Kleinsooge, A , grocer
KNOX, O. S., physician and surgeon , office on Commercial st., over Snowdon's drug store , was born in Bedford, Penn , in 1854, moved to Latrobe, Penn , in 1866, where he enlisted in

Co D, 55th Penn V I , in 1861, and was honorably discharged in 1863. Commenced the study of medicine in his native county, with Dr Harry, and graduated in the University at Albany, N Y , in 1866 , emigrated to Forreston, Ill , in 1867, and in May, 1869, came to Waterloo Married Agnes Manson Nov 12, 1872 , she was born in Rome, N Y , in 1852, Robert Manson and John Otho are their children.
Kramer, Fritz, agricultural
Krapfel, J W , Cashier 1st Nat'l Bank
Kuhn, Jos H , Justice of the Peace
LaBARRE, CHARLES, carpenter

LaBarre, John, laborer
Lampe, H , boot and shoe maker
Lane, Allen T , speculator
Lane, E C , attorney
LANE, H. A., dealer in groceries and provisions, Pardee Block, Fourth st , west side , was born in Belknap Co , N. H , in 1830 Married Harriet C Ordway in 1850 ; she was born in Hampstead, Rockingham Co., N. H Emigrated to Freeport, Stephenson Co , Ill., in 1852, and returned to New Hampshire in Oct , 1854, and came to this city in Oct , 1857, commenced his present business in Chapin's Block in 1874, but came to his present location in 1876. Mrs Ida Mitchel and Albert B are his children
LANE, WILLIAM, Justice of the the Peace , was born in Bradford Co , Penn., Jan 18, 1822 Married Sallie M King in Aug , 1849 , she was born in the State of New York, in 1819. They emigrated to this county in 1855, and moved to Grundy Co , this State, where they resided eight years, and then returned to this county Has held the office of County Treasurer in Grundy Co , over four years , elected Justice of the Peace in the city in 1871. Edgar C and Hattie A are his children.
Lanning, J M , Dr , physician
Lawless, P J , machinist.
LEAVITT, JOHN H., banker, and of the firm of Leavitt & Johnson , born in Franklin Co , Mass., Oct 11, 1831 , emigrated from his native county to this in Sept., 1854, first settling in this city. Married Caroline C. Ware Jan 1, 1858, who was born in Putnam

Co , Ill , Oct 11, 1835   Mr Leavitt commenced the banking business in this city in 1856

Lemper, P P , tinner

Lester, R S , shoemaker.

LIBBY, L., manager of the Grange store, and proprietor of the American House , was born in Waldo Co , Me , April 1, 1837 , moved to Hennepin Co , Minn , in 1858, and in the Spring of 1870, came to this city, taking charge of the store in 1875   Married Missouri Boyer May 14, 1876 , she was born in Pennsylvania , John is their only son

Lichty, C W , cabinet maker

Lichty, E. J , machinist.

Lichty, Lewis, attorney at law

Lincoln, A , plasterer

Lindley, H , lumber merchant

Locke, John, printer.

Logan, John, machinist.

Long, John, machinist.

LUDDEN, GAINES, merchant tailor, East Side , was born in Montgomery Co , N Y., June 10, 1820 , he moved to Onondaga Co , N Y , in 1844. Married Emily Jane Barr Oct. 29, 1851 , she was born in Cayuga Co., N Y , in 1830   After residing in Wayne Co , N. Y., Cayuga and Oswego Counties, they emigrated to this county, settling in this city in Sept., 1877, where he commenced his present business Oct 1, 1877   Harry G is his only son.

Lusch, A. T , lumberman

MᶜCABE, JOHN, merchant

McCORMICK, BERNARD, dealer in flour and feed, Fourth st , was born in Fulton Co , Penn , in 1829   Married Mary Masters in 1854; she was born in Fulton Co , Penn , in 1837 , they emigrated from their native county to this city in 1855, where Mr M was first engaged in running a saw-mill, and after engaging in various kinds of business, commenced his present occupation a short time since   In 1862, he enlisted in 32d Iowa V I , Company C, and was honorably discharged in 1865.   John R , Mary, Emma and Addie are their children

McCullough, J , farmer, Sec 5

McDonald, Robert, painter.

McGaffin, Robert, shoemaker

McIntire, J H , miller

McMurray, H A , miller

McMurray, W B , miller

McNeil, J W , I C R R

McNeal, J , train despatcher, I C R R

MACK, GEORGE J., physician and surgeon , was born in Oakland Co , Mich , Oct. 7, 1850 , commenced medical studies in Bellevue Hospital Medical College, New York, in 1870, and graduated in March, 1872.   Emigrated to this county in 1868, settling in this city   Married, in Monticello, Iowa, Lillian A Kimball, Sept 16, 1872.

Manning, W L , laborer

Manson, Robert, retired.

Manson, Robert M , clerk in bank

Martin, Henry, baker

Mason, George, money lender.

Mason, J W , machinist

Maynard, C J , carpenter

Melendy, O , teamster

Merricle, Amos, laborer

Merrill, O L., painter

Merwin, E S., machinist

Merwin, H E , machinist

Merwin, J. E., machinist

Messick, John, broom maker

Messinger, E. J , retired farmer.

MIDDLEDITCH, ALVARADO, physician and surgeon , was born in Erie Co , N Y , Feb 8, 1829 , in 1844, he with his parents moved to Macomb Co , Mich , returning to his native county, he attended school four years, and commenced his medical studies with Dr. Barber, and in 1854 attended Albany Medical College, where he graduated in May, 1856   Married Paulina Griffith Aug 9, 1856 , she was born in Danbury, Vt ; they emigrated to this county in Sept , 1856, Florence G and Herbert B are their children

Miller, George, laundry

Miller, L B , blacksmith

Miller, Louis, drayman

Miller, O. C , attorney

Miller, Peter, drayman

Miner, John A., farmer, Sec 36

Moran, T , Road Master

Morgadant, Chris , machinist

Moon. William, bookkeeper

MORRILL, A. W., of the firm of Morrill & Co , manufacturers of soap, East Side; was born in Alexander, Grafton Co , N. H., Dec 3, 1830 , moved to Lowell, Mass., in 1851, and emigrated to Rockford, Ill , in 1861 Married Hellen M Richardson Oct 2, 1861 , she was born in Antrim, N. H , in 1833   After manufacturing soap in Rockford until 1871, he sold out and came to this county, arriving August 6

Morrill, C F., merchant

MORRIS, WILLIAM C., jeweler, was born in Oakland Co , Mich , Oct , 1828, moved to Genesee Co., Mich , in 1842, and after two years' residence returned to his native county, where he served four years as an apprentice, learning his trade, he moved to Ovid, N. Y., and to Penn Yan, where he was engaged in business in 1851   Returning to Michigan, he married Sarah Pratt Dec 26, 1854 , she was born in New York May 31, 1829, they came to this State, settling in Independence, Buchanan Co , in 1855 , in the Winter of 1868 they came to this county, and settled in this city

Morrow, Richard, herder

MOSHER, JERRY, meat market, Commercial street, was born in Steuben Co , N Y, May 5, 1827   Married Mary A. Sylvester May 3, 1848 , she was born in Keene, N. A , Sept. 21, 1831   They emigrated to Rockford, Ill , in 1856, and came to this city in 1865, commencing his present business that year   Residence, East Side

Mullin, C W , attorney

MUNGER, J. C., dealer in sewing machines, pianos and organs, was born in Dorchester, Canada West, May 16, 1842   Married Elizabeth A. Jenkins Jan 16, 1867; she was born in Whitbey, C W , July 30, 1841. Emigrated to Scott Co , Iowa, in 1851, and to this county in 1854, settling two miles west of this city , came to Waterloo in 1867, and commenced his present business in 1872 ; handles Haines Bros' of New York, pianos, Mason & Hamlin's, Boston, organs, and the Domestic sewing machines from Newark, N J, keeps all kinds of sewing machine attachments, and genuine needles for all kinds of machines   Mrs Munger is a dressmaker, and has followed the business all her life , she now employs five girls   Isaac E is their only child

Myer, Henry, lime burner.

NAUMAN, HENRY, lumberman

NAUMAN, JOHN, dealer in groceries, Commercial st , opposite Central House, was born in Germany in 1831 , came to this country, first settling in Detroit, Mich , and the same year (1856), came to Waterloo, Iowa, working at the joiner and cabinet maker's trade, commenced his present business three years ago   Married Catherine Betts, from Pennsylvania , they have seven children

NEELY, FRANK, of the firm of Neely & Co , dealers in lumber, shingles and lath, sash, doors, blinds, moldings, etc , Fourth street, West Side   was born in Belvidere, Boone Co , Ill , in 1843, moved to Chicago in 1858, and in 1861, enlisted in Battery I, 1st Ill. Artillery, and was honorably discharged in 1865 , the same year he came to Cedar Falls, and to this city in 1868 , commenced his present business with T A Cobb, in 1865   A T Lust bought out the latters interest in 1877   Mr N. married Mary Sessions in February, 1871, she was born in Warren, Mass , in 1845   Frank B is their only child

Newton, Reuben, conductor

Nugent, Patrick, railroad

OHLER, Adam, carpenter

O'Neal, Arthur, mason

ORDWAY, GEORGE, attorney at law, born in Strafford, N. H , Aug 1, 1829   Married Salone E Fowler Oct 6, 1852, she was born in Springfield, Ill , Aug. 22, 1833   Mr Ordway moved to Springfield, Ill , in 1843, and to this county on April 22, 1854, was admitted to the bar in Freeport, Ill , Oct 13, 1851, and said document was signed by Judge J D. Caton, now of Ottawa, Ill

PAGE, Alvah, fisherman

Palfreyman, John, machinist

Pardee, R H., retired merchant

Park, J L , liveryman

PARKHURST, C. J., wholesale and retail dealer in china, crockery, glass, wooden and willow ware, silver ware and fine table cutlery , also, Ohio stone ware, West Side , was born in Chautauqua Co., N Y , May 19, 1850, he came to this county, settling in this city, Jan. 1, 1869, and has since been engaged in his present business on Commercial st. Married Mary Cluyer on May 13, 1874 , she was born in Pennsylvania

PARROTT, GIRTON & SHERMAN, job printers, manufacturers of blank books, stationers, and publishers of the *Iowa State Reporter*, making a specialty of county offices supplies, East Side, Waterloo, Iowa, the individual members are Matt Parrott, James L Girton and James P. Sherman

PARTRIDGE, MAYNARD, manufacturer and dealer in furniture of all kinds, opposite Logan House, East side , was born in Templeton, Worcester Co , Mass . June 3, 1827 , moved from native county to Lebanon, N H , where he married Harriet Parker on Aug. 12, 1851 , she was born in Canada   Came to Baraboo, Wis , where he resided about four months , after which he moved to Merrimack and Baraboo, Wis , and in June, 1869, settled in this city. Has been engaged in the manufacture and sale of furniture for many years

PATTERSON, J. S., meat market, Fourth st., East Side , born in Monroe Co , N Y , in 1824, emigrated to Fairfield Co , Ohio, in 1838, and then to Highland Co., where he married Katherine Wiley in 1843, she was born in Ross Co , Ohio, in 1820   Mr P went to California in 1853, and returned in 1857 , came to this county, settling in Jessup in 1871, and to this city in 1873, commencing his present business in 1875

Pauling, John, tailor

Peepo, Henry, shoemaker

PEIFER, L. R., of the firm of Peifer & Calladay, dealers in hardware, on Commercial st , was born in Berks Co , Penn , June 22, 1843, went to Lee Co , Ill , in 1863, and after one year's residence, returned to Pennsylvania, where he married Lydia Depper in 1865 , she was born in Berks Co , Penn They emigrated to this county in 1865, settling in Waterloo Tp , on Sec 17 , came to this city in 1864, and in June, 1877, commenced his present business. Edward. aged 13, and Lizzie, 5 years old are their children.

Perry, Wm , R R

Phelps, E S , dry goods.

Pierce, C. W , speculator

PITCHER, S. W., meat market, was born in Bradford Co., Penn., Dec 29, 1835   Married Susan Goodwin in Nov , 1857, she was born in Wayne Co., N Y   Emigrated to this county, settling in this city in the Fall of 1865, and commenced his present business seven years ago   Eveline G. and Nattie are their children

Place, J D , engineer, I C R R

Place, T W , machinist

Polbrook, John, stone cutter

Pollard, J H , machinist

Pomeroy, A T , P O clerk

Ponsford. Joseph, carpenter

Pott, Peter, wagon maker.

Powell, W H , hotel proprietor

Powers, J B , District Attorney

PRATT, HENRY O., born in Foxcroft, Maine, Feb 11, 1838   Married Hala C. Woodward, in Charles City, Iowa. Oct 21, 1865 , she was born in Bloomington, Ind., April 18, 1844   He entered Bowdoin College, Maine, in 1859, in Sept , 1860, he came to Cambridge and studied in Harvard Law School, and graduated in Jan., 1862 ; in March of that year, he came to Iowa, first settling in Nashua, but moved to Mason City, Cerro Gordo Co., Iowa where he enlisted in Company B, 32d Iowa V I , but was discharged in 1863   The Summer of 1863, he taught school in Worth Co , and in the Fall of 1863, went to Charles City, Iowa, where he followed school teaching until 1864, when he commenced the practice of law, and in the Fall of 1869, was elected as a Representative in the State Legislature, and re-elected in the Fall of 1871 , at the general election in the Fall of 1872, was elected to Congress from the Fourth District, and re-elected. He was converted in Charles City, and on coming to Waterloo, was placed in charge of the Jefferson St M E Church as a supply, which position he now holds   His children are Myrta H , Emma G., George W , Harry A. and Ralph.

Preston, J. H.

Pressey, E. H , grain dealer

RAYMOND, E A

Reed, Martin, livery.

Reed, Wm, blacksmith

REED & BIGALOW, feed, board and sale stable, Commercial St. The former was born in Armstrong Co, Penn, in 1821. Married Elizabeth Morrison, who died in this city Again married Theda McGowen After living in Mercer Co, Penn, emigrated to Stephenson Co, Ill, and then came to Cedar Falls, Iowa, in 1870, and to this city in 1872

Remington, G H, gunsmith

RICHARDS, WALTER OSCAR, born in Genesee Co, N. Y, Nov 21, 1820, and was the sixth of a family of nine children, five of whom were boys and four girls When Walter was 8 years of age, his parents moved to Monroe Co., in the vicinity of Rochester, where they resided until 1837, when they moved to Geauga Co, Ohio, in that portion of the State known as the "Western Reserve." Here his mother died, and that Winter, young Walter, when about 17 years of age, taught his first term of school, he soon after went to Farmington Seminary, a branch of Oberlin College. At this institution, he spent about three years, during a greater portion of which time he and John Patchen, now a prominent Congregational clergyman in the Western Reserve, roomed together in a log house, and boarded themselves In 1841, he went to Oberlin College, entering the Freshman class, he remained in this institution nearly three years, and was pursuing the studies of the Junior class when poor health compelled him to leave college, in 1845, he went to Branch Co, Mich, and spent about three years working on a farm with a brother and teaching school during the Winter months. In 1848, he went into the office of Dr. James M Teft, of Sturgis, for the purpose of studying medicine, he remained here three years, and in the Winter of 1850–51, attended one course of medical lectures at the Ann Arbor Medical College. In the Summer of 1851, he was married to Miss Julia A. Bundy, of Ontario, La Grange Co, Ind., and they then went to Huntington in that State, where he obtained the principalship of the Union School with Mrs

Richards in charge of the primary department, in 1852, he returned to Ontario and spent a year in the practice of medicine in partnership with Dr Sargent, in 1854, he returned to Ann Arbor and completed his medical studies, in the Summer of 1855, they came to Waterloo, then a town of between 300 and 400 inhabitants, and have remained here ever since, since residing here, a son and daughter have been born The son graduated in the class of 1876, at the State University of Iowa, and is now city editor *Waterloo Courier* The daughter is still a student at that institution. Dr Richards has been a member of the Congregational Church for the past forty-seven years, has always been a strong advocate of temperance and a member of several temperance organizations In politics, Dr Richards is a Republican with Whig antecedents While at Oberlin, he became thoroughly imbued with the Abolition sentiments of that school, and his first Presidential ballot was cast for J G Birney. Since his residence in Waterloo, he has been Coroner of Black Hawk Co for nearly the entire time. He was one of the five original owners of the Cedar Mills after the death of Miles Spafford, and on the foundation of the Union Mill Company, one of the largest enterprises in the city, he was chosen a member of the Board of Directors, a position he has held ever since. He has never received any pecuniary aid from his parents, and is indebted to his own industry for the measure of success to which he has attained

Rickert, Charles, painter

Rickert, Henry, painter.

Rickert, H F, painter.

RICKER, M., of the firm of Ricker & Lindley, dealers in lumber, lath, sash, doors, blinds, etc ; was born in Waldo, Maine in 1837, went to California in in 1858, and returned to Boston, Mass., in 1865. Came to this county in 1870, where he married Jennie Congar, in 1873, she was born in Dubuque, Iowa, on Dec 12, 1857. Mr. Ricker was engaged in dry goods trade for several years, and commenced his present business in 1874

RIDER, J. Q. A., hardware, Commercial street, was born in Orange Co,

Vt , May 21, 1829   Married Margaret C Grant in 1854 , she was born in Connecticut, emigrated to Grundy Co , Ill , where he was married, and came to this county in February. 1874, commencing his present business   Loren, Dwight and Nelha, the first aged 20, the second 18 and third 14 years, are his children

Rider, S G , retired merchant

Rife, Peter, machinist

Riley, Thomas, Lecture agent

Roberts, G F , Dr., physician

Roberts, Humphrey T., carpenter.

Roberson, F W , druggist

Robinson, G. H , boots and shoes

ROBINSON, WILLIAM S., foundry and machine shop, manufacturer of farmers' boilers   cook stoves, heating stoves, corn shellers, and all kinds of castings, repair shop for machinery, Commercial street, West Side , was born in Cheshire Co , N H., March 22, 1834, learning his trade in Boston, and after spending one year on the lake, he came to this county in October, 1855, settling in this city   Married Sarah Bunnell in June 1877 , she was born in Lake Co , Ohio, in June, 1833

Robson, Andrew, mason

Roby, David, engineer

Roby, Robert, engineer

Rodifer, G W , carpenter

Roe, Charles E , miller

ROEBUCK, C. A., dealer in confectionery, fruits, nuts, cigars, ice cream, etc , East Side , was born in Canada, and came with parents to this city in 1867 , has worked at his trade, that of stone mason, until commencing his present business on May 10, 1878

Roebuck, Nathan, plasterer.

Rose, T A., dentist

Rosgen, Adam, harness maker

Rosgen, H , harness maker.

RENSSELAER, RUSSELL, wholesale and retail dealer in groceries, on Commercial st. , was born in Otsego Co , N Y., June 18, 1828.   Married Caroline M Richards Jan. 12, 1853 , she was born in Paris, Oneida Co., N Y.

SARGENT, CHAS G

Saunders, A., clerk

Saunders, H H , collector.

SEAMAN, B. K., dealer in books and stationery, fancy goods, pictures and picture frames, East Side , was born in Essex Co , N Y , Oct 3, 1807   Married Charlotte H Mead July 7, 1829 ; she was born in Warren Co , N Y, Nov 25, 1807   Mr S commenced life as Steward in Troy Conference Academy, of West Poultney, Vt , and graduated at the State Normal School, of New York, in 1844, and was afterward Principal of Model Department , moved to Clintonville, N. Y., where he was engaged in teaching and mercantile trade, but after nine years' residence moved to Appleton, Wis , purchasing an interest in a flouring-mill , came to this county in 1869, and for several years was Principal of public schools in this city   They have two children living—F D Seaman, at Alma City, Minn , and Mrs C. G Moak, whose husband is a merchant in Sun Prairie, Wis , Mead H died in Andersonville prison during our late war

Seeman, Charles M , machinist

Sellers, George, machinist

Shannon, T F , engineer.

Sharpless, Lewis M

SHAW, SAMUEL D., retired , was born in Rutland Co , Vt , April 19, 1811, emigrated to St Louis, Mo , in 1831, and after eight years moved to Licking Co , Ohio, where he married Elizabeth Stoughton July 16, 1840 , she was born in Greenville, Licking Co., Ohio, Sept. 30, 1819, and they came to this county in 1852, settling in Orange Tp , on Sec. 1   Elected Judge of the County Court in 1862, and moved to this city

Sheever, Nick, blacksmith

SHILLIAM, SAMUEL, livery, sale and feed stable , also dealer in live stock , was born in Mineral Point, Wis , April 9, 1845 , moved to Hazel Green, Wis., when quite young, with parents, where he married Mary H Bates Dec. 11, 1867 , she was born in Vinegar Hill, Jo Daviess Co , Ill., in May, 1850 , in December, 1869, came to this city, where he has been identified as one of the live stock shippers of the city

Shirland, C R , harness maker

SHOOK & WALKER, dealers in groceries, East Side   Daniel Shook was born in Coshocton Co, Ohio, Jan 19, 1845, and came to this county in the Spring of 1869, commenced business in 1870. C Gardner Walker was born in Belvidere, Boone Co, Ill., May 11, 1849, and came to this county in the Spring of 1871, went into the firm in 1873

Shutts, Harvey, druggist

Siberling, P J, retired merchant

Sill, H. W, retired

Sindlinger, Wm M, confectioner

Sine, Edward, carpenter

Sine, John, carpenter

Sine, S G, auctioneer

Singer, Charles, mail agent

Simmons, Charles, hotel

SIMMONS, GEORGE W., proprietor of the New York House, was born in Steuben Co, N Y, Oct 29, 1816 Married Deborah Fulkerson Nov 23, 1839, she was born in Yates Co, N Y., June 9, 1816, Mr. S moved to Yates Co, N Y., where he married, and then in 1843, emigrated to Calhoun Co Mich., and then came in 1854, to this county, settling in this city, and building a portion of his present house twenty years ago, has kept it as a hotel for eleven years

Skillman, Thos B, baggageman.

Slade, Geo W, cracker factory

Slade, S V R, furniture dealer

Smith, Harvey, coal dealer

Smith, H D., miller

SMITH, J. H., general store, Fourth street, born in Cortland Co, N Y, in 1831 Married Martha Jacobs in 1858, who was born in Pennsylvania in 1843, they emigrated to this county in the Fall of 1853, first settling on Sec. 17, in Barclay Tp, came to this city in 1867, and commenced his present busines in 1873 Grant is their only living child, John C died at the age of 19 years, and Freddie, when ten months old

Smith, John, grocer

SNYDER, ADAM, dealer in boot and shoes, repairing of all kinds, East Side, was born in Germany in 1830, emigrated to this country in 1851, settling in New York City in 1852, he went to Canada, and in Oct, 1855, came to Dubuque, Iowa, and came to this county in 1866, settling in this city

Married Sarah Seiffort July 17, 1858, she was born in Vermont, Frank is their only son

Snyder, Daniel, carpenter

SNOWDEN, WILLIAM, dealer in drugs, medicines, paints, oils, glass, dye stuffs, etc, was born in Pittsburgh, Penn, Feb 8, 1834, emigrated to Ogle Co, Ill, in March, 1856, and came to this city in July, 1860, where he married Delia M Evans Aug. 6, 1863, she was born in Edwardsburg, Mich Mr Snowden commenced business on his arrival in this county, and is one of the pioneer business men

Speicher, Ephraim, clerk

Stackpole, J H, laborer

STANLO, DANIEL D., general store, East Side, born in Orange Co, N Y, Aug 28, 1826 Married Sarah A. Green Feb 8, 1851; she was born in Sullivan Co., N Y, June 30, 1831, emigrated to Stephenson Co, Ill, in December, 1855, and to this county June 1, 1860, Mrs Mary A. Boyd, Kate O and Orissa are his children

Stanton, D B, merchant

Stanton, Nath, machinist, I C R. R

Starr, George M

Starr, James, gardener

Stearns, E, engineer, I C R R.

Stearns, John M

Steed, W T, nurseryman

STEINMAYER, C. A., dealer in groceries, crockery and glassware, Commercial st; was born in Germany in 1835 Married Sarah B Bence Emigrated to this country in 1854, settling in Stark Co, Ohio, and then to Waukesha Co, Wis Enlisted in the 2d Wis Lt Art in 1863, and was honorably discharged in 1865, and in August of the same year he came to this city Commenced his present business in 1869

Stevens, John M, retired merchant

Stevens, Reuben, retired merchant

Stewart, Benj, blacksmith

Stilson, C B., Recorder

STOLT, C. F., dealer in boots and shoes, Commercial st, was born in Germany in 1824 Married Mary Wieghlow in 1869 He emigrated to America in 1856; first settled in Williamsburg, N Y, then moved to Milwaukee and Madison, Wis, then to Dubuque and

Dunleith, and in 1866 came to this county

Strayer, Wm , brick yard

Stromgreen, S R , machinist

Sullivan, James, gardener

Sulzer, R F , machinist

Sweeney, J K , Principal of school

Sweet, Richard, barber.

Sweet, Samuel J , prop Commercial Hotel

Sweet, Thomas, laborer

Switzer, John N , carpenter

TARDY, N. C , harness maker

Taylor, M W , blacksmith.

Thee, John, groceries

Thomas, A B , barber

Thompson, Allen, merchant

THOMPSON, ANDREW, of the firm of Thompson Bros , dealers in dry goods, boots and shoes and general stock, Fourth street, was born in Canton, N J , March 30, 1830. He married Elizabeth Goldsworth , she was born in Cornwall, England   Mr. T moved to Galena when quite young, and at the age of 16 he went to Wisconsin, and to Bristol, Conn , from there to this county in 1862, settling in this city

Thompson, John, merchant miller

Thunnison, J , ice merchant.

Titcomb, R D , carpenter

TOWNSEND, A. F., insurance and collecting agency, born in Philadelphia, Penn , May 9, 1834.   After attending public school, he entered as a student at Dickinson College, of Carlisle, Penn , where he graduated in 1856, and emigrated to Dubuque the same year, taking charge of and organizing their present school system in that city , he was afterward Principal of the High School in Galena, Ill   After drifting around for a while on account of his health, he came to Manchester, Iowa, and to this county in 1869 ; was elected County Superintendent of Schools in 1873   Married Sarah P Burn in 1860, who was born in Philadelphia, Penn , they have one child—Sarah

Turner, Isaac, retired

Turner, O F , machinist

Turpening, S P , painter

VAN BUREN, H , laborer.

Van Duyn, C. W., jeweler.

Van Duyn, V. S , jeweler

Vaughn, R , Jr , laborer

Virden, George, livery stable

VIRDEN, JAMES, livery stable , was born in Monroe Co., Ky , Feb 22, 1823 , moved to Wayne Co , Ill, in 1832, and from there to this county, arriving in June 1, 1846, settling in this city, and built the first house in Waterloo Tp   Married Charlotte Pratt Feb. 27, 1851, she was born in Pennsylvania   This was the first marriage in this county

Voorhees, M H , boots and shoes

WAINRIGHT, C , machinist

WALKER, LAFAYETTE, Supervisor of Highways , born in Delaware Co , N Y , Aug 26, 1824   Married E. Edwards in 1847 , she was born in Broome Co., N. Y., Sept 14, 1824   Emigrated to Martinsburg, Bremer Co , Iowa, in 1856, and came to this city in Sept., 1860, was first engaged in meat market , afterward, went into the lumber trade, which he followed ten years.   E B. and Edna are their children

WANGLER BROS., dealers in drugs, books, stationery, paints, oils, etc , Logan House Block   C D Wangler, the senior partner, was born in Germany, Jan 8, 1851, came to Cedar Falls, this county, in Dec , 1866, and March 23, 1868, settled in Waterloo, but returned to Cedar Falls in 1869 , after going to Waverly in 1871, to this city in 1872, and then to Fort Wayne, Ind , in 1873, and to Cincinnati, Ohio, in 1874, he came to this city Jan 1, 1878, buying his present business   Married Katie Landgraf May 5, 1878 , she was born in Cleveland, Ohio, in Feb., 1853   Graduated at College in Cincinnati in 1876.   R. C Wangler was born in Baden, Germany, Aug. 6, 1854 , came to this county in March, 1870, to Cedar Falls, April 1, 1870, and to this city May 28, 1872, in August of the following year. returned to Cedar Falls , Sept 23, 1875, he moved to Cincinnati, Ohio, where he graduated at college in 1877, and came to this city Feb. 1, 1878.

Ward, John, gardener.

Warlich, Charles, grocer.

Watkins, Joseph, carpenter
Watkins, Joseph, Jr, hardware
Watkins, Wm, teamster
Watson, Joseph, laborer
Watson, G H., conductor, I C R R

WEATHERWAX, A. THEO-DORE, dealer in groceries and crockery, was born in Ontario Co, N Y, July 4, 1831, moved in 1840 to Monroe Co, N Y, and to Niagara Co. in 1844, where he married Martha E Albright Oct 20, 1853, she was born in Niagara Co, N Y., in Dec, 1831, came to this county in Nov, 1866, and commenced business on Dec 1, 1866

Weatherwax, H E, merchant
Weaver, Daniel, grocery merchant
Weaver, J D, merchant tailor.

WEIS, KASPER, dealer in dry goods, clothing, hats, caps and furnishing goods, Commercial st., was born in Germany in 1844, emigrated to America in 1860, settling in Goodhue Co, Minn, came to this county in 1871, commencing his business at that time

Wells, Sanford, carpenter
Welsh, W. J.
Westphal, J C, engineer, I C R. R.
Wheeler, John, engineer, I C R. R.
White, C K., vet surgeon
White, Fred, harness maker

WHITAKER, R. A., Grand Recorder of Iowa A. O U W, was born in Oneida Co, N Y, Aug 26, 1828, moved to Jefferson Co, N Y., in 1836 with his parents, and came to this city in Nov, 1855 Married Mary E Clark Sept 17, 1856, who was born in Le Roy, N Y, April 17, 1832 Mr Whitaker has held the office of County Treasurer of this county for eight years, and was the first Mayor of the city, being elected July 21, 1868, elected to his present Masonic position in Feb, 1878. Ardelle G is his only daughter.

Whitney, W. T, liveryman.
Wichman, C F, machinist

Widman, Con, machinist
Widman, William, machinist
Wiley, Tobias, saloon
Willer, Zack, carpenter
Williams, S B., physician
Williams, Henry D, Central House.
Williams John H, prop Central House
Wilson, Norman, drayman
Winnie, Frank, blacksmith
Wood, W J, engineer, I C R R
Woodford, A R, printer
Wooley, J N, sewing machine agent
Worcester, W K., painter

WRIGHT, MAITLAND, with Parrot, Girton & Sherman, was born in Picton, Canada, April 2, 1828, and married Eleanor Nugent Feb, 14, 1849, she was born in Picton, Jan. 5, 1830, after marriage, he emigrated to Belmont, Canada, where he resided until 1865, when he moved to London, Canada. and in 1867, came to this county and settled in this city, where he has since made it his home, they have four children living—Thomas D, Emma A (first daughter, who received her early education in one of the public schools of this city, from which time she has ever taken an active interest in the cause of education, and has been a successful teacher in different village schools since 1874, in September, 1867, she commenced teaching in the branch of the high school, in which position she is still occupied, and is regarded as a thorough and efficient officer), Phœbe J (second daughter, has attained a thorough musical education, and numbers among the finest vocalists in the city), May E, (youngest daughter, also advancing to the attainment of educational qualifications). To this group the writer is greatly indebted for much valuable information, extended courtesy and hospitality during his stay.

YATES, D S, mason

WATERLOO TOWNSHIP.
(P O WATERLOO.)

ADAMS, E , farmer, Sec. 18

Adams, J S , farmer, Sec 18

Aikin, E S , farmer, S 17.

ATCHESON, CHARLES, farmer, Sec. 7 , born in Somerset Co., Penn , in 1821 Married Mary A Shoemaker in 1844 , she was born in same county in 1823, came to this county July 4, 1867, and settled in Waterloo village and has since made this county his home, moved on the present farm he now occupies, of 192 acres, in 1877 , Catherine, Norman and Benjamin are the living children , lost two children—John H , who enlisted in March, 1864, in Indiana, and contracted diseases from which he died at Dallas, Ga , Feb 6, 1865 , last child died in infancy

BRIGGS, Z N , farmer, Sec 2

BEERS, WHITNEY, farmer, Sec 19 , P O Cedar Falls, born in Canada in 1822 Married Triphena Creppen in January, 1843 ; she was born in Canada in 1827 , have two children—George S and Henry J , came to this State in 1869 and settled in Independence, and in 1870 moved to Parkersburg, this State, where he remained until 1877, when he come to this county and settled on his present place of forty acres, valued at $1,200

BUTTERFIELD, E. S., farmer, Sec 31, born in Jefferson Co , N Y , June 11, 1825. Married Mohalia Hilborn in 1852 , she was born in Fayette Co , Penn, in 1831 , they have eleven children—Isabel J , Martha A., Loena, Caroline, James S , Alice, Martha, Franklin, William, George, and Freddie C Came to this county in October, 1863, and settled on his present estate of 220 acres, valued at $35 per acre

CADY, J. F , nurseryman, Sec 5.

Carpenter, S B , farmer, Sec 35

CASE, FREDERICK W., farmer, Sec 34, born in Hartford Co , Conn , in 1834. Married Emma Dewitt in 1856 , she was born in Delaware Co., Ohio, in 1837 , have four children living—Alta, Addie, Mary and Nettie ,

came to this county same year of marriage and settled on the farm adjoining his present estate where he lived until 1877, when he moved on the farm he now owns, consisting of 280 acres, valued at $50 per acre. This family are among the early settlers of this county.

CARR, JAMES I., farmer, S 23 , born in Montgomery Co , N Y , in 1836 , came to this county in 1857, and settled in Waterloo Village, where he lived until 1860, in which year he was married to Elizabeth S Hill , she was born in Massachusetts in 1840 . In 1860, he moved to Windsor, Fayette Co , where he lived until 1865 , returning, settled on his present estate, consisting of 133⅓ acres, valued at $50 per acre Are members of the Congregational Church Was Assessor four years, and is Secretary of the independent school district of Pleasant Hill and Town Trustee Minnie and Willie are their children

CLEMMENS, WILLIAM, farmer, Sec 22 , born in England in 1827. Married Mary Eason in 1852 , she was born in the same place in 1829 , have seven children—William, Mary A , George, Charles, John, Thomas and Frank , lost three children—Elizabeth, James and one that died in infancy. came to this country in 1850, and first settled in Cleveland, Ohio, where he remained until 1870, when he came to the city of Waterloo, and in February, 1877, settled on his present farm, consisting of forty acres, valued at $40 per acre Are members of the Baptist Church

COON, HARMON, farmer, Sec 33 , born in Rensselaer Co , N. Y., in 1821. Married Sarah J Knapp in 1851 , she was born in same county in 1835 , have three children living—Emma J , Mary F and Dolly A. , lost one child—Charles H. Came to this county in 1869, and settled in Lincoln Tp , where he resided until 1874, when he moved to Waterloo Village, and in 1876 settled on his present estate, consisting of forty-two acres, valued at $1,200

COX, SYLVANUS B., farmer, Sec 17 , born in Onondaga Co , N Y., in 1816. Married Sallie M Bement in 1840, she was born in Cayuga Co, N Y., in 1820, they have four children living—Grove B., Acton M, Susan S and Josephine A, lost two children—Acton M. (1st) and Mary Came to this county in 1855, and entered eighty acres in this township and lived until 1865, when he moved to his present place of twenty acres, valued at $40 per acre, is one of the early settlers of this town and county.

DANIEL, H, far., S 22

Downing, John, far S 21
Downing, L, far, S 21
Downing, S L, far S 21

FILKINS, T H, far., S 12
Fisher, Frank, far., S 28

FISHER, W. W., farmer, Sec 34, born in Lake Co, Ohio, in 1840 Married Sarah A Peck in 1861, she was born in the same county in 1843, have five children—Jennie T, Alice, Eva E, Gracie and Nellie Came to this county in 1871, and settled near his present place, where he lived until 1875, when he moved to Waterloo and engaged in commission business until the Spring of 1878, when he moved on his present estate, consisting of eighty acres, valued at $3,000 Member of Masonic fraternity

GLOVER, JOHN, farmer, Sec. 29

GEORGE, JOHN S., farmer, S. 21; P O Waterloo, born in Marshall Co., Ill, Oct 26, 1840 Married Susan Cox Sept 2, 1872; she was born in Kane Co, Ill, Dec 10, 1853, have two children—Walter and Lewis. Came to this State with his parents in 1856, and settled in Benton Co., where he enlisted in the 32d I V. I, Co D, July 6, 1862, participated in the battles of Vicksburg, Lookout Mountain and Atlanta, and was with Sherman on his march to the sea, was honorably discharged in July, 1865, when he came to this county, and in 1872, settled on his present estate, valued at $1,000

GEORGE, PATRICK, deceased, Sec 21, born in Essex Co, Mass, in April, 1804 Married Elizabeth Miller in 1855, she was born in Virginia, Oct. 8, 1817, have two children—Phebe,

born Dec 11, 1856, and Mattie, born Aug 4, 1860, came to this State and settled in Benton Co in 1856, where they lived until 1866, when they came to this county and settled in the city of Waterloo, and in 1871, settled on their present farm, valued at $1,000, Mr George died May 26, 1878 and was beloved by all who knew him

Glover, James, farmer, Sec 20.

HARRIS, JOSEPH, farmer, Sec 28

HANNA, GEORGE W., farmer, Sec 20, born in White Co, Ill, Nov 20, 1817 Married Mary Melrose in 1837, she was born in Edwards Co, in 1821, have seven children living—John K, Emeline, George, Robert W, Philip, Mary and Edith M., lost two children James N., who died Oct 18, 1845, it being the first death of a white person in Black Hawk Co, the second died in infancy Came to this county in July, 1845, and settled near his present farm, where he erected a small cabin on the southeast corner of Section 20, the relics of which are still to be seen was the first permanent white settler in this county, and from Jan, 1845, to September of the same year was, the only white settler living in the county, and Mrs Hanna was the first white woman that ever crossed the Cedar River at Waterloo. Was the first Justice of the Peace elected in this county, and served in that capacity five terms, the family are members of the Free Methodist Church Have 95 acres of land, valued at $75 per acre.

HILL, ELIM, farmer, S 33, born in Genesee Co, N. Y., in 1817 Married Jane A Dewey in 1836, she was born in Pittsfield, Mass, in 1819, and died June 4, 1856, they had three children—Sarah E., Paulina M and James D, his present wife Marietta Williams, was born in New York State in 1832, they were married in 1858, and have three children—Charles, Ada and Eddie He came to this county in the Fall of 1855, and resided in Waterloo village the Winter of that year, when he moved on his present estate, consisting of 200 acres of land, valued at $50 per acre, is among the early settlers of this town and county.

Hunt, C P , nurseryman, Sec. 3.

Huntington, H , far., Sec 3

JENNINGS, CHARLES, far , Sec 22

KIRKWOOD, T J , far , Sec. 21

KNAPP, MARQUIS L., farmer, Sec 20 , born in Stockton, N Y , in 1829 Married Mary Streeter in 1852 , she was born in N Y State in 1832, and died in 1864, they had five children—Martha J , Nettie, Benjamin F , Lucinda and Louisa , his present wife, Mary A Wells, was born in N Y. State in 1829, and have four children— Lilly, Katie, Giles and Ruth Came to this county in the Fall of 1850, and settled in Washington Township, where he entered 280 acres of land, where he remained until 1865, when he moved to Cedar Falls and engaged in grain business and stock buying, and continued in this capacity until 1869, when he settled on his present estate of 285 acres, valued at $40 per acre Are members of the Baptist Church To his father, Benjamin, belongs the honor of naming the towns of Washington and Mt. Vernon, he being one of the earliest settlers.

Knapp, Solomon, far , Sec 7

LANSING, E. D., farmer, Sec 31 , born in Oneida Co , N Y , in 1831, and first settled in Minneapolis, Minn , in 1856, where he lived until 1865 , in which year he married Sarilda Ludlam , she was born in Ohio, in 1833. In 1875, he came to this county after a residence of eight years in Peoria, Ill , and settled on the farm he now occupies, of eighty acres Cornelia, Carlos, Grace, Harry and Adelaide are his children

LATHROP, SARAH J., nursery, Sec. 26 , widow of Lucian Lathrop, who was born in Connecticut in 1829 , her maiden name was Sarah J Hagerty, she was born in Utica, N Y , in 1827, and they were married in July, 1854, and in 1863, settled in Waterloo City, where they resided until 1868, when they moved on their present estate, consisting of ten acres, valued at $3,000, their living children are Susan, Mary and Charles F., who married Cora Hill, and have one child—Perley

McCULLIAN, PATRICK, farmer

McCulian, William, farmer, Sec. 30.

McDowell, S D , far., Sec 21

McDowell, S E , far., Sec. 8.

Merwin, J H W , far., Sec 28

Morris, William P , far , 32.

Myers, J B , far., Sec 34.

PALMER. STEPHEN, far , Sec 36

PARKER, F. H., farmer. Sec 20 ; born in Canada in 1854, and came to this county in 1865, with his parents, who settled near his present home, and where he lived until 1876, when he married Mattie S. Knapp , she was born in this county in 1854, settled on his present farm in 1878 ; farm consists of eighty acres, valued at $2,000

PARKER, LEVI, farmer, Sec. 19 , P O Cedar Falls , born in Berkshire Co , Conn , in 1814 Married Mary Rogers in 1841 , she was born in Cayuga Co , N Y., in 1816, they have lost two children—Samuel M and one that died in infancy Came to this county in Jan , 1866, and settled in Cedar Falls, where he worked at his trade, being a carpenter , in 1867, he purchased his present farm, consisting of forty-two acres, valued at $40 per acre, and settled on the same in 1871

REBER, MICHAEL, farmer, S 34.

Rector, T C , far , Sec 28

Robinson, Wm , farmer, Sec. 36

ROBINSON, WILLIAM A., farmer, Sec 31 , born in Warren Co , Ohio, in 1837. Married Eliza Chaddick in 1857 , she was born in Hopkins Co , Ky , in 1841, their living children are Eugene, Walter, William and Mary, J., they came to this county in 1862, and settled in Cedar Falls, and in 1864 removed to Bremer Co , and resided until 1870, when he emigrated to Harlan Co , Neb , and lived there until 1873 , returned in that year to this county, and settled on the place he now occupies, consisting of seventy acres

Round, Jas. M , far., S. 19 ; P O Cedar Falls

SHUMAKER, J W , farmer, Sec. 29.

SHEHAN, PATRICK, farmer, Sec 21 , P O Cedar Falls , was born in Ireland in 1820. Married Ann McArdle in 1857 ; she was born in

Ireland in 1821, have ten children—John, Mary, Catharine, Patrick, Daniel, Elizabeth, Thomas, William and Margaret (twins), and Maurice Came to this country in 1850, landing in New Orleans; lived in Indiana and Ohio until 1855, when he came to this county and settled in Cedar Rapids, where he engaged at his trade, being a mason, in 1863, he came to this township, and settled on his present estate, consisting of 250 acres—100 acres valued at $50 per acre, and the remainder at $20 per acre Mr S and family are members of the Catholic Church

SPEER, JOHN A., farmer and nurseryman, Sec. 19, he was born in Westmoreland Co, Penn, in 1834, where he enlisted in the 11th Penn. Res. in May, 1861, and was honorably discharged in 1865 Married Sabina Barr in 1866, she was born in Armstrong Co, Penn., in 1840, they have three children—Lola, Victor and Mildred; came to this county same year of marriage, and settled on his present estate, valued at $60 per acre

Speers, Robert, far, S 19

TURNER, MICHAEL V. B., far., S. 36, born in Lycoming Co, Penn, in 1839, and came to this county in 1862, and settled in Waterloo, when in 1863, he enlisted in the 7th Iowa Cavalry, Co. H, and served three years on the plains. Returning to this county, married Helen M. Parker in 1867, she was born in this county in 1837, settled on his present place in 1874, consisting of 11½ acres valued at $100 per

acre They lost their only child—Mary A

VIRDEN, OSCAR, far, S 32, born in Barren Co, Ky, in 1819. Married Love C Powell in 1846, she was born in Berkshire Co, Mass, in 1822 Came to this county July 1, 1851, and settled on his present estate, which he entered and upon which he erected a rude cabin where he lived to enjoy the experience of pioneer life, this rude habitation has long since given place to a large and commodious residence, of which most of the building material was drawn by team from Dubuque Their children are—George D., Charles, Elizabeth and Emma, lost two children—Norman and Willie

WARD, GEORGE F, far, S 29. Weeks, Jas, far, Sec 30.

WALKER, ISAAC, far, S 34, born in Bedford Co., Penn, in 1844. Married Minerva Scroggy in 1866, she was born in Northumberland Co, Penn, in 1843, came to this county the same year of their marriage, and settled in Eagle Township, where he lived one season, when he moved on his present estate of 153 acres, valued at $50 per acre In 1863, he enlisted in the 21st Penn Cav, Co E, and served eight months; re-enlisted in 1864, in the 205th Penn Regt, Co E, and served eleven months, participated in the battles of Fort Steadman, Pittsburg and others and was honorably discharged at the close of the war Charles R., Nettie A, Isaac M, Mollie A and Minerva M are their children

EAST WATERLOO TOWNSHIP.
(P O WATERLOO)

ALBERT, JACOB, farmer, Sec 2, born in Wurtemberg, Germany, in 1818 Married Florence Beptine in 1854 , she was born in Saxony, Germany, in 1830, they have five children—John P , Augusta A , Viola I , George H and Ella M. Came to this country in 1849, and first settled in Rensselaer Co , N Y , and in 1857 emigrated to this county, first settling in Mt. Vernon Tp., and in April, 1865, settled on his present farm of sixty-six acres, valued at $40 per acre Are members of the First Baptist Church

ALDRICH, RELIEF C., farming, Sec 20 , widow of Truman Aldrich, who was born in Utica, N. Y , in November, 1829 , they were married in July, 1873, and he died in September, 1877 , her maiden name was Relief C. Hills, and she was born in Chautauqua Co. N. Y., in 1838 , came to this county in 1872, and settled in the city of Waterloo, where they resided until 1876, when they moved on their present estate, consisting of 120 acres, valued at $35 per acre ; also owns a market in the city, and four dwellings. He was also engaged in the purchase of tax titles, in which he carried on an extensive business. Have one child—Truman, Jr

AKERMEANT, GEO., farmer, Sec 23 , born in England in 1849, and came to this country in 1863, and settled in this county the same year Married Annie Roler in 1868 , she was born in New Jersey in 1850 , have three children—Mary J , born June 9, 1869 , Joseph, born May 10, 1872 , Sarah E., born Sept 25, 1875 Settled on his present place in 1875, where he has since made it his home

Ball, R D , farmer, S 31

BACOM, JESSE, farmer, Sec. 28 , was born in Westmoreland Co., Penn , in 1817 Married Mary Mc-Clintock Feb 18, 1841 , she was born in Allegheny Co , Penn , in 1820 , came to this State in 1858, and settled in Dubuque Co., where he resided until 1863, when he moved to this county, and settled on his present estate of forty acres,

valued at $1,600   Have one adopted daughter—Addie   Mrs B is a member of the Presbyterian Church.

BAILEY, DAVID M., farmer, Sec 34 , born in Niagara Co , N Y , in 1848, where he married Lodena Browning in 1869 , she was born in same county in 1848 ; came to this county in February, 1873, and settled in Waterloo, where he engaged in a meat market, and continued in that capacity until 1874, when he moved on his present estate, consisting of 100 acres, valued at $30 per acre   Seth, Grace and Dewey are their living children , lost two children—Burton, and one died in infancy

BALL, JOHN, farmer, Sec 7 , born in Grafton, N H , July 4, 1814 , moved with his parents to Sharon, Vt., where he resided until 21 years old, and moved to Genesee and Chautauqua Counties, N Y., went down the river to Louisville, Ky , on a raft, took a boat to St, Louis and Tully, Mo , and afterward settled in Louis Co , Mo., in 1837, Married Juliette Polk Dec 20, 1839, she was born in Scott Co., Ky , in 1819, they moved to Sangamon Co , Ill., and after one year, moved to Adams Co., Iowa , in 1845, went to Dubuque, Iowa, and was appointed Government Surveyor. came to this county in 1864, settling on Sec. 26. John P is their only child

Bannister, L. S , farmer, S 31

BARTLETT, A. N., farmer, Sec. 9 , P O Cedar Falls, born in Chenango Co , N Y , in 1826. Married Margaret Anderson in 1854 , she was born in Scotland in 1827 , they have three children—Frank, Tracelia and Willie   Came to this county in 1856, and settled in Washington Tp., and, in 1861, settled on their present farm of sixty acres, valued at $2,500.

Bazeley, B , farmer, Sec. 24
Birdsall, G B , farmer, S. 20.
Brainard, S R , farmer, S 6
Brinker, Henry, farmer, S 3

BROOKS, THOMAS, farmer, S 18 , born in Orange Co , N Y , in 1823   Married Elizabeth King Jan

27, 1853, she was born in the same county in 1825 Emigrated to this county in 1854, and settled in the city of Waterloo, where they resided until May, 1859, when he moved on his present farm of eighty-four acres, valued at $50 per acre, which land he entered, they number among those of the earliest settlers in this town and county Are members of the Methodist Church

BROWN, ALLEN, farmer, Sec 2; born in Litchfield Co, Conn., in 1842, where he married Eliza J Lewis in 1862; she was born in the same county in 1845 Nellie M, George L., Julia L, Fannie M, Lottie L and Harry K are their children They came to this county in 1868, and settled in Mt Vernon Tp, where he resided until 1877, when he settled on his present estate of eighty acres of land, valued at $25 per acre

Brown, Hiram, farmer, S 3

BROWN, STEPHEN, farmer, S 3; born in Litchfield Co, Conn, in 1816 Married Elmira Abbott in 1836, she was born in Berkshire Co, Mass, in 1817, they have five children living —Sarah, Hiram, Luther, Allen, Warren, and lost one child—Myra Came to this county in April, 1868, and settled on his present farm of 148 acres, valued at $40 per acre, also carried on livery business at Waterloo six years of his residence in this county.

BURDEN, WM., farmer, Sec. 18, born in Devonshire, England, in 1812. Married Susanah Chapple in 1837; she died in 1852, they had three children —Sarah, Wm W and George W His present wife, Susannah Burden, was born in Bristol, England, in 1830, they have by this marriage three children—Mary E., Ada S, and Estella J, lost three children—George, Julia and one that died in infancy Came to this country in 1835, and settled in Genesee Co., N. Y, where he resided until 1859, and in 1864, came to this county, and settled on his present farm of 114 acres, valued at $60 per acre. Are members of the M. E Church

CATLING, J M., far, S 1.

Choate, N B., far, S 22
Clark, Wm, far, S 7.

Cobb, E. M, far, S 28
Corbett, Sylvester, far., S 29
Cotton, Enoch, far, S 10
Cotton, John, far, S 9

COWLES, CHARLES C., farmer, S 3, born in Hampshire Co, Mass., in 1836 Married Julia H Andrews in 1862, she was born in Geauga Co., Ohio, in 1841, have two children—Lydia M and Bertie A Came to this county in 1867, and settled in Waterloo City, where he lived until 1875, when he settled on his present farm, where he has since made his home

Crabtree, J A, far., S 11

CROSS, B. N., farmer, Sec 3, born in Licking Co, Ohio, in 1833 Married Mary J Baroff in 1857, she was born near Tiffin, Ohio, in 1835, they have six children—William, Ellsworth, Albert, Eliza, John and Henry, lost three children—Zoloman B., Sarah M and Charles M. Came to this county in 1866, and settled in Mt Vernon Tp, where they resided until 1871, settled on their present estate of 160 acres, valued at $35 per acre Mr. C served sixteen months in the 123d Ohio V I, Co. A Are members of the United Brethren Church

Cross, W A, far, S 20
Crumrine, James, far, S 4
Crumrine, Wm, far, S 2

CURRAN, MICHAEL, farmer, Sec 4, born in Ireland in 1824, and emigrated to this country in 1856 and settled in Stamford, Conn, and in 1858 moved to the West and settled in Winnebago Co, Ill, where he remained until 1866, when he came to this county and settled on his present farm, where he has since made his home Are members of the Catholic Church.

DERRICK, N, far, S 35
Dewey, Earl, far, S. 30

DEWEY, J. D., farmer, Sec 8; P O Cedar Falls, born Nov 1, 1823, in Crawford Co, Penn, in 1849, came to Wisconsin, in 1852, came to his present farm; owns 230 acres, valued at $25 per acre Married Mary E Wykoff Aug 15, 1847; she was born in 1829, in Crawford Co., Penn, had eight children, seven living—Earl, Walter, Mary Ann, Louis, Henrietta, Horace and George

Dewey, Lewis, far , S 31

Dewey, Walter, far S 22

DOBSON, JOHN, farmer, Sec 9 , P O Cedar Falls, born in Ireland in 1810. Married Ann Webster in 1832 , she was born in Ireland in 1812, and died in 1843 by this marriage they have four children—Thomas, William, Elizabeth and James Came to this country in 1832, and settled in Clinton Co , N.Y , where he lived until 1836, when he emigrated to Fairfield Co , Ohio, and resided until 1851, when he moved to Indiana, and in 1853 came to this county and settled on his present estate of 343 acres, valued at $35 per acre   In 1855, he married Emma W Good , she was born in 1825, they have five children—Alice, John, Wesley, Abraham and Francis , lost two—Amos and Eunice.

Dobson, T , far , S 4 , P O Cedar Falls

DONALDSON, WILLIAM, farmer, Sec 4 , born in Canada in 1841. Married Fannie Atkinson in 1866 , she was born in England in 1832 , they have four children—Robert R , Edwin, Annie and Elsie Emigrated to Illinois in 1862, where he resided until 1868, when he came to this county ; settled on his present estate in 1873, where he has since made it his home

Douglas, J. H , far , S 10

Dubois, J S , far , S. 28.

Dunkelberg, S , far., S 16

Dunkelberg, W. B , far , S 16

EASTMAN, H , farmer, Sec 9

Eddy, Milo, far S 18.

Ellis, D G , far , S. 19

Ercanbrack, John, farmer

Evans, John O , far , S 32

FARNSWORTH, L., farmer, Sec. 4 , born in Bradford Co , Penn , April 9, 1821. Married Mary J Rice June 8, 1851, she was born in Bradford Co , Penn , in 1833. Came to this county in 1855, purchasing his present farm from the government, and returned to the East , in 1863, moved with his family and settled in Waterloo, where he resided until 1866, when he settled on his present farm, consisting of 120 acres of land, valued at $25 per acre Is one of the early settlers of this county

FILKINS, THEODORE, farmer, Sec 1 , born in Cayuga Co , N. Y., Oct 18, 1840 , he emigrated with his parents to Iowa and Black Hawk Co in the Fall of 1858 he settled on his present farm in 1869 He was married in 1865, to Miss Elizabeth Trobridge, from New York , they have seven children — John C , William, Cornelius, Charles, Addie, Emily and Ida He has 163 acres of land, valued at $30 per acre   He has held the office of School Director one year   In politics he is Republican.   They are members of the M E Church His parents were among the oldest settlers of Waterloo Township, His house is just across the road in Waterloo Township

FISHER, WILLIAM, JR., farmer, Sec 5 P O Cedar Falls , born in Pendleton Co , Va in March, 1848, and came to this county with parents in Oct , 1853, and resides on a portion of the old homestead   Married Mary E Parker in 1869 , she was born in Clinton Co , N Y , in 1852, they have one child—George B , born Oct. 4, 1870 She is a member of the First Baptist Church

GARRETT, JOHN, far Sec 15

Garrett, W. F , farmer, Sec 18

Gaston, Charles C farmer, Sec 18

Gaston, David, farmer, Sec 21.

Gaston, N P , farmer, Sec 12

GIFFORD, DANIEL A., farmer, Sec 3 , born in Canada West in 1843 and came to this county in 1866, and settled in Poyner Tp , where he married Mary C Fuller in 1872; she was born in Illinois in 1854, and have two children—Nora B and Tabor B Settled on his present farm in the Fall of 1877, consisting of 160 acres, valued at $35 per acre, where he has since made it his home

GILBERT, FRANK, farmer, Sec. 4 , born in Vermont in 1837, and emigrated to the West in 1853, and settled in Kendall Co , Ill Married Henrietta Collins in 1866 , she was born in Kendall Co , Ill., in 1846 , children—Seth, Harriet A., Catherine R , Francis, Edward and Harvey In 1861, he enlisted in the 10th I V I , Co. H, and served three years , participated in battles of Fort Henry, Fort Donelson and others, and was honorably discharged at the close of the war. Settled on his present farm in 1877, where he has 160 acres of land under cultivation.

Grant, J. M , far , Sec 30
Grant, J. M , far , Sec 12
Grant, J B , far., Sec 29
Gulzo, John, far , Sec 32

HAFFA, ABE W , carpenter, Sec. 8

HAGENBAUGH, GILBERT C., farmer, Sec. 14 , born in La Salle Co , Ill , 1852 , came to this county with his parents in 1865, and settled on their present estate of 252 acres, valued at $45 per acre Married Fannie Bell in 1872; she was born in Tyrone, Blair Co., Penn , in 1856 Mary E and Alice E. are their children

HALE MASON, farmer, Sec 14 , born in Rhode Island in 1800 Married Almira King in 1823 , she was born in the State of Connecticut in 1805, and died in 1868 , they have seven children living—Byron, who served in the rebellion, Mandana, Kaziah, Susan Albert, Fidelia and Emma , have lost five children—Charlotte, John, who was killed at Lookout Mountain, and Charles, died from disease contracted in the army , and two that died in infancy. Came to this county in 1853, and set on his present estate, consisting of 115 acres, valued at $40 per acre Mr. H. has been prominently identified with the interests of the county, and numbers among the early settlers

HALL, ARAD, farmer. Sec. 2 , born in Franklin Co , Mass , in 1818 Married Charlotte Fisk in 1842, she was born in same county in 1818, have eight children—Ellen M , Augusta J , Arthur W , J Bordman, Charles F , Frank F , Cirus E and Frederick Came to this county in May, 1866, and settled on his present farm, consisting of 144 acres, valued a $40 per acre Previous to his coming to this county he was engaged for thirty years in the manufacture of Hall's hand rake at Heath, Mass. Mr. H and family are members of the Baptist Church

HALLETT, RICHARD B., farmer, Sec 5 , P O Raymond , born in Barnstable Co , Mass., in 1803 Mar-

ried Marian Baker in 1838 , she was born in St John, N B , in 1810 Came to this county in 1855, and settled in the city of Waterloo, where he remained until 1866, when he moved on his present farm, consisting of 40 acres, valued at $40 per acre Daniel, Sarah A , Martha and Rodman are their living children , they lost one child—Richard, who was drowned in the Cedar River Mr H. is one of the earliest settlers in the county, and is well known throughout

HARRISON, FREDERICK H., farmer, Sec 2 , born in Litchfield Co., Conn , in 1848 Married Martha E Harrison in 1872 , she was born in same county in 1848 , they have two children—William H , born in Feb , 1873 and Charles F , born Aug , 1874 Came to this county, and settled on his present estate, consisting of 160 acres, valued at $40 per acre, in March, 1877 They are members of the Congregational Church

HAWKINS, E., farmer, Sec 15 , born in Grafton Co , N H., in 1818 , came to the West in 1839, and settled in Bureau Co , Ill , where he married Mary J Harmon in 1840 , she died in 1854 , they had four children—Helen A , Alphonso B , Edwin and Amanda. His present wife, Rachel Ginger, was born in Vandalia in 1847, and have three children by this marriage—Albert R., Joseph B and Guy Came to this county in March, 1877, and settled on his present farm, consisting of 160 acres, and where he has since made his home

HAWVER, LOUIS M., farmer, Sec 16 , born in Walworth Co , Wis , in 1850, and came to this county in 1864, settling in the city of Waterloo, where he married Alice Merwin in 1875 , she was born in Pennsylvania in 1852, they have one child—Lizzie M Settled on his present farm, consisting of 130 acres, valued at $40 per acre, in 1876

Hewitt, Daniel, far , S 24.
Hewitt, James, far., S 4

HEWITT, WM. H., farmer, Sec 6 , born in England in 1839, and emigrated to this country in 1858, and settled in Winnebago, Ill., where he married Eliza Gilmore, they have four children—Walter W , Henry F , George A and Albert L   Came to this county in the Fall of 1873, and settled on his present estate in 1878, consisting of forty acres, valued at $30 per acre

Hoffman, John B , farmer, Sec 7

Holtz, Fred, farmer, Sec 23

HOWARD, JACKSON, farmer, Sec 12, born in Pike Co , Ohio, in 1819 Married Edith Brazeton in 1838; she was born in Bean Blossom, Brown Co , Ind in 1822 , came to this county in February, 1866, and settled in Mt Vernon Tp , and in October, 1875, moved to Waterloo City where he resided one year, when he settled on his present estate of forty acres, valued at $1,200 Are members of the United Brethren Church

HUBBART, FRANK, farmer, Sec 9 , born in Broome Co , N Y., in 1834, came to this State in 1854, and settled in Tama Co , where he married Idelia Kellogg in 1857, she was born in Chautauqua Co , N Y , in 1843, they have five children—Ellen, Allen, Fredie, Nettie and Harvey, lost one child— Idelia. In 1862, he enlisted in the 27th I V I , Co I, and served nine months and was honorably discharged on account of sickness , came to this county in May, 1863, and settled on his present estate in November, 1875, consisting of 160 acres, valued at $5,000 Are members of the M E. Church Mr H has held county offices, and has been permanently identified with the interests of the town and county

JOHNSTON, D S , farmer, Sec 31.

Johnston, John, Rev , far , Sec 31

Joyner, A H., farmer, Sec 29

KING, JOSEPH, farmer, Sec. 5; born in Morgan Co , Ohio, March 30, 1830. Married Phœbe Harris in December, 1855, she was born in the same county in 1836, and has two children living—Louisa M and Eldora A , have lost two children—Anna F. and William S   Came to this county in 1854 and purchased his present estate, which he entered, and returned to Ohio , in 1860, he returned to this State and settled in Linn Co , and in 1863 returned to this county and settled on his estate; owns a farm of 144 acres,

valued at $55 per acre. Has been Supervisor and School Director and otherwise prominently identified with the interests of the town and county Are members of the Methodist Church.

LELAND, H. P., farmer, Sec. 5

LELAND, AMBROSE, farmer, Sec 4 , P. O Cedar Falls , born in Middlesex Co , Mass , in 1842, and came to this county in March, 1855, with his parents, who settled on their present estate of eighty acres, valued at $30 per acre. He married Matilda Firman in 1866, and has six children— Maud, Charles, Lovina, John, Bernice and Frank His father died in March, 1865 , his mother is still living at the age of 75 years and resides with him on the homestead , the family numbers among the early settlers of the county.

LELAND, GEORGE, farmer, Sec 10 , P O Cedar Falls, born in New York City in 1837, and came to this county with his parents in 1855, and settled on the farm of which he still occupies and owns a portion, consisting of 258 acres, valued at $30 per acre   Married Floretta E Clark in 1863 ; she was born Rensselaer Co , N Y , in 1842 , they have two children—William C. and Carrie   Held the office of Assessor two terms, Town Trustee four years, and has been identified with the interests of the town and county   Are all members of the Universalist Church.

LUPKIN, CYRUS, farmer, Sec 4, born in Oxford Co , Me , in 1820, and married Mary A. McKellopp in 1849, she was born in Orange Co., Vt , in 1831   Came to this county in the Spring of 1872, and settled on his present farm of 220 acres, where he has since made his home   Emma M , Frederick B , George H , Nellie J , Ida B and Willie are their living children, lost three children—Mary L , John A and Addie L

LYONS, JOHN, farmer, Sec 5, born in Limerick, Ireland, in 1815, and married Johannah Cavanagh in 1852, she was born in Ireland in 1815, they have four children—Michael, Annie, William and Margaret; lost four children—Timothy, James, Katerina and Mary   Came to America in

1846, and landed in Boston, Mass.; came to this county and settled in the city of Waterloo, where he lived until 1870, when he moved on his present estate of 120 acres, valued at $30 per acre Are members of the Catholic Church

McCLELLAND, A. W., farmer, Sec 11

McCullum, J , far , S. 30

McMANUS, ANDREW, farmer, Sec. 17 , born in Trenton, N J , in 1826 Married Bridget Doling in 1856 , she was born in Ireland in 1832. Came to this county in 1857, and settled on his present farm of 137½ acres, valued at $40 per acre Was one of the early settlers of this section Are members of the Catholic Church

MASON, ELIAS F., farmer, Sec 4 , born in Madison Co , N Y , in 1835 , moved with his parents to Wisconsin in 1845, where he enlisted Nov 30, 1861, in Co A, 1st Wis V. C , and served three years, participated in the battles of Chickamauga and Knoxville, and was honorably discharged Returned to Jefferson Co , Wis , where he married Louisa Fleming in March, 1866 , she was born in Racine, Wis., in 1845 Came to this county in 1868, and settled in the city of Waterloo, and in 1871 moved on his present estate of 160 acres, where he has since made his home William F , Benjamin F , Ada F and George H are their children.

ellon, M M , farmer, Sec 16

MERVINE, WILLIAM C., farmer, Sec 15 ; born on board a man-of-war, in Jefferson Co., N Y., in 1816 Married Martha G Sawyer in 1838 , she was born in Maine, and died in 1842 , had one child—Charles E His present wife, Rohana Shirley, was born in Morgan Co , Ohio, in 1826, and they were married in 1844 Came to this county in 1864, and settled in Raymond , in 1868, settled in Waterloo, where he built the Waterloo House, which he conducted until 1875, when he settled on his present farm of ninety-four acres, valued at $35 per acre

Mesenger, Z T , far , S 11 ,

MILES, ANDREW, farmer, Sec 5 , born in Tioga Co., N., Y , in 1809. Married Sabrina Corey in 1830 , she

was born in Vermont in 1811, and died in June, 1855 ; they had ten children—Warner, Willard, William, Hiram, Walter, Joseph, Francis, Rosetta, Mark and James , his present wife, May Esterbrooks, was born in Rutland Co., in 1820, and they were married in 1858, and have two children—H A and Stephen A Came to this county in 1865 and settled on his present estate of 140 acres, valued at $40 per acre

Miller, Owen F , far , Sec 3

MOORE, BENJAMIN, farmer, S 16 , born in Huntingdon Co , Penn., in 1827 Married Thirza McLane in 1848 , she was born in Knox Co , Ohio, in 1827 Came to this county in 1867, and settled in Mt. Vernon Tp , where he resided until 1876, when he moved on his present farm of 160 acrse, also owns 100 acres of land in Buena Vista Co , valued at $10 per acre. Rinaldo, Nancy E , Charles W and Ann M are their children

Mullin, John, far , Sec 21

NIGHTINGALE, JOHN, far., S. 14,

NEWTON, REUBEN, farmer, S. 4, born in England in 1854, and came to this country in June, 1870, and first settled in Darlington, Wis , where he resided until 1874, when he came to this county and settled in Waterloo, where he married Marilla Goodwin in 1876 , she was born in Indiana in 1858, settled on his present farm in the Spring of 1877, consisting of sixty-five acres of land, valued at $30 per acre.

OWENS. J J far., S 32

Owens, Orrin , far , S 32

Owens, Samuel, farmer, S. 32.

PARK, R J , far , Sec. 21.

PARSONS, BENJAMIN B., farmer, Sec 20 , born in Bennington Co , Vt in 1817 Married Polly N Blanchard April 10, 1848 , she was born in Windham Co , Vt , Sept 3, 1813 , first settled in Dodge Co , Wis., where he remained until 1862, when he came to this county and settled in the city of Waterloo, where he resided until 1865 , moved on his present estate, consisting of 440 acres of land, valued $40 per acre Fernando A , born Sept

29, 1849, Winslow R, born April 12, 1851 ; Lonara E, born April 21, 1855, are the names and births of their children

PARSONS, DANIEL, farmer, S 15, born in Winchester Co, N Y, in 1833 Married Jane C Ide, in July, 1854, she was born in Vermont, in 1838. In 1864, he enlisted in the 44th Ill V I, Co H, and served until the close of the war; participated in the the battles Spring Hill, Franklin and Nashville, where he was wounded by a ball passing through his wrist, which has left him with an honorable scar, was discharged from the hospital May 11, 1865 Came to this county April 16, 1866, and settled on his present estate of 240 acres, valued at $35 per acre Emma J, Charles, William, Estella, Abraham, George, Cora and Jessie are their children.

PARSONS, ROSCOE M., farmer, Sec 19, born in Bennington Co, Vt., in 1848, and came to this county with his parents in 1862, and settled in Waterloo, where he resided until 1865, In 1870, married Ella R Spaulding, she was born in Cape May Co, N J, in 1850, have three children—Bell, Percy and one not yet christened Settled on his present farm in 1875, 160 acres, valued at $50 per acre

Peek, G. H., farmer, Sec 18

Pendleton, E. F., farmer, Sec. 12.

Pendleton, E F., Jr, farmer, Sec 35.

Pendleton, E R, farmer, Sec 14

Pendleton, W. A., farmer, Sec 31.

PIERPONT, JOSEPH W., farmer, Sec 1, born in Franklin Co, Mass., in December, 1839. Married Ellen Hall in 1865, she was born in the same county in 1843, they have three children—Mary E, Grace H and Arthur W. Came to this county in 1867, and settled on his present estate of 130 acres, valued at $50 per acre Are members of the Baptist Church

PRICE, JAMES V., farmer Sec 8, P O Cedar Falls, born in Bucks Co, Penn, in 1814, and married Jane Wikoff in 1842, she was born in Crawford Co, Penn, in 1824, William, Julia and Cynthia are their living children, lost two children—Nathan and Martha. Came to this county in 1864, and set-

tled on his present farm in 1876. Are members of the Presbyterian Church

RAUB, C M., farmer, Sec 12

RAUB ANDREW C., farmer, Sec. 19, born in Cattaraugus Co., N. Y, in 1829, and married Sylvia Bishop in 1855, she was born in the same county in 1835, they have two children living —Charles and Lua A, lost one child— Henry. Came to the West in 1855, and settled in Adams Co., Wis., and in the following year moved to Rock Co, Wis, where he remained until 1874, when he came to this county, and on his present farm of sixty five acres, valued at $35 per acre Are members of the M E Church

RICHARDSON, GLEASON P., farmer, Sec 2, born in Chenango Co., N Y, in 1844 Married Emeline Gates in 1867, she was born in the same county in 1847 ; Lenora, Blanche and Levi are their living children, lost one infant Came to this county in January, 1872, and settled on his present place, where he has since made it his home

RICHARDSON, JAMES, farmer, Sec 12, born in Pittsfield, Mass, in 1822 Married Harriet A Park in 1843, she was born in Chenango Co, N. Y in 1824, and died in 1860, by this marriage they had three children— Gleason P, Mary J. and George M His present wife, Jane Gilliland, was born in Chenango Co, N Y, in 1840, and they were married in 1865, and have two children—Elmer and Hattie. Came to this county in 1867, and in 1868, settled on his present farm, consisting of eighty acres, valued at $40 per acre Are members of the Baptist Church

Richardson, James, far, S 18

Rickert, E J, far., S. 21

ROBINSON, GEORGE, farmer, Sec 5, born in Delaware Co, Ohio, in 1837 Married Charlotte A. Brooks in 1857, she was born in Illinois in 1838; they have two children—Flora A and Dora M Came to this State in 1855, and settled in Floyd Co, where he remained until 1862, when he came to this county and settled in the city of Waterloo, where he worked at his trade, being a carpenter, and where he erected many houses and became extensively engaged in real estate transfers, during his residence there, settled on his present farm in March, 1877, consisting of 120 acres, valued at $35 per acre, also owns residence on Main st, in Waterloo, and is well known throughout the county

SAGE, E. A, far, S 16.

SAGE, GEORGE G., farmer, Sec 4, born in Onondaga Co, N Y, in 1824 Married Sarah J. Amidon in 1850, she was born in the same county in 1831, they have six children—Harriet A, Edward A, Orrin G, Frank L, Rosella and Eudora L Came to this county in November, 1864, and settled in Mt Vernon Tp., where he resided until 1877, when he settled on his present place, where he has since made his home.

SECHSER, JOHN, farmer, Sec 16, born in Germany in 1820 Married Elizabeth Collar in 1852, she was born in Germany in 1822, have three children—John, Jr, Frank and Michael Came to this country in 1856, and settled in Dyersville, Delaware Co, where he resided until 1866, when he came to this county, and in 1878, settled on his present estate of 160 acres Are members of the German Meth Church.

Shaw, Arthur, far, S 2
Shaw, William, far, S 1.
Shirley, George, far, S 9.
Smith, A. M., far, S 17
Smith, C D, far, S 9

SMITH, GEORGE W., farmer, Sec. 6, born in Livingston Co, N Y, in 1838, and emigrated to this State in 1854, and in 1861, enlisted in the 9th I V. I., Co D, served one year and was honorably discharged. Married Fannie Flint in July, 1863, she was born in New Hampshire in 1844; they have five children—William, Frederick, Charles, Florence and Franky, lost three children—Benjamin, Dora and one that died in infancy Settled on his present estate of 240 acres in the Spring of 1878, where he has since made his home

SMITH, GEORGE W., farmer, Sec. 4, P O. Cedar Falls, was born in Fulton Co, N Y, in 1807 Married Lorinda Throop in 1827, she was born

in the same county in 1806, they have three children—Angeline, Eliza and Melissa, have lost two children—Enoch T. and George W Came to this county in July, 1855, and settled in Cedar Falls, where he built a grist-mill, and engaged in that business until 1873, when he purchased and settled on his present estate, consisting of seventy-two and one-half acres of land, valued at $2,000 Held the offices of Supervisor, Constable and Sub-Director of Schools, and has been otherwise prominently known and identified with the interests of the county.

Smith, J D farmer, S 18
Smith, J G, farmer, S 10
Sohner, Paul, farmer, S 20
Stoner, Wm, farmer, S 19
Stout, D, farmer, S 36
Streeter, J W, farmer, S 12
Streeter, Z, Jr, farmer, S 8

TIMENS, W. W, farmer, S 17

TAYLOR, ALBERT, farmer, S 34, born in Richland Co., Ohio, in 1827 Married Martha Hampton in in 1852, she was born in Plymouth Co, Ohio, in 1829, and died in Aug, 1872, Came to this Co in 1852, and settled in Poyner Tp, being one of the earliest settlers at that time, in 1871, settled on his present farm of 160 acres, valued at $30 per acre Their children are Mary L., Sylvester, Aseneth and Jesse

TODD, THOMAS, farmer, S 28, born in England in 1830, emigrated to this country in 1852, and settled in Livingston Co., N Y, where he married Sarah P. Hosford in 1859, she was born in Orange Co, Vt, in 1829. He first settled in La Salle Co., Ill., in 1855, and in 1857, came to this county and entered the land of his estate, returned with his family, and settled permanently in 1865, has farm of 160 acres, valued at $30 per acre. Held the offices of Assessor, School Director, Road Supervisor and otherwise prominently known and identified with the interests of the town and county Sarah and Mary are their living children, they lost two children—Joseph and Lucy (twins)

TRAVIS, CHARLES W., far, Sec. 2; born in Onondaga Co, N. Y, in 1842, and came to this county in 1858, and settled in Mt Vernon Tp In Aug, 1861, enlisted in 36th Ill. V. I, Company B, and served until the close of the war, participated in the battles of Stone River, Pea Ridge and others, was taken prisoner and confined in Andersonville and Florence, South Carolina, eight and one-half months In 1877, settled on his present farm consisting of eighty acres, valued at $40 per acre John W, Chloe M, Hiram and Mary A. are his living children, lost one child—Nellie A

VAUGHN, HIRAM, far
    Vaughn, Robert, far.
WALLACE, C J, far, S 13
    Wambaugh, Levi, far, Sec 16.
Ward, Pierson, far, Sec 12.
Wellman, L B, far, Sec 15.
WHITE, JOSEPH P., far, Sec 19, born in Franklin Co., Mass., in 1821, and married Cynthia Reed in 1846, she died in 1871, they had three children who are living—Eliza, Joseph and Edward, his present wife, Martha Reed, was born in Connecticut in 1835 He came to this county in 1854, and returned after a short visit making his home and permanent settlement in 1856, taking up his residence in the city of Waterloo, where he resided until 1870, when he moved to his present estate consisting of 160 acres, valued at $30 per acre. Are members of the Congregational Church, and number among the early settlers of this town and county

Whitney, Allen R., far, S 17
Worden, A, far., S. 21.
Woolwine, J. J, far., S 32.
YOUNG, WILLIAM, far, S. 12.

CEDAR FALLS TOWNSHIP.

(P O CEDAR FALLS)

ADAMS, H M., physician.

ABBOTT, JOHN B., grain, residence cor Washington and Seventh sts, born Sept. 14, 1834, in Rensselaer Co, N Y ; in 1838, came to Wyoming Co, N Y, in 1858, came to Cuyahoga Co, Ohio, and in 1865, removed to Cedar Falls Married Vine H. Day in 1858, she was born in 1837, in Wyoming Co N Y Enlisted in 1861, in the 21st Ohio V I. was detailed as Camp Instructor, by Gen Buel, of a regiment of Alabama troops, then organizing at Huntsville, Ala , the regiment elected him Major of their command, he resigned his position in 1863, he was appointed in 1866, Superintendent of the Iowa Soldiers' Orphans' Home, held his position about eighteen months Mrs A was Matron of the institution during this time. He, in connection with G B Van Saun, is running a line of seven elevators on the B, C R & N R R.

Albrick, Z S , foundry
Alderman, A J , far , Sec 7
Alderman, E A
Amrlin, Joseph, wagon maker
Andrews, O S , live stock.
Andirson, T

ANDERSON, WILLIAM B., groceries and provisions, Main st., residence cor. Eleventh and Washington sts ; born June 4, 1834, in Scotland, in 1836, came to Quebec, in 1841, removed to Lockport, Ill ; on May 4, 1854, came to Cedar Falls, engaged in farming till 1877, when he commenced his present business Married Lavenia Brown Oct 10, 1865, she was born in 1844, in England, have four children—Basiel, Barton, Ina and Rosamund Has been Justice of the Peace and Town Clerk

Armitage, Thomas, R R

ARQUITT, ADOLPHUS, saloon and billiards, cor First and Washington sts., resides on First st , born March 8, 1841, in Syracuse, N. Y , in 1855, came to Dubuque, Iowa, and in 1863, removed to Cedar Falls, and first engaged in the clothing business Married Ella G Phinney in 1865 , she was born in 1851

in Syracuse, N Y., have four children—Edward, Cora, Ella and Charles Are members of the Universalist Church

Aunnin, Thomas, far , Sec 5
Aurger, Thomas, far , Sec 5

BAGLEY, C. S , cooper

Baker, E , grocery
Baker, G A , laborer.
Barnard, Geo W , Overseer Poor
Barns, John, far , S 30
Bartle, H L , restaurant.

BARTLETT, M. W., Professor of Languages at Iowa State Normal School, born Feb 26, 1834, in Bath, N H , in 1857, came to Western College, Linn Co, in 1853, entered Dartmouth College, and graduated in 1857, and taught for a term of ten years, mostly in ancient languages , was President of the school during the years 1866 and 1867, then went to Denmark Academy, in Lee Co , as teacher for six years ; then spent three years teaching in Memphis Academy, Missouri , in the Fall of 1876, was chosen for his present position Married Miss Julia Abbott July 12, 1859 , she was born in Oct , 1837, in Bath, N H , had four children, three living—Elmer E , Willie A and Mary E Are members of the Congregational Church.

Batcheller, A , far , S 9
Batcheller, M K , far , S 9
Batcheler, K , far , S. 9
Beason, R. A
Belden, A N , far , S 5

BELDEN, T., farmer, Sec. 33 , born Oct 2, 1814, in Genesee Co , N Y , in 1857, came to Bureau Co , Ill , in 1867, came to Cedar Falls Tp , owns forty acres of land, valued at $25 per acre Married Cynthia Harding May 21, 1835 ; she was born April 11, 1818, in Livingston Co , N Y , they have three children—Josephine, Harriet and Eugenia Their son-in-law, W V. Hoagland, was born July 11, 1840, in Wyoming Co , N Y , in 1861, he came to Cedar Falls, he owns forty acres of land. He was married in Sept., 1865, to Mary J Belden, she was born Aug. 11, 1845, in New York , they have three children—Fred T , George A and Harry They are all members of the M E Church

Berry, Henry, far , S 8

Beny, Samuel, clothing

Beny, W H , far , S 8

Beswick, T F , grain

Bell, J S , physician

Bintz, H , far , S 16

BINTZ, HENRY, farmer, Sec. 16, born Dec 1, 1816, in Germany, in 1852, came to Wayne Co., N Y ; in 1868, came to Black Hawk Co , Iowa , he owns eighty acres of land, valued at $25 per acre Married Elizabeth Donhour July 26, 1841 , she was born July 26, 1818, in Germany , had eight children, three living—John, Anna and Henry. Are members of M E Church

Bishop, G K , clerk

BISHOP, S. A., nursery , residence on Twelfth street , owns 160 acres of land in Sec. 11, Grundy Co., Iowa , also twenty acres inside the corporation , he was born Sept 4, 1824, in Trumbull Co., Ohio , in 1845, came to Cleveland, Ohio , in 1848, removed to Wooster, Wayne Co , Ohio, and in 1852, came to Cedar Falls , engaged first in land business, and in 1854, commenced the drug business, and continued it about eleven years, and commenced his present business in 1865. which is carried on quite extensively Married Cordelia McCurdy September, 1850 , she was born in 1826 in Wooster, Wayne Co , Ohio, and died in April 1864 ; have four children——Mary E (now Mrs Bœhmler), Geo. K ; Charles W and Edmund A   The second marriage was to Miss Anna M Buchmann in July, 1865 , she was born in 1838 in Germany , have four children by present marriage—John W , Clara M., Bertha A and Nellie M.   Is a Republican

BISHOP & BANCROFT, proprietors of the Twelfth Street Nursery ; dealers in green house and bedding plants, fruit and ornamental trees, evergreens, grape vines and small fruits, hardy herbaceous flowering plants, flowering bulbs, etc , they endeavor to select only the *best* , their plants and ornamental shrubs are unusually thrifty and well grown , their class of foliage plants are of the most brilliant tints and colors, many of them especially adapted for edging beds and borders, planting in vases and for baskets , they have a magnificent display of house plants, some of them remarkable for their varied and beautiful foliage, profusion and splendor of flowers of other varieties , there are to be procured from their collection, some of the most showy plants for blooming in the late Fall and early Winter months, magnificent Winter-blooming plants, vines and climbers in profusion, variegated grasses, etc , customers unacquainted with the different kinds of plants that bloom throughout the season , by stating the object which they wish to effect and the plants they have, and the amount of money they wish to expend, a selection will be made that doubtless will prove satisfactory , when selections are left with the proprietors, persons may rely on being liberally dealt with ; when left to them, they will use their best judgment ; the mails offer good facilities for sending out plants, which are quite safe , all plants distinctly labeled and packed in the best manner for safe carriage , in the fruit department of this nursery, will be found the most select varieties of apples, crabs, cherries, plums, pears, grapes, raspberries, strawberries, currants, rhubarb, etc , in the ornamental department, they have the almond, berberry vulgaris, honeysuckle, deutzia gracilis, lilac, snowball, wiegela rosea, and many other choice varieties , probably no finer selection of evergreens can be found than can be furnished by Bishop & Bancroft , they have the Norway, American and white spruce, Scotch, Austrian and white pine, red and white cedar, Irish juniper, balsam fir, hemlock, American yew, savin, etc , this firm is worthy of the large patronage extended to them, and all orders by mail or otherwise will be promptly and satisfactorily executed , descriptive catalogues, with prices, etc., will be sent on application

Bixby, A L

Bley, A , farmer, Sec 14

Bley, Dan, farmer, Sec 24.

Blood, R., farmer, Sec. 17

Bœhmler, Charles, boots and shoes.

Bœhmler, Philip, tinner

Bœhmler, Theo , hardware.

Peter Melendy

CEDAR FALLS

Bovie, A D , painter.

Bovie, W A , painter

BOZARTH, JOHN P., farmer, Sec. 19, born Aug 4, 1828, in Lewis Co., Va , in 1839, came to Muscatine, Iowa, in 1854, came to Black Hawk Co , in 1868, came to his present farm. Owns 160 acres, valued at $25 per acre. Married Eliza J Miller in December, 1852 , she was born in September, 1833, in Virginia , had eight children, seven living—Charles, Thomas, Mary J , Sarah, John P , Frank and Roy.

Bozarth, Thomas, farmer, Sec. 19.

Briggs, G W , well driller

Brinenstoon, G D , farmer, Sec 9

Bronson, L N , laborer

Bronson, R A , laborer

Brother, Charles, farmer, Sec 5

Brown, William, laborer

Bryant, F A , physician

BRYANT, M. E. MRS., widow of N C Bryant, Captain in the U S Navy , he was born in December, 1826, in Maine, and died Sept 19, 1874 He married Miss Mary E Southall Sept 19, 1858, she was born Aug. 16, 1838, in England , they removed to Cedar Falls in 1863. She owns several stores in the city, as well as residence property , she also owns 800 acres of land, mostly improved, in Spring Creek She has two children—Percy, born April 19, 1862 , Walter, born Oct 1, 1863 Is a member of the Episcopal Church Capt Bryant served in the Mexican war

BRYANT, WM. C., firm of Wise & Bryant, druggists and booksellers ; established in 1867 ; residence, corner of Franklin and Sixth , born April 12, 1841, in Otsego Co , N Y , in 1850, came to Oshkosh, Wis., April 20, 1861, enlisted in Co E, 2d Wis Inf., enlisted as a private, and promoted to several positions, and in 1866 was promoted to Major , left the service Feb. 16, 1867, in Baltimore, Md , participated in the first and second battles of Bull Run, Gainesville, Petersburg, Spottsylvania, Wilderness, Gettysburg and others , in 1867, came to Des Moines, Iowa, and came to Cedar Falls Jan. 15, 1868 Married Vesta A. Bryant June 30, 1869 , she was born Nov 23, 1847, in Massachusetts Are members of the

Congregational Church , is Secretary of the Library Association

Burgess, R , farmer, Sec 26.

BURR, O. L., firm of Burr & Davis, proprietors "Carter House ," born in March, 1839, in Wyoming Co , N Y , in 1861, came to Independence, Iowa, and in 1868, came to Cedar Falls Married Miss Alice Getchell in 1874 , she was born in Waterville, Me

Buhalem, Jacob, lumber

Butler, Daniel, foundry.

Butler, F F , foundry

Butterworth, R , blacksmith

CAMERON, SAM , farmer, Sec 34

Carpenter, Ed . teamster

Carpenter, F A , farmer, Sec 36.

Carpenter, T B , lumber and coal

Carrall, M , laborer

Castello, John, cemetery

Chapman, A G., farmer, Sec. 17

Chapman, C S , insurance

Chapman, M W., retired.

CHASE, W. H., farmer, Sec 26, born Sept 20, 1820, in Portsmouth, R I , in 1848, came to Connecticut , in 1863, came to Illinois , in 1866, came to Grundy Co , Iowa, and opened a farm of 960 acres, in 1869, he sold 640 acres and removed to Cedar Falls , then commenced the grocery business, and continued it about four years ; then returned to Grundy Co., remained there about one year, then sold the balance of his farm (320 acres) and returned to Cedar Falls, in 1875, came to his present farm, consisting of eighty acres, valued at $30 per acre Married, March 27, 1871, Mrs Anna M Barker, daughter of Luther H and Margaret A Barnes , she was born March 27, 1831, in Toronto, Canada , have two children —Anna B and Margaret , she has one child by a former marriage—Fred Barker. Clark Chase was born April 3, 1794, in Portsmouth, R I , in 1876, came to Cedar Falls , he lives with his son He married Eliza Woodman, she was born in 1797, and died in December, 1874, aged 76 years , had six children, four living—W. H , Alfred S , Constant W and Elizabeth (now Mrs. Bordon)

Christenson, P , far , S 30

Christensen, T , far., S 27

3

Church, Hiram, far , S 3

Clark, G H , omnibus line

CLARK, GEORGE W., proprietor of Cedar Falls Omnibus Line, and breeder and shipper of pure-bred Poland-China swine, he was born Aug. 30, 1833, in Monroe Co., N Y , in 1850, came to Janesville, Wis , in 1854, came to Cedar Falls, he owns 120 acres of land in Sec 20, valued at $35 per acre Married Fannie F Streeter in January, 1855 , she was born Aug 9, 1837, in Clifton Springs, N. Y. , had eight children, four living—Clara R. (now Mrs J E Bates), William K., Nettie E. and George B

CLARK, WM. H., firm of Clark Bros , livery. board and sale stables, cor First and Washington sts., born Nov. 7, 1838, in Berkshire Co, Mass , in 1858, came to Freeport, Ill , in 1860, removed to Dixon, Ill , in 1862, returned to Massachusetts, and in 1873, came to Cedar Falls, Iowa Married Alice Conklin March 21, 1878 , she was born in November, 1855, in Iowa ; he owns 6½ acres outside the city limits , also a house and lot in the city

COLE, JACOB, retired , residence corner of Washington and Twelfth sts., born April 12, 1814, in Hunterdon Co, N J , in 1863, he removed to Morgan Co , Ill., the same year, came to Cedar Falls ; he owns 240 acres of land in Sec 26, also property in the city Married Catherine Swayze Sept 5, 1838, she was born April 6, 1821, in Morris Co , N J ; have two children—John L , born in April, 1839, and Martha M (now Mrs. Henry), born in March, 1845

Cook, J G , far , S 9

Cooper, I , teamster

Cornell, M , laborer.

Corrigan, Dan, mason.

Cotton, F , far., S. 26

Cotton, A J , far., S 26.

Cotton, Wm., far , S 26

Coughlin, J., laborer

COX & ANDREWS, dealers in groceries, crockery, boots and shoes, etc., Main st. Francis Cox was born March 1, 1829, in England , in 1852, came to Fayette Co , Ohio , in 1854, came to Cedar Falls, and followed the stone cutting trade till 1876, when he commenced his present business Married Mary Mann April 4, 1852, in London , she was born Aug 21, 1828, in England, and died April 11, 1868, have four children—Thomas, Lizzie, Carrie and William Was a member of the Town Council from 1874 to 1876. Edward L. Andrews was born Jan 28, 1845, in Hartford, Conn., in 1854, came to Whitewater, Wis , in 1866, came to Manchester, Iowa, and in 1872, removed to Cedar Falls , engaged in the printing business till 1876, when he commenced his present business Married Annie L. Hunt Sept 1, 1872, she was born Oct. 25, 1849, in Rolling Prairie, Ind. , have one child—Irving H , born Aug 20, 1874 Enlisted in Co I, 40th Wis V. I., served 100 days.

Cropper, J S , foundry

Crosby, J. Q A , S 7.

Culver, B., grain

Cunningham, M., far , S 16

Currier, G. F , stone cutter

Curtight, J., carpenter

Curtight, T S

DAHL, H , cabinet maker

Davenport, F , retired

Davidson, H , carpenter

Davidson, L , farmer, S. 7

Davidson, Lyman farmer, S 7.

Davis, H G , renter

Davis, M , omnibus driver

Davison, E. B , bakery and confectionery.

Dayton, W. N., merchant milling

Deetrick, R. S , laborer.

Dewey, M , clerk

Dilfill, A. H , farmer, S 36

Doll, G., farmer, S. 10

Doll, P , farmer, S 10.

Doorley, John, mason

DORWIN, W. S., minister of M. E Church, Sec 34, born July 10, 1833, in Franklin Co., Vt. ; in 1855, came to Cedar Falls , has had charges in Butler, Grundy, Franklin, Black Hawk and other Counties , in 1876, he came to his present farm ; they own 200 acres of land, valued at $30 per acre. Married Harriet L. Morris Feb , 1858 , she was born Dec. 15, 1834, in Chemung Co , N. Y , have five children— C. M , T E., Mabel, A. N and A. M D. In 1863, commenced in the regular ministry, and has continued in the work ever since

Doud, A D , laborer

Drohman, F , far , S 18.

Dufoe, N H , far , S 22

Duggau, T , railroad.

Dunsback, Wm., far., S 6

EDDY, H L , far , S 9.

Eckhart, T , clerk

Eiler, George, farmer, Sec 30

Eichnlamb, Henry, miller

EILER, PHILIP, farmer, Sec 30 , born May 20, 1811, in Germany , in 1838, came to Rensselaer Co , N Y , in 1848. he came to Waukesha Co , Wis , in 1868, he came to his present farm , owns 320 acres of land, valued at $30 per acre Married Frederika Knoch Feb 5, 1851, she was born Aug. 11, 1829, in Germany , they have six children—George, Caroline, Daniel, Philip, Mary L and Sarah E Are members of the Evangelical Church

Emerson, Wm A., farmer, S 5

Emerson, W A , farmer, S 5

FABRICK, FRANK, tinsmith

Fabrick, John A , far , S. 27.

Farwell, I N , well driller

Fasdick, J. A , engineer.

FIELDS, C. J., Cashier First National Bank, and firm of W M Fields & Bro , proprietors of the Cedar Falls Stock Farm , born Nov 9, 1844, in England , in 1847, came to Pennsylvania, and in 1873, came to Cedar Falls Married Miss Isabella Cass in 1866 , she was born in England , have three children—Albert M , Isabella F and Violetta M Are members of the M. E Church

FIELDS, W. M., President First National Bank, also firm of W M. Fields & Bro , proprietors of Cedar Falls Stock Farm, Sec 22 , they own 960 acres, and are extensively engaged in fine stock raising, consisting of short-horns, Berkshire, Poland-China swine and Cotswold sheep , this is the largest and one of the best improved farms in the county ; he was born Feb 22, 1841, in England ; in 1847, came to Pennsylvania , in 1873, came to Cedar Falls Married Miss Violetta Cass in 1866 , she was born in England , have three children—J Cass, W. M , and Charles A Are members of the M. E. Church

Filmley, J D , far , S 15.

Ford, C , retired farmer

Ford, Frank, laborer

Fowler, W H , laborer.

Fransen, H , farmer, Sec 33

FRENCH, THEODORE L., agricultural implements , also one of the proprietors of the Adams & French Harvester, residence Cedar Falls , born July 6, 1836, in Chittenden Co , Vt , the same year, he came with his parents to De Kalb Co., Ill. , in 1863, removed to Cedar Falls. Married Miss Mary E Barnes Sept 11, 1862, she was born Sept 11, 1842, in Chemung Co , N Y , have one child—Jesse R., born July 1, 1863, in De Kalb Co., Ill

GARLAND, T J , laborer.

Gates, D , laborer

Gatley, R , farmer, Sec 26

Geyer, Jacob, Jr , laborer

Gibson, Joseph, blacksmith

Gibson, W , farmer, Sec 14

Geddis, S H , carpenter.

GILCHRIST, J. C., Principal of the Iowa Normal School, born May 20, 1832, in Allegheny City, Penn , in 1837, came to Trumbull Co , Ohio , in 1851, attended the Poland Institute in Mahoning Co , Ohio , remained there till 1853, then taught school about two years , in 1855, attended the Antioch College, Ohio, and continued for two years , since 1857, he has been teaching continuously , in June, 1876, he was chosen Principal of the Iowa State Normal School, was three years County Superintendent of Washington Co., Penn , then Principal of the Southwestern State Normal School at California, Washington Co , Penn. , then Principal of the State Normal School at Fairmount, West Va He helped to recruit a company in California, Penn , and spent about one year recruiting and assisting the government Married Hannah Cramer in 1858, she was born April 1, 1835, in Hubbard, Trumbull Co., Ohio, had ten children, six living—Cleland, Maud, Willard C., Fred C , Grace, and infant daughter Are members of the M E Church

Gilispie, M , blacksmith

Glasser, N , stone dealer

Glanvill, A E , farmer, Sec 9

Glasser, Jacob, laborer

Godfrey, J R , builder

GRAHAM, ALEX., merchant and custom milling, resides on South Main street, born April 6, 1816, in Utica, N. Y , in 1820, came to Cortland Co., N Y , with his parents, in 1837, located in Tompkins Co , N Y , and commenced a general merchandise business , in 1858, removed to Janesville, Wis , and came to Cedar Falls in 1876, and established his present business. Was married in September, 1842, to Miss Abigail M , daughter of Gen Martin Keep, of New York , she was born in April, 1816, in Homer, N Y , had three children , lost Richard M in 1846, aged two years, William R and Kate M (now Mrs Cook) W. R. enlisted in 1861 in Co E, 3d Wis. Cav , served about ten days , was promoted to Col Barstow's staff, then transferred to the line and attached to Co. G as Lieutenant Commanding, he was then 18 years of age He was a graduate of the Michigan State University, and admitted to the bar in Janesville, Wis

Graham, W J , far , S 5
Graham, W. R , merchant milling.
Granger, O E , far , S 25
Grus, Fred., laborer
Griffith, J J , far , S 25.
Griffith, W. B , far , S 20
Greene, Abel, far , S 14
HACKEROLT, A , farmer, Sec 6

Hageman, John, painter
Harris, W H , Novelty Works

HALVORSIN, JENS, machinist, Water st , born June 4, 1835, in Norway , in 1857, came to Quebec , then to Boston , then to Chicago, to St. Paul, to St Louis, and to Keokuk , in 1861, returned to Chicago, and in 1862, went to California, in 1865, returned to Chicago , in 1867, removed to Cedar Falls and worked for Overman & Co for about seven years Owns seventy-three acres of land in Butler Co ; also house and lot in the city. He was burned out in 1877 Married Betsey Peterson Jan 9, 1866, she was born Aug 19, 1849, in Wisconsin , had four children, three living—Harry, Arthur and Jessie

amilton, N. T., laborer

HAMMER, A. D., farmer, Sec. 6 , born Feb 14, 1824, in Pendleton Co , Va , in 1851, came to Ohio , in 1855, came to his present farm, owns 216 acres, valued at $25 per acre. Married Malinda Wagner March 18, 1847 ; she was born June 5, 1822, in Pendleton Co , Va , had five children, three living —Elizabeth, William and Louisa   Mr H is Treasurer of the School Board of Cedar City.

Hammond, M , laborer
Hamm, C P , horse trader
Hamm, J C , far , S 7
Hansen, Nels, far , S 19
Hansen, N C , far , S 31
Hardman, D D , far , S 19
Harlacher, G H , furniture
Harrington, Grant, laborer
Harrington, J K , laborer.
Harrington, L L , far , Sec 31
Harris, N. H., manufacturer of pumps and lightning rods.
Harris, S W , wagon manufacturer
Hart, A H , far , Sec. 7

HARTMAN, J., retired , born March 5, 1816, in Union Co , Penn , in 1834, came to Lycoming Co , Penn , served three years at the millwright trade , in 1839, came to Stark Co , Ohio, and followed the millwright trade until 1854, when he came to Cedar Falls, and engaged in the real estate business , he owns thirty acres of land inside the corporation. Married Anna Kleckmar in 1849, she was born in 1820, in Crawford Co , Penn , died in 1852; had one child—Jacob A   Second marriage to Jane Glover in 1856; she was born Nov 18, 1833, in Ohio, have one child —May (now Mrs. Kaynor) Is a Republican

Haskell, B F , far., Sec 6
Haskett, B T , far , Sec 6
Hastroh, D , far , Sec. 21
Hatch, Pat , clerk
Hatfield, James, miller
Hazlett, Theo., general merchandise
Heart, James, far., Sec 20
Hearst, James, far., Sec. 20.
Hedglin, H , laborer
Hedglin, John, laborer
Hemenway, H C , attorney.
Henningson, L. L , far , Sec. 31
HENSLEY, EDWARD, farmer, Sec. 22 , born Jan. 5, 1812, in England ,

in 1832, came to Canada, in 1837 came to Illinois, in 1854 came to Black Hawk Co, Iowa, the same year, returned to Illinois, the following year, came again to Black Hawk Co, and in June, 1866, came to his present farm, owns forty acres of land, valued at $30 per acre. Married Martha Holbrook Dec 28 1857, she was born July 12, 1819, in England, in 1855, she came to Cedar Falls, have two children—Sarah Ann and William H. Mrs. H is a member of the M. E. Church.

Henry, W H, laborer.
Herman, Fred, far, Sec 28
Hewey, S, far, Sec 7
Hewitt, J. N, farmer, S 7
Hilten, H, well driller
Hites, M., farmer, S 22.
Hites, M., farmer, S 22.
Hayland, Peter, grain
Hoagland, P, farmer, S 33
Hoagland, W U, farmer, S 33
Hoagland, W V, farmer, S 33
Hobrón, J M, Prof of Music
Hoeppen, E, blacksmith
Hopkins, H, farmer, S 7
Horty, Pat, horse trader
Hotchkiss, F A, bookkeeper
Houghmaster. G, miller
Houghtaling, J, farmer, S. 28
Houghtaling, James, farmer, S 28
Hoyt, C. L, farmer, S 25

HUBBARD, SOLOMON, far, owns thirty acres of land with his residence in Cedar Falls, also eighty acres in the county, he was born Aug 21, 1827, in New Hampshire, in 1831, came to Wayne Co, Ind., in 1856, removed to Jo Daviess Co., Ill, remained there and in Stephenson County until 1873, when he came to his present home. Married Mary Rathff in Feb., 1852, she was born July 18, 1832, in Wayne Co, Ind., had eight children, four living—Joseph, Edgar, William and Eva. Has been a member of the City Council. Members of the Quaker denomination

HUFFMAN, M. E., painter, shop over Harris' Wagon Mfy., resides corner Clay and Fifteenth sts., born Oct 14, 1849, in Richland Co., Ohio, in 1857, came to Cedar Falls. Married Lucy Wantz June 1, 1874, she was born in Oct, 1852, in Illinois.

Huber, J, farmer, S 18
Hughes, J T, carpenter
HUGHES, OLIVER, farmer, S 29, born Oct 10, 1824, in Salem Co, N J; in 1845, came to Ohio, in 1846, to Wisconsin, in 1849, came to Chicago, in 1852, returned to N J, the same Fall, returned to Chicago, and then to Michigan, in the Fall of 1853, came to Knox Co, Ill, in April, 1854, came to Black Hawk Co., Iowa, in 1866, came to his present farm, owns 420 acres of land, valued at $20 per acre. Married Mary C Hardman in May, 1865, she was born in 1845, in Pennsylvania, have two children—John and Oliver. Has been Township Supervisor and Assessor
Humbert, E C, far, Sec. 7
Humbert, Sol B., farmer, Sec 7.
Humphrey, F, clergyman
Hunt, J. E, prop Monitor House
HURLBUT, M. F., cooper, Mill st, born Jan 5, 1826, in Addison Co, Vt., in 1852, came to DeKalb Co, Ill, in 1861, came to Cedar Falls. Married Almira Fuller in May, 1846, she was born in April, 1828, in Grand Isle, Vt., have two children—Lynda C (now Mrs W M Perkins), Carrie S (now Mrs E L Ross).

INGERSOLL, W. T., farmer, Sec 5
Isamel, Mark, clothing.

JACOBS, A E, farmer, Sec. 7.
Jacob, John, laborer.
Jackson, L L., far, Sec 24
Jaquith, C. F, grain
Jansen, J., farmer, Sec. 7.
Jarnor, Thos., clerk
Jay, Barton, farmer, Sec 7.
Jeffers, C H, farmer, Sec 2
Jennings, J B, meat market
Jeppson, Lawrence, farmer, Sec 5
Jewell, F. L, far, Sec 16.
Johnson, Henry, farmer, Sec 28
Johnson, E, farmer, Sec 31
Joness, R. W., farmer, Sec 31.
Jones, H E, farmer, Sec 4
JORDAN, H. A., photographer, Main st, residence, same place, born Oct 8, 1837, in Norwich, Conn., in 1847, came to New Haven, Conn., in 1863, came to New London, Conn; in 1866, came to Syracuse, N. Y.; in 1874,

removed to Benton Co , in 1876, came to Cedar Falls He commenced his business when a boy, and has followed it since continually , when in Syracuse he was running seven galleries in different cities at the same time , this is the leading gallery in the county Married Mary L Johnson Oct 31, 1858 ; she was born May 2, 1840, in Hartford, Conn , have three children—Eugene H , Cora H and Annie M   Are members of the Congregational Church.

Jassen, Hans, farmer, S 20

Judd, T C , general merchandise

KALLENBACH, C , teaming

Kaymer, C , farmer, S 24

Kaymer, E J , physician

Kehner, Val , laborer

Kerr, John, farmer, Sec 16

King, R. K., farmer, Sec 16

Kirk, E N , laborer

Knapp, J. T , banker

Knapp, L

Knochi, Frederick, milling

Krassman, Charles H , harness.

Kreiger, John, farmer, Sec 35

LAMB, S D , laborer

Lamb, Thomas M , teamster.

Lamb, W J , laborer'

Landis, B. F , school teacher

Langdon, R. H , teamster.

Larsen, C., farmer, Sec 28

Larsen, H. P , laborer

Larsen, J P., harness

Larsen, Peter, farmer, Sec. 28

Lasson, Charles, farmer, Sec 28

Law, William, laborer

Lawrence, Charles, barber

Lawrence, Wm , far., S 18

Leahy, J , far , S 36

Leister, A W , retired.

Lewis, E F , marble worker

Lewis, Warren, marble worker

Lewisson, L , clerk

Lippold, M , barber

Loos, Fred K , gun shop.

Loose, Charles, gun shop.

Love, Wm., laborer

LUND, HANS N., brewer; born July 27, 1848, in Denmark , in 1871, came to Cedar Falls, and commenced his present business in 1877 His father lives in Denmark, aged 67 years, his mother died in Denmark in 1861, aged about 40 years , has a brother and sister living in Cedar Falls.

McBAIN, FRANK, farmer, Sec 36

McCafferty, Charles, R R

McCLURE, WILLIAM H., attorney , resides on Second st , born May 5, 1829, in Watertown, N Y.; in 1836, came to Rochester, N. Y , in 1853, came to Cedar Falls His first wife was Miss Mary Overman, now dead His second marriage, to Miss Olive Merrill, March 29, 1859, she was born in Jamestown, N Y.; had five children, four living—Samuel, Helen, William and Olive He enlisted Aug 8, 1861, in the 3d Iowa Battery, was in the battle of Sugar Creek and was wounded at the battle of Pea Ridge; was senior First Lieutenant commanding, and commissioned Lieutenant Colonel of the Iowa State Militia March 25, 1865 He attended the first jury trial ever tried in this county in a court of record, and was the first attorney admitted to practice in this county

McCowers, J J., agent Singer S Machine

McElwain, I. A., agent Marsh Harvester

McNally, Z , grocer.

McNaughton, Jas , Sup't Public Schools.

MAGGART, JAMES W., blacksmith , residence corner Third and Franklin sts , born Feb 11, 1805, in Monroe Co , Va , in 1841, came to Madison Co , Ind , in 1855, came to Cedar Falls Married Jane Alford in 1827 , she was born April 22, 1805, in Monroe Co., Va , had seven children, two living—Mary J and James M

Mahoney, Daniel, tailor

MARKLEY, CATHARINE, MRS., widow of James Markley , he was born March 25, 1802, in Bedford Co , Penn , in 1867, came to Cedar Falls, and died June 5, 1871, she was born Aug 8, 1817, in Westmoreland, Co., Penn. They own ten acres with their residence in Cedar Falls , also 640 acres in Butler Co   Had ten children—Henry H , Semantha J , Mandy E , Mary L , Lucy, Geo. A , Ida L , John R , James E and Nellie M   Are members of the Baptist Church

Markley, H

Maroney, T , farmer, Sec 34

Mansfield, James, laborer

Marks, A , laborer

Marshall, C. F , carpenter

Martin, James, farmer, Sec 30.

Martin, J. W., farmer, Sec 32

Mason, A W , Ass't Cash First Nat. Bk

Mason, James, laborer.

May, Caleb, farmer, Sec 35

MATTHIAS, FRED., firm of Matthias & Robbins, hardware, Main st , born Sept. 23, 1841, in Hessen, Germany , in 1866, came to Cedar Falls , in 1874, commenced their present business Married Mary Severin Oct 20, 1867 , she was born March 23, 1849, in Germany , have three children—Lily, Mary and Emilie. Are members of the Lutheran Church Has been a member of the City Council two years , was Secretary of the German Aid Society for two and a half years

Mattison, James, cooper.

MAXOM, J. H., Baptist minister , resides in Cedar Falls , born Oct 16, 1817, in England , in 1838, came to Quebec, and was connected with the English army, remained in Canada until 1856, when he removed to Creston, Ill ; in 1858, removed to DeKalb, Ill , and was Pastor of the Baptist Church there. In 1861, he enlisted in Co. B 58th Ill. Inf , as First Lieutenant , then had command of Co. B at Shiloh, where he was severely wounded , remained in the service about two years , in 1863, came to Battle Creek, Mich , and was Pastor of the Baptist Church there, Tecumseh and Bellevue until 1872, when he came to Cedar Falls Married Anna Turner in 1840 , she was born in 1819, in England , had eight children, seven living—Henry, Mary, Philander S., Methlancton, Etta C , Florence M and Ida Z Philander S has been Pastor of the Baptist Church in Mt Morris, N Y , for the past three years

Mead, S. P , retired

Mellen, H., farmer, Sec. 23.

Mendenhall, Isaac

Melendy, C B , art gallery

MELENDY, PETER, agricul urist , residence cor Eleventh and Washington sts , born Feb 9, 1823, in Cincinnati, Ohio , in 1850, removed to Mt Healthy, Hamilton Co , Ohio, and engaged in farming and fine stock raising for breeding purposes, in 1856, came to Cedar Falls, and continued farming till 1860, when he engaged in the agricultural business In 1864, he was appointed U S. Marshal, and held that position for about eighteen months Was elected President of the State Agricultural Society, which position he held for five years He has been connected with the State Agricultural College for the past fifteen years Was appointed by the Governor to settle the Agricultural College lands, consisting of 240,000 acres. Has always been a stanch Republican, and always taken an active interest in politics Was Chairman of the State Central Committee. In 1868, he organized the State Horticultural and Agricultural Societies. Married Martha Coddington in 1847 , she was born in 1832, in Hamilton Co , Ohio, and died in 1866, in Cedar Falls , has two children—Charles B. and Ettie B (now Mrs Dr Bassett.) Second marriage to Mrs McFarland, formerly Mary A Wolson, Dec , 1868 , she was born in Tonawanda, N. Y. , two children by her first marriage—Clark S McFarland and Marion I McFarland Are members of the Presbyterian Church.

Merchant, L S , printer

Merrill, A , lumber

Messier, E , far , Sec 23

Messerly, Godlieb, far., Sec 2

Messerly, John, far , Sec 5

Messerly, Rudolph, far , Sec 7

Meyers, C. H., collector

Miller, August, shoemaker

Miller, Charles, far , Sec. 9.

Miller, George, far , Sec. 9

Miller, John, Sec 32

Mills, Joseph, carpenter

Miner, W. O , farmer, Sec 25

Molloy, John, tailor

Moore, John, farmer, Sec 3

Morgan, George, farmer, Sec 6.

Morgan, Jesse, farmer, Section 6

Morrill, Arthur H , retired.

Mormer, Peter, laborer

Morner, P D , Alderman.

Morris, William, cattle dealer.

Morrison, A , patent right

Morrison, W , farmer, Sec. 21

MULLARKY, ANDREW, deceased; born in the year 1820, in County Mayo, Ireland , came to the United States in 1830, with other members of the family, lived for a time in the States of Rhode Island, Ohio, Indiana and

Wisconsin, from whence he removed to Illinois, where he was married, in 1849, to Ellen Mullarky, and opened one of the first stores in Freeport, from there he removed to Iowa, in 1850, and located where now is the business center of Cedar Falls, then but a remove from a wilderness He built and operated the first store building in the county, in the second story of which the county business was long conducted He was accidentally drowned in the mill race on the evening of the 12th of December, 1863, leaving his wife Ellen and three children, named respectively, Owen Emmett, Lizzie Ellen and Kate Emeline, all of whom are now residing in Cedar Falls Mr M was a man thoroughly imbued with the spirit of Western enterprise, of great force of character, possessed of wide and comprehensive views, and, with full confidence in the successful future of his adopted State, he directed all his energies to the end that Iowa should not be behind in the race for supremacy among the sisterhood of States The now thriving city of Cedar Falls is largely indebted to his ability and untiring exertions in her behalf, for the proud position she occupies to-day And it is the conviction of one and all that had he lived, many other and larger enterprises than are now occupying the attention of the people, would have been successfully inaugurated and vigorously prosecuted Through his mercantile transactions, he amassed a competency. He held many local positions of trust and honor, in the Council, School Board, railroad and other corporations, was Postmaster for a number of years, but never sought prominence in official life. Kind and generous to the deserving, his early death was sincerely regretted by every one, for by by the exertions of his type of man are the resources of a new country fully developed

Mullarky, Charles H , farmer, Sec 23

Mullarky, T , farmer, Sec 23.

Mullarky, O. E., farmer, Sec. 23

Mullhoff, F , farmer, Sec. 35

MUNGER, E. A., firm of E. A. Munger & Co , wind-mills, iron pumps and fixtures, Second st , resides in Cedar

Falls , born Aug 13, 1852, in Canada; in 1854, came to Beloit, Wis., with his parents, and in 1855, came to Cedar Falls, and commenced his present business in 1876 Married Charlotte Odell in 1872 , she was born in 1853, in Michigan , had two children—lost Mabel in infancy, and Maud born July 17, 1875

Murdock, E , far , S 13

Myers, Jacob, far., S 18

Myers, Levi, far , S 18

NOLTE, **CHARLES,** painter

Norris, A. J., far., Sec. 4.

Nye, A H , teacher.

OBERLY, laborer.

O'BRIEN, PETER, tailor, First street, born in Ireland in 1836, in 1852, came to New York City, in 1855, came to Dubuque, Iowa, and from there to Winona, Minnesota; in 1858, went to Chicago Enlisted in the United States service, and went to Salt Lake City , in 1863, came to Cedar Falls and worked for William Ireland about two and a half years ; then worked for Bird, Pickton & Co., for two years, and for Samuel Berry for about two years, and then for the woolen mill company Married Ann Barnes in Dec , 1863 , she was born in 1838, in Ireland, have two children—James P , born April 14, 1865, and William F , born May 2, 1870

O'Connor, O. James, blacksmith.

Oday, Jemy, laborer.

Odell, A J , cabinet maker

ODELL, CHAS. W., firm of Odell & Harlacher, furniture and undertakers, Main st , born Nov 7, 1846, in Essex Co , N Y , in 1864, came to Cedar Falls ; in 1868, commenced his present business. Married Elida A. Odell in Oct., 1868 , she was born May 21, 1850, in Toledo, Ohio , had three children, two living— Harry A , born Sept 4, 1869, and Ed C , born Dec 25, 1873

Oleson, Peter, far , S 32

OLMSTED, F. S., farmer, born April 20, 1825, in Wayne Co , N Y , in March, 1867, came to Cedar Falls , he owns five acres with his residence in the city, also 65 acres in Sec 14, and 160 acres in Sec 16. Married Jane Wells in

1847, she was born in 1828, in Wayne Co ,N.Y., have five children—Helen(now Mrs F H Peabody), Park C., Flora, Bert and George. Are members of the M E Church.

Onan, David, grocer

O'Neil, Patrick, laborer

Osgood, N B, laborer.

Ostegaard, James, farmer, Sec 34.

Ottry, P O, drayman

Overman, E W, gardener

Overman, J M, farmer, S 11.

Overman, W P, retired, S 1

PALMER, Amos, laborer

PACKARD, S. H., attorney, office on Main st, residence on Sixth st; born Sept 10, 1828, in Rochester, N Y, in 1854, came to Cedar Falls, and engaged in law and newspaper publishing Married Z C Barnes April 23, 1857, she was born in 1835, in Rice Lake, Canada, had four children, three living—Clarence W, Jeffrey G and Hellen M Has held nearly all the city offices, has been U S Commissioner and Postmaster In the Winter of 1857 and 1858, he was caught on the prairie in a blinding storm from the northwest, was out for forty-eight hours, and, in consequence, had his right leg amputated above the ankle He is a member of the Episcopal Church.

Palmer, A. H, collector

Patterson, S., farmer, S 20

Peek, E. C., livery.

Pennington, L., agent for Am Ex Co

Perkins, W J, trader

Perry, Marion, prop Monitor House.

Petersen, E. A, laborer

Petersen, F. L., gardener

Peterson, Robert, laborer

Pettit, W. H., physician

Pfeiffer, H, brewer

Pfeiffer, Jacob, brewer,

Philleo, H, farmer, S 1

PHILLEO, MILTON, farmer, S. 1, born March 16, 1816, in Oneida Co, N.Y., came to Will Co, Ill, in 1854; in 1863, came to Cedar Falls Tp; owns 310 acres of land, valued at $40 per acre Married Mary Shaw in 1843, she was born May 16, 1824, in Oneida Co., N Y., had ten children, nine living—Harriet, Ella, Millard, Henry, Halsey, Frank, Grant, Veva

and Alson Has been Justice of the Peace, School Superintendent and Director

PHILPOT, GEORGE, SR., farmer, Sec 11, born June 7, 1817, in Belmont Co, Ohio, in the Spring of 1850, came to his present farm, owns 100 acres of land, valued at $50 per acre Married Charlotte Morrison May 9, 1837, she was born in March, 1815, in Alleghany Co., Md, had thirteen children, seven living—Wm. S., John, James, George, Shepherd, Margaret and Samuel. Has been Justice of the Peace and Constable, also, City Marshal. John, George and Charles P enlisted in the war of the rebellion Chas P enlisted in the 31st Iowa V I, in 1862, served about one year and died in Aug, 1863, at Andersonville, Ga

Philpot, Geo, Jr, far, Sec. 11.

PHILPOT, JOHN W., farmer, Secs 2, 3, 10 and 11, born Jan 14, 1847, in Belmont Co, Ohio, when a child, removed with his parents to Summerfield, Ohio, in 1855, came to Cedar Falls, he owns 320 acres, valued at $75 per acre His father was born Feb 15, 1815, in Barnesville, Ohio, and died April 15, 1877, in Cedar Falls, his mother was born Oct 27, 1816, in Maryland; she lives with her son His father has been Mayor of Cedar Falls and Town Trustee His mother is a member of the M. E Church

Phinney, C C, farmer, Sec 7

Phohl, C, laborer

Pickton, Peter, merchant tailor

Pierce, D R, shoe store

Pierce, S N., physician

PLUMMER, DANIEL, mining operator; born Oct 26, 1818, in Canada, in 1848, removed to Ohio, in 1849, came to Detroit, Mich., from there to Lake Superior, in 1852, returned to Canada, in 1855, returned again to Lake Superior Enlisted in 1863 was Captain of Co A, 27th Michigan V. I, served to the close of the war In 1868, came to Cedar Falls, he owns his residence with about eight acres in the city, also forty-three acres in other parts of the city Married Pauline Alondier Nov 5, 1850, she was born March 17, 1832, in Canada, had ten children, nine living—Elizabeth,

Adelaide, John, Carrie, Charles, Daniel, Alexander, Fannie and Robert. She is a member of the Roman Catholic Church, he is a member of the Episcopal Church. At the age of 18, he enlisted in the British army, and served during the rebellion.

Plummer, John, gardener

Polk, A D , attorney

Pomeroy, A L., farmer, Sec 27

Pomeroy, James T , farmer, Sec 34.

POOLER, O. L., harness and saddlery, on Main street, between Second and Third streets, resides on Twelfth street, born June 12, 1854, in Mineral Point, Wis., in 1855, came to Madison, Wis, in 1858, came to Sparta, Wis, in 1865, came to McGregor, Iowa, in 1866, removed to Rochester, Minn, in 1868, came to Cedar Falls and commenced his present business in 1875. Married Elsie West, Dec, 1872, she was born in 1853, in N Y, have one child—Louie, born Dec. 11, 1877.

Porter, E , farmer, Sec 34

Porter, John R., farmer, Sec. 34

Porter, Thomas, farmer, Sec. 34

Prouty, Joel, bridge builder

Prouty, O K , harness maker

Pruner, T , laborer

RABUCK, L , laborer.

Rakers, H , far., S. 35

Ramback, George, far., S 6

Ramsdell, L. J , omnibus driver

Rarrick, George, far , S 6

Rath, Felix, wagon manufactory

Raymond, A , retired

Raymond, E , far , S 8

Reed, I. M , far , S 5

Reed, J M , far , S 5

REED, T. C., farmer, Sec 5, born April 7, 1814, in Lycoming Co., Penn, Oct 8, 1841, came to Crawford Co, Ohio, April 1, 1857, removed to Cedar Falls, he owns 160 acres of land Married Mary J. Boyd June 29, 1843, she was born Jan. 25, 1822, in Shelby Co., Ky, had five children, three living —Luther T , Jane E. and James B Luther T enlisted in Co B, 31st I V. I , served three years, to the close of the war

Refshange, C , far , S. 14

Reinhart, C , laborer

Reimchusell, Charles, stone mason

Rice, Charles, laborer.

Rice, O B., grocery.

Richardson, J. R , laborer

Ripke, John, laborer

Ritter, Cris, laborer.

Robbins, T R , hardware

Robinson, W A , carpenter

Robinson, Wm , physician

Rodenbach, N , grocer

RODENBERGER, EDWIN, surveyor and civil engineer, resides cor. Ninth and Walnut sts, born Dec 31, 1837, in Lehigh Co, Penn. in 1844, came to Waukesha Co., Wis., in April, 1865, came to Cedar Falls; he has followed this business the past twenty years Married Miss Hannah Martin June 9, 1861, she was born March 27, 1838, in Montgomery Co, Penn.; had five children, two living—Eddie and Frank She is a member of the Evangelical Association. Mr. R. is County Surveyor

Roedhling, Frank, laborer.

Rohrabacher, A., surveyor.

Romhilt, G C , shoemaker.

Rownd, C H , far , S 24

Rownd, C. W , far , S. 24.

Rownd, J Q far , S 15

Rownd, Samuel H , far , S 24

Rownd, S H., Jr., far., S. 24.

Rownd, W. H , far , S. 24.

Rownd, W. M , stock dealer

Rownd, W. S , Sec. 24

Royce, J J., Deputy Sheriff

Ruby, H H , teamster

Rusehling, C , farmer, Sec 14

Ryan, Dan'l, laborer

SAGER, Jeff., ice dealer

Sartori, Anton, druggist.

Sartori, Joseph, farmer, Sec. 2

Savage, Dan'l, laborer.

Savage, E , farmer, Sec 2

Sawyer, F. R , gardener

Sawyer, Mons W , clerk

Schenck, Isaac, farmer, Sec 1

Schmidt, Jorgen, farmer, Sec 28

Seavy, Geo., gardener.

SEAVY, RUFUS, retired, born Aug 9, 1802, in Chester, N. H.. in 1847, came to Lawrence, Mass.; in 1855, came to Butler Co.; in 1866, removed to Cedar Falls; he owns 4½ acres with his residence in this city Married Betsey Smith November 16,

1835, she was born May 2, 1811, in Chester, N. H., had four children —Charles, enlisted in Co B, 31st Iowa Infantry, served about nine months, and died June 21, 1863, at Walnut Hill, Miss, the survivors are Meranda J (now Mrs Speer), Eunice F. (now Mrs Homer Hammond), and George Are members of the M E Church

Secor, A, carpenter

Selby, Chas, laborer

Sessions, Fitzroy, grain dealer

Sessions, W H, retired

Severin, F C., clothing.

SEVERIN, L. H., druggist, Main st, residence, corner Washington and Fourth sts, born Feb 2, 1842, in Germany, in 1853, came to Chicago, in 1855, removed to Elgin, Ill, and was five years apprenticed to the drug business In 1861, enlisted in Co A, 36th Illinois Infantry, served three years and three months, and was honorably discharged in 1865. Came to Cedar Falls and commenced his present business in 1867. Married Celia Zach in 1867, she was born in 1851 in Bridgeport, Conn, have two children—Mary and Celia Are members of the German Lutheran Church Has been four years a member of the City Council

Severin, Wm, grocer

SHAFER, AUGUSTUS, farmer, Sec 6, born Feb 24, 1828, in Penn, in 1834, came to Crawford Co, in 1849, came to De Kalb Co, Ill., in 1852, came to Rockford, Ill, and in 1854, removed to Cedar Falls. He owns 165 acres of land. Married Mary Hammen in 1853, she was born in 1832 in Westmoreland Co, Penn, had nine children, seven living—Emma C, Charles H., Elmer E., Simon W., Irene E, Burton A and Della A

Shaver, H C, printer

Sherburne, J. S, printer.

SHERWOOD, W. A., firm of W B Sherwood & Co, pottery on First street; born April 17, 1842, in Attica, N Y., the same year came with his parents to Whitewater, Wis, in 1858, came to Green Lake Co, Wis, in 1866, came to Eldora, Iowa, in 1867, removed to Cedar Falls Married Josephine Tolman in 1865, she was born April 10, 1846, in Worcester, Mass,

had three children, two living—Hattie and Nellie

Shequin, L., laborer

Shequin, L, Jr., laborer

Shields, Patrick, railroad.

SHOCKEY, C. C., restaurant and confectionery, Main street, born June 29, 1847, in Fountain Co, Ind., in 1856, removed to Iowa City, Iowa, in 1862, came to Danville, Ill, in 1866, returned to Iowa City, in 1867, came to West Liberty, the same year, to Brooklyn, Iowa, in 1868, came to Iowa Falls, and in the Fall removed to Cedar Falls, in 1870, came to Waterloo; in 1872, came to Parkersburg, Iowa, in 1873, came to Eldora, then to Osage, in the Spring of 1874, came to Cedar Falls Married Henrietta F Foss April 23, 1870, she was born Jan 31, 1853, in Janesville, Wis, have one child— Henry C, born June 24, 1876

Shoults, J C, farmer, Sec 31.

Shouse, C, proprietor Farmers' Home.

Showers, Wm, laborer

Shuller, Wm, tailor

Shulz, C C, farmer, Sec 32

Smallpage, S G, clerk

Smilcer, Wm, farmer, Sec 14

Smith, A. S., farmer, Sec 23.

SMITH, A. S., Mayor, and dealer in real estate, residence corner Third and Washington streets, born Aug 24, 1814, in Litchfield, Conn., in 1817, came with his parents to Bradford Co, Penn, in 1841, commenced the general merchandise business, and so continued till 1854, when he removed to New York City and engaged in the commission business for about two years, in 1856, removed to Cedar Falls Married Sarah M Baldwin Oct 10, 1841, she was born in 1819, in Connecticut, have four children—Robert S, Sarah A, Edward P and Ella S Mrs S is a member of the Presbyterian Church

Smith, D W, laborer

Smith, G F., far, S. 25

Smith, John, far, S 20

Smith, Jas, proprietor cheese factory

Smith, J E, clerk

Smith, J. W., clerk

Smith, Luther, laborer

Smith, Stephen, far., S 7

Snow, Geo A., prop Monitor House

Snyder, Charles, engineer

Snyder, C W , Postmaster

SNYDER, E. A., editor *Cedar Falls Gazette.*

Snyder, W C , clerk postoffice

Sondergaard, J., laborer

Sorrenson, C , saloon

Spaulding, A , bridge builder

Stark, E E , laborer.

Stam, C , tinner

Stanley, J H , jeweler

Stead, E M , carriage manufacturer

Stellar, Joseph, carpenter

Stewart, W. B., mail agent.

Stickney, W. H , Alderman

Stillter, D B , laborer.

Stitler, Samuel, laborer

Stitler, W C , carpenter

Stone, C , laborer

Stone, Joel, laborer

Stowe, G. M , speculator.

Strong, Frank, dyer

Sturtevant, I W , dentist.

Sulhvan, Patrick, section boss

Sweet, John, teamster

TAUBMAN, W P , farmer, Sec 15

Taylor, George W., laborer

Taylor, L , bar tender

Thomas, P H , farmer, Sec. 3

Thomas, W H , farmer, Sec 7.

THOMPSON, A. G., firm of Thompson & Co , hardware, Main st. , residence cor Clay and Sixth sts ; born Jan 9, 1831, in Cortland Co , N Y , in 1847, came to Tompkins Co , N. Y., in 1852, removed to New York City , in 1856, came to Chicago, and in the Fall of 1857, returned to New York City , remained there till July, 1862, then returned to Chicago, and in January, 1863, 1863, came to Cedar Falls Married Harriet Huntington June, 1867, she was born in 1840, in Oswego Co , N Y , had four children, three living—Mary H , Bertha May and Harry E Members of the Congregational Church Has been School Director.

Thompson, A J , druggist.

THOMPSON, JOSIAH, firm of Thompson & Co., hardware, Main st ; resides cor Seventh and Washington sts , born Jan. 5, 1829, in Livingston Co , N Y , in 1853, came to Chicago, and in 1863, removed to Cedar Falls and commenced their present business Married Clara Lathrop January, 1856 , she

was born in Massachusetts in 1830 ' have six children—Alice L , Jennie F ' Edwin, Annie, Maud and Madge Alice and Jennie are members of the Presbyterian Church He is a Trustee of the same church Has been Town Trustee and member of the City Council

Thorpe, B., Jr., merchant.

Thorpe, G. H , attorney.

TILLER, H. D., firm of Tiller Bros., blacksmiths, Washington st. ; born June 13, 1845, in Mercer Co , Va. , in 1869, came to Tama Co , Iowa , in 1874, came to Cedar Falls Married Elizabeth Whitteker July 18, 1865 , she was born Jan 14, 1846, in Giles Co , Va , have three children — John A , Thomas J and Nellie V

Tiller, T. J , blacksmith

Tollerton, J J , attorney.

TONDRO, C. H., soap manufactory , born April 27, 1851, in Boone Co , Wis , in 1859, came to Cedar Falls. His father and brother-in-law established this business in 1869 Married Emma Stowell April 27, 1873, she was born in May, 1857, in Manchester, Iowa , have two children—Maud, born May 9, 1875, and Lena, born April 7, 1876 Are members of the Baptist Church.

Torry, A C , cattle dealer.

Townsend, E , grain.

Tucker, George, paper and old iron

VAIL, A T , grocer.

Vanderlip, L. P , retired.

VANDER VAART, S., DR., office in Wise & Bryant's drug store, resides corner Main and Twelfth streets , born Aug 13, 1820, in Holland, in 1861, he came to Milwaukee In 1862, he enlisted in the 26th Wis V I as First Asst Surgeon, and in 1864 was promoted to the Surgeoncy of the same regiment , remained till the close of the war, and was honorably discharged in 1865. Returned to Europe, and came back the same year and settled in Cedar Falls Married Catharine Van Nierop in 1849, in Holland, she was born in Sept., 1832, in Holland, they had six children, five living— Henry W , Simon, Catharine, Cornelius and Sarah Members of the Congregational Church Has been a member of the School Board.

Van Devun, H R , clerk
Van Haser, propr Commercial Hotel
VAN METER I., editor *Record*
Van Norden J J , clerk
Van Saun, G. B , grain
WAGONER, C , laborer.

Wallace, J G , manuf of mattresses
WALLACE, W. W., music dealer and speculator, Main street , was born in St Joseph Co , Mich., in 1832 Married Lovila C Parshal, in 1860 , she was born in Wyoming Co , N Y , in 1842 Came to this county in 1864, settling in Cedar Falls, where he engaged in the livery business, following the same until 1874, when he opened his present music store. Owns farm in Mt Vernon Township of 120 acres in Sec 26, valued at $4,000 They have one child—Indie

Walters, H , farmer, Sec 30
Ward, Warner, laborer
Warner, Joseph laborer
Warren, L W , physician
Waugh, J. H , clerk.
Weisbard, F , carpenter.
West J W , laborer.
WETLANFER, C. W., farmer, Sec 30, born April 1, 1854, in Indiana , in 1874, came to Iowa , works his father-in-law's farm, consisting of 260 acres of land He was married to Elizabeth Martin March 4, 1875 , she was born in 1853, in Wisconsin ; her father, John Martin, was born Feb 14, 1811, in Brandywine Co , Del , in 1814, came to Philadelphia, in 1837, came to Wisconsin , in 1866, came to Cedar Falls Tp. He married Mary M. Liston in 1834 , she was born in 1815, in Pennsylvania , had nine children, seven living — Mary A , Hannah, Louisa, James, Henry, Emma and Elizabeth Are members of the Evangelical Church

Wheeler, H N , laborer
Whitbeck, P , laborer
White, B. F , grain
White, F. O., clerk.
Whitlock, I H., life ins agt
Whitney, Wm , far., S 30
WILLIAMS, DEWITT C., Cedar Falls Nursery, born in Boston, Erie Co , N Y , March 21, 1827 , removed to Chantauqua Co , N Y. in 1835, lived there until 1848, when he removed to Winneba-go Co , Ill , resided in that county three years, then removed to Freeport, Stephenson Co., Ill , where he lived until May, 1861, when he came to Cedar Falls Mr. Williams had been engaged in the nursery business for ten years , previously for eighteen years, he was engaged in the photograph business He married Sarah M. Foye March 23 1869 , she was born in Cattarangus Co , N Y, Mr Williams has, by former marriage, one son—Frank R Mr and Mrs. Williams are members of the First Presbyterian Church of Cedar Rapids

WILLIAMS, D. C & CO., dealers in all kinds of Northern hardy fruit trees—crab apples a specialty, twenty-five kinds of crab apples growing in their nursery, they range in size from the Hyslop to the the Duchesse, or Gross Pomier, twelve Minnesota varieties, all perfectly hardy, ripening in every month of the year, some of the leading crabs are Daomie, Minnesota, Soulard. Gen Grant and Hesper Blush , all of those are as large as common apples The Russian crab is the largest of the Russian family , it will stand fifty to sixty degrees of cold—ripe in July, choice eating and cooking, subacid, good for drying, early and profuse bearer. Pembina crab as large as Gross Pomier , originated in Pembina, British America, cross between Transcendent and Duchess of Oldenberg ; large as the Duchess splashed with red , subacid, and ripe in August and September Pomona Crab is a remarkable Hybrid, a cross between Tetofsky and Pom Royal, an annual and abundant bearer, fruit large, cheese-like in shape, and dark red and hardy as an oak Farmer Crab is a seedling from Hyslop, cross between the Hyslop and Ben Davis, the best winter apple known of crab variety, size of Fameuse The following is a list of some of the delicious crab apples and Hybrid apples or crosses between the crab and apple They ripen in the following order . 1st, Early Strawberry, last of June , 2d, Early Russia, July 15 , 3d, Tetofsky ; 4th, Hesper Blush, September This apple is four times as large as Transcendent, and is a choice eating apple , 5th, Orange Yellow, October to February , fine for cooking, eating and preserves, 6th, Gen Grant, large as Fameuse, a good keeper, and a choice eating apple, will keep until March, 7th, Minnesota, the very best of the winter varieties, for all purposes, January to April, large as E. G Russet, 8th, Daomie. This remarkable crab is a cross between the Hyslop and Yellow Bell Flower, measures twelve inches in circumference, and is as fine a grower and good a keeper as the Yellow Bell Flower; this is the largest and most beautiful crab apple in the world. Quaker Beauty and Soulard are the longest keepers of all the crabs, the Quaker Beauty is fine for cooking and eating, and is very desirable on account of its long-keeping quality, the Soulard is equal to the quince for preserves, every man should have one or more of each of the varieties mentioned, no finer stock can be found to select from than that kept by Mr Williams He deals extensively in other fruit trees, but he is giving his attention largely to bringing before the people the most choice varieties of crab apples It is impossible to give here a complete description of his extensive stock, but the citizens of Iowa would do well to examine the desirable fruit trees, which will be found in this nursery All orders will be filled promptly, correspondence solicited

Wild, Daniel, far., S 16.
Wiler, D., far, S 4
Wiler, H J., far, S 14
Wiler, Noah, far, S 14
Wiler, W F, far, S 14.
Wilhard, Daniel, stone mason.
Williams, D. C, gardener

Williams, W T, merchant
Willie, J W., laborer
Willis, James, laborer
Wilson, G M, far, S 8.
Wilson, James H, wool mills
Wilson, Joseph H, retired
Wilson, M, far, S 8
Wilson, Shephard, dry goods
Winkoop, C, Novelty Works
Winkoop, F G, Novelty Works
Wise, C A, druggist
Wood, O B., mason.
WOOD, SAMUEL H., farmer, Sec 1, also dealer in butter and eggs; born Feb 12, 1856, in Rockford, Ill, 1865, came to Cedar Falls, and removed to his present farm in 1878, owns 100 acres, valued at $30 per acre Married Ellen D Jones Jan 1, 1878, she was born Dec 7, 1858, in Wisconsin His father died in Rockford, Ill, his mother now lives in Cedar Falls
Wood, Wm, far, S 6
Wylde, Thomas, laborer
WYTH, JOHN, merchant tailor and gents' furnishing, Main st., born Dec, 1833, in Dublin, Ireland, in 1861, came to New York City, the same year, came to Cedar Falls Married Anna Bacon Jan. 24, 1864, she was born in 1840, in London, Eng, her cousin, John George Bacon, is Vice-Chancellor of England, they have seven children— Katie, Mathew, Rosanna Margaret, Mary E, George J, Thomas H. and Francis Joseph Is a Republican.
YOCKSTICK, ADAM, farmer

Young, J W, physician
ZEISING, J. F., life ins agt

BIG CREEK TOWNSHIP.
(P O LA PORTE CITY)

ABBOTT, W H , farmer

Adams, J. C. liveryman.
Allen, Smiley, blacksmith.
Amburn, Amos, carpenter.
Anthony, C W , minister
Armstrong, S E , farmer, Sec 21

BAHR, BENJ , farmer, Sec 12

BALLHEIM, JACOB, farmer, Sec. 30, born in Washington Co , Wis , in 1845 Married Eva Fisher in 1868, she was born in Germany in 1845, they have two children—Lizzie and Annie Came to this county in March, 1871, and settled on his present place consisting of eighty acres, valued at $50 per acre Enlisted in Co A, 51st Wisconsin Infantry, in 1865, and served six months, when he was honorably discharged

Bahr, Levi, farmer, Sec 12
Baldwin, J C.. farmer, Sec. 25.
Ballou. Frank, harness maker.
Banman, James C , carpenter
Barnes, B. F , mason
Barnes, Ezra, farmer, Sec 33.
Beedenbender, H , farmer, Sec 30
Belenger, F., farmer, Sec 9
Belzer, L , Sr , farmer, Sec 34.
Benorton, R , farmer, Sec 9
Benson, I , farmer, Sec. 6

BEREND, PETER, merchant tailor, Main street, was born in Germany May 11, 1840, emigrated to this country Dec 18, 1865, first settling in Wood Co , Ohio, and came to this county March 18, 1869, settling in Waterloo, and working at his trade He married Catherine Tont in April, 1866, she was born in Germany Sept 18, 1848. Came and opened his present business in this city Feb 22, 1878, owns farm of eighty acres in Cedar Tp , where his family reside. Nettie, Nicholas, Phrona and Ann are his children

BERRY, DANIEL, farmer, Sec. 30; born in Canada East in 1827, and emigrated to Stephenson Co , Ill , in 1847, where he married Adaline Allard in 1850, she was born in the same place in 1833 George F, Wm H and Cora A. are their children Mr. B

was one of the earliest settlers in Stephenson Co , where, by his industry and earnest perseverance, he has gained his present position in life The estate he now occupies, and upon which he settled, and purchased in April 1870, consists of 1,300 acres of land, valued at $50,000

BISHOP, CHARLES A., attorney, Main st , born in Waukesha Co , Wis , in 1853 Married Mary D Dow in Nov , 1873, she was born in the same county in 1856 , have one child— Alvord L Commenced his studies with Bingham & Weed, at Palmyra, with whom he remained until 1873, when he moved to New London, Waupaca Co , Wis , where he first opened his office, and where he continued until 1875, when he came to this county, and occupied his present place Was elected Mayor in the Spring of 1877, and filled that office one term , upon retiring from that position, was elected City Attorney, and still holds that office

BISHOP, GEORGE S., attorney at law, born in Livingston Co , N Y , May 9 1850 Married Mariah Seaman May 13. 1877 , she was born in Grant Co., Ind , June 11, 1855 Graduated at the Iowa State University at Iowa City, and was admitted to the bar June 25, 1872 Came to this county with his parents in April, 1856, where he has since made his home

Bitterly, S , farmer, S 8

BOYNTON, F. S., druggist , born in Worcester Co , Mass., Oct 19, 1824 , settled with his parents in Essex Co , N Y , in 1832 , emigrated to Francis Co Mo , in 1849 , returned to Troy, N Y , in 1853, and moved to Poweshiek Co , Iowa, in 1856, and settled in this city in 1866, where he opened business in the Fall of that year Married Mariah Tomlinson July 6, 1848 , they have three children—Lettie L , Florence M and Mary M , lost one child In 1863, he enlisted in 44th Iowa V I., Company E, and served about six months

Bradfield, W R., farmer, S 20
Brainard, S P , attorney.

BRAVINDER, ALBERT, farmer, Sec 27, born in Roxhan, C. E, in 1841. Married Lucy Lyon in 1875, she was born in Clayton Co., Iowa, in 1844, have one child—Winfield Came to this county with his parents July 4, 1855, and settled on his present estate of 240 acres, valued at $40 per acre Is one of the early settlers Has held the offices of Assessor and Road Supervisor, and is well known

Brown, F S, farmer, Sec 16
Brown, Joseph L, insurance agent
Brown, Thomas, farmer, Sec 15
Brown, T H., farmer, Sec 7
Bruce, B F, farmer, Sec 1
Buchan, W H, merchant
Bunton, Thos., far. and prop of hotel.
Burnham, F F. agricultural implements
Butler, W H., Principal high school

CALEY, R V S, dealer in stock.

Camp, Asa, farmer, Sec 19
Carney, John, farmer. Sec 10

CHADWICK, DAVID, farmer, Sec 33, born in Berkshire Co, Mass, May 28, 1815. Married Clarinda L Judd June 18 1843, she was born in Trumbull Co, Ohio, March 14, 1824; have six children—John J, Annie J, Lola L, Gilbert L, Jason D and Merrit M. Came to this State and settled in Bremer Co in 1852, settled on his present farm in 1875, consisting of 110 acres, valued at $30 per acre

Champlin, Hiram, farmer, Sec 3

CHAPIN B. A., firm of Bangor & Chapin, dealers in boots and shoes, born in Ashtabula Co, Ohio, Nov 25, 1852, came to this county with his parents in May, 1854 Married Fannie Simmons Jan 4, 1877, she was born near Cleveland, Ohio, Feb 9, 1859 Entered the copartnership Feb 6, 1876

Chapple, H, farmer, Sec 10
Chapple, Wm, expressman
Clinton, B, farmer, Sec 18

CLARK & SUSONG, meat market, the senior of this firm, Wm Clark, was born in Lower Canada, in 1845, and came to this county with his parents in 1856. The junior partner, Henry Sussong, was born in Wyoming Co, N. Y., in 1842, came to Washington Co., Wis., in 1847, with his parents, and to this county April 3, 1863. Dec.

3, 1863, enlisted in Co. D, 32d I V I, and was honorably discharged in June, 1866. Married Mina Young Nov 14, 1866, in Washington Co., Wis, where she was born Sept 20, 1846, their children are Charles and Eddy. Opened their place of business in this village in March, 1875

Clark, Edward W., dentist
Clark, W B, Sr, butcher

COGGINS, H., editor, local.

Colvin, Alvah, farmer, Sec 29
Cooper, H W, farmer, Sec. 35.

COOPER, S. P., farmer, Sec. 35, born in Cuyahoga Co., Ohio, in 1819 Married Lucy E Bonnelle in 1843, she was born in same county in 1823, they emigrated to this county in June, 1854, and settled on his present estate consisting of 240 acres, valued at $40 per acre; was one of the earliest settlers in this town and has experienced all the hardships of pioneer life Has two children—Ward, and Wirt, who married Effie Moon in 1875, she was born in Kane Co, Ill, in 1853, and has one child—Ray Mr. Cooper lost one son, who enlisted in Co D, 31st I V I, and died of disease contracted at Memphis, Tenn, after a service of eight months Has been Justice of the Peace and Assessor, and is well known throughout the town and county.

Cooper, Wirt, farmer, Sec 35
Corkins, C, farmer, Sec 13
Cotton, Allen, hotel proprieter.

COUNTRYMAN, JOHN, farmer, Sec 33, born in Montgomery Co., N Y., in 1807, and married Ellen Christman in 1828, she was born in Herkimer Co, N Y., in 1807, they have seven children living—Nicholas, Henry, Nancy, Isaac, Martha, Sallie and Adelia, lost seven children Came to this county in October, 1867, and settled on his present estate of eighty acres, valued at $30 per acre. Are members of the Evangelical Church.

Cotton, Noah, carpenter
Crowell, Wilbur, carpenter

DARLING, J B., physician.
Day, A. N., carpenter

Deeds, M, carpenter
Depew, M S, millinery merchant
Dodson, Jesse, proprietor La Porte House.
Dolph, E., farmer, Sec 12.

EDWARDS, THOMAS, far, Sec 21

EBERHART, J. S., dealer in hardware, Main street, was born in Fayette Co, Penn., in February, 1841, with parents moved to Rock Island Co, Ill, and to Waterloo, Iowa, in September, 1857. Married Ella Payne Dec 24, 1872; she was born in Ashtabula Co., Ohio, Feb 14, 1849 Enlisted in Co A, 20th I V I, July 24, 1862, was honorably discharged Aug 4, 1865; came to this city, commencing his present business in 1867

ELWELL, J. H., proprietor of the La Porte City Flouring Mill, born in Knox Co., Ohio, Nov 6, 1813 Married Sarah Reed in Union Co, Ohio, in 1847, she was born in the same county Sept. 6, 1823, and after his marriage, engaged in milling at Millford Center for eight years. Came to this county in 1854, and settled in Waterloo, where he engaged in the mercantile business and milling, and in 1863 went to California, returning in 1864, and engaged in business at Waterloo, also purchased his present property the same year, and commenced operations in the mill in 1866. Martha, Ida and Albert are his children

Emmert, David, farmer, Sec 32

Emmert, Sol, farmer, Sec. 32

EVARTS, A. M., physician and surgeon; born in Crittenden Co, Vt, Oct 2, 1843. Married Alice Haddock June 1, 1873; she was born in Waterloo, this county, Aug 11, 1852, graduated at the Louisville Medical School, Louisville, Ky., March 31, 1871; first commenced to practice April 3, 1871. Gracie B, born Nov 6, 1877, is their only child

FEATHERLY, DAVID, contractor

FEGLES, GEORGE W., farmer, Sec. 22, born in Lycoming Co, Penn, in 1820 Married Hannah Edwards in 1851, she was born in the same county in 1831, have four children—Caroline, William, Sylvester and Phœbe, lost one child, which died in infancy, came to this county in September, 1867, and settled on his present farm of 175 acres, valued at $40 per acre Are members of the Evangelical Church.

Fegles, W, far, S 12

Felton, P, speculator

Fisher, J H, carpenter

Foss, B V, far, S 10

Fox, E K, far, S 16

FOX, WILLIAM L., retired landlord, was born in Columbia Co, Penn., Feb 15, 1827 Married Sarah Watts Feb 1, 1845, who was born in the same county Nov 30, 1825, and died Nov 7, 1873, have six children living—Cathran, Syros, Christiana, Mary, John and Jessie Emigrated and settled where this city now stands June 18, 1855, and is one of the pioneers of the township Has held the office of Postmaster four years, and has been prominently identified in the county since he settled here

Fritzsinger, F M., boots and shoes.

Fry, Martin, far, S 14

Fuller, J T, market.

GANNON, JAMES, railroad conductor

Gates, H F, far, S 11

Gill, John, far, S 10

Gohlkie, Wm., merchant

Good, C, far, S 29

Green, John, Chief Engineer.

HAHN, JOHN, harness maker.

Hamilton, W W, far, S 4

HANGER, JOHN S., farmer, Sec 33, born in Somerset Co, Penn, in 1815, and married Harriet Lentin in 1843, she was born in the same county in 1823, have eight children living—Sarah A., Daniel C, Noah, Hiram, Elvira, John W, Michael and William, have lost four children—Siras, Mary J, Lydia and Anna Came to this county in 1866, and settled in Waterloo, where he resided two years, when he moved on his present estate of 400 acres, valued at $30 per acre Is Elder of the Evangelical Church, having filled that position for thirteen years past

Hansel, Geo C, blacksmith

HARMON, WILLIAM, farmer, Sec 30, born in Indiana in 1813 Married Hannah F Thompson in 1832, she was born in Virginia in 1816, and died in 1866. He married Elizabeth Rice in 1868, she was born in Ohio in 1825 Has thirteen children by his first wife—Mary J, James C, William N, Nancy A Richard

4

E., who enlisted in Co E, 32d I. V.
I , and died at Vicksburg, Martha,
Charles, Hiram M , David N , George
W , Sarah E , Hannah P , Albert T ,
lost one child—Elizabeth   Came to this
county in 1856, and settled in Spring
Creek, and in 1855, settled on his present
estate of 155 acres, valued at $60 per
acre

Harvey S , Justice of the Peace.
Hawfas, Frederick, farmer, S 20.
Hayday, O M , farmer, Sec 24.

HEATH, RODOLPHUS, C.,
nurseryman, Sec 26, born in Caledonia
Co , Vt , in 1820   Married Margaret
Allred in 1848 , she was born in Wayne
Co , Ind , in 1840, and died leaving eight children—Emma J , Betty,
Sarah, H   Courtney, Alice J Lea-
vette, and Rodolphus C , Jr., they
have lost two children—Eva and
Gertie E   His present wife, Pris-
cilla A Gee, was born in Delaware
Co , N. Y , in 1835; they were married
in the Summer of 1877 , they have two
children—Maud and Bunn R   Came
to this county in March, 1865, and
settled on his present estate, consisting
of 150 acres, valued at $65 per acre
Are members of the Presbyterian
Church   Held the office of Trustee
two years.

Helm, W R., speculator
Hill, William, bakery
Hock, Martin, farmer

HOFMASTER, A., farmer, Sec
33, born in Prussia in 1842 , emigrated
to this country in 1847, settled in
Stephenson Co , Ill , where he remained
until 1868, when he removed to Ackley,
and resided one year, and moved to
Waverly the same year   Married
Emma Anthony in 1868 , she was born
in Pennsylvania in 1849, they have
four children—Frank E., Jennie A ,
Freddie J and Annie N   From
Waverly he moved to Cerro Gordo Co ,
and in the Fall of 1877 , he came to this
county and settled on his present farm
of eighty acres, valued at $35 per acre.

Horning, James, boot and shoemaker

HUDSON, FREDERICK, far ,
Sec 33, born in London, England, in
1826   Married Catharine Bahr in
1848 , she was born in France in 1828 ,
they have five children—Charles H ,

Albert A., Frederick W , Lydia A. and
Katie J   Emigrated in 1836 with his
father, and settled in New York City,
where he lived until 1836, when he
moved to Jefferson Co , N Y , and in
1849, came West and settled in Brown
Co , Wis , in 1864, he came to this
county and settled in this township,
and on the farm he now occupies in
1875   He owns eighty acres of land
on Sec 28   Members of the Evangelical Church

Hummell, Charles, farmer, S. 21.
Hummell, D J , farmer, S 30
Hungerford, A S , banker
Hunter, Richard, shoemaker.
Hussman, Joseph, farmer, S 16

IGO, JACOB, farmer, Sec. 6

Igo, J H , farmer, S. 13.
Ingersoll, C T , banker, retired

JAMES, ISAAC, people's drug
store , was born in Marshall Co., Ill ,
Sept. 18, 1850   Married Esther Goodrich, of Linn Co , Iowa, May 27, 1874;
born in Vergennes, Vt , Jan 22, 1854 ,
was engaged as drug clerk at the age of 15
years , emigrated to this city June 1,
1872 , commenced his present business
in October, 1873   Eva A , born March
13, 1875, is their only child

KELLER, ADAM, barber

Kennedy, N R , farmer, S 29
Kennedy, Robert, farmer, S 28
Kennicott, Asa, farmer, Sec. 22.
Kennicott, A. J., far , S 31
Kennicott, James, Pound Master.

KENNICOTT, LEVI, retired far ,
born in Montgomery Co , N Y , Jan.
16, 1804 , moved to Cattaraugus Co , N
Y , in 1819   Was married in Canada,
to Abbie Hayes Sept 14, 1828, she was
born in Storman Co , Canada, Nov 22,
1812 , have three children living—Asa
J., Mary J and Esther   Emigrated to
Kenosha Co , Wis., in 1831, and in 1833,
moved to Chicago, and June 16, 1854,
settled in this township, which he has
since made his home.

Kettering, A., far , S. 9
Kettering, Conrad, far , S. 31.

KING, ANDREW J., farmer, S
32, born in Indiana Oct 4, 1834.
Married Olesa A Nolen in 1857 , she
was born in Greene Co , Ind , in 1838 ;

have one child Orren Came to this State in 1852, and settled in Benton Co, and in 1868, came to this county and settled on his farm, consisting of twenty-four acres of land, valued at $850

King, John, far., S 32

Kline, A , far , S. 30

Kline, A E , far., S 11

Kline, Elisha, far , S 10

Kline, W L , far , S 13

Klingaman, J G , lumber merchant

KNOWLES, GEORGE A., farmer, Sec. 35 , born in Hillsboro Co , N H , in 1811, and married Sarah A. Meador in 1836 ; she was born in Newbury, Vt , in 1815 ; have seven living children—Wilbur F , Nancy A , George W , Byron L B , Woodbury A , Emma D and Ada May Came to this county in the Spring of 1854, and settled on Sec. 27, and is one of the earliest settlers in the town, there being but four permanent settlers at that time Dubuque and Muscatine were his nearest markets He has experienced all the hardships of pioneer life , many anecdotes of his early life are interesting Was Justice of the Peace one term, and has been identified with the interests of the town and county Owns 200 acres of land, valued at $60 per acre, and has one of the finest orchards on his place in the county

KREBS, MARTIN, farmer, Sec. 28, born in Wyoming Co, N Y., in 1837 Married Mary C. Reichart in 1861 , she was born in Prussia in 1838 , have eight children—Mary E , George J , Ida May, Emma, Ellen, Mary, Frank R and Gertie J , lost one child—Susan. Came to this county in 1861, and settled on his present estate of forty acres, valued at $40 per acre

LANE, R M , Merchant

Leech, J R., far , S 23

Lesher, J L , far , S 26

Ludlow, George, far , S 24.

Ludlow, W H D., jeweler.

Luneman, H , blacksmith

McFAYDEN, JOHN C., wagon maker

McGrow, John, far , S 27

McKirryher, H , far , S. 26

McQuilkin, R J , far , S. 6

Mayes, Thomas, farmer, Sec 27.

Meeker, Columbus, farmer, Sec 11,

Miles, Oscar farmer, Sec 25

Mitchell, H J , farmer, Sec 29

Moon, O B , retired farmer, Sec 9.

Moore, A Y , farmer, Sec 29

Moore, J E , farmer, Sec 35

Motts, G , farmer, Sec 7.

MOULTON, FREEMAN, farmer, Sec 35 , born in Canada in 1807 Married Louisa Ballard, widow of Erastus Burnham, who was born in Orange Co , Vt., in 1829, was married in 1851, and he died in 1869, they had three children—Leslie A , Silas E and Marcus W Mr Burnham enlisted in Co D, 24th I. V I , Feb. 29, 1862, and served three years, and died from disease contracted from service to his country In August, 1871, she married Freeman Moulton, and first settled in Tama Co. in 1851, where they remained until 1856, when they came to this county and settled on their present estate, valued at $45 per acre Are members of the Free-Will Baptist Church

Mullen, John, farmer, Sec 20.

NICHOLS, JOS H , gardener and mason

NEWTON, MARTIN L., dealer in drugs and medicines, toilet and fancy goods, etc , Main st , born in Freeport, Stephenson Co , Ill , May 27, 1851 Married Sophia Barry Oct 25, 1876 , she was born in Freeport, Stephenson Co , Ill., May 26, 1852 Mr N is the oldest son of Seth Newton, who was born in Canada East Aug 29, 1822, and married Anna M Berry Feb 19, 1848 , she was born near Freeport, Stephenson Co , Ill , Feb 19, 1832, and now resides in Marshall Co , Iowa The subject of this sketch graduated at Ann Arbor, Mich , as civil engineer, June 30, 1875 , came to La Porte City, this county, and was Principal of the High School April 10, 1876 , commenced his present business March 20, 1877

NICHOLS, GEORGE, farmer, Sec 27, born in England in 1803, and married Mary Perfect in 1827 , she was born in England in 1806, have five children living—Eliza, John, William, Joseph and Mary A , lost three children—Mariah, Thomas and George, who died while crossing the sea Emigrated to this country in 1832, and first settled at Rouse's Point, N Y, and after a short residence moved to Perrysville, where he resided until 1856, when he came West and settled on his present farm of sixty acres, valued at $2,500.

Norton, James, grain buyer

OLDS, HARVEY, farmer, Sec 36

Oren, Jesse, farmer, Sec 34
Osborn, John, farmer, Sec 5

PALM, A, stone mason

Parks, Hiram, farmer, Sec 32
Peck, Charles, farmer, Sec 8
Phillips, O. A, farmer, Sec 12

PIERCE, A. G.. Cashier of City Exchange Bank, was born in Nantucket Island, Mass, March 10, 1851; came to this city with parents in 1855, where he married Myrtie Bogart Aug 10, 1876, she was born in Steuben Co, N Y., Aug. 17, 1858; commenced in the bank as clerk, and from that position has risen to Cashier. Gilbert, born May 4, 1877, and died Aug. 27, 1877, are the birth and death of their child

Pray, R J, carpenter.

PREBLE, HARRY J., dealer in groceries and confectionery of all kinds on Main street, was born in Maine, Sept. 27, 1835 Married Emma J. Heath June 1, 1867, he with parents came to Lowell Mass, in 1841, and to Cleveland, Ohio, in 1850, emigrated to LaSalle Co, Ill, in 1856, and to this county in 1859 Enlisted in the 3d Iowa Battery on Sept. 26, 1861, serving four years and two months Commenced business in this city in 1868 Gertrude H, Maggie E, Charles H and Edgar C are their children

QUACKENBUSH, E., far, Sec. 25.

RAVLIN, C. W, agriculturist

Reese, John, farmer, Sec 29
Rice, J C., farmer, Sec 19
Rodman, J F, farmer, Sec. 31.
Rolph, Wm, farmer, Sec. 32.
Rolph, Wm, farmer, Sec. 18.

SALMONS, JOHN, farmer, Sec 33

Sanders, J A, farmer, Sec 21
Sanders, M D, carpenter

Schirer, J T., farmer, Sec. 16.
Schneider, Jacob, carpenter.
Sheffler, Henry, farmer, Sec. 30.
Shirer, John F, farmer, Sec. 22
Shubert, B, coal
Shuck, Nicholas, farmer, Sec 21.
Sigg, B, brewery.
Smelser, Henry, retired.
Smiley, C E, liveryman and blacksmith.
Smith, T J., farmer, Sec 32
Smith, Wm, farmer, Sec 34
Spicer, L D, carpenter.
Stahnke, H, farmer, Sec 19
Stancer, W, farmer, Sec. 34.
Stanton, B. S, hardware.

STEBBINS, JOHN R., Postmaster, was born in Medina Co, Ohio, June 2, 1821 Married Sarah A. Beal June 21, 1853, she was born in New York, June 31, 1823 Mr Stebbens held the office of County Auditor in his native county for sixteen consecutive years. Came to this county, settling in La Porte City April 20, 1870, and appointed Postmaster in the Spring of 1874 Mrs Clara E. Eberhart, Henry E, William A. and George E. are his living children, William H, deceased

STEDMAN, ELIHU H., proprietor National Hotel, born in Meigs Co, Ohio, Dec. 16, 1813, to which county his father—Eli—emigrated from Vermont in the Winter of 1803-4, and traveling to Pittsburgh in sleighs, remaining at this point until the river opened. This small colony secured flatboats, and floated down the Ohio to Point Harmer, from which place they proceeded to Woolf Creek, where they erected the first mill that was ever built in that section of the country. Purchased their land of the Ohio Land Purchasing Company in 1806, his father died in this county in May, 1846 The subject of this sketch married Adeline Elliott May 20, 1837, she was born in Meigs Co, Ohio, March 8, 1819, and died Sept 18, 1854, at which time they were making preparations for their journey to this State In that year, he settled in Cedar Rapids, where he resided until 1865 Eli M, Mary C, Dudley E., Elbert P and Addie are their children His present wife, Sarah J Powell, was born in Washington Co, Ohio, June 27, 1830, and they were married

April 24, 1855, by this marriage, they have three children—Alice, Jennie and Charlie Settled in this village in 1877, he has since made it his home. Has been prominently identified with the interests of the town and county where he resided Served one year in the rebellion as First Lieutenant in Company A, 37th Iowa V. I, and was honorably discharged

Stone, H, mason

STRONG, O., dealer in groceries, Main st, was born in Madison Co, N Y, April 5, 1823 Married Olivia Ellis, she was born in Genesee Co, N Y He moved to Livingston Co, N. Y., and to De Kalb Co., Ill, and to this county in June, 1872, when he commenced his present business Mrs Mary Jarvis and William C are their children

Susong, J D, mason.

Suter, A. L, barber

Scrogges, C B., retired farmer

SOLOMON, CHRISTOPHER, farmer, Sec 19, born in England in 1833, and emigrated to America in 1865, first settling in Michigan, where he resided until 1866, when he came to this county, where he has since made it his home, owns farm of eighty acres of land valued at $1,600, lives in the enjoyment of a bachelor.

TERRY, J R, farmer, Sec 31.

TAYLOR, NELSON, of the firm of Stanton & Taylor, dealers in hardware, Main st.; was born in New Market, York Co, Canada, May 1, 1834, emigrated to Cedar Co, Iowa, in March, 1855, and to Benton Co in the Fall of 1856, settling five miles from La Porte City Married Ann Buchan Oct 26, 1858, she was born in Scotland July 1, 1834. Commenced his present business with Mr Stanton March 1, 1876. William F, born Nov 21, 1864, and Greta, born April 30, 1870, are his children

Thompson, F M, carpenter

TRAST, PETER, harness manufacturer, Main st, was born in Mertan, Germany Jan 18, 1844, came to this country in 1856, settling in Peru, La Salle Co, Ill., and came to this county in January, 1867, settling in Waterloo, where he married Anna Flersner Dec

23, 1867, she was born in Germany Came to this city and commenced his present business May 16, 1872, owns a farm in Cedar Township of 204 acres, on which his family reside Enlisted in Co K. 146th I V I, serving one year, and honorably discharged. Mary A, Josephine, Anna and Elizabeth are his children

TRIEM, HENRY H., farmer, Sec 29, born in Stark Co, Ohio, in 1848 Married Martha Ferry in 1871, she was born in Benton Co., Iowa, in 1857, have one child—Archy E, came to this county in March, 1870, and settled in this township, and in September, 1875, settled on his present estate, consisting of eighty acres, valued at $20 per acre

Triem, L L, far, Sec. 35

Turner, H, far, Sec 31,

URBAN, GEORGE, farmer, Sec 22

VANSCHRAIK, PETER, physician

Volland, John, far, Sec. 22.

Volland, Michael, far, Sec 30

WAGGONER, JACOB, retired farmer

WAGNER, JOHN F., lumber merchant, born in Herkimer Co, N Y., July 23, 1838, where he married Delila Wagoner, who died in 1871, had one child—Frank J His present wife, Eva A Casler, was born in same county in 1853, they were married March 12, 1873, came to this county in 1873 First engaged in dry goods business, selling out to his partner, George Waltz, in 1877, and began his present business Feb 15, 1878 Is also an architect, which profession he carries on in connection with his present business

Wagner, Simon, far, Sec 21.

Wagner, Robert, far, S 21.

WAGNER, ROBERT, farmer, Sec. 19, born in Snyder Co, Penn, in 1834, and emigrated to this county in 1856, and settled near Waterloo, where he married Flora Turner in 1857, she was born in Lycoming Co., Penn, in 1833 Settled on his present farm in 1865, consisting of 110 acres, valued at $40 per acre Are members of the Methodist Church Are numbered among the early settlers of this town and county

WAGNER, W. D., dealer in dry goods, boots, shoes and ready-made clothing, Main st, born in Jefferson Co., N Y, June 17, 1843. Married Mary C Wagoner Jan 8, 1868, she was born in the same county March 1, 1850, have one child—Maud L. Came to this county Nov 8, 1873, and opened his place of business in April, 1877

Wagner, Wm, lumberman

Walker, J. S., far, S 14

Walker, Sanders, far, S 1

WALKER, W. A., Mayor and Justice of the Peace, office Main st, was born in Owen Co, Ind, Jan 25, 1830 Married in Morgan Co, Ind, Sarah J Hogshire Oct 3, 1853, she was born in 1832 in Marion Co, Ind, and died Aug. 10, 1867 They came to this county Oct 20, 1853, and he is one of the old pioneer settlers and business men of this county Columbus, Alonzo, Arminta, Alice A and William R are their children

WALTS, GEORGE, dealer in dry goods, boots and shoes, etc, Main st, was born in Herkimer Co, N Y, March 31, 1825 Married Nancy M Wagner Emigrated to Walworth Co., Wis., in 1846, and to Vernon Co, Wis., in the Spring of 1860; emigrated to this county in March, 1866, commenced his present business July 5, 1866 Edward L and George A. are their children

Waltz, M W, carpenter.

WEISS, CLARLES, of the firm of Fuller & Weiss, meat market; was born in Germany March 20, 1849, and came to America in 1868 Married Sopha Bittiger in Feb, 1869, she was born in Germany May 17, 1854 Came to this city in Sept, 1877, beginning business on Feb 21, 1878 Charles, born Jan 21, 1878

Wheat, C M, Pastor M E Church

Whitcomb, Duane, restaurant

WILL, TILLMANN, farmer, Sec 26, born in Germany in 1817, and came to this country in 1849, and settled in Fond du Lac Co, Wis, where he remained until 1866, where he married Mary Hassick in 1858, she was born in Switzerland in 1820. Has a farm of eighty acres, valued at $40 per acre Are members of the Evangelical Church

Worthing, Charles, far., S. 23

YARROW, CHRISTOPHER, farmer, Sec 20

Yarrow, John, far., S 22

Young, Edward, carpenter.

ORANGE TOWNSHIP.

ALLEN, E A , farmer, Sec 23 , P O Waterloo

ALLEN, A. A., farmer and nurseryman, Sec 13 , P. O Waterloo, born in Lewis Co , N Y., Aug 16, 1841 Married Elizabeth Carpenter Nov 9, 1869, she was born in Pittsburgh, Penn , May 27, 1848, came to this county Jan 13, 1867, owns 160 acres of land, valued at $35 per acre Mrs A is a member of the M E Church Their children are Albert C, born Sept 30, 1870, Nettie M , born May 5, 1872

BEACHLY, MICHAEL, Sec 31 , P O Waterloo

Beachly, W , far , S 29 , P O Waterloo

BEEKLY, SAMUEL B., far , Sec 17 , P O Waterloo, owns 160 acres of land, valued at $40 per acre ; born in Westmoreland Co , Penn, Aug 21, 1848, he with his parents emigrated to Ohio in 1850, and to this county in 1868, where he married Susan Klingamon June 2, 1872, she was born in Somerset Co., Penn., Feb 2, 1848. They are members of the German Baptist Church George E , born Nov 19, 1874, are the name and birth of their only child.

Berkley, J J., far., S 26 , P O Waterloo

Berkley, L , far , S. 10 , P O. Waterloo

Berry, J P , far , S 11 , P O. Waterloo.

BERTCH, ISAAC E., farmer, S 2 , P O Waterloo; born in Union Co , Penn , in 1848 Married Mary Dohmer in 1872, she was born in Snyder Co , Penn , in 1855 , came to this county in 1874, settling on his present farm of ninety acres, valued at $40 per acre Minnie, Emma and William are his children

Braninger, W., far., S 17 , P. O. Waterloo

Brown, A E , far , S 34 ; P O Waterloo

BUECHLEY, ELIAS K., retired farmer and Elder of the German Baptist Church , P O Waterloo, born in Somerset Co., Penn , Dec 9, 1812 Married Barbara Good Nov. 2, 1834 , she was born in the same county Dec 22, 1814, and died Feb. 3, 1851, Anna, born June 26, 1836, Abigail, Sept 7, 1837 ; Amelia, Aug 25, 1840 , Mary E., March 31, 1842 , Barbara, July 16,

1843, William G , Feb 3, 1845 , Sarah, Feb 21, 1847 , Elijah G , Dec 11, 1848, and Jacob G , Jan 23, 1851, are their living children His present wife, Sally Clingaman, was born in Somerset Co , Penn , March 9, 1813 , they were married Nov 9, 1851 , came to this county in March, 1861, where he has since made it his home, and is prominently known and identified among his brethren of the church, and to him the writer is largely indebted for much valuable information regarding the history of the church and facts of the town's early settlement

Bueghley, E G , far , S 17 , P O Waterloo

BUEGHLY, HIRAM, farmer, Sec 10 , P O Waterloo, born in Somerset Co , Penn , Sept. 20, 1852 Married Mary Hosteter Sept 10 1876 , she was born in Somerset Co , Penn., April 26, 1856. Came to this county in 1855 Members of the German Baptist Church

Bueghley, J , far , S. 8 , P O Waterloo

Bueghley, M , far , S 12 , P O Waterloo

BUDD, CHARLES W., far , S 35 , P O Waterloo , born in Columbiana Co , Ohio, Aug. 7, 1839, came to Dubuque Co , Iowa, in 1854, and to this county in 1856 Enlisted in Co E, 27th I V I , Aug 22, 1862, and was honorably discharged Aug, 8, 1865 , was in the battles of Pleasant Hill and Nashville Married Mary A. Warner July 22, 1869, she was born in Alleghany Co., Md , Oct. 16, 1849 , John W , born Aug 4, 1871, Esther M., born March 19, 1876, are their children Mr Budd settled on his present farm, consisting of 100 acres of land, valued at $35 per acre.

BUDD, JOHN C., farmer, S 28 , P O Waterloo, born in Columbiana Co., Ohio, Sept. 25, 1846 , came to this State in 1854, and to this county, settling on his present farm of 160 acres, valued at $35 per acre, in 1865, where he married Jennie Raymond in Sept , 1874, she was born in Indiana, in Dec., 1853, Charles H and William are their children.

BUDD, JACOB J., farmer, S. 35; P O Waterloo, born in Columbiana Co , Ohio, in 1831 Married Elizabeth Atchison in 1873, she was born in Somerset Co , Penn , in 1850, came to this county in 1864, Settled on his present farm of 220 acres, valued at $35 per acre. His wife is a member of the M E Church Olive is their only child

Burgoon, C , far., S 7 , P O Waterloo

Burgoon, F , far , S. 7 ; P. O Waterloo

CAIN, SAMUEL, far , Sec 8 , P O Waterloo

CARPENTER, DAVID H., farmer, S 25 , P O Waterloo, born in Pittsburgh, Penn , in 1851 Married Anna Lee in 1872; she was born in Cedar Co , Iowa, in 1849 Came to this county in 1865, settling on his present farm of 320 acres, which is owned by his father Members of the M E Church Anna S and David M. are their children

Carpenter, Israel S , far., S 25 , P O Waterloo

Carpenter, J H , far , S 25 , P. O. Waterloo

Carpenter, W L , far., S 14 , P O Waterloo

Ceaser, E W , far , S. 24 , P O Waterloo

Ceaser, H., far , S 24 ; P O Waterloo

Ceaser, J , far , S. 24 , P O. Waterloo

Ceaser, Wm , far , S 24 , P O Waterloo.

Clark, Robert, far , Sec. 2 , P O Waterloo.

CLARK, JOHN W., retired farmer, Sec 3 , P O Waterloo, born in Columbia Co , Penn , May 4, 1805, where he married Margaret Derr , she was born in the same county June 12, 1806, died March 9, 1873 , they came to this county and settled on their present farm, consisting of 180 acres, valued at $60 per acre, in 1856 When the rebellion broke out, Mr C sent five of his sons to the army, all of whom returned home Their children are Charles, born March 25, 1832 , Caroline, born June 1, 1833 , Elizabeth, born Sept. 17, 1834 , George, born Dec 7, 1835 ; William, born Aug. 21, 1837 , Robert, born May 14, 1839 , John F , born Aug 8, 1841 , Lyman, born Jan 25, 1843, and Margaret, born Aug. 25, 1848

Clifford, F , far , S 16 , P O Waterloo.

DANE, M E., farmer, Sec 36 , P O. Waterloo

Dane, S D , far , S 36 ; P O Waterloo.

Degering, Henry

Deitrich, Chris , ten far , P O Waterloo.

EASON, J C , far , S 25 , P O Waterloo

EASON, JAMES D., farmer, Sec 25 , P O Waterloo, born in Lycoming Co , Penn , Dec 7, 1820 Married Eliza A Carr Sept. 23, 1841 , she was born in Orange Co., Penn , Dec. 14, 1820, came to this county in 1854, entering his present farm of 160 acres, valued at $40 per acre, and moved on the same in 1866. Are members of the Baptist Church Anna M , Mary F., Joseph C , William H , Maggie E and Ori N are living children , Sarah E , Eliza J , James F. and John K are the names of the deceased , one died in infancy

Eason, W H , far , S 25 , P O Waterloo

Edwards, G W , far , P O Waterloo

FIKE, JOHN, far , S 27 , P O Waterloo

FIKE, JACOB C., far , S 23 , P O Waterloo, born in Somerset Co , Penn , Feb 13, 1821, where he married Elizabeth Blough May 8, 1842 , she was born in the same county April 6, 1820 , they came to this county and settled on their present estate, consisting of 280 acres, valued at $40 per acre, in March, 1869. They are members of the German Baptist Church Their children are Christian, born June 28, 1843 ; Sarah, Oct 13, 1845 , John, Oct 1, 1847 , Susannah, June 26, 1850 , Samuel, June 9, 1859 , Mary Ann, Oct 10, 1862

Fish, D H , far , S 9 , P O Waterloo

FLICKINGER, JONAS, far , S. 26 , P O Waterloo , born in Somerset Co , Penn Married Cornelia Barkey in 1857, she was born in same county in 1836 , came to this county in March, 1860, and settled on his present estate, consisting of 414 acres of land, valued at $40 per acre. Members of the German Baptist Church David C , Marietta E , Lydia L , John H are their children , lost two—Abraham H and Maggie

Forney, Joseph, far , P. O. Waterloo.

GEIST, H H far., S. 12 ; P O. Waterloo

Geist, J. P , far , S 14 , P O Waterloo.

GNAGEY, JOSEPH D., far , S 5, P O Waterloo, born in Somerset Co , Penn , Nov 28, 1854, where he married Anna Blough June 5, 1876 , she was born in Somerset Co , Penn , Dec 3, 1853 , they emigrated to Carroll Co , in the Fall of 1876, and to this county on June 25, 1877. Members of the German Baptist Church

Grady, N far , P O Waterloo.

HOOD, FREDERICK, far , P O. Waterloo.

HAHN, JOHN G., far , S 2 , P O Waterloo, born in Germany in 1834 Married Phœbe Shaffer in 1869 , she was born in Union Co , Penn , in 1838 Came to this country in 1853. settling in Pennsylvania, and in 1868, moved to Elkhart Co., Ind., and in 1869, moved to Minnesota, and in 1876, came to this county, settling on his present farm of ninety acres, valued at $40 per acre. Anna, Charles, Harrie, Cora, Lulu and Eddie are their children

HITTER, THOMAS, farmer, Sec 32, P. O Waterloo, born in Lehigh Co , Penn., March 15, 1830, where he married Elizabeth Wilson March 5, 1856 , she was born in Montour Co , Penn , Dec 9, 1836 Emigrated to Stephenson Co , Ill , in 1848, and to this county March 19, 1869, settling on their present farm of 160 acres, valued at $35 per acre Alice M , born Dec. 28, 1856 , Mrs Emma Miller, Lewis W , born March 29, 1862, and William F., Nov 5, 1870, are their children

HELLER, CHARLES, farmer, Sec 10 , P O Waterloo, born in France April 17, 1836 Emigrated to this country and settled in Lake Co., Ill , in 1846. Married in Chicago Elizabeth Salz Jan. 25, 1859, who was born in Prussia Nov 6, 1839 , came to this county, settling on their present farm consisting of 160 acres, valued at $6,400, on June 22, 1869, seven children—Charles J , born April 21, 1862 , Elanora M , June 27, 1866, Thomas H , Jan. 22, 1868, Sarah C., July 3, 1869 , Henry W , June 16, 1872 , George F , Jan 26, 1874, Anna M , Nov 6, 1875

HILDEBRAND, SYLVESTER, farmer, Sec. 9 , P O Waterloo, born in Cambria Co , Penn., Aug. 8, 1836, where he married Louisa Roberts March 7, 1858 , she was born in same county June 4, 1838 , came to this county, settling on their present farm consisting of eighty acres, valued at $3,200, May 6, 1869 They are members of the German Baptist Church Five children—Edward L , born Nov 17, 1860 , Sarah A , Sept 19, 1866, Charles W., Sept. 24, 1869 , Mary E , May 6, 1872 , John H , April 7, 1874

HILDEBRAND, WILLIAM, farmer, Sec 9 , P O Waterloo, born in Cambria Co , Penn , July 6, 1835, where he married Lavina Horner March 25, 1858 , she was born in Cambria Co , Penn , on Sept 17, 1838 , came to this county May 6, 1869, settling on his present farm consisting of eighty acres, valued at $3,200 They are members of the German Baptist Church. Four children —David M , born May 6, 1867 , Frankie G , April 5, 1869 , Anna B., Jan 25, 1876 , Harry H , Oct. 27, 1877

HOCHSTETTER, A. B., far , Sec 11 , P O Waterloo, born in Somerset Co , Penn., in 1826 Married Rachel Rankin in 1852 , she was born in Westmoreland Co., Penn , in 1833 Came to this county in 1868, first settling in Lester Tp , and, in October, moved to Waterloo, and after one month's residence, came to his present farm of 160 acres of land, valued at $35 per acre Members of the German Baptist Church John R , Harry A , Mary E , George W , Arabella J , Elmer L , David E , William K , Hiram A , Martin B , Samuel J and Susan are his children , one child dead—Arabella

HOFF, ISAAC (deceased) , born in Wayne Co , Ohio, March 5, 1836, and died Dec 18, 1875 Married Sarah Garven in Wayne Co , Ohio, Dec. 20, 1860 , she was born in the same county Feb 7, 1842. Came to this county, and settled on their present farm, consisting of eighty eight acres on Section 5, valued at $40 per acre, April 7, 1865 Mrs. H and her eldest daughter are members of the German Baptist Church They have three children— Rebecca, born May 26, 1863, Jacob A., Jan. 6, 1865, and Susana, Nov 19, 1870.

HOFF, JOHN B., farmer, Sec 6, P O Waterloo, born in Wayne Co., Ohio, March 27, 1833, where he married Mary Beekley Dec 25, 1855, she was born in Westmoreland Co, Penn, June 1, 1836   Came to this county and settled on their present farm, consisting of 233 acres of land, valued at $40 per acre, April 3, 1863   Members of the German Baptist Church.   Their children are Ephraim, born Jan. 29, 1859, Emanuel B, Dec 21, 1861, Sarah D, July 6, 1866, and Mary M, Nov 3, 1875

HOFFMAN, CHARLES E., farmer, Sec 12, P O Waterloo, born in Whiteside Co, Ill, July 7, 1858   Married Flora B Robinson Feb 13, 1878, she was born in Floyd Co, Iowa, May 25, 1858, and came to this county in 1865, settling on his present farm of 140 acres of land, valued at $45 per acre

Hoover, Abe, far, P O Waterloo

HOOVER, DANIEL, farmer, S 22, P O Waterloo, owns 240 acres of land valued at $40 per acre, born in Lancaster Co, Penn., in Dec., 1817   Married Rebecca Hershey in May, 1841, she died in Sept, 1855.   Settled on his present farm April 1, 1866   Lydia, born, March 5, 1842, John, Sept 18, 1843, Samuel, Sept 15, 1845, Sarah, Aug. 15, 1847, Abraham, Aug. 12, 1850, and Daniel, Sept 20, 1853, are their children

Hoover, Eli, far, S 10, P. O Waterloo

HOOVER, EPHRAIM, farmer, Sec 6, P O Waterloo, born in Wayne Co, Ohio, Oct 5, 1850, where he married Elizabeth Pinkerton Dec. 23, 1873, she was born in Wayne Co., Ohio, May 22, 1852, came to this county, settling on their present farm, Sept 23, 1875   Mrs Hoover is a member of the German Baptist Church   Samuel P, born Nov 10, 1874, and Ira, born July 9, 1876, are the names and births of their children

Hoover, H M, far., S 10, P. O. Waterloo

Hoover, M, far, S. 9, P O. Waterloo

HOOVER, SAMUEL, farmer, Sec. 15; P. O. Waterloo, born in Wayne Co., Ohio, in 1845.   Married Martha Hembarger in 1869, she was born in same county in 1846   Came to this

county in 1856, settling on his present farm of eighty acres, valued at $40 per acre   Members of the German Baptist Church   One child—Ephraim B

HORN, ELIAS, farmer, Sec 11, P O Waterloo, born in Pennsylvania in 1823.   Married Mary Ann Menich in 1853, she was born in same State in 1836   Came to this county in 1870, settling on his present estate of eighty acres, valued at $40 per acre   Sarah A and Franklin H are their children

Horner, C W, far, S 33, P. O. Waterloo

Hutzel, Samuel, far. P. O. Waterloo

IKENBERRY, WM, far, S 10; P. O Waterloo

IKENBERRY, BENJAMIN, farmer, Sec 16, P O Waterloo; owns eighty acres of land, valued at $3,500, born in Ohio Aug 13, 1811, moved to Union Co, Ind, in 1832, where he married Catherine Moss Jan 3, 1832, who was born in Union Co, Ind, Nov 22, 1815   Emigrated to this State, settling in Butler Co., May 5, 1856, and in this county, on his present farm, Sept 1, 1871   They are members of the German Baptist Church   Their children are Henry H, born July 4, 1834; William, April 27, 1836, John E., July 20, 1838, Mary, Feb 27, 1843, Elizabeth, March 5, 1846, Sarah, June 4, 1848; Levi, Jan 12, 1851, Harvey, Oct 15, 1853, who married Sarah C Talhelm Feb 21, 1875, she was born in Franklin Co, Ill, Feb 25, 1857; Ephraim M, born Dec 3, 1877—their only son, all members of the German Baptist Church

KLINGAMAN, J. F, far, Sec 29, P. O. Waterloo

Klingaman, S. L, far, Sec 30, P. O Waterloo

LAKE, L H, farmer, P. O Waterloo.

Langdis, C W, farmer, P O Waterloo.

Lichty, A J, farmer, P. O. Waterloo

LICHTY, CHARLES, farmer, S 20, P. O Waterloo, born in Somerset Co., Penn, March 2, 1840, came with his parents to Van Buren Co, Iowa, October, 1856, and to this county in August, 1861, where he married Sarah Beekly Oct. 16, 1866, she was born in Somerset Co, Penn, Nov 15, 1838   Enlisted Dec 4, 1861, in the 16th I.

V I, Co I, where he engaged in the battle of Pittsburg Landing and was honorably discharged Oct 4, 1862 Stanley S, born July 10, 1868, Sanford L, March 20, 1870, Horace G, Aug 18, 1873, Alvin M, June 4, 1877, are their children Members of the German Baptist Church.

Lichty, H J, far., S 28, P O Waterloo

LICHTY, JACOB P., farmer, Sec. 10, P O Waterloo, born in Somerset Co, Penn, April 25, 1824, where he married Sarah Miller April 20, 1848, she was born in Somerset Co, Penn, May 29, 1825 Came to this county, settling on their present farm, consisting of 120 acres, valued at $5,500, Sept. 26, 1877 Their children are Mrs. Lizzie Lent, born March 30, 1850, Peter, Dec 24, 1852, Mary, Dec 27, 1858, Ella N., April 12, 1861, four children deceased Members of the German Baptist Church

Lichty, J M, far, S 11, P O Waterloo

Lichty, J A, far, S 34, P O Waterloo

Lichty, J., far, S 32, P O Waterloo

Lichty, S A, far, S. 26, P O Waterloo

Lichty, S J, far, P O. Waterloo

LICHTY, WILLIAM H., farmer, Sec. 16, P O Waterloo, born in Somerset Co, Penn, Aug 29, 1843, emigrated to this county Aug. 18, 1864, where he married Mary Beekly Jan 8, 1865, she was born in Somerset Co., Penn, March 31, 1842. Members of the German Baptist Church Anna, born April 8, 1866, Elias, Aug. 25, 1872, Joseph, Aug. 31, 1875, Abbie, Dec. 3, 1877, are the names and births of their children

Logan, John, farmer, P O Waterloo

McCARTHY, JOHN, farmer, P O Waterloo

McCARTHY, PATRICK, farmer, Sec 19, P. O Waterloo, born in Ireland, in 1831, and married Jane Shomen in 1854, she was born in Ireland in 1835, John, Mary, Dennis, Ellen, Johana, Patrick, Richard, Timothy and Jane are their children Came to America in 1849, and settled in Rensselaer Co, N Y, and in 1864, came to this county and settled on his present farm of ninety-one acres, valued at $25 per acre Members of the Catholic Church

McDOWELL, JAMES, farmer, Sec. 30, P. O Waterloo, born in Ireland in 1832, and came to this country in 1856, and settled in Winnebago Co, Ill, where he resided until 1864, when he came to this county, where he married Lavina Baldwin in 1867, she was born in Crawford Co, Penn., in 1840, Effie E., John W, Lizzie E and Willie O are their living children. Owns 323 acres of land, valued at $40 per acre

McKEEN, SETH, farmer, Sec. 3, P O Waterloo, born in Oxford, Worcester Co, Mass, April 9, 1836, came to Pennsylvania in 1862, where he married F. Perkins Jan 1, 1863, she was born in Oxford, Worcester Co, Mass, June 10, 1844, came to this county in the Spring of 1864, their children are Byron W, born Nov 10, 1863, Walter, born Aug 30, 1865, Benjamin, born March 18, 1867, Harry, born Feb 9, 1870, Charley, born March 12, 1872, Merton, born June 22, 1874, Lillie E, born Oct. 12, 1877

McMahon, T, far, S 8, P O Waterloo

MILLER, ABRAHAM A., far, Sec 16, P O Waterloo, born in Somerset Co., Penn., Aug 5, 1814, where he married Saloma Forney Nov 13, 1836, she was born in the same county Aug 23, 1817 they emigrated to this county, settling on their present farm of 118 acres, valued at $40 per acre, March 27, 1865. They are all members of the German Baptist Church Perry A, born Dec. 26, 1838, Mary, born Aug 8, 1845, Susan, born March 31, 1847, Matilda, born Nov 18, 1854, Henry F, born Dec 18, 1856, William A, born April 1, 1859, Harvey A, born Jan 14, 1861.

Miller, A W, far., S 4, P O Waterloo

MILLER, CORNELIUS, farmer and dealer in thorough-bred cattle, Sec 21, P O. Waterloo, born in Somerset Co, Penn, March 3, 1833, where he married Elizabeth Bittner June 5, 1853, she was born in Somerset Co, Penn, Jan 9, 1831 They emigrated to and settled in Lake Co, Ill, in the Fall of 1864, and came to this county Sept. 25, 1857, settling on their present farm of 200 acres, valued at $45 per acre A little frame barn into which they moved was all the improvement on their place when they arrived, but now fine buildings and good improvements have taken its place, and are the result of honesty and industry   William was born Feb 24, 1856, and married Emma Heitter July 20, 1876, Cinderella (now Mrs Milo Miller, and married Nov 29, 1877), was born Sept 30, 1858, Mary C, born Jan 7, 1861, Joseph M, born Feb 28, 1863, Minerva, born Jan 27, 1866, Emma, born June 5, 1873, are their children

Miller, Daniel

Miller John H

MILLER, JACOB W., farmer, Sec 21, P O Waterloo, owns 240 acres of land, valued at $10,000, born in Somerset Co, Penn, Feb 8, 1844, came to this county Jan 1, 1863, returning to Pennsylvania in the Fall of the same year, where he married Charlotte Walker Dec 12, 1863, she was born in the same county July 29, 1843, returned to this county with his bride in the Spring of 1864, who died April 4, 1865, has one child by first marriage— Mary E, born March 28, 1865 In the Fall of 1865, Mr M again returned to Pennsylvania, where he married Maggie Maust May 11, 1866, she was born in the same county May 24, 1841; he with his new bride again returned to this county in July, 1866, their children are Madeira, born March 20, 1867, Ulysses C, born July 3, 1869, Norman, born Nov 23, 1870, Calvin J, born Nov 20, 1872, Henry W, born Oct 26, 1874, Anna M, born Nov 10, 1876, and one infant, born March 23, 1878

MILLER, JONAS A., farmer, Sec 15, P. O Waterloo, born in Somerset Co, Penn, Oct 29, 1809   Married Sallie E Horner in 1832, she died in 1850, Married Sallie Saylor in 1852, she was born in Somerset Co, Penn, in 1825; came to this county in 1875, settling on his farm of 250 acres of land, valued at $30 per acre   His children are William H., Mary H, Samuel H, Anna H, Becky H, John H, one dead—Catherine   Are members of the German Baptist Church,

MILLER, LEVI, farmer, Sec 24, P. O. Waterloo, born in Berks Co, Penn, in 1826, emigrated to Stephen-son Co, Ill, in 1849, where he married Caroline Rees in 1851, she was born in 1832, and died in 1855, Frances and Richard are the children by this marriage Came to this county in 1860, and enlisted in Co C, 32d I V I, in August, 1862, and was honorably discharged Sept 1, 1865, engaged in the battles at Nashville, Fort Blakely and others Again married Caroline A. Moody in 1866, she was born in York Co, Penn, in 1835, and died in May, 1869   Married Catherine S. Albright May 19, 1872, she was born in Mifflin Co, Penn, in 1839, settled on their present farm of 160 acres, valued at $50 per acre, in 1877   Members of the M E Church

MILLER, MATHIAS, farmer, Sec 32, P O Waterloo, born in Somerset Co, Penn, July 5, 1822, where he married Mary Berkley March 5, 1848; she was born in the same county Dec 22, 1830   They came to this county, settling on a portion of their present farm, which now consists of 320 acres, valued at $4,500, in August, 1858, most of this land was entered at Government price   They are members of the German Baptist Church   Mrs. Sarah A Lichty, born May 23, 1849, William H, born Nov 17, 1851, Elias, born July 31, 1858, are their living children, Silas B, born Sept 27, 1854, and killed by the cars March 17, 1874

Miller, Noah W, P O Waterloo

Miller, S B, far, S 24, P O Waterloo

MILLER, SAMUEL H., farmer, Sec 17, P O Waterloo, owns 160 acres of land, valued at $6,400, born in Somerset Co, Penn, May 15, 1838, came to this county Dec. 10, 1862 Married Eliza Boechley Sept. 1, 1863, she was born in the same county March 16, 1836, and died Oct 26, 1865, has one child by this marriage—Edwin Stanton, born July 31, 1864 Married again, to Susan Taylor July 9, 1870, she was born in same county, Pennsylvania, Sept. 19, 1845, their children are Gracie, born April 16, 1874, Ira, born April 20, 1876, Howard, Dec 8, 1877. Are members of the German Baptist Church

MILLER, SAMUEL M., farmer, Sec 29, P. O Waterloo, owns 240 acres of land, valued at $45 per acre, born in Somerset Co , Penn , May 15, 1833, where he married Anna Buechley March 4, 1855 , she was born in Somerset Co , Penn , June 26, 1836, they came from their native county to this, and settled on their present farm April 25, 1858 Mr M is one of the Speakers in the German Baptist Church. Mary S., born Aug 3, 1856, John O , June 9, 1859, Abigail, March 22, 1861 , Daniel, Nov 21, 1862, Harvey, Dec 21, 1864 , Richard, Feb. 7, 1867 , Nora, Feb 25, 1875, are their living children This family are all members of the German Baptist Church

MILLER, WILLIAM, farmer, Sec 21; P O Waterloo , owns 280 acres of land, valued at $12,600, born in Somerset Co., Penn , Sept 26, 1827. Married Lydia Fike Jan. 7, 1849 , she was born in the same county in Pennsylvania May 9, 1826, and died March 13, 1862 ; came to this county and settled on their present farm March 24, 1860 Again married Abigail Buechley Aug. 14, 1862 His children by first marriage are Sarah, born June 21, 1855 , Susan, Feb. 19, 1858, and John W , June 10, 1860 , by second marriage, Lewis, born Feb 11, 1866, Myra May, Jan 3. 1869, Alvin B , Aug 1, 1870 , Ada Bell, July 17, 1872 , Silas B., June 2, 1875, and Frank, July 23, 1877. They are members of the German Baptist Church.

MONTAGUE, THOMAS, farmer, Sec 9, P O Waterloo , born in England Jan 25, 1825, where he married Louisa Evans in Aug , 1849 , she was born in England May 15, 1825. They emigrated to America in 1855, first settling in Oneida Co , N Y., where they remained until March 1865, when they removed to this county, and settled on their present estate, consisting of 240 acres, valued at $40 per acre, in 1872 , their children are John T , born April 20, 1853, Mary E , Sept., 21, 1854 , Sarah T., Nov 15, 1856, George H , Jan. 29, 1859 , Emma L , Sept. 15, 1860 , Thomas W., March 2, 1862, and Julia E , Jan 6, 1865

MURRAY, JACOB A., farmer, Sec 29 , P O. Waterloo, owns eighty acres of land, valued at $3,000 , born in Fayette Co , Penn , Oct. 11, 1834, where

he married Sarah Bauders May 3, 1857 , she was born in Fayette Co , Penn , May 22, 1836, they emigrated from native county to this on Aug 25, 1864, and settled on his present farm in the Fall of 1873 They are members of the German Baptist Church, and Mr M is one of the ordained Elders Amzi, born Feb 19, 1858, Naomi, May 19, 1860 , Orpha, Aug 1, 1870 , Verna, April 12, 1872 ; Charlie, Nov. 18, 1874, are their children

PHILIPPI, A L , far , Sec 13, P. O Waterloo

SANER, ANDREW F , far , P O Waterloo.

Saylor, J , far . S. 11 , P O Waterloo

Saylor, J L , far , S 22 , P. O Waterloo

SAYLOR. JOSEPH M., farmer, Sec 11 , P O Waterloo, born in Somerset Co , Penn , Dec 25, 1837 Married Mary Buechly in Dec., 1860 , she was born in Somerset Co., Penn , Jan 21, 1837, they have two living children—Elias B and Daniel , three children dead—William, Emma and Elnora Came to this county in 1862, settling on his present farm of 120 acres, value dat $50 per acre Members of the German Baptist Church

SCHAEFER. JACOB, farmer, Sec 33 , P. O Waterloo, born in Prussia Feb 11, 1846, came to America with his parents in 1854, first settling in Lee Co , Ill , came to this county, settling on his present farm of 120 acres, valued at $35 per acre, March 9, 1871 Married Mary E Amfahr Sept 29, 1871 ; she was born in Prussia Aug 27, 1851. Members of the Roman Catholic Church They have two children—Angeline, born July 9, 1872, and Charles P , born Nov 26, 1877

Schrack. J M , far , S 27 , P.O. Waterloo

Schrock, J J , far , S 28 , P O Waterloo.

Schrock, S S , far., S 27 , P O Waterloo

Schrock, W F , far., S. 27 , P O. Waterloo

Shanlis, E. A , far., S. 35 , P O Waterloo

SHANLIS, NOAH P., far , Sec 35 , P O Waterloo ; born in Somerset Co., Penn , in 1847. Married Hannah Perkins in 1871 , she was born in Maine in 1851, he came to this county in 1867, and in 1871, settled on his present farm of eighty acres, valued at $40 per acre Members of the M E Church Charlotte, Effie and Ammon N. are their children

SHANLIS, SIMON, farmer Sec 16, P O Waterloo, owns 580 acres of land, valued at $40 per acre, born in Penn, Nov 5, 1821, where he married Julian Harsh Oct 20, 1842, she was born in Penn, Feb 2, 1822, they came to this county, settling on their present farm Oct 24, 1867 They are members of the United Brethren Church They have ten children—Elizabeth, born March 18, 1843, Simon, born July 31, 1844, enlisted in the 142d Penn V I Co C, Aug 2, 1862, and discharged May 29, 1865, Caroline, Jan 14, 1846, Noah, Sept 3, 1847, Amanda, Nov 24, 1848, Emanuel E, Dec. 19, 1851; Wesley, May 17, 1854, Charlotte, Nov. 3, 1855, Jacob R, Sept 8, 1859, John R, June 20, 1862

Shanlis, W, far, S 35, P O Waterloo.

SHIMER, JESSE, farmer, Sec 19, P. O. Waterloo, born in Madison Co, Ind, in 1827, and married Eliza Winsett Dec 29, 1849, she was born in Delaware Co, Ind, Feb. 19, 1831, and died June 28, 1859, they have four children—Henry C, born Dec 19, 1850, John A, Jan 26, 1853, William A, March 14, 1857, and James M., March 4, 1859 In 1852, he emigrated to the West, and settled in Linn Co., and in the following year came to this county, and settled in Spring Creek Tp. Married his present wife, Elizabeth Leach, Aug 25, 1859, she was born in Wood Co, Va, July 28, 1840, then children are Elvira J, born Oct 5, 1860, Harvey L, Sept 27, 1862, Jesse M, Nov 23, 1864, Melissa M, Jan 30, 1871, and Hanford A, Jan 5, 1873, have lost three children—Berry E, Irving G, and Effie E Mr. S was largely engaged in the stock business during his residence in Spring Creek, where he resided until 1874, when he removed to La Porte City, and, in 1877, settled on his present farm, where he has since made it his home

HOWALTER, E., farmer and dentist, Sec 15, P. O Waterloo, born in Tuscarawas Co, Ohio, Aug 30, 1839; in 1856, he went to Ashland Co, Ohio, where he attended school until 1859,

in 1862, he moved to Wayne Co., Ohio, where he married, at West Salem, Catherine A Meyers Aug 28, 1862, she was born in the same county June 2, 1841 Emigrated to Van Buren Co, Mich, and came to this county in 1873, settling on their present estate, consisting of forty acres, valued at $40 per acre Are members of the German Baptist Church Their children are Sarah, born Oct 12, 1863, Mahlon F, May 27, 1867, and John, Feb 7, 1875.

Sieglaff, C, far, S 19, P O Waterloo

Smith, Nathan, far, P O Waterloo

Smith, Samuel, far, S 4, P O. Waterloo,

SMITH, WILLIAM, farmer, Sec. 30, P. O Waterloo, born in Ireland in 1818 Married Bessy Glannay in 1842, she was born in Ireland in 1815 Annie, Henry, Richard, Mariah and Jane are their children, lost three children—Isabel, Eliza and Eliza Emigrated to America in 1853, and settled in Winnebago Co, where he resided until 1869, when he moved to this county, and settled on his present farm of eighty-three acres, valued at $40 per acre

SMITH, WILLIAM F., farmer, Sec 35, P O Waterloo, born in Hanover, Germany, in 1835 Married Augusta Kistner in 1859, she was born in the same place in 1836, and died in 1872. Came to this country in 1858, settling in Somerset Co, Penn, and in 1863 came to this county, and settled on his present farm in 1864, it contains 120 acres, valued at $35 per acre Charles, Ida, Anna, John, Emma, Willie and Edward are their children

SPEICHER, JOHN, farmer, Sec. 16, P O Waterloo, owns eighty acres of land, valued at $45 per acre; born in Somerset Co, Penn, Jan. 7, 1816. Married Barbara Saylor Jan 24, 1841, who was born in Somerset Co, Penn, March 12, 1822 Emigrated to Allamakee, Iowa, in the Fall of 1854, and came to this county Oct. 19, 1856 Mr. S is one of the Speakers of the German Baptist Church. Missouria (now Mrs. Louis Libby), born Nov 7, 1841, and William, March 16, 1860, are their children

SPOOR, JACOB, far., S. 25, P. O Waterloo, born in Somerset Co.,

Penn, in 1835   Married Lydia Horner in 1865, she was born in Wayne Co, Ohio, in 1840, came to this county in 1866, settling in Orange Township   Have four children—Lovina, Wilson, Eunice and Mariah

STOKES, WESLEY S., far S 8, P O Waterloo, born in Putnam Co, Ind, April 8, 1844, emigrated with his parents to McDonough Co, Ill, in 1848, where he remained until 1862, when he enlisted in the 124th Ill V I, Co I, engaging in the battles of Champion Hills, siege of Vicksburg and many others, and was honorably discharged Aug 16, 1865, returning to Hancock Co., Ill., and Feb 12, 1868, married Mary C Grigsby, she was born in Muskingum Co, Ohio, July 9, 1848, April 1, 1868, they came to this county and settled on their present farm, consisting of 200 acres, valued at $40 per acre. Their children are—Edward and Ella (twins) born July 6, 1869, Ida M, May 12, 1871, Clara E, Dec. 13, 1872, Arthur E, May, 21, 1876

Stoy, C J., far, S. 26, P O Waterloo

Strickler, J S, far, S 3, P O Waterloo.

SWEITZER, JONAS D., far, S 31, P O Waterloo, born in Somerset Co, Penn, in 1839, and emigrated to this county in 1865, and married Lydia Lichty in 1868; they have three children—Clara, Emma and ——   Settled on his present estate the same year of his coming, consisting of 293 acres, valued at $35 per acre   Was one of the early settlers in this town and is well known throughout   Also are members of the German Baptist Church

WARD, NICOLAS, far, P O. Waterloo

Weigle, John, far, P O Waterloo

Weiner, Samuel, far, P. O. Waterloo

Weller, J J, far, S 13, P O Waterloo

WHITE, SAMUEL, far, S 12, P O Waterloo; born in Clark Co, Ill, in 1835   Married Sendrella Nicholls, in 1856, she was born in Licking Co, Ohio, in 1837   Came to this county in 1851, and settled on their present farm of 300 acres, valued at $25 per acre, in 1856   Hattie, Clara and Lincoln are their children

Williams, J W, far, S. 36, P O Waterloo

MT. VERNON TOWNSHIP.

ADAMS, JOHN, farmer, Sec. 9, P O Cedar Falls

Allen, B., far, S 9, P O Cedar Falls.

Altland, Ed, far, S 3, P O Nautrill.

Anderson, R, far S 20, P O Cedar Falls

Andrews, S, far, S 36, P O Waterloo

BANDFIELD, J M, farmer, Sec. 17, P O Cedar Falls

BAILEY, HIRAM M., farmer, Sec 35, P O Waterloo, born in Rensselaer Co, N Y, April 26, 1831, and Aug 27, 1854, married Mary E Williams, she was born in Nassau, same county, in 1837, in 1854, he came to this county and settled on Sec 24, remaining two years, and removed to Illinois and lived there until 1856, when he returned and settled on his present estate, consisting of 120 acres, valued at $5,000 Was Supervisor and Trustee two terms Emma S, born March 28, 1857, Charles E., born July 2, 1863, are his children Mr B. is a natural mechanic and a self-made man.

Bandfield, C, far, S 17, P O. Cedar Falls

Barclay, H, far, S 36, P O Waterloo

Barclay, M J, far, S 13, P. O. Waterloo

BESH, MICHAEL, farmer, Sec 1, P O Denver, Bremer Co, born in Germany in 1832, came to America in 1850, settling in Rensselaer Co, N Y Married Anna M Rainhart in 1857, she was born in Germany in 1832, in 1864, came to this county and settled on his present farm of 168 acres, valued at $35 per acre, they have five children living—George, Sanford, Ida, Maud and Cora; lost two—Caspar and Anna M.

BRACKENBERRY, BENJAMIN, far, S 12, P O Waterloo, born in Lincolnshire, England, in 1819 Married Rebecca Hollman in 1853, she was born in Wilburncliff Rowe, Eng, in 1816, and died in 1868 Came to this country in 1872 and settled in Cook Co, Ill, removing to this county in 1877, where he owns a farm of 120 acres, valued at $35 per acre. Member of the Church of England William A, Benjamin and Elizabeth are his children

Brandis, C, far, Sec 10, P O Waterloo

Briden, John

Brown, Joseph, far, S 9; P O Nautrill.

Buck, C, far, Sec. 12, P O. Waterloo.

BURK, HENRY, farmer, Sec 1, P O Waterloo, born in Germany, in 1832, and married Juliana Faust in 1859, she was born in Germany in 1836 Came to this county in 1859, settling on his present farm of 320 acres, valued at $30 per acre Are members of the Lutheran Church Charles, Henry, Elizabeth, Juliana, George, Anna and Clara are their living children, they lost three children—May, Adair, and one that died in infancy.

CALLEGHAN, M., far., S 18, P O Cedar Falls.

Coates, G, far., S 8; P O Janesville

Cobb, A., far, S 36, P O. Cedar Falls.

COLE, OSCAR, farmer, Sec. 28, P O Cedar Falls, born in Rensselaer Co., N Y, in 1834. Married Lavantia J. Foote in 1858, she was born in Chenango Co, N Y., in 1836, they have two children—Ellen and Georgia. Came to this county in 1854, and settled on his present estate of 160 acres, which was Government land, and is now valued at $40 per acre He broke the first land in this town, and numbers among those of the earliest settlers.

Cook, A., far, S 33, P O. Cedar Falls.

Cook, Asa, far, S 33, P O Cedar Falls.

DECKEN, RICHARD, farmer, Sec. 6, P O Janesville, Bremer Co.; born in Richmond Co., N. Y, in 1818. Married Elizabeth A Cortelyou in 1840, she was born in same county in 1823 Came to this county in 1855, and settled on his present estate, consisting of eighty acres, valued at $50 per acre, is one of the early settlers of this town Their children are Cornelius L, Albert W., Lincoln H, Robert A, William T S, Freddie R and Evaline A, lost two children—Emma E and John J

DEEMING, GEORGE, farmer, Sec. 27, P O Waterloo, born in Leicestershire, Eng, in 1836, and came to this country in 1850, and settled for a short time in Chicago, when he moved to Will

Co., Ill., and settled on a farm with his father, Thomas Deeming, where he resided until 1858, when he came to this county. In 1861, he enlisted in the 3d Iowa Battery, and served over four years, was in the battles of Pea Ridge, Alma, Sugar Creek and others, and was honorably discharged, when he returned to this county and settled on his farm, consisting of 120 acres, valued at $35 per acre. Married Margaret L. Ellenmitt in 1864, have three children—Freeman J., Isabel B. and Guido H., lost three children—Anna, and two that died in infancy.

DEEMING, THOMAS, farmer, Sec 8, P. O. Cedar Falls, born in England in 1808, and in 1850, came to this country, and first settled in Will Co., on a farm, where he resided until 1854, when he emigrated to Nebraska, took up a claim and lived one year, returning, settled in this county and on his present farm, consisting of eighty acres, valued at $50 per acre. Married Catherine Simpson in 1850, she was born in England and died in 1854, their children—Henry S. is still living, and Nancy A., who died in 1854. When the war broke out, he enlisted in the 19th Illinois Regimental Band, and served six months.

DEEMING, THOMAS C., farmer, Sec 20, P O Cedar Falls, born in England in 1840, and in 1849, came to this country, first settling in Will Co., Ill., where he lived until the war broke out, when he enlisted in the 39th I. V. I., and participated in the battles of Winchester, Blackwater River, and other important battles, also at Pittsburg, and with the forces at the surrender of Lee's army; served over four years, and mustered out Dec 6, 1865. Returning home, married Mary A. Bentley, in 1870, and came to this county and settled on his present farm of eighty acres, valued at $35 per acre, their children are Martha J. and Ruth A.

DEEMING, WILLIAM, farmer, Sec 27, P O Cedar Falls, born in England March 7, 1834. Married Ellen Ford Nov 28, 1858, she was born in Wyandot Co., Ohio, Sept 9, 1838. Came to this country in 1854, and settled in this county where, with the ex-

ception of one year's residence in Missouri, he has since made his home, settled on his present farm in 1855, consisting of eighty acres, valued at $40 per acre. Has been Road Supervisor and Trustee one year. Their children are Nancy N., Josiah, William H., Louisa, Katy M. and Nelhe.

EYESTONE, A L., far., S 26, P O Waterloo.

FISHER, H., far., S 21, P O Cedar Falls.

FITCH, THOMAS H., farmer, S 3, P. O. Nautrill, born in Salisbury, Conn., in 1804. Married Amelia Harwood in 1836, she was born in Bennington Co., Vt., in 1818. Came to this county in June, 1855, and settled on his present farm of 280 acres of land, valued at $40 per acre. Has been Postmaster at Nautrill for seventeen years, and Justice of the Peace for six years. Mary C., Cornelia L., John E., Catherine A., Isabell J., Harriet N., Annie E. and Jessie E. are their living children, lost three children—Henry A., enlisted in the 1st Iowa State Cav., and was killed at the battle of Corinth, Susan L. and Frank A.

GARTON, J., far., S 22, P O Cedar Falls.

GARTON, THOS. H., farmer, Sec 2, P O Nautrill, born in St. Joseph Co., Mich., in 1834. Married Margaret Pashby in 1857, she was born in Yorkshire, England, in 1840, have seven children—Ada F., Fred, Della P., Joe, William H., Nettie G. and Agnes V. Came to this county in the Spring of 1867, and settled on his present place, consisting of 200 acres of land, valued at $40 per acre.

GEYER, ADAM, farmer, Sec 2, P O Naunell, born in Columbus, Ohio, in 1854, and in 1868, came to this county, living with his father until 1876, when he moved upon the present farm, which he carries on in connection with his brother, consisting of 160 acres of land.

GEYER, JOHN C., farmer, Sec 2, P O Nautrill, born in Germany in 1815, and married Margaret Smith in 1838, she was born in Germany in 1821. Came to this country in 1836, settling in New York City, and after

5

seventeen years, removed to Columbus, Ohio, where he remained until he came to this county, and settled on his present estate of 120 acres of land, valued at $30 per acre Andrew George, Adam, Henry, Margaret, Kate, Susan and Ann are his living children, one died—John

GIBBS, CHARLES, farmer, Sec 12, P O Waterloo, born in England in 1830 Married Mary J. Joice March 17, 1856, she was born in England in 1839 Came to America in 1842, and settled in Onondaga Co, N Y, where he lived until 1860, when he emigrated to this county, and settled on his present farm, consisting of 120 acres of land, valued at $37 per acre Is one of the earliest settlers in this town, and both are members of the M E Church Fred J is their only child

Griffin, J K, far, S 23, P O Cedar Falls

HALLOWAY, G, farmer, S 23, P O Waterloo.

Heideman, F, far, S 10, P. O. Janesville

HEIZER, LORENZO, farmer, S 24, P O Waterloo, born in Germany in 1819 Married Christen Hooder in 1851, she was born in Germany in 1825 First settled in Troy, N Y., where he lived until 1861, when he came to this county, and settled on his present farm of 280 acres of land, valued at $30 per acre Has ten children—Phillip, Jacob, John, Emma, Sophia, Charles, Caroline, Libbie, Fred and Henry, and are members of the Lutheran Church

Henry, A, far, S 21, P O Waterloo

Henry, D C, far, S 33, P. O Cedar Falls

Henry, F, far, S 21, P O Cedar Falls

HICKS, WILLIAM, farmer, Sec., 25, P O Waterloo, born in Devonshire, England, in 1806 Married Grace Palmer Dec 27, 1829, she was born in England in 1810 Came to this county in 1857, settling in Lincoln Tp, and after four years residence, came to Black Hawk Tp, remaining six years, when he came to this township, has a farm of 60 acres, valued at $40 per acre, and is one of the oldest settlers in the township, members of the Baptist Church Eliza-

beth, William, Jr, John, Ezekiel, Mary Ann, Stephen, Thomas and Clara are his living children, two dead—Mary Ann and Julia

Hiser, J far, S, 2, P O Cedar Falls

Hiser, Joel, far, S. 4, P O Janesville

HOLLWAY, THOMAS, far, S. 23, P O Waterloo, born in England in 1815, and came to this country in 1852, and settled in Greene Co, N Y, where he remained until 1869, when he came to this county and settled on his present farm, consisting of eighty acres of land, valued at $40 per acre Married Mary Dart, she was born in England in 1820, they have four children—Emma, Jane, Thomas and George H Members of the Free Methodist Church

HOOL, JAMES, farmer, Sec 8, P O Cedar Falls, born in Canada in 1833 Married Nancy N Murray Dec 1, 1857, she was born in Ireland in 1834, came to this county in 1855, and first settled in Cedar Falls, where he lived until 1865, when he moved to this township and settled on his present estate, consisting of eighty acres, valued at $25 per acre

Howard, H, far, S. 36, P O Waterloo.

Howe, W C, far, S 7, P O Cedar Falls

Howe, W J, far, S 7, P. O Cedar Falls.

Hue, H, far, S 14, P O. Waterloo.

HULL, GORDON, farmer, S 28, P. O. Cedar Falls, born in Monroe Co, N Y in 1830, and came to this State in 1866, and settled in Bremer Co, where he resided until 1870, when he moved to this county and on his present estate, consisting of 180 acres of land, valued at $30 per acre. In 1871, he Married Lydia A Herrick, widow of William Randall, she was born in Onondaga Co, N Y, has two children—M E and William

JACOB, FREDERIC, farmer, Sec 11, P. O Waterloo, born in Kent, England, in 1826 Married Mary A Swift in 1851, she was born in Isle of Sheppy, England, in 1823, came to this country in Feb, 1862, settling in Buffalo, N Y, after three years, moved to Rockford, Ill, residing three years and came to Buchanan Co, Iowa, cam.

to this county in the Fall of 1860 Enlisted in Co B, 31st I V. I, Aug 14, 1862, was honorably discharged Jan 31, 1865, was in battles at Vicksburg, and Dallas, Ga, where he was wounded May 27, 1864 Went to England in Dec, 1866, returning in March, 1867, settling on his present farm of 160 acres, valued at $40 per acre, in Nov, 1867 returned to England with his wife in Dec, 1874, came back in 1875 His wife is a member of the M E. Church Having held prominent offices in his township, he is regarded as a prominent man Thomas, Fredoni W, John F, Susannah J, and Morphew are his children

JAQUITH, JEFFERSON, far., Sec. 29, P O Cedar Falls, born in St. Lawrence Co., N Y, in 1826, which State he left in 1851, and settled in Yellow Springs, Ohio, where he lived until April, 1854, when he moved to this county, where he has since made it his home Married Mary J Knapp in November, 1858, she was born in Crawford Co, Ohio, in 1837 In 1860, he moved on his present farm of 160 acres, valued at $30 per acre Has filled the office of Supervisor most of the time since 1861, was also Magistrate one year at Cedar Falls, and is well and prominently known throughout the town and county Their children are Ida L and Lucy May

KIMBERLY, FRED, farmer, Sec 10, P O Nautrill

King, E, far, S. 36, P O Waterloo

King, H, far, S 36, P O Waterloo

KNAPP, DENNIS, farmer, Sec 34, P. O. Waterloo, born in Rensselaer Co, N Y., in 1827 Married Francis Clark in 1854, she was born in same county in 1831; have one child—Ida. Came to this county in 1857, and purchased, and in 1865, settled on his present estate, consisting of eighty acres, valued at $35 per acre. Is one of the early settlers in this town.

Kyler, J, far, S 15, P O Cedar Falls

Kyler, J, far., S 15, P O Cedar Falls

LEEPER, JACOB W., farmer, Sec 27, P O Waterloo

LAWRENCE, JOHN, farmer, Sec. 11, P O Nautrill, born in Washington Co, Ohio, in 1829. Married

Asenith Budd in 1857, she was born in Allen Co, Ohio, in 1832, came to this county in 1858, and settled on his present estate of 160 acres, valued at $50 per acre Are members of the M. E Church. Frank B, Ezra and Edwin (twins) and Emma are their children

LELAND, R. L., farmer, Sec 25, P O Waterloo, born in New York City in 1833 Married Rachel M Cole in 1852, she was born in Rensselaer Co, N Y, in 1829 He came to this county in 1854, where he has since made it his home, owns a farm of 160 acres, valued at $40 per acre Is one of the early settlers in this town George F, eldest son, was the first boy born in this town, and Sarah E are his children, lost one son—Adolphus

Leversee, A W, far, S 30, P. O. Cedar Falls

Leversee, S G, far, S 29, P O Cedar Falls

LYNCH, GEO. W., farmer, Sec 32, P O Cedar Falls, born in Lake Co, Ohio, in 1829. Married Eveline DpKing in 1856, she was born in Erie Co, N. Y., in 1835, they have five children—Clara, John, Burr, Mary and Lena. First settled in La Fayette Co, Wis, in 1853, where he resided until he came to this county in 1864, and settled on his present farm of 200 acres, valued at $35 per acre

McGOURIN, JOHN, farmer, Sec. 25, P O Waterloo

McKinney, Jas, far, S 31, P O Cedar Falls

McKinney, John, far, S 31, P. O Cedar Falls

McKinney, L P, far, Sec 31, Cedar Falls

MARQUIS, GEORGE, farmer, Sec 2, P O Nautrill, born in Miami Co, Ind, in 1841 Married Sarah Ann Carberry in 1867, she was born in Scotland Co, Mo, in 1848, have four children—Clarence D, Cora B, Florence M and George E Settled on his present farm, consisting of eighty acres, valued at $30 per acre, in 1867

Marquis, J., far, S. 11, P O Nautrill.

Mears, W., far, S. 13, P O Waterloo.

Messinger, H. M. C, far, Sec 36, P O Waterloo.

MILLARD, LEONARD B., farmer, Sec 26, P O. Waterloo, born in Kalamazoo, Mich, in 1847. In 1862, he enlisted in Co C, 31st I V I, and served three years, participated in battles of Haines Bluff, Arkansas Post, and was with Sherman on his march to the sea. Married Sarah Blake in 1870, she was born in New York State in 1849. In 1874, he came to this county, and settled in this township. They have two children—Addie and Elias T

Miller, John, far, S 8, P O Janesville

MILLER, WILLIAM, farmer, S. 18, P O Cedar Falls, born in Clark Co, Ohio, in 1813. Married Rebecca A Gordon in 1844, she was born in same county in 1819, they came to this county in 1867, and settled on his present estate, consisting of eighty acres, valued at $35 per acre, their children are Margaret, Mary J, John G, Emma and Ellen, lost one child—Julia. Are members of the Presbyterian Church

Moore, A, far, S 20, P O Cedar Falls.
Moore, B., far, S. 16, P O Nautrill
Moore, H C, far, S 16, P O Waterloo

MOORE, JOHN C., farmer, Sec 15; P O Waterloo, born in Huntingdon Co, Penn., in 1812, and married Mariah Miller in April, 1837, she was born in Shenandoah Co, Va, in 1818, they have eleven children—Elias A, Margaret J, Albert, Henry C, Lydia, William, John W, Benjamin, George, Mary, Laura M,, and Thomas F., they have lost two children—John W and Sarah E. Came to this county in 1860, and settled in this township, moved on his present estate, consisting of 196 acres, valued at $35 per acre, in 1870. Has been Assessor, and is a member of the United Brethren Church

Moore, S J., far, S 31, P O. Cedar Falls
Moore, Wm, far, S 15, P O Waterloo
Munger, A, far, S. 31, P O Cedar Falls.
Munger, T, far, S 33, P O Cedar Falls
Murrey, L, far, S 29, P O Cedar Falls

NATTGER, F, farmer, Sec 12, P Nautrill
Nattger, P, far, Sec. 12, P O. Waterloo.
Nichols, L. F., far, Sec 29, P O Cedar Falls

PATTEE, DAVID, farmer, Sec. 7, P O Janesville

PALMER, W. H., farmer, Sec 4, P O Waterloo, born in Devonshire, England, in 1829. Married Elizabeth Hicks in 1850, she was born in same place in 1830. Mr P came to this country in 1854, and stopped one year in Chicago, when he came to this county and settled in Waterloo, where he resided until 1861, when he moved upon his present farm, consisting of 345 acres, valued at $45 per acre. Is Supervisor. Democrat

PASHBY, THOMAS, farmer, Sec. 11, P O Nautrill, born in Yorkshire, England, in 1835, and in 1852, came to this country, settling in St. Joseph Co, Mich, until 1856, when he went to California, and lived ten months there, and returning, married Jane Forsyth in 1862, she was born in England in 1842. In 1864, came to this county and settled on his present farm of eighty acres, valued at $40 per acre

Pattee, Isaac, far., S 7, P.O Janesville
Pattee, J, far, S. 7; P O Janesville
Pattee, W. O, far, S. 7; P.O Janesville
Paul, C., far, S. 12, P O Nautrill
Paul, G, far, S 13, P O Waterloo
Peck, J A, far, S 6, P O. Janesville
Peck, W H, far, S 6, P O Janesville.

PHELPS, ANDREW, far, Sec 6, P O Janesville, Bremer Co., born in Crawford Co, Penn, in 1848, and emigrated to this county with his father, Edward S, in 1860, and settled in Washington Township, in 1864, he removed to this town, where his father died in 1867. Married Julia Pattee in 1872, she was born in Illinois in 1848, they have two children living—John E. and Sarah J, lost one child—Arthur N. Rents farm of sixty acres

Pixley, D B, far, S 32; P O Cedar Falls
Pixley, F. K, far., S 32, P O Cedar Falls

REINHART, GEORGE A, far, Sec 1, P O Janesville

REINHART, JACOB F., farmer. Sec. 1, P O Denver, Bremer Co, was born in Wurtemberg, Germany, in 1840. Married Emma Valentine in 1876; she was born in Illinois in 1853. He came to this country in 1854, settling in Rensselaer Co, and in 1860, came to this county, settling on his present farm of 190 acres, valued at $35 per acre. Orrin, born Dec., 1876, is their child

ROLPH, LYMAN D., farmer, Sec 23, P O Waterloo, born in Chautauqua Co, N Y, in 1834, and married Hannah M. La Mont in 1865 He emigrated to this county in March of that year, and settled on his present farm of 160 acres, valued at $30 per acre Both are members of the M E Church Edward L, Ruby A., Carrie L and Lou Adell are their children

Rolph, T, far., S 23, P O Waterloo

Rowen, F A, far, S 6, P O Janesville

RUNDLES, JANE, farmer, Sec 4, Janesville, Bremer Co, born in Onondaga Co., N Y., in 1821 Widow of Norman Rundles, who was born in Cortland Co, N Y, in 1819 They were married in March, 1847, and he died in Oct, 1870, their living children are Helen A, Ellci J, Mary E, James E, Ida M and Wilhe L, lost four children—Martha, Eva, Norman and Sarah Came to this county in 1856, and settled on their present estate, living in a rude log house, which has given place to a large and palatial residence, which Mr R partly completed before his death The estate consists of 186 acres, valued at $60 per acre Was one of the earliest settlers in this town, and founder of the first school built in this section of the county, also held prominent offices, and was well and prominently known

SEVERIN, JOHN, farmer, Sec 2, P O. Nautrill

SHAFFER, SAMUEL M., farmer, Sec 19, P O Cedar Falls, born in Carroll Co, Ind., in 1837 Married Nancy Lenhart in Oct, 1861, she was born in the same county in 1842, have three children—William H, James L and John W Came to this county in 1866, and in 1869, settled on his present estate, consisting of eighty acres, valued at $40 per acre Has been Road Supervisor four years, and his family are members of the M E Church

Shields, R, far, S 19, P O Cedar Falls.

SHIELDS, ROBERT R., farmer, Sec 33, P. O Cedar Falls, born in England, July 12, 1809, and married Hannah Johnson in 1832, she was born in England in 1809, and died in 1853, have six children living—Elizabeth, Mary, Isabel, Jane, Samuel and Edward; they have lost six children—Robert,

Edward, Eliza, Sarah, Rosana and Robert Came to America in 1851, and settled in St Joseph Co, Mich, where he resided until 1856, when he came to this county, and in 1873, settled on his present farm of forty acres, valued at $40 per acre

SHIELDS, SAMUEL, farmer and broom manufacturer, Sec 17, P O Cedar Falls, born in Yorkshire, England, in 1841, and came to this country in 1854, with his father Robert, and settled in St. Joseph Co, Mich, where he lived until 1861, when he married Orilla Thomas she was born in Rock Island Co, Ill, in 1843 Resided one year in Chicago, and moved to this county, and in 1864, settled on his present estate of 120 acres, valued at $30 per acre Is Justice of the Peace, School Director and Secretary Has been engaged in the manufacture of brooms for twenty years, and does an extensive business. Their children are Edward V, Melinda E, Emma J, Nellie E and William C

SKOW, PETER, farmer Sec 24, P O Waterloo, born in Denmark in 1852, and married Martha Fillerup in 1874, she was born in Denmark in 1852 Came to this country in 1872, and after one year in Grundy Co, came to this county, settling in this township Anna K and Grace E are his children

SMALLING, IRA, far, S 6, P O Janesville, Bremer Co, born in Greene Co, N Y., in 1818 Married Mary E Peck Feb 2, 1842, and came to this county in April, 1865, and settled on his present farm, consisting of eighty acres of land, valued at $3,000 Are members of the Prebyterian Church. Their living children are Dorrance K. and Eunice C, they lost one child—Harriet B

Stanley, J, far, S. 21, P O. Waterloo

STEARS, HENRY, far, S 6, P O Janesville, Bremer Co, born in Yorkshire, England in 1827, and came to this country in 1835, settling in St Joseph, Mich, where he married Hannah Thurston, in 1855, she was born in St. Joseph County in 1835 In 1853, he moved to Bremer County and resided until 1864, when he came to this township and settled on his present estate, consisting of eighty acres, valued at $35 per acre　Their children are Charles H. and A Genevieve

St. John, M W , far , S 21 , P O Cedar Falls

SUNDERLIN, LETITIA, far , S 5 ; P O Janesville, Bremer Co. , born in Cortland Co., N Y , in 1821, and married William Sunderland in 1872, he was born in Chenango Co , N Y , in 1808　Mrs Sunderland's maiden name was Rohrabacher , her deceased husband had two children by his first marriage—James W , and Martin V　She came to this county, settling on their present farm, consisting of 76 acres, valued at $40 per acre, and where her husband died.

Sunderlin, M V B , far , S 5 ; P O Janesville

Sunderlin, Wm , far , S. 5 , P O. Janesville

THOMPSON, JOSEPH, far., S 13 , P O Waterloo

Timjeon, F , far , S 15 , P O Nautrill

VINCENT, WILLIAM, far , S. 15 , P O. Waterloo, born in England in 1830　Married Elizabeth Salway in 1853 , she was born in England in 1822　Came to this country in 1855, and settled in Cook Co , Ill , where he lived until 1862, when he moved to this county and settled on his present farm of 120 acres, valued at $40 per acre.　Are members of the Methodist Church　William, John and Alice are their children.

WEBSTER, A T , far , S. 4 , P O Janesville

WARREN, CHARLES F., far., S 28 , P O. Cedar Falls, born in Windham Co , Vt , April 5, 1820 Married Nancy Reynolds in 1843 , she was born Sept. 19, 1812 , they emigrated to the West in 1843, settling in Kane Co., Ill , where he lived until September, 1854, when he moved to this county, and settled six miles west of Cedar Falls , in 1860, he settled on his present estate, consisting of 160 acres, valued at $40 per acre　Is one of the early pioneers in this town and county.　Their children were George, born Dec 8, 1845, and died May 29, 1847, and Irving, born Nov 14, 1847, died the same year

WEBSTER, DANIEL, far., S 4 , P O Janesville, Bremer Co., born in Lake Co , Ohio, in 1836, and came to this county in the Fall of 1854, and settled on his present estate, consisting of 120 acres, valued at $40 per acre Married Helen Mills Nov. 22, 1855, she was born in St Joseph Co , ——, in 1836.　Numbered among the early settlers, being one of the five who voted at the first election held in this township　Went to Dubuque to market, and experienced all the difficulties attending early pioneer life.　Their living children are Frank, Fred, Charles, Jessie and Katie, they lost one child—Cappa

Winter, W , far , S 11 , P O Waterloo

Woodbury, Jno , far , S 16 , P O Cedar Falls

Woodbury, Jos , far , S 16 , P O Cedar Falls

WOORE, HENRY, far , S 14 , P O. Waterloo, born in the Island of Jamaica, West Indies, in 1846　In 1861, he enlisted in Co F, 39th Ill Inf , was in the battles of Winchester, Ft Sumter, Deep Bottom, and served three years and one month, and was honorably discharged　Settled on his present farm of eighty acres valued at $40 per acre, in 1871, and in Feb , 1872, married Lydia Moore , she was born in Union Co , Ohio, in 1848 , Cora M , Ira T and Mary J are their living children

WORCESTER, LEVY B., far , S. 32 , P O Cedar Falls, born in Ticonderoga, N Y , in 1820, and married Mary A. Grant in 1844 , she was born in the same place in 1822 ; have three children—Albert T , Myron G and Louisa I　Came to the West in 1855, and settled in Winnebago Co , Ill , where he lived eight months, when he moved to this county and resided nearly one year in Waterloo, when he settled on his present estate, consisting of forty acres, valued at $40 per acre.　Is one of the early settlers in this county. Was Justice of the Peace seven years, and held other town offices, and has been prominently identified with the interests of the town and county

Worcester, M G , far , S 31 , P. O. Cedar Falls.

SPRING CREEK TOWNSHIP.

ASHLEY, C E , far , S 17 , P O La Porte City

Ashley, N F , far , S 8 , P O. La Porte City

BAILEY, C M , far , S 8 , P. O. La Porte City

BAILEY, CHARLES F., farmer, Sec 7 , P O La Porte City, born in Ross Co , Ohio, in 1842, and came to this county with parents in 1858, where he enlisted in the 5th Regt I V I., Co. E, in July, 1861, and was honorably discharged in November, 1865 , participated in the battles of Corinth, Vicksburg and others, and at the close of the war returned to this county, where he married Elizabeth Morris in 1870 , she was born in La Porte Co , Ind , in 1852, have three children—Carrie M , Nellie J and Herbert Owns eighty acres of land, valued at $1,000

Bailey, C P , far., S 8 , P O La Porte City

BAILEY, JOHN M., farmer, S. 8 , P O La Porte City, born in Ross Co , Ohio, in 1832, and married Emily J Stottard in 1854 ; she was born in Erie Co., Ohio, in 1835 , they have six children—Lewis H , Charles M , Lincoln A , Effie E , Edgar and Emma Came to this State with parents in 1850, and settled in Linn Co , where he resided until 1854, and settled in Poyner Tp , and, in 1860, moved on his present farm of 260 acres, valued at $30 per acre , also owns 160 acres in Sioux Co , valued at $2,000 Held the office of Sub-Director and Supervisor, and has been prominently identified otherwise throughout the county

Bailey, J , far., S 8 , P O La Porte City

Bailey, L H , far., S 8 , P O La Porte City

Bannister, A G , far , S 25 , P O Jesup

Bartlett, B. M , far , P O Enterprise

Bartlett, Wm., far., Sec 25 , P O Jesup.

Benorden, W., far., S. 2 , P O Enterprise.

Bingaman, W P , far., S 24 , P. O Jesup

BOEHRINGER, JOHN, farmer, Sec 1 , P. O. Jesup, Buchanan Co , born in Germany in 1817 Married Johana Shoeman in 1842 , she was born in Germany in 1817 , they have

five children—John, Dora, Barbara, John (2d), and Eustine, came to America in 1842, and to this county in 1872, and settled on his present farm of forty-three acres of land, valued at $35 per acre. Are members of the Lutheran Church

Bradfield, C , far , S 9 , P O Enterprise

Bradfield, W R , far., S. 8 , P O Enterprise

Brown, A H., far , S 5 , P. O La Porte City

Brown, G W., far , S 5 , P O La Porte City

BUTLER, WILLIAM, farmer, Sec. 14 , P O La Porte City, born in Germany in 1813 Married Dority Loloff in 1838 , she was born in Germany , have eight children—Frederick, Henry, Albert, Austein, Emma, Harmon, Frank and Bertha , lost four children—Julius, who was killed in the army, Henrietta and two that died in Germany Came to this country in 1867, and settled on his present farm of 275 acres, valued at $35 per acre Are members of the Lutheran Church.

CANADY, ANDREW

Clark, A , far , S 22 ; P O La Porte City

Clark, G , far , Sec 14 , P O La Porte City

Clark, Henry, farmer.

CLARK, JEREMIAH, farmer, Sec 11 , P. O Enterprise , born in Bedford Co , Penn , in 1830 Married Ellen Ritz in 1850 , she was born in the same county in 1831 , Crammel, Sammy, Laura, Belle, Willie and Henry are their children Came to this county in 1866, and settled on his present farm of thirty-eight acres, valued at $25 per acre

Clark, J W., far , S 22 , P O La Porte City.

Clark, L , far , Sec. 24 , P O La Porte City

Clark, W , far , S 13 , P O La Porte City

Conley, Sylvester

Cox, P., far , S. 12 , P. O. Jesup.

Cry, David

FIKE, J L, farmer, Sec 16, P O La Porte City.

FALK, PHELIX, farmer, Sec 6; P O Gilbertville, born in Baden, Germany, in 1827 Married Maggie Zundler in 1858, she was born in the same place in 1836, have six children— Minnie, Rosie, Phœna, Fred, John and Barbara. Came to this country in 1866, and settled on his present farm of ninety acres, valued at $25 per acre

FEHL, JACOB, farmer, Sec. 10, P O Jesup, Buchanan Co, born in Germany in 1837, came to America in 1846, and settled in Washington Co., Wis Married Margaret Lape in 1861, she was born in Germany in 1844. Katie, Jacob, Eliza, Margaret, Mary and George are their living children, have lost two children Came to this county in 1875, and settled on his present farm in May, 1878, consisting of 200 acres, valued at $4 000   Members of the Lutheran Church

Franklin, G., far., S 25, P O Jesup
Franklin, J L, far. S 11, P O Jesup
Franklin, L, far, S. 25, P O Jesup
Franklin, S, far, S 25, P O Jesup
Franklin, Wm., far, S 25, P O Jesup.

GILLEY, S., far, Sec 6, P. O Gilbertville

HAMILTON, E, far, S 6, P O. La Porte City

Hamilton, G, far, S 6, P O La Porte City

HAMILTON, JOHN R., farmer, Sec 6, P O La Porte City, born in Champaign Co Ohio, in 1828 Married Sarah Barton in 1861, she was born in Union Co., Ind, in 1833 Robt G, Madison J, William G and Harry E. are their living children Came to this county in 1855 and, in 1859, returned to Indiana, and settled permanently in this county in 1873, and on his present farm in 1874, consisting of eighty acres of land, valued at $25 per acre.

Hamilton, S, far, S 6, P O. La Porte City

Harmon, C. H, far, S 21, P O Enterprise

Harmon, D, far.; S 20, P O Enterprise

Harmon, G W, far., S 21, P O. Enterprise

Harmon, H N., far, S 21, P O La Porte City

Harmon, W N, far, S 21, P O La Porte City

Haymond, J, far, S 4; P O Enterprise

HEDGE, WILLIAM, farmer, S. 7, P O La Porte City, born in Franklin Co, Penn, in 1842, and married Margaret E. Little in 1875, she was born in Montgomery Co., Penn., in 1853. Feb 4, 1864, he enlisted in 2d Minn Cav., and was honorably discharged in Feb, 1865 Came to this county in 1873, first settling in La Porte City, and in 1874, settled on his present farm, consisting of eighty acres of land, valued at $1,600. Members of Evangelical Church

HOLLENSHEAD, CATHERINE, farming, Sec 23, P O. Enterprise, widow of Levi Hollenshead, who was born in Fulton Co, Penn, in 1821 He married Catherine Giffin in 1842, she was born in the same county in 1822, they have three children living Came to this county in 1854, and settled on their present farm in 1862, consisting of forty acres of land, valued at $1,000   Mr. H enlisted Sept. 1, 1862, and died at Jefferson Barracks Feb 10, 1862, from disease contracted while serving in the cause of his country

Howrey, J A, far, S 21, P O. La Porte City

Howrey, J C, far, P O. La Porte City.

Hower, J, far, S 15, P O. Enterprise.

Howrey, J., far, S 10, P O Enterprise

Howrey, James L., far, S 15, P O Enterprise

KNAPP, JOHN, farmer, Sec 20, P O La Porte City.

Knapp, Judson, far, S. 20, P. O. La Porte City

LANNING, MICHAEL, farmer, Sec 18, P O La Porte City, born in Jackson Co, Ind, in 1830, where he married Martha Sawyer in 1851; she was born in Vigo Co, Ind, in 1833, have six children—William E, Daniel F, Roselbia, J E, Alice A and Laura L, lost one child—Sarah, came to this county in 1852 and settled on his present estate, consisting of 155 acres, valued at $30 per acre   Held the offices of Assessor and Trustee and has been otherwise prominently identified in the interests of the county

LUCAS, PHILLIP, farmer, Sec 19, P O Enterprise, born in Boone Co, Ind, in 1845 Married Mary Ames in 1875 she was born in Randolph Co, Ind, in 1845 Enlisted in 82d Ind V I., Co A, and served one year and was honorably discharged, came to this county in 1873 and settled on his present farm in 1875, of 160 acres, valued at $30 per acre

MASTERS, DAVID, farmer, Sec 13, P. O Jesup
Miller, E, far.,S 16, P O La Porte City,
Miller, M, far, S 17. P O La Porte City
Morris, A, far, S. 6, P O La Porte City
Morris, J, far, S 6, P. O La Porte City.

PLANT, DANIEL R., farmer, Sec 4, P O Enterprise, born in Delaware Co, Ohio, in 1839 Married Mary L Taylor in 1863, she was born in Ohio in 1842, they have two children—Cecelia L. and Thursie R., lost one child—Henrietta Came to this county in 1854 with his parents where he has ever since made it his home, settled on his present farm in the Spring of 1877

RICE, Seth, farmer, Sec 25, P O Enterprise
Rice, M, far, Sec. 25, P O Enterprise
Roberts, E O, far, S 5, P. O Enterprise
Roberts, F P, far, S 9, P O. Enterprise
Roberts, J D, far, S 9, P O Enterprise
Roberts, J J, far., S. 9, P O Enterprise
Roberts, J, far, S 9, P. O Enterprise
SAWYER, EDMOND, SR, far S 7, P. O. La Porte City
Sawyer, E, Jr, far, S. 7, P O. La Porte City.
Sawyer, L D, far, S 7; P. O La Porte City
Schroeder, A., far, S 3, P O Enterprise
Schroeder, N., far, S 3, P. O Enterprise
Shimer, J. P, far, S 21, P O Enterprise.
Smith, G W., far, P O. Enterprise.
Smith, H M., far and P M., S 16, P O Enterprise.
Smith, M H., far and P. M of Enterprise
SPRAGUE, JAMES W., farmer, Sec 5; P O La Porte City, born in Oswego Co., N Y, in 1844. Married Amanda Brown in 1874, she was born in Logan Co, Ohio, in 1846, have one child— Dora M, Mrs S has one child by first marriage—Nellie Hagenbaugh Came to this county in May, 1864, and settled in Poyner Tp, where he still owns a farm of ninety-four acres, valued at $25 per acre He enlisted in the 1st I V C, Co L, in 1864, and was honorably discharged in February, 1865

Stephens, H, far, S 27, P O La Porte

STEVENS, HENRY, farmer, Sec. 20, P O La Porte, born in Waukesha Co Wis, in 1835 and came to this county in July, 1857, where he married Nancy Hammond in 1860, she was born in Indiana July 16, 1841, their children are Alonzo, Sylvester, Clarissa A., Addie, Edith, Alfred, Ellis, Cora and Evalena He enlisted in the 31st I V I, Co D, Aug 8, 1862, and was honorably discharged in August, 1865, engaged in the battles of Lookout Mountain, Vicksburg and others Owns 460 acres of land, valued at $35 per acre Are members of the Church of God

Stephens, S M, far, S 27; P. O. Enterprise
Sutherland, A, far, S 18, P O La Porte
TAYLOR, R C, far, S 17, P O Enterprise
Taylor, F T L, far, S. 17, P O Enterprise

TEETER, DANIEL B., farmer, Sec 15, P O Enterprise, born in Bedford Co, Penn in 1825 Married Emeline Clark in 1850, she was born in same county in 1832, have nine children living—Louis, Hannah R., Nancy M, Thirman D, Dennis A, Susan A, Lucy A, Mahlon H and Thursa, have lost four children—John, David F, Daniel E and Emily J Came to Jefferson Co, Iowa, in 1851, and to this county in 1853, and settled on his present farm, consisting of 200 acres, valued at $30 per acre Mr T was among those of the earliest settlers in this town and county, and has always taken an interest in its public affairs, being well known throughout

WELLS, ABRAMS, far, S 4, P O Enterprise
Wells, H, far, S 4, P O Enterprise
Wells, R, far. S 4; P O Enterprise
WILLIAMS, ABSALOM, farmer, Sec 20, P O La Porte City, born

ın Randolph Co , Ind , in 1833 , came to this county in 1855, and married Sarah Bailey , she was born in Greene Co , Ohio, and dıed in 1871 , they had eıght children by this marriage—Armelıa, Demarquis, Andrew H , Martha H , Lızzıe. Wılhe, Curtıs and Freddie. Hıs present wıfe, Amanda A. Sprague, was born in 1841, and they were married ın 1875 , they have one child Enlısted in the 31st I V I , Co D, ın 1863, and served eleven months, and was honorably dıscharged.   Settled on his present farm ın 1868, of 103 acres, valued at $35 per aore   Are members of the Methodist Church

Wıllıams, I D , far , S 18 , P O. La Porte City.

Wıllıams, M , far , S. 18 , P O La Porte Cıty

Wood, E G., far , S 10 , P. O. Enterprise

Wood, E N , far , S 8 , P O Enterprıse

Woods, E., far., S. 8 , P. O Enterprise

Wood, G N , far , S 10 ; P. O Enterprise

Wood, J. W , far , S 4 , P O Enterprıse

BENNINGTON TOWNSHIP.

ADAMS, J , farmer, Sec 20 , P. O Waterloo

ALLEN, ROBERT, farmer, Sec. 13 , P. O Blakeville, born in Scotland in 1826 , emigrated to this country and Scott Co , Ill , in 1850 , made a trip to California in 1852 , settled on his present farm in 1857 He was married in 1863 to Miss Roxie A Siples, from Canada , they have six children—Edwin G , George W , Jessie A , Ada May, James A., Lewis A He has 180 acres of land, valued at $3,600 He built a large barn in 1875, and a new house in 1877 Mr Allen was among the earliest settlers in this county , he did his trading at Independence for some time after he came to the county , his neighbors were few and far between In politics, Republican.

Appel, Henry, far., S. 19 ; P. O. Waterloo

Appel, John, far , S 19 , P O Waterloo.

BARTH, H , farmer, Sec 15 , P. O. Waterloo

Betts, M W , far , S 26 , P O Waterloo

Biller, A J , far , S 8 , P O Waterloo

Broadbent, B., far , S 16 , P O Waterloo

Brown, A C , far., S 5 , P O Waterloo

Burke, A , far., S. 19 ; P O Waterloo.

Burke, H. B , farmer, Sec. 7 , P O Waterloo

BURK, JOHN, farmer and Justice of the Peace, Sec 6 , P O Waterloo , born in Germany July 30, 1835 , emigrated with his parents to this country and settled in Freeport, Ill , in 1857 , to Iowa and on his present farm in 1858 He was married in 1864 to Miss M C Reinhart, from Germany , she was born Feb 18, 1846 , they have five children —Fred, John, Will, Alfred and Emma L He has 235 acres of land, valued at $25 per acre. He has held the office of Township Trustee three years, Township Assessor two years, Justice of the Peace four years, School Director six years, President of the School Board two years. Mr Burk and his parents were among the earliest settlers in this township They live on Sec. 7 , they are past 75 years of age Mr Burk has always taken a lively interest in his county and township

Burk, J H , far , S. 7 , P O. Waterloo

CAMPBELL, HUGH, farmer, Sec 30 , P O Waterloo

Carigg, S , far , S 14 , P O Waterloo

CASTEEL, PERRY, farmer, Sec 34 , P O Waterloo , born in Coshocton Co , Ohio, in 1830 , he emigrated to Iowa in 1855 , entered a half section of land from the Government the same year , has since sold one-half to his brother , he has 160 acres of land, valued at $4,000 He was married in 1858 to Miss Emeline Herrod, from Knox Co , Ohio , they have eight children—Frank W , Cora A , Bertie M , Minnie E., Carrie A , Thomas L , Walter P and Dora He has held the office of Township Assessor one year, Road Supervisor one year and School Director three years Mr C was among the earliest settlers in the county , he built the second house between Waterloo and Blakeville He built a fine barn, 40x 48, in 1877 He deals quite extensively in cattle and hogs.

CHOATE, NATHAN B., farmer, Sec 20 , P O Waterloo , born in Port Hope, Canada West, June 10, 1832 , emigrated to this country and Wisconsin 1855 , he came to Iowa, and entered his land from the government in 1855, and settled on it in 1856. He was married the same year to Miss E P Leffingwell, from Illinois , she was born in Vermont in March, 1838, her parents emigrated to Ogle Co , Ill., in 1845 ; they were among the pioneers of that county He has 400 acres of land, valued at $12,000, They have two children—Charles S , born Sept 7, 1857, and Charlotte A , born Dec 21, 1863 Mr C. imported to his farm from Canada, in 1872, sixteen head of Devonshire cattle, the pedigree of his herd of thorough-breds shows that they have been carefully selected, he very readily disposes of the increase of his herd. He was among the earliest settlers in the county ; he was present at the meeting for the organization of the county , presented a motion to establish the roads on the section lines, which, though opposed by many, was carried , he has rented his farm the most of the time for the past twelve years, spending his time in Waterloo and Ogle Co , Ill   He is a Republican in politics.

Cleveland, J A , far , S 9 , P O Waterloo

Cone, A , far , S 36 , P O Blakeville.

Cone, G., far , S 35 , P O Blakeville

Cone, L , far , S 36 , P O Blakeville.

CONE, W. A., farmer Sec 26 , P. O Waterloo, born in Pennsylvania in 1816, emigrated with his parents to Connecticut in 1817, and to Wisconsin in 1843, to Iowa in 1869, and on his present farm the same year   He was married in 1841 to Miss Vincy B Mack, from Connecticut , they have had seven children, five living—Augustus, Levi P , Amelia, George and Cynthia   He has 160 acres of land, valued at $4,000   He has held the office of School Director one year, Road Supervisor one year   Mr C has held the position of local preacher for the M E Church for the past thirty-five years , he preaches occasionally now.

COWLISHAW, J. H., farmer S 13 , P O Blakeville, born in England in 1830, emigrated to this country and Pennsylvania in 1830, to Illinois in 1851, across the plains to California in 1852 ; returning, made a trip to England in 1855 , returned and settled on his present farm in 1855   He was married in 1858 to Miss Lucy French, from England , they have had five children, three living—Betsey, Yeoman N and Gertrude   He has 475 acres of land, valued at $15,000   He has held the office of School Director six years, Road Supervisor six years, and Treasurer   Mr S was among the earliest settlers in the county, only two houses being between him and Waterloo at that time   He took another trip to England in 1866.   They are members of the Free-Will Baptist Church , he is a Republican in politics

Cummings, S , far , S 28 , P O Waterloo

DOHNER, JACOB, farmer, S 17 , P O Waterloo.

EICKELBERG, FRED , farmer, S. 10 , P O. Waterloo.

Ennis, Jacob, farmer, Sec 17 , P. O Waterloo

FAUST, HENRY, farmer, Sec. 6 , P O Waterloo

Fink, J , far , S 4 , P. O Waterloo

FOALE, ROBERT S., farmer, Sec 34 , P O. Waterloo , born in Indiana Sept 20, 1833 , emigrated to this State in 1856 , settled on his present farm in 1874   He was married in 1861, to Miss Martha Siple, from Canada , she was born Sept 4, 1843 ; they have four children—Mary A., born July 14, 1863, Joseph L , born March 21, 1865, Eliza J , born June 18, 1869, Elias E , born Aug. 24, 1876 , Eliza died March 18, 1870   He has eighty acres of land, valued at $18 per acre   In politics, Democrat   His parents were among the early settlers in Lester Township

Fritz Conrad, far , S 6 , P O Waterloo

FULLER, D. D., farmer, Sec 21 , P O. Waterloo, born in Vermont Jan. 18, 1828 , moved with his parents to New York in 1834 , he came to De Kalb Co , Ill., in 1855 , to Iowa in 1863, on his present farm in 1865   He was married in 1852, to Miss Abigail J Wordward, from New York , she was born in Chautauqua Co , N Y , Dec 11, 1828   He has 160 acres of land, valued at $4,000   He has made some fine improvements on his farm, among which, is a fine barn, 36x40, built in 1875   He has held the office of Township Assessor three years, Township Treasurer six years, Township Clerk two years, Justice of the Peace two years   They have five children—Katie M , Mary C , Ida E and Fred A , Charles and Katie are dead   Mr F is a Republican in politics   They are members of the Free-Will Baptist Church   He has always taken a lively interest in the affairs of the county and township

Funk, C , far , S 20 , P O Waterloo

GOFF, JAMES, farmer, Sec. 28 , P O Waterloo

Gookins, D J , far , S 17 , P O Waterloo

GRAHAM, HENRY, farmer, Sec. 18 , P O Waterloo   born in Tompkins Co , N Y , in 1836 , he emigrated to Iowa, and on his first farm in 1855   He was married in 1864 to Miss Mary Gibbs, from New York , they have four children—Frances O., Ida, Carrie and Lewis , Frances and Ida are dead   He has 160 acres of land, valued at $4,000   They are members of the Methodist Church   They were among the earliest settlers in the township.

His nearest market was Independence. Politics, Republican

HARDING, E., farmer, Sec 18 , P. O Waterloo

Harding, J , far , S 12 , P O Blakeville.

Hazel, H L , far , S 33 , P O Waterloo

Hecht, Fred., far , S. 23 , P O Waterloo.

Hoffman, J , far , Sec 34 , P O Waterloo.

HOMER, H. P., farmer, Sec 4 , P O. Waterloo, born in Cortland, N Y , in 1836, emigrated to Iowa, and his present farm in 1856 He was married in 1860 to Miss Glorvinia Corwin, from New York, they have three children—Herbert F , Herman C and Adella He has 160 acres of land, valued at $4,000. Mr Homer represented his county in the State Legislature in 1876 , he has held the offices of Justice of the Peace eight years, Township Supervisor two years, Township Trustee five years, Township Clerk two years, and Assessor two years. Mr H is Republican in politics He has always taken a prominent part in the interests of his county and Tp

HUTTON, WILLIAM W., far , Sec 18; P O Waterloo, born in Adams Co , Penn , in 1825, and married Margaret Buck in 1852; she was born in Centre Co., Penn , in 1829, they came to this county in 1856, and now has a farm of 160 acres, valued at $35 per acre, was one of the early settlers in this town and county. Member of the M E Church Has held the offices of Assessor, Township Trustee and Supervisor. Ellen R., Daniel M , Samuel J , Margaret E., William E , Charles W , Ida V and Frank E , are his children

IMMELT, OTTO, farmer, S 16 , P O Waterloo, born in Germany Feb 13 , 1832, emigrated to this country and settled in Chicago in 1852 , he was employed on the construction of the old C & N W R. R for three years , he moved to Kankakee Co in 1855 He was married in 1866 to Miss Mena Dahler, from Germany, she was born Aug. 2, 1844 They came to Iowa, and on his first farm in 1867, he has a fine farm of eighty acres of land, under a good state of cultivation, with fine improvements, which he values at $30 per acre. In politics, he is a Democrat

They are members of the Lutheran Church

JOLLS, D. W., farmer, Sec 30 , P. O Waterloo , born in New York in 1831, emigrated to Michigan in 1853, and to Iowa and Davenport in 1854 , moved to his present farm in 1859 He was married in 1853 to Miss Electa White, from New York ; they have four children—Elva J , Albert W , Edgar and Ida May He has 160 acres of land, valued at $5,000 He has held the offices of Road Supervisor four years, and School Director three years In politics, Republican Mr J erected a fine, large barn (40x60), in 1877 He entered his land from the Government in 1854, he now has one of the finest farms in the Tp He was the earliest settler in the county

KEHE, J C , far., S 2 , P O Blakeville

Kurth, J , far., S 5 , P O Waterloo

LINDSEY, H , far , S 35 , P O Waterloo

Lintred, J., far , S 9 , P O Waterloo

McGINLEY, C

McGinley, H , far , S 8 , P O Waterloo

Michel, J., ret far , S 7 , P O. Waterloo

Millikin, S , far , S 24 , P O Blakeville

Myers, G H , far , S 25 , P O Blakeville

Myers, G K , far , S 15 , P O Waterloo

Myers, H , far , S 2 , P O. Lester

Myers, M , far , S 29 , P O. Waterloo

Myers, S , far , S 24 , P O Blakeville.

NOTTGER, J. PHILLIP, far., S 9 , P. O. Waterloo.

PAUL, C. A , far , Sec 35 , P O Waterloo

Paul, John, far , S. 35 ; P O Waterloo

Potter, W F , far , S. 19 , P O Waterloo

Price, W. H , far , S 11 , P O Waterloo.

REIREL, J M , far , S 11 , P O Waterloo

Ressler, J H., far , S 24 , P O Waterloo

Rhodes, J , far , S 12 , P O. Lester.

Rogers, J., far , S 26 ; P. O. Blakeville.

SAGE G. W , school teacher, Sec. 18 , P O Waterloo

Sage, H , far , S 18 , P O Waterloo

Schenk, C., far , S 21 ; P O Waterloo

SCHENK, JOSEPH, farmer, Sec 19 , P O Waterloo, was born in Germany May 6, 1834, emigrated to this country and Connecticut in 1854 , to

New York in 1855, to Burlington, Iowa, in 1857, he took a trip to California in 1859, returning, he made a trip to Germany in 1863 Was married in 1864 to Miss Mary Gizer, from Germany, she was born Feb 14, 1843 Returning to this country, he settled on his present farm in 1864, he has 240 acres of land, valued at $4,000, they have had seven children—Joseph, John M, Elizabeth, Irwin, Catherine, Lena, Casper W Democrat.

Schutte, H, far, S 4, P O Waterloo.

Smith, Fred, far, S 16, P O Waterloo

SOUTH, CHARLES S., farmer, Sec 25, P O Blakeville, born in Allegheny Co, Penn, Oct 31, 1842, emigrated to this State and his present farm in 1865 He was married, in 1863, to Miss Jane McGill, from Greene Co, Wis, they have five children— John C, Edith R, Harry R, Leonard and Effa He has eighty acres of land, valued at $2,000 He has held the office of School Director one year Mr S enlisted in the army Sept 5, 1861, in the 5th Wis Battery, mustered out March 3, 1863, he was in several severe engagements

Spies, P, far, S 2, P O Lester

Stark, E, far, S 11, P O Waterloo

Stark, M, far, S 2, P O Waterloo

STEELY, JOHN M., farmer, Sec. 10, P O Waterloo, born in Pennsylvania in 1837, came to Iowa, and on his present farm in 1868 He was married in 1859, to Miss Mary Haffa, from Pennsylvania, they have eight children —Allen W, Henry, Ellsworth M., Daniel O, Nelson, John, Joel, Cora E He has 320 acres of land, valued at $6,000 He has held the office of Township Supervisor two years, Township Trustee three years, School Director four years In religion, they are members of the Evangelical Church, in politics, Republican. Mr S has always taken a prominent part in the interests of his county and township

Stickles, S, far, S 3; P O Lester

Stubbs, F W., far, S. 32, P O Waterloo

Stubbs, J. W, far, S 32, P O Waterloo

WARNAKA, JOHN, farmer, Sec 22, P. O Waterloo

Weingarbred, J J., far, Sec 16, P O Waterloo.

WELSTEAD, THOS., farmer, S. 26, P O Blakeville, born in Allegany Co, N Y, in 1838, moved to Illinois in 1863, to Iowa in 1865, and to his present farm in 1869 He was married in 1859, to Miss Lucy Bennett, from New York, she was born April 11, 1836, they have two children— Clarence H., born Aug 19, 1861, Merta B, born Jan 18, 1871 Mr W has 160 acres of land, valued at $4,000 He has held the office of Township Trustee six years, Township Assessor one year, Road Supervisor four years In politics, Republican As a farmer, he has been very successful, and at this time finds himself out of debt and ready to make improvements

Whitney, A, far, S 23, P O Blakeville

Whitney, F A, far, S 23, P O Waterloo

Widdel, C, far., S 27, P O Blakeville

Widdel, H, far, S 5, P O Waterloo

Wilson, J L, P O Waterloo

WILSON, W. A., farmer, Sec 30, P O Waterloo, born in North Carolina in 1834, emigrated to Kossuth Co, Iowa, in 1855; to Mahaska Co. in the Fall of 1859, to this county in 1863, and to his present farm in 1866. He was married in 1858 to Miss Chloe Lawrence, from New York, they have nine children—Barnett A., Ellis E, Mary C, Emma J, William L, Frank G, Edith L, Elsie L and baby He has 240 acres of land, valued at $6,000 He has held the office of Township Trustee two years, Township Assessor one year, School Director five years In politics, he is a Republican

Wining, C, far, S. 4, P. O Waterloo.

YOUNG, J., farmer, Sec 31, P O. Waterloo

UNION TOWNSHIP.

BARKER, R, farmer S. 9, P O. Finchford

BENHAM, WILLIAM, far, S 29, P O. Cedar Falls, born in Aug, 1835, in Brown Co, Ohio, in 1850, came to Stark Co, Ill, in 1854, came to Black Hawk Co, in 1864, came to his present farm, owns forty acres of land, valued at $25 per acre Married Mary Young Nov 20, 1856, she was born in 1840 in Illinois, died April 22, 1863, have three children—E. G, William J, and John S, second marriage to Lucinda Hoesington, June 18, 1865, she was born in 1846, have five children—Hiram, George, Cora, Theodore and Jay

BENNETT, JAMES, farmer, S 16, P O Cedar Falls, born Aug. 14, 1827, in Ireland, in 1840, came to Canada, in 1874, removed to Oswego Co, N Y, in 1850, came to Kane Co, Ill, in 1853, came to his present farm, owns 220 acres of land, valued at $25 per acre Married Elizabeth McNally in 1850, she was born in 1830, in Ireland, had nine children, seven living—Walter J, William A, Lizzie A, Louisa M, Douglas H, Aurrie J and James A He has been Assessor and Road Supervisor.

BOVEE, I. M., farmer, Sec. 21, P O Cedar Falls, born March 6, 1836, in Fulton Co, N Y, in 1851, came to Will Co, Ill, in 1854, came to Black Hawk Co, Iowa, first entered 120 acres of land in Secs 17 and 20, from the Government; now owns 124 acres, valued at $25 per acre His father died in 1854, aged 56 years, his mother died in 1855, aged 54 years. Has been Constable for three or four terms

BOZARTH, CLINTON, farmer, Sec 30, P O Cedar Falls, born April 10, 1830, in Louisa Co, Va., in 1839, came to Muscatine Co, Iowa, in 1850, removed to California; in 1854, came to his present farm, which he entered from the Government, owns 300 acres of land, valued at $30 per acre Married Elizabeth Lane in 1855, she was born April 17, 1833, in Harrison Co, Va, have seven children—Wilford,

Granville, John, Charles, Lee, Harry and Maud He has been School Trustee about five years

BROWN, B. F., agt. B., C R & N R. R., Finchford, born July 14, 1841, in Fulton Co, Ind; in 1869, came to Cedar Falls, Sept 13, 1875, came to his present position Married M E Powers Oct. 13, 1864, she was born May 26, 1845, in Miami Co, Ind; have two children—Charles E and Genevieve Enlisted April 16, 1861, in Co A, 2d Ohio V I, served three months in Co D, 13th Ohio V I, afterward, re-enlisted and served until the close of the war, participated in the battles of Perryville, Ky, Stone River, Chickamauga, Mission Ridge and Lookout Mountain, Allatoona Mountain, Ga, and others, was wounded June 2, 1864, and honorably discharged May 17, 1865

Burke, J.. far., S 7, P O. Finchford

CAMERON, CHARLES, far, S 28, P O Cedar Falls.

Cameron, J R, far., S 28, P O Cedar Falls

Cassaday, W J, Sr far., S 7; P O Finchford

Cassaday, Wm, Jr., blacksmith, Finchford

CHURCHILL, J. P., S 6, P O Finchford

Clark, C, far., S 29, P O Cedar Falls

COLLINS, G. W., S. 6, P O Finchford

Collins, O N, far, S 7, P O Finchford

Corwin, Wm, far, S 7, P. O Finchford

Covey, A H, far., S. 30, P O Cedar Falls

Covey, L W., far, S 30, P O Cedar Falls

Crans, F A, far, S 20, P O. Cedar Falls

Crook, M., far, S 28, P O. Cedar Falls

DEES, M., proprietor mill, Finchford

Deimer, L, prop. Finchford Hotel

Diller, J H, far., S 8, P O Finchford

Dutcher, E, far, S 7, P O Finchford

ELDERKIN, D, far., S 18, P O Cedar Falls

FAIST, C , far , S 18 , P O Cedar Falls

Finch, P. D , merchant, Finchford

Franzkie, H , far., S 9 , P O. Finchford

GERHOLT, C , far , S 20 , P O. Cedar Falls

Gerholt, R , far , S 20 , P. O Cedar Falls

HACKLINGER, F , far , S. 21 , P. O. Cedar Falls

HACKETT, MARY, MRS., daughter of Rosel Lent and widow of John Hackett, Sec 21 , P O. Finchford. He was born in 1804 in Canada, and died in 1863 She was born in 1806 in Clinton Co , N Y Was married in 1831 , they came to their present farm in 1854 , she owns 165 acres of land, valued at $25 per acre, had six children, two living—Alonzo and Delia.

Hammer, A., far., S 9 ; P O Finchford.

Hook, E G , far., S 6 , P O Finchford

JANES, E L , farmer, Sec 21 , P O. Cedar Falls

Janes, H , far , S 21 , P O Cedar Falls

Jones, B , far , S 30 , P O Cedar Falls.

JONES, C. A., farmer, Sec 30 , P. O Cedar Falls , born Dec 14, 1848 Married Emma F Clark April 15, 1874 , she was born April 3, 1855 , have three children—Edith, Emma E and infant His father, Benj Jones, was born Aug 3, 1807, in New Haven , in 1814, came to Windsor Co , Vt , , in 1858, came to Cook Co , Ill , in 1865, came to their present farm they own 320 acres, valued at $25 per acre Married Minerva Smith in 1829, she was born Aug 27, 1811, in Barnard, Vt , had twelve children, three living—Willard S , Mary, Clarence A Elias S. enlisted in 1861, Co. K, 113th Illinois Infantry , served about one year and died of a disease contracted in the army at Vicksburg, Miss

Jones, W , far , S 33 , P O Cedar Falls

KLOCK, P G , farmer, Sec 32 , P. O Cedar Falls.

LANTZ, JOHN, farmer, Sec 5 , P. O Finchford.

McNIEL, JAMES, carpenter, Finchford

March, Jesse, far., S. 6 , P O Finchford.

Marks, L , far , S. 21 , P O. Cedar Falls

Matz, A , blacksmith, Finchford.

Mickley, H , Constable, Finchford

Miller, F., far., S. 8 , P. O. Finchford.

Miller, J M , far , S 9 , P O Finchford.

Miller, M , far , S 9 , P O. Finchford

Miller, Wm , far , S 18 , P O. Cedar Falls.

Margan, A , far , S 21 , P. O Cedar Falls

MORGAN, JNO., farmer, Sec. 16 , P. O. Cedar Falls , born Dec. 14, 1817, in Warren Co., Ohio , in 1849, came to Stark Co , Ill , in 1855, came to Black Hawk Co , Iowa, owns eighty acres, valued at $25 per acre Married Mary A Miller in 1846 , she was born Sept 21, 1829, in Clermont Co , Ohio , have two children—Catharine E. and Andrew

Mulnix, A , far , S 32 , P O Cedar Falls

NEWELL, DAVID, farmer, Sec. 8 , P O Finchford

NEWELL, GEORGE, farmer, Sec 20 , P O Finchford, born Jan 18, 1833, in Wayne Co., Ohio ; in 1836, came to Louisa Co., Iowa ; in 1846, came to Black Hawk Co , in 1856, removed to his present farm , owns 185 acres, valued at $25 per acre Married Adelia Hackett Feb 12, 1856 ; she was born April 19, 1834, in Ohio, have seven children—Alonzo, Mary E , Jennie, Clara, Ernest, Louetta and Louella are twins.

NEWELL, H. J., farmer, Sec. 16 , P. O. Cedar Falls, born Oct 12, 1831, in Wayne Co , Ohio , in 1832, came to Louisa Co , Iowa, in 1846, came to Black Hawk Co , Iowa, in 1856, removed to his present farm , owns 266 acres, valued at $25 per acre. Married Sarah J Benham Nov 20, 1855 , she was born Sept 3, 1840, in Ohio , had seven children, five living—Mary M , Marion F., Florence A., Emmitt M. and Harrison G.

NEWELL, MARION, farmer, Sec. 4 , P. O Janesville, born Jan 21, 1841, in Louisa Co , Iowa , in 1847, came to Black Hawk Co , Iowa, first located a farm in Sec 3, Washington Tp., in 1873, removed to Janesville, and kept the Janesville House , in 1876, removed to his present farm , owns 174½ acres, valued at $25 per acre Married Emily F Webster in 1867 , she was born in March, 1850, in Illinois . had four children, three living—Olive L., May and George H Enlisted in 1862 in Co. B, 38th Iowa V. I , served to the close of the war.

Neswonger, G. W , far , S. 7 , P. O Finch-ford

PASHBY, JOHN, farmer, Sec. 7 , P O Finchford

Peterson, F , far., S 30 , P O Cedar Falls

Plats, J , far , S 5 , P O Finchford

Pound, T R., far , S. 5 , P O Finchford

RANBA, J , farmer, Sec 18 , P O Cedar Falls

Rarick, A., far., S 32 , P O. Cedar Falls

Rich, C , far , S 29 , P O Cedar Falls

Roloff, John, wagon mfr, Finchford

SANDS, GEORGE, farmer, Sec 6 , P O Finchford.

Saul, D , far., S. 32 ; P. O. Cedar Falls

Saul, E , far , S 32 ; P O Cedar Falls

Sharp, J , far , S 7 , P O Finchford

Sohr, C , far., S 9 , P O. Finchford

SMITH, A. L., farmer, Sec 30 , P. O Cedar Falls , born March 31, 1835, in Massachusetts, in 1839, came to Winnebago Co , Ill ; in 1865, came to Black Hawk Co., Iowa ; owns 185 acres, valued at $25 per acre Married Eunice M Wheeler April 2, 1857 , she was born in 1837, in New York , have six children—Fred L , Elsie E., Orvil, Courtney, Orra and Gains Mr S has been three years Assessor

Stanton, E H , far , S 32 ; P O Cedar Falls.

Stanton, L B , far , S. 7 , P O Cedar Falls

Streeter, A , far., Sec 33 , P O Cedar Falls

Streeter, E P , far , S 29 , P. O Cedar Falls

Sturms, H , far , S 9 , P O Finchford

THOMPSON, O S , far., S 9 , P. O Finchford

THOMPSON, HENRY J., farmer, Sec 21 , P O Cedar Falls , born April 6, 1824, near Springfield, Mass , in 1827, came to Washtenaw Co , Mich , in 1833, came to Du Page Co , Ill , in 1854, came to Black Hawk Co , Iowa , owns 120 acres, valued at $25 per acre Married Mary Hawkins in 1858 , she was born in 1839, in New York , have four children—George, William, Clarence and Lillie May

VAN WERT, E A , far , S. 32 , P O Cedar Falls

Van Wert, John, far , S. 32 , P O Cedar Falls

WATSON, U H , far., S 7 ; P O Finchford.

Wood, Samuel, far , Sec 7 , P O. Finchford

POYNER TOWNSHIP.

ALDEN, B D , clergyman, Raymond

Aldrich, D D

Althouse, George, laborer

Ambrose, M , far , S 22 and 23 , P O Gilbertville

Arthur, John, far , P O Gilbertville

BAKER, J. W., far , S 12 , P O Waterloo

BAKER, J. E., farmer, and Local Elder of the M E Church, S 14 , P.O Waterloo , born in Columbia Co , N Y , Dec 6, 1831, moved to New Jersey in 1852 ; to Wisconsin in the Spring of 1857, to Iowa and Black Hawk Co in 1865, on his present farm in 1873 Was married Jan 30, 1855, to Miss Rebecca Robins , they have ten children—Mary, Cathetia, Charlotte R , Richard C , Louisa, Isabella M , Rebecca E , Edwin U , Chas M , Esther He has 280 acres of land in Black Hawk Co , valued at $6,200 ; 160 acres in Grundy Co , valued at $4,000 He was licensed to preach at Freehold, N Y , at the age of 22, and at once entered upon the work of the ministry , at the age of 25, he joined the Wisconsin Annual Conference, in the Fall of 1863, was disabled by sickness , in the Fall of 1866, he was stationed at Buckingham, Tama Co , as a supply , was transferred to the Upper Iowa Conference in 1868, of which he remained a member until the Fall of 1877, when he voluntarily located to attend to the interests of his family and farm , he still preaches occasionally. The daughter, Mary, is a teacher of mathematics at the College for the Blind at Vinton Cathetia and Charlotte are also teachers.

Baker, L , far , Sec 12 , P. O Raymond

Ballow, A , far , Sec 36 , P O Gilbertville.

Ballow, E B , far , S. 12 , P O Gilbertville

Bannister, P , far., S 36 , P O Gilbertville

Barker, J , far , S 36 , P O Raymond

Bell, John, retired, Raymond

Bell, Wm , far , S 14 , P O Waterloo

Bigsby, Levi, far , P O Waterloo.

Bowerman, H K., laborer, Raymond

BROMWELL, J. E., farmer, Sec. 34 , P O Raymond , born in Linn Co , Iowa, March 12, 1847 , moved to Jones Co in 1864, and to his present location in 1865 Married in 1875 to Miss Eliza J Lamb, from England , she was born July 14, 1852 , they have two children—Edward O., born July 6, 1876 , baby, born Feb. 17, 1878 Mr. B held the office of Road Supervisor one year Has eighty acres of land, valued at $2,400 In politics, Republican His mother lives with him , she was born in Kentucky in 1816 , his father died in 1866.

Bronson, F , laborer, Raymond.

Bronson, J. W., far , S 15 , P O Raymond

Bronson, L H , laborer, Raymond

Buchner, J C , far , S 1 , P O Waterloo

BURROUGHS, J. W., clergyman and pub and prop. of *Burroughs' Journal*, Raymond , born in Erie Co , N Y , in 1832 , moved to Pennsylvania in 1837 , to Illinois in 1845 , to Floyd Co , Iowa, in 1853 , settled on his present location in 1874 He was married in 1862 to Miss H A Bockus, from Pennsylvania. Mr B has been in the ministry for the past twelve years, seven years in Illinois and five years in Iowa , he has been the Pastor of the Christian Church at Raymond for four years , published the *Burroughs' Journal* for five years, eighteen months in Streator, Ill., as *Rock of Salvation,* and three years in Raymond as *Burroughs' Journal.* He is also Pastor of the Christian Church at Cedar Falls, has been its Pastor for three years

Butler, R W , physician, Raymond

Butterfield, A., far., S 2 , P. O. Raymond.

CALDWELL, C. C , far , S. 36 , P O Raymond

Call, O , blacksmith, Raymond.

CAMPBELL, C. B., far. and stock raiser S 13 , P. O. Raymond ; born in Columbia Co , N Y , in 1843 , moved to Waterloo, Iowa, in 1865 , settled on his present farm in 1872 , he has 360 acres of land valued at $9,000. He represented his county in the Legislature in 1874-5 ;

Township Assessor one year Mr C is quite extensively engaged in stock raising, he makes blooded hogs a specialty, the Poland-China is his favorite

Carey, A, far, S 12, P O Waterloo.

Carrington, C., farmer, Raymond.

Carroll, H, far, S 35, P O Gilbertville

Carroll, J, farmer, Gilbertville

Chamberlin, C, far., S 36, P O Raymond.

Chapelski, railroad hand, Raymond

Ciegler, C, retired, Raymond

Clark, A D., far, S 2, P O Raymond

CLOSE, J. F., blacksmith, Gilbertville, born in Prussia in 1832, came to this country, and Prairie du Chien, Wis, in 1858, to Iowa and Allamakee Co. in 1859, to McGreger in 1863, and to Black Hawk Co. in 1865 He was married in 1862 to Miss Dora Shroeder, from Prussia, they have two children —Julia, born in 1873, and Anna, born in 1875 He has 160 acres of land, valued at $4,000 He was in the Government employ as blacksmith at Nashville and Chickamauga in the Winter of 1864-5 Mr Close is an A No 1 workman, and thereby secures a large business, he also manufactures " The Freedman Patent Drag "

Collum, J, farmer, Waterloo

Cook, I, far, S. 14, P O Raymond

CORWIN, I. T., farmer, Sec 25, P O Gilbertville, born in Tompkins Co, N Y, in 1827 moved with his parents to Lake Co, Ill., in 1845 He was married in 1853 to Miss Sarah Davis, from Illinois, they moved to Iowa, and located on their present farm in 1854, they have five children—Howard M, Elmer F., Ella J, Fred W, Nettie E They have 380 acres of land, valued at $10,000 He has held the office of County Supervisor seven years, and holds the same by appointment now, Justice of the Peace seven years, Tp Clerk two years, Tp. Assessor two years, and Road Supervisor two years Has always taken a prominent part in the interests of the county and township He moved to this State with an ox team, arriving at Independence, they found the roads so bad, caused by heavy rains, that they were obliged to leave their team and foot it to their present

home, they endured many privations, neighbors very scarce, and Cedar Falls their nearest market, and Independence their nearest mill He assisted in the organization of the Township, and gave to Gilbertville the name of Frenchtown, by which it is now called Going to G one day, he met a neighbor who asked him where he was going, he said "to Frenchtown," by which name it has since been called, except as a Post Office

Corwin, J A, far, S 12, P O Gilbertville

Daniels, C H, farmer, Raymond.

Deisch, J, far, S 14, P. O Gilbertville.

Deisch, N, far, S. 14, P O Gilbertville

Deitrick, W. S, merchant, Raymond

Denniston, M G, far, P O Waterloo

DIXON, T. A., far, Sec 24, P O Gilbertville, born in Columbus, Ohio, in 1845, moved to Illinois in 1851, to Iowa and Black Hawk Co in 1856, on his present farm in 1868 He was married the same Spring to Miss Lucy Wheeler, from Indiana, they have four children—Adda J, Ernest, Willie and Alfred He has 200 acres of land, valued at $6,000 Republican His parents were among the earliest settlers of the county

Douglass, O M, farmer, P O Waterloo

Edgington, G T, farmer, P O Raymond

Edgington, J T, far, S 35, P O Raymond

Edmunds, E B, far, S 23, P O Waterloo

Edwards, J B, far., S 11, P O Raymond.

Eickelberg, C, far., P O Gilbertville

EMERT, J. J., far, S 12, P. O. Waterloo, born in Somerset Co, Penn., May 25, 1837, moved to Illinois in 1857, returned to Pennsylvania in 1859, to Iowa in 1868 He was married Aug 19, 1866, to Miss Elizabeth Maurer from Pennsylvania, she was born Jan 6, 1841 ; they have had four children—Ross W, born Aug. 31, 1867, Clara B, born Nov. 11, 1869, Annie M., born May 25, 1871, Carrie V, born Aug 15, 1877, Clara B and Annie M are dead. Mr. E enlisted in the 2d Ky V C, Co G, August, 1864; mustered out in 1865 He has 360 acres of land, valued at $12,000 He has held the office of School Director three years, Treasurer three years, Road Supervisor two years Mr. Ernest has a beautiful farm, with a fine residence and farm buildings Republican, his wife is a member of the Lutheran Church.

ENGLE, JOHN, far , S 25 , P O Raymond , born in Belmont Co , Ohio, in 1833 , moved with his parents to Morgan Co in 1835 ; to Washington Co in 1839 , to Iowa, and Black Hawk Co , in 1860 , on his present farm in 1865 He was married in 1854 to Miss Louisa Heald from Ohio , they have had five children—Levi H., William W , Rosetta L , Allen W and Ivie L William W is dead Mr Engle served in the army as Quartermaster in Gen Sully's division He has 217 acres of land, valued at $6,000 , he erected a large barn during the past year Republican , he was brought up in the Quaker faith

Engle, Richard, laborer, Raymond
Englert, Herman, farmer.

FAGAN, JOHN, far., Sec 2 , P O Raymond.
Faulk, George, shoemaker, Gilbertville.
Fleming, Matt, wagon maker, Gilbertville
Follett, O , far , S 11 , P O Waterloo.
Fox Jas , far , S. 11 ; P O Waterloo.

FULLER, BENJ., farmer, Sec 35 , P O Raymond , born in Caledonia Co , Vt , Sept 18, 1813 , he moved to Dodge Co , Wis., in 1843 , to Iowa and on his present farm in the Fall of 1867 He was married in 1836 to Miss Betsy Cole, from Vermont , they had one child —Ebenezer , his wife died in May, 1844 He was married again in 1847, to Miss Maria Griffin, from Wisconsin , she died Jan. 31, 1869. He was married again in September, 1869, to Miss Sarah E. Bunbury, from Waterloo , she was born May 23, 1845 , they had two children—Florence, born July 4, 1871 ; baby, born Feb. 2, 1878 He has 100 acres of land, valued at $5,000 He has held the office of School Director two years. Politics, Republican

GAUSCHE, JOHN, farmer, Sec 1 , P. O Gilbertville
GIGER, J. F., farmer, Sec. 26 , P O Gilbertville, born in Perry Co.,

Ohio, in 1842, moved to Iowa, and Tama Co , in 1851 , to his present location in 1875 He was married in 1869 to Miss M Winset, from Indiana , they have had one child—Regina, born Aug 28, 1872 Mr G. enlisted in the 44th I V I , Co. G, in the Spring of 1864 , mustered out in the Fall of 1864 He has eighty acres of land, valued at $2,000 Has held the office of Township Assessor the past two years, School Director two years Mr G took a regular classic course at Cornell College, Linn Co., Iowa, graduated in 1869

Gilley, M , far , S 2 , P O Gilbertville
GILLEY, THOMAS, farmer, Secs. 23 and 24 , P O Gilbertville ; born in Wyoming Co., N Y , in 1845 , moved with his parents to Iowa and this county in 1856 , settled on his present farm in 1873 He was married in 1873, to Miss Aggie Schroder from New York , she died in 1876 He lives with his brother Michael, on Sec 2 , he has ninety-four acres of land, valued at $3,000 His family were among the earliest settlers of the county , his father died in 1862 , his mother still lives, and makes her home at Gilbertville

Girsh, M , far , S 1 , P O Gilbertville
Gould, D W., far , S 10 , P O. Raymond.
Gould, H. D , far., S 10 , P O Raymond
Gray, C., far , S 12 , P O La Porte City

HALLOWELL, A B , school teacher, Raymond.
Hallowell, P , far , S. 26 ; P. O. Raymond
Hallowell, W. A., laborer, Raymond

HANTEN, JOHN, merchant, Gilbertville, born in Luxemburg, Holland, in 1839 , he came to this country and Will Co , Ill , in 1862 , to Iowa in 1865, and to his present location in 1872 He was married in 1865, to Miss Susan Demuth, from Luxemburg , they have had five children—Susan, Michael, Bernard, Helena, Nicholas He has forty acres of land, 150 village lots in Gilbertville, and a mill privilege on the Cedar, adjoining the town. Mr. H enlisted in 1863, in the 2d Ill Art , Co K , mustered out in 1865 He commenced the building of his mill and dam in 1876, but owing to the hard times he did not succeed in its completion. He has lately taken in a partner (Peter Beruner). The company is now incorporated as the Gilbertville Milling Co Mr Hanten keeps a general stock of merchandise The company propose to establish a ferry across the Cedar at this point

Hamilton, W , far , S 11 , P O La Porte City.

Hanton, John, merchant, Gilbertville

HARROD, S. R., far , S 3 , P. O. Raymond, born in Ohio Dec 2, 1846 , moved with his parents to Iowa, and Fox Township, in 1863 , on his present farm in 1878 Was married Oct 10, 1877, to Miss Alice Dixon, from Fox Township, Black Hawk Co He has 150 acres of land, valued at $4,000. He held the office of Assessor one year In politics, Republican

Haynes, W B , far., S 11 , P O Raymond

Healas, R W , far , S. 25 , P O Waterloo

Heathershaw, W , far

Heid, F , carp , Gilbertville

HINEN, HENRY, far , S 12 , P O Raymond , born in Germany in 1835, came to this country and Illinois in 1857 , to Iowa and on his present farm in 1867 Was married in 1862, to Miss Annie Brock, from Indiana, have had five children—Mary S , Jack H , Edna, Fred and William C He has eighty acres of land, valued at $2,500. Mr Hinen worked his way up from nothing to the owner of a good farm all paid for

Heinen, V , far , S 14 , P O Raymond

HEIPLE, N. J., far , S 10 , P O Waterloo ; born in Somerset Co , Penn , in 1828 , moved to Illinois in 1855 , to Iowa and Waterloo in 1867, on his present farm in 1869 He was married in 1849, to Miss Elizabeth J. Lint, from Pennsylvania , they have nine children—John W , Henry F , Everst W , Benj W., William G , Davis S., James I , Hattie A and Mary C He has eighty acres of land, valued at $1,600 He has held the offices of School Director three years and Secretary of the School Board one year.

HIGHSMITH, J. M., far S 11 , P O Waterloo, born in Lawrence Co., Ill., in 1837; moved to La Salle, Ill , in 1849 ; to Iowa, and Tipton in 1854 , to Jackson Co., in 1856 ; on his present farm in 1857. He was mar-

ried in 1862, to Miss Elizabeth Freeborn, from N. Y , they have an adopted son—Clarence S Mr H was engaged in driving the first hack in Waterloo for six months He has 160 acres of land, valued at $4,000 He was among the early settlers of the county, very few in this township when they settled here In politics, Democratic

Hobson, J W , far , S 36 , P O Raymond

HOXIE, A. K., farmer and money loaner, S 36 , P O Raymond; born in Delaware Co , N Y , Nov 30, 1814 , he moved, with his parents, to Cayuga Co., N Y , in 1815 , to Wayne Co , Penn., in 1848 , to Iowa and this county in 1872 , settled on his present farm in 1877 He was married in 1848, to Miss J. E Preston, daughter of the Hon Paul S Preston, from Wayne Co , Penn. , they had three children—Alma A , Paul P and Henryetta M , his wife died in April, 1853 He has sixty acres of land, valued at $1,800 Mr Hoxie was extensively engaged in farming, milling, lumbering and mercantile business in Pennsylvania for several years His son, Paul P , was married to Nora Washburn, from Illinois, in 1877 , he is a miller by trade , he lives with his father on the farm

Hoxie, C H., renter, S 35 , P O Raymond

Hoxie, J J , carp., Raymond

Hoxie, P P , far., S 36 , P O Raymond.

Hunter, C O , far , S 24 , P O Waterloo

JENKINS, WILLIAM, farmer , Sec 2 , P O Waterloo

JOHNSTON, GEORGE, farmer, Sec. 31 , P O Raymond, born in Ireland in 1802 , came to this country and Ohio in 1818 , moved to Iowa and this county in 1856 He was married in 1830 to Miss S Little, from Ireland , they had five children , she died in the Spring of 1841 He was married again in the Fall of 1841 to Mrs. Margrette Simpson, from Pennsylvania , they have had five children — John, Richard, George A , Edward S. and Caroline R He owns 250 acres of land in Barclay Tp , valued at $6,000. He has held the offices of School Director five years, and School Treasurer four years In politics, Republican; religion, Methodist His sons Richard, George A. and James E were in the army. Mrs Johnston was thrown from a carriage in Feb, 1877, and dislocated her hip, by which she is made a cripple for life

KEEFE, D, farmer, Sec 12, P O Raymond

Kelley, E., far, S. 2, P O Gilbertville.

Kelley, J, far, S 2, P O Gilbertville

KIEFFER, J. P., Justice of the Peace, Gilbertville, born in Luxemburg, Holland, in 1849, came to this country and Wisconsin in 1864, to Iowa and Dubuque in 1866, to Waterloo in 1868, to Gilbertville in 1871 He was married in 1873 to Miss Leona Gohmaux, from Cedar Tp, they have one child—Jossie, born Jan. 25, 1875 Mr K was engaged in the mercantile trade for a short time, he now holds the offices of Justice of the Peace, Notary Public and Township Clerk.

Kirsch, M., far., S 23, P O Gilbertville.

LEWIS, G, farmer, Sec 36, P O. Raymond

LEWIS, M. D., farmer, Sec 36, P O. Raymond, born in Tioga Co, Penn, in 1827, he moved to Ogle Co, Ill, in 1854, to Mitchell Co, Iowa, in 1855; to Worth Co., in 1856, to Carroll, Ill, in 1857, to Clinton, Iowa, in 1858, to Iowa and on his present farm in 1866 He was married in 1849 to Miss Margaret Wilson, from Pennsylvania, they have had eight children, four living—George E, Mary J, Wilber W, Charles W He has 200 acres of land, valued at $5,000. Mr Lewis followed millwrighting and carpentering fourteen years His son, George E, lives with him, he has followed the carpenter's trade four years past and is also interested in the farm

MANGRIST, JOHN, farmer, Sec 14, P O Gilbertville

McSHANE, JOHN, farmer, Secs. 11 and 12, P. O La Porte City, born in Scotland in 1825, came to this country and Illinois in 1853, to Iowa and this county in 1857 He was married in 1853 to Miss Margrette Johnston, from Scotland, they have had eight children—John, Henry, James, William, Edward, Joseph, Mary A and Margrette He has 594 acres of land, valued at

$5,000. He has held the office of School Director three years In politics, Democratic

MARBLE, JOHN N., Justice of the Peace, mason and shoemaker, Raymond, born in Unadilla Co, N. Y, in 1818, he moved to Illinois in 1862, returned to New York in 1872, to Iowa in 1873. He was married in 1839 to Miss Martia Barber, from New York, they have had four children—Betsy R, Edmund, Lillie, Thornton, Lillie died. Mr M. has held the office of Justice of the Peace for the past six years In politics, Republican, religion Methodist Mr. M has always taken a great interest in his county and township

Marble, M A, far, S. 11, P O Raymond

Marx, N, far, S 24, P O Gilbertville.

Melich, John, far., S 1, P O Waterloo

Messinger, E J, far, S 15; P O Waterloo

MILLER, C. & M., merchants, Gilbertville, born in Germany. C Miller was born June 12, 1836; came to this country and New York in 1856, to Iowa and his present location in 1869 He was married in 1866, to Miss Elizabeth Welter, from Germany, they have had seven children—five living—Leonard, Matthias, Mary, Maggie and Katie He holds the office of Constable at this time M Miller was born in 1829, came to this country and New York in 1854, to Illinois in the Spring of 1855, to Michigan in the Fall of 1855; to New York, in 1856, to Illinois in 1857, to Iowa and his present location in 1869 He was married Jan 17, 1855, to Miss Mary Gasper, from Germany, they have had ten children, seven living—Maggie, Michael, John, Mary, Catherine M, Christina and William J Mr Miller has held the office of Postmaster for the past eight years The brothers carry a general stock of merchandise, dry goods, groceries, crockery, boots and shoes; the firm name since May 1, 1878, is C & M Miller

Mulqueen, M, sec boss, I C R R., Raymond

NEMMERS, JOHN, REV., Pastor of the "Immaculate Conception" Church, Gilbertville, born in Tete Des Morts, Jackson Co., Iowa, in 1847; he commenced his studies for the ministry at Milwaukee in 1866; completed his course in Dubuque in 1874; he became Pastor of this Church in 1875, which now has a membership of 120 families; they have a fine church building 36x66; he also has charge of the church in Barclay Tp., with a membership of twenty-seven families, with a new church 32x48; they have two private schools connected with the church in Gilbertville, with a membership of 100 pupils

O'NIEL, A G., far, S 36, P O Gilbertville

OWENS, DAVID, farmer, Sec 11, P O Raymond; born in North Carolina in 1825; moved to Bedford Co, Tenn, in 1832; to Indiana in 1835; to Illinois in 1850; to Iowa, and on his present farm, in 1855 He was married in 1843, to Miss Sarah Hollar, from Indiana; they had nine children; his wife died in 1864; married again, in 1866, to Miss Eliza Barker, from Vermont; have had four children—William L, Emery E., Carrie E, Mary A He has held the office of Assessor one year, Secretary of the School Board eight years, School Director six years He has eighty acres of land, valued at $3,000, which he entered and purchased from the Government

PEEK, JOHN, far, S 14, P O Waterloo

PAUL, W. T., far, Sec 2, P O. Waterloo; born in Illinois in 1829; moved with his parents to Iowa and Dubuque in 1830; settled in his present location in 1877; the farm is owned by C F Green Was married in the Spring of 1852, to Miss Lorena Sutherland, from Davenport; have had six children — Alonzo L, William A, Amelia J, John C F, Emma L and Henry W He has held the office of School Director four years. His father, John Paul, was in the Black Hawk war, at Galena; he was among the first who were allowed to cross the river at Dubuque at the close of the war He was engaged in mining for several years, when he moved into the township north and engaged in farming

Poyner, H, far., S 26, P O. Gilbertville
Poyner, J, far, S 25, P O Gilbertville
Poyner, T, far., S 10, P O Raymond

RATHS, CHARLES A, retired, Gilbertville
Reed, I, far, S 14; P O Waterloo
Reed, S W., far, S 12; P O Waterloo
Roberts, N, far, S 23, P O Gilbertville

RUTTER, W. H., farmer, Sec 23, P. O Raymond; born in Pennsylvania in 1831; moved to Jo Daviess Co., Ill, in 1855; to Iowa and Black Hawk Co in 1867; on his present farm in the Fall of 1869 He was married in 1852 to Miss Catherine Grove, from Pennsylvania; they have six children—Samuel G, Rossie J, Louisa E, Francis P, Cora M and Ira E He has 100 acres of land, valued at $3,000 He has held the offices of Township Trustee eight years, Road Supervisor six years In politics, Republican; religion, German Baptist

SAWYER, GEORGE, farmer, Sec 12, P O La Porte
Scott, D H, far, S 11, P O Raymond

SHAW, C. L., farmer, Sec 35, P O Raymond; born in Wyoming Co, N Y, in 1836; moved to Illinois in 1853; to Iowa and Cedar Falls in 1866; on his present farm in 1876 He was married in 1857 to Miss Jeannette Culver, from New York; they have four children, three living—Elmer F., born Sept 28, 1859, Carrie D, born March 31, 1862, Lottie, born April 26, 1869 He has 240 acres of land, valued at $7,000 He enlisted in the 105th I V I, Co A in 1862, mustered out June 20, 1865; he was in sixteen severe engagements He was in the Atlanta campaign with Gen Sherman He has held the offices of Township Assessor, one year; Township Clerk one year

Shimer, I, far., S 35, P O Gilbertville
Sickles, D, rent, S 1, P O Raymond
Smith, A, far, S. 27, P O Waterloo.
Smiley, S, far, S. 12, P O La Porte City
Smiler, J., renter, S 13, P O La Porte City
Sprague, J J, far, S 13, P O. La Porte City

SPRAGUE, THALMA, farmer, Sec 13, P O. La Porte City; born in Oswego Co, N Y, June 19, 1815; moved to Wisconsin in 1845; to Iowa and on his present farm in 1855 He was married in 1837 to Miss Hannah

Baldwin, from New York, born May 2, 1817, they have had nine children, three living—Julius J., born June 20, 1846, Milvina, born April 4, 1852, Lester S, born Dec 17, 1857. He has 200 acres of land valued at $6,000. He has held the office of School Director five years. Mr Sprague is among the pioneers of the county Cedar Falls was the nearest market, Independence the nearest mill Mr S followed the lakes for fourteen years, Oswego to Cleveland his principal route

THELGERN, FRANK, farmer, Sec 3, P O Waterloo

URAN, H, farmer, Sec 13, P O. Gilbertville.

VAN VLACK, JOHN, farmer, Sec 36, P. O Gilbertville.

VAIL, D., farmer, Sec 30, P O Waterloo, born in Coshocton Co., Ohio, in 1810, he moved to New Jersey in Fall of 1828, returned to Ohio in 1832, to New Jersey in 1845, to Iowa, and on his present farm in 1866 Married in 1835 to Miss Phebe Quimby, from New Jersey, they have had eleven children, seven living—Sarah J, Emma E, Theodore M, Isaac Q, William A, Mary I and Louise D H. He has 320 acres of land, valued at $10,000. His son, Theodore M., holds the position of General Superintendent of the Railway Mail Service, which position he has held for the past five years Isaac Q, holds position of Postal Clerk from Ogden to Green River, Utah William A, holds position of Postal Clerk from Dubuque to Chicago Mrs Vail's mother lives with her, she is 84 years old; she has twelve great grandchildren

Veach, John, far., Sec 2; P. O. Waterloo.

Vroom, J, far, S. 12, P O Raymond.

WAGNER, MICHAEL, far, Sec 23, P O Gilbertville

WALLACE, GEORGE T., farmer, Sec 10, P O Waterloo, born in Essex Co, N Y, in 1849, came to Iowa and on the estate in 1868. He was married in 1873 to Miss Sarah Schenk, from New York, they have two children—Eliza and Burt • His father, John Wallace, died in 1873, his mother still lives, her home is in Monticello. George has carried on the estate for the

past ten years. He has held the office of Road Supervisor one year

Walsh, E E, merchant, Raymond.

WALSH, JOHN, merchant and shoemaker, Raymond, born in Pennsylvania in 1831, moved to Ohio in 1843, to Missouri in 1861, to Iowa and his present position in 1871 He was married in 1851 to Miss Martha A Ellis, from Ohio, they have seven children—Alva A, Elva E, Laura M., Charles C., Eddie E, Frances Ida and George P He has held the offices of Township Trustee four years, School Director three years. Mr Walsh is in partnership with his son, Elva E., in the drug, grocery and notion business, he also carries on shoemaking and the sale of agricultural implements Elva E. is Postmaster for Raymond

WATERFIELD, WM., far, Sec 3, P O Raymond, born in New Jersey May 4, 1828; moved to Iowa in the Spring of 1856, and on his present farm the same year He was married in 1850 to Miss Mercy Van Syckle, from New Jersey, they have had two children, both dead, his wife died in 1859 He was married again in September, 1860, to Miss Nancy Hughs, from North Carolina, they have had two children—Geo C., born July 12, 1862, Mary E, born April 26, 1865, he has eighty-three acres of land, valued at $4,000 He has held the offices of Justice of the Peace two years, Township Trustee, three years, and Assessor, one year In politics, Republican Mr W often fills appointments as preacher for the M E Church; he also gives lectures on phrenology

White, J F, far., S. 11, P O La Porte City

White, S D., far, S 11, P O La Porte City

Wheeler, Wm, far., S. 14, P O Raymond.

Wilds, B B, carpenter, Raymond.

Williams, A H., laborer, Raymond.

Winset, B, far, S 26, P O Gilbertville

Winset, B. C, far, S 24, P. O Gilbertville

Winset, J K, far, S. 2; P. O. Raymond.

WINSET, THOS., farmer, Sec. 26, P. O Gilbertville; born in Poyner Tp, Black Hawk Co, in 1854, settled on his present farm in 1876. Married

May 28, 1876, to Miss Ella Herrod, from Fox Tp., Black Hawk Co.; have had one child—Claud L., born March 28, 1877. Mr. W. has held office of Road Supervisor one year. Has eighty acres of land, valued at $2,400. His father, Benj. Winset, was one of the pioneers of the county and assisted in its organization.

ZIMMER, JOHN, farmer, Sec. 1; P. O. Waterloo.

Zimmer, M., far., S. 24; P. O. Gilbertville.

WASHINGTON TOWNSHIP.

ALGIER, JOHN, far , S 2 , P O Janesville

Anderson, J , far , S 27 , P O Cedar Falls

Andrews, S., far , S 36 , P O Cedar Falls

Andrews, Wm , far , S 36 , P O Cedar Falls

Augustson, H , far , S 2 , P O Janesville

BAKER, JAMES, far , Sec 13 , P O Cedar Falls

Baker, R., far , S 15 , P. O Cedar Falls.

Bennett, J , far , S 13 , P O Cedar Falls.

Boomer, D G , far S 12 , P O Cedar Falls

Boomer, M , far , S 12 , P O Cedar Falls

CAMP, A , far , S 25 , P O Cedar Falls

Carroll, F., far , S 26 , P. O Cedar Falls

CRAIL, A. M., farmer, Sec 12 , P O Janesville; born May 29, 1830, in Beaver Co , Penn , March 15, 1854, came to Janesville, Bremer Co, Iowa, in 1857. came to his present farm Owns 160 acres, valued at $35 per acre Married Caroline Mowry Nov. 24, 1853, she was born July 3, 1835, in Beaver Co., Penn ; had seven children, six living—Arlo, Miranda, Martha, Mary, Flora and Wesley. Enlisted Aug 15, 1862, in Co B, 38th I V I, and served to the close of the war Is Township Assessor , has held this position the past five years Are members of the M E Church

Crail, J. A , far , S 12 , P. O. Janesville

COCHONOUR, GEORGE W., farmer, S 26 , P O. Cedar Falls, born April 20, 1844, in Seneca Co , Ohio , in 1856, came to Black Hawk Co , Iowa, in 1872, removed to his present farm Owns forty-five acres, valued at $60 per acre Married Lydia Ford Feb 7, 1867 , she was born April 16, 1846, in Wyandot Co , Ohio, have one child— Nettie L , born June 11, 1868 Are members of the United Brethren Church.

Cochonour, J , far., S 35 , P O Cedar Falls

Cole, B , far , S 2 ; P O Janesville

Cole, C , far , S 3 , P O Janesville

Cook, V., far , S. 26 , P. O. Cedar Falls

Corwin, H E , far , S. 2 , P. O. Janesville

DAVIS, CHAS F , far , S 24 , P. O Cedar Falls

Davis, J W , far , S 24 , P. O. Cedar Falls

Dean, H , far , S 25 , P O. Cedar Falls

Dwight, R , far., S 14 , P O. Cedar Falls

FAIRBROTHER, A., far , S 2 , P. O Janesville

Fairbrother, C M., S 2 , P O Janesville

Fairbrother, M., far., S. 2 , P. O Janesville

FISH, E. W., farmer, blacksmith and wagon maker, S 2 , P O Janesville; born May 31, 1825, in Otsego Co , N. Y , in 1853, came to Bremer County, Penn , in 1867, removed to Black Hawk Co , owns sixty-five acres of land, valued at $30 per acres Married Lorilla Tabor in 1852, she was born May 19, 1827, in Erie Co , Penn., have five children—Harvey E , Horace G , Alice C , Annette L. and Bertha A., have one child by a former marriage— Elizabeth M Has been Township Clerk of Bremer Co , Treasurer of the School Board, Township Trustee and School Director

Fish, H. G , far., S 2 , P O Janesville.

Flickinger, J , far , S 36 , P O. Cedar Falls

Ford, C , far., S. 36 , P. O. Cedar Falls.

Ford, D., far , S 25 , P. O. Cedar Falls.

Ford, F , far , S 26 , P. O. Cedar Falls.

Ford, H D., far., S 23 ; P O Cedar Falls

Ford, J , far , S. 23 , P. O Cedar Falls.

Ford, N , far , S 35 , P. O Cedar Falls

Ford, R , far , S. 26 , P. O Cedar Falls

Ford. R R , far , S 13 , P. O. Cedar Falls

GODFREY, J. A , far , S 3 , P O Janesville

HELFER, J , far , S 26 , P O Cedar Falls

Helfer, Jesse, far , S. 35 , P O Cedar Falls

HELM, ALONZO, farmer, S. 10 ; P O Cedar Falls ; born July 5, 1835, in St Joseph Co , Mich. , in 1836, came to Stephenson Co , Ill , in 1843, came to Benton Co , Iowa, in 1854, removed to Tama Co Iowa, in 1862, returned to

Benton Co., Iowa, and in 1864, came to Black Hawk Co Owns 155 acres of land, valued at $35 per acre. Married Emily Rextrew Sept 7, 1857, she was born Sept. 3, 1837, in Greene Co., Ohio, have nine children—Mary Ann, Wm L, Sarah R. Lucretia J, Lillie E, Nettie C., Charles F, Alonzo R and Frank U. Enlisted in 1861 in Company B, 28th Iowa V I., and served about six months, was discharged on account of sickness

Helm, R, far, S 14, P O Cedar Falls

Helm, V, far, S. 11, P O. Cedar Falls

Helm, W, far, S 11, P O Cedar Falls

Hicock, J D, far, S. 2; P O Janesville.

Hicock, S W, far, Sec. 13, P O Cedar Falls

Houghtaling, W., far, S 34, P O Cedar Falls

Howe, W, Sr, far, Sec 24, P O Cedar Falls

Howe, W., Jr., far, S. 11, P. O. Janesville.

Huckins, J, far, S 2, P O Janesville

JEFFERS, J. H, farmer, Sec 36, P O Cedar Falls

Johnson, D, far, S 13, P O Cedar Falls

Jones, H, far, S. 15, P O Cedar Falls

Jones, W. E, far, S 15, P O Cedar Falls

JORDAN, D. W., far, S 23, P O. Cedar Falls, born Sept 6, 1815, in Steuben Co, N Y, May 14, 1845, left for Ohio, in 1853, came to his present farm, owns 335 acres of land, valued at $35 per acre. Married Harriet Swarthout in 1838, she was born June 19, 1820, in Steuben Co, N Y, had seven children, four living — Henry, Michael, Harrison and Mary Henry enlisted in 1861, in the 10th Kan V. I., Co. K, served about three years and was honorably discharged, Michael enlisted in 1861, in Co. G, 9th I V I, served to the close of the war Mr J. was the first Assessor of this township, the election was held at his house, was for four years Township Superintendent

Jordan, H., far., S 23, P O Cedar Falls.

Jordan, M L, far., S. 22, P O. Cedar Falls

KEYSER, JNO, far, S. 14; P O Cedar Falls.

Keyser, T. H, far, S 15, P O Cedar Falls

Knapp, A, far, S 14, P O Cedar Falls

Knapp, A M, far, Sec 25, P O Cedar Falls.

Knapp, M, far, S 14, P. O Cedar Falls

LARKIN, JOHN, far., S 13, P. O Cedar Falls

Larkin, W D, far, Sec 25; P O Cedar Falls

McMURRAY, JOHN, farmer, Sec 1, P. O Janesville

McMurray, S, far, S 1, P O Janesville

McMurray, M, far, S 2, P O. Janesville

Miller, J, far, S 10, P. O Cedar Falls

Miller, J, far, S 10, P O Cedar Falls

Miller, Jas, far, S 10, P O Cedar Falls

Miller, Wm, far, S 10, P O CedarFalls

MORGAN, NOAH, farmer, Sec 24, P. O Cedar Falls, born Nov 21 1831, in Fairfield Co., Ohio, in 1854, came to his present farm, owns 230 acres, valued at $35 per acre Married Ellen N Bell in 1859, she was born Jan 10, 1837, in New Jersey, had six children, four living—Jesse S, William H, Ida May and D. Clinton He has been Township Clerk and Trustee Are members of the United Brethren Church

Mowry, T, far, S 12, P O Janesville

Mulinix, E, far, S. 15, P O Cedar Falls.

Mulinix, Eli, far, S 15, P O Cedar Falls

Murphy, F, far., S 12, P. O. Cedar Falls

Murphy, S, far., S 1, P. O Janesville

Murphy, O C., far., S. 2, P. O Janesville

NEGLY, J, farmer, Sec 13, P. O. Cedar Falls

NEWELL, NANCY A., MRS., daughter of Daniel Howard, and widow of James Newell, Sec 10, P O Janesville He was born Aug. 11, 1809, in Jeromeville, Ohio; in 1832, came to Louisa Co, Iowa; in 1845, came to Black Hawk Co, Iowa, and located his present farm, afterward bought from the Government, consisting of 514 acres He built the first house in this township, he died May 30, 1875 Mrs N was born June 11, 1824, in Decatur Co, Ind They were married Nov 7, 1847, had seven children, five living—William, Daniel, Millie, Douglas and Joshua A. He had five children by his first marriage—Thomas J, Harrison, George, Jackson and James. He had three children by his second marriage—Marion, C P and Elizabeth. Her father, Daniel Howard, was born July 13, 1798, in Vermont, and at present is living with his daughter here

Newell, W , far., S 10 , P. O Cedar Falls.

Norris, A , far., S 34 , P O. Cedar Falls.

PEARL, JAMES, farmer, Sec 2 , P O. Cedar Falls.

Pierce, G , far., S. 25 , P O Cedar Falls

Pierce, H W , far , S. 24 , P O Cedar Falls.

Prasser, J A , far , S 1 ; P. O Cedar Falls.

REYNOLDS, E , far , S 23 , P. O. Cedar Falls

RHODES, W. H., farmer, S 36 , P. O Cedar Falls , born Aug 5, 1846, in Summit Co , Ohio ; in 1864, came to Plainfield, Ill , in 1867, returned to Ohio , in 1868, moved to Joliet, Ill , in 1869, returned to Ohio , in 1870, came to Cedar Falls, Iowa , in 1875, came to his present farm , owns 129 acres of land, valued at $25 per acre   Married Katie Mc-Culloch in 1873 , she was born in 1851 in Springfield, Mass , have two children— Jessie and Joe

RINKER, C. P., farmer, Sec. 1 , P O Janesville, born Jan 22, 1826, in Louisville, Ky , in 1829, came to Sullivan Co , Ind , in 1834, came to Putnam Co., Ill.; in 1839, removed to Ogle Co , Ill , in 1866, came to Black Hawk Co , Iowa , owns 102 acres of land, valued at $30 per acre   Married Louisa L Turk in 1848 , she was born in July, 1826, in Cayuga Co , N Y , have two children—Mary A and Lorenda   Are members of the M E Church

Riker, C , far., S 23 , P O Cedar Falls

Riker, E , far., S. 23 , P O Cedar Falls.

Roop, H C , far , S 1 , P O Janesville

SHAFFER, AARON, far , S 22 , P O Cedar Falls.

Shaffer, H C , far , S. 22 , P O Cedar Falls

tine, J. M , far , S 13 , P O Cedar Falls

Streeter, N , far , S 23 , P O Cedar Falls.

TAYLOR, M. A , farmer, S 3 , P. O. Janesville

TAYLOR, J. A., farmer, S 3 , P O Janesville, born Feb. 24, 1839, in Miami Co , Ind , in 1854, came to his present farm , there was but one house here at that time west of the Des Moines River , he owns ninety-seven acres land, valued at $3,500   Married Margaret A Woodruff in May, 1867 , she was born in 1848, in Ohio , have five children— Adelbert A , John A., Charles W , James A and Lee   Enlisted in 1864 in

Co E, 7th I. V. C , served to the end of the war   Mrs T is a member of the M E. Church

TENNYSON, JOHN, farmer, S 24 , P O Cedar Falls, born June 21, 1826, in Yorkshire, England , May 19, 1844, left for St Joseph Co , Mich , in 1854, came to Washington Tp , Aug. 16, 1864, removed to his present farm , owns 94 acres of land, valued at $35 per acre   Married Matilda Kelly in March, 1854 , she was born Sept 14, 1835, in Branch Co , Mich   Has been Justice of the Peace, he is Secretary of the School Board , has held the position for the past eleven years , has also been Township Clerk and Constable

THOMAS, V., farmer, Sec 15 , P. O Cedar Falls , born Aug 1, 1812, in Steuben Co , N Y , in 1829, came to Illinois , in 1851, came to Black Hawk Co , Iowa , owns 150 acres of land, valued at $25 per acre   Married Almeda Helm Dec 8, 1838, she was born July 10, 1818, in Chautauqua Co , N Y , had five children, three living—Olive (now Mrs Baker), Orilla (now Mrs. Shields) and Malinda (now Mrs Jones)   He was one of the first Township Trustees, having held this position about fifteen years , also School Director about three years

Thompson, L , far , S 13 , P O. Cedar Falls

True, S W , far , S 2 , P O. Janesville

Tuthill, G., far., S 36 , P O Cedar Falls

ULRICH, J B , far , Sec 11 , P O Janesville

Ulrich, W., far , S 11 , P O Janesville

WATROUS, HENRY, farmer, Sec 23 ; P O Cedar Falls

Weaver, B J , far , S. 12 , P O Cedar Falls.

Weaver, M A., far., S 12 , P. O Cedar Falls

Weatherby, Chas , far , S 24 , P O Cedar Falls

Weatherby, O , far , S. 24 , P O Cedar Falls.

Webster, G , far., S 24 ; P O Cedar Falls.

Wilkins, J. N., far , S 35 , P O Cedar Falls

WILKIN, JOHN W., farmer, Sec 35 , P O Cedar Falls, born March 14, 1822, in Orange Co , N Y ; in 1850, came to Wisconsin, then to Michigan , in 1866, came to his present farm; owns 200 acres, valued at $40 per acre. Married Mary J. Randalph in 1849; she was born in 1830, in Orange Co., N. Y., had three children, two living—Joseph N. and George; lost Reuben in 1876, aged 21 years.

Wilson J., far., S. 26; P. O. Cedar Falls.

Wilson, J. A., far., S. 25; P. O. Cedar Falls.

Wilson, M., far., S. 11; P. O. Janesville.

Wilson, T., far., S. 35; P. O. Cedar Falls.

Wing, L. A., far., S. 24; P O. Cedar Falls.

Wise, C., far., S. 14; P. O. Cedar Falls.

Wise, J., far., S. 14; P. O. Cedar Falls.

Wise, W. B., far., S. 14; P. O. Cedar Falls.

Wyatt, R., far., S. 16; P. O. Reinbeck.

ZIMMERMAN, AUG., far., S. 3; P. O. Janesville.

LINCOLN TOWNSHIP.

ALEXANDER, L , far , S. 10 , P O Waterloo

Auner, O J , far , S. 15 , P O Hudson

BARRETT, J E., far , S. 20 , P O Reinbeck

Beaubien, F , far , S. 26 , P O. Traer

BECKER, CHARLES D., far , S 19 , P O Reinbeck , born in Jefferson Co., N Y , July 12, 1841 , he emigrated to Stephenson Co , Ill , in 1866 , to Iowa and Orange Township in 1865 , to his present farm in 1870 He was married in 1868 to Miss Amanda Sarvay, from Jefferson Co , N Y , they have two children—Mary, born Dec 12, 1870 , Louis, born Sept 6, 1873 He has 120½ acres of land, valued at $30 per acre Mr B enlisted in our late war, in Co D, 10th N Y Heavy Artillery, in 1862, and was connected with the Army of the Potomac, mustered out in 1865 He has held the offices of Township Assessor three years, Township Clerk two years, School Director two years, Clerk School Board three years, Road Supervisor three years In politics he is a Republican They are members of the M E Church His farm was in a raw state when he purchased , he broke it up and has made all his improvements Mr Becker has always taken a deep interest in the affairs of his county and township

Beckwith, H , far , S 24 , P O Waterloo

Bedford, D , far., S 18 , P O Reinbeck

Beistline, D , far , S 30 , P. O Reinbeck

Beistlein, A , far , S 30 , P O Reinbeck

Bly, J H , far , S 12 , P O Waterloo

Brayton, W , far , S 16 ; P O Waterloo.

BROWN, LEVI, far , S 3 , P. O Hudson , born in Schuylkill Co , Penn , March 8, 1823 , he emigrated to La Salle Co , Ill , in 1854 ; to Iowa and Hudson in 1866, Black Hawk Township , he located on his present farm in 1869 He was married in 1844, to Miss Catherine Pofenberger, from Berks Co , Penn. , they have seven children— Mrs Caroline Reed, of Oregon ; Mrs, Mary Dewey, of La Salle Co , Ill., Willabaugh J , Mrs Sarah Hay, who lives at home , Fremont, Lincoln and Daniel J He has 335 acres of land valued at $9,500. Mr. Brown enlisted as a soldier in the late war in the 104th Ill V. I , Co C, in 1862 , he was mustered out in 1863, on account of sickness He is Republican in politics. Has held the offices of Township Trustee three years and School Director two years Mr B 's farm was raw prairie when he settled on it , he has reduced it to a fine state of cultivation, with many fine improvements , he has 140 rods of osage and one mile of willow hedge He is a blacksmith by trade, which he learned in Berks Co , Penn , he followed it three years at Hudson, and eleven years in Illinois They are members of the M E Church

Brown, W , S. 3 , P O Hudson

Brunner, Jos , far., S 24 , P. O Waterloo.

CAMPBELL, WM , farmer, Sec 34 , P O Traer.

Cavanaugh, C., far , S. 36 , P O Traer

Cavanaugh, C , far., S 35 , P O Traer

Chenrey, J , far , Sec 2 , P. O Waterloo.

Coddington, C , far , S 14 , P O Waterloo.

Coddington, O S , far , S 11 , P O. Waterloo

Codling, E , far , S. 15 , P O Reinbeck

Colburn, A. P , far , S 23 , P O Reinbeck.

Cranny, T., far , S 27 , P O Traer

Creswell, J R , far., S. 8 , P. O Hudson

Corey, C , far , S. 16 ; P. O. Hudson

DELMATER, C. A., farmer, Sec 27 , P O Waterloo

Delamater, S , far , S 27 , P O. Waterloo

EASTMAN, G W , farmer, Sec 22 , P O Reinbeck

Emmett, J , far., S 36 , P O Traer

FULLER, E B., farmer, Sec 23 , P O Waterloo

FAULKNER, JAMES, farmer, Sec. 10 , P O Hudson , born in York Co , Penn , Jan 4, 1839 , he emigrated to New York in 1862 , to Iowa and to Black Hawk Township in 1867 , he settled on his present farm in 1869 He was married Oct. 4, 1870, to Miss Marion Halley, from Illinois ; she was born Aug. 11, 1844, they have five children —Charles E., born April 15, 1872 , David H., born Jan. 24, 1874 , John H., born Feb 18, 1876 ; Walter S and William W are twins, born March 2,

1878 He has 280 acres of land, valued at $7,000. He has held the office of Road Supervisor one year In politics, he is a Republican. Mr Faulkner has a very fine farm, and is making some very fine improvements

GILMORE, ROBERT, farmer, Sec 15, P O Hudson

GIBSON, SAMUEL, farmer, Sec 5, P O Hudson, born in Ireland in 1834, he emigrated to this country and Wyoming Co., N Y, in 1850, to Iowa and on his present farm in the Fall of 1853. He was married in 1860 to Miss Mary Wheylen, from New York, they have seven children—Margaret, Mary E, Jennie, Lillie, William S, Dora and Charles He has 547 acres of land, valued at $25 per acre He has held the offices of Justice of the Peace two years, Township Trustee four years, Township Treasurer one year, School Director six years, Road Supervisor ten years Mr. Gibson made a trip to Kansas and Pike's Peak in 1858 and 1859. He was the first and only settler in Lincoln Tp for twenty-seven years He deals quite extensively in cattle, horses and hogs, he has 230 head of hogs at this time In politics, Republican

Gleason, Martin, far, 28, P O Reinbeck.
Gleason, M., far, S 28, P O Reinbeck.
Gleason, P, far., S 28, P O Reinbeck
Greeley, W E, far., S. 2, P. O. Hudson
Gregg, W. H, S 34, P O Traer

GRIFFITH, M. C., farmer, Sec 4, P O Waterloo, born in Montgomery Co, Nov 28, 1843, he moved with his parents to Ohio in 1855, to Rock Co. Wis in 1857, to Iowa and on his present farm in 1871 He was married in 1869 to Miss Isabel Chambers, from Lancaster City, Penn., she was born Aug. 8, 1843, they have three children —John H, born March 9, 1872. Charles C, born June 3, 1874, William H, born April 27, 1876 He has eighty acres of land, valued at $2,000. In politics he is Republican He has held the office of Road Supervisor one year. They are members of the Congregational Church He is adding many fine improvements to his farm

HAYE, JACOB, farmer, Sec. 27, P O Traer

HALLEY, J. S., farmer, Sec 14, P O Waterloo, born in Scotland March 16 1837, he emigrated with his parents to this country and Vermont in 1841 He enlisted in 1861 in Co H, 4th Vt. V I, he was detailed to do hospital service the most of the time, mustered out in 1864, returning, he went to Massachusetts, where he remained until the Spring of 1866, when he went to Illinois, to Iowa, and on his present farm, in the Spring of 1868 He was married in 1861, to Miss Evelina Richardson, from Maine, they had six children, four living. His wife died in 1873. He was married again in Dec, 1875, to Miss Delia Turner, from Oswego Co., N Y., she was born Aug 3, 1840. they have two children—Fred T, born May 3, 1876, Nelson, born March 2, 1878 Mr H has 240 acres of land, valued at $30 per acre He has held the offices of School Director three years, Assessor two years, Road Supervisor one year He is a Republican in politics They are members of the M. E Church

Hicks, W, Sr, far., S 8, P O Reinbeck.
Hoag, H, far, S 28, P O Waterloo
Holmes, J far S 1, P O Waterloo
Humphreys, G W, far., Sec 17, P. O Waterloo
Hunter, J A, far S 3, P O Hudson

IRONS, JOHN, renter, Sec 21, P. O Reinbeck

JACOBSON, JACOB, renter, Sec 19, P O Reinbeck

Jamison, G. C, far, S 25, P O. Waterloo

KELLY, PATRICK, farmer, Sec 26, P O Reinbeck.

KELLY, WILLIAM, farmer, Sec 33, P O Traer, born in Lawrence Co., Penn, July 11, 1828, he emigrated to Iowa and Cedar Rapids in 1856, he was engaged as a sawyer in a mill at that place three years, he moved to Johnson Co. in 1859 He enlisted in the army from that county, in Co A, 14th I V. I in 1861, in 1863, he was transferred to the 7th Iowa Calvary, he was mustered out in 1866, he was five years lacking two months, a soldier. He moved to Black Hawk Co and on his present farm, Sept, 1867. He was married in 1868 to Miss Amanda Johnson, from Illinois, they have two children—

William F , born Aug. 21, 1872, Arthur E , born Feb. 10, 1878   He has 160 acres of land, valued at $30 per acre Has held the offices of Township Trustee three years, School Director seven years.   In politics he is Republican His farm was wild prairie when he purchased , he broke it and made some fine improvements

Klinefelter, J W , far S 5 , P O. Hudson

LAWLER, JOHN, far , S. 20 , P O Reinbeck

Lawler, P , far., S 21 , P O Reinbeck

Lynch, M , far , S 26 , P O Traer

McCRACKEN, R , far , S. 20 , P O Reinbeck

McMahon, J , far., S 34 , P. O Traer

McManus, T P., far , S 17, P O. Reinbeck

McNally, P., far , S 1 , P O Waterloo.

McNally, R , far., S 16 , P O. Hudson

Mahoney, P., far , S 14 , P. O. Waterloo

Millner, G., far , S 25 , P O Waterloo

Molyneaux, W. F , far , S 7 , P O. Reinbeck

Molyneaux, W. S , far , S 7 ; P O Reinbeck.

Moyer, A., far , S 27 , P. O. Reinbeck.

MUELLER, JACOB, farmer, Sec 13 , P O Hudson , born in Switzerland Jan 28 , 1827 , he emigrated to this country, and to Madison Co , Ill , in 1850 , to Iowa and Dubuque in 1852 , to Lincoln Tp., Sec 15 , in 1874 , located on his own farm in 1876   He was married in 1847 to Miss Mary A Schweingruber, from Switzerland , they had one child—John J , his wife died in 1852 ; he was married again in 1855, to Miss Elizabeth Fern, from Dubuque , she is said to be the first white child born in the State , the date of her birth was March 19, 1836 , they have had nine children, seven living—Mary A , William N , John R , Alfred C , Henry, Herman and Franklin   He has 360 acres of land, valued at $20 per acre He has held the offices of School Director one year, and Road Supervisor one year. He is a miller by trade.   In politics, he is a Democrat.

Mueller, J J , Sec 13 , P O Hudson

NOLL, JACOB, Sec 33 , P O Traer Noll. W T., far., S 33 , P O Traer

NORTHWAY, CHARLES H., farmer, Sec 22 , P O Waterloo , born in Onondaga Co , N Y , Feb 5, 1840 , he emigrated to Whiteside Co , Ill , in 1862 ; to Iowa and on his present farm in 1868   He was married in 1867 to Miss Jennie Mosher, from New York , she died June 3, 1867 ; he was married again in March , 1871, to Miss Liddia M D'Lamather, from New York , they have had three children, two living— Homer C , born May 18, 1874 , Edith W., born April 3, 1876   He has 160 acres of land, valued at $30 per acre He has held the offices of Township Clerk for five years, Township Trustee one year   In politics he is Republican , they are members of the M E Church , Mr N takes an active part in the Sabbath school work.   Mr. Northway was engaged in the mercantile trade for four years in Syracuse, N. Y., before he emigrated to the West.

Northway, M. L., far. S 22 ; P. O. Traer

Northway, R H , far S 22 ; P O Traer

RASMUSON, E , farmer, S. 31 , P O Traer

Roberts, S B , far S 3 ; P O Hudson

Ross, P B , far , S 11 , P O Waterloo.

Rousselow, A , far , S 23 , P O Waterloo.

SALISBURY, G. W , far , S 19 , P O Reinbeck.

SARVAY, LOTUS, farmer, Sec 26 ; P O. Traer ; born in Jefferson Co , N Y , July 22, 1846 ; emigrated to Iowa and on to his present farm in 1868   He was married same year to Miss Sarah Colburn, from Jefferson Co., N Y , she was born Aug 22, 1847 , they have two children—Leonard, born Jan 6, 1874 , Elizabeth C , Sept. 7, 1877   He has 160 acres of land, valued at $30 per acre   He has held the offices of Road Supervisor two years   He is quite extensively engaged in stock raising , makes hogs a specialty, of which he keeps a fine herd.   He has made some fine improvements on his farm In politics he is Republican , they are members of the M E Church

Severance, E , far , S 21 , P. O. Reinbeck.

Sherratt, William, far , S 7 , P O Hudson

Smith, Simeon L., far , S. 8 , P. O. Hudson

STEVENS, W. H., farmer, Sec 20 , P O Reinbeck, Grundy Co., he was born in Jefferson Co , Wis , March 17, 1844 , he moved to Iowa and on to his present farm in 1866   He was married in 1863 to Miss Charlotte Barrett, of St. Lawrence Co.,

N Y., they had two children—Silas E and Lena, Lena died His wife died June 8, 1874 He was married again April 5, 1875, to Miss Olive Hoag, from Illinois; they have one child—Alma, born June 17, 1876 He has 120 acres of land, valued at $35 per acre He enlisted in the 1st Wis Heavy Artillery, Co E, in 1864, he was mustered out in July. 1865. He has held the office of School Director three years, Road Superintendent one year. In politics he is Republican Mr. S is among the earliest settlers in the township His farm was in a wild state when he came, he has reduced it to a fine state of cultivation, and made some fine improvements

Stearns, Wm, far, S 21, P O Waterloo.

Switzer, W N, far., S 10, P O Hudson

TAYLOR, H. E., farmer, Sec 5, P. O Waterloo.

Thurber, J, far, S 12, P O Waterloo.

Thompson, R O, far, S 35, P O Traer.

Thornton, T., far, S 26, P O Traer

Thornton, W., far., S 26, P O Traer

THOMPSON, W. P., far, S 1, P O Waterloo, born in McMinn Co, Tenn, Feb 1, 1837, he emigrated to McDonough Co., Ill, in 1854, to Hancock Co. in 1858, to Iowa and on his present farm in 1866. He was married in 1858 to Miss Eliza A Pennington, from Illinois, they have seven children —George A, Ida J, William T., Mary A, Abbie I., Charles M and James R He has 240 acres of land, valued at $30 per acre He has held the offices of Township Trustee one year, Township Treasurer seven years, Township Assessor two years, School Director nine years, School Treasurer seven years Mr Thompson raises and fattens hogs quite extensively, he has made some fine improvements on his farm. They are members of the Baptist Church, Mr T organized and has carried on a Sabbath school in the school house near him for the past ten years, he has also filled the position of Clerk of the church the past eight years, his school numbers forty-five pupils.

Trainor, Henry, farmer

Trainor, James, farmer

Trainor, M, far, Sec 34, P O Traer

Trainor, O, far, Sec. 35, P. O Traer

Trainor, Thomas, farmer

Traites, W, far, S 24, P O Waterloo

VAUGHN, JAMES, farmer, Sec. 12, P O. Waterloo

VITTUM, ALBERT, farmer, Sec 30, P O Reinbeck, born in New Hampshire, Sept 23, 1831, he moved to Massachusetts, then to Iowa in March, 1856, he returned to Boston in December, 1859, remaining there four years in the employ of the Express Co, he returned to Iowa and settled on his present farm in 1863 He was married in 1864 to Miss Mary E Sherrett, from New York, the courts granted him a divorce from her, and he married again in March, 1870, to Miss Martha A Baker, from Canada, he had two children by his first wife — Edgar and Frank; he has four children by his present wife—Arthur, Ernest, Henrietta and Allena. He has 500 acres of land, valued at $25 per acre He has held the offices of Township Supervisor four years, Township Assessor four years, Justice of the Peace past two years, School Director two years, he is now President of the School Board Republican. Mr. Vittum has always been alive to the interests of his county and township

WALKER, JOHN, farmer, Sec. 34, P O Traer

Warner, J, far, Sec 2, P O. Waterloo.

Wilhelm, A. L, far, S. 33, P. O. Traer

Warner, S., far, S 2, P O Waterloo

Wilhelm, H, far, S 33, P O Traer

WILSON, SAMUEL, farmer, Sec. 4, P O Waterloo, born in Herkimer Co, N Y, Sept. 25, 1832, he emigrated to Whiteside Co, Ill, in 1865, to Iowa, and Lincoln Township, in 1874, settled on his present farm in 1875 He was married in 1857 to Miss Marion Sutton, from Oswego Co., N Y, she was born April 7, 1835, they have three children — Ella J, born March 17, 1858, Berton E, born Oct. 13, 1865, Amos A., born May 15, 1871 He has 123 acres of land, valued at $3,000 Republican, they are members of the Congregational Church Mr Wilson was a soldier in our late war, he enlisted in 1861, in the 81st N Y. V I, Co. F, mustered out on account of sickness in 1865

7

BLACK HAWK TOWNSHIP.

ANDORF HENRY, farmer, Sec 7, P O Cedar Falls

Andorf, W , farmer, Sec 7, P O Cedar Falls.

ASQUITH, CHARLES, farmer, Sec 16, P O Cedar Falls, born in Yorkshire, England, May 16, 1823, he emigrated to this country,and Johnstown, Penn, in 1853, to Ohio in 1859, he returned to Pennsylvania in 1861. He enlisted in the Spring of 1863 in the 78th Penn V I , Co C, mustered out in 1865, he was in four severe engagements He was married in 1847 to Miss Mary Stead, from Yorkshire, England, they had three children, one living—Mrs. Mary A Shaw, of Waterloo His wife died in 1851 He was married in 1852 to Miss Mary Sutcliff, from England, they have one child—Robert C He has 120 acres of land, valued at $30 per acre Mr. A has held the offices of Township Trustee two years, Road Supervisor four years and School Director five years. He was ordained as preacher for the German Baptist Church in 1876, he has preached for the church located on Sec 22 for the past two years, they have a membership of eighty.

ASQUITH, JOHN, farmer, Sec 16, P O Cedar Falls, born in Yorkshire, England, June 19, 1835, emigrated to this country and Johnstown, Penn, in 1857, to Braceville, Ill., in 1862 He was married in 1859 to Miss Rebecca Sutcliff, from Johnstown, Penn, they have had ten children, five living—Miriam A , Stead A , Frank R , Anna J and Jessie M. Mr A enlisted in the U S Navy Nov., 1864, in the Mississippi Squadron, mustered out Aug 9, 1865. Came to Iowa, and on his present farm, in the Fall of 1865. He has held the offices of Township Trustee four years, Road Supervisor three years and Secretary of the School Board one year They are members of the German Baptist Church Mr A was engaged as Overseer of worsted spinning in England for thirteen years, he was also engaged as miner in Pennsylvania five years.

BALDWIN, ANDREW, farmer, Sec. 24, P O Waterloo

Baldwin, A T. far , S. 24 , P. O Waterloo.

Baldwin, W., far , S. 24 , P O Waterloo.

Bailey, P , far , S. 29 ; P. O. Hudson

Batterfeldt, J., S. 15 , P O. Hudson

Baxter, D , merchant, Hudson

Beal, J. L , far , S 1 , P O Waterloo

Bluhm, H A., far , S 11 , P.O. Hudson.

Bluhm, W J , far , S 11 , P O Waterloo

Boldt, A T , far , S 30 , P O Hudson

Bonn, J , far , S 10 , P O Cedar Falls

Bonn, J A , far , S 10 , P O Cedar Falls.

Bonn Jos , far , S 4 , P O Cedar Falls

BRANDHORST, C. F., farmer, S 34 , P O Hudson, born in Prussia in 1840. He emigrated to this country and Dane Co., Wis , at the age of 15, alone, in 1855, to Iowa and on his present farm in 1864 He was married in the Fall of 1864 to Mrs Margarette Klinefelter, from Maine, she has one son by her former husband—Horace Klinefelter They have six children by this union—Albert, Charles, Ida, Hattie, Mary, Annie He has 124 acres of land, valued at $40 per acre He has held the offices of Township Trustee five years, Road Supervisor two years, School Director five years, Secretary of the School Board two years, and Treasurer of the School Board one year. His farm was in a wild state when he purchased it, he has since made many fine improvements Mr B is alive to the interests of his township and its schools

Brandhorst, C H , far , S 28; P. O Hudson

Burden, M A , far , S 25 , P. O. Waterloo.

Burger, R , far , S 17 , P O Cedar Falls.

CAREY, R B., far., S. 11 , P O Waterloo.

Chinery, E., far., S. 8 , P O Cedar Falls

Clark, A. J , far., S. 12 , P O Waterloo

Clouse, S , far , S 9 , P O Cedar Falls.

Connerd, D W , far., S. 22 , P.O. Waterloo.

Conners, T , far , S. 35 ; P. O. Waterloo.

COONS, JACOB A., farmer on Sec 16, P. O Waterloo, born in Rensselaer Co , N. Y , Feb 25, 1854, he moved with his parents to Iowa and Waterloo Tp. in 1868; to their present farm in 1869, he, together with his brother, L. B. Coons, has carried on the farm for the past three years Their parents reside in Waterloo, the brothers have lately purchased eighty acres of land in Sec. 16 Jacob A was married in 1877 to Miss Emma M. Virden, from Waterloo Tp , her parents came to and settled in this county in 1849 L B Coons was born in Rensselaer Co, N Y., May 11, 1852, he moved to and settled on his present location in 1869 He was married in 1875 to Miss Susie French from Oneida Co, N Y , they have one child—Lena A, born Nov 3, 1876 The brothers are Republican in politics

Coons, L

Costello, John, Hudson

Costello, John, Jr, far, S 15, P O Cedar Falls

COTTRELL, AMASA, farmer, Sec. 33, P. O. Waterloo; born in Rensselaer Co., N Y, in 1825 Emigrated to Iowa and Black Hawk Co in 1857; he spent three years on rented farms, then took a trip to Pike's Peak in 1860, returned to Iowa and settled on his present farm in the Spring of 1862. He was married May 15, 1847, to Miss Rebecca Deavitt, from New York, they have four children—William A, Louisa J, Warren H, Harmon S Mr C owns 960 acres of·land valued at $25 per acre He has held the offices of Township Trustee one year, School Director eight years, and Secretary of the School Board eight years. He held the office of President of the Black Hawk County Agricultural Society three years, also President of the Patrons' Joint Stock Co two years; also President of the Waterloo, Belle Plaine & North Missouri Narrow-Gauge Railroad two years Mr C has added many fine improvements to his farm—a large barn 60x100; he is now building a fine dwelling 48x56. He is quite extensively engaged in feeding cattle and hogs, during last year, he sold seventy-four head of fat cattle, and 260 fat hogs. The family are among the first and prominent settlers of·the township He was appointed on a committee to assist in the division of Black Hawk Tp into Black Hawk and

Lincoln, giving to each equal territory Their son—William A —has held the office of Deputy Auditor of Black Hawk Co., for the past five years, Louisa J is engaged in teaching school, she has taught in her own and adjoining districts for the past seven years, Warren H attends the Iowa State University at Iowa City, he drew the prizes of his class in 1876-7, Harmon remains at home and attends to the interests of the farm

Cottrell, H , S. 33, P O Waterloo

Crites, J , far, S 20, P O Hudson

Crites, L , far, S 22, P O Hudson

Crites, Wm., far, S 22, P O Hudson

Crow, M , far, S. 31, P O Waterloo

CURTIS, P. B., farmer and Postmaster, Hudson, born in Orleans Co, N. Y, in 1831, he emigrated to Iowa, and Orange Tp in 1857, he sold out and moved to Sioux Co, Iowa, in 1873, returned and settled in Orange Tp the same year, and to Hudson in 1875 He was married in 1854 to Miss Mary Jane Lord, from Monroe Co, N. Y , they have four children—Clara A , Frank W., George W and Ray J His wife died in Dec, 1877 He has seven acres of land in Hudson, valued at $75 per acre He has held the office of Postmaster for three years He was among the earliest settlers in the county H brother, W H Curtis, of Waterloo, is actively engaged in the great temperance reform.

DAGNAN, W, far, S 15, P O Cedar Falls.

Daly, J , far, Sec 6, P. O Cedar Falls.

Davis, E J , far . S. 34, P. O Waterloo.

Day, Benj , renter

Dewey, S., far, S 14, P O Cedar Falls

De Witt H , far , S 1, P. O. Waterloo.

De WITT, H. H., farmer, Sec 1, P O Waterloo; born in Chemung Co, N Y, July 16, 1814, he moved with his parents to Richland Co, Ohio, in 1818. Was married in 1835 to Miss Mary M Caulkins, from New York; she was born March 1, 1812 They moved to Cedar Co., Iowa, in 1852, to Black Hawk Co and their present farm in 1855 They have ten children, four living—Mrs Eunice E Case of Waterloo Tp., Henry C, Edwin M, of Hutchinson, Kansas, Mrs Frances I

Walker, of Kansas Center, Kansas. He has 117 acres of land, valued at $35 per acre He has held the offices of Justice of the Peace three years, Township Trustee seven years, Township Assessor one year, County Supervisor one year, and School Director one year Mr De Witt was among the earliest settlers of the county, he entered his land in 1852 He showed his patriotism by enlisting in the army in the late war, but was rejected on account of age He is carpenter by trade, and also served his apprenticeship at the cabinet maker's trade. His son, Henry C, occupies a part of the house, and assists in carrying on the farm He was married in 1872 to Miss Alice Cole, she died in Sept, 1872 He was married again to Miss M C Hubbard, from Missouri, they have two children—Eunice J and Lenae

Dolan, J, far., S 10, P O Cedar Falls

Dolan, T, far, S 10, P O Cedar Falls

EGERMIRE, JOHN, far, Sec 15, P. O Cedar Falls

Egermire, John W, farmer, S 15, P O Cedar Falls.

Englehart, Paul, far., S 31, P O Cedar Falls

FARALL, PATRICK, renter

Ferris, C, far., S. 36, P. O. Hudson

Ferris Forrest, S 13, P O Waterloo.

FERRIS, JOHN D., farmer, Sec 13, P O. Waterloo, born in Saratoga Co., N Y, Dec 2, 1826; moved with his parents to Orleans Co., in 1837, to Indiana in 1842, to Knox Co, Ill, in 1847, to Iowa and his present farm in 1852. He was married in 1851 to Miss Louisa Jackson, from Illinois, she was born March 6, 1834; they have had eight children—Syntha L, Algenon N, Forest C, John H, Frank E, Mary P, Hattie L and Rosie V Syntha L. is dead. He has 192 acres of land, valued at $40 per acre He has held the offices of Township Trustee four years, Road Supervisor two years, and School Director two years In politics, Mr Ferris is a Republican They are members of the United Brethren Church, located Sec 24; Mr Ferris and family were among the pioneers of Black Hawk Tp, there was no house west of his

and only two between his and Waterloo, there was no Waterloo, only a small cabin, and no family lived in that for some time, there were plenty of deer and elk, and a few buffaloes were killed near him, he built a log cabin 14x 14 and lived the first Winter without a floor Algenon was the second white child born in the township, they were obliged to endure many privations; they have a fine farm now, with many substantial improvements

Ferris, O. B, far, S 11, P O Cedar Falls.

Flynn, M, far, S 15, P O Cedar Falls

Fuller, A, far, S 10, P O Hudson.

GILLEN, ALEX, school teacher; P O Hudson

GILLIN, E., MRS., farmer, Sec 26, P O Hudson, she was born in Bedford Co., Penn., Jan 29, 1826, she moved with her parents to Cambria Co, Penn, in 1840 She was married in 1846 to John Gillin, from Pennsylvania, he was one of the seven children born on the ocean on the passage from Ireland to this country July 18, 1818, he died Oct 1, 1865, she moved with family to Linn Co, Iowa, in 1867; to her present farm in 1870, she has had ten children—Samuel B, Robert J., John E., Alexander S, Mary C., Martha M., William S, Mesach, Frances Jane and Charles W, they have 140 acres of land, valued at $35 per acre Her son, Mesach, died. John E is a physician and located at Reinbeck, Grundy Co Alexander S teaches school Samuel is a farmer in Linn Co The other boys remain at home She is a member of the German Baptist Church

Gillen, R, far, S 26, P O Hudson.

Gilmore, W, far, S. 25, P O Hudson

Gonchnour, S, far, S 22, P O Hudson

Gonchnour, Thomas, miller, Hudson.

Grauickey, David, farmer

Grassley, John, farmer

Gutknecht, F, far, S. 30, P O Huron.

Gutknecht, H, far., S. 19, P O Cedar Falls

HAYENNAN, JOSEPH, far, S 35, P O Waterloo

HALL, GEORGE N., farmer, S. 26, P O Hudson, born in Richland Co, Ohio, April 5, 1834, he lived with his parents until 1849, when they both died with the cholera in Cincinnati, and were buried at the same time; he moved to Ashtabula Co, the same year, to Iowa, and on his present farm in 1855 He was married to Miss Harriet M Hoskins, from Ohio He enlisted in 1861, in the 16th I V I, Co I, he served two years, when he was mustered out, and at once re-enlisted as a veteran at the siege of Vicksburg, he was in the battles of Shiloh, Corinth, Vicksburg, etc, mustered out in July, 1865 He has 100 acres of land, valued at $4,000, they have two children—Juliette A, born Feb. 18, 1853, Alburtus A, born May 21, 1860 In politics he is a Republican

HATHAWAY, THOMAS P., farmer, S 9; P O Cedar Falls, born in Adams, Mass, in 1830, he moved to Iowa and Cedar Falls in 1868, on his present farm in 1869 He was married in 1854 to Miss Amelia Bryant from Adams, Mass, they have had five children, three living—Lawrence B, Mary A. and Martin E He has 160 acres of land, valued at $3,200 He has held the offices of Township Trustee three years, Township Assessor one year, School Director four years, Justice of the Peace four years In politics, he is a Republican Mrs H is a member of the Congregational Church, Cedar Falls Mr H sold the farm he now occupies, to Dr. Bryant of Cedar Falls, in 1877, he still works the farm, he is also fitting up another farm on Sec. 8, of 160 acres His son, Lawrence B is a practicing physician and surgeon at Raymond, Iowa

HESSE, CHARLES A., farmer, Sec 17, P O. Cedar Falls, born in Germany July 26, 1826, he emigrated to this country and Blair Co, Penn., in 1854; to Iowa and Cedar Falls in 1861, he purchased his farm in 1868, he removed and settled on it in 1873 He was married in 1852 to Miss Anna Koehne, from Germany, she was born July 20, 1829; they have six children —Harmon, born in Germany, Aug 13, 1853, Minnie, born May 25, 1856; William, born Oct. 15, 1857, Charles A, born Dec 18, 1859, Lavica, born July 8, 1866, Otto F, born July 15, 1873 He has 240 acres of land, valued at $30 per acre. He has held the offices

of School Director for three years, School Treasurer three years, Road Supervisor one year In politics, votes for the best man

Hesse, H, S 17, P O Cedar Falls
Hildebrand, J, far, S. 36, P O Hudson
Holcomb, L J, carpenter, Hudson

HOLLIS, F. R., farmer, Sec 16, P O Cedar Falls, born in Rensselaer Co, N Y, April 9, 1842, he emigrated to Iowa and settled on Sec 1, Black Hawk Tp, in 1866, to his present location in 1870. He was married in 1865 to Miss Hellen Bly, from New York, she was born April 23, 1843 He has 160 acres of land, valued at $30 per acre They have six children— Charles, Harliu, Iola, Eddie, John and Rienzi He has held the offices of Township Trustee two years, School Director one year and Road Supervisor one year He enlisted in Co E, 125th N Y. V I, in 1862, mustered out in 1865, he was in all the general engagements with the Army of the Potomac In politics, is Republican

Horn, F W, far., S. 15, P O Hudson
Howe J, far, S 6, P. O Cedar Falls

JONES, R. A., farmer, Sec 24, P O Waterloo, born in Edwards Co, Ill, March 24, 1823, moved to Wisconsin in 1849 to Iowa and this county in 1850, he settled on Sec. 7, Orange Tp, the same year, on his present farm in 1862, he has 176 acres of land, valued at $30 per acre. He was married Dec 23, 1843, to Miss Margaret Hunt, from Edwards Co, Ill., she was born April 7, 1825. they have five children—Mrs. Mary E Auner (they live in Lincoln Tp.), Mrs Emeline J Jackson, of Nebraska, Rose, Isabel and Charles M He lives at the Black Hills Mr Jones was among the earliest settlers in the county. He has held the offices of School Director two years, Road Supervisor one year Mrs Jones is a member of the United Brethren Church

KAUTH, JACOB, blacksmith, Hudson
Kelley, F, far, S 30, P O. Hudson

LAMB, IRA, farmer, Sec 32, P. O. Cedar Falls.
Landis, A, far, S 13, P O Waterloo.
Law, M, far, S. 19, P O Cedar Falls

LAW, ROBERT, farmer, Sec 19, P O Cedar Falls, born in Canada in 1846, came to the United States in 1868, and on his present farm the same year. He was married in 1871 to Miss Phebe Collins, from Canada, they have two children—Ira, born July 6, 1872, and Walter, Jan. 27, 1877 Mr Law has eighty acres of land, valued at $25 per acre In politics, Republican

Loeper, A, far, S 4, P O Cedar Falls

Loonan, T, far, S 25, P O Waterloo

McNALLY, JOHN, farmer, Sec. 15, P O Cedar Falls

McCARTNEY, H., blacksmith, Hudson, born in Westmoreland Co, Penn, Nov 5, 1835 He was married in 1867 to Miss Eliza Horner, from Cambria, Penn, they emigrated to Iowa and his present location in 1871, they have had six children—Lorenzo S, Frank H, John G, Nancy M J., Annie May, Carrie Bell Mr M was engaged in the Great Cambria Iron Works as rail heater for ten years, they are the largest railroad iron works in the United States, employing 3,500 men In politics Mr M is Republican They are members of the German Baptist Church He is a first-class worker, and has a good trade

McNally, J., far, S 15, P O Cedar Falls

Maguire, John, far, S 5, P O Cedar Falls

Marston, Chas, far., S 2, P O Waterloo

Marston, G, far, S 25; P O Waterloo

Marston, N, far, S 25, P O Waterloo

Marston, S, far, S 2, P O Waterloo

Matteling James, laborer, Hudson

Melleck, W, far, S 2, P. O. Cedar Falls

Merner, D., far, S 5, P O Cedar Falls

MERWIN, JOSEPH, farmer, S. 10, P O Cedar Falls, was born in Oneida Co, N Y, Oct 6, 1818, he moved with his father to Pennsylvania in 1834 He was married in 1837 to Miss J R Beers, from Pennsylvania, they emigrated to Iowa and Jones Co in 1853, to Black Hawk Co and Lester Tp in 1866, to Bremer Tp in 1867, to Cedar Falls in the Spring of 1868, Dec, 1868, to his present farm, he owns eighty acres of land, valued at $2,000. They have four children—Mary E., Phœbe S, Byron W and Ann M Mr Merwin is a carpenter and wagon maker by trade, he carried on the trade of

wagon maker in Pennsylvania for seventeen years, he has followed the trade of carpenter the most of his time since he lived in Iowa, renting his farm

Merner, John, Sr, retired, Cedar Falls

Merner, J, Jr, far S 5, P.O Cedar Falls

Merner, S, far, S 5, P O Cedar Falls

Metz, O A, far, S 14, P. O Hudson

Metz, S J, far, S. 14, P O. Hudson

Miller, C, far, S 19, P. O Cedar Falls

Miller, J Jr, far., S 35, P O Hudson

Miller, Stephen, miller, Hudson

Milliken, J T., far., S. 9, P O. Cedar Falls

Murray, J, far, S. 29, P O Hudson

Musser, P T, far., S 21, P O Hudson

NAGEL, HENRY, farmer, Sec 17, P. O Cedar Falls

North, G, far, S 32, P O Cedar Falls

OSMAN, G, farmer, Sec 28, P O Hudson

PALMER, JOHN, farmer, Sec 14, P O Cedar Falls

Palmer, S G, Sec 14, P O Waterloo

Parmelee, C. S, far, S 12, P O Waterloo

Patterson, J, far, S 31, P. O Waterloo

Patterson, M, far, S 32, P. O. Cedar Falls

Pratt, O G, far, S 12, P O Waterloo

Price, J, far, S 3, P O. Cedar Falls

Price, R, far, S 21, P O Hudson

Popp, J G, far, S 30, P. O Hudson

Popp, J K, far, S 30, P O Hudson

QUINN, JOHN, farmer, Sec 8, P O Cedar Falls

REKERS, HENRY, farmer, Sec 3, P O Cedar Falls

Rickus, H, far, S 3, P O. Cedar Falls

Rohrer, Jacob, Sec 21, P O Hudson

Rohrer, S, far, S. 21, P O Hudson.

Rugg, C P, far, S 20, P O. Waterloo

SENFFERLIN, FRED, Section 16, P O Cedar Falls

Senfferlin, J, far, S 16, P O Cedar Falls.

SERGEANT, BYRON, farmer, Sec 24, P O Waterloo, born in Pennsylvania Dec. 25, 1829, emigrated to this State, and on his present farm in 1853 He was married in 1855 to Miss Maria Crane, from New York, they have four children—Effa H, Harriet M, George C and Alma B. He has 262 acres of land, valued at $30 per acre. He has held the offices of Township Supervisor four years, Township Trustee one year, Secretary School Board six years. Mr Sergeant was among the earliest settlers in the township, only one when he came, he attended the meeting for the organization of the county in the Fall of 1853 He is a Republican, and attended the first Republican Convention held in the county He has always taken a lively interest in his county and township He also attended the meeting, and assisted in the organizing of the township He was chosen as Clerk of the meeting, and was afterward elected permanent Clerk of the township There were but 11 voters in the township at that time They depended entirely on a home market to dispose of their products for the first three years

SEVERANCE, GEORGE, farmer, Sec 26, P. O. Hudson, born in Greenfield, Mass, in 1827, he moved to East Hartford, Conn, in 1854, and worked at his trade as burnisher until 1856, when he moved to and located in Grundy Co in this State, and to his present location in 1860. He was married in 1848 to Miss Eliza E Backus from Connecticut, they have five children—Annie E, Isabel M, Cora J, Charles F, Virginia I Mr S has held the offices of School Director one year, Road Supervisor three years He was the first Road Supervisor elected in Grundy Co, only two houses in Grundy Center when he came He hauled the lumber from Dubuque, with an ox team, and built the first frame house built in Grundy Center He came through from Chicago to Waterloo with team in 1856, and it rained every day but one while on the way

Schmit, Frank X., far, Sec 8 P. O Cedar Falls

SHAFFNER, P., farmer, Sec 27, P O Hudson, born in Knox Co, Ohio, in 1832, he emigrated with his parents to Clark Co, Ill, in 1848 He was married in 1860 to Miss Malinda Rupp from Ohio They have three children—Ella May, born July 9, 1861, Emma N, born March 1, 1863, Etta D, born Aug 14, 1874 In 1864, he, with his family, moved by team to Anoka, Minnesota, where he was engaged in the grocery and meat trade for four years. Mr Shaffner went to Minnesota for his health The distance

they traveled was 1,100 miles, which took six weeks In 1869, he came to Iowa and settled on his present farm, which consists of 145 acres of land, valued at $35 per acre He has held the office of School Director one year In politics, Republican They are members of the M E Church, but not having any M E. Church near they unite with the United Brethren and worship in their new church on Sec 24

Shank, W, far, S 34, P O Hudson
Shirey, J, renter, S 25, P O Hudson
Shroeder, C, far, Sec 22, P O Hudson
Smith, B, far, S 10, P O Cedar Falls

STRAYER, G. W., farmer, Sec. 22, P O Hudson, born in Cambria Co, Penn, July 12, 1840, emigrated to Iowa and on his present farm in the Spring of 1869 He was married in November 1862, to Miss Barbara Cain from Pennsylvania, she was born Aug 7, 1843, they have five children— Elizabeth A, Joseph W, Lucinda E, Rebecca A and Charles. Mr. S has held the offices of Township Clerk one year, Township Trustee one year, School Director seven years, Treasurer of School Board four years He is adding some fine improvements to his farm, he has just erected a barn, 45x111½. The German Baptist Church is located on his land, i was built last season, it is 36x44, they are members of that church Mr S has held the office of Director of the Farmers' Mutual Fire Insurance Company for four years He has 372 acres of land, valued at $30 per acre

Strayer, Jacob, Sec 28, P O. Hudson

STRAYER, LEVI, farmer, Sec 28, P O Hudson, born in Cambria Co, Penn, in 1844 He was married in 1862 to Miss Lavina Myers, from Somerset Co, Penn, emigrated to Iowa and on his present farm in 1870, they have seven children—Sarah E, Alvin J, Emma E, Huldah S, Martha E, Cyrus T and baby He has 105 acres of land, valued at $3,000 He has held the offices of Township Assessor two years, School Director four years In politics, Democratic They are members of the German Baptist Church His parents emigrated to the State at the same time His father purchased the farm known as the Geo F Ward property—400 acres   They all lived together for five years, when Levi purchased his farm of his father, and moved on to it   His father died in 1875

Struble, J , far   Sec 34, P. O Hudson

Stumphenhausen, H , far , S 6 , P O Hudson

TAYLOR, JOSIAH, far , Sec 29 ; P O Hudson

Tierman, C , far , S 4 , P O Cedar Falls

Trost, J , far , S 17 , P. O Cedar Falls

Tucker, G W., far , S 29 , P O Hudson

Tucker, W A , far , S 29 , P O Hudson

Tullock, H , far , S. 8 ; P O Cedar Falls.

VIEREGGE, HENRY, far., S 17 , P O Cedar Falls.

VINTON, S. B., farmer, Sec 1 , P O Waterloo , born in Canada July 17, 1814 , he emigrated to Watertown, Wis , 1837 , on his route he passed through Chicago, June 6, 1837 , he moved to Minnesota in 1856 ; to Iowa and on his present farm in the Fall of 1869 , he has 100 acres of land, valued at $40 per acre   He was married in November, 1843, to Miss Caroline Owen, from Addison Co , Vt , she died in 1870 , he was married in 1872 to Miss Anna Hall from Herkimer Co , N Y , they have two children—Elvira G , born Oct 21, 1873 ; Esther G , born Aug 5, 1875   Democrat, Mrs Vinton is a member of the Episcopal Church At the time when Mr Vinton settled in Wisconsin, Wisconsin, Iowa, Minnesota and Nebraska composed the Northwest Territory , the seat of government was at Burlington, Iowa , he assisted in building the first frame building in Watertown , Milwaukee was then the nearest market , it was then but a small village , they were obliged to cart their grain fifty miles through the woods with ox teams to mill , he was obliged to pay $5 per bushel for seed potatoes the first season , the next season they were a drug in the market , plenty of Indians all around at that time ; they were obliged to make fish their principal diet for some time , when he moved to Minnesota, Minneapolis had but one small house, St Paul was but a trading post. While in Minnesota, Mr V. held the office of Postmaster at Staunton five years. At this time, he holds the offices

of Treasurer and Director of the Black Hawk Co Mutual Fire Insurance Association

WALKER, JOHN, far , Sec 2 , P O Waterloo

Waltman, G , far , S 9 , P O Cedar Falls.

Washburn, D D , P O Waterloo

WASHBURN, J. H., farmer, Sec 25 , P O Waterloo , born in St. Lawrence Co , N Y , April 30, 1838 , he emigrated to Walworth Co , Wis , in 1856 , to Iowa in the Fall of 1857, and settled on Sec 24 , in 1860 he sold out to his brother, D B Washburn, and settled on his present farm   He was married in 1862 to Miss Margaret E Sergeant, from Pennsylvania , they have two children—Frank S , born Nov 4, 1864 ; Guy, born in August, 1874   He has eighty acres of land, valued at $30 per acre   He has held the offices of Justice of the Peace for six years, Township Assessor, one year, Township Clerk two years, School Director three years.   Mr W is a carpenter by trade, he worked on the Court House at Waterloo, in 1857 , he also assisted in building the two first churches built in Waterloo.   In politics, is a stanch Republican.

Warren, S S , far , S 24 ; P O Waterloo.

WASSOM, D. J., farmer, S 34 , P O Hudson, born in Cambria Co , Penn , Feb 1, 1838 , he emigrated to Indiana in 1843 , in 1864, he returned to Cambria, and was married to Miss Lucinda Cain Nov 6, 1864 , they moved to Iowa and Orange Tp in 1865, and on to their present farm in the Spring of 1868 , they have four children—Francis J , born Aug 7, 1866 , Lorenzo A , born Oct 13, 1869 , Vena V , born Feb 6, 1874, and Clarence W , born Oct 23, 1877   He has eighty acres of land, valued at $3,000. In politics, Republican.   Mrs Wassom is a member of the German Baptist Church.

Mr W. was engaged in teaming supplies for the great Cambria R. R Iron Works for eight years before he came to Iowa

Watters, D., far , S 34 , P O Hudson.

Wilson, A , far , S 24 , P. O Waterloo.

Wilson, Ed , far , S 24 , P. O Waterloo.

Wilson, S , far , S 24 , P. O. Waterloo

YOUNG, M., far., S. 6 ; P. O. Cedar Falls.

Yonkstick, A., far., S. 9; P. O. Cedar Falls.

ZACH, J., far., S. 20; P. O. Cedar Falls.

EAGLE TOWNSHIP.

AMFAHR, WILLIAM, far, S 8, P O Waterloo born in La Salle Co, Ill, in 1857, and came to this county in 1866 and settled on his present farm. Married Ann Reuter in 1877, she was born in Germany in 1854 Are members of the Catholic Church

ARMSTRONG, JAMES, far, S 34, P O Miller's Creek, born in Stark Co., Ohio, in 1811 Married Catharine Shoup in 1834, she was born in Pennsylvania in 1819, and died in 1869, Elizabeth, Amanda, Nancy, Caroline, John, William, Sanford and Isaac are their living children, they lost two children—Catharine and George Came to this county in 1869 and settled on his present farm of eighty acres, valued at $30 per acre

BATEMAN, A, far, S 27, P O Miller's Creek

Bateman, H, far, S. 27, P O Miller's Creek

Bateman, M, far, S 26, P O Miller's Creek

Bauler, William

Beck, Nick

Berry, S, far, S 34, P O La Porte

BLACK, THOMAS, far, S 20, P O Traer, Tama Co, born in New York City in 1853, and emigrated to Stephenson Co in 1865, and to this county in 1871, and settled on his present farm, consisting of eighty acres, valued at $20 per acre, where he has since made it his home He, with others of this township, lives in the full and seemingly perfect enjoyment of bachelorhood

Blitch, John, far, S 29, P O. Miller's Creek

BLOOM, WESLEY, far, S 9, P O Waterloo, born in Greene Co, Wis, in 1856, and came to this county in 1873, and settled on his present place of 160 acres, valued at $30 per acre, in March, 1878, where he has since made it his home

Boor, S. C, far, S 27, P O Miller's Creek

BORY, PETER, far, S 8, P O Waterloo, born in Germany in 1844, and emigrated to America in 1868, and settled in Lake County Ill, where he lived until 1872, when he came to this county, and in 1875, settled on his present farm. Married Katie Shears in 1874, she was born in Germany in 1853, they have two children—Willie and Adam Are members of the Catholic Church

BRONSON ABRAM, far., S. 16; P O Waterloo, born in Greene Co, N Y, in 1835, and settled in La Salle Co, Ill, in 1854, where he married Mary Humphrey in 1859, she was born in Oneida Co, N. Y., in 1839 Came to this county in 1862, and settled on his present farm of 240 acres, valued at $35 per acre Has held the office of Constable for thirteen consecutive years, and has filled nearly every town office during his residence in the county Charles, Hugh E, Della, Albert, Eddy, Ettie, Winnie and Frank are their living children, lost one child—Annie Are members of the Methodist Church

BURGER, GEORGE, farmer, S 17, P O Waterloo, born in Germany in 1832, and emigrated to America in 1854, and settled in La Salle Co, Ill, where he married Mary Offerman in 1861, she was born in Germany in 1841, they have seven children—Anton, Katie, John, Annie, William, Frank and Josephine, have lost four children—William, John, Henry and Louis Came to this county in 1868, and settled on his present estate of 160 acres, valued at $30 per acre Members of Catholic Church

Burns, J, far S 16, P. O Waterloo

BUXTON, JOHN, farmer, S 20, P O. Waterloo, born in Yorkshire, England, in 1822, and married Mary Pratt in 1848, she was born in same place in 1830 Came to America in 1859, and settled in Dubuque Co., Iowa, where he lived until 1876, when he came to this county, and settled on his present farm of 160 acres, valued at $30 per acre Their children are Ann E, John H., Agnes, Christina, Addie, Hannah, Mary J, Margaret P, Eliza, Thomas and William, lost two children

—Elizabeth and Mary J Are members of the M E Church

CAHILL, T, farmer, Sec 19, P O Waterloo

Clark, M, far, S 25, P O La Porte City

Conner, A, far, S 10, P O Miller's Creek

Conner, J M, far, S 19, P O Miller's Creek

Conner, J O, far, S 10, P O Miller's Creek

Conner, T, far., S 11, P O Miller's Creek

COVER, E. MERRICK, farmer, Sec 24, P O La Porte City, born in Johnstown, Penn, in 1851, and came to this county in May, 1874, and settled on his present farm of eighty acres, valued at $30 per acre Married Martha Jewell in Jan, 1875, she was born in Wilmington, Delaware, in 1856 Addie B and infant son not yet christened are their children

DILGER, A, far, S 14, P O Miller's Creek

EIGHMEY, P P, farmer, Sec 9, P O Waterloo

EASHAR, JOSEPH, farmer, S 21, P. O. Waterloo, born in Herkimer Co, N Y, in 1842, emigrated to De Kalb Co, Ill, where he enlisted in the 105th Ill V I, Company A, in 1862, and served three years; participated in all the battles of that regiment, and was with Sherman on his march to the sea, and honorably discharged at the close of the war He came to this county in 1865, and settled on his farm of 160 acres, valued at $50 per acre, where he lives in the full enjoyment and blessedness of bachelorhood

EIGHMEY, C. W., far, Sec 10, P O Waterloo, born in Saratoga Co., N Y, in 1832, and emigrated to La Salle Co. with parents in 1846, settling in La Salle Co, Ill, from which place he moved to Dubuque, Iowa, in 1856, came to this county, and settled on his present farm of 160 acres, valued at $35 per acre He married Catherine Penne in 1854, she was born in Germany in 1834, they have four children—Nettie, William, Frank and Charles, lost one child—Jessie Was Justice of the Peace two terms, and

Trustee a number of years, and is one of the early settlers of this town

EIGHMEY, HIRAM B., far, Sec 4, P O Waterloo, born in Saratoga Co, N Y, in 1838, came to La Salle Co, Ill, with his parents in 1846, and to Dubuque in 1850, where he lived until 1867 He married Lizzie Long in 1872, she was born in Pennsylvania in 1849, they have four children —Orvie, Grace, Clyde and Ralph He settled on his present farm, consisting of 160 acres, valued at $30 per acre, in 1868 Served four years in the army, and was honorably discharged

EIGHMEY, ORSON, farmer, S 10, P O Waterloo, born in Dubuque, Iowa, in 1849, came to this county in 1868, and settled on his present estate of eighty acres, valued at $35 per acre Married Mary Hopkins in 1877; she was born in Waterloo, Iowa, March 6, 1857, they have one child—Edith, born Dec 26, 1877 Mr E is Republican

FITZSIMMONS, NANCY, farming, Sec. 29, P O Waterloo, widow of Benard Fitzsimmons, who was born in Ireland in 1803, and came to America in 1840, settling in Cincinnati, Ohio, where he married Nancy McCoy, she was born in Ireland in 1825, she has six children — Edward, Mary, Thomas, Bernard, John, Ellen Mr F. dropped dead on the streets of Cincinnati, from heart disease, Feb 1, 1870, she with her family came to this county the same year, where they have since made it their home.

FIKE, JACOB M., farmer, Sec 23, P O Miller's Creek, born in Somerset Co, Penn, in 1843, where he married Catharine Muller, Dec 24, 1863, she was born in same county in 1841, they have seven children—Emanuel, Mary, Orphy, Eliza, Edwin, Sadie and Arthur They came to this county in March, 1865, and settled on his present farm, consisting of 160 acres, valued at $4,000 They are members of the German Baptist Church

GUNN, J C, farmer, Sec 33, P O Miller's Creek

GARDNER, A. W., farmer, Sec 26, P O La Porte City, born in Jefferson Co, N Y, Feb 26, 1829, he emigrated to Licking Co, Ohio, in Sept.

1852, where he married Clarisa A King Dec 19, 1853, she was born in same county Dec 12, 1832, Burton F and Eugene A are their living children. Mr G came to this county in June, 1864, and in Dec, 1866, settled on his present estate, consisting of 160 acres, valued at $35 per acre Held the offices of Assessor and Justice of the Peace, and has been otherwise prominently identified with the interests of the town and county

GARDNER, GILSON, farmer, Sec 35, P O. La Porte City, born in Jefferson Co, N Y., in 1830, and emigrated to Licking Co, Ohio, in 1851, where he married Margaret Humphrey in 1855, she was born in same county in 1832, came to this county in 1855, and entered the land comprising his present estate, upon which he permanently settled with his family in 1860, his farm consists of 240 acres, valued at $46 per acre   Frank P, William T; Fred H, Numan A and Birdie J are their living children

HERRICK, L D, far, S 33, P O. Waterloo

Herrick, L L, far, S 33, P O Waterloo

HERRMAN, NIKOLAUS, farmer, Sec 5, P O. Waterloo, born in Germany in 1836   Married Johanna Long in 1853, she was born in Germany in 1818, they have four children—Catherine, Barbara, Angeline and John, lost one child in Germany   Came to America in 1862, and settled in Wood Co, Ohio, and in 1866, moved to Dayton, Ohio, where he lived until 1868, when he came to this county and settled near Waterloo, and in 1873 settled on his present farm of eighty-eight acres, valued at $35 per acre   Are members of the Catholic Church

HOLMES, JOHN, farmer, Sec. 6, P. O. Waterloo, born in England in 1822, and emigrated to America in 1854, and in 1864, settled in this township   In 1876, married Mary Smith, she was born in Clermont Co, Ohio, in 1831   Owns eighty-five acres, valued at $35 per acre, upon which he settled after marriage, where he has since made it his home

Hughes, D L, far, S 30, P O Miller's Creek.

Humphrey, T. J, far., Sec. 16; P O. Waterloo

KELROY, BRUNO, farmer, Sec 28, P O Miller's Creek, born in Canada in 1835, and emigrated to Stephenson Co, Ill, in 1856, where he married Martha J Galbraith Oct 14 1860   Came to this county in 1870, and in 1871 settled on his present farm of 120 acres, valued at $40 per acre   Are members of the Advent Church

KISTNER, FREDERICK, farmer, Sec 2, P. O Waterloo, born in Hanover, Germany, in 1833, and came to America in 1845, and settled in Somerset Co, Penn, where he married Frederica Meckey, in 1856, she was born in Germany in 1832. they have four children—Augusta, Ella, Dora and Mary. Came to this county in 1864, and settled in the city of Waterloo, where he lived until 1877, when he settled on his present estate of 160 acres, valued at $25 per acre   Are members of the Christian Church

KISTNER, GEORGE, farmer, Sec 10, P O Waterloo, born in Hanover, Germany, in 1843, and came to America in 1849, and settled in Somerset Co, Penn, where he married Elizabeth Shaulls, in 1865, she was born in Somerset Co, Penn, in 1843   Came to this county in 1865, and settled on his present estate of 200 acres, valued at $20 per acre, in 1872, where they have since made it their home.

LICHTY, DAVID, far, S 3, P. O. Waterloo.

Lilley, J, far, S. 16, P.O. Miller's Creek.

McGARVEY, PAT, far, S 9, P O Waterloo

McKinster, G, far, Sec 3, P O Miller's Creek

McKinster, Wm, far., S. 3, P. O. Miller's Creek

McManus, F, far., S 29; P. O. Miller's Creek

McManus, O, far, S 26, P O Miller's Creek.

Marshall, G, far, S 30, P O Miller's Creek

Meredith, T, far., S. 10, P. O. Miller's Creek

Mitchell, M, far, S 14, P O. Miller's Creek

Miller, P, far, S. 12, P O Miller's Creek.

MOORE, LORENZO, farmer, Sec. 35, P O Miller's Creek; born in Columbia Co, Penn, in 1821, and came with his parents when quite young and settled in St Joseph Co, Mich, where he married Hannah Good in 1844, she was born in Bucks Co, Penn, in 1822, they have nine children living—Rebecca, Clara, Edward, Emily, Oliver, Mary, Kent, Annie and Harry Moved to Cass Co., Mich, in 1850, where he resided until the Spring of 1865, when he came to this county, and settled on his present estate, consisting of 240 acres, valued at $35 per acre. Is a Republican

MOTT, DAMON, farmer, Sec. 33, P O Miller's Creek, born in Oswego Co., N. Y, Feb 17, 1837. Married Lucy M Dye in 1860, she was born in Oneida Co, N Y, July 17, 1837 Came to this county in March, 1861, and on May 2, the same year, settled on his present estate, consisting of 640 acres of land, valued at $30 per acre Mr M. is one of the heaviest stock raisers in the county Addie E, their only child, was born March 29, 1865 Are members of the M. E. Church

Myers, N., far, S 28, P O Miller's Creek.

NENISER, FRANK, farmer, Sec 11, P O Miller's Creek

O'NEIL, ALEX, farmer, Sec. 21, P O. Miller's Creek

O'Neil, S., far, S 21; P O Miller's Creek

O'Neil, W., far, S 21; P O. Miller's Creek.

PENNE, PETER, farmer, Sec 15, P O Waterloo.

PECK, JERRY J., farmer, Sec. 3; P O Waterloo, born in Somerset Co, Penn, in 1854, came to this county in 1874, and married Lizzie Lichty in 1876, she was born in the same county in 1855 Owns eighty acres of land, valued at $30 per acre. Are members of the German Baptist Church

Penne, W. J, far, S 5, P O Waterloo

ROBERTS, THOMAS, farmer, Sec 26, P O Miller's Creek

RIETER, HENRY, farmer, Sec. 7, P O Waterloo, born in Germany in 1818. Married Catherine Schenkelberg in 1850, she was born in Germany in 1822, have four children—Elizabeth, Annie, Katherina and Christina. Came to this country in 1866, and settled in Illinois, and in 1867, settled on his present farm of eighty acres, valued at $35 per acre

Rodamer, B J, far, S. 27; P O Miller's Creek

ROTH, MATHIAS, farmer, Sec 20, P O Waterloo, born in Germany in 1812. Married Susan Zemith in 1848, she was born in Germany in 1816, came to this country in 1864 and settled in Chicago, Ill, where he lived until 1869, when he came to this county and settled on his present farm of eighty acres, valued at $30 per acre Nicholas, John and Michael are their children Members of the Catholic Church

SHAFFER, PETER, farmer, Sec 17, P. O Miller's Creek.

SCHRADER, WILLIAM, far, Sec 9, P O Waterloo; born in Germany in 1816, and emigrated to America in 1845, and settled in La Salle Co, Ill. Married Seble Sebelee in 1859, she was born in Germany in 1826, and have four children—Mary, Henry, Annie and Katie, lost one infant daughter. Came to this county in 1867, and settled on his present farm of eighty acres, valued at $30 per acre Are members of the Catholic Church

SHEAN, JAMES, farmer, Sec 14, P O Waterloo, born in Ireland in 1815. Married Mrs Elizabeth Kelley in 1862, she had three children by first marriage who are still living—Mary A, Maggie and Elizabeth A Came to this county in 1852 and settled on his present estate of eighty acres, valued at $30 per acre. They have one child—Rosa, and are members of the Catholic Church

Shenkelberg, G, far., Sec 7, P O Miller's Creek

Smith, B, far, S. 21, P. O Miller's Creek

Smith, E J, far, Sec 21, P O Miller's Creek

STRUBEL, CHARLES J., far, Sec 4, P O Waterloo, born in Germany in 1830, emigrated to America in 1849, and settled in Bureau Co, Ill Married Eva Fullin in 1856, she was born in Germany in 1833, and have eight children—Eva, Charles, Josephine, Fred, Adam, Christie, Annie and Willie Came to this county in 1866 and settled on his present farm of 164 acres, valued at $35 per acre   Was Town Trustee three years   Are members of the Catholic Church.

STEIMEL, WILLIAM, farmer, Sec. 15 , P O Waterloo , born in Germany in 1829, and emigrated to this country in 1854, and settled in La Salle Co , Ill., and in 1856 came to this county and settled on his present farm of 180 acres, valued at $45 per acre Married Ann E. Penne in 1859, she was born in Germany in 1838; they have nine children—Adaline E , Mary B , Emma K , William E , Clara H , Edgar, Joseph F , John A. and Theodore   Held the office of Assessor six years, Town Clerk two years, and otherwise prominently identified.   Are members of the Catholic Church

TAGGERT, JAMES, Sr., farmer, Sec. 10 , P O Miller's Creek

Taggert, James, Jr , far., S 10 , P O. Miller's Creek

Trost, Philip, far , S 29 , P O Miller's Creek.

VAN BUREN, M , far , Sec 9 , P. O Miller's Creek

WAGER, CHARLES, farmer, Sec. 21 , P. O. Miller's Creek

Whipkey, I., far., S. 30 , P O. Miller's Creek.

Whipkey, S A., far., S. 30 , P. O Miller's Creek.

Williams, J , far., S. 20 , P O. Miller's Creek.

YUCKER, S , farmer, S. 35 , P O. Miller's Creek.

CEDAR TOWNSHIP.

ASH, JOHN, farmer, S 18, P O La Porte City

BLATHERWICK, H , farmer, Sec 6, P. O La Porte City

Blatherwick, J H , S. 6 , P O La Porte

BROWN, HORNER, farmer, Sec 8 , P O La Porte City, born in Ireland, in June, 1820, and in 1846, married Ann J Marshall, she was born in Clinton Co , N Y , in August, 1821 , have ten children—Thomas, George, Elizabeth, Maria, James, John, Mary A , Robert, William and Fletcher E , lost one—Delia Came to this country when a child and settled in Canada, where he lived until 1853, when he moved to Ogle Co , Ill , and lived there until 1856, when he traveled to this county with oxen, and settled on his present estate, consisting of 120 acres, valued at $30 per acre Is one of the early settlers of this town and county. Are members of the M. E Church.

Brown, James, far , S 17 , P O La Porte City

Brown, John, far , S. 17 , P O La Porte City

Brown, Wm., far., S 8, P. O La Porte City.

Buechley, M , far., S. 7 , P. O Waterloo

CLOSE, CICERO, far , S. 33 , P O. Cedar Falls

Close, E. T., far , S 7 , P O La Porte City

Close, G. E H , far., S 33 ; P O Cedar Valley.

Close, J. A , far , S. 7 , P. O. La Porte City.

Conner, J , far., S. 3 , P. O Cedar Valley.

Countryman, Wm , La Porte City.

Costetter, John, farmer

DOUD, J., far , Sec 6 ; P O Cedar Valley

DOBSHIRE, JOHN, farmer, Sec 9 , P. O Cedar Valley , born in Ireland in 1808 Married Ellen Clinghan in 1855 , she was born in Ireland in 1807 ; have one child living—Mary , lost one child—Thomas. Came to this country in 1843, and enlisted in Co B 1st Artillery and served through the Mexican war, and served as teamster in the regular army eighteen years, after which he

went to California and lived there two years , returning, went to New Orleans, where he resided until 1852, when he came to this county and entered the land of his estate , has a farm of 120 acres, valued at $35 per acre , is one of the earliest settlers in the county, and are members of the Catholic Church

Doud, J , Jr , far , S 6 , P O Cedar Valley

Doud, T , far , S 6 , P O Cedar Valley

DOXEY, THOMAS B., farmer, Sec 20 , P O Cedar Valley , born in the city of Baltimore, Md , Aug 17, 1820 He married Margaret Henry, of Wayne Co , Ind., Oct 7, 1847 , she was born in Lewis Co., N Y , Dec 27, 1825 , they have seven children—Ella, Boyd, Mrs Ida Geist, Mrs May Edwards, Loren B , Willie S. and Della They emigrated to this county May 12 1855 , they settled on their present farm in March, 1870 , they have 320 acres of land, valued at $30 per acre Mr. D enlisted Oct 6, 1862, in Co C, 32d I V. C , was engaged in battles at Pleasant Hill, Nashville and others , was honorably discharged Oct. 6, 1865, His family are members of the Presbyterian Church

EASTMAN, GEORGE, farmer, S 8 ; P. O. La Porte City.

FAEUK, L F , farmer, S 3 , P O Cedar Falls

FOULK, PETER, farmer, S. 31 , P O Cedar Valley ; born in Perry Co , Penn , Jan 25, 1803, moved to Freeport, Ill , in 1852 , to De Kalb Co , Ill , in 1855 , to Iowa and his present farm in 1865 He was married to Miss Susan Showalter from Pennsylvania, born Dec 9, 1805 , they have had eleven children, seven of whom are living—Mrs Matilda Mythaler, Mrs Mary M Gordon, Mrs Lyle B Brown, Mrs Sarah J Hess, Mrs Susan C Dener, William H and Levi F Mr F owns 120 acres of land, valued at $3,000 Politics, Republican , religion, Disciples

Fauek, W. H , far., S. 31, P. O Cedar Valley.

Felton, N., far., S 21 , P O. Cedar Valley

Flaherty, M , far , S. 7 , P O La Porte

Frost, H , far , S 8 , P O La Porte City.

Frost, M , Jr , far., S 17 , P. O La Porte City

Frost, M , far , S 17 , P O La Porte City

Frost, N , far , Sec 17 . P O La Porte City

GAY, J., farmer, S 33 , P O. Cedar Valley

Gay, L , far , S 33 ; P O Cedar Valley

GOLINVANE, MARY B., MRS., farmer, S. 21 , P O. Gilbertville , she was born in France Feb 10, 1827. She was married to August Golinvean April 15, 1850 They emigrated to this country, arriving in New Orleans in July, 1854 , left New Orleans in 1857 and came to Iowa, and Dubuque, where they lived eleven years ; settled on their present farm in March, 1868, they have had nine children—Joseph P , Mary P , Lewis J , Emele P , Gust D , August, Mary M., Julia, Eugene, Mary P ; Eugene and Joseph P , died Mr Golinvean died Aug 31, 1870 The estate contains 400 acres of land, valued at $25 per acre. They age members of the Cathole Church.

HAMMER, S., far., Sec 3 , P O La Porte City

Hilts, J M , far., S 4 , P O La Porte City

HOSMAN, ISAAC, farmer, Sec. 18 , P O Waterloo, born in Richland Co., Ohio, Jan 20, 1829 , emigrated from his native State to Linn Co., Iowa, Oct. 6, 1853 In the same year he was married to Susanuah Kistler, from Ohio, she was born in Fairfield Co., Ohio, June 9, 1830 , resided in Linn Co. one year , moved to Waterloo in 1854, and was engaged in general merchandise , in October, 1864, he settled on his present farm, consisting of 120 acres, valued at $30 per acre, his children are Thomas D. and Elmer E They are members of the M E Church , in politics, Republican He has held the office of Township Supervisor , also School Director

Hubbard, A , far S. 15 ; P O. La Porte City

Hubbard, D , far , S 15 , P O La Porte City

Hubbard, L , far., S 15 , P O La Porte City

Hummel, F M , far , S 3 , P O La Porte City

Hummel, J. V , far., S. 3 , P O La Porte City

ISENHOWER, JOHN, farmer, Sec 17 , P O. Waterloo, born in Lincoln Co , N. C , in April, 1807 He was married June 1, 1854, to Miss Anna Ketring, from Tennessee , she was born Aug. 7, 1825 Emigrated to Black Hawk Co , Iowa, settling on their present farm, consisting of 100 acres of land, valued at $38 per acre, in 1868 They are members of the Presbyterian Church ; politics, Democrat. He was formerly married to Pursis Hinkle, by which marriage he has four living children, three sons were in the army , one died ; his children are Destamona, Mary J , William R , Saphrona E , Sylvester J , Selrenus K , Jessie A. and Sarah May

KEYSER, D., far., S. 20 ; P. O. La Porte City.

Koch, H , far , S 7 ; P. O. Waterloo

Koch, J , far , S 18 , P. O Waterloo

LEEKINGTON, A , far., S 19 , P O. Waterloo.

Leekington, D , far., S 19 , P O Waterloo

McCLURE, G B , far., S 17 , P O La Porte City

McClure, Geo. E., far , S 17 , P O La Porte City

McDonald, T., far , S 6 ; P O La Porte City

McKELLAR, NELSON, farmer, Sec 16 , P O Waterloo, born in Scotland Feb 7, 1830 , he emigrated to this country, and Elgin, Kane Co , Ill., where he was married on Oct 20, 1857 ; moved to Iowa, and this county on his present farm Nov 24, 1857 , they have had eleven children—John A , Daniel B., Edward A , Eva J , Frank, Alexander H , Nelson P , Jennie E., Joel H , Vernon and baby died. He owns 320 acres of land, valued at $25 per acre His wife is a member of the Presbyterian Church. , in politics, Republican He has held the office of Road Supervisor

McKevitt, J , far , S 12 , P O La Porte City

McNaughton, A , far , S 3 , P O Cedar Valley.

Marshall, H , far , S 17 ; P O La Porte City.

Marshall, W , far., S 31 , P O Cedar Valley

Mead, J H , far , S 20 , P. O Waterloo

Miles, J , far., S 10 , P. O. La Porte City

Morris, G , far , S 5 , P O La Porte City.

Mullar, P., far , S 18 , P O La Porte City

MYTHALER, FREDRICK, farmer, Sec 32 , P O. Cedar Valley , born in Germany March 6, 1835, came to this country and Pennsylvania in 1853 , to Ohio, to Black Hawk Co , in 1864 , to his present farm same year He was married Nov 25, 1860, to Miss Matilda Foulk, from Perry Co , Penn , born Oct 23, 1830 , they have five children—Minnie J., Emma L., George F , William E and David F He has 255 acres of land, valued at $7,000 Member of the Christian Church , politics, Republican.

Mythaler, J , far , S. 8 ; P O Cedar Valley.

NICHOLS, ANSON, far , Sec 20 ; P. O Waterloo.

NICHOLS, CLARK, P., farmer, Sec 20 , P O Waterloo , born in Windsor Co , Vt , Dec. 10, 1809. He married Sallie Stoughton Dec 23, 1834, she was born in Johnson Co , Vt , Feb 17, 1817 ; they have six children—Sarah E , Amos P , Matilda E , Naomi A , Mariam S and Edwin S , they have lost three children—Clark P , Patwin S and an infant son. In 1856, he emigrated and settled in Orange Township , came to his present farm in 1868 , he has 260 acres of land, valued at $25 per acre Member of the Presbyterian Church.

Nichols, E S , far , S 20 , P O Waterloo

OPPLE, JOHN, farmer, Sec. 27 , P. O Gilbertville

Osmon, J. S , far , S. 1 , P O La Porte City

OSBORN, WILLIAM, farmer, Sec 18 , P O La Porte City , born in England in 1830, and emigrated to America in 1832 with his parents, who settled in Erie Co., N Y , in the Fall of 1853, moved to De Kalb Co , Ill , where he resided until 1855, when he came to this county and settled in the city of Waterloo, settled on his present farm in 1857, consisting of 120 acres, valued at $30 per acre, where he lived in the enjoyment of single blessedness until 1860, when he married Sophia Dobney ; she was born in England in 1830 , their children are Hattie S , Ella E , William H , John T , Charles J and May.

PAUL, FRANK, farmer, Sec 13 , P O. Gilbertville.

Peck, A , far , S 4 ; P O. Gilbertville

Peck, G , far , S. 4 , P. O Gilbertville

ROBERTS, D A , farmer, Sec 6 , P O Cedar Valley

RIPPEL, JACOB, farmer, Sec 9 , P O La Porte City, born in Germany in 1838 Married Henrietta Steinke in 1862, she was born in Germany in 1844, have two children living—Annie and Ida Came to this country in 1850, with his father, William, and settled in Waukesha Co , Wis , resided in that State until 1874, when he came to this county, and settled on his present farm of 125 acres, valued at $40 per acre Member of the Evangelical Church

ROBERTS, ROBERT D., farmer, Sec 30 , P O Cedar Valley , born in Oneida Co , N Y , in 1827, and in 1865, came to this county, where, in 1868, he married Sarah McArthur , she was born in Scotland in 1846, have three children—Ella, Archibald and John, lost one child—Grace After marriage, settled on his present farm of 240 acres, valued at $45 per acre Members of the Presbyterian Church

SCROGGY, ISRAEL, farmer, Sec 18 , P O Waterloo

Shields, S.. far , S 9 P O Cedar Valley

Shoop, A. L , far , S. 2 , P O Cedar Valley

Sisson, W W , far., Sec 29 ; P O Cedar Valley.

Smith, Geo H , far , Sec 9 , P. O Cedar Valley

Smith, L O., far , S. 9 , P O Cedar Valley

Smith, S G , far , S 10 , P. O. Cedar Valley

STUHLMILLER, JOHN, farmer, Sec 17 , P O Waterloo, born in Canada, July 28, 1858 Emigrated to this country, settling in Erie Co , N Y , where he married Annie Kuhn July 5, 1861 , she was born in Wurtemberg Aug 9, 1838. In Nov, 1862, they emigrated to Black Hawk Tp, this county, in a short time to Waterloo, where he was the proprietor of the Pennsylvania House, and returned

8

to Black Hawk Tp, then to this township, settling on his present farm, consisting of 240 acres of land, valued at $30 per acre, Sept. 12, 1876. Margarett E., Charles W., Mary E., Julia C. and Louis G are their children Congregationalists in religion; in politics, Democratic

TROST, Peter, farmer, Sec 6, P. O. Cedar Valley.

TOURNIEN, THEOPHILE C., farmer, Sec. 22; P. O. Cedar Valley, born in France March 21, 1814. He was married Nov 28, 1846, to Miss Florentine Letevere, she was born in Paris Dec. 30, 1823. They emigrated to this country and Dubuque, Iowa, in the Spring of 1860, to their present farm in 1867 He owns 180 acres of land, valued at $15 per acre They are members of the Catholic Church. In politics Democratic. They have had six children — Pona, Theophile, Louis,

Mykey, Gust and Florentin; Gust and Florentin are dead

TURNER, ABRAHAM, farmer. Sec. 18, P. O Waterloo, born in Northumberland Co, Penn., March 3, 1827 He married Mary Tallman Sept 29, 1852, she was born in Pennsylvania March 19, 1834. Emigrated and settled in Cook Co., Ill., in 1847; came to Iowa and on his present farm April 10, 1854, he erected a log house 18x 24, which was the second house built in that part of the township; it is now replaced by fine substantial improvements, his farm has 248 acres, valued at $40 per acre They have eight children— Lyman, Joseph, Levi, Sarah, Chrislyan, Charles, Ellen, Mary A, have lost two children—Susan and Flora.

WALDMAN, H, farmer, Sec 12, P O Gilbertville

Watson, T, far, S 7; P O. Gilbertville

BARCLAY TOWNSHIP.

ATWELL, ALLEN, farmer, Sec 28, P. O Jesup

BAKER, J H., farmer, Sec 29, P O. Raymond

Baldwin, C W., far., S. 12, P O Jesup

BASSE, EDWARD, Postmaster, Sec 13, owns forty-nine acres, probable value $2,000, born June 14, 1833, in the Province of Westphalia, Prussia, Germany, where he attended school until he was 15 years old, he intended to study for the ministry, but the death of his father caused him to turn his thoughts in another channel. When 13 years old, he began to learn the trade of gold and silver smithing, and has continued at that business off and on to the present time, he came to the United States, arriving in New York City in February, 1855, and immediately went to Philadelphia, where he stayed a short time, and then moved to Stephenson Co, Ill., where he was engaged a this trade, and part of his time at farming, for about three years, in 1858, he came to Black Hawk Co., Iowa, and located in Barclay Tp, he lived here until 1861, when he started for Colorado with an ox team, and eight dollars in his pocket to pay expenses, but returned with a couple of thousands of dollars, a top carriage and two ponies, he lived in Central City, Colorado, pursuing his business of jeweler for six years, his establishment was known as the "Crystal Palace," in 1867, he returned to Black Hawk Co., and finally settled in Barclay Tp., where he now resides He was married Sept 16, 1866, to Lydia N, daughter of Peter and Mary Trumbauer, of this township, she was born Feb 29, 1844; they have six children—Lottie M, born July 8, 1867, Ida, Nov 14, 1868, Dora, Aug 16, 1870, Ella, Feb 19, 1871, Charley Nov 28, 1872, and Frances, Jan. 13, 1877, they lost one child—Hattie, born Oct. 14, 1874, died Sept. 16, 1875. Mr Basse was appointed Postmaster of this township in 186~ He is a Republican in politics and was Township Constable eight years, Township Collector one year, and Road Supervisor one term He is a member of No 133, Jesup Lodge of I O O F., and also a member of the Blue Ribbon Temperance Reform Society of Barclay Township

Bratnober, A. C, far, S. 19; P O Waterloo

Brennen, W., far, S. 33, P O Jesup.

Brown, A, far., S 22, P O. Jesup

Brown, F, far, S 21, P O Jesup

Brunn, D, far, S 5, P. O Waterloo

Buss, H. D, far, S 12, P O Barclay

CAMPBELL, D, far, S 16 and 20, P O. Barclay.

Chaplin, A, far, S 33, P O Raymond

CHATFIELD, G. W., farmer, Sec 18, P O Waterloo, born in DuPage Co, Ill, 1837, moved to Iowa, and on his present farm in 1864 He was married in 1869 to Miss Elizabeth Wood, of Wisconsin Mr C enlisted October, 1861, in the 33d I. V I., Co B, under Col Hovey; mustered out in 1862, on account of sickness Has 160 acres of land valued at $5,000 He has held the office of Justice of the Peace for the past two years He was elected Captain of the Township Militia during the war after his return

Chaplin, Wm. L, far, S 28 and 33, P O. Raymond.

Clark, E, far, S 32, P. O. Raymond.

Colson, J, far, S 25, P O Jesup

Cowan, W., far, S 12, P. O Barclay

Craton, J B, far., S. 21, P O Jesup.

Cunningham, M, far, S 12, P O Barclay

CUNNINGHAM, THOMAS, farmer, Sec 1, P O Barclay, owns 440 acres, probable value $8,800, born in 1833, in County of Clare, Ireland, where he attended school and worked at farming until he emigrated with his parents (Michael and Hannah Cunningham) to Quebec, Canada, in 1851, after spending about a year in the Dominion, he came to Portage Co, Ohio, where he lived until 1854, and in August of that year, he came to Black Hawk Co, Iowa, and settled in Barclay Tp, where he now resides He was married in the Fall of 1856 to Margaret, daughter of Michael and Bridget Meaney, of County Clare, Ireland, where she was born in

1828, they have four children—Mary A, born July 4, 1857, Daniel, May 15, 1860, John, June 20, 1862, and Thomas, July 11, 1867 When Mr Cunningham came to settle in this township, there were but very few settlers, the whole country was an unbroken tract of prairie, no schools, no laid-out roads, no bridges, in those days were to be seen, the land he now owns was entered in 1854, at $1 25 per acre He is Democratic in politics, and is School Director now serving his third term; he is also Road Supervisor, and his family are members of the Catholic Church

Cunningham, T, far, S 1, P O Barclay

DENNISTON, HENRY B., far, S. 20, P O Waterloo, owns 360 acres of land, valued at $8,300, born April 5, 1833, on Grand Island, Niagara River, N Y, and, when an infant, moved with his parents (John and Margaret Denniston) to Wayne Co., Mich, where he assisted his father, who was engaged in the lumber and saw mill business In 1852, he came West to Illinois, and lived in Leaf River Tp for about four years, where he was married Oct 15, 1854, to Amanda, daughter of David and Sarah Hunter, of the same place, Mrs Denniston was born March 6, 1832, they have seven children—Emma N, born Feb. 25, 1856, Mary C, Dec. 21, 1861, Artaxa A., Dec 19, 1864, Harriet A, March 11, 1867, Clara B, Feb 1, 1869, Albert H., Nov 5, 1871, and Frank E, Oct 27, 1873. In the Spring of 1857, he came to Black Hawk Co, and settled in Barclay Tp, where he now resides From the time he left Michigan to the present, he has been engaged in farming, he has one acre of peat bog on his farm, which affords, when used as fuel, a very fine fire, and will prove a very good substitute for wood and coal, he says that when he first came to this township there were not more than 300 acres of land broken He is a Republican, and is now serving his fourth term as Township Trustee, was Township Constable one term, Township Collector one term, and School Director about six years He is a member of the Wesleyan Methodist Church, and is class leader in the same, he is also President of the Blue Ribbon Temperance Reform Society, of Barclay Tp.; this is the first society of the kind ever organized here. Mrs Denniston is also a member of the Wesleyan Methodist Church

EGGE, A, far, S. 15, P O. Barclay.

Elliott J., far.. S. 26, P. O Jesup

Ellis, A J, far, S. 3, P. O. Barclay

FENTON, A. C, far., S. 19; P O Waterloo

FENTON, ALVIN W., farmer, Sec. 19; P O. Raymond, owns 248 acres of land, probable value $6,200, born April 15, 1836, in Allegany Co., N Y, and went from there with his parents (Franklin and Levina Fenton), to Chautauqua Co, N Y, where he lived until he was 13 years old, and he then moved to Erie Co, and engaged in the business of carpenter, in which he assisted his father until he was 18 years old, and then moved West to Ogle Co, Ill, where he engaged in farming, and has followed that business ever since, excepting some short intermissions that occurred through temporary absence from his home In 1864, he enlisted in the 142d Iowa V I., and at the expiration of his term of service, was honorably discharged Was married Jan 19, 1866, to Lottie, daughter of Anson and Sarah Ingham, formerly of Franklin Co, Ohio, and at present of this county, she was born July 3, 1847, they have three children—Edwin, born April 21, 1867, Horace, Sept. 24, 1869, and Mary L, Oct 29, 1871 Mr Fenton made two trips to Colorado; the first trip was spent in prospecting, and the second time he went there, he spent all his time in Denver City, he also visited the " Gregory Diggings," on Clear Creek, in the mountains, about thirty miles distant from Denver In June, 1855, he came to Black Hawk Co, and settled in Barclay Tp, where he now resides, he says that Barclay Tp has about doubled its population since he came here In politics, he is a Republican, and is a member of the Church of Christadelphians

Fenton, A. W., far, S. 19, P O. Waterloo

Forbes, F, far, S 9, 10, 15 and 16; P O. Barclay.

Fritz, F , far., S 3, 7, 8 and 17, P O Waterloo

GEISER, A., far , S. 12 , P O. Barclay

Gibbons, J , far , S 29 , P O Raymond

Gibson, D , far , S 28 , P O Jesup

Gibson, J , far , S 28 , P. O Jesup

Graham, J. T , far, S. 11 , P O Barclay.

HALLMAN, S , far, S 12 , P O Jesup.

Hepshire, D , far , S 1 , P O Barclay.

Hoffman, G W., far., S 13 , P. O Barclay

Holliday, Wm , far., S 30 , P. O. Raymond.

Hull H., far , S 30 , P O Raymond

JOHNSON, E , far , P O Raymond

Johnson, G , far , S 30 , P O Raymond

Johnson, Wm , far., S. 31 , P O Raymond

KEEFFE, J O , far., S 31 , P O Raymond

Keeffe, T. O , far., S 33 , P O Raymond

LABOR, P., far , S 36 , P O Jesup

Lewin, J , far , Secs 2 and 3, P O Barclay.

LEWIS, LYMAN, farmer and bee keeper Sec 22 , P O. Jesup, Buchanan Co , owns 160 acres, probable value $3,500 , born Nov 18, 1819, in Erie Co , Ohio , his parents were Samuel Lewis and Elizabeth Hall, of the State of New York , his father participated in many of the hard-fought battles and privations of the war of 1812. Lyman, from his boyhood has been engaged in farming, and was married Feb 20, 1843, to Drusilla, daughter of Amos and Flora Brown, of Erie Co., Ohio , she was born Aug 16, 1826 , they have four children —Rachel, born Dec 10, 1844, Charles, Dec 19, 1847, Melissa, March 12, 1849, and Elizabeth, Dec. 28, 1865 , they lost five children—Sarah, born March 22, 1850. died in 1851 , Calista, born in 1846, died in 1847 , Royal A , born Aug 22, 1853, died Jan 25, 1856 , Harriet E., born June 19, 1854, died Jan 31, 1856, and Marion, born Jan 18, 1863, died Sept. 14, 1865. Mr Lewis came to Black Hawk Co in the Spring of 1855, and settled in Barclay Tp., where he now resides ; the township, he says, was but sparsely set-

tled at that time , the principal trading points were Waterloo and Independence, where wheat was sold for twenty-eight cents a bushel, and hardly could sell it at that Mr L is quite extensively engaged in the raising of bees , at present he has thirty hives, and it is his intention to increase his stock in that direction , he is now engaged in perfecting a new double dividing hive, which it is hoped may prove a success, as he claims it will safely preserve bees through our long, cold winters In politics, Mr L is Republican, and is now serving his fourth term as Township Trustee , he was School Director for four terms He says that in early days his team got so poor for want of corn that he could not trust them to haul a load , no not even to carry himself. and he was obliged to go on foot to Gilbertville, in Poyner Tp , to invest his last twenty-five cents for meal to provide food for his family, such an incident is but an example of the hardships which the pioneers had to undergo

Lloyd, F , far , Sec. 27 , P O Jesup.

McMANN, M , far., S 1 , P O Barclay

May, D , far , S 27 , P O Jesup

Martin, J A , far , S 23 , P. O. Barclay

Meehlig, M , far , Secs 5 and 6 , P. O Waterloo

Metcalf, M , far , S 18 , P O Waterloo

Metchler, P , far , Sec 14 , P O Barclay.

Moyer, Geo , far , S 28 , P O Jesup.

NEIBEL, PAUL, far , S 3 , P. O Barclay

NIETH, GREGORY, farmer, Sec. 13 , P O Barclay, owns 121½ acres, probable value $3,050 , born March 10, 1818, in Baden, Germany, where he attended school between the ages of 6 and 14 years , in July, 1833, he came with his parents (Joseph and Mary Nieth) to the United States, arriving in New York City, and went directly to Northampton Co , Penn , where he assisted his father, who engaged in lime burning and farming , when 18 years old, he began to learn the trade of blacksmithing, and has followed that business in connection with farming, to the present time In December, 1841, he married Susan, daughter of John and Catherine Heller, of Bucks Co , Penn , she was born May 1,

1820, they have seven children—Mary, born Jan 5, 1843; James E, April 9, 1851, Sarah, Nov. 23, 1853, Joseph M, Nov 19, 1855, Alice, Nov 28, 1857, Emma, April 2, 1859, and Arthur G, June 20, 1866, they lost four children—Henry E, Maria, Matilda and Margaret In 1845, Mr Nieth moved to Lehigh Co, Penn, and lived there eleven years, in 1856, he came to Black Hawk Co, Iowa, and settled in Barclay Tp., where he now resides, there were but very few settlers here then He is a Republican, Mr Nieth and wife are members of the Methodist Church.

esbit, J, far, S 16, P O Waterloo

ORTNER, JOHN, farmer, Sec 8, P. O. Waterloo, owns sixty acres, probable value $1,100, born Sept 9, 1851, near Wels, Upper Austria, and when an infant was brought by his parents (Joseph and Theresa Ortner) to the United States, arriving in New York City in December, 1853, they at once came West as far as Freeport, Ill., thence to Ridout Tp, Stephenson Co, Ill, and lived there two years, thence to Foreston Tp, Ogle Co, Ill, where they lived three years, and went thence to Carroll Co., Ill, where they lived until 1864 From the time he was old enough to work, the subject of this sketch assisted his mother on the farm, and in 1864, he came to Black Hawk Co, Iowa, and settled in Barclay Tp, where he now resides He was married Feb 6, 1877, to Mary A., daughter of Jacob and Eva Schneck, formerly of Germany, and now of Grundy Co, Iowa, she was born March 5, 1852, in La Salle Co, Ill, they have one child—Margaret Theresa, born Dec. 9, 1877. In politics, Mr Ortner is a Democrat, and is Township Assessor, he is also Secretary of the School Board, and is now serving his sixth term as School Director, was Township Trustee one term and Road Supervisor one term. He and his wife and mother are members of the Catholic Church His mother was born near Wels, Upper Austria, in 1810, and although having completed her 68th year, is still a healthy, active lady, she is living with her son John, and owns 160 acres, the probable value of which is $4,000

PATTEN, CHARLES, far., S 22, P O Jesup

Prangley, E, far., S 32, P. O. Raymond

Purtin, P, far., S. 1, P. O. Barclay

REESE, N., far., S. 7; P. O. Waterloo

RICE, THOMAS F., farmer, Sec 2, P O Barclay, owns 1,000 acres of land, probable value $25,000, born March 23, 1828, in Camden Co, N J, where his father (Thomas Rice) was engaged in editing a newspaper that was known as the *West Jerseyman*, the subject of this sketch attended school in Philadelphia until he was nearly 20 years old, and then turned his attention to the practice of chemistry in his native county, and followed that profession for seven years. He was married March 23, 1850, to Sarah, daughter of John and Ann Cummings, of Camden Co, and formerly from Ireland, Mrs. Rice died Oct 12, 1854; there was one child by that marriage—Martha A, born June 10, 1852 In May, 1854, Mr. Rice went to Ogle Co, Ill, and lived there until October, 1856, he then came to Black Hawk Co., Iowa, and settled in Barclay Tp., where he now resides. He was married to Catherine, daughter of John J and Catherine Schott, of Dauphin Co, Penn.; she was born Sept. 18, 1826; they have four children—Ellen, born Dec 10, 1856, Elijah, Nov 13, 1858, Ada, April 14, 1861, and Elizabeth, June 27, 1863 Mr Rice says there was but one school in his district when he came here in 1856, and not until ten years after was there a school in his sub-district for children to attend The nearest mill was at Waverly, Bremer Co, and not a bridge anywhere to cross streams in going to and from Waterloo In politics, he is Republican, and was Justice of the Peace for ten or twelve years, and School Director about ten years. He was engaged in teaching school in Illinois for four or five years, and taught school in this county three or four years In connection with farming, he is extensively engaged in real estate transactions, and the buying and selling of cattle.

Robertson, J. L, far, S 23, P. O Jesup

Rosborough, W, far, S 22, P. O. Jesup

Roy, J., far., S. 27, P. O. Jesup

SCHMIDT, CASPER, Sr , Sec 4, P. O Barclay

SCHMITT, CASPER, Jr., far., S 6, P O Waterloo, owns 120 acres of land in Black Hawk Co , and eighty in Buchanan Co., probable value $4,-000 , born Sept 21, 1829, in Bavaria, Germany, where he attended school between the ages of 6 and 14 years , he then turned his attention to farming, and followed that business until he came to the United States, arriving in New York City Oct 1, 1853 , he then went to Seneca Co , Ohio, where he engaged in various occupations until April, 1856, when he went to Stephenson Co , Ill., and worked there by the month until the Spring of 1857; he then began the cultivation of a piece of land for himself, which was leased him by his former employer, and in that way he continued until the Fall of 1860, when he came to Black Hawk Co , Iowa, and was married in November of that year to Helena Berger of this county, she died in Jan., 1864 , in Feb , 1865, he went back to Seneca Co , Ohio, and stayed there until April, 1867, and then moved to Freeport, Ill., where he was married May 7, 1867, to Matilda, daughter of Adam and Anna Maria Kungel, of Bavaria, Germany , she was born Sept 12, 1841; they have five children—Francis, born March 23, 1868 , Theresa, born March 12, 1870 , Henry, born Oct 15, 1872 , Edward, born Oct 12, 1874, and Albert, born Nov. 15, 1876 , there is also one child, Kasper, born of his first wife, Nov 3, 1863   In the Spring of 1867, Mr Schmitt again returned to Barclay Tp , and finally settled here and engaged in farming   He is Democratic, and he and his wife and children are members of the Catholic Church.

Shane, T J , far , S 27 , P O Jesup
Sherman, J F , far , S 24 , P. O Jesup
Shuler, J , far , S. 6 , P O Waterloo.
Smith, Austin M , Sec 8; P O Waterloo
Smith, Clayton C , S. 17 , P O Waterloo

SMITH, THOMAS L., farmer, Sec 17 , P. O Waterloo, owns 170 acres of land, probable value $4,300, born Oct 8, 1830, in Cortland Co., N Y , and when old enough to work, assisted his father (Abraham Smith), to work the farm, until he was 21 years of age; in 1851, he went to Galena, Ill , he lived there for about six months, and then went to Wisconsin, where he engaged in various occupations until 1853, when he went to the pineries of that State and superintended the running of the lumbering shanties until 1859, during that time he did considerable rafting on the Mississippi River , he came to Black Hawk Co , Iowa, and settled in Barclay Tp., in 1859, and on Dec. 26 of that year, was married to Henrietta, daughter of Cyrus and Catharine Smith, of this township , she was born Dec 26, 1842 , they have five children—Frank M , born Dec 26, 1860 , Rachel, born Sept. 6, 1865 , Owen A , born March 6, 1866, Elias P , born March 17, 1868 and Jennie L., born July 12, 1872   Mr Smith had entered eighty acres of land here in 1855, four years before he became a settler , when he arrived in Galena in 1851, he had not a cent in his pocket, and now is the owner of a nice home and farm free from debt   In politics, he is a Democrat, and was Road Supervisor three or four terms, Mrs Smith is a member of the Wesleyan M E Church. Her father was one of the first settlers of this township, having came here in 1856 , he died Nov 21, 1874

Smith William, far , Sec 24 , P O Jesup
Starbell, F , far , S 4 , P O Waterloo
Stewart, J , far , S 9 , P O. Waterloo
Stewart, J M , far , S 17 , P O Waterloo

ST. JOHN, ELON, farmer, S 19 , P O. Waterloo, owns sixty acres of land, probable value, $1,500, born May 9, 1816, in Cayuga Co , N. Y , when 6 years old, he moved with his parents (Joshua and Rebecca St John) to Wayne Co , N. Y , where he assisted his father on the farm and went to school between times   He was married Dec 23, 1837, to Julia, daughter of Benjamin and Anna Burton, of Saratoga Co., N Y , she was born Jan 14, 1814 , they have three children—Philo, born Sept 12, 1851 , Lilla, born Feb 7, 1850 , Perry, born Feb. 27, 1855 ; lost seven children—Josiah, Adelia, Burton, John, Alice, Esther and Ella   Mr St John was engaged in the saw-mill business from 1845 to 1867 in Wayne Co , N Y , and in 1868, he came to Black

Hawk Co , Iowa, and settled in Barclay Tp , where he now resides He is a Republican, and is serving his second term as Township Clerk, and is also serving his ninth consecutive term as School Treasurer , he was Township Trustee two terms, and Assessor three terms While in New York, he took an active part in the completion of the Erie Canal, having been engaged in extensive contracts on that work from 1855 to 1867, when it was completed , in 1866, he was appointed Superintendent of Section 10, on the Erie Canal, and served in that capacity one year , in 1857, he was Commissioner of Highways in the town of Arcadia, Wayne Co , N Y , for four consecutive terms , in 1860, he was elected Supervisor for the same town for three years, and again for two years, in 1862, was Chairman of the Board of Supervisors of the same town for three years, and again for two years was Chairman of the Board of Supervisors , in 1863, he was appointed Commissioner of Excise for Wayne Co , and filled that office for three years. His son John was born Oct 28, 1844, and enlisted in Sept., 1864, in the 18th N Y V Battery, and was in several engagements, amongst which was the reducing of Mobile and its capture , he died at Cape Hatteras June 4, 1865, from disease contracted by exposure while in active service.

Sweely, J , far , S, 36 , P O. Jesup

THAYER, J P , far , S 23 ; P. O Jesup

Thayer, W D , far , S 13 ; P O Barclay

Thompson, J , far., S. 26 ; P O Jesup

Trumbauer, P P , far., S 27 , P O Jesup

Tunks, L , far , S 26 , P O Jesup

WITHEY. ELIAS, farmer, S 13; P O Barclay

WALKER, WILLIAM, farmer, Sec 25 , P O Jesup, born in Buchanan Co , owns 360 acres, probable value, $10,800 , born June 14, 1827, in Ayrshire, Scotland, and his mother (Janet Patten) died there in 1832 In company with his father, William Walker, Sr , he came to the United States, arriving in New York City in 1847 and immediately came West and located in Kane Co., Ill , where he resided until 1852 engaged in farming , he then

moved to McHenry Co , Ill , and lived there five years In 1857, he came to Black Hawk Co , Iowa, and settled in Barclay Tp Was married June 19, 1852, to Elizabeth, daughter of John and Jane Paul, of Ayrshire, Scotland , she was born Sept 22, 1832 , they have seven children—Eliza J , born March 14, 1853 , Agnes C , Dec. 17, 1854 , John L., July 1, 1859 ; William P , May 28, 1862 Franklin C , Feb 3, 1866 , Mary J , July 13 , 1868, and George G., Nov 8, 1871 , they lost two children—Franklin C , born Dec 24, 1856, died Oct. 7, 1859, and Mary J., born July 30, 1864, died March 12, 1865. When Mr Walker came to Barclay Tp, there were but two houses to he seen from where he now resides , the surrounding country was an unbroken tract of prairie He had a few cattle when the first assessment was made, and the Assessor said he had more cattle than could be found in the whole township at that time He says that on July 31, 1859, they were visited by a terrific hail-storm that completely destroyed the first crop that he had planted in Iowa, and as he was trusting to its success to enable him pay his bills and buy provisions for the second year, the disappointment at that time was very hard, to say the least , but such were the trials the early settlers had to undergo To-day, Mr Walker is one of the most solid men in Barclay Tp , and is the owner of as handsome a house and farm as can be found anywhere He is truly one of the representative men of Black Hawk Co He is a Republican, and was School Director two or three terms and Road Supervisor two or three terms He and his wife are members of the Presbyterian Church.

WHITNEY, AZRO B., farmer, Sec. 10 , P. O. Jesup, Buchanan Co , owns forty acres, probable value $700 , born March 11, 1840, in Orange Co., Vt , was engaged in farming Enlisted Sept 11, 1861, for three years during the war of the rebellion , was honorably discharged March 31, 1862, by reason of disability, near Hampton, Va Married Emma A. Hackett, of Orange Co., Vt., Nov 1, 1865 , she was born Aug.

4, 1845; they have four children—Myron A., born Jan. 7, 1867; Cora M., Jan. 10, 1869; Aurie E., March 27, 1871, and Mark H., April 13, 1876. Mr. W. left his native county in February, 1868, and went to Jefferson Co., Wis., thence to this county and settled in Barclay Tp. He is a Republican, and was Justice of the Peace two years and Township Assessor two terms. He has a very handsome testimonial presented to him by the Governor (John W. Stewart) of Vermont, for the honorable part he bore as a volunteer in the war of the rebellion —his courage, patriotism and fidelity to the Union being fully established thereby.

White, John, far., S. 15; P. O. Barclay.
White, Wm., far., Secs. 2, 10, and 15; P. O. Barclay.

LESTER TOWNSHIP.

ADAMS, A. P., far, S 14, P. O. Fairbank

Adams, R, far, S. 19, P O Lester Center

Alderman, C, far, S 13, P. O Fairbank

BARBER, A W, far., S 8, P O Lester

Barker, J, far, S 16, P O Lester.

BARTHOLOMEW, ALFRED, farmer and stock raiser, Sec. 20, P O. Lester Center, owns 650 acres, probable value $13,000, he was born Oct 27, 1831, in Cattaraugus Co, N Y, and moved at a very early age with his parents (Daniel and Minerva Bartholomew) to Chautauqua Co, N Y, and lived there until the year 1846 or 1847, when he moved to Cuyahoga Co, Ohio, where he lived until 1849, his father was engaged in farming, stock raising and speculating, while Alfred attended school; in 1848 or '49, his father died of cholera, and with his mother and two sisters he went to the southern part of Wisconsin to an uncle who lived there at that time, in the Spring of 1849 or 1850, he rented a farm in Lake Co, Ill, and in the following year went to Cook Co, Ill, where he bought a farm and lived there until 1862. He was married Jan. 1, 1855, to Margaret, daughter of Benjamin and Eliza Butterfield, of Cook Co, she was born Nov. 20, 1832, they have eight children—Dan, born May 27, 1860, Alice, born March 31, 1862, Martha, born Dec. 18, 1865, Earl, born March 4, 1868; Eliza, born July 12, 1870, Minnie, born March 25, 1873, Albert, born March 29, 1875, and Gertrude, born April 30, 1877, they lost three children—Benjamin, born Oct 3, 1856, died April 25, 1859, Ellen, born April 26, 1858, died Oct. 11, 1860; Clara, born Feb. 16, 1864, died March 13, 1865 In 1862, Mr B came to Black Hawk Co. and located in Waterloo Tp, where he was engaged in farming until 1867; he then went to the city of Waterloo and engaged in various speculations, and lived there until the Spring of 1870, when he came to Lester Tp and settled here, in connection with his farm, he is engaged in stock raising to a considerable extent; since he came here he has made more improvements than any one in the township, he has an orchard of 300 apple trees, and the finest artificial grove in Lester Tp. In politics he is a Republican, and is now serving his third year as District Township Treasurer, and serving his second year as Road Supervisor, he was Township Assessor two years in this township; School Director for six years in this and Waterloo Tps, and was Road Supervisor three years in Waterloo Tp He was appointed in July, 1875, to carry the United States mails between Blakeville and Jesup, and is still holding that position and is a member of the Masonic Order, Victor Lodge, of Waterloo

Beeghley, C, far, S 18, P O. Blakeville

Bentley, L A, far, S 11; P O Fairbank

Beyersmith, J., far., Secs 2 and 10, P. O Fairbank.

BLAKE, THOMAS, farmer, Sec 19, P O Blakeville, owns 250 acres, probable value $5,000, was born Dec 2, 1828, in Somersetshire, Eng, where he learned the trade of blacksmith from his father, Jacob Blake, who followed that vocation He was married March 14, 1850, to Isabella, daughter of William and Sarah Tucker, of Butley, Eng, she was born Dec 29, 1824, they have seven children—William J., born Jan 18, 1853; George H, born March 22, 1855, Emma C, born May 24, 1857, Leonard, born March 13, 1860; Sarah A, born Oct 13, 1862, Isabella, born July 10, 1868, and Kate May, born April 16, 1872, they lost two children in infancy. On his arrival in New York City from England in 1850, he went to Seneca Co., N. Y., and in 1855, he came to Black Hawk Co and entered lands in Lester, having done this, he went back to Seneca Co, and, in January, 1856, returned with his family, in the Spring of the latter year, he went to Bennington Tp and established himself at his trade in the village of Blakeville, which takes its name from the subject of this sketch, and his cousin (Thomas C. Blake), who resided there at that time   In 1858, he moved to Lester Tp., where he has since resided   He is a Republican, and was Township Trustee one or two years, School Director three terms, and was Road Supervisor for a year in Blakeville   Is a member of the Old School Baptist Church, and Mrs. Blake is a member of the same denomination.   Mr. B and two of his children (Miss Emma and his son George) are Bible-class teachers in the Sunday school of School District No 7, of this township, and Mr Blake was Superintendent of the same for two years   In connection with farming, he is engaged in stock raising to a considerable extent, and devotes more or less of his time to blacksmithing to accommodate neighboring farmers, and to do his own repairs, he is also agent for the lands owned by Adjt -Gen A C Fuller, Belvidere, Ill, which are situated in Lester and Bennington Tps and adjoining Mr. Blake's own farm, he has broken 275 acres of it, and is still breaking

BONESTEEL, PHILIP, farmer, Sec 19, P O Lester, owns 360 acres, probable value $9,000, was born Jan. 10, 1838, in Cattaraugus Co, N Y, when quite young moved with his parents (Henry and Irena) to Racine Co., Wis, thence to Lake Co., Ill., where he farmed for six years, in 1850, moved to Lake Co, Ind, and in 1854, came to Black Hawk Co., Iowa, and located in Orange Tp, where he assisted his father on the farm.   Nov. 6, 1862, he married Harriet, daughter of John and Charlotte E Parker, of Marion Co, Ohio, she was born Nov 16, 1838, in 1865 (April), Mr B went to Ohio, and the Spring of 1866 returned to Black Hawk Co and settled in Lester Tp., where he now resides   In politics, he is a Democrat, and was Township Trustee two terms, and is now School Director, having been elected the Spring of 1878   When he came to this county, in 1854, there were only six log houses in Waterloo City, his father built the first frame house in Orange Tp, and hauled the lumber from Davenport, the studding and rafters were cut by the first saw-mill (a horse-power concern) erected in Waterloo in 1854.

Boyle, J W, far., Secs 21 and 22, P. O Lester.

Brenizer, E. K, far, Secs 21 and 23, P O Lester.

Brown, A, far., S 22, P O. Lester

Brown, B. E., far, Secs 26 and 27, P O Lester

Bucher, H W, far., S 18, P O Lester.

BUCHNER, JOHN, retired farmer, Sec 6, P O Waterloo, owns 112 acres in Lester and twenty acres in Bremer Co, probable value $3,300; he was born July 20, 1813, in Bavaria, Germany, where he attended school from 6 to 14 years of age, and then learned the trade of blacksmith, which business he followed until he came to the United States, arriving in New York City July 12, 1843, from there he went to Lehigh Co., Penn, and worked at various occupations for five years   He was married Feb 12, 1844, to Adelaide, daughter of John and Barbara Buchner, of Bavaria, they have three children—Anna E, born June 29, 1847, John, born Jan. 16, 1852, Matilda, born Nov 13, 1853, they lost seven children—Louis, Matilda and five children, who died in infancy   In 1848, Mr B. went to Stephenson Co, Ill, and in 1849, to Winnebago Co, Ill, where he worked at his trade until 1856, he then came to Black Hawk Co, Iowa, and located in Barclay Tp., in 1865, he settled in Lester Tp   He is a Republican, and was School Director one year, is also a member of the Evangelical Association of North America, and Mrs Buchner is a member of the same Association.

BUTZ, AARON K., farmer, Sec 6, P O Waterloo, owns twenty acres of land in this township, and forty acres in Bennington Tp, probable value $1,300, he was born Oct 28, 1817, in Lehigh Co, Penn, and worked at farming until he was 24 years old   Was married Nov 14, 1839, to Ellen, daughter of Daniel and Elizabeth Klopp, of Berks Co, Penn, she was born Jan 16, 1819, and died May 29, 1862, they had five children, one of whom, Ellen Nora, born April 12, 1862, died Sept 16, 1862, the names of those living are Sarah A, born April 21, 1844, Caroline L., June 26, 1846; Henry S,

April 21, 1850, and Franklin J , April 29, 1854   In 1845, he went to Du Page Co , Ill , thence to Carroll Co , in 1853, and in 1856, came to Black Hawk Co., Iowa, and located in Bennington Tp., where he was engaged in farming until he came to Lester Tp in June, 1877   His present wife was Mrs. Johanna Wagner, maiden name, McKesson, daughter of Samuel and Catharine McKesson, of Centre Co, Penn , she was born Jan. 15, 1815, and by her former husband had seven children—Mary J , born Dec 9, 1840 , Catharine A , March 21, 1843 ; Elizabeth, May 22, 1845 , Jemima, May 2, 1847 ; Emeline, Feb 25, 1849 ; John F , June 22, 1851, and Cynthia M , Nov 19, 1854, the last named is living in Bennington Tp.   Mr. Butz is a Republican   Was Road Supervisor one term, and is a member of the Evangelical Association   Mrs. Butz is also a member of the same society

CAMPBELL, C , far , S 3 , P O Fairbank.

Campbell, R , far , S 3 , P O Fairbank
Canfield, P S , far., S 9 , P O Lester.
Canfield, S C , far , S. 21 , P O Lester
Carucross, J , far , S 8 , P O Lester
Carnes, J E., far , S 10 , P O. Lester.
Centlivre, D , far , S 24 , P. O. Fairbank
Cook, Chas , Jr., far , S 17 , P O Lester.

DERR , J , far., S 34 , P O Lester.

De Graff, J., far , S 3 , P O Lester
Duffy, F , far , S. 13 , P O Fairbank
Duffy, H., far , S 24 , P O Fairbank
Duffy J , far , S. 13 , P O Fairbank
Duffy, P , far., S 23 , P O Fairbank
Duffy, T , far , S 23 , P O Fairbank
Dunkerston, J , far , S 28 , P O Lester.

ELLIS, J. M , far., S. 12 , P. O. Fairbank.

Elliott, A , far , S 12 , P O. Fairbank

FENTIMAN, J , far , S 29 , P O Lester

Finch, Wm B , far , S. 24 , P. O. Fairbank
Fisher, D., far., S 28 , P O Lester
Foale, P., far., S 25 , P O Barclay
Freedman, C , far , S 14 , P. O. Fairbank

FRENCH, EDMUND, farmer, S 27 , P. O. Lester ; owns 160 acres of land, probable value $4,000 , was born March 1, 1803, in Helhdon, Northamptonshire, England, but from infancy lived in Banbury, Oxfordshire, until 1845 , he is a shoemaker by trade, having been bound as an apprentice, when 15 years old, to serve seven years.   He was married July 17, 1824, to Ann Humphries, of Kingsutton, Northamptonshire , she was born May 7, 1804 , they have six children—George born Feb 25, 1827 , Esther, Dec 31, 1828 , Caleb, April 26, 1831 ; Ephraim, March 14, 1834 , Lucy V C , Jan 20, 1842, and Emily S , Dec 8, 1844 , they lost two children—Ezra J , born May 7, 1836, and died July 29, 1872, and Leah H , born Jan 24, 1839, died in Feb , 1866   In April, 1845, Mr F came to the United States, and arrived in New York City, where he worked at his trade, and in Feb , 1846, his family joined him , in the Fall of 1846, he went to Trumbull Co., Ohio, and in 1854, came to this county, settled land, and returned to Trumbull Co , Ohio, in the Fall of 1855, came back here and settled in Lester Tp   He is a Republican, and was Township Trustee three or four years , County Supervisor one year, Road Supervisor two or three terms and School Director about three years.   He is one of the very few now remaining of the first settlers of Lester, and he and his wife are now *fifty four years married, both are very happy,* and in the comparative enjoyment of good health

GALIVAN, JAMES, farmer, Sec 23 , P O Lester

GREEN, LIONEL, farmer, Sec 34 , P. O. Lester ; owns 160 acres of land, probable value $3,200 ; he was born June 4, 1814, in Leicester, England, and emigrated with his parents (George and Sarah Green) to the United States, arriving in New York City in Sept , 1836 , his father was engaged in general grocery business in England, and previous to their coming to this country, he took his family to France, and traveled through a great portion of that country   At a place near Paris, he met with some Americans, who advised him to come to this country, and on receiving letters of introduction to some parties in New York City from friends in Havre de Grace, he sailed from the last mentioned port for the United States, on arriving in New York, he started at once to Milwaukee, Wis, where he still lives Lionel lived in Milwaukee until 1843, and then went to Naperville, Ill., where he learned the trade of carpenter and joiner, and followed that business until 1852, when he went to California, arriving in "Hangtown ' in Sept of the latter year, he worked at mining until Dec, 1853, went thence to San Francisco, where he sailed, via Panama, to New York City, thence to Naperville, Ill He was married Dec 30, 1846, to Polly Ann, daughter of Roswell and Hulda Hyde, of Naperville, Ill, she was born Dec 4, 1824, in Cattaraugus Co, N. Y, they have six children—George L, born Sept. 25, 1847, Harriet N., Nov. 26, 1849, Edgar, June 8, 1858, Ida, Aug. 11, 1860, Adelaide, April 5, 1863, and Lydia, July 6, 1865 In May, 1855, Mr Green came to Black Hawk Co., and settled in Lester Tp, there was only one house between the place where he now resides and Independence, they were obliged to drive stakes to serve as guideposts to and from Waterloo, no schools, roads or bridges in those days, he says that game abounded in this county at that time, and deer tracks were to be seen all around the country In politics, he is a Republican, and was Justice of the Peace two years, Township Clerk one term, School Director two or three terms, and Road Supervisor three or four terms He is a member of the Free-Will Baptist Church

Guyer, Joseph, far, S. 17, P O. Lester

Guyer, Samuel, far, S. 17, P O. Lester.

HARN, P, farmer, Sec 22, P O Lester.

Hetherington, G, far., S. 1 P. O Fairbank

Hickox, John, far, S. 21, P O Lester

Hogan, John, far, S 3, P O Lester

Holdeman, J, far, S 32, P O Waterloo.

Hoofnagle, H., far, S 33, P O Lester

Horn, August, far., S 36, P O. Barclay.

Howard, S, far S 2, P. O Fairbank

Hyde, G B, far, S 2, P O Fairbank

INGRAHAM, WALLACE, farmer, Sec 8, P. O Lester.

JOHNSON, F, farmer, Sec. 14, P O Fairbank

JOHNSON, JOHN W., farmer, Sec 9, P. O Lester, owns eighty acres of land, probable value $2,000, was born Sept 6, 1814, in Leicester, England, came to the United States, arriving in Philadelphia in 1828, and went to learn the trade of jeweler, but resigned on account of poor health, having his indentures canceled, went to Schuylkill Co, Penn, and worked at the coal trade, and also boating on the Schuylkill canal, in 1832, went to Lycoming Co, and engaged in various occupations and helped his father, who was conducting a saw-mill, in 1833, went to Kentucky, and was overseer on a plantation in the Spring of 1834, came to Iowa, which was not then a State in the Union, but known as the Black Hawk Purchase, having traveled two years through Iowa, Illinois, Indiana and Michigan, prospecting, went back to Pennsylvania, Clinton Co., which formerly was part of Lycoming Co Was married Sept 24, 1840, to Mary, daughter of Henry and Nancy Brown, of Clinton Co., Penn, she was born Aug 23, 1821, they have ten children—Sarah A, born May 16, 1841, Fanny E, Sept. 6, 1845, Mary M., Dec 16, 1846, John M, March 27, 1848, Nancy M, Sept 5, 1849, Catharine A, March 7, 1851, George W, May 17, 1852, Tacy R., Sept 5, 1853, Nathan P, May 25, 1860, Olive L, Aug. 24, 1861, they lost four children—Maria J., Joseph N, Ida A. and one not named Joseph N enlisted early in Oct, 1861, in Co. E, 12th Iowa V. I, was severely wounded in the arm at Shiloh, taken prisoner by the rebels and died in prison at Macon, Ga., Sept. 11, 1862, aged 18 years 4 months and 7 days Mr J was principally engaged in farming from 1840 until he came to Black Hawk Co and settled in Lester Tp in 1855, and except three years spent in Bremer Co, has lived in Lester ever since. He spent the most of the first year here hunting, and supported his family in that way, they were very poor, and were obliged to live in their wagon until the snow fell. He attended the Fourth of July celebration in Waterloo in 1855, and heard the first sermon preached in Lester by Rev. Mr Ritchey, who was a member of the U B Church Mr. J is a Republican, and was Township Trustee two or three terms, Road Supervisor once or twice, School Director two or three terms, and is a member of the Free-Will Baptist Church, of which denomination Mrs. Johnson and three of their children—Sarah A , Nancy M and Tacy R —are likewise members

KAYLOR, SAMUEL H , farmer, Sec. 8 , P O Lester

Keames, J , far , S 10 , P O Fairbank

Kelinski, S , far , S 25 , P. O. Barclay

Knepper, D J , far , S. 19; P O Blakeville

Kingley, J , far , S 13 ; P. O. Fairbank

Kraft, F , far , Secs 1, 12 and 13 , P O Fairbank

LAMB, HOSEA, farmer, Sec. 4, P. O Lester.

LAMB, NORMAN F., farmer, S 6 ; P O Lester, owns 160 acres of land in Bennington Tp , probable value, $1,800 , was born Jan 27, 1845, in Ontario Co , Upper Canada, where he worked at farming until he was 23 years old , in 1868, he came to Black Hawk Co., settled in Lester Tp., and engaged in farming Was married Dec. 23, 1875, to Eva C , daughter of Samuel and Mary J. Neil, of Stephenson Co., Ill , she was born June 4, 1855 , they have one child—Alice May, born Oct 28, 1876.

Lamphret, J., far , S 24 , P O. Lester.

Lanagan, L , far , S. 33 ; P. O Waterloo.

Law, G., far , S 36 , P O Barclay

Law, M., far , S. 24 , P. O Fairbank

Lenius, J , far , Sec 3 , P. O. Fairbank

Leibenan, A , far , S 11 , P O Fairbank

Leibenan, F , far , S 24 , P O Fairbank

McGRANNAHAN, S B , far , Sec. 25 , P O Barclay

McNellis, Wm , far , Sec. 20 , P.O. Lester

MAGEE, EDWARD W., far , Sec 5 , P O. Lester , owns 320 acres, probable value $8,000 ; was born Oct 22, 1837, in Franklin Co , Penn , in 1842, he went with his parents, James and Elizabeth, to McHenry Co., Ill and lived there farming until 1867 . Was married July 4, 1861, to Sarah J Davis, who was born in McHenry Co., Ill , Jan 14, 1839 , her parents were

Martin and Mary A Davis Mr and Mrs Magee have nine children—James, born May 1, 1862, Cora, Aug. 28, 1863 , Frank, Sept 3, 1865 , Charles, March 26, 1868, Eddie, July 14, 1869, Adell, April 28, 1871 , Carrie, April 16, 1873 , William, March 28, 1875 , and Alice, Feb 18, 1877. In 1867. Mr Magee left his home in Illinois and came to Black Hawk Co , and settled in Lester Tp He is a Republican, and was School Director two terms , at present he is Township Assessor

Moynihan, J , far., S 23 , P O Lester

Milks, Luke, far , S 2 , P O Fairbank.

Miller, Geo , far , S 14 , P O Lester.

Miller, J , far , S 12 . P. O Fairbank

Monroe, Sam'l, far , S 12 , P O. Fairbank

NEIBUHR , P W , farmer, Sec 3 ; P O Fairbank.

Northrup, G M , far , Secs 7, 18 , P. O. Lester

OWEN, CHARLES, farmer, Sec 5 , P O Lester.

OCHS, JACOB, farmer, Sec 8 ; P O. Lester Centre, owns 160 acres, probable value $4,000 , he was born March 4, 1825, in Berks Co , Penn , when very young he moved with his parents, Charles and Mary Ochs, to Lehigh Co , where he lived until he was 10 years old , moved thence to Northampton Co., Penn , and assisted his father, who was engaged in the tobacco trade, was engaged on the Pennsylvania and Delaware Canal about four years, and followed steamboating on the Delaware River from Philadelphia about four years , about the year 1843, he went to Du Page Co , Ill , and, because of fever and ague, returned in about a year to Lehigh Co , Penn., and lived there about six years , he then went to Stephenson Co , Ill , thence back to Pennsylvania, and West again, via Dubuque, Iowa, to this county, with a view of seeing the country , after visiting different places, and spending about a year in Kansas, he eventually came back to Black Hawk Co , Iowa, and settled in Lester Tp , where he now resides He was twice married; his first wife was Charlotte Smiley, she died Jan. 11, 1857; there were four children by that marriage, two of whom, James and Jacob, are living He was afterward married Oct. 28, 1858, to Mary Jane, daughter of Samuel and Catharine Mihken, of Centre Co., Penn; she was born July 5, 1835; they have five children—Lizzie M, born May 15, 1864; Lottie, Feb 29, 1868; Minnie, July 29, 1869; Frank, March 23, 1874, and George, Feb 5, 1876; they have lost two children—Freddie, born March 15, 1871, died Aug. 15, 1872, and Grace, born March 25, 1873, died Aug. 25, 1873. In politics, Mr. Ochs is Independent, and was School Director two terms; he is a member of the Free-Will Baptist Church, and Mrs. Ochs is also a member of the same denomination.

Owen, Eli, far, Secs. 3, 5, P. O Lester

Owen, Henry, far., S 16; P O Lester

PAGE, SEWALL, farmer, Sec. 16, P O Lester

Perry, Allen, far, Sec 28, P. O Lester

PERRY, ALFRED B., farmer, Sec 21, P O Lester, owns 200 acres, probable value, $4,000; he was born Nov. 30, 1822, in Cayuga Co, N. Y, but spent much of his time in Cortland Co, N. Y, until he was 21 years old. He worked at the trade of tanner and currier from the time he was 11 until he was 18 years of age and then temporarily abandoned that profession In 1844, he went to Tecumseh, Lenawee County, Mich, and resumed his trade. In 1845, he went to Illinois and Wisconsin, thence to Valparaiso, Ind, and engaged as a Superintendent of a tannery and held the position for two years, then betook himself to work on the Michigan Central and Michigan Southern Rys, moved thence to Mineral Pt, Wis, and worked in lead mines, back to Porter Co., Ind., where he had a farm, and worked at his trade three years in Terre Coupee, St Joseph Co, Ind, where he was married Nov 25, 1852, to Lydia, daughter of James and Hannah Smith, of Hamilton Co, Ohio, she was born March 1, 1832, and died Jan. 25, 1861, there were five children by that marriage—Wm. W., born Aug 16, 1853, Silas S, Oct. 26, 1854; George T., Jan. 22, 1856; John L., Oct. 7, 1857, and Mary H, Sept. 1, 1859. On the 2d of August, 1857, Mr. P

arrived in Lester Tp., Black Hawk Co., Iowa, and engaged in farming He married his present wife, Emily, daughter of John E and Margaret Carnes, of this township, May 23, 1861, she was born Feb. 20, 1841, in Chippewa Tp, Wayne Co, Ohio, they have six children—Ida I, born April 27, 1862, Robert I, Jan 14, 1867, Frederick N, July 11, 1869, Thomas A, Dec 9, 1871, Franklin S, July 9, 1874, and Lydia B, Sept 3, 1877 Mr. Perry enlisted Oct. 12, 1861, in the 12th I V. I, Co E, for three years, or during the war, and was engaged in the battles of Fort Donelson, Shiloh, siege of Vicksburg (where he spent forty-two days), Jackson and Brandon, Miss., Tupelo Woodstock and Nashville, Tenn, and Spanish Fort, Ala He was captured by the rebels at Shiloh and dragged around to the rebel prisons of Montgomery, Ala, Griffin and Macon Ga, and was at last sent to Libby Prison, Richmond He was paroled Oct 17, 1862, and sent to Annapolis, Md, thence to St. Louis, Mo, and was exchanged in the Winter of 1862-3 He helped guard a lot of rebel prisoners that were sent from St Louis to Columbus, Ohio, before he was exchanged himself, he participated in all the engagements his regiment took part in, and was honorably discharged Jan 20, 1866, at Memphis, Tenn, and then returned to his home and family in Lester Tp, since which time he has been engaged in the peaceful pursuit of farming. He is a Republican and was School Director and President of the School Board three or four terms, was elected Justice of the Peace, but declined to serve. He is a member of the Free Will Baptist Church

Polk, Fred, far, S 34, P O Barclay.

Potts, J H, far, S. 11, P. O Fairbank.

Presha, Wm C, far., S 7, P. O. Lester

REYNOLDS, WM H, farmer, Sec 29, P O Waterloo.

Richards, J, far, S 11, P O Fairbank

Robinson, J, far, S 14, P O Fairbank

SANDOE, JACOB, D, farmer, Sec 9, P O. Lester.

Sauer, L., far., S 3, P O Fairbank

Schrack, John, far, Sec 6, P O Lester.

Shafler, J., far, S. 16 and 17, P O Lester.

Shannon, F., far., S. 36 ; P. O. Barclay.
Shannon, P., far., S. 36 ; P. O. Barclay.
Shillington, T., far., S. 28 ; P. O. Lester.
Sholes, E., far., S. 2 ; P. O. Fairbank.
Shuler, Geo., far., S. 31 ; P. O. Waterloo.
Shuler, J., far., S. 31 ; P. O. Waterloo.
Sigglekow, J., far., S. 3 ; P. O. Fairbank.
Sipel, Elias, far., S. 27 ; P. O. Lester.
Spicher, D. J., far., S. 20 ; P. O. Lester.
Strempkie, J., far., S. 25 ; P. O. Fairbank.
TREBON, S., far., S. 25 ; P. O. Fairbank.
Trumbauer, J., far., S. 35 ; P. O. Barclay.

Tucker, L. H., far., S. 3 and 6 ; P. O. Lester.
VAN ETTEN, M. C., far., Sec. 20 and 21 ; P. O. Lester.
WAGONER, WM., far., S. 14 ; P. O. Lester.
West, J. S., far., Sec. 2 ; P. O. Fairbank.
Wilhelm, A., far., S. 23 ; P. O. Waterloo.
Willey, W., far., S. 11 ; P. O. Fairbank.
Willner, Jos., far., Secs. 9 and 10 ; P. O. Lester.
Wood, E., far., Secs. 4 and 5 ; P. O. Lester.

FOX TOWNSHIP.

AHLES, J , far , Sec 19 , P O Gilbertville

ARTHUR, GEORGE W., far., S 31 , P O Gilbertville , owns 125 acres, probable value $3,750 , he was born Oct 4, 1828, in Knox Co., Tenn , when but 7 years old, he moved with his parents, William and Lydia Arthur, to Vigo Co , Ind , when 13 years old, he went to Clark Co , Ill , and lived with his uncle, Jacob Long, until he was 23 years old, engaged in farming, in 1851, he came from Indiana to Dubuque, Iowa, by team, and pushed on to Linn Co , near Marion, but because of constant rains and swollen streams, went back to Muscatine Co , and lived there for a year or more He was married Aug 21, 1851, to Nancy Peery, of Jackson Co , Ind., she was born Oct 27, 1831, in Clark Co , Ill , they have seven children—John, born June 12, 1852 , William A , July 27, 1854, David, Aug 25, 1856 , James E , July 15, 1860 , George E , May 26, 1865 , Mary E , July 23, 1867, and Sylvester, Oct 27, 1868 In 1852, Mr Arthur came to Black Hawk Co , and in the Spring of 1853, he came to Fox Tp , and settled here In politics he is a Republican, and was School Director for seven or eight years, and Road Master for several years He and his wife are members of the M. E Church

Arnold, J. D , far , S 34 and 35 , P. O Jesup

BAHL, B , far , S. 17 , P O Gilbertville.

Baysinger, C , far , S 16 , P O Jesup

Baysinger, J , far , S 16 , P O. Jesup

Beckley, H , far , S 6 , P O Raymond

Benorden, C F. W , far , S 35 , P O Jesup.

Benorden, F , far , Sec 34 , P. O Jesup and Enterprise

Bernardy, H , far , S 33 , P O Enterprise.

Bernardy, Wm , far S 32 , P. O. Enterprise

BETAR, HIRAM, farmer, Sec 11 , P O. Jesup, Buchanan Co , owns 120 acres land, probable value $3,600 , he was born May 12, 1839, in Prussia, Germany, where he attended school between the ages of 7 and 14 years , he then turned his attention to farming, which occupation he followed until he came to the United States, arriving in New York City November, 1856 , he immediately went to Lockport, N Y where he worked until the Spring of 1858, and then came West to Burlington, Iowa, where he lived until 1860, when he went to St Louis, Mo , and stayed there three years , in 1864, he came to Black Hawk Co , and settled in Fox Tp He was married Sept 28, 1858, to Mary, daughter of Isaiah and Mary Thompson, of Des Moines Co , Iowa , she was born Dec. 17, 1817, and died May 21, 1877, he was afterward married Sept 12, 1877, to Ricky, daughter of Frederick and Hannah Bremer, formerly of Hanover, Germany, and now of Fox Tp in this county , she was born Oct 26, 1860. Mr Betar is Republican in politics and was Road Supervisor for two years He and his wife are members of the Lutheran Church

Bole, Ed , far , S 16 , P. O. Jesup

Bole, M A , far , S 15 , P O. Jesup

BOYLE, THOMAS, farmer, Sec. 6 , P O Raymond, has eighty acres of land (in his wife's name), probable value $1,600 , he was born March 20, 1804, in Brook Co , Va ; when quite young, moved with his parents, Jonathan and Elizabeth Boyle, to Knox Co , Ohio, where he helped on the farm for his mother (his father having died one year after his arrival there), until he was married April 26, 1827, to Mary, daughter of James and Mary McCamant, of Brook Co , Va , she was born Feb 26, 1804, in September, 1831 , they had two children— Charlotte, born Jan. 21, 1828, and Louisiana, April 8, 1830. He followed farming until 1851, when he engaged in running a saw-mill, which he conducted until 1866 , then came to Iowa and settled in Black Hawk Co., in November, 1836 He married Susannah, daughter of Ephraim and Mary Drake, of Pittsburgh, Penn , she died in 1842, there were two children by that marriage—

9

Ephraim D , born Oct 15, 1837 , enlisted in the 43d Ohio V I , September, 1861, and died in June, 1862, from the effects of inflammatory rheumatism, at Cincinnati, Ohio , John, born Nov 27, 1839, died the 6th of August, 1843. Mr B was married to Mrs Julia E. Lewis, daughter of Uzziel and Mary Stevens, of Litchfield Co , Conn , she was born Aug 28, 1806, in Washington Co , N. Y , have two children—James S , born May 30, 1844, and Josephine M , Jan 18, 1850 , they lost one child —Mary E , born July 25, 1846, died Aug 3, 1862. James S enlisted May 13, 1864, in the 142d Ohio V I , and saw service at Cold Harbor, Bermuda Hundreds, and near Petersburg , he was honorably discharged Sept. 2, 1864, and returned to his home in Knox Co , Ohio, and has since followed farming Mr Boyle and his son James S are Republican in politics He was Road Supervisor for two years in Fox Tp Mr and Mrs Boyle are members of the Christian Church

Blakeman, A J., far , S 12 , P O Jesup
Blakeman, T , far , S 25 , P O Jesup
Bloes, N , far , S 33 , P. O Enterprise
Brady, J , far , S 14 , P. O. Jesup
Bremer, F , far , S 13 , P O Jesup.
Brubaker, D , far , S 17 , P O Gilbertville
Bruche, A , far , S 7 , P O Raymond
Buchelee, J , far , S 27 , P. O Jesup
Buttke, H , far , S 28 ; P O Gilbertville.

BYERS, WILLIAM, farmer, S. 36 , P O Jesup, Buchanan County, Iowa , owns 120 acres of land, valued at $4,000, he was born March 25, 1825, in Dauphin County, Penn.; in 1836, he came West with his parents (Robert and Elizabeth Byers), to Putnam Co., Ill., where he assisted his father on the farm, and went to school between times until he was 22 years of age He was married May 20, 1847, to Lydia A , daughter of John and Elizabeth Plank, of Dauphin Co , Penn , she was born Aug. 26, 1826 , they have seven children—John, born Sept 16, 1848, Oella, April 28, 1850, Robert E , May 14, 1852 ; Wm A , Sept 3, 1854, Emma M , Aug 24, 1859 , Eva O , July 8, 1862, and Geo. F., July 24, 1866 , they lost two chil-

dren—Rudolph, born Dec 27, 1846, and died July 10, 1847, and Walter C , born April 28, 1864, died April 8, 1865 In the Fall of 1860, he came to Black Hawk Co., Iowa, and settled in Fox Tp., where he has since resided. His son, Wm A., graduated at Baylie's Commercial College at Dubuque, Iowa, in 1874, and is now attending College at Valparaiso, Ind , with a view of preparing for admission to the bar , he has taught school for about five years in Fox Tp and other places Mr Byers is a Republican in politics, and was School Director four years, and Road Supervisor three years

CALDWELL, J D , far , S 5 , P O. Raymond

Corton, John, far., S. 23 and 26 ; P O. Jesup

DEMUTH, B , far., S 28 , P. O Enterprise

Demuth, P., far., S 33 , P O Enterprise.

DICKERSON, ALBERT L., farmer, Sec 7 , P O Raymond, owns eighty acres of land, probable value $3,200, he was born Sept 26, 1836, in Steuben Co , N. Y., and in 1848, he moved with his parents (Jeremiah and Hannah Dickerson) to Chemung Co , N Y , where he assisted his father on the farm, and went to school between times, until he was 21 years old , he attended school at Starkey Seminary, in Yates Co , N Y , one year, and then engaged in teaching school, which vocation he has followed in connection with farming until the present time , he came to Black Hawk Co., Iowa, and settled in Fox Tp. in 1859 He was married Nov 27, 1862, to Eliza, daughter of Archibald and Lois Dixon, of Fox Tp.; she was born in 1839 In politics, he is a Republican, and was Township Clerk two or three years , Township Assessor three or four years , Secretary of School Board one term, School Director one term, and Justice of the Peace one term. He and his wife are members of the Christian Advent Church.

Dickenson, J W , far , S 19 and 25 , P O Gilbertville

EHRET, M , far., S. 24 and 25 , P O. Jesup.

Ehr, P , far , S 20 ; P O Gilbertville

FALK, A., far , S. 29 , P O Gilbert-
ville
Falk, G , far , S 29 and 30 , P. O Gil-
bertville.
Flood, M , far , S. 8 . P O Raymond.
Frost, J , far . S. 5 , P. O Raymond

GALES, J , far., S 32 , P O En-
terprise
Gifford, A B , far , S. 25 , P O Jesup.
Gouche, D , far , S 17 , P. O. Jesup

HANSEN, M , farmer, S. 22 , P O
Jesup
Harrod, A & S R , fars , S. 20 , P O
Gilbertville.
Harrod, L , far , S. 19 , P. O. Gilbertville
High, C H., far , S. 36 , P O Jesup
Hoffman, D , far , S. 25 , P. O. Jesup
Hook, T , far , Secs 26, 27, 34, 35 , P
O. Jesup
Hubbard, E B , far , S 25 , P O. Jesup.
Hubbard, G W , far , S. 14 , P O Jesup
Hubline, A , far , S. 34 , P O Jesup
Huck, Chas , far , S. 27 , P O Jesup.
Hyde, N., far , S 25 ; P O Jesup.

JOHNSON, N F , far , S 8 , P O
Raymond.

KASCHT, WILLIAM, farmer, Sec.
30 , P. O Gilbertville
Kimble, A , far., S 7 , P. O Raymond
Koob, E , far., Secs 26, 35 , P. O Jesup
Krantz, J. H , far., S. 32 , P O Enter-
prise
Kyrk, Wm , far., S. 22 , P O Jesup

LIES, NICHOLAS, far , Sec 22 ; P
O Jesup

**LICHTENBERG, CHARLES
L.,** farmer, Sec. 35 , P O Jesup,
Buchanan Co , owns 220 acres in Black
Hawk Co and 160 acres in Buena Vista
Co , Iowa, probable value $7,600 , he
was born Dec 1, 1828, in Prussia, Germany, where he attended school between
the ages of 7 and 14 years , he then
turned his attention to farming until he
came to the United States ; he spent
one year in sailing from Amsterdam,
Holland, to other ports, in 1839. his
father (Ernest H Lichtenberg) came to
the United States, intending to procure
a home for his family, but died about
one year after his arrival in this country
The subject of this sketch arrived in
New York City in Oct , 1849, and went
at once to Indianapolis, Ind , where he
lived nine months, and from there went

to Sandusky, Ohio, where he lived for
eighteen months, excepting one season
that he spent sailing on Lake Erie , in
1852, he went back to Indianapolis, and
engaged in the repairs of the Indianapolis & Bellefontaine Ry , and was soon
given charge of a section ; he served
that company one year, and then worked
for the Indianapolis & Madison Ry Co
one year , in 1854, he came to Davenport, Iowa, and went thence to Iowa
City, and thence to Cedar Rapids, but
not being pleased with the country
through which he traveled, he came to
Black Hawk Co , and entered eighty
acres in Fox Tp. and purchased forty
acres second hand , he then went back
to Indianapolis, and lived there three
years   On Feb 25, 1855, he was married to Engel, daughter of Charles and
Bina Harting, formerly of Schomberg,
Germany, and now of Spring Creek Tp
in this county , Mrs L was born Nov
8, 1827, they have eight children—
Charles W , born March 10, 1856 ,
Frederick, May 24, 1858 , Henry, Dec
11, 1860, Caroline, June 19, 1862 ,
Christina, Oct 21, 1863 , William, May
7, 1865, John, Oct 21, 1867, and
Louis, Oct 30, 1871 In the Summer
of 1856, he returned to Black Hawk
Co , and settled in Fox Tp He is a
Democrat, and is now School Treasurer,
was Road Supervisor five years, Township Trustee five years, Trustee of the
Select School of the Zion Lutheran
Church, Spring Creek Tp , for eight
years   Mr and Mrs L are members
of Zion Lutheran Church. When Mr
L first came here there were but two
houses within twenty miles of where he
located , to-day he is one of the representative men, respected by all who know
him   The name that this township now
bears was suggested by one of the first
settlers, named Murphy, and seconded
by Mr. Lichtenberg, and through these
two men the township bears the name
of Fox

Lingwood, Wm., far., S 36 , P O Jesup
Loeb, P V., far , S 34 ; P O Jesup.
Lowe, A , far., S. 8 , P. O. Raymond
Lowe, L B , far , S 5 , P O Raymond

McCORD, H J., farmer, Sec. 35 ,
P O Jesup.
Mai, W., far , Secs 21, 22 ; P O Jesup.

Miller, J , far , Secs. 9, 4 · P. O Jesup

MILLER, ROMANZO R., dairyman and farmer, Sec 1 , P O Jesup, Buchanan Co , owns 299 acres, probable value $12,000 , he was born Dec 26, 1832, in Windham Co , Vt , where he assisted his father on the farm and went to school between times, until he was 21 years old , in 1857, he came West to Livingston Co., Ill , where he engaged in farming ; in 1865, he went to Wisconsin, and in 1866, returned to his home in Vermont ; in 1867, he came to Black Hawk Co., Iowa, and settled in Fox Tp , where he now resides . in 1873, he engaged in dairying with twenty cows, and in April, 1878, in company with F W Harris, of Perry Tp , Buchanan Co., built a new dairy which they are now running on a large scale ; it is known as the " Big Spring Creamery " in Buchanan Co , they handle from 6,000 to 7,000 lbs of milk daily, and manufacture about 240 lbs. of butter per day , the creamery butter commands the highest market price, and in course of time the proprietors intend to enlarge their factory, so that this concern is another important addition to the industries of Iowa , Mr Miller also owns 144 acres of land in Westburg Tp , Buchanan Co., the probable value of which is $2,800 He was married March 24, 1857, to Amanda, daughter of Joseph and Rhoda Wright, of Westminster, Vt , she was born April 6, 1830 , they have an adopted child— Florence W Miller born Nov 4, 1874 Mr and Mrs. Miller are members of the Baptist Church , in politics Mr M. is a Republican.

Mullony, P , far., S 3 , P O. Jesup

Mythaler, J J , farmer, Sec. 16 , P O. Jesup.

NIE, JOHN, far , S. 33 , P. O. Enterprise

Nosbisch, J., far , S 28 , P O Jesup.

PENOYER, IRA C far , S 9 , P O Jesup

Perry, O R , far , S 12 , P O Jesup

Perry, S , far , S 20 , P. O. Gilbertville.

Peyson, A M., far , S 21 , P. O Jesup

Pint, L , far , Secs. 18 and 19 , P O Gilbertville.

Phillips, F., far , S 28 , P. O. Jesup.

Phillips, H., far , S 21 , P. O Jesup.

RANDALL, G. H , far., S. 16 , P O. Jesup

Renche, Wm , far , S 26 , P O Jesup

Robe, A A , far., S 24 , P. O. Jesup.

Robe, W M , far., S. 13 , P. O. Jesup.

SAUERBREI, A , far., S. 27 ; P. O Jesup

Schmitz, J., far , Secs. 29 and 32 , P. O. Gilbertville

SCHOMMER, PETER, school teacher, Sec 22 , P O Gilbertville , owns forty acres, probable value $1,200 , he was born June 26, 1851, in the province of Rhine, Germany, where he attended school from the time he was 6 years until he was 18 years old , having passed successfully through his common school and academical courses, he engaged in teaching school for one year and nine months, and in January, 1872, he came to the United States, arriving in New York City on the 6th of that month , he went immediately to Milwaukee, Wis , where he stayed a short time, and then came to Black Hawk Co , Iowa, and settled in Fox Tp. ; during his first year in this township he was engaged in farming, and in the following year, he again engaged in school teaching, which vocation he has since continued to follow . he attended a course of studies at the " Western Waterloo College," and also at the " Mt Vernon Institute," Linn Co., Iowa, so as to try and perfect his knowledge of the English language , he is a close student, and never fails to avail himself of a favorable opportunity to improve his already well-stored mind, the youth of the county, and very many others, too, would do well to emulate his example in this respect   He was married May 27, 1877, to Anna, daughter of John and Margaritta Nosbisch, of Rhine Province, Germany. In politics Mr S is a Democrat, he and his wife are members of the Catholic Church

Schroeder, W.. far , S. 28 , P. O. Jesup.

Shares, W., far , S. 31 , P O Gilbertville.

Smith, W , far , S. 19 ; P O Gilbertville.

Starkhart, H , far , S 20 . P O Gilbertville

TAYLOR, S. S , far , S. 30 , P O. Gilbertville.

Tennant, J., far., S. 23 , P O Jesup

Theilen, J , far , S. 20 , P O. Gilbertville.

Tillen, J , far , S 17 , P O Jesup

Tschanbenz, M , far , S. 32 ; P O Enterprise.

Tunis, M , far , S. 17 , P. O. Jesup

WEBER, JOHN, far , S 29 , P O Gilbertville

Weber, Peter, far., S 28 , P. O Enterprise

Weiers, J. M , far , S 21 , P O. Gilbertville

Wellman, A , far , S 27 , P O Jesup

Werser, B , far., S 9 , P O Jesup

Wheland, D , far., S 26 , P O Jesup

Wirtz, J , far , S 18 , P. O. Gilbertville

WOOSTER, ROLLIN S., farmer, Sec. 12 , P O Jesup, Buchanan Co , owns 181 acres of land, probable value $5,500 , he was born Nov 25, 1824, in Bethlehem, Litchfield Co , Conn , where he attended school at the Warren Institute, until he was 17 years old, he then turned his attention to learning the trade of a stone mason, and followed that business about six years , in 1849, he engaged in traveling for a manufacturer of surgical instruments, and traveled throuh all the Western and Southwestern States for about three years He was married Jan 31, 1854, to Charlotte L , daughter of Zalmond and Elizabeth Miller, of Cornwallbridge, Conn , she was born Feb 22, 1827 ; Mrs Wooster's family date back to the earliest settlers of Connecticut. In 1854, Mr Wooster went to Rock Co , Wis , and in 1855, he engaged in farming, in 1857, he added to his business the raising of the improved American Merino sheep, in which he is now extensively engaged, he also taught school for ten terms in Rock Co , Wis , in 1864, he came to Black Hawk Co , and settled on a piece of land in Fox Tp , which he had entered ten years previously , he says that surrounding him was but sparsely settled at that time, there were only a few houses anywhere near him, and they were a mile apart In politics, he is a Republican, and is Township Clerk, now serving his eighth consecutive term , was Justice of the Peace one year, County Supervisor one year, School Director three years, Secretary of the School Board three years , he and his wife are members of the M E. Church of Jesup , he was one of the first Trustees of that

organization and has continued a such to the present time , is also Recording Steward, and Sunday School Superintendent, now serving his seventh term in both positions

YOUNG, O G , farmer, Sec 5 , P O Raymond

YOUNG, WALLACE M., S 2 , P O Jesup, Buchanan Co , owns 938 acres of land, probable value, $23,450, and 154 acres in Buchanan Co , probable value $4,000 , he was born Jan. 1, 1827, in Monroe Co , N Y , where he worked on a farm and went to school between times, until he attained his 17th year , his father, Eliphet T Young, was born Aug. 27, 1786, in Rensselaer Co , N Y., and was married twice, the first wife was Mary Udell, born in Rensselaer Co , Jan 22, 1788, died Feb 13, 1824, and his second wife was Mary Maxfield, who was born March 20, 1799, died Jan 25, 1865 ; the latter was the mother of Wallace M. Young, who in 1844, left his native county and went to Branch Co , Mich , where he became engaged in farming and real estate transactions , he resided in Branch Co (with the exception of about four years that he lived in Cass Co) until 1869 On the 1st of Jan , 1851, he married Miranda, daughter of John and Miranda Allen, of Brandon, Vt , she was born Sept 20, 1826, and died Jan 14, 1852 , there was one child by that marriage — John, born Nov 22, 1851, died April 8, 1852 , Mr. Y was afterward married Dec 4, 1852, to Catharine, daughter of Henry and Sabra Wells, of St Lawrence Co , N Y , she was born April 9, 1832, they have seven children — George W , born Jan 26, 1856 , Martha, born May 8, 1858 , John, born June 2, 1860 , Mary, born Aug 20. 1861 , Elizabeth, born May 1870 , Manly, born Dec. 26, 1871, and Bertha, born July 17, 1876 , they lost two children — Miranda, born April 16, 1854, died March 1, 1869, and Freddie, born Oct 7, 1866, died Feb 15, 1867. In 1869, Mr Young came West to Buchanan Co , Iowa, and lived there for about twenty or twenty-one months, and on March 6, 1871, he came to Fox Tp , where he now resides. In politics, he is Independent, and is now serving his second term as President of the

Board of School Directors, and was School Director for four years; he was also Justice of the Peace for one year, and is a member of Siloam Lodge, No. 222, of Jesup, Buchanan Co., Iowa.

ZIMMERMAN, J., far., S. 20; P. O. Gilbertville.

TABULAR STATEMENT,

Showing the totals of Real and Personal Property assessed for taxation in Black Hawk County, Iowa, for the year 1877.

PERSONAL PROPERTY	Number	Average Valuation	Assessed Value
Horses of all ages . . . . . ◄	10,179	$16 48	$167,753
Cattle of all ages	21,080	6 02	126,910
Mules of all ages	316	21 40	6,761
Sheep of all ages	2,183	87¾	1,918
Swine of all ages	28,725	1 69	48,545
Other taxable property not enumerated . . .	. . .	288,485
Total assessed value of personal property ..			$640,642
REAL ESTATE			
Aggregate value of realty in towns . .	.	.. ..	$1,084,771
Aggregate value of railroad property, as assessed			300,380
Land, 3,524 55/100 acres	. . ..	$9 02	3,181,899
Total value of all taxable property in county . .			$5,207,692
Polls	4,557		

POPULATION OF BLACK HAWK COUNTY IN 1875.

Compiled from the State Census of Iowa for 1875.

TOWNSHIPS	WHITE INHABITANTS			NATIVITY OF INHABITANTS				BIRTHPLACE OF VOTERS					
	Male	Female	Total	No born in Iowa	No born in the U S but not in Iowa	No born in foreign countries	No of Voters	No born in United States	Do in British America	Do in England and Wales	Do in Ireland	Do in Scotland	Do in Germany
Barclay	463	360	768	301	320	142	157	103	2	6	21	4	16
Bennington	409	326	735	256	334	145	131	89	3	5	2	2	27
Big Creek... .. .	385	308	693	227	367	99	168	123	...	8	6	..	23
Black Hawk	413	250	768	258	358	52	166	103	14	9	13	2	23
Cedar	339	296	635	269	242	124	119	78	6	4	13		15
Cedar Falls .	639	584	1223	477	590	157	206	136	.	7	11	.	24
Eagle . . .	380	309	689	223	239	177	116	55	8	1	16	.	36
East Waterloo . .	476	407	883	289	483	111	190	157	4	11	8	1	7
Fox	418	412	830	311	304	215	152	128	1	3	2		23
Lester	501	446	947	388	400	159	192	182	5	11	21	.	20
Lincoln	333	235	568	168	300	106	116	83	4	11	11	2	3
Mt Vernon	472	438	910	381	369	160	199	129	13	27	13	2	15
Orange	431	353	784	292	453	39	175	168	1	1	..	.	5
Poyner	531	512	1043	365	519	159	203	165	3	3	3	2	26
Spring Creek	359	321	680	340	310	30	146	135	.		1	1	8
Union	205	222	427	165	227	39	90	83		1		..	6
Washington ...	239	206	445	156	253	36	118	99	2	7	4	2	4
Waterloo	222	224	446	185	204	57	100	79	4	3	8	2	3
Cedar Falls City	1577	1689	3226	1052	1554	661	680	494	6	24	46	13	76
Laporte City (Incorp'n)	374	341	715	223	421	71	154	134	5	4	2	...	9
Waterloo City	2753	2749	5502	1747	2909	852	1289	973	43	32	64	16	121
Total	11809	11088	22897	8068	11151	3691	4877	3641	124	198	265	49	489

CPSIA information can be obtained
at www.ICGtesting.com
Printed in the USA
BVHW011837190319
543108BV00005B/158/P

9 781296 485887